Contemporary Authors®

ISSN 0010-7468

# Contemporary
# Authors®

A Bio-Bibliographical Guide to
Current Writers in Fiction, General Nonfiction,
Poetry, Journalism, Drama, Motion Pictures,
Television, and Other Fields

*volume* **210**

GALE®

GALE™

Detroit • New York • San Diego • San Francisco • Cleveland • New Haven, Conn. • Waterville, Maine • London • Munich

# THOMSON

## GALE

### Contemporary Authors, Vol. 210

**Project Editor**
Scot Peacock

**Editorial**
Katy Balcer, Shavon Burden, Sara Constantakis, Anna Marie Dahn, Alana Joli Foster, Natalie Fulkerson, Arlene M. Johnson, Michelle Kazensky, Julie Keppen, Joshua Kondek, Thomas McMahon, Jenai A. Mynatt, Judith L. Pyko, Mary Ruby, Lemma Shomali, Susan Strickland, Anita Sundaresan, Maikue Vang, Tracey Watson, Thomas Wiloch, Emiene Shija Wright

**Research**
Tamara C. Nott, Nicodemus Ford, Michelle Campbell

**Permissions**
Lori Hines

**Imaging and Multimedia**
Dean Dauphinais, Robert Duncan, Leitha Etheridge-Sims, Mary K. Grimes, Lezlie Light, Dan Newell, David G. Oblender, Christine O'Bryan, Kelly A. Quin, Luke Rademacher

**Composition and Electronic Capture**
Carolyn A. Roney

**Manufacturing**
Stacy L. Melson

**LIBRARY OF CONGRESS CATALOG CARD NUMBER 62-52046**

ISBN 0-7876-5203-2
ISSN 0010-7468

# Contents

**Indexing note:** All *Contemporary Authors* entries are indexed in the *Contemporary Authors* cumulative index, which is published separately and distributed twice a year.

**As always, the most recent Contemporary Authors cumulative index continues to be the user's guide to the location of an individual author's listing.**

# Preface

*Contemporary Authors* (*CA*) provides information on approximately 115,000 writers in a wide range of media, including:

- Current writers of fiction, nonfiction, poetry, and drama whose works have been issued by commercial publishers, risk publishers, or university presses (authors whose books have been published only by known vanity or author-subsidized firms are ordinarily not included)

- Prominent print and broadcast journalists, editors, photojournalists, syndicated cartoonists, graphic novelists, screenwriters, television scriptwriters, and other media people

- Notable international authors

- Literary greats of the early twentieth century whose works are popular in today's high school and college curriculums and continue to elicit critical attention

A *CA* listing entails no charge or obligation. Authors are included on the basis of the above criteria and their interest to *CA* users. Sources of potential listees include trade periodicals, publishers' catalogs, librarians, and other users of the series.

## How to Get the Most out of *CA*: Use the Index

The key to locating an author's most recent entry is the *CA* cumulative index, which is published separately and distributed twice a year. It provides access to *all* entries in *CA* and *Contemporary Authors New Revision Series* (*CANR*). Always consult the latest index to find an author's most recent entry.

For the convenience of users, the *CA* cumulative index also includes references to all entries in these Gale literary series: *Authors and Artists for Young Adults, Authors in the News, Bestsellers, Black Literature Criticism, Black Literature Criticism Supplement, Black Writers, Children's Literature Review, Concise Dictionary of American Literary Biography, Concise Dictionary of British Literary Biography, Contemporary Authors Autobiography Series, Contemporary Authors Bibliographical Series, Contemporary Dramatists, Contemporary Literary Criticism, Contemporary Novelists, Contemporary Poets, Contemporary Popular Writers, Contemporary Southern Writers, Contemporary Women Poets, Dictionary of Literary Biography, Dictionary of Literary Biography Documentary Series, Dictionary of Literary Biography Yearbook, DISCovering Authors, DISCovering Authors: British, DISCovering Authors: Canadian, DISCovering Authors: Modules* (including modules for Dramatists, Most-Studied Authors, Multicultural Authors, Novelists, Poets, and Popular/ Genre Authors), *DISCovering Authors 3.0, Drama Criticism, Drama for Students, Feminist Writers, Hispanic Literature Criticism, Hispanic Writers, Junior DISCovering Authors, Major Authors and Illustrators for Children and Young Adults, Major 20th-Century Writers, Native North American Literature, Novels for Students, Poetry Criticism, Poetry for Students, Short Stories for Students, Short Story Criticism, Something about the Author, Something about the Author Autobiography Series, St. James Guide to Children's Writers, St. James Guide to Crime & Mystery Writers, St. James Guide to Fantasy Writers, St. James Guide to Horror, Ghost & Gothic Writers, St. James Guide to Science Fiction Writers, St. James Guide to Young Adult Writers, Twentieth-Century Literary Criticism, 20th Century Romance and Historical Writers, World Literature Criticism,* and *Yesterday's Authors of Books for Children.*

### A Sample Index Entry:

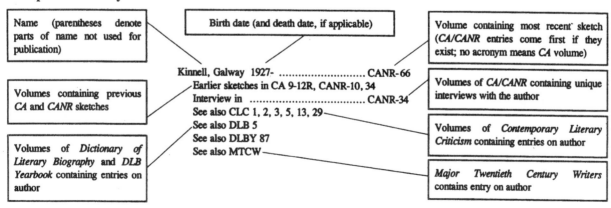

vii

# How Are Entries Compiled?

The editors make every effort to secure new information directly from the authors; listees' responses to our questionnaires and query letters provide most of the information featured in *CA*. For deceased writers, or those who fail to reply to requests for data, we consult other reliable biographical sources, such as those indexed in Gale's *Biography and Genealogy Master Index,* and bibliographical sources, including *National Union Catalog, LC MARC,* and *British National Bibliography.* Further details come from published interviews, feature stories, and book reviews, as well as information supplied by the authors' publishers and agents.

*An asterisk (\*) at the end of a sketch indicates that the listing has been compiled from secondary sources believed to be reliable but has not been personally verified for this edition by the author sketched.*

# What Kinds of Information Does An Entry Provide?

Sketches in *CA* contain the following biographical and bibliographical information:

- **Entry heading:** the most complete form of author's name, plus any pseudonyms or name variations used for writing

- **Personal information:** author's date and place of birth, family data, ethnicity, educational background, political and religious affiliations, and hobbies and leisure interests

- **Addresses:** author's home, office, or agent's addresses, plus e-mail and fax numbers, as available

- **Career summary:** name of employer, position, and dates held for each career post; resume of other vocational achievements; military service

- **Membership information:** professional, civic, and other association memberships and any official posts held

- **Awards and honors:** military and civic citations, major prizes and nominations, fellowships, grants, and honorary degrees

- **Writings:** a comprehensive, chronological list of titles, publishers, dates of original publication and revised editions, and production information for plays, television scripts, and screenplays

- **Adaptations:** a list of films, plays, and other media which have been adapted from the author's work

- **Work in progress:** current or planned projects, with dates of completion and/or publication, and expected publisher, when known

- **Sidelights:** a biographical portrait of the author's development; information about the critical reception of the author's works; revealing comments, often by the author, on personal interests, aspirations, motivations, and thoughts on writing

- **Interview:** a one-on-one discussion with authors conducted especially for *CA*, offering insight into authors' thoughts about their craft

- **Autobiographical essay:** an original essay written by noted authors for *CA*, a forum in which writers may present themselves, on their own terms, to their audience

- **Photographs:** portraits and personal photographs of notable authors

- **Biographical and critical sources:** a list of books and periodicals in which additional information on an author's life and/or writings appears

- **Obituary Notices** in *CA* provide date and place of birth as well as death information about authors whose full-length sketches appeared in the series before their deaths. The entries also summarize the authors' careers and writings and list other sources of biographical and death information.

## Related Titles in the *CA* Series

*Contemporary Authors Autobiography Series* complements *CA* original and revised volumes with specially commissioned autobiographical essays by important current authors, illustrated with personal photographs they provide. Common topics include their motivations for writing, the people and experiences that shaped their careers, the rewards they derive from their work, and their impressions of the current literary scene.

*Contemporary Authors Bibliographical Series* surveys writings by and about important American authors since World War II. Each volume concentrates on a specific genre and features approximately ten writers; entries list works written by and about the author and contain a bibliographical essay discussing the merits and deficiencies of major critical and scholarly studies in detail.

## Available in Electronic Formats

**GaleNet.** *CA* is available on a subscription basis through GaleNet, an online information resource that features an easy-to-use end-user interface, powerful search capabilities, and ease of access through the World-Wide Web. For more information, call 1-800-877-GALE.

**Licensing.** *CA* is available for licensing. The complete database is provided in a fielded format and is deliverable on such media as disk, CD-ROM, or tape. For more information, contact Gale's Business Development Group at 1-800-877-GALE, or visit us on our website at www.galegroup.com/bizdev.

## Suggestions Are Welcome

The editors welcome comments and suggestions from users on any aspect of the *CA* series. If readers would like to recommend authors for inclusion in future volumes of the series, they are cordially invited to write the Editors at *Contemporary Authors*, Gale Group, 27500 Drake Rd., Farmington Hills, MI 48331-3535; or call at 1-248-699-4253; or fax at 1-248-699-8054.

# Contemporary Authors Product Advisory Board

The editors of *Contemporary Authors* are dedicated to maintaining a high standard of excellence by publishing comprehensive, accurate, and highly readable entries on a wide array of writers. In addition to the quality of the content, the editors take pride in the graphic design of the series, which is intended to be orderly yet inviting, allowing readers to utilize the pages of *CA* easily and with efficiency. Despite the longevity of the *CA* print series, and the success of its format, we are mindful that the vitality of a literary reference product is dependent on its ability to serve its users over time. As literature, and attitudes about literature, constantly evolve, so do the reference needs of students, teachers, scholars, journalists, researchers, and book club members. To be certain that we continue to keep pace with the expectations of our customers, the editors of *CA* listen carefully to their comments regarding the value, utility, and quality of the series. Librarians, who have firsthand knowledge of the needs of library users, are a valuable resource for us. The *Contemporary Authors* Product Advisory Board, made up of school, public, and academic librarians, is a forum to promote focused feedback about *CA* on a regular basis. The seven-member advisory board includes the following individuals, whom the editors wish to thank for sharing their expertise:

- **Anne M. Christensen,** Librarian II, Phoenix Public Library, Phoenix, Arizona.

- **Barbara C. Chumard,** Reference/Adult Services Librarian, Middletown Thrall Library, Middletown, New York.

- **Eva M. Davis,** Youth Department Manager, Ann Arbor District Library, Ann Arbor, Michigan.

- **Adam Janowski, Jr.,** Library Media Specialist, Naples High School Library Media Center, Naples, Florida.

- **Robert Reginald,** Head of Technical Services and Collection Development, California State University, San Bernadino, California.

- **Katharine E. Rubin,** Head of Information and Reference Division, New Orleans Public Library, New Orleans, Louisiana.

- **Barbara A. Wencl,** Media Specialist, Como Park High School, St. Paul, Minnesota.

# International Advisory Board

Well-represented among the 115,000 author entries published in *Contemporary Authors* are sketches on notable writers from many non-English-speaking countries. The primary criteria for inclusion of such authors has traditionally been the publication of at least one title in English, either as an original work or as a translation. However, the editors of *Contemporary Authors* came to observe that many important international writers were being overlooked due to a strict adherence to our inclusion criteria. In addition, writers who were publishing in languages other than English were not being covered in the traditional sources we used for identifying new listees. Intent on increasing our coverage of international authors, including those who write only in their native language and have not been translated into English, the editors enlisted the aid of a board of advisors, each of whom is an expert on the literature of a particular country or region. Among the countries we focused attention on are Mexico, Puerto Rico, Germany, Luxembourg, Belgium, the Netherlands, Norway, Sweden, Denmark, Finland, Taiwan, Singapore, Spain, Italy, South Africa, Israel, and Japan, as well as England, Scotland, Wales, Ireland, Australia, and New Zealand. The sixteen-member advisory board includes the following individuals, whom the editors wish to thank for sharing their expertise:

- **Lowell A. Bangerter,** Professor of German, University of Wyoming, Laramie, Wyoming.

- **Nancy E. Berg,** Associate Professor of Hebrew and Comparative Literature, Washington University, St. Louis, Missouri.

- **Frances Devlin-Glass,** Associate Professor, School of Literary and Communication Studies, Deakin University, Burwood, Victoria, Australia.

- **David William Foster,** Regent's Professor of Spanish, Interdisciplinary Humanities, and Women's Studies, Arizona State University, Tempe, Arizona.

- **Hosea Hirata,** Director of the Japanese Program, Associate Professor of Japanese, Tufts University, Medford, Massachusetts.

- **Jack Kolbert,** Professor Emeritus of French Literature, Susquehanna University, Selinsgrove, Pennsylvania.

- **Mark Libin,** Professor, University of Manitoba, Winnipeg, Manitoba, Canada.

- **C. S. Lim,** Professor, University of Malaya, Kuala Lumpur, Malaysia.

- **Eloy E. Merino,** Assistant Professor of Spanish, Northern Illinois University, DeKalb, Illinois.

- **Linda M. Rodríguez Guglielmoni,** Associate Professor, University of Puerto Rico—Mayagüez, Puerto Rico.

- **Sven Hakon Rossel,** Professor and Chair of Scandinavian Studies, University of Vienna, Vienna, Austria.

- **Steven R. Serafin,** Director, Writing Center, Hunter College of the City University of New York, New York City.

- **David Smyth,** Lecturer in Thai, School of Oriental and African Studies, University of London, England.

- **Ismail S. Talib,** Senior Lecturer, Department of English Language and Literature, National University of Singapore, Singapore.

- **Dionisio Viscarri,** Assistant Professor, Ohio State University, Columbus, Ohio.

- **Mark Williams,** Associate Professor, English Department, University of Canterbury, Christchurch, New Zealand.

# *CA* Numbering System and Volume Update Chart

Occasionally questions arise about the *CA* numbering system and which volumes, if any, can be discarded. Despite numbers like " 29-32R," " 97-100" and "209," the entire *CA* print series consists of only 255 physical volumes with the publication of *CA* Volume 210. The following charts note changes in the numbering system and cover design, and indicate which volumes are essential for the most complete, up-to-date coverage.

| | |
|---|---|
| *CA* **First Revision** | • 1-4R through 41-44R (11 books)<br>*Cover:* Brown with black and gold trim.<br>There will be no further First Revision volumes because revised entries are now being handled exclusively through the more efficient *New Revision Series* mentioned below. |
| *CA* **Original Volumes** | • 45-48 through 97-100 (14 books)<br>*Cover:* Brown with black and gold trim.<br>101 through 210 (110 books)<br>*Cover:* Blue and black with orange bands.<br>The same as previous *CA* original volumes but with a new, simplified numbering system and new cover design. |
| *CA* **Permanent Series** | • *CAP*-1 and *CAP*-2 (2 books)<br>*Cover:* Brown with red and gold trim.<br>There will be no further Permanent Series volumes because revised entries are now being handled exclusively through the more efficient *New Revision Series* mentioned below. |
| *CA* **New Revision Series** | • CANR-1 through CANR-118 (118 books)<br>*Cover:* Blue and black with green bands.<br>Includes only sketches requiring significant changes; **sketches are taken from any previously published CA, CAP, or CANR volume.** |

| If You Have: | You May Discard: |
|---|---|
| *CA* First Revision Volumes 1-4R through 41-44R and *CA Permanent Series* Volumes 1 and 2 | *CA* Original Volumes 1, 2, 3, 4 Volumes 5-6 through 41-44 |
| *CA* Original Volumes 45-48 through 97-100 and 101 through 210 | **NONE:** These volumes will not be superseded by corresponding revised volumes. Individual entries from these and all other volumes appearing in the left column of this chart may be revised and included in the various volumes of the *New Revision Series*. |
| *CA New Revision Series* Volumes *CANR*-1 through *CANR*-118 | **NONE:** The *New Revision Series* does not replace any single volume of *CA*. Instead, volumes of *CANR* include entries from many previous *CA* series volumes. All *New Revision Series* volumes must be retained for full coverage. |

# A Sampling of Authors and Media People
# Featured in This Volume

## William J. Broad

Broad has enjoyed a long career as a science reporter for the *New York Times*. He has been honored with two shared Pulitzer prizes, and in addition to his reportage has written several well-received books. *Betrayers of the Truth: Fraud and Deceit in the Halls of Science*, coauthored with Nicholas Wade, exposes several cases of scientists who lose their purely scientific pursuit of the truth in favor of the more compelling drive to prove a favorite theory or make a name for themselves. Broad is also coauthor of 2001's *Germs: Biological Weapons and America's Secret War*.

## Nilo Cruz

Cruz shot to national prominence in 2003 when he won the Pulitzer Prize for his play *Anna in the Tropics,* a Depression-era tale about migrant Cubans working in a Tampa, Florida, cigar factory. Though several of his works have been staged by the Joseph Papp Public Theater in New York, Cruz is one of the few playwrights to win a Pulitzer without having a major presence on the New York theater scene. He is often praised by critics for his poetic language and his ability to weave strains of other literary traditions, such as magic realism, into his works.

## Tod Goldberg

Goldberg, a frequent contributor of short stories to literary magazines, gained widespread recognition with his first novel *Fake Liar Cheat*, which he wrote when he was twenty-seven years old. The novel provides a satirical look at Generation-X characters living in southern California. His 2002 novel, *Living Dead Girl,* is a psychological thriller about a professor in Southern California whose ex-wife goes missing. *Living Dead Girl* received a nomination for the *Los Angeles Times* Book Award for best mystery.

## Amira Hass

Israeli journalist Amira Hass based her debut book, *Drinking the Sea at Gaza: Days and Nights in a Land under Siege,* on her experiences reporting about the plight of the Palestinian people who have lived for many years under Israeli occupation. Hass has been a reporter for one of Israel's most respected daily newspapers, *Ha'aretz,* since 1989. One of Hass's main contentions since she first began reporting from Gaza is that few Israelis truly understand the plight of the Palestinian people, largely out of fear and prejudice.

## Nigella Lawson

Lawson's passion for food has catapulted her to the top of the culinary world. Starting with columns in several British newspapers, Lawson has written books and hosted television shows devoted to the enjoyment of food and cooking. She is best known in the U.S. for the television show *Nigella Bites*. In the book *How to Be a Domestic Goddess,* Lawson explains how to cook to bring out your personality, not necessarily your culinary expertise, and emphasizes the fun in preparing food and sharing it with those you love.

## Lyn Lifshin

One of the most prolific contemporary poets in the United States, Lifshin has contributed to hundreds of anthologies and appeared in many poetry and literary magazines. In addition to publishing more than ninety collections of her own work, an autobiography, and a "how-to" book for other writers, she is also recognized for editing several critically acclaimed collections of women's writings and for her many poetry readings and writing workshops. An autobiographical essay by Lifshin is included in this volume of *CA.*

## Mike McAlary

McAlary was a Pulitzer Prize-winning journalist who began his career as a sports writer with the *Boston Herald.* McAlary wrote for several New York City papers and became a columnist with the *Daily News* in 1988. His articles often reflected the heroism of the police, but he also exposed the failures within the system. His book *Buddy Boys: When Good Cops Turn Bad* is an account of a 1986 police scandal. He is also the author of *Good Cop, Bad Cop: Detective Joe Trimboli's Heroic Pursuit of NYPD Officer Michael Dowd* as well as the novel *Sore Loser.* McAlary died of colon cancer, at age forty-one, on December 25, 1998.

## Martha Sears

Sears, usually in conjunction with her husband, pediatrician William Sears, is best known for her well-regarded advice on parenting, through a series of books covering a range of issues, including the fussy eater, the high-need child, pregnancy and toilet training. Together, they have developed the method of parenting known as "attachment parenting." In *The Baby Book: Everything You Need to Know About Your Baby from Birth to Age Two* Martha and William Sears cover all aspects of child care. In 2002 the Sears, along with Elizabeth Pantley, authored *The Successful Child: What Parents Can Do to Help Kids Turn Out Well.*

# Acknowledgments

Grateful acknowledgment is made to those publishers, photographers, and artists whose work appear with these authors' essays. Following is a list of the copyright holders who have granted us permission to reproduce material in this volume of *CA*. Every effort has been made to trace copyright, but if omissions have been made, please let us know.

## Photographs/Art

**Richard Grayson:** All photos reproduced by permission of the author.

**Michael Heller:** All photos reproduced by permission of the author.

**Lyn Lifshin:** All photos reproduced by permission of the author.

# A

## ABZUG, Martin 1916-1986

*PERSONAL:* Born 1916, in New York, NY; died of a heart attack July 18, 1986, in New York, NY; married Bella Savitsky (a politician and feminist).

*CAREER:* Worked in his family's garment business, New York, NY, 1934-60; worked as a stockbroker for more than 20 years; associated with brokerage firm Philips, Appel & Walden.

*WRITINGS:*

*Spearhead* (novel), Dial (New York, NY), 1946.
*Seventh Avenue Story* (novel), Dial (New York, NY), 1947.

Author of articles on economic issues.

*SIDELIGHTS:* Martin Abzug, husband of outspoken feminist and New York congresswoman Bella Abzug, worked as a stockbroker for more than twenty years. An associate of the Philips, Appel & Walden brokerage firm at the time of his death, Abzug once worked in his family's New York garment business and wrote freelance articles about economic issues. Just before he died, Abzug completed a book of fiction about a man's lifelong search for his Nazi persecutor.

*Spearhead,* one of Abzug's two published novels, follows Lieutenant Knupfer, an average military man, and Captain Hollis, a once-timid man who became a killer, for several days during the U.S. Army artillery battery retreat during the Battle of the Bulge. According to John Barkham in *Saturday Review of Literature,* the book is "an honest, unpretentious, sometimes moving novel whose sober worth well merits recognition." A reviewer for the *New York Times* contended: "*Spearhead* is a well-paced novel, cleanly written. But dramatically, it fails to achieve its purpose. . . . Abzug makes his captain talk sensibly but act like a fool, while his lieutenant acts sensible and talks like a fool. The reader will be more than a little confused trying to keep up with them." "It would be a great pity if the current prejudice against war books were to deny this promising young writer the encouragement he deserves," Barkham said. "The story is lean and alive, stripped of everything but life-in-the-instant." "In showing how they act in a crisis, and how the men under them react, Mr. Abzug makes a grim and graphic contribution to war fiction," wrote Lisle Bell in *Weekly Book Review.* "Unfortunately," wrote *San Francisco Chronicle* contributor George Snell, "the novel does not do well by its theme, although it contains many good scenes and all the realistic detail one could wish."

*Seventh Avenue Story,* published a year after *Spearhead,* features a young man who founds a garment business in New York. *Library Journal* reviewer Anne Whitmore called the novel is "not an important book, but an interesting picture of a unique section of America." Merie Miller's judgment was less favorable in a *Saturday Review of Literature* assessment: "I'm afraid his is just a plain bad book. . . . Abzug has unquestionably done a lot of research; he seems to know the industry, but his style is so turgid, so dull, so filled with cliches that it fails completely." Richard

Spinney commented in the *New York Herald Tribune Weekly Book Review:* "Seventh Avenue Story, in spite of its tough, accurate dialogue and concise form, reminded me less of recent American work of the same genre (dealing with mankind under economic pressure) than of novels that came out of Europe after the first world war and in the '30s. . . . One feels that Mr. Abzug's attention is directed less toward literary effect than toward a deep and just penetration of the individuals about who he writes."

*BIOGRAPHICAL AND CRITICAL SOURCES:*

PERIODICALS

*Book Week,* October 6, 1946.
*Library Journal,* August, 1946; August, 1947.
*New York Herald Tribune Weekly Book Review,*
    September 7, 1947.
*New York Times,* September 29, 1946.
*San Francisco Chronicle,* November 3, 1946.
*Saturday Review of Literature,* October 5, 1946;
    August 30, 1947.
*Weekly Book Review,* November 3, 1946.

*OBITUARIES:*

PERIODICALS

*Chicago Tribune,* July 21, 1986.
*New York Times,* July 19, 1986.*

\*          \*          \*

**ACHTEMEIER, Elizabeth (Rice) 1926-2002**

*OBITUARY NOTICE*—See index for *CA* sketch: Born June 11, 1926, in Bartlesville, OK; died October 25, 2002, in Richmond, VA. Minister, educator, and author. Achtemeier was a Presbyterian minister, Bible scholar, and professor who wrote on issues such as abortion, suicide, and euthanasia. She received her associate's degree from Stephens College, her bachelor's degree in 1948 from Stanford University, and her M.Div. from Union Theological Seminary in 1951. Ordained a minister in the United Church of Christ, she then taught at Lancaster Theological Seminary as a visiting

lecturer from 1959 to 1971 and as an adjunct professor of the Old Testament from 1971 to 1973. In 1973 she joined the faculty of Union Theological Seminary as visiting professor of homiletics, during which time she also was a visiting professor at Presbyterian schools around the United States. During her career she sometimes drew criticism from feminists as a result of her stand on women's issues, such as her pro-life stance, but was credited by many for her strongly held principals on this and other serious moral issues. Well known for her oratory skills as a preacher, Achtemeier retired in 1997. Among the over two dozen books to her credit are *Creative Preaching* (1980), *Nature, God, and Pulpit* (1992), *The Right Choice* (1997), and the autobiography *Not til I Have Done: A Personal Testimony* (1999).

*OBITUARIES AND OTHER SOURCES:*

PERIODICALS

*Richmond Times-Dispatch,* October 28, 2002, obituary by Jenifer V. Buckman, p. B5.

OTHER

*Presbyterians Pro-Life,* http://www.ppl.org/ (February 3, 2003).

\*          \*          \*

**ACSADI, Gwendolyn**
    **See JOHNSON-ACSADI, Gwendolyn**

\*          \*          \*

**ADAMS, Bernard (Paul Fornaro) 1915-2002**

*OBITUARY NOTICE*—See index for *CA* sketch: Born June 26, 1915, in Carshalton, Surrey, England; died December 10, 2002. Librarian and author. Adams was an authority on the architecture of London, England. After his education at Westminster School and a stint in the Royal Air Force, he worked as a library assistant at Cambridge University. Most of his career, however, was spent at the British Council in London, where he was the librarian from 1946 until his early retirement in 1976. While working at the British Council library, Adams became fascinated with the history of London's topography, a subject he was better able to pursue after retirement. His extensive research resulted in the book *London Illustrated, 1604-1851: A Survey and Index of Topographical Books and Their Plates* (1983). In addition to his interest in London, Adams was also a scholar of the Italian Renaissance.

*OBITUARIES AND OTHER SOURCES:*

*PERIODICALS*

*Times* (London, England), January 28, 2003, p. 30.

\*     \*     \*

**ADLER, Elmer 1884-1962**

*PERSONAL:* Born July 22, 1884, in Rochester, NY; died January 11, 1962.

*CAREER:* Collector of books and fine prints. Pynson Printers, New York, NY, founder and director, 1922-40; Random House, New York, NY, co-founder and first vice president; Princeton University, research associate of graphic arts, professor and curator, established department of graphic arts. *Colophon: A Quarterly for Booklovers,* founder and editor, c. 1930-40; *The New Colophon: A Book-Collectors' Miscellany,* editor, c. 1948-50.

*WRITINGS:*

*An Informal Talk by Elmer Adler at the University of Kansas, April 17, 1953,* University of Kansas (Lawrence, KA), c. 1953.
*Breaking into Print,* Simon & Schuster (New York, NY), c. 1937.

Contributor of articles and reviews to various periodical publications.

*SIDELIGHTS:* Elmer Adler collected books and fine prints. Before establishing and editing the periodicals *Colophon: A Quarterly for Booklovers* and *The New Colophon: A Book-Collectors' Miscellany,* Adler started Pynson Printers to produce books with high-quality graphics. Pynson adopted the slogan, "we will do no work in which quality must be sacrificed to exigencies of time and cost." Adler was also a founding vice president of the Random House publishing company.

Adler in 1940 attached himself and his collection to Princeton University, where he founded the department of graphic arts and became a professor and curator. There, he conducted seminars in collecting, commenced a print loan program and invited marquee speakers. An Adler Book Collecting Prize is awarded annually to a Princeton student.

Adler edited *Breaking into Print,* "a compilation of papers in which each of a select group of authors tells of the difficulties of authorship and how such trials are met, also about their first published work," a reviewer wrote in *Saturday Review of Literature.* Among the authors contributing to the collection are Pearl Buck, Sinclair Lewis, and Edith Wharton. "Most of the papers . . . have a rather self-conscious air," Louis Kronenberger said in the *New York Times.* "Nobody has wanted to be pompous or self-important, but in trying not to be, many people have been a little arch."

Other reviews of *Breaking into Print* were more positive. A *Saturday Review of Literature* critic maintained that "all in all, [it is] a successful experiment." L. E. Stoyle wrote in *Boston Transcript,* "It is a profoundly interesting book and one that anyone interested in writing should read."

*BIOGRAPHICAL AND CRITICAL SOURCES:*

*BOOKS*

McAllister, Coleman, *An Appreciation of the Work of Elmer Adler,* William Edwin Rudge (Mount Vernon, NY), 1920.
Thompson, Lawrence Roger, *Elmer Adler at Princeton: A Tribute on the Occasion of His Retirement from the Princeton Faculty and from the Curatorship of the Graphic Arts Division of the Library,* Princeton University Press (Princeton, NJ), 1952.

*PERIODICALS*

*Booklist,* October 1, 1937.
*Books,* September 12, 1937, William Soskin, review of *Breaking into Print,* p. 6.
*Boston Transcript,* October 9, 1937, L. E. Stoyle, review of *Breaking into Print,* p. 1.
*New York Times,* September 19, 1937, Louis Kronenberger, review of *Breaking into Print,* p. 2.
*Saturday Review of Literature,* October 2, 1937, review of *Breaking into Print.*

*OTHER*

*Princeton University Web site,* http://www.princeton.edu/, "For the Love of Books and Prints: Elmer Adler and the Graphic Arts Collection at Princeton University Library," 2001.*

\* \* \*

## AGENT ORANGE
### See MOSELEY, James W(illett)

\* \* \*

## ALLAUN, Frank (Julian) 1913-2002

*OBITUARY NOTICE*—See index for *CA* sketch: Born February 27, 1913, in Manchester, England; died after a series of strokes November 26, 2002, in Manchester, England. Politician, journalist, and author. Allaun was a newspaper editor and leftist member of Parliament known for his vehement support of the lower classes and strong anti-nuclear and anti-military stance. A graduate of the University of London, he took a correspondence course in accountancy, which he completed in 1934. He then worked in various types of jobs, including as an engineer, a tour guide, a shop assistant, and a lecturer for the Workers' Educational Association. A member of the Communist Party until 1944, his politics were definitely left wing. After abandoning Communism, Allaun became editor of the Labour Party newspaper the *Northern Voice,* where he worked from 1945 to 1967; he was also a northern industrial correspondent for the *Manchester Evening News* from 1947 to 1951 and for the *London Daily News* during the 1950s. Allaun was elected to the House of Commons in 1955 as a member of the Labour Party representing Salford East. While a member of Parliament, he was parliamentary private secretary to Colonial Secretary Anthony Greenwood from 1964 until his resignation in 1965, and was on the Labour Party's national executive committee from 1967 to 1983, serving as deputy chairman in 1977 and 1978 an as chairman from 1978 to 1979. Allaun's political career was fraught with contention, and he often found himself opposing the more popular views in Parliament. As an organizer of the Campaign for Nuclear Disarmament, for which he became vice president in 1983, and as president of the Labour Action for Peace from 1965 to 2001, he argued against Britain's more militant stances on such issues as the Suez Crisis of 1957. He was an advocate for better housing for the poor, arguing that it was more important to build decent homes than it was to build bombs to make war abroad, and he constantly pressed for Britain's withdrawal from the European Economic Community, calling the Europeans "warmongers." Furthermore, he was one of the participants in the 1974 Commons revolt, which consisted of Labour Party members who opposed the government's plans for military spending. In addition to his anti-war and pro-housing causes, Allaun was a supporter of reform in the media, and he chaired a Labour committee that proposed a "right to reply" reform which was ultimately unsuccessful. With the rise of a more conservative government under Prime Minister Margaret Thatcher, Labour's influence waned, and Allaun retired from Parliament in 1983. However, he remained politically active and continued to serve as president of Labour Action for Peace until 2001, when he stepped down from president to vice president. Allaun's political beliefs led him to write a number of pamphlets and books, including *Your Trade Union and You* (1950), *Heartbreak Housing* (1968), *No Place like Home: Britain's Housing Tragedy* (1972), *Nuclear Weapons: Questions and Answers* (1981), *Spreading the News: A Guide to Media Reform* (1988), and his last work, *The Struggle for Peace* (1992). In addition to his many achievements, Allaun was also a champion ballroom dancer.

*OBITUARIES AND OTHER SOURCES:*

*BOOKS*

*Who's Who 2002,* Palgrave (New York, NY), 2002.

*PERIODICALS*

*Daily Telegraph* (London, England), November 29, 2002.
*Guardian* (London, England), November 27, 2002, p. 24.
*Independent* (London, England), November 29, 2002, p. 22.
*Times* (London, England), November 27, 2002, p. 33.

\*    \*    \*

## ALLEN, Debbie 1953-

*PERSONAL:* Born May 7, 1953, in Gary, IN; daughter of John R. Lahaie (in auto sales) and Nancy C. Dault (in clothing sales).

*ADDRESSES: Office*—131 West Sunburst Lane, Tempo, AZ 85284; fax 480-831-8334. *E-mail*—debbie@debbieallen.com.

*CAREER:* Professional speaker, entrepreneur, and author. Small-business owner of in car rental company, storage facilities, and retail stores; Allen & Associates Consulting, Inc., Tempe, AZ, president, 1996; speaker on sales topics internationally; has appeared on radio and television talk shows.

*MEMBER:* National Speakers Association (past president, AZ chapter), American Speakers Association, ABPA, SPAN.

*AWARDS, HONORS:* Blue Chip Enterprise Award, National Chamber of Commerce, 1997.

*WRITINGS:*

*Trade Secret of Retail Stars,* Publisher Success Showcase Publishing (Scottsdale, AZ), 1996.
*Confessions of Shameless Self-Promoters,* Publisher Success Showcase Publishing (Scottsdale, AZ), 2001.
*Confessions of Shameless Internet Promoters,* Publisher Success Showcase Publishing (Scottsdale, AZ), 2002.

Contributor to periodicals, including *Entrepreneur, Selling Power, Franchise,* and *Sales and Marketing Excellence.*

*BIOGRAPHICAL AND CRITICAL SOURCES:*

*OTHER*

*Debbie Allen Web site,* http://www.debbieallen.com (April 19, 2003).

\*    \*    \*

## ALMOND, Gabriel A(braham) 1911-2002

*OBITUARY NOTICE*—See index for *CA* sketch: Born January 12, 1911, in Rock Island, NY; died December 25, 2002, in Pacific Grove, CA. Political scientist, educator, and author. Almond was a respected political scientist who took a multidisciplinary approach to his writings, incorporating psychology, sociology, economics, and anthropology into his theories. He was a graduate of the University of Chicago, where he earned a Ph.D. in 1938. His thesis paper, *Plutocracy and Politics in New York City,* went unpublished until 1997 because the university's administrators did not appreciate its criticism of what Almond called "the idle rich" and its author's unflattering portrait of John D. Rockefeller, who was a major benefactor of the university at the time; however, for decades the thesis remained a kind of cult classic among students. Almond's first academic post was as an instructor in political science at Brooklyn College. World War II saw him serving as chief of the Office of War Information, where he analyzed propaganda and worked on the U.S. Strategic Bombing Survey, the purpose of which was to analyze the psychological effects of carpet bombing. Returning to academia in 1947 after working for the U.S. War Department in Washington, D.C., Almond joined the faculty at Yale University, teaching political science there until 1951. He spent the 1950s at Princeton University, returned to Yale in the early 1960s, and then moved to California. He was a professor at Stanford University from 1963 until 1976, and was head of the political science department from 1964 to 1968. Throughout his career, Almond pursued his interests in post-colonial nations, the effects of public opinion and religion on politics, Communism, and the study of political science. He wrote or edited about two dozen books on these and other topics, including *The American People and Foreign Policy* (1977), *A Discipline Divided: Schools and Sects in Political Science* (1990), and *Ventures in Political Science: Narratives and Reflections* (2002). The eighth edition of his *Comparative Politics Today: A World View,* first published in 1974, was scheduled for publication in 2003.

## OBITUARIES AND OTHER SOURCES:

BOOKS

*Writers Directory,* 17th edition, St. James Press (Detroit, MI), 2002.

PERIODICALS

*Los Angeles Times,* January 8, 2003, p. B11.
*New York Times,* January 13, 2003, p. A22.
*Times* (London, England), January 17, 2003.
*Washington Post,* January 13, 2003, p. B7.

\*     \*     \*

## AL SIDDIK
    See ROLFE, Frederick (William Serafino Austin Lewis Mary)

\*     \*     \*

## ARGYLE, (John) Michael 1925-2002

*OBITUARY NOTICE*—See index for *CA* sketch: Born August 11, 1925, in Nottingham, England; died following a swimming accident September 6, 2002, in England. Psychologist, educator, and author. Argyle is best remembered for his contributions to the field of social psychology and was the coiner of the phrase "social skills." He studied at Emmanuel College, Cambridge, and when World War II broke out he trained in Canada as a navigator for the Royal Air Force. Returning to England, he worked as a fireman in London and in radio in Berlin, Germany. After the war he returned to Cambridge, where he completed his master's degree in psychology in 1952. Beginning

that year, he joined the faculty at Oxford University as university lecturer. He spent the rest of his academic career there, being promoted to reader in social psychology in 1969 and retiring as emeritus reader in 1992. Among his many contributions to the university, Argyle was a founding fellow of Wolfson College, where he was vice regent from 1989 to 1991, and he also served as acting head of the department of experimental psychology from 1978 to 1980. A teacher beloved by his students, Argyle was a ground-breaking researcher in such areas of psychology as non-verbal behavior, social interaction, interpersonal relationships, and the effects of work, entertainment, and religion on people's mental health. Perhaps his most significant breakthrough, however, was his discovery that many behavioral disorders have their roots not in mental illness but in poorly learned social skills, a theory that has since gained wide acceptance and about which he wrote in his best-known book, *The Psychology of Interpersonal Behaviour* (1967). Devoutly religious, Argyle was also interested in how people's religious beliefs affect them mentally, a topic he wrote about in *Religious Behaviour* (1959). In addition to these works, Argyle was a prolific producer of other psychology books, publishing over twenty works during his lifetime, including *Social Interaction* (1969), *Bodily Communication* (1975), *The Psychology of Happiness* (1987), and, with Adrian Furnham, *The Psychology of Money* (1998). He also was a former editor of the *British Journal of Social and Clinical Psychology.* Among other honors awarded him for his contributions to the field of psychology, Argyle received a Distinguished Career Contribution Award from the International Society for the Study of Personal Relationships in 1990.

## OBITUARIES AND OTHER SOURCES:

BOOKS

*Writers Directory,* 16th edition, St. James Press (Detroit, MI), 2001.

PERIODICALS

*Guardian* (London, England), October 3, 2002, p. 22.
*Independent* (London, England), September 30, 2002, p. 16.
*Times* (London, England), September 13, 2002, p. 39.

## ARRIZÓN, Alicia

*PERSONAL:* Born in San Luis, AZ; daughter of Francisco and Ofelia (Peña) Arrizón; companion of Gina Ong (an attorney). *Ethnicity:* "Mexican/American." *Education:* Arizona State University, B.A., 1984, M.A., 1986; Stanford University, Ph.D., 1992. *Politics:* "Radical Democrat." *Religion:* "Believe in many Gods and Goddesses." *Hobbies and other interests:* Arts.

*ADDRESSES: Home*—Temple City, CA. *Office*—University of California—Riverside, Riverside, CA 92521. *E-mail*—alicia.arrizon@ucr.edu.

*CAREER:* University of California—Riverside, Riverside, CA, associate professor of American studies, 1992—.

*MEMBER:* American Studies Association, Association in Theater for Higher Education, Modern Language Association of America.

*WRITINGS:*

*Latina Performance,* Indiana University Press (Bloomington, IN), 1999.
*Latinas Onstage,* Third Woman Press (Berkeley, CA), 2000.

*WORK IN PROGRESS: Transculturation and Performance,* completion expected in 2004.

*SIDELIGHTS:* Alicia Arrizón told *CA:* "My primary motivation for writing is the dissemination of knowledge marginal to mainstream society. The work of many Latino/a artists (and many other subjects) and historical facts influence my work. My writing process is an accumulation of many things: research and original thinking. My passion for the theater and performance culture inspired the writing of my two books."

\*     \*     \*

## ASEN, Robert 1968-

*PERSONAL:* Born July 12, 1968, in New York, NY; son of Allen and Fela Asen; married Rochelle Klaskin, July 7, 1996; children: Simone Hadora. *Ethnicity:* "Polish/Russian." *Education:* University of Illinois—Urbana-Champaign, B.A., 1991; University of North Carolina—Chapel Hill, M.A., 1994; Northwestern University, Ph.D., 1998. *Religion:* Jewish.

*ADDRESSES: Home*—2604 Kendall Ave., Madison, WI 53705. *Office*—Department of Communication Arts, University of Wisconsin—Madison, Madison, WI 53705. *E-mail*—rbasen@facstaff.wisc.edu.

*CAREER:* Educator and author. University of North Carolina—Chapel Hill, instructor in communication studies, 1992-94; Northwestern University, Evanston, IL, instructor in communication studies, 1996-99; University of Wisconsin—Madison, assistant professor of communication arts, 1999—, and affiliate of Institute for Research on Poverty.

*MEMBER:* National Communication Association, American Forensic Association.

*AWARDS, HONORS:* Daniel Rohrer Research Award, American Forensics Association, 2001.

*WRITINGS:*

(Editor, with Daniel C. Brouwer, and contributor) *Counterpublics and the State,* State University of New York Press (Albany, NY), 2001.
*Visions of Poverty: Welfare Policy and Political Imagination,* Michigan State University Press (East Lansing, MI), 2002.

Contributor to books; contributor of articles and reviews to academic journals, including *Text and Performance Quarterly, Rhetoric and Public Affairs, Philosophy and Rhetoric,* and *Political Communication.* Coeditor of special issue, *Argumentation and Advocacy,* 2003. Member of editorial board, *Controversia,* 2001—, and *Communication Theory,* 2001-02.

*WORK IN PROGRESS:* A book on market-based appeals in public policy debates.

*SIDELIGHTS:* Robert Asen told *CA:* "I have just begun research on a book-length project exploring the influence and significance of market-based appeals in public policy debates. The book will focus on the areas of public assistance, social insurance, and education policy.

"Contemporary policy debates in these three areas exhibit fundamental reversals in the aims and purposes of public policies when compared to debates that occurred during the founding era of the U.S. welfare state in the mid-1930s. These reversals have proceeded in part through participants' portrayals of markets as reliable producers of social outcomes and governments as inept institutional actors unable to alleviate lingering social ills. The widespread use of market language in social-welfare policy debates has established a framework for deliberation that, prior to consideration of any specific policy initiative, narrowly restricts appropriate aims of public policy, populations served by public policies, and expectations of policy beneficiaries. Moreover, debating public policies through market-based evaluative standards invites a recasting of citizens as consumers.

"A consumer orientation to citizenship discounts the importance of public discourse for determining social goods and denies the possibility that people can gain an appreciation of one another's values and beliefs through debate, insisting instead that diverse interests can be adjudicated only by processes of bargaining."

\*     \*     \*

## AUGSTEIN, Rudolf (Karl) 1923-2002

*OBITUARY NOTICE*—See index for *CA* sketch: Born November 5, 1923, in Hannover, Germany; died of pneumonia November 7, 2002, in Hamburg, Germany. Journalist and author. Augstein was best known as the founder and publisher of the respected Germany news magazine *Der Spiegel*. He finished school just before World War II and worked briefly for a small newspaper before being drafted into the German army. Fighting on the Eastern Front as a telegraph operator and then artillery observer, he was wounded and sent home. With the victory of Allied forces, Augstein was briefly held prisoner by the U.S. forces and then released in 1945. He joined the staff of the newspaper *Hannoversches Nachrichtenblatt* in 1945. In 1946 he took a job as a reporter for *Diese Woche*, a newspaper run by British occupation forces that he took over in 1947 and turned into *Der Spiegel*. Under Augstein's leadership *Der Spiegel* became a powerful voice for the new democracy in Germany, and its circulation grew from 65,000 subscribers to over one million. As editor and chief editorial writer, Augstein held considerable sway over public opinion in Germany, and he became a symbol for freedom of the press for his war-weary nation. This freedom, however, was challenged in 1962 when he was put in prison for over three months for criticizing the North Atlantic Treaty Organization (NATO). A flood of protests erupted against this action; Augstein was freed, and Defense Minister Franz-Josef Strauss, who ordered the arrest, was forced out of office in the ensuing scandal. Augstein returned to his newspaper, helping his country to navigate through the cold war years. However, after the fall of the Berlin Wall and the reunification of East and West Germany, *Der Spiegel* lost influence as a political voice as other newspapers and magazines began to compete for its readership. Augstein turned over editorship of *Der Spiegel* to Stefan Aust in 1995, but continued to serve as publisher until his death. For his important work in journalism, he was made an honorary citizen of Hamburg in 1994, received the Commander's Cross of the Order of Merit of the Federal Republic of Germany in 1997, and earned the Ludwig-Borne award in 2000. In addition to his work as an editor, Augstein was the author of several books, including *Konrad Adenauer* (1964), *Spiegelungen* (1964), *Meinungen zu Deutschland* (1967), and *Jesus Menschensohn* (1972), which was translated in 1977 as *Jesus, Son of Man*.

### OBITUARIES AND OTHER SOURCES:

*BOOKS*

*Who's Who in the World,* 18th edition, Marquis (New Providence, NJ), 2000.

*PERIODICALS*

*Chicago Tribune,* November 9, 2002, section 2, p. 11.
*Los Angeles Times,* November 9, 2002, p. B21.
*New York Times,* November 8, 2002, p. C11.
*Times* (London, England), November 8, 2002.
*Washington Post,* November 10, 2002, p. C11.

\*     \*     \*

## AUSTIN, Frederick
See ROLFE, Frederick (William Serafino Austin Lewis Mary)

# B

## BARBER, Willard F(oster) 1909-2002

*OBITUARY NOTICE*—See index for *CA* sketch: Born March 21, 1909, in Mitchell, SD; died of cardiopulmonary arrest December 3, 2002, in Greenwich, CT. Government official, educator, and author. Barber had a long and distinguished career in the U.S. Department of State. A bright student, he graduated from Stanford University with a master's degree in international relations in 1929, at the young age of nineteen. After working as an instructor in government for the City College of the City University of New York for nine years, he was hired by the U.S. Department of State in 1938, where he worked until 1962. While a government officer, he served in posts in countries around the world, including Peru, Columbia, and Warsaw. He returned to Washington, D.C., in 1957 as director of senior officer training at the Foreign Service Institute, and in 1960 was made chairman of Mutual Security evaluation teams in Turkey, Iran, and Pakistan. The remainder of his career was spent at the University of Maryland, where he lectured in international affairs from 1962 to his retirement in 1977. Barber was the coauthor of *American Government* (1935) and *Internal Security and Military Power: Counter Insurgency and Civic Action in Latin America* (1966).

*OBITUARIES AND OTHER SOURCES:*

*PERIODICALS*

*Washington Post,* December 8, 2002, p. C8.

## BARON CORVO
### See ROLFE, Frederick (William Serafino Austin Lewis Mary)

\*     \*     \*

## BARR, Anthony 1921-2002
### (Tony Barr)

*OBITUARY NOTICE*—See index for *CA* sketch: Original name, Morris Yaffe; born March 14, 1921, in St. Louis, MO; died December 19, 2002, in Palm Desert, CA. Media executive, educator, actor, director, producer, and author. Barr was the founder of the Film Actors Workshop and a former television executive at ABC and CBS. A graduate of Washington University in St. Louis, where he earned his B.S. in 1942, he was an actor for two years in New York City, spent a year as stage manager of the Katherine Dunham Dancers, and then worked from 1947 to 1952 as an actor in Hollywood. A job as a stage manager for CBS-TV led to his first directing work, for the television series *Climax,* which he later worked on as associate producer in the mid-1950s. Barr went on to work as a director and producer for ABC and Metro-Goldwyn-Mayer during the early 1960s. Then, in 1963, he was hired as a program executive for ABC-TV, becoming vice president of prime-time series in 1973. CBS hired him in 1976 to be their vice president of dramatic programs, and he helped produce such popular programs as *Magnum P.I.* and *Simon & Simon.* He retired in 1987. Other than his television work, Barr was a highly regarded acting coach, founding the Film Actors Workshop in 1960. His acting advice is published in his only book, *Acting for the Camera* (1981).

*OBITUARIES AND OTHER SOURCES:*

*BOOKS*

*Who's Who in Entertainment,* third edition, Marquis
(New Providence, NJ), 1997.

*PERIODICALS*

*Los Angeles Times,* December 23, 2002, p. B9.

\*        \*        \*

**BARR, Tony**
  **See BARR, Anthony**

\*        \*        \*

**BARRY, Dana (Marie Malloy) 1949-**

*PERSONAL:* Born May 26, 1949, in Utica, NY;
daughter of Daniel S. and Celia (Sacco) Malloy; married James F. Barry (a teacher), July 3, 1971; children:
James Daniel, Brian Patrick, Daniel Thomas, Eric
Michael. *Ethnicity:* "White." *Education:* State University of New York-Potsdam, B.A., 1971, M.S.
(education), 1972; Clarkson University, M.S.
(chemistry), 1974; Columbia Pacific University, Ph.D.,
1985. *Hobbies and other interests:* Trumpet player,
singer, and keyboard player in community bands and
orchestras; ice skating, cooking, walking, swimming.

*ADDRESSES: Home*—46 Farmer St., Canton, NY
13617. *Office*—Box 5665, CAMP, Clarkson University,
Potsdam, NY 13699. *E-mail*—dmbarry@clarkson.edu.

*CAREER:* Author, certified chemist, and educator.
State University New York-Potsdam, member of
Education Department faculty, 1987-89; Center for
Advanced Materials Processing (CAMP), Clarkson
University, Potsdam, NY, technical writer and editor,
1993—, Horizons Program (for gifted seventh- and
eighth-grade girls), staff member, 2002—. Ansted
University, Malaysia, visiting and external professor,
2001—; Suzuka National College of Technology,
Japan, visiting professor, 2002. Has worked as a chem-
ist and chemical consultant. Organizer of World's First

MoonLink Mission (educational component to NASA's
Lunar Prospector Mission), 1998, World's First
NEARLink Mission (educational component to
NASA's NEAR Mission), 1998, and World's First
MarsLink Mission (educational component to NASA's
Global Surveyor Mission), 2000. Member of People to
People Ambassador program in Asia, 2002.

*MEMBER:* National Science Teachers Association,
American Institute of Chemists, American Chemical
Society (officer), Cameroon Ozone Club (honorary
member).

*AWARDS, HONORS:* APEX Awards for Publication
Excellence, Communications Concepts (VA), 1996-
2002; permanent certification by NASA to borrow
lunar rocks, 1999; honorary doctorate from Ansted
University (Malaysia), 2001; Outstanding Achieve-
ment Award for Promoting Chemistry to Youths of All
Ages, American Chemical Society (Northern New
York section), 2002; Science Fair Judge Service
Award, 2003.

*WRITINGS:*

*Innovative Activities for Elementary and Middle
    School Science,* Burgess International (Minnesota),
    1992.
*Simple Chemistry,* Teacher Created Materials
    (Huntington Beach, CA), 1994.
*Easy Chemistry,* Teacher Created Materials
    (Huntington Beach, CA), 1994.
(With James F. Barry) *Modern Chemistry Experiments,*
    Barry (Massena, NY), 1996.
*Science Fair Projects: Helping Your Child Create a
    Super Science Fair Project,* illustrated by Howard
    Chaney, Teacher Created Materials (Huntington
    Beach, CA), 2000.

*Simple Chemistry* and *Easy Chemistry* have been
published in Spanish; *Science Fair Projects* has been
published in Japanese. Author of numerous articles in
professional publications, including *Chemist, Journal
of Chemical Education,* and *Bulletin of the Tokai Ka-
gaku Kougyoukai.* (Japan). Script writer, host, and co-
producer of *Sensational Science*( television series),
1996; author and composer of *Chemical Sensation
with the Barry Tones* (CD and audio cassette), 1996;
script writer and presenter for *Science Connected to
Other Areas of the Curriculum for Elementary Children*
(video series), 1998.

*WORK IN PROGRESS:* Chemistry research, "including an acid rain simulation project with professors in
the United States and Japan," and a collaborative

chemistry education project with a university in Japan; continuation of the World's First MarsLink space mission; two romance mysteries, *Mail Mystery* and *Mind Games Plus.*

*SIDELIGHTS:* "I love to write for children (people) of all ages," Dana Barry told *CA.* "My writing topics are diverse and my audiences are at all levels of learning. I write journal features and books for elementary, middle school, and high school science teachers and their students. Also I write video scripts and journal features that relate science to other areas of the curriculum such as English, art, and music.

"In addition, I present many hands-on science workshops for teachers and students in the United States and in other countries. Science excites and motivates me in such a way that I am able to transfer the excitement to students in my workshops. I have also been able to turn their parents and young siblings on to science at the same time. My outstanding success in this endeavor has allowed me to have my own science education television series, called *Sensational Science.* I served as script writer, host, and co-producer for the shows.

"The great honor and pleasure of organizing three Worlds First space missions has been a wonderful opportunity for me. The missions, sponsored by NASA and Space Explorers, Inc. (with support from the Clarkson Space Grant Program and the Northern New York section of the American Chemical Society), provide ideas and information for my features about space and space science. Some of my articles target students and their teachers, while others are written for chemists and scientists.

"In my position as technical writer and editor at Clarkson University's Center for Advanced Materials Processing (CAMP), I write about leading-edge research. My audience includes professors, their industrial collaborators, and scientists throughout the world. I have received many prestigious awards for this work.

"One of my great loves is music. I sing, play keyboard, and am an avid trumpet player. I wrote the lyrics and composed the music for the science education music CD and cassette *Chemical Sensation with the Barry*

*Tones.* These chemistry songs, which cover the chemistry curriculum, are written in rhyming poems and have diverse music styles (e.g., rock, rap, blues). My music is being incorporated into a collaborative chemistry education project that I have with three professors at Suzuka National College of Technology in Japan. Our unique multisensory project uses music and chemical experiments (which I prepared) to teach college and high school chemistry in a very interesting and meaningful way.

"For fun I am writing two short love mysteries, which I hope to have published in the near future. One is titled *Mail Mystery.* It is about a college student and the danger that awaits her while she works as a mail carrier during her summer vacation.

"The other mystery is called *Mind Games Plus.* It is about a newly hired school teacher who encounters many strange people and events, and then mysteriously disappears. My son Eric Michael Barry (hopefully an up-and-coming TV/movie star) wrote a forward to this book.

"Also, I plan to write a science education book with professor Hideyuki Kanematsu from Suzuka National College of Technology in Japan. I was recently featured in a cover story for Japan's *Journal for the Association of Colleges of Technology* and featured on CNS Television News in Suzuka City, Japan."

*BIOGRAPHICAL AND CRITICAL SOURCES:*

*PERIODICALS*

*Science Books & Films,* September-October, 2001, Charles Hibberd, review of *Science Fair Projects,* p. 219.

\*     \*     \*

**BARTON, Marlin 1961-**

*PERSONAL:* Born October 25, 1961, in Montgomery, AL; son of Marlin C., Jr. and Jeannine (Beinert) Barton; married Rhonda Goff, October 12, 2001. *Ethnicity:* "White." *Education:* University of Alabama, B.S., 1985; Wichita State University, M.F.A., 1990.

*ADDRESSES: Home*—2822 Biltmore Ave., Montgomery, AL 36109. *Office*—Alabama Writers' Forum, Alabama State Council on the Arts, 201 Monroe St., Montgomery, AL 36130.

*CAREER:* Educator and fiction writer. Auburn University—Montgomery, Montgomery, AL, lecturer, 1991-92; Clemson University, Clemson, SC, instructor, 1992-96; Alabama State Council on the Arts Writers' Forum, Montgomery, teaching writer with "Writing Our Stories" project for juvenile offenders, 1997-2000, master teacher and assistant program director, 2000—. Huntingdon College, lecturer, 1991-92, 1999-2000; Auburn University—Montgomery, lecturer, 1997-99.

*AWARDS, HONORS:* Individual artist fellow in literature, Alabama State Council on the Arts, 1992-93; O. Henry Award, 1994; Andrew Lytle Prize, *Sewanee Review*, 1995; Theodore Christian Hoepfner Award, *Southern Humanities Review*, 2000.

*WRITINGS:*

(Editor, with Jeanie Thompson) *Open the Door: An Anthology of Poems and Stories from the "Writing Our Stories" Project*, Alabama Writers' Forum (Montgomery, AL), Volume 1, 1998, Volume 2, 1999, Volume 3, 2000, Volume 4, 2001.
*The Dry Well* (short stories), Frederic C. Beil (Savannah, GA), 2001.
*A Broken Thing* (novel), Frederic C. Beil (Savannah, GA), 2002.

Work represented in anthologies, including *Prize Stories, 1994: The O. Henry Awards*, Doubleday (New York, NY), 1994. Contributor of short stories to magazines, including *Apalachee Review, Virginia Quarterly Review, Sewanee Review, Southern Humanities Review, Alabama Literary Review, American Literary Review, Amaryllis, Shenandoah, Crescent Review*, and *South Carolina Review*.

*SIDELIGHTS:* Marlin Barton told *CA*: "It's difficult to say why I'm motivated to write fiction, but I think all of us have a desire to tell stories and to hear them. It's a very natural impulse, I think. We like to be entertained, and we're curious about other people's lives. For some reason, after I took a poetry-writing class as an undergraduate, I began to wonder if I could write a story. I'd always loved to read, and maybe once I discovered that I wasn't a poet, the impulse to write moved into the direction of fiction. Perhaps I wanted to see if I could create something that had some sense of shape and meaning. Maybe I wanted to see if I could write something similar to the stories I'd read in English classes and on my own. Stories, I think, help us to see who we are; they help us examine ourselves—our fears, longings, needs—and our world. Perhaps on some intuitive level I understood this and wanted to examine human nature more deeply.

"Other than such writers as Sherwood Anderson, William Faulkner, Flannery O'Connor, and Madison Jones, I think the biggest influence on my writing has been place. I'm originally from Montgomery, Alabama, but I grew up in rural Greene County in west central Alabama. At the time that I was growing up there it was the fifth poorest county in the nation, and I met a wide variety of people, many of whom I saw come in and out of my grandfather's country store. When I first moved there it was as if I had entered another world, one that was vastly different from the middle-class neighborhood I'd known in Montgomery. And, years later, when I began to write, I found myself drawn to characters and stories that were similar to the people I'd met and whose stories I'd listened to. I didn't consciously decide to write out of the place I was from—it happened naturally. Maybe the best way I can say it is that the place where I grew up gave me my stories."

\*    \*    \*

## BATTAGLIA, Pasqual
(Pat Battaglia)

*PERSONAL:* Born in Niagara Falls, NY. *Education:* University of Notre Dame, B.S., 1960; State University of New York at Buffalo, M.S., 1968.

*ADDRESSES: Office*—International Puzzle Features, 4507 Panther Place, Charlotte, NC 28269. *E-mail*—Author@CleverPuzzles.com.

*CAREER:* ISO9000 Documentation Service, Charlotte, NC, owner; industry documentation specialist, 1991—.

*MEMBER:* American Society for Quality.

*WRITINGS:*

*UNDER NAME PAT BATTAGLIA*

*If You're So Smart . . .*, Maralee Enterprises, 1976.
*So You Think You're Smart: 150 Fun and Challenging Brain Teasers,* TAB/McGraw-Hill, 1988.
*The Practical Guide for Marketing to Syndicates: Your Key to Unlocking Syndication Wealth,* Syndicate Publications, 1996.
*Self-Syndication: Is It for You? Everything You Wanted to Know about Self-Syndication but Didn't Know Who to Ask,* Syndicate Publications, 1996.
*Are You Smart, or What? A Bizarre Book of Games and Fun for Everyone,* International Puzzle Features, 2001.

Author of "If You're So Smart . . ." (syndicated newspaper column of international puzzle features), 1982-87, 1990—.

*WORK IN PROGRESS:* Developing clever word games/puzzles to continue book series.

*SIDELIGHTS:* Pasqual "Pat" Battaglia became a fan of collecting and solving puzzles early on. He began collecting puzzles that were especially clever and fun on and would share them with his friends, teasing them with hints until they found the correct answers. Eventually, he put together the book *If You're So Smart . . .*, containing his extra-special favorites, as a way to share the fun on a wider scale. His book simply increased his craving for more puzzles and not finding them, he began developing them himself.

Battaglia launched his "If You're So Smart . . ." newspaper puzzle column in 1982 and he continues it to this day. He creates word puzzles with surprising and sometimes even amusing answers. Spurred on by letters from column readers, he compiled a second book of unusual word games in 1988. Many people wrote to tell him that working on his games has made them alert. This led Battaglia to author his third book, *Are You Smart, or What?,* which contains still more fun and challenge from Battaglia.

**BATTAGLIA, Pat**
**See BATTAGLIA, Pasqual**

\*          \*          \*

**BATTLE-WALTERS, Kim(berly A.)**

*PERSONAL:* Born in Los Angeles, CA; daughter of Randall and Janet Walters. *Ethnicity:* "African American." *Education:* Southern California College, B.A., 1989; Temple University, M.S.W., 1991; University of Florida, Ph.D., 1997. *Politics:* Democrat. *Religion:* "Christian-Charismatic."

*ADDRESSES: Office*—Azusa Pacific University, 901 East Alosta Ave., Azusa, CA 91702. *E-mail*—kwalter@apu.edu.

*CAREER:* Ordained minister, United Church of the Living God, Los Angeles, CA. Azusa Pacific University, Azusa, CA, assistant professor of social work, 1997—. International missions work in Africa, Australia, Asia, Europe, and South, Central, and North America.

*MEMBER:* BPD, NCFR.

*AWARDS, HONORS:* Azuza Pacific University black faculty fellowship, 1994-97, and Provost Award, 1999-2000.

*WRITINGS:*

*Sheila's Shop: The Experiences and Realities of Working-class African-American Women,* Rowman & Littlefield (Totowa, NJ), 2000.

Contributor to *Family Relations Journal and Journal of Marriage and the Family;* contributor to *African-American Encyclopedia Supplement,* 1997.

*SIDELIGHTS:* Kim Battle-Walters told *CA:* "I have been writing since I was a little girl. I would give my handwritten books to my parents and they would always encourage me (even when it wasn't good). My writing interest areas are issues regarding race and ethnic relations, marriage and family, singleness, urban sociology, social work, and religious issues. I am inspired to write because of my faith in God."

\*     \*     \*

### BEATTY, William K(ave) 1926-2002

*OBITUARY NOTICE*—See index for *CA* sketch: Born February 5, 1926, in Toronto, Ontario, Canada; died of a heart attack December 9, 2002, in Evanston, IL. Historian, librarian, educator, and author. Beatty was an authority on the history of medicine. After serving in the 617th Field Artillery Observation Battalion in northern Italy during World War II, he attended Harvard University for three years and obtained his master's degree in library science from Columbia University in 1952. Beatty became interested in medical history while working as a circulation assistant and then assistant librarian at the College of Physicians of Philadelphia during the early 1950s. This led to his appointment as a professor of medical bibliography at the University of Missouri—Columbia, where he worked until 1962. He next moved to Northwestern University, where he was a librarian and taught medical history and bibliography until his retirement in 1994. He was the author of several medical history books with Geoffrey Marks, including *The Story of Medicine in America* (1973) and *Epidemics* (1976), and more recently published *Professional Reading for Library Staff Members in Hospital Libraries* (1980). Beatty was also a regular contributor to journals such as the *Journal of Medical Education* and was a consultant to *Stedman's Medical Dictionary.*

*OBITUARIES AND OTHER SOURCES:*

BOOKS

*Who's Who in America,* 56th edition, Marquis (New Providence, NJ), 2001.

PERIODICALS

*Chicago Tribune,* December 14, 2002, section 2, p. 11.

### BELLIN, Andy 1968(?)-

*PERSONAL:* Born c. 1968. *Education:* Attended Vassar College.

*ADDRESSES: Home*—New York, NY. *Office—The Paris Review,* 541 East 72nd St., New York, NY 10021.

*CAREER: Paris Review,* New York, NY, editor. Has worked as a professional poker player and journalist.

*WRITINGS:*

*Poker Nation: A High-Stakes, Low-Life Adventure into the Heart of a Gambling Country,* HarperCollins (New York, NY), 2002.

Author of articles for magazines, including *Esquire, Details, Maxim* and the *Atlantic.*

*WORK IN PROGRESS:* A book about horse racing for HarperCollins.

*SIDELIGHTS:* Andy Bellin is a former professional poker player and journalist whose book *Poker Nation: A High-Stakes, Low-Life Adventure into the Heart of a Gambling Country* explores those who inhabit the American subculture of gambling. Without sugarcoating the experience of living among the high rollers, *Poker Nation* is a "travelogue to the quirky world of competitive poker," wrote Karen Dukess in *USA Today,* "an exploration of poker obsession and addiction (not necessarily the same thing) and a primer on mathematics, poker lingo and technique." The book focuses on the characters who play the game, as well as on the game itself.

Bellin's career began early; he started playing poker as a child, using marshmallows as chips. In high school he played to show off among his peers and rebel against his father. In college he studied physics and mathematics, which further honed his card-playing skills, and quit graduate school in order to turn semipro. For several years he played poker six nights a week for hours at a time and augmented his income by working as a journalist during the day. It was a lifestyle that had a negative impact on his relationships with women, among other things, Bellin writes in *Poker Nation*, but after a while poker became more work than fun. He found a way to merge his careers by writing a book about poker, with the result being the critically acclaimed *Poker Nation*.

The game is much more than numbers and odds, Bellin explains in *Poker Nation*. Players must become memory experts and learn how to read unconscious signals—known as "tells"—given off by other players; they must know how to bluff, cheat, and strategize. Bellin relates humorous stories of those who never learn these lessons, like the friend who slapped him on the back when he was dealt a flush, and writes of the game's philosophy and the psychological toll it can take on those who devote their lives to it. "Texas Hold 'Em," a form of poker fast growing in popularity among medium-stakes players— those who buy into a game for less than $10,000—is especially attractive to Bellin, and its rules are featured in the chapter about Benny Binion, the Las Vegas casino owner who popularized tournament poker. "The most appealing passages revolve around the bad boy's tiny mistakes," wrote James McManus in the *New York Times Book Review,* "and colossal howlers at the table, which he constructively appraises instead of just licking his wounds."

*Poker Nation* grew out of an article Bellin wrote for *Esquire* magazine that traced his participation in poker from private poker clubs in New York to the World Series of poker in Las Vegas. Another chapter in the book was also published as an article in the *Atlantic*. "It's a winning read for poker experts and newcomers alike," observed a reviewer for *Publishers Weekly*. Other critics offered similar praise. Bellin represents the viewpoint of a "player madly devoted to the insidious card game," noted a *Kirkus Reviews* critic, "from the world of scarred and victorious veterans." Troy Patterson of *Entertainment Weekly* called *Poker Nation* "a first-person case study of a talented, masochistic, monomaniacal freak."

Since Bellin left the world of professional poker, he has become an editor with the *Paris Review* in New York, and plays only recreationally a couple times a week. He told Dukess, "I love playing poker again. It's pure pleasure." More specifically, Bellin told *Beatrice* writer Ron Hogan that poker is "the perfect combination of everything that I love: it's math, competition, money."

*BIOGRAPHICAL AND CRITICAL SOURCES:*

PERIODICALS

*Entertainment Weekly,* May 2, 2002, Troy Patterson, review of *Poker Nation: A High-Stakes, Low-Life Adventure into the Heart of a Gambling Country.*
*Kirkus Reviews,* February 1, 2002, review of *Poker Nation*, p. 172.
*Library Journal,* March 15, 2002, Harold D. Shane, review of *Poker Nation*, p. 86.
*New York Times Book Review,* April 7, 2002, James McManus, "All the Man's Kings," p. 27.
*Publishers Weekly,* February 25, 2002, review of *Poker Nation*, p. 53.
*USA Today,* March 12, 2002, Karen Dukess, "High-Stakes Gamble Pays Off."

OTHER

*Beatrice,* http://www.beatrice.com/ (May 2, 2002), interview with Ron Hogan.*

\* \* \*

## BERRIGAN, Philip (Francis) 1923-2002

*OBITUARY NOTICE*—See index for *CA* sketch: Born October 5, 1923, in Two Harbors, MN; died of cancer December 6, 2002, in Baltimore, MD. Priest, political activist, and author. Berrigan was a famous anti-war protestor who was especially prominent for his activities during the Vietnam War. As a young man, Berrigan was not the protester he was in later life; he served courageously in the U.S. Army infantry and artillery during World War II, but became disgusted by the carnage he witnessed. Returning home, he studied to become a priest and graduated from the College of the Holy Cross in 1950. Ordained as a priest in the Josephine order in 1955, he later went on to earn a B.S. from Loyola University in 1960 and a master's degree from Xavier University in 1963. Berrigan's first jobs included being an assistant pastor in Washington, D.C., in 1955 and working as a high school counselor in New Orleans from 1956 to 1963. It was while in New Orleans that he first became incensed by the racism he witnessed in the schools and communities; he began to view the U.S. government as an active agent of this racism, and he became involved in the civil rights movement. His radicalism grew in the 1960s while he was in New York City, first as director of promotion at St. Joseph's Society of the Sacred Heart and then as an English instructor at Epiphany College in Newburgh, New York. Berrigan witnessed further racial injustices while serving as curate of the St. Peter Claver Church in Baltimore, and his loud protestations against racism became so pronounced that Catholic Church officials told him to cease his troublemaking. Ignoring his superiors, Berrigan became more vocal in his stance against war during the late 1960s. In Baltimore he founded Peace Mission, an anti-war protest group, and in 1967 the group's actions became radicalized when they destroyed draft records at the Baltimore Customs House, for which action Berrigan was sentenced to six years in prison. Before he was sentenced, however, Berrigan and several other Peace Mission members, including his brother, the Reverend Daniel J. Berrigan, carried out another raid. They went to the draft board office in Catonsville, Maryland, and destroyed more draft records, an act that became the subject of a 2001 film. The Catonsville raid inspired Vietnam War protests around the country. Berrigan was put on trial, and, after a lengthy appeal process, sentenced to jail in 1970. He and his brother escaped authorities before actually being put in custody, and were briefly on the F.B.I.'s Most Wanted list before being captured. Berrigan did not mind being imprisoned; in fact, he considered it an honor to be jailed for his beliefs. He got into more hot water in 1972 for writing letters in which he outlined his plans to kidnap government officials—specifically, Henry Kissinger—and sabotage government buildings. The letters were intercepted by an F.B.I. agent. However, a trial in which Berrigan was accused of conspiracy ended in a hung jury. After serving his sentence, Berrigan—who was excommunicated in 1973 after announcing publicly that he had married nun Elizabeth McAlister in 1970—earned his living by giving lectures, painting houses, and writing. He also opened Baltimore's Jonah House, a commune and meeting place for anti-war activists, with his wife. Berrigan continued to mount protests through the rest of his life, including a raid in 1980 on a General Electric plant, but his activities would never again draw as much attention as they did during the Vietnam era. He was the author of several books, including *Prison Journals of a Priest Revolutionary* (1970), *Of Beasts and Beastly Images: Essays under the Bomb* (1978), *Whereupon to Stand: The Acts of the Apostles and Ourselves* (1993), and, with his wife, *The Time's Discipline: The Beatitudes and Nuclear Resistance* (1993).

*OBITUARIES AND OTHER SOURCES:*

BOOKS

*Contemporary Heroes and Heroines,* Gale (Detroit, MI), 1990.
Kohn, George Childs, editor, *The New Encyclopedia of American Scandal,* Checkmark Books (New York, NY), 2001.
*Religious Leaders of America,* Gale (Detroit, MI), 1991.
Toropov, Brandon, *Encyclopedia of Cold War Politics,* Facts on File (New York, NY), 2000.

PERIODICALS

*Chicago Tribune,* December 8, 2002, section 4, p. 11.
*Los Angeles Times,* December 7, 2002, p. B23.
*New York Times,* December 8, 2002, p. A36.
*Times* (London, England), December 9, 2002, p. 8.
*Washington Post,* December 8, 2002, p. C11.

*       *       *

**BISS, Eula 1977-**

*PERSONAL:* Born August 9, 1977, in Rochester, NY; daughter of Roger (a doctor) and Ellen (an artist; maiden name, Graf) Biss. *Education:* Hampshire College, B.A., 1999. *Politics:* "Radical."

*ADDRESSES: Home*—322 East 11th St., No. 8, New York, NY 10003. *E-mail*—eularuth@hotmail.com or eulabiss@yahoo.com.

*CAREER:* DreamYard Project, New York, NY, teacher, 2000-02; writer, 2002—. V-Day Youth Initiative, teacher, 2001-02. Gives readings of her works throughout the northeastern United States.

*WRITINGS:*

*The Balloonists* (prose), Hanging Loose Press, 2002.

Contributor of poetry and essays to periodicals, including *Both, Massachusetts Review, Rattapallax, Hanging Loose,* and *Race Traitor.*

*WORK IN PROGRESS: How to Love a Bicycle* (tentative title), a collection of personal essays; research on revolutionary or unusual marriages, with a book expected to result.

*SIDELIGHTS:* Eula Biss told *CA:* "On my twentieth birthday I wrote a list of things to do that year. The first was: learn how to talk. I sat in silence under a flickering lightbulb before going out in the boat with my father, where we sat in silence. On my twenty-first birthday I wrote another list that also began with: learn how to talk. I recognized that my silence was a liability. I was perceived to be meek, weak, and willing. My answer was to write. By my twenty-second birthday I had written my first book and had, to some extent, learned how to talk.

"I am often praised for the distinct 'voice' in my writing. My writing has voice simply because it is my voice. The fact that my writing is an essential act of communication has determined how I write. I cannot afford to be impenetrable and obtuse. It is as dangerous and isolating for me to be inaccessible as a writer as it is for me to be silent as a young woman.

"I write primarily in the overlapping genres of prose poetry and creative nonfiction. My interest in prose poetry is due to its potential to be more accessible than poetry. Prose, no matter how blurred its genre, is intrinsically easier to read than verse. We learn to read by reading prose. It is the beautifully mundane form of instructions, letters, and textbooks.

"I assimilate the everyday life of prose into my writing. In one essay that incorporates personal ads from the newspaper, my desire is to frame familiar prose in a new context. In the same essay I work to frame a familiar detail of life—the romantic relationship—in a new context. In both form and content, I want to borrow from the everyday, the banal elements of life, and display them in a new light.

"I want, more than anything, to tell new stories. And I want to tell these stories with nonfiction because the allure of a 'true' story is specifically that it is possible. I believe that one way to change the way people live is to illustrate what is possible.

"I write both for and about life. My writing is not auxiliary to my own life. Like my voice, it is integral."

\*     \*     \*

**BLAESER, Kimberly M. 1955-**

*PERSONAL:* Born 1955, in Billings, MT; daughter of Anthony Peter and Marlene Dawn (Antell) Blaeser; married Leonard Joseph Wardzala, August 17, 1985; children: Gavin Leonard. *Education:* College of St. Benedict, B.A., 1977; Notre Dame University, M.A., 1982, Ph.D., 1990.

*ADDRESSES: Home*—2431 Partridge Woods Court, Burlington, WI 53105-9098. *Office*—Curtin Hall 572, University of Wisconsin, Milwaukee, Department of English, P.O. Box 413, Milwaukee, WI 53201-0413. *E-mail*—kblaeser@uwm.edu.

*CAREER:* Thief River Falls (MN) *Times,* reporter and photographer, 1977-79; University of Notre Dame, teaching fellow, 1981-84, information systems staff, 1983; *Daily Courier News,* Elgin, IL, reporter, 1986-87; University of Wisconsin, Milwaukee, professor of English and comparative literature, 1987—.

*MEMBER:* Native American Literary Prize Commission (1988-91), Native American International Prize in Literature (member of governing board, 1991-94), Indian Relief, Inc (board of directors, 1983-84), American Studies Association, Modern Language Association, Association of Studies in American Indian Literature.

*AWARDS, HONORS:* North American Native Authors First Book Award and Diane Decorah First Book Award for Poetry, 1993, for *Trailing You;* Francis C. Allen fellowship, Darcy McNickle Center for the History of the American Indian, the Newbery Library, 1985; fellowship from the Center for Twentieth Century Studies, University of Wisconsin, Milwaukee, 1993-94; research award from Institute on Race and Ethnicity, University of Wisconsin, 1992, George Miller American Indian Scholar, Squaw Valley Community of Writers, 1994; Wordcraft Circle Storyteller of the Year Award, 1999.

*WRITINGS:*

*Trailing You: Poems,* Greenfield Review Press
     (Greenfield Center, NY), 1994.
*Gerald Vizenor: Writing in the Oral Tradition,*
     University of Oklahoma Press (Norman, OK),
     1996.
*Stories Migrating Home: A Collection of Anishinabe
     Prose,* Loonfeather Press, 1999.
*Absentee Indians And Other Poems,* Michigan State
     University Press (East Lansing, MI), 2002.

*SIDELIGHTS:* Born in Billings, Montana, and raised
on the Chippewa White Earth Reservation in northern
Minnesota, Kimberly Blaeser is a woman of mixed
Anishinabe and German heritage who writes about
what life is like as a Native American in contemporary
times. She does this, through her poetry, essays, short
fiction, journalism, and scholarly articles. As stated at
the Web site *Voices from the Gaps,* she does this by
uniting "the stranger with the relative, the far-away
with the near, the dream with the direction." By
superimposing varied and oppositional elements, she
examines how differences are merged. She accomplishes this by focusing on the little things that occur
every day, thus expressing, through her writing, a
celebration of "life's common moments."

Although she writes in many different genres, Blaeser
is most noted for two books, *Trailing You,* an award-
winning 1994 collection of poems, and her critical
study of fellow White Earth author Gerald Vizenor,
*Gerald Vizenor, Writing in the Oral Tradition,* who
was one of the most prolific Native American writers
of the twentieth century.

In her poetry collection *Trailing You,* as stated in a
*Publishers Weekly* review, her writing is "informed by
the natural world." However, Blaeser does not only
focus on nature. Although she is very well aware of
her natural surroundings, *Library Journal* reviewer
Louis McKee stated, "she acknowledges more openly
the outside world, full of its own ritual and tradition."
In other words, she is informed not only about nature
or the wilderness, but about city life as well. She
knows as much about the complexities and challenges
of living in an urban setting as she does about living
in the country and on the reservation. She also
recognizes the dichotomy present in the general

struggle to maintain a relationship with her Native
culture while attempting to build bridges to that
outside, urban, white society. She often does this by
creating images that help her explore her ambivalent
emotions, such as her description of her jewelry. She
writes, for instance, that on one arm, she wears the
traditional Native jewelry of turquoise and silver;
while on the other arm, she wears traditional European
jewelry—diamonds and gold and a brand-name watch.
Thus, she becomes a living metaphor for the different
cultural forces that often pull in opposite directions.

McKee further described Blaeser's wide-angled view
of the world as both Native and American by stating:
"Blaeser's place includes the rivers and trees and
wondrous wildlife but also Barbie dolls, the 4-H, and
awareness of the bomb." McKee recommended
Blaeser's poetry as one way to better understand the
lives of Native Americans and to dispel "the myths"
that many non-Native people continue to hold about
them. Blaeser has received several literary awards for
*Trailing You* as well as critical acclaim, such as from
Charles G. Ballard, writing for *American Indian
Culture and Research Journal,* who stated, "The
overall impression is that the mainstream society has
passed her by, which, of course, may be a point in her
favor. Certainly she is pleasant company, and I, for
one, enjoy seeing a few out-of-the-way places through
her eyes."

During her doctoral studies at the University of
Wisconsin, Milwaukee, Blaeser analyzed Gerald
Vizenor's extensive body of work. *Gerald Vizenor:
Writing in the Oral Tradition* was praised by critic
Linda Rouse, writing for *MELUS,* as a "valuable
study." Rouse found that Blaeser's "careful research
connects the threads of the oral tradition that run
throughout Vizenor's writing and illuminates Vizenor's
aspirations for and practical uses of the written word.
Most importantly, Blaeser underscores the 'challenge
of Vizenor's writing' as 'he offers new ways to think
about reading, writing, speaking, and being.'"

Baleser's second book contains detailed analyses of
Vizenor's work as well as informative material that
she gathered from personal interviews with Vizenor,
which offer insights into the author's writing. "Blaeser
does an excellent job of showing the development of
Vizenor," wrote reviewer B. Hans for *Choice;* and
Robert Allen Warrior, a critic for *World Literature
Today,* found Blaeser's book to be a "well-executed,

deeply learned introduction to the Anishinaabe writer's complex oeuvre."

Vizenor is noted for his fiction, nonfiction, screenplays, and poetry, which includes poems influenced by the Japanese haiku. His writing spans more than thirty years, and Warrior praised Blaeser's ability to find an overall theme in Vizenor's extensive work. Warrior wrote: "What Blaeser finds as she reads across three decades of Vizenor's work is a consistent commitment to overturning entrenched images of Native people."

Because Vizenor's work is mostly experimental, critic James A. Gray, writing for *Contemporary Literature,* recommended that readers of Vizenor's works "might benefit from an orientation to what is going on, and for that purpose Blaeser's book is an indispensable and long-needed source." Vizenor, despite his prolific writing, does not enjoy a wide readership due in part to his "self-conscious intellectualism," Gray wrote, "and in part because of his willingness to upset complacencies of both white liberals and Indian activists." Blaeser helps to illuminate Vizenor's writing, analyzing some of his ambiguities as well as examining some of his metaphors. Gray continued, "[Blaeser] turns her attention most fully to the particular 'strategies of a revolutionary style' that Vizenor uses to 'reanimate' tradition and to pull his readers toward active participation in completing the meaning of the text." Blaeser has written, according to Gray, "by far the most complete study to date of the most challengingly experimental and perhaps most influential of today's leading American Indian writers."

*BIOGRAPHICAL AND CRITICAL SOURCES:*

*PERIODICALS*

*American Indian Culture and Research Journal,* 1995, Charles G. Ballard, review of *Trailing You,* pp. 305-307.
*Choice,* January, 1997, B. Hans, review of *Gerald Vizenor: Writing in the Oral Tradition,* p. 791.
*Contemporary Literature,* spring, 1998, James A. Gray, review of *Gerald Vizenor: Writing in the Oral Tradition,* pp. 146-154.
*Library Journal,* March 15, 1995, Louis McKee, review of *Trailing You,* p. 73.

*Melus,* summer, 1999, Linda Rouse, review of *Gerald Vizenor: Writing in the Oral Tradition,* p. 198.
*World Literature Today,* winter, 1998, Robert Allen Warrior, review of *Gerald Vizenor: Writing in the Oral Tradition,* p. 181.

*OTHER*

*Voices from the Gaps,* http://voices.cla.umn.edu/ (April 7, 2002), "Kimberly M. Blaeser."*

\*　　　\*　　　\*

**BLAIR, Toni**
　　**See BLAKE, Toni**

\*　　　\*　　　\*

**BLAKE, Toni 1965-**
　　**(Toni Blair)**

*PERSONAL:* Born October 16, 1965, in Covington, KY; daughter of Talc (a construction worker) and Rita (a homemaker; maiden name, Blevins) Brewsaugh; married September 23, 1989; husband, a computer programmer. *Ethnicity:* "White." *Education:* Attended Northern Kentucky University, 1983-84. *Hobbies and other interests:* Genealogy, "scrapbooking", cross-stitch embroidery, snow skiing.

*ADDRESSES: Home*—P.O. Box 17835, Covington, KY 41017. *Agent*—Deidre Knight, Knight Agency, P.O. Box 550648, Atlanta, GA 30355. *E-mail*—toni@ toniblake.com.

*CAREER:* Novelist.

*MEMBER:* Romance Writers of America.

*AWARDS, HONORS:* Fellowship for Kentucky women writers, Kentucky Foundation for Women, 1996.

*WRITINGS:*

*ROMANCE NOVELS*

*The Cinderella Scheme,* Kensington (San Diego, CA), 1998.
*Baby Love,* Kensington (San Diego, CA), 1998.

*October Moon,* Kensington (San Diego, CA), 1998.
*Hotbed Honey,* Harlequin (New York, NY), 2000.
*Seducing Summer,* Harlequin (New York, NY), 2001.
*Something Wild,* Harlequin (New York, NY), 2002.
*Mad about Mindy . . . and Mandy,* Harlequin (New York, NY), 2003.

OTHER

Contributor of short stories to periodicals. Some writings appear under the pseudonym Toni Blair.

*SIDELIGHTS:* Toni Blake told *CA:* "I have been writing since my childhood, but it was only around 1992 or 1993 that I began seriously to pursue publication. I originally intended to write literary fiction and succeeded in having several short stories published in literary journals, one of which garnered a nomination for the Pushcart Prize.

"Around 1995 I changed directions and began targeting the romance industry. I hadn't read a romance in many years. A friend and fellow writer shoved a couple of romance novels into my hand, and I was amazed to discover how smart, funny, and compelling they were. After reading them, I knew this was a genre I wanted to be a part of. Like every other market, competition is stiff when breaking into romance, but three years later I made my first sale and was lucky enough to have three books out in 1998.

"For me, writing romance is about giving women heroines they can relate to and heroes they can fall in love with—stories that take them away from their everyday troubles. I write sexy stories with a touch of humor, and I hope that if there is a message in my work, it is to encourage women to embrace their sensuality, to make women understand that you can be smart, capable, responsible, funny, and sexy—all at the same time."

\*    \*    \*

**BLAKELY, Gloria 1950-**
**(Glori Ann)**

*PERSONAL:* Born 1950, in PA; daughter of Andrew and Mildred Blakely. *Ethnicity:* "African American." *Education:* Howard University, B.S. (psychology; with honors), 1972; George Washington University, graduate study. *Hobbies and other interests:* Reading, scuba diving, white-water rafting, traveling, history.

*ADDRESSES: Agent*—c/o Author Mail, Chelsea House, 1974 Sproul Road, Suite 400, Broomall, PA 19008. *E-mail*—blake100@voicenet.com.

*CAREER:* Executive in corporate brand management, including posts at CIGNA Insurance Company and General Mills, 1976-98; freelance author and journalist, 1998—; consultant, 1999—; copywriter and copyeditor, 2000.

*MEMBER:* Philadelphia Association of Black Journalists, Greater Philadelphia Chamber of Commerce.

*AWARDS, HONORS:* Black Achievers Award, Black Achievers Association, 1982.

*WRITINGS:*

*Black Americans of Achievement: Danny Glover,* Chelsea House (Philadelphia, PA), 2002.

Contributor to *Profiles of Great African Americans* and *African-American Perpetual Calendar,* Publications International (Lincolnwood, IL), 2002. Contributor, sometimes under pseudonym Glori Ann, to numerous periodicals, including *Benefits Quarterly, Philadelphia Sunday Sun, Philadelphia Tribune, Pathfinders Travel,* and *Upscale.*

*WORK IN PROGRESS:* (Under pseudonym Glori Ann) *An African Safari for Jarvis; Getting a Clue: Centenarian Chronicles,* an anthology of life lessons related to centenarians; *I Am a People: The Keepers of Our Story,* a documentary.

*SIDELIGHTS:* Gloria Blakely told *CA:* "My path to literary expertise has been unconventional. I became hooked on writing while volunteering African-American history briefs to an employee newsletter during my last year at CIGNA Insurance Company. I then left a twenty-five-year commitment to brand management in corporate America for a career in literature. Starting with contributions to *Pathfinders*

*Travel* magazine, I have augmented my travel summaries with articles on topics as varied as history, entertainment, health, beauty, technology, architecture, politics, and business. Some were published in *Essence, Heart and Soul, Upscale,* and *Black Diaspora* magazines, but most were seen in the *Philadelphia Sun* newspaper. Additional articles appeared in the *Philadelphia Tribune,* as well as in local newspapers in Orlando and Los Angeles, including a series on African-American contributions to the twentieth century.

"I have written a yet-to-be produced documentary, *I Am a People: The Keepers of Our Story,* a study inspired by the exploding number of African-American historic sites and stories about slavery that their keepers preserve. My first book was completed in 2001, a work-for-hire biography of Danny Glover for Chelsea House written in order to provide a positive role model for teens. I continue making inroads into the book marketing by contributing historical tidbits and profiles respectively to a perpetual calendar and an updated book on great African Americans. I have also extensively edited an autobiography of a Philadelphia independent filmmaker and completed writing a children's book. Altogether, my published works total one hundred and counting."

*       *       *

## BLAUNER, Bob 1929-

*PERSONAL:* Born May 18, 1929, in Chicago, IL; son of Samuel (a lawyer and poet) and Esther (a librarian; maiden name, Shapiro) Blauner; married, 1962; wife's name, Rena K. (marriage ended, 1980); married Karina Epperlein (a filmmaker), July 12, 1992; children: Marya Blauner Jensen, Jon. *Ethnicity:* "Jewish." *Education:* University of Chicago, A.B., 1948, M.A., 1950; University of California, Ph.D., 1962. *Politics:* "Independent, left-liberal anarchist." *Hobbies and other interests:* Chess, the Oakland A's baseball team, men's groups.

*ADDRESSES: Home*—641 Euclid Ave., Berkeley, CA 94708. *Office*—c/o Department of Sociology, University of California—Berkeley, Berkeley, CA 94720-1980; fax: 510-527-8650. *Agent*—Andrew Blauner, Blauner Books, 12 East 86th St., Suite 633, New York, NY 10028. *E-mail*—kebb@uclink4.berkeley.edu.

*CAREER:* San Francisco State College (now University), San Francisco, CA, assistant professor of sociology, 1961-62; University of Chicago, Chicago, IL, assistant professor of sociology, 1962-63; University of California—Berkeley, assistant professor, 1963-67, associate professor, 1967-78, professor of sociology, 1978-93, professor emeritus, 1993—. Consultant to poverty programs c. 1960s and 1970s.

*WRITINGS:*

*Alienation and Freedom: The Factory Worker and His Industry,* University of Chicago Press (Chicago, IL), 1964.
*Racial Oppression in America,* Harper & Row (New York, NY), 1972.
*Black Lives, White Lives: Three Decades of Race in America* (oral history), University of California Press (Berkeley, CA), 1989.
*Our Mothers' Spirits: On the Death of Mothers and the Grief of Men* (memoir), HarperCollins (New York, NY), 1997.
*Still the Big News: Racial Oppression in America,* Temple University Press (Philadelphia, PA), 2001.

Contributor to periodicals, including *Psychiatry.*

*WORK IN PROGRESS: Good Days, Bad Days: A Memoir of Anxiety and Depression;* a book of poetry; research for *Claudia,* an oral history of a twenty-first-century immigrant cleaning woman from Brazil; research for *Friday Night Chess: Why Your Average Club Player Is in Love with a Game,* a collection of interviews.

*SIDELIGHTS:* Bob Blauner told *CA:* "Writing is my creative expression, my art form. Since I learned the craft at thirteen as a sports writer for my high school paper, I've loved to write. Often I've regretted not getting an M.A. in journalism and going into newspaper work. My thirty-five-plus years in sociology and the academic world was frustrating because the demands of teaching left me too little time to write, and I always thought that academic writing, especially in the social sciences (history may be an exception) was not 'real writing.'

"To retire at sixty-four in 1993 was a liberation. Since then I've written every day, first thing in the morning, until two cups of tea before breakfast make me sluggish (usually no more than two hours). I always have from two to four writing projects going, and my unpublished manuscripts have piled up over the years, in part because I'm (too much of) a perfectionist. But I'm not discouraged and, although I'm still hoping for fame and fortune, it's the process itself that drives me—the satisfaction in the work—a good sentence, a completed chapter. During those weeks when I'm reading and not writing, I feel restless, and I hope to write every day until I die.

"A few months ago I began writing poetry seriously and think I'm getting good at it. Poetry is something I drew back from trying all my life, despite a lifetime of reading and loving it. Why? My father and older sister are both poets.

"I write with a pen on yellow, lined pads. Only when I have a chapter drafted do I go to the computer. The computer is for storage, for printing out a first draft and then making corrections to it. I will never do fresh creative writing on my computer, except letters of recommendation for students and certain memoranda. For me creativity comes out of the organic connection between mind, hand, pen, and paper. Years ago I seemed to be able to write well on my old Royal Standard, but typewriters have souls, computers don't. I also used to write with an actual fountain pen, but I found I was always spilling ink on desk, hands, and clothes.

"The subjects I've written on all come out of my life history, and this I know is true for everyone, even the most 'scientific' scholars. I wrote on factory workers and their work because I spent five years in factories as a communist in my twenties. I've written three books on race in America because the issue of racial justice has spoken to me since I was seventeen, perhaps even earlier. I wrote a 'seminal' article on death because I had suffered from death anxiety at age thirty-two, which was really fear about losing my father. I edited a book about the death of mothers because I wrote a great piece about my own mother three years after she died, and no one would publish it; I also taught a course on men's lives for twenty years and found *all* the focus was on sons and fathers, nothing on mothers!

"I've been writing a memoir about depression for years now, trying to get it right. Because I suffered from it for almost two years, I hope I have something to add

to the fine books on male depression by Styron, Terrence Real, and Andrew Solomon. I'm also writing a book about our cleaning woman, because she thinks she has a uniquely interesting life (she does) and because it's a challenge. I want to write a book on why my co-players at the Berkeley Chess Club are fascinated by the game because I love chess, and all the books have been written by 'the greats,' not 'the ordinaries.'"

*BIOGRAPHICAL AND CRITICAL SOURCES:*

*PERIODICALS*

*American Visions,* August, 1989, review of *Black Lives, White Lives: Three Decades of Race Relations in America,* p. 41.

*British Journal of Sociology,* December, 1990, Michael Banton, review of *Black Lives, White Lives,* p. 577.

*California Lawyer,* September, 1989, Beret E. Strong, review of *Black Lives, White Lives,* p. 98.

*Contemporary Sociology,* July, 1990, Walter R. Allen, review of *Black Lives, White Lives,* p. 524.

*Entertainment Weekly,* November 21, 1997, review of *Our Mothers' Spirits: On the Death of Mothers and the Grief of Men,* p. 120.

*Ethnic and Racial Studies,* January, 1990, Ken Plummer, review of *Black Lives, White Lives,* p. 125.

*Journal of American Ethnic History,* winter, 1992, Jack Bloom, review of *Black Lives, White Lives,* p. 86.

*Journal of Southern History,* November, 1990, Linda Reed, review of *Black Lives, White Lives,* p. 784.

*Library Journal,* March 15, 1989, Suzanne W. Wood, review of *Black Lives, White Lives,* p. 79.

*National Black Law Journal,* winter, 1993, Cranston Williams, review of *Black Lives, White Lives,* pp. 255-258.

*Oral History Review,* fall, 1990, Cary D. Wintz, review of *Black Lives, White Lives,* p. 160.

*Publishers Weekly,* March 10, 1989, review of *Black Lives, White Lives,* p. 68.

*Review of Black Political Economy,* fall, 1990, Harold E. Cheatham, review of *Black Lives, White Lives,* p. 75.

*Social Forces,* March, 1990, Charles Jaret, review of *Black Lives, White Lives,* p. 997.

*Social Service Review,* March, 2002, review of *Still the Big News: Racial Oppression in America,* p. 198.

## BLISS, Edward, Jr. 1912-2002

*OBITUARY NOTICE*—See index for *CA* sketch: Born July 30, 1912, in Foochow, China; died of respiratory failure November 25, 2002, in Washington, DC. Journalist, educator, and author. Bliss was a television writer, producer, and editor who worked with such famous broadcasters as Edward R. Murrow and Walter Cronkite. Born in China as the son of a missionary—about whom he would later write in his 2001 book *Beyond the Stone Arches: An American Missionary Doctor in China, 1892-1932*—Bliss first intended to become a doctor like his father, but switched to journalism while studying at Yale University, graduating in 1935. From 1935 to 1943 he worked as a newspaper reporter in Ohio before being hired by the Columbia Broadcasting System (CBS) as a reporter, writer, and editor. He remained with CBS until 1968, working on such programs as *CBS Reports* and *CBS News with Walter Cronkite* before joining the faculty at American University as a journalism professor. He founded the university's School of Communications, teaching there until his retirement in 1977. Bliss then spent the remainder of his career as a consultant to various broadcasting companies in the United States and Canada, retiring in 1997. For his television work he was awarded the Paul White Award from the Radio-Television News Directors Association in 1993. Among his publications are *In Search of Light: The Broadcasts of Edward R. Murrow, 1938-1960* (1967), which he edited, and the books *Writing News for Broadcast* (1971), written with John M. Patterson, and *Now the News: The Story of Broadcast Journalism* (1991). At the time of his death Bliss had just completed a book about his wife's struggle with Alzheimer's disease, that was scheduled to be published in 2003. Among his other accomplishments, Bliss successfully worked to have the image of Murrow placed on a U.S. postage stamp.

*OBITUARIES AND OTHER SOURCES:*

BOOKS

Murray, Michael D., editor, *Encyclopedia of Television News,* Oryx Press (Phoenix, AZ), 1999.

PERIODICALS

*Chicago Tribune,* November 29, 2002, section 3, p. 7.
*New York Times,* November 28, 2002, p. C11.
*Times* (London, England), December 11, 2002.
*Washington Post,* November 28, 2002, p. B6.

*       *       *

## BLOMAIN, Karen 1944-

*PERSONAL:* Born March 26, 1944, in Scranton, PA; daughter of Thomas K. (an insurance executive) and Lucille (a singer; maiden name, Watkins) Blomain; married (divorced); married Michael Downend (a writer), January 4, 1992; children: (first marriage) James T. McHale III, Karen Kielty Turner, D. Brett McHale. *Education:* Marywood College, B.A., 1975; University of Scranton, M.A. (English), 1978; Columbia University, M.F.A. (creative writing), 1987.

*ADDRESSES: Home*—Village of the Four Seasons, R. R. #2, Box 3352, Uniondale, PA 18470. *Office*—Department of English, Kutztown University, Lytle Hall, Kutztown, PA 19530. *Agent*—Lisa Bankoff, ICM, 40 West 57th St., New York, NY 10019. *E-mail*—lefloog@aol.com.

*CAREER:* Educator and poet. Kutztown University, Kutztown PA, professor of English and professional writing, 1992.

*WRITINGS:*

POETRY, UNLESS OTHERWISE NOTED

*Black Diamond,* Foothills Publishing, 1988.
*The Slap,* Nightshade Press, 1990.
*Borrowed Light,* Nightshade Press, 1992.
(Editor) *Coalseam: Poems from the Anthracite Region,* University of Scranton Press (Scranton, PA), 1996.
*Normal Ave.,* Nightshade Press, 1998.
*A Trick of Light* (novel), Toby Press, 2001.

*SIDELIGHTS:* Karen Blomain told *CA:* "For me, writing is an act of uncovering what was there all along. My poems tend toward the narrative, the accessible, focusing on the emotional truth of a particular experience. I write about ordinary people who find themselves in extraordinary situations. I'm interested in setting events in motion and finding out what happens. Most of my fiction and poems have a strongly developed setting. When I write fiction my characters live with me for a time before I begin to tell their stories. I get to know them, to develop a kind of sympathy for their lives and their efforts. I see them struggling with problems of moral dimension. I cheer for them, but don't make them behave in any particular way. By the time I finish writing a book, the world of those events, that time and place, have become my own. I hope to transmit that same feeling to my readers. I enjoy reading and talking about my work and about writing in general. In addition to my teaching, I conduct workshops and seminars on the writing process and journal writing."

*       *       *

## BLUM, Louise A(gnes) 1960-

*PERSONAL:* Born 1960; married Connie Sullivan; children: Zoë. *Education:* Graduate of Iowa Writer's Workshop.

*ADDRESSES: Office*—Mansfield University, Department of English, Mansfield, PA 16933. *E-mail*—lblum@mnsfld.edu.

*CAREER:* Worked as an inmate advocate and community organizer in low-income neighborhoods in Columbus, OH, Pittsburgh, PA, and Atlanta, GA, 1982-85; University of Iowa, Iowa City, teaching assistant and instructor of creative writing, 1987-88; University of Nebraska, Lincoln, assistant professor of creative writing, 1988-89; Mansfield University, Mansfield, PA, associate professor of English, 1989—.

*AWARDS, HONORS:* Best Lesbian Fiction finalist, Lambda Literary Award, 1996, for *Amnesty;* Nonfiction Honor Book, American Library Association GLBT Round Table, 2002, for *You're Not from around Here, Are You?*

*WRITINGS:*

*Amnesty* (novel), Alyson (Boston, MA), 1995.
*You're Not From Around Here, Are You?: A Lesbian in Small-Town America* (autobiography), University of Wisconsin Press (Madison, WI), 2000.

Also author of *Good Girls,* 1993. Contributor of short stories and poems to numerous journals and anthologies.

*SIDELIGHTS:* Louise Blum writes what she knows. A lesbian who has gotten married, had a baby, and is raising a family in rural America, she has a life perspective that deviates from what society considers the norm. And her writing reflects that perspective. While the short story "Good Girls" explores life "in the closet" in God's country, her memoir *You're Not from around Here, Are You?: A Lesbian in Small-Town America* is a portrait of a more mature woman, one who has come out to the world and proclaimed her lesbianism. Blum paints a picture for the reader that chronicles her life as she lives it on a daily basis. The reader experiences Blum's wedding to her wife Connie, her pregnancy and ultimate delivery of a healthy daughter, and her attempt to gain tenure at Mansfield University, where Blum is an associate professor.

Her life is much like anyone else's in its daily struggles and triumphs, but with a twist. We see small-town America's prejudices and intolerances through the eyes of Blum, whose comedic retelling of her community's response to her and Connie's relationship doesn't overlook the sadness of it all. Blum and her family encounter obscene phone calls, vandalism of their home, and insensitive comments from neighbors. Their mere existence is the catalyst for the formation of a local chapter of the Christian Coalition.

Because of its detailed exploration of conception, pregnancy, and birth, *You're Not from around here, Are You?* has been recommended to any lesbian considering birthing a baby. *Curve* reviewer Rachel Pepper wrote that "this is a very honest book, and readers will come to know Blum and her partner very well by book's end. . . . I hope Blum's account leads to other first-person narratives about the honest hardships and joys of becoming a lesbian mother." Julia Willis, reviewer for the *Lambda Book Report,* praised the book as well. "Now I will say in letters writ large that Louise is a very fine and often funny writer. . . . She excels in scenes of comic relief." The critic added: "I marvel (and grudgingly admire) how Louise can subject herself and her family to the everyday off-the-cuff bigoted remarks against all minorities while appreciating her little town's charm."

*You're Not From Around Here, Are You?* was included in the University of Wisconsin Press's series "Living Out: Gay and Lesbian Autobiography". The press was honored with the Lambda Literature Foundation's 2002 Publisher's Service Award, given to recognize organizations that have done exemplary work in the field of gay, lesbian, bisexual, and transgendered literature. The book itself was also a Lambda Literary Award finalist.

Blum's first novel, *Amnesty,* is about a young girl named Maura Jaeger. When Maura is ten, her older brother escapes the draft for the Viet Nam War by fleeing to Canada. Her father's wrath reflects the family's shame, and Maura is transformed from a golden child into a rebellious student. She eventually seeks refuge in drugs and a lesbian affair. The next decade finds Maura estranged from her parents, until her father's death brings both her and her brother home.

Gale Harris praised the book's "lyricism," and added in *Belles Lettres* that "Blum's first novel heralds an emerging and already formidable talent." A *Publishers Weekly* critic, however, called the work "uneven" and commented that it "fails to achieve its potential but is distinguished by a stylistic fierceness that commands attention. . . . After setting up a classic family confrontation through a wealth of background and impassioned writing, Blum winds up showing us not much more than emotionally wounded people whom time has done little to change or heal." *Lambda Book Report* reviewer Charlotte Innes similarly remarked that "the major flaw in this tightly written (if occasionally clichéd) exploration of 'the kingdom of the fathers' is that the father himself is one-dimensional. . . . I wish Blum had made us (and her heroine) struggle more." Nevertheless, the critic concluded, Blum "has written a powerful story, with many moments of insight, even humor, on the private origins of the patriarch."

*BIOGRAPHICAL AND CRITICAL SOURCES:*

PERIODICALS

*Belles Lettres,* January, 1996, Gale Harris, review of *Amnesty,* pp. 2-3.
*Booklist,* April 1, 1995, Whitney Scott, review of *Amnesty,* p. 1377.
*Curve,* May, 2001, Rachel Pepper, "Baby Dykes to Baby's Mamas," p. 42.
*Lambda Book Report,* May-June, 1995, Charlotte Innes, review of *Amnesty,* pp. 17-18; May, 2001, Julia Willis, "The Dykes Next Door," p. 29.
*Library Journal,* April 15, 1995, Lisa Nussbaum, review of *Amnesty,* p. 111; May 1, 2001, Ina Rimpau, review of *You're Not from around Here, Are You?: A Lesbian in Small-Town America,* p. 115.
*Publishers Weekly,* March 13, 1995, review of *Amnesty,* p. 60; February 26, 2001, review of *You're Not from around Here, Are You?,* p. 67.

OTHER

*Wisconsin Press Web site,* http://www.wisc.edu/ wisconsinpress/ (October 1, 2002), "Living out: Gay and Lesbian Autobiography."*

\*      \*      \*

**BORMAN, Fred**
**See MOSELEY, James W(illett)**

\*      \*      \*

**BOSTROM, Kathleen (Susan) Long 1954-**

*PERSONAL:* Born November 1, 1954, in Los Angeles, CA; daughter of Myron C. (an aeronautical engineer) and Mary Virginia (a homemaker; maiden name, Anderson) Long; married Greg Richard Bostrom (a minister), June 27, 1981; children: Christopher Richard, Amy Kathleen, David Michael. *Education:* California State University—Long Beach, B.A. (psychology), 1976; Princeton Theological Seminary, M.A. (Christian education), 1980, M.Div., 1983; McCormick Theological Seminary, D.Min. (preaching), 2000. *Religion:* Presbyterian (U.S.A.). *Hobbies and other interests:* Reading, walking, writing, yoga.

*ADDRESSES: Home*—33392 North Mill Rd., Wildwood, IL 60030. *Office*—Wildwood Presbyterian Church, 33428 N. Sears Blvd., Wildwood, IL 60030. *E-mail*—KGB81@msn.com.

*CAREER:* Author, minister. Church of the Covenant, Washington, PA, associate pastor, 1983-91; Wildwood Presbyterian Church, Wildwood, IL, co-pastor, 1991—. Guest speaker at Presbyterian conferences.

*MEMBER:* Society of Children's Book Writers and Illustrators, Authors Guild, Society of Midland Authors, Presbyterian Writers Guild (president, 2001-04), Presbytery of Chicago.

*AWARDS, HONORS:* Gold Medallion Award finalist, Evangelical Christian Publishers Association, 2000; Retailer's Choice Award finalist, 2001; recipient of several awards for sermon writing.

*WRITINGS:*

*The World That God Made,* illustrated by Peter Adderley, Tyndale House Publishers (Wheaton, IL), 1997.

*What Is God Like?* illustrated by Elena Kucharik, Tyndale House Publishers (Wheaton, IL), 1998.

*The Value-able Child: Teaching Values at Home and School,* Good Year Books (Glenview, IL), 1999.

*Who Is Jesus?* illustrated by Elena Kucharik, Tyndale House Publishers (Wheaton, IL), 1999.

*What about Heaven?* illustrated by Elena Kucharik, Tyndale House Publishers (Wheaton, IL), 2000.

*Are Angels Real?* illustrated by Elena Kucharik, Tyndale House Publishers (Wheaton, IL), 2001.

*God Loves You* (board book), illustrated by Elena Kucharik, Tyndale House Publishers (Wheaton, IL), 2001.

*Song of Creation,* illustrated by Peter Fasolino, Geneva Press (Louisville, KY), 2001.

*What Is Prayer?* illustrated by Elena Kucharik, Tyndale House Publishers (Wheaton, IL), 2002.

*Thank You, God!* (board book), illustrated by Elena Kucharik, Tyndale House Publishers (Wheaton, IL), 2002.

*Papa's Gift,* illustrated by Guy Porfirio, ZonderKidz (Grand Rapids, MI), 2002.

*The Snake in the Grass: The Story of Adam and Eve,* illustrated by Dennis McKinsey, Geneva Press (Louisville, KY), 2003.

*Green Plagues and Lamb; The Story of Moses and Pharaoh,* illustrated by Dennis McKinsey, Geneva Press (Louisville, KY), 2003.

*Mary's Happy Christmas Day,* ZonderKidz (Grand Rapids, MI), 2003.

*Winning Authors: Profiles of Newbery Award Winners,* Libraries Unlimited (Westport, CT), 2003.

*How Paul Became Christian: The Story of the Apostle Paul,* Geneva Press (Louisville, KY), in press.

*OTHER*

Articles published in *Presbyterian Outlook, inSpire, Christian Ministry,* and *Horizons.* Contributor to *These Days: Daily Devotions for Living by Faith,* Presbyterian Publishing Corporation (Louisville, KY), 1999, 2000; *Voice of Many Waters: An Anthology of Sacred Literature,* About Words, 1997; and *The Greatest Gifts Our Children Give to Us,* by Stephen Vannoy, Simon and Schuster (New York, NY), 1997. Author of the 2005-06 Presbyterian Women's National Bible Study. Contributor of sermons to *This Call's for You: A Christian Vocation Workbook for Congregations,* Christian Vocation and Enlistment Services (Louisville, KY), 1993, and *Shining Lights: Mon Valley Ministries 1992 and 1993 Small-Church Preaching Awards,* Mon Valley Ministries (Dravosburg, PA), 1993, 1994.

*WORK IN PROGRESS: Sunrise Hill: An Easter Story,* and *Pete's Dad Got Sick* ("Love Makes Me Strong" series), both for ZonderKidz (Grand Rapids, MI), 2004; *Josie's Gift,* for Broadman and Holman Publishers (Nashville, TN); (with Cathy Hoop and Elizabeth Caldwell) *Making Worship a Welcome Place,* for Geneva Press (Louisville, KY); an Easter board book.

*SIDELIGHTS:* Kathleen Long Bostrom told *CA:* "I was born and raised in southern California, and grew up in the same town where Newbery Medalist Scott O'Dell once lived: San Pedro. A shy child, I clammed up when introduced to strangers, but had no problem being vocal around people I knew. My mother used to wonder if I'd ever stop chattering! She couldn't believe that the same loquacious child at home was seen by schoolteachers as quiet and reserved.

"I had a lot of energy and enthusiasm for life, and I knew my own mind. I insisted on wearing a cowboy hat and holster while I was still in diapers, and Zorro later became my favorite hero. Yet I wore white gloves while riding my tricycle around the driveway. I loved playing outdoors and was good at sports, and kept up with my younger brother and his friends until they hit puberty and could hit a baseball further than I.

"Although many authors know from an early age that they want to grow up and make writing into a career, I had no such aspirations. I wanted to be a teacher, and get married and have fourteen children. I even had names picked out for all those kids! Most of the writing I did was in my daily diaries, which were very boring. I got up, I went to school, I did my homework, I went to bed, stuff like that. They became more in-depth as the years went on, and I still have them tucked away, although I don't keep diaries or journals like I once did.

"I wrote my first book in sixth grade, coauthored and co-illustrated by my best friend. We called it 'Two Girls on Fantasy Island' and we populated our imaginary island with talking animals. My friend and I also wrote a radio show that we would broadcast to our friends at the lunch table. I kept the manuscript for that first book, and I am certain that it will never be found on a bookstore shelf!

"I grew up, decided to attend seminary and become a minister, married a fellow classmate, and had three children (not the fourteen I originally imagined!).

"My first serious thoughts about being a writer came in 1992. I was thirty-eight years old, married with three young children, and the co-pastor of a church. I worked part time at the church in order to be at home with the children. I also suffered from chronic pain due to a condition diagnosed as fibromyalgia, and so I began walking in the mornings to try to relieve some of the stiffness in my muscles.

"The town we live in is built around a beautiful lake. It is an older community and trees abound. As I enjoyed my morning walks, thoughts and images began to dance around in my mind. How could I describe the bark on that tree without just calling it bark? What thoughts did I have as I walked through a snowstorm of cottonwood seeds on an early June morning? I would hurry home to write down what I had seen, felt, and heard, relishing the challenge of finding a new and different way to describe the ordinary. I had no goal other than to write for the fun of it, and the thought of publication had not yet crossed my mind.

"The writing fever began to spread to other areas of my life. As I worked on sermons, drove in the car, or rocked my children to sleep at night, words continued to tumble and tangle within me. And, being a mother, it was a natural progression that soon these words began forming into stories to tell my children.

"So I began to write: lullabies, poems, tales of dogs finding their way in the world—everywhere I looked, I found a story waiting to be put to words. My children, of course, thought my stories were wonderful. Although I knew that their enthusiasm was biased, their delight in listening to stories that were inspired by pieces of their own lives stirred my creative juices until I began spending every free moment writing. Those free moments were hard to come by: early in the morning, during nap time, and eventually, while the kids were in school. My family got used to the sight of Mom sitting with paper and pen in hand, or typing away at the computer.

"I've always loved to read, and from the time my children were born, I read to them. As I sat with a child snuggled in my lap, reading beloved books, I began to think: Wouldn't it be wonderful to publish a book that a parent and child would read and cherish together? I knew that as I read to my children, we were building some of our most precious memories. To be a part of that memory-building for other adults and children seemed like a gift beyond compare.

"These thoughts launched me into my quest to become a published author. I read books about publishing, joined organizations such as the Society of Children's Book Writers and Illustrators. I attended workshops and retreats, joined a writer's critique group, and took a writing class at the local junior college. I did research, seeking to discover which publishers were looking for children's books, and then began submitting manuscripts to publishing houses. I felt certain that some wise editor would snatch my first stories from the dreaded 'slush piles' and that I would get a phone call saying, 'Kathy Bostrom—we want to publish everything you write!'

"Along the way, I began writing children's books with theological content. I listened to the questions the children of the church asked. 'Where does God live?' 'Is God a boy or a girl?' As I wrestled with providing answers to these questions at a level the young children would understand, books began to take shape. I discussed with an editor the possibility of writing a book for young children that would deal with these very basic and practical questions, and to write the book in verse, since children love rhyme. The editor seemed enthusiastic and encouraged me to write the book.

"After spending six months writing the book, I submitted it to this editor, only to receive a form-letter rejection. Discouraged, I set the manuscript aside, not sure what to do with it. Several months later, a friend suggested that I send the manuscript to Tyndale House, a religious publishing house based in Wheaton, Illinois, about an hour from where we lived. I wrote one of the editors and received a reply: 'We are not doing many children's books at this time, but I will take a look at your manuscript.'

"I didn't hold out much hope, but mailed the manuscript to the editor in March of 1996. I waited. And waited. Meanwhile, I continued to submit other manuscripts to other publishers. The rejections piled up—over 250 during the course of four years. That August, I heard back from the editor who told me that they were interested in my book but that the manuscript had to be approved by several other committees. I tried not to get my hopes up too high. I had come close to publication before, only to have it all fall through. But on September 23, 1996, the editor called me and said, 'I think we have good news for you. We want to publish your book.'

"I cannot describe my elation! Even for a writer, words are inadequate. After all those years of hard work, persistence, anonymity, hours of writing and mailing and rejection, I felt like Cinderella at the ball. The glass slipper fit! I had found my editor and my publisher—and they had found me.

"When I announced to my family that I had a book accepted for publication, their reactions varied from my husband's and oldest son's enthusiastic, 'Hooray for you!' to my daughter's supportive, 'I knew you could do it!' to my youngest son, the would-be publisher's, sigh of relief: 'Finally!' Now he was free to pursue other career options.

"Two months later, Tyndale House called to offer me a contract on another book. The floodgates began to open. The original book they accepted, *What Is God Like?,* became the first in a series of five books. Eventually, I placed manuscripts with various publishers, hired an agent, and continued to write—and sometimes, to be rejected. Yet plenty of my books were being published, so even though the rejections still hurt, they no longer had any power over me.

"Through the years of rejections I never gave up. I had sermons and articles published, but I never let go of my wish to publish books for children. All along,

my writing felt to me like a 'call', just as my 'call' to ministry came quite unexpectedly. There was a force, greater than my own will, urging me on. I sensed a deeper purpose to my obsession with the written word, that somehow God would use my books to reach out to children and adults and answer their questions about faith. I see my books as an extension of my ministry as an ordained pastor. Several of my books have been published in ten foreign languages. The outreach is even greater than I could have imagined when I first put pen to paper and thought about how wonderful it would be to write a book that would create a memory between an adult and a child.

"I believe that it is my responsibility as an author to encourage young writers. I speak to classes at schools and without shame tell the kids about my many rejections. My message to them: Don't give up! Read! Write! Follow your heart! Not everyone wants to be a writer/author, but for those of us who do, it is well worth the wait. There's nothing like walking into a bookstore or library and seeing a book with your name on it. But even better is getting a letter from someone whose life has been touched by one of my books. I've had letters from people telling me that a book I wrote helped a terminally ill child die in peace, or gave a family comfort when they lost a baby. There are no words to say how much that means. For me, it's what being an author is all about."

*BIOGRAPHICAL AND CRITICAL SOURCES:*

*PERIODICALS*

*Christian Parenting Today,* January-February, 2002, Jennifer Mangan, review of *God Loves You,* p. 44.

*          *          *

**BOYER, Pascal (Robert)**

*PERSONAL:* Male. *Education:* Received Ph.D. from Paris university, 1986.

*ADDRESSES: Office*—Washington University, Box 1114, St. Louis, MO 63130. *E-mail*—pboyer@artsci. wustl.edu.

*CAREER:* Anthropologist and educator. King's College, Cambridge, junior research fellow, 1986-90, senior research fellow in anthropology, 1990-93; Centre National de la Recherche Scientifique, Lyon, France, senior researcher, 1993-99, director of research, 1999-2000; Stanford University, Stanford, CA, Center for Advanced Study, fellow, 1995-96; Washington University, St. Louis, MO, Henry Luce Professor of Individual and Collective Memory, 2000—. Visiting fellow, Center for Psychology, University of California, Santa Barbara, 1999-2000; executive editor, *Journal of Cognition and Culture,* 2001—.

*AWARDS, HONORS:* MacArthur fellowship, 1995; research grant from French Ministry of Technology, 1997, and French Ministry of Research, 2000.

*WRITINGS:*

*Tradition as Truth and Communication: A Cognitive Description of Traditional Discourse,* Cambridge University Press (New York, NY), 1990.

(Editor) *Cognitive Aspects of Religious Symbolism,* Cambridge University Press (New York, NY), 1993.

*The Naturalness of Religious Ideas: A Cognitive Religion,* University of California Press (Berkeley, CA), 1994.

*Religion Explained: The Evolutionary Origins of Religious Thought,* Basic Books (New York, NY), 2001.

Contributor to books, including *The M.I.T. Encyclopedia of the Cognitive Sciences,* MIT Press, 1999, and *Debated Mind: Evolutionary Psychology and Ethnography,* Oxford University Press, 2001. Contributor to research journals, including *Cognitive Development, Philosophical Psychology, American Behavioral Scientist,* and *Anthropological Theory Today.*

*SIDELIGHTS:* Pascal Boyer is a cognitive anthropologist whose publications explore how and why people obtain their cultural beliefs. His main question, as he states on his Web site, is "what cognitive processes are engaged in the acquisition, use and transmission of cultural knowledge?" Toward this end, Boyer's research has resulted in several books, including *Tradition as Truth and Communication: A Cognitive*

*Description of Traditional Discourse* and *Religion Explained: The Evolutionary Origins of Religious Thought.* Pascal, who was educated in England and France, has studied at Stanford University and the Centre National de la Recherche Scientifique in Lyon, France, and was awarded a MacArthur fellowship, the prestigious so-called "genius grant," in 1995.

Boyer's first book-length work to concentrate specifically on religion is *The Naturalness of Religious Ideas: A Cognitive Theory of Religion.* In it, he explains how similarities in world religions are due to the limitations of the human brain, and then he uses cognitive psychology to explain religious differences between various cultures. Ideas common to all religions, Boyer says, include belief in gods and ghosts, the idea of an eternal soul, the belief that some people can communicate with gods and spirits, and the belief that performing rituals can have an effect on a person's spiritual state. Cultural transmission—the method by which beliefs are passed from one generation to the next—do not sufficiently explain the stability of religious ideas across time, Boyer maintains. As Rem B. Edwards explained in a review of the book in the *Review of Metaphysics,* "these intuitive beliefs are too impressively widespread to be mere products of social teaching." Also of interest to Boyer is how children learn, and the relationship between language and religious concepts. Critics noted Boyer's insistence in challenging previously well-accepted notions of cultural transmission. Robert Nossen of the *International Journal of Comparative Sociology* wrote that Boyer "is constantly challenging anthropological theories about cultural transmission, and he has no hesitation in further challenging academic fields, such as psychology and other social sciences." Nossen concluded by calling *The Naturalness of Religious Ideas* "a demanding study" that requires "patience and dedication." And Don Gardner of the *Journal of the Royal Anthropological Institute* called Boyer's thesis "a powerful confection of psychological research, philosophical analysis and ethnographic evidence," which makes for a "splendid, substantial book."

In *Religion Explained,* Boyer elaborates on his theory of how and why the world's major religions have evolved and credits the idea of an omniscient being on the biological architecture of the brain. Religion, Boyer asserts, began to emerge between 100,000 and 50,000 years ago, as the brain evolved in a manner that was conducive to the construct of a god, or a "full-access strategic agent," as he calls it. Boyer uses his research among the Kwaio tribes of the Solomon Islands and the Fang of Cameroon as the basis for his conclusions. Contrary to what most philosophers have long believed—mainly that religion arose in order to give people an explanation for the mysteries of life and to appease their fear of death—Boyer believes that religion is more biologically based. "Cultural memes," as he calls the predisposed beliefs of religion, are passed down through generations much like genes, and the surviving mutations involve "supernatural concepts" like death and demons that are common to all world religions. "Evolution by natural selection gave us [humans] a particular kind of mind so that only particular kinds of religious notions can be acquired. Not all possible concepts are equally good. The ones we acquire easily are the ones we find widespread the world over; indeed, that is why we find them widespread the world over," Boyer states.

Critical reaction to *Religion Explained* was mixed. Paul J. Griffiths, writing in the journal *First Things*, felt that Boyer's theory is marred by the "blithe confidence," that fuels Boyer's assertion that "the explanations offered by Catholics for why they go to Mass cannot be right, whereas his explanations are." Moreover, continued Griffiths, Boyer "fails to establish the unacceptability of religious people's explanations for their religion; the possible validity of his own explanation is thus irrelevant. And what's worse, he apparently fails even to see what he would need to do in order to establish what he claims to have established." Still, Griffiths concluded, the book "is breezily written, ascending at times to the eloquence of the revivalist preacher." Other critics appreciated Boyer's emerging theories. "If he isn't altogether successful (who could be?)," wrote Tom Flynn in *Free Inquiry*, "he magnificently summarizes what cognitive science has learned about the reasons humans believe as they do." But David Sharp pointed out in *Lancet* what he viewed as a major flaw in Boyer's thinking: "Boyer fails to explain why, with this same mental architecture, many of us end up agnostic or go the whole way to atheism, a word that does not even rate a place in the index." But Steven Schroeder, in a review for *Booklist*, commented that though "Boyer's argument that 'religious concepts are parasitic upon other mental capacities' may offend some . . . it is critical to this fascinating book, and it doesn't in any way demean religion."

In *Tradition as Truth and Communication: A Cognitive Description of Traditional Discourse*, Boyer

explains how tradition and ritual function in a society. He seeks to create new theories concerning tradition, rituals, and other cultural performances, an area he believes has been overlooked by most anthropologists. Contrary to popular belief, he sees most traditions as important to their practitioners not because of their actual meaning, but because they are conveyed with a sense of authority. Claudia Strauss, reviewing the book in *Ethnohistory*, complimented Boyer for his "fresh approach to hoary questions about the status of magical knowledge—an approach that takes seriously the truth claims made by the practitioners themselves." O. Pi-Sunyer of *Choice* called the book "a challenging work for the informed professional," and Lawrence A. Hirschfeld, writing in *American Anthropologist*, faulted Boyer for his lack of examples and proof but nonetheless called *Tradition as Truth and Communication* "an exceptional work, both in terms of the scope of its well-crafted and ingenious arguments and the specific empirical consequences of its claims."

## BIOGRAPHICAL AND CRITICAL SOURCES:

*BOOKS*

Boyer, Pascal, *Religion Explained: The Evolutionary Origins of Religious Thought*, Basic Books (New York, NY), 2001.

*PERIODICALS*

*American Anthropologist*, September, 1991, Lawrence A. Hirschfeld, review of *Tradition as Truth and Communication: A Cognitive Description of Traditional Discourse*, pp. 730-731.

*American Ethnologist*, August, 1995, Victor C. De Munck, review of *Cognitive Aspects of Religious Symbolism*, p. 639.

*Booklist*, June 1, 2001, Steven Schroeder, review of *Religion Explained: The Evolutionary Origins of Religious Thought*, p. 1803.

*Choice*, December, 1990, O. Pi-Sunyer, review of *Traditional as Truth and Communication*, p. 666; January, 2002, R. F. White, a review of *Religion Explained*, p. 842.

*Commonweal*, January 25, 2002, John F. Haught, "The Darwinian Universe: Isn't There Room for God?," p. 12.

*Ethnohistory,* fall, 1992, Claudia Strauss, review of *Tradition as Truth and Communication,* p. 565.

*First Things,* January, 2002, Paul J. Griffiths, review of *Religion Explained,* p. 53.

*Free Inquiry,* spring, 2002, Tom Flynn, "Religion Explained? Maybe So," p. 65.

*International Journal of Comparative Sociology,* June, 1995, Robert Nossen, review of *The Naturalness of Religious Ideas,* p. 101.

*Journal for the Scientific Study of Religion,* March, 1994, William M. Wentworth, review of *Cognitive Aspects of Religious Symbolism,* p. 83.

*Lancet,* March 2, 2002, David Sharp, "Science, Faith, and Gods," p. 806.

*Library Journal,* August, 2001, H. James Birx, review of *Religion Explained,* p. 120.

*National Review,* October 1, 2001, David Klinghoffer, "Faith No More?"

*Publishers Weekly,* May 28, 2001, review of *Religion Explained,* p. 84.

*Review of Metaphysics,* December, 1995, Rem B. Edwards, review of *The Naturalness of Religious Ideas,* p. 400.

*Science,* September 28, 2001, John Polkinghorne, review of *Religion Explained,* p. 2400.

*Times Literary Supplement,* March 29, 2002, David Martin, "It Used to Be Catching," p. 7.

*OTHER*

*Pascal Boyer Home Page,* http://www.artsci.wustl.edu/ ˜anthro/ (May 2, 2002).*

\*     \*     \*

### BREMNER, Robert H(amlett) 1917-2002

*OBITUARY NOTICE*—See index for *CA* sketch: Born May 26, 1917, in Brunswick, OH; died September 7, 2002, in Columbus, OH. Bremner was a history professor at Ohio State University. A graduate of Baldwin-Wallace College, where he earned his B.A. in 1938, he went on to complete a Ph.D. at Ohio State University in 1943. He spent his entire academic career at Ohio State, rising from instructor in 1946 to professor of American history from 1960 until his retirement as professor emeritus in 1980. He was the editor or author of several history books, often focusing on philanthropy, poverty, and welfare. Among these works are

*American Philanthropy* (1960), *Philanthropy and Social Welfare in the Civil War Era* (1981), and *The Discovery of Poverty in the United States* (1992), as well as edited works that include *Essays on History and Literature* (1966) and the multi-volume *Children and Youth in America: A Documentary History* (1970-74).

*OBITUARIES AND OTHER SOURCES:*

*BOOKS*

*Directory of American Scholars,* tenth edition, Volume 1: *History, Archaeology, and Area Studies,* Gale (Detroit, MI), 2002.

*PERIODICALS*

*Chronicle of Higher Education,* November 8, 2002, p. A43.

\*     \*     \*

### BRENTANO, Robert 1926-2002

*OBITUARY NOTICE*—See index for *CA* sketch: Born May 19, 1926, in Evansville, IN; died after an asthma attack November 21, 2002, in Berkeley, CA. Educator and author. Brentano was an authority on medieval European history, but taught a wide range of university history courses. Receiving his bachelor's degree from Swarthmore College in 1949, he was awarded a Rhodes scholarship to Oxford University, where he completed his D.Phil. in 1952. After graduating, he joined the faculty at the University of California at Berkeley and enjoyed the institution so much that he never left (he was still teaching there when he passed away). Brentano was a favorite teacher among Berkeley students; he was named Professor of the Year by the Council for the Advancement and Support of Education in 1986, and in 1991 was awarded the Clark Kerr Medal from the Academic Senate for Distinguished Leadership in Higher Education. He was, furthermore, active in the Academic Senate and was chairman of that organization in 1999. Brentano was the author of five books, including *Early Middle Ages*

(1964), *Rome before Avignon* (1974), and *A New World in a Small Place: Church and Religion in the Diocese of Rieti, 1188-1378* (1994).

*OBITUARIES AND OTHER SOURCES:*

*BOOKS*

*Directory of American Scholars,* tenth edition, Volume 1: *History, Archaeology, and Area Studies,* Gale (Detroit, MI), 2002.

*PERIODICALS*

*Los Angeles Times,* November 27, 2002, p. B10.
*San Francisco Chronicle,* November 23, 2002, p. A19.

\*  \*  \*

## BROAD, William J.

*PERSONAL:* Born in Milwaukee, WI. *Education:* Attended University of Wisconsin.

*ADDRESSES: Home*—Larchmont, NY. *Office*—c/o *New York Times,* Science Desk, 229 West 43rd St., New York, NY 10036.

*CAREER: New York Times,*New York, NY, science reporter, 1983—.

*AWARDS, HONORS:* Pulitzer Prize for explanatory journalism (with fellow *New York Times* reporters,) 1986, for six-part series on the Strategic Defense Initiative ("Star Wars"), and 1987 for national reporting (with fellow *New York Times* reporters), for coverage of the Challenger space shuttle disaster.

*WRITINGS:*

(With Nicholas Wade) *Betrayers of the Truth: Fraud and Deceit in the Halls of Science,* Simon & Schuster (New York, NY), 1983.
*Star Warriors: A Penetrating Look into the Lives of the Young Scientists behind Our Space-Age Weaponry,* Simon & Schuster (New York, NY), 1985.

(With others) *Claiming the Heavens: The "New York Times" Complete Guide to the Star Wars Debate,* Times Books (New York, NY), 1988.
*Teller's War: The Top-Secret Story behind the Star Wars Deception,* Simon & Schuster, (New York, NY), 1992.
*The Universe Below: Discovering the Secrets of the Deep Sea,* Simon & Schuster (New York, NY), 1997.
(With Judith Miller and Stephen Engelberg) *Germs: Biological Weapons and America's Secret War,* Simon & Schuster (New York, NY), 2001.

*SIDELIGHTS:* With a degree in the history of science, William J. Broad has enjoyed a long career as a science reporter for the *New York Times.* He has been honored with two shared Pulitzer prizes, and in addition to his reportage has written several well-received books.

His first book, coauthored with Nicholas Wade, is *Betrayers of the Truth: Fraud and Deceit in the Halls of Science.* In this work, the authors expose several cases of scientists who, for one reason or another, lose their purely scientific pursuit of the truth in favor of the more compelling drive to in some way prove a favorite theory of theirs (despite empirical evidence) or to make a name for themselves. As P. B. Medawar wrote in *London Review of Books,* "I do not suppose that personal advancement is a principal motive for cheating in science: rather it is the hunger for scientific reputation and the esteem of colleagues." Whatever the reason for the fraud, *Betrayers of the Truth* details some of the more famous cases. "It is not the authors' intention to shock," wrote Medawar, "though in fact they do so: no, the purpose is rather to show that research is not a wholly rational and explicitly logical procedure but subject to the confinements and constraints that afflict other professional men trying to make their way in the world."

Two years later, Broad published his *Star Warriors: A Penetrating Look into the Lives of the Young Scientists behind Our Space-Age Weaponry,* which Michael Riordan, for the *Technology Review,* referred to as "a remarkable, riveting book." The book relates the story of a small team of young scientists working at Lawrence Livermore Laboratories in California. These scientists had, at that time, developed many of the designs and conceptions employed by the Strategic

Defense Initiative (SDI, popularly known as "Star Wars"), a program involved in, according to Riordan, "a 'third generation' of nuclear weaponry—the 'directed-energy' weapons based on X-ray lasers that their creators expect will render offensive missiles obsolete."

The title of Broad's book comes from President Reagan's promotion of the "Star Wars" technology that would supposedly save the United States from nuclear attack. Broad challenges this assumption as he exposes the philosophies of the young scientists, who in general believed, as stated by Riordan, that the world is "without complexity, of black and white, of good and evil, with absolutely no middle ground." Riordan also added that these young scientists could not "imagine that their inventions might make nuclear warfare more likely, not less."

Broad spent a week at Livermore, a huge laboratory created by Edward Teller, a principal developer of the hydrogen bomb; Broad's book is an attempt to explain what the scientists do there. Broad "paints with rough, impressionistic strokes," wrote Washington Monthly critic Paul M. Barrett. He "succeeds in combining a comprehensible explanation of SDI with a lively diary of a week-long visit to the Livermore lab, one of the government's two main nuclear weapons design facilities." Barrett praised Broad for his "considerable insight into the origins and purposes of strategic defense." However, Barrett concluded that Broad's work "also poses the troubling question of whether we ought to view advances in nuclear technology as necessary or inevitable simply because people at places like Livermore may have the brainpower and bravado to accomplish them."

Continuing along the same theme, Broad, together with several colleagues from the New York Times, published Claiming the Heavens: The "New York Times" Complete Guide to the Star Wars Debate in 1988. This book is an expanded version of a Pulitzer Prize-winning series of articles that ran in the New York Times in March, 1985. The book, as stated in a Publishers Weekly review, answers very critical questions about President Reagan's Star Wars plan and provides "an objective survey of Star Wars, in which basic questions are asked and either answered or intelligently speculated upon."

In a review for Business Week, Dave Griffiths related a quote from the book as stated by Teller, whom Griffiths referred to as "father of the hydrogen bomb" and "SDI cheerleader." Teller reportedly said that without a nuclear missile defense plan, such as Star Wars, "a billion lives could be lost in a global war." Teller then added: "Defense might reduce that to 'only' 100 million." Griffiths pointed out that as "grotesque and appalling" as that statement might be, at least some lives might be saved with such a plan. Griffiths then concluded: "Such are the extraordinary stakes in the Star Wars game. . . . So far, nobody has set forth the dimensions and rules of that game with more clarity than the team behind Claiming the Heavens."

In his next book Teller's War: The Top-secret Story behind the Star Wars Deception, Broad turns his full focus on the Hungarian-born Teller, whom a Chicago Tribune Books reviewer described as a scientist who continually went "over the heads of scientific colleagues and into the corridors of Washington to lobby for some pet scheme: the hydrogen bomb in 1950, a weapons laboratory of his own in 1952, the so-called 'clean bomb' in 1957." Each time he did so, Teller "frightened his auditors by telling them" that the Soviets were ahead in the arms race. "And nearly every time he got what he was campaigning for."

It is through this book about Teller that Broad relates the story behind the Star Wars program. In the Chicago Tribune Books review, a critic described Broad's book as "a story that must surely spell the end of the Teller saga." It does not read as a diatribe against the aging scientist, however, but rather as "a carefully researched and documented account." Because of his careful research and objective reporting, the reviewer held, Teller's War "is a devastating indictment of Teller—and of Ronald Reagan, the president he seduced."

Although G. Allen Greb, writing for Science, also praised Broad's book, Greb wrote that Broad may have overemphasized Teller's influence. "Certainly, this is a good book to learn more about the secret and largely closed world of the national laboratories and their relationship to Washington, D.C.," Greb stated. However, "Broad's ultimate fascination with Teller—key figure to be sure—really prevents us from getting a clear picture about the true dynamics of the arms race, arms development, and arms control." A Publishers Weekly reviewer, on the contrary, found Broad's work to be "investigative journalism at its finest."

In 1997, Broad turned to a less controversial topic with his book The Universe Below: Discovering the Secrets of the Deep Sea. In it, Broad reports that new discoveries have shown that life is much more abundant in the ocean than previously thought. The number of species found in the depths of the ocean might actually constitute more than all the creatures found on land, scientists are now surmising. Broad's book explores these new developments, as well as the political debates that occurred during the Cold War surrounding the military's involvement in developing submersibles that were capable of searching the bottom of the ocean. At the end of the Cold War, the technology the U.S. Navy produced was declassified and put to use by private and scientific industries.

"Broad tells absorbing stories of the investigators who unravel secrets of the deep ocean," wrote reviewer Laurence A. Marschall for *Sciences;* while a *Booklist* reviewer reported that "Broad gives readers a transfixing and creepy glimpse into the perpetual darkness of inner space." In even greater appreciation was David Pawson, writing for the *Washington Post Book World.* Pawson, a deep-sea diver himself, having made "hundreds of dives in manned submersibles," stated that he "welcomed" Broad's book. "The author has performed a valuable service by summarizing the current state of our knowledge of the deep sea, by identifying the rewards that deep sea exploration can offer, and by making an eloquent plea for more intensive research in the future."

Broad's *Germs: Biological Weapons and America's Secret War* was published in 2001. It is a joint effort by the *New York Times* staff members who made a study of bio-terrorism. One of the members of the writing team, Judith Miller, was a victim of bio-terrorism, having received a letter laced with anthrax following the attack on the World Trade Center. *Germs* made the *New York Times* bestseller list, eventually hitting the number one position.

In the book, the three reporters cover the history of bio-terrorism, such as a detailed account "of bioweapons programs, including the United States' largely secret experiments during and after World War II, the former Soviet Union's massive buildup after signing a ban on such weapons in 1972 and Saddam Hussein's push to develop a smorgasbord of deadly pathogens in Iraq," wrote Michael Massing for the *Nation.* Although the book fascinated the public, critics have provided mixed reviews. Thomas R. Eddlem, writing for *New American,* stated: "For the critical reader capable of discounting the terrible policy recommendations at the end of the book, *Germs* serves as a helpful and well-written primer on the 20th-century history of biological weapons." An *Economist* reviewer did not find fault with the author's proposals and instead concluded that the book contained "well informed reporting."

*BIOGRAPHICAL AND CRITICAL SOURCES:*

*PERIODICALS*

*Atlantic Monthly,* December 2001, Bruce Hoffman, "One-Alarm Fire," p. 137.

*Booklist,* April 15, 1997, Gilbert Taylor, review of *The Universe Below: Discovering the Secrets of the Deep Sea,* p. 1370.

*Business Week,* March 21, 1988, Dave Griffiths, "Star Wars: Is the Force with Us?" pp. 10-11.

*Economist,* October 20, 2001, "Topical Treatment: Germ Warfare."

*Harper's,* March 2002, Howard Market, review of *Germs: Biological Weapons and America's Secret War,* pp. 65-70.

*London Review of Books,* November 17, 1983, P. B. Medawar, "Scientific Fraud," pp. 5-7.

*Nation,* December 21, 1985, Peter Pringle, review of *Star Warriors: A Penetrating Look into the Lives of the Young Scientists behind Our Space-Age Weaponry,* pp. 686-688; December 17, 2001, Michael Massing, "Where Germs Rule," p. 7.

*New American,* January 14, 2002, Thomas R. Eddlem, review of *Germs,* pp. 25-26.

*Publishers Weekly,* December 18, 1987, review of *Claiming the Heavens: The "New York Times" Complete guide to the Star Wars Debate,* p. 48; January 13, 1992, review of *Teller's War: The Top-secret Story behind the Star Wars Deception,* p. 44; February 24, 1997, review of *The Universe Below,* pp. 776-777.

*Science,* March 25, 1983, review of *Betrayers of the Truth,* pp. 1417-1418; May 15, 1992, G. Allen Greb, review of *Teller's War,* pp. 1043-1044.

*Sciences,* May, 1997, Laurence A. Marschall, review of *The Universe Below,* p. 43.

*Sierra,* January, 2000, Jennifer Hattam, review of *The Universe Below,* p. 115.

*Technology Review,* July, 1986, Michael Riordan, review of *Star Warriors,* pp. 76-77.

*Tribune* (Chicago, IL), March 1, 1992, "Cold War Science," pp. 5, 9.

*Washington Monthly,* January, 1986, Paul M. Barrett, review of *Star Warriors,* pp. 50-52; April, 1992, James Fallows, review of *Teller's War,* pp. 44-48.
*Washington Post Book World,* David Pawson, "Plumbing the Depths," p. 7.*

\*   \*   \*

## BRODMAN, James W(illiam) 1945-

*PERSONAL:* Born December 9, 1945, in Rochester, NY; son of Adolph and Margaret (Laukaitu) Brodman; married Marian Masiuk, January 5, 1980; children: James C., Margaret M. *Education:* Canisius College, B.A., 1967; University of Virginia, M.A., Ph.D., 1974. *Religion:* Roman Catholic. *Hobbies and other interests:* Sailing, bread-making.

*ADDRESSES: Home*—1209 Dogwood Trail, Conway, AR 72032. *Office*—Department of History, University of Central Arkansas, Conway, AR 72035; fax: 501-450-5617. *E-mail*—jimb@mail.uca.edu.

*CAREER:* University of Central Arkansas, Conway, assistant professor, 1972-77, associate professor, 1977-84, professor of history, 1984—. Library of Iberian Resources Online, director.

*MEMBER:* American Academy of Research Historians of Medieval Spain (president, 1994-2000), Society of Spanish and Portuguese Historical Studies.

*WRITINGS:*

*Ransoming Captives in Crusader Spain: The Order of Merced on the Christian-Islamic Frontier,* University of Pennsylvania Press (Philadelphia, PA), 1986.
*Charity and Welfare: Hospitals and the Poor in Medieval Catalonia,* University of Pennsylvania Press (Philadelphia, PA), 1998.

*WORK IN PROGRESS:* A Book on opera caritatis in medieval Europe.

\*   \*   \*

## BROWN, John L(ackey) 1914-2002

*OBITUARY NOTICE*—See index for *CA* sketch: Born April 29, 1914, in Ilion, NY; died of congestive heart failure November 22, 2002, in Washington, DC. Educator, diplomat, and author. Brown was a profes-

sor of comparative literature whose extensive diplomatic experience in countries throughout Europe gave him a particularly diverse perspective on American and European literature. He graduated in 1935 with an A.B. from Hamilton College before studying for a year at the École des Chartes in Paris. Receiving his doctorate from the Catholic University of America in 1939, he then taught for two years at Catholic University of America in Washington, D.C. before World War II broke out. During the war he worked for the Office of Strategic Services, afterwards embarking on a career as a cultural attaché in Paris, Brussels, and Rome. During the 1960s Brown was counselor for cultural affairs at the U.S. Embassy in Mexico City; he then joined the faculty at Catholic University of America, where he was a professor of comparative literature from 1968 until 1979, retiring as professor emeritus. Brown authored several nonfiction books during his career, among them *Discovering Belgium* (1957), *Hemingway* (1961), and *Valery Larbaud* (1981), as well as several poetry collections, including *Numina* (1969), *Shards* (1982), and *Celebrations* (1990).

*OBITUARIES AND OTHER SOURCES:*

BOOKS

*Directory of American Scholars,* tenth edition, Volume II: *English, Speech, and Drama,* Gale (Detroit, MI), 2002.

PERIODICALS

*Washington Post,* November 27, 2002, p. B5.

\*   \*   \*

## BUCHANAN, Sue 1939-

*PERSONAL:* Born July 7, 1939, in Charleston, WV; parents named Maynard and Mary Jane; married Wayne Buchanan (a consultant); children: two daughters. *Ethnicity:* "White." *Education:* Attended Kings College (Briarcliff Manor, NY) and Northwestern University. *Politics:* Republican. *Religion:* Presbyterian.

*ADDRESSES: Home*—6545 Brownlee Dr., Nashville, TN 37205. *Agent*—Alive! Communications, 7680 Goddard, Suite 200, Colorado Springs, CO 80920. *E-mail*—suebue@aol.com.

*CAREER:* Dynamic Media, Nashville, TN, vice president, 1978-96; author and speaker, 1995—.

*AWARDS, HONORS:* Christian Booksellers Association bestseller selection, and Silver Award, Excellence in Media, both for *Mud Pie Annie: God's Recipe for Doing Your Best;* Children's Choice list, International Reading Association and Children's Book Council, 2002, Christian Booksellers Association bestseller selection, Gold Medallion finalist, Evangelical Christian Publishers Association, and Silver Award, Excellence in Media, all for *I Love You This Much: A Song of God's Love.*

*WRITINGS:*

*Love, Laughter, and a High Disregard for Statistics,* Thomas Nelson Publishers (Nashville, TN), 1994, also published as *I'm Alive and the Doctor's Dead: Surviving Cancer with Your Sense of Humor and Your Sexuality Intact,* Zondervan (Grand Rapids, MI), 1998.

(With Gloria Gaither, Peggy Benson, and Joy MacKenzie) *Friends through Thick and Thin,* Zondervan (Grand Rapids, MI), 1998.

*Duh-votions: Words of Wisdom for the Spiritually Challenged,* Zondervan (Grand Rapids, MI), 1999.

*Girls Gotta Have Fun!: 101 Great Ideas for Celebrating Life with Your Friends,* Zondervan (Grand Rapids, MI), 2000.

*A Party Begins in the Heart,* Word Publishers (Nashville, TN), 2001.

(With Gloria Gaither, Peggy Benson, and Joy MacKenzie) *Confessions of Four Friends through Thick and Thin,* Zondervan (Grand Rapids, MI), 2001.

(With Dana Shafer) *Mud Pie Annie: God's Recipe for Doing Your Best,* illustrated by Joy Allen, ZonderKidz (Grand Rapids, MI), 2001.

(With Lynn Hodges) *I Love You This Much: A Song of God's Love,* illustrated by John Bendall Brunello, ZonderKidz (Grand Rapids, MI), 2001.

Regular contributor to *Homecoming* magazine.

*WORK IN PROGRESS:* With Lynn Hodges, *Dear God, It's Me* and *Count Yourself to Sleep,* publication for both expected in 2004.

*SIDELIGHTS:* Sue Buchanan told *CA:* "Twenty years ago I was a busy executive, when suddenly, I was diagnosed with breast cancer—with a not-too-positive prognosis. The doctor wrote on my report that he didn't expect me to live through the year. The journal I kept during that time of ups and downs became my first book, *I'm Alive and the Doctor's Dead: Surviving Cancer with Your Sense of Humor and Your Sexuality Intact.*

"Next my agent suggested that I write a book of devotions, 'because devotionals are hot!', he said. 'But I'm spiritually challenged,' I replied. Out of that conversation came *Duh-votions: Words of Wisdom for the Spiritually Challenged,* and later, *A Party Begins in the Heart.*

"As a speaker and author, my message is this: when I thought I was at the end of my life, I found that instead it was a whole new beginning! I encourage my readers and listeners to take steps (sometimes leaps!) to reclaim their lives after crises.

"When I had the chance to write children's books, the responsibility weighed heavily on my mind. 'You can tell adults any ole thing,' I thought, 'and they can sort it out, but children are impressionable and parents need to be able to trust me for solid truths when their kids are concerned.' With that in mind, I wrote a simple mission statement.

"It is my intention, in everything I write, to, number one: Show that there are absolutes in life, that those truths are found in Holy Scripture, that following Biblical principles can be part of everyday life, and that those lessons can begin at an early age. Number two: I intend to include some 'crossroads' where the character has to think and has to make a decision for right or wrong. Number three: Because I believe children can grasp much bigger concepts than we give them credit for, I intend to write to that end. Number four: Read-aloud ability is always an important factor."

Buchanan's books for children include *Mud Pie Annie: God's Recipe for Doing Your Best* and *I Love You This Much: A Song of God's Love,* both picture books that deal with issues that are important to children. For example, in *Mud Pie Annie*, a little girl delights in her ability to create fantastic culinary creations out of mud, even as her efforts are criticized by the adults around her. Her skill in making mud pies and cookies convince Annie that despite the disbelievers around her, she has a special gift that needs to be celebrated with joy. In *I Love You This Much*, Buchanan focuses on conveying feelings of love to young children via the story of a young bear cub and his parent. In a brief essay about both books posted on her Web site, Buchanan explained that she hopes Annie will "introduce" her young fans "to new things that are just beyond the reach."

*BIOGRAPHICAL AND CRITICAL SOURCES:*

PERIODICALS

*Today's Christian Woman*, September, 2001, "Girlfriend's Guide to Giggling," p. 58.

OTHER

*Sue Buchanan Web site*, http://www.suebue.com (February 28, 2003).

\*   \*   \*

**BURDON, Eric 1941-**

*PERSONAL:* Born May 11, 1941, in Newcastle upon Tyne, England. *Education:* Attended Newcastle College of Art.

*ADDRESSES: Home*—CA. *Agent*—c/o Author Mail, Thunder's Mouth Press, 161 William St., 16th Floor, New York, NY 10038; Raven, P.O. Box 26811, Richmond, VA 23261.

*CAREER:* Musician and singer. Alan Price Combo, vocalist, 1962, band changed name to the Animals, 1963-65; New Animals, vocalist, 1966-68; War, vocalist, 1970; Fire Dept., vocalist, c. 1970s. Actor in films, including *The Eleventh Victim*, 1979, *Comeback*, 1981, *Movin' On*, 1987, and *The Doors*, 1990.

*AWARDS, HONORS:* Inducted into Rock and Roll Hall of Fame as a member of the Animals, 1994.

*WRITINGS:*

*I Used to Be an Animal but I'm All Right Now*, Faber (London, England), 1986.
(With Craig J. Marshall) *Don't Let Me Be Misunderstood*, Thunder's Mouth Press (New York, NY), 2002.

Albums include *Eric Burdon and the Animals; Animalization*, MGM Records; *Eric Is Here*, MGM Records; *Winds of Change*, MGM Records, 1967; *Every One of Us*, MGM Records, 1968; *Eric Burdon Declares War*, Polydor, 1970; *Black Man's Burdon*, Liberty, 1971; (with Jimmy Witherspoon) *Guilty!*, United Artists, 1971; *Before We Were So Rudely Interrupted; Ring of Fire*, Capitol, 1974; *Sun Secrets*, Capitol, 1975; *Stop*, Capitol, 1975; *Love Is All Around*, ABC, 1976; *Survivor*, Polydor, 1978; *Darkness—Darkness*, Polydor, 1980; (with Fire Dept.) *The Last Drive*, Ariola, 1980; *Comeback* (soundtrack to movie of same title), Blackline, 1983; *Power Company*, Carrere, 1983; *That's Live*, In-Akustik, 1985; *I Used to Be an Animal*, Striped Horse, 1988; *Wicked Man*, GNP Crescendo, 1988; *Roadrunners*, Raven, 1990; (with Robby Kreiger) *The 1990 Detroit Tapes*, 1991; *The Unreleased Eric Burdon*, Blue Wave, 1992; *Crawling King Snake*, Thunderbolt, 1992; (with Brian Auger) *Access All Areas*, SPV, 1993; *Misunderstood*, Aim, 1995; *Live at the Roxy*, Magnum, 1997; *Official Live Bootleg 2000*, Flying Eye Records, 2001; and *Night*, One Way Records, 2001.

*SIDELIGHTS:* As the lead singer for the British blues band the Animals, Eric Burdon first came to prominence as part of the British Invasion in 1964 with the hit record "House of the Rising Sun." With the trademark of Burdon's gravely voice, the Animals melded blues and soul with the psychedelic sounds of the 1960s, a combination that garnered the band several hit records and a permanent place in the annals of rock history. But the Animals' union was tumultuous; they soon broke up and Burdon continued his music career as the front man for War, a progressive rock band whose sound was infused with funk. Throughout the years, Burdon continued to record with various configurations of musicians, maintaining his reputation as one of the foremost white singers of blues-influenced music. He recounts his front-row seat to the madness of rock stardom in the 1960s in two memoirs, *I Used to Be an Animal but I'm All Right Now* and *Don't Let Me Be Misunderstood.*

Burdon grew up in Newcastle upon Tyne, England, an industrial town far removed from cosmopolitan London. It was there that he developed a fondness for African-American singers such as Chuck Berry and Otis Redding, who proved to be big influences when he formed the Animals. Originally, Burdon attended art school and wanted to become a filmmaker; music was his second career choice. But the Animals found fame nearly instantaneously, and perhaps unprepared for the rigors of stardom, they soon self-destructed and became entangled in legal problems. By 1967, Burdon had reformed the band, now called the New Animals, and wound up performing at the legendary Monterey Pop Festival. Burdon soon moved to California and immersed himself in the vibrant subculture of music and drugs that permeated San Francisco at the time, and the Animals went their separate ways again. Burdon became a fixture on the scene, mingling with the likes of John Lennon, Jim Morrison, and Jimi Hendrix. Once again he tried to launch a film career, the highlight of which was his starring role in the semi-autobiographical movie *Comeback.* In the early 1980s, Burdon gave in to the mania for reunion tours and reformed the Animals. The band's line-up included original members Alan Price, Chas Chandler, Hilton Valentine, and John Steel, and the idea, perhaps, was better than the execution. Burdon called the tour "purgatory since day one" in an interview with *Rolling Stone* reporter Steve Pond.

In *I Used to Be an Animal but I'm All Right Now,* Burdon concentrates on the triumvirate of sex, drugs, and rock and roll during his days of stardom. Among other things revealed in the book, Burdon claims to be the fabled "eggman" in the Beatles' song "I Am the Walrus," and recounts the mysterious circumstances surrounding the death of Jimi Hendrix, who was a close friend. He also writes about his first impressions of the United States, including his visit to the Apollo Theater in Harlem and his tour of the deep South amidst the racial strife of 1965. Though the book was called "poorly written" and "sometimes contradictory" by a *Listener* reviewer, Jim Weir in the *Times Educational Supplement* commended it for revealing "a genuine, if inarticulate, empathy and a deep-seated

sense of guilt" over Burdon's obsession with "the black experience," as Weir calls it. A *Publishers Weekly* reviewer noted the book's unflinching look into the sometimes violent world of rock music—Burdon was familiar with Hell's Angels and was a neighbor of Sharon Tate at the time of her murder by the Charles Manson family—and pointed out Burdon's "considerable writing skill" that "captures the winding down of the psychedelic era with hauntingly descriptive details." Other critics noted the cautionary tone of the memoir as well; rather than relating a life of rock and roll excess, Burdon's book underscores the tragic side of fame, and his tales "should dispel any illusions readers may have about the romance of being a rock star in the 1960's," wrote Andrea Barnet in the *New York Times Book Review,* who concluded that the book "stands as a vivid record of what has now become pop mythology."

In *Don't Let Me Be Misunderstood,* Burdon's days as a rock star, amid the ubiquitous drugs and booze, are recounted again, covering territory not included in *I Used to Be an Animal.* His resentment at the music industry is palpable, even thirty years later. He states that "the Animals never had a chance when it came to protecting ourselves from the vampires in the music business," and tells how a record company executive admitted that the company had bought enough copies of their hit single "The House of the Rising Sun" to put it on top of the music charts, thereby artificially manipulating the Animals' status as rock stars. The book is a "surprisingly literate chronicle," said Mike Tribby of *Booklist.* Tales include Burdon's time in a German prison, his pilgrimage to the actual House of the Rising Sun brothel in New Orleans, and the shady music business practices that cheated him out of millions of dollars. The absurdity of the music industry is further conveyed through his discovery that one of Burdon's actual gold records was an old Connie Francis album, a fact ascertained when he took it out of the frame and played it on his stereo. Like his first memoir, and Burdon's music in general, noted a critic for *Kirkus Reviews, Don't Let Me Be Misunderstood* contains a "theme of haunted survival," a theme which also "epitomizes Burdon's life."

## BIOGRAPHICAL AND CRITICAL SOURCES:

### BOOKS

Burdon, Eric, and Jeff Craig, *Don't Let Me Be Misunderstood,* Thunder's Mouth Press (New York, NY), 2001.

Egan, Sean, *Animal Tracks,* Helter Skelter, 2001.

*PERIODICALS*

*Booklist,* December 1, 2001, Mike Tribby, review of *Don't Let Me Be Misunderstood,* p. 621.

*Kirkus Reviews,* November 1, 2001, review of *Don't Let Me Be Misunderstood,* p. 1528.

*Library Journal,* December 2001, Lloyd Jansen, review of *Don't Let Me Be Misunderstood,* p. 126.

*Listener,* November 6, 1986, review of *I Used to Be an Animal but I'm All Right Now,* p. 36.

*New York Times Book Review,* May 3, 1987, Andrea Barnet, review of *I Used to Be an Animal but I'm All Right Now,* p. 45; February 10, 2002, Margaret Hundley Parker, review of *Don't Let Me Be Misunderstood,* p. 23.

*Publishers Weekly,* February 6, 1987, review of *I Used to Be an Animal but I'm All Right Now,* p. 92; October 22, 2001, review of *Don't Let Me Be Misunderstood,* p. 59.

*Rolling Stone,* October 27, 1983, Steve Pond, "Eric Burdon and Co.: Behaving like Animals," p. 91.

*Times Educational Supplement,* November 21, 1986, Jim Weir, "War Baby," p. 29.


OTHER


*Eric Burdon's Web site,* http://www.ericburdon.com (May 2, 2002).*


\*      \*      \*

**BURKE, Janine 1952-**

*PERSONAL:* Born March 2, 1952, in Melbourne, Australia; daughter of Brian Burke and Joyce (Hamilton) Kelly. *Education:* Melbourne University, B.A. (with honors); La Trobe University, M.A.; Deakin University, Ph.D.

*ADDRESSES: Agent*—Bryson Agency, 1/313 Flinders Ln., Melbourne, 3000, Australia. *E-mail*—jcbb@ bigpond.com.

*CAREER:* Author. Victorian College of the Arts, lecturer in art history, 1977-82; Heide Museum of Modern Art, director, 1997—. Member of programming committee, Melbourne Writers Festival, 1994-97.

*MEMBER:* Greenpeace, Amnesty International.

*AWARDS, HONORS:* Victorian Premier's Award for Fiction, 1987, for *Second Sight;* Book of the Year Award shortlist, *The Age* (Melbourne, Australia), 1989, and Miles Franklin Award shortlist, 1990, both for *Company of Images.*

*WRITINGS:*

*ADULT FICTION*

*Speaking,* Greenhouse (Richmond, Victoria, Australia), 1984.

*Second Sight,* Greenhouse (Richmond, Victoria, Australia), 1986.

*Company of Images,* Greenhouse (Elwood, Victoria, Australia), 1989.

*Lullaby,* Picador (Chippendale, Sydney, Australia), 1994.

*ADULT NONFICTION*

*Australian Women Artists, 1840-1940,* Greenhouse (Collingwood, Victoria, Australia), 1980.

*Joy Hester,* Greenhouse (Richmond, Victoria, Australia), 1983.

*Field of Vision: A Decade of Change: Women's Art in the Seventies,* Viking (Ringwood, Victoria, Australia), 1990.

(Editor) *Dear Sun: The Letters of Joy Hester and Sunday Reed,* William Heinemann Australia (Port Melbourne, Victoria, Australia), 1995.

*The Eye of the Beholder: Albert Tucker's Photographs,* Museum of Modern Art at Heide (Bulleen, Victoria, Australia), 1998.

*Australian Gothic: A Life of Albert Tucker,* Knopf (Milsons Point, New South Wales, Australia), 2002.

*YOUNG ADULT FICTION*

*Journey to Bright Water,* Mammoth (Port Melbourne, Victoria, Australia), 1994.

*The Blue Faraway,* Addison Wesley Longman (Melbourne, Victoria, Australia), 1996.

*The Doll,* illustrated by Shaun Tan, Lothian (Port Melbourne, Victoria, Australia), 1997.

*Our Lady of Apollo Bay,* Lothian (Port Melbourne, Victoria, Australia), 2001.

Contributor of book reviews to *Australian Book Review* and scholarly articles to journals, including *Hecate.*

## BIOGRAPHICAL AND CRITICAL SOURCES:

*PERIODICALS*

*Magpies,* May, 2001, Alison Gregg, review of *Our Lady of Apollo Bay,* pp. 37-38.

*Meanjin,* September, 2002, John Thompson, "Burke's Backyard: or, Just Good Friends," p. 42.

*OTHER*

*Bryson Agency Australia Web site,* http://www.bryson. com.au/ (March 3, 2003), profile of Janine Burke.

\*     \*     \*

## BUTLER, Iris (Mary) 1905-2002

*OBITUARY NOTICE*—See index for *CA* sketch: Born June 15, 1905, in Simla, India; died November 9, 2002, in North Walsham, Norfolk, England. Author. Butler was born and spent much of her early life in India while that country was still part of the British Empire. Her father was a British governor of the Central Provinces, and his work allowed her to be exposed to the people and culture of India, which she grew to love. With the onset of World War II she worked as a nurse in Delhi and Burma, but was finally compelled to return to England in 1943. When her husband, Gervas Portal, died in 1961, Butler turned her attentions to writing. She was the author of three biographies: *The Rule of Three: Sarah, Duchess of Marlborough, and Her Companions in Power* (1967), *The Viceroy's Wife: Letters of Alice, Countess of Reading, from India, 1921-25* (1969), and *The Eldest Brother: The Marquess Wellesley, the Duke of Wellington's Eldest Brother* (1973), the last two of which drew considerably on her impressive knowledge of India.

## OBITUARIES AND OTHER SOURCES:

*BOOKS*

*International Authors and Writers Who's Who,* 11th edition, International Biographical Center (Cambridge, England), 1989.

*PERIODICALS*

*Daily Telegraph* (London, England), November 22, 2002, p. 1.

*Times* (London, England), November 12, 2002, p. 34.

# C

## CACH, Lisa

*PERSONAL:* Born in Portland, OR. *Hobbies and other interests:* Reading, playing the piano, travel, hiking.

*ADDRESSES: Home*—Portland, OR. *Office*—c/o Dorchester Publishing Co., Inc., 276 Fifth Ave., Suite 1008, New York, NY 10001. *Agent*—Linda Kruger, Fogelman Literary Agency, 919 Third Ave., Suite 2700, New York, NY 10022. *E-mail*—Lisa@lisacach.com.

*CAREER:* Writer. Has worked at a zoo, a bookstore, and a crisis hotline; taught English in Japan; studied marine life in the Caribbean.

*WRITINGS:*

*The Changeling Bride,* Love Spell (New York, NY), 1999.
*Bewitching the Baron,* Love Spell (New York, NY), 2000.
*Of Midnight Born,* Love Spell (New York, NY), 2000.
*The Mermaid of Penperro,* Love Spell (New York, NY), 2001.
*The Wildest Shore,* Love Spell (New York, NY), 2001.
*Dating without Novocaine,* Red Dress Ink (New York, NY), 2002.
*George and the Virgin,* Love Spell (New York, NY), 2002.
*Dr. Yes,* Love Spell (New York, NY), 2003.

Contributor of novellas to anthologies, including "A Midnight Clear" in *Mistletoe and Magic,* Love Spell, 2000; "Eliza's Gateau," in *Seduction by Chocolate,* Love Spell, 2000; "Puddings, Pastries, and Thou," in *Wish List,* Love Spell, 2001; and "The Breeding Season," in *A Mother's Way,* Love Spell, 2002.

*SIDELIGHTS:* Lisa Cach is a historical romance novelist whose breakout book, *Dating without Novocaine,* explores the love life of twenty-nine-year-old Hannah O'Dowd, a seamstress living in Portland, Oregon. Hannah is tormented by the thought of turning thirty and having so many unanswered questions in her life, including the identity of Mr. Right. Through her friends, she meets Scott, a dentist, and Hannah is forced to confront her fear of sitting in the dentist's chair. But happily-ever-after is a complicated concept in the twenty-first century, and Hannah concludes that it is more important to create a satisfying life than to merely find a satisfying man. *Dating without Novocaine* is Cach's first contemporary romance, a contender in the fast-growing "chick lit" phenomenon spawned by the success of Helen Fielding's *Bridget Jones's Diary.* Concentrating on the dating foibles of the twentysomething set, *Dating without Novocaine* has "a certain outlandish charm," according to *Romance Reader* reviewer Susan Scribner, who summarized the book's moral as the sage and oft-stated advice to "live your own life and be happy without a man."

Cach began her writing career with the time-travel romance *The Changeling Bride.* The book takes place in 1790s England and was inspired by Jude Deveraux's *A Knight in Shining Armor.* In the novel, Wilhelmina March, a typical 1990s woman, finds herself magically transported to eighteenth-century England, and into the body of Eleanor, a young maiden betrothed to the handsome Henry Trevelyan, the Earl of Allsbrook. Henry is befuddled—but quite smitten—with the sudden, bizarre personality change the formerly recalcitrant Eleanor has undergone and does his best to seduce her. Wilhelmina, on the other hand, is consumed by the culture clash and with getting back to her normal life. Even though Henry is everything she has ever wanted in a man, her attention is diverted by issues of antiquated plumbing, birth control and corsets. Cathy Sova of the *Romance Reader* called *The Changeling Bride* an "excellent debut novel—cleverly plotted, genuinely funny, and featuring two endearing leads."

*The Mermaid of Penperro* is a similarly exotic tale, inspired by local lore Cach uncovered on a trip to Cornwall, England, that tells of a church frequented by a mermaid. In Cach's story, set in the early nineteenth century, the mermaid is actually Konstanze Bugg, a woman taking a quiet holiday to escape her wretched and overbearing husband. While sunbathing in the altogether, she flexes her operatic vocal chords to serenade herself and is overheard by Foweather, a hapless tax collector staying in town to investigate allegations of illegal activities among the townspeople. Foweather assumes her to be the town's legendary mermaid, an assumption that is reinforced when the town's smugglers convince her to play the part of the mermaid to divert Foweather's attention from their business. One of the smugglers, the handsome Tom Trewella, takes an interest in Konstanze, and helps her thwart her conniving stepson, who has just learned that she is the sole heir to his father's fortune. *Booklist* reviewer Diana Tixier Herald praised *The Mermaid of Penperro* for its "beautifully crafted, erotically charged scenes and light humorous touch." Wendy Crutcher, writing in the *Romance Reader,* called it a "fun romance, the perfect cure for when you have had a bad day."

In *The Wildest Shore,* a Regency-period romance, shipwrecked lady's maid Anne Hazlett is rescued by homeward-bound army officer Horatio Merivale. As they face disaster and adventure while trying to find their way to safety from their cobbled raft adrift in the Indian Ocean, Horatio finds himself enraptured by Anne, who is not so quick to return the sentiment. Rather than sailing back home to England, Anne insists that the raft sail east, toward an island in the South Seas she believes is her destiny.

Cach's novel *Bewitching the Baron* features a heroine, Valerian, who possesses healing powers and a talking pet raven. But when townspeople suspect her of being a witch, she is delivered from harm's way by the dashing Baron Ravenall. Their romance has trouble getting off the ground, however, when Valerian refuses to give in to his advances in order to guard her secret powers. The novel prompted Sova to call Cach "an author of ingenuity when it comes to plotting and characters."

Cach is a lifelong resident of Portland, Oregon, who began writing seriously while working the night shift at a crisis hot line. In addition to her historical romance novels, she has published novellas in several anthologies, including *Mistletoe and Magic, Seduction by Chocolate, Wish List,* and *A Mother's Way.*

*BIOGRAPHICAL AND CRITICAL SOURCES:*

*PERIODICALS*

*Booklist,* May 1, 2001, Diana Tixier Herald, review of *The Mermaid of Penperro,* p. 1670.
*Publishers Weekly,* February 25, 2002, review of *Dating without Novocaine,* p. 41.

*OTHER*

*Lisa Cach Web site,* http://www.lisacach.com (May 2, 2002).
*Romance Reader,* http://www.theromancereader.com/ (June 13, 2002), Cathy Sova, review of *Bewitching the Baron* and *Of Midnight Born;* Susan Scribner, review of *Dating without Novocaine;* Wendy Crutcher, review of *The Mermaid of Penperro;* Nancy J. Silberstein, review of *The Wildest Shore.*\*

\*            \*            \*

**CARDINAL, Douglas J(oseph) 1934-**

*PERSONAL:* Born March 7, 1934 in Calgary, Alberta, Canada. *Education:* Attended University of British Columbia, Vancouver, 1953-54; University of Texas, Austin, B.Arch. 1963.

*ADDRESSES: Office*—Douglas J. Cardinal Architect Ltd., 10160 112th Street, Edmonton, Alberta T5K 2L6, Canada.

*CAREER:* Design architect, Bissell and Holman, Red Deer, Alberta, Canada, 1963-67; Principal, Douglas J. Cardinal Architect, Red Deer, 1964-67, then Edmonton, Alberta, 1967—.

*AWARDS, HONORS:* Honor award, Alberta Association of Architects, 1968; honor award, 1969 and Award of Excellence, 1978, both from the City of Red Deer, Alberta; Award of Excellence, *Canadian Architect,* 1972; member, Royal Canadian Academy of Arts, 1974; Achievement of Excellence Award in Architecture, Province of Alberta, 1974; fellow, Royal Architectural Institute of Canada, 1983; Banff Centre National Arts Award, 1990; Canada Council Molson Prize for the Arts, 1993; Aboriginal Achievement Award, 1995; honorary doctorates, University of Windsor, Ontario, University of Calgary, Alberta.

*WRITINGS:*

*Of the Spirit,* NeWest Press (Edmonton, Alberta, Canada), 1977.
(With Trevor Boddy) *The Architecture of Douglas Cardinal,* NeWest Press (Edmonton, Alberta, Canada), 1989.
(With Jeanette C. Armstrong) *The Native Creative Process,* Theytus Books, 1994.

*SIDELIGHTS:* Douglas J. Cardinal is an architect who was born in the village of Red Deer in Alberta, Canada. His father was a member of the Blackfeet tribe. He began studying architecture at the University of British Columbia, but was asked to withdraw because of his radical designs and ideas about creating buildings. Cardinal finished his degree at the University of Texas and went on to become one of the most famous and well-respected Native American architects in North America. He is especially recognized for his innovative and enterprising use of technology, such as computer-drawn blueprints. Cardinal has designed prominent buildings, such as The Institute of American Indian Arts in Santa Fe, New Mexico and the National Museum of the American Indian in Washington, D.C.

Cardinal maintains close contacts with his family and tribal elders, claiming that these relationships nurture and influence his work. He often manages to combine modern ideas about architecture with certain ancient traditions, such as his emphasis on the circle and curvilinearity in his designs. These concepts are distinctly Native American, honoring the sacred hoop of creation.

Cardinal is also the author a collection of writings published in 1977, titled *Of the Spirit.* He has also contributed personal essays to the book *The Architecture of Douglas Cardinal.*

*BIOGRAPHICAL AND CRITICAL SOURCES:*

BOOKS

*Native North American Artists,* St. James Press (Detroit, MI), 1998.

PERIODICALS

*Architecture,* May, 1998, Heidi Landecker, "American Indian Museum Ousts Architect," p. 38; December, 1999, Michelle Patient, "Court Fines Indian Museum: Grant Cardinal Shared Authorship," p. 39.
*Financial Post,* April 27, 1996, Peter Morton, "Designs on America," p. 27.
*Maclean's,* July 10, 1989, Pamela Young, "Showcasing Canada," p. 38; June 3, 1996, "Home on the Mall," p. 13.
*Progressive Architecture,* September, 1989, Adele Freedman, "'Right-sided' Museum for Ottawa," p. 21.
*Time,* July 10, 1989, Kurt Anderson, "A Grand Folly in Ottawa: Canada's Newest Museum Is Costly, Controversial, and Curious," p. 64.*

*      *      *

**CARROLL, Vinnette (Justine) 1922-2002**

*OBITUARY NOTICE*—See index for *CA* sketch: Born 1922 in New York, NY; died November 5, 2002, in Lauderhill, FL. Director, actress, and author. Carroll was a trailblazing theater director and the first African-American woman to direct a play on Broadway. In college she originally worked toward a degree in psychology because her father wanted her to be a doctor. After earning a bachelor's degree from Long Island University in 1944 and a master's degree in psychology from New York University in 1946, she studied at Cambridge University before deciding to switch careers to pursue her real love: the theater. She studied at the New School of Social Research's Erwin Pescator dramatic workshop and then found work as an actress with the Harlem YMCA and other venues; for a time, during the 1950s, she starred in her own one-woman show, which she also wrote. Carroll began to gain recognition in the 1960s as an actress in *Moon over a Rainbow Shawl,* for which she received an Obie Award in 1962; she was acclaimed for her role in *Trumpets of the Lord;* and in 1964 she received an Emmy Award for her performance in *Beyond the Blues* and *Jubilation.* By the 1960s Carroll was also directing such plays as *Prodigal Son,* in which she also acted, and in 1967 she founded and became artistic director of the Urban Arts Corps, an organization that trained black and Hispanic actors and produced plays written by minorities. During the 1970s Carroll again gained praise for conceiving the musical plays *Don't Bother Me, I Can't Cope* (1970), for which she won a Drama Desk award, a Tony award, an Image award from the National Association for the Advancement of Colored People, and a Los Angeles Drama Critics Circle award for directing, and *Your Arms Too Short to Box with God* (1975), for which she was nominated for a Tony award. Both plays enjoyed long Broadway runs and revivals. Carroll was also the author of such plays as *Step Lively, Boy* (1973), *I'm Laughin' but I Ain't Tickled* (1976), and *What You Gonna Name That Pretty Little Baby?* (1978). As an actress, she also appeared in several films, including *Up the Down Staircase* and *Alice's Restaurant.* After buying a home in Florida, Carroll split her time in the 1980s between New York City and Florida, where she founded the Vinnette Carroll Repertory Company in Fort Lauderdale. Among Carroll's other awards are a Audelco Achievement Award for outstanding contribution to black theatre and a Black Filmmakers Hall of Fame award.

*OBITUARIES AND OTHER SOURCES:*

BOOKS

*Contemporary Black Biography,* Volume 29, Gale (Detroit, MI), 2002.
*Who's Who among African Americans,* 14th edition, Gale (Detroit, MI), 2001.

PERIODICALS

*Chicago Tribune,* November 8, 2002, section 3, p. 13.
*Los Angeles Times,* November 7, 2002, p. B25.
*New York Times,* November 7, 2002, p. A27.

\*      \*      \*

## CHEE, Alexander 1967-

*PERSONAL:* Born 1967, in South Kingston, RI. *Education:* University of Iowa Writers Workshop, M.F.A.

*ADDRESSES: Agent*—c/o Author Mail, Welcome Rain Publishers/Stewart, Tabori & Chang, 115 West 18th St., New York, NY 10011. *E-mail*—unstricken@aol.com; achee@wesleyan.edu.

*CAREER:* Writer. Wesleyan University, Middletown, CT, visiting writer.

*AWARDS, HONORS:* Michenor Prize for *Edinburgh.*

*WRITINGS:*

*Edinburgh,* Welcome Rain Publishers (New York, NY), 2001.

Contributor of stories and essays to anthologies and periodicals.

*SIDELIGHTS:* Alexander Chee's debut novel, *Edinburgh,* addresses the painful subject of child abuse. "If a story about child molestation could ever be beautiful, this first novel comes very close to that unusual mark," wrote Michael Spinella in *Booklist.* In the story, Aphias Zee, nicknamed Fee, is a young Korean American in a professional boys' choir, whose director turns out to be a serial child molester. "Big Eric"'s sexual assaults have devastating results on Fee and his friends, especially his first love, Peter, who kills himself rather than live with the shame and the pain of what happened to him. Even after the choir director's arrest and conviction, Fee's life continues to spiral out of control. "Chee is a gifted, poetic writer who takes big risks, from the background and sexual orientation of his protagonist to the chapters dealing with drugs, pedophilia and casual sex with grace and unflinching honesty," wrote a reviewer for *Publishers Weekly.*

Ann Abel, writing in the *New York Times,* also noted this poetic quality. "If his metaphors occasionally seem more sophisticated than his teenage narrators, it's forgivable because they're generally so evocative . . . Chee frequently says volumes with just a few incendiary words." These incendiary words are not incidental. As Chee told a *Publishers Weekly* interviewer, "I'd been writing *Edinburgh* around the unanswered question of why a boy might set himself on fire." The result, according to a *Kirkus Reviews* contributor, is a "complex story told with skill and intensity, but also filled with moments when agony and extraordinary beauty somehow coexist."

*BIOGRAPHICAL AND CRITICAL SOURCES:*

*PERIODICALS*

*Booklist,* November 15, 2001, Michael Spinella, review of *Edinburgh,* p. 550.
*Kirkus Reviews,* October 1, 2001, review of *Edinburgh,* p. 1379.
*New York Times,* January 20, 2002, Ann Abel, "In Destiny's Choir," p. 19.
*Publishers Weekly,* October 8, 2001, review of *Edinburgh,* p. 43; November 8, 2001, interview with Alexander Chee.*

\*      \*      \*

**CHESLER, Bernice 1932-2002**

*OBITUARY NOTICE*—See index for *CA* sketch: Born October 3, 1932, in New Bedford, MA; died of cancer September 4, 2002, in Newton, MA. Author. Chesler was renowned for her popular books on bed-and-breakfast inns. She was a graduate of Northeastern University, where she earned her B.A. in 1955. After graduating, she worked in public relations for WBGH-TV and WGBH-FM in Cambridge, Massachusetts for two years. During the early 1970s she also worked as a research and publications coordinator for the children's television program *Zoom* and edited

the spin-off book *Do a Zoom Do* in 1975). However, Chesler is best remembered for her books about B & B's, which not only told travelers the basic facts about small inns across America, but also tried to inform readers about the inns' hosts and atmosphere. These books include *Bed and Breakfast in the Northeast* (1983), *Bed and Breakfast Coast to Coast* (1986), *Bed and Breakfast in New England* (1987; seventh edition, 2000), and *Bed and Breakfast in the Mid-Atlantic States: Delaware, District of Columbia, Maryland, New Jersey, New York, Pennsylvania, Virginia, West Virginia* (1987; fifth edition, 1997). She was also the author of *In and out of Boston, with Children* (1966; fifth edition, 1992) and coauthor of *The Family Guide to Cape Cod: What to Do When You Don't Want to Do What Everyone Else Is Doing* (1976).

*OBITUARIES AND OTHER SOURCES:*

*PERIODICALS*

*New York Times,* September 16, 2002, p. A19.

\*      \*      \*

**CHESTER, May**
**    See ROLFE, Frederick (William Serafino Austin Lewis Mary)**

\*      \*      \*

**CLEMENT, Charles B(axter) 1940-2002**

*OBITUARY NOTICE*—See index for *CA* sketch: Born March 27, 1940, in Memphis, TN; died of heart failure September 14, 2002, in Milwaukee, WI. Businessman, attorney, and author. Clement had an eclectic career in the hotel business, antiques, venture capitalism, and literature. He graduated from Princeton University with a bachelor's degree in comparative literature in 1962, followed by a law degree from the University of Virginia Law School in 1965 and a master's degree in law from the University of Heidelberg in 1967. Admitted to the Bar of Tennessee in 1966 and the Bar of Illinois in 1976, Clement practiced law only briefly before becoming involved in building hotels. Hired by Kemmons Wilson, founder of the Holiday Inn chain, and later working for Armand Hammer, he traveled throughout northern Africa and Europe, building hotels on both sides of the Iron Curtain. Returning to the United States, he opened an antiques store in Memphis called Old World Tiles, which he later moved to Chicago. In Chicago Clement next started the New South Venture Capital Company and joined the Chicago Board of Trade. In between his many business enterprises, Clement somehow also found time to write, and is the author of two novels: *The Fairy Godmother* (1981) and *Limit Bid! Limit Bid!* (1984).

*OBITUARIES AND OTHER SOURCES:*

BOOKS

Roberts, Nancy L., *American Peace Writers, Editors, and Periodicals: A Dictionary,* Greenwood Press (New York, NY), 1991.

PERIODICALS

*Chicago Tribune,* September 22, 2002, section 4, p. 9.

\*          \*          \*

## COBBING, Bob 1920-2002

*OBITUARY NOTICE*—See index for *CA* sketch: Born July 30, 1920, in Enfield, England; died September 29, 2002, in London, England. Publisher, educator, painter, and author. Cobbing was an innovative poet of the modernist school who was known for his concrete, sound, and visual poetry and for heading the Writers' Forum press. He began his career, however, as an accountant, civil servant, and farmer before World War II, switching to teaching art, literature, and music in Swindon, England from 1944 to 1948. After receiving his teaching certificate from Bognor Training College in 1949, Cobbing taught in London schools until 1964, when he became manager of the city's Better Books Poetry Bookshop. The Bookshop, where he worked until 1967, was well known for carrying underground literature and for helping to publish the early works of Allen Ginsberg and P. J. O'Rourke. All the time he was pursuing these other careers, Cobbing was also writing poetry, often in the style of the concrete move-

ment popular in the 1950s and 1960s. Interested in going beyond the limitations of the printed word, he explored the relationship between language, art, and music, and often performed his pieces on British and Swedish radio, then live performances. Working in publishing as joint editor of the magazine *And* in the 1950s and then founding Writers Forum in 1963, Cobbing experimented with visual poetry—he was an abstract painter—sometimes using shapes and patterns rather than words to blend art and poetry, and experimenting with type in an attempt to convey visceral meanings. This blending of art forms was also employed in his live performances, and Cobbing organized workshops through Writers' Forum where poets could come together and share their ideas. He also organized the International Sound Poetry Festivals and was an active member of the Poetry Society. Publishing dozens of poetry collections in his lifetime, some of his more recent verse works include *Circuit* (1998), *Voices* (1999), and *Shrieks and Hisses: Collected Poems* (1999). Many of Cobbing's best-known poems were collected in *Bill Jubobe* (1976) and *Bob Jubile* (1990), while a third collection of his most important verses was planned for publication in 2003. Cobbing also edited, with Peter Mayer, the study *Concerning Concrete Poetry* (1976).

*OBITUARIES AND OTHER SOURCES:*

BOOKS

*Contemporary Poets,* seventh edition, St. James Press (Detroit, MI), 2001.

PERIODICALS

*Guardian* (London, England), October 7, 2002, p. 20.
*Independent* (London, England), October 2, 2002, p. 22.
*Times* (London, England), November 7, 2002.

\*          \*          \*

## COHEN, Josh 1970-

*PERSONAL:* Born 1970.

*ADDRESSES: Agent*—c/o Author Mail, Pluto Press, 22883 Quicksilver Dr., Sterling, VA 20166-2012.

*CAREER:* Academic and author.

*WRITINGS:*

*Spectacular Allegories: Postmodern American Writing and the Politics of Seeing,* Pluto (Sterling, VA), 1998.

*SIDELIGHTS:* American scholar and author Josh Cohen published his debut work, *Spectacular Allegories: Postmodern American Writing and the Politics of Seeing,* in 1998. The highly academic book, which was influenced by the work of Walter Benjamin and his "politics of seeing," discusses the manner in which television and film have impacted the way American authors write. In fact, Cohen believes that contemporary American novels and films have become a "simulatory universe." Cohen's main thesis is that the consumerist nature of film, with its sight and sound, have become overwhelming influences on the novel in postmodern America and that writers are weighted down by the politics of correctness. Cohen is particularly critical of consumerism, which he describes as "a condition in which the narrating subjects' eroding authority reproduces the political importance of the collective."

In an attempt to prove his hypotheses, Cohen makes references to recent American literary works. For example, he refers to Norman Mailer's *The Deer Park* as "a symbolic repository of American mass culture's fetish of surfaces." Furthermore, Cohen feels the works of novelists such as Robert Coover, Stephen Dixon, and Jerzy Kosinski have become "cinematographic fiction" because of their reliance on visuality. To show how this trend seems to be unique to American writing, Cohen compares and contrasts writings from America with those from the German district of Northumbria. Rather than consumerism, Cohen believes the Northumbrian writers are more driven by empiricism, which he explains as actual reality versus the perception of reality. By contrast, in America the politics of seeing has skewed the perception of reality. Feeling the effort "deserves applause," *Times Literary Supplement* critic A. Robert Lee called the work "a genuine and timely attempt to find a new grammar for a new American writing."

*BIOGRAPHICAL AND CRITICAL SOURCES:*

BOOKS

Cohen, Josh, *Spectacular Allegories: Postmodern American Writing and the Politics of Seeing,* Pluto (Sterling, VA), 1998.

PERIODICALS

*Times Literary Supplement,* December 18, 1998, p. 21.*

\*    \*    \*

## COHEN, Randy 1948-

*PERSONAL:* Born July 12, 1948, in Charleston, SC; son of Harry and Irma (Greenberg) Cohen; children: one daughter. *Education:* State University of New York—Albany, B.A., 1971; California Institute of Arts, Los Angeles, CA, M.F.A., 1973.

*ADDRESSES: Home*—New York, NY. *Agent*—c/o Author Mail, Random House, 1540 Broadway, New York, NY 10036.

*CAREER:* Freelance writer, New York, NY, 1974-84; *Late Night with David Letterman,* New York, NY, staff writer, beginning 1984; *Rosie O'Donnell Show,* head writer; *TV Nation,* writer. *New York Times Magazine,* columnist, "The Ethicist."

*AWARDS, HONORS:* Emmy Awards Late Night with David Letterman, 1985, 1986, 1987, TV Nation, 1995.

*WRITINGS:*

*Easy Answers to Hard Questions,* Fawcett (New York, NY), 1979.
(With Alexandra Anderson-Spivy) *Why Didn't I Think of That?,* Fawcett (New York, NY), 1980.
*Modest Proposals: The Official Correspondence of Randy Cohen,* St. Martin's Press (New York, NY), 1981.
*Diary of a Flying Man,* Knopf (New York, NY), 1989.
*The Good, the Bad, and the Difference: How to Tell Right from Wrong in Everyday Situations,* Doubleday (New York, NY), 2002.

Contributor of column "The Ethicist" to *New York Times Magazine.*

*SIDELIGHTS:* From television sketch comedy to wrestling with serious ethical issues, Randy Cohen's varied writing career has generally focused on everyday concerns, but with a distinctive, often absurdist twist. In 1979 he published *Easy Answers to Hard Questions,* which addresses questions drawn from popular culture, including songs and clichés. Questions such as "How clean is a whistle?" and "Why must I be a teenager in love?" get real answers, and according to a reviewer in *Kliatt,* "This unique, imaginative book will fascinate every reader."

In 1981, Cohen went from answer man to unsolicited-advice man, collecting the results in *Modest Proposals: The Official Correspondence of Randy Cohen.* The "modest proposals" are actually ridiculous suggestions sent to public figures, such as a letter advising New York Mayor Ed Koch to allow prostitution on city buses as a means of increasing fares and "keeping crime off the streets." A *Kliatt* contributor wrote, "The zaniness is not just with the proposals themselves, but in the elaborate cleverness of the letters and even in the answers which are sent to him." A *New York* reviewer advised people to be careful where they read the book, as "it can make you fall, giggling, out of the hammock."

In *Diary of a Flying Man,* Cohen dispenses with quips, questions, and letters to skewer the everyday in a series of fictional stories. In these pieces, ordinary characters find themselves dealing with ridiculous situations, either of their own making or not. The stories are "well-crafted, highly conceptual (sometimes too conceptual) and play off cultural trends and journalistic styles," according to Leah Rozen in the *Los Angeles Times Book Review.* In the title story, a man miraculously given the power of flight finds he still can't escape the day-to-day frustrations of a typical New Yorker. In another, parents train their toddlers for the Kentucky Derby. (The rules specify that entrants must be three-year-olds, but they don't say which species.) The everyday details are every bit as important as the oddities. "Throughout, Cohen has perfect pitch when reproducing newspaper cant or the flak-talk of public relations pros who are expert only in gilding the silly," wrote a *Kirkus Reviews* contributor. For Ed Weiner, writing in the *New York Times Book Review,* "He forces us to ponder a scary question: which is the more absurd—the real world or Randy Cohen's version of it?"

In a sense, Cohen comes full circle as writer of the *New York Times Magazine*'s "The Ethicist" column, but unlike *Easy Answers to Hard Questions,* both the questions and the answers are serious. The column addresses ethical issues that arise in the course of ordinary life, such as whether one should tell a friend that their spouse is cheating or whether it is okay to profit from a class-action lawsuit if the product did not hurt you personally. In 2002 Cohen published *The Good, the Bad, and the Difference: How to Tell Right from Wrong in Everyday Situations,* a collection of his columns with a great deal more on his theory of ethics, some follow-up with people who took his advice, and even a chapter on columns he has changed his mind about. As Cohen himself told a *Publishers Weekly* reviewer, "it's a chance to write about my background, how the column developed, what I hope to accomplish in it. And in a more theoretical way, how I think about ethics."

Jesse Berrett, critiquing the book for the *New York Times Book Review,* wrote, "While Cohen himself occasionally reverts to tiresome one-liners, for the most part he is cleareyed, reasonable and engaging." A *Booklist* reviewer called it "a very handy guide to some tricky everyday problems," and a *Publishers Weekly* contributor wrote, "Cohen's weekly fans will want this for their reference shelves; word of mouth should take it much further."

*BIOGRAPHICAL AND CRITICAL SOURCES:*

*PERIODICALS*

*Booklist,* February 15, 2002, David Pitt, review of *The Good, the Bad, and the Difference,* p. 972.
*Kirkus Reviews,* September 15, 1989, Leah Rozen, review of *Diary of a Flying Man,* p. 1372.
*Kliatt,* January, 1980, review of *Easy Answers to Hard Questions,* p. 70; September, 1981, review of *Modest Proposals,* pp. 73-74.
*Los Angeles Times Book Review,* November 26, 1989, review of *Diary of a Flying Man,* p. 33.
*New York,* July 6, 1981, Rhoda Koenig, review of *Modest Proposals,* p. 90.
*New York Times Book Review,* March 24, 2002, Jesse Berrett, review of *The Good, the Bad, and the Difference,* p. 21.
*Publishers Weekly,* February 18, 2002, review of *The Good, the Bad, and the Difference,* p. 87, and Lynn Andriani, "PW Talks with the Ethicist," p. 88.*

## COHEN, William B(enjamin) 1941-2002

*OBITUARY NOTICE*—See index for *CA* sketch: Born May 2, 1941, in Jakobstad, Finland; died after a fall November 25, 2002, in Bloomington, IN. Historian, educator, and author. Cohen was a noted historian who taught Western civilization and was considered an expert on French colonial history. The son of a physician with the World Health Organization, he spent much of his childhood in Ethiopia, moving to the United States in 1957 after his father died. He earned his B.A. from Pomona College in 1962 and attended graduate school at Stanford University, where he received his Ph.D. in 1968. Except for a year spent teaching at Northwestern University from 1966 to 1967, Cohen spent his entire academic career at Indiana University in Bloomington, teaching history there from 1967 until his untimely death. He was promoted to professor of history in 1980 and was chairman of West European studies from 1978 to 1980 and chairman of the department of history from 1980 to 1987. Cohen specialized in French colonial history, writing several books on the subject, among them *Rulers of Empire: The French Colonial Service in Africa* (1971), *The French Encounter with Africans: White Response to Blacks, 1530-1880* (1980), and *Urban Government and the Rise of the French City: Five Municipalities in the Nineteenth Century* (1998). At the time of his death he was at work on a book to be titled *The Algerian War and French Memory, 1962-2002*.

*OBITUARIES AND OTHER SOURCES:*

*BOOKS*

*Writers Directory,* 17th edition, St. James Press (Detroit, MI), 2002.

*OTHER*

*Indiana University Web site,* http://www.indiana.edu/ (February 3, 2003), "William B. Cohen, in Memoriam."

\*      \*      \*

## COLBERT, Nancy A. 1936-

*PERSONAL:* Born February 2, 1936, in Cedar Rapids, IA; daughter of George and Eleanor A. (Dvorak) Shearer; children: James T., Susan Colbert Hyler, Sally J. Kenney, Mary Ellen Lancaster, Martin J. Colbert.

*Education:* Kirkwood Community College, A.A., 1976; University of Iowa, B.A. (summa cum laude), 1992. *Politics:* Democrat. *Religion:* Catholic. *Hobbies and other interests:* Tent camping, fishing, reading.

*ADDRESSES: Home and office*—228 Wilson Ave. SW, Cedar Rapids, IA 52404. *E-mail*—nacwrites@aol.com.

*CAREER:* Homemaker, 1954—. Collins Radio Co., Cedar Rapids, IA, secretary, 1954-57; Kirkwood Community College, Cedar Rapids, department secretary, 1971-74; Kudart & Holmes (law firm), Cedar Rapids, legal secretary, 1974-81. St. Ludmila Catholic Church, member of parish council, liturgy committee, and worship space committee and lay minister.

*WRITINGS:*

*Lou Henry Hoover: The Duty to Serve,* Morgan Reynolds Publishing (Greensboro, NC), 1998.
*The Firing on Fort Sumter: A Splintered Nation Goes to War,* Morgan Reynolds Publishing (Greensboro, NC), 2001.
*Great Society: The Story of Lyndon Baines Johnson,* Morgan Reynolds Publishing (Greensboro, NC), 2002.

*WORK IN PROGRESS:* Research on U.S. President Harry S Truman.

*SIDELIGHTS:* Nancy A. Colbert told *CA:* "Writing, for me, has always been an outlet for thoughts and emotions. Although I've never been a faithful journal writer—I have numerous spiral notebooks, fancy diaries, and binders, enthusiastically begun but never filled—to prove that. But for years I have jotted thoughts and poems and observations and whatever entered my head . . . on nearby scraps of paper. I have perfected the ability to write in the dark while in bed on a three-by-four [inch] scratchpad and have it readable in the morning. These bits and pieces convinced me that I might be able to be a writer, a real writer. I worked at perfecting my craft, publishing a couple of poems, a short story, and articles in small publications."

Colbert chose as the subject for her first biography the wife of one of the least popular presidents in U.S. history, Herbert Hoover, who has been criticized for the ineffectual approach to economic recovery after the stock market crash of 1929 that began the Great Depression. In *Lou Henry Hoover: The Duty to Serve,* Colbert reveals that the future president met Lou Henry while both were attending Stanford University; after their marriage Lou Henry Hoover concluded her studies by becoming the first woman to earn a degree in geology from an American university. Her life was studded with other stellar achievements, as she and her husband, a mining engineer, traveled all over the world, living through the Boxer Revolution in China and staying on in Europe during World War I to aid in the war effort. Colbert emphasizes Hoover's scholarship, including her co-translation (with her husband) of a sixteenth-century mining book in Latin and her penchant for speaking Chinese to husband Herbert when discretion demanded it, as well as her good works, including her role in the Girl Scouts of America. While a contributor to *Kirkus Reviews* called the work "a serviceable biography of one of the unsung women of the era," for GraceAnne A. DeCandido, writing in *Booklist, Lou Henry Hoover: The Duty to Serve* is "a fascinating life that puts a very different perspective on the Depression and the years before and after."

Colbert explained to *CA* how she decided to write about Lou Henry Hoover: "After writing seven middle-grade and young adult novels and not finding a home for any of them at a publishing house, I turned to non-fiction. A first lady of the United States had caught my attention and admiration. Lou Henry Hoover, Mrs. Herbert Hoover, was born and lived part of her childhood in Iowa. The Herbert Hoover Presidential Library is at West Branch, Iowa, and is within driving distance of my home. I made the trip many times to research this important woman. From this interest came my first published book, *Lou Henry Hoover: The Duty to Serve.* The excitement of the editor's telephone call offering me a contract goes down in my personal history as one of the highlights of my life. Holding that first book when my box of author's copies arrived sold me on the writing life. No matter how much work, time, or heartache it required, this was what I wanted to do. Write."

In her second book, *The Firing on Fort Sumter: A Splintered Nation Goes to War,* Colbert details the events that immediately preceded the onset of the U.S. Civil War. "The writing is lively and interesting, and the information is presented clearly and in detail," remarked Gillian Wiseman in *Voice of Youth Advocates.* For Jack Forman, who reviewed the book for the *Horn Book Guide,* the key to the success of Colbert's second work is her "sharply etched characterizations" of the decision-makers on both sides of the issue.

According to Colbert, *The Firing on Fort Sumter: A Splintered Nation Goes to War* "was written with a much cooler head but no less impassioned heart because of the story itself. I felt this was a story that needed to be told. The terrible 'what if' stood before me as I wrote. Could the Civil War have been averted? If so, how? These are questions for young (and older) minds to grapple with. I believe that looking at history teaches us about life and helps us live today. I hope to help history to be part of my readers' lives with my books."

A single individual is at the center of Colbert's third biography for young adults, *Great Society: The Story of Lyndon Baines Johnson.* The author's focus here is on a president who is remembered for his vision of his country as a "Great Society" and for allowing the United States to become inextricably entangled in the Vietnam War. Colbert presents a portrait of Johnson that takes into account all sides of his personality: his facility for politicking, his immoderate temper, and his generosity of spirit, demonstrated in the pivotal role he played in the fight for civil rights for African Americans and for the poor. *Booklist*'s Kay Weisman characterized Colbert's effort as "a solid, readable introduction for both report writers and history buffs."

When asked why she writes, Colbert told *CA:* "I write because it is part of me. I feel being able to express ideas in the written word is a gift I have been given and that it is my responsibility to use it to the best of my ability. Life itself often takes precedence over writing—husband, family, friends, church—but this is what provides the base to all writing. And when I'm not writing, I'm reading."

*BIOGRAPHICAL AND CRITICAL SOURCES:*

*PERIODICALS*

*Booklist,* February 15, 1998, GraceAnne A. DeCandido, review of *Lou Henry Hoover: The Duty to Serve,* p. 1002; April 15, 2002, Kay Weisman, review of *Great Society: The Story of Lyndon Baines Johnson,* p. 1396.

*Horn Book Guide,* spring, 2001, Jack Forman, review of *The Firing on Fort Sumter: A Splintered Nation Goes to War,* p. 156.

*Kirkus Reviews,* October 15, 1997, review of *Lou Henry Hoover,* p. 1579.

*School Library Journal,* March, 1998, Susan R. Farber, review of *Lou Henry Hoover,* p. 230; August, 2002, Andrew Medlar, review of *Great Society,* p. 204.

*Voice of Youth Advocates,* June, 2001, Gillian Wiseman, review of *The Firing on Fort Sumter,* p. 139.

\*　　\*　　\*

## CONLON-McKENNA, Marita 1956-

*PERSONAL:* Born November 5, 1956, in Dublin, Ireland; daughter of Patrick J. (a businessman) and Mary (Murphy) Conlon; married James David McKenna, August, 26, 1977; children: Amanda, Laura, Fiona, James. *Education:* St. Nicholas Montessori College, diploma, 1983. *Religion:* Roman Catholic.

*ADDRESSES: Home*—Homewood, 50 Stillorgan Grove, Blackrock, County Dublin, Ireland.

*CAREER:* Writer. Fund raiser for Mount Anville N.S. parents council; affiliated with Kilmacud Children's Summer Project.

*AWARDS, HONORS:* Reading Association of Ireland Award, 1991; International Reading Association Award, 1991; Irish Arts Council Bursary award, 1991; Bisto Book of the Year, 1991-92, 1992-93; Irish Children's Book Trust Award, 1992, for historical fiction, and Book of the Year award, 1993; Osterreichischen Kinder und jugendbuchpreis, 1993.

*WRITINGS:*

'CHILDREN OF FAMINE' TRILOGY

(Illustrated by Donald Teskey) *Under the Hawthorn Tree,* Holiday House (New York, NY), 1990.

(Illustrated by Donald Teskey) *Wildflower Girl,* Holiday House (New York, NY), 1992.

(Illustrated by Donald Teskey) *Fields of Home,* Holiday House (New York, NY), 1996.

OTHER

*My First Holy Communion,* Veritas (Ireland), 1990.

*The Blue Horse,* O'Brien Press (Dublin, Ireland), 1992.

(Illustrated by Christopher Coady) *Little Star,* Little, Brown (Boston, MA), 1993.

(Illustrated by Christopher Coady) *The Very Last Unicorn,* Little, Brown (Boston, MA), 1994.

*Safe Harbor,* O'Brien Press (Dublin, Ireland), 1997.

*No Goodbye,* O'Brien Press (Dublin, Ireland), 1998.

*Granny MacGinty,* O'Brien Press (Dublin, Ireland), 1999.

*In Deep Dark Wood,* O'Brien Press (Dublin, Ireland), 1999.

*The Magdalen,* Forge (New York, NY), 2002.

*Promised Land,* Severn House (New York, NY), 2002.

*SIDELIGHTS:* An award-winning children's book author, Marita Conlon-McKenna is probably best known for her "Children of Famine" series, a trilogy of young adult novels about the Irish Potato Famine and its effects on three young children. In the first of these, *Under the Hawthorn Tree,* the O'Driscoll family faces starvation when their potato crop fails. After burying her dead baby, the mother sets out to find the father, who has left the farm to seek work as a roadbuilder. When Mother fails to return, twelve-year-old Eily is forced to take on the responsibility of her younger brother, Michael, and their younger sister, Peggy. When the local bailiff threatens to send them to the disease-ridden workhouse, they must undertake a harrowing journey to find their great aunts, living many miles away in Castletaggart. A *Junior Bookshelf* reviewer praised it as "A vivid recreation of the Ireland of the Great Famine of 1845-50," and a *School Library Journal* contributor found, similarly, that "The horrors of the potato famine in Ireland vividly leap from the pages of this first novel." Betsy Hearne wrote in the *Bulletin of the Center for Children's Books* that "The historical situation is projected through credible characterizations and brisk action that will sustain readers' interest to a fortuitous ending." *School Librarian* contributor Maggie Bignell remarked "I shall certainly welcome the book into the library for those pupils who want a break from stories about peer-group problems in this century. It may make some of them think again about their own materialistic values."

In the sequel, *Wildflower Girl,* the children have survived the famine, but poverty still haunts them, and when passage to America is offered, the youngest sister, Peggy, takes advantage of it. "Readers will feel the enormity of her decision and the pain of leaving loved ones behind," noted Renee Steinberg in the *School Library Journal.* Similarly, Jane Van Wiemokly wrote in the *Voice of Youth Advocates,* "Young readers can learn a lot of the plight of immigrants during this time in history, along with all they had to endure." Once ashore, Peggy finds herself enduring a "boozy landlady" running a boardinghouse and then long hours and hard work as a scullery maid for a wealthy family. This is "dramatic history individualized through the action of a determined survivor," wrote Betsy Hearne in the *Bulletin of the Center for Children's Books.* "One thing is certain," concluded a *Junior Bookshelf* contributor. "Marita Conlon-McKenna has a deep understanding of Irish history and character which she writes of with an engaging clarity and non-partisan point of view."

In the concluding volume of the trilogy, *Fields of Home,* the original children have grown up, and Eily has children of her own. Still, life is not settled. Eily and her husband might lose their tenant farm. Michael, training as a horseman, loses his position when angry Irish tenants burn down the property where he works. And Peggy must decide whether to stay on as a maid or take a chance on life in the Wild West. A *Booklist* reviewer felt that "much of this reads like an add-on to the taut narratives of the first two books." *Bulletin of the Center for Children's Books* reviewer Betsy Hearne wrote, the "depictions of socioeconomic upheaval are accurate, honest, and nuanced," but felt "the narrative, though absorbing . . . suffers from shifts in place and focus." Not all critics shared these trepidations. *School Library Journal* reviewer Elaine Fort Weischedel felt that the "transitions between the intertwined lines are handled nicely, avoiding confusions." According to a *Kirkus Reviews* contributor, "Every character in the book is believable, and every line is beautifully written; still, it's the powerful sense of the importance of family that makes this tale singular."

In addition to this historical trilogy, Marita Conlon-McKenna has written a number of other children's books, including *Little Star,* about a star that gets trapped in a little boy's room and starts to dim until the boy figures out what he must do to save it. *School Library Journal* Christine A. Moesch called it a "nice book, and a good bedtime story," but with "the potential to be so much more." In *No Goodbye,*

Conlon-McKenna tells the story of a mother who suddenly abandons her family, and how the children cope with this tragedy. While noting that the author had "captured and encapsulated many of the practical difficulties and touched on the emotional turmoil," a *Magpies* reviewer felt that the story "doesn't quite convince," particularly when comparing the devastating actions of the mother with her children's fond memories.

Returning to historical fiction, Conlon-McKenna published *Safe Harbor,* the story of two children caught in the London Blitz of World War II, who must flee to their paternal grandfather in Ireland. "The main characters are somewhat stereotypical, but *Safe Harbor*'s strength lies in its evocation of this period of English and Irish history." *In Deep Dark Wood* trades real history for fantasy, telling the story of eleven-year-old Mia, who tries to convince her family that the old woman next door keeps baby dragons. When Bella, the old woman, takes Mia away to learn witchcraft and dragon training, her brother Rory must rescue her. *School Librarian* reviewer Audrey Laski wrote that the story "takes a little while to get going, but becomes quite exciting and has some original touches." Even more whimsical is *Granny MacGinty,* a picture book about a family that keeps buying unsuitable pets for their supposedly lonely grandmother. "Full of warmth and humour, this is a wonderful picture book that will be immensely popular," predicted *School Librarian* contributor Sarah Reed.

*BIOGRAPHICAL AND CRITICAL SOURCES:*

*PERIODICALS*

*Booklist,* April 15, 1997, Hazel Rochman, review of *Fields of Home,* p. 1420.

*Books for Keeps,* November, 1999, Valerie Coghlan, review of *Safe Harbor,* p. 28.

*Bulletin of the Center for Children's Books,* December, 1990, Betsy Hearne, review of *Under the Hawthorne Tree,* p. 81; January, 1993, Betsy Hearne, review of *Wildflower Girl,* p. 142; July, 1997, Betsy Hearne, review of *Fields of Home,* p. 390.

*Junior Bookshelf,* August, 1991, review of *Under the Hawthorn Tree,* p. 172; August, 1993, review of *Wildflower Girl,* p. 160.

*Kirkus Reviews,* March 15, 1997, review of *Fields of Home,* p. 459.

*Magpies,* March, 1997, review of *No Goodbye,* p. 32.

*School Librarian,* August, 1991, Maggie Bignell, review of *Under the Hawthorn Tree,* p. 113; summer, 2000, Audrey Laski, review of *In Deep Dark Wood,* p. 79; summer, 2000, Sarah Reed, review of *Granny MacGinty,* p. 74.

*School Library Journal,* December, 1990, Renee Steinberg, review of *Under the Hawthorn Tree,* pp. 100-101; November, 1992, Renee Steinberg, review of *Wildflower Girl,* p. 88; April, 1993, Christine A. Moesch, review of *Little Star,* p. 94; June, 1997, Elaine Fort Weischedel, review of *Fields of Home,* p. 114.

*Voice of Youth Advocates,* April 1993, Jane Van Wiemokly, review of *Wildflower Girl,* p. 24.*

\*     \*     \*

## COOK, Terrence E. 1942-

*PERSONAL:* Born July 28, 1942, in Washington, DC; son of Calvin E. (a civil engineer) and M. Delores (a homemaker) Cook; married Annabel Kirschner (separated, 2001); children: Andrew, Eryn. *Ethnicity:* "White, anglo." *Education:* University of Wisconsin—Madison, B.A., 1964; Princeton University, M.A., 1966, Ph.D., 1971. *Politics:* "Left-liberal." *Hobbies and other interests:* Kayaking, fly-fishing, poetry.

*ADDRESSES: Home*—440 North St., Pullman, WA 99163. *Office*—Department of Political Science, Washington State University, Pullman, WA 99164-4880. *E-mail*—tcook@wsu.edu.

*CAREER:* Washington State University, Pullman, professor of political science, 1967—. Senior lecturer in international relations at a university in Slovakia, 1993.

*MEMBER:* American Political Science Association, Pacific Northwest Political Science Association (past president), American Civil Liberties Union (member of state board of directors, 1999-2000).

*WRITINGS:*

(Editor, with Patrick M. Morgan) *Participatory Democracy,* Canfield Press (San Francisco, CA), 1971.

*The Great Alternatives of Social Thought: Aristocrat, Saint, Capitalist, Socialist,* Rowman & Littlefield (Savage, MD), 1991.

*Criteria of Social Science Knowledge: Interpretation, Prediction, Praxis,* Rowman & Littlefield (Savage, MD), 1994.

*The Rise and Fall of Regimes: Toward Grand Theory of Politics,* Peter Lang Publishing (New York, NY), 2000.

*Nested Political Coalitions: Nation, Regime, Program, Cabinet,* Praeger (Westport, CT), 2001.

Contributor to academic journals, including *Journal of Politics* and *Political Quarterly.*

*WORK IN PROGRESS:* Research on Dutch seeds of classical liberalism and on ethnic minority policy alternatives.

*SIDELIGHTS:* Terrence E. Cook told *CA:* "My primary motive is understanding. Writing, communicating what I have learned to others, is a secondary motive. Yet anticipating that communication sharpens my inquiries.

"Although I could mention specific teachers who have awakened my interests, such as Michael Walzer (Princeton) in normative political theory or Charles Anderson and Bernard Cohen (Wisconsin) in empirical questions, what most guides my writing is an attempt to understand in a comprehensive way, proceeding by exercises in comparisons and contrasts.

"I usually first try out some ideas about a subject in a conference paper, then I keep coming back to it as I learn more about a subject. As John Dewey once noted, it is not induction or deduction so much as a recurrent dance between the particular and the general, which he called abduction. In reading a book or a newspaper about politics, I often ask the query recommended by James Rosenau, 'Of what is that an instance?'

"One topic connects me into another. Thus, if I recently wrote of the large processes of the rise and fall of political communities and regimes, I found that I had to think about coalition mechanisms as part of the understanding. Those two books have led me also to think broadly of minority policy, which I am now examining under the heads of segregation, assimilation, and accommodation, viewed in each case as a strategy of the stronger group and as a strategy of the weaker. It seems to be pointing into the next book. Against the grain of current tendencies to microspecialization, I believe that one must think of the whole to really understand a part."

\* \* \*

## COWEN, John (Edwin) 1940-

*PERSONAL:* Born September 3, 1940, in Jersey City, NJ; son of John E. Cowen, Sr. (a business owner) and Edna May O'Donnell Doerflein; married Jay Totten Miesegaes (a special education teacher), June 28, 1964; children: Jill Totten, Juliet Totten. *Education:* Attended St. Peter's College, 1962; New Jersey City University, M.A., 1965; Columbia University Teachers College, Prof. Dipl., 1971, Ed.D., 1973.

*ADDRESSES: Home*—1081 Trafalgar St., Teaneck, NJ 07666-1929. *Office*—Fairleigh Dickinson University, 1000 River Street, T-BH 2-01, Teaneck, NJ 07666. *E-mail*—cowtra@aol.com

*CAREER:* Educator, editor, publisher, and author. Pinellas Park Junior High School, Pinellas Park, FL, teacher, 1962-63; New York University Reading Institute, NY, reading instructor, 1965-73; St. Petersburg Junior College, St. Petersburg, FL, instructor in Directed Studies Department, 1966-67; University of South Florida, Tampa, adjunct professor, 1967; New Jersey City University, adjunct professor, 1968-69; William Paterson University, adjunct professor in graduate division, 1974; King & Cowen Publishing, publisher and editor, 1977-83; Bravo Editions, New York-New Jersey, publisher and managing editor of *Bravo: The Poet's Magazine,* 1980-97, publisher and editor, 1998-2000. Fairleigh Dickinson University, Teaneck, NJ, adjunct professor in Center for Clinical Teaching, 1980-82, assistant professor of education and reading, School of Education, coordinator of New Jersey State Reading Specialist Certificate program and Graduate Elementary Education Master of Arts in Teaching program, 1995—. Judge, *Teaneck Poetry Anthology,* 1983; literary trustee for estate of Jose Garcia Villa, 1997—.

*MEMBER:* United Nations Society of Writers, Academy of American Poets, e e cummings Society, American Literature Association, Bergen County Poets, International Reading Association, New Jersey Reading Association, National Council for the Teachers of English, Association for Supervisors and Curriculum Developers Association of Teacher Educators.

*WRITINGS:*

*Human Reading Strategies That Work,* New Jersey Department of Education, 1979.
(Editor and contributor) *Teaching Reading through the Arts,* International Reading Association (Newark, DE), 1980.
(Editor and contributor) *English Teacher's Portfolio of Multicultural Activities,* Center for Applied Research in Education/Simon & Schuster, 1996.
(Editor) Jose Garcia Villa, *Parlement of Giraffes: Poems for Children, Eight to Eighty,* Anvil (Metro Manila, Philippines), 1999.

Poems anthologized in *Contemporary American Thoughts,* Wingate (New York, NY), 1967; *National Poetry Anthology,* National Poetry Press, 1966, 1968, 1969; *Teaneck Poetry Anthology,* Teaneck Advisory Board on the Arts (Teaneck, NJ), 1983; and *Best Poems of 1995,* National Library of Poetry, 1995. Poetry published in periodicals, including *Poetic License, Café Solo, New York Quarterly, Bravo, Atavist, Reading Instruction Journal, Parnassus, Spring, Literary Pursuits,* and *Reflections. Journal of Reading,* member of editorial advisory board, 1983-85; *Reading Instruction Journal,* editor-in-chief, 1980-83.

Essays published in *Life, Journal of the e e cummings Society, Reading Instruction Journal, Review* (Manila), and *Manila Times.*

*WORK IN PROGRESS: The Nude Eye: Poems,* completed 2000; *Bugs to Butterflies* (haiku), illustrated by Dana Snider, seeking publication; editor, with Mort Malkin, *Jose Garcia Villa's "Xoce'risims": Poetic Aphorisms.* Research on e e cummings/Garcia Villa connection and on Garcia Villa's theory of poetry.

*SIDELIGHTS:* John Cowen told *CA:* "The Philippine/ American poet, critic, and teacher Jose Garcia Villa has been the greatest influence on my thinking and poetry writing. Villa was my mentor, friend, and poetry associate for more than three decades before he died in 1997. The poet who had the greatest influence on Villa's poetry was e e cummings, who befriended Villa for more than two decades, writing a poem about him and using his pseudonym—'Doveglion'—for its title. I became familiar with cummings's poetry years before I encountered Villa, and I was delighted with his sheer joy of language, lyricism, technique, and mastery of experimental form. Therefore, it was no wonder that I found Villa's poetry and mentoring to be a perfect match with my developing interest in the duality of lyricism and experimentation.

"Dylan Thomas's lyricism and his 'art and sullen craft' also seduced me to poetry forever. Robert Bly, with whom I corresponded sporadically over two decades, has also influenced my writing style, and, today, I find the writing of Dana Gioia and X. J. Kennedy to be uplifting and in concert with these earlier poetic influences mentioned above. Today, the poet I enjoy reading most is Seamus Heaney, whose poetry, I believe, resonates with the lyricism and craft that form a classical, yet modern, tradition."

"To express my views on poetry and how I write my own poems—I am going to take the liberty to paraphrase and quote from an article of mine written about cummings in *Spring* (1996): 'I believe that a poem should transcend meaning; and that its magical elements include such techniques as the vivid first line, the intricacies of versification, metaphor, economy, the element of surprise, and the implosive drama of the last line, all couched within the ambience of the poet's transcendental vision. The prose meaning of the poem, therefore, is subsidiary; just as the poet discovers meaning through the writing of the poem, so will the reader discover "how the poem means." The lyrical poet can swing a line, and it is the swing of the line that creates musical chords as well as metaphysical essence. I believe poems require first lines that "jump-start" the poem and are energized from start to finish by a language of action, so that the verb dances, sings, weaves, jumps, flies, and leaves the reader staggering. The poet must trust language, and in return, language will entrust the poet to discover new ways of expressing things and to discover new ways of understanding them, and if you are lucky enough, perhaps, your poems may help you to discover yourself.'"

## CRAIG, David A.

*PERSONAL:* Married; wife's name Linda; children: David Thomas, Jude Francis, Bridget Jean. *Education:* Cleveland State University, B.A., 1980; Colorado State University, M.A., 1984; Bowling Green State University, M.F.A., 1986, Ph.D., 1997.

*ADDRESSES: Home*—690 Overlook Dr., Wintersville, OH 43953. *Office*—Department of English, Franciscan University of Steubenville, Steubenville, OH 43952-1763; fax: 740-283-6401. *E-mail*—dcraig@franuniv.edu.

*CAREER:* Cleveland State University, Cleveland, OH, lecturer in English, 1986-88; Franciscan University of Steubenville, Steubenville, OH, professor of English, 1988—. Cuyahoga Community College, lecturer, 1986-88. Presenter of workshops; judge of poetry contests; gives readings from his works.

*MEMBER:* Academy of American Poets, South Central Conference on Christianity and Literature, Midwestern Conference on Christianity and Literature, Mideastern Conference on Christianity and Literature.

*AWARDS, HONORS:* Pulitzer Prize nomination, 1991.

*WRITINGS:*

*The Sandaled Foot* (poetry), Writing Center, Cleveland State University (Cleveland, OH), 1980.
*Psalms* (poetry chapbook), Park Bench Press (Cleveland Heights, OH), 1982.
*Peter Maurin and Other Poems,* Writing Center, Cleveland State University (Cleveland, OH), 1985.
*Like Taxes: Marching through Gaul* (poetry), Scripta Humanistica (Washington, DC), 1990.
*Only One Face* (poetry chapbook), White Eagle Coffee Store Press (Chicago, IL), 1994.
(Editor, with Janet McCann, and contributor) *The Odd Angles of Heaven,* Harold Shaw Publications (Wheaton, IL), 1994.
*The Cheese Stands Alone* (novel), CMJ Press (Chicago, IL), 1997.
*The Roof of Heaven* (poetry), Franciscan University Press (Steubenville, OH), 1998.

*Mercy's New Face: New and Selected Poems, 1980-2000,* Franciscan University Press (Steubenville, OH), 2000.

*Our Lady of the Outfield* (fiction), CMJ Press (Chicago, IL), 2000.

(Editor, with Janet McCann, and contributor) *Place of Passage,* Story Line Press (Brownsville, OR), 2000.

*When All the Flowers Grew* (novella), CMJ Press (Chicago, IL), in press.

Work represented in anthologies, including *A Widening Light,* Harold Shaw Publishers (Wheaton, IL), 1984; *Claresong,* Ottocento Press (Cincinnati, OH), 1994; *Upholding Mystery,* Oxford University Press (New York, NY), 1997; and *From the Dark Forest,* Malpais Press (Bowling Green, OH), 1997. Editor of poetry chapbook series, Franciscan University of Steubenville. Contributor of poetry, fiction, and reviews to periodicals, including *Christianity and Literature, American Literary Review, Ancient Paths, Bloomsbury Review, Burning Light, Windhover, North Coast Review, Christian Century, Franciscan Way,* and *Home Planet News;* contributor to Library of Congress recording *Upholding Mystery.* Member of editorial staff, *Colorado State Review, Dark Tower,* and *Colorado State Review.*

\*      \*      \*

## CRONIN, Justin

*PERSONAL:* Male; children: Iris. *Education:* Attended Harvard University; and Iowa Writers' Workshop.

*ADDRESSES: Office*—La Salle University, English Department, Olney Hall 161, 1900 West Olney Avenue, Philadelphia, PA, 19141. *E-mail*—cronin@lasalle.edu.

*CAREER:* Writer. La Salle University, Philadelphia, PA, associate professor of English.

*AWARDS, HONORS:* National Novella Award, Arts and Humanities Council of Tulsa, 1990, for *A Short History of the Long Ball;* Hemingway Foundation/PEN Award for First Fiction, 2002, for *Mary and O'Neil.*

*WRITINGS:*

*A Short History of the Long Ball,* Council Oak Books (Tulsa, OK), 1990.

*Mary and O'Neil,* Dial Press (New York, NY), 2001.

*SIDELIGHTS:* A graduate of the Iowa Writers' Workshop, Justin Cronin published *A Short History of the Long Ball* in 1990. It is the story of two childhood friends, Jake and Donny, one good, one bad. Told from Jake's perspective, the book recounts his own rather conventional life as a journalist and father, contrasted with Donny's slide into heroin addiction and his ultimately painful recovery. While the book won the National Novella Award of the Arts and Humanities Council of Tulsa, Oklahoma, it also garnered somewhat mixed reviews. Joyce M. Latham wrote in the *Library Journal,* "While the prose is comfortable and the construction artful, this character study remains basically shallow." A *Kirkus Reviews* contributor concluded it was "At best, a lyrical ode to small pleasures."

A decade later, Cronin published *Mary and O'Neil,* a "novel in stories." "Delicate, dreamy and yet grounded in a crystalline world of the real, 'Mary and O'Neil' offers many pleasures to its readers, not least the melancholic sense of the ways an early loss reverberates throughout even a happy life," wrote Sylvia Brownrigg in the *New York Times.* That early loss concerns O'Neil's parents, who die in the first story. "Playing out variations on the theme of the inability of parents and children to truly know one another, Cronin is capable of creating fresh poignancy," commented a *Publishers Weekly* reviewer. Other stories concern Mary's decision to abort an early pregnancy, O'Neil's and his sister Kay's struggles to cope with the loss of their parents, and Kay's own struggles with cancer. Other stories are happier, of course, including the meeting and subsequent marriage of Mary and O'Neil. Ann Patchett, in Chicago's *Tribune Books,* commended Cronin's development of minor characters, such as O'Neil's first love, the au pair who helps Kay's family through her bout with cancer, and an old roommate of Mary's. "There is a real generosity in a writer who takes his minor characters as seriously as he takes the major ones," she wrote.

Writing in *Book,* Beth Kephart noted that much of the action, such as it is, occurs offstage, and that "the revelations are summarized, made retrospective. . . .

In their stead are elegant passages about everyday life, the vital ways in which we can and must care for one another's souls." While criticizing the book for relying on "the utilization of worn-out ideas" like fidelity, maturation, and cancer, *Booklist* reviewer Jeff Snowbarger noted that "Cronin's use of language, when crisp and inventive, allows the characters a freedom to develop within the tired concepts." In a different way, Ann Patchett also noted this use of language in providing deep emotional resonance "while working with what appears to be little material." "So how does a story about average people leading average lives turn into such a good book?" she asked. "It is the writing, pure and simple."

*BIOGRAPHICAL AND CRITICAL SOURCES:*

*PERIODICALS*

*Book,* March, 2001, Beth Kephart, review of *Mary and O'Neil,* p. 80.
*Booklist,* January 1, 2001, Jeff Snowbarger, review of *Mary and O'Neil,* p. 914.
*Kirkus Reviews,* April 1, 1990, review of *A Short History of the Long Ball,* p. 448.
*Library Journal,* May 15, 1990, Joyce M. Latham, review of *A Short History of the Long Ball,* p. 93.
*New York Times Book Review,* February 18, 2001, Sylvia Brownrigg, "From Cradle to Grave," p. 14.
*Publishers Weekly,* December 11, 2000, review of *Mary and O'Neil,* p. 63.
*Tribune Books* (Chicago, IL), January 28, 2001, Ann Patchett, "Just Plain Folks," p. 2.*

\*   \*   \*

**CRUZ, Nilo 1961?-**

*PERSONAL:* Born c. 1961, in Matanzas, Cuba; immigrated to the United States, 1970; son of Nilo and Tina Cruz; divorced; children: Chloe Garcia-Cruz. *Ethnicity:* "Cuban-American." *Education:* Brown University, M.F.A., 1994.

*ADDRESSES: Home*—New York, NY. *Agent*—Peregrine Whittlesey, Peregrine Whittlesey Agency, 345 East 80th St., New York, NY 10021.

*CAREER:* Playwright. McCarter Theatre, Princeton, NJ, playwright-in-residence, 2000; New Theatre, Coral Gables, FL, playwright-in-residence, 2001-02. Has taught drama at Brown University, University of Iowa, and Yale University.

*MEMBER:* New Dramatists.

*AWARDS, HONORS:* Grants from National Endowment of the Arts, Rockefeller Foundation, and Theatre Communications Group; W. Alton Jones Award for *Night Train to Bolina;* Kennedy Center Fund for New American Plays award for *Two Sisters and a Piano;* American Theatre Critics/Steinberg New Play Award, Humana Festival for New American Plays, and Pulitzer Prize for drama, both 2003, both for *Anna in the Tropics.*

*WRITINGS:*

*PLAYS*

*A Park in Our House,* produced in San Francisco, CA, at the Magic Theatre, 1996.
*Dancing on Her Knees,* produced in New York, NY, at the Joseph Papp Public Theater, 1996.
*A Bicycle Country,* produced in Manalapan, FL, at the Florida Stage, 1999.
*Two Sisters and a Piano,* produced in Princeton, NJ, at the McCarter Theater, 1999.
(Adapter) Gabriel García Marquéz, *A Very Old Man with Enormous Wings,* produced in Minneapolis, MN, at the Children's Theater, 2002.
*Anna in the Tropics,* produced in Coral Gables, FL, at the New Theatre, 2002.
*Beauty of the Father,* produced in Coral Gables, FL, at the New Theatre, 2003.
*Lorca in a Green Dress,* produced at the Oregon Shakespeare Festival, 2003.

Also author of the plays *Night Train to Bolina,* produced in San Francisco, CA, *Hortensia and the Museum of Dreams,* and *Graffiti.* Translator of Federico García Lorca's *The House of Bernarda Alba* and *Dona Rosita, the Spinster.*

*SIDELIGHTS:* Nilo Cruz shot to national prominence in 2003 when he won the Pulitzer Prize for drama for his play *Anna in the Tropics,* a Depression-era tale about migrant Cubans working in a Tampa, Florida, cigar factory. The play "is about the power of art and how art can actually change your life," Cruz told Michael Kuchwara in a *Boston Globe* article. Cruz's tale of the Cuban-American experience centers on the "lector" of the factory, a man hired to provide cultural enrichment to the workers as they toil. The lector chooses to read Leo Tolstoy's *Anna Karenina* to the workers, and as the play progresses their lives come to mirror those of the characters in the Russian classic. The immigrant experience is a common theme in many of Cruz's plays. "He gives voice to the stories, the struggles and the sensibilities of the Cuban-American," Rafael de Acha, the director of *Anna in the Topics*, was quoted as saying in the *Miami Herald*, "with grace, sensitivity, imagination and immense theatricality." In addition, Cruz is often praised for his poetic language and his ability to weave strains of other literary traditions, such as magic realism, into his works.

Cruz was born in Matanzas, Cuba, and for the first few years of his life, his father was in jail for attempting to emigrate. When Cruz was nine, his family successfully fled to the United States and settled in the Little Havana area of Miami. He became interested in theater in the early 1980s as an actor, and in 1988 he directed *Mud*, by playwright Maria Irene Fornés, who in 1990 became the only other Latin American ever nominated for a Pulitzer Prize for drama. Fornés invited Cruz to join her Intar Hispanic Playwrights Laboratory, and it was there that he began writing plays in earnest. Cruz's plays were soon produced in theaters across the country, from San Francisco to Princeton. Though several of his works have been staged by the Joseph Papp Public Theater in New York, Cruz is one of the few playwrights to win a Pulitzer without having a major presence on the New York theater scene. In fact, none of the Pulitzer judges had seen a performance of *Anna in the Tropics;* it won on the strength of its script alone.

In 2001, Cruz served as the playwright-in-residence for the New Theatre in Coral Gables, Florida, which commissioned *Anna in the Tropics.* The main action of the play pits the women against the men, with the dashing lector as the central figure of both admiration and contempt. The impoverished women, led by Ofelia and her two daughters, Conchita and Marela, are mesmerized by Juan Julian and are swept away from their dreary Ybor City lives by his recitation of *Anna*

*Karenina.* But the men feel differently. Some, like Ofelia's brother-in-law Cheche, view Juan with ambivalence, but others, like Conchita's unfaithful husband, see him as unwelcome competition. Tensions mount when attempts to keep their tight-knit community together are imperiled by encroaching industrialization; cigar-making machines are on the horizon, and soon the lector—not to mention the workers' own positions—may be obsolete. The play opened to good reviews for both the playwright and the cast. Despite the characters' flaws, wrote Christine Dolen of the *Miami Herald,* "each of Cruz' characters commands attention and elicits empathy." Bruce Weber of the *New York Times* called it "a lyrical paean to a lost pocket of culture and a lost way of life," which exudes "the romance and tragedy of Tolstoy."

One of Cruz's first plays to be produced, the semi-autobiographical *A Park in Our House,* harkens back to the playwright's youth in Cuba, when Fidel Castro rolled out his "Ten Million Tons of Sugar Harvest" program in 1970. When a Russian botanist comes to stay with a Cuban family as part of an exchange program, the family is distracted from their economic deprivations by his presence. The mother of the family, Ofelina, is the emotional fulcrum of the play; she dreams of a romantic reconciliation with her husband, Hilario. But Hilario, a low-ranking government official, is obsessed with his desire to build a park in order to boost his reputation within the administration. The allegorical nature of the play is borne out through those who share their house. Ofelina and Hilario's gay nephew, Camilo, regains his voice after years of being mute; their niece, Pilar, longs to seek happiness in the Soviet Union. Their cousin, Fifo, a photographer, captures the symbolism of their predicament through his photographs. According to Cruz, the play attempts to understand the human reaction to oppression: "They take flight and move into the imagination in order to transcend their immediate reality," he said in *American Theater.* In terms of its autobiographical elements, Cruz said that writing *A Park in Our House* "helped me understand my own loss of innocence."

Another of Cruz's early plays, *A Bicycle Country,* takes place on a raft manned by three refugees, known as *baseleros,* who are making the treacherous journey from Cuba to Florida. They pass the time by telling the stories of their lives, and as their situation becomes more desperate, their stories take on mythical and hallucinatory qualities. Julio is a wheelchair-bound widower recovering from a stroke who is sure that all the misfortunes of his life will evaporate once he sets foot on American soil. Julio's gloom is tempered only moderately by his traveling companions: Ines, the nurse who cares for him, and his friend Pepe. Like Cruz's other plays, *A Bicycle Country* concerns both the prisons of the physical world and the psychological shackles the human spirit seeks to overcome in order to be free. According to Diane Thiel of *Brown Alumni Magazine,* "the waters of the Straits of Florida seem to have their own role" in the play as the metaphorical walls of the jail that must be breached for the characters to gain their freedom. Other reviewers also noticed the play's use of water as a symbol. Madeleine Shaner of *Back Stage West* wrote that "Cruz's language is uncluttered, simplistic, sometimes banal, but informed by an unpretentious poetry that rocks with the inevitable bonding of the first act and the rhythm of the unforgiving ocean in the second."

*Two Sisters and a Piano,* though not autobiographical, features characters based on Cruz's sisters as well as on the Cuban poet Maria Elena Cruz Varela, who was imprisoned by Castro for her writings. The play is set in Havana in 1991, where the sisters Maria, a romance novelist, and Sofia, a pianist, are under house arrest following Maria's release from prison. Her crime was writing a letter to Castro urging him to support the Soviet reforms known as *perestroika.* In order to get her hands on the letters her exiled husband has mailed to her from Europe, Maria offers to tell some of her romantic stories to her police protector. The sympathetic policeman, Lieutenant Portuondo, is secretly a fan of Maria's novels, and eventually he seduces her. Sofia's romantic interest is the piano tuner, Victor, who flirts with her as he tunes her piano, but their relationship goes stale when Sofia's house arrest prevents her from seeing him on a regular basis. Above all, the sisters are tied to each other in their isolation and in their memories, as the regime's grip around their lives tightens.

Critics recognized *Two Sisters and a Piano* as a mature continuation of Cruz's earlier works. Robert L. Daniels of *Variety* called it "a provocative observation of the snail-paced changes of Cuba's political landscape" that is "layered with lyrical flights of romanticism." Ben Brantley of the *New York Times* noted parallels to Anton Chekhov's *Three Sisters,* saying that Cruz's play "somehow seems more old-fashioned than its Russian antecedent," even though it "fitfully evokes a poetic appreciation of the visions of phantom lives bred in circumscribed existences." David A. Rosenberg of *Back Stage* praised the play, calling it an "affecting piece, even if stronger on releasing passion than explaining politics." Similarly, noted Daniels, "there is a restless ambiguity in the narrative, and an undercurrent of tragedy that is never fully realized." Survival instincts are more the point than politics, according to Cruz, who told Randy Gener in the *New York Times* that "*Two Sisters and a Piano* is about two women who, even though they live in very harsh condition, make the best of their lives. They create a little paradise in their house. Even though they are under house arrest, they bring out the beautiful china and use a tablecloth. It's the integrity of that, the dignity of it, that moves me."

In 2002, Cruz adapted Colombian author Gabriel García Marquéz's short story "A Very Old Man with Enormous Wings" as a musical that premiered at the Children's Theatre in Minneapolis. The story concerns an injured angel who falls to earth and is nursed back to health by two children. Though the children try to protect him, the adults in their village see the old man as a curiosity to be exploited. Soon he is caged and put on display where he is at the mercy of people's misguided desire to be cured of all their physical and spiritual pain. Rohan Preston of the Minneapolis *Star Tribune* wrote that the play "is full of the layering common in Caribbean and Latin American cultures," in which ancient Earth-based religions coexist with Christianity. While Marquéz's story is steeped in his trademark blend of magic realism, Cruz told Preston that for him, the question is not so much magic as it is religion: "It's this mesh of Catholicism and Yoruba religions, for example—that's reality." Or, as Robert Simonson of *Playbill* quoted Cruz as saying, his plays are "realism that is magical."

Consistently, critics have commented favorably on Cruz's poetic language. "The words of Nilo Cruz waft from a stage like a scented breeze," wrote Dolen in the *Miami Herald;* "they sparkle and prickle and swirl, enveloping those who listen in both a specific place and time." In addition, Cruz's works are steeped in his cultural heritage. His plays are "imagistic dramatic poems," wrote John Williams of *American Theatre,* that are "rich in myth, symbol and metaphor." Commenting on *A Bicycle Country,* Thiel similarly wrote that Cruz's "language becomes increasingly rich with [the characters'] 'hallucinations' and evocative surreal visions."

Though Cruz is acknowledged as a rising star of the Cuban-American literary scene, he says he doesn't aim to speak for the community as a whole, nor is he trying to advocate for political change in his homeland. As he told Gener: "Ultimately my plays are about being an individual. Belong to a particular group, left or right, entails a political loss. When you embrace your whole being and all that you can be in this world, that's the strongest position."

*BIOGRAPHICAL AND CRITICAL SOURCES:*

PERIODICALS

*American Theatre,* July-August, 1996, John Williams, "A Lens on Cuba's Past," p. 8.

*Back Stage,* March 15, 1996, David Sheward, review of *Dancing on Her Knees,* p. 60; March 3, 2000, David A. Rosenberg, review of *Two Sisters and a Piano,* p. 56.

*Back Stage West,* April 12, 2001, Madeleine Shaner, review of *A Bicycle Country,* p. 16.

*Boston Globe,* April 7, 2003, Michael Kuchwara, "A Cuban Cigar Factory Tradition Sparks the Winner of the 2003 Pulitzer Prize for Drama."

*Brown Alumni,* March-April, 2001, Diane Thiel, "Drifting from Cuba: The Ocean Can Be a World of Uncertainty and Love."

*Miami Herald,* October 14, 2002, Christine Dolen, "Cruz's Poetry in Motion in Passionate 'Anna.'"

*New York Times,* February 16, 2000, Ben Brantley, "Clinging to Fantasy behind Cuban Walls," p. E1; February 27, 2000, Randy Gener, "What It Means to Be Both Cuban and American," pp. 8, 22; April 9, 2003, Bruce Weber, "Tapping Cuban Roots for American Drama."

*Playbill,* April 7, 2003, Robert Simonson, "Nilo Cruz's *Anna in the Tropics* Wins the 2003 Pulitzer Prize for Drama."

*Star Tribune* (Minneapolis, MN), September 6, 2002, Rohan Preston, "With Syncretic 'Very Old Man,' CTC Swings and Zings."

*Variety,* March 1, 1999, Robert L. Daniels, review of *Two Sisters and a Piano,* p. 93.

OTHER

*Pulitzer Prize Web site,* http://www.pulitzer.org/ (April 9, 2003), "The Pulitzer Prize Winners: 2003."*

## CULLUM, Paul

*PERSONAL:* Born in Austin, TX.

*ADDRESSES: Office*—*L.A. Weekly,* P.O. Box 4315, Los Angeles, CA 90078.

*CAREER: L.A. Weekly,* Los Angeles, CA, writer; *Film Threat,* managing editor.

*WRITINGS:*

(With Harry Knowles and Mark Ebner) *Ain't It Cool? Hollywood's Redheaded Stepchild Speaks Out,* Warner Books (New York, NY), 2002.

*SIDELIGHTS:* A film reviewer and former managing editor of *Film Threat,* Paul Cullum, along with Mark Ebner, teamed up with Harry Knowles to help the Web pioneer tell the story of aintitcoolnews.com. By 2002 the Web site had become well-known as a place for movie lovers to congregate, share opinions, and read scoops on upcoming projects, results of private screen tests, and other Hollywood secrets. *Ain't It Cool? Hollywood's Redheaded Stepchild Speaks Out* tells the story of the Knowles family's Hollywood memorabilia business and the accident—involving a cartload of movie collectibles—that left him bedridden and free to start a Web site about his passionate interest in movies. Other "insider" tales include Knowles' split from his original mentor, Matt Drudge, and an exposé of the National Research Group's methods for test marketing movies. "Even more intriguing, however, is the story of the Internet's democratizing power. . . . To his credit, Knowles has given a great deal of thought to this process, and his reflections on the fun and responsibility of being a cyber pioneer illuminate this memoir," wrote a *Kirkus Reviews* contributor. *New York Times* reviewer David Edelstein, who was more ambivalent, wrote of the book coauthored by Cullum, "The realest deal is that what Knowles presents as the democratization of taste is actually the democratization of hype: thanks to the Internet, any little guy can write ad blurbs."

"Knowles presents himself as a hard-boiled, scrappy underdog working on behalf of the public; largely this works," wrote a *Publishers Weekly* contributor. "Film lovers, however, will probably most appreciate Knowles's exuberant, knowledgeable paeans to his celluloid favorites."

*BIOGRAPHICAL AND CRITICAL SOURCES:*

*PERIODICALS*

*Kirkus Reviews,* January 15, 2002, review of *Ain't It Cool?,* p. 87.
*New York Times Book Review,* April 28, 2002, David Edelstein, "Revenge of the Nerd," p. 26.
*Publishers Weekly,* February 18, 2002, review of *Ain't It Cool?,* p. 86.*

*        *        *

## CUSTANCE, Olive 1874-1944

*PERSONAL:* Born February 7, 1874, in Weston Hall, Norfolk, England; died February 12, 1944, in East Sussex, England; daughter of Colonel Frederik Hambledon and Eleanor (Jolliffe) Custance; married Alfred Douglas, March 4, 1902; children: Raymond Wilfrid Sholto.

*CAREER:* English poet.

*WRITINGS:*

*Opals,* John Lane (London, England), 1897.
*Rainbows,* John Lane (London, England), 1902.
*The Blue Bird,* Marlborough (London, England), 1905.
*The Inn of Dreams,* John Lane (London, England), 1911.
*The Selected Poems of Olive Custance,* edited by Brocard Sewell, Cecil Woolf (London, England), 1995.
*Opals; with Rainbows,* edited by R. K. R. Thornton and Ian Small, Woodstock (New York, NY), 1996.

Custance's poems have been included in several anthologies, as well as in Douglas Murray's *Bosie: A Biography of Lord Alfred Douglas,* Hyperion Press, 2000. Custance's letters and diaries, along with many

of her husband's letters and manuscripts, are housed in the Henry A. and Albert W. Berg Collection at the New York Public Library.

*SIDELIGHTS:* The British poet Olive Custance published four volumes of poetry that gained her a moderate amount of notoriety during her lifetime. Scholars and literary critics usually associate Custance with the group of writers and artists that emerged during the decadent era of the 1890s and created works dealing with the fin de siècle, its members including the artist Aubrey Beardsley, the poet Richard Le Gallienne, and the publisher John Lane, who published three of Custance's books.

Custance was more renowned, however, for her marriage to Lord Alfred Douglas, a minor writer who was himself famous for his personal relationship with homosexual writer Oscar Wilde. Wilde, who was convicted of sodomy and sentenced to two years of hard labor, later addressed his confessional letter, *De Profundis,* to Douglas. The letter was published in 1905, after Wilde's death. Throughout the remainder of his days Douglas was never able to escape the dubious notoriety of that relationship.

Custance's indirect relationship with Wilde dates back to the days before her marriage to Douglas. When she was sixteen, Custance met and fell in love with John Gray, who was the model for the main character in Wilde's classic 1891 novel *The Picture of Dorian Gray.* Although their relationship never went beyond corresponding by letter on literary matters, Custance expressed her love for Gray in the 1892 poem "The Prince of Dreams." Later renamed "Ideal," the poem was included in Custance's first book, *Opals,* which was published in 1897. One of sixteen poems Custance dedicated to Gray, "Ideal" describes her first and only face-to-face meeting with Gray at a party: "You were indifferent . . . and I may forget / Your profound eyes, your heavy hair, / your voice / So clear, yet deep and low with tenderness."

Custance's other collections of poetry include *Rainbows, The Blue Bird,* and *The Inn of Dreams.* Brocard Sewell, a Custance biographer, has stated that the poet was not too shy to write to the people whose work she admired. In addition to Gray, Custance often wrote to the poet Le Gallienne, who was so enamored of her that he referred to her "flower-like loveliness" in his 1926 book *The Romantic '90s.*

Some evidence suggests that Custance was bisexual, and many of her poems describe being trapped in a male-dominated world. For these reasons, some literary scholars have labeled her as an early feminist writer. Other critics, however, including Michelle L. Whitney, who wrote an essay about Custance's life for the *Dictionary of Literary Biography,* feel that the renewed interest in Custance's work will show that her craft was more diverse. "With increased critical attention, Custance's status as a 'girl-poet' of the 1890s is likely to change," Whitney wrote.

Custance was born into an aristocratic family on February 7, 1874, in Weston Hall, Norfolk, a region in eastern England along the North Sea. Her father was Colonel Frederic Hambledon Custance, a justice of the peace and an English military leader during the Boer War. Custance's childhood was a privileged one. In one of her diaries that she kept as an adult, Custance wrote that she had been "a naughty . . . funny . . . fat little child, with pink cheeks and short brown hair, and big blue eyes." According to her diary, she had a flair for the dramatic and for attracting attention very early on. "My great amusement was 'acting' . . . pretending to be someone else," she wrote. "And it was not only one person that I acted but a whole crowd. The first thing I remember acting was Robin Hood and his merry men. I did not do it as a play. . . . I entered as it were into the words."

Custance's first published poem was "Twilight," which appeared in an October, 1894, issue of *The Yellow Book,* a controversial literary journal published by Custance's good friend John Lane. Le Gallienne and Beardsley were both regular contributors to the publication. Several years later, in 1897, Lane published *Opals,* a title derived from Custance's fondness for the stone as well as the fact that she had nicknamed herself "Opal." According to Whitney, many reviewers pointed to Custance's "simplistic, almost childish themes, trite language, and exaggerated use of punctuation." These were labels that would stick with Custance throughout her career. However, as Whitney pointed out, even the most critical reviewers "acknowledged that Custance's poems had an ineffable charm and moments that pointed toward a bright potential." Certainly Le Gallienne appreciated *Opals,* calling it "the best poetry written by a woman in a long time." The poems in the collection declare a yearning for freedom. "The trees look sad—sad—I long for the leaves, / Green leaves that shimmer—and

shelter the nests that the / song-birds make, / The earth is glad—glad—but my spirit grieves. / Break forth from your buds and awake / O! leaves!" The same poem is also a good example of why some critics decried her use of punctuation. For example, a reviewer for the *Times Literary Supplement* wrote, "If Miss Custance will realize that one full stop can do quite as much work as three, the look of her pages would be improved."

Custance's correspondence with Douglas began in 1900, when she wrote to the young and handsome poet. He was the son of John Sholto Douglas, who was the eighth marquis of Queensberry. When the two met the following year, they fell for each other almost immediately. Although their relationship grew very passionate, marriage did not seem like an option for them because of the feelings Custance's family harbored toward Douglas owing to his notorious past. The two separated when Douglas briefly moved to America in hopes of finding and marrying a rich heiress. During his absence Custance had an intimate relationship with lesbian writer Natalie Clifford Barney before agreeing to marry George Montagu, who later became the ninth earl of Sandwich. However, Douglas returned to England in 1902, and Custance broke her engagement so that the two could resume their relationship. Knowing her father would never agree to let her marry Douglas, she eloped with him. They were married March 4, 1902, and in November of the same year Custance gave birth to the couple's only child, Raymond Wilfrid Sholto.

In 1902 she also published *Rainbows,* her second volume of poetry, which a contributor for *Academy and Literature* called "markedly sincere." In her essay Whitney described the poems in the book as an improvement over what Custance had written before. "*Rainbows* shows significant growth in poetic style and thematic content. Among the new themes are disillusionment with love, gender roles within relationships, and self-analysis," Whitney wrote. It was around this time that monetary considerations and a dimming of the spark in their relationship caused Custance to begin to regret marrying Douglas. In the period between 1904 and 1907 she barely wrote anything. Poems she had written earlier, however, were compiled and published as *The Blue Bird,* her third book, in 1905.

Again, disillusionment plays a pivotal role in much of the verse. "The poems . . . are not the childishly innocent love poems of her earlier two volumes," Whitney wrote. "The unhappiness and regret that were hinted at in *Rainbows* have grown into disillusionment; the theme of love grown bitter is repeated throughout the collection." In the poem "A Memory" Custance wrote, "You never saw the prisoned soul / Behind the windows of my eyes, / Frantic to break from fate's control." As monetary and marital problems only worsened for Custance and Douglas, relations with Custance's father became even more strained. Despite the problems, Custance published her fourth and final book, *The Inn of Dreams,* in 1911. Of the thirty-nine poems in the volume, twenty had already been published in *The Blue Bird,* which had sold poorly. Many critics noted that the new book lacked the qualities that had made Custance's earlier work appealing. For example, a contributor for the *Times Literary Supplement* felt Custance's verse had lost the "freshness and the buoyancy" it once had shown. The poem "Prisoner of God" gives insight into Custance's

mental state at the time: "Once long and long ago I did rejoice, / But now I am a stone that falls and falls. / A prisoner, cursing the blank prison wall."

The remainder of Custance's marriage to Douglas was tumultuous, and the two separated for good in 1920. In 1932 Custance moved to a cottage in Hove in East Sussex, not far from the apartment in which Douglas lived. Although the two admitted that they could not live with one another, they did see each other often and remained friends. Custance was ill for much of 1943, and she died in February of the next year, with Douglas at her bedside. He would follow her in death a month later after a bout with congestive heart failure.

*BIOGRAPHICAL AND CRITICAL SOURCES:*

*BOOKS*

*Dictionary of Literary Biography,* Volume 240: *Late Nineteenth-Century and Early Twentieth-Century British Women Poets,* Gale (Detroit, MI), 2001.*

# D

## DAVIS, Claire

*PERSONAL:* Born in Milwaukee, WI; children: Brian. *Education:* University of Montana, M.F.A., 1993.

*ADDRESSES: Home*—Idaho. *Office*—English Dept., Lewis-Clark State College, 500 Eighth Ave., Lewiston, ID 83501. *Agent*—George Witte, Picador USA, 175 Fifth Ave., New York, NY 10010. *E-mail*—cdavis@ lcsc.edu.

*CAREER:* Lewis-Clark State College, Lewiston, ID, assistant professor of English, 1994—; has also worked as a farmer and bookseller.

*AWARDS, HONORS:* Associated Writing Program Award for poetry; "Balance" named to Best American Short Stories List of 100, 1994; Pushcart Prize, 1997, for short story "Grounded"; Foundation Award, Lewis-Clark State College, 2000, for teaching; Pacific Northwest Booksellers Association Book Award, 2001, for *Winter Range.*

*WRITINGS:*

*Winter Range,* Picador USA (New York, NY), 2000.

Contributor of stories and poems to journals, including *Gettysburg Review, Shenandoah,* and *Southern Review.*

*WORK IN PROGRESS: Black Dogs,* a novel; *Labors of the Heart,* a short-story collection; and *Flying Changes: Menopause on Horseback,* essays.

*SIDELIGHTS:* Born and raised in Milwaukee, Wisconsin, short story writer and novelist Claire Davis, like many women busy with their daily lives, postponed her writing dreams until she was in her mid-thirties. In 2000 she made a strong debut on the literary scene with the novel *Winter Range,* which won a Pacific Northwest Booksellers Association award the following year.

While earning her master's degree in fine arts at the University of Montana, Davis worked at an independent bookstore in Missoula, an experience she later realized was important to her career as a writer. "It occurs to me only years later," she wrote in "The Work Ahead," her 2001 Pacific Northwest Booksellers Association award acceptance speech, "how integral that entire experience was to my writing career. . . . I have read more work, become more aware of what the world of books encompasses in the small upper loft of that bookstore than I ever learned in a classroom." While a student, Davis had been writing poetry and short stories, one of which, "Grounded," won a Pushcart Prize in 1997. "I'd been writing short story up to this point—learning the art of compression, control, learning to recognize the elegant possibilities of the sentence," Davis recalled in her speech.

Davis discussed the inspiration for *Winter Range* in an interview with Cindy Heidemann for the *Pacific National Booksellers Association Web site.* "I was in graduate school in Montana when a particularly ugly case of abuse was prosecuted in the eastern part of the state. It was a couple who, it turned out, had a history of starving their horse herds. It started me thinking about who would do such a thing, and what the reaction would be in a community so invested in the idea of independence and personal property. And what if someone 'outside' of that community was faced with the dilemma." Drawing on her experience as a transplanted Midwesterner as well, Davis first put all of these "what ifs" together into a not-so-short story which begged to become a novel. It eventually became *Winter Range,* which recounts the tale of Chas Stubblefield, a rancher who is too proud to ask for help when he faces bankruptcy and the starvation of his cattle and horses. Ike Parson, the sheriff and a newcomer to Montana, having married local woman Pattiann, tries to deal with the situation and faces new challenges within the community.

Reviewers found much to like in *Winter Range,* particularly Davis's portrayal of the Montana landscape. Karen Anderson, writing in *Library Journal,* described Davis's integration of quotidian details of ranching and small-town life as "brilliant" and her descriptions of place as "breathtaking." Likening her prose to crystalline, clean snow, a *Publishers Weekly* reviewer added: "Crisp details establish place and characters with authoritative clarity." In *Booklist,* Bill Ott noted that *Winter Range* contains "stylistic and thematic connections to both [Larry] Watson and [Ivan] Doig but is in no way derivative of either" and that Davis ensures that her lyrical prose serves the story. In the *Denver Post,* Ron Franscell also compared Davis's work favorably with that of her western contemporaries: "Davis' literary ethos rivals Larry Watson, Kent Haruf and Ivan Doig. And *Winter Range* might be an even more poetic example of the new Western literature, in which landscape, climate and the earth make an indelible mark upon the human character. Its vivid details . . . prove Davis is a writer who both embraces and transcends the boundaries of Western regional literature."

Several reviewers voiced opinions about Davis's characterizations. In the *Boulder News,* Clay Evans remarked that "the characters in *Winter Range* remain mostly at arm's length, and their decision-making is so misguided that readers may wish they could shake the players by the scruff of the neck." Conversely, Ron Charles, writing in the *Christian Science Monitor,* claimed that the relationship between Ike and Pattiann is "drawn perfectly," that "Davis captures the complexity of this tragedy in all its personal and social dimensions," and that she "brands these characters with rich psychological clarity." Calling *Winter Range* "brilliant,

and beautifully written," a *Kirkus Reviews* critic concluded, "Davis's skill brings wintery Montana alive—predictably bleak, unexpectedly vibrant."

*BIOGRAPHICAL AND CRITICAL SOURCES:*

*PERIODICALS*

*Booklist,* July, 2000, Bill Ott, review of *Winter Range,* p. 2007.
*Boulder (CO) News,* September 24, 2000, Clay Evans, "A Novel as Grim, Brutal, and Cold as Montana Winter."
*Capital Times,* September 15, 2000, Heather Lee Schroeder, "Similar Books? Look between the Covers."
*Christian Science Monitor,* September 7, 2000, Ron Charles, "Winter Is No Paradise on the Montana Range."
*Denver Post,* September 10, 2000, Ron Franscell, "Paradise Frozen."
*Kirkus Reviews,* July 1, 2000, review of *Winter Range,* p. 903.
*Library Journal,* September 15, 2000, Karen Anderson, review of *Winter Range,* p. 111.
*Publishers Weekly,* July 10, 2000, review of *Winter Range,* p. 42.
*Washington Post Book World,* September 8, 2000, Carolyn See, "Welcome to Montana, Where Paranoia Runs Deep," p. C2.

*OTHER*

*Pacific National Booksellers Association Web site,* http://www.pnba.org/ (January 2, 2002), Claire Davis, "The Work Ahead," and Cindy Heidemann, "Author Interview."*

\*       \*       \*

### de HARTOG, Jan 1914-2002
### (F. R. Eckmar)

*OBITUARY NOTICE*—See index for *CA* sketch: Born April 22, 1914, in Haarlem, Netherlands; died September 22, 2002, in Houston, TX. Author. De Hartog was a novelist and playwright most noted for his sea adventure stories and for the Broadway hit comedy *The Fourposter.* He had an early love for the sea, and at the age of ten ran away from home to work as a cabin boy. His minister father found him, however, and brought him back home, only to have him run away again two years later. Growing up to be an experienced salt, de Hartog attended the Netherlands Naval College, but did not graduate. Instead, he began writing detective novels under the name F. R. Eckmar. His first publishing success, however, came not in the detective genre but with the adventure novel *Hollands Glorie* (1940), later translated into English as *Captain Jan* (1976), which was a bestseller in the Netherlands. From 1932 to 1937 de Hartog also gained a love for theater, and worked as an actor in Amsterdam. With the onset of World War II he worked with the Dutch Resistance and consequently had to flee from the Nazis. Hiding in Amsterdam, he wrote his play *The Fourposter* before escaping to England. While in England de Hartog penned more novels based on his ocean adventures; the first of these to be translated into English was *The Lost Sea* (1951). A string of books in the same mode followed, including *The Little Ark* (1953), *The Captain* (1966), and *The Outer Buoy: A Story of the Ultimate Voyage* (1994). Many of these books were later adapted as movies, including *The Spiral Road, The Inspector, Stella,* and *The Little Ark.* As a dramatist, de Hartog's biggest success was with the Tony Award-winning *The Fourposter,* which had its Broadway debut in 1951 with a production starring Hume Cronyn and Jessica Tandy and was later adapted as the musical *I Do! I Do!* Some of de Hartog's other plays include *Skipper Next to God* (1945) and *William and Mary* (1963). De Hartog moved to Texas in the 1960s, where he lectured for a year at the University of Houston and also volunteered at a local hospital. This experience led him to write *The Hospital* (1964), an exposé on the terrible overcrowding occurring at a big-city charity hospital and the attendant lack of sufficient staffing. In addition, de Hartog was the author of a book about his escape from the Nazis that was published only in his native Dutch.

*OBITUARIES AND OTHER SOURCES:*

BOOKS

*Who's Who in America,* 56th edition, Marquis (New Providence, NJ), 2001.

PERIODICALS

*Los Angeles Times,* September 26, 2002, p. B13.
*New York Times,* September 24, 2002, p. A28.
*Washington Post,* September 27, 2002, p. B5.

\*   \*   \*

## DeKOVEN EZRAHI, Sidra

*PERSONAL:* Female. *Education:* Hebrew University of Jerusalem, B.A., 1965; Brandeis University, M.A., 1968, Ph.D., 1976.

*ADDRESSES: Office*—84 Prescott St., #31, Cambridge, MA 02138; The Hebrew University of Jerusalem, Mount Scopus, Jerusalem 91905, Israel.

*CAREER:* Hebrew University of Jerusalem, Jerusalem, Israel, professor, 1978—. Princeton University, visiting professor, 1997; Duke University, visiting assistant professor, 1984-84; Susquehanna University, visiting associate professor, 1998; Dartmouth College, visiting professor, 1999; Yale University, visiting fellow, 2000.

*MEMBER:* Modern Language Association, American Comparative Literature Association.

*WRITINGS:*

*By Words Alone: The Holocaust in Literature,* foreword by Alfred Kazin, University of Chicago Press (Chicago, IL), 1980.
*Booking Passage: Exile and Homecoming in the Modern Jewish Imagination,* University of California Press (Berkeley, CA), 2000.

*SIDELIGHTS:* Sidra DeKoven Ezrahi is the author of *By Words Alone: The Holocaust in Literature,* an "academic stud[y] of Holocaust literature," according to Robert Leiter in *Commonweal. Library Journal* contributor James B. Street referred to *By Words Alone* as "a courageous and intellectually rigorous study . . . a detached critical evaluation [that is]. . . terribly important but difficult." Avoiding works written at the time of the Holocaust by those directly involved, "Ezrahi is concerned primarily with creative responses to the Holocaust; and she is unshakable in her belief that there have been great successes in the genre," stated Leiter. To classify the body of literature connected to the Holocaust, Ezrahi creates a continuum divided into six types of relationship with the holocaust: "documentary art of. . . . 'concentrationary realism'. . . . literature of survival. . . . [as] depicted as a Jewish tragedy. . . . [as] reduced to myth. . . . [and affect] on American literature," specified Alan Mintz in *Commonweal.* "Although the main business of the book is classification, her occasional analyses of specific texts are always insightful and well handled. Her essays in literary evaluation are also worthwhile," praised Mintz, determining that the flaws in the text "stem from the model itself, which like all models, is limited in its explanatory power." However, maintained Mintz, the faults of *By Words Alone,* "take little away from the value of this admirable book." This "map of Holocaust literature" contains "well-reasoned discriminations" and, asserted Mintz, "Ezrahi writes with authority and sensitivity about material that is too commonly treated with theatricality."

*BIOGRAPHICAL AND CRITICAL SOURCES:*

PERIODICALS

*Commonweal,* January 16, 1981, Alan Mintz, review of *By Words Alone: The Holocaust in Literature,* p. 27; July 31, 1981, Robert Leiter, review of *By Words Alone,* p. 438.
*Library Journal,* June 1, 1980, James B. Street, review of *By Words Alone,* p. 1309.
*Publishers Weekly,* April 11, 1980, review of *By Words Alone,* p. 70.*

\*     \*     \*

**DENDEL, Esther (Sietmann Warner) 1910-2002**

*OBITUARY NOTICE*—See index for *CA* sketch: Born February 2, 1910, near Laurel, IA; died August 24, 2002, in Costa Mesa, CA. Craftswoman, educator, and author. Dendel was a respected craftswoman who wrote about Liberia and owned and operated Denwar

Studios in Costa Mesa, California, with her husband, creating ceramic and textile art. Fascinated by crafts at a young age, after high school she taught arts and crafts in West Virginia for six years before going to college. She earned her B.S. from Iowa State University in 1938 followed by a master's degree from Columbia University in 1939. Inspired by African art, she decided to travel to Liberia to study the crafts of the African people there and teach crafts to them as well. She supported this endeavor by training and selling chimpanzees to Americans. Dendel remained in Africa from 1941 to 1944 and turned her experiences into the books *New Song in a Strange Land* (1948), *Seven Days to Lomaland* (1954), *The Crossing Fee: A Story of Life in Liberia* (1968), and the novel *The Silk-Cotton Tree* (1958); in 1995 she also published the collection *You Cannot Unsneeze a Sneeze and Other Tales from Liberia* (1995). While in Liberia she met her future husband, Jo Dendel. After their return to the United States and Jo's service in the U.S. military, the couple opened Denwar Studios together. There they created ceramics, mosaics, and, later, fiber artworks. Dendel also taught classes in the studio and at high schools and universities, such as the University of Minnesota, the University of California at Irvine, and Orange Coast College. She wrote about arts and crafts in such books as *The Basic Book of Fingerweaving* (1974), *The Basic Book of Twining* (1978), and *Design from Nature: A Source Book for Artists and Craftsmen* (1978). Dendel was a supporter of the arts throughout her life, and founded the Dendel Scholarship Fund for artists and craftspeople.

*OBITUARIES AND OTHER SOURCES:*

PERIODICALS

*Los Angeles Times,* August 30, 2002, p. B13.

\*     \*     \*

**DENNIS, John V(alue) 1916-2002**

*OBITUARY NOTICE*—See index for *CA* sketch: Born November 9, 1916, in Princess Anne, MD; died of cancer December 1, 2002, in Princess Anne, MD. Ornithologist and author. Dennis was a well-known bird expert who helped make bird-watching more popular in the United States. Originally studying political science at the University of Wisconsin in Madison, Dennis was turned on to bird-watching by a friend and he decided to pursue a degree in ornithology. After earning his bachelor's degree at Wisconsin, he enlisted in the U.S. Army and during World War II was stationed in China. When he returned stateside, Dennis found a job as the sanctuary director for the Massachusetts Audubon Society, where he worked until 1949. In 1951 he completed his master's degree in ornithology at the University of Florida in Miami; he also worked on a doctorate at the University of Illinois, but never completed that degree. Dennis headed the Nantucket Ornithological Station during the early 1950s, and was a biologist for Koppers Co. in Pittsburgh and the American Petroleum Institution during the 1960s and early 1970s. While in Pittsburgh he invented a bird repellent that kept woodpeckers from damaging telephone poles. He also worked as a field researcher for the Nature Conservancy from 1977 to 1979. Dennis was best known as the author of bird-watching guides and guidebooks for maintaining bird feeders and gardens. His books include *A Complete Guide to Bird Feeding* (1975; revised, 1994), *Wildlife and Garden Plants* (1983), *Summer Bird Feeding* (1988), and a volume focusing on his beloved region of Maryland, *The Pocomoke: History and Natural History of Maryland's Most Scenic River* (2000).

*OBITUARIES AND OTHER SOURCES:*

PERIODICALS

*New York Times,* December 9, 2002, p. A27.
*Washington Post,* December 7, 2002, p. B6.

\*   \*   \*

**de RICARDI, Uriele**
    See **ROLFE, Frederick (William Serafino Austin Lewis Mary)**

\*   \*   \*

**de TOTH, Andre 1913-2002**

*OBITUARY NOTICE*—See index for *CA* sketch: Born May 15, 1913 (some sources say 1910), in Mako, Hungary; died of an aneurysm October 27, 2002, in Burbank, CA. Director and author. Though he rarely received critical acclaim for his film work, most of which consisted of Hollywood "B" movies in the crime and western genres, de Toth was highly respected by his fellow directors and became famous for his 3-D horror film *House of Wax.* As a youth in Hungary, his original interest was in the theater, and he wrote several stage plays. Although these efforts went unproduced, they led to an acquaintance with Hungarian playwright Ferenc Molnar, who provided the young de Toth with many contacts in theater and film circles. De Toth became interested in film, and directed the first of his five Hungarian films in 1938. With the onset of World War II he was compelled by the Germans to make propaganda movies, and he consequently recorded a number of battles during the war before fleeing to England in 1939. Once in England, de Toth found work writing and directing films for Alexander Korda. Three years later he moved to the United States, where he became associated with director David O. Selznick and Hunt Stromberg; his first film in America was the war drama *Passport to Suez* (1943). De Toth worked for several film companies, directing and often penning scripts, among them Enterprise, Twentieth Century-Fox, Columbia, Warner Brothers, and Horizon Pictures. In the 1950s, with the brief rise in popularity of 3-D films, de Toth made what has been credited as one of the best movies in the 3-D genre, *House of Wax* (1953), starring Vincent Price. The fact that the movie used 3-D technology is somewhat ironic, given that its director, who was missing an eye, lacked depth perception. Most of de Toth's other films were crime dramas and westerns. Although some of these proved quite successful—including *Pitfall* (1948); *The Gunfighter,* for which de Toth was nominated for an Academy Award for writing; *Springfield Rifle* (1952); *Carson City* (1952); *The Bounty Hunter* (1954); and *Crime Wave* (1958)—film critics always considered him a "B"-movie director. Late in his career, de Toth also directed episodes in television series such as *Maverick,* and directed his final film, *Play Dirty,* in 1968. He wrote about his filmmaking experiences in his 1994 autobiography *Fragments: Portraits from the Inside.*

*OBITUARIES AND OTHER SOURCES:*

PERIODICALS

*Chicago Tribune,* November 4, 2002, section 1, p. 10.
*Los Angeles Times,* October 30, 2002, p. B10.

*New York Times,* November 1, 2002, p. C12.
*Times* (London, England), November 1, 2002.
*Washington Post,* November 1, 2002, p. B6.

\*      \*      \*

## DINCULEANU, Nicolae 1925-

*PERSONAL:* Born February 26, 1925, in Padea, Romania; son of Nicolae and Frusina (Lusca) Dobrescu; married Elena Constantinescu, 1959. *Ethnicity:* "Romanian." *Education:* Polytechnical Institute of Bucharest, engineering degree, 1950; University of Bucharest, license, 1951, Ph.D., 1957, Doctor Docent, 1966.

*ADDRESSES: Home*—610 Northwest 22nd St., Gainesville, FL 32603. *Office*—Department of Mathematics, University of Florida, Gainesville, FL 32611; fax: 352-392-8357. *E-mail*—nd@math.ufl.edu.

*CAREER:* University of Bucharest, Bucharest, Romania, began as assistant, became professor of mathematics, 1950-76; University of Florida, Gainesville, professor of mathematics, 1977—. Queen's University, Kingston, Ontario, Canada, visiting professor, 1966-67; University of Pittsburgh, Distinguished Mellon Visiting Professor, 1970-71; guest speaker at colleges and universities throughout the world.

*MEMBER:* Romanian Academy (honorary member; deputy director of Mathematical Institute, 1965-75).

*AWARDS, HONORS:* Stoilov prize, Romanian Academy, 1964; grants from University of Liége, 1968, University of Rennes and University of Erlangen, 1970, National Science Foundation, 1972, 1973, 1974, National Research Council of Italy, 1986, École Polytechnique (France), 1987; University of Rome, 1996, University of Palermo, 1998, 2000, and University of Madrid, 1999; honorary doctorate, University of Craiova, 1995, and University of Bucharest, 2001.

*WRITINGS:*

(With E. Radu) *Manual de Analiza Matematica,* Didactica (Bucharest, Romania), 1959.
(With M. Nicolescu and S. Marcus) *Manual de Analiza Matematica,* Didactica (Bucharest, Romania), Volume 1, 1962, Volume 2, 1964.
*Textbook of Mathematical Analysis* (in Romanian), Gil (Zalau, Romania), 1966.
*Vector Measures* (monograph), Pergamon Press (Oxford, England), 1967.
*Integration on Locally Compact Spaces* (monograph), Nordhoff (Leiden, Netherlands), 1974.
*Vector Integration and Stochastic Integration in Banach Spaces* (monograph), Wiley Publishing Group (New York, NY), 2000.

Author of other monographs published in Romanian. Contributor to scientific journals.

\*      \*      \*

## DONOUGHUE, Carol 1935-

*PERSONAL:* Born December 22, 1935, in London, England; daughter of Abraham (a civil servant) and Diana Young Goodman (a homemaker); married Bernard Donoughue (divorced); children: four. *Education:* Oxford University, B.A. (honours), M.A.; National Froebel Foundation, diploma and postgraduate certificate of education; Institute of Education, London, diploma in educational administration. *Hobbies and other interests:* Life drawing, music, theater.

*ADDRESSES: Home*—19 Wood Ln., London N6 5UE, England. *E-mail*—cdonoughue@aol.com.

*CAREER:* Lesley College Laboratory School, Cambridge, MA, teacher, 1958-59; primary grade school teacher, England, 1959-60; BBC TV, London, England, producer of educational programs, 1960-65; part-time teacher in primary schools, 1965-75; National Union of Teachers Research, officer, 1976-79; Open University, lecturer in language development, 1979-81; Middlesex University, research fellow, 1981-83; inspector of schools for Her Majesty, Queen of England, 1983-93, head of inspection unit at Institute of Education, 1993-96; consultant in the field of education, 1996-2000. Serves as governor of Phoenix High School and Bedales School.

*WRITINGS:*

*The Development of Writing,* Cape (London, England), 1967, Grossman Publishers (New York, NY), 1969.

*Everest,* Jackdaw (London, England), 1968, Grossman Publishers (New York, NY), 1975.

(Editor) *In-service: The Teacher and the School,* Kogan Page and Open University Press (London, England), 1981.

(With Elizabeth Jane Goodacre) *Local Authority Support for Language Post-Holders in Primary Schools,* Middlesex University (Barnet, England), 1984.

*The Mystery of the Hieroglyphs: The Story of the Rosetta Stone and the Race to Decipher Egyptian Hieroglyphs,* Oxford University Press (New York, NY), 1999.

Contributor of articles to various education journals.

*WORK IN PROGRESS: A History of Writing,* for British Museum Press; various books on other history topics for nine to eleven year olds.

*SIDELIGHTS:* Carol Donoughue told *CA* "I have spent most of my professional life writing one thing or another, mostly to do with education and always for adults. I was at home for ten years, looking after my four children, and during that time I wrote two short nonfiction books for nine to eleven year olds. I really enjoyed the effort of presenting sometimes-complex information in a way that would interest and excite children of that age. Now that I have retired from the world of education, I have taken up writing for children again with much pleasure.

"Books should still be an important source of information for children, but the competition from television and the Internet means that you have to fight for their attention. That should not lead to poor imitations in book form of what they receive on screen. When I was writing *The Mystery of the Hieroglyphs: The Story of the Rosetta Stone and the Race to Decipher Egyptian Hieroglyphs,* I took a draft into a class of nine year olds and tried it out on them. They were very helpful! I shall do the same again with *The History of Writing.* If I can grab the interest of the boys, particularly, then I'll know I'm on the right lines."

According to Mark Dressman and Janet Gaffney, Donoughue did not miss her mark in *The Mystery of the Hieroglyphs.* Writing in the *New Advocate,* both critics praised Donoughue for the information contained in her book as well as the "readable and engaging" way in which she packages the topic for her young readers. Similarly, Mary J. Neale of *School Librarian* not only lauded Donoughue's presentation of the facts, but the attractive layout of the book as well, while *Booklist*'s Carolyn Phelan characterized the work as "an excellent introduction to the subject."

*BIOGRAPHICAL AND CRITICAL SOURCES:*

*PERIODICALS*

*Booklist,* December 1, 1999, Carolyn Phelan, review of *The Mystery of the Hieroglyphs: The Story of the Rosetta Stone and the Race to Decipher Egyptian Hieroglyphs,* p. 698.

*New Advocate,* winter, 2001, Mark Dressler and Janet Gaffney, review of *The Mystery of the Hieroglyphs,* p. 96.

*New Statesman,* November 7, 1975, Eric Korn, review of *Everest,* p. 585.

*School Librarian,* autumn, 2000, Mary J. Neale, review of *The Mystery of the Hieroglyphs,* pp. 148, 151.

\*     \*     \*

**DURING, Simon 1950-**

*PERSONAL:* Born February 3, 1950; son of Peter (a research scientist) and Zoe (a medical doctor) During; married Lisa O'Connell, 2002; children: Nicholas (first marriage). *Education:* Victoria University, New Zealand, B.A., 1970; University of Auckland, New Zealand, M.A. (first class honors), 1975; Cambridge University, England, Ph.D., 1982.

*ADDRESSES: Office*—700 Washington Place, 5B, Baltimore, MD 20201.

*CAREER:* Robert Wallace professor of English, University of Melbourne, 1994—; John Hopkins University, Baltimore, MD, professor of English, 2002—.

*MEMBER:* Australian Academy of the Humanities, International Association for Literary Theory and Criticism (vice president, 2000—).

*AWARDS, HONORS:* Honorary professor, Shandong University.


*WRITINGS:*


*Foucault and Literature: Towards a Genealogy of Writing,* Routledge (New York, NY), 1992.

(Editor) *The Cultural Studies Reader,* Routledge (New York, NY), 1993.

*Patrick White,* Oxford University Press (New York, NY), 1996.

*Modern Enchantments: The Cultural Power of Secular Magic,* Harvard University Press (Cambridge, MA), 2002.


*WORK IN PROGRESS: Out of Life: Literature in the Modern World.*


*SIDELIGHTS:* A professor of cultural studies, Simon During attempted something of a cultural revolution with *Foucault and Literature: Towards a Genealogy of Writing.* According to *Modern Language Review* contributor Nick Groom, this "is a promising idea: an introduction to the influence of Michel Foucault on literary studies, and the first step towards a Foucauldian analysis of the institution of literature itself." The first part summarizes Foucault's major arguments and discusses their relevance to the works of Samuel Johnson, George Eliot, Henry James, and other literary giants. "The application of Foucault to English writing is a productive enterprise, and the author initiates discussion of work as diverse as *What Maisie Knew, Hamlet, Middlemarch* and the novels of Theodore Dreiser by way of generally helpful illustration," commented *Times Educational Supplement* reviewer Edward Neill. The second half of the book attempts a Foucauldian analysis of literature itself, exploring the power relationships in the literary canon and its transmission over the years. "Unfortunately, his attempts to document this massive field persistently muddle his excellent little summaries and put his modest examples under impossible strain," wrote Nick Groom. "During's style, it has to be said, also ensures a level of difficulty that would undermine any confidence that the text could introduce this work to anyone not already familiar with it," commented Ian Saunders in the *Review of English Studies.* But Saunders concluded, "That aside, this is a substantial book, and on account of both its range of reference, and provoca-

tion within the contemporary debate, no doubt will become one of the more enduring texts that continue to circulate around the name of 'Foucault.'"

During's next project, *The Cultural Studies Reader,* cast a much wider net. Contributors such as Pierre Bourdieu, Cornel West, and Andrew Ross explore numerous topics, including the development of the culture industry, image marketing across national lines, and the many ways in which power relationships influence mass culture. *College Literature* reviewer Adam Katz felt that there "seems to be no particular effort to represent specific tendencies, stages of development, or theoretical problematics, in any productive relation to one another. For this reason, its usefulness even for those supportive of the politics articulated by the anthology is probably limited." *Canadian Literature* reviewer Alison Blunt faults the work for marginalizing some important developments, such as postcolonialism, but wrote that it "is a valuable introduction and resource for anyone with an interest in cultural studies."

From the large and amorphous field of cultural studies, During turned next to the influence of a particular writer in *Patrick White.* During explores the life and influence of this giant of Australian literature, focusing in particular on White's homosexuality and how it affected his writing. Not all critics were pleased. *Quadrant* contributor Richard Bell remarked, "White's novels are far from perfect, but as deeply felt works of art they deserve better than this silly, infuriating book." Similarly David Coad wrote in *World Literature Today,* "During's little book reeks of the jealousy and bitterness of the engage critic. It reveals a smoldering academic propped up by the latest critical fad." Surveying the firestorm that During's "little book" kicked up, *Australian Literary Studies* contributor Ian Syson felt that "The biggest surprise is how unremarkable and uncontroversial this book is." For Syson, "During's underlying argument . . . is a fairly sound one: Patrick White is less than relevant today because he was too relevant and perhaps too influential at his peak."

During next jumped to a very different subject: the cultural influence of magicians. In *Modern Enchantments: The Cultural Power of Secular Magic,* he describes the development of magic from a dark and unsavory subject to a modern entertainment, and the ways in which this "secular magic" has found its way into the wider culture. "Well researched and clearly written in academic prose, this study nevertheless comes to grief by the sheer range of material it attempts to digest," wrote a *Publishers Weekly* reviewer. But for *Financial Times* reviewer Marina Warner, During is a "most curious and learned and thoughtful guide" and "the book is richly informed" and "warmly argued."

*BIOGRAPHICAL AND CRITICAL SOURCES:*

*PERIODICALS*

*Australian Literary Studies,* May, 1997, Ian Syson, review of *Patrick White,* p. 94.

*Canadian Literature,* autumn, 1995, Alison Blunt, review of *The Cultural Studies Reader,* p. 156.

*College Literature,* June, 1994, Adam Katz, review of *The Cultural Studies Reader,* p. 157.

*Financial Times,* May 22, 2002, Marina Warner, review of *Modern Enchantments.*

*Modern Language Review,* October, 1996, Nick Groom, review of *Foucault and Literature,* pp. 946-949.

*Publishers Weekly,* February 18, 2002, review of *Modern Enchantments,* p. 84.

*Quadrant,* July, 1996, Richard Bell, review of *Patrick White,* pp. 88-89.

*Review of English Studies,* August, 1995, Ian Saunders, review of *Foucault and Literature,* p. 448.

*Times Educational Supplement,* June 11, 1993, Edward Neill, review of *Foucault and Literature,* p. 10.

*World Literature Today,* fall, 1996, David Coad, review of *Patrick White,* p. 1025.

# E-F

**E. A.**
   See ESDAILE, Arundell (James Kennedy)

\*   \*   \*

**ECKMAR, F. R.**
   See de HARTOG, Jan

\*   \*   \*

**ESDAILE, Arundell (James Kennedy) 1880-1956**
   **(E. A.)**

*PERSONAL:* Born April 25, 1880, in London, England; died June 22, 1956, in London, England; son of James Kennedy Esdaile (a justice of the peace); married Katharine Ada McDowall (a scholar and historian), 1902; children: three. *Education:* Lancing College, received degree; Magdalene College, Cambridge, M.A.

*CAREER:* Librarian, bibliographer, nonfiction writer, essayist, editor, lecturer, and poet. British Museum, assistant second class, 1903-13, assistant first class, 1913-26, secretary, 1926-40. Lecturer in bibliography at the University of London; held Sandars Readership in Bibliography at Cambridge University; served on library committee of the Institute of Intellectual Cooperation of the League of Nations.

*MEMBER:* Library Association (president, 1939-45), Malone Society (honorary secretary, 1907-24), English Association (chairman, 1944-46), Bibliographical Society, Sussex Archaeological Society, Johnson Society of Lichfield, Johnson Club (prior, 1925-26).

*AWARDS, HONORS:* D.H.L., University of Liverpool, 1939; honorary fellowship, British Library Association, 1946; Commander of the Order of the British Empire, 1952. The Library Association Council and the English Association established the Arundell Esdaile Memorial Lectures in 1958.

*WRITINGS:*

*NONFICTION*

*Bibliography of the Writings in Prose and Verse of George Meredith,* Spencer (London, England), 1907, Folcroft Press (Folcroft, PA), 1969.

(With Alfred W. Pollard, Victor Scholderer, and others) *Catalogue of Books Printed in the XVth Century Now in the British Museum,* Volumes 1-4, British Museum (London, England), 1908-16.

(Editor) Samuel Daniel and Michael Drayton, *Daniel's Delia and Drayton's Idea,* Chatto & Windus (London, England), 1908.

(With Alfred W. Pollard and J. A. Herbert) *Catalogue of the Fifty Manuscripts and Printed Books Bequeathed to the British Museum by Alfred H. Huth,* British Museum (London, England), 1912.

*A List of English Tales and Prose Romances Printed before 1740,* Blades & East, (London, England), 1912, Folcroft Press (Folcroft, PA), 1970.

(Editor) *The Age of Elizabeth (1547-1604)* ("Bell's English History Source Books" series), Bell (London, England), 1912, Folcroft Library Editions (Folcroft, PA), 1972.

(Translator) Wilhelm Busch, *Max and Moritz,* Routledge (London, England), 1913.

*The Lancing Register: A New Edition, Revised and Continued to 1912*, Meyers, Brooks (Enfield, England), 1913.

*A Chronological List of George Meredith's Publications, 1849-1911*, Constable (London, England), 1914.

(Editor) Henry R. Plomer, H. G. Aldis, E. R. McC. Dix, G. J. Gray, Ronald B. McKerrow, *A Dictionary of the Booksellers and Printers Who Were at Work in England, Scotland and Ireland from 1668 to 1725*, Bibliographical Society (Oxford, England), 1922.

*Bath in Art and Literature: An Address*, Chronicle & Herald Press (Bath, England), 1927.

*The Sources of English Literature: A Guide for Students, Sandars Lecture 1926*, Cambridge University Press (Cambridge, England), 1928, Franklin (New York, NY), 1969, revised edition published as *The Sources of English Literature: A Bibliographical Guide for Students, Sandars Lecture 1926*, Cambridge University Press (Cambridge, England), 1929.

*A Student's Manual of Bibliography*, Scribners (New York, NY), 1931, revised edition edited by Roy B. Stokes, Allen & Unwin (London, England), 1954, Barnes & Noble (New York, NY), 1955.

(As E. A.) *Bibliography for Babes: Being Aids to Memory for Young Learners by an Old Forgetter*, Bibliographical Press (New Haven, CT), 1934.

*Boswell in His Diaries: A Paper Read to the North Midland Branch of the Library Association*, Simson (London and Hertford, England), 1934.

*National Libraries of the World: Their History, Administration and Public Services*, Grafton (London, England), 1934, revised edition edited by F. J. Hill, Library Association (London, England), 1957.

*Lancing: An Address*, privately printed (London, England), 1938.

(Editor) *The Journals, Letters, and Verses of Marjory Fleming in Collotype Facsimile from the Original Manuscripts in the National Library of Scotland*, Sidgwick & Jackson (London, England), 1934.

(Author of introduction) Margaret Burton, *Famous Libraries of the World: Their History, Collections and Administrations*, Volume 2: *The World's Great Libraries Surveyed by Arundell Esdaile*, Grafton (London, England), 1937.

*The British Museum Library: A Short History and Survey*, Allen & Unwin (London, England), 1946, Greenwood Press (Westport, CT), 1979.

Contributor to periodicals, including *Library, Library Quarterly,* and *Library Review.*

*POETRY*

*Poems and Translations*, Mathews (London, England), 1906.

*Autolycus' Pack, and Other Light Wares: Being Essays, Addresses and Verses*, Grafton (London, England), 1940, Books for Libraries Press (Freeport, NY), 1969.

*Four Poems of the Second World War*, privately printed (Winchester, England), 1945.

*Wise Men from the West, and Other Poems*, Dakers (London, England), 1949.

*Scala Sancta Amoris*, Bumpus (London, England), 1955.

*SIDELIGHTS:* Arundell Esdaile was recognized as an eminent bibliographer and librarian. His scholarship, dedication, and enthusiasm for his profession, which is evinced through his writings, helped shape the field for the generations of librarians who followed him.

In October 1903, after graduating from Lancing College near the Sussex coast and earning an M.A. from Magdalene College, Cambridge, Esdaile was hired in the Department of Printed Books at the British Museum. He was assigned to help in the admissions office and the reading rooms. Soon after he started, however, the man who had been working on the *Catalogue of Books Printed in the XVth Century Now in the British Museum* passed away, and the task of compiling the first four volumes of the bibliography (1908-16), which covered early German and Italian printing, fell to Esdaile.

Esdaile edited several literary works and was involved in numerous other bibliographical projects. For example, he undertook a survey of literature on Shakespeare that was published in the journal *The Library* in 1906. He also completed both the *Bibliography of the Writings in Prose and Verse of George Meredith* and *A Chronological List of George Meredith's Publications, 1849-1911*. He would take on the task of editing a volume containing Samuel Daniel's *Delia* and Michael Drayton's *Idea*. They were published together as *Daniel's Delia and Drayton's Idea* in 1908.

During his early years at the British Museum, he compiled *A List of English Tales and Prose Romances Printed before 1740*, which was published in 1912.

"This area of English literature had been largely unexplored," noted David A. Stoker in the *Dictionary of Literary Biography,* "and Esdaile's book remained the only satisfactory treatment of the subject for decades to come."

In 1926, Esdaile was appointed to the distinguished Sandars Readership in Bibliography at Cambridge. In 1928, his lectures, which were designed to help inexperienced students use bibliographic resources, were published by the Cambridge University Press in *The Sources of English Literature: A Guide for Students.* G. M. Troxall, writing about the book in the *Saturday Review of Literature,* stated that "to have made available in one place so much specialized information that ordinarily is to be found only within the brains of the best reference librarians, and to have done it with clearness and distinction, is an achievement of which Mr. Esdaile may be distinctly proud—his book is consistently useful and interesting."

After World War I, Esdaile helped found the first British school of librarianship at University College, London. He contributed to the development of the curriculum and, in 1919, became a part-time lecturer in bibliography, a position he held for two decades. His lectures were published as *A Student's Manual of Bibliography,* one of the earliest guidebooks in a series published for people studying for the Library Association exam. However, it was written as an aid not only for library students but also for book collectors and conservators. The manual delves into the history of printing and publishing and describes bookmaking processes, including binding and illustration. In a review in *Spectator,* S. Gaselee noted that "Mr. Esdaile has produced a readable, workmanlike handbook, which does credit both to himself and to the British Museum where he has learned his art, and to this country which has been the pioneer in these studies. I don't see how any library, book-seller or individual collector can afford to be without it."

Appointed secretary of the British Museum in 1926, Esdaile represented the organization at conferences throughout the world. He collected information from the global contacts he made and wrote *National Libraries of the World: Their History, Administration and Public Services.* It explores the operations of about thirty prominent institutions. A reviewer in the *Times Literary Supplement* wrote that "as a first attempt to describe a special class of libraries, which has always been of great importance and relatively to every other becomes more so every decade, the book deserves high praise."

In preparation for a sequel, Esdaile gathered information on other famous libraries, but poor health forced him to turn over the project to Margaret Burton, his assistant. With an introduction by Esdaile, Burton's *Famous Libraries of the World: Their History, Collections and Administrations* was published as the second volume in a series called "The World's Great Libraries Surveyed by Arundell Esdaile."

Poor health also forced Esdaile to cut down on the scope of the history of the British Museum he wrote after he retired in 1940. In the preface to *The British Museum Library: A Short History and Survey,* he wrote that his goal was to provide only "a summary account, historical and descriptive, which shall be full enough to be useful for reference and information, and at the same time to bring out the true significance of the collections and of the tale of their gathering—in a word, to be readable." Although he finished the history in 1943, wartime shortages of paper prevented publication until 1946.

During retirement Esdaile also wrote several articles for professional and bibliographic journals. He died in London in 1956. Obituary notices praising his accomplishments were published in both professional journals and the popular press.

Besides his other achievements, Esdaile served the British Library Association with distinction for several decades. He joined in 1919, a time when the organization was struggling with financial problems. Within a year, Esdaile was elected to the governing council, and he helped revive the organization as a viable professional association. In 1922, he assumed editorship of the *Library Association Record* and was instrumental in its development as a respected publication. He also edited the annual review and served as chief examiner of bibliography. In 1927, he helped establish the association's University and Research Section, for which he served as chairman until his death. In 1939, he was elected Library Association president, a title usually held for a year, but when war broke out in September, he was asked to continue to serve. Ultimately, he served six years.

Esdale belonged to numerous other professional organizations. For example, he had a particular interest in the work of Samuel Johnson and served as prior of the Johnson Club from 1925 to 1926. He was president of the Johnson Society of Lichfield from 1926-1927. In the *Dictionary of Literary Biography,* Stoker maintained that Esdaile's "essays on Johnson are among his best works."

Esdaile also wrote poetry meant mostly for his own pleasure, and he printed many poems privately. A few were published commercially, however, including *Poems and Translations, Autolycus' Pack, and other Light Wares: Being Essays, Addresses and Verses, Wise Men from the West, and Other Poems,* and *Scala Sancta Amoris.* Esdaile is not considered an especially accomplished poet, but according to James Olle, who wrote a tribute to Esdaile in the *Journal of Librarianship,* many of his artistic works were "surely among the best written by any librarian."

*BIOGRAPHICAL AND CRITICAL SOURCES:*

*BOOKS*

*Dictionary of Literary Biography,* Volume 201: *Twentieth-Century British Book Collectors and Bibliographers, First Series,* Gale (Detroit, MI), 1999.
*Encyclopaedia of Library and Information Science,* Volume 38, Dekker, 1985.

*PERIODICALS*

*Journal of Librarianship,* Volume 12, 1980, pp. 217-228.
*Library Association Record,* Volume 58, 1956, pp. 321-325, 410-411.
*Library Review,* Volume 15, 1956, pp. 474-477.
*Library World,* Volume 58, 1956, pp. 25-28.
*Saturday Review of Literature,* August 25, 1928, p. 76.
*Spectator,* October 24, 1931, p. 544.
*Times Literary Supplement,* August 20, 1931, p. 631; November 1, 1934, p. 750.*

\* \* \*

**EZRAHI, Sidra DeKoven**
**See DEKOVEN EZRAHI, Sidra**

**FELIX, Charles Reis 1923-**

*PERSONAL:* Born 1923, in New Bedford, MA; married; wife's name, Barbara. *Education:* Stanford University, B.A., 1950.

*ADDRESSES: Home*—CA. *Agent*—c/o Author Mail, Burford Books, 32 Morris Ave., Springfield, NJ 07081.

*CAREER:* Writer and high school teacher. *Military service:* U.S. Army, 1940s.

*WRITINGS:*

*Crossing the Sauer: A Memoir of World War II,* Burford Books (Springfield, NJ), 2002.

*SIDELIGHTS:* Charles Reis Felix was a young, raw recruit in the closing stages of World War II. In *Crossing the Sauer: A Memoir of World War II,* Felix tells of his part in those dramatic days. In December of 1944, he was sent to the Western Front as an infantry replacement, and soon found himself part of Patton's Third Army moving through France and on to victory in Germany. He later remarks that he and his fellow recruits soon realized that Patton's famous nickname "Blood and Guts" really meant "his guts, our blood." *Library Journal* contributor Robert J. Andrews wrote, "For anyone wanting to know how it felt to participate in the events of World War II, this memoir is highly recommended." Through his memories and reconstructed conversations, Felix recounts life at the front and behind the lines in occupied France and Germany. "What really distinguishes this account is the quality of those conversations and of Felix's interior observations," noted a *Publishers Weekly* reviewer. Felix's observations take in petty and tyrannical noncoms, grandstanding and incompetent officers, and encounters, sometimes comic, sometimes violent, between the American soldiers and French and German civilians. Still, years later, Felix still sees his war years as a good experience still "casting its shadow over everything." "One need not be an enthusiast to enter that shadow's den, making this book a good experience by any measure," concluded the *Publishers Weekly* reviewer.

*BIOGRAPHICAL AND CRITICAL SOURCES:*

*PERIODICALS*

*Library Journal,* April 1, 2002, Robert J. Andrews, review of *Crossing the Sauer: A Memoir of World War II.*
*Publishers Weekly,* February 18, 2002, review of *Crossing the Sauer,* p. 85.*

## FERGUSSON, Peter (J.)

*PERSONAL:* Male. *Education:* Michigan State University, B.A., 1960; Harvard University, M.A., 1961, Ph. D., 1967.

*ADDRESSES: Office*—Wellesley College, Jewett Art Center 267, 106 Central St., Wellesley, MA 02481. *E-mail*—pferguss@wellesley.edu.

*CAREER:* Wellesley College, Wellesley, MA, professor of art, member of faculty, 1966—.

*MEMBER:* Society of Antiquaries of London, fellow; Save Venice (Boston chair, 1980-86; vice-chair, 1986—.

*AWARDS, HONORS:* Charles Rufus Morey Book Award, College Art Association of America, 1986, for *Architecture of Solitude;* Alice Davis Hitchcock prize, Society of Architectural Historians of Great Britain, 2001, for *Rievaulx Abbey.*

*WRITINGS:*

*Architecture of Solitude: Cistercian Abbeys in Twelfth Century England,* Princeton University Press (Princeton, NJ), 1984.
(With Stuart Harrison) *Rievaulx Abbey: Community, Architecture, Memory,* Yale University Press (New Haven, CT), 2000.

*SIDELIGHTS:* A longtime professor of art with a particular interest in the architecture of medieval Cistercian abbey, Peter Fergusson published *Architecture of Solitude: Cistercian Abbeys in Twelfth Century England* in 1984. In 2000, he teamed up with Stuart Harrison to produce a history of the most prestigious of these structures. *Rievaulx Abbey: Community, Architecture, Memory* tells the story of the founding, dissolution, and restoration of this remarkable monastery. Built in 1131-32, in a northern England still reeling from William the Conqueror's campaigns, it was rebuilt and expanded by the third abbot, Aelred, who governed it from 1147-1167. Like all monasteries, it was suppressed in the reign of Henry VIII and passed ultimately into the Earls of Fersham, and gradually fell into ruins.

"The final chapters . . . are among the most interesting; here, the authors and their collaborators chronicle the rediscovery of Rievaulx by nineteenth century antiquarians, and the campaign . . . to prise protection of the standing remains away from the Fevershams," wrote Simon Pepper in the *Times Literary Supplement.* That effort was successful, and today 100,000 visitors come to the site every year. "This book represents a magisterial achievement in archaeological and architectural analysis and reconstruction," concluded *Catholic Historical Review* contributor Bennett Hill.

*BIOGRAPHICAL AND CRITICAL SOURCES:*

PERIODICALS

*Catholic Historical Review,* January, 2001, Bennett Hill, review of *Rievaulx Abbey: Community, Architecture, Memory,* p. 92.
*Times Literary Supplement,* February 8, 2002, Simon Pepper, "Care of the Community," p. 20.\*

\*        \*        \*

## FEUER, Lewis S(amuel) 1912-2002

*OBITUARY NOTICE*—See index for *CA* sketch: Born December 7, 1912, in New York, NY; died November 24, 2002, in Newton, MA. Educator and author. Feuer was a professor of sociology, government, and philosophy. After earning his undergraduate degree from City College of the City University of New York, he attended graduate school at Harvard University, where he earned his doctorate in philosophy in 1935. Feuer was an instructor at City College until the war started. During World War II he was an army sergeant who was demoted to private after standing up for workers in New Caledonia by helping them to organize against what they considered slave-labor practices in building air strips. Returning home to academia, Feuer accepted a post as an associate professor of philosophy at Vassar College, but he quit after a personality conflict with another professor led to a fist fight. He then moved to the University of Vermont as a professor of philosophy and, in 1957, to the University of California at Berkeley where he taught philosophy and sociology. From 1966 to 1976 Feuer taught sociology at the University of Toronto; he finished his academic career at the University of Virginia, where he taught sociology and the humanities until his retirement as emeritus professor in 1983. As a philosophical thinker, Feuer at first espoused Marxist ideals, but this gradually changed following his disillusionment over the Soviets' signing of the Ribbentrop-Molotov Pact with Germany in 1939. In 1963, when he had the opportunity to lecture on Marxism in the USSR, his opinions displeased the Soviet government and students were instructed not to attend his sessions. Feuer created his next stir in 1969 when his book *The Conflict of Generations: The Character and Significance of Student Movements* was released. Holding that the conflicts between students and university administrators had Oedipal-like routes, the book was criticized by some reviewers who felt it trivialized students' political idealism. Among Feuer's other writings are *Spinoza and the Rise of Liberalism* (1958; revised edition, 1983), *Marx and the Intellectuals: A Set of Post-Ideological Essays* (1969), and *Imperialism and the Anti-Imperialist Mind* (1986). A fan of British novelist Sir Arthur Conan Doyle, Feuer was also the author of the novel *The Case of the Revolutionist's Daughter: Sherlock Holmes Meets Karl Marx* (1983).

*OBITUARIES AND OTHER SOURCES:*

*BOOKS*

*Who's Who in America,* 46th edition, Marquis (Wilmette, IL), 1990.

*PERIODICALS*

*New York Times,* November 30, 2002, p. A32.

\*    \*    \*

## FILBY, P(ercy) William 1911-2002

*OBITUARY NOTICE*—See index for *CA* sketch: Born December 10, 1911, in Cambridge, England; died of a stroke November 2, 2002, in Laurel, MD. Historian, librarian, and author. Filby was an authority on genealogy, calligraphy, and the history of the "Star-spangled Banner." After completing high school in Cambridge,

England, he was a librarian at Cambridge University, where he worked in the rare books division from 1930 until 1937 and was director of the science library until 1940. With the onset of World War II Filby joined the British Army and served in the Intelligence Corps, working as a cryptographer and helping to break the Nazi's ULTRA code. He was also head of the German Diplomatic Section from 1943 until 1946 and attained the rank of captain. Following the war Filby became senior researcher and archivist for the British Foreign Office, remaining there until 1957. That same year he married an American and moved with his wife to Baltimore, Maryland where he found work as assistant director for the Peabody Institute. Filby's deep interest in history led to a job as librarian and assistant director of the Maryland Historical Society in 1965, and he became its director from 1972 until his retirement in 1978. During his tenure as director he helped make the Maryland Historical Society an institution of national importance. In retirement, Filby remained active as an historian and headed the genealogical effort at the Gale publishing house, editing books on passenger immigration and heraldry. As an expert on calligraphy, he was the author of *Calligraphy and Handwriting in America, 1710-1962* (1963), and his book *Star-spangled Banner: Books, Sheet Music, Newspapers, Manuscripts, and Persons Associated with the "Star-spangled Banner"* (1972), written with Edward G. Howard, dispelled some common myths about the U.S. national anthem.

*OBITUARIES AND OTHER SOURCES:*

*BOOKS*

*Writers Directory,* 17th edition, St. James Press (Detroit, MI), 2002.

*PERIODICALS*

*Baltimore Sun,* November 9, 2002, p. 4B.

\*    \*    \*

## FJELDE, Rolf (Gerhard) 1926-2002

*OBITUARY NOTICE*—See index for *CA* sketch: Born March 15, 1926, in Brooklyn, NY; died September 10, 2002, in White Plains, NY. Educator and author. Fjelde is perhaps best remembered for his work as a translator of the plays of Henrik Ibsen. He was a student at

Yale University, where he received his bachelor's degree in 1946 before going to Cambridge University to earn his master's degree in 1947. He also attended the Pratt Institute, Copenhagen University, and the University of Heidelberg during the early 1950s, and the University of Oslo in 1965. Fjelde began his career as an advertising copywriter in New York City from 1948 to 1950, followed by two years as a senior copywriter and editorial assistant for *Outdoor Life* magazine. In 1954 he joined the Pratt Institute's faculty as a teacher of English and drama, an association that would last more than forty years. He also taught at Juilliard beginning in 1973. Of Norwegian ancestry, Fjelde became fascinated by the plays of Ibsen, first translating *The Wild Duck* in 1956 for a production at the Pratt Institute. This first success led to two translations of Ibsen's *Peer Gynt* (1964 and 1980), and the translated volumes *Four Major Plays* (Volume 1, 1965, Volume 2, 1970) and *The Complete Major Prose Plays* (1978). In addition to his translation work, Fjelde edited collections of Ibsen's writings and was the founding president of the Ibsen Society and editor of its newsletter. A lover of poetry, he also wrote such verse as *The Rope Walk* (1967), *Rafferty One by One* (1975), and *The Bellini Look* (1982), and was the founding editor of the *Yale Poetry Review* and *Poetry New York*. For his work in promoting Norwegian literature, Fjelde received the Norwegian Royal Medal of St. Olaf in 1991.

## OBITUARIES AND OTHER SOURCES:

### BOOKS

*Writers Directory,* 17th edition, St. James Press (Detroit, MI), 2002.

### PERIODICALS

*Los Angeles Times,* September 14, 2002, p. B21.
*New York Times,* September 13, 2002, p. A22.
*Washington Post,* September 14, 2002, p. B7.

\* \* \*

## FOLLETT, Beth

*PERSONAL:* Female. *Education:* McGill University, degree in social work, 1992.

*ADDRESSES: Agent—* Press, 401 Huron St. . Canada.

*CAREER:* Novelist and pub. onto, Ontario, Canada, owner, editor, 1996—.

*WRITINGS:*

*Tell It Slant,* Coach House Press, (To. Canada), 2001.

*SIDELIGHTS:* Beth Follett began her own in. literary publishing house in 1996. She is . proprietor, publisher, and editor. In 2001, she . first novel published.

*Tell It Slant* is the story of Nora Flood, a charact. taken from a 1930s novel by Djuna Barnes calle. *Nightwood*. The plot line also closely follows that of *Nightwood* and Barnes even shows up in this book as a minor character. The title is derived from an Emily Dickinson poem, which reads "Tell the Truth but tell it slant / Success in Circuit lies." Nora is a young, insecure lesbian, living in Montreal with a dysfunctional past and an unfaithful lover. As the story opens, she decides to leave her partner and begin a journey of self-discovery. Emily Pohl-Weary, a reviewer for *Now Toronto* felt that the best part of the novel is Follett's "heady portrayal" of the main character's "pathological hunger for self-acceptance." The novel was called "a classic tale of love and loss," by an *Exread.* reviewer, who also acknowledged that Follett "navigates the slippery line between poetry and prose with dexterity and grace, and unfolds a text that is muscular and startling." Michael Basilieres in the *Danforth Review* agreed by stating, "This is a novel written from the inside out."

## BIOGRAPHICAL AND CRITICAL SOURCES:

### PERIODICALS

*Performing Arts & Entertainment in Canada,* autumn, 2001, Beth Follen and John Degan, "Portrait of the Artist as . . . Publisher," p. 13.

*House Press Web Site,* http://www.chbooks.
m/ (May 6, 2002), review of *Tell It Slant.*
*rth Review,* http://collection.nlc-bnc.ca/ (May 6,
002), Michael Basilieres, review of *Tell It Slant.*
*d,* http://www.exread.com/ (May 6, 2002), review
of *Tell It Slant.*
*Toronto Online,* http://www.nowtoronto.com/
(May 6, 2002), Emily Polh-Weary, review of *Tell
It Slant.*
*ream in High Park Biography,* http://www.
thescream.ca/ (May 6, 2002).*

\*　　\*　　\*

**FORSTER, Gwynne**
**See JOHNSON-ACSADI, Gwendolyn**

\*　　\*　　\*

**FRAGOULIS, Tess**

*PERSONAL:* Born in Heraklion, Crete, Greece. *Ethnicity:* Greek. *Education:* Attended Concordia College.

*ADDRESSES: Home*—Montreal, Quebec, Canada. *Agent*—c/o Author Mail, Thistledown Press, 633 Main St., Saskatoon, Saskatchewan S7H 0J8, Canada.

*CAREER:* Writer and creative writing teacher.

*AWARDS, HONORS:* QSPELL First Book Award nomination, 1998 for *Stories to Hide From Your Mother.*

*WRITINGS:*

*Stories to Hide From Your Mother,* Arsenal Pulp Press (Vancouver, British Columbia, Canada), 1997.
*Ariadne's Dream,* Thistledown Press (Saskatoon, Saskatchewan, Canada), 2001.

*SIDELIGHTS:* Tess Fragoulis was born in Greece, but moved to Montreal, Quebec, Canada as an infant. She is a writer and creative writing teacher who discovered her own personal connection to Greek mythology later in life.

Her first work, a collection of short stories titled *Stories to Hide From Your Mother,* is labeled as post-punk modernism. Fragoulis focuses on the condition of being a woman, as all of her main characters are female and tend to be outsiders in society. The protagonists also seem to struggle with reality. For example, in "Swan Dive," an artist/porn star dreams of killing herself in front of everyone she knows, and in "Day Two Last Twenty-Four Hours," a mother fantasizes about devouring her children in an effort to survive menstruation. Nadia Halim, reviewing for the *Canadian Forum,* pointed out that while Fragoulis has indeed "embraced and internalized the persona of the mad, suffering artist," she has also marginalized these characters and "the mad-artist myth quarantines her, preventing her from really challenging the status quo." Britta Santowski, a writer for the *Canadian Book Review Annual,* found this collection to be "extraordinary," and noted,"Fragoulis uses language like a knife, slicing through flimsy surfaces and exposing profound alternative perspectives."

In Fragoulis's second book, *Ariadne's Dream,* she returns to the land of her ancestors: Greece. The novel is set in modern times, but incorporates the occasional appearance of mythical creatures, such as Persephone and Hades. It seems that the main character, Ariadne, may be fashioned after the Fragoulis herself, as she is a young Montrealer of Greek descent who returns to her native country. She falls in love with a heroin addicted rock star, Yannis, and the affair turns sour. It is then that the main character begins to journey through something akin to the mythological stages of Hell. Ariadne then ends up on the island of Nysas, working in a bar and fighting off male tourists as she tries to forget her lover. Joel Yanofsky, writing for the online *Montreal Review of Books,* called this book a "story of sex, drugs, obsessive love and unkind fate, played out against the backdrop of ancient history." Yanofsky also admitted that while the novel is a bit "short on action," Fragoulis makes up for it with the wonderful atmosphere she creates and her "mischievous, chatty, and omniscient narration."

*BIOGRAPHICAL AND CRITICAL SOURCES:*

*PERIODICALS*

*Canadian Book Review Annual,* 1998, Britta Santowski, review of *Stories to Hide From Your Mother,* p. 209.
*Canadian Forum,* March, 1998, Nadia Halim, review of *Stories to Hide From Your Mother,* p. 42.

*OTHER*

*Thistledown Press Web site,* http://www.thistledown. sk.ca/ (May 6, 2002).

*Montreal Review of Books,* http://www.aelaq.org/ (May 6, 2002), Joel Yanofsky, review of *Ariadne's Dream.**

\*        \*        \*

## FRESCHET, Gina 1960-

*PERSONAL:* Born March 9, 1960, in San Francisco, CA; daughter of Ferucio (an educator) and Berniece (an author, maiden name Speck) Freschet; married Steve Cieslawski (an artist), November 27, 1997. *Education:* School of Visual Arts (New York, NY), B.F.A.

*ADDRESSES: Home and office*—34 East 4th St., New York, NY 10003.

*CAREER:* Freelance author and illustrator.

*WRITINGS:*

*The Lute's Tune,* illustrated by Steve Cieslawski, Doubleday (New York, NY), 1992.
(And illustrator) *Naty's Parade,* Farrar, Straus &Giroux (New York, NY), 2000.
(And illustrator) *Beto and the Bone Dance,* Farrar, Straus & Giroux (New York, NY), 2001.
(And illustrator) *Winnie and Ernst,* Farrar, Straus & Giroux (New York, NY), 2003.

*ILLUSTRATOR*

Berniece Freschet, *Bernard Sees the World,* Scribner (New York, NY), 1976.
Berniece Freschet, *Bernard of Scotland Yard,* Scribner (New York, NY), 1978.
Berniece Freschet, *Bernard and the Catnip Caper,* Scribner (New York, NY), 1981.

Contributor of illustrations to various periodicals, including the *New York Times, New York Magazine, Esquire, Psychology Today, Ms.,* and others.

*WORK IN PROGRESS:* Two new picture books for children; a young adult novel for teenagers about E.S.P. and the occult.

*SIDELIGHTS:* Gina Freschet told *CA:* "My mother wrote children's books so I remember from an early age spending hours in the library and checking out dozens of books for her research and our pleasure.

"I remember writing and illustrating my first little book when I was in third grade—so I guess I was about nine years old. The book was about a horse, of course—a little black foal who would grow up to become a sort of Pegasus. I was under the influence of Walter Farley's *Big Black Horse* and *Black Beauty* at the time.

"While growing up, I continued writing and illustrating my own stories, often about virtuous maidens who loved unwisely and expired of unrequited affection. In my early teens, I was under the influence of Arthurian romances by Howard Pyle and admired the classics of Arthur Rackham, N. C. Wyeth, Edmund Dulac, John Tenniel, and E. H. Shepard.

"Coming from a big, boisterous family, I often escaped by immersion in [Laura Ingalls Wilder's] 'Little House' books; I was fascinated by the work of Garth Williams. As a lifelong admirer and collector of children's books, I'm delighted to be a creator of them as well. I only hope to be as imaginative as my idols."

In *Naty's Parade,* one of her first self-illustrated picture books for children, Freschet writes about the Mexican dance festival of Guelaguetza. The festivities, including descriptions of music, color, and dance, are relayed to the reader via Naty, a young girl who is participating in the celebration dressed in a mouse costume. In a text accompanied by lively and colorful pictures, Freschet skillfully conveys the "surrealism" of the "wild parade," effectively blending the two to convey Naty's fright as she gets separated from her father, noted a *Kirkus Reviews* critic. She finds him in time, however, and the pictures in the book, along with the words, subside to a more gentle representation, leaving readers resonating with "melodies and bright hues," concluded the same reviewer. A writer for *Publishers Weekly* was also appreciative of Freschet's "dreamlike, folk-art-inspired imagery," coupled with her "accessible travelogue" detailing the sights and sounds of this colorful Mexican carnival.

In *Beto and the Bone Dance*, Freschet returns to Mexico once again, this time celebrating the Day of the Dead, known in Mexico as el dia de los muertos. As Beto and his father wander the colorful marketplace gathering supplies for the festival, Beto thinks about what gifts he can offer with his prayers for his recently deceased grandmother. As the day passes, he is unable to think of anything suitable until later that night. While waiting to participate in the midnight bone dance, the young boy falls asleep, and in his dream, Beto becomes aware of his grandmother's spirit as she cradles him in her otherworldly arms. When he awakens, Beto now knows exactly what his grandmother would want, something no one else has considered, a picture of the young boy. Writing in *Booklist*, Annie Ayres thought that "Freschet's festive illustrations add a happy sparkle to a simple story." *School Library Journal* contributor Ann Welton called *Beto and the Bone Dance* "a sprightly, informative tale," going on to note that Freschet's palette of rich golds and reds in her illustrations "gives the slightly scary tale a reassuring and joyful look."

*BIOGRAPHICAL AND CRITICAL SOURCES:*

PERIODICALS

*Booklist*, May 15, 2000, Helen Rosenberg, review of *Naty's Parade*, p. 1747; August, 2000, Isabel Schon, review of *Naty's Parade*, p. 2155; October 15, 2001, Annie Ayres, review of *Beto and the Bone Dance*, p. 401.
*Kirkus Reviews*, March 15, 2000, review of *Naty's Parade*, p. 382; October 1, 2001, review of *Beto and the Bone Dance*, p. 1422.
*Publishers Weekly*, February 7, 2000, review of *Naty's Parade*, p. 84; October 22, 2001, "Seasonal Celebrations," p. 79.
*School Library Journal*, June, 1992, Jane Marino, review of *The Lute's Tune*, p. 92; May, 2000, Maria Otero-Boisvert, review of *Naty's Parade*, p. 190; October, 2001, Ann Welton, review of *Beto and the Bone Dance*, p. 118.*

*       *       *

**FRY, Stephen 1957-**

*PERSONAL:* Born August 24, 1957, in London, England; son of Alan John (a physicist and inventor) and Marianne Eve (Newman) Fry. *Education:* Qeen's College, Cambridge, B.A. (English), 1981. *Politics:* Labour Party. *Hobbies and other interests:* Pressing wild flowers, cricket.

*ADDRESSES: Agent*—Hamilton Hodell Management, Ground Floor, 24 Hanway St., London W1T 10H, England.

*CAREER:* Actor and writer. *The Listener,* columnist, 1988-89; *Daily Telegraph,* columnist, 1990-91. Dundee University, rector.

*MEMBER:* Amnesty International, Comic Relief, Groucho Club.

*AWARDS, HONORS:* Antoinette Perry (Tony) Award nomination, best book (musical), 1987; three Tony Awards and Olivier Award for *Me and My Girl* (with others); honorary LL.D, Dundee University, 1995; Golden Space Needle Award, Seattle International Film Festival, best actor, 1998, Golden Globe Award nomination, best performance by an actor in a motion picture—drama, Golden Satellite Award nomination, best actor in a motion picture—drama, 1999, all for *Wilde;* Golden Globe Cast Award for *Gosford Park.*

*WRITINGS:*

BOOKS

(With Hugh Laurie) *A Bit of Fry & Laurie,* Mandarin (London, England), 1990.
(With Hugh Laurie) *A Bit More Fry & Laurie,* Mandarin (London, England), 1991.
*The Liar,* Heinemann (London, England), 1991.
(With Hugh Laurie) *Three Bits of Fry & Laurie,* Heinemann (London, England), 1992.
*Paperweight,* Heinemann (London, England), 1992.
*The Hippopotamus,* Hutchinson (London, England), 1994; Random House (New York, NY), 1995.
*Fry & Laurie: Bit Number Four,* Mandarin (London, England), 1995.
*Making History: A Novel,* Hutchinson (London, England), 1996, Random House (New York, NY), 1997.
*Moab Is My Washpot: An Autobiography,* Hutchinson (London, England), 1997; Random House (New York, NY), 1999.

*The Stars' Tennis Balls,* Hutchinson (London, England), 2000.

*Revenge: A Novel,* Random House (New York, NY), 2002.


OTHER


*Gossip* (screenplay), 1983.

*Me and My Girl,* adapted from Noel Gay's 1937 musical, produced 1984.


*WORK IN PROGRESS:* Director, *Bright Young Things,* a film adaptation of Evelyn Waugh's *Vile Bodies.*


*SIDELIGHTS:* While he isn't as familiar in America, British-born actor and author Stephen Fry attained tremendous success in his native land. Although he is most known for his work in television, film and on the stage, Fry considers himself a writer first and foremost. His published books include several novels, an autobiography, a collection of columns, and four volumes of scripts from his popular sketch comedy television series, *A Bit of Fry and Laurie.* Fry's success came early when he adapted Noel Gay's 1937 musical *Me and My Girl* in 1984, when he was still in his mid-twenties. The adaptation earned Fry numerous awards, including three Antoinette Perry Awards (Tony's) and an Olivier Award. In addition to writing for both radio and television, Fry worked as a columnist from 1988 to 1991 for several British periodicals, including *The Listener* and the London *Daily Telegraph.* His 1992 book, *Paperweight,* is a collection of many of the columns he wrote during the period. Fry published his first novel, the highly autobiographical *The Liar,* in 1991. His other novels include *The Hippopotamus, Making History,* and *The Stars' Tennis Balls.* Despite Fry's affinity for comedy in other areas of his career, he has shown a more sober side with his novels. "His . . . novels are witty and imaginative and show a deep concern for serious ideas," literary critic Merritt Moseley wrote of Fry in the *Dictionary of Literary Biography.* As with most of his other work, Fry received accolades for his witty and intelligent autobiography, *Moab Is My Washpot,* which appeared in 1999. "If there is one trait that runs through almost all of Fry's writing, including his columns, his autobiography, and his novels, it is cleverness," Moseley wrote in the *Dictionary of Literary Biography.*

Although he has earned much praise for his writings, Fry's literary work has been somewhat overshadowed by his acting and comedic work. Throughout the 1980s and 1990s, he was a familiar face in English theaters, appearing in productions of a number of plays, including *Forty Years On, The Common Pursuit* and *Cell Mates.* He has also appeared in several well known movies, including *The Good Father, A Fish Called Wanda, I.Q.,* and *The Wind in the Willows.* He played major supporting roles in the 1995 film, *Cold Comfort Farm,* and in the 2001 film *Gosford Park.* Perhaps his most well known cinematic role was his portrayal of Oscar Wilde in the 1998 film, *Wilde.* Between 1989 and 1995, Fry teamed up with fellow comedian Hugh Laurie to write and perform in the hit sketch comedy series *A Bit of Fry and Laurie.* Fry also played the character of Jeeves in the popular British television series *Jeeves and Wooster, based on the novels by P.G. Wodehouse*

Fry was born August 24, 1957, in the Hampstead section of London, though he grew up in the rural town of Norfolk. His father, Alan Fry, was a creative man, who worked as a self-employed physicist and inventor. His mother, Marianne, was Jewish, a heritage Fry has always closely associated himself with. Although he was not deprived as a child, Fry led a troubled childhood. While enrolled at a public school in Uppingham, Fry began a pattern of lying to teachers and stealing money from classmates, which often landed him in trouble, and once led him to attempt suicide. After serving a jail sentence for stealing, Fry enrolled himself at Norwich City College. He was eventually accepted into Queens' College at Cambridge University, where he earned an English degree in 1981. It was at Cambridge where he first got involved with theater and where he met Hugh Laurie.

Fry's first novel, *The Liar,* is largely based on his experiences at the school in Uppingham. The protagonist in the story is a troubled schoolboy named Adrian Healey, who is outwardly homosexual. Fry has said that he also discovered his own homosexuality while at Uppingham. After Healey moves on to Cambridge, he comes under the tutelage of a homosexual professor, who encourages him to write a concocted lost manuscript of Charles Dickens—a pornographic work called "Peter Flowerbuck." Literary critic Richard Davenport-Hines, who reviewed *The Liar* for the *Times Literary Supplement,* felt the work contained "some funny opening passages," but ultimately called the book "a great disappointment." Fry's next novel, *The Hippopotamus,* appeared some four years after *The Liar.* Fry, who took the title from a T. S. Eliot poem, uses the book to explore elements of British anti-Semitism. Part of the plot concerns the difficulties of a Jewish boy in an English school, which may allude to some of Fry's troubles at Uppingham. Even more so than in *The Liar,* Fry writes about homosexual sex, and even delves into bestiality. According to literary critic Merritt Moseley in the *Dictionary of Literary Biography,* the book allowed Fry to "explore several themes of interest to him, including the proper role of spirituality." Michiko Kakutani, writing in the *New York Times,* called the work "a deliciously wicked and amusing little fable."

Fry grew more satirical with his next novel, *Making History,* which appeared in 1996. The book contains elements of science fiction, which was something new for Fry. The plot revolves around the efforts of a Cambridge student and a physicist, who together learn how to manipulate time and space, and attempt to erase the Holocaust by going back in time to prevent the rise of Adolf Hitler. The book is narrated by the student, Michael Young, whose post-graduate work is spent studying Hitler's early life. The physicist Young meets at Cambridge wants desperately to change history because his father, a Nazi physician, committed terrible acts against Jews. As the story progresses, the two men go back in time and sterilize Hitler's mother drinking well, so she can never give birth to the future German leader. In a cruel twist of fate, Hitler's birth is prevented, but the Holocaust isn't. In fact, there is a Holocaust that is much worse, as a man named Rudi Gloder rises to power in Germany, and even uses the water from Hitler's mother's well to sterilize Jews. Realizing the mistake, Young once again goes back in history and changes it back, allowing Hitler to be born. Elizabeth Mellet of *Library Journal* called the work an "intelligent and gripping tale."

*Moab Is My Washpot* appeared a year after *Making History.* As he explained to Simon Bell in an interview for the London *Telegraph,* Fry found it much more difficult to write an autobiography than his previous fiction. "In an autobiography, you have to remember things you've forgotten, conceal names, try to work out and remember motives," he told Bell. "The messiness of real life, its woolliness, is such that it's harder to get the truth across." At more than 400 pages, the book only includes aspects of Fry's life from his childhood until the age of eighteen, when he was accepted to Cambridge. The title, which Fry took from Psalm 108 of the Bible, is a reference to God's disdain for all the enemies of Israel and the Jews. In the book, Fry describes his early youth as a time of privilege and relative happiness. But the period gives way to the difficulties of his juvenile years. Fry discusses his thoughts about his general cockiness during those years. "The moment I began to speak I found I became more than simply nerveless. I became utterly confident and supremely myself. It was as if I had discovered my very purpose in life," Fry writes, describing his propensity to tell fibs and steal as a child. "I am trying hard, even now, to forgive myself for these years of stealing." In addition to describing his own life, the book offers observations about the British education system, as well as Fry's feelings about sexuality. *Moab is my Washpot* was lauded by numerous literary critics, including a contributor for *Publishers Weekly,* who called it "witty, intelligent and honest." Jonathan Cecil, who reviewed the book for *Spectator,* referred to the book as "a meticulously recalled narrative of youth, a ruthless self-examination, and a maniacally clever literary stand-up comedy routine."

Fry also earned critical praise for *The Stars' Tennis Balls,* a novel published in 2000 and later released on audio. As in *Making History,* the book's plot contains its share of absurd elements. It is also Fry's most violent book, containing numerous scenes of physical brutality. The book revolves around young protagonist Ned Maddstone's odyssey of revenge against a group of jealous classmates, who, early on in the book, conspire to ruin his life. Referring to the work as "stylish," a contributor for *Spectator* felt *The Stars' Tennis Balls* to be "a page-turner and full of fun."

*BIOGRAPHICAL AND CRITICAL SOURCES:*

*BOOKS*

*Contemporary Theatre, Film, and Television,* Volume 27, Gale (Detroit, MI), 2000.
*Dictionary of Literary Biography,* Volume 207, Gale (Detroit, MI), 1999.

*PERIODICALS*

*Advocate,* June 8, 1999, p. 79.
*Booklist,* February 1, 1998, p. 896; December 15, 1998, p. 760; May 15, 1999; October 15, 1999, p. 467.

*Kirkus Reviews,* March 15, 1993, p. 321.

*Lambda Book Report,* March-April, 1995, pp. 17-18; June, 2000, p. 31.

*Library Journal,* February 1, 1998, p. 110; June 15, 1999, p. 80; March 1, 2002, pp. 78-79.

*National Review,* May 31, 1999, p. 67.

*Newsweek,* March 13, 1995, p. 69.

*Publishers Weekly,* February 22, 1993, p. 81; October 31, 1994, p. 42; January 26, 1998, p. 70; May 17, 1999, p. 62.

*Spectator,* October 14, 2000, pp. 54-55.

*Telegraph* (London, England), August 30, 1997, interview with Simon Bell.

*Time,* February 20, 1995, p. 79.

*Times Literary Supplement,* September 20, 1991, p. 23; October 20, 2000, p. 23.*

\*        \*        \*

## FRY, Ying Ying

*PERSONAL:* Born in China; adopted daughter of Amy Klatzkin (a writer and editor) and Terry M. Fry. *Education:* Attended Chinese American International School, San Francisco, CA. *Hobbies and other interests:* Girl Scouts, soccer, drawing, reading.

*ADDRESSES: Home*—San Francisco, CA. *Agent*—c/o Yeong and Yeong, 1368 Michelle Dr., St. Paul, MN 55123-1459.

*CAREER:* Student and writer.

*MEMBER:* Girls Scouts of America.

*WRITINGS:*

(With mother, Amy Klatzkin) *Kids Like Me in China,* Yeong and Yeong (St. Paul, MN), 2001.

*SIDELIGHTS:* Ying Ying Fry attends the Chinese American International School in San Francisco where she studies all subjects in English and Mandarin. Outside of school, which takes up much of her day, Fry likes to play soccer, draw, and read. Despite her busy schedule, Fry found time to pen her debut book, an adoption story. Ying Ying Fry was just eight years old when she wrote *Kids Like Me in China.*

Having spent part of her childhood in an orphanage in Changsha, Hunan province, Fry was curious to go back and visit, reunite with her loving caregiver, and spend time with the other children there. She is fortunate enough to have parents who are not only willing, but have the ability to take her back to her birthplace. What she experiences on this pilgrimage is the subject of *Kids Like Me In China.*

Her book is the first of its kind—an adoption story, a tale of reconnecting and reuniting—written by a child. Written with the help of her mother, the book is in first person and illustrated with color photographs, some of which were taken by Ying Ying herself. Fry wanted to write this book so that other adopted children could understand where they came from. Rose Lewis, praised the book on the Yeong and Yeong Web site. "Every adopted child will love to read this book again and again. It is their story too."

Although Ying Ying was adopted by her American parents while still an infant, she still recalls Li Ayi, the caregiver who showered her with love and attention. Their reunion is one of the highlights of *Kids Like Me.* Ying Ying visited not only the orphans while on her adventure, but other children as well—in their homes, on playgrounds, at school. Her new friendships helped her see her life from a brand new perspective, one she shares forthrightly and with great enthusiasm in her book. And the author doesn't shy away from the tougher issues—the birth control policy in China, the fate of the disabled children living at the orphanage, the feelings of not belonging to anyone. Her message is one of hope, of awakened identity, and of realizing that a person can belong to two families at one time.

Amy Klatzkin, Ying Ying's mother, called the book "our quilt." In an essay on *Chinasprout.com,* she explained the process. "During our two weeks in Changsha, Ying Ying kept a journal, and we took lots of video and more than 1,300 photographs. My job was to provide structure and flow to the narrative. The book was our quilt. Ying chose what pieces to put in it, and I trimmed them and sewed them together, one piece at a time. Her most important personal discoveries of the trip remain private."

Upon returning home from her overseas trip, Ying Ying consented to an interview with Suzanne Lee of *AsianWeek.* When asked if she'd ever return to China, the young Ying Ying informed her interviewer that she'd be returning in ten days. "I'm giving eye exams to the kids in the orphanage," she explained. Her father, who took many of the photos for *Kids Like Me in China,* filled in the details. Using some of the royalties from the book sales, Ying Ying is providing eye exams for the children of the orphanage. She noticed during her visit that none of them were wearing glasses.

*BIOGRAPHICAL AND CRITICAL SOURCES:*

*PERIODICALS*

*Women's Review of Books,* January, 2002, Anita D. McClellan, "Bridging the Ocean," pp. 7-9.

*OTHER*

*AsianWeek,* http://www.asianweek.com/ (April 9, 2002), Suzanne Lee, "Kid by Day, Author by Night."

*China Daily Online,* http://www.chinadaily.com/ (April 9, 2002), synopsis of *Kids Like Me in China.*

*Chinasprout.com,* http://www.chinasprout.com/ (April 9, 2002), Amy Klatzkin, "Making Kids Like Me in China."

*Families With Children from China,* http://www.fwcc. org/ (April 9, 2002), review of *Kids Like Me.*

*Yeong and Yeong Web site,* http://www.yeongandyeong. com/ (April 9, 2002), review and synopsis of *Kids Like Me in China.*\*

# G

## GABORI, Susan 1947-

*PERSONAL:* Born June 17, 1947, in Putnok, Hungary; daughter of George (operator of a knitting factory and a taxicab business) and Judith (a drafter; maiden name, Varadi) Gabori; married second husband, Dani Hausmann (a photographer), August 10, 1991. *Education:* McGill University, B.A., 1970; Hornsey College of Art, London, England, M.A. *Religion:* Jewish.

*ADDRESSES: Home and office*—655 Bloomfield Ave., Outremont, Québec, Canada H2V 3S2. *E-mail*—sgabori@securenet.net.

*CAREER:* National Film Board of Canada, Montreal, Québec, Canada, camera operator, 1973-75; CTV (television network), Toronto, Ontario, Canada, director of documentary programs, 1975; filmmaker and writer. Québec Writers' Federation, instructor in dramatic nonfiction writing, 2001.

*MEMBER:* Canadian Writers' Union, Québec Federation of Writers.

*AWARDS, HONORS:* Joseph Brant Award, Ontario Historical Society, c. 1993, for *In Search of Paradise: The Odyssey of an Italian Family.*

*WRITINGS:*

*In Search of Paradise: The Odyssey of an Italian Family,* McGill-Queen's University Press (Montreal, Canada), 1993.

*Blind Sacrifice: Portrait of Murderers* (second part of a trilogy), Gordon Shillingford Publishing (Winnipeg, Manitoba, Canada), 2000.

*A Good Enough Life* (first part of a trilogy), Goose Lane Editions, 2002.

Film scripts include *Stripping,* Persis Films; *Symbiosis,* National Film Board of Canada; *Mrs. Mudrick* (television play), Canadian Broadcasting Corp. (CBC); *Limits* (anthology of one-hour television dramas), CBC; and *When Evils Were Most Free* (television miniseries). Writer and director of television documentaries, including *Survival; Dundas Project,* Toronto Board of Education; *Open Doors; Shared Destiny,* CTV Television; *New Romance,* National Film Board of Canada; *Black Business Women in Montreal,* CBC; *Prenatal Diagnosis,* CBC; *Étape travail,* National Film Board of Canada; *Half Way; Pat; John, John,* National Film Board of Canada; and *Being Human,* CTV Television. Work represented in anthologies, including *Fruits of Experience,* Emanation Press (Toronto, Ontario, Canada), 1980. Contributor of short stories and articles to periodicals, including *Canadian Woman Studies, Nightshift, Today, Broadcaster, Cinema Canada,* and *Catholic Digest.*

*WORK IN PROGRESS: Home Again?* (working title), the third part of a trilogy.

*SIDELIGHTS:* Susan Gabori told *CA:* "I am presently researching the third part of a trilogy. The first part, *A Good Enough Life,* is about the dying. A terminal illness is a very dramatic, cathartic event on an individual level, and the person must face his/her life and his/her coming end. The second part, *Blind Sacrifice,* is about murderers—about a dramatic event that takes place between the murderer and the murdered, one which the murderer must face. *Home Again?* will be about people's experiences in World War II and how they have lived with these horrors over the succeeding years. I am interviewing Germans who were in Germany at the time of the war, European Jews who were taken to the concentration camps, a couple of Jewish children who had to hide during the war, a composer who left Germany in 1934 for Singapore and then Shanghai, then landed in Canada, an artist, a Greek Jew who moved to Israel and then to Canada. My own father went through Dachau and was jailed by the Russians when the war was over, and my mother had to hide in the countryside outside of Budapest, Hungary, with my grandmother and her younger sister.

"The book will be divided into five or six sections, and the characters will relate their experiences in each section. Sometimes one character will only talk in one section. The divisions will tentatively cover home before the war, the chaos of the war, liberation, home again, wandering, and setting down roots. I hope my readers will be historians and those interested in what social upheaval can do to a person."

Gabori described herself as "a former documentary filmmaker who has brought her interviewing and editing skills to the written word. I use only ten percent of the interview material from each person, sometimes only one percent. I do a lot of choosing, moving around, throwing out—exactly like in the editing room. However, the interviews I am doing for books run over sixteen hours; this kind of in-depth work cannot be done for films."

"I must write," Gabori added. "I have no choice. Subjects alight in my brain, take root, and seduce me. They demand my attention. They are like jealous lovers. I must do the research and the writing. I have no choice. I can find a rational explanation for what I write, but sometimes the more subtle reasons come at least a year or more after I finish writing a book. I begin to understand what I have written after it is done. It is a wonderful process because I keep learning.

"The early fiction of V. S. Naipul, *The 42nd Parallel* by John Dos Passos, *The Executioner's Song* by Norman Mailer, *The Right Stuff* by Tom Wolfe, and David

Malouf's *An Imaginary Life, Remembering Babylon,* and *The Great War* have each had their influence on me in subtle ways. The strongest influence on me has been my work as a documentary film director and having edited all my own films. I edit my interviews much like I edited films. My respect for structure comes from having written film scripts.

"There is a certain idealism that drives my writing. I try to find and show people the hope, beauty in dirt, chaos."

*          *          *

## GAFFANEY, Timothy J. 1966-

*PERSONAL:* Born March 1, 1966, in San Jose, CA. *Education:* University of California—Los Angeles, B.A., 1988, M.A., 1994, Ph.D., 1997. *Politics:* Democrat.

*ADDRESSES: Office*—Department of Government, Georgetown University, Washington, DC 20057-1034. *E-mail*—gaffanet@georgetown.edu.

*CAREER:* Georgetown University, Washington, DC, adjunct assistant professor of government, 1998—.

*MEMBER:* American Political Science Association, Western Political Science Association.

*WRITINGS:*

*Freedom for the Poor: Welfare and the Foundations of Democratic Citizenship,* Westview Press (Boulder, CO), 2000.

Contributor to periodicals, including *Pacific Studies* and *Polity.*

*WORK IN PROGRESS:* A book on the democratic conception of political freedom; research on "the transition the Roman Catholic church has made to fully endorsing democratic regimes."

*BIOGRAPHICAL AND CRITICAL SOURCES:*

*PERIODICALS*

*Contemporary Sociology,* September, 2001, Ruth Sample, review of *Freedom for the Poor: Welfare and the Foundations of Democratic Citizenship,* p. 509.

\*     \*     \*

## GARDINER, George (Arthur) 1935-2002

*OBITUARY NOTICE*—See index for *CA* sketch: Born March 3, 1935, in Witham, Essex, England; died November 16, 2002, in London, England. Politician, journalist, and author. Gardiner was a conservative Member of Parliament and an avid supporter of Prime Minister Margaret Thatcher. He was a 1958 graduate of Balliol College, Oxford, who began his career as a political correspondent for the *Conservative News,* the London *Sunday Times,* and Thomson Regional Newspapers during the 1960s and early 1970s. Gardiner had an unsuccessful run for Parliament in 1970 that was followed, in 1974, with his election to the House of Commons, representing Reigate, Surrey. A extreme right-wing politician, he supported such causes as re-institution of the death penalty, British support of white rule in South Africa, strengthened anti-immigration laws, and economic reforms to aid the middle classes. He was particularly adept at backroom dealings, actively garnering support for his conservative agenda through his position on various committees, as well as through his editorial writings in the *Sunday Express.* Although Prime Minister Thatcher never awarded Gardiner a posts in her government, in appreciation for his work she arranged for him to be knighted before she left office. With the election of Prime Minister John Major in 1990, Gardiner worked to block the government's more liberal reforms, especially with regard to Major's advocacy of increased economic cooperation with Europe. By the late 1990s even Tory Party right-wingers were growing frustrated with Gardiner's controversial politics. Gardiner reacted by joining the Referendum Party, but he subsequently lost his seat in the 1997 elections. He was the author of four books: *A Europe for the Regions* (1971), *The Changing Life of London* (1973), *Margaret Thatcher: From Childhood to Leadership* (1975), and *A Bastard's*

*Tale: The Political Memoirs of George Gardiner* (1999). During the 1990s he was also editor of *Forward* magazine.

*OBITUARIES AND OTHER SOURCES:*

*PERIODICALS*

*Guardian* (London, England), November 18, 2002, p. 24.
*Independent* (London, England), November 19, 2002, p. 18.
*Irish Times* (Dublin, Ireland), November 23, 2002, p. 14.
*Times* (London, England), November 18, 2002.

\*     \*     \*

## GARRETT, Greg

*PERSONAL:* Male. *Education:* Oklahoma State University, Ph.D.

*ADDRESSES: Home*—Austin, TX. *Office*—Baylor University, English Department, Waco, TX 76798. *E-mail*—greg_garrett@baylor.edu.

*CAREER:* Author and educator. Baylor University, Waco, TX, associate professor of English, 1989—. Taught creative writing at the University of Central Oklahoma and University of Oregon.

*AWARDS, HONORS:* William Faulkner Prize for Fiction; regional CASE Gold Medal for Nonfiction.

*WRITINGS:*

*Free Bird,* Kensington Books (New York, NY), 2002.

Contributor to periodicals, including *High Plains Literary Review, Grain, South Dakota Review,* and *Writers' Forum.*

*SIDELIGHTS:* After years of contributing short stories to literary journals and magazines, American author and educator Greg Garrett published his debut novel,

*Free Bird,* in 2002. An associate professor of English at Baylor University in Texas, Garrett has earned accolades for his work in the classroom. He has also taught creative writing at the University of Central Oklahoma and the University of Oregon. Before completing *Free Bird,* Garrett had published more than forty short stories in such publications as *Writers' Forum, High Plains Literary Review,* and *South Dakota Review.* His stories have also appeared in literary journals outside of the United States, including in Canada, Australia and New Zealand. A contributor for *Publishers Weekly,* after reviewing *Free Bird,* called Garrett "a fine storyteller with a deft comic touch."

*Free Bird* revolves around protagonist Clay Forester, and the demons that haunt him. Once a promising lawyer working for one of Washington D.C.'s most prestigious law firms, Forester finds his life beginning a downward slide when his beautiful wife and young son are killed in an automobile accident in which he was driving while intoxicated. Blaming himself and ridden with guilt, Forester quits his job and moves back to his small hometown of Robbinsville, North Carolina, where he now lives with his mother and stepfather. In addition to striking up a noncommittal romance with an old high school flame, Forester spends his time singing and drinking in redneck bars. His only possession in life is a 1961 Triumph once owned by his biological father, who abandoned the family when Forester was just a young child. The car is the only reminder Forester has of his father, and he refuses to drive it.

Forester's life takes a turn when he receives a phone call and learns his father, Steve Forester, has passed away in New Mexico and the last thing he said was Clay's name. Clay blows off the news until he walks outside to find the Triumph's engine mysteriously running. Unable to ignore the coincidence, he decides to drive the old car to New Mexico for the funeral. The rest of the book follows him on his odyssey, as he picks up a three-legged dog and meets a number of strange, down-and-out characters that teach him lessons about life. They also make him confront the realities of his own life that he has tried so hard to suppress. At one point, Forester runs into an old classmate from law school who has become a priest and political protester. "Forgiveness is easier than hatred in the long run," the man tells Forester. When he arrives in Santa Fe, Forester is surprised to learn of his father's legacy as a renowned artist and philan-

thropist. In the end, he accepts the advice of his old classmate and reconciles himself to his father, as well as to himself. The contributor for *Publishers Weekly* called the book an "entertaining debut" with "well-drawn characters."

*BIOGRAPHICAL AND CRITICAL SOURCES:*

PERIODICALS

*Publishers Weekly,* February 18, 2002, review of *Free Bird,* pp. 74-75.

OTHER

*California State University, Northridge Web site,* http://www.csun.edu (July 28, 2002), Greg Garrett biography.*

\* \* \*

## GARRISON, Cal 1948-

*PERSONAL:* Born September 18, 1948, in Milton, MA; daughter of Robert L. (a school administrator) and Eva (a social worker; maiden name, Carlson) Filbin; children: Eliza, Julia, Johanna Garrison Souza. *Ethnicity:* "Swedish." *Education:* Massachusetts College of Art, B.F.A. *Religion:* Wiccan. *Hobbies and other interests:* Geo-biology, dowsing, metaphysics, meditation, crystals, the Tarot, the occult, planetary healing work, herbalism.

*ADDRESSES: Home and office*—2710 Main St., P.O. Box 14, West Pawlet, VT 05775; fax: 802-645-0049. *E-mail*—minerva@sover.net.

*CAREER:* Professional astrologer, c. 1972—. Also Reiki master and "Flower of Life" facilitator.

*MEMBER:* American Society of Dowsers.

*WRITINGS:*

*The Old Girls' Book of Spells,* Red Wheel/Weiser (York Beach, ME), 2002.
*The Old Girls' Book of Dreams,* Red Wheel/Weiser (York Beach, ME), 2003.

*WORK IN PROGRESS: Astrology 101,* completion expected in 2004; research on alchemy, "free energy," and physics of light.

\* \* \*

## GATES, Bea(trix)

*PERSONAL:* Female. *Education:* Sarah Lawrence College, M.F.A.

*ADDRESSES: Office*—Goddard College, MFA Program, 123 Pitkin Rd., Plainfield, VT 05677. *Agent*—Sydelle Kramer, c/o Frances Goldin Agency, 57 East 11th St., Ste. 5B, New York, NY 10003.

*CAREER:* Teacher and author. Goddard College, Plainfield, VT, currently member of MFA faculty; Granite Press, Penobscot, ME, founder, 1973-1989. Freelance editor, designer, and publishing consultant; former teacher at New York University, Hampshire College, and the New School.

*AWARDS, HONORS:* MacDowell Colony fellow; finalist, Lambda Book Award, for *In the Open;* Puffin Foundation grant, 2000; The Open Meadows' Patsylu Fund, 2002; National Endowment for the Arts, 2003.

*WRITINGS:*

*Native Tongue,* Hopalong Press (Monterey, MA), 1973.
*Shooting at Night,* Granite Press (Penobscot, ME), 1980.
(Editor) *The Wild Good: Lesbian Photographs and Writings on Love,* Anchor Books (New York, NY), 1996.
*In the Open: Poems,* Painted Leaf Press (New York, NY), 1998.

Translator, with Electa Arenal, of *Like the Oar That Cuts the Current: Poems of Vikram Babu* by Jesus Aguado, 2002. Contributor of poems to anthologies and literary journals, including *Kenyon Review* and *The World In Us: Lesbian and Gay Poetry of the Next Wave;* contributor of book reviews to *Lambda Book Report* and *Nation.* Contributor to *A Woman Like That: Lesbian Writers Tell Their Coming Out Stories.*

*WORK IN PROGRESS:* A libretto for *The Singing Bridge,* an original opera with composer Anna Dembska. A translation with Electa Arenal of a selection of poems by Spanish poet, Jesus Aguado called "What You Say About Me."

*SIDELIGHTS:* Bea Gates is a writer whose poems have been described as "shocking in their nakedness," according to author Jaime Manrique on the *Painted Leaf Press Web site.* Her themes are contemporary—child abuse, AIDS, friendship, homelessness—and explored without cliché. Gates' 1998 collection, *In The Open,* was a finalist for the Lambda Book Award.

Gates also edited the collection *The Wild Good: Lesbian Photographs and Writings on Love.* The anthology includes poetry and essays written by authors such as Adrienne Rich, Muriel Rukeyser, Kate Rushin, Audre Lorde, and Pat Califia. It also includes photographs by artists such as Berenice Abbott, Luz Maria Gordillo, and Zoe Leonard, Lucy Winer, and Barbara Hammer. Gates told CA: "The contributors range from world-famous and award-winning artists to emerging and unkown photographers; film-makers, videographers, and mixed media installation artists, most of whose chosen work has never been reproduced in book form." Pauline Klein, a reviewer for *Library Journal* wrote, "The last three sections are particularly strong, but the writing is uneven, and the reader occasionally wonders what the point is."

Gates' own poetry collection, *In the Open,* received a warm welcome. Fellow writer Grace Paley, gave the book a thumbs-up on the *Painted Leaf Press Web site:* "These are some of the strongest poems I know—tough without meanness or complaint, new knowledge and the language to carry it." Also, on the *Painted Leaf Press Web site,* Marie Ponsot said: "Bea Gates is a discoverer. Her poems of the lost and the found are transparently true to the time we live in. They move us because she has endured until she found words steady enough to present them." Sue Russell, reviewer for *Lambda Book Report,* praised the collection's content. "*In the Open* is a book that dares much, offers moments of great lyric beauty, and raises interesting questions about the nature of art."

Gates regularly offers a mixed-genre workshop, "The Words to Say It: Fiction, Poetry, and Autobiography," in New York city. She also travels nationally offering readings and workshops.

*BIOGRAPHICAL AND CRITICAL SOURCES:*

PERIODICALS

*Lambda Book Report,* January, 1997, Jeannine De-Lombard, review of *The Wild Good: Lesbian Photographs and Writings on Love,* p. 12; April, 1999, Sue Russell, review of *In the Open,* p. 11.

*Library Journal,* February 1, 1997, Pauline Klein, review of *The Wild Good,* p. 98.

OTHER

*Goddard College Web site,* http://www.goddard.edu/ (October 2, 2002), professional profile of the author.

*Painted Leaf Press Web site,* http://www.paintedleaf. com/ (October 10, 2002).

\*    \*    \*

## GAWANDE, Atul A. 1965-

*PERSONAL:* Born November 5, 1965; in Brooklyn, NY; son of Atmaram (a physician) and Sushila (a physician) Gawande; married Kathleen Hobson, November 28, 1992; children: three. *Education:* Stanford University, B.A., B.S., 1987; Balliol College, Oxford, M.A., 1989; Harvard Medical School, M.D.; Harvard School of Public Health, M.P.H.

*ADDRESSES: Home*—Newton, MA. *Office*—Senior Adviser to Assistant Secretary for Planning & Evaluation, Office of Secretary, U.S. Department of Health and Human Services, 200 Independence Ave. SW, Hubert H. Humphrey Building, Room 424-E, Washington, DC 20201.

*CAREER:* Harvard University, Cambridge, MA, teaching assistant, 1991, research assistant, 1991-92; Boston University, Boston, MA, teacher, 1991-92; Clinton-Gore Campaign, health and social policy adviser, 1992; Clinton's Presidential Transition Team, deputy director for health policy, 1992-93; U.S. Department of Health and Human Services, senior advisor to assistant secretary, 1993—. *New Yorker,* staff writer.

*WRITINGS:*

*Complications: A Surgeon's Notes on an Imperfect Science,* Metropolis (New York, NY), 2002.

Contributor to *The Best American Science and Nature Writing 2000,* and *In Sickness and in Health,* as well as to the periodical *Slate.*

*SIDELIGHTS:* American author Atul A. Gawande utilized his experiences as a medical resident when writing his debut book, *Complications: A Surgeon's Notes on an Imperfect Science.* The critically lauded effort is a collection of Gawande's essays, which detail his observations about the state of medical science in America.

Born in Brooklyn, New York, Gawande has made a name for himself in several fields. Before beginning his medical residency at a Boston hospital, Gawande completed an exemplary academic career as a Rhodes Scholar at Oxford University. He has also served in the political arena, first as an advisor to former president Bill Clinton, and, beginning in 1993, as a senior advisor for the U.S. Department of Health and Human Services. Gawande used his medical and political experiences while writing articles for numerous publications and periodicals, which eventually led to him becoming a staff writer on medicine and science for the *New Yorker.* His book, which *Time* critic Lev Grossman called "riveting," is both a memoir of Gawande's experiences in the medical profession and a critical look at how surgeons are trained in America. The book's main theme is that surgeons often make mistakes because they lack the necessary training to perform certain surgeries. In a 2002 interview with *U.S. News & World Report* reporter Linda Kulman, Gawande provided some insight into the problems that he addresses in his book. "Science and technology move so fast you have to learn on the fly or what you're doing becomes outdated. The way we learn is to do things once or twice with some supervision. Then it's time to give it a try on someone," he said. "We want perfection without practice, yet everyone is harmed if no one is trained for the future."

Numerous literary critics lauded *Complications* for its honest yet compassionate look at the medical profession. For example, a contributor to *Publishers*

*Weekly* called the book a "distinguished debut." In the book's thirteen essays, some of which had previously appeared in periodicals, Gawande examines a number of issues faced by medical professionals. According to William Beatty of *Booklist,* Gawande does so in a "smooth, engaging style." In the book, Gawande describes his profession as an "enterprise of constantly changing knowledge, uncertain information, fallible individuals, and at the same time lives on the line." In several of the essays, Gawande probes the prevailing ethics of medicine, and criticizes doctors and medical organizations for failing to police themselves properly. For example, in the book's first essay, Gawande describes numerous errors he has personally witnessed in the operating room, which he blames on a number of factors, including the inexperience of younger doctors and burnout or depression of veteran physicians. In other essays, he delves into how the human psyche often affects how a doctor treats a patient.

While he is often critical, Gawande is also very sympathetic to the plight of medical professionals, who often deal with life-or-death situations. "Good doctoring is all about making the most of the hand you're dealt," he writes in the book. Critic Barron H. Lerner, who reviewed the book for the *Nation,* felt Gawande was able to get his points across in a clear manner. "He is a deft writer, telling compelling stories that weave together medical events, his personal feelings and answers to questions that readers are surely pondering," Lerner wrote. Other critics had similar opinions of the book. "*Complications* impresses for its truth and authenticity, virtues that it owes to its author being as much [a] forceful writer as [an] uncompromising chronicler," wrote F. Gonzalez-Crussi in the *New York Times.*

*BIOGRAPHICAL AND CRITICAL SOURCES:*

*PERIODICALS*

*American Scientist,* May, 2002, review of *Complications: A Surgeon's Notes on an Imperfect Science,* p. 269.
*Booklist,* March 1, 2002, review of *Complications,* p. 1075.
*Entertainment Weekly,* April 26, 2002, review of *Complications,* p. 140.
*Kirkus Reviews,* February 1, 2002, review of *Complications,* pp. 158-159.
*Nation,* May 6, 2002, review of *Complications,* p. 35.
*New York Times,* April 7, 2002, review of *Complications,* section 7, p. 10.
*Publishers Weekly,* February 25, 2002, review of *Complications,* p. 50.
*Time,* April 15, 2002, review of *Complications,* p. 72.
*US News & World Report,* April 15, 2002, review of *Complications,* p. 76.*

\*     \*     \*

## GEARIN-TOSH, Michael 1940-

*PERSONAL:* Born 1940, in Nambour, Australia. *Education:* University of Oxford, England, B.A., 1961; M.A., 1964. *Hobbies and other interests:* Garden design, theatre.

*ADDRESSES: Office*—c/o St. Catherine's College, University of Oxford, Manor Rd., Oxford, 0X1 3UJ, England. *E-mail*—gearin@lineone.net.

*CAREER:* English professor and writer. Ford Foundation research fellow, lecturer in English literature, 1966—; Oxford School of drama, director, 1984—; University of Oxford, assessor, 1986-87; St. Catherine's College, vice-master, 1988-90; Stanford University, California, visiting professor, 1991—; Russian Academy of Theatre Arts, Moscow, visiting professor, 1993-94; University of Oxford, St. Catherine's College, Oxford, England, lecturer in English literature.

*AWARDS, HONORS:* Kindred Spirit International Award, 2002, for best book on complementary medicine.

*WRITINGS:*

*Living Proof: A Medical Mutiny,* Scribner (New York, NY), 2002.

*WORK IN PROGRESS:* A sequel to *Living Proof: A Medical Mutiny.*

*SIDELIGHTS:* Diagnosed in 1994 with an incurable cancer of the blood and immune system called multiple myeloma, Oxford English professor Michael Gearin-

Tosh gambled and decided not to have chemotherapy. Instead, he decided to pursue an alternative approach. The odds were approximately one in 20,000 that he would survive. In 2002, eight years after his decision, Gearin-Tosh saw his book *Living Proof: A Medical Mutiny* published.

As he explains in his book, Gearin-Tosh decided to forego conventional treatment for a number of reasons. He begins his story in journal form with an almost lighthearted account about his learning of his illness and the impact it has on him. The overwhelming advice from medical experts was that he receive chemotherapy as the only chance for possibly prolonging his life. But Gearin-Tosh did not panic. Similar to the training he had received in studying literature, he mulled the situation over as he would the subtext of a classic novel. The author felt at times like he was being pushed into a specific treatment with little consideration for his own wishes or his ultimate fate, and he began to analyze the experts' words and the meaning behind their medical jargon. For example, one doctor who recommended chemotherapy related that his own wife died from myeloma and then added that "she died not of the cancer, but of an opportunistic pneumonia just after she had responded very successfully to treatment." For Gearin-Tosh, the question immediately came to mind: "What gave an opportunity to the opportunistic pneumonia? Cancer? But she was just given very successful treatment for cancer. So it was not the cancer." The conclusion that Gearin-Tosh comes to is that she died from the treatment. Ernst Wynder, a cancer expert who had worked at the Sloan-Kettering Hospital, also raised the author's suspicions when he stood out as the lone voice in the medical establishment to warn one of the author's friends, "If your friend touches chemotherapy, he's a goner," as Sandra Goodman related on the *Positive Health* Web site.

Eventually, Gearin-Tosh sets out on a therapeutic regimen that includes orthomolecular medicine, Eastern breathing and visualization, mega doses of vitamins, acupuncture, coffee enemas, and the Gerson diet. The author devotes a large portion of the book to explaining why he and some others believe the alternative regimen was the most likely reason for his cure and that he is the "living proof." However, the author is careful and smart enough to note that there is no absolute or irrefutable evidence that his alternative treatments were the reason for his survival.

In the book, Gearin-Tosh also discusses some of the universal challenges that cancer patients must face, including promises by research that have yet to be fulfilled and the difficulty of the doctor-patient relationship. Goodman noted: "However, what ought to make the medical establishment cringe with embarrassment and take note are that certain of its practitioners were guilty of abruptness, rudeness, bullying attempts to force treatment and insensitivity in discussing life and death matters with patients." The book also includes an appendix of the author's medical history; a list of the specialists he consulted, including a discussion of the author's case by his primary physician, Oxford University's senior professor of Medicine, Sir David Weatherall and also by the Mayo Clinic's senior professor of Myeloma, Robert Kyle; and a peer-reviewed case history by Carmen Wheatley.

As should probably be expected, reviews and comments about the book have varied greatly. Some in the medical establishment have been quick to point out that Gearin-Tosh's book is not scientific proof that these regimens work because cancers that are believed to be fatal can go into spontaneous remission. Ross Camidge, writing in the *British Medical Journal*, called the author's insistence that patients should be supported by the medical establishment in trying alternative approaches as being "zealously impractical" and that the author "is often wooed more by narrative than by scientific argument." Nevertheless, Camidge noted, "Despite these faults *Living Proof*'s assertion that we should investigate those who do well and not dismiss them as quirks is undeniable." Brian Drurie, writing in *Myeloma Today,* calls the book "inspiring . . . powerful and thought-provoking." In a review in *Booklist,* William Beatty remarked that "Gearin-Tosh provides pertinent information about the unusual treatment of a devastating malady in a context that resembles a good novel." *Library Journal* contributor Valeria Long called the book a "captivating, detailed, and enlightening account." As the critic concluded: "It all comes together in an intelligent, beautifully written narrative sprinkled liberally with humor and aplomb."

*BIOGRAPHICAL AND CRITICAL SOURCES:*

*BOOKS*

Gearin-Tosh, Michael, *Living Proof: A Medical Mutiny,* Scribner (New York, NY), 2002.

*PERIODICALS*

*Booklist,* April 1, 2002, William Beatty, review of *Living Proof: A Medical Mutiny,* p. 1286.

*British Medical Journal,* April 6, 2002, Ross Camidge, review of *Living Proof,* p. 855.

*Daily Telegraph,* February 16, 2002, Rachel Cusk, "Imagination is a Blessing," p. 58.

*Kirkus Reviews,* February 15, 2002, review of *Living Proof,* p. 235.

*Library Journal,* March 15, 2002, Valeria Long, review of *Living Proof,* p. 101.

*Myeloma Today,* February 2002, Brian Drurie, review of *Living Proof: A Medical Mutiny,* p. 4.

*New England Journal of Medicine,* December 12, 2002, James Spencer Malpas, review of *Living Proof,* p. 1986.

*New York Times,* May 12, 2002, Natalie Angier, "Physician, Take a Hike," review of *Living Proof,* p. 10.

*Publishers Weekly,* April 1, 2002, review of *Living Proof,* p. 71.

*Spectator,* February 9, 2002, Francis King, review of *Living Proof,* p. 43.

*Times* (London, England), February 5, 2002, Nigel Hawkes and Giles Whittell, "A Question of Survival," includes an interview with Michael Gearin-Tosh, p. S2.

*Townsend Letter for Doctors and Patients,* June, 2002, Irene Alleger, "The case of the .005 Percent Survivor," p. 127.

*OTHER*

*Positive Health Web site,* http://www.positivehealth.com (June 3, 2002), Sandra Goodman, Ph.D., review of *Living Proof: A Medical Mutiny.*

\*    \*    \*

## GEISSMAN, Grant 1953-

*PERSONAL:* Born April 13, 1953, in Berkeley, CA.

*ADDRESSES: Office*—General Confusion Music, P.O. Box 56773, Sherman Oaks, CA 91413-0773.

*CAREER:* Writer. Affiliated with General Confusion Music, Sherman Oaks, CA.

*AWARDS, HONORS:* Nominated for Eisner Awards, 1995, 2000, and Harvey Award, 2000.

*WRITINGS:*

*Collectibly Mad,* Kitchen Sink Press, 1995.

(Compiler and annotator) *Mad about the Fifties,* Little, Brown (Boston, MA), 1997.

(With Fred von Bernewitz) *Tales of Terror! The E. C. Companion,* Gemstone/Fantagraphics Books (Seattle, WA), 2000.

\*    \*    \*

## GEISST, Charles R. 1946-

*PERSONAL:* Born November 18, 1946, in Newark, NJ; married Margaret Kramer, January 29, 1972; children: Margaret Ann. *Education:* University of Richmond, B.A., 1968; New School for Social Research, M.A., 1970; London School of Economics, Ph.D., 1972.

*ADDRESSES: Home*—453 Grant Avenue, Oradell, NJ 07649-1815. *Office*—Department of Economics and Finance, Manhattan College, Riverdale, NY 20471. *E-mail*—charles.geisst@manhattan.edu.

*CAREER:* City University of New York, New York, NY, assistant professor, 1972-75; Cazanove & Company, London, England, consultant, 1978-79; Orion Bank, London, England, analyst, 1979-81; Bank of America, London, England, associate director, 1981-83; CIBC Ltd., London, England, associate director, 1983-84; Hudson Institute, consultant, 1984; Manhattan College, Riverdale, NY, professor of finance, 1985—, Louis Capalbo chair, 1992—. J. P. Morgan, New York, NY, consultant, 1996. Visiting scholar, Yale Law School, 1973-74, and Oxford University, 1977-78.

*MEMBER:* Yale Club.

*WRITINGS:*

*Raising International Capital: International Bond and the European Institutions,* Saxon House (Farnborough, England), 1980.

*A Guide to the Financial Markets,* St. Martin's (New York, NY), 1982.

(With Brendan Brown) *Financial Futures Markets,* St. Martin's (New York, NY), 1983.

*The Political Thought of John Milton,* Macmillan Press (London, England), 1984.

*A Guide to Financial Institutions,* St. Martin's (New York, NY), 1988.

*Visionary Capitalism: Financial Markets and the Dream in the Twentieth Century,* Praeger (New York, NY), 1990.

*Entrepot Capitalism: Foreign Investment and the Dream in the Twentieth Century,* Praeger (New York, NY), 1992.

*Exchange Rate Chaos: Twenty-five Years of Finance Consumer Democracy,* Routledge (New York, NY), 1995.

*Investment Banking in the Financial System,* Prentice Hall (Englewood Cliffs, NJ), 1995.

*Wall Street: A History,* Oxford University Press (New York, NY), 1997.

*Monopolies in America: Empire Builders and Their Enemies, from Jay Gould to Bill Gates,* Oxford University Press (Oxford, MA), 2000.

*One Hundred Years of Wall Street,* McGraw-Hill (New York, NY), 2000.

*The Last Partnerships: Inside the Great Wall Street Dynasties,* McGraw-Hill (New York, NY), 2001.

*Wheels of Fortune: The History of Speculation from Scandal to Respectability,* John Wiley & Sons (New York, NY), 2002.

*SIDELIGHTS:* Charles R. Geisst is a professor of finance at Manhattan College and the author of books on Wall Street and finance. In *Wall Street: A History* Geisst discusses the major historical events that occurred on Wall Street from 1879 to the 1990s and the impact Wall Street has had on the history of the United States. He also provides information on the major investors that played a role in the market during this time period. *Social Science Journal* contributor R. William Weisberger noted, "Geisst's book is a splendid synthesis of this field and assuredly will be recognized as a classic in it."

Booklist contributor David Rouse called Geisst's book *One Hundred Years of Wall Street* "an excellent companion" to *Wall Street.* In *One Hundred Years of Wall Street* Geisst tells the history of Wall Street through 150 photographs and illustrations, along with short quotes and stories.

In *The Last Partnerships: Inside the Great Wall Street Dynasties* Geisst continues his history of Wall Street by focusing on investment banking. Investment banks first began as partnerships between two or more individuals, and later turned into large corporate run businesses. Geisst discusses the partnerships involved in many early investment banks, including Clark Dodge and Jay Cooke; J. P. Morgan and Morgan Stanley; Merrill Lynch and E. F. Hutton, and more.

*BIOGRAPHICAL AND CRITICAL SOURCES:*

*PERIODICALS*

*American Historical Review,* June, 1993, Thomas W. Zeiler, review of *Entrepot Capitalism: Foreign Investment and the Dream in the Twentieth Century,* p. 980.

*Booklist,* August, 1997, David Rouse, review of *Wall Street: A History,* p. 1859; December 1, 1999, David Rouse review of *Monopolies in America: Empire Builders and Their Enemies, From Jay Gould to Bill Gates,* p. 665; January 1, 2000, David Rouse, review of *One Hundred Years of Wall Street,* p. 844; May 15, 2001, David Rouse, review of *The Last Partnerships: Inside the Great Wall Street Dynasties,* p. 1715.

*Business History,* January, 1999, R. C. Michie, review of *Wall Street,* p. 1152; July, 2001, Margaret Levenstein, review of *Monopolies in America,* p. 163.

*Business History Review,* spring, 1992, George D. Green, review of *Visionary Capitalism: Financial Markets and the Dream in the Twentieth Century,* p. 203; autumn, 1993, Mira Wilkins, review of *Entrepot Capitalism,* p. 509; spring, 2000, Maury Klein, review of *Monopolies in America,* p. 127.

*Business Library Review,* Volume 16, issue 4, 1991, review of *A Guide to the Financial Institutions,* p. 322.

*Choice,* October, 1982, review of *A Guide to the Financial Markets,* p. 316; June, 1991, S. P. Ferris, review of *Visionary Capitalism,* p. 1678; October, 1992, T. E. Sullivan, review of *Entrepot Capitalism,* p. 350; May, 1996, R. Grossman, review of *Exchange Rate Chaos: Twenty-five Years of Finance Consumer Democracy,* p. 1524.

*Economic Journal,* July, 1996, Forrest Capie, review of *Exchange Rate Chaos,* p. 1132.

*Economist,* June 30, 2001, Benjamin M. Cole, "You Need a Friend; Wall Street; Wall Street, Past and Present," p. 7.

*Historian,* fall, 1999, Douglas Karsner, review of *Wall Street,* p. 149.

*Journal of Economic History,* March, 1992, review of *Visionary Capitalism,* p. 303; March, 1993, Larry Schweikart, review of *Visionary Capitalism,* p. 208.

*Journal of Economic Literature,* December, 1988, review of *A Guide to the Financial Institutions,* p. 1834; June, 1990, review of *A Guide to the Financial Markets,* p. 760; June, 1993, review of *Entrepot Capitalism,* p. 992; June, 1996, review of *Exchange Rate Chaos,* p. 858.

*Library Journal,* October 1, 1997, Charles A. Shewis, review of *Wall Street,* p. 96; November 15, 1999, Richard S. Drezen, review of *Monopolies in America,* p. 78; May 15, 2001, Steven Silkunas, review of *The Last Partnership,* p. 136.

*Management Today,* June, 2001, Martin Vander Weyer, "The Rogues of Wall Street," p. 43.

*Publishers Weekly,* April 30, 2001, review of *The Last Partnership,* p. 71.

*Social Science Journal,* January, 2000, R. William Weisberger, review of *Wall Street,* p. 158.

*Strategic Finance,* November, 1999, "Tools of the Trade," p. 87.

OTHER

*Management Today,* http://www.clickmt.com/ (April 10, 2002), Martin Vander Weyer, review of *The Last Partnerships.*

*Manhattan College Web site,* http://www.manhattan. edu/ (April 10, 2002), "Charles R. Geisst."

*Oxford University Press Web site,* http://www.oup-usa. org/ (April 10, 2002), review of *Wall Street.**

\* \* \*

## GIFFIN, Mary (Elizabeth) 1919-2002

*OBITUARY NOTICE*—See index for *CA* sketch: Born March 30, 1919, in Rochester, MN; died of complications from heart surgery October 25, 2002, in Evanston, IL. Psychiatrist, educator, and author. A specialist in child and adolescent psychiatry, Giffin once served as medical director for the Josselyn Center in Illinois. Suffering from polio as a child, she overcame her illness and excelled in school. She earned a B.S. from Smith College in 1939, followed by her medical degree from Johns Hopkins University in 1943, and a master's degree in psychiatry and neurology from the University of Minnesota—Minneapolis in 1948. Giffin was also a graduate of the Chicago Institute of Psychoanalysis. During the 1940s Giffin worked at the Mayo Clinic. She switched to teaching in 1948, becoming an instructor in psychiatry for Johns Hopkins Hospital and then in 1949 joining the faculty at the University of Minnesota, where she taught psychiatry for almost a decade. In 1958 she was appointed medical director of the Irene Josselyn Clinic (later the Josselyn Center), where she remained until her retirement as director emeritus in 1989, though she continued to work as a psychiatrist in private practice thereafter. Giffin's interest in child and teenage psychiatry led her to do volunteer work at community centers and schools and to write a book on teenage suicide, *A Cry for Help* (1983), with Carol Felsenthal. Giffin was also the author of *Her Doctor, Will Mayo.*

*OBITUARIES AND OTHER SOURCES:*

BOOKS

*Who's Who in the Midwest,* 28th edition, Marquis (New Providence, NJ), 2001.

PERIODICALS

*Chicago Tribune,* November 4, 2002, section 1, p. 9.

\* \* \*

## GILMAN, Phoebe 1940-2002

*OBITUARY NOTICE*—See index for *CA* sketch: Born April 4, 1940, in New York, NY; died of leukemia August 29, 2002, in Toronto, Ontario, Canada. Educator and author. Gilman was a popular author and illustrator of children's picture books and was best known for her series character Jillian Jiggs. In love with art and illustration since she was a child, Gilman studied at the Art Students' League and Hunter College in New York during the late 1950s. She then moved to Israel, where she lived for four years and continued her studies at the Bezalel Academy in Jerusalem. Instead of returning to the United States, she next moved to Toronto and taught at the Ontario College of Art and Design from 1975 to 1990. Gilman did not try her hand at children's books until later in life, publishing her first picture book, *The Balloon Tree,* in 1984. Her popular character Jillian appeared in her next book, 1988's *Jillian Jiggs.* Jillian would appear in four more books, the last of which was *Jillian Jiggs and the Great Big Snow* (2002). Some of her other books include *Something from Nothing* (1990) and *The Gypsy Princess* (1995). At the time of her death Gilman was working on a manuscript for another children's book, *The Blue Hippopotamus,* and had just completed a short autobiography.

*OBITUARIES AND OTHER SOURCES:*

BOOKS

*Writers Directory,* 17th edition, St. James Press (Detroit, MI), 2002.

PERIODICALS

*Quill & Quire* (Toronto, Ontario, Canada), October, 2002, p. 11.
*Toronto Star,* October 21, 2002.

\*      \*      \*

# GILMAN, Rebecca (Claire) 1965-

*PERSONAL:* Born 1965, in AL. *Education:* Attended iddlebury College and Birmingham Southern College; University of Virginia, M.A.

*ADDRESSES: Home*—Columbus, OH. *Agent*—c/o Author Mail, Faber and Faber, 19 Union Square West, New York, NY 10003.

*CAREER:* Playwright.

*AWARDS, HONORS:* Scott McPherson Award, Goodman Theatre; Joseph Jefferson citation and After Dark Award for New Work, both 1997, and Osborn Award, American Theatre Critics Association, 1998, all for *The Glory of Living; Evening Standard* Award.

*WRITINGS:*

*Spinning into Butter: A Play,* Faber and Faber (New York, NY), 2000.
*Boy Gets Girl: A Play,* Faber and Faber (New York, NY), 2000.
*The Glory of Living: A Play,* Faber and Faber (New York, NY), 2001.
*Blue Surge: A Play,* Faber and Faber (New York, NY), 2001.

Author of the plays *The American in Me, The Land of Little Horses,* and *My Sin and Nothing More.*

*SIDELIGHTS:* Rebecca Gilman started writing plays while in college. She has won numerous awards, including a Scott McPherson Award, and she was the first American playwright to win an *Evening Standard* Award.

*The American in Me* tells the story of Ben and Jeannie, a married couple. Ben, originally from Boston, moves to Jeannie's hometown in the South. Ben is unhappy with his life: he feel he doesn't fit in and he hates his job as a financial analyst at a company owned by Jeannie's father. They have borrowed from his father-in-law, creditors are hounding him, and they are living far grander than they can really afford. Even though they are having problems conceiving, Jeannie is adamant about having a child, no matter what the cost, which adds to Ben's problems.

In *Spinning into Butter,* Sarah Daniels, a white woman and dean of Belmont College in charge of race relations, finds her life falling apart. Her career is going nowhere, her boyfriend has left her, and she is dealing with racist feelings. A black student receives hate mail containing threats, and during the investigation of the case Sarah learns that she was hired because everyone thought she was black. "*Spinning into Butter* addresses a pervasive and troubling American problem and does so in a serious and often thoughtful way," observed Richard Scholem in a *Long Island Business News* review. *New York* contributor Joanne Kaufman claimed, "*Spinning into Butter* begins loosely but coils tighter and tighter as we're drawn in."

In *Boy Gets Girl: A Play,* Theresa, a single magazine reporter, goes on a blind date with Tony. She agrees to go to dinner with him again, but Theresa finds she has no interest in Tony. He keeps calling, sending flowers, and showing up at her office, and soon begins stalking Theresa. "One of the finest, most disturbing American plays in years," concluded Richard Zoglin in a *Time* review. *Library Journal* contributor Howard Miller noted that it is "brilliant and thought-provoking."

Gilman's *The Glory of Living: A Play* has won awards such as a Joseph Jefferson citation, an After Dark Award, and an Osborn Award from the American Theatre Critics Association. *The Glory of Living* tells the story of Lisa and Clint, a poor young couple from the South. Lisa, who is still a teenager, was raised by a single prostitute mother in a one-room apartment. Clint has been in jail on auto theft charges. They live in a dirty hotel room and to pass the time they kill young girls. Lisa soon feels guilty and calls the police to confess to their crimes, and her lawyer tries to understand why Lisa committed such brutal crimes.

*Blue Surge: A Play,* set in the Midwest, tells the story of two cops, Curt and Doug, who try to shut down a house of prostitution that fronts as a massage parlor. The cops get involved in the lives of the two prostitutes after their failed arrest. Doug begins a sexual relationship with one of the prostitutes, while Curt and the other prostitute become friends. Curt tries to get her to quit prostitution. *Library Journal* contributor J. Sara Paulk called it a "great work by an upcoming playwright." *Variety* contributor Chris Jones wrote, "A racy, smart piece of gritty social realism that's alternately funny and politically provocative."

*BIOGRAPHICAL AND CRITICAL SOURCES:*

PERIODICALS

*American Theatre,* March, 2000, Chris Jones, "A Beginner's Guide to Rebecca Gilman," p. 79; February, 2002, "Twenty Questions," p. 88.

*Back Stage,* August 11, 2000, Julius Novick, review of *Spinning into Butter: A Play,* p. 48; April 20, 2001, Michael Sander, "Twin Cities," p. 15.

*Back Stage West,* September 7, 2000, David Sheward, "Goodbye, Summer," p. 16; September 13, 2001, Kristina Mannion, review of *Spinning into Butter,* p. 14.

*Booklist,* April 15, 2000, Jack Helbig, review of *Boy Gets Girl: A Play,* p. 1516; June 1, 2000, Jack Helbig, review of *Spinning into Butter,* p. 1806; December 15, 2001, Jack Helbig, review of *Blue Surge: A Play,* p. 698.

*Crain's Chicago Business,* November 6, 2000, Brian McCormick, "Rebecca Gilman 36; Playwright Provocateur," p. E8.

*Entertainment Weekly,* March 2, 2001, Melissa Rose Bernardo, Ty Burr, Gillian Flynn, "Stage," p. 61.

*Knight-Ridder/Tribune News Service,* February 13, 2002, "Female Playwrights Are Getting More Work Produced, Finally," p. K5262.

*Library Journal,* July, 2000, Howard Miller, review of *Boy Gets Girl,* p. 90; July, 2000, Howard Miller, review of *Spinning into Butter,* p. 90; February 1, 2002, J. Sara Paulk, review of *Blue Surge,* p. 98.

*Long Island Business News,* September 8, 2000, Richard Scholem, "Worthy Tale Probes Self-denial of Racism in U.S.," p. 49A.

*New Criterion,* April, 2001, Mark Steyn, "Policy Paper Plays," p. 38.

*New York,* July 10, 2000, Joanne Kaufman, "She Said What?," p. 38.

*New York Times,* September 28, 2001, Jesse McKinley, "From Film to Stage," p. E2; November 16, 2001, Ben Brantley, "In Her World, Normalcy Includes the Grotesque," p. E3.

*Time,* June 7, 1999, Richard Zoglin, review of *Spinning into Butter,* p. 82; April 10, 2000, Richard Zoglin, "The Date from Hell: Boy Meets Girl. Boy Stalks Girl. Rebecca Gilman Puts Us on Edge," p. 134E.

*Times Literary Supplement,* November 23, 2001, Robert Shore, "Funny, Like, in an Offensive Way," pp. 28-29.

*Variety,* February 26, 2001, Charles Isherwood, review of *Boy Gets Girl,* p. 51; July 16, 2001, Dennis Harvey, review of *The American in Me,* p. 26; July 23, 2001, Chris Jones, review of *Blue Surge,* p. 23; November 19, 2001, Charles Isherwood, review of *The Glory of Living: A Play,* p. 48; November 19, 2001, Matt Wolf, review of *Boy Gets Girl,* p. 48.

OTHER

*American Library Association Web site,* http://www.ala.org/ (April 10, 2002), Jack Helbig, review of *Boy Gets Girl.*

*Center Stage Chicago,* http://centerstage.net/ (April 10, 2002), "Rebecca Gilman."

*Chicago Business,* http://www.chicagobusiness.com/ (April 10, 2002), Brian McCormick, "Rebecca Gilman: Playwright."*

## GIRARD, Danielle

*PERSONAL:* Born in CA; daughter of a physician. *Education:* Cornell University, B.A., 1992. *Hobbies and other interests:* Hiking, skiing, biking, and reading.

*ADDRESSES: Agent*—c/o Author Mail, Penguin Putnam, 375 Hudson St., New York, NY 10014. *E-mail*—danielle@daniellegirard.com.

*CAREER:* Fiction author.

*WRITINGS:*

*Savage Art,* Onyx (New York, NY), 2000.
*Ruthless Game,* Onyx (New York, NY), 2001.
*Chasing Darkness,* Onyx (New York, NY), 2002.
*Cold Silence,* Onyx (New York, NY), 2002.

*SIDELIGHTS:* Since publishing her debut work in 2000, Danielle Girard has made a name for herself in the police procedural and detective/mystery genre. Born and raised in northern California, Girard grew up with the intention of becoming a physician like her father. However, after she graduated from Cornell University, her love of literature pulled at her. Admiring such writers as Patricia Cornwell, Michael Connelly, and Tami Hoag, she chose to forego a life in medicine, deciding instead to become a writer. Ironically, Girard feels the two professions have numerous similarities. "Writing is mathematical and scientific in nature . . . plotting a chapter is like working out a large equation," Girard said on her Web site. Girard's novels are similar in the fact that they all revolve around strong-willed female protagonists. For example, in Girard's first novel, *Savage Art,* central character Casey McKinley, a former FBI agent, must track the same serial killer who once maimed her so badly, she had to quit the bureau. After *Savage Art* was published in 2000, some literary critics recognized talent in Girard's work. Critic Jennifer Monahan Winberry, who reviewed the book for *Mystery Reader,* called it "a skillfully written first novel that leaves nothing to chance." Girard's more recent works, *Ruthless Game* and *Chasing Darkness,* also earned her praise.

Called "a tautly written thriller" by Winberry, *Savage Art* begins with a depressed Casey McKinley living in San Francisco, a year after being savagely beaten by a killer she was tracking for the FBI and a continent away from her family in Virginia. Depressed by the fact her body was maimed and she had to quit her job, she left her family and went to San Francisco to try rehabilitate her spirit. She awakens from her depression, however, when the same killer, known as Leonardo for the way he carves up bodies in an almost artistic manner, begins killing little girls in the San Francisco area. McKinley joins forces with a local detective named Jordan Gray, who is already working on the case. Together they track down the serial killer.

In *Ruthless Game,* the female protagonist is Alex Kincaid, a rookie police officer in Berkeley, California. The book begins when Kincaid awakens from a sleep, only to find herself mysteriously in her car, parked away from her home. Not knowing how she got there, Alex goes to work that morning only to be sent to the same location to investigate a murder that had taken place the night before. To make matters worse, her partner finds one of her earrings at the crime scene. From there, more and more evidence points to Alex as the killer, and she must solve the case before being charged for the crime. "Girard knows how to keep the suspense so high the audience never leaves until the book is finished," wrote Harriet Klausner, in reviewing *Ruthless Game* for *BookBrowser.*

With *Chasing Darkness,* Girard creates another critically lauded detective story. This time, however, she also decides to tackle a serious social issue, as much of the book deals with the problems of child abuse. The book's female protagonist, Sam Chase, is a former homicide detective who chose to transfer to California's Department of Justice because she could no longer deal with being around death all the time. With her new job, Sam mainly works to apprehend child abusers. Sam's life takes another turn when she becomes the guardian of her twin eight-year-old nephews after their parents are killed. The main theme of child abuse first becomes evident when Sam must work on one of her old cases involving the mother of a child-abuse victim who is found murdered. She teams up with her old partner from the sheriff's department, Derek Thomas, and the two try to solve the case. Just as in Girard's previous work, the protagonist is linked to the main crime, and must prove her innocence by catching the real murderer. As the story unfolds, Sam discovers some disturbing facts about the abuse her nephews endured before coming to her. The tale sheds light on how child abuse affects its victims long after the actual abuse took place. Impressed by Girard's attempt to address the seriousness of that subject, a contributor for *Publishers Weekly* called *Chasing Darkness* "a compelling thriller and a skillful treatment of a difficult topic." Harriet Klausner, writing for *BookBrowser,* referred to the book as "a tightly woven thriller." Klausner also made reference to Girard's attempt to bring awareness to a tough topic, feeling the book "entertains as well as educates."

## BIOGRAPHICAL AND CRITICAL SOURCES:

PERIODICALS

*Publishers Weekly,* February 18, 2002, p. 81.

OTHER

*Danielle Girard Web site,* http://www.daniellegirard. com (November 8, 2002).
*Book Browser,* http://www.bookbrowser.com/ (August 1, 2002), Harriet Klausner, reviews of *Chasing Darkness* and *Ruthless Game.*
*Mystery Reader,* http://www.themysteryreader.com/ (August 1, 2002), Jennifer Monahan Winberry, review of *Savage Art.*\*

\*          \*          \*

## GLORI ANN
**See BLAKELY, Gloria**

\*          \*          \*

## GODKIN, E(dwin) L(awrence) 1831-1902

PERSONAL: Born October 2, 1831, in County Wicklow, Ireland; died May 21, 1902; son of James (a Protestant minister and editor) and Sarah Lawrence Godkin; married Frances Elizabeth Foote, July 27, 1859 (died 1873); married Katharine Sands, June 14, 1884; children: Lawrence, Elizabeth, Ralph. *Education:* Queen's College, received degree, 1851; studied law at the Middle Temple. *Politics:* Liberal. *Religion:* Protestant.

CAREER: American journalist and essayist. Worked as subeditor for the *Workingmen's Friend,* special correspondent for the *London Daily News,* and editor of the *Sanitary Commission Bulletin;* cofounder and founding editor of *Nation* (magazine), 1865-99; *Evening Post,* former editor-in-chief.

AWARDS, HONORS: M.A., Harvard University, 1871; honorary doctorate of civil laws, Oxford University, 1897.

WRITINGS:

*The History of Hungary and the Magyars from the Earliest Times to the Close of the Late War,* Montgomery (New York, NY), 1853.
*The Morals and Manners of the Kitchen, and Baby Suffrage,* Tompkins (New York, NY), 1875.
*The Question of Elections, and of the Separation of Municipal Elections Read January, 1876,* Hamilton Steam Printers (New York, NY), 1876.
*The Danger of an Office-Holding Aristocracy,* Putnam's (New York, NY), 1882.
*Henry G. Pearson: A Memorial Address Delivered June 21, 1894,* privately printed (New York, NY), 1894.
*The Triumph of Reform: A History of the Great Political Revolution, November Sixth, Eighteen Hundred and Ninety-four,* Souvenir Publishing (New York, NY), 1895.
*Reflections and Comments, 1865-1895,* Scribners (New York, NY), 1895.
*Problems of Modern Democracy: Political and Economic Essays,* Scribners (New York, NY), 1896.
*Unforeseen Tendencies of Democracy,* Houghton (Boston, MA), 1898.
*A Letter on Lincoln,* Hillacre Bookhouse (Riverside, CT), 1913.
*The Gilded Age Letters of E. L. Godkin* (correspondence), edited by William M. Armstrong, State University of New York Press (Albany, NY), 1974.

Also contributor to periodicals, including *North American Review, Century Magazine, Atlantic Monthly, New York Times, New York Evening Post, Knickerbocker, North American Review,* and *Forum.* Contributing editor, *Northern Whig.*

*SIDELIGHTS:* When Irish-born E. L. Godkin arrived in the United States to report on the South for the London *Daily News,* few would have predicted that he would become one of America's most influential journalists. Godkin helped found the journal *Nation,* which soon became an authority on politics and culture in America. He served as its editor from 1865 to 1899. With Godkin's nineteenth-century American liberalism and passion for politics, the *Nation* became an even more powerful shaper of national thought than any of its founders could have hoped for, especially given its small circulation. Later in life Godkin joined the *Nation* with the *New York Evening Post,* and became the *Evening Post*'s editor-in-chief.

Born Edwin Lawrence Godkin on October 2, 1831, in County Wicklow, Ireland, he was the oldest of James and Sarah Lawrence Godkin's five children. John Godkin was a Protestant minister who moved the family around as he took assignments all over Ireland. He also worked as an editor. At the age of nine Edwin Godkin enrolled at a prestigious grammar school at Armagh, the Belfast Royal Academical Institution. His parents transferred him to Silcoates, a school emphasizing classics for the sons of Congregational ministers, located in Leeds, outside Yorkshire, England (he may have also attended Belfast Academy, according to some sources). Godkin started taking classes in Queen's college in Belfast in 1846. There he was elected president of the college literary and scientific society. Queen's college fostered an atmosphere in favor of utilitarianism, as *Dictionary of Literary Biography* essayist Terry Hynes quoted Godkin as explaining: "John Stuart Mill was our prophet, and Grote and Bentham were our daily food . . . but America was our promised land." After graduating in 1851 he studied law at the Middle Temple in London.

Godkin's law studies were abandoned before long; he decided on a career in journalism instead. He solicited a job from his father's friend, the radical publisher John Cassell. Cassell found him a position as subeditor at one of his new magazines, *Workingmen's Friend.* This was a penny weekly with fiction, poetry, home instruction, and travel essays, and featuring contributors such as Jules Verne and Harriet Beecher Stowe. Godkin wrote a series of historical sketches on Hungary for the winter issues of 1851 and 1852, which he later enlarged in his first book, *The History of Hungary and the Magyars,* published in 1853. In this book Godkin established his trademark passionate writing style as he railed against Austria's tyrannical reign over Hungary.

In 1853 Godkin was made a special correspondent covering the Crimean War for the London *Daily News.* He was one of the first English journalists to witness the war. He wrote his reports as a series of letters, and returned to England in October of 1855. Later he said of this period, "If I were asked now what I thought the most important result of the Crimean war, I should say the creation and development of the 'special correspondents' of newspapers." When he returned to Belfast a year later he delivered lectures on the War. He was hired as a contributing editor to the *Northern Whig,* a mostly liberal paper which remained conservative about property rights and social revolutions. In the autumn of 1856 Godkin left for the United States, planning to tour the South for a series of articles for the London *Daily News.* Before traveling south he stayed in New York with Frederick Law Olmstead, who was revising a book of his letters about his own travels through the South while reporting for the *New York Times.* Godkin arrived in Mississippi in November 1856 and returned to New York in January 1857. He was ambivalent on the issue of slavery. In an early letter to the *Daily News* he wrote, "Their [slaves'] only refuge or consolation in this world is in their own stupidity and grossness. The nearer they are to the beast, the happier they are likely to be." But in a letter printed in March he wrote, "I have never passed them [slaves], . . . staggering along in the rear of the wagons, at the close of a long days' march, the weakest furthest in the rear, the strongest already utterly spent, without wondering how Christendom . . . can so long look calmly on at so foul and monstrous a wrong as this American slavery."

Godkin remained in New York, passing the state's bar exam in 1858, and practicing by 1859. But the confines of the courtroom and office made him restless. He continued as a freelance correspondent for the *Daily News,* and contributed to the *New York Times,* the *New York Evening Post,* and the *Knickerbocker.* Godkin spent at least four hours each day writing, a habit he maintained for the rest of his life. While visiting Yale University president Theodore Woolsey in 1857, Godkin met Frances Elizabeth Foote. She was a cousin to Harriet Beecher Stowe and Henry Ward Beecher. Godkin and Foote married in New Haven, Connecticut on July 27, 1859. With a new wife to support, Godkin began working excessively, and worried that he was due for an emotional breakdown. Soon after his first son, Lawrence, was born in 1860, the Godkins left for Ireland. They wintered in Paris, spent the spring in London, and summered in Switzerland. For two years Godkin published only two unsolicited letters to the *Daily News.*

The Godkins returned to New York in 1862. Godkin was made a special correspondent for the *Daily News* and resumed writing for the *New York Times.* He edited the *Sanitary Commission Bulletin* for a few months until the publication was moved to Philadelphia. Godkin was writing for the *North American Review* when Charles Eliot Norton and Major George Searns contacted him about planning a new magazine called the *Nation.* They invited Godkin to edit this in April 1865, and Godkins agreed on the condition that he be given editorial freedom. He commenced to fundraising in New York and organized the legal organization for the magazine. The first issue of the *Nation* appeared on July 6, 1865, despite dissention among the magazine's financial backers. The *Nation* focused on improving conditions in the South, discussing public affairs accurately, supporting democratic principles and the importance of public education, and providing intelligent literary and art criticism. The magazine featured a host of illustrious contributors such as James Russell Lowell, Henry James, Yale president Noah Porter, Johns Hopkins founder Daniel Gilman, and British correspondent Leslie Stephen. According to Hynes, "Godkin earned a reputation as an exacting, even ruthless editor. He encouraged the *Nation* contributors to write with a straightforwardness and wit similar to his own style and, in the process, showed that serious writing could be lively and readable as well as informative and profound." He was mostly a moderate upper-middle-class liberal who supported business over labor, property rights over human rights; the content of the magazine reflected his mercurial political temper. By its third issue the *Nation* had a circulation of five thousand, and by the mid-1870's it had more than doubled. However, the magazine's circulation never rose above twelve thousand during Godkin's lifetime.

In 1881 Godkin was hired as associate editor of the *New York Evening Post,* newly purchased by Henry Villard. That same year Godkin sold the *Nation* to the *Evening Post,* and the magazine became in effect the paper's weekly edition. Villard's brother-in-law, Wendell Garrison, took over the editorship of the *Nation*

and Godkin was later made editor-in-chief of the *Evening Post.* Frances Godkin died in 1873. She had suffered two tragedies: her second son Ralph died in infancy in 1868, and her daughter Elizabeth died after a brief illness in 1873. Nearly a decade after his first wife's death, Godkin married thirty-eight-year-old Katharine Sands. From 1889 he began taking annual trips to England and Europe. His paid vacations from the *Evening Post* grew longer and longer, up to five months by 1897, as his rheumatism grew more debilitating. He retired in 1899, though he was allowed to retain the title of editor-in-chief until January 1900.

With the dawning of the twentieth century, Godkin's life drew to a close. In February 1900 he suffered a stroke, and on May 21, 1902, at Greenway House, Brixham, England, Godkin suffered a second stroke and died. The recipient of honorary degrees from Harvard and Oxford, he was remembered by *Nation* contributor William James—as cited by Hynes—as a journalist who left behind a rich legacy: "To my generation his was certainly the towering influence in all thought concerning public affairs, and indirectly his influence has certainly been more pervasive than that of any other writer of the generation, for he influenced other writers who never quoted him, and determined the whole current of discussion."

## BIOGRAPHICAL AND CRITICAL SOURCES:

*BOOKS*

Armstrong, William M., *E. L. Godkin: A Biography,* State University of New York (Albany, NY), 1957.
Armstrong, William M., *E. L. Godkin and American Foreign Policy, 1865-1900,* Bookman Associates (New York, NY), 1957.
Christman, Henry M, editor, *One Hundred Years of The Nation,* Macmillan (New York, NY), 1965.
*Dictionary of Literary Biography,* Volume 79: *American Magazine Journalists, 1850-1900,* Gale (Detroit, MI), 1989.
Grimes, Alan P., *The Political Liberalism of the New York Nation, 1865-1932,* University of North Carolina Press (Chapel Hill, NC), 1953.
Haskell, Daniel C., *The Nation: Indexes of Titles and Contributors,* New York Public Library (New York, NY), 1951-53.

Knightley, Phillip, *The First Casualty,* Harcourt (New York, NY), 1975.

Mott, Frank Luther, *A History of American Magazines, 1865-1885,* Harvard University Press (Cambridge, MA), 1938.

Nevins, Allan, *The Evening Post: A Century of Journalism,* Boni & Liveright (New York, NY), 1922.

Ogden, Rollo, editor, *Life and Letters of Edwin Lawrence Godkin,* Macmillan (New York, NY), 1907.

Parrington, Vernon L., *Main Currents in American Thought,* Volume 3: *The Beginnings of Critical Realism in America, 1860-1920,* Harcourt (New York, NY), 1930.

Pollack, Gustav, *Fifty Years of American Idealism: The New York Nation, 1865-1915,* Houghton (Boston, MA), 1915.

*PERIODICALS*

*Bulletin of the New York Public Library,* April, 1969.

*Historian,* autumn, 1954; August, 1968.

*Journalism History,* autumn, 1974.

*Nation,* July 22, 1950; February 15, 1965; January 3, 1966; May 5, 1898.

*South Atlantic Quarterly,* July, 1907; October, 1931; autumn, 1973.\*

\*      \*      \*

## GOLD, Kenneth M. 1966-

*PERSONAL:* Born May 21, 1966, in North Plainfield, NJ. *Education:* Princeton University, B.A., 1988; University of Michigan, M.A., Ph.D., 1997.

*ADDRESSES: Office*—College of Staten Island of the City University of New York, 2800 Victory Blvd., Staten Island, NY 10314; fax: 718-982-3743. *E-mail*—gold@postbox.cs.cuny.edu.

*CAREER:* College of Staten Island of the City University of New York, Staten Island, NY, associate professor of education, 1995—.

*MEMBER:* American Historical Association, History of Education Society, American Educational Research Association.

*WRITINGS:*

*School's In: The History of Summer Education in American Public Schools,* Peter Lang Publishing (New York, NY), 2002.

*WORK IN PROGRESS:* Research on the history of school-community organizations.

\*      \*      \*

## GOLDBERG, Myla 1972(?)-

*PERSONAL:* Born c. 1972 in MD; married Jason Little. *Education:* Oberlin College, B.A., 1993. *Religion:* Jewish. *Hobbies and other interests:* Playing pinball; playing the accordion, banjo, flute, and other instruments; foreign and independent films.

*ADDRESSES: Home*—Brooklyn, NY. *Agent*—c/o Doubleday Publicity, 1745 Broadway, New York, NY 10019.

*CAREER:* Writer. Has worked as an English teacher in Prague, Czech Republic, and as a freelance reader for a film production company.

*WRITINGS:*

*Bee Season,* Doubleday (New York, NY), 2000.

Contributor of short stories to literary journals and anthologies, including *Post Road 3,* Aboutface, 2001.

*WORK IN PROGRESS:* A novel set in 1918 revolving around the influenza epidemic.

*SIDELIGHTS:* Spelling the word "tomorrow" incorrectly in her fourth-grade spelling contest is the extent of Myra Goldberg's experience with spelling bees. Yet Goldberg's claim to fame is a book titled *Bee Season,* the story of the Naumann family, which consists of siblings Eliza and Aaron and their parents. Their father is a cantor devoted to the study of Jewish mysticism; their mother is a practicing lawyer without whom the family would probably starve. Aaron is a gifted sixteen-year-old whose father hopes will follow in his own footsteps and become a scholar, while nine-year-old Eliza is an average student of whom no one expects much. Eliza suddenly finds herself the focus of her father's attention and love when she takes first place in district and then state spelling competitions. Aaron becomes jealous and rebels by becoming involved with the Hare Krishnas. Meanwhile, hard-working Miriam goes on a crime spree for which she is arrested and committed to a mental institution. As the family falls apart, Aaron finds the courage to declare his intentions to follow his own path, and Eliza risks losing the affection of her demanding father when she finds her own voice and uses it. What looks on the surface to be tragedy for the Naumann family actually turns out to be exhilarating and emancipating for its members.

Goldberg got the idea for *Bee Season* when she read an essay about how spelling bees prolong the act of losing. She then, coincidentally, had dinner with a friend who regaled her with stories of her own experiences in a family dedicated to spelling bees. In an interview with Laura Buchwald of *Boldtype,* Goldberg explained, "She was telling me these stories, and I was simultaneously fascinated and repulsed. Eventually that clicked with Jewish mysticism, which has been a semi-obsession of mine for quite some time. . . . One morning I woke up and the two ideas had combined."

One of the highlights of the novel that is consistently praised is the realistic voice of nine-year-old Eliza. In an interview with Linda M. Castellitto of *Booksense. com,* Goldberg mused: "The good voice has in part to do with the fact I haven't quite figured out I'm a grownup yet. I remember very clearly what it was like to be a child."

In researching her book, Goldberg attended the National Spelling Bee in Washington, D.C. She told Buchwald, "I interviewed kids and I sat in the auditorium and watched the whole thing—it was intense! . . . It's an alternate universe; there's just so much there. For me it became a microcosm of the childhood experience, for just about everyone that I know. You grow up, you have parents who have expectations of you, who want certain things, and you try really hard to fulfill them. And then you realize that you can't always. That kind of moment is defining for a lot of people."

*Bee Season* was praised by many critics, despite the flaws they mentioned. Dwight Garner wrote in his review for the *New York Times Book Review* that "*Bee Season* is so smart, and frequently so charming, that you wait for Goldberg to begin making mistakes. She makes some big ones." His review ends by saying, "For a novel that's partly about transcendence, however, *Bee Season* keeps its feet planted in the earth. . . . [It] flickers past like a dream, and it is artful indeed."

*Newsweek* reviewer Jeff Giles noted, "It is amazing how quickly a true talent can announce itself. In the case of Myla Goldberg, it is not even a matter of pages, but of sentences." And *Booklist* contributor Bill Ott observed that "there is something of Holden Caulfield in Eliza, the same crazed determination to saved her loved ones from themselves." The critic concluded by calling *Bee Season* "an impressive debut from a remarkably talented writer."

### BIOGRAPHICAL AND CRITICAL SOURCES:

*PERIODICALS*

*Booklist,* May 15, 2000, Bill Ott, review of *Bee Season,* p. 1729.

*Harper's Bazaar,* June, 2001, Laurel Narersen, "Write Guard: Bazaar Asks Five Fiction Masters about the Agony and Ecstasy of Modern Literary Life," pp. 116-117.

*Library Journal,* April 15, 2000, Kimberly G. Allen, review of *Bee Season,* p. 122.

*MacLean's,* June 11, 2001, "The Sting of a Spelling Bee," p. 56.

*Newsweek,* May 29, 2000, Jeff Giles, "E Is for Eliza, a Speller at Heart: A Debut That Succeeds Far beyond the Simple ABCs," p. 70.

*New York Times,* June 12, 2000, Christopher Lehmann-Haupt, "Seeking Transcendence through Proper Spelling," p. B7.

*New York Times Book Review,* June 18, 2000, Dwight Garner, "Spellbound," p. 5.

*Publishers Weekly,* April 17, 2000, review of *Bee Season,* p. 50; July 10, 2000, Daisy Maryles, "To Bee or Not to Bee," p. 13.

*School Library Journal,* November, 2000, Molly Connally, review of *Bee Season,* p. 182.

*Time,* July 3, 2000, Paul Gray, "From A to Z: All the Letters Fall into Place in *Bee Season,*" p. 62.

*Wall Street Journal,* June 16, 2000, Erica Schacter, "A Letter Perfect Debut," p. W9.

*Washington Post,* August 13, 2000, Louis Bayard, "Buzz Words," p. X5.

OTHER

*Booksense,* http://www.booksense.com/ (October 1, 2002), Linda M. Castellitto, interview with Myla Goldberg.

*FluxFactory,* http://www.fluxfactory.org/ (October 1, 2002), brief profile of Myla Goldberg.

*Grendel,* http://www.grendel.org/milgeek/ (October 1, 2002), interview with Myla Goldberg.

*Random House Web site,* http://www.randomhouse.com/ (October 1, 2002), Laura Buchwald, "A Conversation with Myla Goldberg."

*Salon.com,* http://www.salon.com/ (April 10, 2002), Gavin McNett, review of *Bee Season.\**

\*    \*    \*

## GOLDBERG, Tod 1971-

*PERSONAL:* Born January 10, 1971 in Berkeley, CA; son of Alan Goldberg and Janice Curran; married; wife's name, Wendy. *Education:* California State University.

*ADDRESSES: Home*—La Quinta, CA. *Agent*—Jennie Dunham, Dunham Literary, 156 Fifth Avenue, Suite 625, New York, NY 10012-7002. *E-mail*—tod@todgoldberg.com.

*CAREER:* Writer. Teacher of creative writing, University of California, Los Angeles Extension Writers' Program; has also taught at California State University, Fullerton, and California State University, Northridge. Worked as an advertising account executive in Santa Monica, CA, and as an employment consultant with a staffing service.

*AWARDS, HONORS: Los Angeles Times* Book Award finalist for best mystery/thriller, 2002, for *Living Dead Girl.*

*WRITINGS:*

*Fake Liar Cheat* (novel), MTV Books (New York, NY), 2000.

(Editor) *Hungry? Thirsty? Las Vegas,* Really Great Books (Los Angeles, CA), 2002.

*Living Dead Girl* (novel), Soho (New York, NY), 2002.

(Editor with Andrew Kiraly) *Horny? Las Vegas: A Sexy, Steamy, Downright Sleazy Guide to the City,* Really Great Books (Los Angeles, CA), 2003.

Weekly columnist, *Las Vegas Mercury.* Contributor of short stories to numerous literary magazines.

*ADAPTATIONS: Fake Liar Cheat* was optioned for film by Miramax.

*WORK IN PROGRESS: Comeback Special,* a collection of short stories, *The Low Desert,* a novel.

*SIDELIGHTS:* Although Tod Goldberg has had numerous short stories published in literary magazines, he gained widespread recognition with his first novel *Fake Liar Cheat,* which he wrote when he was twenty-seven years old. The novel provides a satirical look at Generation-X types and life in southern California. The novel's hero, twenty-five-year-old Lonnie Milton, works for a temporary staffing agency as a headhunter. In the book, Goldberg describes Lonnie as "an up-and-coming star." Lonnie eventually meets Claire Goodens in a bookstore and is charmed by the beautiful and rebellious young woman. Clearly under Claire's spell, Lonnie begins accompanying her to fancy restaurants, where they run up huge tabs and then skip out without paying and without the slightest guilt that they are stealing and ruining lives, as in the instance of the waiter who gets fired after they skip out on a bill totaling hundreds of dollars. Eventually, things turn bad. Lonnie embarks on a blackmail scheme with Claire, loses his job, and becomes a murder suspect.

Writing in the *Los Angeles Times Book Review,* Mark Rozzo called *Fake Liar Cheat* an "amiable, wafer-thin Hollywood send-up." He also said, "In true B-movie fashion, Goldberg isn't fussy about causality, and he delivers his big theme—Hollywood is bad and will eat you up—with all the subtlety of a jumbo concession-stand Pepsi being spilled in your lap." A *Publishers Weekly* critic was less kind, calling the novel "smarmy, [and] self-congratulatory." However, a *Kirkus Reviews* critic took a more qualifying viewpoint, calling the book an "entertaining, movie-thin comedy not out to change your life, only to offer an amusing read, which it does with high success."

In an interview with Jon Jordan on the *Books Bytes* Web site, Goldberg, whose mother, brother, and uncle are writers, talked about his next novel: "When I set out to write my second novel, which became *Living Dead Girl*, my goals had changed: I wanted to write a book that challenged me, that challenged what I held true, and what ultimately touched on strong emotional ideas and instances—a novel not about a human life, but about humans life."

*Living Dead Girl* focuses on Paul Luden, an anthropology professor living in southern California whose ex-wife goes missing from their log cabin at Granite Lake in Washington. Luden travels to Granite Lake to see what is going on when he receives a call from neighbor saying his wife has disappeared. Traveling with him is Ginny, one of his nineteen-year-old students as well as his lover. As the story unfolds, we learn of Paul's failed marriage and how his young daughter died from brain and body tumors. The Ludens had tried to have children previously, but both pregnancies failed. These failures bolster their mutual feelings of guilt about the child who was born and died so soon afterwards, which is the primary cause leading to their divorce. A psychological thriller, *Living Dead Girl* intimates that Paul, a manic depressive, may have killed his ex-wife Molly, as it also explores Paul's madness and the story of a couple's love and loss.

*Living Dead Girl* received a more favorable reception from critics, as well as a nomination for the *Los Angeles Times* Book Award for best mystery. Although a *Publishers Weekly* reviewer called the novel "painfully drawn out," the writer also noted that "Goldberg shows plenty of promise and may yet become a leading suspense writer." A *Kirkus Reviews* critic said, "Goldberg rises above the sleazy glamour of his well-received debut . . . and takes a far deeper cut into his material." In a review in *Booklist*, Jenny McLarin called the book "both a page-turner and a complex study of human relationships."

*BIOGRAPHICAL AND CRITICAL SOURCES:*

*PERIODICALS*

*Booklist*, March 1, 2002, Jenny McLarin, review of *Living Dead Girl*, p. 1095.
*Kirkus Reviews*, June 1, 2000, review of *Fake Liar Cheat*, p. 737; February 15, 2002, review of *Living Dead Girl*, p. 208.

*Library Journal*, April 1, 2002, Rex E. Klett, review of *Living Dead Girl*.
*Los Angeles Times Book Review*, July 23, 2000, Mark Rozzo, review of *Fake Liar Cheat*, p. 10.
*Publishers Weekly*, June 5, 2000, review of *Fake Liar Cheat*, p. 73; February 25, 2002, review of *Living Dead Girl*, p. 45.

*OTHER*

*Books 'n' Bytes*, http://booksnbytes.com/ (June 3, 2002), Jon Jordan, "Interview with Tod Goldberg."
*Tod Goldberg Web site*, http://todgoldberg.com (June 3, 2002).

\*　　\*　　\*

**GOLDBLATT, Mark (Meyer) 1957-**

*PERSONAL:* Born June 8, 1957, in New York, NY; son of Morris and Leona (Meyer) Goldblatt. *Education:* Queens College, B.A., 1979, City University of New York, Ph.D., 1990.

*ADDRESSES: Office*—Fashion Institute of Technology, 227 West 27th St., New York, NY 10001-5902.

*CAREER:* Educator and writer. Queens College, Queens, NY, adjunct lecturer, 1982; Queensborough Community College, Queens, adjunct lecturer, 1982-91; Fashion Institute of Technology, State University of New York, adjunct assistant professor, 1989—.

*WRITINGS:*

*Africa Speaks* (novel), Permanent Press (Sag Harbor, NY), 2002.

Contributor of columns, articles, and book reviews to periodicals, including *New York Post*, *New York Times*, *USA Today*, *Reason*, *Newsday*, *National Review Online*, *Daily News*, and *Travel and Leisure*.

*SIDELIGHTS:* Mark Goldblatt is a white author who slips into the skin of a black character in his debut novel, *Africa Speaks*. The protagonist is Kevin

"Africa" Ali, an intelligent but confused twenty-three year old who in interviews with an anonymous white sociologist reveals his most intimate feelings and the details of his life. Africa is the son of a teacher father he considers to be an Uncle Tom and with whom he no longer keeps in touch. His mother is deceased, and his brother, Dexter, died of a gunshot wound. Africa hasn't seen his young son since the baby's mother had him removed from the delivery room when he refused to tell her he loved her. He is a small-time drug dealer, peddling nickel and dime bags in his 149th Street neighborhood while his friend Hercules deals hard drugs. Africa beats and robs gays, collects and disrespects women, and hates whites, Jews, and homosexuals. Another friend, Fast Eddy, is working toward a career in sales and is disappointed that Africa isn't pursuing a degree at Columbia. Jerome is a political college friend, who tells Africa that Cleopatra, Jesus, and Socrates were black and that Aristotle stole all his writings and ideas from the library in Alexandria. At various points, these friends and Africa's girlfriend Keisha take over the monologue. Jerome reveals how Dexter was killed, and Fast Eddy talks about Africa's recovery from a self-inflicted gunshot wound.

Africa falls in love with Liang, a Chinese immigrant, but their relationship ends when she tells him not to back up Hercules in a dangerous situation. A *Publishers Weekly* reviewer felt that the relationship between Africa and Liang provides some of the story's "more profound passages," but added that Goldblatt "ultimately does more to perpetuate longstanding stereotypes than to push readers to the brink of new understanding."

Africa describes the difference between black sex and white sex and his sexual adventures with Keisha. J. Stefan-Cole wrote for *Free Williamsburg* online that "the physical part is important. Africa, besides believing that ancient whites stole knowledge from ancient blacks—a wrong that will someday be put right when black men rule in a world free of wars, a brotherhood of harmony—reveals his almost bodily contempt for white society. He doesn't want to be pale and always looking out for money with lawyers and power deals and always fearing death. The white man is disconnected from himself, but the black man is whole—only his self-esteem has been robbed, humiliated by his manipulating oppressor."

Stefan-Cole felt that "there is a lot of sadness in this book, the sort of sadness you hear about in the news.

Babies beaten by their mother's boyfriend, kids with no idea who their fathers are, physical violence. But there is also a lot of very funny writing. Mark Goldblatt has a gifted ear for the vernacular of his subject, no doubt about that." "This book should encourage debate," concluded Stefan-Cole. "And the debate should not center on a white guy daring to write in a black guy's idiom. . . . There is a dark idea afloat, largely unconscious, that something is basically wrong with being black, and whites and blacks believe it, and this needs badly to be brought out and questioned. *Africa Speaks* is a start."

Goldblatt noted in a *National Review Online* article that getting this book in which he satirizes African Americans published was difficult and that his first agent felt he'd "wind up with Al Sharpton picketing my house." Permanent Press published *Africa Speaks,* but Goldblatt wrote that there have been few reviews of the novel, which he also noted is not readily available in bookstores. "As far as I can tell," he said, "I'm being whiteballed. Which is a shame. Not just for me (though of course for me especially) but for African Americans."

Goldblatt said that "less than half a century ago, African Americans—like the Jews of the Old Testament—were emerging from centuries of enslavement and subjugation with a culture that was stirring in its resilience, rich in its subtleties and epic in its scope. They were turning out a generation of national heroes like Jackie Robinson and Thurgood Marshall and Rosa Parks—a generation crowned by the towering world figure of Martin Luther King." "African-American political leaders are, nowadays, with rare exceptions, a ragtag crew of racial arsonists, conspiracy mongers, and corporate shakedown artists," continued Goldblatt, who noted that hip hop is "the black obsession with blackness." Not the crossover hip hop, but conscious rap, which Goldblatt described as "a noxious brew of racist delusions skimmed from the diverse streams of black separatist rhetoric, Afrocentric propagandizing, Nation of Islam theology, and a kind of Cliff Notes Marxism."

"What's significant," said Goldblatt, "is not the fact that hip-hop stars, in their ongoing attempts to 'keep it real,' are walking around expressing pinheaded, or even racially incendiary, ideas—which of course is their constitutional right—but the impact of such ideas on their fans. The thesis of my novel *Africa Speaks* is that hip hop instills in young black people a self-destructive us-against-them mindset in which pathological behavior is equated with black authenticity."

Goldblatt noted that he once taught remedial English to a young black woman who sabotaged her own progress because "her 'peeps' were telling her that going to college was turning her white." He said that he wrote *Africa Speaks* with that young woman in mind.

"It takes chutzpah for a nonblack to write something like this," said a *Kirkus Reviews* writer, "but some risks are worth the effort for what they reveal of essential humanity. This is one."

### BIOGRAPHICAL AND CRITICAL SOURCES:

*PERIODICALS*

*Kirkus Reviews,* December 1, 2002, review of *Africa Speaks,* p. 1631.
*Publishers Weekly,* November 26, 2001, review of *Africa Speaks,* p. 37.

*OTHER*

*Free Williamsburg,* http://www.freewilliamsburg.com/ (June, 2002), J. Stefan-Cole, review of *Africa Speaks.*
*National Review Online,* http://www.nationalreview.com/ (April 24, 2002), Mark Goldblatt, "On Being Whiteballed."*

\*     \*     \*

### GOLDENTHAL, Peter 1948-

*PERSONAL:* Born 1948; married; children: two. *Education:* University of Southern Maine, undergraduate degree (summa cum laude); Cornell University, A.M. (psychology), 1980; University of Connecticut, Ph.D. (clinical psychology).

*ADDRESSES: Agent*—c/o Wiley, 909 Third Avenue, New York, NY 10022. *E-mail*—dr.goldenthal@mindspring.com.

*CAREER:* Psychologist and author. Has taught psychology at Bryn Mawr College, the University of Pennsylvania, Jefferson Medical College, and the Children's Hospital of Philadelphia; has served as director of Valley Forge Contextual Therapy Institute.

### WRITINGS:

*Contextual Family Therapy: Assessment and Intervention Procedures,* Professional Resource Press (Sarasota, FL), 1993.
*Doing Contextual Therapy: An Integrated Model for Working with Individuals, Couples, and Families,* Norton (New York, NY), 1996.
*Beyond Sibling Rivalry: How to Help Your Children Become Cooperative, Caring, and Compassionate,* H. Holt (New York, NY), 1999.
*Why Can't We Get Along?: Healing Adult Sibling Relationships,* J. Wiley (New York, NY), 2002.

*SIDELIGHTS:* A specialist in pediatric and family psychology who has been in practice for more than twenty years, Peter Goldenthal is board certified both in clinical and child psychology. He is often consulted on parenting and family issues by writers for articles in such publications as the *Wall Street Journal, Parenting,* and *Time* magazine. Goldenthal has also appeared on television's *Today* show and on National Public Radio. The author of books aimed at colleagues and the general public, Goldenthal writes primarily about the relationships of siblings, both as children and as adults, for his lay audience.

In *Beyond Sibling Rivalry: How to Help Your Children Become Cooperative, Caring, and Compassionate,* Rosenthal parts company with those who hold the common view that sibling relationships are inevitably difficult and nearly impossible to control. In his book, Rosenthal delves into practical ways parents can help their children have better relationships with their brothers and sisters. Through an examination of sibling relationships within the family, Rosenthal provides parents with both theories and advice on how they can learn more about their children's needs and the roots of sibling rivalries. Contrary to another popular notion, Rosenthal points out that the source of sibling battles is often not competitiveness or jealousy but rather is more likely to stems from issues like problems at school, poor communications between siblings, and a lack of effective communication on the parents' part. Goldenthal also writes that how children get along with each other is influenced by how the parents got along with their parents and siblings when they were children. He discusses both common sibling rivalries and how they can be prevented and predicted as well as more serious problems, such as one or more siblings suffering from attention deficit hyperactivity disorder, or ADHD. Goldenthal also provides practical advice for dealing with problems between siblings by showing parents how to implement child-rearing techniques that will lessen and possibly even prevent future sibling conflicts. Brian McCombie, writing in *Booklist,* said, "Helpful and compassionate, it should be a fine addition to parenting collections."

In his next book, Goldenthal moves from children to adult siblings. *Why Can't We Get Along?: Healing Adult Sibling Relationships* focuses on siblings who have gone through decades of mutual jealousy, anger, and tension towards each other. Pointing out that these problems often hide the true love that siblings may feel for each other, Goldenthal speaks directly to those brother and sisters who want to move beyond their problems and reestablish a strong bond with their siblings. In the book, the author provides dramatic anecdotes from case histories within his own practice and specific steps that siblings can take to develop a healthy relationship, despite years of antagonism. Chapter titles include "Five Myths about Sibling Rivalry," "How to Talk—and Listen to—Your Sibling," and "Advice for Spouses, Partners, and Other Innocent Bystanders." *Library Journal* contributor Pam Matthews said the book "lacks focus" but also commented: "The most compelling [part] of the book is an appendix-like chapter that lists ways for parents to reduce sibling conflict."

*BIOGRAPHICAL AND CRITICAL SOURCES:*

*PERIODICALS*

*Booklist,* February 1, 1999, Brian McCombie, review of *Beyond Sibling Rivalry: How to Help Your Children Become Cooperative, Caring, and Compassionate,* p. 952.
*Contemporary Psychology,* December, 1994, review of *Contextual Family Therapy: Assessment and Intervention Procedures,* p. 1123.

*Library Journal,* January, 1999, Kay L. Brodie, review of *Beyond Sibling Rivalry: How to Help Your Children Become Cooperative, Caring, and Compassionate,* p. 130; March 15, 2002, Pam Matthews, review of *Why Can't We Get Along?: Healing Adult Sibling Relationships,* p. 97.
*Publishers Weekly,* December 21, 1998, review of *Beyond Sibling Rivalry,* p. 61.

*OTHER*

*Family Resources Web site,* http://www.family resources.com/ (June 3, 2002).*

\* \* \*

## GOLDFINCH, Shaun 1967-

*PERSONAL:* Born June 27, 1967, in Te Awamutu, New Zealand. *Ethnicity:* "Pakeha." *Education:* University of Otago, B.A., B.Com., postgraduate diploma, 1990; University of Melbourne, Ph.D., 1994.

*ADDRESSES: Office*—Department of Political Science, University of Canterbury, Private Bag 4800, Christchurch, New Zealand.

*CAREER:* University of Canterbury, Christchurch, New Zealand, lecturer in political science, 1998—.

*WRITINGS:*

*Remaking New Zealand and Australian Economic Policy,* Georgetown University Press (Washington, DC), 2000.

*WORK IN PROGRESS:* Research on computer systems failure, conflict, and political theory.

\* \* \*

## GORMAN, R(udolph) C(arl) 1931-

*PERSONAL:* Born July 26, 1931, in Chinle, AZ; son of Carl Nelson (an artist) and Adelle Kathern (Brown) Gorman. *Ethnicity:* Native American. *Education:* Attended Guam Territorial College, Arizona State College, San Francisco State University, and Mexico City College.

*ADDRESSES: Home*—P.O. Box 1756, Taos, NM 87571-1756.

*CAREER:* Artist; Navajo Gallery, Taos, NM, owner, 1967—. *Military service:* U.S. Navy, 1952-56.

*AWARDS, HONORS:* Honorable mention, New Mexico Fiesta Biennial, 1969; first prize, Tanner's All Indian Invitational Pottery and Painting Show, 1974; Key to cities of El Paso, San Antonio and Houston, TX, 1988; R.C. Gorman Day named in his honor, State of New Mexico, 1979; Humanitarian award in Fine Art, Harvard University, 1986.

*WRITINGS:*

*The Man Who Sent Rainclouds,* Viking (New York, NY), 1974.
*Nudes and Foods: Gorman Goes Gourmet,* Northland Press (Flagstaff, AZ), 1981.
*R. C. Gorman's Nudes and Foods in Good Taste,* Clear Light Publishers (Santa Fe, NM), 1994.

*SIDELIGHTS:* R. C. Gorman is one of the most celebrated and well-known Native American artists of the twentieth century. He was born on a Navajo reservation in Chinle, Arizona, where he had a traditional Navajo childhood, living in a hogan and herding sheep.

Though he always showed talent as a writer, Gorman chose to follow in his father's footsteps and pursue a career in art. The subject of his painting is often Native American, but his style fairly non-Indian. His work is very abstract and he has even been called a modern Picasso. One of the greatest recognitions of his talent occurred in 1973, when Gorman was the only living Native American artist whose work was chosen for inclusion in the Metropolitan Museum of Art exhibit "Masterworks of the Museum of the American Indian." Two of his pieces were also selected for the musuem's magazine cover.

Gorman has written two books that combine his art with his love for literature and food. *Nudes and Foods: Gorman Goes Gourmet* and *R. C. Gorman's Nudes and Foods in Good Taste* contain many of Gorman's drawings, as well as short stories and anecdotes about all things culinary. The recipes in the book are among Gorman's favorites, collected from family and friends. The food and the stories are mostly native to the Taos, New Mexico area.

*BIOGRAPHICAL AND CRITICAL SOURCES:*

OTHER

*Kiva Publishing,* http://www.kivapub.com/ (July 6, 2002).*

*        *        *

## GOROSTIZA, Carlos 1920-

*PERSONAL:* Born 1920.

*ADDRESSES: Agent*—c/o Author Mail, Planeta Argentina, Av Independencia 1668, 1100, Buenos Aires, Argentina.

*CAREER:* Puppeteer, poet, playwright, theater director, and television producer. Professor of Theater Arts, University of Indiana, 1965-66, and Escuela Nacional de Arte Dramatico, Buenos Aires, Argentina; operated private school for actors.

*WRITINGS:*

*El puente* (title means "The Bridge"; play), El Junco (Buenos Aires, Argentina), 1949, reprinted, Ediciones Colihue (Buenos Aires, Argentina), 1993, translation by Louis Curcio published as *The Bridge: A Drama in Two Acts,* S. French (New York, NY), 1961.
*El reloj de Baltazar; comedia en tres actos,* Ediciones de Losange, 1955.
*El lugar,* Editorial Sudamericana (Buenos Aires, Argentina), 1972.
*¿A qué jugamos?* (title means "What Shall We Play?"), Editorial Sudamericana (Buenos Aires, Argentina), 1974.
*Los cuartos oscuros,* Editorial Sudamericana (Buenos Aires, Argentina), 1976.

*Juana y Pedro,* Monte Avila Editores (Caracas, Venezuela), 1976.

(With Roberto Cossas) *Los hermanos queridos* (title means "Beloved Brothers"), Sociedad General de Autores de la Argentina (Buenos Aires, Argentina), 1980.

*Cuerpos presentes,* Editorial de Belgrano (Buenos Aires, Argentina), 1981.

*Hay que apagar el fuego; Matar el tiempo,* Ediciones Paralelo 32 (Rosario, Argentina), 1983.

*Papi,* Ediciones Paralelo 32 (Rosario, Argentina), 1985.

*La basural,* Editorial Sudamericana (Buenos Aires, Argentina), 1988.

*El pan de la locura* (title means "Bread of Madness") [and] *Los prójimos* (title means "The Neighbors"), Editorial Abril (Buenos Aires, Argentina), 1988.

(With Luis Ordaz) *Páginas de Carlos Gorostiza,* Editorial Celtia (Buenos Aires, Argentina), 1988.

*Teatro,* Ediciones de la Flor (Buenos Aires, Argentina), 1991.

*Vivir aquí,* Talía (Buenos Aires, Argentina), 1993.

*El patio de atrás* (play), Ediciones de la Flor (Buenos Aires, Argentina), 1996.

*Vuelan las palomas,* Planeta Argentina (Buenos Aires, Argentina), 1999.

*La buena gente,* Planeta Argentina (Buenos Aires, Argentina), 2002.

Also author of *El juicio,* 1954, and *150 años de motocicleta,* (Madrid, Spain), 1954.

*FOR CHILDREN*

*La clave encantada; obras de títeres, algunas para niños y todas para grandes,* Talía (Buenos Aires, Argentina), 1970.

*El gran circo,* illustrated by Blanca Medda, Editorial Kapelusz (Buenos Aires, Argentina), 1977.

*La calle del "Mucho-que-hacer,"* illustrated by Blanca Medda, Editorial Kapelusz (Buenos Aires, Argentina), 1977.

*Pelusa en la Argentina,* illustrated by Blanca Medda, Editorial Kapelusz (Buenos Aires, Argentina), 1977.

*Trotín nos lleva a la pampa,* illustrated by Blanca Medda, Editorial Kapelusz (Buenos Aires, Argentina), 1977.

*Pipo conductor,* illustrated by Blanca Medda, Editorial Kapelusz (Buenos Aires, Argentina), 1978.

*¡Todos al zoologico!* (title means "All to the Zoo!"), illustrated by Blanca Medda, Editorial Kapelusz (Buenos Aires, Argentina), 1978.

*Los días de fiesta* (title means "The Holidays"), illustrated by Blanca Medda, Editorial Kapelusz (Buenos Aires, Argentina), 1978.

*El barquito viajero* (title means "The Traveling Little Boat"), illustrated by Blanca Medda, Editorial Kapelusz (Buenos Aires, Argentina), 1978.

*SIDELIGHTS:* In 1930, the Argentinian foundation Theater of the People gave rise to the Independent Theater, a movement in Buenos Aires seeking to fight against commercial theater. As a part of this process quite a number of innovative playwrights emerged, among them Carlos Gorostiza, Aurelio Ferreti, Osvaldo Dragún, Andrés Lizarraga, and Agustín Cuzzani. Gorostiza has remained active in the movement as an actor, director, and author. The theme of this "off Broadway" style was the creation of a legitimate theater built from Argentine and other Latin American plays to compete with the superficial popular hits and translations of uninspiring foreign imports. Not the most avant-garde or iconoclastic of the group, Gorostiza watched his first success, *El puente,* span the gap between the independent theater and the large commercial theaters in Buenos Aires. Merlin H. Forster wrote in *Dramatists in Revolt: The New Latin American Theater,* "*El Puente* is one of Gorostiza's most important plays, both for its notable box-office success and as the beginning of the naturalistic-realistic portrayals that are most typical of Gorostiza."

The 1950s and 1960s were Gorostiza's most influential and prolific period. Postwar Italian neo-realism greatly influenced the Argentine artistic community and Gorostiza's major works, including *El pan* and *Los projimos. El pan* is set amid the banal and everyday. What happens in the play breaks through the flat reality and exposes underlying social tensions. The play takes place in a bakery where the customers begin going mad because of contaminated flour used in baking the bread. Bread, one of the basic symbols of Western culture, becomes the symbol around which human responsibility is judged.

In *Los projimos,* written in 1967, Gorostiza incorporates elements of the absurd into the neo-realism of his earlier plays. The play is based on the infamous Kitty Genovese murder in New York. This case became symbolic in the public mind of the dark side of urban life and made the public aware of the growth of a dehumanizing urban environment in which existed neighbors who were too indifferent or too frightened or too alienated to "get involved" in helping a fellow human being in dire trouble. Gorostiza sets the scene in a Buenos Aires apartment. As in the real crime in New York, a woman is killed in full sight of the fellow occupants of the woman's building.

*¿A que jugamos?* takes place in a middle-class apartment in Buenos Aires. Five people find out more and more about each other in a strange parlor game. They agree to imagine that the end of the world is only minutes away and to act on how they feel. As the play progresses, the players become more agitated and their reactions more violent. As the alarm clock sounds, signifying the end of the game and the "end of the world," the characters have revealed things about themselves that can never be hidden again. As Forster noted in *Dramatists in Revolt: The New Latin American Theater,* in *¿A que jugamos?* "Gorostiza suggests that superficial relationships between people can be fairly cordial, but a more profound involvement becomes taxing and uncertain."

Gorostiza's career also includes children's literature. Through the 1940s the author wrote and performed works for the puppet theater. In the 1970s, in collaboration with artist Blanca Medda, Gorostiza wrote a successful series of children's books, including *¡Todos al zoologico!, El barquito viajero,* and *La calle del "Mucho-que-hacer,"* which were recommended by Isabel Schon for special consideration in *Booklist.*

### BIOGRAPHICAL AND CRITICAL SOURCES:

*BOOKS*

Banham, Martin, Editor, *Cambridge Guide to World Theater,* Cambridge University Press (Cambridge, England), 1988.

Lyday, Leon F., and George W. Woodyard, editors, *Dramatists in Revolt: The New Latin American Theater,* University of Texas Press (Austin, TX), 1976.

Williams, David, editor, *A Dictionary of Latin American Authors,* Centre for Latin American Studies, Arizona State University (Tempe, AZ), 1975.

*PERIODICALS*

*Booklist,* June 15, 1982, reviews of *El barquito viajero, Los Días de fiesta,* and *¡Todos al zoologico!,* p. 1373.

*Cuadernos Americanos,* May, 1979, Eugene Moretta, "Villaurrutia and Gorostiza: Hacia una vision amplia de los poetas 'contemporaneos', " pp. 71-115.

*Latin American Theater Review,* spring, 1980, Eugene L. Moretta, "Spanish American Theater of the 50's and 60's: Critical Perspectives on Role Playing," pp. 5-30.

*Top of the News,* spring, 1986, review of *¡Todos al zoologico!,* p. 269.*

\*    \*    \*

## GOTHARD, Jan 1955-

*PERSONAL:* Born December 22, 1955 in Canberra, Australia. *Education:* Australian National University, B.A., 1977; Murdoch University (Murdoch, Western Australia), Ph.D., 1992.

*ADDRESSES: Office*—History Programme, Murdoch University, South Street, Murdoch, Western Australia 6150, Australia. *E-mail*—J.Gothard@murdoch.edu.au.

*CAREER:* School of Social Inquiry at Murdoch University (Murdoch, Western Australia), currently senior lecturer; Center for West Australia History, University of Western Australia, general editor; Council on International Education, regional director in Australia; Wofford College, Spartanburg, South Carolina, visiting professor of history, 2002.

*MEMBER:* Oral History Association of Australia, Society for the Study of Labour History, Australian Historical Association, History Teachers Association of Western Australia, History Council of Western Australia.

*AWARDS, HONORS:* Western Australian Premier's Book Award for nonfiction, Library and Information Service of Western Australia; shortlisted for the A.K. Hancock Prize for Australian history, 2001; Centenary

Medal, for service to society and literature by the Australian government, 2002, all for *Blue China: Single Female Migration to Colonial Australia.*

*WRITINGS:*

(Editor) *Asian Orientations,* Centre for Western Australian History, University of Western Australia (Nedlands, Western Australia), 1995.

(Editor with Jane Long and Helen Brash) *Forging Identities: Bodies, Gender, and Feminist History,* University of Western Australia Press (Nedlands, Western Australia), 1997.

*Blue China: Single Female Migration to Colonial Australia,* Melbourne University Press (Carlton South, Victoria, Australia), 2001.

(Editor with Laksiri Jayasuriya and David Walker) *Legacies of White Australia: Culture, Race, and Nation,* University of Western Australia (Nedlands, Western Australia), 2002.

Also contributor to scholarly periodicals and anthologies.

*SIDELIGHTS:* Australian scholar Jan Gothard's interest in history has taken her around the world, and she has spent time working in Japan, the United Kingdom, and the United States. Her research interests include migration, disability, and women's history, and all of these areas are addressed in her numerous articles, essays, and books.

One of Gothard's books, of which she is coeditor, is *Forging Identities: Bodies, Gender, and Feminist History.* This collection of essays explores the complexities of femininity, the construction of gender and gendered identities, and the complicated relationship between identity and embodiment. The collection is a direct result of the 1994 Australian Historical Association Conference Women's Network sessions, of which Gothard was a participant. Celia Winkler, writing in *Women's Studies International Forum,* while suggesting that the volume "could have used more judicious editing to ensure that non-Australian readers could understand the Australian references," nonetheless judged the volume to be worthwhile. "Overall," Winkler noted, "the collection makes a significant contribution to women's comparative history, and I can imagine using the preface, introduction, and es-

says in women's studies, history, and historiographic methodology courses." *Journal of Australian Studies* contributor Mary Spongberg called *Forging Identities* "perhaps one of the most important collections to come out in Australian women's history in a long time."

Gothard's next major work is *Blue China: Single Female Migration to Colonial Australia.* The book, which was awarded the prestigious Western Australian Premier's Book Award for nonfiction, is a carefully researched book that began as a thesis. *Blue China* is the story of almost one hundred thousand single women who emigrated from Britain to the Australian colonies between 1850 and 1900. Told through Gothard's narrative as well as authentic journal and diary entries, the author lays to rest the popular myth surrounding this group of women, whose passage was paid for by the colonial government. She establishes that, rather than immigrating in order to find husbands, the primary objective of the women was to improve their own lives through employment. The British government viewed the migration as a way to ease the shortage of domestic servants in Colonial Australia.

Regardless of motive, the oppressive attitudes toward women during that era put a serious limitation on their mobility and initiative. In an effort to "protect" their investment, the government employed shipboard matrons whose sole duty it was to keep the women away from men. Once to shore, they were again confined and isolated, the result being an overall ignorance of the wages they could have demanded in Australia's labor-hungry market. Gothard's research also explores and assesses the notion of women workers as commodities whose value was considered directly in line with their ability to maintain bourgeois values of family and nation. *Blue China* is the first book of its kind to present a treatment and analysis of this theory.

The title is a reference to flow blue china, which becomes worthless if damaged. *Blue China* analyzes the women's experiences from screening and selection to transition. In the end, Gothard determines that the women did what women have always done: they used to their own advantage the very institutions designed to control them.

*BIOGRAPHICAL AND CRITICAL SOURCES:*

*PERIODICALS*

*Journal of Australian Studies,* March, 1999, Mary Spongberg, review of *Forging Identities: Bodies, Gender, and Feminist History,* p. 193.

*Rostrum,* December, 2001, review of *Blue China: Single Female Migration to Colonial Australia.*

*Times Literary Supplement,* November 23, 2001, Andrew Hassam, review of *Blue China,* p. 30.

*Women's Studies International Forum,* March-April, 1999, Celia Winkler, review of *Forging Identities,* pp. 268-269.

OTHER

*Murdoch University Web site,* http://wwwsoc.edu.au/history/staff/ (July 25, 2002), "Jan Gothard."

*State Library of Western Australia Web site,* http://www.liswa.wa.gov.au/ (July 25, 2002), "Western Australian Premier's Book Awards—2001 Winners."

\*     \*     \*

## GOUGH, Julian 1966-

*PERSONAL:* Born 1966.

*ADDRESSES: Home*—Galway, Ireland. *Agent*—Jessica Sutton, Fraser & Dunlop Group Ltd., Drury House, 34-43 Russell St., London WC2B 5HA, England.

*CAREER:* Writer and musician; cofounder of underground rock band *Toasted Heretic.*

*WRITINGS:*

*Juno & Juliet: A Novel,* Nan A. Talese/Doubleday (New York, NY), 2001.

*SIDELIGHTS:* In his first novel, *Juno & Juliet,* Irish writer and rock musician Julian Gough has created a romance set amid university life in his native Ireland. Although Gough claims to have set out to write a contemporary version of a Jane Austen novel, the inspiration was much closer to home. As Gough told Kelley Kawano in a *randomhouse.com* interview, "I was trying to understand women at the time. I'd fallen in love with a beautiful, fascinating, intelligent woman. When she left the county, I was left with this beautiful-woman-shaped hole in my life. I suppose I explored that, mapped it, filled it in by writing *Juno & Juliet.* . . . I was absolutely astonished it turned out funny."

The plot is simple and straightforward: two beautiful twin sisters, Juno and Juliet, leave their provincial home for college. What follows is an optimistic and warmhearted account of their first year at a Galway university. They make friends, have love affairs, and even manage to attend classes. The ethereal Juno finds her friends and lovers—and a stalker—in the theater department. Juliet finds her way into the world of modern English literature, with all its convoluted, high-minded theory.

Characterization is the strength of the novel more than plot, and Gough has created a cast happily free of the usual stereotypes seen in "campus" novels. Even though the characters sometimes border on caricature, the light and breezy tone of the book makes them welcome. As *Los Angeles Times* reviewer Mark Rozzo commented, "it's the most brutally—and hilariously—real depiction of Irish undergraduate life since *The Gingerbread Man.*"

Gough is especially successful in narrating from the female perspective: Juliet manages to be young, sarcastic, and sentimental at the same time. Commenting on a classmate, she remarks, "I'd always found her as brittle as our grandmother's right hip and as artificial as its replacement." Or further along, "Ah, the old make us so philosophical. No wonder we avoid them."

In the world of Irish literature, comparisons are inevitable. *Washington Post* contributor Carolyn See felt Gough wrote as well as author Roddy Doyle, but without the morbidity and gloom that is often part and parcel of the Irish novel. "Gough's Ireland is a place you pine for, a place you can't wait to visit. His women are beautiful and kind; the men—except for one pathetic villain—chivalrous and witty. Even the criminals have good hearts and are overly generous, though they're giving away mostly stolen goods. And that traditional curse of the Irish turns out not to be a curse: when people get drunk in this novel, they have the time of their lives."

*BIOGRAPHICAL AND CRITICAL SOURCES:*

BOOKS

Gough, Julian, *Juno & Juliet,* Nan A. Talese/Doubleday (New York, NY), 2001.

*PERIODICALS*

*Booklist,* May 1, 2001, Kristine Huntley, review of *Juno & Juliet,* p. 1665.

*Entertainment Weekly,* July 27, 2001, review of *Juno & Juliet,* p. 66.

*Library Journal,* May 1, 2001, Karen T. Bilton, review of *Juno & Juliet,* p. 126.

*Los Angeles Times,* July 29, 2001, Mark Rozzo, review of *Juno & Juliet,* p. 10.

*New York Times,* July 17, 2001, Richard Eder, "Ready for Double Trouble in the Big City of Galway," p. E8.

*New York Times Book Review,* August 26, 2001, William Ferguson, review of *Juno & Juliet,* p. 20.

*Publishers Weekly,* May 14, 2001, review of *Juno & Juliet,* p. 49.

*Washington Post,* July 13, 2001, Carolyn See, "Irish Eyes That Are Actually Smiling," p. C08.


*OTHER*       .


*Bookreporter,* http://bookreporter.com/ (February 1, 2002), Jana Siciliano, review of *Juno & Juliet.*

*Literalmind,* http://literalmind.com/ (February 1, 2002), Susan Miller, review of *Juno & Juliet.*

*Random House Web site,* http://www.randomhouse.com/ (March 20, 2003), Kelley Kawano, "A Conversation with Julian Gough."*

*    *    *

## GRANGÉ, Jean-Christophe 1961-

*PERSONAL:* Born 1961, in Paris, France.

*ADDRESSES: Agent*—c/o Author Mail, Éditions Albin Michel, 22, rue Huyghens, Paris 75014, France.

*CAREER:* Journalist, author, and screenwriter; founder of news agency.

*WRITINGS:*

(With Christian de Rudder) *Made in Space,* Editions Syros-Alternatives (Paris, France), 1992.

*Le vol des cigognes,* Albin Michel (Paris, France), 1994, translation by Ian Monk published as *The*

*Flight of the Storks,* Harvill Press (London, England), 2000.

*Les rivières pourpres,* Albin Michel (Paris, France), 1998, translation by Ian Monk published as *Blood-Red Rivers,* Harvill Press (London, England), 2000.

*Le concile de pierre,* Albin Michel (Paris, France), 2000, translation by Ian Monk published as *The Stone Council,* Harvill Press (London, England), 2000.

*L'empire des loups: roman,* Albin Michel (Paris, France), 2003.


Also author of the screenplay *Vidocq,* a co-production of RF2K, Studio Canal, TF1 Groupe, 2000.


*ADAPTATIONS: Blood-Red Rivers* was adapted to film as *The Crimson Rivers* (*Les rivières pourpres*), Columbia TriStar Home Entertainment Video, 2001.


*WORK IN PROGRESS:* Movie adaptation of the cult series *Vidocq,* a fantasy thriller mixing history with the supernatural.


*SIDELIGHTS:* Jean Christophe Grangé is at the forefront of new French "Polar" writers (the French name for crime/detective fiction). Born in Paris, Grangé wrote for magazines worldwide before becoming an investigative reporter and setting up his own news agency. During his ten years as a journalist, research into the paranormal and a lengthy study on the nomads of Mongolia left lasting impressions on him, and he was determined to incorporate them into his books. While Grangé's first novel, *Flight of the Storks,* published in 1994, was largely unnoticed, *Blood-Red Rivers,* published in 1998, became an international bestseller and later a film directed by Mathieu Kassovitz.

The plot of *The Flight of the Storks* follows the storks' incredible 12,000-mile annual migration from Northern Europe to Central Africa. When, one year, they do not return, wealthy Swiss ornithologist Max Boehm hires Louis Antioch, a young French academic, to make the journey tracing the flight of the storks in an attempt to solve the mystery of the birds' disappearance. Before Antioch can begin his trip, Boehm dies of a heart attack under suspicious circumstances. The police suspect murder, and diamond smuggling is involved.

From there, the plot follows the storks' flyways through a Bulgarian Gypsy encampment to an Israeli Kibbutz and into the jungles of Central Africa. Soon after the book's publication, Grangé was contacted by the movie industry to write screen adaptations because of the novel's cinematic qualities.

In *Blood-Red Rivers,* a mutilated corpse is found wedged in a crevice on a rock face outside Guernon, a university town in the French Alps. Superintendent Pierre Niemans is sent from Paris to investigate. He is an ex-commando with a brilliant mind, but cursed with violent fits of temper. At the same time, another rogue cop, Karim Abdouf, who was brought up on the rough streets of Nanterre, is investigating the desecration of a child's grave in a local cemetery. When a third body is found, high up on a glacier, the paths of the two men cross. "Abdouf . . . takes a scientific approach to certain genetic clues, while the abrasive Niemans . . . dives into deep emotional waters," wrote Marilyn Stasio in the *New York Times Book Review* about Grangé's charting of the separate investigative routes directing these unorthodox cops to Guernon. Nothing is what it seems. As Niemans says early on, "When a murder has been committed, you have to look at every surrounding detail as though it were a mirror . . . somewhere inside one of those mirrors, in a dead angle, the murderer is hiding." Ranti Williams, writing in the *Times Literary Supplement,* noted that "each corpse is first discovered by means of its reflection—in ice, in glass and in water . . . two-thirds of the way through the novel . . . each detective's case is a reflection of the other, and it is only when they finally come together that the 'dead angle' becomes apparent."

In *The Stone Council,* Grangé incorporates his passion for the nomads of Mongolia into a story that leaves the thriller genre and ventures into the fantastic. Grangé had traveled the Mongolian-Siberian border following an indigenous tribe, which was so isolated that it managed to escape the repression of both the Soviet and communist Chinese governments. Grangé was especially interested in the shamans and their ritual healing magic. *The Stone Council* begins when Diane Thiberge adopts a little boy in Thailand. Soon, there are attempts on the boy's life and encounters with the paranormal. As Diane follows the thread of circumstances that lead to the past, and to the Mongolian taiga, she begins to understand the Law of the Stone Council, the point of original combat where man, animals, and the universal spirit are one.

*BIOGRAPHICAL AND CRITICAL SOURCES:*

*PERIODICALS*

*French Review,* May, 2000, Kathryn M. Bulver, review of *Les rivières pourpres,* p. 1260.
*New Statesman,* October 11, 1999, Sebastian Shakespeare, review of *Blood-Red Rivers,* p. 57.
*New York Times Book Review,* September 24, 2000, Marilyn Stasio, review of *Blood-Red Rivers,* p. 29.
*Times Literary Supplement,* October 8, 1999, Ranti Williams, review of *Blood-Red Rivers,* p. 24; September 29, 2000, Hugh MacPherson, review of *Flight of the Storks,* p. 26.*

\*     \*     \*

## GRAY, Ed(ward Emmet) 1945-

*PERSONAL:* Born March 7, 1945, in Honolulu, HI; son of L. Patrick III (a lawyer) and Beatrice Castle (Kirk) Gray; married Rebecca Crawford (a writer and cook), December 6, 1975; children: Caroline, Douglas, Hope, Samuel, William. *Ethnicity:* "Caucasian." *Education:* Dartmouth College, A.B., 1967, M.B.A., 1971. *Politics:* Independent. *Hobbies and other interests:* Active outdoor pursuits.

*ADDRESSES: Office*—Gray Books, P.O. Box 69, Lyme, NH 03768; fax: 413-812- 6149. *E-mail*—edwardegray@earthlink.net.

*CAREER:* Writer and publisher. *Gray's Sporting Journal,* founding editor, 1975-91; freelance writer, Lyme, NH, 1991—. Connecticut River Watershed Council, trustee, 2002—. *Military service:* U.S. Navy, 1968-70; became lieutenant junior grade.

*WRITINGS:*

*Gray's Journal: The First Collection,* GSJ Press (Lyme, NH), 1982.
*Gray's Journal: The Second Collection,* GSJ Press (Lyme, NH), 1984.
(Editor) *Tales from Gray's: Selections from Gray's Sporting Journal, 1975-1985,* GSJ Press (Lyme, NH), 1986.

*Flashes in the River: The Flyfishing Images of Arthur Shilstone and Ed Gray,* illustrated by Arthur Shilstone, Willow Creek Press (Minocqua, WI), 1996.

*Wings from the Cover: The Upland Images of Robert Abbett and Ed Gray,* illustrated by Robert Abbett, Willow Creek Press (Minocqua, WI), 1996.

*Shadows on the Flats: The Saltwater Images of Chet Reneson and Ed Gray,* illustrated by Chet Reneson, Willow Creek Press (Minocqwa, WI), 1997.

*The Lake of the Beginning: A Fable of Salmon, Northern Lights, and an Old Promise Kept* (fiction), Willow Creek Press (Minocqua, WI), 1998.

(With Benjamin Kilham) *Among the Bears: Raising Orphan Cubs in the Wild* (nonfiction), Henry Holt (New York, NY), 2002.

*Flights on the Wind: Waterfowl Images,* Willow Creek Press (Minocqua, WI), in press.

Also author of the novel *The Bretton Woods Incident.*

*BIOGRAPHICAL AND CRITICAL SOURCES:*

*PERIODICALS*

*Publishers Weekly,* January 21, 2002, review of *Among the Bears: Raising Orphan Cubs in the Wild,* p. 74.

*OTHER*

*Gray Books Web site,* http://www.graybooks.net/ (January 11, 2003).

\*    \*    \*

**GRAY, James P. 1945-**

*PERSONAL:* Born February 14, 1945, in Washington, DC; son of William P. (a judge) and Elizabeth (Polin) Gray; married Grace Walker (a physical therapist), September 17, 2000; children: Edward K., William P., Jennifer Marie. *Ethnicity:* "Caucasian." *Education:* University of California—Los Angeles, B.A., 1966; University of Southern California, J.D., 1971. *Politics:* Republican. *Religion:* Protestant. *Hobbies and other interests:* Songwriting, tennis, travel.

*ADDRESSES: Home*—2531 Crestview Dr., Newport Beach, CA 92663. *Office*—Department 16, Superior Court, 700 Civic Center Dr. W., Santa Ana, CA 92663.

*CAREER:* Office of the U.S. Attorney, Los Angeles, CA, attorney, 1975-78; Office of Wyman Bantler, Newport Beach, CA, attorney, 1978-83; Municipal Court, Santa Ana, CA, judge, 1983-89; Superior Court, Santa Ana, judge, 1989—. Chapman University, professor, 1989. Orange County Peer Court, founder; William P. Gray Inn of Court, founder and president. *Military service:* U.S. Navy; served in Vietnam. U.S. Naval Reserve, Judge Advocate General's Corps, 1972-75.

*MEMBER:* Orange County Bar Association.

*WRITINGS:*

*Why Our Drug Laws Have Failed and What We Can Do about It: A Judicial Indictment of the War on Drugs,* Temple University Press (Philadelphia, PA), 2001.

*WORK IN PROGRESS: Americans All,* a musical.

*SIDELIGHTS:* James P. Gray told *CA:* "Based upon my experience as a federal prosecutor in Los Angeles, a criminal defense attorney in Navy JAG, and a trial judge in Orange County, California since 1983, I had seen firsthand how our laws of drug prohibition not only had failed, but actually were hopeless. We were unnecessarily churning numbers of nonviolent drug offenders through the criminal justice system for no good purpose whatsoever, which resulted in the United States leading the world in the incarceration of its people, mostly minorities. We had lost more of our civil liberties due to the war on drugs than anything else in our nation's history. We had directly been funding terrorism all around the world due to the sale of illicit drugs. We had exacerbated the AIDS epidemic due to the deprivation of clean needles to drug-addicted people; we had actually put them in harm's way due to the profit motive in selling these dangerous drugs. What our society had not focused upon, however, was that we have viable options to this failed system, and these options are being used successfully in other countries around the world.

"But no one particularly was talking about this critical issue.

"Since I am a conservative Republican from a conservative county, I have never used any of these illicit drugs, and I am a veteran trial judge who has nothing personal to gain by discussing this issue publicly, I determined that there were few people better placed in our society than I to discuss the possibility of change.

"Writing my book, documenting every assertion of fact with footnotes, proofreading the entire work numbers of times, and obtaining a publisher and endorsements for the book made it the most difficult and time-consuming project I had ever undertaken. However, if by my efforts I am able to assist in changing away from this hopeless system, I believe that I will have helped to save hundreds of lives, kept thousands of others from being ruined, and saved the taxpayers hundreds of millions of dollars."

## BIOGRAPHICAL AND CRITICAL SOURCES:

PERIODICALS

American Prospect, January 28, 2002, Emily Parsons, review of Why Our Drug Laws Have Failed and What We Can Do about It: A Judicial Indictment of the War on Drugs, p. 43.
Journal of Policy Analysis and Management, spring, 2002, Philip J. Cook, review of Why Our Drug Laws Have Failed and What We Can Do about It, p. 303.
Publishers Weekly March 26, 2001, review of Why Our Drug Laws Have Failed and What We Can Do about It, p. 80.

OTHER

Judge Jim Gray Web site, http://www.judgejimgray.com (December 5, 2002).

\*　　\*　　\*

## GRAY, Penny 1957-
### (Nadia Nichols)

PERSONAL: Born December 19, 1957, in Gloucester, MA; daughter of Richard Paul (an innkeeper) and Nancy (an innkeeper; maiden name, Dyer) Gray. Education: Essex Agricultural College, A.A.S.; also attended University of Maine. Hobbies and other interests: Dog sledding, hiking, camping.

ADDRESSES: Office—Harraseeket Inn, 162 Main St., Freeport, ME 04032; fax: 208-865-1684. E-mail—Harraseeke@aol.com.

CAREER: Harraseeket Inn, Freeport, ME, assistant manager, 1985—. Ridge Runner Kennel (for racing Alaskan husky dogs), owner, 1983—; registered Maine guide.

MEMBER: National Wildlife Rehabilitation Association.

WRITINGS:

UNDER PSEUDONYM NADIA NICHOLS

Across a Thousand Miles (romance novel), Harlequin (Don Mills, Ontario, Canada), 2002.
Montana Dreaming (romance novel), Harlequin (Don Mills, Ontario, Canada), 2002.

WORK IN PROGRESS: Buffalo Summer, a romance novel, under pseudonym Nadia Nichols, for Harlequin.

## BIOGRAPHICAL AND CRITICAL SOURCES:

PERIODICALS

Boston Herald, February 14, 2002, Rosemary Herbert, "Maine Dogsled Racer Teachers Romance Genre New Tricks," p. 53.

\*　　\*　　\*

## GRAYSON, Richard (A.) 1951-

PERSONAL: Born June 4, 1951, in Brooklyn, NY; son of Daniel (in business) and Marilyn (a retailer; maiden name, Sarrett) Grayson. Ethnicity: "White/Jewish." Education: Brooklyn College of the City University of New York, B.A., 1973, M.F.A., 1976; Richmond College of the City University of New York, M.A., 1975; University of Florida, J.D., 1984.

*Richard Grayson*

*ADDRESSES: Home*—2701 Southwest 79th Ave. #204, Davie, FL 33328. *Office*—Nova Southeastern University, Shepart Broad Law Center, 3305 College Ave., Fort Lauderdale, FL 33314. *E-mail*—graysonric@ yahoo.com.

*CAREER:* Fiction Collective, Brooklyn, NY, editorial assistant, 1975-77; Long Island University, Brooklyn, NY, lecturer in English, 1975-78; City University of New York, lecturer in English at Kingsborough Community College, Brooklyn, NY, 1978-81, Brooklyn College, Brooklyn, NY, 1979-81, John Jay College of Criminal Justice, New York, NY, 1984-86, and Bernard M. Baruch College, New York, NY, 1985-86; The School of Visual Arts, New York, NY, lecturer in humanities, 1979-1980; Tuoro College, New York, NY, lecturer in English, 1979-1980; Broward Community College, Fort Lauderdale, FL, instructor in English, 1981-84, 1987-91; Florida International University, Miami, FL, lecturer in computer education and English, 1986-90; Nova Southeastern University, Fort Lauderdale, instructor in business, liberal arts, and legal studies, 1992-2000; Florida Atlantic University, Boca Raton, FL, lecturer in English, 1997-98;

Mesa Community College, Mesa, AZ, lecturer in English, 2000-01; Nova Southeastern University, Fort Lauderdale, FL, director of academic resource program at Shepart Broad Law Center, 2001—. University of Florida, staff attorney in social policy at Center for Governmental Responsibility, 1994-97. Rockland Center for the Arts, writer-in-residence, 1988-89. Brooklyn College Alumni Association, member of board of directors, 1973-81; Human Rights Council of North Central Florida, member of board of directors, 1995-97.

*MEMBER:* International PEN, Association of Computer Educators, Authors Guild, Authors League of America, Associated Writing Programs, Lambda Legal Defense and Education Fund, South Florida Peace Council, Phi Beta Kappa, Coif, Mensa.

*AWARDS, HONORS:* Scholar of National Arts Club at Bread Loaf Writer's Conference, 1977; scholar at Santa Cruz Writing Conference, 1978; residencies at MacDowell Colony, 1980 and 1987, Virginia Center for the Creative Arts, 1981 and 1982, Millay Colony for the Arts, 1984, Ragdale Foundation, 1997 and 2001, Villa Montalvo Center for the Arts, 1998, Ucross Foundation, 1998, and Writers' Colony at Dairy Hollow, 2001; fellowships from Florida Division of Cultural Affairs, 1981, 1988, and 1998; writer-in-residence award from New York State Council on the Arts, 1988-89; fellow-in-residence, Center for Mark Twain Studies, Elmira College, 1990.

*WRITINGS:*

*Disjointed Fictions,* X Archives (Harrisburg, PA), 1978.
*With Hitler in New York and Other Stories,* Taplinger (New York, NY), 1979.
*Lincoln's Doctor's Dog and Other Stories,* White Ewe (Havre de Grace, MD), 1982.
*Eating at Arby's: The South Florida Stories* (pamphlet), Grinning Idiot Press (Brooklyn, NY), 1982.
*I Brake for Delmore Schwartz,* Zephyr Press (Somerville, MA), 1983.
*The Greatest Short Story That Absolutely Ever Was,* Lowlands (New Orleans, LA), 1989.
*Narcissism and Me,* Mule & Mule (New York, NY), 1990.

*I Survived Caracas Traffic: Stories from the Me Decades,* Avisson (Greensboro, MA), 1996.

*The Silicon Valley Diet and Other Stories,* Red Hen Press (Los Angeles, CA), 2000.

Contributor of short stories to more than a two hundred periodicals, including *Epoch, Texas Quarterly, Confrontation, Shenandoah, Carleton Miscellany,* and *Transatlantic Review;* contributor of nonfiction to magazines and newspapers, including *People, New York Times, Miami Herald, San Jose Mercury News, Orlando Sentinel, Arizona Republic,* and *Tampa Tribune.* Humor columnist, *Hollywood Sun-Tattler,* 1986-87, *New Jersey Online,* 1995-97, and *Boca Raton* (FL) *News,* 1997-99.

*WORK IN PROGRESS:* A collection of related short stories.

*SIDELIGHTS:* Unconventional, imaginative, and possessed by an offbeat sense of humor, Richard Grayson is the author of several collections of short stories that examine life from a perspective many critics find refreshingly different. Originally published in a variety of small magazines, his stories "are full of insanity, nutty therapists, cancerous relatives, broken homes, fiction workshops, youthful theatricals at Catskill bungalow colonies and the morbid wizardry of telephone-answering machines," according to Ivan Gold in the *New York Times Book Review.* Some also feature such unlikely "characters" as the voice of the cold that "assassinated" President William Henry Harrison in 1841 and Sparky, Abraham Lincoln's doctor's puppy, who grows up to become a successful politician and lecturer (the latter story was inspired by an article Grayson once read that stated most recent bestsellers have dealt with presidents, diseases, or animals—hence, "Lincoln's Doctor's Dog"). As Mark Bernheim observed in *Israel Today,* "Grayson is able to create a full range of masks from behind which the artist peers out to make his criticisms of artificial modern life."

Commenting in *Best Sellers,* Nicholas J. Loprete, Jr., asserted that Grayson's stories "display a versatility which commands attention. [The author] can parody human excess and human frailty, parent-child relationships, and recreate a 1960's scene with poignancy. He is serious and comic, charming, given to outrageous

puns, and a sharp-eyed observer of and participant in Life's absurdities." Lynne Gagnon wrote in the *Ventura County News,* "Richard Grayson gets the prize for making us laugh about the ridiculous insaneness surrounding our lives. But the award is two-fold; he also forces us to examine people and what they do to us. And more importantly what we do to them."

Grayson once told *CA:* "Writing has been the primary way I've defined myself; at first it was therapy, but now, I hope, it has become something more. I see the writer's first job as giving the lowdown on himself, and through himself, on humanity. As I reluctantly leave the longest adolescence in history, I find myself happily becoming less self-conscious, more patient. I would like to avoid becoming pompous, but I'm afraid statements like these are among the mine fields on the road to absurd self-importance. I have a lot to learn about writing (and other things)."

*AUTOBIOGRAPHICAL ESSAY:*

Richard Grayson contributed the following autobiographical essay to *CA:*

### A WRITER IN SPITE OF MYSELF

"You should call it 'A Writer in Spite of Himself,'" said my current therapist—my seventh since I was a teenager—of this autobiographical essay. "You know, like Moliere's *A Doctor in Spite of Himself.* Tell how despite your distractions and your self-doubts, your lack of confidence and your extreme self-consciousness—your *mishigass,* as we say in New York—you managed to become and remain a writer."

We were sitting in Dr. Koncsol's office of The Psych Team in Davie, Florida, and I had been telling him how I had this mass (and mess) of "and then this happened, and then this happened" material but my that essay needed a theme.

I had been thinking of calling it "Travels of an Agoraphobic"—after a book by another neurotic, Oscar Levant's *Memoirs of an Amnesiac,* because in many ways I am still that anxiety-ridden seventeen year old who barely left his room for a year.

*Age four, at Rockaway Beach, 1955*

But perhaps my therapist's idea is better than mine. After all, his title does come closer to the sensibility of the self-conscious fiction I write, about the impossibility and desperate necessity of telling stories and the overriding fear that I'm not going to get it right.

I was born Richard Arnold Ginsberg in Brooklyn on June 4, 1951, two years after my parents, Marilyn and Daniel, had married. When I was six months old, Mom and Dad changed our Jewish last name to the ethnically neutral Grayson.

My parents had met as teenagers in the bungalows of Rockaway Beach, Queens, where their parents were summer neighbors and friends. My grandparents—Nathan and Sylvia Ginsberg, Herbert and Ethel Sarrett—had spent most of their lives in Brooklyn, but all had been born in the shtetls of Eastern Europe and had immigrated as children.

Both sets of grandparents had known each other a long time; as a boy, Grandpa Herb lived with his family next door to the family of Grandma Sylvia, many years before they would become *machetunim* (Yiddish for "co-parents-in-law").

When I was born, my mother was twenty, my father twenty-four, and my grandparents in their forties.

As the psychologist who interviewed me at fifteen said, first memories are often unreliable but revealing. My first memory, I told Dr. Machover, was being held up to the window and watching cars go by on Ocean Parkway. I guessed that meant I saw myself as an observer.

A story my mother tells:

When I was two, Mom left me alone with the TV on in our apartment's "front room." She returned to find the word *Tide* written in crayon on a piece of construction paper.

"What's that?" Mom asked, startled.

"It's *Tide,*" I said. "I saw it on TV." I had copied the word from a commercial for the detergent.

My mother read to me constantly, mostly little Golden Books like *The Tawny, Scrawny Lion.* I would make her read them aloud over and over until I could interrupt her and recite the rest of the story from memory.

A neighbor who was a first-grade teacher brought me schoolbooks, and somehow I taught myself to read—or so I was told.

I loved books and was crazy about maps. My Uncle Matt Sarrett had given me his boyhood set of the Britannica Junior Encyclopedia and a world atlas as big as I was—an edition published during World War II which featured a large Nazi Germany which took up much of central Europe.

I memorized the capitals of the forty-eight states and then foreign countries. In restaurants, Grandpa Herb would show off my talents to the other diners. He wanted me to go on the kid quiz show *Take a Giant Step,* but I was too nervous.

I was always "nervous." I was afraid of school, traveling, dentists, swimming, vomiting, bridges, airplanes, suffocation, and getting up on stage. My problem with anxiety is probably partly genetic, and partly a result of my overprotective family. It resulted in a fearful childhood, panic attacks and agoraphobia in adolescence, and a diagnosis of generalized anxiety disorder when I was almost fifty.

In the fall of 2000, the nurse-practitioner in Arizona who diagnosed me said, "I think you've had this your whole life."

My two brothers are Marc, born in 1955, and Jonathan, born in 1961. Since coming to America at the start of the twentieth century, our family had worked in New York's garment industry. My father and Grandpa Nat owned Art Pants Company, manufacturers of men's dress slacks. My maternal grandparents met in an underwear factory where Grandpa Herb was the foreman and Grandma Ethel sewed. My great-grandfather Max Shapiro was a furrier; my great-uncle Harry Ginsberg manufactured men's clothes; and my first job as a teenager was in The Slack Bar, a downtown Brooklyn pants store owned by Uncle Matt and his father-in-law, where Grandpa Herb worked as a tailor.

We spent summers at the beach in Rockaway bungalow colonies, where within one block I could find all four grandparents, my step-great-grandmother, several sets of great-aunts and great-uncles, and various in-laws of other relatives. After the bungalows were torn down in 1968, my grandparents moved from their apartments in Brooklyn to oceanfront high-rises in another part of Rockaway, across the street from one another.

In 1957, my parents moved us to a small, newly built brick row house on East 56th Street and Avenue O, where we'd stay for the next twenty-two years. In 1970, New York City's first enclosed shopping center, Kings Plaza, opened a few blocks away, and our mostly Italian and Jewish neighborhood took the name of the mall. My mother worked there, in The Pants Set, a women's clothing store owned by Dad and Uncle Matt.

I went to New York public schools, first P.S. 244, then P.S. 203 and Junior High School 285, where I was in the SPE (Special Progress Enrichment) program. I met my friend Linda Konner, an author and literary agent, in second grade, and we were in the same classes through our graduation from Midwood High School in

*Richard's sixth-grade class at P.S. 203 in Brooklyn (the author is seated on the floor to the right of the sign)*

1968, except for tenth grade, which I spent at a private school on Manhattan's Upper West Side. Nearly always the shortest boy in the class, I was considered a gifted student—besting sixth-graders in geography quizzes when I was in kindergarten, reading at a tenth-grade level at age seven, writing a seventy-page research paper in ninth grade—until my emotional problems caused my marks to slip into the high 80s.

When I was fifteen, I began having severe panic attacks daily. I would get nauseated, my heart would beat wildly, I'd sweat and shake and feel like the world was ending. The term "panic disorder" was not then known, but I realized that my problem was psychological, so I asked my parents if I could see a psychiatrist.

In the late 1960s, anxiety disorders and depression were rarely treated with medication; instead, psychoanalysis was the norm. Although I learned a lot about myself in sessions with Dr. Lippman, my panic attacks kept getting worse and more frequent. I soon began avoiding going out in public and skipped events like family weddings and my own high school graduation. The traumatic national events of my last year at Midwood H.S.—the turmoil of the Vietnam war, the assassinations of my heroes Martin Luther King, Jr. and Robert Kennedy—only made things harder.

I had been accepted to Brooklyn College, which then had free tuition like all City University of New York campuses. I never considered going anywhere else. I knew I could not leave my parents' home, and BC seemed as safe as any college could be, since I walked through its campus on my way to high school.

But as it turned out, I couldn't even handle BC. In late August, after watching antiwar protestors get beaten in the streets of Chicago during the 1968 Democratic convention, I was unable to sleep for days and began to shake uncontrollably. Mom called my pediatrician, who made a house call and prescribed the tranquilizer Librium.

A couple of weeks later, on the first day of classes, I just couldn't face the nausea and panic I knew I'd have to endure, and I told my parents that I wasn't well enough to go to college. I then entered a period where I gradually cut myself from the world. I stopped taking phone calls from friends, as I was too ashamed to tell anyone about my panic disorder. My agoraphobia got more severe as winter came and I rarely left the house. Yet even the safety of my little bedroom didn't stop the panic attacks from occurring several times a day. My main refuge from anxiety was reading.

I had always loved books. Starting when I was about nine, I began collecting a huge number of paperbacks, which were then available for 25 or 50 cents. On my birthdays my parents would give me $20, which I'd take to a bookstore and buy an armful of Bantam and Signet and Pocket Books. I read voraciously—everything from books about psychology and history to trashy potboilers to classic literary works to American fiction writers I idolized: Salinger, Roth, Pynchon, Vonnegut, Updike, Mailer, Malamud, Bellow, Cheever, Baldwin, Vidal, Flannery O'Connor, John Rechy, Carson McCullers.

I also was a big fan of superhero comic books. I proudly possessed the early issues of Justice League of America, Green Lantern, Spider-Man, and Daredevil. At eleven, I would pretend to be The Flash—Fastest Man Alive—as I bicycled around the neighborhood, playing hooky from Hebrew school. (The one kind of reading I did not like was in Hebrew, since we were not given the English translations for the prayers we had to recite. Reading without meaning seemed totally pointless, especially since I was an atheist like Grandpa Herb).

By the end of high school, I outgrew comics, and Mom threw out my carefully catalogued collection. I held on to the paperbacks and the hardcovers from the Book-of-the-Month Club and the Literary Guild.

*Working on a play, age seventeen, 1968*

I also adored movies and plays, but my panic attacks eventually stopped me from going to theaters. One of the last films I went to see before that time was *Who's Afraid of Virginia Woolf?*, the adaptation of Edward Albee's drama. The movie was considered so "adult" that even in those pre-rating days Dad needed to accompany me to the Canarsie Theater.

Housebound by agoraphobia, I was forced to get my dose of dramatic narrative from TV. Starting in junior high, I got caught up in the convoluted plots of soap operas, which have remained a guilty pleasure. I have watched some daytime dramas for over thirty years, and as a teenager I developed the theory that these slow-moving shows were the form of narrative that most closely resembled real life—except, perhaps, for the diary.

My panic attacks reached a crescendo in February 1969, and Mom insisted that my psychiatrist prescribe some medication. Although at the time it seemed a coincidence, Triavil—a combination of a tricyclic antidepressant and a tranquilizer—slowly helped relieve the anxiety. As spring approached, I started going out little by little. I still had panic attacks, but every day I would force myself to ride buses and then subways, seeing how far I could go before anxiety overwhelmed me. Eventually I could go all the way to Manhattan.

By summer, soon after my eighteenth birthday—when I had to register for the draft—I was well enough to start college. It was as if I had been re-hatched into a world that was new and exciting in the summer of Woodstock and the Stonewall riot.

Not only did I get an *A* in political science that summer, but I worked in New York Mayor John Lindsay's re-election campaign and in the Manhattan headquarters of the Vietnam War Moratorium Committee. I saw plays like *The Boys in the Band, The Indian Wants the Bronx,* and *The Toilet.* I went to movies like *Easy Rider, Alice's Restaurant,* and *Midnight Cowboy.* I discovered Greenwich Village and psychedelic music and love beads and incense. I read *Ramparts, The Village Voice,* and *The East Village Other.* My hair grew long and I hung out with hippies by the fountain in Washington Square Park. I got my driver's license and explored New York's art museums and parks. A twenty-three-year-old guy from the neighborhood fell in love with me. I wore fringed vests and tie-dyed shirts and a pair of bellbottom pants that my parents got for me on London's Carnaby Street. I was still something of a nervous wreck, but even that seemed normal and maybe something to be proud of in the summer of '69.

Of all the new things I did that summer, maybe the most important was to start a writing habit that would last a lifetime.

On Friday, August 8, 1969, I went with Jeanette, the eight-year-old daughter of our Haitian cleaning woman, Jusele Feron, to watch a young street theater group perform on the BC campus. As we walked back to Flatbush Avenue, I saw a red, book-like 1969 diary on sale at a college bookstore. Because the year was more than half over, it was cheap.

That evening, over a cup of tea, I wrote my first diary entry, and I also went back over the first seven days of August and wrote what had happened on those days and how I had felt about it. For over a third of a century, I've been writing daily diary entries in the same format. The diary company has changed hands several times, but the product is still basically the same one it was in 1969.

For me, what's neat about the diary is that I'm able to go back to any day and see what happened then and what I was feeling. Sometimes I use the diary to work out ideas for stories and article ideas, though I usually use notebooks, and more recently, computer files, for that purpose. In 1980, I experimented for a while writing my diary entries in the third person ("Grayson walked across Miami Gardens Drive to Grandma Sylvia's car; he loved being in Florida in January"), but mostly I've kept pretty much to the style (or lack thereof) I had in 1969. Although I wince at some of the observations of my eighteen-year-old or twenty-five-year-old or forty-two-year-old selves, the artless, spontaneous writing in the diaries has been an important part of my life. Currently I store the diaries—now totaling over six million words—in boxes in the walk-in closet in my parents' house in Arizona. I will eventually use them as reference material for a series of memoirs.

It took me a while to adjust to Brooklyn College, but by the end of my freshman year in the spring of 1970, I had gotten involved with student government and the newspaper. When the invasion of Cambodia and the killings of student protestors at Kent State University led to a nationwide student strike, we took over the BC campus, ending the semester prematurely and staging a series of teach-ins and "liberation classes" about the war in Southeast Asia, feminism, racism, and the capitalist system. Things petered out as summer approached and students fled to the beach and cheap trips to Europe. Of course, my phobias prevented me from taking my backpack across the Atlantic, so I stayed in summer school that year.

At BC I met many of the people who would become my lifelong friends. Although it was a commuter school with no dormitories, I spent most of the day hanging out in LaGuardia Hall with other students who were active in politics, journalism, and cultural affairs. For the first time since junior high school, I had peers with whom I shared nearly everything—from my panic attacks to my desire to be a writer, from tips on how to fail the draft physical (a letter from the psychiatrist did the trick for me) to the marijuana we passed around at gatherings like the Flat Earth Party, the Safari Awards, and the J. Edgar Hoover Death Celebration. (Alcohol was not a big part of our socializing, and I've always been a teetotaler.)

While I learned a lot and got good grades in my undergraduate classes, the more important discoveries I made involved my relationships with my fellow students and that my peculiarities were welcome among a community for whom the word "freak" was a high compliment. Although I knew I was mostly attracted to other guys, I found myself in deep relationships with women—some as close friends, but others as girlfriends who didn't mind having a bisexual boyfriend as long as he was monogamous, which I was.

A breakup with a girlfriend at the beginning of my junior year put me into a funk—she left me for a friend she married a few months later (he, too, would later turn out to be gay)—but I eventually recovered from adolescent melancholy and began dating other people. In my senior year started seeing a girl I had been friends with for a while; we dated for two years before going back to being just friends.

Like many of the people I hung out with in LaGuardia Hall, Randy is still very much in my life—along with her husband and children. Luckily, my college friends have never given me too much flak for appropriating events in their lives for my fiction. To them, I was "Richie the writer" even before I'd published a single word.

When I was in high school, plays seemed easier to write than fiction because I didn't have to deal with long passages of description. My stories have never been heavy on description of people and places. Rarely do I say what my fictional characters look like. Except for some stage directions, plays were pure dialogue and easier for me to write.

Most of my teenage plays were outright homages to Albee. A long one-act play I wrote at fifteen, *Have You Seen Grandma Since She Got Rich?,* featured a vulgar old lady—nothing like my beloved but prudish Grandma Sylvia and Grandma Ethel—and her teen-aged granddaughter and grandson, the latter a vaguely effeminate intellectual. As a college senior in 1973, I submitted the play to the Ottillie Grebanier Drama Award competition and won first prize and a $150 check. Jack Gelber, the playwright/professor who judged the contest, said I should think about getting the play workshopped somewhere, but I assumed he was only being polite, and somehow I ended up throwing out my only manuscript. Other plays I wrote as a teenager were based on my dreams or on exaggerations of my family life, with sons who were afraid to leave the bathroom or parents who installed velvet ropes so that no one could come in their living rooms.

By the time I got to college, I had pretty much abandoned writing plays for fiction. In my freshman and sophomore years, I wrote a series of representational short stories about an extended family in Brooklyn, which were mostly autobiographical and mostly awful. Only one story remains from that group: "Reflections on a Village Rosh Hashona 1969," an early version of which appeared in Brooklyn College's undergraduate literary magazine at the end of my freshman year. Later, I revised it, and after garnering twenty-four rejections, it appeared in the London-based *Transatlantic Review.* It was the only undergraduate story in which I managed to attain an anecdotal, conversational, rambling style that was not dead on the page.

When I took my first creative writing class in college, I was so nervous about the class's reaction to my work that I made sure I was absent on the day when the class was to go over my story. I later found out that the reactions had been generally positive, and my professor, Saul Galin, urged me to continue with creative writing courses.

Although I remained a political science major, I was soon taking more literature and writing courses. My fiction writing class with Jonathan Baumbach introduced me to the wonderful stories of Donald Barthelme and the start of my leanings toward "experimental" fiction. I discarded vague plans to attend law school and decided to apply for the first class of BC's new M.F.A. program in creative writing, to begin in September 1974.

I decided that in the year between my graduation with a B.A. in June 1973 and then, I needed to learn more about literature if I was going to be a writer. So I became a student in the M.A. program in English at Richmond College, a CUNY school then located in an office building near the ferry terminal in Staten Island. Given a new Mercury Comet for graduation, I learned to overcome my terror of driving over the monumental Verrazano-Narrows Bridge.

Richmond, now part of the College of Staten Island, was an innovative institution that didn't have letter grades—just Pass, Fail, or Honors. All my courses were in the late afternoons and evenings, and during the day I hung out in Brooklyn College's LaGuardia Hall, where my girlfriend was managing editor of the student newspaper and where my other undergraduate friends still congregated.

*Family portrait, 1974; clockwise, from left: Richard, father Daniel, brother Marc, brother Jonathan, mother Marilyn*

I owed this luxury of time to Dad, who was still paying my expenses. Although tuition for graduate school at CUNY was not free, my parents told me I didn't need to work.

My friend Jerry Weinberger and I were two of the seven students in the first fiction writing class of Brooklyn College's M.F.A. program, where Jonathan Baumbach and John Ashbery were the directors in fiction and poetry. The first stories I handed in for our workshop were fairly traditional, like the ones I'd written as an undergraduate, but as I became influenced by metafictionists like Borges, Barth, Barthelme, Hawkes, Cortazar, Coover, and Gass, my work began to loosen up, play with narrative, and comment on the process of writing fiction.

While our workshops and my tutorials with Baumbach that fall were interesting, what I loved most about the M.F.A. program was being in a community of fledgling writers, where students took their literary aspirations seriously.

I decided that to succeed as a short story writer, I would have to produce a story a week. Terribly lazy about editing—except in my head—I wrote most of my stories in one sitting, on the floor of my little bedroom, using the Smith-Corona electric typewriter I'd gotten in high school. I almost never rewrote my stories, even if I realized they didn't work; instead, I'd just incorporate the best elements into a new story.

I jumped at the opportunity when Baumbach asked me to work as an editorial assistant at the Fiction Collective, an authors' book publishing cooperative he had founded along with another of our M.F.A. professors, Peter Spielberg, and such experimental writers as Ronald Sukenick, Steve Katz, and Raymond Federman.

At the Fiction Collective I dealt with everything from handling queries from authors and writing catalog copy to planning publication parties and sending out review copies. Another aspect of my job was running the system that selected new books for publication. In order to be published, a manuscript had to get four "yes" votes from the various author-members. I sent the manuscripts out a maximum of seven times, and sometimes books were published that had gotten three "yes" votes and three "no" votes and got a final deciding "yes." I read all the manuscripts myself to find out what other writers were doing.

I was also the preliminary judge for the Fiction Collective's First Novel Contest. At the Manhattan office of our distributor, the publisher George Braziller, I found an office stacked top to bottom with over four hundred manuscripts. My task was to whittle them down to fifty for the three final judges. Most of the novels were so badly written that I could put them aside after the first few pages, but it took weeks to cull the manuscripts. A few were so atrocious that they were actually funny. Our ultimate winner turned out to be a woman who'd recently been released from a mental hospital.

In addition to working at the Collective that first year of the M.F.A. program, I also held a series of minimum-wage "real" jobs to help my parents defray expenses, as Dad could no longer afford to be as generous as he had been. The recession of 1974 had hit his business hard, and Art Pants ultimately couldn't survive in the face of cheap imports and the trend toward jeans and casual pants.

I found I didn't have the patience to stay in any of these jobs very long, but despite the bad economy, it was easy to find work for $2 an hour. I worked in the law library of the white-shoe Wall Street firm of Sullivan & Cromwell and in a Rockaway adult home for the mentally disturbed; sold pants (the same cheap double-knit polyester imports that were killing our family business) at Alexander's Department Store in Kings Plaza; was a deliveryman for Midtown Florist and Canarsie Laundry and a messenger for the display advertising department of the Village Voice; and I shelved books in the Flatbush branch of the Brooklyn Public Library.

In March 1975, I was working in the library when I got a phone call from Eric Spector, a friend from high school and college, who said his father wanted to speak to me. Dr. Spector, chairman of the English Department at Long Island University in downtown Brooklyn, explained that a professor had died a few nights earlier on his way home from an evening composition class. Knowing I had finished my coursework for my M.A. in English, Dr. Spector thought I might take over the professor's class and asked me to come in for an interview.

Wanting to make a good impression so I could get the job, I feverishly did everything I could to learn about teaching writing, from rereading Jonathan Baumbach's book *Writers as Teachers/Teachers as Writers* to consulting Susan Fromberg Schaeffer, the novelist and poet who was my M.F.A. adviser that term. But it turned out that I needn't have bothered: I already had the course. When I walked into the chairman's office at LIU, Dr. Spector said, "Mr. Grayson, your students are going to eat you alive!" That was my introduction to the main criteria for hiring adjunct instructors for freshman English: one needed a master's degree and a body temperature approaching 98.6 degrees.

My class met on Tuesdays and Thursdays after our afternoon fiction writing workshop at Brooklyn College. My students were all working adults older than I. At twenty-three, I still looked very young, but that might have been a plus: at the end of the semester, a student told me the class assumed I had to be brilliant to be a teenaged professor.

Like many college instructors, I had no training at all in teaching methods, and I was incredibly nervous the first few sessions. At first I sat behind the desk, needing a barrier between the class and myself. Gradually I started standing up in front of the desk and relied less on *The Harbrace Handbook* to rule my lesson plans. Over the next three years, working at LIU, as I learned to trust my instincts and that sometimes the best classes came out of spontaneous "teachable moments," I gradually gained confidence and began to enjoy teaching more than I'd ever thought possible.

That first semester of teaching I decided to keep my morning job at the library although it was jarring to be treated like a high school kid at one menial job and respected as a college professor at another. The dissonance finally became too much to bear one Saturday when one of my students came in to do a research paper I had assigned. A librarian ordered me over to fetch a book for my puzzled student. When I quit later that day, the head librarian said, "I guess you're leaving to take a job at the new McDonald's."

LIU never paid me more than $600 per course, and given preparation time, office hours, and time spent grading papers, I sometimes wondered if flipping burgers actually was a better deal than being an adjunct. I'm sure that even today, many part-time college teachers have the same thought.

In the spring of 1975, not only did I start teaching college English, but I also had my first story published in a literary magazine, *New Writers,* which featured work by students in graduate writing programs. For weeks, I walked around with the letter accepting "Rampant Burping," which said that the editors liked it "although it is a bit artsy-craftsy."

Most of my stories were from four to twelve pages. From *Writers Market* I learned the format for fiction manuscripts, and from *The International Directory of Little Magazines and Small Presses,* I gathered the names of places to send them to. Although most magazines said they did not accept simultaneous submissions, I figured the odds of two magazines accepting the same story were very slim. So, upon finishing a new story, I'd take it over to the Flatbush Copy Center near BC, and for a nickel a page, I'd make five copies, which I'd then send out in manila envelopes, including the all-important stamped, self-addressed envelope.

I often tried the *New Yorker* or the *Atlantic* or *Harper's* first, but except for an occasional handwritten comment on a rejection notice, I knew my chances of my getting noticed by the slick magazines were not good because of the number of submissions they received and the quirkiness and quality of my fiction. I have never fooled myself about my place in the literary food chain, and I knew I didn't match up to "real" writers like those published in the *New Yorker.*

My strategy, therefore, was based on quantity rather than quality. I'd read how William Saroyan once had written thirty stories in a month, sending each one of them out to a magazine. While I couldn't be that prolific, I tried my best. In the late 1970s there were numerous literary journals, thanks to generous government arts funding. Sometimes instead of just getting copies of the issue my story appeared in—the usual remuneration—I received checks of $25 or $50, because grants from the National Endowment of the Arts required payment to contributors.

I didn't distinguish between the more prestigious university-sponsored journals and the homemade little magazines of cranky or brilliant individual editor-publishers. I got tons of rejections—many form rejections, others cruel or condescending, some encouraging—sometimes as many as ten a day, but eventually there were a lot of acceptances, too.

So I published in places as relatively well-known as *Epoch, Shenandoah,* and *Texas Quarterly* and as obscure as *Nausea Review, Street Bagel,* and *Coffee Break.* I had stories in *Webster Review, Westbere Review,* and *Westerly Review*; *Canadian Jewish Dialog, Mississippi Mud,* and *Nantucket Review*; *Writ, Iron, Mati,* and *Ataraxia.*

By my second year of the M.F.A. program, I was no longer writing for my classmates. It took the sting out of negative criticism of my work when I could end the workshop by telling my classmates that the story they had just disparaged had already been accepted by *California Quarterly* or *Panache.*

Within a few years, I had published over one hundred stories in little magazines and caught the attention of people in the small press scene, which in the 1970s was largely a counterculture movement whose Woodstock was the annual New York Book Fair, held in places like the old Customs House downtown, the Huntington Hartford building on Columbus Circle, the

basement of Lincoln Center, and the Seventh Regiment Armory on Park Avenue. I loved these events, as I got to meet the poets and fiction writers and editors with whom I'd corresponded or whose works I'd found in the same journals I had been published in.

Year-round there were good places in New York to find little magazines and small press books, giving me an advantage over fledgling writers in other parts of the country. I would often prowl the shelves of Frances Steloff's Gotham Book Mart on West 47th Street, on a block otherwise filled with diamond merchants; E.S. Wilentz's Eighth Street Bookshop, owned by the father of a Midwood classmate; and the free library in the offices of the Coordinating Council of Literary Magazines, where I worked in the summer of 1976 as the preliminary judge of their college literary magazine awards.

Publishing in obscure magazines gave me a sense of freedom. I didn't really think anyone would actually read my work, so I could make embarrassing revelations about myself or avoid changing the names of my friends and family. I could take my stories in crazy directions, like admitting at the end of one that the story was falling apart and asking the editor to take pity on me and publish it anyway. The playfulness and vitality in my naïve early work would become hard to replicate once I began thinking of myself as an "author."

Although I'd driven to Miami Beach with friends for the 1972 Democratic convention and to a Washington, D.C., vacation with Randy, I still had fears of traveling and rarely left the New York metropolitan area. But in 1977 I got a National Arts Club scholarship to the Bread Loaf Writers Conference in Middlebury, Vermont. A year out of the M.F.A. program, I sort of missed writing workshops, and I was looking forward to attending classes with famous authors like led by John Gardner and Stanley Elkin.

However, I got off to a bad start when, following Elkin's lecture on the craft of fiction, I piped up from the audience of a hundred novice writers to ask, "Mr. Elkin, does a story need a beginning, a middle and an end, and if so, should they be in that order?"

"That's the stupidest question I've ever gotten in all my years of teaching writing," Elkin replied, and the crowd snickered.

*Photo rejected for back cover of* With Hitler in New York, *because "I looked too young"*

Given the fiction I'd been writing, the question had seemed eminently reasonable to me.

While I thrilled to hear John Irving and Toni Morrison read from the novels-in-progress that would eventually become two of my favorite books, *The World according to Garp* and *Song of Solomon,* I was too socially inept to make any connections with the established writers at Bread Loaf.

I felt more comfortable with my peers in the small press world. In the summer of 1978, George Myers, Jr., who had published one of my pieces in his *X: A Journal of the Arts,* wanted to use some grant money to do a special issue of his magazine devoted to my work. The magazine—six stories I called *Disjointed Fictions*—was rather raggedy-looking, but I was still proud of it. A few years later, George reprinted the issue as a chapbook with a more professional-looking typeface and format.

As I was typing up *Disjointed Fictions,* I got a letter from Louis Strick, the president of Taplinger, a commercial publisher in Manhattan. He had read one of my stories in *Epoch* and asked if I had a book manuscript. I wrote back that I assumed he was interested only in a novel and that unfortunately, I wasn't a novelist—but that I did have about 150 stories of varying quality.

Mr. Strick replied to what he called my "diffident" letter—I had to explain to my parents what "diffident" meant—by asking to see a manuscript. I then sent him all the stories I'd ever published: photocopied pages from the magazines, in different typefaces, plus the typed manuscripts of the stories I hadn't yet placed. Not discouraged with this unprofessional-looking mass, Mr. Strick told me he'd turn it all over to his son, Wesley, who had just graduated NYU's publishing program and was joining the firm as an editor.

Wesley Strick called in September and asked to meet me. By then I'd left LIU to teach remedial writing at CUNY schools. On Rosh Hashona, as I climbed the stairs to Wes's Upper East Side apartment, I had the irrational thought, "This could be a trap." At a nearby restaurant, Wes showed me a paper containing title *With Hitler in New York and Other Stories* and the table of contents for the stories he'd selected for the book. I was flabbergasted.

When our waiter came to take our order, I recognized him as a former P.S. 203 classmate. After telling him who I was, I introduced Wes as "my editor." I felt foolish, but saying it made it sound slightly more real to me.

Over the next month or so, Wes and I worked on the manuscript sentence by sentence. One disadvantage of publishing in little magazines was that the editors almost always took the stories as I'd written them. No one before Wes had pointed out the problems in my published fiction, like the way I often didn't know how to end a story. During the editing and book production process, afraid of disappointment, I wouldn't let myself believe it was really happening—despite evidence such as the whimsical cover designed by Wes's sister Ivy, the promotional copy in Taplinger's spring catalog, and the payment of my $500 advance in two installments.

One May afternoon, after I'd given my spring remedial writing course at Brooklyn College its final exam, Wes called to say that the book was in. I zoomed into Manhattan. Upon seeing a copy of *Hitler,* I blurted out, "It looks like a real book."

"We've cleverly disguised it," Wes told me.

The back cover was blank, because other Taplinger editors thought my photograph made me look too babyish—a drawback at a time when publishers rarely emphasized the youth of their new authors. Wes gave me the six author's copies specified in my contract, and in my room that night, I put them on my shelves among books by what I still thought of as "real" authors.

On June 15, I went to the beach in Rockaway with some lesbian friends. "Today's the book's official publication date," I told them. "Don't you think something should be happening to me today?"

"It is," one friend said. "You're getting sunburned."

When *Hitler* came out in 1979, publishers brought out only one-third the number of books published today. *The New York Times* then published a listing of "Recently Published Books,"—which now seems as musty a relic as its daily listing of ocean liners' arrivals and departures. (I've been a *New York Times* reader ever since ninth grade, when our English teacher, Mrs. Sanjour, regularly quizzed us on the Sunday paper's contents.) The listing was the only mention my book got in the *Times,* but—shy only in person and not in letters—I pestered gossip columnists and book editors at other papers to mention or review *Hitler.* Taplinger was not a major publisher, and I wanted to make sure my book got noticed.

Late one night, my friend Stephen LiMandri, who ran the newsstand at the Abbey-Victoria Hotel, called to tell me I was in Liz Smith's column in the next day's *Daily News.* Liz Smith called my book "really funny" and compared me to Steve Martin. Quoting my letter, she said she couldn't resist an author who said he lived with in Brooklyn with his family, "poor but honest and gossip-loving people." Unfortunately, the plug didn't help sales, as *Hitler* was not yet in any stores.

When my book finally arrived in the Waldenbooks in Kings Plaza, my parents kept going into the store and buying copies, believing it would somehow stimulate demand.

Following a series of business reverses—the demise of Art Pants Company and The Pants Set stores, bad investments in a racehorse that constantly needed surgery and a Catskills hotel my parents had to sell for a dollar to the Mafia (who made them an offer they couldn't refuse)—Dad was hired as the Florida sales

rep for a clothing company owned by the father of one of my friends. Grandma Sylvia and Grandpa Nat had moved to their South Florida condo several years before, and in 1979 my parents decided to sell our Brooklyn house and buy a townhouse in Davie, a Fort Lauderdale suburb.

I had to figure out what to do with my life, as my prolonged adolescence seemed over. I applied for full-time positions as an English professor, but the only job offer I got was for a one-semester gig as a visiting writer-in-residence at Texas Women's University. I probably should have taken it, but I was too scared to go off by myself to Denton, Texas, even for six months.

I decided to stay in New York City, where part-time teaching jobs were plentiful. In the fall of 1979, I found a studio for $240 a month right on the boardwalk in Rockaway. It was far from Manhattan—where I'd be working at the School of Visual Arts—but it was in familiar territory, with Grandpa Herb and Grandma Ethel less than a mile away. My brother Marc rented a basement in Brooklyn, near Kingsborough Community College, where I was also teaching. Jonathan, who had just graduated from high school, went to Florida with our parents to start Broward Community College.

Although I was twenty-eight years old, in many ways I was still a boy, and it was hard for me to live on my own that fall. After spending my Christmas vacation at my parents' new townhouse in Davie, I returned to the cold winter of New York and developed labyrinthitis, an ear infection, which left me with severe vertigo for months. Expected courses hadn't materialized for the spring term, and I was teaching only one course each for the School of Visual Arts and for Touro College, where my paychecks bounced. Money was scarce, and as the summer of 1980 approached, I was dizzy, depressed, unemployed, on food stamps, and unable to write.

A welcome respite was a residency for June at the MacDowell Colony in Peterborough, New Hampshire. My studio in the woods was the same one where Thornton Wilder had composed *Our Town.* After a rocky start in which I could not write at all the first week—and gnashed my teeth so much that I had to see a local dentist—I dreamed an eighteen-page story which later won a magazine contest and then produced a story a day for the next seven days. I also had the stimulating company of other writers, as well as composers, painters, sculptors and filmmakers. Mac-Dowell made me feel like a creative artist and not a poverty-stricken nobody. Future residencies at Mac-Dowell and other artists' colonies continued to have that nurturing effect.

But the rest of the summer of 1980 was difficult, and in the fall, to aid my finances, I took on as many adjunct courses—all in remedial writing—as I could. On Thursdays, for example, I would leave my apartment in Rockaway at 7 a.m., drive over the bridge to teach an 8 a.m. class at Brooklyn College, take the subway to teach two classes at John Jay College of Criminal Justice in Manhattan, return to BC to teach a class in the early evening, and then drive to a Brooklyn high school to teach a continuing education course for Kingsborough, getting home after 11 p.m. By then I was used to the low level of my students' writing— that term I had to explain the difference between *a, an,* and *and*—but I was constantly grading papers and did not have time to write.

By then *With Hitler in New York* was long out of the stores, and Wes was leaving his father's publishing company to work on his own career as a writer. (He would eventually have great success in Los Angeles as the screenwriter of such movies as *Cape Fear, Arachnophobia,* and *Return to Paradise.*) On one of his last days on the job, Wes told me that Taplinger's scheduled trade paperback edition of *Hitler* had been canceled. That was the day I decided to leave New York and move to Florida once the hectic fall semester was over. I needed a change and I missed my family.

In January 1981, my friend Nina Mule threw me a surprise farewell party in her Manhattan apartment. I handed in my final grades, put my furniture on a truck headed for Florida, and left Rockaway to join my parents in the Fort Lauderdale suburbs.

I'd always hated the cold and snow of winters, so I was thrilled to be in South Florida. My room at my parents' house had a screened-in terrace overlooking a brace of palm trees. Davie was then more rural than suburban, an old cowboy town filled with rednecks and horse farms. Jewish senior citizens and snowbirds dominated neighboring towns.

I somehow walked into a job teaching composition at Broward Community College, taking over a class a few weeks after the semester began. The pay was minimal, but so were my expenses. I still enjoyed teaching, but now I also had time to work on the collection of stories that Kevin Urick—another writer/editor who'd published my fiction in his literary magazine—was considering for his White Ewe Press.

Florida was glorious in the winter, but the heat and humidity were less attractive by May, when the term at BCC ended. I returned to New York and spent two months at Marc's apartment in Brooklyn and Nina's on the Upper West Side before a July residency at the Virginia Center for the Creative Arts.

I'd been applying to universities for creative writing jobs, but the only job offer I had for the fall was as my friend Tom Whalen's half-time assistant at New Orleans' arts high school, NOCCA, where I'd guest-taught in his rigorous creative writing program. In early August, I returned to Florida, uneasy about my prospects.

A few days after my arrival at my parents' house, I was reading *The Miami Herald* at breakfast and spotted a news item announcing state arts council fellowship winners. When I saw "Richard Grayson, Davie, $3,000," I started jumping around and yelling so much, Mom thought I was having some kind of attack. I had forgotten I'd applied for the Florida fellowship, assuming I'd have no more success than I had in my many grant applications in New York State.

I would have to remain in the state to accept the fellowship money, but giving up the part-time job in New Orleans was no problem. After reading a newspaper interview with me about my grant, the BCC English Department head offered me a one-year position as a full-time instructor. With the fellowship and my $13,000 teaching salary, I could afford to get my own place, a rented condo among elderly neighbors in Sunrise Golf Village.

I stayed on at Broward Community College for three annual temporary contracts. As an English instructor, I taught twelve classes a year, almost all of freshman composition or remedial writing, with nearly thirty students in each class. I sometimes felt as if I was constantly grading essays. I loved the classroom, but marking papers infringed on much of my free time.

Because I still thought of myself as a writer, I chose not to apply for BCC's permanent full-time English Department positions. I lived one year at a time, with

*At a publication party for* I Brake for Delmore Schwartz *at B. Dalton Bookstore in Greenwich Village, March 22, 1983*

at least part of the summer off, to spend in New York or at artists' colonies. The early 1980s were a fairly stable period in my life, but the deaths of Grandma Sylvia and Grandpa Herb made me realize that I needed to stop thinking of myself as a kid.

In 1982 White Ewe Press brought out my second hardcover collection, *Lincoln's Doctor's Dog.* Later that year, Jerry Weinberger's Grinning Idiot Press published my satiric chapbook, *Eating at Arby's: The South Florida Stories.* I provoked some outrage by using my fellowship money to fund these banal vignettes critical of South Florida told in the style of a first-grade primer. Generally, however, local readers got the joke, and the book sold out after I appeared on Neil Rogers's popular radio show.

The next year, Zephyr Press—run by my friends Ed Hogan and Miriam Sagan from the Boston literary magazine *Aspect*—published *I Brake for Delmore Schwartz.* I flew to New York in March 1983, staying in Rockaway with Grandma Ethel, for my first publication party and reading at the B. Dalton store in the Village. Seeing a whole window display dedicated to my book and having Dad and so many friends from all different parts of my life at the party made me feel blessed.

In New York in the late 1970s, I had started doing what I called "publicity art" by sending out press releases commenting on issues in the news. In 1979, I filed with the Federal Elections Commission to run for

vice president of the United States, a stunt that got me into the *New York Times* and the *National Enquirer.* NBC president Fred Silverman and Gloria Vanderbilt tried to sue me when I formed political committees touting them as candidates for, respectively, the presidency and the United State Senate.

Other publicity stunts followed. When New York Mayor Ed Koch prevailed on the city's public radio station to air "The John Hour," in which men arrested for soliciting prostitutes would have their names read over the air, the *New York Post* printed the story of how I wanted my name read on the show despite not having been arrested "because I deserve to be publicly humiliated." In another self-manufactured scandal, the *Post* supposedly exposed me as a "literary imposter" trying to publish a defamatory article about respected authors called "The Weird Sex Lives of Jewish-American Novelists." The *Post*'s Page Six gossip column soon began referring to me as "playful prankster Richard Grayson."

While my grandparents were still alive, I formed "international" fan clubs for them and sent out press releases that resulted in media attention. Grandpa Herb and Grandma Ethel told their life stories on Barry Farber's nationally syndicated radio program. The *Miami News* published a story on the Sylvia Ginsberg International Fan Club on its front page while the *Miami Herald* printed a photo of me kissing Grandma Sylvia—who hated to be kissed, believing it spread germs.

Campaigning for the Davie Town Council in 1982, I advocated giving horses the right to vote. My platform consisted mainly of bad puns, like pledging to vote "neigh" on everything till horse suffrage was passed, offering the town a "more stable" form of government, and in the end forgoing campaign speeches because I had "become a little hoarse myself." I got 26% of the vote as the media routinely covered my antics.

In 1983, I registered as a presidential candidate, and articles about me appeared in dozens of periodicals, from *People* and *USA Today* to *Time* and *The Wall Street Journal.* I churned out one press release after another: starting the Committee for Immediate Nuclear War (which for years was listed in the reference book the *Encyclopedia of Associations*); advocating that the U.S. capital move to Davenport, Iowa; supporting the admission of El Salvador as the 51st state; proposing a Devil Broadcasting Network to compete with religious TV stations. On the Florida primary ballot as a candidate for delegate to the Democratic convention (supporting myself), I received over 2,000 votes—but Mom, whose name I had put on the ballot as a candidate for alternate delegate, got twice as many votes as I did.

As the decade wore on, my publicity stunts dealt more and more with the economy. In 1988, I panhandled in front of the New York Stock Exchange, begging for $27.5 billion dollars so I could launch a hostile takeover bid for RJR Nabisco; *Business Week* called my stunt "social commentary on Wall Street." Two years later, I appeared on CNN and in the *New York Times,* touting my *Pauper Magazine,* the poor man's answer to all the "lifestyles of the rich and famous" publications. I also got media exposure as the head of the Donald Trump Rescue Fund, formed to help out the real estate magnate during his time of financial difficulty.

A prank in the spring of 1984—a letter I'd written to Florida state senators on Broward Community College stationery asking for their participation in an academic study I called "Legislators in Love"—led to political outrage, threatened cuts to BCC's budget, and a banner headline in the *Orlando Sentinel* ("Prof's Love Quiz Stirs Only a What's That?!"). Knowing I wouldn't be asked back to teach at BCC in the fall, I gave up my apartment in North Miami Beach at the end of May, put my stuff in storage, and went to Manhattan to apartment-sit for Nina for six weeks while she toured Europe.

Those six weeks turned into six years, as 350 West 85th Street became my part-time address for the rest of the decade. The Upper West Side in the 1980s was an exciting place, and Nina was an incredibly generous host and roommate. Since she spent most of the summer at her beach house in Fire Island, I had the apartment to myself much of the time. When she was home, I slept on the living room couch or a futon on the floor.

Congenitally lazy, I spent the rest of my thirties like the retired South Florida snowbirds who came to Fort Lauderdale to escape the Northern winters but who returned to New York when the summer heat and humidity started to get uncomfortable.

I survived financially by relying on income from adjunct courses, student loans, unemployment insurance, state arts council awards from Florida and New York, and credit card cash advances. At one time I had over forty MasterCards and Visas; I wrote articles about this ("You've Got to Give Me Credit" and "Guess How I Got Rich Without Working") for national magazines under the pen name Gary Richardson.

I had my New York City life and my South Florida life. I taught English courses part-time in both places, more because I enjoyed teaching writing than because of the still-pitiful adjunct pay. I even went back to BCC in 1987, teaching in the evenings and later as an occasional full-time substitute instructor for professors on sabbatical.

My first stint at BCC had given me the opportunity to learn how to use personal computers. As my interest in using computers in education grew, I started taking graduate courses in the subject. From 1984 to 1990, I earned over fifty graduate credits in educational technology from Teachers College at Columbia University and two Florida universities.

This interest led to a part-time job as a facilitator of teacher training workshops in computer education in the Miami public school district. I traveled to schools in Little Havana, Miami Beach, Coral Gables, and Liberty City to instruct teachers on the use of the Apple IIe and the IBM PC computers. I taught word processing, spreadsheets, databases, and educational software as well as programming in the Basic and Logo computer languages.

It was a thrill to empower computer-shy teachers who started off worried they would break the machines by turning them on. These workshops didn't require me to mark papers or give final grades, so I had the pleasure of teaching without the drudgery.

I took less pleasure in writing fiction. It seemed easier and more rewarding to write a satirical *People* article on an alleged celebrity shortage or my humor column for the *Hollywood Sun-Tattler.* Still, I managed to produce occasional stories when I felt I had something to say. For a computers and writing course at Teachers College, I wrote a long story about an AIDS death, "I

Survived Caracas Traffic," which appeared in the *Florida Review* and helped get me a second individual artist fellowship from the state of Florida in 1988.

That same year I scored a Writer-in-Residence Award from the New York State Council on the Arts. Working for the Rockland Center for the Arts, I went into schools in suburban Rockland County and experienced the joy of teaching children. My second-graders produced delightful, cleverly naïve stories that we collected into a book.

The late 1980s were fun-filled years. My father was doing well as a salesman for such designer labels of men's clothing as Sasson, Bugle Boy, and Guess. Mom and Dad bought a large four-bedroom house. They also followed my brother Jonathan's lead and became strict vegetarians and animal rights enthusiasts who gradually acquired a dog, three cats, and two rabbits. When I was in New York, I made regular visits to Rockaway to spend weekends with Grandma Ethel, and I was an unofficial member of Nina's close Italian family and got to share in their celebrations of holidays, birthdays, and anniversaries.

But these fun years were coming to an end. I realized that my credit card chassis—paying off one card with a cash advance from another—would ultimately end and I'd have to declare bankruptcy during the next recession. I assumed—correctly, as it turned out—that I could do so in a time when so many others were going broke that my filing would hardly be noticed. Nina had decided to give up her Manhattan apartment and move to Long Island. Grandma Ethel also was moving to Long Island, into an adult home in the Five Towns where she lived out her life happily, her lifelong depression successfully treated with medication. Watching Grandma Ethel establish new friendships after age eighty convinced me that it's never too late to make a new life.

In the fall of 1990, I moved in with my parents again and declared bankruptcy. My computer training jobs had dried up, but I got a full-time position back at BCC, taking over for a professor on sick leave. I attended a series of Fort Lauderdale obscenity trials involving the rap group 2 Live Crew, an experience that led to an article in *New York Newsday,* kindled an interest in hip-hop culture, and revived an ambition I had put aside years before: attending law school.

In April 1991, while I was on my first trip to California, visiting friends and teaching at a Long Beach State writers' conference coordinated by Linda Konner, Dad called with the news that the University of Florida law school had accepted me. Luckily, I managed to get a scholarship that would help defray expenses.

I spent one last summer in New York. Grandma Ethel had held on to her subsidized apartment in Rockaway, and I lived there for several months, visiting her at the adult home and taking the long subway ride into Manhattan to visit friends. I was very nervous about moving to Gainesville in North Central Florida, but every change in my life—even short trips—had engendered anxiety.

At dinner at a sidewalk café in the Village, I told Linda I had no intention of ever practicing law.

"Then why are you going to law school?" she asked me

"To have fun," I replied.

Linda looked dubious, and frankly, I shared her skepticism. But I figured I would try one semester of law school and leave if I didn't like it.

Law school turned out to be more fun than I could have imagined, and somehow I easily adjusted to life on my own in a classic college town. The life of a new law student is so hectic, I had no time to think about being away from my friends or family or have regrets about not being a writer anymore.

Law school courses were harder than any I'd ever taken—often I had trouble keeping up with class discussions—yet they provided incredible intellectual stimulation. I also liked being in a community of students again.

After the first semester, returning from a three-week Christmas vacation in New York, I discovered that my grades were good. I won book awards, prizes for the highest grade on a final exam, in criminal law and jurisprudence.

While I loved law in a theoretical, intellectual sense, this didn't mean I wanted to practice law. I didn't want to dress up in a suit and tie, putting in long hours doing what seemed like drudgery. In spite of myself, I still longed for the life of a writer.

Near the end of my first year in law school, in response to a call for stories about Barbie for an anthology edited by my friends Rick Peabody and Lucinda Ebersole, I produced "Twelve Step Barbie," the first fiction I'd written in two years. When *Mondo Barbie* received enthusiastic reviews, some of which singled out my story, I realized I could still be a writer—sort of.

In my second year of law school, I began teaching courses in writing and literature for Nova Southeastern University and Santa Fe Community College. It was good to get on the other side of a classroom again. My law school grades continued to put me near the top of my class, but I made no attempt to interview for any legal jobs. Never one to give much thought to the future, I concentrated on enjoying my law school classes, my teaching, and my writing and new publicity projects.

Several newspapers covered my plan, proposed before the state reapportionment commission, to draw legislative districts in the shape of an alligator, a palm tree, and Mickey Mouse. I also wrote a couple of new stories, contributed op-ed pieces to the *Gainesville Sun,* and wrote about the "Legislators in Love" scandal for the *Miami Herald*'s Sunday magazine section.

In May 1994, I graduated with high honors from UF law school, but I merely continued teaching my adjunct courses for NSU and SFCC. Although I'd moved to increasingly smaller, cheaper apartments during my three years in Gainesville, money was still tight.

Luckily, in October 1994, I got a position at the Center for Governmental Responsibility, the think tank at UF law school headed by one-time Florida House Speaker Jon Mills. Hired as a staff attorney in the Center's social policy division, I had a grant-funded position as a consultant on legal issues in educational technology to Schoolyear 2000, a program of the state Department of Education. It seemed like an ideal way to combine my interests in the law and computer education.

Although this was my first full-time office job, the atmosphere at CGR was informal and friendly, and I worked with people dedicated to public policy research on the environment, health care, and other important issues. I enjoyed churning out memoranda on education law and computer law, and I also branched out to work on fields like historic preservation, genome sciences, and water management. We got many requests from the local media, and since I was a whiz at doing research, I became a short-notice expert on a variety of subjects. Often quoted in newspapers and a guest on radio and television, I became an "authority" on affirmative action, the legalization of marijuana, Presidential disability, anti-tobacco legislation, and the rising influence of Hispanic voters.

Since part of my job was covering the new Republican majority in the state legislature, I found myself opposing many of their conservative initiatives, such as mandatory drug testing for public school students, forbidding gay student groups at state universities, making welfare recipients refund any state lottery winnings, bringing back prison chain gangs, and making it harder for people to declare bankruptcy—and I was not shy about expressing my opinions in the op-ed pages of Florida newspapers.

My work at CGR did not stop me from engaging in my other interests. Excited about the possibilities of the Internet, I got a part-time gig writing weekly humor columns for *New Jersey Online,* the website of several Garden State newspapers. I also returned to teaching NSU classes on weekends and evenings. Because of my varied background, I was able to teach numerous subjects; I'd be the business law or public policy professor one night and then return on Saturday to teach the very same students American literature or essay writing.

In the 1994 election, I ran as the only opponent to Congressman Mike Bilirakis in a write-in campaign. I called my political action committee God Hates Republicans. Although endorsed by the National Organization for Women and an African-American newspaper, I received less than two hundred votes.

Meanwhile, religious right activists in Gainesville had placed a referendum on the ballot to repeal the county's gay rights law. Their TV commercials presented vicious stereotypes and lies about gay and lesbian people. I felt I couldn't ignore this, so I became a volunteer in the "No on 1" campaign.

After our election defeat, I was asked to be a board member of the local gay rights group, the Human Rights Council of North Central Florida. Once I was surprised to see myself on the 11 p.m. news with the label "Gay Activist" under my name. We were ultimately successful in getting a pro-gay rights majority elected to the Gainesville city commission.

As I abandoned some of my earlier experimental strategies, my short stories began to be more about gay relationships. In Gainesville, for the first time I had close friends who were African-American, Latino, Asian-American, and Arab-American, and my characters were no longer all white. My fiction also began to deal with food and diet—I had successfully lost nearly fifty pounds by completely changing my eating habits—and the new culture of the Internet. I started submitting my fiction to Web-based literary magazines, where I didn't have to deal with manuscript hard copies, postage, and envelopes, and where I could sometimes send a story on Tuesday and find it "in print" in a webzine a few days later.

I found a publisher for my next book of stories, *I Survived Caracas Traffic,* mostly pieces that had been published years before. Martin Hester, the founder of Avisson Press in Greensboro, North Carolina, had known my work from literary magazines. After thirteen years, it gave me a thrill to again publish a hardcover book, but even a fairly favorable review in the *New York Times Book Review* didn't sell many copies.

Always restless—if not anxious—I left Gainesville and my job at CGR in the spring of 1997, moving my raggedy furniture to my parents' garage in Fort Lauderdale while I spent a few years in flux. I taught some classes in creative writing and literature for NSU and other universities in South Florida. In 1998, Florida awarded me a third fellowship in fiction writing for $5,000. I wrote a monthly column for the *Boca Raton News,* and after countless attempts, finally managed to sell my first op-ed article to the *New York Times.*

Because I could leave most of my belongings with my parents, I was able to travel a good deal as my desire to live in different parts of the country trumped my fears. I spent long periods living with Nina and her husband in their home on Long Island and mooching off other friends and relatives in Brooklyn, Phoenix, Los Angeles, and Philadelphia. I also took advantage of residencies at artists' colonies in suburban Chicago,

in Silicon Valley outside San Jose, and on a cattle ranch in northeast Wyoming. At these places I managed to complete a new collection of gay-themed stories that would be collected in *The Silicon Valley Diet,* published by Los Angeles's Red Hen Press in the summer of 2000.

In the fall of 1999, I began a one-year visiting professorship teaching undergraduate legal studies at NSU's main campus in Davie. It was probably the happiest year of my teaching career, as I was able to teach courses like Constitutional History, Private Law and Modern American Thought, and Political and Civil Rights, as well a multicultural studies class in which I taught the fiction of Edwidge Danticat, Junot Diaz, Bharati Mukherjee, Gish Jen, and Sherman Alexie. I would have loved to apply for a permanent full-time position, but I didn't have the necessary Ph.D.

That same year, my parents and Jonathan left South Florida and moved to Arizona to join Marc, who had gone there two years earlier. The four of them bought a house in Apache Junction, at the eastern edge of the Phoenix metro area, right by the Superstition Mountains.

I was unsure what to do when my year as a visiting professor was up, so I relied on a formula that had worked for me in the past: return to school and follow my family. After a summer with friends in the suburbs of New York and Los Angeles, I found an apartment in Mesa, about twenty miles from my family's house and an equal distance away from my old college friend Satnam Khalsa in Phoenix. My plan was to get yet another graduate degree, this time at the Walter Cronkite School of Journalism at Arizona State University. I'd also be teaching two sections of composition at ASU and one at Mesa Community College, up the street from my apartment.

But adjustment to a new life in the desert was difficult, and I soon found myself waking up at 2 a.m. with uncontrollable worries. I had severe insomnia, trembling, sweaty palms, agitation, and other symptoms. Except for a course in Arizona Media Law, I didn't enjoy my graduate classes, and while I still liked teaching, I felt faceless on the vast ASU campus. Working as just another drudge teaching composition—a job also performed by twenty-two-year-old teaching assistants just starting graduate school—I was isolated in an English Department that housed a respected program in creative writing that I could not be part of. Although *The Silicon Valley Diet* had gotten the best reviews of any of my books, it didn't achieve my overblown hopes that it would be a breakthrough for me.

Diagnosed with generalized anxiety disorder and "adjustment disorder," I entered therapy again and was treated with a variety of drugs that didn't seem to help. Being mugged and beaten outside my apartment one night exacerbated my anxiety. At times I felt quite desperate and began to experience panic attacks like the ones I had as a teenager. Finally, I stabilized with the help of one medication that worked—the Triavil that was first prescribed for me in 1969. I realized that at fifty, I was too old to be a student again and was not cut out to be a journalist.

When the academic year in Arizona ended in May 2001, I put my things in storage and traveled for six months, hoping to heal. I went to the artists' colonies of Ragdale in Lake Forest, Illinois, and Dairy Hollow in Eureka Springs, Arkansas, where I met the young novelist Brian Pera, who cheered me by telling me how important my books had been to him. I also stayed with my parents and brothers in Apache Junction and with Aunt Violet Anenberg in Miami. Old friends—the Sawyers in Los Angeles, the Cirellis on Long Island, the Tunkels in Philadelphia—allowed me to be part of their families for unconscionably long periods of time. I am nobody's father or uncle, but I have been lucky enough to share good times with my friends' children. I've always been crazy about kids.

Unable to get a full-time job teaching college English—I feared I was too old to be hired as a full-time instructor—I got lucky and in December 2001 landed a position as director of the academic resources program at Nova Southeastern University's law school. I supervise teaching assistants who help law students navigate the difficulties of first-year courses; conduct workshops on such skills as briefing cases, taking notes, and writing essay exams; help prepare graduates for the bar exam; and tutor and counsel students having academic difficulties.

I am back in the land of almost-perpetual summer, South Florida, living in a rental complex where I had four previous apartments during my nomadic 1980s

*With a friend's baby, Arizona, 2000*

and 1990s. I live just across the street from where my parents owned their townhouse, and within walking distance of the NSU and BCC campuses. In this quasi-urban sprawl, I feel like an old-timer who remembers the town of Davie's rural past.

The adjustment to a new life in the law school environment caused me renewed problems with anxiety, but time, therapy, and medication have all helped. So has the ritual I began 'as a boy in Brooklyn at eighteen: confiding in my diary every night.

A good sign is that I have begun to write fiction again. Although I have accepted the fact that my talents are modest, I'm proud that I haven't given up writing despite the many real, imagined, and self-inflicted obstacles in my path. I've traveled further than an agoraphobic has a right to expect.

Somehow I managed to publish books in the 1970s, 1980s, 1990s, and 2000s. My goal is to publish another book—even if it's not a literary masterpiece—in a fifth decade, the 2010s.

Inshallah and in spite of myself, I may do just that.

*BIOGRAPHICAL AND CRITICAL SOURCES:*

*BOOKS*

*Contemporary Literary Criticism,* Volume 38, Gale (Detroit, MI), 1986.

*PERIODICALS*

*Aspect,* number 72/73, 1979.

*Athens Daily News,* July 18, 1983.

*Best Sellers,* May, 1982.

*Des Moines Register,* October 21, 1983.

*Israel Today,* May 8, 1983.

*Kings Courier,* August, 1978.

*Library Journal,* April 15, 1983, review of *I Break for Delmore Schwartz,* p. 839.

*Los Angeles Times,* July 17, 1979.

*Miami News,* April 13, 1984.

*New York Times Book Review,* August 14, 1983; March 17, 1996, Sally Eckhoff, review of *I Survived Caracas Traffic: Stories from the Me Decades,* p. 20.

*Orlando Sentinel,* April 18, 1982; January 14, 1984.

*Publishers Weekly,* April 9, 1982, Barbara A. Bannon, review of *Lincoln's Doctor's Dog and Other Stories,* p. 42; March 4, 1983, review of *I Break for Delmore Schwartz,* p. 95; January 8, 1996, review of *I Survived Caracas Traffic,* p. 60; May 15, 2000, review of *The Silicon Valley Diet,* p. 91.

*Ventura County News,* February 4, 1980.

## GREEN, K. Gordon 1934-

*PERSONAL:* Born October 27, 1934, in London, England; son of Kenneth (a portrait painter) and Miriam (an actress; maiden name, Lehmann-Haupt) Green; married Diana B. Douglas, July 7, 1962; children: Douglas M., Andy Blair. *Education:* University of British Columbia, B.S.F., 1961; Harvard University, M.B.A., 1967. *Politics:* Conservative. *Religion:* Anglican. *Hobbies and other interests:* Music (opera), gardening, fishing, boating, wind surfing.

*ADDRESSES: Home*—895 Towner Park Rd., Sidney, British Columbia, Canada V8L 5L6; fax: 250-656-9961. *E-mail*—ravengreen2@shaw.ca.

*CAREER:* Nesbitt Thomson Securities, Inc., Toronto, Ontario, Canada, vice president, 1968-73; Morgan Stanley Canada Ltd., Montreal, Quebec, Canada, managing director, 1974-80; RBC Dominion Securities, Inc., Toronto, Ontario, Canada, vice president and director, 1980-93; writer. British Columbia Hydro, member of board of directors and chair of finance committee; Ainsworth Lumber Co. Ltd., member of board of directors. Pacific Opera, member of board of directors and past president; Canadian Stage Company, member of board of directors.

*WRITINGS:*

*The Raven and I* (humor), General Store Publishing House (Burnstown, Ontario, Canada), 1999.

*WORK IN PROGRESS: Of Moose and Men,* a work of humor.

# H

## HABER, Barbara (Lubotsky) 1934-

*PERSONAL:* Born April 1, 1934, in Milwaukee, WI; daughter of John and Belle (Goldberg) Lubotsky; married Herbert Robert Haber (a professor), August 24, 1959; children: Jonathan, Nicholas. *Education:* University of Wisconsin, B.S., 1955; University of Chicago, M.A., 1957; Simmons College, M.L.S., 1968; attended Boston College. *Politics:* Democrat. *Hobbies and other interests:* Culinary history.

*ADDRESSES: Home*—5 Woodside Road, Winchester, MA 01890. *Office*—Schlesinger Library, Radcliffe Institute for Advanced Study, 10 Garden Street, Cambridge, MA 02238. *E-mail*—b_haber@radcliffe. edu.

*CAREER:* Wayne State University, Detroit, MI, instructor, 1961-63; Highland Park Community College, Highland Park, MI, instructor, 1964-66; Schlesinger Library, Radcliffe Institute for Advanced Study, Cambridge, MA, curator of books, 1968—. Harvard Divinity School, women's studies in religion advisor committee member, 1981—; Business and Professional Women's Foundation, trustees committee member, 1982—.

*MEMBER:* Organization of American Historians, National Women's Studies Association, Culinary Historians, Women's Culinary Guild, 9 to 5.

*AWARDS, HONORS:* Fellow, Harvard University, 1975; Radcliffe Scholar, 1979; Harvard University grantee, 1979; named to Who's Who in American Food and Beverages, James Beard Foundation; M. F. K. Fisher Award, Les Dames d'Escoffier.

*WRITINGS:*

*Women in America: A Guide to Books, 1963-1975,* G. K. Hall (Boston, MA), 1978.
(Editor) *The Women's Annual, the Year in Review,* G. K. Hall (Boston, MA), 1981-1982.
(Editor) *The Women's Annual,* G. K. Hall (Boston, MA), 1983-1985.
*From Hardtack to Home Fries: An Uncommon History of American Cooks and Meals,* Free Press (New York, NY), 2002.

*SIDELIGHTS:* Barbara Haber is curator of books at the Schlesinger Library, a women's history research center, at Radcliffe College. Under Haber's care the Schlesinger library expanded from just 8,000 books in 1968 to over 60,000 books, including 14,000 cookbooks. With her special interest in culinary history and women's issues, according to *Ms.* contributor Christina Robb, Haber "may well know more than anyone else about American women in the twentieth century."

Haber's book, *Women in America: A Guide to Books, 1963-1975,* is a bibliography of 450 books published from 1963 to 1975, covering eighteen women's issues, including abortion, education, work, popular culture, and rape. Included are reviews by Haber of the top three books listed for each issue. *American Reference Books Annual* contributor Susan C. Holte commended the book as "An excellent reference work which reflects her knowledge of the literature on American women."

In *From Hardtack to Home Fries: An Uncommon History of American Cooks and Meals* Haber provides numerous stories on the history of American food and cooking from the 1840s to 2002. Stories include the diets of prisoners of war during World War II, the origination of the graham cracker, and why meals were so bad in Franklin Delano Roosevelt's White House. *Booklist* contributor Mark Knoblauch wrote, "Haber's wonderfully readable, intelligent, and eclectic history of cooking in America sheds new light on women's achievements and relates stories sure to delight."

## BIOGRAPHICAL AND CRITICAL SOURCES:

*PERIODICALS*

*American Reference Books Annual,* Volume 13, 1982, review of *Women in America: A Guide to Books, 1963-1975,* p. 389.

*Bon Appetit,* November, 2000, Rand Richards Cooper, "Hosts of Kitchens Past," p. 72.

*Booklist,* April 1, 2002, Mark Knoblauch, review of *From Hardtack to Home Fries: An Uncommon History of American Cooks and Meals,* p. 1286.

*Choice,* February, 1979, review of *Women in America,* p. 1642.

*Library Journal,* December 1, 1978, Esther Stineman, review of *Women in America,* p. 2405; December 1, 1981, Diane K. Harvey, review of *The Women's Annual, 1980: The Year in Review,* p. 2302; March 15, 2002, Mary Russell, review of *From Hardtack to Home Fries,* p. 102.

*Los Angeles Times,* May 8, 2002, Charles Perry, "History in the Kitchen: Tales of American Cooks," p. H8.

*Ms.,* September, 1982, Christina Robb, "Barbara Haber: Arbiter of Women's History," p. 10.

*Newsweek,* October 17, 1988, Katrine Ames, "The Scholar's Joy of Cooking," p. 82.

*Publishers Weekly,* March 25, 2002, review of *From Hardtack to Home Fries,* p. 57.

*Wilson Library Bulletin,* January, 1979, review of *Women in America,* p. 410.

*OTHER*

*Radcliffe Institute Web site,* http://www.radcliffe.edu/ (August 6, 2002), "Schlesinger Library: Overview of Collections."*

## HADOT, Pierre 1922-

*PERSONAL:* Born February 21, 1922, in Paris, France; son of Henri and Marianne (Meyer) Hadot; married Illsetraut Ludolff, August 3, 1966; children: Karla. *Education:* École Pratique des Hautes Études, diploma, 1962; Sorbonne University, Ph.D., 1968.

*ADDRESSES: Home*—2 rue Tolstoi, 91470 Limours France.

*CAREER:* Centre National de la Recherché Scientifique, Paris, France, researcher, 1949-64, 1970-74, decision committee in philosophy member, 1972—; École Pratique des Hautes Études, Paris, France, professor, 1964-84; Religions du Livre, research center director, 1972-84; College de France, Paris, France, professor, 1982-91, chairman of department of history of Hellenistic and Roman thought, 1983-1991, professor emeritus, 1991—.

*MEMBER:* Akademie der Wissenschaften und der Literatur, Mainz, Association des Etudes Grecques, Commission of Philology.

*AWARDS, HONORS:* Prix Saintour, Academy of Inscriptions and Beautiful Letters, 1969; silver medal, Centre National de la Recherché Scientifique, 1976; Money Medal, Centre National de la Recherché Scientifique, 1979; honorary doctorate, University of Neuchâtel, 1985; Dagnan-Bouveret prize, Acad&eacutemie des Sciences Morales et Politiques, 1990; Academie Française award, 1992; Great Prize of Philosophy, French Academy, 1999.

*WRITINGS:*

*Plotin ou la Simplicité du Regard,* 1963, translated by Michael Chase as *Plotinus; or The Simplicity of Vision,* introduction by Arnold I. Davidson, University of Chicago Press (Chicago, IL), 1993.

(Editor) Marius Victorinus, *Christlicher Platonismus,* Artemis Verlag (Zurich, Switzerland), 1967.

*Porphyre et Victorinus,* Études Augustiniennes (Paris, France), 1968.

*Le Neoplatonisme. Royaumont, 9-13 Juin 1969,* Editions du Centre National de la Recherché Scientifique (Paris, France), 1971.

Marius Victorinus, *Recherches sur sa vie et ses oeuvres,* Études Augustiniennes (Paris, France), 1971.

(Author of notes) Ambroise de Milan, *Apologie de David,* Éditions du Cerf (Paris, France), 1977.

*Exercices spirituels et philosophie antique,* Études Augustiniennes (Paris, France), 1981, translated by Michael Chase as *Philosophy as a Way of Life: Spiritual Exercises from Socrates to Foucault,* edited by Arnold Davidson, Blackwell (New York, NY), 1995.

*Zur Idee der Naturgeheumnisse: Beim Betrachten des Widmungsblattes in den Humboldtschen "Ideen zu einer Geographie der Pflanzen,"* F. Steiner (Wiesbaden, Germany), 1982.

*La citadelle interieure: introduction aux pensées Aurele,* Fayard (Paris, France), 1992, translated by Michael Chase as *The Inner Citadel: The Meditations of Marcus Aurelius,* Harvard University Press (Cambridge, MA), 1998.

(Author of introducton and commentary) *Commentario al "Parmenide" di Platone,* Vita e Pensiero (Milan, Italy), 1993.

*Eloge de la philosophie Antique: leçon inaugurale de la chaire d'histoire de la pensée Hellenistique et Romaine faite au college de France, le vendredi 18 fevrier 1983,* Allia (Paris, France), 1999, translated by Michael Chase as *What Is Ancient Philosophy?,* Harvard University Press (Cambridge, MA), 2002.

*La philosophie comme maniere de vivre,* A. Michel (Paris, France), 2001.

*SIDELIGHTS:* Pierre Hadot, retired professor emeritus at the College de France, was described as "one of the most significant and wide-ranging historians of ancient philosophy writing today," by *Critical Inquiry* executive editor Arnold I. Davidson.

Hadot's *Plotinus; or The Simplicity of Vision,* is a study of the philosophy and spirituality of Plotinus. Hadot also discusses Plotinus's life and activities. "Anyone interested in late Roman philosophy should read this book. It is a delight," commented Edgar M. Krentz in a review for *Religious Studies Review.*

In *The Inner Citadel: The Meditations of Marcus Aurelius,* Hadot provides a look at the philosophy of Marcus Aurelius, a Roman emperor, who wrote down his beliefs on how to live a good life in a text known as *Meditations. Choice* contributor P. A. Streveler commented, "This is an excellent study of the Meditations, certainly itself one of the great books of Western civilization." A *Virginia Quarterly Review* contributor concluded, "This is the kind of book that can grab your attention and hurl you through several hundred pages."

In *What Is Ancient Philosophy?* Hadot provides a look at ancient philosophy and shows it in use during everyday life. Ancient philosophy's goal was to achieve happiness in life and people are still trying to attain that goal. Hadot provides information on why ancient philosophy is not used in the Western world as he believes it should be. *Library Journal* contributor Terry Skeats called *What Is Ancient Philosophy?,* "Quite possibly one of the best one-volume works on the subject to have appeared in English."

*BIOGRAPHICAL AND CRITICAL SOURCES:*

*PERIODICALS*

*Choice,* January, 1996, H. L. Shapiro, review of *Philosophy as a Way of Life: Spiritual Exercises from Socrates to Foucault,* p. 806; December, 1998, review of *The Inner Citadel: The Meditations of Marcus Aurelius,* p. 701.

*Critical Inquiry,* spring, 1990, Arnold I. Davidson, "Spiritual Exercises and Ancient Philosophy: An Introduction to Pierre Hadot," pp. 475-482.

*Journal of the History of Philosophy,* October, 1997, François Renaud, review of *Philosophy as a Way of Life,* pp. 637-640.

*Library Journal,* April 1, 2002, Terry Skeats, review of *What Is Ancient Philosophy?,* p. 111.

*Philosophical Quarterly,* July, 1997, Lloyd P. Gerson, review of *Philosophy as a Way of Life,* pp. 417-420.

*Political Theory,* February, 1999, Thomas Augst, "Composing the Moral Senses: Emerson and the Politics of Character in Nineteenth-Century America," pp. 85-120.

*Publishers Weekly,* March 25, 2002, "Thinking It Through," p. 58.

*Religious Studies Review,* July, 1992, Alexander L. Khosroyev, review of *Plotin,* p. 230; October, 1995, Edgar M. Krent, review of *Plotinus; or The Simplicity of Vision,* p. 329.

*Review of Metaphysics,* September, 1995, Eric D. Perl, review of *Plotinus; or The Simplicity of Vision,* p. 138; December, 1999, Marcelo D. Boeri, review of *The Inner Citadel,* p. 449.

*Southern Humanities Review,* winter, 1996, David Bradshaw, review of *Plotinus; or The Simplicity of Vision,* p. 77.

*Virginia Quarterly Review,* winter, 1999, review of *The Inner Citadel,* p. 14.

OTHER

*College de France Web site,* http://www.college-de-france.fr/ (June 3, 2002), "Pierre Hadot."

*Harvard University Press Web site,* http://www.hup.harvard.edu/ (June 3, 2002), review of *What Is Ancient Philosophy?* and review of *The Inner Citadel.**

\*    \*    \*

## HALL, Tarquin 1969-

*PERSONAL:* Born 1969.

*ADDRESSES: Home*—London, England. *Agent*—c/o Author Mail, Atlantic Grove Press, 841 Broadway, New York, NY 10003.

*CAREER:* Journalist and writer. *Associated Press,* New Delhi, India, reporter.

*WRITINGS:*

*Mercenaries, Missionaries, and Misfits: Adventures of an Under-age Journalist,* Muncaster Press [England], 1995.

*To the Elephant Graveyard,* Atlantic Monthly Press (New York, NY), 2000.

*SIDELIGHTS:* Journalist Tarquin Hall has "seen some really awful things" during his career. While spending more than ten years living in the United States, Africa, and Asia he has witnessed death and violence in Sudan, Somalia, and Afghanistan. "But I have to say," Hall told an interviewer for London's *Independent Sunday,* "India has had the most effect on me. It makes you stop and think at every turn. You never get used to the shocks of India which at least serves to bring out the philosopher in you." Hall was referring to the experience of observing an elephant being tracked and shot in Assam, a remote, forested region on the northeastern frontier of India, while doing research for his first book. As Hall commented, "It really brought home the harsh realities that face both animal and human communities."

The result of Hall's research in India was the book *To the Elephant Graveyard.* Robert Carver, reviewing it in the *Times Literary Supplement,* called the work a "vivid and energetic debut as a travel writer—an authentic tale from the hills." Carver further described Hall's account as "a lively, engaging and often exciting Indian travel book." Vicki Croke, writing for the *Houston Chronicle,* noted that "what had started as a naive empathy for the elephant marked for execution deepens, with understanding and appreciation during this slow march, into a real dread over the task at hand." Robert Twigger, writing in the *Spectator,* commended Hall's book as one that "takes a wildlife narrative and fuses it with a true crime story, whilst retaining all the qualities of good travel writing." Commenting on Hall's writing style, Twigger stated, "We remain surprised and interested in our narrator who is at his best in this insightful, yet unforced observation of people." Twigger concluded, "Hall is to be congratulated on writing a book that promises humour and adventure, and delivers both." Holly Smith, reviewing *To the Elephant Graveyard* in *Geographical,* noted that Hall provides descriptive insight into the members of a disappearing profession, the mahout, or elephant keeper: "The time that Hall spends with these men makes for fascinating and moving reading."

*BIOGRAPHICAL AND CRITICAL SOURCES:*

PERIODICALS

*Booklist,* September 1, 2000, Gilbert Taylor, review of *To the Elephant Graveyard,* p. 50.

*Geographical,* May, 2000, Holly Smith, review of *To the Elephant Graveyard,* p. 93.

*Houston Chronicle,* November 12, 2000, Vicki Croke, "The Difficult Journey to Find a Murderous Elephant," p. 17.

*Independent Sunday* (London, England), April 23, 2000, Tarquin Hall, "The Place That Changed Me," p. 11.

*Library Journal,* September 15, 2000, Harold M. Otness, review of *To the Elephant Graveyard,* p. 104.

*Publishers Weekly,* August 7, 2000, review of *To the Elephant Graveyard,* p. 82.

*Spectator,* May 6, 2000, Robert Twigger, "No Innocent Trumpeter," p. 38.

*Times Literary Supplement,* July 28, 2000, Robert Carver, "Awfully Big Adventures," p. 5.*

*       *       *

## HAMLIN, Catherine 1925-

*PERSONAL:* Born c. 1925 in Sydney, New South Wales, Australia; married Richard Hamlin (a doctor), 1946 (died, 1993); children: Richard. *Education:* University of Sydney, M.D., 1946.

*ADDRESSES: Home*—Ethiopia. *Office*—Addis Ababa Fistula Hospital, P.O. Box 3609, Addis Ababa, Ethiopia.

*CAREER:* Gynecologist, researcher, and author. Princess Tsahai Hospital, Addis Ababa, Ethiopia, physician, teacher, 1959-74; Fistula Hospital, Ethiopia, co-founder and co-director, then director, 1975—.

*AWARDS, HONORS:* Rotary Award for World Understanding, Rotary International, 1998, for groundbreaking work in the treatment of vaginal fistula; Nobel Peace Prize nomination, 1999; ESR Hughes Award, Royal Australasian College of Surgeons, 2000, for contributions to surgery; Haile Selassie Humanitarian Award; Companion of the Order of Australia; ANZAC Peace Prize.

*WRITINGS:*

(With John Little) *The Hospital by the River: A Story of Hope,* Pan Macmillan (Sydney, New South Wales, Australia), 2001.

*SIDELIGHTS:* In 1958 Catherine Hamlin and her husband Reginald, both gynecologists and children of missionaries, responded to an advertisement in the medical journal *Lancet* to establish a school for midwives at the Princess Tsahai Hospital in Ethiopia. In 1959 they signed a contract with the Ethiopian government and arrived in the country's capital city of Addis Ababa. What the two doctors found there would lead them to dedicate their lives to helping thousands of Ethiopian women over the following decades. They would never return to their homeland of Australia to live.

In her book, *The Hospital by the River: A Story of Hope,* Catherine Hamlin and coauthor John Little recount the Hamlins' extraordinary lives. Shortly after arriving in Ethiopia, the Hamlins' were changed forever when they encountered their first fistula patient, a seventeen-year-old woman who had undergone labor for five days. As a result, the woman suffered from a condition called obstetrical, or vaginal, fistula. The problem is typified by abnormal openings between the bladder and/or the vagina and rectum, which usually includes severe internal injuries and leads to various degrees of pain and incontinence. Soon, the couple would learn that this condition, which had become relatively rare and was routinely treated in most developed countries, occurred often in young Ethiopian woman and that it often went untreated. The couple were also deeply troubled by the fact that the young Ethiopian women who suffered from this problem were routinely treated as outcasts who lived the remainder of their lives incapacitated and in shame.

The problem, as Hamlin recounts in her book, stems from a centuries-old practice in which young girls, many under the age of ten, are sold into marriage to adult males. Their small, still immature bodies are often not capable of giving birth without suffering fistulas, which often cripples them from nerve damage that occurs during a labor process that can sometimes last for days. As a result, the child they carry is usually born dead. Their bladders burst and, in extreme cases, their bowels also drip almost continuously. The ultimate emotional insult comes when these women are then abandoned by their husbands and ostracized by the rest of the community.

As the news spread that the Hamlins were treating fistula patients, more and more women from all over the country began to seek their help. The Hamlins would soon begin calling these women the "fistula pilgrims." Being in a Third-World country did not make the Hamlins' job any easier. Civil unrest abounded, supplies were often limited, and blood shortages were common. The Hamlins, however, were determined and even conducted research to refine the surgical procedures needed to relieve the incontinence and pain these women suffered. They ultimately revolutionized the procedure and reached a ninety-percent success rate with the operations. In 1975, after raising money, the two co-founded the Addis Ababa Fistula Hospital, which would provide care for some 18,000 fistula patients over the next three-plus decades. Although Hamlin's husband died in 1993, she continued to direct the hospital and treat patients while living in a small traditional Ethiopian house made of mud and stone.

Although many people told Hamlin that she should write a book about her and her husband's work and lives, she thought few people would be interested in the tale. Finally, Australian writer John Little convinced her to do it. In a review of *The Hospital by the River* that appeared in the Australian newspaper the *Age,* Anne Crawford wrote, "She writes with compassion and a natural restraint but pulls no punches when she wants to make a point." Writing for the Web site *The Blurb,* Michele Perry said, "Read this book and your outlook on life could change dramatically."

As for Hamlin, she writes in her book, "Never for a moment have I felt like retiring or wanted to change my life or my work. The joy I receive from working for these patients is something for which I thank God every day."

*BIOGRAPHICAL AND CRITICAL SOURCES:*

BOOKS

Hamlin, Catherine, with John Little, *The Hospital by the River: A Story of Hope,* Pan Macmillan (Sydney, New South Wales, Australia), 2001.

PERIODICALS

*Age* (Melbourne, Australia), August 14, 2001, Anne Crawford, "Emissary of Hope."
*Nursing Times,* April 15, 1998, Daloni Carlisle, "Silent Suffering," pp. 63-65.

OTHER

*Blurb,* http://www.theblurb.com.au/ (May 7, 2002), Michele Perry, "Heartbreak Hospital."
*Fistula Hospital Web site,* http://www.fistulahospital. org/ (May 7, 2002).*

## HAMM, Mark S.

*PERSONAL:* Male.

*ADDRESSES: Home*—Bloomington, IN. *Office*—Department of Criminology, 255 Reeve Hall, Indiana State University, Terre Haute, IN 47809. *E-mail*—m-hamm@indstate.edu.

*CAREER:* Criminologist. Indiana State University, Terre Haute, IN, professor of criminology.

*WRITINGS:*

*American Skinheads: The Criminology and Control of Hate Crime,* Praeger Publishers (Westport, CT), 1993.
*The Abandoned Ones: The Imprisonment and Uprising of the Mariel Boat People,* Northeastern University Press (Boston, MA), 1995.
*Apocalypse in Oklahoma: Waco and Ruby Ridge Revenged,* Northeastern University Press (Boston, MA), 1997.
(Editor, with Jeff Ferrell) *Ethnography at the Edge: Crime, Deviance, and Field Research,* Northeastern University Press (Boston, MA), 1998.
*In Bad Company: America's Terrorist Underground,* Northeastern University Press (Boston, MA), 2001.

*SIDELIGHTS:* An expert on right-wing hate groups, according to Suzy Hansen at *Salon.com,* Mark S. Hamm is a criminology professor at Indiana State University. Hamm stated in an interview with Hansen, "I spent thirteen years working in prisons so I've been around inmates and violent men. And I've been studying and interviewing skinheads for a good ten years."

*American Skinheads: The Criminology and Control of Hate Crime* examines the subculture, origin, ideology, and activities of the white supremacist, Nazi-inspired groups known as skinheads. In researching the book, Hamm interviewed or distributed questionnaires to skinheads to gather information about them and their beliefs and activities, including their background and families, organizational structure, crimes they had committed, recruitment methods, and views of Nazism. The first part of the book discusses the history of the movement, which began in London, England, and spread to the United States in the late 1970s. The second part of the book examines the skinheads and their lifestyle, and the third offers recommendations for preventing the hate crimes skinheads sometimes commit. Betty A. Dobratz in the *Journal of Criminal Justice* noted the work includes "an important section on the cultural legacy of Reaganomics and another on the future of American Neo-Nazism and domestic terrorism."

Hamm's research revealed the surprising fact that despite their commission of crimes, most skinheads "are employed, are good workers, and are responsible students," according to Robert D. Billingsley in *Federal Probation*. Billingsley noted that "this book demands that the reader reconsider some of the stereotypes of Skinheads and encourages the reader to consider what factors have created these hard-working, responsible student thugs."

In *The Abandoned Ones: The Imprisonment and Uprising of the Mariel Boat People,* Hamm considers the 1980 migration of about 120,000 Cubans from the port of Mariel, Cuba, to the United States. Most found new lives, but about 7,600 of the refugees were detained by the U.S. government at federal penitentiaries in Atlanta, Georgia and Oakdale, Louisiana; they were imprisoned without due process of law. In November 1987, these prisons exploded with violence instigated by the angry refugees. Hamm discusses how immigration laws, combined with the actions of Immigration and Naturalization Service officials, deprived these people of their rights and contributed to the uprising. In 1988 Hamm was hired by a coalition in support of the detainees to train legal representatives for the detainees, and thus became what he called "a witness to a chronicle of massive political corruption and administrative bungling," which he describes in the book.

A critic for *Reference Services Review* called *The Abandoned Ones* "a fascinating study . . . which reveals the incredible injustices the USA government inflicted on many of the single, male, black participants of the Mariel boatlift." "A devastating narrative of homegrown human rights violations," wrote Mary Carroll in *Booklist*. A *Choice* reviewer said that while the theories Hamm expresses in the book may prove "controversial," the work is "a significant study essential to understanding the history of U.S.-Cuban

relations." In *Library Journal,* Philip Y. Blue stated the book is "excellent for students of criminal justice and/or Cuban American relations."

*Apocalypse in Oklahoma: Waco and Ruby Ridge Revenged* describes the events that led to the Oklahoma City bombing in 1995. Drawing on newspaper and television accounts, Hamm describes the story of bomber Timothy McVeigh as well as the social factors of the American militia movement that inspired McVeigh to commit his crime. Hamm also considers the 1992 FBI assault on Ruby Ridge, Montana, and the 1993 burning of the Branch Davidian compound in Waco, Texas. Hamm's thesis is that the actions of the federal government fueled these situations, making them worse than they would have been without government action.

In the *American Journal of Criminal Law,* Mike Leitch noted that *Apocalypse in Oklahoma* is "exceptionally detailed," but that it is occasionally marred by Hamm's speculations about the men involved and his inclusion of his own opinions of the events. A *Kirkus Reviews* critic expressed a similar opinion, noting the work is "serviceable as a reconstruction of a national disaster, but it fails to substantiate the conspiracy theories that inform it." B. Weston in *Choice* called the book "thoroughly researched and well-written," and evidence "of an extended period of study."

In *Ethnography at the Edge: Crime, Deviance, and Field Research,* Hamm and fellow editor Jeff Ferrell present a collection of eleven articles about the problems inherent in researching the lives and subcultures of drug producers and dealers, prostitutes, the homeless, terrorists, property offenders, and others. Sudhir Venkatesh in the *American Journal of Sociology* explained that the contributors' "argument, which is a provocative one, is that a true ethnographic study of a crime . . . involves some type of complicit behavior, often a performance of the very transgression one is studying." Venkatesh found the work "unique" and "compelling." In *Choice,* D. O. Friedrichs called this a "valuable, often fascinating" account of "criminological research at the edge." In *Contemporary Sociology,* William Shaffir wrote that the book is "an exceptionally well-crafted volume. Issues are raised clearly, and the articles are interesting and readable."

In *Bad Company: America's Terrorist Underground* Hamm explores the culture of the Aryan Republican Army, a white supremacist group that the author suspects aided Oklahoma City bomber McVeigh. Hamm interviewed group leader Pete Langan at great length, and much of his book is based on Langan's perspective. Hansen said of the book: "Hamm builds a convincing case for the widely held theory that McVeigh couldn't have pulled off the bombing alone." *Booklist* reviewer Mike Tribby noted that the book contains "more oblique twists and turns than fiction could sustain." A *Publishers Weekly* reviewer wrote that Hamm's portrait of the eccentric Langan is "overly simplistic," but praised Hamm's wealth of information about the group's subculture.

*BIOGRAPHICAL AND CRITICAL SOURCES:*

PERIODICALS

*American Journal of Criminal Law,* fall, 1997, Mike Leitch, "Not McVeigh, It's the Government's Fault," p. 187.
*American Journal of Sociology,* July, 1999, Sudhir Venkatesh, review of *Ethnography at the Edge: Crime, Deviance, and Field Research,* p. 284.
*Booklist,* June 1, 1995, Mary Carroll, review of *The Abandoned Ones: The Imprisonment and Uprising of the Mariel Boat People,* p. 1703; December 1, 2001, Mike Tribby, review of *In Bad Company,* p. 612.
*Choice,* June, 1993, R. T. Sigler, review of *American Skinheads: The Criminology and Control of Hate Crime,* p. 1710; December, 1995, F. Cordasco, review of *The Abandoned Ones,* p. 677; October, 1997, D. Harper, review of *Apocalypse in Oklahoma,* p. 379; November, 1998, D.O. Friedrichs, review of *Ethnography at the Edge,* p. 607.
*Contemporary Sociology,* May, 1999, William Shaffir, review of *Ethnography at the Edge,* p. 363.
*Federal Probation,* September, 1993, Robert D. Billingsley, review of *American Skinheads,* pp. 88-89.
*Journal of American Studies,* April, 1999, Charles H. Lippy, review of *Apocalypse in Oklahoma,* p. 138.
*Journal of Criminal Justice,* November-December, 1996, Betty A. Dobratz, review of *American Skinheads,* pp. 563-565.
*Journal of Criminal Law and Criminology,* spring, 1999, Bard R. Ferrall, review of *Ethnography at the Edge,* p. 1158.
*Kirkus Reviews,* February 1, 1997, review of *Apocalypse in Oklahoma,* p. 195.

*Library Journal,* May 15, 1995, Philip Y. Blue, review of *The Abandoned Ones,* p. 82.
*Michigan Journal of International Law,* summer, 1997, Richard A. Boswell, review of *The Abandoned Ones,* pp. 689-711.
*Publishers Weekly,* November 12, 2001, review of *In Bad Company,* p. 51.
*Reference Services Review,* 1999, review of *The Abandoned Ones,* pp. 196-197.

OTHER

*Salon.com,* http://www.salon.com/ (January 17, 2002), Suzy Hansen, "America's Homegrown Terrorists."*

\*    \*    \*

## HAMMER, Michael 1948-

*PERSONAL:* Born 1948. *Education:* Massachusetts Institute of Technology, B.S., M.S., Ph.D.

*ADDRESSES: Office*—Hammer and Company, One Cambridge Center, Cambridge, MA 02142. *E-mail*—mhammer@hammerandco.com.

*CAREER:* Author, lecturer and consultant. Hammer and Company, Cambridge, Massachusetts, president; Massachusetts Institute of Technology, Cambridge, MA, professor of computer science.

*WRITINGS:*

(With James A. Champy) *Reengineering the Corporation: A Manifesto for Business Revolution,* HarperBusiness (New York, NY), 1993, second edition with new prologue, 2001.
(With Steven Stanton) *The Reengineering Revolution: A Handbook,* HarperBusiness (New York, NY), 1995.
*Beyond Reengineering: How the Process-centered Organization Is Reshaping Our Work and Our Lives,* HarperBusiness (New York, NY), 1996.
*The Agenda: What Every Business Must Do to Dominate the Decade,* Crown Business Publications (New York, NY), 2001.

Also author of articles in professional journals, including *Harvard Business Review* and *Leader to Leader.*

*SIDELIGHTS:* Because of the influence of his management books, Michael Hammer was ranked by *Business Week* as one of the top four preeminent management thinkers of the 1990s. He was also selected by *Time* as one of America's twenty-five most influential individuals. John Byrne, writing in *Business Week,* called Hammer's first book, *Reengineering the Corporation: A Manifesto for Business Revolution,* "the best-written, most well-reasoned business book for the managerial masses since *In Search of Excellence.*"

Hammer shows companies how to redesign their organization completely to improve productivity, quality and profits, and provides case studies to show how many top corporations have done so. Hammer and Champy take the point of view that "American corporations must undertake nothing less than a radical re-invention of how they do their work" as its central thesis. They argue that significant changes in the "three Cs (Customers, Competition and Change)" now render obsolete the traditional organizational arrangements based on extreme division of labor and pyramidal organizational structures. Their solution to this crisis is "reengineering"—fundamental, radical, and dramatic changes to business procedures to achieve better performance on measures such as cost, quality, service, and speed.

In *The Reengineering Revolution: A Handbook,* the sequel to *Reengineering the Corporation,* Hammer focuses on the experiences of organizations that implement reengineered concepts. The book follows some of the corporations that have tried the reengineering concepts laid out in *Reengineering the Corporation* and examines some of the successes, traps, and failures associated with implementing these efforts. Much attention is paid to the role of top leadership and the type of team needed for successful organizational change. At the same time, reengineering has become synonymous with a less popular form of reorganization, notably downsizing, where CEOs fire workers wholesale to make a company more "efficient." The first book was blamed, in part, for the wave of downsizings in the early 1990s. Hammer says that the goal is not to eliminate people. The author contends that a reengineered company initially requires fewer workers, but that as the rejuvenated firm grows, its growth creates more jobs.

*Beyond Reengineering: How the Process-centered Organization Is Reshaping Our Work and Our Lives* is the second sequel to *Reengineering the Corporation.* In *Booklist* Barbara Jacobs noted the "basic shift in the concept of reengineering, from 'radical redesign' (i.e. 'let's throw everything out') to 'process-centered' ('what combination of tasks comprises this project') is a challenge to contemporary corporate mind-set, forcing a reexamination of the very soul of a company."

*The Agenda: What Every Business Must Do to Dominate the Decade* heralds what the author calls the new "customer economy" where "sellers have become supplicants for scarce buyers." As a self-styled diagnostician to the ills of corporate America, Hammer sets out in each of the nine chapters in *The Agenda* to examine a corporate "disease," offer a cure, and provide brief case histories of companies undergoing treatment.

*BIOGRAPHICAL AND CRITICAL SOURCES:*

*BOOKS*

Hammer, Michael, *The Agenda: What Every Business Must Do to Dominate the Decade,* Crown Business Publications (New York, NY), 2001.

*PERIODICALS*

*American Banker,* May 30, 1996, John Kimmelman, interview with Michael Hammer, p. 4.

*Architects Journal,* December 15, 1993, Ken Allinson, review of *Reengineering the Corporation: A Manifesto for Business Revolution,* p. 42.

*Artforum International,* September, 1995, Brian Massumi, review of *Reengineering the Corporation,* p. 16.

*Association Management,* August, 1997, Ann I. Maloney, article on Michael Hammer, p. 133.

*Booklist,* June 1, 1996, Barbara Jacobs, review of *Beyond Reengineering: How the Process-centered Organization Is Reshaping Our Work and Our Lives,* p. 1654; September 15, 2001, Barbara Jacobs, review of *The Agenda: What Every Business Must Do to Dominate the Decade,* p. 170.

*Business Credit,* September, 1993, Cindy Tursman, review of *Reengineering the Corporation,* p. 35.

*Business Horizons,* September, 1993, Henry Beam, review of *Reengineering the Corporation,* p. 90.

*Business Week,* May 24, 1993, John A Byrne, review of *Reengineering the Corporation,* p. 12; December 13, 1993, Denise DeMong, review of *Reengineering the Corporation,* p. 15; October 29, 2001, review of *The Agenda,* p. 21.

*Challenge,* November, 1994, Steven Pressman, review of *Reengineering the Corporation,* p. 62.

*Chemical Week,* May 24, 1995, Rick Mullins, review of *The Reengineering Revolution: A Handbook,* p. 57.

*Christian Science Monitor,* May 2, 1996, Donald Coolidge, review of *The Reengineering Revolution,* p. 9.

*Competitive Intelligence Review,* summer, 1994, Giuliana Lavandel, review of *Reengineering the Corporation,* p. 73.

*Computer System News,* October 8, 1990, Christina Van Horn, interview with Michael Hammer, p. 8.

*Computerworld,* January 24, 1994, Joseph Maglitta, interview with Michael Hammer, p. 8.

*Fortune,* January 24, 1994, review of *Reengineering the Corporation,* p. 111; August 19, 1996, Thomas A. Stewart, review of *Beyond Reengineering,* p. 197.

*Governing,* March, 1993, John Martin, interview with Michael Hammer, p. 29.

*Government Finance Review,* June, 1996, Kenneth L. Barber, review of *Beyond Reengineering,* p. 66.

*Hospitals & Health Networks,* October 5, 1997, interview with Michael Hammer, p. 74.

*HR,* July, 1995, review of *The Reengineering Revolution,* p. 149; December, 1996, Ira Stuart Katz, review of *Beyond Reengineering,* p. 124.

*Inc.,* June, 1993, review of *Reengineering the Corporation,* p. 48.

*Information Age* (London, England), December 10, 2001, review of *The Agenda.*

*InfoWorld,* August 9, 1993, Robert Metcalf, review of *Reengineering the Corporation,* p. 48.

*Internal Auditor,* June, 1998, Christy Chapman, interview with Michael Hammer, p. 38.

*Journal of Business Strategy,* September, 2001, Bristol Lane Voss, review of *The Agenda,* p. 43; November, 2001, interview with Michael Hammer, p. 11.

*Knight-Ridder/Tribune Business News,* October 14, 2001, Richard Pachter, review of *The Agenda.*

*Library Journal,* April 15, 1995, Jane Kathman, review of *The Reengineering Revolution,* p. 88; September 1, 1996, Dale F. Farris, review of *Beyond Reengineering,* p. 77.

*Management Today,* July 1993, Robert Heller, review of *Reengineering the Corporation,* p. 74; September, 2001, profile of Michael Hammer, p. 50.

*Midrange Systems,* August 4, 1992, John Kador, interview with Michael Hammer, p. 38.

*Nation's Restaurant News,* August 23, 1993, Michael Schrader, review of *Reengineering the Corporation* p. 22.

*New Statesman,* January 17, 1998, Howard Davies, review of *Beyond Reengineering,* p. 45.

*New York Times,* April 18, 1992, Glenn Rifkin, article on Michael Hammer, p. 17; November 25, 2001, Williams J. Holstein, review of *The Agenda,* p. BU6.

*Optimum,* winter, 1993, Andre deCarufel, review of *Reengineering the Corporation,* p. 105.

*PC,* November 9, 1993, Mathew Ross, review of *Reengineering the Corporation,* p. 71.

*PC Week,* November 18, 1996, Rusty Weston, review of *The Reengineering Revolution,* p. E10.

*Physician Executive,* October, 1994, Robert H. Hodge, Jr., review of *Reengineering the Corporation,* p. 44.

*Public Manager,* winter, 1993, A. C. Hyde, review of *Reengineering the Corporation,* p. 61.

*Publishers Weekly,* March 29, 1993, review of *Reengineering the Corporation,* p. 40; June 17, 1996, review of *Beyond Reengineering,* p. 53; October 1, 2001, review of *The Agenda,* p. 52.

*Reason,* December, 1993, Paul H. Weaver, review of *Reengineering the Corporation,* p. 51.

*Supply Chain Management Review,* November, 2001, Francis J. Quinn, review of *The Agenda,* p. 36.

*Time,* June 17, 1996, p. 73.

*Training,* November, 2001, Jane Bogart, review of *The Agenda,* p. 69.

*Wall Street Journal,* June 1, 1993, Stanley W. Anfrist, review of *Reengineering the Corporation,* p. A10; May 19, 1994, Gilbert Fuchsberg, article on Michael Hammer and James Champy, p. A1; January 24, 1995, Hal Lancaster, interview with Michael Hammer, p. B1; October 23, 2001, Paul Carroll, review of *The Agenda,* p. A24.

*Washington Business Journal,* July 27, 2001, p. 49; October 19, 2001, review of *The Agenda,* p. 31.

*Washington Post,* July 25, 1993, Steven Pearlstein, review of *Reengineering the Corporation,* p. H1; May 7, 1995, Steven Pearlstein, review of *The Reengineering Revolution,* p. H5.*

## HAMMETT, Jo(sephine)

*PERSONAL:* Daughter of Samuel Dashiell (an author) and Josephine (a nurse; maiden name: Dolan) Hammett.

*ADDRESSES: Agent*—c/o Author Mail, Carroll & Graf Publishers, 161 William St., 16th Floor, New York, NY 10038.

*CAREER:* Author.

*WRITINGS:*

*Dashiell Hammett: A Daughter Remembers,* Carroll & Graf, 2001.

*SIDELIGHTS:* Jo Hammett's first published work was a fairly short book containing her thoughts and recollections concerning her famous father, Dashiell Hammett, who authored several classic detective novels, including *The Maltese Falcon.* Hammett was urged to write *Dashiell Hammett: A Daughter Remembers* after finding a cache of her father's old letters and photographs in a garage, where they had remained undisturbed since his death in 1961. In the diminutive 172-page book, published in 2001, Jo Hammett discusses her remembrances of the man who abandoned her, as well as her mother and sister, when she was just three years of age. The book was edited by the team of Richard Layman and Julie M. Rivett, who also collaborated to edit a related book called *Selected Letters of Dashiell Hammett, 1921-1960,* which was based on the collection of letters Hammett found in the garage with the photos. In fact, Hammett contributed an introduction to the work, which contains letters to and from most of the women in her father's life, including his longtime lover, actress Lillian Hellman.

Several literary critics who reviewed *Dashiell Hammett: A Daughter Remembers* described it as an uncritical look at Dashiell Hammett's life. In fact, Jo Hammett describes it as such in the book's preface. "It is not a biography. It is what the title says: what I remember—impressions that are imperfect, imprecise, biased, maybe even poorly interpreted," she writes. "It is not true. But it is as true as I can make it."

Containing many of the photographs found in the garage, the book also includes previously unknown information about Dashiell Hammett's personal background. He was born in 1894 in a rural Maryland town. At the age of twenty-one, he landed a job as a detective for the Pinkerton agency, and began writing detective stories for the pulp magazines of the time. In a short span, Hammett wrote five major detective novels, including *The Maltese Falcon,* which many critics consider one of the finest hard-boiled detective stories ever written.

While Jo Hammett includes information about her father's successes, she also describes the bitter period that followed, which was marked by heavy drinking, gambling, and womanizing. As is well known, the period also saw his literary output nearly disintegrate. However, according to his daughter, Hammett did begin writing novels during his later years, he just had a difficult time completing the projects. "He didn't stop writing. Not until the very last," Jo Hammett writes of the long drought. "What he stopped was finishing."

Due to his association with the Communist Party of America during the late 1930s, Hammett was blacklisted during the "red scare" era of the 1940s and 1950s. The Internal Revenue Service also went after him for back taxes, and seized many of his assets. By the time of his death at the age of sixty-six, Hammett was a broken man. As his second daughter, Jo Hammett did have contact with her father in his later years, and she describes their relationship up until his death. While much has been written about Dashiell Hammett, many literary critics enjoyed *Dashiell Hammett: A Daughter Remembers* because it was written from the viewpoint of a loved one. "Jo Hammett writes concisely, with much personal anecdote and wry observation. She sees her father from a necessarily intimate angle," Margaret Atwood wrote in a review reprinted in the London *Guardian.* "This is a perfect book for the Hammett enthusiast," a *Publishers Weekly* contributor added, while also referring to the book as a "compelling memoir." A *Kirkus Reviews* critic was particularly impressed with Hammett's portrayal of her father's faults, believing "she candidly relates his drinking, gambling, [and] womanizing."

*BIOGRAPHICAL AND CRITICAL SOURCES:*

*BOOKS*

Hammett, Jo, *Dashiell Hammett: A Daughter Remembers,* Carroll & Graf (New York, NY), 2001.

*PERIODICALS*

*Guardian*, February 16, 2002, Margaret Atwood, "Mystery Writer."
*Kirkus Reviews*, September 1, 2001, p. 1265.
*Publishers Weekly*, October 29, 2001, review of *Dashiell Hammett: A Daughter Remembers*, p. 51.
*Wall Street Journal*, December 7, 2001, Diane Scharper, review of *Dashiell Hammett: A Daughter Remembers*, p. W16.*

*       *       *

## HAMMOND, Michelle McKinney 1957-

*PERSONAL:* Born 1957, in London, England; daughter of George Hammond. *Ethnicity:* "African American."

*ADDRESSES: Home*—Chicago, IL. *Office*—HeartWing Ministries, P.O. Box 11052, Chicago, IL 60611. *Agent*—c/o Author Mail, Harvest House Publishers, Inc., 900 Owen Loop N., Eugene, OR 97402-9173.

*CAREER:* Author. Worked in television as co-host of *Aspiring Women*; Burrell Advertising, Chicago, IL, associate creative director; has appeared on radio, the stage and as a public speaker. Founder and president of HeartWing Ministries, Chicago, IL; singer and voiceover announcer.

*AWARDS, HONORS:* U.S. Television Award, for a commercial; Creative Excellence in Black Advertising awards; Golden and Bronze ITVA-Philco awards.

*WRITINGS:*

*What to Do until Love Finds You*, Harvest House Publishers (Eugene, OR), 1997.
*Secrets of an Irresistible Woman*, Harvest House Publishers (Eugene, OR), 1998.
*The Genius of Temptation*, Harvest House Publishers (Eugene, OR), 1998.
*His Love Always Finds Me*, Harvest House Publishers (Eugene, OR), 1999.
*The Power of Femininity*, Harvest House Publishers (Eugene, OR), 1999.

*Get a Love Life*, Harvest House Publishers (Eugene, OR), 2000.
*If Men Are like Buses, then How Do I Catch One?*, Multnomah Publishers (Sisters, OR), 2000.
*Prayer Guide for the Brokenhearted: Comfort and Healing on the Way to Wholeness*, Vine Books (Ann Arbor, MI), 2000.
*How to Be Blessed and Highly Favored: Living Richly under the Smile of God*, WaterBrook Press (Euless, TX), 2001.
*Intimate Thoughts Whispered Prayers: Meditations for the Single Heart (Matters of the Heart)*, Harvest House Publishers (Eugene, OR), 2001.
*What Becomes of the Brokenhearted*, Harvest House Publishers (Eugene, OR), 2001.
*Where Are You, God?*, Harvest House Publishers (Eugene, OR), 2002.
*Why Do I Say "Yes" When I Need to Say "No"?*, Harvest House Publishers (Eugene, OR), 2002.
*Wounded Hearts—Renewed Hope*, Harvest House Publishers (Eugene, OR), 2002.
*Get over It and on with It!: How to Get up When Life Knocks You Down*, WaterBrook Press (Colorado Springs, CO), 2002
(With Joel A. Brooks, Jr.)*The Unspoken Rules of Love: What Women Don't Know and Men Don't Tell You*, WaterBrook Press (Colorado Springs, CO), 2003.
*Sassy, Single & Satisfied*, Harvest House Publishers (Eugene, OR), 2003.
*101 Ways to Get and Keep His Attention*, Harvest House Publishers (Eugene, OR), 2003.
(With Holly Virden) *If Singleness Is a Gift, What's the Return Policy?*, T. Nelson (Nashville, TN), 2003.

Also author of the play *Love Talk*, performed by Chicago Theater Company.

*SIDELIGHTS:* Michelle McKinney Hammond was born in London, England, but when she was two years old her parents divorced, and she was sent to Barbados to live with her maternal aunt and uncle and her grandmother. She lost contact with her father, George Hammond, during this time and would not see him again for many years. Hammond's mother, who had gone to England to finish her education, returned to Barbados for her daughter five years later, having married William McKinney. The family then moved to Michigan, where Hammond grew up. When she was fourteen years old, a family member coincidentally bumped into Hammond's father during a trip to Africa. Hammond has been in touch with him ever since, often visiting him in Africa where he resides. She later moved to Chicago, where she attended college and began her professional career. Chicago continues to be her home base.

From the time of adolescence and into later years, Hammond went through many difficult relationships, with men whom she hoped, according to her interview with Camerin Courtney in *Christianity Today,* would "validate my existence." She desperately wanted a husband. The relationships ultimately would end, and she would find herself alone again and miserable. "But, eventually," Hammond continued in her interview, "I got tired of being sick and tired. . . . So I started consciously choosing happiness every day."

It is by building upon this premise, as well as her strong religious beliefs, that Hammond has created a ministry that focuses on helping women, especially single women, to appreciate their own worth. With this concept in mind, she created a Web site, maintains a very full schedule as a motivational speaker, and has written several books. One of the main themes in all of her endeavors can be found in her statement to Courtney: "Finding a mate becomes less important when we find joy and meaning. . . . It's about fulfilling our God-given purpose—what we were created to do and be. Only then will you find true peace and satisfaction—whether you're married or not."

Prior to founding HeartWing Ministries, Hammond won several awards for her work in the largest minority-owned advertising agency, Burrell Advertising, in Chicago, Illinois. Later she founded McKinney Creates, through which she produced short films and television advertisements. She has worked in television in a variety of ways, including her current role as co-host on the Emmy-nominated television talk show *Aspiring Women.* She is also much sought after by television and radio commercial producers for her voiceover talent.

Hammond wrote her first book, *What to Do until Love Finds You,* during a four-year period of rehabilitation in which she was mostly immobile, after being hit by a van. She chose to write on this topic because she herself had been unable to find a satisfactory book with a religious perspective that addressed the difficulties of being single. The only books she could find

"were so spiritual, they weren't *practical,"* she said. So she started writing the kind of book that she had "always wanted someone to write for me."

One year later, Hammond wrote *Secrets of an Irresistible Woman,* the theme of which, Hammond told Courtney, was "Get a life!" Instead of waiting for a man to fulfill a woman, Hammond suggested, women should make their lives as interesting as possible on their own. Only then will they attract someone who is equally exciting. When people get married, she stated, they "strengthen each other," by blending their "talents and interests." She goes on to suggest that women should try to discover what their talents are before they get married.

When she was asked how a person discovers what her talent is, Hammond responded, "Ask yourself, 'What do I do that amazes people and I think is absolutely nothing?' That thing is your gift."

In 2000, Hammond published three books. One of her more memorable titles, *If Men Are Like Buses, then How Do I Catch One?,* teaches single women how to stay balanced while looking for a mate. Her teachings in this book reflect her philosophy of life: strive for personal integrity and self-responsibility and don't ever forget the old adage that all that glitters is not gold. Although Hammond enjoys a large following of admirers, especially among Christian women, one reviewer for *Publishers Weekly* commented negatively on Hammond's reference to the importance of women "having beautifully groomed hair" as a means of finding a man, as well as her warning that women must be careful not to go beyond "their biblical role as followers."

*What Becomes of the Brokenhearted* was published the following year. In an interview with Christin Ditchfield for *Christian Single,* Hammond talked about how she could relate to women whose hearts were broken because, as she said, "Been there, done that." Hammond wrote the book because she has learned, through her own sufferings, that if women do not take time to fully heal themselves, they will only find themselves in the same position, over and over again. "The biggest mistake I've ever made," Hammond told Ditchfield, "was to sweep my tears under a rug, square my shoulders, and move on." She did this, she says, thinking that it was what she was supposed to do to show strength. However, this attitude did not allow for a time of reflection, a time to learn the lesson of the whole situation. "For every lesson I refused to learn, every heartache I refused to process, the backlash was worse than the original occurrence." During the interview, Ditchfield found Hammond radiated "an unshakable peace and confidence. It's something she longs to impart to others."

Hammond has continued to publish books as well as travel widely as a motivation speaker and produce audio cassettes of essays and music. In response to the question of what she thought was the biggest challenge facing Christian women, Hammond stated that women need to keep their balance, "Living in the world without being seduced by it."

### BIOGRAPHICAL AND CRITICAL SOURCES:

*PERIODICALS*

*Black Issues Book Review,* July, 2001, Johnnie Roberts, "Healing for Those Hurt by Love," p. 64.
*Publishers Weekly,* April 10, 2000, review of *If Men Are like Buses, then How Do I Catch One?,* p. 95; July 23, 2001, review of *How to be Blessed and Highly Favored,* p. 71.
*Today's Christian Woman,* September, 2001, "Five Minutes with Michelle McKinney Hammond," p. 136.

*OTHER*

*CBN.com,* http://www.parable.com/cbn/ (March 2, 2002), "Michelle McKinney Hammond: Exclusive Interview."
*Christian Single Online,* http://www.lifeway.com/ (October 7, 2001), Christin Ditchfield, "Michelle McKinney Hammond: Straight Talk."
*ChristianityToday.com,* http://www.christiantitytoday.com/ (October 7, 2001), Camerin Courtney, "*Sassy, Single, & Satisfied:* Author Michelle McKinney Hammond Dishes on Men, Marriage, and Why She Loves Being a Woman"; (March 2, 2002), "Five Minutes with. . .Michelle McKinney Hammond."
*Crosswalk,* http://women.crosswalk.com/ (March 2, 2002), Lori Smith, "Michelle McKinney Hammond Speaks."*

\*   \*   \*

### HANAN, Stephen Mo 1947-

*PERSONAL:* Born January 7, 1947, in Washington D.C..

*ADDRESSES: Agent*—c/o Smith & Kraus Publishers, P.O. Box 127, Lyme, NH 03768.

*CAREER:* Singer, dancer, actor, and author. Has acted in numerous plays in New York City and other U. S. cities, and London, including *Cats, Sex,* and *Peter Pan,* all New York, NY. Has appeared in film and television productions, including *Malcolm X,* 1992.

*AWARDS, HONORS:* Antoinette Perry ("Tony") Award nomination for best actor in a featured role—musical, 1983, for *Cats;* Carbonell Award, Florida Drama Critics, for appearance in *A Funny Thing Happened on the Way to the Forum.*

*WRITINGS:*

(With Jay Berkow) *Jolson & Co.* (play), first produced in New York, NY, 1999.
*A Cats Diary: How the Broadway Production Was Born,* Smith & Kraus (Hanover, NH), 2001.

Author of plays produced in San Francisco, East Hampton, Louisville, and Palm Beach County. Also author of book, music, and lyrics for *An Underground Revue.* Author of essays appearing in the *Washington Post, Harvard Magazine, Tikkun, Sun, Western Humanities Review,* and *New Age Journal.*

*SIDELIGHTS:* Longtime New York stage actor Stephen Mo Hanan originated the roles of Asparagus, Growltiger, and Bustopher in the first American production of the musical fantasy *Cats* in the early 1980s. As a part of this unique production, Hanan kept a diary throughout rehearsals as the production made its way to Broadway. Although he never intended for it to be published, his journal, called *A Cat's Diary: How the Broadway Production of Cats Was Born,* made it to bookstores in 2002 and provides an inside look at developing a smash musical hit on Broadway.

"I came home so tired I can hardly find my way to bed," writes Hanan of one day during his work in the musical. Not only were rehearsals tough in terms of the long, demanding hours put in to rehearse dancing and singing, but, as Hanan points out, the emotional toll was just as difficult. The actor/dancers/singers needed to be highly improvisational in their work and, under the direction of Trevor Nunn, endured a good bit of psychological inquiry as they progressed into a tight-knit, seamless performing troupe. For Hanan's part, he wrote often about being on the verge of tears. The author also reveals much about his relationships with others in the production and details many of the technical aspects of producing such a difficult musical. In addition to his writing about *Cats* in particular, Hanan reflects on the art of acting and on theatre in general. Hanan also waxes philosophical, as when he writes, "The life that the theatre seeks to illuminate rests upon ever-shifting foundations of achievement and regret. But the world turns forward only; the past recedes, the future approaches."

Laura W. Ewald, writing in the *Library Journal,* called *A Cat's Diary* a "personable day-by-day account" and "an insightful look at both the highly improvisational nature of the rehearsal process and [Hanan's] . . . personal interactions with fellow artists." *Bookreporter. com* reviewer Jesse Kornbluth noted, "Hanan's account of opening night is appropriately triumphant." He also commented that "*Cats* lovers will enjoy it. Actors, if they are smart, will turn it into gold."

Hanan has also written several plays and essays for various newspapers and magazines. Of special note is his musical play *Jolson & Co.,* which he coauthored with Jay Berkow. Through songs, monologues, and various dramatic scenes, *Jolson & Co.* reveals the life of the renowned musical entertainer Al Jolson. The musical, in which Hanan plays Jolson, provides a look at the entertainer from his boyhood in Lithuania to his Broadway success to his sagging career and comeback in the 1930s. Reviewer John Simon noted in *New York* magazine that "it does a pretty fair job of giving you the man, warts and all, and generally avoids sappi-

ness." Writing in the *New York Times,* reviewer Lawrence Van Gelder observed: "As portrayed in the book by Mr. Hanan and Jay Berkow, Jolson emerges as a man whose unshakable loneliness and insecurity . . . fed his deep hunger for the love of his audiences while it crippled many of his personal relationships." Van Gelder concluded by calling the play "intelligent, informative and winning."

BIOGRAPHICAL AND CRITICAL SOURCES:

PERIODICALS

*Library Journal,* March 15, 2002, Laura A. Ewald, review of *A Cat's Diary: How the Broadway Production of Cats Was Born,* p. 83.
*New York,* January 17, 2000, John Simon, "Laughing Gasbag," pp. 51-52.
*New York Times,* October 8, 1982, Frank Rich, "Theater: Lloyd Webber's *Cats',*" p. C3; December 23, 1999, Lawrence Van Gelder, "Jolson, Obnoxious Guy Who Missed His Mother," p. E5.
*Variety,* January 10, 2000, review of *Jolson & Co,* p. 119.

OTHER

*Bookreporter.com,* http://www.bookreporter.com/ (June 3, 2002), Jesse Kornbluth, review of *A Cat's Diary: How the Broadway Production of Cats Was Born.*

\*        \*        \*

## HANDY, Charles 1932-

PERSONAL: Born July 25, 1932, in Kildare, Ireland; son of Brian Leslie (an archdeacon) and Joan Kathleen (Herbert) Handy; married Elizabeth Ann Hill, 1962. *Education:* Oriel College, Oxford, B.A., 1956; M.A., 1966; Massachusetts Institute of Technology, M.B.A., 1967.

ADDRESSES: Agent—c/o Author Mail, Harvard Business School Press, Soldiers Field, Boston, MA 02163.

CAREER: Businessman and author. Shell International Petroleum Co., 1956-65; Charter Consolidated Ltd., 1965-66; Massachusetts Institute of Technology, Sloan School of Management, International faculty fellow, 1967-68; London Business School, 1968-94, professor, 1972-77, visiting professor, 1977-94, fellow, 1994; St George's House, Windsor Castle, warden, 1977-81. Royal Society for Encouragement of Arts, Manufactures and Commerce, 1987-89. FCGI, 2000.

AWARDS, HONORS: Honorary Fellow at Institute of Education, London, 1999, St. Mary's College, Twickenham, 1999; honorary D.Litt., Bristol Polytechnic, 1988, Open University, 1989, University of East Anglia, 1993, QUB, 1998, Middlesex University, 1998, Exeter University, 1999, and Essex, Hull, and Durham universities, 2000.

WRITINGS:

Understanding Organizations, Penguin Books (Harmondsworth, England), 1976.

Gods of Management: How They Work and Why They Will Fail, Souvenir Press (London, England), 1978, revised as Gods of Management: The Changing Work of Organizations, Oxford University Press (New York, NY), 1995.

The Future of Work: A Guide to a Changing Society, B. Blackwell (Oxford, England), 1984.

Understanding Schools as Organizations, Penguin Books (Harmondsworth, England),1986.

Understanding Voluntary Organizations, 1988.

The Age of Unreason, Business Books (London, England), 1989.

Inside Organizations, 1990.

Waiting for the Mountain to Move: and Other Reflections on Life, Arrow Books (London, England), 1991, published as Waiting for the Mountain to Move: Reflections on Work and Life, Jossey-Bass (San Francisco, CA), 1992.

The Age of Paradox, Harvard Business School Press (Boston, MA), 1994.

The Empty Raincoat: Making Sense of the Future, Hutchinson (London, England), 1994.

Beyond Certainty: The Changing Worlds of Charles Handy, Harvard Business School Press (Boston, MA) 1995.

The Search for Meaning, Lemos & Crane (London, England), 1996.

The Hungry Spirit beyond Capitalism: A Quest for Purpose in the Modern World, Broadway Books (New York, NY), 1998.

The New Alchemists, Hutchinson (London, England), 1999.

Thoughts for the Day, Arrow Books (London, England), 1999.

Twenty-one Ideas for Managers: Practical Wisdom for Your Company and Yourself, Jossey-Bass (San Francisco, CA), 2000.

The Elephant and the Flea: Looking Backwards to the Future, Hutchinson (London, England), 2001, published as The Elephant and the Flea: Reflections of a Capitalist, Harvard Business School Press (Boston, MA) 2002.

SIDELIGHTS: Charles Handy has been a professor, an oil executive, and an economist, but he is most well known for the numerous books he has written on business organization and management. He is often called a social philosopher and is considered one of the most prominent management thinkers of the late twentieth century. Handy has impressed many influential people in the business world with his practical, yet humanitarian ideas and his accurate predictions. His central belief, which is the thesis driving all of his writings, is that companies are not set apart from society, and business is a fundamental part of human life.

Handy's first book, Understanding Organizations, was published in 1976. In it, Handy teaches managers to apply what they know to be true about human behavior to organizational structures. He looks at motivation, theories about leadership, power, and politics. Thomas Patten, reviewing Understanding Organizations for the Wall Street Review of Books, called it "a fresh perspective on . . . managing people at work," and said that "the presentation is lucid and informed." Handy continued to write about organizations with Gods of Management: The Changing Work of Organizations, Understanding Schools as Organizations, and Understanding Voluntary Organizations. The last two apply Handy's business theories to the classroom and volunteer groups, promoting the teacher or leader as manager. He also touts the theory that neither institution can run on good intentions alone, but must be managed and organized. Gods of Management takes a slightly humorous look at the roles people play within institutions. Handy assigns each role the name of a Greek god, based on similar characteristics. According to Joan Warner in Business Week, the author asserts that managers invite trouble "when they try to impose the culture of one god in an organization built to worship another." A reviewer from *Choice* called this book "entertaining and highly readable."

Handy attempts to predict the future in *The Future of Work,* where he argues that without significant change, unemployment, or lack of full-time employment will continue to rise as the level of technology increases. He proposes a radical shift in the way we think about and value work, encouraging readers to entertain the ideas of less time spent at the office and placing more importance on domestic and voluntary work. These ideas were fairly revolutionary when the book was published in 1984. Paul Blyton of the *British Book News* commented, "Handy deals with these (issues) in a thoughtful and thought-provoking way. This is an optimistic book,"

Moving to a more personal style in his collection of essays, *Beyond Certainty: The Changing Worlds of Organizations,* Handy stays with the same themes, but puts an individual spin on them. A reviewer for *Library Journal* thought that this book proved Handy to be "one of the most graceful and articulate writers on the business scene." The author asks the question, What is the purpose of companies? He answers his own question in his essays, asserting that companies must learn to operate as communities. However, there is also a tone of uncertainty in this book, as Handy ponders the culture of work and challenges facing the economy and education.

In 1989 Handy published a book that addresses the manner in which work has changed over the years and is still shifting. *The Age of Unreason* argues that the industrial workplace is well on its way to becoming obsolete, along with the traditional educational path which prepares one to spend a lifetime at a single career. Handy offers the notion of individuals possessing a portfolio of skills and life experiences, making them more generalists than experts. This would make workers much more adaptable and able to work at a variety of jobs. Handy's 1994 book, *The Age of Paradox,* is an expansion on these ideas. He describes nine global paradoxes that plague organizations and the employed and also further develops his portfolio theory, stating that every worker would also need an agent. Examples of the paradoxes include: the paradox of aging, wherein every generation distinguishes itself as very different from the preceding generation,

however, government and educational organizations plan for the future as if the next generation will be exactly the same. The paradox of riches describes a world of extreme economic growth where people desire more and more material possessions. This means that there must also be more and more customers, yet the rich are living longer and having fewer children. Edward Cornish of the *Futurist* stated that this book "brims with the choice anecdotes, sharp insights, and ironical humor of one of the liveliest minds of our time." Cornish also found that though Handy has many stimulating ideas to share, he "can't take much time with any one of them before rushing on to the next." Martin M. Greller of *Human Resource Planning* felt that while the book's "arguments are often less well-supported than one would hope," it is "interesting even with its flaws." The same reviewer noted that "many of the paradoxes are not paradoxical, instead they are competing forces or issues requiring balance,"

*The New Alchemists* is Handy's collection of biographies, which features people who have essentially built their careers from the ground up. The title refers to these individuals as alchemists because they have made something out of nothing. In the spotlight are people such as Dee Dawson, who started Britain's first anorexia treatment center. She had previously applied to the London Business School and medical school. When both turned her down, she managed to talk her way in to the schools. Other biographies include those who work in business, the arts, education and social services. Winston Fletcher, reviewing for the *Times Higher Education Supplement* found that this book was not quite as "radical and original" as some of Handy's earlier works. He also thought that not enough space was devoted to each person, but that it still makes a beautiful coffee table book with its "delightful" photography.

In 2001, Handy took a good, long look at his own life and career and decided to write about it. *The Elephant and the Flea: Reflections of a Capitalist* is mostly autobiography and part social commentary. Handy uses his own experiences in the work force to examine how the nature of work has evolved in the late twentieth century. He also points out the advantages and disadvantages of working within an organization. To describe the workplace, Handy uses the metaphor of "elephants" for large corporations and "fleas" for independent entrepreneurs. He explains how elephants must find a way to expand, while maintaining personal relationships and originality and vision, while fleas should focus on making better connections. Robert Ayling, writing for *Management Today,* called the author's style "easy" when compared to other management texts on the market. He also commented, "Like all good teachers, he (Handy) makes difficult stuff seem easy."

BIOGRAPHICAL AND CRITICAL SOURCES:

PERIODICALS

*Booklist,* February 1, 1977, Lonnie Fletcher, review of *Understanding Organizations,* p. 788; February 15, 1994, David Rouse, review of *The Age of Paradox,* p. 1040; November 1, 1995, David Rouse, review of *Gods of Management,* p. 443; February 15, 1996, David Rouse, review of *Beyond Certainty,* p. 974; April 1, 1999, David Rouse, review of *Waiting for the Mountain to Move,* p. 1368; February 1, 2002, David Siegfried, review of *The Elephant and the Flea,* p. 911.

*Books,* January, 1994, review of *The Empty Raincoat,* p. 15.

*British Book News,* September, 1984, Paul Blyton, review of *The Future of Work,* p. 536; December, 1986, D. G. Lewis, review of *Understanding Schools as Organizations,* p. 699; March, 1987, Prabhu S. Guptara, review of *Gods of Management,* p. 111.

*Business Week,* November 13, 1995, Joan Warner, review of *Gods of Management,* p. 27.

*Choice,* September, 1985, review of *The Future of Work,* p. 174; May, 1996, review of *Gods of Management,* p. 1521.

*Economist,* April 22, 1989, review of *The Age of Unreason,* p. 84; February 19, 1994, review of *The Empty Raincoat,* p. 103; September 6, 1997, review of *The Hungry Spirit,* p. S16; January 8, 2000, review of *The New Alchemists,* p. 81.

*Electronic News,* April 11, 1994, Robert Sobel, review of *The Age of Paradox,* p. 38.

*Fortune,* February 11, 1991, Richard I. Kirkland, Jr., review of *The Age of Unreason,* p. 139; January 27, 1992, Brian Dumaine, review of *The Age of Unreason,* p. 113; April 4, 1994, Brian Dumaine, review of *The Age of Paradox,* p. 141; October 31, 1994, Carla Rapoport, "Charles Handy Sees the Future," p. 155.

*Futurist,* October, 1986, Burnham P. Beckwith, review of *The Future of Work,* p. 42; 1994, Edward Cornish, review of *The Age of Paradox.*

*Human Resource Planning,* September, 1991, Daniel C. Feldman, review of *The Age of Unreason,* p. 235; March, 1995, Martin M. Greller, review of *The Age of Paradox,* p. 48.

*Industry Week,* April 18, 1994, Sue Gibson, review of *The Age of Paradox,* p. 31.

*International Small Business Journal,* January-March, 1998, Graham Beaver, review of *The Hungry Spirit,* p. 114.

*Ivey Business Journal,* May, 2000, Carl Honore, interview with Charles Handy, p. 52; July, 2000, Carl Honore, interview with Charles Handy, p. 30.

*Kliatt Young Adult Paperback Book Guide,* September, 1987, Everett M. Woodman, review of *Understanding Schools as Organizations,* p. 46.

*Library Journal,* February 1, 1996, review of *Beyond Certainty,* p. 85.

*Los Angeles Times Book Review,* May 19, 1996, G. J. Meyer, review of *Beyond Certainty,* p. 1.

*Management Review,* June, 1998, Perry Pascarella, interview with Charles Handy, p. 52.

*Management Today,* May, 1989, Terry Maher, review of *The Age of Unreason,* p. 173; August, 1990, Tom Kempner, review of *Inside Organizations,* p. 94; June, 1994, Francis Kinsman, review of *The Empty Raincoat,* p. 107; October, 1999, John Kay, "The Glittering Upstarts," p. 46; September, 2001, Robert Ayling, "The Free Corporate Spirit," p. 46.

*Marketing,* November 11, 1999, Charles Barraclough, review of *The New Alchemists,* p. 68.

*National Productivity Review,* summer, 1994, Earle Hitchner, review of *The Age of Paradox,* p. 439.

*New Statesman,* October 10, 1997, Ben Pimlott, review of *The Hungry Spirit,* p. 43.

*New Statesman & Society,* September 1, 1995, Bob Tyrell, review of *Beyond Certainty,* p. 32; March 11, 1994, Denis MacShane, review of *The Empty Raincoat,* p. 38.

*Organizational Dynamics,* summer, 1996, Barbara Ettorre, "A Conversation with Charles Handy on the Future of Work and an End to the 'Century of the Organization,'" p. 15.

*Publishers Weekly,* February 7, 1994, review of *The Age of Paradox,* p. 81; November 3, 1997, review of *The Hungry Spirit,* p. 71; February 18, 2002, review of *The Elephant and the Flea: Reflections of a Reluctant Capitalist,* p. 91.

*South,* July, 1989, Paul Godfrey, review of *The Age of Unreason,* p. 73.

*Times Educational Supplement,* August 24, 1984, Joe Benjamin, review of *The Future of Work,* p. 19; March 17, 1989, Catherine Dawson, review of *Understanding Voluntary Organizations,* p. B43; September 24, 1999, Geraldine Brennan, review of *The New Alchemists,* p. 11.

*Times Higher Educational Supplement,* March 24, 2000, Winston Fletcher, review of *The New Alchemists,* p. 24.

*Times Literary Supplement,* February 7, 1992, review of *Waiting for the Mountain to Move,* p. 25; September 26, 1997, Amitai Etzioni, review of *The Hungry Spirit,* p. 6.

*Wall Street Review of Books,* fall, 1978, Thomas H. Patten, Jr., review of *Understanding Organizations,* p. 289.

*Washington Post Book World,* January 25, 1998, Steven Pearlstein, review of *The Hungry Spirit,* p. 6.*

*　　*　　*

## HANLON, Joseph

*PERSONAL:* Male.

*CAREER:* Writer. Former journalist for *New Scientist;* Correspondent for the British Broadcasting Corporation and the London *Guardian* in Mozambique from 1979-84.

*WRITINGS:*

*Mozambique: The Revolution Under Fire,* Zed (Towata, NJ), 1984.

*Apartheid's Second Front,* Penguin Books (New York, NY), 1986.

*Beggar Your Neighbors,* Indiana University Press (Bloomington, IN), 1986.

(With Roger Ormond) *The Sanction Handbook,* Penguin Books (New York, NY), 1987.

*Mozambique: Who Calls the Shots?,* Indiana University Press (Bloomington, IN), 1991.

*Peace without Profit: How the IMF Blocks Rebuilding in Mozambique,* African Institute/James Currey Publishers (Oxford, England), 1996.

(With Frances Christie) *Mozambique and the Great Flood of 2000,* Indiana University Press (Bloomington, IN), 2001.

Contributor to books, including *Guia basico sobre as autarquias locais* (title means Local Guide to Land Law and Local Government), Ministerio de Administracao Estatal e Associacao de Parlamentares Europeus for Southern Africa (Maputo, Mozambique), 1997; *Guia sobre a assembleia da republica,* European Parliamentarians for Africa (Maputo, Mozambique), 1997; *SADDC: Progress, Projects, and Prospects: The Trade Investment Future of the Southern African,* Economic Intelligence (London, England), 1984; *Christian Aid* [Maputo, Mozambique], 1995; *Mozambique Process Bulletin,* European Parliamentarians (Amsterdam, Netherlands), 1993; and *SADCC in the 1990s: Development on the Front Line,* Economist Intelligence (New York, NY), 1989.

*SIDELIGHTS:* Joseph Hanlon was the correspondent in Mozambique for the British Broadcasting Corporation and the London *Guardian* from 1979 through 1984. As an acknowledged expert on southern Africa, he has written five books and many important articles about the region. Throughout his career, he has fought against apartheid with writings that are often carefully documented indictments of the West's destabilization of Third-World countries as punishment for their experiments in socialist governments. According to Hanlon, this has taken the form of aid packages with so many conditions that it is de facto recolonization.

In his 1991 book *Mozambique: Who Calls the Shots?,* Hanlon reported that Mozambique is the world's poorest, hungriest, most indebted, most aid-dependent country, according to the World Bank's World Development Report of 1990. The book explains how this happened and how the process of recolonization began.

The International Monetary Fund (IMF) and the World Bank are specifically indicted as the principal cause of the poverty and indebtedness of the region. In a *Journal of Development Studies* review of *Peace without Profit: How the IMF Blocks Rebuilding in Mozambique,* Bridget O'Laughlin concurred that "sharp limits on domestic credit have undercut the marketing of peasant produce and investment in locally owned industry, in clear contradiction to the programme traced by the World Bank for economic recovery. He [Hanlon] shows how limitations on public sector wages have undercut essential public services and fueled corruption, contrary to stated aims of poverty alleviation and promotion of a favorable business environment."

In his 1986 book *Apartheid's Second Front,* Hanlon argues that the South African government ruthlessly and effectively used its military and economic superiority to repress any resistance to apartheid in the region. He shows that South Africa, along with international corporations based in South Africa, have control over virtually all regional transport, oil and electricity. Hanlon also discusses the roles of Britain, the United States, Japan, and West Germany as South Africa's largest trading partners. In a review in *British Book News,* Chris Allen said, "There are . . . very few books in English that provide a full account and assessment. . . . This one is comprehensive, judicious, accessible to a wide range of readers—and cheap."

Hanlon's *Mozambique and the Great Flood of 2000* documents the flood that made international headlines and provoked a huge international relief effort. Hanlon and Frances Christie, who co-authored the book, examine the natural and man-made causes of the flood and the nature of the relief work that followed. A description of the book on the Web site of publisher Indiana University Press noted, "*Mozambique and the Great Flood of 2000* probes the effectiveness of various forms of aid ....Documenting the experience of the floods, the authors provide important insights for future emergency planning and management in Mozambique and elsewhere."

*BIOGRAPHICAL AND CRITICAL SOURCES:*

*BOOKS*

(With Frances Christie) *Mozambique and the Great Flood of 2000,* Indiana University Press (Bloomington, IN), 2001.
Hanlon, Joseph, *Beggar Your Neighbors,* Indiana University Press (Bloomington, IN), 1986.
Hanlon Joseph, *Mozambique: Who Calls the Shots?,* Indiana University Press (Bloomington, IN), 1991.
Hanlon, Joseph, *Peace without Profit: How the IMF Blocks Rebuilding in Mozambique,* African Institute/James Currey Publishers (Oxford, England), 1996.

*PERIODICALS*

*Africa Today,* winter-spring 1992, Loretta J. Williams, review of *Mozambique: Who Calls the Shots?,* p. 135.

*American Academy of Political and Social Science,* March, 1993, Brian Winchester, review of *Mozambique: Who Calls the Shots?,* p. 209.
*Black Scholar,* winter, 1994, Chalis Johnson, review of *Mozambique: Who Calls the Shots?,* p. 65.
*Booklist,* February 1, 1987, *Mozambique: The Revolution under Fire,* p. 812.
*British Book News,* February, 1985, Chris Allen, review of *Mozambique: The Revolution under Fire,* p. 127.
*Choice,* March, 1987, J. S. Uppal, review of *Beggar Your Neighbors,* p. 1147; April, 1985, C. E. Welch, *Mozambique: The Revolution under Fire,* p. 1224.
*Journal of Development Studies,* December, 1997, Bridget O'Laughlin, review of *Peace without Profit: How the IMF Blocks Rebuilding in Mozambique,* p. 192.
*Kliatt Young Adult Paperback Book Guide,* April, 1988, review of *The Sanction Handbook,* p. 42; spring, 1987, review of *Apartheid's Second Front,* p. 43.
*Library Journal,* October 15, 1986, J. Grotpeter, review of *Beggar Your Neighbors,* p. 85.
*Listener,* November 6, 1986, review of *Apartheid's Second Front,* p. 36.
*New Statesman,* October 26, 1984, Basil Davidson, p. 29; May 30, 1986, Paul Martin, review of *Apartheid's Second Front,* p. 26.
*New York Review of Books,* October 23, 1986, Leonard Thompson, review of *Beggar Your Neighbors,* p. 3.
*Political Studies,* June, 1991, G. R. Berridge, review of *The Sanctions Handbook,* pp. 381-382.
*Times Literary Supplement,* January 16, 1987, Arthur Sheps, review of *Beggar Your Neighbors,* p. 54; June 22, 2001, Nicola Walker, review of *Mozambique and the Great Flood of 2000,* p. 32.

*OTHER*

*Indiana University Press Web site,* http://www.indiana.edu/ (December 2, 2001).*

\*　　\*　　\*

**HARKNESS, Joan**

*PERSONAL: Female. Education:* Graduated from University of Kansas and Juilliard School of Music.

*ADDRESSES: Office*—Flying Leap Music, 1348 71st St., Brooklyn, NY 11228. *E-mail*—joan@fleap.com.

*CAREER:* Pianist, teacher, and lecturer. Brooklyn Friends School, Brooklyn, NY, piano teacher.

*MEMBER:* New York State Music Teachers Association.

*WRITINGS:*

(With Anna Dembska) *You've Got Rhythm: Read Music Better by Feeling the Beat,* three volumes, Flying Leap Music (Brooklyn, NY), 2000.

*ADAPTATIONS: Play the Piano,* a book with Anna Dembska featuring a new method for adults to learn to play the piano.

*SIDELIGHTS:* Joan Harkness is a pianist who has performed throughout the United States and Mexico, including performances at Alice Tully Hall, Weill Recital Hall, and the Spanish Institute in New York City. She also teaches piano and has lectured extensively throughout the United States, including lecture/workshops on meter rhythm and lecture-recitals featuring Mexican and Spanish music. Her performances include numerous premieres of contemporary musical works by Leroy Jenkins and Anna Dembska. In 1999 Harkness and Dembska teamed up to form Flying Leap Music. As music teachers and performers, the authors found that children and adults desire a way to learn music that is not intimidating. Flying Leap Music is devoted to creating new materials for music education that focus on activating and integrating the senses, intellect, and imagination.

*You've Got Rhythm: Read Music Better by Feeling the Beat,* coauthored by Harkness and Dembska, focuses on a new approach for reading rhythm in music. The approach integrates both "Talking Music," that is, compositions of spoken words that have diverse rhythms and various lyrics. These are studied with hand-clapping patterns designed to coincide with the meter, that is, a measured rhythm in verse. "It's the body that feels the groove, and therefore it's the body that needs to learn a meter and its metric accents," Harkness wrote in an article for the Pennsylvania Music Teachers Association Web site. She pointed out that the approach creates "a way to link reading with physical movement." She explained: "When students move their hands through slap, clap, and tap patterns while reading music, movement and reading are integrated to deepen a student's intuitive and analytic understanding of music notation."

In the article, Harkness explained the "slap/clap/tap" pattern as being based on the metric accents formed by groups of two and three beats found in meters. "The first metric accent is the downbeat, and its weight is indicated by a Slap on the legs," wrote Harkness. "Clap is strong, but lighter than the downbeat, and is used on any secondary metric accent, i.e., the beginning of any other groups of two or three within a measure." She continued, noting that the "weakest beat" is the "Tap," which is a "silent weightless tap of the index finger and thumb together."

The book is arranged into three volumes: *Notes, Rests, and Simple Meter; Compound Meter and Syncopation Between the Beats; Tuplets, Double Dots, Suspending the Meter, No Meter, and Irregular and Shifting Meters.* The rhythm-teaching process, which is suitable for students 9 years old and older, takes the student step-by-step from basic music notation to college-level music reading. The authors also include short biographies of American composers and brief commentaries on music, as well as literary quotations, nineteenth-century advertising copy, and even a few recipes. Writing for the *Shareware Music Machine* Web site, a reviewer called the teaching method "simple but profound" and added that it "makes sight-reading intuitive, instantly understandable, and best of all, fun." On the *Piano Pedagogy Plus!* Web site, a reviewer commented that the authors avoid both "boredom" and "over-explaining." Janet Brewer, writing in the *Library Journal,* called the guide "fresh and unique."

*BIOGRAPHICAL AND CRITICAL SOURCES:*

PERIODICALS

*Library Journal,* March 15, 2002, Janet Brewer, review of *You've Got Rhythm: Read Music Better by Feeling the Beat,* p. 82.

OTHER

*Flying Leap Music Web site,* http://www.fleap.com (June 3, 2002).
*Piano Pedagogy Plus! Web site,* http://www.pedaplus. com (June 3, 2002), review of *You've Got Rhythm.*

*Pennsylvania Music Teachers Association Web site,* http://www.pamusicteachers.org (September 20, 2002), Joan Harkness, "Meter: The Classical Musician's Groove."

*Shareware Music Machine Web site,* http://www.hit squad.com/smm/ (June 3, 2002), review of *You've Got Rhythm.**

* * *

## HARRIS, Chris 1951-

*PERSONAL:* Born April 11, 1951, in New Westminster, British Columbia, Canada; son of Bruce Goodall (a mill worker) and Nora Virginia (an artist; maiden name, Springer) Harris; married Birte Soegaard (deceased); married Charmaine Lila Illig, September 14, 1996; children: Aron Christopher, Amelia Florence. *Ethnicity:* "Mongrel." *Education:* Vancouver School of Art, graduated (with honors), 1975. *Politics:* "Socialist." *Religion:* Christian.

*ADDRESSES: Home*—2603 Reef Rd., Pender Island, British Columbia, Canada V0N 2M2. *E-mail*— chrisharris@gulfislands.com.

*CAREER:* Sculptor, author, landscape designer, and painter. Lighthouse keeper at Egg Island, British Columbia, Canada, 1974-76; president of landscape design company, New York, NY, 1987-92.

*AWARDS, HONORS:* Named world champion sand castle builder, British Columbia Writers Group; fine arts award, Canada Council.

*WRITINGS:*

*How to Paint* (poetry), New Star Books, 1998.

Contributor of poetry to *Exile: Literary Quarterly.*

*WORK IN PROGRESS: Job's Curse; The Chameleon.*

*BIOGRAPHICAL AND CRITICAL SOURCES:*

OTHER

*Chris Harris Web site,* http://pender.gulfislands.com/ chrisharris/ (December 9, 2001).

## HARRIS, Judith (Lynn) 1955-

*PERSONAL:* Born 1955; married; children: one daughter. *Education:* Brown University, A.M., 1980; George Washington University, Ph.D. (rhetoric/ composition, creative writing, poetry), 1993. *Religion:* Jewish.

*ADDRESSES: Home*—Washington, DC. *Office*— George Washington University, English Dept., 2121 Eye St. NW, Washington, DC 20052. *E-mail*—jlha@ gwu.edu.

*CAREER:* Writer, and poet. George Washington University, Washington, DC, adjunct assistant professor of English.

*WRITINGS:*

*Poppies* (poems), Washington Writers Publishing House (Washington, DC), 1981.
*Song of the Moon,* Orchises Press (Washington, DC), 1982.
*Signifying Pain: Constructing and Healing the Self through Writing,* State University of New York Press (Albany, NY), 2000.
*Pearls for My Birthday: A Gift from Cancer*, iUniverse (Lincoln, NE), 2000.
*Atonement: Poems,* Louisiana State University Press (Baton Rouge, LA), 2000.

Contributor to anthologies, including *Her Face in the Mirror: Jewish Women on Mothers and Daughters,* Beacon, 1994; *Hungry as We Are,* Washington Writers Publishing House (Washington, DC), 1995; *Altered States: Uneasy Transitions into Wedded Bliss,* edited by Virginia Hartman and Barbara Eastman, 1997; *A More Perfect Union: Poems and Stories About the Modern Wedding,* edited by Virginia Hartman and Barbara Eastman, St. Martin's Press (New York, NY), 1998; and *Storming Heaven's Gate: Women's Spiritual Journeys,* edited by Patrice Vecchione and Amber Coverdale Sumrall, Penguin (New York, NY), 1997.

*SIDELIGHTS:* Judith Harris's poetry explores a variety of themes within the framework of family life and remembrance. A review in *Library Journal* commended Harris's first poetic work *Poppies* for its "gift for feeling." *Pearls for My Birthday: A Gift from Cancer* addresses personal family challenges involved in coping with loss and grief. And likewise *Atonement: Poems* is described by the publisher as a "poetic family album, a scrapbook of remembrances of a privileged suburban Jewish upbringing and reflections of motherhood and family life." Michael S. Harper, reviewing the book in *American Poet,* stated that within Harris's poems "strength shines forth in playful energy." Harris's contributions to anthologies are also characterized by these same themes of remembrance and family experiences.

*BIOGRAPHICAL AND CRITICAL SOURCES:*

PERIODICALS

*American Poet,* winter, 2000-2001, Michael S. Harper, review of *Atonement,* p. 43.
*Library Journal,* December 15, 1981, review of *Poppies,* p. 2357.

OTHER

*Brown University Web site,* http://www.brown.edu/ (March 2, 2002).
*Louisiana State University Press Web site,* http://www.lsu.edu/ (September 15, 2002). *

\*     \*     \*

**HART, William 1945-**

*PERSONAL:* Born January 27, 1945, in Wichita, KS; son of W. J. (a banking executive) and Louise (an elementary school teacher; maiden name, Loy) Hart; married Carole Welsch, 1963 (divorced, 1975); married Melissa Mellor Renner, 1979 (divorced, 1981); married Jayasri Majumdar (a filmmaker), July 13, 1986; children: Lynda Jane (first marriage). *Education:* University of Kansas, B.A., 1967; Wichita State University, M.A., 1979; University of Southern California, M.P.W., 1985, Ph.D., 1985. *Politics:* "Far left." *Religion:* "Agnostic; philosophy: Buddhist." *Hobbies and other interests:* Hiking, walking, travel.

*ADDRESSES: Home and office*—2721 Piedmont #3, Montrose, CA 91020. *E-mail*—hartsarts@earthlink.net.

*CAREER:* Teacher and writer. University of Southern California, Los Angeles, instructor in English, 1981-85; California State University, Los Angeles, instructor in English, 1984-2000.

*MEMBER:* Teachers of English to Speakers of Other Languages, PEN, Phi Beta Kappa.

*AWARDS, HONORS:* Second place, *Chiron Review* poetry contest, 1996 for *Mansion of Dead Animals,* Merit Book Award, Haiku Society of America, 1997, for *Paris;* Second place, California Writers' Roundtable Poetry Contest, Women's National Book Association, Los Angeles chapter, 1998, for "Tourist Bus"; second place, Gertrude Dole Memorial Poetry Content, Massachusetts Poetry Society, 1998, for "Moles of the Air"; Silver Apple Award, National Educational Media Network, 1999, for film *Roots in the Sand;* Swan Duckling Press Chapbook Competition, 2000, for *Hard Bucks.*

*WRITINGS:*

*Dream Machine* (television script), USC Cinema/TV, 1984.
*Danger: USA* (television script), Ford International Productions, 1989.
*Monsoon* (poetry chapbook), Timberline Press (Fulton, MO), 1991.
*Durga Puga* (television documentary,) K-Pas Cable Channel, 1992.
*Paris* (poetry chapbook), Timberline Press (Fulton, MO), 1996.
*Wildcat Road* (poetry chapbook), Timberline Press (Fulton, MO) 2000.
*Roots in the Sand* (documentary film), Hart Films, 1998, broadcast on PBS-TV, 2000.
*Hard Bucks* (poetry chapbook,) Swan Duckling Press (Cypress, CA), 2000.
*Journeyman's Dues* (poetry chapbook,) Musclehead Press (Russell, NY), 2002.
*Factory Stiff* (poetry chapbook), Pitchfork Press (Austin, TX), 2002.
*Never Fade Away* (novel), Daniel & Daniel (Santa Barbara, CA), 2002.
*On Cat Time* (poetry chapbook), Timberline Press (Fulton, MO), 2003.

Contributor of hundreds of poems and short stories to various periodicals and anthologies, including *Cicada, Black Bear Review, Blue Collar Review, Florida Review, Honolulu Advertiser, Mainichi Daily News, Modern Haiku, Potomic Review,* and *Quixote.*

*WORK IN PROGRESS: Calcutta: Cauldron of the Gods,* a poetry collection about "street life and the infinite in India's former capital"; *Iceland Speed Club,* poems about "roller speed skating and teenage love"; *Ruled by the Moon,* a collection of short stories; *Plunderland Goes to War,* a black comic novel about the aftermath of September, 11.

*SIDELIGHTS:* William Hart published his first novel, *Never Fade Away,* in 2002. Prior to that, Hart wrote and published hundreds of poems and short stories, many of which have been anthologized. He has also published numerous poetry chapbooks. *Hard Bucks,* published in 2000, won the Swan Duckling Press Chapbook Competition of that year.

*Hard Bucks* is a collection of poetry centered on the topic of work, something familiar to Hart. As he told *Contemporary Authors:* "During college and for ten years after I worked mainly as a laborer: sheet metal, welding, house painting. I worked on a ranch, dug ditches, planted trees, and much more." This background gave Hart the authority necessary to make the poems in *Hard Bucks* resonate. Tim Scannell, writing in the *Small Press Review,* remarked that "*Hard Bucks* is a golden arrow which flies straight to the core of work qua work; its tedium, joy, and very often, its genuine metaphysical mystery." He highly recommended it.

Another poetry chapbook, this one titled *Wildcat Road,* was illustrated by Hart's wife, artist and filmmaker Jayasri Majumdar. Kevin Bailey reviewed the book for *Haiku Quarterly.* and noted: "Even if the poems were pure nonsense, this would be a fine thing to own, but thankfully the poetry, all haiku, is Bill Hart on his best form."

An earlier chapbook bearing the title *Paris* garnered a Third Place Merit Book Award in 1997. In his *Next* review, Richard Modiano wrote: "Mr. Hart shows himself to be an accomplished haiku/senryu poet. . . . The effect of haiku is rather like throwing a pebble into a still pond: if thrown with sufficient force, ripples of association spread across the mind of the reader, deepening and enriching the reader's awareness of the natural world or the folly or pathos of human behavior. Mr. Hart manages this difficult feat in several fine poems." Hart finds his writing is deeply influenced by his beliefs, as he explained to *CA:* "I am influenced by the belief that, in some regards, literature can describe nature better than science. The only type of writing I don't use notes or an outline for is the haiku. In the case of haiku, one has to wing it."

*Never Fade Away,* Hart's debut novel, revolves around a student who signs up for an English as a Second Language class taught by a psychologically damaged Vietnam veteran. The story is about the teacher-student relationship and their eventual, evolving love for one another. A *Publishers Weekly* writer praised the novel for avoiding clichés while exploring the nuances of the transforming relationship, but the reviewer felt that Hart "misses numerous opportunities to delve deeper into his characters' motivations and add atmospheric details that would have made this a deeper, richer book. Still, this is a solidly impressive debut by a writer worth watching."

Again, Hart drew on his own experiences to write *Never Fade Away.* He told *CA:* "My life experiences, including things I've witnessed, typically are the source of my writings. My novel *Never Fade Away* is a good example. It arose from a terribly unjust academic situation I lived through, only to recreate the essentials as fiction." Helen Heightsman Gordon, writing in the *Midwest Book Review,* made a prediction about the book: "Someone will probably make a movie out of this book, and that would be unfortunate. Bill Hart's prose is snappy and incisive; his deft turns of phrase provide a treat even apart from the story." As the critic concluded: "This is Hart's first novel, but his poetic artistry serves him well in fiction. Already he has me looking forward to the next one."

*BIOGRAPHICAL AND CRITICAL SOURCES:*

PERIODICALS

*Frogpond,* number 1, 2001, Jim Kacian, "Books Received," p. 78.
*Haiku Quarterly,* numbers 19-20, 1997, Kevin Bailey, review of *Paris,* pp. 69-70; number 25, 2001, Kevin Bailey, review of *Wildcat Road,* pp. 47-48.
*Midwest Book Review,* April, 2002, Helen Heightsman Gordon, review of *Never Fade Away.*
*Modern Haiku,* winter-spring, 2001, Robert Spiess, review of *Wildcat Road,* p. 101.

*Next,* January, 1998, Richard Modiano, review of *Paris,* p. 19.

*Publishers Weekly,* December 3, 2001, review of *Never Fade Away,* p. 38.

*Small Press Review,* March-April, 2001, Tim Scannell, review of *Never Fade Away,* p. 11.

\*     \*     \*

## HARTMAN, David 1931-

*PERSONAL:* Born 1931, in Brooklyn, NY; son of Shalom Hartman. *Education:* Received degree from Yeshiva University; attended Fordham University, Bronx, NY.

*ADDRESSES: Home*—Jerusalem, Israel. *Office*—Shalom Hartman Institute, 12 Gedalyahu Alon, P.O. Box 8029, Jerusalem 93113, Israel. *Agent*—c/o Jewish Lights Publishing, P.O. Box 237, Sunset Farm Office, Rt. 4, Woodstock, VT 05091.

*CAREER:* Author and rabbi. McGill University, Montreal, Quebec, Canada, philosophy instructor; Hebrew University, Jerusalem, Israel, professor emeritus; Shalom Hartman Institute, Jerusalem, founder and director.

*AWARDS, HONORS:* National Jewish Book Award for *Maimonides: Torah and Philosophic Quest, A Living Covenant: The Innovative Spirit in Traditional Judaism* and *A Heart of Many Rooms: Celebrating the Many Voices within Judaism.*

*WRITINGS:*

*Maimonides: Torah and Philosophic Quest,* Jewish Publication Society of American (Philadelphia, PA), 1976.

*Joy and Responsibility: Israel, Modernity, and the Renewal of Judaism,* Ben-Zvi-Posner (Jerusalem, Israel), 1978.

*The Breakdown of Tradition and the Quest for Renewal: Reflections on Three Jewish Responses to Modernity, J B. Soloveitchik, M. M. Kaplan and A. J. Heschel,* Gate Press (Montreal, Quebec, Canada), 1980.

(With Noam Zion) *Responses to Suffering and Tragedy,* Shalom Hartman Institute for Advanced Judaic Studies (Jerusalem, Israel), 1981.

(With Noam Zion) *Human Renewal: The Courage to Change,* Shalom Hartman Institute for Advanced Judaic Studies (Jerusalem, Israel), 1982.

*Interfaith Pluralism: A Jewish Viewpoint,* Shalom Hartman Institute for Advanced Judaic Studies (Jerusalem, Israel), 1983.

(With Tzvi Marx and Noam Zion) *The Dynamics of Tzedakah,* Shalom Hartman Institute for Advanced Judaic Studies (Jerusalem, Israel), 1985.

*A Living Covenant: The Innovative Spirit in Traditional Judaism,* Free Press (New York, NY), 1985.

*Conflicting Visions: Spiritual Possibilities in Modern Israel,* Schocken Books (New York, NY), 1990.

(With David Dishon) *Education for Inter-Dependence in the Jewish Family,* Shalom Hartman Institute for Advanced Judaic Studies (Jerusalem, Israel), 1995.

*Shabbat and the Human Experience of Labor,* Shalom Hartman Institute for Advanced Judaic Studies (Jerusalem, Israel), 1995.

*A Heart of Many Rooms: Celebrating the Many Voices within Judaism,* foreword by Shlomo Pines, Jewish Lights (Woodstock, VT), 1999.

*Israelis and the Jewish Tradition: An Ancient People Debating Its Future,* Yale University Press (New Haven, CT), 2000.

*Love and Terror in the God Encounter: The Theological Legacy of Rabbi Joseph B. Soloveitchik,* Jewish Lights (Woodstock, VT), 2001.

Also author of articles published by Shalom Hartman Institute for Advanced Judaic Studies (Jerusalem, Israel) and of *Rabbinic Responses to History as Mirrored in Hanukkah and Purim,* Shalom Hartman Institute for Advanced Judaic Studies.

*SIDELIGHTS:* David Hartman is a philosopher and social activist, as well as a respected theologian and author. He is also very active in the Shalom Hartman Institute, which he founded and now directs. The institute, which Hartman named after his father, is a kind of think tank of intellectuals dedicated to comprehending classical Judaism in such a way that it might be applied to the challenges of the modern world.

Born and raised in the United States, in the Brownsville section of Brooklyn, Hartman grew up near poverty. Although his family had few possessions, there was never a shortage of books in his home. The intellectual environment may have been a bit daunting for young Hartman, who was held back once in elementary school and once in high school. According to an article in *Time* by Michael Kramer, there was a time in his youth when he was advised to go into carpentry or plumbing.

One of Hartman's great influences in the philosophical and religious world is his belief in pluralism, a concept that is very difficult, at times, for many people in his adopted country of Israel to accept. Hartman states that he first grasped the concept from his neighborhood, where he grew up with an ethnically mixed population.

Later, he attended Yeshiva University, where, upon graduation, he became a rabbi, at the age of twenty-three. For graduate school, he chose the Jesuit sponsored Fordham University. Here, his concepts of pluralism blossomed as he "encountered the great Roman Catholic philosopher, Robert C. Pollack," Kramer reported.

In 1971, after living in Montreal, where he worked both as a rabbi and as an instructor of philosophy at McGill University, Hartman, his wife, and their five children immigrated to Israel. Upon arrival in Israel, Hartman discovered that his luggage had been stolen. As quoted in Kramer's article, Hartman's response was: "A perfect metaphor for the transition between dreams and reality."

Besides his own studies and his teaching, Hartman has been both spiritual and political adviser to Shimon Peres, former Israeli prime minister. He has also provided his services and intellectual thought to many other political figures, both in Israel and abroad.

Hartman claims it is difficult to find stories or examples of tolerance in the Bible, so he relies heavily on the Talmud, Judaism's oral tradition, which, as Kramer stated, "mediates . . . biblical literalism." Similarly, Hartman is doing his best to mediate the differences between traditional and modern Jews, between the political and the philosophical, as well as between the Israelis and the Palestinians, a job that he admits may take decades.

The first book Hartman published, *Maimonides: Torah and Philosophic Quest,* won the National Jewish Book Award. Living in the twelfth century, Moses Mai-

monides was the foremost intellectual force of medieval Judaism. He was a dedicated scholar and author, and his writings have influenced philosophy, religion, and medicine ever since. The scope of Maimonides's writing is vast. Of his most influential writings are *Commentary to the Mishne,* which has become a code of Jewish law, and *Guide of the Perplexed.*

Many modern Jewish philosophers have argued that Maimonides's two works stand opposed to one another: one endorses the way of reason and action, while the other the path of contemplation. Hartman's book contends Maimonides in no way contradicts himself. As a reviewer for *Choice* put it, Hartman "contends that Maimonides linked action based on Jewish lay (Halakhah) with a philosophical understanding and love of God." Hartman's attempts at integrating Maimonides's thoughts on both topics have won not only the National Jewish Book Award, but also the recommendation of many critics. *Commentary* reviewer David Singer called Hartman's book a "fresh and quite fascinating attempt to solve a long-standing riddle," while Gerda Haas, for *Library Journal,* wrote that Hartman's "explanations are both profound and clear."

In 1990, Hartman published *Conflicting Visions: Spiritual Possibilities in Modern Israel,* a series of essays analyzing religion's role in the state of Israel, which Carol R. Glatt of *Library Journal* described as having been written with "a sane voice among the many discordant sounds emanating from Israel." Although Hartman's philosophy has gone through various changes over the years, his ideal of pluralism remains the same. In this book, he attempts to point out the problems that are facing Israel, with its potentially volatile mix of what Glatt called "messianic right-wing groups and ghettoized religious extremists."

In 1999 Hartman wrote *A Living Covenant: The Innovative Spirit in Traditional Judaism,* for which he won another National Jewish Book Award. Here again Hartman attempts to bridge philosophical divides. In this interpretation of Jewish teachings, Hartman tries to create a relationship between divine demand and human response, between traditional religious thought and modernity. His basic argument is that, as he interprets Judaic law, he sees no need for blind obedience and complete resignation. Rather, he suggests that there is room for individuality and freedom of expression. Hartman is concerned that the movement among Orthodox Jews in Israel will not be able to properly answer the modern needs of Jews. Hartman would like to see the Torah faithfully observed. He believes that if Jews truly understood the traditional lessons of the Torah, there could be a return to both a deeply religious state, as well as a modern one. If this could be done, Israel would stand as a model for all Jews in the Diaspora.

*Christian Century* contributor John T. Pawlikowski opened his review with this statement: "David Hartman is bent on stirring up all sectors of contemporary Judaism and, by implication, Christians and other religious people as well." Further explaining himself, Pawlikowski stated that Hartman believed that Judaism is in "a delicate stage of transition." If Judaism can see its way successfully through this transition, "Judaism might help spur the equally necessary renovation of Christianity."

Hartman published a collection of essays in 1999 for which he received yet another National Jewish Book Award, *A Heart of Many Rooms: Celebrating the Many Voices within Judaism.* This time, Hartman contemplates the spiritual and philosophical questions that face all Jews as they watch their religion broken apart into a variety of practices. A secondary question addressed is how Jews can relate to people of other religions. Hartman, through his sixteen essays, calls upon all Jews to help create a shared spiritual language and a tolerance of the diversity that they find both among themselves and along their borders. A *Publishers Weekly* contributor noted Hartman's efforts by stating, "Hartman's incisive wit, passionate heart and loving soul animate his desire for religious diversity and understanding." And S. T. Katz for *Humanities* remarked, "Given its subject matter, the intelligence and learning represented by these essays, and the generous and humane spirit that energizes them, this is an important collection."

In 2000 Hartman completed *Israelis and the Jewish Tradition: An Ancient People Debating Its Future.* Putting this book into an interesting perspective, Arnold Ages, for *Midstream,* critiqued the work by first commenting about the difficulty of Jewish philosophers, in comparison to gentile or secular counterparts. The difference, Ages stated, is that other philosophers can "sit tranquilly in their libraries and studies and dissect the meaning of meaning and other esoterica of metaphysics and logic." Unfortunately for Jewish philosophers, Ages contended, their lot is not so easy, since, historically, Jews have had to deal with "continual confrontation with history from the time of Abraham, through Moses, to the settlement of Eretz Israel, and beyond—to the cataclysms of pogrom, ghetto, and the Holocaust." Since the founding of the State of Israel, Ages stated, the "philosophical problems have become even more complex." In his attempts to confront these complex issues, Hartman has written his "most controversial contribution to the religious meaning of Jewish history and its unfolding in the Jewish state during the past 50 years."

## BIOGRAPHICAL AND CRITICAL SOURCES:

*PERIODICALS*

*Booklist,* March 1, 1999, George Cohen, review of *A Heart of Many Rooms: Celebrating the Many Voices within Judaism,* p. 1129; October 15, 2000, Mary Carroll, review of *Israelis and the Jewish Tradition: An Ancient People Debating Its Future,* p. 394.

*Choice,* September, 1977, review of *Maimonides: Torah and Philosophic Quest,* p. 876; February, 1999, Z. Garber, review of *A Living Covenant: The Innovative Spirit in Traditional Judaism,* p. 1077; November 1999, S. T. Katz, review of *A Heart of Many Rooms,* p. 556.

*Christian Century,* July 2, 1986, John T. Pawlikowski, review of *A Living Covenant,* pp. 623-624.

*Commentary,* December, 1977, David Singer, review of *Maimonides,* p. 90.

*Judaism,* summer, 1993, Arnold Eisen, review of *Conflicting Visions: Spiritual Possibilities in Modern Israel,* p. 378.

*Library Journal,* May 15, 1977, Gerda Haas, review of *Maimonides,* p. 1196; August, 1990, Carol R. Glatt, review of *Conflicting Visions,* p. 115; May 15, 1998, Michael Rogers, review of *A Living Covenant,* p. 121; August, 1999, review of *A Heart of Many Rooms,* p. 100.

*Midstream,* November, 2000, Arnold Ages, review of *Israelis and the Jewish Tradition,* p. 73.

*New York Times Book Review,* November 10, 1985, Hyam Maccoby, "Overruling the Voice from Heaven," p. 24.

*Perspectives on Political Science,* winter, 2001, Benjamin Scolnic, review of *Israelis and the Jewish Tradition,* p. 55.

*Publishers Weekly,* March 8, 1999, review of *A Heart of Many Rooms,* p. 62; November 1, 1999, review of *A Heart of Many Rooms,* p. 51; September 25, 2000, review of *Israelis and the Jewish Tradition,* p. 109; July 23, 2001, review of *Love and Terror in the God Encounter: The Theological Legacy of Rabbi Joseph B. Soloveitchik,* p. 73.

*Tikkun,* November, 1994, interview with David Hartman, p. 57.

*Time,* April 30, 1990, Michael Kramer, "Sage in a Land of Anger: Teaching Tolerance and Pluralism, Israeli Philosopher David Hartman Seeks to Heal Israel's Trauma," pp. 90-92.

OTHER


*Jewish Lights Publishing Web site,* http://www.jewishlights.com/ (October 7, 2001).*

\*    \*    \*

# HASS, Amira 1956-

*PERSONAL:* Born 1956, in Jerusalem, Israel. *Education:* Studied history at Hebrew University and the University of Tel Aviv.

*ADDRESSES: Agent*—c/o Author Mail, Henry Holt and Co., 115 West 18th St., New York, NY 10011. *E-mail*—amira@haaretz.co.il.

*CAREER:* Journalist and author. *Ha'aretz,* Israel, staff editor, 1989—. Worked as a teacher before beginning journalism career.

*AWARDS, HONORS:* Robert F. Kennedy Award nomination for *Drinking the Sea at Gaza: Days and Nights in a Land under Siege.*

*WRITINGS:*


*Li-shetot meha-yam shel 'Azah,* Sifre Siman (Tel Aviv, Israel), 1996 translated by Elana Wesley and Maxine Kaufman-Lacusta as *Drinking the Sea at Gaza: Days and Nights in a Land under Siege,* Metropolitan (New York, NY), 1999.

*SIDELIGHTS:* Israeli journalist Amira Hass based her debut book, *Drinking the Sea at Gaza: Days and Nights in a Land under Siege,* on her experiences reporting about the plight of the Palestinian people who have lived for many years under Israeli occupation. Hass has been a reporter for one of Israel's most respected daily newspapers, *Ha'aretz,* since 1989. In 1991 the paper assigned Hass to cover life in the Gaza Strip, which is one of the territories occupied by Israel. As a result of spending time in Gaza and coming to know its people, Hass became empathetic to their fight for independence. She eventually moved to Gaza in 1993, becoming the first and only Israeli journalist to live in one of the Palestinian territories. One of Hass's main contentions since she first began reporting from Gaza is that few Israelis truly understand the plight of the Palestinian people, largely out of fear and prejudice. In fact, few of her countrymen understood why she would want to live in Gaza. "To most Israelis, my move seemed outlandish, even crazy, for they believed I was surely putting my life at risk," Hass wrote in *Drinking the Sea at Gaza.*

One of the major themes Hass discusses in her book is that Israel has continued to rule over Gaza with an iron fist, despite the fact that Israel signed over sovereignty to the territory as part of the Israeli-Palestinian Peace Accord of 1993. Numerous literary critics lauded *Drinking the Sea at Gaza* for its honest portrayal of the political realities and daily tribulations faced by the Palestinian people living in the occupied territories, especially by those living in Gaza. "Few writers have exposed the prison-like wretchedness, and dangers, of Gaza life with the vehemence and precision of Ms. Hass," wrote a contributor for the *Economist.* The work also earned Hass a nomination for the Robert F. Kennedy Award. Because of her criticisms, many Israelis have viewed Hass as somewhat of a traitor. She dispelled this notion in a 2002 interview with Marjorie Miller of the *Los Angeles Times,* when she suggested that she was just doing her job as a journalist. "Journalism is not about telling people what they like to hear," Hass said. "The task of journalists is to monitor power and, in the relations between Israelis and Palestinians, Israel is certainly the center of power." The daughter of two Holocaust survivors, Hass moved to the Palestinian town of Ramallah in 1997, when she began covering the West Bank, another occupied territory.

Originally published as *Li-shetot meha-yam shel 'Azah* in 1996, Hass's book was translated to English by

Elana Wesley and Maxine Kaufman-Lacusta, and published in America three-years later. Despite the three year span, many literary critics felt the work was still pertinent to the political events taking place in Israel, because the Israeli government's policies toward the occupied territories had not changed significantly during the period. The book includes vivid descriptions of what it is like for the average person to live in Gaza. For example, in the chapter titled "Gaza Prison" Hass discusses how Palestinians are only allowed to leave Gaza with a permit given by the Israeli government, which she believes is an arbitrary process with no clear guidelines. Hass describes how this process hinders Palestinian businessmen and workers alike, who must overcome the obstacle to earn a living. Throughout the book, Hass decries the prevailing Israeli stereotypes of the Gazan people as "savage, violent and hostile to Jews." However, she doesn't put all the blame on the Israelis for the hostilities between the two peoples, or the sorry state of the Palestinians. In the book's concluding chapter, Hass blasts the cruel and repressive governing tactics of the Palestinian Authority, led by Yassir Arafat, and charged with administering the territories as part of the Israeli-Palestinian Peace Accord. In fact, Hass describes how many of her Palestinian friends decry Arafat's authoritarian leadership, which many believe has only worsened the Palestinian's crumbling economy. Jennifer Mitchell, who reviewed *Drinking the Sea at Gaza* for *Washington Report on Middle East Affairs,* was just one of the many literary critics who lauded Hass's effort. "Throughout the book, she expertly blends her encounters with Gaza residents with a consistently astute analysis, in a style both insightful and captivating," Mitchell wrote. "Hass ably dissects and explicates the individual elements of a generally difficult and evolving political problem," Gilbert Taylor of *Booklist* similarly wrote. A contributor for *Publishers Weekly* felt *Drinking the Sea at Gaza* would be a particularly beneficial read for Americans. "Hass's book offers a much closer look at life on the ground in Gaza than American readers are used to receiving from newspapers and television," the contributor wrote.

*BIOGRAPHICAL AND CRITICAL SOURCES:*

*BOOKS*

Hass, Amira, *Drinking the Sea at Gaza: Days and Nights in a Land under Siege,* Metropolitan (New York, NY), 1999.

*PERIODICALS*

*Booklist,* May 1, 1999, Gilbert Taylor, review of *Drinking the Sea at Gaza: Days and Nights in a Land under Siege,* p. 1575.
*Economist,* September 18, 1999, p. 11.
*Journal of Palestine Studies,* spring, 2000, Sara Roy, review of *Drinking the Sea at Gaza,* p. 98.
*Library Journal,* April 15, 1999, Nader Entessar, review of *Drinking the Sea at Gaza,* p. 124.
*Los Angeles Times,* March 15, 2002, p. A1.
*Middle East Policy,* June, 2000, Al J. Venter, review of *Drinking the Sea at Gaza,* p. 191.
*Publishers Weekly,* May 3, 1999, review of *Drinking the Sea at Gaza,* p. 55.
*Washington Report on Middle East Affairs,* April, 2002, Jennifer Mitchell, review of *Drinking the Sea at Gaza,* pp. 103-104.

*OTHER*

*IPI Press Homepage,* http://www.freemedia.at (August 1, 2002), profile of Amira Hass.*

\*     \*     \*

## HAWASS, Zahi A. 1947-

*PERSONAL:* Born May 28, 1947, in Damietta, Egypt. *Education:* Cairo University, B.A. (Greek and Roman archaeology), 1967; Cairo University, diploma (Egyptology), 1980; University of Pennsylvania, M.A. (Egyptology and Syro-Palestinian archaeology), 1983; University of Pennsylvania, Ph.D. (Egyptology), 1987.

*ADDRESSES: Agent*—c/o Publicity Director, Harry N. Abrams, Inc., 100 Fifth Ave., New York, NY 10011.

*CAREER:* Educator, writer, Egyptologist, and archaeologist. Inspector of antiquities at various Egyptian sites, 1969-75; first inspector of antiquities at Giza Pyramids, Embaba, and Bahriya Oasis, 1974-79; chief inspector at Giza Pyramids, Cairo, 1980; general director at Saqqara and Bahriya Oasis, 1987-97; general director of Giza Pyramids excavation, 1996—; undersecretary of the state for the Giza Monuments, 1998—. Associate director of excavations at Kom

Abou Bellou and Ashmuneim, 1968-74; director of preliminary excavations at Merimdeh Beni Salama, 1976; director of excavations and director of conservation and restoration at various Egyptian sites, including the Sphinx, the Sphinx Temple, Khufu's Pyramid, the Temple of Khufu, the Tombs of the Overseers of the Pyramid Builders, the Great Pyramid, the Pyramid Complex of Teti at Saqqara, the Third Pyramid at Giza, and the Valley of the Golden Mummies, 1975—. Site manager of Memphis and the Giza Plateau, 1987—. Consultant, lecturer, university instructor and media commentator on Egyptology and Egyptian culture and archaeology.

Member of committee,foreign exhibits committee, and fellowship committee of the Egyptian Antiquities Organization, and board of trustees, 1992-93; Committee for the Protection of the Monuments of the Giza Pyramids; National Specialist Committee in Egypt for Archaeology and Tourism; Committee for the Restoration of the Sphinx; Tourist Promotion Committee for Giza Government; Sound and Light Company (board of trustees, 1990); High Council of Culture (history and archaeology) of the Ministry of Culture; and German Archaeological Institute: member of the board Cairo Museum..

*AWARDS, HONORS:* Fulbright scholarship, 1980; University of Pennsylvania scholarship, 1986; Pride of Egypt Award, Cairo Foreign Press Association, 1998; Egypt Presidential Award: First Class in Arts and Sciences, 1998; Golden Plate Award, American Academy of Achievement, 2000; Distinguished Scholar, Egyptian Scholars Association, 2000.

*WRITINGS:*

*The Pyramids of Ancient Egypt,* Carnegie Museum of Natural History (Pittsburgh, PA), 1990.
*The Secrets of the Sphinx: Restoration Past and Present,* American University in Cairo Press (Cairo, Egypt), 1998.
*Silent Images: Women in Pharaonic Egypt,* Harry N. Abrams (New York, NY), 2000.
*Valley of the Golden Mummies,* Harry N. Abrams (New York, NY), 2000.
*The Mysteries of Abu Simbel: Ramesses II and the Temples of the Rising Sun,* forword by Farouk Hosni, American University in Cairo (Cairo, Egypt), 2000.
*Secrets from the Sand: My Search for Egypt's Ancient Past,* Harry N. Abrams (New York, NY), 2003.

Also contributor of articles to periodicals, including *National Geographic Traveller.*

*SIDELIGHTS:* Zahi A. Hawass was born in Egypt to a prosperous family. At the age of sixteen, he left home to attend law school in Alexandria, but he quickly discovered that his heart was not in studying law. With mixed feelings, he pursued his second choice, Greek and Roman archaeology, and after experiencing his first archaeological dig, Hawass realized that he had found his life's work. After earning a diploma in Egyptology at Cairo University, he traveled abroad and attained more education in the United States. He returned to Egypt to oversee excavations and conservation projects at many sites before becoming the general director of the Giza Pyramids at the age of forty—the youngest person to attain that position. Hawass's first priority was to put an end to unrestricted access to the monuments. As the work at the site progressed, he turned his attention to the restoration of the three Pyramids and the Sphinx.

*Silent Images: Women in Pharaonic Egypt* is one of Hawass's first books looking at the ancient culture of the people of the area. Mary Morgan Smith, reviewing the book in *Library Journal,* commented, "The book's color photographs of wall painting, statues, and landscapes are wonderful in their own right." Stephen Williams, reviewing *Silent Images* in *African Business,* called it "a superb book" and noted that Hawass "suggests that the balance between the very different roles of men and women created a stable society."

The discovery of hundreds of mummies at the Bahriya Oasis made headlines around the world. Field director Hawass informed the world about the discovery in his book *Valley of the Golden Mummies.* In *Booklist* Brad Hooper called it a "book to be savored by readers of all ages and interests." Edward K. Werner, writing in *Library Journal,* described the book as "well suited to general readers and . . . and will be quality additions to any library's holdings in ancient history and archaeology." Rabiya S. Tuma, reviewing *Valley of the Golden Mummies* in *Discover,* described it as an "evocative narrative [that] weaves together stories of the upper-middle-class families buried in the Valley with tales of modern Egyptians who dwell in the villages nearby." Brian Fagan, writing in the *Los Angeles Times Book Review,* commented, "*Valley of the Golden Mummies* has all the allure and fascination of classic

Egyptology: a chance for spectacular discovery, of gold and mummies peering from the soil, archaeologists brushing sand from richly adorned burial mounds, the thrill of mummy eyes peering from the dirt." Fagan concluded, "The Bahariya cemetery has come along at an opportune moment, for a revolution in our knowledge of mummies is unfolding in quiet, air-conditioned laboratories."

*BIOGRAPHICAL AND CRITICAL SOURCES:*

*PERIODICALS*

*African Business,* July, 2000, Stephen Williams, review of *Silent Images: Women in Pharaonic Egypt,* p. 42.

*Atlantic,* January, 1985, Katie Leishman, "The Future of the Past: Egypt Would Like to Solve Its New Archaeological Crisis Alone—But Non-Egyptians Have the Expertise," p. 21.

*Booklist,* August, 2000, Patricia Monaghan, review of *Silent Images,* p. 2084; September 1, 2000, Brad Hooper, review of *Valley of the Golden Mummies,* p. 4.

*Choice,* March, 2001, J. Pollini, review of *Valley of the Golden Mummies,* p. 1324.

*Current Events,* October 29, 1999, "Ancient Faces: Valley of the Golden Mummies Discovered in Egyptian Desert," p. 2A.

*Discover,* October, 2000, Rabiya S. Tuma, review of *Valley of the Golden Mummies,* p. 102.

*Library Journal,* October 1, 2000, Mary Morgan Smith, review of *Silent Images,* p. 121; November 15, 2000, Edward K. Werner, review of *Valley of the Golden Mummies,* p. 80.

*Los Angeles Times Book Review,* December 24, 2000, Brian Fagan, "Mummy Dearest: A Lost World Emerges from the Sand,"p. 6

*Publishers Weekly,* October 2, 2000, review of *Valley of the Golden Mummies,* p. 74.

*Time,* September 6, 1999, Andrea Dorfman, "Valley of the Lost Tombs: A Cache of Pristine Mummies Offers a Look at Egyptian Life and Death around the Time of Jesus," p. 62.

*Time for Kids,* September 29, 2000, Kathryn Hoffman, "City of the Dead: The Latest News from the Biggest Mummy Cemetery Ever Found," p. 4.

*Time International,* September 18, 2000, Andrea Dorfman, "City of Mummies: A First Look at Ancient Egyptian Treasures from One of the Richest Finds since King Tut's Tomb," p. 48.

*OTHER*

*E-Museum,* http://www.emuseum.mnsu.edu/ (September 15, 2001).

*The Plateau, Web site of Zahi Hawass,* http://www.guardians.net/hawass/ (September 15, 2001).*

\*    \*    \*

**HEIGHTON, Steven 1961-**

*PERSONAL:* Born 1961, in Toronto, Ontario, Canada. *Education:* Queen's College, B.A., 1985, M.A., 1986.

*ADDRESSES: Home*—P.O. Box 382, Kingston, Ontario, K7L 4W2 Canada.

*CAREER:* Writer. Teacher in Japan, mid-1980s.

*AWARDS, HONORS:* Air Canada Award, 1989; Gerald Lampert Award for best poetry debut, 1990, for *Stalin's Carnival;* first prize in short fiction, *Prism International,* 1991; gold medal for fiction, National Magazine Awards, 1992; finalist, Trillium Award, 1993, for *Flight Paths of the Emperor;* finalist, Governor General's Award, 1995, for *The Ecstasy of Skeptics.*

*WRITINGS:*

*Stalin's Carnival* (poetry), Quarry Press (Kingston, Ontario, Canada), 1989.

*Foreign Ghosts* (poetry), Oberon Press (Ottawa, Ontario, Canada), 1989.

*Flight Paths of the Emperor* (short stories), Porcupine's Quill (Erin, Ontario, Canada), 1992.

*The Ecstasy of Skeptics* (poetry), Anansi (Concord, Ontario, Canada), 1994.

*On Earth as It Is* (short stories), Porcupine's Quill (Erin, Ontario, Canada), 1995.

*The Admen Move on Lhasa: Writing and Culture in a Virtual World* (essays), Anansi (Concord, Ontario, Canada), 1996.

*The Shadow Boxer* (novel), Knopf Canada (Toronto, Ontario, Canada), 2000, Houghton Mifflin (Boston, MA), 2002.

Work represented in anthologies, including *The Journey Prize Anthology,* McClelland & Stewart (Toronto, Ontario, Canada). Contributor to periodicals. Editor, *Quarry,* 1991-94.

*SIDELIGHTS:* Steven Heighton is a Canadian writer who has distinguished himself in both poetry and fiction. He began his literary career in 1989 with *Stalin's Carnival,* a poetry collection that Maurice Mierau, writing in *Books in Canada,* described as "a promising if uneven debut." In the central portion of this volume, Heighton explores the psychology of Soviet dictator Josef Stalin, and he even presents English renderings of works attributed the onetime leader. Mierau proclaimed the Stalin-related verse "interesting and uneven," and he concluded that "Heighton is already an ambitious and very accomplished writer."

In 1992 Heighton published *Flight Paths of the Emperor,* a collection of short stories that Ann Copeland, in her *Books in Canada* appraisal, found "sophisticated and elegantly told." Some of the tales in this volume reflect Heighton's experiences as a teacher in Japan during the mid-1980s. "A Man away from Home Has No Neighbors," for example, concerns a Japanese soldier's love for a Chinese peasant, and "An Apparition Play" relates a father's alienation from his daughter while in Japan to conduct a burial service. Another tale, "On Strikes and Errors in Japanese Baseball," chronicles an attempt to uncover information on the atomic bombing of Hiroshima. Copeland proclaimed *Flight Paths of the Emperor* "a memorable collection," and she praised it as "larger and deeper than any one of its fascinating parts." Another reviewer, Mark Ford, wrote in the *Times Literary Supplement* that Heighton's tales "are nearly all vivacious, purposeful, and entertaining," and Tom McCarthy, meanwhile, noted in the London *Observer,* "Technically, the best pieces are little short of brilliant."

Heighton followed *Flight Paths of the Emperor* with *The Ecstasy of Skeptics,* an ambitious collection of poems expressing both the Apollonian and Dionysian aspects of his own life. "As you might guess, this is ambitious stuff," acknowledged Scott Ellis in *Books in Canada,* adding that "Heighton almost always pulls it off." Less impressed, Bert Almon wrote in the *Canadian Book Review Annual* that *The Ecstasy of Skeptics*

"arouses more skepticism than ecstasy," and he contended that "this is not a powerful collection of poems." He conceded, however, that "Heighton has talent."

After issuing *The Ecstasy of Skeptics,* Heighton produced his *On Earth as It Is,* his second collection of short stories. Notable tales in this volume include "Translations of April," wherein a translator relates tales written by a dead loved one, and "To Everything a Season," in which, as Sheryl Halpern observed in *Books in Canada,* eight individuals "play out the different seasons of lovemaking and leavetaking." Stephen Smith, in his *Quill & Quire* assessment, summarized the tales in *On Earth as It Is* as "real and rooted and vital," and Tamas Dobozy added in *Canadian Literature* that "the book delivers." Another reviewer, Henry Hitchings, noted in the *Times Literary Supplement* that "Heighton explores the failure of our attempts to communicate—both with others and with ourselves—and the way reality cannot sustain the fantasies we attempt to imprint on it."

Heighton next published *The Admen Move on Lhasa: Writing and Culture in a Virtual World,* a collection of essays on subjects ranging from the essence of art to the nature of contemporary life. Zsuzsi Gartner, writing in *Quill & Quire,* deemed Heighton's book "passionate, honest, and somewhat noble," and Lawrence Mathews, in his *Essays on Canadian Writing* analysis, praised it as "passionate, generous-spirited . . . , blessedly anachronistic." Even Patricia Morley, who concluded that "some of the individual pieces attempt more than they achieve," considered Heighton "an accomplished writer of fiction and poetry," and she added, in her *Canadian Book Review Annual* consideration, that *The Admen Move on Lhasa* "is ambitious in scope and brilliant in parts."

Among Heighton's other writings is *The Shadow Boxer,* a novel about an aspiring writer who attempts to complete his first novel while overcoming both personal inadequacies and family problems. *Times Literary Supplement* reviewer Margaret Stead called *The Shadow Boxer* "an energetic, fluent and interesting novel," and a *Publishers Weekly* critic hailed it as "remarkable."

Heighton's fiction is also included in *The Journey Prize Anthology.* In *Canadian Literature,* Jim Snyder described Heighton as "the most obviously gifted technician" among the eleven writers represented in the volume.

## BIOGRAPHICAL AND CRITICAL SOURCES:

PERIODICALS

*Books in Canada,* January, 1990, Maurice Mierau, "Man of Steel," pp. 46-47; April, 1995, Scott Ellis, "The New Lyricism," pp. 49-50; September, 1995, Sheryl Halpern, "Lingering Refrains," pp. 35-36; December, 1992, Ann Copeland, "Senses of Strangeness," pp. 38-39.

*Canadian Book Review Annual,* 1995, Bert Almon, review of *The Ecstasy of Skeptics,* p. 3173; 1998, Patricia Morley, review of *The Admen Move on Lhasa: Writing and Culture in a Virtual World,* p. 268.

*Canadian Literature,* fall-winter, 1993, Jim Snyder, "Claims of Loneliness," pp. 158-160; summer, 1998, Tamas Dobozy, "Approaching Earth," pp. 176-178.

*Essays on Canadian Writing,* spring, 1998, Lawrence Mathews, "Beautiful Downtown Lhasa," pp. 167-171.

*Kirkus Reviews,* December 15, 2001, review of *The Shadow Boxer.*

*Library Journal,* December, 2001, Jim Dwyer, review of *The Shadow Boxer,* p. 172.

*Observer* (London, England), February, 1997, Tom McCarthy, "Change at Japan for All Points West," p. 17.

*Publishers Weekly,* February 18, 2002, review of *The Shadow Boxer,* p. 77.

*Quill & Quire,* December, 1992, Stephen Smith, "Remarkable First Flight," p. 15; July, 1995, Stephen Smith, review of *On Earth as It Is,* p. 51; March, 1997, Zsuzsi Gartner, "Life Is Short and Literature Matters," p. 74.

*Times Literary Supplement,* February 7, 1997, Mark Ford, review of *Flight Paths of the Emperor,* p. 21; September 19, 1997, Henry Hitchings, "Rudderless in Kathmandu," p. 21; August 11, 2000, Margaret Stead, "Leaving the Soo," p. 24.

OTHER

*Pagitica,* http://www.pagitica.com/ (May 6, 2002), review of *The Shadow Boxer.**

## HELLER, Michael (David) 1937-

*PERSONAL:* Born May 11, 1937, in New York, NY; son of Peter Frank (a publicist) and Martha (Rosenthal) Heller; married Doris C. Whytal, June 10, 1962 (divorced March 23, 1978); married Jane Augustine (writer), March 5, 1979; children: (first marriage) Nicholas Solomon. *Education:* Rensselaer Polytechnic Institute, B.S. Eng., 1959; New York University, M.A., 1986; graduate study at New School for Social Research.

*ADDRESSES: Office*—P. O. Box 1289, Stuyvesant Station, New York, NY 10009. *E-mail*—mh7@nyu.edu.

*CAREER:* Norelco, New York , NY, chief technical writer, 1963-65; private teacher of English in Spain, 1965-66; freelance industrial and advertising writer, 1966-67; New York University, American Language Institute and Washington Square College, New York, NY, master teacher in English, 1967—, acting director, 1986-87, academic coordinator, 1987-92. Lecturer, New York City Community College, 1973. Curator, "Poetry—An Exhibition," City University of New York, 1977. Participant in Poetry-in-the-School programs in New York and Wyoming; member of advisory panel, New York Poetry-in-the-School, 1970—; Naropa Institute, summer faculty in M.F.A. program; Keystone College, PA, poet-in-residence, 1979. Has lectured on poetry and poetics at numerous universities and has given readings at many universities across the United States and Europe.

*MEMBER:* PEN (member of Freedom to Write committee), American Language Institute, Academy of American Poets, Poetry Society of America, Poets and Writers, Modern Language Association, National Book Critics Circle, New York State Poets in the Schools, Poets House (advisory board member).

*AWARDS, HONORS:* Coffey Poetry Prize, New School for Social Research, 1964; poetry fellowship, New York State Creative Artists Public Service, 1975; Poetry in Public Places award, 1975; grants from National Endowment for the Humanities, 1979, 1986; Alice Fay di Castagnola Award, Poetry Society of America, 1980; Yaddo fellow, 1989; New York Foundation for the Arts fellow, 1989.

*Michael Heller*

## WRITINGS:

*Conviction's Net of Branches: Essays on the Objectivist Poets and Poetry,* Southern Illinois University Press (Carbondale, IL), 1984.

(Editor) *Carl Rakosi: Man and Poet,* National Poetry Foundation (Orono, ME), 1993.

*Living Root: A Memoir,* State University of New York Press (Albany, NY), 2000.

*POETRY*

*Two Poems,* Perishable Press , 1970.

*Accidental Center,* Sumac Press (Fremont, MI), 1972.

*Figures of Speaking,* Perishable Press, 1977.

*Knowledge,* SUN (New York, NY), 1979.

*Marginalia in a Desperate Hand,* Staple Diet Pig Press, 1985.

*In the Builded Place,* Coffee House Press, 1989.

*Six Poems,* Hot Bird MFG, II(15), 1993.

*Wordflow: New and Selected Poems,* Talisman House (Jersey City, NJ), 1997.

*Exigent Futures: New and Selected Poems,* Salt Publishing (Cambridge, England), 2003.

Also author of the libretto for the opera *Benjamin,* with music composed by Ellen Fishman Johnson. Contributor of articles and poems to literary journals and national publications, including *Nation, Caterpillar, Sumac, Paris Review, Extensions, Ohio Review, Ironwood,* and *Parnassus.* Editor of *Origin: Fifth Series;* former contributing editor, *Montemora;* advisory editor, *Pequod;* contributing editor, *Sagetrieb.*

*SIDELIGHTS:* Michael Heller, according to Burt Kimmelman in the *Dictionary of Literary Biography,* "has staked out a territory all his own. His is the most important of many attempts to elaborate an 'Objectivist' poetics, first described as such by Louis Zukofsky in a 1931 issue of *Poetry* magazine. Heller is faithful to the Objectivist desire for a poetry deriving from the senses, from fact and directness, yet he aspires to a more complex aesthetic. His poems are marked by an acute and highly original sensitivity to contemporary concerns about voice, language, history and knowledge."

In a discussion of *Accidental Center,* Robert Vas Dias in *Contemporary Poets* called Heller "an authentic, hard-edged, meditative poet of truly contemporary sensibility." Further, Vas Dias noted the parallel between Heller's work as a physicist and his approach to words as shifts in matter. The poems in *Accidental Center* focus on images, often paradoxical, formed from precise observation. Heller utilizes scientific terminology to form links to tradition and even religion. In "Meditation on the Coral," Heller describes the lives of city-dwellers in terms of the structure and origins of coral. The style of the poetry is short and spare and the content frequently acknowledges the negative capabilities of things, ideas, and feelings. Heller does not oversimplify the nature of his subjects, but instead acknowledges their mystery with the understanding that what we know is a function of how we know.

*Knowledge* is more leisurely and digressive than *Accidental Center.* Having found a comfortable, yet serious, style, Heller is able to explore more personal themes. He draws on occasions and events in his life and creates poetry that contains both the literal and the figurative. To Vas Dias, *In the Builded Place* represents "the poet at the height of his powers, in his willingness in many of the poems to take risks and therefore to say more than he otherwise might have." In this collection, Heller shows various traditions rivaling one another (such as urban angst and the Asian poetic), resulting in a unique poetic structure and outlook. The poems express the ambiguity and potential of a single person's existence at a certain point in time. Heller depicts city life, but not in a sterile, fabricated way. Instead, he demonstrates that even in the bustle of urban life, there is a human heart at the center, as in the buildings that seem to be little more than a composite of angles and planes, but hold within them the diversity of human life and experience. "One of Heller's chief concerns throughout his poetry," wrote Kimmelman, "is the act of perception. He often speaks of perception as an act in which the world impinges on a consciousness that continually interprets a sensorium of act and event."

Kimmelman concluded: "Heller's poetry, especially when appreciated in conjunction with his prose, has created a system of signs complexly wrought and freighted with human history and desire. His extraordinary achievement is that he handles both language and the notion of language with great intellectual rigor and equally great tenderness and compassion. His poems communicate his rigor of thought in the most human of terms. Heller's poetry and prose are noble in gesture and intent, superbly rich and profoundly emotional. They should be considered a unique and vital part of the contemporary canon. Widespread recognition of his accomplishments can only sustain a healthy literary culture."

Combining his poetry and prose, Heller's 2000 book *Living Root: A Memoir* presents "poems, notes on poems, journal entries, poignant descriptions, and philosophical thoughts" about his family's history, according to Gene Shaw in *Library Journal*. While tracing his Jewish family back to its roots in Poland, then to their immigration to Brooklyn, Heller chronicles the lives of his mother and father, his grandfather and aunts, while delineating the family and its memories. The critic for *Publishers Weekly* found that *Living Root* "is as much about [Heller] as it is about the importance of memory." Shaw praised the book's "seamless joining of personal tone and historic incident."

Heller once told *CA:* "My formal education has been in science and engineering, and recently, in philosophy, interests which continually play a great part in my thinking and writing. Science, thought—these later gods—deny the comforts of the old animisms; they too, however, are in need of demystification, not because they are wrong, but because they are not sufficient. I try to pose something as language which gives more force to a human argument of the world. Nevertheless, I would not want to call it a "fine art."

*AUTOBIOGRAPHICAL ESSAY:*

Michael Heller contributed the following autobiographical essay to *CA:*

I blundered into poetry, into being a writer, around 1959 shortly after college. I'd written school assignments, short funny poems, book reports, sketches, lots of things before that time, as did almost everyone I knew. But these bits of writing were either school assignments or toss-offs, jokey-hokey things. Nothing I had an urge to stand behind or imagine being in print. I did not conceive of myself as a "writer." What impelled me into poetry was a series of encounters and near-inexplicable choices, almost all of which occurred in the short space of time between 1959 and 1966.

As well, I ought not discount genetic disposition, even a subtle pressure as though an inscribed destiny already existed for me arising out of family background. My grandfather had been a writer as well as a rabbi. His Talmudic studies and his children's stories were published in German in Munich and in Yiddish in Bialystok, where he lived until immigrating to the United States in 1912. I knew little of this while I was young and remember him mostly as a cheek-pinching, sweet old man. But there had been a stern streak in my grandfather's character which drove my father from his house at the age of fifteen. My father was running away, as though from real life into something confected out of literature. From the family's doorstep in Brooklyn, he went to sign up as a cook's mate on a Grace Lines freighter sailing to European, Latin, and South American ports. After a year and a half of travels, and as though impelled by half the young man's romantic fiction in the world, he launched himself into a Gatsby-like American life, assuming the roles of railway detective, soldier, newspaperman, filmmaker, lawyer, politico, finally a public relations counselor looking for the "big deal."

*The author's grandfather, Zalmon Heller, 1940*

In the family archive, which I inherited when my parents died, I discovered that my father had written two or three letters a day during those long intermittent periods over the years when he and my mother were living apart. When he could finally move to Florida in 1957, he stumbled into a public relations career, writing press releases, sales letters, advertising proposals and, two or three times a week, penning a new poem to my mother. In his many careers, in his day-to-day life, the employment of language was central.

Along with all this writing came another essential character trait of my father's. Whether proposing love or pushing a product, my father was more soft-hearted than intellectual. He was sentimentally disposed toward life, seeing it in either rosy or maudlin tones, and some of that coloration may have rubbed off on me. For my father, characteristically, wanted to believe in what he wrote; it was absolutely crucial to his self-image and to his work, as it is, in some sense, to the poet who must lay down words not only with art and purpose but with faith in them as well. In my memoir, *Living Root,* I exfoliate my father's life and its many impingements on me, finding it most perfectly realized, sometimes damningly so, in my father's own words. Writing was my father's essential *tic,* and my background, as I look back, is drenched with torrents of words.

I must also add the fact that my mother in her late sixties took up "creative writing" typing up short stories that were really thinly disguised bits of autobiography. She, in contrast to my father, had a more sardonic view of human relations, and so these little snippets of story often turned on a hilarious embarrassment or *faux pas,* my father being the suffering butt of most of them. But my mother could also reach back in time and pinpoint, in excoriating fashion, her own mother and siblings. Of course, my mother's taking up writing came much too late to be considered an influence. Rather, I think that like me she had surrendered to the family's propensity for making verbiage the way farmers make hay.

Yet to take this family history as solely determinative would be, as literary critics call it, "back-shadowing." For when I look to the past, I see myself already laying out my own pathways and traceries. As a child, I made up stories for myself and others, and also experienced the absorption and thrills of a reader. But

My father throughout his entire life was also something of a poet manqué, writing sentimental poems to my mother from before they were married until his Parkinson's disease rendered writing and then speech impossible. In the late 1930s, he "inherited" the firm of Rosenthal Brothers from my mother's mother, Grandma Rose, a stern, well-to-do businesswoman. The firm, located on Lower Broadway in Manhattan, made braids and trimmings for draperies. From what I understand, the business had been imposed upon him by my mother's family, not only to give him a stable source of income so as to provide for my mother, but to smother his own deeply held romantic inclinations to live a carefree, irresponsible life.

Then, in 1941, my mother developed heart trouble, and the main cure suggested by her various doctors was to live in a warm climate. From 1942 to the mid-1950s, my mother lived in the Miami area of south Florida, and my father commuted once or twice a month to see her and us, the children.

*The author's parents, Pete and Martha Heller, Miami Beach, FL, 1952*

possibly my first sustained literary effort involved my being on the radio as a young child. In the third grade, I was selected by one of my teachers, Miss Shiner, to be an actor in a children's radio program. As a young boy, I fell in love with at least three of my female teachers, and Miss Shiner was the focus of one of my early if distant longings, always smelling, when I was near her, like a fresh bar of soap. She must have still been in graduate school when I was a pupil in her classroom, for she was involved with a number of the instructors from the drama and radio department of the University of Miami. They had asked her to find a student who could play a part in a children's drama they had written. Miss Shiner chose me.

The University of Miami radio department and its studios were located in one of the towers of the university library, a beautiful building faced with white coral surrounded by rows of stately Royal Palms. Its offices were accessible only by a steep, winding staircase up and down which rushed anxious students carrying clipboards, stopwatches, and roles of magnetic wire. I remember, however, that there was an eerie claustrophobic feeling to the studio, with its hanging microphones and control room window, and the deadening claustrophobic effect of the sound-proofed walls. The radio play was called, *The Sasparilla Kid,* the "Kid" to be played by me. Despite the innocuous title, the play was actually quite scary. In it, the hero, the Kid, confronts and overcomes strange leathery beings who climb out of the depths of the earth and threaten to take over the planet. The evil creatures were rendered quite powerfully in the script and have populated my dreams ever since.

But this show was only to be a beginning, for over the next few weeks after this broadcast, the young teachers invented a radio program entitled *Unfinished Fables* and found a local ice-cream company to sponsor it. It was broadcast live on Saturday mornings from the stage of the Royal Theater, a movie house in downtown Miami, to be followed by a kiddie show of seven cartoons and two full-length adventure films, thus guaranteeing something of a live audience.

The format of the show represented my first challenge with literary form. The program began with an adult moderator reading half of a short story written by one of the instructors to three school-age children, one of them being me. There was a commercial break for the ice cream, then, one by one, we kids offered our own continuings and endings. Throughout, the moderator would help us along, suggesting how to finish a sentence or a thought, asking questions when what we said was unclear. The stories were supposed to be completed spontaneously on the air, but in fact, an hour before airtime, we arrived at the theater and were read the story and given an opportunity to make some notes for our endings. After the show, and before the cartoons began, the sponsors passed out free ice cream to the participants and to the audience in the movie theater.

Those programs also ushered in glorious childhood Saturday afternoons, as I recall. For after the show and the cartoons and the double bill, my younger sister, Tena, and I walked into downtown Miami and saw at least another double bill, often two Charlie Chan movies, at the Olympia theater. We'd spend what little money we had left on White Castle hamburgers and Birch Beer served in glistening, frosted mugs. In the late afternoon, sated and with our eyes red from so many hours in front of movie screens, we hitched a ride home on the causeway, often picked up by one of the old, beat-up jitneys that brought black people to and from their jobs on Miami Beach.

As I look back, I see that, as with the children's books my mother read to me, I was being imprinted with narratives, with the egg-perfect plots of the detective movies we saw or of the radio fables that I finished with so much satisfaction as though I, too, had solved a puzzle. When I wasn't playing sports, I went over to the public library. I loved the solitary afternoons there in the cool, high-ceilinged reading room with its hushed quiet and the faint smell of the whitewashed walls. I was an avid reader of science and science-fiction books, and already felt a strong attraction to science with its pure symmetries and unexpected discoveries. Even then, I had thought that being a scientist or engineer, handling beautifully polished objects or working on elegant equations, was my ideal. Such inclinations were reinforced by the suspense-filled shapeliness of the films and fables I was exposed to.

Later, as I described in *Living Root*, my family adopted my cousin Arthur who, after his parents died, came to live with us. Arthur was six years older and precociously well-read, and at night while I lay in bed he read aloud to me classical poetry, *The Iliad* and Dante, before I fell asleep. During the day he talked about his desires to be a biochemist. As if through his example, the love of words and of science were fused in my mind. And while I had no thought to be a writer nor did I reflect deeply on language, these formative experiences exposed me to a kind of intellectual wonder. It was only much later that I came to understand what words could catch and bring to light.

\*

The impulse to take myself seriously as a writer came as a sort of late and mostly post-college phenomenon, one not without serious obstacles. My engineering degree from Rensselaer was a job passport of sorts, but was also, if anything, an anti-certificate of entrée into a writing community. C. P. Snow's two cultures of science and humanities had had little to do with each other on the Rensselaer campus. English was an elective, and Rensselaer, a land-grant college, required all physically able students to take ROTC, substituting courses in military strategy and leadership for anything like English or the humanities. Although I was required to enroll in the program, I hated ROTC and the commandant, Colonel X, a regular army career officer, who wandered the halls with a swagger stick. On the parade grounds, during inspection, my answer to the loudly shouted "Do you want to be an officer in this man's army?" was an equally loud "No!" The first time, I astounded the cadet officer who had shouted the question and then paused to check the cleanliness of my rifle. He managed to mouth an expletive under his breath before handing it back. Often, I showed up for Parade unshaven and in wrinkled clothes, turned left when I was supposed to turn right, thus knocking the rifles off the shoulders of my fellow cadets. It was all amusing, fueled by a few drinks before drill or class. At the end of my sophomore year, I was called in by the commandant and told that I could either sign up for the following two years or be flunked out of the program. I chose the latter, and during my next two summers, while living at home in Miami Beach, took make-up English courses at the University of Miami.

I account those early evening summer classes an odd, dreamlike interlude, almost untouched by the rest of my life at that time. Perhaps the long rides through the dusk over the MacArthur Causeway, the wave tops of the bay glittering with the setting sun, cast a spell, or was it that the long, white buildings of the university, nestled in flowers and with a veranda outside of every classroom, so sharply contrasted with the brick and grime of my Rensselaer surroundings? I was also reminded of my radio days, feeling that I was reentering those unfinished fables of my childhood but on a higher, more complex plane.

Professor Wadsworth, fittingly Byronic in appearance with a long, leonine mane of hair and a smiling mouth filled with gleaming white teeth, taught the Introduction to English classes both summers. An expert in Blake and the early Romantics, he discoursed on the emergence of the Romantics, took us through Dryden's dramas *All for Love, Absalom and Achitophel,* even *Mac Flecknoe,* with their backbiting satires on politics at the court, including the office of poet laureate which Dryden both held and lost. The classes on Blake, especially those on the Prophetic Books, those raging worlds seemingly apart from the life I was living, further added to the semi-unreal quality of those summer learning experiences. Still, when we got to Wordsworth and the dailiness of *The Prelude,* the words in Book I "Fair seed-time had my soul, and I grew up / Fostered alike by beauty and by fear" suddenly flooded me with a feeling of life not yet lived, of a longing previously unknown washing over me.

Back at Rensselaer, I brushed up against literary matters in an almost accidental fashion. I'd always been a reader and hung around with a group of students who worked on the humor magazine, *Bachelor,* and also

*RPI Engineer,* the school's science and technical writing magazine. I later became the managing editor of the *Engineer* and for my efforts was given a gold-capped Shaeffer pen with my name inscribed on it. I still use the pen to sign my letters.

Working on *Bachelor* was a great deal of fun. We reviewed movies and local concerts, campus theatrical productions, and wrote satiric pieces about college life. The magazine was nearly banned after we published an article titled "Architectural Sights of the Tri-State Area" that included photographs of Albany's Green Street brothels, local bars, and Pete Simonian's Pleasure Show Boat, an old paddle-wheeler moored in the Hudson much favored for wine, women, and song by members of the New York State Assembly and Senate.

One semester, in one of our free periods, I and a few fellow classmates gathered with a couple of English professors who were putting together a textbook collection of short stories. The professors were testing out their critical apparatus, and we were the guinea pigs, fed the typical, slightly absurd questions at the backs of college readers. Our discussions were animated, although not very helpful to the professors. Amidst the cultural deserts of RPI, we, at least, read the stories. In regular coursework, I was an indifferent student, spending most of my evenings in bars or playing bridge at the frat house.

I had come to Rensselaer with great enthusiasm to be an engineer or physicist. My childhood fantasies had been nurtured on science-fiction novels, tinkering with mechanical gadgets and even miniature rockets which I set off on the abandoned municipal golf course across the street from where I lived on Miami Beach. But I wasn't up to the math for high physics, and the sterile, anti-intellectual life of the campus had a corrosive effect on my hopes and dreams. I had drifted into fraternity life, become a Deke (Delta Kappa Epsilon), one of the few Jews in an otherwise Waspy, preppy club. In my short novella, *Marble Snows,* written in 1979, I describe the dark side of this life, the sadism and contempt of the initiations, the drinking. I tried to capture the disillusionment that I was feeling at the time.

From Rensselaer, we made forays to Bennington College, mostly to meet young women, who teased anyone from RPI as "tools," the expression then in place for "nerds." But I also sat in on Kenneth Burke's lectures. These impressed me deeply, though at times, Burke himself seemed embattled, for no sentence he uttered went unchallenged by the smart, sassy students, especially those from the Bronx and Manhattan.

There was, as well, a tradition of seeming sophistication in our fraternity house. Before party weekends, when dates arrived from Vassar and Skidmore, and occasionally from Bennington, some of us would memorize scraps of dialogue from Huxley novels or snippets of poetry. Wearing our J. Press suits and armed with an amazingly small amount of literature in our heads, we sallied forth to impress the beautiful liberal arts majors circulating at the cocktail parties. We were trying to create an effect, but it often backfired. I remember one late fall weekend when Ken Gangemi and I (he was one of my fraternity brothers and later went on to become a well-regarded fiction writer) walked into the house living room, spouting from Ginsberg's "Footnote to Howl." When we came to the line "Holy, the cocks of the grandfathers of Kansas!" all talking in the room stopped, and for the briefest of moments, the Vassar and Bennington girls sat there with their jaws dropped. It was short-lived, for within a few moments our dates were all swearing like sailors. Among ourselves, we made no pretense of being intellectuals. We were "gentlemen," many of us, like myself, with the requisite *Cs* to prove it, even if we were nerds as well.

In 1959, I graduated with less-than-exemplary grades, to say the least. I headed for New York City without any particular plan and ended up renting my old summer room from my Aunt Jen in Island Park, New York. The pine riser walls of the unfinished attic room where I had stayed while working at a Long Beach bathing club after my freshman year had been enclosed with dry wall sheeting and plaster. It had been freshly painted, and in addition to the bed, there were now a desk and small bookcase. From Island Park, I went job hunting. I rode the Long Island Railroad into the city or drove the fifteen-year-old Plymouth I bought for five hundred dollars out to the eastern end of Long Island, looking for work. I chalked up a long string of failed interviews. I remember one for a small firm that designed garbage incinerators. I met the chief engineer of the firm in a grimy downtown office off Lower Broadway, not far from my father's old business. Could I get excited writing about incinerators, he asked? Controlled conflagrations of greasy kitchen waste, newspapers, tin cans, and thrown-out children's toys? I searched the bottom of my heart, ready to tell a lie, but the chief, seeing my hesitation, had already dismissed me as a candidate.

My next interview was mysterious. It was held in a small suite of rooms on a high floor in Rockefeller Center. A portly gent (I say "gent" because he spoke with a distinct, clipped British accent) in a three-piece suit and old school tie meandered around the subjects of jet airplanes, security, foreign correspondence, but never got to the point of telling me what job I was being interviewed to do. I loved the surroundings, leather chairs and mahogany desks and wonderful views of other skyscrapers swirled in clouds. I wasn't hired here either, but I think the cause was as much the typically English vagueness on my duties as it was my failure to give an account of myself and of what qualities I might bring to an undefined job. I thought that perhaps I had been invited so that I might be looked over by some intelligence agency or government bureau, some organizational front, and not being Ivy League enough in either appearance or diction, had not been let in on the secret needs of the place.

Ironically, given my rebellious ROTC days, I finally got a job with a large defense contractor, an aviation plant out in Farmingdale, Long Island. This was at the height of the era of defense spending. Korea was over, and Vietnam had not yet happened. But there was McCarthy and the missile gap and the Rosenbergs, sufficient scare stories to fuel funding for the military industrial complex. Contractors for the Pentagon were operating on a "cost-plus" basis. The fatter the payroll, the more money the company would earn. Better to hire someone as an engineer, with the inflated salary that went along with the title, even if the work to be done was something a clerk out of high school could manage. I was taken on as a management engineer and would be asked to evaluate various aircraft building operations for cost analysis and efficiency. This sounded good, but, as I later learned, ran counter to the "cost-plus" culture of the company. What benefit would it be to the bottom line to reduce expenses? In those halcyon days of overcharging with no questions asked, most of my work was relegated to the wastebasket.

I left after three months to go to work for Sperry Gyroscope as a publication engineer (the company's glorified name for a technical writer), and looking back, I see this as the first step on the path I sort of sidestepped into. Sperry was headquartered in the old United Nations building at Lake Success. Here, where diplomats had once sought for a world without war, plowshares were being beaten back, rather expensively, into electronic gear for bombers: the company's main contract was to build equipment for the B-58 Hustler, at that time the most formidable airplane in the U.S. arsenal, designed for precise delivery of nuclear weapons, including the hydrogen bomb, to any place in the world. The publications division where I worked was housed in a small building in Garden City, halfway between Lake Success and Syosset, where Sperry also built electronic gear for the Polaris submarines.

Within the engineering community, technical writers compose an odd, less-than-glamorous subset of ex-humanities majors, scientists who've fallen from the exalted levels of researcher, mathematical grammarians, and individuals like myself who can read both blueprints and prose. The writing group at Garden City had more than its share of would-be poets, novelists, playwrights, and science writers. And there was one man obsessed with both the philosophy of Henry George and the Flat Earth Society—he spent his lunch hours in the cafeteria challenging us to disprove his theory that gravity didn't exist, that bodies didn't fall to the earth, but that the universe was in a constant state of expansion so that objects grew toward each other until they touched. Among this motley group I found companions.

The first day I walked into the office, I ran into Terry, "TK" for short, a friend of one of my Rensselaer fraternity brothers. TK had studied civil engineering at Clarkson, a school about a hundred miles from RPI. But he was a well-known character at my college, showing up at our big weekend parties in the dead of winter wearing Bermuda shorts, tuxedo jacket, and top hat. When he arrived for a party, all of us locked our rooms, for TK when drunk had the habit of throwing people's possessions—their books, papers, clothes, and even furniture—down into the parking lot. He then descended to the parking lot and picking them up one by one from the asphalt, tried to throw them back into the rooms through the half-open windows.

Over lunch, we resumed our friendship and decided to look for an apartment we could share somewhere in Manhattan. Soon we found a garden apartment on

Charles Street in Greenwich Village and began throwing parties. We invited some people from Sperry, and at one of these gatherings I got to talking with Ernie, another publications engineer. Ernie had graduated from Brooklyn Polytechnic; he'd been a student of the poet Louis Zukofsky and had worked on the college literary magazine, *Counterpoint,* which Zukofsky advised. Ernie's roommate, Dick, was also a former student of Zukofsky, as was Hugh Seidman, whom I met briefly in those days and who later became one of my closest friends. Poetry and talk about poetry filled much of our conversation.

When we met, Ernie brought books of poetry for me to read: Zukofsky's *"A"* published in a small red-covered edition by Cid Corman's Origin Press, Robert Creeley's *For Love,* Charles Olson's *Maximus,* and George Oppen's *The Materials.* The last poems I had read were Wordsworth and Longfellow, and some of the other Romantics like Keats and Shelley. I can't fully articulate why, but my experience of reading the books that Ernie gave me was almost overwhelming. The clean language of these poets, the absence of the usual metaphoric material or traditional rhymes and meters, made me feel as if I was not reading poetry at all but something immediate and intense: less pleasurable than the poetry I was familiar with but cutting directly to the point where word and emotion seemed joined. I suddenly felt that I wanted that energy. I wanted to eat up and possess the power of those poems which were not art and not about the making of art but about the sudden apprehension of a person's truth. This feeling, thoroughly naive in a way I still admire, was occurring in a person, myself, who was only half-serious about anything.

I was not so much confused as noncommittal, and this was reflected in my day-to-day living. On any given night, for instance, I might be in a Village coffeehouse listening to a poet read. But it was just as likely I'd be hanging out with some of my old fraternity brothers who'd moved to the city. We'd booze it up at the Plaza bar or sip Samoan Fog Cutters at Trader Vic's. In our business clothes, we were figures right out of that Ferlinghetti poem about Cock Robin, "you killed him, you in your Brooks Brothers suits." Flush with money, I bought a sleek sports car, an Elva Courier, which could turn on a dime. I loved racing it, listening to the motor roar, as I sped around Central Park's inner roadway in the early hours of the morning.

Art, *la vie sentimentale,* or wanting to be an *homme d'affaires,* all these currents roiled in me, though in

*The author leaning against his Elva Courier, Bridgehampton Raceway, New York, 1964*

another way it felt marvelous, in the New York of the early sixties, to have one's life composed of a series of secret compartments. Only the young women I dated knew, as if instinctively, that I was a creature of two worlds. They sort of held my hand as I shamefully crossed the waters between the two, and not without a bit of a smirk on their faces over the pretentiousness of both.

At this time, the world of poetry, at least in America, was in tremendous ferment. The Beats and then the Black Mountain poets, among others, were challenging the hegemony of mainstream academic poetry. Our little group of unknown, would-be poets, far out on the periphery of the literary scene, was yet a microcosm of the arguments and tensions that were going on in the world of poetry at large. What was that world but the substance of the conversations about poetry and the poems themselves? In my mind, I was beginning to feel part of a community, one from which I could step out further into increasingly larger and more complex groupings of contemporary poets and poetry. This feeling was very tentative, propelled by curiosity and by the friendships with Ernie and others. I was beginning to scribble things, to participate hesitantly in the writing of poetry.

Behind this immediate scene loomed the person and intellect of Zukofsky, who while known to very few

people outside the literary world, had been a major figure in poetry for years. In the 1920s and 1930s, he had engaged deeply with poets like Pound and Williams, editing and publishing their work. He had not only coined the term Objectivist and gathered poets such as Charles Reznikoff, Carl Rakosi, Lorine Niedecker, and Oppen into the group, he had also been their chief theorizer. In the 1960s, at Brooklyn Polytechnic, he taught in semi-obscurity, but left a mark on the students who went through his classes. Of the poetry Ernie thrust upon me, Zukofsky's work was the first that I seriously considered. Its complexity and musicality seemed like an enormous lyric puzzle. The long sections of Zukofsky's epic *"A,"* neither clearly narrative nor associatively linked, were written with an amazing intensity and concentration. Both intimate and formally distant, the poems hovered before one on the page like galaxies or constellations.

Through Ernie, I met Zukofsky the night of the debut at Carnegie Recital Hall of Zukofsky's son Paul, aged fourteen and already an impressive violinist. Zukofsky had "papered the house," giving tickets away to his students by the dozens for them then to give to friends so that there would be a semblance of an audience at the debut. Later I was a visitor to the Zukofsky apartment on Seventh Avenue where Louis chain-smoked through enormously erudite discussions of Shakespeare and music. He sat beside a desk, where he could prop his elbow, a cigarette dangling in his elegant, thin fingers. He spoke just barely above a whisper, but the voice did not seem frail or indistinct. One could imagine him speaking, as he put it, "out of deep silence." His art was domestic, turning the materials of his life, his readings, and his family into his masterpiece, *"A"*.

I was still sharing an apartment with TK, this one on Cornelia Street, just over Joe Chino's theater cafe. It was an old walk-up with a tub in the kitchen, but the rent was only twenty-nine dollars a month. By then, I knew young painters and poets and was dating Doris, an aspiring actress and dancer who I had met at Sperry, and who later became my wife. With her, I was attending performances by Yvonne Rainer and Merce Cunningham. As with poetry, this was a period of great ferment in all the other arts. One saw it in Cunningham's work, which was cool, pure movement, beautiful and haunting in its mathematical precision and wry use of the dancer's body. Rainer's dances explored erotic and social relationships with an intensity that threatened to ignite both audience and the gray boards her company danced on. Twyla Tharp, whom Doris briefly danced for, had introduced ordinary movement as the basis of performances. In music, in the visual arts, as in literature, the air was rife with a giddy sense of revolution and experimentation, all of it honed to a fine edge by occurring within and against the more conservative traditions of the mainstream fifties and early sixties.

TK, who was out of work, formed a small painting and fix-up company with Chuck, one of our painter friends, and Dick, Ernie's roommate, another poet who, like Ernie, had been a student of Zukofsky's. On days when I could find an excuse for being out of the office, I'd work with them. They didn't have a truck or car but used the subway to get to their jobs, transporting all their paint and supplies with them. Each morning, it was Chuck's job to carry the company ladder, and when a train pulled in, prop it so as to jam open the car doors. While people on the train yelled at us, the rest of us swiftly loaded our buckets of paint, drop cloths, and painting gear onto the train. Then Chuck removed the ladder, and we were off. The same precision drill happened on our return home in the evening.

Our "accountant" was a beautiful ex-Bennington student, a philosopher who'd been Stanley Edgar Hyman's protégé. She kept telling us that we bid too low on the jobs and were in fact losing money with every contract. Depending on where the work was being done, the crew, sometimes including me, ended each day at a local bar in the neighborhood, drinking away whatever profits we might have made. One afternoon, after completing a paint job at a Yorkville apartment, we dropped into a saloon on East 86th Street. As we sat there sipping boilermakers, most of the German-speaking clientele eyed us with suspicion. One man came up to Dick's stool and began cursing him in German. Dick was so drunk by this time that he just looked at the man with a silly grin on his face. The man reared back and threw a solid right punch to Dick's chest. Dick, seated on his barstool, fell back in slow motion as though he were glued to the stool and crashed to the floor. Chuck and I gently righted Dick, the stool still under him, and the man threw another punch, knocking Dick back, again as though in slow motion. Dick just lay there still grinning amid the sawdust and cigarette butts, and his assailant, in disgust, walked away. Chuck and I kept on drinking as

if nothing had happened. That night ended our work as contractors.

I took only one course in poetry writing in my life, with Kenneth Koch at the New School in 1964. Much of what Kenneth taught were the "exercises" that he later incorporated into his famous books on teaching children to write poetry, *Wishes, Lies, and Dreams* and later *Rose, Where Did You Get That Red?* What he said was designed to shake up the minds of those in the class still clinging to traditional notions of poetry current in academe. Having come from a scientific and engineering background and having already leapt unknowingly—I emphasize, *unknowingly*—over much poetry history as a result of Ernie's exposing me to the work of the Objectivists and the Black Mountain poets, I did not experience the feudal tensions of the class as did others. But when Kenneth talked about French poetry or about O'Hara and Ashbery, all the newness possible in the poem radiated in his words.

It was in this class that I met Hannah Weiner, whose friendship, like Ernie's, was decisive for me as a writer. Hannah, working as a lingerie designer at the time, was eager to be a poet; her early attempts at writing verse were criticized by Kenneth as both unclear and old-fashioned. His words to her were a tremendous impetus. She often came away from his class in tears but also with a fierce determination to change her style. We sat up late at one of the coffee shops near the New School talking about the class, about poetry, and about a life as a poet, an idea which had not yet occurred to me.

I was reading poetry intensively, Creeley, Olson, Duncan, and Oppen especially, whose work was so spare and deep that I began to memorize his poems and recite them to myself as I walked around Manhattan. I bought books by Charles Reznikoff and William Bronk at the old eigth Street Bookstore on the corner of MacDougal. Ted Wilentz, sweet *mensch,* publisher, and patron saint of poets, showed me works by Ed Dorn and the then LeRoi Jones, now Amiri Baraka. His own Corinth Press brought out books by Gil Sorrentino, Diane di Prima, and Michael McClure. Wilentz gave me these books and thrust Denise Levertov's writings into my hands as well. Reading these, I was creating my own canon, one owing nothing to the usual academic list of great poets. Rather, the authority of these works was something *I* granted them, giving them more power over my understanding of poetry than anything I had been taught. Their hold on me still astonishes. And it might be imagined that mysteriously, in this period, I crossed over a certain line, suddenly finding for myself that whatever else I might do, poetry would now matter greatly, matter more to me than I could ever explain.

\*

How to circle back to those days of blunder and trial, of forming out of the unformed? The streets of Manhattan, saturated with literature and poetry, were always a background. I can walk down Second Avenue today and mark out the site of the old Café Metro, the corner near Auden's broken down residence, remember his ghostly appearances in bedroom slippers and robe, the Monday night open readings at St. Marks in the Bowery where Paul Blackburn taped endless sessions of poetry. I met Louis Ginsberg there, Allen's father, long before I met Allen. He was a fixture, reciting his formally crafted stanzas into Paul's microphone, complaining affectionately about the "loose" lines of his now-famous son's work. I remember Ted Berrigan holding court at a cafe on the Avenue, his flip takes on poetry occasionally enraging me, though later I was to discover that I was more of his party than I realized.

Kenneth Koch's class was coming to an end, but Hannah and I continued to meet. She created a marvelous and funny performance piece called *Code of Flag Behavior,* based on the U.S. Navy ship-to-ship flag signals. All dialogue for the work was taken out of the signal manual, the characters in the piece having to "communicate" to each other using the appropriate flag positions. The code, primarily concerned with nautical events or military action, was full of unintended puns and innuendoes. Lines such as "I am following your bottom" or "Can I speed up screw?" transported the audience into gales of laughter as Hannah's piece tried to dramatize an absurd love story using only the language from the manual.

It was 1964, and to my surprise, I won one of the end-of-year poetry prizes given by the New School. There wasn't much money, a few hundred dollars to the prize, but this competition had been open to many young and, in some cases, published poets. Happiness and strangeness! The prize sat in my consciousness, indicating a possible turn in the road for me.

By this time, I was working at a gigantic international corporation headquartered on East 42nd Street. But the office in which I worked had become an odd phantomlike place, or better to say, I felt like a ghost in it. My substance had fled, was suddenly enmeshed with words and literature in a way I had never imagined. I was the corporation's chief technical writer, my office cubicle and desk in the advertising department across the hall from the head of the department. The corporation was Dutch based, and most of the time, my job was to "translate" the texts of Dutch English instruction manuals and promotional materials written by my counterparts in Holland into better-sounding English. Occasionally, I'd make up and approve the layouts of the instruction booklets that came with the products. But by now, I'd been bitten with the bug of poetry and of art in general. On many days, I'd sit at my desk with a legal-sized yellow pad in front of me. On the top line, in bold caps, in case any nosy employee peered into my cubicle, I'd print out the name of the product I was supposed to be writing about, then below it, in longhand, sketch out poems and ideas for poems down the page. Often at lunchtime, I told the secretary I had an appointment to see a printing vendor and wandered on up Madison Avenue to look at the newest painting and sculpture in the galleries. I rarely made it back to the office. Nights were a buzz of running from one reading or art opening to another, with coffee and a snack at the Krazy Kat cafe off MacDougal Street. There, still in my three-piece Brooks Brothers suit, an undercover agent even unto myself, I drew the glare of other would-be bohemians. But my Deke days had given me the gift of intellectual name-dropping, not to mention a pretend *hauteur,* that I could easily unveil if circumstances warranted.

Doris and I had been married for a couple of years, and we both wanted a change in our lives. We began to put money aside for a stay in Europe. Was more of a life in poetry a possibility? I had published nothing, but via some inarticulate internal rebellion, a rebellion which had been stamped and sanctified by that minuscule poetry prize, I was ready to throw economic cautions to the wind. While we stored up our funds, I followed the routines of work and play, not half-heartedly but with a renewed vigor. More jazz, more concerts and performances, more gourmet restaurants and dinners at our apartment on Horatio Street, even more attendance to my duties at work. I sensed that the last "big" salary in my life was shortly to disappear. In a slightly maniac way, I wanted to do it and my current life justice. I was in my late twenties, with no excuse for indulging in the madnesses of youth, yet that is exactly what I was suddenly doing. And when one afternoon, I told my older brother, a division manager for Western Electric in New Jersey, of my plans to quit and spend a year or so abroad, he looked at me as though I'd lost my mind. "What will you put on your resume," he angrily asked?

By 1965, we had saved over four thousand dollars, enough we thought to last us at least a year abroad if we found someplace cheap to live. I gave notice at work, but no one would believe my reasons for leaving. My boss called me in. "Look," he said, "we like you here. I'll give you a raise of ten percent more than *they* are offering you." I tried to explain that there was no "they," that I'd decided to try something else in my life. It was incomprehensible to him, and perhaps it was testimony to the effectiveness of my chameleon-like existence at work. I'd never given an outward sign of anything other than being a good "organization man." After all, I'd worn my suits and ties, had placed a dark beige homburg on my head when I left for the day, and got tipsy at the Christmas party and kissed Rosie, my secretary, and cracked jokes with the CEO. And despite my late afternoon forays to the galleries and my secret poetry sessions at my desk, I'd done all my work and on time, and indeed, didn't truly regret being there until this other option suddenly stared me in the face.

We started packing our possessions for storage, driving them out to my brother's place in New Brunswick. He seemed always to be shaking his head as though in disbelief as I covered our Danish modern couch and table with old sheets. One day, I left the car with him to sell. It was the last piece of the former life's bric-a-brac to go, and I suddenly felt as though Sisyphus had been relieved of his rock. My business suits and paisley ties I gave to the super. I began to grow a beard. These gestures and dispossessions were a kind of shriving by which I confessed my desire for a new life.

That same week, I bought a small, blue travel trunk with brass clasps and lock and started to pack it. Copies of Shakespeare and Dante, some back issues of *Kulchur,* a magazine I much admired, my compact, metal-green-cased Hermes portable typewriter, books by Oppen and Creeley and Duncan. When I think back now, I realize what a paltry hoard I was collecting to shore against my ruins.

The cheapest transport to Europe then was on a freighter, and the least expensive of these was on a

Yugoslav line. I bought us tickets to leave in the first week of June on the *Novi Vinadolski*; for $250 round trip, we'd be taken to Tangier and brought back from there to New York when we wanted.

In the late morning of June 5th, a taxi deposited us at the *Novi*'s dockside in Brooklyn's Erie Basin. TK and another old friend, Ed, had accompanied us out for our send-off. A little later, Ernie and some of my old college friends arrived. The ship was still being loaded, so we all went up to the cabin and sat around drinking delicious Yugoslav beer and munching on little snacks brought in by a solicitous purser. By late afternoon, we were all rather soused, but there had been no calls for visitors to leave. Passport officials came around and examined our documents. At about 7 p.m., warnings were given to clear the ship. Departure was imminent. Our friends said their good-byes and tottered down the gangplank, hands on the rails to steady themselves. The horns blew as a tug came alongside, and slowly we were eased out into the East River and Lower New York Bay. The Verranzano Bridge was under construction. The steel arc of the bridge was in place but the roadbed still unfinished. Long graceful lines of electric lights had been strung along its length. They came on just as we were sailing beneath the bridge.

\*

That night we watched the lights of the bridge for miles, slowly receding over the horizon. The red glow of New York filled the sky until we were way out in the Atlantic. By morning, the *Novi* was dipping and rolling in the gentle seas. Flying fish leapt in parallels with our course, which lay along the calm Southern route and which accounted for the bilious clumps of seaweed and the pink stains of algae that grazed against the ship's hull in our passage. The gulls and the scavenger fish ate the garbage thrown over the side each evening by the cook's mate. There were no entertainments on the freighter, so one was left pretty much to oneself, to lean over and look at the foam or scan the horizon. By the end of the first day, I felt as though I were losing the traces of being as surely as the waves rolled over and flattened the ship's wake. At sunset, the first mate appeared on the bridge with his sextant to shoot the horizon and the evening's first star. It was almost as if the only thing anchoring us to the world was the imaginary line from the star to the ship's position. For the next three days, the radio in the ship's lounge offered nothing but the groans of the empty air waves.

To add to the unreality, there was Madame Ravicic, an elderly woman returning to her home in Belgrade. All day, she sat in her deck chair squinting at the ocean, then looking at her square of canvas. On some days, she painted blue horses on green fields and on others, green horses on blue fields. She sold two or three pictures to the other passengers, mostly returning Hungarians and Yugoslavs. One afternoon, she dressed Doris in one of her native costumes, and the two danced around the deck to Yugoslav music piped over the ship's intercom.

Though a couple of the crew members spoke a bit of broken English, we were in a linguistic limbo. At night, one of the sailors came around to our cabin with a bottle of powerful *slivovitz* and a handful of miniature beer mugs. We nibbled rather than sipped at the fiery liquid while he demarcated the ethnic divisions of the crew, the Serbs who barely spoke to the Macedonians, the Russian-trained officers, mostly Slavs, who were feared and yet held in contempt by the below-decks crew. Old stories about World War II poured out of him, not stories really but justifications, who sided with whom, a litany of deceits and betrayals. A couple of days into the voyage, it was announced that our port of call in Morocco would be Casablanca rather than Tangier.

On that voyage, we met Antonio, a literary critic and translator, who was traveling to do research on Spanish and Portuguese literature in Lisbon under a grant from the Gulbenkian Foundation. He tutored us in day-to-day Spanish phrases and taught us how to count in Portuguese as well. To practice, I tried to write short poems in Spanish; their defective syntax and misused vocabulary kept him in stitches.

It was only as we approached the coast of Morocco that the air of unreality began to lift. The purser called us into the lounge and gave us back our passports and customs papers. He reminded us that the Moroccan stevedores would be coming aboard soon. We should lock our cabins, he told us, as we were no longer sea voyagers but back among our own kind, corrupt and untrustworthy landlubbers. Before we knew it, Casablanca loomed off our forequarters, a dull grey city of small buildings and minarets punctuated here and there by a large office tower.

We took the morning train from Casablanca to Tangier, then the ferry over to Algeciras. A bus conveyed us to Malaga, where we spent a week in a pension, sightseeing and deciding what to do. The trunk with my books and papers was deposited in an old warehouse by the Malaga cathedral, and we took off for three months of seeing Europe, Lisbon, London, Paris, Amsterdam, Barcelona, slowly working ourselves back to the Costa del Sol.

On our return, we searched Malaga's streets for a place to live that we liked and could afford. Nothing seemed to turn up. One day, we took a bus out to Nerja to look at the famous caves just outside of the town with their primitive drawings and powerful rock formations. Walking back into the town, we came to the Paseo, the *Balcon de Europa* as it was called, a plaza built on a bluff overlooking the Mediterranean with twenty-mile views up and down the coast. I walked into a local bank and asked if they knew anyone who had a house for rent.

A woman came and showed us a two-story house with a rooftop terrace overlooking the sea and the mountains. We took the place immediately, went back to Malaga that afternoon and retrieved our baggage and my trunk from the warehouse. By that evening, we were back in Nerja, the first night in our own place since we had left New York.

In a way, the first few weeks in Nerja resembled an extension of our times aboard the *Novi,* our old Yugoslav freighter. The unreality of our existence, our lack of ties to anyone, the freedom we had to do as we chose, the separation from the English language, which was barely heard in Nerja—all these while liberating, also threw one back on oneself. I began devoting my time to reading the poets I had brought. The experience of otherness, as embodied in the quaint strangeness of Nerja, gave the language of these American poets a powerful yet curious impact. The words felt newly minted out of both distance and nostalgia, and as I held a book in my hands, I wasn't sure whether a poem's effect were near or far, whether I was, in the instant, homesick for New York or for a desire to be at one with the words and lines before me. And also, after New York and the other large cities we had recently visited, the day-to-day quiet of Nerja was sometimes startling, as when suddenly the sound of my pen scratching the paper on the desk sounded as though an animal were thrashing about nearby in my room.

*At the Alhambra Café, Neria, Spain, 1966*

For diversion, we went in the cool early evenings to the Paseo to sit under the flapping umbrellas of the cafés, the Alhambra or the somewhat fancier Balcon de Europa, part of the hotel by that name which drew a few English tourists. From the cafés, one could see the low, mounded foothills of the Sierra Morenos or watch the light play across the Mediterranean till darkness fell. Then the sea became a deep black punctuated by large spotlights used by the fishing boats to draw the fish to the surface. Miguel, the thin, almost toothless waiter of the Alhambra, played at being a confidant to the *estranjeros*; he told us stories about the civil war period, including one concerning the anti-Franco owner of the Alhambra whose friend, the mayor, put him in an insane asylum to keep him from being caught in a roundup of Republicans. In Nerja, the effects of the civil war were everywhere. Those loyal to Franco held power and much of the wealth. But there were now, in the mid-sixties, expressions of

dissent. Locals were heard to hiss at celebrations on the Paseo for Jose Antonio, one of the Fascist heroes of the civil war era, a young handsome *pistolero* who'd been transformed into a martyr by Franco's propagandists. And most locals would tell you that they did not believe what they read in the newspapers, least of all about the amelioration of poverty or about the many amnesties declared for former opponents of Franco.

Our house, it turned out, was owned by a former peasant, Domingo Platero, an informer for Franco's men, who'd been rewarded for his services with many acres of sweet potato fields. He regularly sold the harvest to the U.S. Air Force based near Cadiz down the coast. With his profits, he'd bought up property, like the house we lived in, and was now one of the wealthiest men in Nerja. Many of the houses were managed by his two daughters, Estrella and Margo. Both women were well-educated, mostly in finishing schools in Malaga and Madrid, but neither had found a husband. They were too sophisticated for the Nerja peasants and shopkeepers, and yet, coming themselves from peasant stock, they would not be considered for marriage into the aristocratic or business classes that flourished under Franco's rule. In our sixth month in Nerja, the father finally arranged a marriage for Estrella, the younger of the two, to an elderly but wealthy peasant who had the round bulbous face and physique of Nikita Khrushchev. The morning she was to be married she came to our house full of tears, crying that she'd been sold into slavery.

Slowly, we discovered that there were a few other non-Spaniards in the town. Among the first people we met were the English playwright and poet Bernard Kops and his wife, Erica. I gave him a sheaf of my poems to read and invited him to dinner. Doris and I went up to the market and bought a chicken, the first one we'd ever bought, and one of the most expensive items sold among the stalls. It turned out to be a very leathery old bird. Kops said to me at that dinner, as he worked very hard sawing away with his knife, "I won't be as tough on your poems as this chicken."

Later, we met the Irish novelist Aidan Higgins and his wife, Jill, who were living on Carrebeo, a rock-strewn road on the cliff above the beach. A Swedish painter, Jan Olaf, and his girlfriend, Elsa, also lived in Carrebeo. One failed poet and playwright, Lyle, who'd abandoned his family to be a writer, lived a few doors down from us on Calle de la Cruz. Lyle drank all day at the Alhambra, then went home and wrote a few words of dialogue into his play, and then returned to the Paseo to continue his drinking. Other writers moved in and out of the town at various times, including the novelist John Deck and his wife, and a Rhodesian novelist, Leon Whiteson. Rhodesia was in the midst of breaking away from England, and Leon was leaving shortly to return to London, ruing the fact that he had a Rhodesian passport and that, on his arrival, he would have to swear fealty to the queen and the Commonwealth.

Higgins and I often drank together at El Molino, a working-man's bar hidden back in the old streets of Nerja. An old mill converted into a tavern, its interior was always dark and cool. In the bar was the only Scopitone in Nerja, a juke box with a video screen that matched tapes to the songs. The fishermen put their hard-earned coins into the machine to play "Yellow Polka Dot Bikini" over and over again, leering and cracking jokes at the scantily attired Swedish model in her polka dots and not much else gyrating across the screen. Here Higgins introduced me to the work of European writers I had only vaguely heard of: Robert Musil, Walter Benjamin, Hermann Broch. For me, this was a tremendous education, long before these writers were wellknown or even spoken about in America. Benjamin, not just his writing but his strange, doomed exemplary life, has been central to my thinking and writing since those days. We talked about poetry, American, English, and Irish, as well. Higgins, a powerful stylist, often held up before me writers like Djuna Barnes or Beckett, whom he knew, insisting that the sentences they wrote were his models and ought to be mine as well.

Midway in our year in Nerja, a friend of Aidan's, Trevor, a heavy, burly South African, arrived and with him his American wife, Anne Marie. Trevor was even more of a drinker than either Aidan or myself and often walled himself up in his pension with a bottle of scotch only to arise each morning bellowing about his hangover. He was extremely strong, and when sober spent his afternoons scuba diving after moray eels and sharks in the Mediterranean with a captain of the Guardia Civil. When he was drunk, Trevor's eyes filled with tears, and he sobbed over his failures as a writer, spouting Irish poetry between every self-tirade.

About this time, Jan Olaf seemed to be having a nervous breakdown. He told me that one of the paintings he made "frightened him." He talked to us about the "evil of certain letters" in the alphabet, and had as Elsa told me, lost the capacity to have sex with her. Trevor took up with Elsa, the painter's girlfriend. The affair and Jan Olaf's deterioration went on for some weeks, until it was decided that he should be taken back to Sweden. On the morning she and the painter were going back, Trevor fell into a black drunk, seeing Elsa and Jan Olaf off at the bus stop, then crawling on all fours back down Calle de la Cruz to our doorway. He began banging on the heavy wooden door, awakening us and drawing a crowd in the street. Anne Marie came rushing to our house where, with the help of some local workers, she carried the bawling Trevor back to her house.

It was while we were in Nerja that Hannah Weiner came to visit. We took the bus to the Malaga airport to pick her up. She was on her way to Paris but spent a few days lazing on Nerja's beaches. When she left, she took a group of my poems and showed them to Maxine Grofsky at the *Paris Review.* About a month later, I received a letter from Grofsky telling me that my poems were to be published in the magazine. A few months after that, the issue was in my mail with a cover, a red, white, and blue abstraction, by the painter Jack Youngerman. These were my first published poems. As it turned out, there was an excerpt from Higgins's novel, *Balcony of Europe,* in the same issue. Later, I remember the dazzling feeling of happiness as I sat at the Alhambra, the bright Spanish sun shining down on the white pages and the crisp black print.

*

In late 1966, Doris and I returned to New York on the Yugoslav freighter the *Klek.* The ship arrived in New York Harbor after dark, too late in the evening for the vessel to be berthed. It was autumn, but an unusually warm night as we walked the decks in our shirtsleeves looking at the skyline drawing near. The ship was anchored till dawn off the docks of the Erie Basin. Far away I could hear horns tooting and even threads of music floating over the water. We had eight hundred dollars left in our bank account, no jobs, and no plans. Ahead lay unforeseen things, books published, readings, a broken marriage, and then new lives for the both of us. But that evening, the pilot who took the ship's helm from the Narrows up Lower New York Bay and into the East River had come aboard just in front of the Verranzano Bridge. As we turned in for the last time aboard, we could hear his thick Brooklyn accent as he shouted out orders to the crew, his "dem" and "dose" ringing out on the night air. From the streets of Brooklyn, coming to us across the water, there were more scraps of speech, of radios playing, and even the occasional wail of a police car siren. Somehow these reminded me of my own crude beginnings as a poet, of a return home in the most acute and poignant sense, a fitting chorus to our reentry to the New World.

*BIOGRAPHICAL AND CRITICAL SOURCES:*

*BOOKS*

*Contemporary Poets,* 6th edition, St. James Press (Detroit, MI), 1996.

*Dictionary of Literary Biography,* Volume 165: *American Poets since World War II, Fourth Series,* Gale (Detroit, MI), 1996.

Finkelstein, Norman, *Not One of Them in Place,* State University of New York Press (Albany, NY), 2001.

*PERIODICALS*

*Choice,* April, 1985.

*Contemporary Literature,* fall, 1991, Thomas Gardner, "An Interview with Michael Heller," pp. 297-311.

*Contemporary Poetry,* spring, 1978, Thomas H. Johnson, "An Interview with Michael Heller," pp. 1-24.

*Library Journal,* August, 2000, Gene Shaw, review of *Living Root,* p. 102.

*New York Times Book Review,* January 27, 1991.

*Parnassus,* fall/winter, 1972, James Guimond, "Moving Heaven and Earth," pp. 106-115; fall/winter, 1981, Alan Williamson, "At, Borders, Think," pp. 247-254.

*Publishers Weekly,* May 26, 1997; June 26, 2000, review of *Living Root,* p. 66.

*Reflector,* 1992, Keith Baughman, "Michael Heller: Interview," pp. 16-29.

*Sagetrieb,* spring, 1980, Laszlo K. Géfin, review of *Knowledge,* pp. 143-147.

*Talisman,* fall, 1993 (special Michael Heller issue), Edward Halsey Foster, "An Interview with Michael Heller," pp. 48-64.

*Voice Literary Supplement,* March, 1985; February, 1986.

*       *       *

## HEMON, Aleksandar 1964-

*PERSONAL:* Born 1964, in Sarajevo, Bosnia-Herzegovina; immigrated to United States, 1992; son of Petar Hemon and Andja Zivkovic; married Lisa Stodder (a freelance journalist), 1998. *Ethnicity:* "Bosnian." *Education:* Northwestern University, M.A., 1995; Loyola University, Chicago, IL, pursuing Ph.D., 1997—. *Politics:* "Left." *Hobbies and other interests:* Soccer, film.

*ADDRESSES: Agent*—Nicole Aragi, Watkins Loomis, 133 East 35th St., New York, NY 10016. *E-mail*—Sorgespy@hotmail.com.

*CAREER:* Author. Worked variously as a journalist, kitchen worker, bicycle messenger, Greenpeace canvasser, bookstore clerk, and teacher. *Military service:* Served one year in the Yugoslav army, as a conscript.

*MEMBER:* PEN American.

*AWARDS, HONORS:* Named one of twenty-one writers for the twenty-first century by the London *Observer;* notable book designation, *New York Times,* best books of the year designation, *Esquire; Village Voice; Los Angeles Times Book Review,* 2000, all for *The Question of Bruno; Nowhere Man* nominated for National Book Critics' Circle Award and *Los Angeles Times* Book Award, both in 2002.

*WRITINGS:*

*Zivot i djelo Alphonsea Kaudersa,* Bosanska knj. (Sarajevo, Bosnia-Herzegovina), 1997.
*The Question of Bruno,* Nan A. Talese (New York, NY), 2000.
*Nowhere Man: The Pronek Fantasies,* Nan A. Talese (New York, NY), 2002.

Contributor to publications, including *Ploughshares, New Yorker, Granta, Esquire, Triquarterly,* and *Baffler.* Work included in *Best American Short Stories,* Houghton Mifflin, 1999, 2000. Writes a bi-weekly column for the Sarajevo magazine, *Bhdani.*

*SIDELIGHTS:* Aleksandar Hemon, Bosnian author, came to Chicago from Sarajevo in 1992 for a short journalist exchange program armed with a few hundred dollars and two suitcases. When war erupted at home, Hemon sought asylum in the United States as a political refugee, and his application was accepted. Hemon worked at a variety of jobs while improving his English, including two years of door-to-door fundraising for Greenpeace, during which time he estimates he spoke with 5,000 people. Within three years, Hemon was writing in his adopted language. *The Question of Bruno,* Hemon's first English-language offering, consists of seven short stories and a novella. *Esquire* contributor Sven Birkerts called the stories "subtly braided, just enough link and suggestion between one and the next to make you feel as you do when you slip from one uncanny dream to the next."

*Lancet* reviewer Daniel Davies wrote that "if some of the language is stilted and clumsy, much of it is startling in its virtuosity. . . . At a time when so much new fiction in English centres around the metropolitan adventures of trendy twenty/thirty somethings in London/New York, Hemon's stories turn over a very different side of life—full of fear, isolation, brutality, and bloodshed. . . . Yet the collection is far from relentlessly grisly. Hemon is a playful and experimental writer, whose favourite trick is to intertwine fact and fiction." In *Review of Contemporary Fiction,* Paul Maliszewski pointed out that Hemon has been compared to Vladimir Nabokov and Joseph Conrad, both of whom wrote in English as a second language. Maliszewski noted that Nabokov learned English and French from an early age, while Conrad, who also learned English as an adult, never wrote in another language. Maliszewski felt that although comparisons can be drawn between the writing of Hemon and Nabokov, "Hemon's closest literary compatriot is really Danilo Kis. Like Kis, Hemon writes fiction that uses autobiography as a starting point from which to elaborate."

"Hemon handles English as though each sentence were an incendiary device, beautifully made but volatile," wrote Donna Seaman in *Booklist.* The opening story, "Islands," is about a young boy who visits his uncle on an island where mongooses imported to eliminate snakes are also killing the domestic animals. "This is a funny and horrifying child's perspective of a dread vacation," commented Daniel Orozco in the *San Francisco Chronicle.* "The beaches are gravelly; the tourists are repellent, old men with puckered skin and doughy breasts; and Uncle Julius regales the boy with stories of his torture in Stalin's labor camps. . . . Like the boy, we hear more than we ever wanted to, and this darkly comic story suddenly shifts into even darker territory, with the brutalities of Stalin's regime casting a deep disquieting pall."

Scott Blackwood wrote in the *Austin Chronicle* that "in Hemon's stories, as in Kafka's, fantasy and suffering are intertwined." Blackwood noted that in "The Sorge Spy Ring," "this mixture of fantasy and suffering is evoked again . . . when a boy imagines that his father is a spy based on the strange toys he brings home from his business trips to the Soviet Union. And, as if the objective world has conspired to solidify the boy's fantasy, his father is soon arrested." This story contains photographs and details about real-life Soviet spy Richard Sorge.

Richard Eder wrote in the *New York Times Book Review* that "the novella and one of the stories evoke the displacement felt by a young Bosnian—a partly fictional version of the author—who finds himself struggling to get by in Chicago while so many terrible things are happening in Sarajevo. How can you be an island when the bell incessantly tolls 5,000 miles away and makes all American sounds a meaningless cacophony? The novella labors over the theme. . . . The story, 'A Coin,' accomplishes it dazzlingly. It is a series of undelivered, perhaps unwritten letters, between the Chicago expatriate and Aida, who edits film for the foreign television crews in Sarajevo." *Observer* contributor Tim Adams said "The Coin" "finds pathos and absurdity among the detritus of life and death. . . . But if the terrain of many of Hemon's stories is the banal cartography of war, the substance is often fantastical. 'The Life and Work of Alphonse Kauders' is a bullet-point biography of a Yugoslavian Zelig, bee-keeper, pornographer, and statesman, each 'fact' of whose life is more outlandish than the last."

Eder observed that in the novella "Blind Jozef Pronek & Dead Souls," "the barely sketched exile with an unforgettable voice becomes a longer but not well fleshed-out version. Flesh muffles spirit." Jozef Pronek has escaped the siege of Sarajevo and watches his homeland burn on CNN. The reader sees America through Pronek's eyes, as when he is at JFK Airport and pictures it shaped like John F. Kennedy's "supine body, with his legs and arms outstretched, and leech-like airplanes sucking its toes and fingers." Pronek lives on Snickers and Twinkies and greets the cockroaches in his apartment when he returns home from work. Orozco wrote that "at times scathingly funny, the humor nonetheless highlights Pronek's absolute isolation, cut off from home and family. We are laughing, yes. But Pronek is not. Again and again in these astute and keenly imagined stories Hemon brings us up short and startles us into sharing his characters' vision, seeing what we haven't seen before. The effect is unsettling and illuminating."

*Time Europe* writer Susan Horsburgh said in an interview with Hemon that "'Blind Jozef Pronek' reads like a scathing critique of Americans and American culture. Was that the intention?" Hemon said: "No, it's a critique of a layer of American culture. This self-contained, bourgeois, ahistorical layer. American culture is much more than that. American culture is African-American culture, a culture of immigrants and refugees, a culture of the working class. . . . Half of the text in the *New Yorker* talks about this allegedly self evident 'we'—'we' like books like this, 'we' think this. There's a problem here. Hip-hop is also American culture—just as much, if not more, than any John Updike book."

*Salon.com* reviewer George Packer wrote that "in Hemon's stories, comedy and cruelty always run close together, passing equally under the narrator's detached and exacting gaze. . . . Reinvention, fluid identity, imagined surveillance, historical coincidences and mysteries—these elements recur throughout the stories." Packer called "Blind Jozef Pronek & Dead Souls" "the collection's strongest piece," and said that it "has all the brilliant whimsy of the shorter pieces, but where some of them remain interesting conceits from which the reader is held at a certain distance, over its longer span the novella gathers a powerful emotional resonance of anger and self-disgust and grief. It feels directly drawn from life—the picaresque and ghostly half-life an exile—and it suggests that this talented writer's next English-language operation will be a remarkable novel."

Hemon brings back Josef Pronek in the 2002 novel, *Nowhere Man.* "Vivid depictions" of Josef's youth in Sarajevo are revealed, according to *Booklist*'s Donna Seaman. The novel follows Pronek through adolescence and his formation of a rock band, to his move to Chicago shortly before war erupts in Yugoslavia. In Chicago, Pronek struggles to adapt to American life—finding odd jobs and living with his father. A *Kirkus Reviews* critic wrote, "This vivid tragicomedy of alienation and assimilation is further enlivened by the freshness of Hemon's figurative language." A *Publishers Weekly* contributor noted that *Nowhere Man* "should cement his reputation as a talented young writer."

*Salon.com* contributor Craig Offman noted that Hemon grew up "as a middle-class kid, reading Carver and J. D. Salinger in Serbo-Croatian. . . . The influence of Raymond Carver here is unmistakable." Hemon said in an interview with *Feed* online: "Well, I liked Salinger when I was a teenager. I just reread *Catcher in the Rye,* and it's still a good book. I liked *Nine Stories* too. And I liked Raymond Carver, although the consequences of Raymond Carver have been kind of disastrous for American fiction. It is that kind of minimalist tradition, and now, a lot of stories are Raymond Carver minus the working-class background—and minus the talent." Hemon told *Bomb* interviewer Jenifer Berman: "I love books more than ever. Because I learned that books don't represent 'truth.' Rather they open a space, a public space, in which that truth can be negotiated. With books you are never alone, never isolated."

A *Guardian* contributor said that "everything Hemon writes is unmistakably flavoured by Bosnia in all its modern ages—from the assassination of Archduke Ferdinand through the long years of Tito's rule to a gold period of a few brief years between the extinction of communism and the explosion of rabid nationalism, when Sarajevo flowered as an exciting and magnetic cultural centre." A *Publishers Weekly* reviewer wrote that "generously endowed with pathos, humor, and irony, and written in an off-balance, intoxicating English, this collection announces a talent reminiscent of the young Josef Skvorecky." *Library Journal* contributor Mirela Roncevic called Hemon's fiction "clearheaded" and "sensible, with a hint of satire . . . heavily based on wistful description rather than farfetched dialog." In an *Entertainment Weekly* review, Vanessa V. Friedman remarked that Hemon "is an original voice, and he has an imagination and talent all his own."

*BIOGRAPHICAL AND CRITICAL SOURCES:*

*PERIODICALS*

*Austin Chronicle,* July 21, 2000, Scott Blackwood, "By the Book."
*Booklist,* May 1, 2000, Donna Seaman, review of *The Question of Bruno,* p. 1651; August, 2002, Donna Seaman, review of *Nowhere Man,* p. 1920.
*Chicago Tribune,* September 12, 1999, Stephen Franklin, "Marking His Place: rising literary Star Aleksandar Hemon Learned English by writing it—and He Learned to Love the Chicago Immigrant Experience by Living It."
*Entertainment Weekly,* June 2, 2000, Vanessa V. Friedman, "The Week," p. 74.
*Esquire,* May, 2000, Sven Birkerts, "And English Isn't His First Language," p. 36.
*Guardian,* April 8, 2000, Julian Borger, "Brave New Words."
*Kirkus Reviews,* August 1, 2002, review of *Nowhere Man,* p. 1061.

*Lancet,* December 2, 2000, Daniel Davies, "The Half-Lives of Immigrants," p. 1937.
*Library Journal,* July, 2000, Mirela Roncevic, review of *The Question of Bruno,* p. 144.
*London Review of Books,* July 7, 2000, review of *The Question of Bruno,* p. 30.
*Los Angeles Times,* October 3, 2002, Carmela Ciuraru, review of *Nowhere Man,* p. E-2.
*Los Angeles Times Book Review,* June 18, 2000, review of *The Question of Bruno,* p. 10.
*National Review,* October 23, 2000, review of *The Question of Bruno,* p. 79.
*New York Times Book Review,* July 30, 2000, Richard Eder, review of *The Question of Bruno,* p. 12; August 6, 2000, review of *The Question of Bruno,* p. 22; September 15, 2002, Gary Shteyngart, review of *Nowhere Man,* p. 1920.
*Observer* (London, England), June 20, 1999, Robert McCrum, "Tomorrow's Worldbeaters"; April 16, 2000, Tim Adams, "Is This the New Kundera?"; July 2, 2000, review of *The Question of Bruno,* p. 5.
*Publishers Weekly,* May 15, 2000, review of *The Question of Bruno,* p. 87; September 2, 2002, review of *Nowhere Man,* p. 55.
*Review of Contemporary Fiction,* fall, 2000, Paul Maliszewski, review of *The Question of Bruno,* p. 151.
*San Francisco Chronicle,* June 4, 2000, Daniel Orozco, "Funny, Startling Stories of War and Loneliness."
*Yale Review,* July, 2000, Meghan O'Rourke, "Fiction in Review," p. 159.

*OTHER*

*Bomb,* http://www.bombsite.com/ (April 19, 2001), Jenifer Berman, interview with Hemon.
*Feed,* http://www.feedmag.com/ (April 19, 2001), interview with Hemon.
*Salon.com,* http://www.salon.com/ (April 16, 1999), Craig Offman, "Bosnian Writer Prefers Chicago, Thanks"; (April 27, 2000) George Packer, "Espionage and Exile."
*Time Europe,* http://www.time.com/time/europe/ (April 26, 2000), Susan Horsburgh, "Crossing Borders" (interview).

\*　　\*　　\*

## HEMPHILL, Ian

*PERSONAL:* Born in Australia; son of John and Rosemary Hemphill; married; wife's name, Elizabeth; children: three daughters.

*ADDRESSES: Office*—Herbie's Spices, 745 Darling Street, Rozelle, New South Wales, Australia 2039; fax: (02) 9555-6037. *E-mail*—herbie@herbies.com.au.

*CAREER:* Managed a spice company in Singapore; senior manager for a multinational food company in Australia; Herbie's Spices (specialty spice shop), Sydney, New South Wales, Australia, owner, 1997—.

*WRITINGS:*

*Spice Notes: A Cook's Compendium of Herbs and Spices,* 2000.
*The Spice and Herb Bible: A Cook's Guide,* Firefly Books (Toronto, Ontario, Canada), 2002.

*SIDELIGHTS:* Ian Hemphill began learning and working with spices as a young child. His parents owned and ran a spice farm in Australia. To help out he would gather and dry spices and flowers, prepare and pack spices, and assist in the mixing and blending of the spices. He is now the owner of Herbie's Spices, a specialty spice shop in Sydney, Australia.

In *Spice Notes: A Cook's Compendium of Herbs and Spices* Hemphill provides a history of spices and gives a detailed look at a variety of spices from all over the world. Hemphill's *The Spice and Herb Bible: A Cook's Guide* is an alphabetic guide to approximately one hundred spices. Hemphill provides information such as the common and botanical name of the spice, its history, and suggestions on buying, storing, and using the spice. *Library Journal* contributor Judith Sutton noted, "This invaluable reference is essential for most collections."

*BIOGRAPHICAL AND CRITICAL SOURCES:*

*PERIODICALS*

*Library Journal,* March 15, 2002, Judith Sutton, review of *The Spice and Herb Bible: A Cook's Guide,* p. 103.
*Publishers Weekly,* April 1, 2002, review of *The Spice and Herb Bible: A Cook's Guide,* p. 75.
*Winston-Salem Journal,* May 29, 2002, "*Spice and Herb Bible* a Key to Heavenly Food," p. E2.

*OTHER*

*Herbie's Spices,* http://www.herbies.com.au/ (August 6, 2002), "About Us."
*Perry Middlemiss Homepage,* http://www.middlemiss. org/ (June 3, 2002), review of *Spice Notes: A Cook's Compendium of Herbs and Spices.**

\* \* \*

## HENDEL, Yehudit 1926-

*PERSONAL:* Born 1926, in Warsaw, Poland; daughter of Akiva (a rabbi) and Nehama Hendel; married Zvi Mairovich, 1948; children: Dorit, Joshua. *Education:* Attended Levinski Sem, Tel Aviv, Israel. *Religion:* Jewish.

*ADDRESSES: Home*—Tel Aviv, Israel. *Agent*—c/o Author Mail, University Press of New England, 23 South Main St., Hanover, NH 03755.

*CAREER:* Author.

*AWARDS, HONORS:* Jerusalem Prize; Newman Prize; Bialik Prize, 1996.

*WRITINGS:*

*Anashim aherim hem: sipurim* (title means "They Are Different People"), Sifriyat po'alim (Merhavyah, Israel), 1950, reprinted, Hotsa'at ha-Kibuts ha-me'uhad (Tev Aviv, Israel), 2000.
*Rehov ha-madregot, roman,* 'Am 'Oved (Tel Aviv, Israel), 1954, published as *Street of Steps,* Herzl Press (New York, NY), 1963.
*he-Hatser shel Momo ha-gedolah* (title means "Courtyard of Momo the Great"), 'Am 'Oved (Tel Aviv, Israel), 1969, published as *ha-Hamsin ha-aharon, o, he-Hatser shel Momo ha-gedolah,* 1993.
(With Tsevi Me'irovits and Marc Scheps) *Me'irovits,* Muze'on Tel-Aviv (Tel Aviv, Israel), 1979.
*ha-Koah ha-aher: Tsevi Me'irovits ve-Yehudit Hendel* (title means "The Other Power"), ha-Kibuts ha-me'uhad (Tel Aviv, Israel), 1984, reprinted, Muze'on Tel-Aviv le-omanut (Tel-Aviv, Israel), 1999.

*Le-yad kefarim sheketim: 12 yamim be-Polin,* ha-Kibuts ha-me'uhad (Tel Aviv, Israel), 1987.

*Kesef katan: mahazor sipurim,* ha-Kibuts ha-me'uhad (Tel Aviv, Israel), 1988, translation by Dalya Bilu, Barbara Harshave, and Marsha Pomerantz published as *Small Change,* Brandeis University Press/University Press of New England (Hanover, NH), 2002.

*Har ha-to'im* (title means "Mountain of Losses"), Ha-Kibuts ha-me'uhad (Tel Aviv, Israel), 1991.

*Aruhat boker temimah: mahazor sipurim* (title means "An Innocent Breakfast"), ha-Kibuts ha-me'uhad (Tel Aviv, Israel), 1996.

Has also contributed to film documentaries such as *Tzilia Khozereth.* Author's work translated into Chinese, French, German, Hindi, Hungarian, Italian, Portuguese, Russian, Spanish, and Ukrainian.

*ADAPTATIONS:* Many works have been adapted to stage, screen, radio and television.

*SIDELIGHTS:* Yehudit Hendel was born in Warsaw, Poland, to a rabbinic family. While she was still very young, her family immigrated to Haifa, Israel. Hendel began publishing books in 1950, and her work has been translated from Hebrew into numerous languages, including English, Chinese, and French. Hendel has also been the recipient of various prestigious literary awards.

Hendel's writings deal primarily with people and their reactions to what life has thrown their way. *Small Change,* a short-story cycle, explores themes such as loneliness, regret, and the complexity of relationships. What makes Hendel's treatment of these universal themes unique is her close attention to detail and lack of sentimentality.

In her novel *The Other Power,* however—a fictional account of the author's life and that of her husband's—reviewer and instructor A. B. Yehoshua in *Modern Hebrew Literature* discussed the obvious lack of details in the book. "If, having finished the book, you ask yourself about this woman—her traits, character, loves, hates, desires, interaction with her children, etc.—you cannot in fact extract any clear details which add up to a portrait of a woman." Yehoshua praised the novel as a treatise on the act of artistic creation, made stronger and more purposeful by its lack of detail.

Many of Hendel's works have been translated into other languages, thereby allowing her voice to be heard throughout the world. Hendel considers the act of translation a double-edged sword. Agreeing with fellow Hebrew writer Chaim Bialik, she was quoted by Wendy Gold of *Writing the Jewish Future* online as "Translation is like kissing a bride through a veil."

*BIOGRAPHICAL AND CRITICAL SOURCES:*

*PERIODICALS*

*Ah'shav,* 1985, Amnon Navot, review of *Ha Ko'ah ha-Aher.*

*Booklist,* March 1, 1989.

*Modern Hebrew Literature,* spring-summer, 1986, A. B. Yehoshua, review of *The Other Power.*

*Variety,* February 17, 1982, movie review of *Tzlila Khozereth.*

*OTHER*

*Dartmouth College Web site,* http://www.dartmouth.edu/ (July 5, 2002), review of *Small Change.*

*Institute for the Translation of Hebrew Literature,* http://www.ithl.org.il/ (July 5, 2002), author biography.

*Writing the Jewish Future,* http://www.jewishculture.org/ (July 8, 2002), Wendy Gold, "Translation: Like Kissing a Bride through a Veil?"*

*      *      *

## HERBERT, Janis 1956-
(Janis Martinson)

*PERSONAL:* Born February 10, 1956, in Chicago, IL; daughter of Sherwynne Martinson (a telecommunications engineer) and Ruth Volkman Martinson Ross (in customer relations); married Jeff Herbert (a chiropractor), July 26, 1997. *Education:* Attended DePaul University. *Politics:* "Very liberal." *Hobbies and other interests:* Hiking, camping, bird watching, reading, baking, and attending U.S. Civil War reenactments.

*ADDRESSES: Home*—Oak Park, IL. *Agent*—c/o Independent Publishers Group, 814 North Franklin St., Chicago, IL 60610. *E-mail*—jmartins@juno.com.

*CAREER:* Author, 1996—. Worked variously as a secretary, bartender, booking agent, salesperson, and in the field of public relations.

*AWARDS, HONORS:* Best Book selection, *Smithsonian* magazine, 2002, for *The American Revolution for Kids: A History with Twenty-one Activities.*

*WRITINGS:*

(Under name Janis Martinson) *The World Don't Owe Me Nothing: The Life and Times of Delta Bluesman Honeyboy Edwards,* Chicago Review Press (Chicago, IL), 1997.

*Leonardo da Vinci for Kids: His Life and Ideas,* Chicago Review Press (Chicago, IL), 1998.

*The Civil War for Kids: A History with Twenty-one Activities,* Chicago Review Press (Chicago, IL), 1999.

*Lewis and Clark for Kids: Their Journey of Discovery with Twenty-one Activities,* Chicago Review Press (Chicago, IL), 2000.

*Marco Polo for Kids: His Marvelous Journey to China,* Chicago Review Press (Chicago, IL), 2001.

*The American Revolution for Kids: A History with Twenty-one Activities,* Chicago Review Press (Chicago, IL), 2002.

Contributor to various blues and literary periodicals.

*WORK IN PROGRESS:* An article on wolves; researching the history of Native Americans and their relationship with French explorers and missionaries, focusing on the Great Lakes region.

*SIDELIGHTS:* Janis Herbert told *CA:* "Though I'm a lifelong, passionate reader, I'm surprised to find myself a writer. This unplanned career began with my friendship with blues musician Honeyboy Edwards. On hearing the story of his life, I resolved to get it written and published—even if I had to do it myself. After accomplishing this goal, my publisher gave me the opportunity to share my love of history by writing books for children. Sometimes I feel like I won the lottery— I'm so lucky to spend my time researching and writing about my favorite topics.

"With each of my children's books, I have tried to share exciting moments in human history while presenting ideas and messages for children to consider.

For example, young readers of my Lewis and Clark book will learn about ecology and the ways of Native peoples while crossing North America with the brave members of the Corps of Discovery. I wrote *Marco Polo for Kids: His Marvelous Journey to China* hoping to educate children about cultural diversity, world religions, and the history of ancient civilizations while following Marco on his journey."

As Herbert shared with *CA,* her children's books focus on significant moments in history, with the aim of educating her young readers in various facets of these interesting developments. Her first effort in this arena is *Leonardo da Vinci for Kids: His Life and Ideas.* Accompanying the text are twenty-one activities and ideas for projects, as well as a list of relevant Web sites. In this "lively biography" noted Michele Snyder in *School Library Journal,* Herbert combines an "interesting text" with great illustrations to "give readers a full picture of this truly amazing man."

In *The Civil War for Kids: A History with Twenty-one Activities,* Herbert follows the same formula she used for her previous work for children, combining pertinent illustrations, maps, project ideas, and facts to help children understand the events of the American Civil War. Also included in this "fun as well as informative" book, related Tricia Finch in *Kliatt,* are maps, a timeline, and a glossary. Reviewing the work for *School Library Journal,* Sarah Smith also noted with appreciation Herbert's inclusion of material on "the contributions of women, African Americans, and even children."

Other books by Herbert include *Marco Polo for Kids,* which tells the story of the famous explorer's journey into Asia and includes phrases in several languages in addition to a mixture of facts, pictures, and a list of projects. Herbert has also issued *The American Revolution for Kids: A History with Twenty-one Activities,* a narrative, including sidebars, biographical entries, and activities to help young readers understand the struggle for independence. Writing about this work in *Booklist,* Roger Leslie said that the variety of projects included, such as how to make root beer at home, will "give young people a hands-on view of colonial life."

*BIOGRAPHICAL AND CRITICAL SOURCES:*

*PERIODICALS*

*Booklist,* March 1, 1999, Susan Dove Lempke, review of *Leonardo da Vinci for Kids: His Life and Ideas,*

p. 1208; October 1, 2002, Roger Leslie, review of *The American Revolution for Kids: A History with Twenty-one Activities,* p. 316.

*Kliatt,* May, 2000, Tricia Finch, review of *The Civil War for Kids: A History with Twenty-one Activities,* p. 34.

*Publishers Weekly,* December 13, 1999, "Do It Yourself," p. 85; August 6, 2001, "Back to School," p. 91.

*School Library Journal,* April, 1999, Michele Snyder, review of *Leonardo da Vinci for Kids,* p. 148; December, 1999, Sarah Smith, review of *The Civil War for Kids,* p. 152; November, 2002, Lynda Ritterman, review of *The American Revolution for Kids,* p. 188.

*Skipping Stones,* November-December 2001, review of *The American Revolution for Kids,* p. 34.

\*        \*        \*

## HERBERT, Victor (Daniel) 1927-2002

*OBITUARY NOTICE*—See index for *CA* sketch: Born February 22, 1927, in New York, NY; died of cancer November 19, 2002, in New York, NY. Physician, educator, researcher, and author. Herbert gained renown for proving that a lack of folic acid in one's diet would lead to anemia, a finding especially important to the health of pregnant women and their fetuses. He was an alumnus of Columbia University, where he received his medical degree in 1952, as well as a law degree in 1974. His military service included four years with U.S. Army Special Forces (1944-46 and 1952-54), and he was in the Army Reserves from 1946 to 1970, achieving the rank of lieutenant colonel. Herbert's career as a doctor included working as an assistant instructor and research fellow at Albert Einstein College of Medicine from 1955 to 1957, as a research assistant in hematology at Mount Sinai School of Medicine from 1958 to 1959 (he was also a professor of medicine there in 1964), and as an instructor and associate professor at the Thorndike Laboratory at Harvard University from 1959 to 1964. He joined the faculty at Columbia University as an associate clinical professor in 1964, becoming a clinical professor of medicine and pathology from 1970 to 1972; and in 1976 he became professor, vice chairman of the department of medicine, and attending physician at the State University of New York Downstate Medical Center. He retired in 1984. Herbert's key discovery about the benefits of folic acid came while he was a researcher at Thorndike Laboratory. To prove his theories that lack of this nutrient due to a dietary deficiency led to anemia, he deprived himself of folic acid until he developed the symptoms of anemia himself. Since the success of his experiment, physicians now know that pregnant women need folic acid supplements to ensure the health of their babies. Interested in the benefits of diet throughout his career, Herbert was chief of the hematology and nutrition research lab at the Bronx Veterans Affairs Medical Center in the early 1970s. He also worked to disprove myths about supposedly helpful health foods through authorship of such books as *Nutrition Cultism: Facts and Fictions* (1980; revised, 1982) and, with Stephen Barrett, *Vitamins and "Health" Foods: The Great American Hustle* (1981). More recently, Herbert also authored *Genetic Nutrition: Designing a Diet Based on Your Family Medical History* (1993; republished as *The Healing Diet,* 1995) and *The Vitamin Pushers: How the Health Food Industry Is Selling America a Bill of Goods* (1994), and wrote and edited *The Mount Sinai School of Medicine Complete Book of Nutrition* (1990) and *Total Nutrition: The Only Guide You'll Ever Need* (1995).

*OBITUARIES AND OTHER SOURCES:*

*BOOKS*

*American Men and Women of Science,* 20th edition, Bowker (New Providence, NJ), 1998.
*Who's Who in America,* 56th edition, Marquis (New Providence, NJ), 2001.

*PERIODICALS*

*Chicago Tribune,* November 22, 2002, section 1, p. 11.
*Los Angeles Times,* November 25, 2002, p. B9.
*New York Times,* November 21, 2002, p. A29.

\*        \*        \*

## HERD, David

*PERSONAL:* Male.

*ADDRESSES: Office*—School of English, Rutherford College, University of Kent, Canterbury, Kent CT2 7NX, England. *E-mail*—D.Herd@ukc.ac.uk.

*CAREER:* Literary critic. University of Kent, Canterbury, England, lecturer in English and American literature.

*WRITINGS:*

*John Ashbery and American Poetry,* Palgrave (New York, NY), 2000.

Also author of articles on contemporary poetry. Coeditor of *Poetry Review.*

*WORK IN PROGRESS:* Book considering the relationship between poetry and democracy.

*SIDELIGHTS:* In his debut book *John Ashbery and American Poetry* literary critic and academic lecturer David Herd provides clarity of thought and straightforward use of language to elucidate Ashbery's poetry and help the reader appreciate its beauty and complexity. In a quote from Herd's book, Ashbery says of himself, "On the one hand, I am an important poet, read by younger writers, and on the other hand, nobody understands me." Throughout *John Ashbery and American Poetry* Herd attempts to bring understanding and appreciation to this self-proclaimed paradox.

Much of Herd's book is dedicated to understanding Ashbery's diverse influences. Herd explores writers as farflung across the literary spectrum as Blasé Pascal and Frank Kermode, as well as William James and Boris Pasternak. Herd shows Ashbery to be both an American pragmatist, in the tradition of James and, at the same time, a committed internationalist, heavily influenced by Pasternak and the Russian avant-garde. Herd plots Ashbery's career as a series of phases, which allow Herd to follow the poet's evolution through his lengthy career.

"Accounting for the unpredictability and variety of Ashbery's own poetry is the aim of David Herd's book," wrote John Palatella in *London Review of Books.* Palatella continued, "Ashbery is concerned about more than the poem and its formal progress: he is a pragmatist, who wants a poem to show that it owes its existence to nothing more than attention to the current moment and all its tangled, muddy, painful and perplexing details, both private and public."

As Robert Potts commented in the *Guardian,* "Herd provides points of access for the reader. He does so with an enthusiasm and humor that courteously matches his subject's own." Potts concluded that "in this spirit, what Herd offers is not a reading of Ashbery, but a way of reading Ashbery. . . . This is one of the most entertaining, lucid, witty, generous and hospitable works of criticism I have had the pleasure of reading. Like all good critics, Herd sends us back to the poems; prepared for the adventurous journey ahead, but not saddled with someone else's luggage."

*BIOGRAPHICAL AND CRITICAL SOURCES:*

*BOOKS*

Herd, David, *John Ashbery and American Poetry,* Palgrave (New York, NY), 2000.

*PERIODICALS*

*Guardian,* (London, England), March 10, 2001, Robert Potts, review of *John Ashbery and American Poetry,* p. 10.
*Library Journal,* June 1, 2001, David Kirby, review of *John Ashbery and American Poetry,* p. 160.
*London Review of Books,* June 7, 2001, John Palattella, "Heavy Lifting," p. 36.
*Publishers Weekly,* August 20, 2001, review of *John Ashbery and American Poetry,* p. 73.
*Times Literary Supplement,* May 11, 2001, Geoff Ward, review of *John Ashbery and American Poetry,* p. 13.*

*       *       *

**HILLS, George 1918-2002**

*OBITUARY NOTICE*—See index for *CA* sketch: Born June 6, 1918, in Mexico City, Mexico; died September 13, 2002. Journalist, educator, and author. Born of English parents, Hills spent his youth in Mexico and Argentina, becoming an expert on South America and Spain. His knowledge of these cultures was widely sought after by politicians and broadcasters in England and other countries. He was a graduate of Kings College, London where he earned his B.A. in 1939. During World War II he served in the Royal Artillery and was an intelligence officer in Asia until 1947. Returning to England, Hills was hired by the British Broadcasting Corporation (BBC), working as the Malay-Indonesian program organizer and then as program organizer for the Spanish and Latin-American Spanish Services. He became an expert trainer in broadcast media, teaching courses in Canada and setting up training facilities in Spain where he helped to found the University of Francisco de Vitoria in Madrid. Hills' interest in Latin America and Spain led to his writing several books, including *Latin America and Communism* (1964), *Franco: The Man and His Nation* 1968), *Spain* (1970), and *The Battle for Madrid* (1976). His final book, *Los informativos en radiotelevision,* was published in 1981.

## OBITUARIES AND OTHER SOURCES:

*BOOKS*

*Writers Directory,* 17th edition, St. James Press (Detroit, MI), 2002.

*PERIODICALS*

*Times* (London, England), October 30, 2002, p. 31.

*       *       *

## HOFFMAN, Yoel

*PERSONAL: Born* in Romania. *Education:* Attended Tel-Aviv University, and Kyoto University. *Religion:* Jewish.

*ADDRESSES: Home*—Israel. *Office*—c/o Department of Philosophy, Eshkol Tower, 19th Floor, University of Haifa, Haifa, Israel, Mount Carmel Haifa, 31905, Israel. *E-mail*—Hoffman@research.haifa.ac.il.

*CAREER:* Translator, and novelist. Department of Philosophy, University of Haifa, instructor.

*WRITINGS:*

(Translator) Hau Hoo, *The Sound of One Hand: 281 Zen Koans with Answers,* Basic Books (New York, NY), 1975.

*Christus shel Daggim,* Keter (Jerusalem, Israel), 1991.
*Bernard,* New Directions (New York, NY), 1998.
*Katschen, and The Book of Joseph (novellas),* New Directions (New York, NY), 1998.
(Compiler) *Japanese Death Poems: Written by Zen Monks and Haiku Poets on the Verge of Death,* Tuttle (North Clarendon, VT), 1998.
*The Heart Is Katmandu,* New Directions (New York, NY), 2001.

*SIDELIGHTS:* Yoel Hoffman's early work as a translator of poetry and Zen koans has informed his more recent novels, the first of which had its American debut in 1998. Though he translates other works into English, he has written his novels in his native Hebrew. The first of his works to be translated into English was the pair of novellas, *Katschen* and *The Book of Joseph. The Book of Joseph* tells the story of a Jewish tailor named Joseph who flees the cossacks of Russia only to find himself pursued by the Nazis in Berlin. Joseph and his son Yingele are killed on Kristallnacht by Siegfried Stopf. Their story is continued by Gurnisht, Joseph's Polish apprentice, who comes to Berlin after spending the war in London and is devastated to find Joseph and Yingele gone. Reviewing the book for the *New Leader,* Betty Falkenberg compared Hoffman's work in *The Book of Joseph* to that of Italo Calvino and William Blake, observing the author's talent for using telling details and noting the connection between personal tragedy and world events. Falkenberg wrote, "The result, dreamlike and precise, wrenches your heart."

Published with, *The Book of Joseph, Katschen* tells the story of a young boy bereft of family connections who is finally sent to work on a kibbutz. Unable to bear the dehumanizing regimen, Katschen seeks out his father, who has been institutionalized for insanity, and breaks him out of his mental asylum. Though Hoffman intimates that "a great disaster" lies ahead for the pair, the novella ends with Katschen's father asserting his recognition of his son. About *Katschen,* Falkenberg wrote, "It meanders through terrain heavily studded with Zen riddles and images from the Kabbalah. At times funny and always engrossing, it is full of intriguing interlingual word play." Though Falkenberg found *Katschen* less compelling than *The Book of Joseph,* she called the book a "stunning . . . debut."

Hoffman's 2001 novel *The Heart Is Katmandu* also won praise for its explorations of the possibilities of words. The book is highly experimental, with both characters and authors sometimes addressing the readers. The layout of the text is also unusual, with blank space representing the distance between the main characters, Batya and Yehoahim, and divisions not by chapter but by 237 frames that counter the traditional linear movement of a story. Reviewer Irving Malin addressed Hoffman's innovations in the *Review of Contemporary Fiction,* writing that "Hoffman's wonderful book is both a love story and a meditation on the words love and story."

*BIOGRAPHICAL AND CRITICAL SOURCES:*

PERIODICALS

*Choice,* September, 1976, review of *The Sound of One Hand,* p. 844.

*Library Journal,* February 1, 1976, M. V. W. Wolfe, review of *The Sound of One Hand,* pp. 537-38.

*New Leader,* May 4, 1998, Betty Falkenberg, review of *Katschen, and The Book of Joseph,* pp. 16-17.

*Publishers Weekly,* October 13, 1975, review of *The Sound of One Hand,* p. 108.

*Review of Contemporary Fiction,* fall, 2001, Irving Malin, review of *The Heart Is Katmandu,* p. 206.

*World Literature Today,* winter, 1992, Dov Vardi, review of *Christus shel Daggim,* p. 198.*

\*   \*   \*

**HOLLAND, Merlin**

*PERSONAL:* Married Sarah Parker; children: Lucian.

*ADDRESSES: Home*—London, England. *Agent*—c/o Author Mail, Henry Holt & Company, 115 West 18th St., New York, NY 10011.

*CAREER:* Journalist and author.

*WRITINGS:*

*The Wilde Album,* Fourth Estate (London, England), 1997, Henry Holt (New York, NY), 1998.

(Author of foreword and revisions) Vyvyan Holland, *Son of Oscar Wilde,* (memoir), Carroll & Graf Publishers (New York, NY), 1999.

(Editor, with Rupert Hart-Davis) *The Complete Letters of Oscar Wilde,* Henry Holt (New York, NY), 2000.

*WORK IN PROGRESS: After Oscar* (working title), about Holland's father and uncle and their lives, and about Wilde's friends Robbie Ross and Frank Miles and their squabbles.

*SIDELIGHTS:* Merlin Holland, a journalist, is Irish writer Oscar Wilde's grandson. Holland has spent twenty years researching his grandfather's life, and his research has produced two books of photographs and previously unpublished letters that provide an important addition to the Wilde canon. Much of the work, Holland says, involved "charming [the letters] out of private collectors who had paid silly money for a bit of the true cross." In *The Complete Letters of Oscar Wilde,* he includes the full texts of several letters previously published only as fragments; to complete the historical record, he has added "trivial letters" omitted from the previous Hart-Davis edition. Holland also expand the footnotes to help identify the correspondents.

These letters are, as Holland explains in *The Complete Letters of Oscar Wilde,* "the autobiography he never wrote. . . . they show that the perception of Wilde as the lightweight author of society comedies, a few memorable poems and some fairy stories must finally make room for Wilde as a hard-working professional writer, deeply interested in the issues of his day and carrying in his intellectual baggage something that we all too frequently overlook, a quite extraordinary classical, literary and philosophical education."

The span of the letters follows Wilde's path from an Irish nursery school through undergraduate work at Trinity College, Dublin and Magdalen College, Oxford, his tour of America, success in London, and his now-famous imprisonment, disgrace, and exile.

"The Oscar Wilde who emerges, in these more than 1,200 pages of missives to friends, protests to newspaper editors, instructions to theatrical producers, actors and actresses, and, of course, letters to the love of his life and the cause of his downfall, Lord Alfred Douglas, is a serious, learned and civilized man," wrote Richard Bernstein in the *New York Times,* "not just a famously witty and clever one." Richard Whittington-Egan, in a review of *The Complete Letters of Oscar Wilde,* for *Contemporary Review,* concluded that "Oscar Wilde was a man worth knowing. There is no better way of getting to know him than listening to him speak for himself in this most attractive volume, addressed to the general reader and the scholar alike."

## BIOGRAPHICAL AND CRITICAL SOURCES:

*BOOKS*

Holland, Merlin, *The Wilde Album,* Henry Holt (New York, NY), 1998.

*PERIODICALS*

*Advocate,* January 30, 2001, Sarah E. Chinn, review of *The Complete Letters of Oscar Wilde,* p. 66.

*American Scholar,* winter, 2001, Adam Kirsch, review of *The Complete Letters of Oscar Wilde,* p. 142.

*American Theater,* March, 2001, Steven Drukman, review of *The Complete Letters of Oscar Wilde,* p. 58.

*Booklist,* March 15, 1998, Ray Olson, review of *The Wilde Album,* p. 1196.

*Bulletin with Newsweek,* January 9, 2001, p. 88.

*Christian Science Monitor,* June 25, 1998, Merle Rubin, review of *The Wilde Album,* p. B8.

*Contemporary Review,* June, 2001, Richard Whittington-Egan, "Oscar Wilde according to the Epistles," p. 375.

*Daily Telegraph* (London, England), November 4, 2000, Claudia FitzHerbert, review of *The Complete Letters of Oscar Wilde,* December 30, 2000, James Davidson, review of *The Complete Letters of Oscar Wilde,*

*Library Journal,* April 15, 1998, Eric Bryant, review of *The Wilde Album,* p. 77; November 15, 2000, Denise J. Stankovics, review of *The Complete Letters of Oscar Wilde,* p. 69.

*London Review of Books,* April 19, 2001, Colm Tóibín, "Love in a Dark Time," p. 11.

*Newsweek International,* November 27, 2000, Anna Kuchment, "Surviving a Legend," (interview with Merlin Holland), p. 4.

*New York Times,* May 28, 1998, Mitchell Owens, "Understanding a Grandfather and the Importance of Being Honest" (interview with Merlin Holland), p. B9; December 13, 2000, Richard Bernstein, "Behind the Wit, a consummate Intellect," p. L11.

*New York Times Book Review,* May 28, 1998, Evelyn Toynton, review of *The Wilde Album,* p. 20; June 14, 2001, Connolly Cole, "Buried in Oscar's Tomb," p. L15.

*People,* June 15, 1998, Nina Biddle and Christina Cheakalos, "Walk on the Wilde Side" (interview with Merlin Holland), p. 95.

*Publishers Weekly,* March 23, 1998, review of *The Wilde Album,* p. 89; October 23, 2000, review of *The Complete Letters of Oscar Wilde,* p. 65.

*Times Literary Supplement,* October 24, 1997, John Stokes, review of *The Wilde Album,* p. 20.*

\*    \*    \*

## HOLLON, Frank Turner 1963-

*PERSONAL:* Born 1963; married; wife's name, Allison. *Education:* Louisiana Tech University, B.S., 1985; Tulane Law School, law degree, 1988. *Hobbies and other interests:* Whiffle Ball, running, literary classics.

*ADDRESSES: Home*—Baldwin County, AL. *Office*—Hoiles, Dasinger & Hollon, 18410 Pennsylvania Street, Robertsdale, AL 36567.

*CAREER:* Hoiles, Dasinger & Hollon (law firm), Robertsdale, AL, attorney.

*WRITINGS:*

*The Pains of April,* Macadam/Cage (San Francisco, CA), 2002.
*The God File: A Novel,* Macadam/Cage (San Francisco, CA), 2002.
*A Thin Difference,* Macadam/Cage (San Francisco, CA), 2003.

*SIDELIGHTS:* Lawyer Frank Turner Holland began writing when he was a teenager. His first novel *The Pains of April* was written while he was in law school, and he didn't show it to a publisher for over ten years.

*The Pains of April* is narrated by an eighty-seven-year-old man who lives in a nursing home. As he thinks about the past and the position he is in now, he tells stories of events that have happened in his lifetime. The man is terribly afraid of being left in the dining room all alone and hates being in the nursing home. "The style, the originality of language, the believable characters, the narrator with his burden of human freedom, the humor, the wit, and the message make this a remarkable debut for Hollon," noted *Harbinger* contributor Kay Kimbrough.

In *The God File: A Novel*, Gabriel Black takes the blame for his girlfriend when she shoots and kills her husband. He never hears from her again after he is sentenced to life in prison without parole. While in prison he searches for God and works on his "God" file, in which he collects information on occurrences in the jail, stories, and quotes that relate to God. With his God file he hopes to prove whether God exist. *Library Journal* contributor Melanie C. Duncan claimed, "Not for the faint of heart, this is an outstanding example of the continuing exploration of gritty reality in spiritual fiction."

*BIOGRAPHICAL AND CRITICAL SOURCES:*

*PERIODICALS*

*Kirkus Reviews*, February 15, 2002, review of *The God File: A Novel*, p. 220.

*Library Journal*, April 1, 2002, Melanie C. Duncan, review of *The God File*, p. 88.

*Publishers Weekly*, March 11, 2002, Bridget Kinsella, "McPublishing, It's Not: To Break out New Authors, Three-Year-Old MacAdam/Cage Will Try Almost Anything," p. 20.

*OTHER*

*American Center for Artists*, http://www.americanartists.org/ (June 3, 2002), John Sledge, "Frank Turner Hollon Interview."

*Book Reporter*, http://www.bookreporter.com/ (June 3, 2002), Sarah Rachel Egelman, review of *The God File*.

*Harbinger*, http://www.theharbinger.org/ (June 3, 2002), Kay Kimbrough, review of *The Pains of April*.

*Over the Transom*, http://www.overthetransom.com/ (June 3, 2002), review of *The Pains of April*.\*

## HORSLEY, Kate 1952-

*PERSONAL:* Born April 17, 1952, in Richmond, VA; daughter of Joseph C. (a physician) and Alice Cabell (an artist) Horsley; married Rhodes Green Lockwood, November 15, 1981 (divorced); married Morgan Davie; children: Aaron Heath Parker Lockwood. *Ethnicity:* "Anglo." *Education:* University of Richmond (Richmond, VA), B.A.; Western Kentucky University (Bowling Green, KY), M.A.; University of New Mexico, Ph.D. (American studies), 1984. *Politics:* Socialist. *Religion:* Zen Buddhist. *Hobbies and other interests:* Cello, drawing.

*ADDRESSES: Office*—TVI Arts and Sciences, 525 Buena Vista SE, Albuquerque, NM 87108.

*CAREER:* Albuquerque TVI, English instructor, 1987—, chair, English department, 1998-2000. Creative writing workshops.

*AWARDS, HONORS:* City of Albuquerque Citizenship Award, 1994; Albuquerque Bravo Award, Albuquerque Arts Alliance, 1996; Western States Arts Federation Award for Fiction, 1996, for *A Killing in New Town,*; New Mexico Press Women's Award, 1996.

*WRITINGS:*

*Crazy Woman*, La Alameda Press (Albuquerque NM), 1992.

*A Killing in New Town*, La Alameda Press (Albuquerque NM), 1996.

*Confessions of a Pagan Nun*, Shambhala Press (Boston, MA), 2001.

*Careless Love; or, The Land of Promise*, University of New Mexico Press (Albuquerque NM), 2003.

*WORK IN PROGRESS:* Research on the Pythagorean cult of the sixth century B.C.

*SIDELIGHTS:* Kate Horsley began creating a character caught in a world of fierce cultural conflict in her first novel, *Crazy Woman*, published in 1992. The novel follows the story of Sara Franklin who is captured by the Apaches. Sara must first learn to survive as a slave and, then, as a woman who must earn the respect and trust of the tribe. Horsley explores the idea of captivity from the point of view of a woman in both her native culture and in her life among the Indians.

*A Killing in New Town* also profiles the life of a strong woman in a period of cultural change and conflict. Eliza Pelham lives in a town divided between the Old Town, where the railroad was supposed to help support the indigenous people, and the New Town, where the whites built their hotels and businesses and then had the railroad stop there. Eliza, a woman grown tired of small-town closed-mindedness, dreams of living in the open country. In her loneliness and depression, Eliza seeks escape through alcohol and an affair. Her life is suddenly transformed by the kidnapping of her two children. When they are stolen, she sets out with her unlikely allies, Bridle O'Doonan, the consumptive saloon girl and an Eastern-educated Apache, Robert Youngman. "The most unforgettable section of the book comes with Eliza's quest for her kidnapped children that leads to a small mining camp in the mountains. No one is accountable for their actions, and whiskey, gambling, prostitution and death by gunfire are the only constants," wrote David Farmer in the *Dallas Morning News.* A reviewer for *Publishers Weekly* said, "The title implies a murder story, and though the story is about murder, Horsley's intention is a double meaning that refers largely to the 'killing' that settlers hope to make in New Town. Small daily details and larger ideas make this unconventional western a truly compelling blend of adventure, Southwestern mythology and reality."

Horsley's novel *Confessions of a Pagan Nun* is set in fifth-century Ireland. Although Christianity is already the dominant religion throughout Western Europe, Ireland still clings to its pagan beliefs. This novel is a fictional memoir of Gwynneve who, after losing her mother, joins a troupe of traveling entertainers and later apprentices herself for many years to Giannon, one of the last surviving Druids. Later in life, though remaining secretly unbaptized, she enters a convent where her literacy gets her a job as a translator of Christian theology. In St. Bridget's Gwynneve copies the gospels and the writings of St Augustine—(with whom she carries on a running intellectual battle)—in the script she learned from Giannon and records her recollections of village and convent life for posterity.

Gwynneve contrasts the waning Druid influence and the emergent Christianity as she tells her story. One religious concept melds into the other. But she is not blind to the disappointing materialism the church brings with it. As Michael D. Langan wrote in the *Buffalo News,* "In the end, Gwynneve is alone. . . . She recognizes the consolation of nature, but lacks a full understanding of the new Christian law of love." Wendy Bethel commented in *Library Journal,* "Her story is not just that of a strong woman making her way in a hostile world. It is also the story of what happens to a country when a new religion takes the place of the old. A beautiful and thought-provoking book." "Poetically written and marvelously researched, the novel offers complex theological arguments wrapped in a compelling story about memorable characters,"wrote Booklist contributor Patricia Monaghan about *Confessions of a Pagan Nun.*

Recording a period of dramatic historical change within a work of fiction proved inspiring for Horsely. Who once told *CA:* "The powerful and challenging times in history compel me to look at the human struggle from the point of view of the average man or woman—the person who, though average, reacts with integrity and strength to seemingly crushing events or pervasive ignorance."

Horsley once told *CA:* "I want to try to communicate the truth in a powerful and absorbing way that encourages compassion and integrity. I want to do for readers what writers have done for me—made me feel that I was not alone and given me a worthwhile means of escape from this cynical world: entertainment that absorbs and challenges. . . .Writers such as Hesse, Tolkein, and Kerouac have influenced my quest for depth and freedom in my own writing."

*BIOGRAPHICAL AND CRITICAL SOURCES:*

*PERIODICALS*

*Booklist,* September 9, 1996, review of *A Killing in New Town,* p. 79; June 1, 2001, Patricia Monaghan, review of *Confessions of a Pagan Nun,*

*Buffalo News,* September 2, 2001, Michael D. Langan, review of *Confessions of a Pagan Nun,* p. F7.

*Dallas Morning News,* April 6, 1997, David Farmer, review of *A Killing in New Town,* p. 8J.

*Library Journal,* August, 2001, Wendy Bethel, review of *Confessions of a Pagan Nun,* p. 161.

*Publishers Weekly,* September 9, 1996, review of *A Killing in New Town,* p. 79.

*School Library Journal,* November, 2001, Christine C. Menefee, review of *Confessions of a Pagan Nun,* p. 191.

\* \* \*

## HOWLETT, David Robert 1944-

*PERSONAL:* Born January 3, 1944, in Streator, IL; son of John Francis (a clergyman) and Jean Elizabeth (a school principal; maiden name, Worden) Howlett; naturalized English citizen; married Phyllida Ruth Gosset, September 26, 1970 (divorced, 1987); children: Michael David Merlin, Katherine Eve Elizabeth, Rachel Anne Ruth. *Ethnicity:* "Scottish, Irish, English." *Education:* University of Montana, Missoula, B.A. (high honors), 1966; University of Oxford, B.A. (honors), 1968, M.A., 1972, D.Phil., 1975.

*ADDRESSES: Home*—50 Godstow Rd., Wolvercote, Oxford OX2 8NZ, England. *Office*—302 Clarendon Bldg., Bodleian Library, Broad St., Oxford OX1 3BG, England. *E-mail*—david.howlett@bodley.ox.ac.uk.

*CAREER:* Professor, editor, writer, and linguist. Oxford University, Oxford, England, tutor and lecturer, 1970-74, lecturer in English language and literature, medieval and modern European languages and literatures, modern history, and music, 1979—; Education Center, RAF Upper Heyford, Oxfordshire, England, administrative assistant, 1974-75. Oxford University Press, assistant editor for *A Supplement to the Oxford English Dictionary,* 1975-79, editor for *Dictionary of Medieval Latin from British Sources,* 1979—, associate editor for *New Dictionary of National Biography,* 1997—; Royal Irish Academy, Dublin, Ireland, consultant responsible for *Dictionary of Medieval Latin from Celtic Sources, Medieval Latin Lexicon from Celtic Sources,* and other publications, 1979—; member of editorial board (chairman, 1990—) responsible to the Royal Irish Academy, the Irish Biblical Association, and the publisher Brepols for *Scriptores Celtigenae,* 1987—. Committee member of British Academy responsible for *Auctores Britannici Medii Aevi* and for digitization of entire corpus of British medieval Latin literature and archives, 1994.

*MEMBER:* Many professional and academic societies, including Phi Beta Kappa, Classics Association of Ireland, Society of Antiquaries of London, Origen Society, and Medieval Society.

*AWARDS, HONORS:* danforth Foundation fellowship; Woodrow Wilson fellowship; F. W. Bateson Prize in English, Oxford University; Council of the Humanities, Princeton University, Old Dominion fellow and senior visiting fellow, 1989-90; Distinguished Alumnus Award, University of Montana, 1991; faculty research fellow of it, University of Oxford. *Literae Humaniores*

*WRITINGS:*

(Editor and contributor, with G. Cigman) *Birthday Celebration for Naky Doniach O.B.E.,* Oxford Centre for Postgraduate Hebrew Studies (Yarnton Manor, Oxford, England), 1991.

(Editor and translator) *Liber Epistolarum Sancti Patricii Episcopi: The Book of Letters of Saint Patrick the Bishop,* Four Courts Press (Dublin, Ireland), 1994.

*The Celtic Latin Tradition of Biblical Style,* Four Courts Press (Dublin, Ireland), 1995.

(Translator) *The Confession of St. Patrick,* Ligourian Press (Ligouri, MO), 1996.

*The English Origins of Old French Literature,* Four Courts Press (Dublin, Ireland), 1996.

*British Books in Biblical Style,* Four Courts Press (Dublin, Ireland), 1997.

*Cambro-Latin Compositions: Their Competence and Craftsmanship,* Four Courts Press (Dublin, Ireland), 1998.

*Sealed from Within: Self-authenticating Insular Charters,* Four Courts Press (Dublin, Ireland), 1999.

*Caledonian Craftsmanship: The Scottish Latin Tradition,* Four Courts Press (Dublin, Ireland), 2000.

*Insular Inscriptions,* Four Courts Press (Dublin, Ireland), 2001.

*Pillars of Wisdom: Irishmen, Englishmen, Liberal Arts,* Four Courts Press (Dublin, Ireland), 2002.

*Dictionary of Medieval Latin from British Sources,* Volumes 2-6, Oxford University Press (Oxford, England),1981-2002.

Contributor of numerous articles, reviews, and music, literary, and linguistic studies to scholarly journals and books.

*SIDELIGHTS:* David Robert Howlett has enjoyed a distinguished career as a linguist and author, working diligently to uncover the mysteries of many languages, including English, Old English, Latin, medieval Latin, and French. As a Rhodes Scholar, Howlett went to Corpus Christi College, Oxford, earned three degrees there, and has remained a resident of the United Kingdom ever since. His academic career has included multiple positions, including tutor in medieval Latin for historians at Worcester College; assistant editor of the *Supplement to the Oxford English Dictionary,* associate editor of the *New Dictionary of National Biography,* and, since 1979, both a faculty and research fellow of Oxford's *Literae Humaniores.*

Of all his scholarly achievements as a teacher and writer, the one that has perhaps brought Howlett the most renown is his insight into the Beowulf code. He devised a mathematical method to establish the names of historical authors who disguised their names within their writings. In his book *British Books in Biblical Style* Howlett proclaim that he had solved what has long been a mystery among scholars: The author of *Beowulf,* Howlett maintain, was Aethelstan, chaplain to Alfred the Great, writing *Beowulf* "as a court etiquette instruction manual for the young king," according to John Dugdale in the *New Yorker.* Other scholars have disputed Howlett's findings.

His book *Sealed from Within: Self-authenticating Insular Charters,* Howlett explain, "is offered as an introduction, a challenge to abler linguists and better diplomatists, an invitation to those of sharper sight and keener hearing, pleas to those of deeper insight, to recover more of an intellectual inheritance that is already rich, but less precious than it was once and might be again." J. C. Crick in his review of the book for the *English Historical Review* noted that "discerning readers are thus encouraged to discard the old orthodoxy that, in the absence of seals, autograph crosses, or other visible signs of authentication, Insular charters were guaranteed by divine providence alone." In *Sealed from Within,* Howlett pursues his longtime research interest: the so-called "biblical style" of prose in the early Latin and British Isles. He utilizes his mathematical method in examining the documents, including charters from England, Wales, Cornwall, Ireland, Scotland, and the Hebrides.

Another of Howlett's books, *Cambro-Latin Compositions: Their Competence and Craftsmanship,* offers a series of "interlocking short studies of Latin authors from Pelagius to Gerald of Wales," according to David N. Dumville, writing for the *English Historical Review.*

Acknowledging the controversial nature of Howlett's methods of study, Dumville nevertheless praised Howlett's results: "The first great gain from the outpouring of Howlett's quite exceptional erudition is that many texts have appeared in new editions with accurate, indeed faithful, yet elegant translations." Again writing in the *English Historical Review,* Dumville also reviewed Howlett's book *Caledonian Craftsmanship: The Scottish Latin Tradition,* which he called an "exciting and useful book."

While much of Howlett's scholarly work might be of particular interest to those with an extensive background in Latin, his research has also provided crucial enlightenment into the history of language and how it was formed.

*BIOGRAPHICAL AND CRITICAL SOURCES:*

*PERIODICALS*

*English Historical Review,* April, 2001, David N. Dumville, review of *Cambro-Latin Compositions: Their Competence and Craftsmanship,* p. 405, and *Caledonian Craftsmanship: The Scottish Latin Tradition,* p. 455; September, 2001, J. C. Crick, review of *Sealed from Within: Self-Authenticating Insular Charters,* p. 925.
*Journal of Ecclesiastical History,* July, 1997, Gernot Wieland, review of *The Celtic Latin Tradition of Biblical Style,* p. 532.
*Medium Aevum,* spring, 2001, review of *Caledonian Craftsmanship,* p. 178.
*New Yorker,* December 23, 1996, John Dugdale, "Who's Afraid of Beowulf?," p. 50.
*Speculum,* April, 2001, Scott Gwara, review of *Cambro-Latin Compositions,* p. 472.
*Times* (London, England), October 13, 1996, Stuart Wavell, "Word Sleuth Cracks Beowulf Code," p. 7.

\*   \*   \*

## HUFFEY, Rhoda 1948-

*PERSONAL:* Born 1948. *Education:* University of California, Irvine, M.F.A.

*ADDRESSES: Home*—Venice Beach, CA. *Agent*—c/o Author Mail, Delphinium Books, 63 East Ninth St., New York, NY 10003.

*CAREER:* Novelist and magazine writer. Performs with tap ensemble *Rhythm Rascals.*

*AWARDS, HONORS:* Recipient of PEN/Hemingway Award for Best First Fiction, 1999, for *The Hallelujah Side.*

*WRITINGS:*

*The Hallelujah Side,* Delphinium Books (Harrison, NY), 1999.

Also contributor to periodicals, including *Ploughshares.*

*SIDELIGHTS:* Rhoda Huffey's debut novel, *The Hallelujah Side,* is described as a funny and heartwarming story of a little girl growing up in 1950s Iowa. Fish, the nine-year-old protagonist, comes from a Pentecostal family, and her father is pastor of a church in Ames, Iowa. The centerpiece of the conflict is Roxanne's fear that the world will end before she is saved. A reviewer in *Publishers Weekly* commented that Huffey's "light touch with her material, and her sensitive rendering of a religious youngster's matter-of-fact-belief that the world may end any minute, move her story from the paradoxical to the plausible."

*BIOGRAPHICAL AND CRITICAL SOURCES:*

*PERIODICALS*

*Publishers Weekly,* September 20, 1999, review of *The Hallelujah Side,* p. 72.*

\*　　\*　　\*

**HUFSTADER, Jonathan 1939-**

*PERSONAL:* Born May 2, 1939, in Trenton, NJ. *Education:* Yale University, B.A., 1960; Pontificio Ateneo di Sant'Anselmo (Rome, Italy), Licentiate in sacred theology, 1968; Harvard University, M.A., 1991, Ph. D., 1993.

*ADDRESSES: Office*—University of Connecticut, Department of English, Box U-4025, 215 Glenbrook Road, Storrs, CT 06269-4025. *E-mail*—jonathan. hufstader@uconn.edu.

*CAREER:* Portsmouth Abbey School, Portsmouth, RI, teacher of French and religion, 1968-86, college advisor, 1970-75, school chaplain, 1975-83, headmaster, 1983-86; Dana Hall School, Wellesley, MA, teacher of French and English, 1986-90, academic dean, 1987-89; Framingham State College, Framingham, MA, visiting lecturer in English, 1992-93; University of Connecticut, Storrs, assistant professor of English, 1993—, honors program director.

*MEMBER:* Modern Language Association, American Conference for Irish Studies.

*WRITINGS:*

*Tongue of Water, Teeth of Stones: Northern Irish Poetry and Social Violence,* University Press of Kentucky (Lexington, KY) 1999.

Contributor to academic journals, including *Colby Quarterly, Essays in Criticism, Studies in the Renaissance, Irish University Review* and *Downside Review.*

*SIDELIGHTS:* American academic Jonathan Hufstader has written a number of essays on Irish poets, and in 1999 he published *Tongue of Water, Teeth of Stones: Northern Irish Poetry and Social Violence.* In this study of seven major poets, including Seamus Heaney, Paul Muldoon, and Medbh McGuckian, Hufstader seeks, in his own words, "to determine how poetry has most effectively dealt with violence within its artistic domain." In doing so, he "walks a thin line that avoids the dominant critical strategies of placing Irish poetry into the larger contexts of postcolonial debate on the one hand and a mode of deconstructive revisionism on the other," according to Garland Kimmer, writing in the *South Atlantic Review.* Kimmer added that his "emphasis on the poetic voice and persona provides a fascinating read that forces me to reassess my own approaches to reading these poets." *Choice* reviewer W. E. Hall noted that while actual historical events are mentioned in the text, "Hufstader's recurring context is essentially a literary one." Hall further commented that "Hufstader's own elegant writing conveys some of the lyric power found in the poetry."

BIOGRAPHICAL AND CRITICAL SOURCES:

PERIODICALS

*Choice,* January, 2000, W. E. Hall, review of *Tongue of Water, Teeth of Stones,* p. 932.

OTHER

*South Atlantic Review,* http://www.samla.org/ (February 14, 2002), Garland Kimmer, review of *Tongue of Water, Teeth of Stones.**
*University of Connecticut Department of English Web site,* http://www.english/uconn.edu/ (February 14, 2002), "Jonathan Hufstader."*

\*　　\*　　\*

## HUGHES, Matthew 1965-

PERSONAL: Born 1965, in England.

ADDRESSES: *Office*—University of Salford, Salford, Greater Manchester M5 4WT, England. *E-mail*—j.blackbourne@salford.ac.uk.

CAREER: Educator and author. University of Salford, Salford, England, senior lecturer in military and international history and director of Centre for Conflict Studies; University College, Northampton, England, professor of modern history; visiting scholar, American University in Cairo, Cairo, Egypt, 2000.

AWARDS, HONORS: Elie Kedourie Fellow, Moshe Dayan Centre, Tel Aviv University, 2000; Royal Historical Society fellow.

WRITINGS:

*Allenby and British Strategy in the Middle East: 1917-1919,* Frank Cass (Portland, OR), 1999.
(With Chris Mann and Roger Ford) *The T-34 Russian Battle Tank,* MBI Publishing (Oxceola, WI), 1999.
(With Chris Mann) *Fighting Techniques of a Panzergrenadier: 1941-1945,* MBI Publishing (Oxceola, WI), 2000.
(With Stephen Hart and Russell Hart) *The German Soldier in World War II,* MBI Publishing (Oxceola, WI), 2000.
(Editor, with Matthew Seligman) *Leadership in Conflict: 1914-1918,* Leo Cooper, Pen & Sword Books (South Yorkshire, England), 2000.
(With Chris Mann) *The Panther Tank,* MBI Publishing (Oxceola, WI), 2000.
*Fools Errant: A Fantasy Picaresque,* Warner (New York, NY), 2001.
*Fool Me Twice,* Warner (New York, NY), 2001.
(With Chris Mann) *Inside Hitler's Germany,* MJF Books (New York, NY), 2003.

Contributor to periodicals and academic journals, including *London Review of Books, BBC History Magazine, History Today, Journal of the Australian War Memorial, Journal of Strategic Studies, Imperial War Museum Review, Journal of the Royal United Services Institute,* and *International Journal of Iberian Studies.*

SIDELIGHTS: Author of both nonfiction and fiction, Matthew Hughes teaches military and international history at the University of Salford, England. His first book, *Allenby and British Strategy in the Middle East: 1917-1919* examines the much-touted Palestine Campaign of 1917-1918, in which the Allies employed new leadership and mobility to recapture Jerusalem and the Holy Land. The aggressive operation helped bring about the fall of the Ottoman Empire and empowered British military negotiation during wartime. Hughes aims to understand the importance of this campaign in defeating the Central Alliance, and to estimate and analyze the significance of the victory for the British Empire, as well as British motives throughout the period.

Hughes follows General Sir Edmund H. H. Allenby from 1917, when Allenby assumed command of the Egyptian Expeditionary Force, to the 1919 British withdrawal from Syria. The book consists of two sections: Allenby's imperfect leadership strategies as well as the campaign's specific operations, and the successful end of the Palestine Campaign, its ultimate value, and examples of Britain's significant postwar bargaining power.

Harold E. Raugh, Jr. wrote in the *Middle East Journal,* "Hughes . . . effectively reevaluates a number of long-held misconceptions and inaccuracies about the Palestine Campaign and reexamines Allenby's generalship." In the book's long first section, for example, Hughes explains that the Third Battle of Gaza was not as much a success as the British claimed, thanks to poor planning on Allenby's part. Raugh wrote, "The numerous planning, operational and strategic shortcomings of the Palestine Campaign elucidated in this study strongly suggest that the author is correct in his assessment that Allenby 'was not one of the great generals of history,' even though Allenby was clearly a better-than-average general and . . . an improvement over his predecessor" Sir Archibald Murray.

Reviewing *Allenby and British Stratgey in the Middle East* for *Middle Eastern Studies,* a writer said Hughes is also "especially concerned with discovering Palestine's importance in the war and in the subsequent peace process, examining the political and military aspects of British strategy and of the campaign in Palestine as a 'tool.'"

In the first portion of the book, Hughes compares Allenby's confident soldier-bolstering leadership to Murray's less-dramatic style; he pits Prime Minister David Lloyd George's support of the Palestine Campaign against Chief of the Imperial Staff General Sir William Robertson's outspoken disapproval.

The book's second section emphasizes the outcome of the campaign, analyzes the placement of the Hashemites in Damascus and portrays Lloyd George's newfound boardroom prowess, following the Palestine Campaign. Thanks to the outcome, Hughes asserts, Britain convinced France to adjust the border of Palestine to include Galilee. In addition, because military air power was becoming more crucial, Britain continued to fight for and gain French claims in the Middle East. "That top-level decisions were influenced by military events and military needs and plans is well argued," the *Middle Eastern Studies* writer said.

Conversely, Briton C. Busch wrote in the *Journal of Military History,* "The real problem is that the last part of the book has little to do with Allenby or military strategy, aside from the fact that the British forces under the general's command had taken Palestine and Syria, and thus gave Britain the leverage of possession over the ground."

Finally, Hughes deems the Palestine Campaign "a waste of scarce British resources." *The Middle Eastern Studies* reviewer added, "Hughes . . . contributes toward the understanding of the role of the Palestinian Campaigns and the British push into the Middle East . . . though the reader has to be aware of the author's lapses into strongly expressed personal opinion."

A *Contemporary Review* critic said, "This is a very thoughtful and well researched study which helps us to understand a war that appears almost incomprehensible to modern Englishmen."

Hughes also published *The T-34 Russian Battle Tank.* Written with Chris Mann and Roger Ford, the book examines the role of the Russian T-34 tank in the defeat of Germany during World War II.Hughes and his cowriters define all aspects of T-34 development and service histories, from design and armaments to crews and armor. Hughes explains how the machine's innovative yet basic design, its efficient mobility, and its strength of armor helped secure an Allied victory in Europe.

Huges's *Fighting Techniques of a Panzergrenadier: 1941-1945,* written with Chris Mann, provides an overview of the training, techniques, and weapons infantry and armored troops used in Germany during World War II. (The Panzergrenadier supported the German tank division.) Hughes and Mann teamed again to write *The Panther Tank,* which narrates the history and features of Germany's heavily-armed Panther tank, and discusses tank commanders' World War II strategies.

Written with Russell Hart and Stephen Hart, Hughes's *The German Soldier in World War II* portrays the German infantryman's daily routine. Following a typical soldier from 1939 through war's end in 1945, it examines military training, indoctrination, brutal circumstances on the Russian front and imprisonment in Prisoner of War camps. Hughes and his fellow authors collect numerous first-person accounts of wartime life, including detailed experiences of life in the Third Reich, and paste together a collage of experiences and photographs.

Edited with Matthew Seligman, *Leadership in Conflict: 1914-1918,* presents an array of wartime leaders, including former ambassadors, a doctor, two field marshals, and several heads of state. Hughes and Seligman analyze the function of a leader's personality in wartime affairs.

In the *Journal of Military History,* Douglas V. Johnson II commended the book's thorough footnotes and said, "The two essays devoted to senior Germans are really interesting pieces of high staff intrigue and both reflect the tension between the Easterners and Westerners. . . . Comparing Eastern and Western factions across several armies would have been more useful." Reviewing *Leadership in Conflict* for *Parameters,* Johnson added, "There are good authors in this book, and their research is extensive and well documented."

Hughes's first fantasy novel, *Fools Errant: A Fantasy Picaresque,* tells the story of young, underachieving Filidor Vesh, nephew of Archon ("absolute ruler") of Old Earth. At story's opening, Filidor and his mentor Gaskarth begin to make their winding way to Archon with a special delivery. Along the path, Filidor and Gaskarth encounter new peoples and travel through to strange, often dangerous lands. Filidor encounters extremist groups, solves their troubles, and move on to new challenges. A *Publishers Weekly* writer said, "Hughes thankfully breaks from this cycle toward the end of the book when the true nature of Filidor's quest is revealed," and called *Fools Errant* reminiscent of *Gulliver's Travels.*

Marsha Valance, reviewing the novel for *Voice of Youth Advocates,* compared the story to classic works *Lazarillo de Tormes* and *Tristam Shandy,* and commented, "This first novel will do very well in any collection where literate fantasy in enjoyed." Hughes has followed up *Fools Errant* with a sequel, *Fool Me Twice.*

## BIOGRAPHICAL AND CRITICAL SOURCES:

*PERIODICALS*

*Analog of Science Fiction & Fact,* October, 2001,Tom Easton, review of *Fools Errant: A Fantasy Picaresque,* p. 132.

*Contemporary Review,* December, 1999, review of *Allenby and British Strategy in the Middle East: 1917-1919,* p. 332.

*Journal of Military History,* January, 2000, Briton C. Busch, review of *Allenby and British Strategy in the Middle East,* pp. 221-222; July, 2001, Douglas V. Johnson II, review of *Leadership in Conflict: 1914-18,* p. 817.

*Library Journal,* January 1, 2001, Jackie Cassada, review of *Fools Errant,* p. 163.

*Locus,* May, 2001, Dawn Castner, review of *Fools Errant,* p. 31.

*Magazine of Fantasy and Science Fiction,* August, 2001, James Sallis, review of *Fools Errant,* p. 43.

*Middle Eastern Studies,* January, 2001, review of *Allenby and British Strategy in the Middle East,* p. 240.

*Middle East Journal,* winter, 2001, Harold E. Raugh, Jr., review of *Allenby and British Strategy in the Middle East,* p. 158.

*Parameters,* autumn, 2001, Douglas V. Johnson II, review of *Leadership in Conflict,* p. 179.

*Publishers Weekly,* February 26, 2001, review of *Fools Errant,* p. 65.

*Voice of Youth Advocates,* April, 2001, Marsha Valance, review of *Fools Errant,* p. 53.

*OTHER*

*Institute of Historical Research Web site,* http://www.history.ac.uk/ (July, 2000) Peter Simkins, review of *Allenby and British Strategy in the Middle East.**

# I-J

## ICHIOKA, Yuji 1936-2002

*OBITUARY NOTICE*—See index for *CA* sketch: Born June 23, 1936, in San Francisco, CA; died of cancer September 1, 2002, in Los Angeles, CA. Historian, educator, and author. Ichioka is credited with coining the term "Asian American," and he worked to bring Asian immigrants of all nationalities together in the United States and foster an understanding of Asian-American history. He was a graduate of the University of California at Los Angeles (UCLA), where he earned his B.A. in 1962, going on to earn a master's degree from the University of California at Berkeley in 1968 and also doing graduate work at Columbia University. Joining the faculty at UCLA, he was a history professor for his entire career and founded the Asian-American Studies Center on the Los Angeles campus in 1969. He was also an important contributor to the Japanese-American Research Project Collection at UCLA and became known as a social activist who fought not only for the rights of Asian American but for those of all minorities. Toward this end, Ichioka founded the Asian-American Political Alliance in 1968. An expert on the history of the Japanese in America, his research shattered stereotypes of these immigrants by showing that they were not simply passive, hard-working laborers; instead, they often fought against social injustices by holding demonstrations and labor strikes. He published his research in *The Issei: The World of the First-Generation Japanese Immigrants, 1885-1924* (1988), which won the National Association for Asian American Studies' U.S. History Book Award in 1989, as well as *A Buried Past: A Bibliography of the Japanese-American Research Project Collection* (1974) and *A Buried Past II: A Sequel to the Annotated Bibliography of the Japanese American Research Project Collection, 1973-1998* (1999).

*OBITUARIES AND OTHER SOURCES:*

PERIODICALS

*Los Angeles Times,* September 7, 2002, p. B16.
*Washington Post,* September 8, 2002, p. C7.

\* \* \*

## INGRAM, Martha R(obinson) 1935-

*PERSONAL:* Born August 20, 1935, in Charleston, SC; daughter of John Minott and Martha Elizabeth (Robinson) Rivers; married E. Bronson Ingram, October 4, 1958; children: Orrin Henry III, John Rivers, David Bronson, Robin Bigelow. *Education:* Vassar College, B.A. (history), 1957.

*ADDRESSES: Office*—Ingram Industries, Inc., One Belle Mead Pl., 4400 Harding Rd, Nashville, TN 37205-2244.

*CAREER:* Kennedy Center for the Performing Arts, Washington, DC, advisory board member, 1972-80; Ingram Industries, Inc., Nashville, TN, vice president for public affairs, 1979, member of board, 1981, chairman, 1995—. Tennessee Performing Arts Center, chairman; board member for Tennessee Repertory Theatre, Nashville City Ballet, Nashville Opera Association, Nashville Institute for the Arts, Nashville Symphony Orchestra Baxter International, Inc., First American Corporation, and Weyerhaeuser Company; board of directors for Spoleto Festival U.S.A.; Vanderbilt University Board of Trust, chairman. Trustee of Ashley Hall School and Vassar College.

*AWARDS, HONORS:* First living woman and first daughter of a laureate to be inducted into South Carolina Business Hall of Fame, 1999; inducted into Junior Achievement National Business Hall of Fame, 1999; recipient of the Mary Harriman Community Leadership Award, Junior League International, Inc.

*WRITINGS:*

*E. Bronson Ingram: Complete These Unfinished Tasks of Mine,* Hillsboro Press (Franklin, TN), 2001.

*SIDELIGHTS:* Martha Rivers Ingram grew up in Charleston, South Carolina where she received an excellent education, graduating from Ashley Hall School. She continued her education at Vassar College, where she developed an interest in the arts. She went on to marry E. Bronson Ingram, who developed Ingram Industries, "the world's largest wholesale distributor of technology products and services," according to *South Carolina ETV.* Martha Ingram is probably best known in Nashville for her work developing the Tennessee Performing Arts Center (TPAC). TPAC needed $3.5 million to defray operating losses and fund programs for future performances, and Ingram surpassed that goal by raising over $5 million for the cause. Due to her success, her husband invited her to work for Ingram Industries where she became the vice president of public affairs in 1979 and a member of the board in 1981. Five days preceding his death she took on the role of chariman of the board as his successor.

In an interview for *Business Wire,* Ingram stated she was "very excited about the continuing growth and success of Ingram Industries." "She has demonstrated her strong business sense," stated Anne Faircloth for *Fortune.* Faircloth continued, "She was the quintes-

sential steel magnolia . . . willing to stand up to those who thought her husband's death would create a power vacuum at Ingram Industries. . . . Martha Ingram was perhaps the country's most anonymous billionaire and most under appreciated businesswoman." In the interview with Faircloth, Ingram said, "Young women who come in for advice are usually very disappointed to learn all I wanted to do was be a wife and mother." Ingram elaborated on her experience of being a women in the business world: "my father never said anything to me about being a woman or how odd it would be to be in the business world. . . I was part of a team with Bronson. . . . . I definitely shared with my husband the sense of wanting to win, of wanting to accomplish whatever it was we set out to do."

Martha Ingram wrote a biography of her husband's success story in *E. Bronson Ingram: Complete These Unfinished Tasks of Mine. Library Journal*'s Dale Farris commented that the book "presents the life of a successful businessman" and went on to say that Martha Ingram "offers a succinct history of the Ingram family tree." Farris expressed that "she shows how his unwavering commitment to integrity, his devotion to his four children, and their success in the expanding Ingram enterprises form the basis for the 14th-largest private company in the United States." Farris wrote, "this personal story of a thriving business is highly recommended for all libraries."

*BIOGRAPHICAL AND CRITICAL SOURCES:*

*PERIODICALS*

*Business Wire,* June 22, 1995, "Martha R. Ingram Named Chairman, Linwood A. 'Chip' Lacy, Jr., CEO of Ingram Industries Inc."
*Fortune,* September 29, 1997, Anne Faircloth, "Minding Martha's Business," p. 173.
*Library Journal,* March 1, 2002, Dale Farris, review of *E. Bronson Ingram: Complete These Unfinished Tasks of Mine,* p. 116.
*Publishers Weekly,* July 10, 1995, Bob Summer, "Martha Ingram, Lacy, New Execs at Ingram Industries," p.10.
*Time,* July 24, 2000, "A New Way of Giving," p. 48.

*OTHER*

*South Carolina ETV,* http://www.scetv.org/ (April 10, 2002).
Providence House Publishers Web Site, http://www.providencehouse.com/ (April 10, 2002).*

## JACKSON, H(eather) J.

*PERSONAL:* Female. *Education:* University of Toronto, B.A., M.A., Ph.D.

*ADDRESSES: Office*—c/o Department of English, 7 King's College Circle, University of Toronto, Toronto, Ontario M55 3K1, Canada. *E-mail*—heather.jackson@ utoronto.ca.

*CAREER:* University of Toronto, Toronto, Ontario, Canada, professor of English.

*MEMBER:* Modern Language Association, member, committee on scholarly editions.

*AWARDS, HONORS:* National Book Critics Circle Award for Criticism nomination for *Marginalia,* 2001.

*WRITINGS:*

(Editor) Samuel Taylor Coleridge, *Selections,* Oxford University Press, (Oxford, England), 1985.
(Editor) Samuel Taylor Coleridge, *Selected Letters,* Oxford University Press (Oxford, England), 1988.
(Editor) Samuel Taylor Coleridge, *Marginalia,* three volumes, part of "Collected Works of Samuel Taylor Coleridge," Princeton University Press (Princeton, NJ), 1992-2001.
(Editor, with George Whalley) Samuel Taylor Coleridge, *Shorter Works and Fragments,* part of "Collected Words of Samuel Taylor Coleridge," Princeton University Press (Princeton, NJ), 1995.
*Marginalia: Readers Writing in Books, 1700-2000,* Yale University Press (New Haven, CT), 2001.

*WORK IN PROGRESS:* A book about reading in the Romantic period.

*SIDELIGHTS:* Professor H. J. Jackson of the University of Toronto worked in the largely anonymous field of scholarly editing, producing several volumes of the minor and unpublished writings of the Romantic poet Samuel Taylor Coleridge before releasing a work of academic criticism that also crossed over to appeal to a general audience. Jackson's efforts in *Marginalia: Readers Writing in Books, 1700-2000* examined how

readers read books at various points in history. A reviewer for the *Economist* wrote, "Ms. Jackson wishes ostensibly to alert scholars and librarians to the importance of marginalia. But the warmth and humour of *Marginalia* reach beyond to the lay reader." Peter Porter, reviewing the book for the *Spectator,* wrote, "Mrs. Jackson's pages demand to be read for pleasure rather than for enlightenment."

Jackson's initial subject, Coleridge, was a prolific writer of marginalia; of a twelve-volume collection of his works, fully three are devoted to his extensive commentary in the margins of books. As one of the principal editors of these volumes, Jackson brought together his commentary on Kant and several other German scholars, German philospher Immanuel Wordsworth's *Prelude,* a variety of literary journals, and the works of Shakespeare. Coleridge is perhaps the exception to most readers due to the depth and detail of his marginalia. Reviewing the second volume of Coleridge's *Marginalia,* in *Essays in Criticism,* Mark Allen described Coleridge's incidental commentary on Shakespeare as "stunning diagnoses of language of behavior," adding that "if there is really anyone who doesn't believe that Coleridge was a great reader of Shakespeare he or she ought to look at the commentaries on the early scenes of *Macbeth* in copies C and D." And unlike most readers who write in the margins, Allen suggested, "Coleridge knows perfectly well he will be read."

In *Marginalia: Readers Writing in Books, 1700-2000,* Jackson expands her study to readers of Samuel Johnson, including his friends Boswell and Hester Thrale-Piozzi, the romantic poet John Keats' famous comments on Milton, T. H. White's notes on Karl Jung, Horace Walpole's copious marginal scribblings, and twentieth-century literary critic Northrop Frye's notes on John Bunyan and Marianne Moore. She also takes into account anonymous marginalia writers, whose notes range from detailed claims of ownership and requests for a book's safe return to personalized indexes to written conversations among friends sharing the book. Tracing these developments through time, Jackson argues, reveals the relationship between publishing and reading practices, as well as changes in the status and function of the author, to whom marginalia is often addressed. In addition, Jackson concludes her study by calling for a greater respect for marginalia, including the preservation of handwritten annotations, larger margins in newly published books, and the sharing of books among friends, in order to expand the conversation in the margins beyond the reader and author.

Reviewers observed that Jackson's work recalls some of the heightened pleasures of reading. In the *Spectator,* Porter concluded his review by saying, "*Marginalia* reminds us of those confident and heartfelt times when a book was an oracle which expected to be answered back. I am looking at my shelves and planning retaliation on some of those well-ruled margins, flamboyant frontispieces and handsome end-papers." Frank Kermode, reviewing *Marginalia* in the *New Republic,* noted that Jackson's book highlights the fact that "reading . . . remained until the early twentieth century, a more social activity than it is now." For the author's thoroughness, humor, and solid argumentation, Kermode wrote, "My respect for Jackson is measureless."

*BIOGRAPHICAL AND CRITICAL SOURCES:*

*PERIODICALS*

*Economist,* June 16, 2001, "Scribble, Scribble; Reading Habits; Readers' Scribbles," p. 6.
*Essays in Criticism,* January, 1994, Mark Allen, review of *Marginalia,* Vol. 3, pp. 60-68; October, 1999, Mark Allen, review of *Marginalia* Vol. 4, pp. 369-374.
*Library Journal,* March 1, 2001, Ali Houissa, review of *Marginalia: Readers Writing in Books, 1700-2000,* p. 86; January, 2002, review of *Marginalia,* p. 50.
*Nation,* March 24, 1997, Alexander Cockburn, review of *Shorter Works and Fragments,* p. 10.
*New Republic,* March 26, 2001, Frank Kermode, "Homo Scriblerus," p. 27.
*Notes and Queries,* June, 1993, E. D. Mackerness, review of *Marginalia* Vol. 3, pp. 255-256; June, 1997, J. D. Gutteridge, review of *Shorter Works and Fragments,* pp. 279-280.
*Publishers Weekly,* January 22, 2001, "Librarians Beware!" p. 236.
*Review of English Studies,* August, 2001, Neil Vickers, review of *Marginalia* Vol. 5, pp. 457-458.
*Spectator,* August 4, 2001, Peter Porter, review of *Marginalia,* p. 31.
*Studies in English Literature,* autumn, 1988, David G. Riede, review of *Samuel Taylor Coleridge: Selected Letters,* p. 723.
*Time,* January 29, 2001, Roger Rosenblatt, "Life in the Margins," p. 76.

*OTHER*

*Fabula,* http://www.fabula.org/ (March 21, 2001), Rene Audet, review of *Marginalia.*
*University of Toronto Web site,* http://www.news andevents.utoronto.ca/ (February 25, 2002), Michah Rynor, "Three Killams for U of T."*

\*　　\*　　\*

## JACKSON, Julian 1954-

*PERSONAL:* Born 1954. *Education:* Received B.A., Ph.D.

*ADDRESSES: Office*—University of Wales, Swansea, Department of History, Singleton Park, Swansea SA28PP, England *E-mail*—J.T.Jackson@swansea.ac.uk

*CAREER:* Author; professor of history, University of Wales, Swansea.

*WRITINGS:*

*The Politics of Depression in France, 1932-1936,* Cambridge University Press (New York, NY), 1985.
*The Popular Front in France: Defending Democracy, 1934-38,* Cambridge University Press (New York, NY), 1988.
*France: The Dark Years, 1940-1944,* Oxford University Press (New York, NY), 2001.
(Editor) *Europe, 1900-1945* Oxford University Press (New York, NY), 2002.
*The Fall of France: The Nazi Invasion of 1940,* Oxford University Press (New York, NY), 2003.

Also contributor to books, including *De Gaulle and Twentieth-Century France,* by Hugh Gough and John Horne, Edward Arnold, 1994; *Writing National Histories,* by S. Berger, M. Donavan, and K. Passmore, Routledge, 1999; and *The French and Spanish Popular Fronts,* by Martin S. Alexander and Helen Graham, Cambridge University Press, 1989.

*WORK IN PROGRESS:* Paper on the French homosexual movement, "Arcadie"; paper on the French economist, Francois Perroux; book on the myth of De Gaulle; history of France, 1914-1940.

*SIDELIGHTS:* Julian Jackson is a Professor of History at the University of Wales, Swansea, with a particular interest in twentieth-century France. His first book, *The Politics of Depression in France, 1932-1936,* published in 1985, clearly shows how and when the Great Depression affected France during 1930s. Jackson shows that although the Depression struck France later and more mildly than it did Germany or the United States, it persisted longer. An important reason for this, according to Jackson, was the almost hysterical resistance in France to the devaluation of the franc. As E. P Fitzgerald noted, in a review for *Choice,* "Memories of the devaluation of 1926 kept alive the mystique of the franc's gold value, thereby postponing for three years the inevitable devaluation required to render French exports competitive."

The political class in France was almost completely ignorant of economic theory. "More important," wrote Nathanael Green in the *American Historical Review,* "was the pleasure they took from their ignorance, for it permitted them to look almost exclusively to political solutions to economic and financial problems." The 1930s was marked by one failed policy after another, which, Jackson writes, sapped the country's vitality and its ability to resist the aggression of Nazi Germany. Neither the Right nor the Left were able to come up with any sort of economic stimulus plan, and the governments (there were eleven cabinets from 1932 to 1936) opted for a program of economic stagnation as the only way out of the economic downturn.

The Popular Front, an anti-Fascist coalition of communists, socialists, and radicals formed in February of 1934. In *The Popular Front in France: Defending Democracy, 1934-38,* Jackson traces the movement from its origins in 1936 to its collapse on the eve of the Anschlus in March of 1938. Douglas Johnson of *New Statesman and Society* wrote, "one of the merits of this judicious book is his [Jackson's] refusal to confine himself to the political, economic and diplomatic aspects of government. He describes how the Popular Front was born in the streets, especially in the Republican heartland of Paris, by the squares of the Bastille, the Nation and the Republic. . . . He describes, too, the 'cultural explosion' associated with the Popular Front, when Renoir set about making his film on the Revolution." Jackson also provides fresh insight into Léon Blum's period in office, including France's choice of nonintervention in the Spanish Civil War and the important changes in workers' conditions.

*The Popular Front* is the first English language study of the movement. Jackson's work, wrote Jack Hayward, in the *Times Literary Supplement,* is a compendium of secondary material that provides a comprehensive and detached history of the period "from the moderation of the Socialists, determined to establish their liberal democratic credentials, to the Communists, prepared to sacrifice social and economic reform to the tactical requirements of extending support for the party at home and for the Soviet Union abroad, to the extreme left's belief that 'everything is possible.'" Through numerous examples, Jackson shows that the seeds of failure were present from the beginning. In retrospect, however, Jackson does feel that the Popular Front was not a complete failure. "The Popular Front did not fundamentally change the world, but it briefly and deeply illuminated the lives of many who had participated in it."

*France: The Dark Years, 1940-1944,* published in 2001, is the first comprehensive study of the German occupation of France. Jackson examines the nature and the extent of collaboration and resistance, the persecution and deportation of Jews, and the cultural life in France under the occupation. "In 1939," writes British historian Mark Mazower in the *New York Times,* "there was only one France. Within a year," Julian Jackson notes, "it had given way to not less than six distinct zones of occupation. Defeat by the German Army led to the country's territorial division and administrative disintegration. By 1943, at least three governments claimed to embody French sovereignty: Marshal Petain's Vichy, General Charles de Gaulle in London and General Henri Giraud's in Algiers. It is hardly surprising, then, that President Franklin D. Roosevelt concluded that France had ceased to exist." France did exist, however, and Jackson has exhaustively researched these years. He describes his book as "a new interpretive synthesis" of the work that has been published in France during the last two decades of the twentieth century.

Patrick Marnham wrote in the *Spectator,* "The history of the wartime Occupation has recently become a French national obsession. . . . Nobody wished to challenge the convenient consensus that the military defeat in 1940 was followed by four years of collaboration imposed by Marshal Petain, until France, represented by the Free French and the Resistance and led by General de Gaulle, joined in its own liberation and eventual defeat of the Nazi regime." This myth, now held up to such intense national scrutiny, began with de Gaulle's suggestion, in 1945, that France had never been defeated at all. "The French, it was said, had fought on, either as resisters or as Gaullists," continued Marnham. This myth served to legitimize de Gaulle's new government, as well as to unite a country that, in 1945, was dangerously divided. It also, along with the idea that the French Communists had been the most important factor in the anti-Nazi resistance, became the accepted version of events for postwar French historians.

In *France: The Dark Years,* Jackson methodically goes about exploring not only the events of wartime France, but also the roots of the Vichy government and the Resistance. As a reviewer for *Publishers Weekly* noted, "Between these endpoints lies a convoluted landscape bearing little resemblance to the usual simplistic picture. . . . Beginning his history with the formation of the politics and society of the Third Republic, he exposes France's past in all its contradictions and complexities: the Resistance forces' diverse membership, including women, Jews, farm workers and foreigners; the latent forces in French government and culture that allowed for an easy transition to the Vichy government, and Marshal Petain's increasing popularity while support for Vichy flagged." Jim Doyle, writing in *Library Journal,* added that "Jackson thoroughly dissects the multi-layered complexities of a nation at war with itself and shows how, in the final analysis, it was the persevering spirit of the average French citizen that prevailed during those dark years."

In 2003 Jackson published *The Fall of France: The Nazi Invasion of 1940.* A reviewer in *Atlantic Monthly* wrote that although Jackson presents equally all sides in the debate of this topic, he takes the revisionist stance that France's fall should be "attributed not to the systemic weaknesses of the Third Republic's decadent political culture but, rather, to discrete intelligence failures and to the army's somewhat inflexible mindset."

## BIOGRAPHICAL AND CRITICAL SOURCES:

### BOOKS

Jackson, Julian, *France: The Dark Years, 1940-1944,* Oxford University Press (New York, NY), 2001.

### PERIODICALS

*American Historical Review,* February, 1987, Nathanael Greene, review of *The Politics of Depression in France, 1932-1936,* p. 148.

*Atlantic Monthly,* October, 2001, Eugen Weber, review of *France: The Dark Years, 1940-1944;* April, 2003, review of *The Fall of France: The Nazi Invasion of 1940,* p. 92.

*British Book News,* David Englander, review of *The Politics of Depression in France, 1932-1936,* p. 26.

*Canadian Journal of History,* April, 1990, Kenneth Moore, review of *The Popular Front in France: Defending Democracy, 1934-38,* p. 135.

*Choice,* June, 1986, C. Fink, *The Politics of Depression in France, 1932-1936,* p. 1589; June, 1986, E. P. Fitzgerald, review of *The Popular Front in France,* p. 1589; fall, 1989, C. Fink, review of *The Popular Front in France.*

*Economist,* July 14, 2001, review of *France: The Dark Years, 1940-1944,* p. 1.

*English Historical Review,* July, 1989, D. R. Watson, review of *The Popular Front in France,* p. 706; January, 1988, François Crouzet, review of *The Politics of Depression in France, 1932-1936,* p. 147.

*International Affairs,* spring, 1989, P. M. H. Bell, review of *The Popular Front in France,* p. 340.

*Journal of Economic History,* December, 1987, Stephen A. Schuker, review of *The Politics of Depression in France, 1932-1936,* p. 101.

*Journal of Interdisciplinary History,* summer, 1989, Robert O. Paxton, review of *The Popular Front in France,* p. 151.

*Journal of Modern History,* December, 1990, Robert Soucy, review of *The Popular Front in France,* p. 872; March, 1988, Bradford A. Lee, review of *The Politics of Depression in France, 1932-1936,* p. 148.

*Library Journal,* July, 2001, Jim Doyle, review of *France,* p. 107.

*New Statesman & Society,* July 29, 1988, Douglas Johnson, review of *The Popular Front in France,* p. 42.

*New York Times Book Review,* July 22, 2001, Mark Mazower, "Gaul Divided: A History of Wartime France Examines the Country's Political Partitioning," p. 27.

*Spectator,* (London, England), July 7, 2001, Patrick Marnham, review of *France,* p. 29.

*Times Educational Supplement,* (London), August 18, 1989, Anne Corbett, review of *The Popular Front in France,* p. 17.

*Times Literary Supplement,* October 2, 1988, Roy Mc-Nab, review of *The Popular Front in France,* p. 1130; September 26, 1986, Douglas Johnson, review of *The Politics of Depression in France, 1932-1938,* p. 27; October 7, 1988, Jack Hayward, review of *The Popular Front in France,* p. 1130.

OTHER

*University of Wales, Swansea Web site,* http://www.swan.ac.uk/ (December 2, 2002) "Julian Jackson."*

\*   \*   \*

**JANESICK, Valerie J.**

*PERSONAL:* Born in Detroit, MI. *Education:* Eastern Michigan University, B.S., 1970; Bowling Green State University, M.A., 1971; University of Michigan, graduate study, 1971-72; Michigan State University, Ph.D., 1977. *Politics:* Democrat. *Religion:* Buddhist. *Hobbies and other interests:* Travel, languages, the arts.

*ADDRESSES: Home*—Chicago, IL. *Office*—College of Education, Roosevelt University, 430 South Michigan Ave., Chicago, IL 60605.

*CAREER:* Elementary school teacher in Detroit, Albion, and Clawson, MI, 1966-69; Lansing Community College, Lansing, MI, instructor in dance, 1976-78; California Polytechnic State University, San Luis Obispo, assistant professor of education, 1978-79; State University of New York—Albany, assistant professor of education and director of Migrant Tutorial Outreach Program, 1979-86; Gallaudet University, Washington, DC, associate professor of educational foundations and research and department chair, 1986-90; University of Kansas, Lawrence, associate professor of curriculum and instruction, 1990-97; Florida International University, Miami, professor of educational leadership and policy, 1997-99; Roosevelt University, Chicago, IL, professor of educational leadership and organizational change, 1999—, depart-

ment chair, 2000—. University of Regina, visiting professor, 1982; University of Hawaii—Hilo, visiting professor, 1987.

*MEMBER:* American Educational Research Association, American Evaluation Association, John Dewey Society.

*AWARDS, HONORS:* Fulbright fellow at Kanagawa University, 1992.

*WRITINGS:*

*Stretching Exercises for Qualitative Researchers: A Sourcebook for Improving Interview and Observation Skills,* Sage Publications (Thousand Oaks, CA), 1998.
*The Assessment Debate: A Reference Handbook,* American Bibliographical Center-CLIO Press (Santa Barbara, CA), 2001.
*Curriculum Studies: A Reference Handbook,* American Bibliographical Center-CLIO Press (Santa Barbara, CA), 2003.

Contributor to books, including *Exceptional Children and Youth,* edited by Ed Meyen and Thomas Skrtic, Love Publishing (Denver, CO), 1988, revised edition, 1993; *Toward Effective Public School Programs for Deaf Students,* edited by Thomas N. Kluwin, Donald F. Moores, and Martha Gunter-Gaustad, Teachers College Press (New York, NY), 1992; *Exploring Collaborative Research in Primary Care,* edited by Benjamin Crabtree, William L. Miller, and others, Sage Publications (Thousand Oaks, CA), 1994; and *Perspectives in Critical Thinking: Theory and Practice in Education,* edited by Dan Weil, Peter Lang (New York, NY), 1999. Contributor of articles and reviews to professional journals, including *Review of Education, Pedagogy, and Cultural Studies, Qualitative Inquiry, Secondary Education Today, Curriculum Inquiry, Studies in Art Education, Anthropology and Education Quarterly, Educational Horizons, Educational Researcher, Journal of Issues in the Education of Minority Language Students,* and *International Journal of Educational Reforms.*

*WORK IN PROGRESS: John Dewey's Influence on British Education: A Historical Perspective,* completion expected in 2004.

*SIDELIGHTS:* Valerie J. Janesick told *CA:* "I write because I love it. I began to keep a journal in high school days and have never stopped writing. My greatest teachers inspired me to write. I set aside two hours per day, six days per week, and write.

"My deep commitment to education as a means of changing the world inspires me every day. I was always influenced by the writing of Shakespeare, Barbara Tuchman, Charles Dickens, and many others. This led me to my career focus in education. In my field, the work of John Dewey has prompted me to look for ways to improve my own teaching and writing. My love for the arts, dance, and music keep me energized."

*BIOGRAPHICAL AND CRITICAL SOURCES:*

PERIODICALS

*Choice,* July-August, 2002, G. E. Hein, review of *The Assessment Debate: A Reference Handbook,* p. 2010.
*School Library Journal,* May, 2002, Linda Greengrass, review of *The Assessment Debate,* p. 95.

\*        \*        \*

## JANKOWSKI, Paul F. 1950-

*PERSONAL:* Born July 8, 1950, in New York, NY; son of Paul (a United Nations civil servant) and Louise (Welsh) Jankowski; *Ethnicity:* "Caucasian". *Education:* Balliol College, Oxford, B.A., 1970, D.Phil., 1987.

*ADDRESSES: Office*—History Department, MS 036, Brandeis University, Waltham, MA 02454. *E-mail*—jankowski@brandeis.edu.

*CAREER: Time,* New York, NY, research assistant, 1971-72; DuPont Company, Wilmington, DE, public and international affairs consultant, 1973-82; Brandeis University, Waltham, MA, visiting assistant professor, 1987-88, lecturer, associate professor, currently assistant professor, 1990—; Stanford University, Palo Alto, CA, visiting assistant professor, 1988-1990.

*AWARDS, HONORS:* Camargo Foundation fellowship, 1995.

*WRITINGS:*

*Communism and Collaboration: Simon Sabiani and Politics in Marseille, 1919-1944,* Yale University Press (New Haven, CT), 1989.
*Cette vilaine affaire Stavitsy: histoire d'un scandale politique,* Fayard (Paris, France), 2001, published as *Stavisky: A Confidence Man in the Republic of Virtue,* Cornell University Press (Ithaca, NY), 2002.

Also author of articles and book reviews.

*WORK IN PROGRESS:* "Scandals in French History. A study of contemporary political scandals in long-term historical perspective."

*SIDELIGHTS:* Paul Jankowski is a historian of twentieth-century France, well known both in the United States and in France. His deeply researched histories of French political figures, Simon Sabiani and Alexandre Stavisky shed new light on this period of French history and draw strong parallels between the end of the Third Republic of France and contemporary liberal society in Europe and the United States.

In *Communism and Collaboration: Simon Sabiani and Politics in Marseille, 1919-1944,* Jankowski explores the career of Simon Sabiani, who, beginning as a Corsican neighborhood boss in Marseille after World War I, went on to forge a populist career and cult of personality not unlike the Louisiana dynasty of Huey Long. He began his political career as a pacifist communist in Marseilles and, in 1922, became the first communist elected to a city office. After only one year, Sabiani became discontented with the Party's dogmatism and founded his own party, the Parti Socialiste-communiste. He consolidated his power in the poorer quarters of the city, founded a newspaper, and was an important figure in city politics. He ruled over his empire from his favorite bar, like the godfather figures of his native Corsica.

Sabiani's political enemies were his old allies, the Communists and the members of the liberal Popular Front, which represented the progressive middle class.

The Popular Front won the city elections of 1935, putting an end to Sabiani's political power. During this period, he formed a friendship with Jacques Doriot, who led the proto-fascist party, the Parti Populaire Français, from the working class Parisian neighborhood of St. Denis. Sabiani's politics now were a mix of populism, neutralism and anti-communism.

After the defeat of France by Germany in 1940, Sabiani openly criticized the Vichy regime for not embracing Hitler's New Europe more enthusiastically. In 1942, when the Germans occupied the South of France, Sabiani was back in power. He worked for the Germans, supplying them with goods, services, and agents through his comprehensive, if unsavory, network of underground connections. When the allies liberated Marseille in 1942, Sabiani fled to Barcelona, Spain where he died in exile in 1956.

Toward the end of communism and collaboration, Jankowski sums up the essential aspects of Sabiani: "Throughout his career, Sabiani was an outsider. He belonged to a small, rough, inarticulate politics of the clientele, he never outgrew the camaraderie of the trenches; he was at home among small groups of men. . . . He was a political nomad who had many friends but never found a home. . . . He was only at home with his followers and dependents, whoever they were and wherever he found them. He was not very discriminating; he did not mind who they were as long as they were loyal to him."

Jankowski is always aware of the gray areas of history, especially with respect to collaborationism in France. He shows that the motivation of men like Sabiani is most often a combination of personal ambition and Mediterranean culture. Richard Cobb, writing in *Spectator,* noted that an important factor of the story is the city of Marseille itself where "fraud, corruption, clannishness and a good deal of underlying violence are leavened with meridianal cynicism and light-headedness, as if it were all sort of a game, including the killing."

Robert O. Paxton, in the *New York Review of Books,* commented that "Paul Jankowski's gritty, street-level perspective on collaboration and resistance plants us in the middle of a hot debate about who sided with the Nazis in occupied countries such as France, and why." Cobb of *Spectator* added, "This is probably one of the most sophisticated books ever written about the elusive, constantly shifting, frontierless subject of Collaboration and Collaborationism. It is a study of marginality, deeply researched, and written with compassion, an observantly wry humour, and a serene wisdom that is never taken by surprise by any unexpected twist or turn."

Jankowski's *Stavisky: A Confidence Man in the Republic of Virtue* was originally published in French as *Cette vilaine affaire Stavitsy: histoire d'un scandale politique. Stavisky* examines the financial scandal that virtually brought down the Third Republic. Not even the Panama Canal Affair, although involving much more money, escalated into a scandal of such magnitude. As Eugen Weber commented in the *Times Literary Supplement,* "The Russian-born con man and his dirty tricks set off convulsions that had little to do with the scale of his misdoings."

Jankowski traces the career of Alexandre Stavisky from his humble beginnings swindling old women, marketing a nonexistent soup, and selling defective refrigerators and stolen bonds to the scandal that rocked France. As a man who loved the lavish lifestyle, he soon saw that it was easier—and more profitable—to issue his own bonds with official blessings than to traffic in counterfeits.

In the late 1920s, Stavisky gained control of the Crédit Municipal de Orléans and began issuing commercial paper. Much like the U.S. savings and loan scandals of the 1980s, noncollateralized securities became the order of the day. Soon, France was flooded with fake vouchers, which eventually closed the banks, started riots, in which fifteen died and 1,500 were wounded, and brought down the government and finally the Third Republic. "The venality and ineptitude revealed by Stavisky's crash and by the subsequent trial of his accomplices, accessories and associates confirmed the drumbeat denunciation of the 'Established Disorder,'" concluded Weber in a *Times Literary Supplement* review.

Jankowski concludes that the Stavisky scandal, much like the 1980s scandals of the Socialist party in France or the Craxi Socialist machine in Italy, included many members of the liberal professions, especially journalists, lawyers and public officials. Such a scandal is often far-reaching in its consequences. The credibility of not only certain individuals, but also of the institutions to which they belong disintegrates. By showing how the elites of the Third Republic brought down the government by their own personal conduct, Jankowski cautions a liberal society about the dangers posed by unethical principals.

BIOGRAPHICAL AND CRITICAL SOURCES:

BOOKS

Jankowski, Paul F., *Communism and Collaboration: Simon Sabiani and Politics in Marseille, 1919-1944,* Yale University Press (New Haven, CT), 1989.

Jankowski, Paul F., *Cette Vilaine Affaire Stavitsy: Histoire d'un scandale politique,* Fayard (Paris, France), 2001, published as *Stavitsky: A Confidence Man in the Republic of Virtue,* Cornell University Press (Ithaca, NY), 2002.

PERIODICALS

*American Historical Review,* October, 1990, John F. Sweets, review of *Communism and Collaboration,* p. 1219.

*Choice,* October, 1989, C. Fink, review of *Communism and Collaboration,* p. 370.

*Economist,* March 9, 2002, "Pro and Con: Financial Swindlers."

*French Politics, Culture, and Society,* spring, 2002, Michael Miller, review of *Cette vilaine affaire Stavitsy: histoire d'un scandale politique,* p. 132.

*Historian,* August, 1990, Robert J. Soucy and John F. Sweets, review of *Communism and Collaboration,* p. 657.

*History: The Journal of the Historical Association,* October, 1990, J. F. V. Keiger, review of *Communism and Collaboration,* p. 422.

*Journal of Modern History,* June, 1992, Julian Jackson, review of *Communism and Collaboration,* p. 408.

*Library Journal,* April 1, 2002, Mary Salony, review of *Stavitsky: A Confidence Man in the Republic of Virtue,* p. 124.

*New York Review of Books,* April 27, 1989, Robert O. Paxton, review of *Communism and Collaboration,* p. 42.

*Publishers Weekly,* April 1, 2002, review of *Stavitsky: A Confidence Man in the Republic of Virtue,* p. 63.

*Spectator,* November 4, 1989, Richard Cobb, review of *Communism and Collaboration,* p. 25.

*Times Literary Supplement,* June, 22, 2001, Eugen Weber, review of *Cette vilaine vffaire Stavitsy: histoire d'un scandale politique,* p. 25; July 28, 1989, Jack Hayward, review of *Communism and Collaboration,* p. 821.

\*   \*   \*

**JARAMILLO, Mari-Luci 1928-**

*PERSONAL:* Born June 19, 1928; daughter of Maurilio Autuna and Elvira Ruiz; children: Ross, Richard, Carla. *Ethnicity:* "Mexican-American." *Education:* New Mexico Highlands University, B.A. (magna cum laude), 1955, M.A. (with honors), 1959; University of California—Los Angeles, attended Teaching English as a Second Language Institute, 1964; University of New Mexico, Ph.D., 1970. *Politics:* Democrat. *Religion:* Roman Catholic.

*ADDRESSES: Home*—4829 Mesa Prieta Court, Albuquerque, NM 87120.

*CAREER:* Diplomat, educator, and author. Worked as a teacher in Albuquerque, NM, and Las Vegas, NM, 1955-65; University of New Mexico, Albuquerque, professor, 1960—, other positions held include department chair, associate dean, vice president, and assistant to the president, 1981-87; curriculum, teacher training, and school reform consultant for schools, colleges, and universities, 1960—. U. S. Ambassador to the Republic of Honduras, 1977-80; Department of State, Washington, D.C., deputy assistant secretary for inter-American affairs, 1980-81, member of Council of Ambassadors, 1983—, minority recruiter, 1990—. Educational Testing Service, Emeryville, CA, assistant vice president for field service, 1987-93; California Commission of Post-secondary Education, Sacramento, commissioner, 1990-93. Member of board of trustees for Tomas Rivera National Policy Center, Claremount Graduate School, 1985-93; member of board of directors, Children's Television Workshop, New York, NY, 1982—, National Institute against Prejudice and Violence, 1984-86, International House, University of California—Berkeley, 1989-93, and Latin American Scholarship Program for American Universities, Boston, MA, 1992—. National Latino Communications Center, Los Angeles, CA, scholar panelist, 1990—.

*MEMBER:* National Association of Latino Elected and Appointed Officials, Golden Key Honor Society (honorary member).

*AWARDS, HONORS:* Cubberly Award, Stanford University, 1975; Outstanding Chicana Award, McGraw-Hill Publishing Company, 1975; New Mexico Distinguished Service Award, 1977; Order of the Great Silver Cross, Order of Francisco Morazan (Honduras), 1980; honorary Honduran citizenship, 1980; "Distinguished Woman of the Year," Mortar Board Alumni Association, University of New Mexico, 1985; Anne Roe Award, Harvard Graduate School of Education, 1986; Distinguished Hispanic Lecturer at California State University—Fullerton, 1988; PRIMERA Award, Mexican American Women's National Association, 1990; Outstanding Leadership to Education in the Hispanic Community Award, 1991.

*WRITINGS:*

*Madame Ambassador, the Shoemaker's Daughter,* Bilingual Press (Tempe, AZ), 2001.

Contributor to books, including *Pluralism in a Democratic Society, Ghosts in the Barrio, Mexican-Americans and Educational Change,* and *Multicultural Education through Competency Based Teacher Education.* Contributor to periodicals, including *Journal of the National Education Association, TESOL Quarterly, Educational Leadership,* and the *New Mexico School Review.*

*SIDELIGHTS:* Mari-Luci Jaramillo told *CA:* "I began writing *Madame Ambassador, the Shoemaker's Daughter* because I wanted to reach young people who might be thinking about quitting their schooling. Although they may think that there are too many strikes against them, I wanted my experience to demonstrate that there are many ways to overcome adversity. I knew I had a strong message to share with those students. I wanted to motivate them to stay in school and value education.

"I write by hand on a lavender lap desk that a close friend gave to me many years ago. She knew I didn't like desks and that I loved the color purple. I sit in the living room, either on the sofa or on a big chair, surrounded by my many plants. As I write on scratch paper, I listen to the television. During my beginning efforts, I care nothing about format; I just jot down ideas as they come to my head. However, if I happen to see a plant with a dry leaf or a dead blossom, I'm off to that cleaning task for a while. Then I return and hit the story again. My plants are a great distraction to my writing efforts.

"I am a poor typist, and even though I've somewhat learned to use the word processor, I stay away from it as long as I can. I write and rewrite the story in longhand, sometimes even three drafts before I go to the computer. I have substantial calluses on two fingers on my right hand that show the intensity with which I work.

"Once the story is on the computer, I start adding or deleting as it suits me. The computer is of tremendous help, but I can't seem to compose my original thoughts on the PC. If I am passionate about the story, I stay with the task for hours. If it has not jelled yet, I keep finding excuses for not writing.

"My advice to people who have no writing experience is to go to a comfortable place and write whatever comes to their mind. We all have lots and lots of stories to tell. I think it best to write about what you know extremely well before attempting to create new characters or write about events you know little about. It just gets you into a relaxed mode and writing becomes easier.

"I have recently started keeping a journal with all the ideas that pop into my head, even if they are not fully developed. Those ideas might become kernels for future writing. Nevertheless, this is a brand-new activity for me, and I cannot vouch for it yet.

"This book is my first attempt at writing a non-academic piece. I am well into a second effort that I am finding much easier to do."

\*       \*       \*

**JEAN D'ARC**
**See WOOD, Joanna E.**

## JENKINS, Lee 1942-

*PERSONAL:* Born 1942; married; children: one son. *Education:* Fisk University (Nashville, TN), B.A.; Columbia University (New York, NY), Ph.D. (English and comparative literature).

*ADDRESSES: Home*—New York, NY. *Office*—John Jay College of Criminal Justice, 1235 North Hall, City University of New York, 899 Tenth Avenue, New York, NY 10019. *E-mail*—cosjenk@msn.com.

*CAREER:* Poet and psychoanalyst. John Jay College of Criminal Justice, City University of New York, New York, NY, professor of English.

*MEMBER:* Phi Beta Kappa.

*WRITINGS:*

*Faulkner and Black-White Relations: A Psychoanalytic Approach,* Columbia University Press (New York, NY), 1981.
*Persistence of Memory: Poems,* Aegina Press (Huntington, WV), 1996.

Also contributor to collections, including "Black-Jewish Relations: A Social and Mythic Alliance" in *Blacks and Jews on the Couch: Psychoanalytic Reflections on Black-Jewish Conflict,* edited by Alan Helmreich & Paul Marcus, Praeger (Westport, CT), 1988; and *African American Identity and Its Social Context to Race, Ethnicity, and Self,* edited by Elizabeth Pathy Salett and Diane R. Koslow, NMCI Publications (Washington, DC), 1994.

*SIDELIGHTS:* Lee Jenkins is both a professor of English and a psychoanalyst who has written extensively on Afro-American identity and the application of psychoanalysis to culture and literature. His 1981 work, *Faulkner and Black-White Relations: A Psychoanalytic Approach,* adds a challenging psychoanalytic addition to the body of Faulkner criticism. Jenkins's theories are also, according to a reviewer in *Choice,* "meant to shock those who believe that Faulkner's fiction is free of the racial confusion that his public statements often reveal. *Light in August, The Unvanquished, The Sound and the Fury, Absalom, Absalom!,*

*Go Down, Moses* and *Intruder in the Dust* are handled chiefly as records of progressive understanding, on Faulkner's part, of how to treat black characters as something other than reflections of the needs and failures of their white companions." In *Modern Fiction Studies,* Stephen M. Ross wrote, "Jenkins discusses the six novels in ways that show him to be a perceptive reader. He unearths the paradoxes in Faulkner's portrayal of blacks without over praising Faulkner's understanding of blacks or over condemning Faulkner for being a white Mississippian."

*BIOGRAPHICAL AND CRITICAL SOURCES:*

*PERIODICALS*

*Choice,* July, 1981, review of *Faulkner and Black-White Relations: A Psychoanalytic Approach,* p. 1546.
*Modern Fiction Studies,* April, 1981, Stephen M. Ross, review of *Faulkner and Black-White Relations: A Psychoanalytic Approach,* p. 729.
*Times Literary Supplement,* July 10, 1981, C. W. E. Bigsby, review of *Faulkner and Black-White Relations: A Psychoanalytic Approach,* p. 796.

*OTHER*

*John Jay College of Criminal Justice Web site,* http://www.jjay.cuny.edu/ (February 14, 2002), "Lee Jenkins."*

\*    \*    \*

## JENKINS, Victoria 1945-

*PERSONAL:* Born May 6, 1945, in Austin, TX; daughter of Allen B. (a psychoanalyst and writer) and Joyce Margaret (Mitchell) Wheelis. *Ethnicity:* "Caucasian."

*ADDRESSES: Home*—2525 Ninth Ave. W., Seattle, WA 98119. *Agent*—Marty Shapiro, Shapiro Lichtman, 8877 Beverly Blvd., Los Angeles, CA 90048.

*CAREER:* Writer.

*AWARDS, HONORS:* Screenwriting fellow, Sundance Film Institute, 1984, 1988.

*WRITINGS:*

*Stacking* (screenplay), Spectra Films, 1987.
*Relative Distances* (novel), Peregrine Smith, 1990.
*Cruise Control* (novel), Permanent Press (Sag Harbor, NY), 2002.

Author of screenplays and screen adaptations, including *West with the Night, Persian Nights,* and *1933 Was a Bad Year.* Contributor of articles, short stories, and reviews to periodicals, including *Chicago Tribune, Outside, Seattle Weekly,* and *Seattle's Child.*

*BIOGRAPHICAL AND CRITICAL SOURCES:*

PERIODICALS

*Publishers Weekly,* June 15, 1990, review of *Relative Distances,* p. 55; January 14, 2002, review of *Cruise Control,* p. 37.

\*      \*      \*

**JEROME, Fred 1939-**

*PERSONAL:* Born February 10, 1939, in New York, NY; son of Victor Jeremy and Alice Rose (Hamburger); married Jocelyn Beatrice Boyd, May 1, 1963; children: Rebecca, Mark, Daniel. *Education:* City College of New York, B.A. (magna cum laude), 1960.

*ADDRESSES: Home*—230 West 79th Street, New York, NY 10024-6210. *Office*—Scientists' Institution of Public Information, 355 Lexington Avenue, New York, NY 10017-6603. *E-mail*—jerome@theeinstein file.com.

*CAREER: Wilmington Star News,* Wilmington, NC, staff writer, 1961; *Augusta Herald,* Augusta, GA, staff writer, 1962; *Public Employee Press,* New York, NY, associate editor, 1963; *Newsweek,* New York, NY, editorial assistant, 1964-66; St. Luke's Hospital, New York, NY, public relations writer, 1975; Associated

Press, San Francisco, CA, staff writer, 1967-71; Scientists' Institution of Public Information, New York, NY, public information director, 1975-80, director of media resource service, 1980-92, vice president, 1988—; *SIPIscope,* editor, 1975—; Gene Media Forum, Newhouse School of Communications, Syracuse University, Syracuse, NY, senior consultant; Media Resource Center, founder. University of California, advisory committee on occupational safety and health project, member, 1974; State University of New York (SUNY)—Empire State College, lecturer, 1975, adjunct professor, 1994—; SUNY—Stony Brook, adjunct professor, 1976; CUNY, adjunct professor of writing, 1981; School of Visual Arts, professor of journalism, 1982; New York University, adjunct professor of journalism, 1983; Columbia Journalism School, adjunct professor of environmental reporting, 1991, 1994.

*MEMBER:* International Science Writers Association, National Association of Science Writers, National Association of Science Broadcasters, American Institute of Physics, Society of Profl. Journalists, New York Academy of Scientists, Institute of Medicine.

*AWARDS, HONORS:* Lewis Thomas Scientific Writing Award.

*WRITINGS:*

*The Einstein File: J. Edgar Hoover's Secret War against the World's Most Famous Scientist,* St. Martin's (New York, NY), 2002.

Contributor to *New York Times, Technology Review, Newsweek,* and *Channels.* Associate editor of *Environment.*

*SIDELIGHTS:* In *The Einstein File: J. Edgar Hoover's Secret War against the World's Most Famous Scientist,* Fred Jerome provides the story behind Edgar J. Hoover's investigation and surveillance of Albert Einstein. J. Edgar Hoover disliked Einstein because he supported civil rights, was friends with top African Americans, and because of his views on government. Hoover's file on Einstein included 2,000 pages, mostly comprised of falsehoods, accusations, and rumors. Hoover's goal was to prove Einstein was a Nazi or a spy and have him deported, which never happened. A *Kirkus Reviews* contributor called *The Einstein File* "A well-written, provocative account that could alter our views of both Hoover and Einstein."

*BIOGRAPHICAL AND CRITICAL SOURCES:*

PERIODICALS

*Kirkus Reviews,* March 1, 2002, review of *The Einstein File: J. Edgar Hoover's Secret War against the World's Most Famous Scientist,* p. 310.
*Library Journal,* April 1, 2002, Stephen L. Hupp, review of *The Einstein File,* p. 124.
*Publishers Weekly,* April 22, 2002, review of *The Einstein File,* p. 61.

OTHER

*Denver Post Web site,* http://www.denverpost.com/ (June 3, 2002), Steve Weinberg, "Another Hoover Enemy: Einstein."*

\*          \*          \*

**JEWELL, Lisa 1968-**

*PERSONAL:* Born July 19, 1968, in London, England; daughter of Anthony (a textile agent) and Kay (a secretary) Jewell; married. *Education:* Attended Barnet College and Epsom School of Art and Design.

*ADDRESSES: Home*—West Hampstead, England. *Agent*—c/o Publicity Director, Plume, Penguin Putnam, Inc., 375 Hudson St., New York, NY 10014-3658. *E-mail*—author@lisa-jewell.co.uk.

*CAREER:* Novelist. Worked in the fashion industry, London, England, for five years.

*WRITINGS:*

*Ralph's Party,* Plume (New York, NY), 2000.
*Thirtynothing,* Plume (New York, NY), 2001.
*One-Hit Wonder,* Dutton (New York, NY), 2002.

*SIDELIGHTS:* After attending college to pursue a career in art, design, and fashion, British writer Lisa Jewell became disillusioned with the "cut-throat" world of fashion and eventually began taking evening classes in creative writing at her local adult education college in London. It was here that she discovered her "true passion."

Although Barbara Sutton, writing in the *New York Times Book Review,* referred to Jewell's debut novel, *Ralph's Party* as a "sitcom novel," it gained international success as a best seller. A contributor to *Kirkus Reviews* described *Ralph's Party* as "a shameless flirt of a first novel that traces the roller-coaster lives of six people sharing the same London brownstone." The reviewer commented that "the author casts a perceptive eye on the difficulty of relationships." A reviewer in *Publishers Weekly* called the book a "light delight" that comes to "an amusing denouement."

Jewell followed *Ralph's Party* with *Thirtynothing,* "another hip and happening comic love story," wrote a contributor to *Kirkus Reviews,* complete with "endearing characters and fine comic timing." Two friends, Digby and Nadine, are thirty-year-old Londoners whose relationships with others have all been casual. When an old love comes back into Digby's life, Nadine begins to realize that her friend is the man she has loved all along. Jennifer Wulff, reviewing the novel in *People,* described *Thirtynothing* as a "witty British import" that tells the story of Digby and Nadine in a way that "is not in the least predictable" and includes "dozens of laugh-out-loud moments." A reviewer in *Publishers Weekly* stated that the book's best attribute might be "Jewell's keen observation of British pop culture." Whitney Scott, writing in *Booklist,* wrote that "Jewell's latest saucy and slangy love story should entertain audiences beyond the U.K."

In 2002 Jewell followed up *Thirtynothing,* with *One-Hit Wonder,* which a *Library Journal* contributor called "an engaging coming-of-age tale skillfully told by interweaving the past and present." *Booklist* contributor Kathleen Hughes labeled it "part mystery, part Brit-pop fiction," noting Jewell's "masterful way of unraveling a story bit by bit to pique the reader's interest."

*BIOGRAPHICAL AND CRITICAL SOURCES:*

PERIODICALS

*Booklist,* December 1, 2000, Whitney Scott, review of *Thirtynothing,* p. 694; May 1, 2002, Kathleen Hughes, review of *One-Hit Wonder,* p. 1507.

*Kirkus Reviews,* November 1, 1999, review of *Ralph's Party,* p. 1667; November 1, 2000, review of *Thirtynothing,* p. 1507.

*Library Journal,* May 1, 2002, May Brozio-Andrews, review of *One-Hit Wonder,* p. 133.

*New York Times Book Review,* January 9, 2000, Barbara Sutton, review of *Ralph's Party,* p. 20.

*People,* February 12, 2001, Jennifer Wulff, review of *Thirtynothing,* p. 41.

*Publishers Weekly,* October 18, 1999, review of *Ralph's Party,* p. 68; November 6, 2000, review of *Thirtynothing,* p. 69; May 27, 2002, review of *One-Hit Wonder,* p. 38.


OTHER


*All about Romance,* http://www.likesbooks.com/ (September 15, 2001), Maria K., review of *Thirtynothing.*

*Lisa Jewell Web site,* http://www.lisa-jewell.co.uk (September 15, 2001).*

*          *          *

## JOHNSON, Elmer W. 1932-

*PERSONAL:* Born May 2, 1932, in Denver, CO; married Connie D. Mahon, 1955; children: three. *Education:* Yale University, B.A., 1954; University of Chicago Law School, J.D., 1957. *Hobbies and other interests:* Golf, skiing, philosophy.

*ADDRESSES: Office*—c/o Jenner & Block, One IBM Plaza, Chicago, IL 60611.

*CAREER:* Kirkland and Ellis (law firm), Chicago, IL, attorney, 1956-99, partner, 1962-99; General Motors Corporation, legal and operating offices, 1983-87, executive vice president and director, 1987-88; Aspen Institute, president and CEO, 1999-2002; Jenner & Block, partner, 2002—. Legal Advisory Committee of the New York Stock Exchange; Detroit Symphony Orchestra, vice-chairman,; United Way of Detroit, general campaign chairman; University of Chicago, trustee; University of Chicago Hospitals and Clinics Board, chairman; Lyric Opera Association of Chicago, trustee; Children's Memorial Hospital of Chicago,

trustee; Chicago Council on Foreign Relations, director; Fourth Presbyterian Church of Chicago, trustee; Metropolitan Planning Council (vice-chairman and governor).

*MEMBER:* American Academy of Arts and Sciences (fellow), Economic Club of Chicago (director), Commercial Club of Chicago (member of executive and civic committees).

*AWARDS, HONORS: Crain's Chicago Business* Executive of the Year, 1999 (with Commercial Club of Chicago).

*WRITINGS:*

*The U.S. Business Corporation: An Institution in Transition,* Ballinger Publishing Company (Cambridge, MA), 1988.

*Avoiding the Collision of Cities and Cars: Urban Transportation Policy for the Twenty-first Century,* American Academy of Arts and Sciences (Cambridge, MA), 1993.

*Chicago Metropolis 2020: The Chicago Plan for the Twenty-first Century,* University of Chicago Press (Chicago, IL), 2001.

*SIDELIGHTS:* Attorney Elmer W. Johnson seemed to have reached the pinnacle of his career in 1987, when he was named one of the three executive vice presidents of General Motors. That position itself was highly prestigious, and an unusual accomplishment for an attorney with limited connections to the automotive industry, but Johnson's promotion from the corporation's lead counsel to one of four potential successors to then-chairman Roger B. Smith made the achievement even more notable. He stayed in that position for only one year, frustrated by GM's bureaucracy. By the time he published his second book, a 1993 study of urban transportation policy, Johnson was also frustrated with the excesses of automotive culture. In his ambitious plan for the future of Chicago, he calls for large taxes on the use of automobiles—one of several recommendations for innovative urban planning outlined in his 2001 book *Chicago Metropolis 2020: The Chicago Plan for the Twenty-first Century.*

The common thread of Johnson's career has been an overriding concern with ethics. While a partner at the Chicago law firm of Kirkland and Ellis, Johnson worked with companies including Amoco, Westinghouse, International Harvester, Firestone Tire & Rubber, and Baxter-Travenol as legal counsel, assisting in investigations of illegal payments and bribery and creating programs for cleaning up their financial and management practices. He also supported research in Judeo-Christian ethics and wrote articles on the issues of corporate responsibility. In signing on with General Motors, Johnson hoped to work on preventing legal problems rather than settling them through the courts. As quoted in the *New York Times,* Johnson said, "I think there's a great opportunity at G.M. to think deeply about ethical issues and come up with some guidelines on them." Among his chief accomplishments at General Motors were his work in labor relations, overseeing talks between the corporation and the auto workers' union, and compelling H. Ross Perot, who would later become a presidential candidate for his own Reform Party, to sell his shares of GM stock. Perot, the largest individual holder of GM stock at the time, had been "flouting corporate governance standards," Johnson said in the *New York Times;* an observer said of Johnson, "Elmer helped crystallize the problem for the board . . . and then he went out and did what had to be done. That's what Elmer does, he helps solve problems."

With the 2001 publication of *Chicago Metropolis 2020,* Johnson presents his broadest effort at problem solving, addressing social and ethical issues on a significantly larger scale. The work, sponsored by the Commercial Club of Chicago, is in some ways a follow-up to architect Daniel Burnham's equally ambitious 1909 plan for Chicago that the Commercial Club had sponsored nearly a century earlier. Burnham had a vision for making Chicago, a Midwestern boomtown at a crucial turning point in its growth, a global center of business and culture on par with London, New York, or Paris. Though not much of the plan was ever realized, Burnham's vision was the impetus for the Chicago lakefront, Michigan Avenue, and several other features of the metro area's infrastructure. Johnson picks up where Burnham left off, seeking solutions to suburban sprawl and substandard education that could make the Chicago area "one of the ten or fifteen great metropolitan centers of the world economic order that is emerging." *Chicago Metropolis 2020* calls for a mix of public and private effort, cooperation between business and civic leaders, and an awareness of the "strong moral component" in urban planning a reflection of Johnson's concern with bringing opposing parties together and practicing tough-minded but ethical capitalism.

Critics responded to *Chicago Metropolis 2020* with both praise and skepticism. Writing for the journal *Planning,* Harold Henderson called *Chicago Metropolis 2020* "handsomely produced," and remarked that Johnson's vision is "distinguished by a willingness to correct . . . problems using incentives rather than command-and-control." The challenge of such an approach, however, lies in the effectiveness of the incentives, as Witold Rybczynski wrote in the *Times Literary Supplement.* Commenting on Johnson's plan for suburban development in concentrated nodes to better suit the parallel development of mass transit, Rybczynski said, "This is a good idea, although it is unclear exactly how the necessary exclusionary zoning and restrictions . . . would be put into effect." Similarly, Paul Glassman in *Library Journal* found Johnson's book full of "laudable goals," but concluded that "this work labors under the same delusional spirit of boosterism as Burnham's plan, namely, that architecture and design can transform society."

Nonetheless in Chicago Johnson's report has attracted a following, including the establishment of the Chicago Metropolis 2020 organization, a group that has raises funds for the implementation of Johnson's proposals and encourages companies to commit to socially responsible development, including locating any new facilities in towns whose zoning codes match with the *Chicago Metropolis 2020* recommendations. Johnson may also be on the right side of a growing trend. In *Crain's Chicago Business,* Anthony Downs of the Brookings Institution, a political think tank, said that Johnson's work is "somewhat ahead of the curve on suburban-sprawl issues that have begun to pick up momentum nationally."

*BIOGRAPHICAL AND CRITICAL SOURCES:*

*PERIODICALS*

*Crain's Chicago Business,* June 7, 1999, Greg Hinz, "Reinventing the Metropolis: Bold, Regional Vision Lands Commercial Club Executive of the Year Award," p. 1.
*Library Journal,* October 15, 2001, Paul Glassman, review of *Chicago Metropolis 2020,* p. 72.
*New York Times Biographical Service,* December, 1985, Steven Greenhouse, "G.M.'s Chief Counsel: Elmer W. Johnson, Limiting the Auto Giant's Liability," pp. 1521-1523; October, 1987, John Ho-

lusha, "Corporate Facilitator: Elmer W. Johnson, Why G. M.'s Rising Star Wants to Shine in the Labor Talks," pp. 1005-1007.

*Planning,* December, 2001, Harold Henderson, "The City: Half Full or Half Empty?" pp. 38-40.

*Times Literary Supplement,* November 2, 2001, Witold Rybczynski, "Hopes and Dreams," pp. 13-15.

OTHER

*Aspen Institute Web site,* http://aspeninstitute.org/ (February, 2002), biography of Elmer W. Johnson.

*New York University Center for Law and Business,* http://www.stern.nyu.edu/clb/ (May, 1998), biography of Elmer W. Johnson.

*University of Chicago Press,* http://www.press. uchicago.edu/ (April 10, 2002), description of *Chicago Metropolis 2020.**

*        *        *

## JOHNSON, Kevin R. 1958-

*PERSONAL:* Born June 29, 1958, in Culver City, CA; married Virginia Salazar, October 17, 1987; children: Teresa, Tomás, Elena. *Ethnicity:* "Mexican-American." *Education:* University of California—Berkeley, A.B., 1980; Harvard University, J.D., 1983. *Politics:* Democrat. *Religion:* Roman Catholic. *Hobbies and other interests:* Running.

*ADDRESSES: Office*—School of Law, University of California—Davis, Davis, CA 95616; fax: 530-752-7279. *E-mail*—krjohnson@ucdavis.edu.

*CAREER:* Educator, corporate lawyer, and author. Law clerk to Stephen Reinhardt, Los Angeles, CA, 1983-84; Heller Ehrman, White & McAuliffe (law firm), San Francisco, CA, attorney, 1984-89; University of California—Davis, professor of law, 1989—. Legal Services of Northern California, vice president, 2000—.

*WRITINGS:*

*How Did You Get to Be Mexican? A White/Brown Man's Search for Identity,* Temple University Press (Philadelphia, PA), 1998.

*A Reader on Race, Civil Rights, and the Law,* Carolina Academic Press, 2001.

*Mixed Race America,* New York University Press (New York, NY), 2002.

## JOHNSON-ACSADI, Gwendolyn
## (Gwendolyn Acsadi; Gwynne Forster, a pseudonym)

*PERSONAL:* Born in Burgaw, NC; daughter of King D. (an entrepreneur) and Vivian (a school principal; maiden name, Williams) Johnson; married G. T. Acsadi (a demographer), December 22, 1970; children: Peter (stepson). *Ethnicity:* "African American." *Education:* Howard University, A.B., M.A. (sociology), 1960; American University, M.A. (economics and demography), 1961; attended Columbia University, 1962. *Religion:* Protestant. *Hobbies and other interests:* Gardening, gourmet cooking, singing, listening to music, reading.

*ADDRESSES: Home*—New York, NY. *Agent*—James B. Finn, James B. Finn Literary Agency, Inc., P.O. Box 28227A, St. Louis, MO 63132. *E-mail*—Gwynne F@aol.com.

*CAREER:* United Nations, New York, NY, chief of fertility and family planning research for Population Division, Department of Economic and Social Affairs, 1962-84; novelist. Community Library of Roosevelt Island, New York, NY, vice president.

*MEMBER:* Romance Writers of America, Authors Guild, Altrusa International.

*AWARDS, HONORS:* Awards for best multicultural romance of the year, *Affaire de Coeur,* 1997, for *Ecstasy,* 1998, for *Naked Soul,* 1999, for *Fools Rush In,* and 2000, for *Swept Away;* named author of the year, *Romance in Color* (Internet Web site), 1999, for *Against the Wind;* Gold Pen Award, Black Writers Reunion and Conference, 2001, for *Beyond Desire.*

*WRITINGS:*

FICTION; UNDER PSEUDONYM GWYNNE FORSTER

*Sealed with a Kiss* (romance novel), Kensington (New York, NY), 1995.

*Against All Odds* (romance novel), Kensington (New York, NY), 1996.

*Ecstasy* (romance novel), Kensington (New York, NY), 1997.

*Obsession* (romance novel), Kensington (New York, NY), 1998.

*Beyond Desire* (romance novel), Kensington (New York, NY), 1999.

*Naked Soul* (romance novel), Genesis Press (Columbus, MI), 1999.

*Fools Rush In* (romance novel), BET Books (Washington, DC), 1999.

*Against the Wind* (romance novel), Genesis Press (Columbus, MI), 1999.

*Swept Away* (romance novel), BET Books (Washington, DC), 2000.

*Secret Desire* (romance novel), BET Books (Washington, DC), 2000.

*Midnight Magic* (romance novel), Genesis Press (Columbus, MI), 2000.

*Scarlet Woman* (romance novel), BET Books (Washington, DC), 2001.

*When Twilight Comes* (novel), Dafina Books (New York, NY), 2002.

*Blues from down Deep* (novel), Dafina Books (New York, NY), 2003.

*If I Ever Love You* (romance novel), BET Books, in press.

Work represented in anthologies, including *I Do,* Kensington, 1997; *Silver Bells,* Kensington, 1997, and *Wedding Bells,* BET Books, 1999.

OTHER

Author of nearly thirty works on demography, under name Gwendolyn Acsadi or Gwendolyn Johnson-Acsadi. Contributor to periodicals.

*WORK IN PROGRESS:* Research for a third mainstream novel, publication expected in 2004.

*SIDELIGHTS:* Gwendolyn Johnson-Acsadi, who pens fiction under the pseudonym Gwynne Forster, told *CA:* "I write because it is all I have ever done, first as a research demographer and now also as a fiction writer. I love using the English language, creating people and bringing them to life. I write because I love to read and because these stories pop up in my head. I have been reading since I was four years old. The written word is my love.

"I begin with an idea, let it simmer for a couple of weeks until I feel I have to write about it. I do whatever research is needed. I develop the major characters by interviewing them for what may be thirty or more handwritten pages of answers. I figure out what the story is about and what I wish to tell my reader; that is, the theme and premise. I don't plot. The characters tell the story. I know the beginning and the end when I start. I may write out seventy to eighty scenes, or I may not. It isn't a matter of inspiration, but of what I perceive, hear, imagine, see. The picture of a waterfall, a lighthouse, a mountain scene can set my imagination on a junket.

"There have been changes in my writing. It is less gentle, I would say, and more down to earth. I love happy endings, but life isn't always like that. I want my writing to be relevant, to allow the reader to find in it something that jerks her out of lethargy or complacency. And I want my readers to recognize themselves. Most of all, I want to write about life without being circumscribed by formula."

*BIOGRAPHICAL AND CRITICAL SOURCES:*

PERIODICALS

*Black Issues Book Review,* May-June, 2002, Ursula Hill, review of *When Twilight Comes,* p. 43.

*Publishers Weekly,* March 27, 2000, review of *Swept Away,* p. 58; May 21, 2001, review of *Scarlet Woman,* p. 87; January 7, 2002, review of *When Twilight Comes,* p. 48.

\* \* \*

## JOHNSTON, Victor S.

*PERSONAL:* Male. *Education:* Queens University (Belfast, Northern Ireland), B.Sc., 1964; University of Edinburgh, Ph.D., 1967.

*ADDRESSES: Office*—Psychology Department, New Mexico State University, Las Cruces, NM 88003. *E-mail*—vic@crl.nmsu.edu.

*CAREER:* Yale University of Medicine, codirector of Yale in Holloman Research Facility, 1967-69; New Mexico State University, Las Cruces, assistant professor, 1969-80, associate professor, 1980-87, professor of psychology, 1988—.

*AWARDS, HONORS:* Stanford University, postdoctoral fellow, 1970-71.

*WRITINGS:*

*Why We Feel: The Science of Human Emotions,* Perseus Books (Reading, MA), 1999.

*SIDELIGHTS:* As a professor of psychology, Victor S. Johnston deals with the complexities of human emotions. But why do emotions exist in the first place? In *Why We Feel: The Science of Human Emotions* he sets forth to answer to that question by showing the value of human emotions in helping us to adapt and pass on our genes. "But unlike other evolutionary explanations of behavior that may degenerate into 'just so' stories, Johnston's perspective provides exceptional insight into why feelings are adaptive," wrote W. F. Sternberg in *Choice.* Using computer models and simulations, he shows that computers can actually develop preferences. By analogy, he demonstrates how such things as taste and color have developed to draw humans toward what is good for us and away from what is bad. A reviewer for *Publishers Weekly* wrote, "Johnston does an impressive job of explaining how millions of years of evolution are capable of yielding complex behaviors." In addition to tastes and preferences, in Johnston's view, emotions like fear and sadness, joy and anger emerge from the brain as ways of dealing with complex and unstable environments. *Booklist* contributor Gilbert Taylor wrote, "Ably argued, his work is a provocative exploration of the emotional component of the mystery of consciousness."

*BIOGRAPHICAL AND CRITICAL SOURCES:*

PERIODICALS

*Booklist,* April 1, 1999, Gilbert Taylor, review of *Why We Feel: The Science of Human Emotions,* p. 1373.
*Choice,* November, 1999, W. F. Sternberg, review of *Why We Feel,* p. 624.
*Publishers Weekly,* April 12, 1999, review of *Why We Feel,* p. 65.

OTHER

*New Mexico State University Department of Psychology Web site,* http://www-psych.nmsu.edu/ (February 24, 2000), faculty profile of Victor S. Johnston.*

## JOLLY, Margaretta 1965-

*PERSONAL:* Born February 21, 1965. *Education:* University of Cambridge, B.A. (honors), 1987; University of York, M.A., 1989; University of Sussex, Ph.D., 1996.

*ADDRESSES: Office*—School of English, University of Exeter, Northcote House, Queen's Dr., Exeter EX4 4QJ, England. *E-mail*—m.jolly@ex.ac.uk.

*CAREER:* University of Sussex, Sussex, England, lecturer in English, 1999-2000; University of Exeter, Exeter, England, lecturer in twentieth-century literature and culture, 2000—; writer.

*MEMBER:* International Auto/Biography Association, Association Interdisciplinaire de Recherche sur l'Epistolaire.

*AWARDS, HONORS:* Associate Award, University of Exeter, 2000-01; award for outstanding reference series, American Library Association, for *Encyclopedia of Life Writing: Autobiographical and Biographical Forms.*

*WRITINGS:*

(Editor) *Dear Laughing Motorbyke: Letters from Women Welders of the Second World War,* Scarlet Press (London, England), 1997.
(Editor) *Encyclopedia of Life Writing: Autobiographical and Biographical Forms,* Fitzroy Dearborn (London, England), 2001.

Work represented in anthologies, including *The Uses of Autobiography,* edited by Julia Swindells, Taylor & Francis, 1995; *War and Memory,* edited by Martin Evans, Berg, 1997; and *Women's Lives, Women's Times,* edited by Linda Anderson and Treva Broughton, New York University Press (New York, NY), 1997. Contributor to books, including *Telling Lives: Interviews on Southern African Auto/biography,* edited by Stephan Meyer, Judith Lutge Coullie, and Thengani Ngwenya; *Arms and the Self,* edited by Alex Vernon, Kent State University Press (Kent, OH); *Gender, the Letter and Politics, 1750-2000: From the Local to the Global,* edited by Marie Cross, Ashgate. Contributor to periodicals, including *Auto/Biography, Literacy Review, New Formations, Sexualities, Women's History Review,* and *Women: A Cultural Review.*

*WORK IN PROGRESS:* Editor, with others, *The Pat Barker Reader;* a book on feminism as reflected in correspondence since the 1970s.

*SIDELIGHTS:* Margaretta Jolly is a University of Exeter lecturer who is known for her work on autobiographical and biographical writing. She served as editor of *Encyclopedia of Life Writing: Autobiographical and Biographical Forms,* a 2001 publication that includes more than six hundred entries. "The aim," declared a *Booklist* reviewer, "is to provide an overview of central genres or themes and shed light on the significance of important individual writers and works in the field of life writing, all across an international and historical perspective." Mary Beard, writing in the *Times Literary Supplement,* described *Encyclopedia of Life Writing* as "a vast compendium . . . from the classical world to the present day." She noted that the volume is "committed to female traditions in life writing," and she affirmed that it is intended "to give due weight to pre-modern and non-Western cultural traditions." Another reviewer, in a *Choice* assessment, acknowledged Jolly's book as "well constructed" and added that "time will decide whether this work makes a lasting or meaningful contribution to scholarship."

Among Jolly's other books is *Dear Laughing Motorbyke: Letters from Women Welders of the Second World War,* a 1997 publication that includes correspondence stored at the Mass-Observation Archive. In addition, she has supplied essays to various books and periodicals, and she has seen her work included in anthologies such as *The Uses of Autobiography* and *War and Memory.*

*BIOGRAPHICAL AND CRITICAL SOURCES:*

PERIODICALS

*Booklist,* February 1, 2001, review of *Encyclopedia of Life Writing: Autobiographical and Biographical Forms.*
*Choice,* March, 2002, C. V. Stanley, review of *Encyclopedia of Life Writing: Autobiographical and Biographical Forms,* p. 1208.

*Times Literary Supplement,* February 15, 2002, Mary Beard, review of *Encyclopedia of Life Writing: Autobiographical and Biographical Forms,* p. 10.*

\*      \*      \*

## JONES, Quincy (Delight) 1933-

*PERSONAL:* Born March 14, 1933, in Chicago, IL; son of Quincy Delight (a carpenter and baseball player) and Sarah Jones; married Jeri Caldwell (divorced); married Ulla Anderson (divorced, 1974); married Peggy Lipton, 1974 (divorced, 1986); children: Jolie, Martina-Lisa, Quincy III, Kidada, Rashida, Rachelle, Kenya (with Nastassja Kinski). *Education:* Seattle University; Berklee School of Music; Boston Conservatory.

*ADDRESSES: Office*—Quincy Jones Music Publishing, 3800 Barham Blvd., #503, Los Angeles, CA 90068. *E-mail*—info@quincyjonesmusic.com.

*CAREER:* Producer, arranger, composer, and musician. Lionel Hampton Orchestra, trumpeter and arranger, 1950-53; Dizzy Gillespie Orchestra, organizer and trumpeter, 1956; Barchlay Disques, Paris, France, music director; Mercury Records, music director, 1961, vice president, 1964; Qwest Records, founder, 1981; QDE, co-founder and co-CEO, 1993—; QD7, founder, 1996; Qwest Broadcasting, co-founder and co-CEO, 1996—; *Vibe* magazine, founder. Has written scores for numerous movies.

*AWARDS, HONORS:* German Jazz Federation Award; Edison International Award (Sweden); *Down Beat* Critics Poll award; *Down Beat* Readers Poll award; Image Award, National Association for the Advancement of Colored People, 1974, 1980, 1981, 1984, 1990, 1991; Hollywood Walk of Fame Star, 1980; Golden Note Award, 1982; City of Hope, Man of the Year Award, 1982; *Billboard* Trendsetters Award, 1983; producer of the year, *Rolling Stone* reader's poll, 1983; Whitney Young, Jr. Award, Urban League, 1986; Martell Foundation Humanitarian Award, 1986; National Academy of Songwriters, Lifetime Achievement Award, 1989; Trustee Award, National Academy of Recording Arts and Sciences, for nonperforming contributions, 1989; French Legion of Honor, 1990; named *U.S.A. Today* and *Financial News Network*

Entrepreneur of the Year, 1991; Scopus Award, Hebrew University, 1991; People for the American Way, Sons of Liberty Award, 1992; Jean Hersholt Humanitarian Award, National Academy of Motion Picture Arts and Sciences, 1995; multiple Grammy awards, including best instrumental arrangement, 1963, for "I Can't Stop Loving You," best instrumental arrangement, 1978, for *The Wiz,* best arrangement on an instrumental recording and best instrumental arrangement accompanying vocal(s), 1981, for songs from *The Dude,* producer of the year, 1981, 1983, 1990, record of the year, 1983, for "Beat It," album of the year, 1983, for *Thriller,* record of the year, 1985, for "We are the World," best music video, 1985, for *We Are the World—The Video Event,* album of the year and best rap performance, 1990, for *Back on the Block,* and best jazz instrumental, 1994, for *Miles and Quincy: Live at Montreux.*

*WRITINGS:*

*Listen Up: The Lives of Quincy Jones,* Warner Books (New York, NY), 1990.

*Q: The Autobiography of Quincy Jones,* Doubleday Publishers (New York, NY), 2001.

*SIDELIGHTS:* Producer Quincy Jones has written two autobiographies documenting the events of his life, perhaps because just one book could not hold all the significant details. Born the grandson of a slave, Jones befriended some of the biggest names in jazz before going on to produce some of the biggest pop recordings of all time, after which he turned to film, television, and print media. In 1985 he produced *The Color Purple,* a nominee for eleven academy awards and the birthplace of the acting careers of Whoopi Goldberg and Oprah Winfrey. By 1990 he was the Bel-Air neighbor of former president Ronald Reagan, and in 1991 he was named Entrepreneur of the Year by *U.S.A. Today.* In February 2002 he won another Grammy award, putting him near thirty over the course of his career, for best spoken world album for *Q: The Autobiography of Quincy Jones.*

Jones was born in the black ghetto of Chicago. His father was a carpenter who played semi-professional baseball, and his mother, who still spoke the African dialect of her father, had a severe emotional disorder not then understood by medical professionals. Jones's grandfather taught him how to catch and cook rats. By

the time Jones was ten, his mother had been institutionalized and his father remarried and took the family to Bremerton, Washington, on the outskirts of Seattle. By age thirteen, Jones was playing the trumpet in Seattle clubs, where he met Ray Charles, then only sixteen, and jazz greats including Count Basie, Charlie Parker, Duke Ellington, and Dizzy Gillespie. Basie in particular took an interest in Jones. Speaking to Steve Dougherty in *People,* Jones recalled, "Basie was like my daddy. I don't know why he took me in like he did. I guess he liked me because I was thirsty to learn." Years later, his friendship with Basie would earn Jones his first Grammy award, for the 1963 instrumental arrangement of "I Can't Stop Loving You," which Basie recorded.

After a brief stint at the prestigious Berklee School of Music, to which he had won a scholarship, Jones began his music career in earnest, touring with his jazz idols as both musician and conductor. Despite his musical successes, by 1959 he was deep in debt and in need of steady work, which he found at Mercury Records as the first black vice president. The job lasted six years, until Jones moved to scoring Hollywood films—early film scores include those for *The Pawnbroker* (1965), *In Cold Blood* (1967), *In The Heat of the Night* (1967), *Bob and Carol and Ted and Alice* (1969), and *The Out-of-Towners* (1970)—in addition to arranging and producing. An early high point of his career came when Frank Sinatra called to ask him to conduct his collaboration with Count Basie, *Sinatra at the Sands* (1966). Discussing the project in an interview for *Down Beat,* Jones said working on that project was "as good as it gets."

Nonetheless, the stress of constant work on arrangements, recordings, film scores, and television music lead to a near-fatal aneurysm in 1974. The event was a watershed for Jones: he married for the third time, determined to pull his life together, and he stopped playing the trumpet, which could damage the clips that repaired his brain. Jones continued his film work, earning his third Grammy award in 1978 for his work on the film version of the musical *The Wiz,* an all-black version of *The Wizard of Oz* starring Diana Ross and Michael Jackson. Jones continued working with Jackson, producing songs for his album *Off the Wall* (1979), and then the groundbreaking best-seller *Thriller* (1982), which became the highest-selling record in history and earned Jones three more Grammys. *Thriller* was one of two works that defined

Jones's producing career; the second was the song "We Are the World" (1984), a collaboration of forty-six of America's best-known recording artists that eventually raised $60 million for famine relief in Africa and another Grammy award for Jones. He also kept up his jazz ties, producing for Lena Horne and Frank Sinatra. During the early eighties Jones was also working on *The Color Purple* with Steven Spielberg, which earned Academy Award nominations for best picture, best original music score, and best song, among others. Still, his personal life remained rocky: in 1986 he divorced Peggy Lipton and suffered a nervous breakdown, spending a month on Marlon Brando's private island to recover.

By 1990, Jones was ready for a substantial comeback. He published his first book, *Listen Up: The Lives of Quincy Jones,* which later became a critically acclaimed documentary. His 1989 album *Back on the Block* won the 1990 Grammy awards for best rap performance and album of the year. He also helped create the NBC sitcom *The Fresh Prince of Bel-Air* for NBC; Jones acted as executive producer, and Will Smith starred as the Fresh Prince, effectively launching his acting career under Jones's auspices. The next year, in 1991, Jones collaborated with Miles Davis for a Gil Evans tribute concert at the famous Montreux jazz festival, only two months before Davis's death. Reflecting on the opportunity with *Down Beat,* Jones said, "Claude Nobs, the founder of Montreux, had been after me to be his primary co-producer for three years, but I never had the time, until that year when we had Miles. I had no idea that Miles was ill." The resulting album from the concert, *Miles and Quincy: Live at Montreux* (1993), won a Grammy for best jazz instrumental. In 1993 Jones merged his company, Qwest Records, which he had founded in 1981, with David Salzman Entertainment, creating QDE. In concert with Time-Warner, Inc., QDE continued the production of *The Fresh Prince of Bel-Air* and other shows for NBC and Fox, developed film projects, and launched the magazine *Vibe,* focusing on urban popular culture. On the 1995 album *Q's Jook Joint,* Jones collaborated with some of the biggest names in music again: U2's Bono, Ray Charles, Coolio, Gloria Estefan, Herbie Hancock, Brian McKnight, Barry White, Nancy Wilson, Stevie Wonder, and dozens more. In 1996 and 1997, Jones started two additional media ventures, QD7 (with David Salzman and 7th Level) and Qwest Broadcasting, one of the largest minority-owned broadcasting companies in America.

For his 2001 autobiography *Q: The Autobiography of Quincy Jones,* Jones covers this territory in addition to his private life and his relationships with family. Reviewing the book for *Variety,* Jon Burlingame wrote, "It's clear that creating this book was a soul-searching, often painful process for the man." In telling his life story, Jones is honest in detailing his numerous affairs, his failures as a father during his children's early years, his problems with prescription tranquilizers, and his breakdown. Jones also practices the collaborative method of his music in presenting an honest picture of his life, including chapters written by friends and family: his brother Lloyd discusses Jones's decision to break with his family when moving from Seattle, Ray Charles tells stories of their early years performing together, his third wife Lipton recalls the failure of their relationship, and two of his children relate the difficulties of establishing a relationship with a busy, famous—and at times irresponsible—father. For many critics, Jones's personal life made an even more interesting read than the details of his relationships with Michael Jackson, Frank Sinatra, Oprah Winfrey, and other big names. Writing for *Library Journal,* Beth Farrell commented, "by far the most compelling part of this autobiography explores his relationships with his family." A reviewer for *Publishers Weekly* concluded, "With the help of his friends, Jones has composed a life story that gives much more than the typical celebrity memoir." Glenn Townes, in *Black Issues Book Review,* found Jones's autobiography "a solidly written book that offers an extremely personal look at one of America's most revered musical gurus."

Musically, Jones has said he is interested in working on new forms and trends, particularly rap and hip-hop. In his 1990 interview for *People,* Jones said, "I'm hearing music in my head all the time. . . . I got millions of pieces of paper, napkins, matchbooks, where I've scratched down ideas, scraps of songs. I hope it never stops. When I get to be eighty, I want to write street ballets, street operas."

*BIOGRAPHICAL AND CRITICAL SOURCES:*

*PERIODICALS*

*Black Issues Book Review,* November-December, 2001, Glenn Townes, review of *Q: The Autobiography of Quincy Jones,* p. 70.

*Booklist,* August, 2001, Mike Tribby, review of *Q: The Autobiography of Quincy Jones,* p. 2046.

*Down Beat,* November, 2001, Eliot Tiegel, "The Touch: Quincy Jones Discusses the Jazz Roots of his Charmed Musical Life," p. 24.

*Ebony,* January, 2002, Charles Whitaker, "Q on Camera: Music Man Celebrates Years in Show Business with Tell-All Book," p. 58.

*Entertainment Weekly,* September 26, 1997, Lisa Schwarzbaum, "The Color of Money," p. 71.

*Library Journal,* September 15, 2001, Lloyd Jansen, *Q: The Autobiography of Quincy Jones,* p. 82; March 1, 2002, Beth Farrell, review of *Q: The Autobiography of Quincy Jones,* p. 162.

*People,* October 15, 1990, Steve Dougherty, "Quincy Jones," p. 103.

*Publishers Weekly,* July 23, 2001, *Q: The Autobiography of Quincy Jones,* p. 57.

*Variety,* November 26, 2001, Jon Burlingame, *Q: The Autobiography of Quincy Jones,* p. 33.

OTHER

*January Magazine,* http://www.januarymagazine.com/ (April 10, 2002), Tony Buchsbaum, "The Ride of His Life."

*Q's Page,* http://www.duke.edu/ (April 10, 2002), biography of Quincy Jones.*

\*     \*     \*

## JONES, Susanna 1967-

*PERSONAL:* Born 1967, in Yorkshire, England. *Education:* Received degree in drama, London University; Manchester University, M.A.

*ADDRESSES: Home*—Brighton, England. *Agent*—c/o Author Mail, Warner Books, Inc., 1271 Avenue of the Americas, New York, NY 10020.

*CAREER:* Author and English instructor. Radio script editor, technical editor, and English instructor in Japan.

*AWARDS, HONORS:* James Creasey Memorial Dagger, Crime Writers' Association, 2001, for *The Earthquake Bird.*

*WRITINGS:*

*The Earthquake Bird,* Mysterious Press/Warner Books (New York, NY), 2001.
*Water Lily,* Mysterious Press/Warner Books (New York, NY), 2003.

*SIDELIGHTS:* Susanna Jones's first novel, *The Earthquake Bird,* has been compared favorably to the works of critically acclaimed British crime writers Minette Walters and Josephine Hart for its assured craftsmanship and dark, psychological suspense.

The novel's central character is Lucy Fly, a young British woman living and working in Tokyo as a technical translator. As the novel begins, Lucy's friend, Lily, has been found dismembered and floating in Tokyo Bay. Police investigating the murder pull Lucy from her office for questioning. The psychological drama unfolds as Lucy, although she insists she is innocent of any wrongdoing, evades the investigators' questions and digresses to memories of her native Yorkshire, her arrival in Japan, her love affair with a photographer named Teiji and her difficult friendship with Lily. During the interrogation, she gradually recalls the events that led to Lily's murder.

"This is a tale of treacherous modern loving, played out by three wounded souls, not the least Teiji, who prefers to live behind his camera lens obsessively documenting water, smoke and his girlfriends," wrote Paul Tebbs in *Spectator.* London *Daily Telegraph* critic Lisa Allardice commented, "This spare, urgent debut is not only a polished crime novel, but a hymn to Tokyo and an awkwardly tender love story."

Published in 2003, Jones's second novel, *Water Lily,* is another psychological thriller set in Japan. *Water Lily* revolves around the character of Runa, an English teacher, and Ralph, an English shopkeeper. *Library Journal* contributor Stacy Alesi summarized the theme as "the seamy underside of Asian matchmaking gone awry." "Jones is at her best when she puts us inside the heads of unbalanced people who cling to their fantasies even as real life rips them away," wrote Frank Sennett in *Booklist,* calling *Water Lily* a "dark tale of longing, self-deception and murder."

*BIOGRAPHICAL AND CRITICAL SOURCES:*

BOOKS

Jones, Susanna, *The Earthquake Bird,* Mysterious Press/Warner Books (New York, NY), 2001.

PERIODICALS

*Booklist,* August, 2001, Carrie Bissey, review of *The Earthquake Bird,* p. 2097; February 15, 2003, Frank Sennett, review of *Water Lily,* p. 1054.

*Daily Telegraph* (London, England), May 19, 2001, Lisa Allardice, review of *The Earthquake Bird.*

*Library Journal,* September 1, 2001, Michele Leber, review of *The Earthquake Bird,* p. 233; February 1, 2003, Stacy Alesi, review of *Water Lily,* p. 116.

*New Statesman,* July 9, 2001, Vicky Hutchings, review of *The Earthquake Bird,* p. 56.

*Publishers Weekly,* August 27, 2001, review of *The Earthquake Bird,* p. 55.

*Spectator,* June 30, 2001, Paul Tebbs, review of *The Earthquake Bird,* p. 43.

*Times,* (London, England), May 30, 2001, James Eve, review of *The Earthquake Bird,* p. 11.

OTHER

*Bookbrowswer,* http://bookbrowser.com/ (December 2, 2001), review of *The Earthquake Bird.*

*Girlposse,* http://girlposse.com/ (December 2, 2001), review of *The Earthquake Bird.*

*Time Warner Bookmark,* http://twbookmark.com/ (December 2, 2001), review of *The Earthquake Bird.**

\* \* \*

## JONSSON, Erik 1922-

*PERSONAL:* Born August 9, 1922 (one source says 1920), in Ostersund, Sweden; son of Erik Petter and Stina J. Jonsson. *Education:* Royal Institute of Technology, M.A., 1944.

*ADDRESSES: Home*—San Diego, CA. *Agent*—c/o Author Mail, Simon & Schuster, 1230 Avenue of the Americas, New York, NY 10020.

*CAREER:* Public Works Department, Stockholm, Sweden, engineer, 1944-46; VBB Vattenbyggnadsbyran, Stockholm, engineer, 1946-70; Department of Water Supply and Environmental Control, engineer, 1970-80s.

*MEMBER:* Swedish Society of Civil Engineers, Swedish Association of Conservation Engineers, Swedish Association of Water Hygiene (secretary, 1953-64), Institute of Water Engineers and Scientists, Water Pollution Control Federation.

*AWARDS, HONORS:* Arthur Sidney Bedell award, Water Pollution Control Federation, 1964.

*WRITINGS:*

*Inner Navigation: Why We Get Lost and How We Find Our Way,* Scribner (New York, NY), 2002.

*SIDELIGHTS:* Erik Jonsson had a long career as an engineer in Sweden before publishing his first book in English at the age of eighty. In *Inner Navigation: Why We Get Lost and How We Find Our Way,* he explores a different topic: disorientation. Drawing from his own experience and other anecdotal evidence, Jonsson develops a hypothesis of cognitive mapping, or human's mental picture of their physical space. Jonsson's examples focus on people's inner sense of such mental landmarks as the angle of sun or the smell of the ocean. When someone changes coasts or moves to a different part of a river, their sense of direction will be off.

Critics suggested that, scientifically, Jonsson relies too heavily on anecdotes to make a strong argument. The anecdotes are nonetheless a fascinating read, they added. Jonsson begins by telling a story about his trip to Cologne, Belgium, when he embarked facing the Rhine in one direction but arrived (after sleeping through the night) approaching from another. For the rest of the trip Jonsson confused east and west to the extent that he thought the Rhine seemed to flow in the wrong direction, and he became so uncomfortable that he soon left for home. In the case of two travelers from San Diego to San Francisco, the smell of salt water from the north and east, in addition to the familiar sense of the ocean to the west, created a kind of geographical anxiety. That anxiety, Jonsson proposes, occurs because humans tend to put their faith in those cognitive maps rather than the reality surrounding them.

Some readers cited the repetition of so many anecdotes as a flaw of the book. Writing for the *New York Observer,* Jennifer Egan stated, "Mr. Jonsson's method is so exhaustive as to be exhausting." A reviewer for *Publishers Weekly* found that the repetition was "flirting dangerously with tedium." Nonetheless, Egan called *Inner Navigation* "illuminating," noting that Jonsson "makes salient points about the challenge modern life poses to our spatial abilities, with its dislocations and paucity of context." Gilbert Taylor, writing for *Booklist,* called the book "an interesting, offbeat ramble," and the *Publishers Weekly* reviewer concluded that although the evidence for Jonsson's theories is largely anecdotal, "he defends them convincingly, and one hopes that future experiments will bear them out."

*BIOGRAPHICAL AND CRITICAL SOURCES:*

PERIODICALS

*Booklist,* February 15, 2002, Gilbert Taylor, review of *Inner Navigation: Why We Get Lost and How We Find Our Way,* pp. 972-973.
*Kirkus Reviews,* December 15, 2001, review of *Inner Navigation,* p. 1739.
*Publishers Weekly,* January 28, 2002, review of *Inner Navigation,* p. 282.

OTHER

*New York Observer Online,* http://www.nyobserver. com (April 10, 2002), Jennifer Egan, "Sense of Where You Are Turns Out to Be Metaphorical."*

\* \* \*

**JORDAN, A(rchibald) C(ampbell) 1906-1968**

*PERSONAL:* Born October 30, 1906, in Mbokoth-wane, Cape Province, South Africa; died, October 20, 1968, in Madison, WI; married Phyllis P. Ntantlala (a writer); children: four. *Education:* Attended St. John's College, Umtata, South Africa; Fort Hare University College, B.A., 1934; University of Cape Town, South Africa, M.A., 1943, Ph.D., 1957.

*CAREER:* Novelist, short story writer, poet, teacher, and African literature scholar. Bantu High School Kroonstad, Orange Free State, South Africa, teacher, 1936-44; University of Cape Town, Cape Town, South Africa, lecturer, 1944-61; University of California—Los Angeles, visiting lecturer, 1962; University of

Wisconsin, Madison, Institute for Research in Humanities, 1963, Department of African Languages and Literature, professor, 1964-68.

*MEMBER:* Cape African Teachers Association, Orange Free State African Teachers Association (president, 1943-44), Society of Young Africa (founding member).

*WRITINGS:*

*Ingqumbo Yeminyanya,* Lovedale Press (Lovedale, South Africa), 1940, revised and translated in English by Jordan as *The Wrath of the Ancestors,* 1980.
*A Practical Course in Xhosa,* Longmans (Johannesburg, South Africa), 1966.
(Translator and reteller), *Tales from Southern Africa,* University of California Press (Berkeley, CA), 1973.
(Translator) *Towards an African Literature; The Emergence of Literary Form in Xhosa* (Nomabhadi and Mbulu-Xhosa folktales), University of California Press (Berkeley, CA), 1973.
*Kwezo mpindo zeTsitsa* (short stories; title means "Along the Bends of the Tsitsa"), Lovedale Press (Lovedale, South Africa), 1975.

Also author of several unpublished manuscripts, including *Ulub-helu-ndongana* and *Ookhetshe bab-hazalele* (title means "The Hawks Abroad"), both novels, and *Imihobe* (title means "Songs"), poems.

*SIDELIGHTS:* A. C. Jordan is best known in literary circles for his 1940 novel *Ingqumbo Yeminyanya,* which is considered a classic African language novel. Jordan wrote the novel in Xhosa, a language spoken by approximately 6.5 million people in southeastern South Africa. A Latin scholar who also studied Greek mythology, Jordan was a South African high school teacher of English and English literature when white missionary friends encouraged him to write the book.

After the publication of his novel, Jordan joined a number of organizations focusing on the rights of native Africans, including the Non-European Unity Movement. His militant stance on the rights of native Africans is often reflected in his poetry, including the poem "Uthi mandiyeke" ("You Tell Me to Sit Quiet").

Jordan was eventually forced into exile because of his political involvements to fight South African apartheid, and eventually came to the United States and taught African languages and literature at the University of Wisconsin.

Although many of Jordan's poems were published in a number of literary journals, much of his work never went beyond the manuscript stage. His collection of verse, *Imihobe,* was never published, and he wrote two more novels in Xhosa that were never published. His collection of short stories, *Kwezo mpindo zeTsitsa,* was published nearly eight years after his death. Jordan also wrote a book on teaching Xhosa.

As pointed out by Daniel P. Kunene in his essay in *African Literature Studies: The Present State,* Jordan's novel *Ingqumbo Yeminyanya* follows the tradition of African oral narratives that feature "child heroes" who must flee their village or homeland, grow up in another culture or setting, and then return home. In this case, the hero Zwelinzima is rescued from being killed by his uncle Dingindawo, who wants to usurp Zwelinzima as the future king. Zwelinzima goes away, grows up in another culture, and eventually returns to be installed as king. Nevertheless, the novel is tragic and reflects the difficulties faced by oppressed people. Having received a Western education before he returns to his village, Zwelinzima tries to develop a new life for his people. Although he only wishes the best for his people, Zwelinzima is doomed to failure. "There is a tragic irony in everything he does," wrote Kunene in his analysis of the book, "and we can say truly that every step he takes in the belief that he will earn himself gratitude, love and loyalty from his people, achieves the exact opposite effect."

In 1980, more than a decade after Jordan's death, *Ingqumbo Yeminyanya* was published in English as *The Wrath of the Ancestors.* Translated by the author with the help of his wife, the book is the result of several attempts at a translation by the author and ultimately ended up with new characters and several alterations to the story. Kunene, this time writing in *Connections: Essays on Black Literature,* noted, "*The Wrath,* while also having moments of high achievement which show Jordan to be a master of the English language, is encumbered by the extra duty to instruct a foreign audience that is to varying degrees hostile and reluctant." Nevertheless, Kunene noted that Jordan's craftsmanship as a writer still shines through. "Yet even in this translation as it now stands," added Kunene, "Jordan now and again treats the reader to a taste of his superior talent" one that can reach "poetic heights."

## BIOGRAPHICAL AND CRITICAL SOURCES:

### BOOKS

Arnold, Stephen H., editor, *African Literature Studies: The Present State/L'etat Present,* Three Continents (Washington, DC), 1985, pp. 189-215.

Herdeck, Donald E., *African Authors, A Companion to Black African Writing, Volume I: 1300-1973,* Black Orpheus Press (Washington, DC), 1973.

Nelson, Emmanuel S., editor, *Connections: Essays on Black Literatures,* Aboriginal Studies (Canberra, Australia), 1988, pp. 75-87.

### PERIODICALS

*South African Journal of African Languages/Suid-Afrikaanse Tydskrif vir Afrikatale,* July, 1987, W. M. Kwetana, "A Reconsideration of the Plot Structure of A. C. Jordan's *Ingqumbo Yeminyanya,*" pp. 77-81; February, 1997, S. J. Neethling, "On Translating A. C. Jordan's *Ingqumbo Yeminyanya* into Afrikaans," pp. 18-22.*

# K

## KABOTIE, Michael 1942-

*PERSONAL:* Born September 3, 1942, in Keams County, AZ; son of Fred (an artist) Kabotie. *Education:* Southwest Indian Art Project, University of Arizona, 1960; attended Haskell Institute, Lawrence, KS, 1961; University of Arizona, 1964-65, studied studio arts.

*ADDRESSES: Agent*—c/o UCLA, American Indian Studies Center, 3220 Campbell Hall, Los Angeles, CA 90095.

*CAREER:* Artist, writer, and lecturer. Hopi Arts & Crafts Co-Op Guild, Second Mesa, AZ, president, board of directors, 1970-74, and manager, 1976-78; Artist Hopid, cofounder, 1973-80s; Hopi Cultural Center Museum, muralist, 1975, consultant, 1977, task team chairman, 1978—; California Academy of Sciences, consultant, 1979-80; Indian Arts & Crafts Association, Albuquerque, NM, member of board of directors, 1975-80; American Indian Art Magazine, member of editorial advisory board, 1975—.

*MEMBER:* Wuwuchim (Hopi Men's Society).

*AWARDS, HONORS:* Honored at Inter Tribal Indian Ceremonials, 1968-70, 1978; honored at fairs at Museum of Northern Arizona, 1970, Heard Museum, 1969-70, and Philbrook Museum of Art, 1969-70.

*WRITINGS:*

(With Dawakema) *Two Hopi Song Poets of Shungo-pavi,* Hopi Arts and Crafts Co-op Guild (Second Mesa, AZ), 1978.

(And illustrator) *Migration Tears: Poems About Transition.* American Indian Studies Center (Los Angeles, CA), 1987.

*SIDELIGHTS:* Michael Kabotie is a Native American belonging to the Hopi tribe of Arizona. In addition to writing two books of poetry, he is also a renowned Hopi painter, lithographer, and a silver and gold smith.

Kabotie's father was also an artist and greatly influenced his son's career. From an early age he was exposed to many Western painting styles, as well as traditional Native American art. Kabotie's art reflects the struggle of his people and also combines Hopi mythology and legend with modern themes. He is concerned with the destructive effects of modern technology of the Hopi lifestyle. These themes are also prevalent in his books of poetry.

*Migration Tears: Poems about Transition* contains Kabotie's original poetry, complemented by six plates of his graphic artwork. Contrary to what one may assume, the "tears'" mentioned in the title is not a direct reference to the "trail of tears" associated with Native American people. The poet is more specifically referring to the transitions that his people have been forced to make in their lives since the Indian Wars, and their continuing struggle between destruction and renewal in contemporary times. Donald W. Tyree, reviewing the book for *MELUS,* acknowledged that these poems "remind us that the spirit never really perished." He also noted that the book is "traditional, yet wry and immediate" and is rooted in the modern day, but is at the same time "resonantly Hopi." An example of this is in his poem "Transistor Windows," in which the narrator is looking out the window at his village, Shungopavi, reflecting on nature and watching the sun sink into "the deep abyss of the Grand Canyon." At the same time, his relatives are seated in the next room, laughing over their burned supper and watching the news of the day on television. Kabotie writes, "Caught between two windows, I ponder the / confusions and hunger of the modern transistor Hopi." Tyree related that by the time the reader completes this volume of poetry, Kabotie's world has "become a place in our literary memory and perhaps even in our hearts."

*BIOGRAPHICAL AND CRITICAL SOURCES:*

*BOOKS*

*Native North American Artists,* St. James Press (Detroit, MI), 1998.

*PERIODICALS*

*American Indian Quarterly,* fall, 1992, Paul G. Zolbrod, review of *Migration Tears: Poems about Transitions,* p. 533.
*MELUS,* spring, 1996, Donald W. Tyree, review of *Migration Tears: Poems about Transitions,* p. 136.*

\* \* \*

## KAHF, Mohja 1967-

*PERSONAL:* Born 1967, in Damascus, Syria; immigrated to United States, 1971; married Najib Ghadbian; children: two. *Ethnicity:* "Arab-American." *Education:* Rutgers University, B.A. (comparative literature and political science; with honors), 1988, Ph.D. (comparative literature), 1994. *Religion:* Muslim.

*ADDRESSES: Office*—Department of English, 333 Kimpel Hall, University of Arkansas, Fayetteville, AR 72701. *E-mail*—mkahf@comp.uark.edu.

*CAREER:* Rutgers University, New Brunswick, NJ, instructor, 1994-95; University of Arkansas, Fayetteville, AR, assistant professor, 1995-2000, associate professor of English, 2001—.

*MEMBER:* Ozark Poets & Writers Collective, Radius of Arab-American Writers, Association of Middle East Women's Studies, Syrian Studies Association, Phi Beta Kappa, Pi Sigma Alpha National Political Science Honor Society, Phi Beta Delta Honor Society for Internation Scholars.

*AWARDS, HONORS:* First-place award, New Jersey Institute of Technology, 1983, for best college poetry in New Jersey; Garden State fellowship, 1988-92.

*WRITINGS:*

*Western Representations of the Muslim Woman: From Termagant to Odalisque,* University of Texas Press (Austin, TX), 1999.
*E-mails from Scheherazad* (poetry), University of Florida Press (Gainesville, FL), 2003.

Contributor of articles to books and anthologies, including *Radius of Arab American Writers Anthology,* RAWI, 1999; *The Space between Our Footsteps: Poems and Paintings from the Middle East,* edited by Naomi Shihab Nye, Simon & Schuster (New York, NY), 1998; and *Windows of Faith: Muslim Women's Scholarship and Activism,* edited by Gisela Webb, Syracuse University Press (Syracuse, NY), 2000. Contributor of poetry to journals, including *Exit 9, Exquisite Corpse,* and *Vision International.* Contributor to periodicals, including *Arab Studies Quarterly, Banipal, Cyphers Literary Journal,* and *World Literature Today.*

*WORK IN PROGRESS:* Short stories.

*SIDELIGHTS:* Mohja Kahf's first book, *Western Representations of the Muslim Woman: From Termagant to Odalisque,* examines the changing representation of Muslim women in literature. She takes examples from medieval chansons, Renaissance drama, Enlightenment prose, and romantic poetry of the early nineteenth century. She shows the changing images of Muslim women in relationship to Western interactions with the Islamic world. Rachel Simon in *MELA Notes Book Reviews* commented, "This book adds an important dimension to the study of Western attitudes towards the Muslim world."

In 2003 Kahf published a collection of poetry titled *E-mails from Scheherazad.* In a *Booklist* review of this work, Donna Seaman described Kahf as "whimsical, colloquial and disarmingly witty," calling some of her poems "brilliantly wry and utterly irresistible."

*BIOGRAPHICAL AND CRITICAL SOURCES:*

*PERIODICALS*

*Arkansas Times,* February 25, 1998, p. C4.
*Booklist,* March 1, 2003, Donna Seaman, review of *E-mails from Scheherazad,* p. 1141.
*Choice,* January 2000, A. Mahdi, review of *Western Representations of the Muslim Woman: From Termagant to Odalisque,* p. 992.
*University of Arkansas Journal,* fall, 1998.

*OTHER*

*MELA Notes Book Reviews,* http://www.lib.umich.edu/ (October 23, 2001), Rachel Simon, review of *Western Representations of the Muslim Woman: From Termagant to Odalisque.*
*Muslim Women's League Newsletter,* http://www.mwlusa.org/ (January, 1999).

*       *       *

**KANFER, Frederick H. 1925-2002**

*OBITUARY NOTICE*—See index for *CA* sketch: Born December 6, 1925, in Vienna, Austria; died of respiratory failure October 18, 2002, in Urbana, IL. Psychologist, educator, and author. As an advocate of having patients actively participate in their own treatments, Kanfer was a highly influential figure in the field of clinical psychology. After earning his bachelor's degree from Long Island University in 1948, Kanfer, a naturalized U.S. citizen after his family fled to the United States from Austria, fought in Europe with the U.S. Army. He then completed his doctorate at Indiana University in 1953. During the 1950s and 1960s he taught at various universities, including Washington University, Purdue University, and the University of Oregon. He received his diplomate in clinical psychology from the American Board of Examiners in Professional Psychology in 1969, after which he was a professor at the University of Cincinnati, joining the University of Illinois at Urbana-Champaign in 1973 and retiring as professor emeritus in 1995. From 1995 to 1998 he worked as a senior fellow in the University of Minnesota's psychology department. During his lengthy career Kanfer earned a reputation as someone

who went against empiricist orthodoxy in developing the theory that patients could actively participate in overcoming negative behaviors. When he developed his theories in the 1960s they were considered revolutionary; they have since become widely accepted by psychologists. Kanfer published several books on behavior therapy, including coauthoring *Helping People Change: A Textbook of Methods* (1975; fourth edition, 1991) and *Guiding the Process of Therapeutic Change* (1988), as well as writing *A Mentor Manual: For Adults Who Work with Pregnant and Parenting Teens* (1995). He was also an associate editor of *Psychological Reports* from 1961 to 1999 and a frequent contributor to other professional journals and textbooks.

*OBITUARIES AND OTHER SOURCES:*

*BOOKS*

*Who's Who in America,* 56th edition, Marquis (New Providence, NJ), 2001.

*PERIODICALS*

*Chicago Tribune,* November 16, 2002, section 2, p. 11.

*       *       *

**KAVANAGH, Ed 1954-**

*PERSONAL:* Born 1954. *Education:* Memorial University of Newfoundland, B.A. (with honors); Carlton University, B.M., B.E.

*ADDRESSES: Home*—St. John's, Newfoundland, Canada. *Agent*—c/o Author Mail, Creative Book Publishing, P. O. Box 8660, 36 Austin St., St. John's, Newfoundland A1B 3T7, Canada. *E-mail*—edk@nfld.com.

*CAREER:* Musician and writer.

*AWARDS, HONORS:* Award for best short story, Newfoundland Arts and Letters Competition, 1984; award for best drama, Newfoundland Arts and Letters Competition.

*WRITINGS:*

(Editor) *The Cat's Meow: The Longside Players Selected Plays, 1984-1989,* Creative Publishers (St. John's, Newfoundland, Canada), 1990.
*The Confessions of Nipper Mooney* (novel), Killick Press (St. John's, Newfoundland, Canada), 2001.

*"AMANDA GREENLEAF" CHILDREN'S BOOKS*

*Amanda Greenleaf Visits a Distant Star,* illustrations by Tish Holland, Moonstone Press (London, Ontario, Canada), 1987.
*Amanda Greenleaf and the Spell of the Water Witch,* illustrations by Janice Udell, Moonstone Press (London, Ontario, Canada), 1990.
*Amanda Greenleaf and the Boy Magician,* illustrations by Janice Udell, Moonstone Press (London, Ontario, Canada), 1991.

*SIDELIGHTS:* Ed Kavanagh's writings include both children's books and a mainstream novel. In 1987 he published *Amanda Greenleaf Visits a Distant Star,* the first of three tales recounting the phenomenal exploits of a young girl who guards a waterfall on a faraway planet. Betty M. Brett, who described the Greenleaf series as "books of fantasy which . . . take the reader into other worlds," commented in *Canadian Children's Literature* that the first volume constitutes "the best" of the three stories.

In the second Greenleaf entry, *Amanda Greenleaf and the Spell of the Water Witch,* Kavanagh's plucky heroine persuades an evil witch to abandon a life of malicious behavior. Eva Martin, writing in *Canadian Children's Literature,* contended that Kavanagh's second Greenleaf tale is "too sweet for those children who enjoy the tough standards of the traditional fairy tales," but Christine Buchanan, in an appraisal for *Canadian Materials,* deemed the book "a good introduction to fantasy." In addition, Buchanan declared that the book "will probably appeal to children who have enjoyed myths, legends, and hero stories."

*Amanda Greenleaf and the Boy Magician,* concluding volume in the Greenleaf trilogy, finds the heroine aiding a pair of friends whose mother has been imprisoned on another planet. Adele M. Fasick, writing in *Canadian Materials,* noted the book's "ingenious twists of magic," and Elizabeth Anthony, in her *Books in Canada* review, affirmed that Greenleaf's rescue missions lead to "unpredictable and sometimes hilarious adventures." Colleen Butt, meanwhile, wrote in *Canadian Children's Literature* that *Amanda Greenleaf and the Boy Magician* serves as "enjoyable fantasy."

Kavanagh's writings also include *The Confessions of Nipper Mooney,* a novel about a youth's schooldays and his encounters with the supernatural.

*BIOGRAPHICAL AND CRITICAL SOURCES:*

*PERIODICALS*

*Books in Canada,* November, 1991, Elizabeth Anthony, "Mutual Cares," pp. 35-37.
*Canadian Children's Literature,* 1990, Eva Martin, "Fairy Tales Retold or Newly Created," pp. 116-118; 1992, Betty M. Brett, "Breaking the Vacuum: Children's Books from Newfoundland," pp. 45-58; 1993, Colleen Butt, "A New Amanda Greenleaf," p. 57.
*Canadian Materials,* May, 1988, Christian Buchanan, review of *Amanda Greenleaf and the Spell of the Water Witch,* p. 88; September, 1991, Adele M. Fasick, review of *Amanda Greenleaf and the Boy Magician,* p. 219.*

\*     \*     \*

## KAYE, Buddy 1918-2002

*OBITUARY NOTICE*—See index for *CA* sketch: Given name, Jules Leonard Kaye; born January 3, 1918, in New York, NY; died November 21, 2002, in Rancho Mirage, CA. Songwriter, musician, producer, educator, and author. Kaye was best known as the author of popular songs performed by such artists as Perry Como and Frank Sinatra. He began his career as a jazz saxophonist with his Buddy Kaye Quintet, which played in clubs and on cruise ships. Finding he had a gift for song writing, he began to publish his lyrics in the late 1930s, writing over 400 songs during his career. Some of the most popular of these include "Thoughtless," "A—You're Adorable (The Alphabet

Song," "Til the End of Time," "Full Moon and Empty Arms," "Little by Little," and "The Old Songs," which were performed by such singers as Dinah Shore, Tony Bennett, Pat Boone, Dusty Springfield, Sarah Vaughan, and Barry Manilow. During the 1960s and 1970s Kaye also wrote lyrics for television programs such as *I Dream of Jeannie* and the Humphrey Bogart film *The Treasure of the Sierra Madre.* As a producer, he won acclaim for directing and producing the recording *The Little Prince,* which received a Grammy Award for best children's record in 1975. Toward the end of his career, Kaye taught songwriting at the University of California at Los Angeles for eleven years, as well as at the College of the Desert. He was also the author of several books, among them *The Complete Songwriter* (1978), *Method Songwriting: The Method Used by Professionals* (1988), and *A You're Adorable* (1994), the last cowritten by Sidney Lippman and Fred Wise. At the time of his death Kaye had just finished writing the book and lyrics for a musical about actress Greta Garbo.

*OBITUARIES AND OTHER SOURCES:*

BOOKS

Harrison, Nigel, *Songwriters: A Biographical Dictionary with Discographies,* McFarland (Jefferson, NC), 1998.

PERIODICALS

*Chicago Tribune,* November 25, 2002, section 1, p. 11.
*Los Angeles Times,* November 24, 2002, p. B17.
*New York Times,* November 23, 2002, p. A17.
*Washington Post,* November 24, 2002, p. C11.

\*     \*     \*

## KEARNEY, Lawrence 1948-

*PERSONAL:* Born 1948, in Brooklyn, NY. *Education:* Attended State University of New York, Binghamton

*ADDRESSES: Home*—Larkspur, CA. *Office*—c/o Hazelden Information and Educational Services, 15251 Pleasant Valley Rd., Center City, MN 55012.

*CAREER:* Poet and novelist.

*WRITINGS:*

*Fifteen Poems,* White Rabbit Press (San Francisco, CA), 1964.
*Kingdom Come,* Wesleyan University Press (Middletown, CT), 1980.
(As Larry Kearney, with Jack Erdmann) *Whiskey's Children,* Vernal Press, 1995.
(As Larry Kearney, with Jack Erdmann) *A Bar on Every Corner: Sobering Up in a Tempting World,* Hazelden Information and Educational Services (Center City, MN), 2001.

Also author of *Streaming,* Trike Publishing, 1998. Contributor to *Finding God When You Don't Believe in God: Searching for a Power Greater than Yourself,* by Jack Erdmann and Anne Lamott, Hazelden Information Education (Center City, MN), 2003.

*SIDELIGHTS:* Larry Kearney translated his struggles with alcoholism into two books, written with Jack Erdmann, that offer an unflinching look at the misery of addiction as well as the potential for hope. Before working with Erdmann on those memoirs, Kearney was a highly regarded poet who had been connected with Jack Spicer's so-called "Jesuits," a circle of young writers who had moved from New York to San Francisco, some of whom grew up as Catholics.

Spicer, who was gay, fell in love with Kearney, who is straight, and acted as an early supporter for the young poet. Stan Persky, who edited the Spicer circle's magazine *Open Space,* called Spicer a Colonel Tom Parker to Kearney's Elvis Presley. When Kearney got an offer to publish his poems with White Rabbit Press, however, Spicer became angry, telling Kearney that he was not ready to publish. Lewis Ellingham, interviewing Kearney for the *Chicago Review,* reported their reconciliation: "A few weeks after *Fifteen Poems* appeared, Larry was sitting at the bar in Gino's and Jack said, 'There are two real poems in your book. I'm not going to tell you which ones they are.' This was, realized Larry, Spicer's way of burying the hatchet."

Though he wrote throughout the 1960s and 1970s, Kearney did not have a major nationwide release until *Kingdom Come,* in 1980. *Kingdom Come* features poems written from the perspective of different characters that Kearney describes as "people whose chief dread—that nothing will work out—has come true." James Campbell reviewed the book for the *Times Literary Supplement,* remarking that although Kearney's poetry is "sincere," the poet "failed to explore his characters' troubled lives sufficiently." A reviewer for *Booklist,* however, noted Kearney's "brilliant handling of their dramatic monologues," calling him "a talent of extraordinary perception and expressive power."

Kearney later used his talents to help another writer. Jack Erdmann was an alcoholic salesman who lost everything, gradually regained his life during twenty years of sobriety, and then chose to tell his story to give hope to others. Erdmann and Kearney's first collaboration was *Whiskey's Children,* which begins with Erdmann's childhood in a violent, alcoholic family and then details Erdmann's helpless repetition of his father's mistakes with his own wife and children. Readers were struck by the truth of the story. A reviewer for *Publishers Weekly* wrote, "With wonderful emotional honesty and precision, Erdman and Kearney offer up Erdmann's own suffering as a powerful source of healing and hope." Kearney also worked with Erdmann on his next book, *A Bar on Every Corner: Sobering Up in a Tempting World.* This work focuses on Erdmann's first year of recovery, outlined according to the twelve steps of Alcoholics Anonymous. Erdmann and Kearney show Erdmann's struggles returning to a society where most everyone drinks, including his mother and his coworkers. In *Publishers Weekly,* a reviewer called *A Bar on Every Corner* a "timeless tale" that offers "hope, encouragement and insight for recovering alcoholics, their families and friends, as well as for anyone concerned about the cultural impact of alcoholism."

*BIOGRAPHICAL AND CRITICAL SOURCES:*

*PERIODICALS*

*Booklist,* October 15, 1980, review of *Kingdom Come,* pp. 300-301; September 15, 1997, Brian McCombie, review of *Whiskey's Children,* p. 184.
*Chicago Review,* fall, 1997, Lewis Ellingham and Kevin Killian, "Ducks for Grownups: Jack Spicer, Larry Kearney, Jamie MacInnis 1964," pp. 44-61.

*New York Times Book Review,* January 18, 1998, Leslie Chris Feller, review of *Whiskey's Children,* p. 16.
*Publishers Weekly,* September 29, 1997, review of *Whiskey's Children,* p. 81; July 23, 2001, review of *A Bar on Every Corner,* p. 60.
*San Francisco Chronicle,* February 15, 1996, Patricia Holt, "Surviving Early Terror of Alcohol and Abuse," review of *Whiskey's Children,* p. D5.
*Times Literary Supplement,* February 20, 1981, James Campbell, "Agony and After," p. 208.

*OTHER*

*BookPage,* http://www.bookpage.com/ (March 19, 2002), "BookPage Talks to Jack Erdmann."*

\*      \*      \*

## KELLY, Michael 1957-2003

*PERSONAL:* Born March 17, 1957, in Washington, DC; died in a military vehicle accident April 3, 2003, near Baghdad, Iraq; son of Thomas (a journalist) and Marguerite (a journalist and author) Kelly; married Madelyn Greenberg (a news producer); children: Tom, Jack. *Education:* University of New Hampshire, B.A. (history), 1979. *Religion:* Catholic.

*CAREER:* Journalist and author. American Broadcast Company, Inc. (ABC), New York, NY, researcher, booker, and associate producer for *Good Morning America,* 1979-83; *Cincinnati Post,* Cincinnati, OH, feature writer, 1983-86; *Baltimore Sun,* Washington, DC, reporter, 1986-89; freelance writer and reporter, 1989-92; *New York Times,* New York, NY, political reporter, 1992-93, reporter for *New York Times Magazine,* 1993-94; *New Republic,* Washington, DC, editor, 1996-97; *National Journal,* Washington, DC, editor, 1998-2000; *Atlantic Monthly,* Boston, MA, editor, 2000-02, editor-at-large, 2002-03.

*AWARDS, HONORS:* National Magazine Award, American Society of Magazine Editors, 1992, and Overseas Press Award, Overseas Press Club of America, both for dispatches to *New Republic* during the Gulf War; PEN/Martha Albrand Award for First

Nonfiction, PEN American Center, 1994, and *New York Times* Notable Book designation, both for *Martyrs' Day: Chronicle of a Small War.*

*WRITINGS:*

*Martyrs' Day: Chronicle of a Small War,* Random House (New York, NY), 1993, with new foreword and afterword, Vintage (New York, NY), 2001.
*The Siege,* Random House (New York, NY), 1996.

Author of columns "Letter from Washington" in *New Yorker,* 1994-96, "TRB" in *New Republic,* 1996-97, and columns in *National Journal,* 1997-98, and *Washington Post,* 1997-2003. Contributor to periodicals, including *Boston Globe, GQ,* and *Esquire.*

*SIDELIGHTS:* Until his untimely death at age forty-six, Michael Kelly had a rich and varied career as a journalist. Kelly made a name for himself while covering the Gulf War in Iraq in 1991, but unfortunately his name became even more well know during the second war in that region when he became the first American journalist to die during America's 2003 war against terrorism. Kelly was best known for penning frequently razor-edged political commentary often espousing a more conservative viewpoint than the publications he edited.

Kelly was born and raised in Washington, D.C., the only son of journalists Thomas and Marguerite Kelly. His father covered politics for the now-defunct *Washington Daily News* and Michael often accompanied him to the office on Saturdays. His mother authored a book on child-rearing and wrote the syndicated column "Family Almanac." His parents' careers were a large influence on Kelly's decision to become a journalist himself.

Kelly obtained a degree in history at the University of New Hampshire. He then worked his way through a variety of jobs at ABC's *Good Morning America* before becoming a reporter and feature writer for the *Cincinnati Post,* which at times included coverage of state and local politics. He moved to national politics, which was to become his forte, when he took a job at the *Baltimore Sun.* It was during his tenure in Baltimore that Kelly met his future wife Madelyn

"Max" Greenberg on a bus of reporters covering the Michael Dukakis presidential campaign. In 1989 he turned to freelance writing and moved to Chicago.

When the Gulf War broke out in 1991, Kelly convinced several publications, including the *New Republic,* to let him submit dispatches independently. While reporting from the front lines at risk to himself, Kelly remained unharmed, and gained respect for his insightful, hard-hitting articles. As then-*New Republic* editor Hendrik Hertzberg recalled to Jack Shafer of *Slate,* Kelly "'was just incandescent. War was the perfect subject for him. He was so full of emotion and yes, anger, too. And war was the subject that gave that its fullest scope.'" Daniel Pipes, writing for *Middle East Quarterly,* noted that Kelly "seemed to be everywhere at the right moment (Iraq when the war started, Tel Aviv as the Scuds fell, Kuwait at liberation) and he wrote with a golden pen." Mike Hoyt commented of Kelly in the *Columbia Journalism Review:* "It was in the weekly rhythms of *The New Republic* that he hit his stride, turning out searing and lush accounts of the war, from the liberation of Kuwait City to the carnage along the Iraqi retreat route to the redecorating of the emir's palace in Kuwait."

After the war, Kelly compiled his war-time dispatches as *Martyrs' Day: Chronicles of a Small War.* As *Library Journal* reviewer Nader Entessar noted, "This eyewitness account . . . deals primarily with human-interest elements rather than military matters. Kelly . . . chronicles the vagaries of the war and its impact on the lives of the people in a revealing and disturbing text." Reviewer Pipes recorded a similar sentiment, noting that, "While *Martyrs' Day* deals with highly political topics at a moment of extreme crisis, the book is essentially apolitical. . . . [Kelly's] reports . . . have a positive, humane quality, sometimes quite at odds with the bellicose rhetoric and nasty actions he witnesses." Concluding that *Martyrs' Day* "not only brings back the tumultuous days of 1991 but his keen insights, his intrepid search for the story, and his ability to turn a phrase," Pipes dubbed the work "the best first-hand account of the entire Kuwait crisis."

After returning from the Gulf War, Kelly covered politics for the *New York Times,* penning profiles of President Bill Clinton, Clinton aide David Gergen, and First Lady Hillary Clinton and holding back few biting words in all three cases. His next assignment, as columnist for the *New Yorker*'s "Letter from Washington," allowed him to continue expressing his opinions about those on Capitol Hill. As Shafer noted, "Unlike most Washington journalists, Kelly wrote about federal politics with the nonchalance of a homeboy, which he was. Congressmen, senators, and presidents—especially President Clinton—didn't impress him much." It was his blunt and often unflattering coverage of the Clinton administration, including Vice President Al Gore, that led to Kelly's firing at his next job as editor of the *New Republic* after less than a year.

Calling Kelly "a conservative in the older, cultural sense," Peter Beinart commented in the *New Republic* that the late journalist "wanted to preserve the unwritten rules, built up imperceptibly over time, that define morality in most people's lives. . . . He judged politicians as human beings. His politics were less ideological than characterological. He believed that some people acted with honor, and others did not. And the people who acted without honor in their private lives would act without honor in their public lives, especially toward the weak." His sensitivity to moral lapses was especially acute during the Yugoslav war of the early 1990s, and prompted his 1996 book *The Siege,* in which he profiles the Bosnian Muslims who rose up to defend themselves against Serbian attempts at ethnic cleansing.

After a stint as editor of *National Journal,* Kelly accepted an editorship at the *Atlantic Monthly* in early 2000. He is credited with revitalizing the time-honored periodical, which won four National Magazine Awards in 2002. To the surprise of many, in the fall of 2002 he became an editor-at-large, planning to use his free time to write a book on the steel industry. However, the looming war against terrorism would change those plans. David Carr explained in the *New York Times,* "As war with Iraq loomed, he decided to return to reporting. . . . 'I am interested in a very specific story,' Mr. Kelly said. . . . 'I want to tell the story of this division at war in a comprehensive way.'" Despite his relatively safe position as an embedded reporter in Iraq, on April 3, 2003, Kelly and a soldier he was accompanying were killed when the Humvee they were riding in rolled into a canal while the driver attempted to evade Iraqi bullets.

Recalling Kelly's career, Beinart noted, "In his columns, Mike could be combative, aggressive, unyielding. In life, he was gentle, warm, playful. And

so, people who loved him have emphasized the distinction between the way he viewed politics and the way he lived his life." "Michael always seemed to be in the right place at the right time to get the best quote and the best story, the best jobs and the best life," added Maureen Dowd of her late colleague in the *New York Times.*

*BIOGRAPHICAL AND CRITICAL SOURCES:*

*PERIODICALS*

*Columbia Journalism Review,* March-April, 1997, Mike Hoyt, "The New *New Republic*: Meet Michael Kelly, Some Kind of Liberal," pp. 40-46.

*GQ,* April, 1997, Martin Beiser, "A Cacophony of Voices," pp. 208-209.

*Library Journal,* February 15, 1993, Nader Entessar, review of *Martyrs' Day: Chronicle of a Small War.*

*Middle East Quarterly,* June, 1994, Daniel Pipes, review of *Martyrs' Day.*

*Washingtonian,* June, 1997, Diana McLellan, "In This Corner . . . ," pp. 72-76.

*OTHER*

*Atlantic Unbound,* http://www.theatlantic.com/ (April 10, 2003), "Michael Kelly."

*New York Times,* http://www.nytimes.com/ (April 7, 2003), "Michael Kelly."

*OBITUARIES:*

*PERIODICALS*

*Chicago Tribune,* April 4, 2003, Michael Tackett, "Atlantic Monthly Editor-at-Large Michael Kelly Killed in Iraq Crash," p. K3202.

*OTHER*

*CNN.com,* http://www.cnn.com/ (April 4, 2003), "U.S. Journalist Killed Covering War."

*New Republic Online,* http://www.tnr.com/ (April 9, 2003), Peter Beinart, "TRB from Washington: Personal Best."

*New York Times,* http://www.nytimes.com/ (April 7, 2003), Jane Perlez, "American Journalist and Soldier Killed in Crash outside Baghdad", Maureen Dowd, "The Best Possible Life," and David Carr, "Michael Kelly, 46, Editor and Columnist, Dies in Iraq."

*Slate,* http://politics.slate.msn.com/ (April 4, 2003), Jack Shafer, "Michael Kelly (1957-2003): Husband, Father, Journalist."

*Washington Post,* http://www.washingtonpost.com/ (April 4, 2003), Howard Kurtz, "Atlantic Monthly Editor Killed in Iraq."*

* * *

## KHAIR, Tabish 1966-

*PERSONAL:* Born 1966, in Ranchi, Bihar, India. *Education:* Magadh University, M.A.; Copenhagen University, Ph.D.

*ADDRESSES: Office*—Department of English/Humanities, Njalsgade 80, University of Copenhagen, 2300 Copenhagen S, Denmark. *E-mail*—tabish.khair@get2net.dk.

*CAREER:* Educator, critic, writer, journalist, and activist. *Times of India,* Delhi, India, reporter; University of Copenhagen, Coenhagen, Denmark, department of English, assistant professor.

*AWARDS, HONORS:* All India Poetry competition winner, 1995.

*WRITINGS:*

*My World,* Rupa & Company (Calcutta, India), 1991.

*The Book of Heroes,* Rupa & Company (New Delhi, India), 1995.

*An Angel in Pyjamas,* HarperCollins Publishers India (New Delhi, India), 1996.

*Where Parallel Lines Meet,* Viking (New York, NY), 2000.

*Babu Fictions: Alienation in Contemporary Indian English Novels,* Oxford University Press (New York, NY), 2001.

Also contributor of articles to newspapers, including *The Hindu* and *Daily Mail & Guardian.*

*WORK IN PROGRESS:* A collection of poems based on "Shakuntalam" and a collection of academic essays.

*SIDELIGHTS:* Tabish Khair was born in a small rural town in India, a fact that critic Maia V. Fallesen, writing for the online publication *INDOlink,* believed will save Khair's writing from the "superficial facility of certain major Indian English authors." Khair himself often criticizes the misrepresentations that some major Indian-English writers offer of life in India. However, as Fallesen pointed out, it is the books of "diasporic" Indian-English authors that most Europeans read. Fallesen reported that one of the reasons for this is that literature written by Indian writers who live in India is often neglected. "The majority of Indian critics," Fallesen explained, are unwilling to review "'local' Indian English novels" and have so far been unable to develop "a critical discourse which will be appropriate to these novels." A case in point is Khair's first two books, for which there has been little critical response.

Since Khair entered the University of Copenhagen in Denmark to work on his doctorate and to take on the role of professor of research there, his books have gained a better critical response. In other words, as Fallesen noted, since Khair is now living in Copenhagen, he, too, will be considered a "diasporic" writer in the future, that is, an emigrant, writing outside of his own country.

An *India Today* reviewer called Khair's first novel, *An Angel in Pyjamas,* "the calling card of an author with the power to fascinate." The fact that an Indian newspaper was willing to review Khair's novel was a sure sign that Khair was well on the road to at least some degree of notoriety.

*An Angel in Pyjamas* is told through two alternating narrators. The "Phansa" section is voiced through a third-person narrator, who lives in a rural section of India. The section referred to as "Dilli/Delhi" is written in a more intellectual style, by a first-person narrator who often seems confused and sometimes speaks ironically, which led Fallesen to believe that Khair was making fun of other "diasporic" writers, such as Rushdie. On the whole, the novel follows the lives of people living in rural sections of India, as well as the lives of a group of reporters living in Delhi. Toward the end of the novel, a couple from the country migrate to Delhi, thus bringing the circumstances of the two alternating sections of the book together for a conclusion. Two of the main themes of the book are the conflict in India between Hindus and Muslims and the influence of English colonization.

Khair's next book, *Where Parallel Lines Meet,* is a collection of poetry. Indrajit Hazra, writing for the *Hindustan Times Online,* found Khair's poems refreshing. Hazra, commenting on the modern television culture of India, feared that poetry in India was becoming "confined to the narrow ledges of academia." Hazra hoped that Khair's collection might bring poetry back to the general reading public. In *Where Parallel Lines Meet,* Khair "gives a rare instance of poetry working as it should: without the millstone of Engl. Lit. hanging around its neck," Hazra wrote, then added that Khair's poetry contains fresh images that are "startling and, on most occasions, kinetic." Another critic, Kala Krishnan Ramesh of *India Writes,* was not quite as enthusiastic, but still admitted that Khair's poems are busy with life, "but in ordinary bite size pieces." Ramesh also believed that Khair's poems have a "tangible quality of innocence . . . as if they are being written in the process of experiencing and learning."

*Babu Fictions: Alienation in Contemporary Indian English Novels* focuses on a topic that Khair takes quite seriously: that of Indian authors writing in English, a language that is understood, spoken, and read by only an elite portion of the Indian population. In an article that Khair wrote for *The Hindu,* he states that "less than four per cent [sic] of the population of India is supposed to speak English." Khair points out that because only this small fraction of the population is literate in English and yet Indian-English literature is quite broadly distributed throughout India, there exists a "huge linguistic and socio-economic chasm" between those people who can and cannot "read and write in English." Khair points out that because of this, there exists a habit in English-Indian literature of either completely ignoring Indians who live in rural areas (where the majority of the people do not speak English) or creating "largely idealised versions" of life in these areas.

The underlying purpose of Khair's book, *Babu Fictions,* is to study whether or not it is even possible for

authors to write about India, its culture, and the life of its people, in a language that most of the population does not understand. Khair looks at the writings of such Indian authors as Raja Rao, Anita Desai, K. K. Narayan, and Salman Rushdie, as well as others. In his search to understand how the body of work presented by these authors communicates, in English, the essence of his native culture, Khair begins by first focusing on general topics, such as power, industrialization, caste, gender and multilingual issues, and the differences between urban and rural populations.

The term "Babu," as used in the title of Khair's book, refers to the middle and upper classes in India, the majority of whom live in urban areas, are very much aware of Western culture, and speak English. However, the term also has a pejorative insinuation. During the colonization of India by England, the word "Babu" was used by Indian people to address English men of power. Thus, Khair is also interested in the effects of colonization in India, as practiced through the use of language.

Michael Wood, who reviewed *Babu Fictions* for the *London Review of Books,* called it an "intelligent and argumentative book." Wood also pointed out that most books written by Indian authors in English are written for non-Indian people, as a way of opening a door to their culture. A review posted on the online *Vedams Books* notes that "Khair presents a reading of contemporary Indian fiction in English that sets out to study whether it is possible to write in English about people who often speak little or no English."

More recently, Khair has moved away from linguistic battles and turned to more explosive issues, writing several articles on the topic of terrorism. In October, 2001, he wrote "Bombing Is the Easy Way Out" for the *Daily Mail & Guardian,* in which he argues, from his own Muslim point of reference, that he has "no intention of backing the Taliban's fight." He maintains that the Taliban's call for all Muslims to unite against the "terrorism" of the United States has no pull on his sentiments. Khair declared that the Taliban has no right to accuse another of terrorist acts, since they have plagued their own people with a "longer and more brutal reign of terror."

In another article written for *The Hindu,* Khair condemns the attack on India's parliament on December 13, 2001. "Often," Khair writes, the people of

India "fail to take enough pride in the one thing that every Indian has good reason to celebrate: our democracy." Although corruption exists in Indian politics, Khair reminds his readers, even in the United States there is corruption. This is no reason to dismiss Indian political affairs. It was, Khair contends, "democracy that the terrorists attacked." Although that democracy is not perfect, he continues, it is "a democracy that all Indians should be proud of."

*BIOGRAPHICAL AND CRITICAL SOURCES:*

PERIODICALS

*London Review of Books,* April 19, 2001, Michael Wood, review of *Babu Fictions: Alienation in Contemporary Indian English Novels,* p. 28.
*World Literature Today,* spring, 1992, John Oliver Perry, review of *My World,* p. 404.

OTHER

*Hindustan Times Online,* http://www.hindustantimes.com/ (February 27, 2002), Indrajit Hazra, "The Invisible Engl. Lit. Machine and Beyond."
*India Writes,* http://www.indiawrites.com/ (December 2, 2001), Kala Krishnan Ramesh, "The Wordless Cook and Kabir's Couplet."
*INDOlink,* http://www.indolink.com/ (February 27, 2002), Maia V. Fallesen, review of *An Angel in Pyjamas.*
*Vedams Books Web site,* http://www.vedamsbooks.com/ (February 27, 2002), review of *Babu Fictions.**

\*     \*     \*

## KIERANS, Eric (William) 1914-

*PERSONAL:* Born February 2, 1914, in Montreal, Quebec, Canada; son of Hugh and Lena (Schmidt) Kierans; married Teresa Catherine Whelan, November 12, 1938; children: Thomas Edward, Catherine Anne. *Education:* Loyola College, B.A., 1935; McGill University, graduate study, 1947-51. *Politics:* Liberal. *Religion:* Roman Catholic. *Hobbies and other interests:* Sports.

*ADDRESSES: Home*—3200 Cedar Ave., Westmount, Quebec H3Y 1Z2, Canada.

*CAREER:* McGill University, Toronto, Canada, professor of communication and finance and director of School of Communications, 1953-60, professor of economics, 1972-80; Montreal and Canadian Stock Exchanges, Montreal, Canada, president, 1960-63; Quebec Legislature, Quebec, Canada, elected member, 1963-68; House of Commons, Ottawa, Canada, elected member, 1968; Canadian Postmaster General, Ottawa, 1968-69; Department of Communications, Ottawa, minister, 1969-71; Dalhousie University, Halifax, Nova Scotia, Canada, professor of economics, 1983-84; writer. Consultant to Manitoba Government, 1972; director, Sidbec-Dosco Ltée, 1978-80, and Caisse de Dépôt, 1979-80; Canadian Adhesives Ltd., chairman, 1980; Kara Investments Ltd., president, 1982; director, Lester Pearson Institute for International Development, and Dalhousie Medical Research Foundation. Dal Grauer Memorial Lecturer, University of British Columbia, 1984; David Alexander Memorial Lecturer, Memorial University, 1985; fellow-in-residence, Institute for Research on Public Policy, 1985-90. *Military service:* Victoria Rifles of Canada, 1942-46; became lieutenant.

*MEMBER:* Nova Barristers Society (council member).

*AWARDS, HONORS:* LL.D., St. Thomas University, 1979; LL.D., McGill University, 1981; D.C.L., Bishops University, 1983; D.C.L., King's College; LL. D., McMaster University; LL.D., Concordia College, 1987; LL.D., Dalhousie University, 1991; officer, Order of Canada, 1995.

*WRITINGS:*

*Challenge of Confidence: Kierans on Canada,* McClellan & Stewart (Toronto, Ontario, Canada), 1967.
*Report on Natural Resources Policy in Manitoba,* 1973.
(With Walter Stewart) *Wrong End of the Rainbow: The Collapse of Free Enterprise in Canada,* Collins (Toronto, Ontario, Canada), 1988.
(With Walter Stewart) *Remembering* (memoir), Stoddart (Toronto, Ontario, Canada), 2001.

*SIDELIGHTS:* Eric Kierans is a notable figure in Canadian politics. In 1963, after stints as an economics professor and president of the Montreal and Canadian stock exchanges, he began his political career by winning election to the Quebec legislature, where he subsequently distinguished himself as an outspoken critic of conservative economics. In 1968 he gained election to the Canadian House of Commons, and he was eventually appointmented to the cabinet of Canadian Prime Minister Pierre Trudeau. Kierans remained a fixture in Canadian politics until 1972, when he resumed his teaching career at McGill University. Eight years later, he left McGill for a brief term as professor of economics at Dalhousie University. After leaving Dalhousie, Kierans continued to provide caustic assessments of economic developments in Canada. "Our place in any kind of global system controlled by the United States is going to be merely as a supplier of raw materials," he told Peter C. Newman in *Maclean's.* "We are being ground right into a mould."

Kierans's writings include *Wrong End of the Rainbow: The Collapse of Free Enterprise in Canada,* which characterizes Canadian capitalism as opportunistic and anti-social. Peter C. Newman, writing in *Maclean's,* praised *Wrong End of the Rainbow* as "provocative and intelligent," and Stan Persky, in a *Books in Canada* analysis, described the book as "biting." Similarly, David Chadwick affirmed in *Canadian Materials* that *Wrong End of the Rainbow*—which Kierans wrote with Walter Stewart—constitutes a "lively and well-written book."

Kierans is also the author, with Walter Stewart, of a memoir, *Remembering,* which Pamela Wallin proclaimed in *Globe Books* as "a fascinating story." John Richards noted in *Inroads* that Kierans's memoir is "an important book for anyone thinking about the governing of a country with 'huge geography [and] clearly distinct regions.'"

*BIOGRAPHICAL AND CRITICAL SOURCES:*

*PERIODICALS*

*Books in Canada,* March, 1989, Stan Persky, "Capital Offenses," pp. 31-32.
*Canadian Materials,* March, 1989, David Chadwick, review of *Wrong End of the Rainbow: The Collapse of Free Enterprise in Canada,* p. 91.

*Inroads,* 2001, John Richards, "Remembering Kierans."
*Maclean's,* August 19, 1985, Peter C. Newman, "Concerns of a Liberal Patriarch," p. 42; November 28, 1988, Peter C. Newman, "Culling the Autumn Book Harvest," p. 42; May 7, 2001, Anthony Wilson-Smith, "The Lessons of Remembering," p. 2.
*Quill & Quire,* December, 1988, Doug Bell, review of *Wrong End of the Rainbow: The Collapse of Free Enterprise in Canada,* p. 24.

*OTHER*

*Globe Books Web site,* http://www.globebooks.com/ (May 6, 2002), Pamela Wallin, "Don't Forget History's Lessons."*

\*       \*       \*

## KINDER, Charles Alfonso II 1946-
## (Chuck Kinder)

*PERSONAL:* Born October 8, 1946, in Montgomery, WV; son of Charles Alfonso and Eileen Reba (Parsons) Kinder; married Diane Cecily Blackmer, March 22, 1975. *Education:* West Virginia University, B.A. (English), 1967, M.A. (English), 1968; Stanford University, M.A. (writing), 1973. *Politics:* Democrat. *Religion:* Methodist. *Hobbies and other interests:* White water rafting, cooking, fishing.

*ADDRESSES: Office*—University of Pittsburgh, English Department CL 526, 4200 Fifth Ave., Pittsburgh, PA 15260.

*CAREER:* Waynesburg College, Waynesburg, PA, instructor of English, 1968-70; Stanford University, Palo Alto, CA, Jones lecturer of fiction, 1973-76; University of California, Davis, writer-in-residence, 1979; University of Alabama, Tuscaloosa, writer-in-residence, spring 1980; University of Pittsburgh, Pittsburgh, PA, associate professor of English, 1980—.

*WRITINGS:*

*UNDER NAME CHUCK KINDER*

*Snakehunter,* Knopf (New York, NY), 1973, revised, Gnomon Press (Frankfort, KY), 1991.

*The Silver Ghost,* Harcourt Brace (New York, NY), 1979.

*Honeymooners: A Cautionary Tale,* Farrar, Straus & Giroux (New York, NY), 2001.

SIDELIGHTS: Charles Alfonso Kinder II is considered by many to be a throwback to early 1960s pranksters such as Jack Kerouac and his group, and is most closely related to Kinder's fellow-writer and best friend Raymond Carver, the noted short story author. Kinder's book, *Honeymooners: A Cautionary Tale,* is based on Carver and Kinder's relationship, a story that took Kinder more than twenty years to write. Prior to *Honeymooners,* Kinder wrote two coming-of-age novels about a young boy in West Virginia, *Snakehunter* and *The Silver Ghost,* both published under the name Chuck Kinder.

Both Kinder and Carver were students in writing classes at Stanford when they met. At first, Kinder shied away from Carver because he "dressed like a big goofy guy, like some kind of nerd," as Kinder told Dennis Loy Johnson in an online interview for *Moby Lives.* Carver had already published his first collection, *Will You Please Be Quiet Please,* and Kinder published his first novel the same year he completed his master's degree and began teaching at Stanford.

Kinder's unusual first novel, *Snakehunter,* chronicles the life of a young, fatherless, West Virginian boy by reminiscing through stories of his relatives and old fables and myths. Kinder uses the memories and fables to try to explain the joys and sorrows of life as experienced by a young boy moving toward adulthood. Kinder relates several deaths, beginning with the death of Speer Whitfield's, the protagonist's pet turtle, Snakehunter. Later, readers learn of the deaths of his father, sister, aunt, grandmother and grandfather. John S. Boudreaux, writing for *Review of Contemporary Fiction,* called Kinder's book "a catharsis, an education in world folklore, a lesson in lyrical language, and a paradigm of how to live without whining." A possible reason why Boudreaux referred to this novel as a catharsis could be that, as Martin Levin, a reviewer for *New York Times Book Review,* made clear, Kinder's book is "a harsh memoir in which the fact of death dramatizes the facts of life."

After his job as lecturer at Stanford ended, Kinder moved back to the east coast in 1979, the same year his second book, *The Silver Ghost* was published. This novel is also set in West Virginia, and the protagonist, Jimbo Stark, is a troubled teen. Jimbo steals his father's miniature World War II soldier set to buy an engagement ring for his girlfriend, and then the real trouble begins. He is kicked out of his father's house and sent to live with his grandmother. The distance between his grandmother's home and his girlfriend's leads to his losing her, and because of this loss, as a writer for *Kirkus Reviews* described it, "Jimbo does a James Dean, a Kerouac, in retaliation." In other words, Jimbo becomes a rebel.

Jimbo leaves West Virginia and hooks up with a gangster who sets him on a path of crime. *Library Journal* contributor Samuel Simons also saw a connection between Kinder's book and the writing of Kerouac, and Simons described Kinder's book as "a swift-moving novel that, despite its overblown and self-conscious prose, manages to read like an updated version of Kerouac's *On the Road.*"

After his first two books were published, Kinder settled down into a teaching job at the University of Pittsburgh. While there, he began to try to capture the story of his relationship with Carver on paper. At one point, ten years before actual publication, Kinder had written almost three thousand words on the subject. "By the time Ray died in '88," Kinder told Johnson in their interview, "I had a stack of manuscripts. But I really got off track, man. I was too influenced at some points by academia, trying to be artsy fartsy and write metafiction. . . . At one point I looked at it and I thought, God, what is this, man? It's sort of 'Ulysses' meets 'Dune'—I even had science fiction crap in there." So Kinder put the manuscript away for five years. Then one day he took it out and started hacking away at it. On the advice of Turow, Kinder cut the material down to about nine hundred pages. Turow persuaded his publishers to look at the finished product, and out of that came Kinder's third novel, *Honeymooners.*

*Honeymooners* recounts the relationship between Kinder and Carver, their carousing, their marriages, their struggles with alcohol and drugs, and their early writing. Although the book is classified as fiction, Kinder confessed to Johnson, "the plot line kind of unfolds pretty much, I guess, as our lifelines." Nevertheless, Kinder stated that the book is "a work of imagination." He labeled it "faction," a cross between fiction and fact.

The main characters in the book are Ralph Crawford (the Raymond Carver substitute) and Jim Stark (the Kinder alias). Jay McInerney, writing for the *New York Times,* found both characters quite enjoyable. "I commend *Honeymooners* to nearly everyone except possibly the parents of young men with literary ambitions. . . . If *Honeymooners* doesn't make you laugh, cry and cringe with sympathetic embarrassment, then you should probably adjust your medication immediately." McInterney also praised Kinder's writing, describing it as having "the range to encompass the tenderness of romantic love and the longing for the infinite that haunts these men." That longing may have driven the young authors to alcohol, as John Freeman, for the *Atlanta Journal-Constitution* wrote: "As far back as Poe, American readers have nurtured a soft spot for self-destructive genius. From the work of Kerouac and Hemingway to Dorothy Parker and Hart Crane, inspiration, this tradition tells us, lies at the bottom of a bottle or at the end of a Benzedrine-fueled binge." Freeman praised Kinder's *Honeymooners* as "a long, garrulous celebration of life that embraces greed and envy and lust, while absorbing them into a larger vision that forgives us our frailties."

*BIOGRAPHICAL AND CRITICAL SOURCES:*

PERIODICALS

*Atlanta Journal-Constitution,* August 26, 2001, John Freeman, "On the Road of Many Rocky Relationships," p. F4.
*Booklist,* June 1, 2001, Bill Ott, review of *Honeymooners: A Cautionary Tale,* p. 1845.
*Choice,* March 1974, review of *Snakehunter,* p. 90.
*Kirkus Reviews,* May 15, 1979, review of *The Silver Ghost,* p. 593.
*Library Journal,* June 15, 1979, Samuel Simons, review of *The Silver Ghost,* p. 1358; June 1, 2001, Reba Leiding, review of *Honeymooners,* p. 217.
*New York Times Book Review,* November 18, 1973, Martin Levin, review of *Snakehunter,* p. 55; July 22, 2001, Jay McInerney, "*Honeymooners*: Please Say Who This Book Is About, Please."
*Publishers Weekly,* May 14, 1979, review of *The Silver Ghost,* p. 206; May 7, 2001, review of *Honeymooners,* p. 220.
*Review of Contemporary Fiction,* summer, 1992, Joan S. Boudreaux, review of *Snakehunter,* p. 223.

*San Francisco Chronicle,* June 28, 2002, David Kipen, "Profile; Chuck Kinder; Pulitzer Material; Writer Who Inspired Chabon's Prize-winning Novel about Writers Finally Publishes His Own about Writers," p. D1.
*Washington Post,* August 5, 2001, Jonathan Yardley, review of *Honeymooners.*
*Washington Post Book World,* December 23, 1973, review of *Snakehunter,* p. 4.

OTHER

*BookBrowser,* http://www.bookbrowser.com/ (December 2, 2001), review of *Honeymooners.*
*Moby Lives,* http://www.mobylives.com/ (February 8, 2002), Dennis Loy Johnson, "The Real Wonder Boy."
*University of Pittsburgh Department of English Web site,* http://www.english.pitt.edu/ (December 2, 2001), "Charles Kinder."*

\*     \*     \*

**KINDER, Chuck**
**See KINDER, Charles Alfonso II**

\*     \*     \*

**KING, J. Robert**

*PERSONAL:* Married; children: three sons. *Education:* Christ College, graduated, 1988.

*ADDRESSES: Home*—Burlington, WI. *Agent*—c/o Author Mail, Tor Books, 175 Fifth Ave., New York, NY 10010.

*CAREER:* Writer.

*MEMBER:* Alliterates.

*AWARDS, HONORS:* Origins Award, 1995, for *Dragonlance: Preludes 2: Planar Powers.*

*WRITINGS:*

ARTHURIAN FANTASY SERIES

*Mad Merlin,* Tor (New York, NY), 2000.
*Lancelot du Lethe,* Tor (New York, NY), 2001.

*"FORGOTTEN REALMS" FANTASY SERIES*

(With Brian M. Thomsen) *Realms of Magic,* Wizards of the Coast (Renton, WA), 1995.

*Realms of the Underdark,* Wizards of the Coast (Renton, WA), 1996.

(With Brian M. Thomsen) *Realms of the Arcane,* Wizards of the Coast (Renton, WA), 1997.

*"MAGIC, THE GATHERING" FANTASY SERIES*

*Invasion,* Wizards of the Coast (Renton, WA), 2000.

*Planeshift,* Wizards of the Coast (Renton, WA), 2001.

*Apocalypse,* Wizards of the Coast (Renton, WA), 2001.

*Artefacts,* Volume 3: *Time Streams,* Wizards of the Coast (Renton, WA), 1999.

*The Thran,* Wizards of the Coast (Renton, WA), 1999.

*The Secrets of Magic,* Wizards of the Coast (Renton, WA), 2002.

*Legions,* Wizards of the Coast (Renton, WA), 2003.

*OTHER FANTASY NOVELS*

*Ravenloft,* Volume 2: *Heart of Midnight,* Tor (New York, NY), 1992.

*Ravenloft: Carnival of Fear,* Tor (New York, NY), 1993.

*Rogues to Riches,* Tor (New York, NY), 1995.

*Dragonlance: Preludes II: Blood Hostages,* Wizards of the Coast (Renton, WA), 1996.

*Dragonlance: Preludes II: Abyssal Warriors,* Wizards of the Coast (Renton, WA), 1997.

*Dragonlance: Preludes II: Planar Powers,* Wizards of the Coast (Renton, WA), 1997.

*Dragonlance: Lost Legends,* Volume 1: *Vinas Solamnus,* Wizards of the Coast (Renton, WA), 1997.

*Onslaught,* Wizards of the Coast (Renton, WA), 2002.

*Scourge,* Wizards of the Coast (Renton, WA), 2003.

*OTHER*

(Editor) *Dragons of Magic,* Wizards of the Coast (Renton, WA), 2001.

*SIDELIGHTS:* J. Robert King is a fantasy novelist who states that his works deal with profound themes. He notes that theology, his major in college, introduced him to considerations of life's essential aspects. "In any culture, there are three foundational questions:

Why do I live? Who will I love? How will I die?," he told an interviewer in the *Valparaiso Theology Alumni/ae Newsletter.* "Theology addresses those questions." He added, "If you don't know why you live, no salary in the world can save you." In the same publication, he described his audience as "young spiritually-open students entering college and striving to understand the relationship between the sacred and the profane." He added: "Anybody who fits that profile should pick up one of my books. That's what they're all about"

King's publications include tales inspired by the Arthurian legends. *Mad Merlin,* the first of these novels, depicts the title character as a wizard who suffers from insanity and an inability to recall his own past. While raising Arthur, however, Merlin eventually begins to overcome his madness, and comes to a surprising recollection of his own past. Writing in *Voice of Youth Advocates,* Libby Bergstrom affirmed that *Mad Merlin* "has fully developed characters and plenty of action," and a *Library Journal* reviewer noted that the novel constitutes "an unusual blend of history and legend." A *Publishers Weekly* critic, meanwhile, declared that King "gives a distinctive and often agreeable spin to the story of Camelot." The same reviewer concluded that *Mad Merlin* "will appeal to those who like their Arthurian tales on the zany side."

*Lancelot du Lethe,* the second of King's Arthurian chronicles, concerns the knight who became King Arthur's greatest friend before betraying that trust by entering into a love affair with the king's wife, Queen Guinevere. A *Library Journal* reviewer praised *Lancelot du Lethe* as further evidence of King's "fresh approach to the Arthurian legend," and a *Publishers Weekly* critic, while contending that the book is "unfocused," conceded that King shows "flashes of brilliance."

King's other publications include entries in the *Ravenloft* series of fantasy tales. His contributions to the series include *Heart of Midnight,* in which the protagonist attempts to destroy his father, a werewolf. In another entry, *Carnival of Fear,* members of a carnival troupe attempt to uncover a murderer considered responsible for dozens of deaths. Marlyene E. Schwartz, writing in the *Kliatt Young Adult Paperback Book Guide,* described *Carnival of Fear* as an "interesting blend of fantasy and horror" and added that "the characters are interesting and diverse." A

*Publishers Weekly* reviewer also praised the novel, noting its "momentum" and its "simple but effective messages about the evils of scapegoating."

Another fantasy novel, *Rogues to Riches,* relates the escapades of two teenagers who attempt to hoodwink knights and rescue a princess held captive by a wicked witch. Hugh M. Flick, Jr., in a review for the *Kliatt Young Adult Paperback Book Guide,* called *Rogues to Riches* "an amusing fantasy tale," and a critic in *Locus* found the novel "cute, but sophomoric."

*BIOGRAPHICAL AND CRITICAL SOURCES:*

PERIODICALS

*Kliatt Young Adult Paperback Book Guide,* November, 1993, Marlyene E. Schwartz, review of *Ravenloft: Carnival of Fear,* p. 16; July, 1995, Hugh M. Flick, Jr., review of *Rogues to Riches,* p. 16.

*Library Journal,* June 15, 2000, review of *Mad Merlin,* p. 121; December, 2001, Jackie Cassada, review of *Lancelot du Lethe,* p. 181.

*Locus,* January, 1995, review of *Rogues to Riches,* p. 35.

*Publishers Weekly,* November 2, 1992, review of *Ravenloft,* Volume 2: *Heart of Midnight,* p. 67; June 14, 1993, review of *Ravenloft: Carnival of Fear,* p. 65; July 3, 2000, review of *Mad Merlin,* p. 53; November 19, 2001, review of *Lancelot du Lethe,* p. 52.

*Voice of Youth Advocates,* February, 2001, Libby Bergstrom, review of *Mad Merlin,* p. 433.

OTHER

*Alliterates,* http://www.alliterates.com/ (April 17, 2002).

*Valparaiso Theology Alumni/ae Newsletter,* http://www.valpo.edu/ (March, 2001), "Fantasy Novelist Alumnus."*

\*　　　\*　　　\*

## KOHANOV, Linda

*PERSONAL:* Married Steve Roach (a composer and musician).

*ADDRESSES: Home*—Tucson, AZ. *Office*—Epona Equestrian Services, 4551 North Oraibi Place, Tucson, AZ 85749. *E-mail*—eponaquest@ix.netcom.com.

*CAREER:* Public speaker, horse trainer and riding instructor, journalist, music critic, and radio producer and announcer. Epona Equestrian Services, Tucson, AZ, founder, 1997—.

*WRITINGS:*

*The Tao of Equus: A Woman's Journey of Healing and Transformation through the Way of the Horse,* New World Library (Novato, CA), 2001.

Contributor to periodicals, including *CD Review, Down Beat, JAZZIZ, Jazz Times, Pulse!,* and *New Age Journal.*

*SIDELIGHTS: The Tao of Equus: A Woman's Journey of Healing and Transformation through the Way of the Horse,* is Linda Kohanov's debut book describing her unique experiences working with horses. In addition to being a riding instructor, Kohanov is a horse trainer specializing in equine experimental learning and equine facilitated psychotherapy. Much of her research in this field is done through Epona Equestrian Services, a group Kohanov founded in 1997 in Tucson, Arizona. The aim of the group, which is a collective of riding instructors and counselors, is to determine the healing effects humans can experience through working with horses. The members of Epona also believe that relationships with horses can reduce stress, teach leadership and parenting skills, and foster creativity and even female empowerment. Kohanov explores many of these theories in *The Tao of Equus,* which also includes details about her own experiences working with horses and general information about members of the equine family.

Early in *The Tao of Equus,* Kohanov explains that the title means "the way of the horse." In her opinion, horses are highly evolved beings capable of communicating with humans on a spiritual level. Kohanov reveals that the impetus to write the book came while working with one of her hobbled horses, a black mare named Rosa. During this period, Kohanov admits to readers that she experienced a number of strange, paranormal dreams. In an effort to better understand Rosa, and what ailed her, Kohanov immersed herself into the daily activities of the animal and her other horses. In the process, she realized that horses share a number of characteristics with humans, including tremendous intelligence and intuition. Armed with this knowledge,

Kohanov began exploring how traumatized and unhappy people could benefit through bonding with the animals. She acknowledges that her methods may not be taken seriously, especially because of her discussion of her paranormal experiences. "I wouldn't be surprised if some people use elements of what I divulge in this book to try to discredit anything else I have to say about the potential of the horse-human relationship," she writes.

Despite her fears, the book received its share of favorable reviews. Mimi Pantelides of *BookPage.com* thought it was "insightful" and "a journey worth taking." Similarly, Ariele M. Huff in the *New Times* called the book "compelling and well written. A good entertainment book as well as an excellent source of inspiration and support." Even critics who tended to express uncertainty about the book's subject matter still praised Kohanov's writing ability. "Kohanov's tale will be greeted with skepticism by many readers, but her sure writing should turn a few of them into believers," wrote a contributor for *Publishers Weekly.*

*BIOGRAPHICAL AND CRITICAL SOURCES:*

PERIODICALS

*Publishers Weekly,* July 23, 2001, review of *The Tao of Equus: A Woman's Journey of Healing and Transformation through the Way of the Horse,* p. 62.

OTHER

*BookPage,* http://www.bookpage.com/ (April 12, 2002), Mimi Pantelides, review of *The Tao of Equus.*
*Epona Equestrian Services,* http://www.taoofequus.com/ (June 24, 2002).
*New Times,* http://www.newtimes.org/ (April 12, 2002), Ariele M. Huff, review of *The Tao of Equus.*
*New World Library Web site,* http://www.nwlib.com/ (April 29, 2002), biography of Linda Kohanov.*

*     *     *

**KRAMM, Joseph 1907-1991**

*PERSONAL:* Born September 30, 1907, in Philadelphia, PA; died May 8, 1991; married Isabel Bonner (an actress). *Education:* University of Pennsylvania, B.A., 1928.

*CAREER:* Actor, director, and playwright. Actor in stock company, Philadelphia, PA, 1928; Civic Repertory Theatre, Philadelphia, actor, 1929-35; actor with theatre companies, including Federal Theatre Project of the WPA, c. 1930s; acting teacher and director in New York City, beginning in 1946. Has performed in stage productions, including *Six o'Clock Theatre, Trojan Incident, Processional, Bury the Dead, Prelude, Alice in Wonderland, Dear Jane, Liliom, Two Seconds, Camille, Siegfried, Romeo and Juliet,* and *The Green Cockatoo. Military service:* U.S. Army, 1936-43.

*AWARDS, HONORS:* Pulitzer Prize, two Donaldson awards, and Page One Award, Newspaper Guild of Philadelphia, all 1952, all for *The Shrike.*

*WRITINGS:*

PLAYS

*The Cry of the Watchman,* first produced, 1947.
*The Shrike,* first produced, 1952.
(And director) *Giants, Sons of Giants,* first produced, 1962.

Also author of produced play *The Gypsies Wore High Hats.*

*SIDELIGHTS:* Philadelphia-born playwright, director and actor Joseph Kramm wrote several plays, including the Pulitzer Prize-winning *The Shrike.* Kramm chose theatre after his mother took him to plays when he was child, and acted throughout high school and college. He first worked professionally as an actor in 1928, for a Philadelphia stock company; by 1929 Kramm began a six-year stretch with the Civic Repertory Theatre, also in Philadelphia. He worked for various theatre companies in the 1930s, including the Federal Theatre Project of the Works Progress Administration. He also performed in several plays for the armed forces during World War II. After the war, Kramm headed for New York, where he acted in and, from 1946 on, directed many plays.

While Kramm had begun writing plays during the 1930s, his first successful work was *The Cry of the Watchman.* He made his mark, however, with *The Shrike* (1952), the drama of a man who attempts suicide to escape a domineering wife—a role actor José Ferrer starred in during the show's Broadway run. Among Kramm's other plays is *Giants, Sons of Giants.**

# L

## LALIĆ, Ivan V. 1931-1996

*PERSONAL:* Born June 8, 1931, in Belgrade, Yugoslavia; died of heart failure July 28, 1996; married; wife's name, Branka; children: Vlajko, Marko. *Education:* Received law degree in Zagreb, Croatia.

*CAREER:* Poet and translator. Radio Zagreb, correspondent, editor and senior editor, beginning 1955; Jugoslavija (publishing house), Belgrade, Yugoslavia, editor, beginning 1964; Nolit (publishing house), Belgrade, editor, 1979-93; Yugoslav Writers Union, general secretary, 1961-64, 1975-79.

*AWARDS, HONORS:* Yugoslavian Tribine Mladih prize, 1960; Yugoslavia Zmaj prize, 1961; Yugoslavia Branko Miljkovic Prize, 1985; *Pro litteris hungaricis,* 1970; Thornton Wilder Prize, 1990; British European Poetry Translation Prize, 1991; runner-up, British Comparative Literature Association Translation Awards, 1994.

*WRITINGS:*

*Bivši dečak* (title means "One-Time Schoolboy"), Lykos (Zagreb, Croatia), 1955.

*Vetrovito proleće* (title means "Windy Spring"), Drutvo knjievnica Hrvatske (Zagreb, Croatia), 1956.

*Velika vrata mora* (title means "Great Gate of the Sea"), Nolit (Belgrade, Yugoslavia), 1958.

(Editor, with Josip Pupačić) *Vrata vremena* (title means "The Door of Time"), Poslijeratni Jugoslavenski Pjesnici (Zagreb, Croatia), 1958.

*Melisa,* Lykos (Zagreb, Croatia), 1959.

*Argonauti i druge pesme* (title means "The Argonauts and Other Poems"), Naprijed (Zagreb, Croatia), 1961.

*Vreme, vatre, vrtovi* (title means "Time, Fire, Gardens"), Matica Srpska (Novi Sad, Yugoslavia), 1961.

*Čin* (title means "Act"), Prosveta (Belgrade, Yugoslavia), 1963.

*Istria and Kvarner* (title means "Istria and the Quamero"), Jugoslavija (Belgrade, Yugoslavia), 1966.

*Krug* (title means "Circle"), Nolit (Belgrade, Yugoslavia), 1968.

*Izabrane i nove pesme* (title means "Selected and New Poems"), Srpska književna zadruga (Belgrade, Yugoslavia), 1969, translated, edited, and with introduction by Francis R. Jones as *A Rusty Needle,* Anvil (London, England), 1996.

*Kritika i delo,* Nolit (Belgrade, Yugoslavia), 1971.

(Editor) *Milutin Bojić,* Narodna (Belgrade, Yugoslavia), 1974.

*Smetnje na vezama* (title means "Trouble on the Line"), Srpska književna zadruga (Belgrade, Yugoslavia), 1975, translated and with an introduction by Francis R. Jones as *Fading Contact,* Anvil (London, England), 1997.

(Editor) Aleksandar Spasov, *Studije, ogledi i kritike* (title means "Studies, Essays, and Criticism"), Narodna (Belgrade, Yugoslavia), 1978.

*O poeziji dvanaest pesnika* (title means "The Poetry of 12 Poets"), Slovo Ljubve (Belgrade, Yugoslavia), 1980.

*Strasna mera,* Nolit (Belgrade, Yugoslavia), 1984, portions translated by Francis R. Jones as *Last Quarter,* Anvil (London, England), 1987, entire book translated, and with introduction, by Francis R. Jones, as *The Passionate Measure,* Anvil (London, England), 1989.

*Pesme* (title means "Poems"), selected and with an introductory essay by S. Velmar-Jankovic, Prosveta (Belgrade, Yugoslavia), 1987, second enlarged edition, Prosveta (Belgrade, Yugoslavia), 1995.

*Vizantija,* Gradska biblioteka (Cacak, Yugoslavia), 1987.

*Pismo* (title means "Script"), Srpska Knjizevna Zadruga (Belgrade, Yugoslavia), 1992, second edition, 1993.

*Cetiri kanona* (title means "Four Canons"), Srpska Knjizevna Zadruga (Belgrade, Yugoslavia), 1996.

*TRANSLATOR*

K. Acz, *Pesme umesto tisine,* Prosveta (Belgrade, Yugoslavia), 1965.

Sandor Weores, *Preobrazenja,* Forum (Novi Sad, Yugoslavia), 1965.

*Antologija moderne francuske lirike* (title means "Modern American French Poetry"), Prosveta (Belgrade, Yugoslavia), 1966.

Pierre Jean Jouve, *Pesme,* Prosveta (Belgrade, Yugoslavia), 1967.

(And selector) Friedrich Hölderlin, *Odabrana dela,* Nolit (Belgrade, Yugoslavia), 1969.

(And selector, with Branka Lalić) *Antologija moderne americke poezije* (title means "Anthology of Modern American Poetry"), Prosveta (Belgrade, Yugoslavia), 1972.

Alfred Bosquet, *Beleske za jednu samocu,* Bagdala (Kragujevac), 1972.

Walt Whitman, *Vlati trave,* BIGZ (Belgrade, Yugoslavia), 1974.

(With others, and editor with B. Zivojinović) *Antologija nemacke lirike XX veka,* Nolit (Belgrade, Yugoslavia), 1976.

(And author of introductory essay) T. S. Eliot, *Izabrane pesme,* BIGZ (Belgrade, Yugoslavia), 1978.

(And editor) Silvije Strahimir Kranjcevic, *Pjesme,* Slovo Ljubve (Belgrade, Yugoslavia), 1978.

(And selector, with J. Ribnikar) Jaroslav Seifert, *Izabrane pesme,* Srpska Knjizevna Zadruga (Belgrade, Yugoslavia), 1984.

Charles Simic, *Avenija Amerika,* Knjievna Optina Vrac (Vrsac, Yugoslavia), 1992.

David Gascoyne, *Pesme,* Matica Srpska (Novi Sad, Yugoslavia), 1993.

(With Branka Lalić) Christopher Marlowe, *Tamerlan Veliki,* Srpska Knjizevna Zadruga (Belgrade, Yugoslavia), 1995.

*IN ENGLISH TRANSLATION*

*Fire Gardens,* selected and translated by C. W. Truesdale and Charles Simic, New Rivers Press, (New York, NY), 1970.

(Contributor) *Four Yugoslav Poets: Ivan V. Lalić, Brank Miljković, Milorad Pavić, Ljubomir Simović,* edited and translated by Charles Simic, Lillabulero (Northwood Narrows, NH), 1970.

*The Works of Love: Selected Poems of Ivan V. Lalić,* selected and translated, with an introductory essay, by Francis R. Jones, Anvil (London, England), 1981.

*Roll Call of Mirrors: Selected Poems of Ivan V. Lalić,* selected and translated by Charles Simic, Wesleyan University Press (Middletown, CT), 1989.

*OTHER*

*Majstor Hanuš* (radio play; title means "Master Hanuš"), LMS, 1965.

(And narrator, with others) *CD Poets 2* (sound recording), translated by Francis R. Jones, Bellew (London, England), 1995.

*SIDELIGHTS:* Ivan V. Lalić, considered one of the greatest poets of the former Yugoslavia, is also acknowledged worldwide as a master of formally rhymed and metered verse, as well as modernist blank verse. A major theme of his work is the value of memory. Still universally appealing, his poems are more poignant, given the cruel dissolution of his homeland in the 1990s.

Lalić, who was born in Belgrade, divided his youth between the city and his family's second home on the slopes of Mount Maljen, a few hours to the south. During World War II the Allied air raids on Belgrade during Easter 1944 were particularly traumatic for Lalić, who saw many school friends die. In 1946 his family moved to the Croatian capital of Zagreb, and soon after his mother died. Lalić, after graduating from high school, studied law at the university. During this time his poems began appearing in literary magazines, and in 1955 his first volume, *Bivši dečak,* was published.

In the opening poem of the volume, "Zardjala igla" ("A Rusty Needle"), Lalić attempts to reconcile the conflicting familial bliss and wartime horror of his youth. Recalling his nights on Mount Maljen, he writes, "Then I came to love the night, to love it for the wind teased / Through the dark needles . . . / . . . / When the wind was gone, the crickets remained, / And my mother's breath, . . . ." Of his classmate killed in Belgrade, he asks "Did they really come of age in an instant, just / Before they crumpled like poppies . . . ?" He answers: "I don't know. But I remained, to grow on / With their gaze in the nape of my neck, like / A rusty needle under the skin; but also, slowly, / To come to love the night and her soft stars again."

The early 1950s were crucial to Yugoslavian poetry as writers, primarily the academic *avante garde,* struggled to end the Communist Party's control over literature. In the late 1950s creativity blossomed in all genres of literature and a "second generation" of gifted Yugoslavian poets emerged. Lalić was neither an avante garde nor a bucolic lyric, the latter more popular with the public. His poetry conformed, rather, to the timeless style of controlled meter and rhyme. Still, by 1964 he had published seven volumes of poetry, won two of his country's major literary prizes, and been appointed general secretary of the Yugoslavian Writers Union.

In his early work, Lalić explored episodes and characters from classical, national and literary history. Francis R. Jones, who translated much of Lalić's work into English, wrote in the *Dictionary of Literary Biography* that Lalić saw history as "a network of threads that link one not only back to a personal and collective past but outward, to a wider geographical space than that of one's birth." "Smederevo," an early work reprinted in *Izabrane I nove pesme,* tells of the medieval Serbian soldiers who defended their last fortress against the unstoppable Ottoman invaders. The poem, like the rest of Lalić's historical works, emphasizes the personal rather than the political. The poem's narrator is an Everyman, waiting "beneath the indifferent stars," hoping "never to be forgotten." *Melisa* examines death and memory in an entire volume of hexameter sonnets based on the Greek legend of a woman, first torn to pieces for refusing to divulge the secrets of the goddess Demeter, and then turned into a swarm of bees by the grateful deity.

After *Melisa,* Lalić abandoned strict meter and rhyme for creative blank verse. His imagery became more spare and clearly defined, although his language remained musical. Though he changed his poetic form, Lalić was still devoted to historical and classical subjects. For *Izabrane i nove pesme,* Lalić wrote two cycles of poems, one around the city of Dubrovnik and one around Byzantium. Dubrovnic was the gateway to Western Europe, through which came the influence of the Italian Renaissance. Byzantium, which opened to the East, symbolized Yugoslavia's classical Grecian heritage. In his introduction to *Izabrane i nove pesme,* Jovan Hristic wrote of Byzantium, "It is a sign of our belonging to and participating in Mediterranean culture, the touchstone of all European Culture. . . . Byzantium is a route by which we can renew classical values in a way both completely natural and spontaneous."

*Smetnje na vezma* appeared in 1975, when the Yugoslavian Writers Union named Lalić general secretary a second time. Again he uses largely historical subjects, but with more of a personal touch. For instance, "Atos u pet Pevanja" ("Athos in Five Songs") is a five-poem cycle about Mt. Athos, the symbolic epicenter of the Greek Orthodox Church. Yet the poems are as contemporary, and about personal memory, as about the culture Mt. Athos represents. Bernard Johnson, in *Contemporary World Writers,* noted that, for Lalić, the act of "creating a verbal image of the poet's own reaction to a scene" was an element of his "self-imposed poetic task, of condensing the very essence of such beauty and thus enhancing its chance of survival." Indeed, in "Mnemosina" ("Mnemosyne"), a cycle dedicated to the Greek goddess of memory and mother of the muses, Lalić writes, "our task is to remember, . . . / The task of the peach is to blossom."

Jones wrote of *Strasna mera,* "Though culture and memory still exist as themes, there are no more historical tableaux: in the rudderless drift into disaster of the Yugoslavia of the 1980s, it is the present, not the past, that is under threat." Lalić, in "Poslednja cetvrt" ("Last Quarter"), warns that "the century is waning fast, making for / The delta, headlong down the slope."

During the late 1980s Lalić returned to formal meter and rhyme. *Pesme* contained a cycle of sonnets, "Deset Soneta nerodjenoj kceri" ("Ten Sonnets to an Unborn

Daughter"), and all poems in *Pismo* are in strict syllabic meter, most using complex rhyme schemes. In his final work, *Cetiri kanona,* he employed the Byzantine kanon form, a cycle of poetic meditations upon a selected set of biblical quotations.

Lalić died of heart failure after a brief illness in 1996. By then he had achieved international stature. Booklength volumes of his poetry had appeared in six languages and individual poems had been anthologized in more than twenty. Though his poetry plumbed all of Western civilization, it remained intensely personal. "My childhood and boyhood in the war," he once told Jones, "marked everything I ever wrote as a poem or poetry."

*BIOGRAPHICAL AND CRITICAL SOURCES:*

*BOOKS*

*Contemporary World Writers,* second edition, St. James (Detroit, MI), 1993.
*Dictionary of Literary Biography,* Volume 181: *South Slavic Writers since World War II,* Gale (Detroit, MI), 1997, pp. 142-149.
Mikasinovich, Branko, *Proceedings: Pacific Northwest Conference on Foreign Languages,* edited by Walter C. Kraft, Oregon State University (Corvallis, OR), 1972, pp. 217-221.

*PERIODICALS*

*Comparative Criticism,* Volume 16, 1994, pp. 105-125.
*Tracks,* Volume 2, 1982, pp. 31-34.*

\* \* \*

**LANCASTER, Lynne C.**

*PERSONAL:* Married; children: (stepchildren) two. *Education:* University of Minnesota, B.A. (summa cum laude).

*ADDRESSES: Home*—Sonoma, CA. *Office*—P. O. Box 1637, 19201 Seventh St. East, Sonoma, CA 95476-5819. *E-mail*—info@generations.com.

*CAREER:* Lancaster Consulting Group, president; writer. Co-founder, BridgeWorks. Member of adjunct faculty, University of Minnesota.

*WRITINGS:*

(With David Stillman) *When Generations Collide: Who They Are, Why They Clash, How to Solve the Generational Puzzle at Work,* HarperCollins (New York, NY), 2002.

Contributor to newspapers and periodicals, including *Futurist, Los Angeles Times, Minneapolis Star Tribune, National Business Review,* and *Nation's Business.* With David Stillman, author of column "Generations," *Twin Cities Business Monthly.*

*SIDELIGHTS:* Lynne C. Lancaster is a business consultant who serves as president of the Lancaster Consulting Group and teaches at the University of Minnesota. With David Stillman, she founded Bridge-Works, a consulting firm designed to address generational differences in business and the work environment. "Lancaster initially was a career counselor for Stillman, who previous worked in the high-tech field," noted a writer in *Entrepreneur.* "They started becoming friends and learning something about each other's age groups along the way." The writer added that Lancaster, when asked which of the team held "better values," responded: "Neither one of us. They're just different."

Lancaster eventually teamed with Stillman in writing *When Generations Collide: Who They Are, Why They Clash, How to Solve the Generational Puzzle at Work,* which discusses issues that result as a consequence of cross-generational interaction. In the book, Lancaster and Stillman divide the workforce into four generations: Traditionalists, born before the end of World War II, constitute the oldest generation, and they are characterized by their desire to establish individual legacies; Baby Boomers, born between 1946 and 1964, are either peaking professionally or preparing for early retirement; Generation Xers, born between 1965 and 1980, fill the voids left by departing Baby Boomers but show less inclination to make the same personal sacrifices that mark the professional devotion shown by the two preceding generations; and Millennials, born between 1981 and 1999, who will enter the workforce as subordinates to Xers and demonstrate a keen desire to maintain employment in an increasingly competitive business world.

Lancaster and Stillman contend that the forthcoming mix of individuals from widely divergent generations will likely constitute a remarkable period in American business. In addition, as a writer in *Community Banker* observed, Lancaster and Stillman believe that "different approaches appeal to different age generations because of their differing experiences and world views," and they caution "against lumping potential customers and applying one marketing campaign, offending and excluding some while attracting others."

*When Generations Collide* has been acknowledged as a valuable analysis of the American workforce. In *Futurist,* the book won recognition for its "insights into the value differences underlying [generational] conflicts," and in *Library Journal,* reviewer Richard Drezen deemed it "a book every corporate human resources department would want on the bookshelf." A *Publishers Weekly* critic, however, charged Lancaster and Stillman with dangerous stereotyping and concluded that they "disappoint in failing to supply specifics for what to do about [generational] differences." *Booklist* reviewer Brad Hooper, meanwhile, ranked *When Generations Collide* among "outstanding business books" and hailed it as "wise and personable." Another enthusiast, Josh Hafetz, wrote in the *Washington Business Forward* that "Lancaster and Stillman have taken what could have been yet another dry workplace advice book and transformed it into a lively read about a subject with implications stretching far beyond the world of cubicles and casual Fridays. In the end, what Lancaster and Stillman preach above all is a mix of open communication, accommodation and a drive for mutual understanding."

Lancaster and Stillman also collaborate in writing "Generations," a column that appears in *Twin Cities Business Monthly.*

*BIOGRAPHICAL AND CRITICAL SOURCES:*

*PERIODICALS*

*Booklist,* November 1, 2001, Brad Hooper, review of *When Generations Collide: Who They Are, Why They Clash, How to Solve the Generational Puzzle at Work,* p. 450.

*Community Banker,* December, 2000, "Generational Customer Service Tips."
*Futurist,* March-April, 2002, review of *When Generations Collide,* p. 59.
*Library Journal,* December, 2001, Richard Drezen, review of *When Generations Collide,* p. 140.
*Publishers Weekly,* November 19, 2001, review of *When Generations Collide,* p. 54.

OTHER

*Entrepreneur,* http://entrepreneur.com/ (May 13, 2002).
*Washington Business Forward,* http://bizforward.com/ (May 13, 2002), Josh Hafetz, "Clashpoint."*

\*    \*    \*

**LAWRENCE, Rae**
    **See LIEBMAN, Ruth**

\*    \*    \*

**LAWSON, Nigella 1960-**

*PERSONAL:* Born 1960; daughter of Nigel (former conservative chancellor) and Vanessa (Salmon) Lawson; married John Diamond (deceased), 1989; children: Cosima, Bruno. *Education:* Graduated from Oxford University.

*ADDRESSES: Home*—227 Golhawk Rd., Shepherd's Bush, London W12 8ER, England.

*CAREER:* Journalist. *Spectator,* columnist, 1985; *Sunday Times,* deputy literary editor, 1986; columnist for *Observer,* and *Times;* host of television shows, including *Nigella Bites.*

*WRITINGS:*

*Il Museo Immaginario della Pasta,* U. Alle mandi (Turin, Italy), 1995, translated by Ros Schwartz as *The Musee of Pasta.*
*How to Eat: The Pleasures and Principles of Good Food,* John Wiley (New York, NY), 2000.

*How to Be a Domestic Goddess: Baking and the Art of Comfort Cooking,* Chatto & Windus (London, England), 2000, Hyperion (New York, NY), 2002.

SIDELIGHTS: Nigella Lawson, who grew up as the daughter of Britain's Chancellor of the Exchequer, has had a somewhat privileged, but bumpy, life. She struggled in school, but ended up graduating from Oxford University. From there she went on to be a columnist for several publications. Not only has she made her mark in the written world, but has laid her sights on the small screen. She has hosted several cooking shows in the UK, and now is known in the States for her show, *Nigella Bites.* Chris Jones with *BBC News* stated, "Writer and TV cook Nigella Lawson has the talent, looks and success to attract the envy of millions." In an interview with Jones, Lawson stated, "food is a narcotic." It is this passion she has for food that has catapulted her to the top of the culinary world. It is not that she has any new, earth shattering recipes, but her sheer indulgence and delight in every morsel of what she prepares captivates viewers.

Overweight and insecure at one time, Lawson has evolved into a self-assured, talented success. Her husband, John Diamond's last words to her before his death were, "How proud I am of you and what you have become," according to Jones' article. Jones continued, "Diamond opened her eyes to her full potential." Diamond's death was not Lawson's only loss to cancer. She also lost her mother and sister, Thomasina. Jones stated, "The brightest light and darkest shade of Nigella Lawson's life has taught her to make the most of her many talents." As Lawson stated to Jones, "I suppose I do think that awful things can happen at any moment, so while they are not happening you may as well be pleased."

Lawson's 2000 book was *How To Eat.* Suzanne Moore wrote in *New Statesman* that "*How To Eat* was a lovely book and contains her best writing." Moore went on to discuss how Lawson's articles on current affairs seem reasonable, but when she begins to speak or write about food, "she goes into drool mode and provides knowledgeable and chatty commentary about food culture. She comes across as a fan, which is always endearing." Victoria Clarke in *Spectator* stated that Lawson's "book is fabulously chatty with a wealth of personal and family detail, the language oozing and

unctuous." Clarke noted that the recipes in the books are laid out as menus rather than by ingredients, which leads readers to use the impressive index quite often. "Nothing is too complicated or fussy, all the timing is accurate, and there are even instructions for order and companionship in the oven." David Sexton in the *Times Literary Supplement* observed that "there is a great eater speaking. . . . There are lots of verbal feasts in which adjectives of sensation in the mouth have been attached to the food itself." Sexton continued, "Her food is all about such feelings of security, comfort and solidity." Clarke was enamored with Lawson's chapter titled "Low Fat," noting that "the mouth-watering recipes are charmingly described as 'Templefood,' very attractive to the potential healthy eater." Clarke finished her review of *How To Eat* by stating "I believe Nigella Lawson may have come up with the domestic bible for the millennium generation. I do not use the word cookbook, as this is something more. It is not just about 'how to eat,' but how seriously to enjoy the food that fuels our bodies."

In *How to Be a Domestic Goddess,* Lawson explains how to cook to bring out your personality, not necessarily your culinary expertise. She makes it quite clear that this book is not about keeping you in the kitchen, but enjoying the creating of food and sharing it with those you love. Bee Wilson in the *Times Literary Supplement* wrote, "the book consists of a collection of recipes for breads, cakes, pies, biscuits and other baked goods, with paragraphs of recommendation in between. . . . descriptions of the food are style-conscious and opinionated." In an interview with Harriet Lane with *Guardian Unlimited,* Lawson stated, "food is better left to its own devices. . . . things do go wrong in cooking, and generally, you can live with them." Lawson explained to Lane how she used green food coloring for the lime-curd filling on one of her cakes for the photo in the book, and she lamented that action as "the cake does look fairly unappetizing—the sort of thing Morticia Addams might have whipped up." Lane commented, "it offers the cheering knowledge that cookery writers have off days, too." "Cooking is not a precise art," Lawson said in the interview. "There's a science that dictates what happens to certain ingredients at certain temperatures, but nevertheless you can't have absolute control over the outcome. You have enough control to be interested, but you're allowing yourself to dabble in the chaos, dip your foot into it without feeling there's a risk of drowning in it."

## BIOGRAPHICAL AND CRITICAL SOURCES:

*PERIODICALS*

*New Statesman,* June 25, 2001, Suzanne Moore, "Pure Oral Fantasy," p. 50; December 18, 2000, Bee Wilson, "Fatuous Foodies," p. 54.

*Spectator,* October 31, 1998, Victoria Clarke, "Inspiring an Unholy Greed," p. 48; November 11, 2000, Digby Anderson, "The Morality of the Omelette," pp. 60-61.

*Times Literary Supplement,* November 27, 1998, David Sexton, "Pudding's Proof," p. 6; December 8, 2000, Bee Wilson, "Angel Cakes," p. 27.

*OTHER*

*BBC News Web site,* http://news.bbc.co.uk/ (July 19, 2002), Chris Jones, "Nigella Lawson: A Sweet and Sour Life."

*Guardian Unlimited,* http://books.guardian.co.uk/ (April 16, 2002), Harriet Lane, "An Angel at Our Table."*

\*   \*   \*

## LAW-YONE, Wendy 1947-

*PERSONAL:* Born in Mandalay, Burma (now Myanmar), April 1, 1947; daughter of Edward Law-Yone; married an American journalist (divorced, 1975), second marriage to Charles A. O'Connor III (an attorney); children: twins from first marriage, two children from second marriage. *Education:* Eckerd College, St. Petersburg, FL, B.A., 1975.

*ADDRESSES: Agent*—c/o Author Mail, Random House, 299 Park Ave., New York, NY 10171-0002.

*CAREER:* Writer for *Washington Post,* Washington, DC, 1975.

*WRITINGS:*

*Company Information, a Model Investigation,* Washington Researchers (Washington, DC), 1980.

*The Coffin Tree,* Beacon Press (Boston, MA), 1983.

*Irrawaddy Tango: A Novel,* Knopf (New York, NY), 1993.

*SIDELIGHTS:* Wendy Law-Yone was born in Mandalay, but was raised in Rangoon. Law-Yone's father was a political activist as well as a newspaper publisher, which caused many problems for the family, leading to his arrest in 1962. A myriad of events followed his arrest and imprisonment, including Law-Yone's own capture and detainment in 1967. She was released two weeks later, after which she fled to Southeast Asia, where she resided until moving to the States in 1973. It was in America where she was able to leave her tumultuous past behind and forge ahead as a successful journalist and writer.

Law-Yone's first novel was titled *The Coffin Tree.* A reviewer from *Voices from the Gaps* described the book as "a remarkable depiction of the fears, rootlessness, and alienation of recent immigrants to this country." Although *The Coffin Tree* is a fictional story, it is clear that Law-Yone hones in on some of her own experiences of being displaced from a country who "disowned" her, and coming to a country where foreigners are often ostracized. The reviewer noted that "Law-Yone's skillful characterization in this novel allows readers to develop an empathy with the narrator and . . . experience first-hand the indifference, or utter cruelty of an American society ill-equipped to deal with difference." The book is about a young woman who is brought up by a bitter and insane grandmother, as well as two flaky aunts, due to the absence of her father. Her father is off fighting for leftist political causes, which eventually lead to him becoming a target of the same party he worked to build up. Due to this, the family is sent to the hills to hide out for many years until a coup occurs. To keep the narrator and her half-brother, Shan, out of danger, they are sent off to America with no money and only one phone number, from which they only get a recording. The rest of the book chronicles the events that lead to Shan's eventual death and the narrator's insanity. The narrator tells the book from the mental hospital ward, as she relives the memories from her lifetime she has worked so hard to shut out. "In a crisp, no-nonsense style that contrasts effectively with her melancholy subject matter, Ms. Law-Yone describes the lonely bewilderment of a young Burmese woman." Edith Milton in the *New York Times* explained that *The Coffin Tree* discovers "a more universal despair and pain, perseverance and adjustment, in their exploration disruption and personal isolation." It "combines the exquisite palpability of dreams with an earthy sense of irony," Milton continued, "this is, in fact, a novel about madness—not just the hospitalized, contained madness . . . but the universal unreason that casts its heavy shadows over the narrator's childhood." Laura Marcus with the *Times Literary Supplement* noted that "The narrator's problems can begin to seem a little overdetermined." Marcus wrote that "*The Coffin Tree* has too much of the feel and structure of an autobiography." Nancy Forbes of *Nation* stated, "The caricatures of family members are often too intense to be comic." Forbes is touched by the narrator's memories of her mother and believes that in the narrator's recollection "all these people shimmer in the high relief of a child's perception." Although Forbes found Law-Yone's writing style a bit "choppy," she said that she "writes with a cool sense of incongruity. . . . it's one of her many gifts, which, taken together, promise much for the future."

Over ten years later Law-Yone delivered her second novel, titled *Irrawaddy Tango*. In this book she writes of a young girl called Tango, who is named such for her skill at performing the dance. When performing in a talent contest she is spotted by an official who quickly woos her and they marry shortly after. She spends several years under his rule, as he takes over the country known as Daya, until one day she is captured by rebel forces. She ends up being a voice for their cause, and disowned by her husband. Her days with the rebel leader do not last long either, as she ends up being shipped off to America, where she faces a cruel existence. While in America she marries a citizen who ultimately perishes at her psychotic hands. The theme of this book, much like Law-Yone's first work, is how the perils in life can cause wounds so deep, they ultimately lead to psychosis. Renee Hausmann Shea in *Belles Lettres* spoke of Tango's torment, stating, "For nearly 50 years, men alternately are the means and reason for her abuse, imprisonment, rescue and vengeance." Hausmann commended the book, writing, "A skillful stylist, Law-Yone weaves a narrative of time shifts, dreams, and madness." *Booklist*'s David Cline noted that "Law-Yone's prose, while developing a frighteningly familiar scenario, is delightful and witty, and Tango is a lively, smart wisecracker who, despite the gravity of her world, keeps us laughing." Jacqueline Trescott in *Washington Post* stated that *Irrawaddy Tango* "is the internal battle of reserving and then releasing self-revelations."

In an interview with Trescott, Law-Yone explained that in Asian countries, "The self is not important, it is the community that is important." Her novel shows how that mindset can send someone spiraling into the quagmire of self-hatred and discontent due to denying the needs of the individual. "It takes a certain kind of introspection to be an interesting character," she added. Shashi Tharoor in the *Washington Post Book World* stated that *Irrawaddy Tango* "is clearly the work of an exceptional talent." He noted, though, that "the novel seems to be building up to an intriguing climax. But it is kept in abeyance, and the narrative goes astray." He finished his review on a positive note, however, stating, "Law-Yone's intimate evocations of place and mood convey a palpable sense of experience relived." Trescott concluded that "the story moves quickly from a coming-of-age saga to a chase." A critic for *Publishers Weekly* wrote that "the novel's final section is gripping, but the bulk of it reads like a first draft." While noting that "Tango's first-person narration quickly wears thin," the critic added, "Law-Yone tackles a worthy theme the inevitable, destructive alienation felt by thoughtful Third World exiles both abroad and at home."

## BIOGRAPHICAL AND CRITICAL SOURCES:

*PERIODICALS*

*Atlantic,* June, 1983, Phoebe-Lou Adams, review of *The Coffin Tree,* p. 105.

*Belles Lettres,* summer, 1994, Renee Hausmann Shea, "Perigrinations of the Rebel Queen," p. 17.

*Booklist,* February 1, 1994, David Cline, review of *Irrawaddy Tango,* p. 995.

*Nation,* April 30, 1983, Nancy Forbes, "Burmese Days," p. 551.

*New York Times,* May 15, 1983, Edith Milton, "Newcomers in New York," p. 12.

*Publishers Weekly,* November 22, 1993, review of *Irrawaddy Tango,* p. 48.

*Times Literary Supplement,* March 9, 1984, Laura Marcus, "Ghosts on the Ward," p. 252.

*Washington Post,* March 16, 1994, Jacqueline Trescott, "Tango of Emotions," p. C1.

*Washington Post Book World,* Shashi Taroor, "The Most Dangerous Dance," pp. 1, 10.

*OTHER*

*Voices from the Gaps,* http://voices.cla.umn.edu (April 16, 2002).*

## LAZARUS, Richard S(tanley) 1922-2002

*OBITUARY NOTICE*—See index for *CA* sketch: Born March 3, 1922, in New York, NY; died following a fall November 24, 2002, in Walnut Creek, CA. Psychologist, educator, and author. As a psychologist, Lazarus was noted for his research into human emotions, particularly in the areas of stress and coping. He earned his undergraduate degree from City College of the City University of New York in 1942, and his doctorate, after serving in the U.S. Army during World War II, from the University of Pittsburgh in 1948. Lazarus's first job was at Johns Hopkins University, where he was an assistant professor from 1948 to 1953; during the mid-1950s, he was associate professor and director of clinical training at Clark University. The rest of his academic career was spent at the University of California, Berkeley, where he was a professor from 1957 until his retirement in 1991. In an era when B. F. Skinner's ideas on behaviorism were gaining wide acceptance among psychologists, Lazarus went against the grain in his belief that human behavior cannot be reduced to minimalist ideas such as anticipation of reward or punishment. Instead, he argued that human beings are much more complex, that their behavior can not be fully understood simply by analyzing the makeup of the brain, and that emotions are a valid and key part of who we are. He backed up his theories with research on how people cope with stress, discovering that those who are more realistic about their problems are often subject to greater feelings of depression and hopelessness, which can lead to their being at greater risk of illness, while those who allow themselves to be uplifted by hope and optimism are more capable of dealing with dire problems. Although he acknowledged that people should not be entirely unrealistic—for example, they should seek a doctor's help if ill—he believed positive emotions have a definite benefit for people's health. Lazarus wrote about his findings in many books he authored or edited, among them *Adjustment and Personality* (1961; third edition, 1976), *Stress, Appraisal, and Coping* (1984), and *Stress and Emotion: A New Synthesis* (1999). He also shared his knowledge of psychology as an investigator on stress for the U.S. Air Force in the early 1950s and for the U.S. Public Health Service. For his work he received a Guggenheim fellowship in 1989 and was awarded the Distinguished Scientific Contribution to Psychology Award from the American Psychological Association.

*OBITUARIES AND OTHER SOURCES:*

BOOKS

*Writers Directory,* 17th edition, St. James Press (Detroit, MI), 2002.

PERIODICALS

*Los Angeles Times,* December 8, 2002, p. B20.
*New York Times,* December 16, 2002, p. A29.
*Washington Post,* December 9, 2002, p. B7.

\*     \*     \*

## LEAHY, Donna 1961-

*PERSONAL:* Born May 15, 1961; married Robert Leahy (a professor and photographer). *Hobbies and other interests:* Cooking.

*ADDRESSES: Office*—Inn at Twin Linden, 2092 Main St., Narvon, PA 17555.

*CAREER:* Innkeeper, chef, and writer.

*AWARDS, HONORS:* Best Cookbook of 2003, *Bed and Breakfast Journal,* for *Recipe for a Country Inn: Fine Food from the Inn at Twin Linden.*

*WRITINGS:*

*Morning Glories: Recipes for Breakfast, Brunch, and Beyond from an American Country Inn,* photography by husband, Robert Leahy, and Jerry Orabona, Rizzoli (New York, NY), 1996.
(Compiler) *Wisdom of the Plain Folk: Songs and Prayers from Amish and Mennonites,* photographs by R. Leahy, Penguin Studio (New York, NY), 1997.
*Recipe for a Country Inn: Fine Food from the Inn at Twin Linden,* photographs by R. Leahy, Morrow (New York, NY), 2002.

*SIDELIGHTS:* In her life before innkeeping, Donna Leahy was a self-employed video producer whose hobby was tending to a bed and breakfast on the coast of Maine. But that was just practice. When she and husband Bob decided to find an inn they could also call home, they traveled west and found just that, in a small town outside Philadelphia called Churchtown. Today the Leahys own and operate the Inn at Twin Linden, an establishment known for its luxurious yet homey atmosphere, friendly owners, and above all, delicious fine food.

Leahy's experience at the Inn was the catalyst for the writing and publishing of her cookbooks. The first, *Morning Glories: Recipes for Breakfast, Brunch and Beyond from an American Inn,* was published in 1996. That was followed closely by *Wisdom of the Plain Folk: Songs and Prayers from Amish and Mennonites.* The book was inspired by the culture which surrounds Leahy. Churchtown is located in Lancaster County, the heart of Pennsylvania Amish country.

Leahy's third book, *Recipe for a Country Inn: Fine Food from the Inn at Twin Linden,* is the culmination of years of adventurous cooking. The book contains 125 recipes as well as an informal behind-the-scenes look at the history and day-to-day running of the inn. In an interview with Barbara Hough Roda of the Lancaster *Sunday News,* Leahy explained that this most recent venture into publishing is her life story. With no formal culinary training or experience, Leahy armed herself with food magazines and cookbooks and set to work, learning by doing, undoing, and overdoing. "I start out with really good ingredients and high quality. I try to get the best of everything," she told Roda. Dishes served at the inn and presented in *Recipe for a Country Inn* take diners from morning to night. The dishes are simple, yet elegant, designed to make people feel special. According to reviewer Judith Sutton, Leahy is successful in this area. "Leahy's highly readable, engaging style reflects the warmth and hospitality that have contributed to the success of the inn," she wrote in *Library Journal.*

Photographs enhance the book's appeal, thanks to Leahy's husband. His work also gives the Inn character and atmosphere, as it is displayed on the walls throughout. Although Bob doesn't photograph food, his slices-of-life from the nearby countryside and portraits of Amish folk give *Recipe for a Country Inn* a personal touch that was acknowledged by critics.

"Husband Robert Leahy's striking photographs of local scenery and Amish and Mennonite neighbors supply an intimate portrait of a weekend in the country," said a review in *Publishers Weekly.*

More than a mere cookbook, *Recipe for a Country Inn* is riddled with sidebars and mini-essays that address issues pertinent to running a successful inn. These "Notes from the Inn" include essays such as "The Difficult Guest" and "Rising with the Chickens." Readers are taken into the confidences of these innkeepers and learn not only the highlights of the lifestyle but also the challenges that confront them on a daily basis. Leahy explained this approach on the HarperCollins Web site: "I felt that sharing my personal view of innkeeping is the best way to have my reader share the experience. I want the readers to feel as if they are living through the process of opening the inn with me and learn first-hand what my life as innkeeper is like—I want them to feel they are part of the moment."

Leahy has appeared on CBS and NBC morning talk shows, where she used her recipes to delight staffers and hosts alike. Leahy was also featured in a James Beard Foundation cooking series on country inn chefs held in New York.

## BIOGRAPHICAL AND CRITICAL SOURCES:

### PERIODICALS

*Library Journal,* March 15, 2002, Judith Sutton, review of *Recipe for a Country Inn: Fine Food from the Inn at Twin Linden,* p. 103.

*Publishers Weekly,* January 21, 2002, review of *Recipe for a Country Inn,* p. 83.

*Sunday News* (Lancaster, PA), April 28, 2002, Barbara Hough Roda, "A Chef Who's in the Know; Donna Leahy's New Book Sheds Light on the Life of an Innkeeper."

### OTHER

*HarperCollins Web site,* http://www.harpercollins.com/ (June 4, 2002), synopsis of *Recipe for a Country Inn* and interview with author.

*Inn at Twin Linden Web site,* http://wwwinnattwinlinden.com/ (June 4, 2002), author's Web site.

*WritersWrite,* http://www.writerswrite.com/ (June 4, 2002), review of *Recipe for a Country Inn.**

## LEBERT, Stephan 1961-

*PERSONAL:* Born 1961; son of Norbert Lebert (a journalist). *Education:* Attended German Journalism School (Munich, Germany).

*ADDRESSES: Agent*—c/o Publicity Director, Little, Brown, 1271 Avenue of the Americas, New York, NY 10020.

*CAREER:* Journalist and author. Worked for *Süddeutsche Zeitung* and *Der Spiegel*; *Berliner Tagesspiegel*, Berlin, Germany, editor-in-chief, 1999—.

*WRITINGS:*

(With Norbert Lebert) *Denn du trägst meinen Namen: das schwere Erbe der prominenten Nazi-Kinder*, K. Blessing (Munich, Germany), 2000, English translation by Julian Evans published as *My Father's Keeper: The Children of the Nazi Leaders—An Intimate History of Damage and Denial*, Little, Brown (Boston, MA), 2001.

*SIDELIGHTS:* Stephen Lebert, was made known to American readers with the publication of *My Father's Keeper: The Children of the Nazi Leaders—An Intimate History of Damage and Denial*, coauthored by his father, Norbert Lebert. The book is based on a number of interviews that the senior Lebert conducted forty years earlier with the children of former high-ranking Nazi officials from Germany's Third Reich. After his father's death in 1993, Stephan, also a journalist, found the manuscripts from the 1959 interviews, which originally had been published in 1961 as a series in the magazine *Zeitbild*. "When I discovered my father's typescript about the Nazi children among other piles of papers in his work room," he wrote in *My Father's Keeper*, "it didn't take long for the idea to form: the idea that I would search out these people once more, forty years later, those who were still alive and were willing to meet their former interviewer's son."

With the exception of Gudrun Himmler, the daughter of Heinrich Himmler, and Hermann Göring's daughter Edda, everyone agreed to the second round of interviews. Most interviewees felt sympathy for their Nazi fathers and some nostalgia for Germany's Nazi past. Stephan Norbert then juxtaposed his interviews with those his father had conducted to create a book many American literary critics have praised. "This is a powerful book, masterfully conceived, brilliant and devastating," a contributor to *Publishers Weekly* wrote.

*My Father's Keeper* was first published in Germany in 2000. In addition to the interviews, the book also includes twenty black-and-white photographs. American critics praised the volume for making readers ponder larger questions about life. "It isn't often that a book can work its way into the minds and souls of its readers and ask them to pose their own questions," Marc P. Smith wrote in *Forward*. Sandy Asirvatham, who reviewed the book for the *Baltimore City Paper Online*, called it "a fascinating, chilling 'insider' account of Germany's violent past and haunted present."

*BIOGRAPHICAL AND CRITICAL SOURCES:*

*PERIODICALS*

*Booklist*, August, 2001, George Cohen, review of *My Father's Keeper: Children of Nazi Leaders—An Intimate History of Damage and Denial*, p. 2081.
*Contemporary Review*, November, 2001, review of *My Father's Keeper*, p. 316.
*Publishers Weekly*, July 30, 2001, review of *My Father's Keeper*, p. 75.

*OTHER*

*Baltimore City Paper Online*, http://www.citypaper. com/ (January 30, 2002), Sandy Asirvatham, review of *My Father's Keeper: Children of Nazi Leaders—An Intimate History of Damage and Denial*, October 17-23, 2001.
*Forward: Arts and Letters*, http://www.forward.com/ (September 14, 2001), Marc P. Smith, "Reckoning the Sins of the Fathers, the Suffering of the Daughters."
*Jewsweek*, http://www.jewsweek.com/ (January 30, 2002), review of *My Father's Keeper*.
*Learning from History*, http://history.zkm.de/news/ (January 30, 2002), "For You Bear My Name."
*Time Warner Bookmark*, http://www.twbookmark.com/ (January 1, 2002), author profile of Stephan Lebert.*

## LEE, Helie 1964-

*PERSONAL:* Born 1964, in Seoul, South Korea; immigrated to the United States, 1969; daughter of Jae Hak (an electrical engineer) and Lily (a homemaker) Lee; married Peter Yum (a special-effects film editor), 2002. *Education:* Attended University of Santa Barbara; University of California-Los Angeles, graduated, 1986.

*ADDRESSES: Home*—Los Angeles, CA. *Office*—c/o Harmony Books Publicity, 1745 Broadway, New York, NY 10019.

*CAREER:* Writer. Lectures on North Korean history and politics at colleges and universities.

*WRITINGS:*

*Still Life with Rice: A Young American Woman Discovers the Life and Legacy of Her Korean Grandmother,* Scribner (New York, NY), 1996.
*In the Absence of Sun: A Korean American Woman's Promise to Reunite Three Lost Generations of Her Family,* Harmony Books (New York, NY), 2002.

*SIDELIGHTS:* When Helie Lee and her family immigrated to Los Angeles while Helie was still a preschooler, she had no idea of the family that was left behind in Korea. Lee was a typical five-year-old, interested in friends and school and having fun. Her family settled in a community primarily comprised of Caucasian Jewish Americans, and she told *People*'s Galina Espinoza: "My parents said you can be anything you want in America. I really wanted to be a white Jewish girl." She went so far as to bleach her black hair blonde, learn to ska to the music of the Police, and Scotch-tape her eyes to crease the lids. She did not want to be Korean; she wanted to be "American." Her past was nothing but the past to her then. It wasn't until after graduation, at which time Lee felt her life lacked direction, that she discovered the life she left behind all those years ago. "My eyes opened for the first time," she told *Chimes Online* writer Joo Eun Kim. Her experiences resulting from that first trip are the subject of her first book, *Still Life with Rice: A Young American Woman Discovers the Life and Legacy of Her Korean Grandmother.*

The book, which is a fictionalized account of Lee's actual journey, begins with Lee's visit to Korea. Once back in Los Angeles, Lee recorded her grandmother's life on paper. This life, complete with all the hardships integral to an oppressed wartime culture, is brought to life through documentation of events both great and small. Gretchen Dent reviewed *Still Life with Rice* for *Bookshelf,* and wrote, "The whole book, from the opium smuggling to the punishing wartime flight across the country, was very interesting. Sometimes a touch too melodramatic, sometimes shockingly callous, the character is always compelling."

Lee gives readers much to digest in the novel. Hongyong Baek, her grandmother, survives the tumultuous times of the Japanese occupation and the division of North and South Korea. She grows into womanhood in a time of intense male dominance, when female identity is severely suppressed. Hongyong's willful spirit keeps her alive as her family escapes the Japanese and immigrates to China, where they encounter great prosperity. Hongyong becomes ill and seeks help in the city's foreign hospital. The doctors are unable to help her, so she teaches herself the ancient practice of ch'iryo, in which one beats the area around the heart to the point of bruising. This is said to improve circulation. This lesson—that Western culture cannot feed the Korean soul—is one of the themes of *Still Life with Rice.* Hongyong eventually returns to Korea after 36 years of Japanese occupation has ended, and in 1972 she immigrates to the United States to be with her family.

Lee uses the novel to explore the generation gap between her and her beloved grandmother. By writing about her experiences with this relationship, Lee acknowledges the symbolism in many of the behaviors of her grandmother, and she comes to appreciate the meaning behind the rituals. In the end, the novel is a sort of coming-of-age story, only one that involves embracing and accepting one's past in order to move into the future with dignity and a sense of self. *Booklist* contributor Mary Ellen Quinn noted the novel was "written with great narrative power and attention to detail," while a *Publishers Weekly* critic called it "a captivating memoir of a courageous survivor."

Lee's second book, *In the Absence of Sun: A Korean-American Woman's Promise to Reunite Three Lost Generations of Her Family,* is a continuation of Hongyong's life. When she left North Korea, Hongyong left behind one son, sixteen-year-old Lee Yong Woon. Forty-one years later, while living in Los Angeles, Hongyong received a letter from a granddaughter she didn't know existed. The letter told her that Lee Yong Woon and his family were living in exile in remote Hyesan City, North Korea. The news stunned not only Hongyong, but Lee as well; she never knew she even had an uncle. She also never knew that her parents and grandmother had been writing to the Korean government seeking information on Yong Woon. Her family kept this information from her to save her heartache. But upon learning about it, she decided to take action, and this journey is the basis for *In the Absence of Sun.*

Lee, her father, and her grandmother visited China in the summer of 1997 in hopes of bringing the "lost" son and uncle home. While Hongyong—in frail health at the time—waited in a hotel, father and daughter went to the border of Hyesan City, hoping to bring Yong Woon to the hotel for a reunion. But that was not meant to be, for Yong Woon was on the brink of starvation and suffering from a heart condition that had gone untreated. So the Lees returned to Los Angeles and began planning a rescue mission. Four months later, Lee and her father, with the help of a Korean guide, assisted Yong Woon and three relatives into China; twenty days later they rescued five more relatives. After two weeks of hiding out in China, the group made it to the South Korean embassy and was granted asylum. Four months after that, the Lee family was reunited with their North Korean relatives in Seoul. Yong Woon told his incredible, painful story of how he had been captured in the 1950s for forming an anticommunist youth group. He was sent to a detention center, and then he and his wife were exiled to Hyesan City in the 1970s for being Christian and coming from a family of landowners. Hongyong's tears fell as she listened to her son's life story; she died shortly thereafter, the pain of the past released.

*Publishers Weekly* reviewed the book and found it "gripping and inspiring," adding that "Lee's prose resonates with a poetic sensibility." While the critic thought that Lee's asides about her own experiences occasionally slowed the story, *In the Absence of Sun* is nevertheless "an all-out thrilling escape story, complete with dangerous border crossings, unexpected romance and touching family moments [that] makes for a terrific and beautiful chronicle." *Booklist's* Quinn praised the book for its portrayal of cultural differences: "The book is important for the glimpse it offers into a closed and oppressive society, as eye-opening for us as the Lee Yong Woon family's first exposure to even the moderate freedoms and comforts of China is for them."

Lee travels the country giving lectures about her experiences in hopes of bringing attention to North Korea. She hopes to create awareness of the oppression that is the way of life there. As she explained to Kim, "America is very powerful. Anywhere America looks, everybody looks."

*BIOGRAPHICAL AND CRITICAL SOURCES:*

*PERIODICALS*

*Booklist,* March 15, 1996, Mary Ellen Quinn, review of *Still Life with Rice: A Young American Woman Discovers the Life and Legacy of Her Korean Grandmother,* p. 1237; April 1, 2002, Quinn, review of *In the Absence of Sun: A Korean-American Woman's Promise to Reunite Three Lost Generations of Her Family,* p. 1300, "Read-Alikes: Ancestral Stories," p. 1301.
*Commonweal,* September 13, 1996, Heather King, review of *Still Life with Rice,* pp. 34-36.
*English Journal,* April, 1997, Ellen Shull, review of *Still Life with Rice,* p. 85.
*Kirkus Reviews,* February 1, 1996, review of *Still Life with Rice,* p. 200; February 15, 2002, review of *In the Absence of Sun,* p. 237.
*Korean Quarterly,* winter, 1997, Andrea Lee, review of *Still Life with Rice.*
*Library Journal,* March 15, 2002, Kitty Chen Dean, review of *In the Absence of Sun,* p. 89.
*Los Angeles Times,* June 26, 2002, Ruth Andrew Ellenson, "A Journey of the Heart and Soul," p. E1.
*People,* June 17, 2002, Galina Espinoza, "Profile in Courage: To Heal Her Grandmother's Heart, Writer Helie Lee Freed Her Uncle from North Korea," p. 105.
*Publishers Weekly,* February 5, 1996, review of *Still Life with Rice,* p. 72; April 1, 2002, review of *In the Absence of Sun,* p. 72.

*OTHER*

*Chimes Online,* http://www-stu.calvin.edu/chimes/ (October 3, 2002), Joo Eun Kim, "Helie Lee Talks on Reuniting Three Lost Generations of Her Family."*

## LEFKOVITZ, Lori Hope 1956-

*PERSONAL:* Born May 6, 1956, in New York, NY; daughter of Rudolf and Lola (Weinstein) Lefkovitz; married Leonard David Gordon, January 9, 1977; children: Royna Heleni, Samara Esther. *Education:* Hebrew University, 1977-79; Brandeis University, A.B., 1977; Brown University, M.A., 1982, Ph.D., 1984.

*ADDRESSES: Office*—Reconstructionist Rabbinical College, 1299 Church Rd., Wyncote, PA 19095-6143. *E-mail*—llefkovi@rrc.edu.

*CAREER:* Brown University, teaching assistant, 1979-82; City University of New York, Queens College, lecturer, 1983-86; Kenyon College, Gambier, OH, assistant professor, 1986-91, associate professor, beginning 1991; lecturer in field; Gottesman Kolot Professor of Gender and Judaism, Reconstructionist Rabbinical College, Wyncote, PA.

*MEMBER:* Institute of Philadelphia Association for Psychoanalysis (fellow), Phi Beta Kappa.

*AWARDS, HONORS:* Golda Meir post-doctoral fellowship, Hebrew University, Jerusalem, 1988-89; Fulbright Scholar, Hebrew University, Jerusalem, 2003.

*WRITINGS:*

*The Character of Beauty in the Victorian Novel,* UMI Research Press (Ann Arbor, MI), 1987.
(Editor) *Textual Bodies: Changing Boundaries of Literary Representation,* State University of New York Press (Albany, NY), 1997.
(Coeditor) *Shaping Losses: Cultural Memory and the Holocaust,* University of Illinois Press (Urbana, IL), 2001.

*SIDELIGHTS:* Lori Hope Lefkovitz specializes in topics of gender and Judaism, having written numerous articles for various publications. She was editor of *Textual Bodies: Changing Boundaries of Literary Representation* and co-editor of *Shaping Losses: Cultural Memory and the Holocaust.* In addition to editing she wrote her own book called *The Character of Beauty in the Victorian Novel.*

*Shaping Losses* describes how memories are used as the heirlooms that Holocaust survivors pass down to their family members in place of all they lost. Arwen Donahue of *Women's Review of Books* stated, "The word love, in this context, celebrates the people whose lives have been incredibly marked by the Nazi genocide." Donahue admitted her admiration of Lefkovitz's view, stating that she is "a person [who] recognizes that she would not exist were it not for that loss." In the introduction Lefkovitz describes cultural memory as "ethnic group consciousness of the past. . . . it refers to the legacy of history as history retains its ability to affect everyday lives by the determining weight of the past." Donahue describes the premise of the books as "those who have suffered traumatic loss . . . cannot claim an identity if they cannot give shape to what they have lost."

"*Textual Bodies* is a collection of essays that examine depictions of the human body in literature," according to Carol Horwitz of *NWSA Journal.* Horwitz found that the book would be useful as "a course text using the female body as the organizing principle." Horwitz closed her review stating, "The female body is a topic worthy of serious study, not just medical management! These texts insist on the significance of the social meanings of the construction of the female body." The majority of reviewers deemed *Textual Bodies* an excellent addition to libraries and a wonderful source for education on the female form.

In *The Character of Beauty in the Victorian Novel* Lefkovitz examines the role that society's depiction of beauty has played in our evolving perception of self. J. Sudrann of *Choice* felt, "despite the wealth of materials Lefkovitz has poured into this book, she does not yet have it under sufficient control." Thais Morgan in *Tulsa Studies in Women's Literature* wrote that Lefkovitz makes "important contributions to our understanding of the inscription of cultural values onto the female body." Morgan also pointed out that the book indicates "the crucial relation between beauty and character." Morgan felt this book "should be read as important feminist work toward examining the sexual politics of representation." Dierdre David, reviewing the work in *Victorian Studies,* noted that Lefkovitz "splendidly incorporates her firm grasp of Hebrew and Midrash interpretation into literary analysis, showing . . . how problematically attractive biblical heroines such as Esther, Judith, Dinah, and Susanna are paradigmatic 'types' of beauty." David stated that Lefkovitz could have done better in demonstrating "how physical descriptions, both express and constitute ideologies of 'loveliness,' (but) plays it safe with a critically undemanding 'survey.'" Sudrann went on to state that *The Character of Beauty in the Victorian Novel* "remains useful to students sufficiently advanced to find in it the right suggestions to spark theses of their own."

*BIOGRAPHICAL AND CRITICAL SOURCES:*

PERIODICALS

*Choice,* May, 1987, J. Sudrann, review of *The Character of Beauty in the Victorian Novel,* p. 1397; May, 1997, R. R. Warhol, review of *Textual Bodies,* p. 1492.
*NWSA Journal,* summer, 1998, Carol Horwitz, review of *Textual Bodies,* p. 154.
*Poetics Today,* 1987, Martin Melaver, review of *The Character of Beauty in the Victorian Novel,* p. 753.
*Tulsa Studies in Women's Literature,* spring, 1989, Thais Morgan, review of *The Character of Beauty in the Victorian Novel,* pp. 140-142.
*Victorian Studies,* winter, 1989, Deirdre David, review of *The Character of Beauty in the Victorian Novel,* p. 231.
*Women's Review of Books,* January, 2002, Arwen Donahue, "Mirror Images," p. 20.

OTHER

*Reconstructionist Rabbinical College Web site,* http://www.rrc.edu/ (April 16, 2002), "Lori Hope Lefkovitz."
*University of Illinois Press Web site,* http://www.press.uillinois.edu/ (April 16, 2002), review of *Shaping Losses.*
*State University of New York Press Web site,* http://www.sunypress.edu/sunyp/ (April 16, 2002), review of *Textual Bodies.*

\*     \*     \*

## LEMELIN, Roger 1919-1992

*PERSONAL:* Born April 7, 1919 in Québec, Canada; died 1992; son of Joseph and Florida (Dumontier) Lemelin.

*CAREER:* Novelist, journalist, essayist, and screenwriter. Journalist for *Time, Life,* and *Fortune* 1948-52; began writing for television, 1951; *La Presse,* Montréal, Québec, Canada, president and publisher, beginning 1972.

*MEMBER:* Royal Society of Canada, Académie Goncourt.

*AWARDS, HONORS:* Prix David and Prix de la Langue Française de l'Académie Française for *Au pied de la pente douce,* 1946; Guggenheim fellowships, 1946 and 1947; Rockefeller fellowship, 1953; Prix de l'Académie des Arts et des Lettres, 1954; Prix de Paris, 1965, for *Pierre le magnifique*; Laurentian University, honorary degree in literature, 1976; Canadian News Hall of Fame, elected 1978; companion of the Order of Canada, 1980.

*WRITINGS:*

*Au pied de la pente douce,* Editions d'Arbre (Montréal, Québec, Canada), 1944, translation by Samuel Putnam published as *The Town Below,* Reynal & Hitchcock (New York, NY), 1948.
*Les Plouffe,* Belisle (Québec, Canada), 1948, translation by Mary Finch published as *The Plouffe Family,* McClelland & Stewart (Toronto, Ontario, Canada), 1950.
*Fantaisies sur les péchés capitaux,* Beauchemin (Montréal, Québec, Canada), 1949.
*L'homme aux oiseaux* (screenplay), National Film Board, 1952.
*Pierre le magnifique,* Institut Littéraire du Québec (Québec, Canada), 1952, translation by Harry Lorin Binsse published as *In Quest of Splendour,* McClelland & Stewart (Toronto, Ontario, Canada), 1955.
*The Stations of the Cross,* translation by Mary Finch, of "Le Chemin de la croix" from *Fantaisies sur les péchés capitaux,* Irwin (Toronto, Ontario, Canada), 1967.
*Langue, esthétique et morale,* La Presse (Montréal, Québec, Canada), 1977.
*L'Ecrivain et le journaliste,* La Presse (Montréal, Québec, Canada), 1977.
(Contributor) *Divided We Stand,* edited by Gary Geddes, PMA (Toronto, Ontario, Canada), 1977.

*Les voies de l'espérance,* La Presse (Montréal, Québec, Canada), 1979.

*La culotte en or,* La Presse (Montréal, Québec, Canada), 1980.

(With Gilles Carle) *Les Plouffe* (screenplay; adapted from Lemelin's novel), International Cinema, 1981.

*Le crime d'Ovide Plouffe,* ETR (Québec, Canada), 1982, translation by Alan Brown published as *The Crime of Ovide Plouffe,* McClelland & Stewart (Toronto, Ontario, Canada), 1984.

Contributor to periodical publications *Regards, L'Action Nationale,* and *Queen's Quarterly.*

*ADAPTATIONS: Les Plouffe* was made into a television series.

*SIDELIGHTS:* Roger Lemelin's writing reflects his life and complements his satire. His writing is characterized by empathy amid social and individual farce, and his paternalism in presenting his well-rounded characters established Lemelin as one of Canada's most acclaimed twentieth-century writers. Seemingly absurd qualities give Lemelin's characters depth and likeable animation, and also allow them to serve in the author's relevant social and political commentary. Lemelin emphasized family life and old-fashioned value systems and social institutions. According to Allison Mitcham in *Dictionary of Literary Biography,* Lemelin's devotion to the vitality and singularity of French Canada, "his understanding of ordinary people, and his ability to portray them vividly paved the way for others and gave him an important place in Canadian letters."

Lemelin, the first of ten sons, was born in the Saint-Sauveur district of Québec City. The economic depression of the 1930s victimized his family economically, so despite his intelligence, he had to drop out of high school in 1934 at age fifteen to help support his family. His first two novels portrayed this period. Anger over a more personal setback, however, fueled his writing. Lemelin, who in the early 1940s wanted to win the Canadian downhill skiing championships, broke his ankle in an accident. Confined to bed and forced to surrender his dream, he first wrote to channel his frustrations.

*Au pied de la pente douce* is arguably his venting of anger over the skiing accident. Mitcham wrote, "The vivid and moving depiction of the agony which one of the characters undergoes because of a knee injury in this novel likely owes much to Lemelin's own suffering while writing this book." Translated as *The Town Below,* Lemelin's first novel involves the frustration of young love, economic disparity, and a sentimentalized version of twentieth-century Canadian youth. The novel contrasts nineteenth-century simplicity with twentieth-century urbanization.

Critics generally praised Lemelin's debut novel. Although a *Canadian Forum* writer said the novel lacks "precision, both in perception and in style," the critic said a poor English translation likely contributes. Recognizing that "in intention, [it is] a serious novel," the critic praised Lemelin for his honesty and for avoiding clichés. A *Christian Century* critic said that "the picture of life in the poverty-stricken and narrow-minded little parish is well worth examining," and added, "Lemelin shows indications of making a genuine contribution to [the] growth and development" of the French-Canadian novel. Mason Wade, writing for *Commonweal,* called *Au pied de la pente douce* "the first French Canadian novel to deal realistically with the urban life of a region which has only recently become more urban than rural, and which has persisted in confining its literature to idealistic pictures of an outmoded agricultural way of life."

Several critics also praised Lemelin's raw talent for style and description. Iris Barry of the *New York Herald Tribune Weekly Book Report* said Lemelin "draws richly and arrestingly upon real-life material observed with rare compassion and tinctured with youthful bitterness, and its author's name is emphatically one to note for the future." Charles Lee of the *New York Times* declared that "few will deny [Lemelin's] gift of characterization, his vigor of style, and his power to give sight and sound to a boisterously live world."

*Les Plouffe* is considered Lemelin's masterpiece. Hailed as "one of Canada's great comic novels" by Mitcham, *Les Plouffe* introduced Canada to the idiosyncrasies and laughable shortcomings of family life. Lemelin playfully introduces frailties and celebrates individual victories in making this family endearing. For example, the matriarch of the large family, Mme. Plouffe, a sixty-year-old robust housewife, absurdly compares her uninspiring life with that of legendary heroine Joan of Arc. In fact, every challenge, no matter how minute, overwhelms her. Both she and her husband, Théophile, intensely dislike the English, and much of their humorous political commentary and not-so-humorous conflicts evolve from their prejudices. Théophile dislikes the English so much he avidly roots for the Germans to defeat "les Anglais" during World War II.

Lemelin leaves no family member unscathed as he plays with the peculiarities and insufficiencies of the Plouffe children, ranging from the youngest at nineteen to the oldest daughter who struggles as a middle-aged spinster. She is still single as Mme. Plouffe's coddling keeps her homebound. Her former suitor enhances her misery, visiting the household daily to discuss politics with Théophile, despite having married someone else. Mme. Plouffe favors her youngest child, Ovide, as she was sure he was destined for priesthood. Ultimately, he breaks his mother's heart by marrying a substandard woman and remaining unhappy.

Lemelin wrote two more novels and a variety of short stories, essays, and news articles. His political shift over the years from liberal to conservative was evident. He often espoused his conservatism in magazines, newspapers, and journals. He became president and publisher of *La Presse,* a Montréal French-language daily newspaper, in 1972. He favored federalism and tempered reformation politics, though much of his work was ignored between 1952 and 1979. He returned from virtual hibernation in 1982, reintroducing the Plouffe family with *Le crime d'Ovide Plouffe.* Though his comedy was still strong, his novel writing evolved little over twenty-plus years. Still, the public was pleased to welcome back the Plouffes. In 1981 Lemelin collaborated with Gilles Carle to produce a screenplay based on *Les Plouffe,* and the family also enjoyed a run as the basis for a series on radio and television. Lemelin's characters, Mitcham said, "are sympathetic figures because of their vigor and valor. Absurd they may sometimes be, but they are rarely cold and never self-pitying. It is perhaps for these reasons especially that—animated on television and film—they attracted such an empathetic audience."

*BIOGRAPHICAL AND CRITICAL SOURCES:*

*BOOKS*

*Dictionary of Literary Biography,* Volume 88: *Canadian Writers, 1920-1959,* Gale (Detroit, MI), 1989.

*PERIODICALS*

*Canadian Forum,* spring, 1948.
*Christian Century,* spring, 1948.
*Commonweal,* spring, 1948.
*New York Herald Tribune Weekly Book Report,* May 16, 1948, p. 12.
*New York Times,* April 18, 1948, p. 7.*

\*          \*          \*

## LERNER, Jimmy

*PERSONAL:* Born in Brooklyn, NY; married (divorced, 1998); children: two daughters. *Education:* Golden Gate University, M.B.A.

*ADDRESSES: Home*—Reno, NV. *Agent*—c/o Author Mail, Random House, 1540 Broadway, New York, NY 10036.

*CAREER:* Writer. A. T. & T. (now Pacific Bell), San Francisco, CA, marketing analyst. *Military service:* Served with the U.S. Army in Panama.

*WRITINGS:*

*You've Got Nothing Coming: Notes from a Prison Fish* (memoir), Broadway Books (New York, NY), 2001.

*WORK IN PROGRESS: It's All Part of the Punishment,* poems.

*SIDELIGHTS:* Jimmy Lerner is a former marketing analyst who wrote *You've Got Nothing Coming: Notes from a Prison Fish,* a memoir of his stint in a Nevada prison, where he was sentenced after receiving a conviction for murder. Lerner claims that he was already wrestling with marital problems, substance abuse, and tenuous employment when he met Mark A. Slavin at an Alcoholics Anonymous meeting. Slavin, described by John Strausbaugh in *New York Press* as "one of those really scary losers—bad coke habit with the accompanying fits of violent rage and a closetful of weapons; pathological liar; porn-devouring loner;

one step ahead of the repo man," eventually accompanied Lerner to a Reno hotel, where the two men indulged in drugs and alcohol. Lerner claimed that he killed Slavin, referred to in *You Got Nothing Coming* as Dwayne Hassleman, in self-defense, strangling him with a belt after being attacked with a knife. On the advice of his attorney, Lerner pled guilty to two counts of manslaughter, and he received consecutive sentences running one to six years.

The aforementioned events constitute what Chris Lehmann, writing in the *Washington Post,* described as "an afterthought to *You Got Nothing Coming.*" He noted that most of Lerner's memoir concerns "his initiation into prison life, from his panicked hazing into the protocols and jargon of the Big House" to his present standing as a "'righteous con,' plying a sinecure in the prison law library while welcoming new generations of rookie inmates . . . onto the yard." In prison, Lerner's sense of humor endears him to other inmates, and his relatively advanced age—late forties—spares him from the violence of sexual exploitation. He even wins the nickname O.G., an abbreviation of Original Gangster, for the grim nature of his crime, As Lehmann noted: "He proves himself useful to a number of otherwise intimidating prison hands: Guards come to him to fill out divorce forms on their behalf; old-time cons appreciate his prowess as a chess partner; and even inmates who'd sworn to pummel him end up prevailing on him for help in contesting disciplinary actions."

After serving three years of imprisonment, Lerner received his release. He soon found a publisher for his manuscript, which he had originally produced on what Joe Schoenmann, writing in *Las Vegas Weekly,* described as "scraps of paper and . . . the margins of pages torn out of the Bible—and mailed out every day to a friend."

When *You Got Nothing Coming* appeared in 2001, it readily won praise as a compelling document. Lehmann acknowledged the book as "a tale steeped in harrowing detail," while Schoenmann described it as a "harsh . . . indictment of the Nevada prison system." A *Kirkus Reviews* critic, meanwhile, deemed Lerner's book "a jolting, unusual memoir" and concluded that it is "hard to put down, harder to forget." A *Publishers Weekly* reviewer summarized it as "the most gripping, and most inviting, prison memoir in years." Still another critic, writing in *Entertainment Weekly,* af-

firmed that *You Got Nothing Coming* "depicts the remnants of humanity."

*BIOGRAPHICAL AND CRITICAL SOURCES:*

*BOOKS*

Lerner, Jimmy, *You've Got Nothing Coming: Notes from a Prison Fish* (memoir), Broadway Books (New York, NY), 2001.

*PERIODICALS*

*Las Vegas Weekly,* April 17, 2002, Joe Schoenmann, "Surviving Prison in Nevada."
*Publishers Weekly,* December 3, 2001, review of *You've Got Nothing Coming: Notes from a Prison Fish.*
*Washington Post,* March 3, 2000, Chris Lehmann, "A Con's Inside Story."

*OTHER*

*New York Press Online,* http://www.nypress.com/ (May 13, 2002), John Strausbaugh, "Making a Killing."*

\*   \*   \*

## LeSUEUR, William Dawson 1840-1917

*PERSONAL:* Born February 19, 1840 in Québec, Canada; died September 23, 1917; son of Peter and Barbara (Dawson) LeSueur; married Ann Jane Foster, 1867; children: Ernest Arthur, Beatrice. *Education:* Attended Osgoode Hall Law School; University of Toronto, received degree, 1863.

*CAREER:* Critic, essayist, biographer, journalist, and philosopher. Canadian post office, department secretary, 1888-1902; editorial writer for *Montreal Star, Montreal Gazette,* and *Ottawa Citizen.*

*MEMBER:* Royal Society of Canada (president, 1912), Literary and Scientific Society of Ottawa (nine-time president).

*AWARDS, HONORS:* LL.D., Queens University, Kingston, Ontario, Canada, 1900; fellowship, Royal Society of Canada, 1903.

*WRITINGS:*

*Count Frontenac,* Morang (Toronto, Ontario, Canada), 1906.

*A Critical Spirit: The Thought of William Dawson LeSueur,* edited by A. B. McKillop, McClelland & Stewart (Toronto, Ontario, Canada), 1977.

*William Lyon Mackenzie: A Reinterpretation,* edited by A. B. McKillop, Macmillan (Toronto, Ontario, Canada), 1979.

Also contributor to periodicals, including *Westminster Review* and *Rose-Belford's Canadian Monthly and National Review. Popular Science Monthly,* contributing editor, beginning 1882.

*SIDELIGHTS:* Canadian essayist and civil servant William Dawson LeSueur advocated rational thought over organized religion. LeSueur featured tempered yet honest criticism, inspired essays, candid biographies, and historical reassessment. Though he used such pseudonyms as "A Radical" and "Loan," before 1876, LeSueur trusted his methodical approach. In his 1875 essay "The Intellectual Life," LeSueur lamented over people avoiding the truth. According to Clifford G. Holland in *Dictionary of Literary Biography,* LeSueur said, "That truth may be on the other side they cannot help at times suspecting, but they are determined never to be brought face to face with the proof."

LeSueur's father was French, while his mother had emigrated from northern England. As a child, LeSueur learned both French and English. His family moved from Québec to Montreal while he was a teenager, and the young scholar studied Greek and Latin in high school. At age sixteen, LeSueur began working as a public servant, and in 1888 he was appointed secretary of the post office department. He also studied law.

LeSueur identified intelligent, logical thinking as the means to a moral life. His first literary breakthrough was an essay he wrote in 1871 supporting Sainte-Beuve, a prominent and gifted French poet and critic. The essay hailed Sainte-Beuve's notion of social criticism only if approached rationally. This countered prevailing contemporary thought. LeSueur, then just thirty-one, lauded Sainte-Beuve for being "less a judge than an enquirer who tells us of his discoveries, and invites us to verify them for ourselves."

LeSueur's frequently targeted organized religion, politics, and selective documentation. Late in the nineteenth century, religious beliefs clashed with theories of evolution and Darwinism. According to Holland, LeSueur "denied that evolutionism sought to subvert belief in God or that science was materialistic, for he felt it could exert a moral influence." In "Ex-President Porter on Evolution," an essay appearing in *Popular Science Monthly* in September 1886, LeSueur exclaimed that the real battle, "however some may try to disguise it, is between dogma on the one hand and the free spirit of scientific inquiry on the other." He wrote many articles on the subject, among which included "Materialism and Positivism," "The Scientific Spirit," "Science and Materialism," and "Morality and Religion."

In his essay "Party Politics," he vehemently opposed rigid party lines, what he called "partyism." He strongly believed such a practice separates an individual from his own moral code. According to Holland, LeSueur said partyism imposed "a ban on the free exercise of a man's mind" and ultimately forced people "to conceal or misrepresent their real opinions." LeSueur urged Canada to stand alone, but also lobbied for an amicable reconciliation between English and French factions.

Early in the twentieth century, the publishers of the "Makers of Canada" series approached him to write a biography of William Lyon Mackenzie, a radical Canadian journalist. LeSueur wrote what Holland called "the first truly critical biography in Canada." Not surprisingly, Mackenzie's heirs were enraged, and set out to prevent the book's publication. Mackenzie's family had expected a complimentary biography, given its willingness to provide LeSueur private papers and information. The heirs, who included eventual Prime Minister Mackenzie King, succeeded temporarily, but the work was published in 1979, with A. B. McKillop as editor.

According to Holland, John Reade, who wrote LeSueur's obituary, praised him for "recogniz[ing] at once the significance of the new science and its destined ultimate effects on religious and philosophic thought." As LeSueur once inquired rhetorically: "Shall we idealize life, or shall we vulgarize it? . . . [I]f we choose the former we choose struggle, but the struggle will be ever upward, and our last days shall be our best."

*BIOGRAPHICAL AND CRITICAL SOURCES:*

*BOOKS*

*Dictionary of Literary Biography,* Volume 92: *Canadian Writers, 1890-1920,* Gale (Detroit, MI), 1990, pp. 198-200.

McKillop, A.B., *A Disciplined Intelligence: Critical Inquiry and Canadian Thought in the Victorian Era,* McGill-Queen's University Press (Montréal, Québec, Canada), 1979.*

\*    \*    \*

## LI, Xiaobing 1954-

*PERSONAL:* Born February 5, 1954, in Beijing China; naturalized U.S. citizen; son of Wei-ying (a petroleum engineer) and Xiao-yi (a petroleum engineer; maiden name, Zhang) Li; married Tran Lai (a homemaker), July 23, 1988; children: Kevin, Christina. *Ethnicity:* "Asian American." *Education:* Nankai University, B.A., 1982; Carnegie-Mellon University, M.A., 1985, Ph.D., 1991.

*ADDRESSES: Home*—2525 Brenton Dr., Edmond, OK 73003. *Office*—Department of History, University of Central Oklahoma, 100 North University Dr., Edmond, OK 73034; fax: 405-974-3823. *E-mail*—bli@ucok. edu.

*CAREER:* Phillips University, Enid, OK, assistant professor of history and director of Asian studies, 1991-93; University of Central Oklahoma, Edmond, assistant professor, 1993-98, associate professor, 1998-2002, professor of history, 2002—, adjunct professor of Asian studies, 1996—, associate director of Western Pacific Institute, 1993—.

*MEMBER:* Association of Chinese Professors of Social Sciences in the United States (organizational director and member of board of directors, 1995-97; president,

1997-99), Association of Chinese Historians in the United States (president, 1995-97), Sino-American International Strategic Research Society (president, 1996—), Oklahoma Chinese Professionals and Scholars Association (vice president, 1997-98).

*AWARDS, HONORS:* Grants from Woodrow Wilson International Center for Scholars, 1995, 1996, Center for Naval Analyses, 1998-99, U.S. Department of Defense, 1999-2000.

*WRITINGS:*

*Diplomacy through Militancy in the Taiwan Straits: Crisis Politics and Sino-American Relations in the 1950s,* China Education Press (Beijing, China), 1993.

(Editor, with others) *Major Events in the Twentieth Century* (in Chinese), China's Broadcasting and Television Press (Beijing, China), 1994.

(Editor, with Hongshan Li, and contributor) *China and the United States: A New Cold War History,* University Press of America (Lanham, MD), 1997.

(Editor, with Ziaobo Hu and Yang Zhong) *Interpreting U.S.-China-Taiwan Relations: China in the Post-Cold War Era,* University Press of America (Lanham, MD), 1998.

(Editor, with Jie Zhang) *Social-Economic Transition and Cultural Reconstruction in China,* University Press of America (Lanham, MD), 1998.

(Editor, with Walter Jung, and contributor) *Korea and Regional Geopolitics,* University Press of America (Lanham, MD), 1999.

(With Peng Deng and Guoli Liu) *U.S. Diplomacy and U.S.-China Relations* (in Chinese), CASS Press (Beijing, China), 2000.

(Editor, with Walter Jung, and contributor) *Asia's Crisis and New Paradigm,* University Press of America (Lanham, MD), 2000.

(Editor, with Allen Millett and Bin Yu) *Mao's Generals Remember Korea,* University Press of Kansas (Lawrence, KS), 2002.

Contributor to books, including *Confucianism and Modernization,* China Education Press (Beijing, China), 1994; *Image, Perception, and the Making of U.S.-China Relations,* edited by Hongshan Li and Zhaohui Hong, University Press of America (Lanham, MD), 1998; and *Chinese Warfighting: The PLA Experi-*

*ence,* edited by Mark A. Ryan and Michael McDevitt, M. E. Sharpe (Armonk, NY), 2002. Contributor of articles, translations, and reviews to scholarly journals, including *Chinese Historians, Cold War International History Project Bulletin, Journal of Chinese Political Science,* and *American Journal of China Studies.* Executive editor, *Western Pacific Journal,* 1993—; editor, *American Review of China Studies,* 1999—; member of editorial board, *Modern China Studies,* 1995—.

WORK IN PROGRESS: *Voices from the Korean War: Personal Stories of the American, Korean, and Chinese Soldiers,* with Richard Peters; *Voices from the Vietnam War: Personal Stories of the American, South and North Vietnamese Soldiers,* with Terry May; *The Making of Mao's Modern Army: The Korean War's Impact on the PLA Reconstruction; Chinese Military Intelligence Operations.*

BIOGRAPHICAL AND CRITICAL SOURCES:

PERIODICALS

*China Review International,* fall, 2000, Danny S. L. Paau, review of *Interpreting U.S.-China-Taiwan Relations: China in the Post-Cold War Era,* p. 490.

\*      \*      \*

## LIEBMAN, Ruth
## (Rae Lawrence)

PERSONAL: Female. *Education:* Attended Radcliffe College.

ADDRESSES: *Agent*—c/o Author Mail, Crown Publishers, 201 East 50th St., New York, NY 10022.

CAREER: Writer. Viking Penguin Press, New York, NY, assistant editor; Random House, New York, NY, worked in sales department.

WRITINGS:

(Under pseudonym Rae Lawrence) *Satisfaction* (novel), Poseidon Press (New York, NY), 1987.
(Under pseudonym Rae Lawrence; with Jacqueline Susann) *Jacqueline Susann's Shadow of the Dolls: A Novel,* Crown (New York, NY), 2001.

SIDELIGHTS: When Ruth Liebman, writing under the pseudonym Rae Lawrence, published her first novel, *Satisfaction,* she also created a fictitious life for her literary alter ego in an article that ran in the *New York Times.* According to this piece, Lawrence was a New Jersey secretary who overcame the obstacles of the publishing world to make it big with her first book. Liebman was soon outed as the real author, her literature major from Radcliffe and background in publishing revealed. Mimi Avins noted in a *Los Angeles Times* article, "Rae writes books in the catty voice of a third wife dumped the day before a pre-nup expires. Ruth works in the sales department at Random House in New York and won't dish about other pop writers. 'God bless everyone who figures out how to finish a novel and get it published,' she says. 'I guess I consider my real competition to be the mall. On a Saturday afternoon, people can decide to read a book or go shopping.'"

*Satisfaction* is a beach book, a genre described by *Los Angeles Times* book reviewer Karen Stabiner as "stories [that] rev at higher r.p.m.s in settings that are even more outlandish than usual." Four Radcliffe freshmen, all daughters of famous men, make up the cast of *Satisfaction.* Stabiner listed them as "Rosaline, the sheltered sweet rich girl; Marinda, the dark, insecure ethnic binge eater; Katie Lee, the conniving Southerner; and December, the free spirit with the horrible secret." Rosaline marries first, wedding a wealthy social-register type like herself. Marinda, whose family has organized crime ties, engages in various complicated relationships, including one with a drug addict. Katie Lee, heir to a Hiltonesque dynasty, becomes a successful though scheming businesswoman. And December uses her beauty to achieve supermodel status and Hollywood starlet fame. Having little in common other than their school tie, the women's lives remain connected by their love for Schuyler Smith, a Montana-born writer they met when he was a student at Harvard and with whom each has had a relationship over the years. One marries him at the book's outset, and the rest of the novel flashes back over the women's lives to reveal the lucky bride.

Regina Weinreich wrote in *American Book Review,* "As it turns out, *Satisfaction* is a pretty good book, in fact a page-turner." The critic added, "You like this book despite yourself. Rae Lawrence is a deft story-teller with a hip sensibility." A *Publishers Weekly* reviewer observed, "There are no huge surprises here, but juicy scandal and engaging rough-edged characters will keep readers turning pages far into the night." Although *Chicago Tribune* book reviewer Roger Davis Friedman found the content of the book to be "fairly mundane," the critic praised the ending, where "the sluggish action gets a kick in the pants, and there is some question as to how it will all turn out."

Friedman cites Liebman's literary precursors as Harold Robbins, Judith Krantz, and Jacqueline Susann. In fact, Susann's literary manager and agent contacted Liebman's editor about her completing the rough draft Susann had written of a sequel to her 1966 bestseller *Valley of the Dolls.* Liebman took the two-hundred-page manuscript and spent two years turning it into *Jacqueline Susann's Shadow of the Dolls: A Novel.* When discussing the process in an interview on *Randomhouse.com,* Liebman said, "The main characters—Anne, Neely and Lyon—are one hundred percent Jackie's. And the big question that drives the plot is from her draft too. In order to make the story contemporary, I had to add things that didn't exist in Jackie's day. For example: the Hamptons is now a celebrity hot spot, but back then it was pretty much one big potato farm. So those settings are mine. And the pages I worked from were rough draft, so the finished sentences are mine too. But if any of my old English teachers are reading this, I want to make sure they know that the exclamation points are Jackie's! I was very lucky to have some Jackie expert read through the draft. When they said 'This is so Jackie!' I knew that where Jackie left off and I began was as seamless as possible."

The three main characters—model Anne Wells; her husband, director Lyon Burke; and singer Neely O'Hara—last seen in the late 1960s, are reintroduced in the late 1980s but have aged only ten years. *Booklist* reviewer Ilene Cooper felt that one of the problems with the sequel is that attitudes and actions that were once shocking in the 1960s, when the original was published, "just seem silly here." However, Cooper allowed that Liebman does a great job of imitating Sussan's style, and "the flow of dialogue still turns the pages." Kathy Ingels Helmond, on the other hand, observed in *Library Journal,* "Fans of *Valley of the Dolls* will enjoy reading about Anne and Neely O'Hara and Lyon Burke and their teenage children." Linda Richard similarly remarked in *January Magazine* that Liebman has successfully "cloned the essential emptiness of Susann's characters. Some of the poignancy

derives from the nonjudgmental way she tells her story." In a *Bookreporter.com* review, Addelaide Hayes concluded that Liebman "can be hilarious, her dialogue is over-the-top in a terribly Susann way, and her acid observations about tricoastal (Manhattan, Los Angeles, the Hamptons) life are right on target."

## BIOGRAPHICAL AND CRITICAL SOURCES:

### PERIODICALS

*American Book Review,* November-December, 1987, Regina Weinreich, "Genuine Fraud," p. 19, 23.

*Booklist,* April 1, 2001, Ilene Cooper, review of *Jacqueline Susann's Shadow of the Dolls: A Novel,* p. 1428.

*Chicago Tribune,* August 16, 1987, Roger Davis Friedman, "Upper Crass," pp. 5, 9.

*Cosmopolitan,* July, 1987, review of *Satisfaction,* p. 200.

*Entertainment Weekly,* May 4, 2001, Karen Valby, "Tome Raiders: Reports of Their Demise Are Greatly Exaggerated: How Dead Authors Are 'Writing' New Books," p. 20.

*Library Journal,* July, 1987, Rosellen Brewer, review of *Satisfaction;* June 15, 2001, Kathy Ingels Helmond, review of *Jacqueline Susann's Shadow of the Dolls: A Novel,* p. 104.

*Los Angeles Times,* June 14, 1987, Karen Stabiner, "Literary Lotions for July," p. 13; July 6, 2001, Mimi Avins, "'Valley of the Dolls' Retains Its Chemistry," p. E1.

*National Review,* November 20, 1987. Jeffrey Giles, "The Selling of the Young," p. 64.

*New York,* June 1, 1987, Susan Squire, "Cliffie Notes," p. 24.

*New York Times,* July 22, 2001, Tom Kuntz, "Sex and the Purple Prose," p. WK2.

*Publishers Weekly,* May 22, 1987, Sybil Steinberg, review of *Satisfaction,* p. 68; April 23, 2001, review of *Jacqueline Susann's Shadow of the Dolls,* 45.

*Savvy,* July, 1987, Jane Goldman, review of *Satisfaction,* p. 40.

*Time,* July 16, 2001, Michele Orecklin, "More Pills, Fewer Thrills: One Trip through the Valley Was Enough," p. 72.

*US Weekly,* June 11, 2001, Francine Prose, review of *Jacqueline Susann's Shadow of the Dolls,* p. 96.

*Wall Street Journal,* July 29, 1987, Joanne Kaufman, review of *Satisfaction,* p. 16; July 13, 2002, Kate Flatley, review of *Jacqueline Susann's Shadow of the Dolls,* p. W16.

OTHER

*Bookreporter,* http://www.bookreporter.com/ (December 31, 2001), Addelaide Hayes, review of *Jacqueline Susann's Shadow of the Dolls.*

*January Magazine,* http://www.januarymagazine.com/ (August 1, 2001), Linda Richards, "Shadow of the Author."

*Randomhouse.com,* http://www.randomhouse.com/ (December 31, 2001), "A Conversation with Rae Lawrence, Author of *Jacqueline Susann's Shadow of the Dolls.*"*

\*    \*    \*

## LIEL, Alon 1948-

PERSONAL: Born October 31, 1948, in Tel Aviv, Israel; son of Pinchas and Daniela Liel; married March 8, 1977; wife's name Rachel (a director); children: Ori, Karen, Daphna. *Education:* Hebrew University of Jerusalem, B.A., M.A., Ph.D. *Religion:* Jewish.

ADDRESSES: *Home*—6/2 Haefroni St., Mevaseret Zion, Israel. *Office*—P.O. Box 1845, Mevaseret Zion, Israel 90805. *E-mail*—alonliel@netvision.net.il.

CAREER: Israeli Ministry of Foreign Affairs, staff member, including assignment in Turkey, 1971-92, ambassador to South Africa, 1992-94; Israeli Ministry of Economy and Planning, director general, 1994-97; Israeli Ministry of Foreign Affairs, director general, 2000-01. *Military service:* Israel Defense Forces, 1966-69.

WRITINGS:

*Turkey in the Middle East,* Lynne Reinner (Boulder, CO), 1994.

*Black Justice: The South African Upheaval* (in Hebrew), Hakkibutz Hameuchad (Israel), 1997.

WORK IN PROGRESS: Research on Turkish politics and foreign affairs.

SIDELIGHTS: Alon Liel told *CA:* "My writing is a result of ongoing work as an Israeli diplomat in Turkey and later in South Africa. I also earned a doctorate on the Turkish economy and foreign policy."

\*    \*    \*

## LIFSHIN, Lyn (Diane) 1944-

PERSONAL: Born July 12, 1944, in Burlington, VT; daughter of Ben and Frieda (Lazarus) Lipman; married Eric Lifshin, 1963 (divorced 1975). *Education:* Syracuse University, B.A., 1960; University of Vermont, M.A., 1963; also attended Brandeis University and State University of New York—Albany.

ADDRESSES: *Home*—2142 Apple Tree Lane, Niskayuna, NY 12309-4714; and 2719 Baronhurst Dr., Vienna, VA 22181; fax: 703-242-0127. *E-mail*—onyx velvet@aol.com.

CAREER: Poet and writing instructor. State University of New York—Albany, teaching fellow, 1964-66; educational television writer, Schenectady, NY, 1966; State University of New York, Cobleskill, NY, instructor, 1968, 1970; writing consultant to New York State Mental Health Department, Albany, NY, 1969, and to Empire State College of the State University of New York, 1973; poet-in-residence, Mansfield State College, 1974, University of Rochester, 1986, Antioch Writers' Conference, 1987, and Glenwood College, 1994 and 1998; Union College, part-time instructor, 1980-85; has also taught at Cornell University, Dartmouth College, University of Chicago, University of New Mexico, and Syracuse University.

AWARDS, HONORS: Hart Crane Award; Bread Loaf scholarship; Harcourt Brace poetry fellowship; Boulder poetry award; San Jose Bicentennial Poetry Award; Yaddo fellowships, 1970, 1971, 1975, 1979, and 1980; MacDowell fellowship, 1973; Millay Colony fellowships, 1975 and 1979; New York Creative Artists Public Service grant, 1976; Jack Kerouac Award, 1984, for *Kiss the Skin Off; Centennial Review* poetry prize, 1985; Madeline Sadin Award,

*Lyn Lifshin*

*New York Quarterly,* 1986; *Footwork* (magazine) Award, 1987; Bring Back the Stars Award, 1987; Estersceffler Award, 1987, for poem "Hiroshima"; Peterson Award, 1999, for *Cold Comfort,* and 2001, for *Before It's Light.*

*WRITINGS:*

POETRY COLLECTIONS

*Why Is the House Dissolving?,* Open Skull Press (San Francisco, CA), 1968.

*Femina 2,* Abraxas Press (Madison, WI), 1970.

*Leaves and Night Things,* Baby John Press (West Lafayette, IN), 1970.

*Black Apples,* New Books, 1971, revised edition, Crossing Press (Trumansburg, NY), 1973.

*Lady Lyn,* Morgan Press (Milwaukee, WI), 1971.

*I'd Be Jeanne Moreau,* Morgan Press (Milwaukee, WI), 1972.

*The Mercurochrome Sun,* Charas Press (Tacoma, WA), 1972.

*Tentacles, Leaves,* Hellric Publications (Bellmont, MA), 1972.

*Moving by Touch,* Cotyledon Press (Traverse City, MI), 1972.

*Undressed,* Cotyledon Press (Traverse City, MI), 1972.

*Love Poems,* Zahir Press (Durham, NH), 1972.

*Lyn Lifshin,* Zahir Press (Durham, NH), 1972.

*Poems by Suramm and Lyn Lifshin,* Union Literary Committee (Madison, WI), 1972.

*Forty Days, Apple Nights,* Morgan Press (Milwaukee, WI), 1973.

*Museum,* Conspiracy Press (Albany, NY), 1973.

*The First Week Poems,* Zahir Press (Durham, NH), 1973.

*All the Women Poets I Ever Liked Didn't Hate Their Fathers,* Konglomerati Press (Gulfport, FL), 1973.

*The Old House on the Croton,* Shameless Hussy Press (San Lorenzo, CA), 1973.

*Poems,* Konglomerati Press (Gulfport, FL), 1974.

*Selected Poems,* Crossing Press (Trumansburg, NY), 1974.

*Thru Blue Post, New Mexico,* Basilisk Press (Fredonia, NY), 1974.

*Blue Fingers,* Shelter Press (Milwaukee, WI), 1974.

*Mountain Moving Day,* Crossing Press (Trumansburg, NY), 1974.

*Plymouth Women,* Morgan Press (Milwaukee, WI), 1974.

*Walking thru Audley End Mansion Late Afternoon and Drifting into Certain Faces,* M.A.G Press (Long Beach, CA), 1974.

*Shaker House,* Tideline Press (New York, NY), 1974.

*Blue Madonna,* Shelter Press (Milwaukee, WI), 1974.

*Green Bandages,* Hidden Springs (Genesco, NY), 1975.

*Upstate Madonna: Poems, 1970-1974,* Crossing Press (Trumansburg, NY), 1975.

*Old House Poems,* Capra Press (Santa Barbara, CA), 1975.

*Paper Apples,* Wormwood Review Press (Stockton, CA), 1975.

*North Poems,* Morgan Press (Milwaukee, WI), 1976.

*Shaker House Poems,* Sagarin Press (Chatham, NY), 1976.

*Naked Charm,* Fireweed Press, 1976, revised edition published as *Op 15 Second Ed,* Illuminati (Los Angeles, CA), 1984.

*Some Madonna Poems,* White Pine Press (Buffalo, NY), 1976.

*Crazy Arms,* Ommation Press (Chicago, IL), 1977.

*The January Poems,* Waters Journal of the Arts (Cincinnati, OH), 1977.

*More Waters,* Waters Journal of the Arts (Cincinnati, OH), 1977.

*Pantagonia,* Wormwood Review Press (Stockton, CA), 1977.

*Mad Girl Poems,* Out of Sight Press (Wichita, KS), 1977.

*Leaning South,* Red Dust (New York, NY), 1977.

*Lifshin & Richmond,* Bombay Duck (Oakland, CA), 1977.

*Poems with John Elsberg,* Fiasco (Filey, Yorkshire, England), 1978.

*Blue Dust, New Mexico,* Basilisk Press (Fredonia, NY), 1978.

*Glass,* Morgan Press (Milwaukee, WI), 1978.

*Early Plymouth Women,* Morgan Press (Milwaukee, WI), 1978.

*35 Sundays,* Ommation Press (Chicago, IL), 1979.

*More Naked Charm,* Illuminati (Los Angeles, CA), 1979.

*Doctors,* Mudborn (Santa Barbara, CA), 1979.

*Men and Cars,* Four Zoas Press (Ware, MA), 1979.

*Lips on the Blue Rail,* Lion's Breath (San Francisco, CA), 1980.

*Doctors and Doctors of English,* Mudborn Press (Santa Barbara, CA), 1981.

*Colors of Cooper Black,* Morgan Press (Milwaukee, WI), 1981.

*In the Dark with Just One Star,* Morgan Press (Milwaukee, WI), 1982.

*Want Ads,* Morgan Press (Milwaukee, WI), 1982.

*Mad Girl,* Blue Horse Publications, 1982.

*Lobsters and Oatmeal,* Pinchpenny (Boston, MA), 1982.

*Finger Prints,* Wormwood Review Press (Stockton, CA), 1982.

*Reading Lips,* Morgan Press (Milwaukee, WI), 1982.

*Hotel Lifshin,* Poetry Now (Eureka, CA), 1982.

*Leaving the Bough,* New World Press (New York, NY), 1982.

*Madonna Who Shifts for Herself,* Applezaba (Long Beach, CA), 1983.

*The Radio Psychic Is Shaving Her Legs,* Planet Detroit (Detroit, MI), 1984.

*Matinee,* Ommation Press (Chicago, IL), 1984.

*Remember the Ladies,* Ghost Dance Press (East Lansing, MI), 1985.

*Kiss the Skin Off,* Cherry Valley Editions (Silver Spring, MD), 1985.

*Blue Horses Nuzzle Thursday,* Illuminati (Los Angeles, CA), 1985.

*Camping Madonna at Indian Lake,* M.A.F (Portlandville, NY), 1986.

(With others) *Eye of the Beast,* Vergin Press (El Paso, TX), 1986.

*Madonna* (bound with *Vergin Mary* by Belinda Subraman), Vergin Press (El Paso, TX), 1986.

*Red Hair and the Jesuit,* Trout Creek Press (Parkdale, OR), 1987.

*Raw Opals,* Illuminati (Los Angeles, CA), 1987.

*Rubbed Silk,* Illuminati (Los Angeles, CA), 1987.

*The Daughter May Be Let Go,* Clock Radio Press (Harbor Beach, FL), 1987.

*Many Madonnas,* Kindred Spirit Press (St. John, KS), 1988.

*Dance Poems,* Ommation Press (Chicago, IL), 1988.

(With Belinda Subraman) *Skin Divers,* Krax (Leeds, Yorkshire, England), 1989.

*The Doctor Poems,* Applezaba (Long Beach, CA), 1989.

*Blood Road,* Illuminati (Los Angeles, CA), 1989.

*Under Velvet Pillows,* Four Zoas Press (Ashvelot Village, NH), 1989.

*Reading Lips,* Morgan Press (Milwaukee, WI), 1989.

*Not Made of Glass: Poems, 1968-1988,* edited by Mary Ann Lynch, introduction by Laura Chester, Combinations Press (Greenfield Center, NY), 1989.

(With Belinda Subraman) *The Innocents,* Buzzard's Roost Press, 1991.

*Sulphur River Lifshin Edition,* Sulphur River, 1991.

*The Jesuit Is Dying,* Big Head Press, 1992.

*Tammy Says,* Big Head Press, 1992.

*Apple Blossoms,* Ghost Dance Press (East Lansing, MI), 1993.

*Marilyn Monroe,* Quiet Lion Press (Portland, OR), 1994.

*Feathers on the Water,* Tazzerine Press, 1994.

*Parade,* Wormwood Review Press (Stockton, CA), 1994.

*Shooting Kodachromes in the Dark,* Penumbra Press, 1994.

*Blue Tattoo,* Event Horizon (Desert Hot Springs, CA), 1995.

*The Mad Girl Drives in a Daze,* JVC Books, 1995.

*Pointe Shoes,* JVC Books, 1995.

*Mad Girl Poems,* Morgan Press (Milwaukee, WI), 1995.

*Color and Light,* Lilliput Press, 1996.

*Mad Girls, Dead Men,* Lilliput Press, 1996.

*Madonna and Marilyn,* Taggerzine Press, 1996.

*Cold Comfort: Selected Poems, 1970-1996,* Black Sparrow Press (Santa Rosa, CA), 1997.

*Jesus Alive in the Flesh,* Future Tense Press, 1997.

*My Mother's Fire,* Glass Cherry, 1997.

*Before It's Light,* Black Sparrow Press (Santa Rosa, CA), 1999.

*A New Film by a Woman in Love with the Dead,* March Street Press, 2002.

*Another Woman Who Looks Like Me,* Black Sparrow Press (Santa Rosa, CA), 2003.

*OTHER*

(Editor) *Tangled Vines: A Collection of Mother and Daughter Poems,* Beacon Press (Boston, MA), 1978, new edition, Harcourt (San Diego, CA), 1992.

(Editor) *Ariadne's Thread: A Collection of Contemporary Women's Journals,* Harper (New York, NY), 1982.

(Editor) *Lips Unsealed,* Capra, 1990.

*Lyn Lifshin Reads Her Poems* (recording), Women's Audio Exchange, 1977.

*Offered by Owner* (recording with booklet of poems), Natalie Slohm Associates (Cambridge, NY), 1978.

*Some Voices,* 1993.

*The 375th Poem about Me Comes in the Mail,* Impetus Press, 1994.

*Mint Leaves at Yappo* (prose), Writers Digest (Cincinnati, OH), 1994.

*Hints for Writers* (prose), Writers Digest (Cincinnati, OH), 1995.

*On the Outside* (autobiography), 1995.

Also author of *The Jesuit Poems, Between My Lips, White Horse Café, The Radio Shrink, Sunday Poems, More Madonnas, He Wants His Meat, Appletree Lane, Sotto Voce,* and *Mad Windows.* Contributor to anthologies, including, *New American and Canadian Poetry,* edited by John Gill, Beacon Press, 1971; *Writing While Young and Seeing thru Shucks,* Ballantine (New York, NY), 1972; *Rising Tides,* Simon & Schuster (New York, NY), 1973; *Psyche,* Dell (New York, NY), 1974; *In Youth,* Ballantine (New York, NY), 1974; *Pictures That Storm inside My Head,* Avon (New York, NY), 1975; *I Hear My Sisters Saying,* Crowell (New York, NY), 1976; *Six Poets,* Vagabond (Ellensburg, WA), 1978; *Editor's Choice,* Spirit That Moves Us (Jackson Heights, NY), 1980; *Woman: An Affirmation,* Heath (Lexington, MA), 1980; *Contents under Pressure,* edited by Fred H. Laughter, Moonlight Publications, 1981; *Poetry: Sight and Insight,* Random House (New York, NY), 1982; and *Deep Down,* Dutton (New York, NY), 1988. Contributor to several hundred publications, including *Chicago Review, Rolling Stone, Ms.,*

*Chelsea, American Poetry Review,* and *Massachusetts Review.* Manuscript collection held at the University of Texas, Austin.

*SIDELIGHTS:* One of the most prolific contemporary poets in the United States, Lyn Lifshin has contributed to hundreds of anthologies and appeared in "virtually every poetry and literary magazine," as she once told *CA.* A critic for the *San Francisco Review of Books* called Lifshin "one of the most distinctive, prolific, and widely published poets of all time . . . and very popular with readers." In addition to publishing more than ninety collections of her own work, an autobiography, and a "how-to" book for other writers, she is also recognized for editing several critically acclaimed collections of women's writings and for her many poetry readings and writing workshops. Essayist Joseph Bruchac in *Contemporary Poets* contended that the very quantity of Lifshin's output has sometimes had a negative effect in terms of "overshadow[ing] the true range and significance of her work."

A typical Lifshin poem is small, consisting of a few words per line and rarely more than thirty lines in length. Her poems, Gerald Burns commented in the *Southwest Review,* are "long thin things." Enjambed phrases intensify the single emotion or event with which each poem is concerned, and humor is never far from the surface. Lifshin's poems, a writer for the *San Francisco Review of Books* believed, are "a quick, fun read, and [she] seems to strive for that effect." Kenneth Funsten of the *Los Angeles Times Book Review* explained that Lifshin "writes poems both spontaneous and sure of their mark." A critic for the *North American Review,* speaking of the speed with which a Lifshin poem can be read, called her "Queen of the quickies." Bruchac found irony in the fact that although Lifshin's poems are seldom more than a page, their cumulative "result is a body of work which is impressive in its size, almost epic in proportion." He also observed that "she seems to reach many of the final versions of her poems not so much by rewriting and reworking a single poem as by producing a series of poems which gradually—or even cumulatively—reach the desired effect."

Lifshin began to read "very, very early" and was writing by the age of three. She "skipped several grades in elementary school," where she was "unable . . . to do long division but . . . [was] pretty good at writing poetry." She grew up in Vermont, not far from the home of American poet laureate Robert Frost, who used to shop at her grandfather's department store. "I used to see Frost," Lifshin noted in the *Contemporary Authors Autobiography Series,* "wandering around Middlebury in baggy green pants, carrying strawberries." Lifshin continued writing poetry as she grew up, and when she first began publishing in literary magazines in the late 1960s her father showed one of her poems to Frost. "Very good sayeth Robert Frost," Frost wrote upon it, telling her father that he liked its striking images.

Lifshin's first poetry collection, *Why Is the House Dissolving?,* appeared in 1968. According to Hugh Fox in the *Greenfield Review* it is "a scathing, angry, iconoclastic, shocking, vituperative book." Part of this early anger was caused by Lifshin's failure to pass her oral examination for a doctorate degree in English literature, Fox believed. This anger led her to reject formal, academic writing—and the formal academic world, to which she has never returned—in favor of personal poetry. "She maintains," Fox wrote, "a high degree of *voluminous spontaneity* . . . [because she] doesn't see poetry as academic watch-making, but rather [as] an important expression of a primal interior *howl.*"

Speaking to Fox about her views on poetry, Lifshin explained that in the Eskimo language "the words 'to breathe' and 'to make a poem' are the same. I mean poetry is that central, essential, as much a part of me as breathing is." She told Theodore Bouloukos II in *Albany* that "when a great deal of time goes by and I haven't written, I begin to feel edgy. I think it's probably like somebody who has an addiction or an obsession." Writing in *Contemporary Poets,* Lifshin commented: "It seems to me that the poem has to be sensual . . . before it can be anything else. So rhythm matters a lot to me, more, or at least first. Before images even." She went on to single out "old black and country blues rhythms" as particularly influential on her voice. She likes to think of her poems as "strong, tight, real, startling, tough, tender, sexy, physical, controlled." In an online interview for *Amazon.com,* she revealed herself as an eclectic and nearly obsessive reader, and noted that her tastes and consequently the influences on her writing range widely from Dylan Thomas to Emily Dickinson to Charles Bukowski.

Similar to haiku and other short poetic forms, Lifshin's lean and concise poems are especially suited for re-creating a single moment or emotion, or describing a

particular place. Her best work, many critics believe, is found in her poems about historical subjects. Some of these pieces are collected in *Shaker House Poems,* in which Lifshin writes about the women of the Shaker religious communities of early America, having visited many of the original historical settlements. A *Choice* critic remarked, Lifshin "very successfully captures the spirit, the mood, the mystique of the Shakers, through magnificently crafted poems, terse as needlework." Her collection *Leaning South* contains poems about sites in New England and about the early Eskimo culture of the Arctic. Peter Schjeldahl, reviewing the book for the *New York Times Book Review,* found the Eskimo poems to be especially well done. These poems, Schjeldahl wrote, evoke "in fantasy, but with a lot of anthropological detail, the world of the ancient Eskimos. Here [Lifshin's] clipped line takes on a chantlike undertone, as of native voices themselves singing from the beyond, that is very pleasing." Fox explained that what Lifshin is doing in her historical poems is "creating a psycho-historical large canvas that traces the evolution of woman within the Occident."

Lifshin's feminist concerns are also evident in her popular "Madonna" poems, each of which describes a modern female archetype in a terse, often humorous manner. Titles in the series include *Madonna Who Shifts for Herself, Many Madonnas,* and *More Madonnas.* Speaking to Bouloukos, Lifshin explained: "Sometimes to be a little more flippant or satirical I use the Madonna as a metaphor. I'm relying on some of my own feelings and reactions which are often totally fictionalized and fantastic." A critic for the *Small Press Review* said of the "Madonna" poems: "Many have the quick, throw-away humor of the epigram, the pun," but also possess "the irony and resentment that provides much of the energy of Lifshin's poetry." Bruchac noted a greater depth and emotional impact in Lifshin's contemporary feminist poems, contending that "one would be hard-pressed to find another writer who has done as thorough a job of evoking the despair of a woman caught in the traps which social restrictions and marriage create for women." Yet more than dealing exclusively with a feminist perspective, Bruchac stressed that "few have written more bitingly or more tenderly about modern sexual mores" than Lifshin. "In her poems of sexuality," he stated, "both the emotional and physical relationships between men and women are laid bare."

In addition to writing poetry, Lifshin teaches classes and workshops in journal and diary writing. She keeps a diary herself and has drawn upon its entries for some of her poems. In 1982 she edited *Ariadne's Thread: A Collection of Contemporary Women's Journals,* which presents a wide spectrum of women's emotions and ideas on such subjects as relationships, work, families, death, and birth. "Most of the journals," Ursula Hegi wrote in the *Los Angeles Times,* "are spontaneous, fascinating, and often painfully honest. . . . Lifshin has woven a living tapestry of women's voices—often angry and sad, sometimes joyful and content, yet never self-pitying."

Lifshin has emerged as one of the most recognized woman poets in the United States. She has given many hundreds of poetry readings and participated in mixed media theater performances as well. In 1988 Karista Films released a documentary on Lifshin, *Not Made of Glass,* which shows her typical working day, a visit she made to the Yaddo artist colony, and a reading she gave at a local coffeehouse. Lifshin also appears on the *First American Poetry Disc,* a Laserdisc recording of readings given by contemporary American poets. Her manuscripts are being collected by the University of Texas at Austin and by Temple University.

A *Choice* reviewer claimed that Lifshin "has slowly moved up among the ranks of her peers . . . until . . . she comes practically to the top." Janice Eidus noted in the *Small Press Review* that Lifshin "continues to explore her poetic obsessions with her unique poetic voice and her unique sensibility." Speaking of Lifshin's writing career, Fox described it as "an artistically rich embattled journey into the fragile clarity of the Here and Now." Citing her rejection and condemnation of formal academia, a significant distinction among contemporary poets of renown, along with the ever-increasing range of subject matter she has addressed with intensity and honesty in her writing, Bruchac viewed Lifshin as "a risk taker. . . . Continually searching for meaning and identity. . . . One whose journey takes us along and teaches us as we go."

*AUTOBIOGRAPHICAL ESSAY:*

Lyn Lifshin contributed the following autobiographical essay to *CA:*

### *LIPS, BLUES, BLUE LACE: ON THE OUTSIDE*

There are only three things I clearly remember my father saying to me, all began with "Don't." Don't wear light pink lipstick, it makes your teeth look grey,

he told me at twelve or thirteen when I discovered Milkmaid's creamy gloss. "Don't invite me to your wedding, I don't want to be involved, or come. Or pay," a few years later, just days before that August 25, on the phone. And then, in the post office, the last words he'd say to me, "Don't do anything you don't want to." When I was born my mother says he was thrilled at my long legs and thought I looked like Ann Miller. Those first years I've heard he played with me every night. I remember none of that. Only how he sat quietly in the gold chair listening for the Dow-Jones average, rarely smiling. And the stain where his head touched that chair when he was gone. But he did one thing never maybe imagining its impact, something that has stayed with me as long as all he never did or said.

Born in Russia, my father had many qualities typical of Vermonters: he was quiet, frugal, taciturn. Maybe it was that lack of warmth, that withdrawn, brooding, often depressed mood, a dark coldness, that endeared my father and Robert Frost to each other. I used to see Frost wandering around Middlebury in baggy green pants, carrying strawberries. He bought those pants in Lazarus Department Store, my grandfather's store, and he would let only my father wait on him. At Syracuse, still afraid I couldn't write enough to take a creative-writing course, I submitted two of the only poems I'd written since high school to *Syracuse 10,* where Joyce Carol Oates published often. One was published. My father, without telling me, got a copy of that poem and showed it to Frost, who wrote on it, "Very good sayeth Robert Frost," and told my father he liked the striking images and wanted me to come and visit him, bring him more.

But, before then . . .

Like me, I think my mother married because she felt she ought to, at a time when there wasn't anything in the next couple of months she wanted to do. Then, on July 12, exactly nine months after my mother first slept with my father, I was born. They'd been married three months and she was beginning to wonder what kind of marriage this would be. They'd eloped July 1 in his brother's borrowed Chevy and went right to one sister's in Maiden, Massachusetts. My father didn't introduce my mother as his wife and slept in a separate room, as he would as they slid between various sisters' houses in Maiden, Winthrop, and Brookline, as unused condoms spilled from a bulging suitcase and he didn't touch her, even when they were alone. When he did, before she had time to think how to deal with the brother-in-law who blew up, sure the car was stolen, or get used to writing her name as Lipman, or had a day to think about what brides buy or the apartment, she was pregnant.

I was born in Bishop de Gosbriand Hospital in Burlington, Vermont. It must have been a beautiful day, my mother said yesterday when I asked her what the weather was, what songs were popular. "Everything about having you was wonderful," she tells me on the phone, that umbilical cord I've struggled to break from and always worry, dream, and dread, since I was five or six, about the time she won't be at the end of. "First," she says, "since it happened after the first time and I wasn't ready, I did panic and ask what I could take to stop it. But I felt great," she says, "not like when I was carrying your sister. With you, no morning sickness." The only bad dreams, she says, were those of war and a terror of Hitler. Even in the middle of the day she'd check the carriage I was in, swathed in cotton netting to keep spiders out, near the apartment I once tried, unsuccessfully, to find when I read at Norwich, near Barre. Perhaps she picked 23 Hill Street as higher, harder to get to should Hitler drift over the Atlantic to snatch me. In photographs of my first birthday party there, I'm the only girl clutching a huge black stuffed animal half dog, half horse.

My mother was the oldest girl, as I am. Only she'd been a disappointment, she always felt. I'm taping stories of her childhood and it always comes back to her father saying, "I wouldn't take a thousand dollars for her but you couldn't give me another for the world." With the smallest, unheated bedroom, my mother felt second-rate and for that reason always wanted daughters. She has few memories of getting attention or feeling special. Probably, tho she didn't even think of having children until she had them, this is why she went to the opposite extreme with my sister and me. She chose not to marry the man I think she cared most for, a non-Jewish law student she spent delicious college days at Simmons with. They went to lectures, on boat rides on the Charles River, laughed and danced until he did a Charlie Chaplin imitation of an old Jewish man and my mother, who never had much patience with acts or comments she considered symbolic, was horrified, knew then she'd have to forget him. She didn't become a librarian, an early choice, because friends said that was too prudish, too

unexciting for her. Instead, she left to work in New York City, in bookstores, Macy's, a credit agency she said was ghastly, any place bustling and alive. On October 9, 1936, she gave a cousin a first-edition copy of Margaret Mitchell's *Gone with the Wind* for her birthday, the address of the apartment they shared with two other young women on the frontispiece, apt. 4J, 53 West Seventy-second Street. Within weeks of moving in, my mother knew the neighbors on all the floors so fast the owner and landlord offered her a job collecting rent. My mother loved to dance, jitterbugged, loved plays, saw *Tobacco Road, a* number of musicals, Cab Calloway, and discovered a lovely French restaurant, Fleur de Lis, where they served multicourse dinners for fifty cents during the week, including shrimp cocktail, seventy-five cents on Sunday. Often she had three dates a day tho she was never a beauty, "except for good legs," she says. Even at seventy she could walk in three-inch heels up Boylston. My mother loved the city, travel, adventure, new people. Even now she's more apt to talk to people on the bus than I am. In her college yearbook people wrote, "For Frieda, get your own phone, so someone else can get messages." Others said her room always had the most girls, in their pleated skirts, midi blouses, cropped hair, and Clara Bow lips, giggling. Bubbly, fun, full of joie de vivre were the words most used.

My father came from Russia, from a town near Kovno in what was Lithuania. He was probably ten. No one is sure of his age. I always heard he was ten years older than my mother, and yet getting my birth certificate for a passport this week, he's listed as thirty-four when I was born, my mother twenty-eight. Even the day of his birth is unknown, and at one time May 10 was picked somewhat arbitrarily. His past, even his presence in the house with us, was shadowy, unreachable, a little dark. Unlike drawers of photographs of my mother and her three brothers and stories I'm still taping, of her birth in Mineville, New York, and the move to the house with crystal and ruby glass beads on Elm, to the house with the Chinese chair, still on North Pleasant, where she peeled barrel rings for hoops, hid china dolls so her younger brothers wouldn't smash them, and, when the family changed their name from Lazarovitz to Lazarus, heard her violin teacher say because of this she'd never become a famous violinist, what I remember of my father's childhood is fragmented and skimpy. Either he told me or I made up feather beds, chickens in the house, and tremendous pines, images I held on to, retold myself in an early poem where I imagine him coming

*The author as a child, with her father*

to this country "riding a gull's back." In photographs he seems to be touching my sister and me lightly, ghostly, as if not sure we were real. Or I was on the beach, fat, trying to catch a ball he'd never throw. My mother says he cherished me, read to me every night. I wish I remembered more than him sitting, a stranger, in that yellow chair, listening to stock reports. Or taking pills on the steep stairs up from Main Street. And how, just before my parents divorced, he'd made plans to have his stocks, on his death, go not to my mother or sister or me, but, like an eternal flame, or astronauts whose spaceship loses power, circle indefinitely. Coldly and untouchably. To this day, I'm drawn to inaccessible, cold men, those uncomfortable and awkward about intimacy.

My mother, all thru my childhood and teens, looked for a house, not an apartment. She wanted my father to want a house my sister and I would be proud to bring friends and dates back to. For twenty years she went out with real-estate agents, still lives in the apartment we moved into when I was six, a flat she never fixed up, certain they'd move soon. No accident that a house is important to me, that it is in the title of my first book, *Why Is the House Dissolving*, and that so many other books are about houses—*Shaker House*

*Poems, Old House Poems, The Old House on the Groton, Leaning South, Audley End*—and many series of poems are about old houses in New York, Vermont, Nantucket, Philipsburg Manor, or that so many of my dreams involve houses.

My father was good looking, quiet, probably intelligent. Unlike my mother, he didn't go to college, and he couldn't dance. My own ex-husband said, "To dance is the same as to have sex." He probably said fuck. My father must have found my mother's joie de vivre, her energy, laughter, and daring irresistible. I wish I'd known her then. She'd suggest friends drive at midnight to Boston, New York, or Montreal for a cup of coffee or crash customs because they were, coming back, low on gas. My mother loved Cab Calloway, danced in jazz clubs in Harlem. Somewhere she'd heard that the Lipmans made good husbands and at twenty-six or twenty-seven resigned herself to giving up a life of adventure.

I don't know if I got my tendency to do things to an extreme from my parents, but my mother went from having no use for kids—she'd say, "Use it well," at a howling baby—to making my sister and me her life. In the cellar, in a box of musty carbons, interviews, news clips, letters, I found a twenty-five-page outline for an autobiographical novel for a Chicago press I never wrote. It tells of my grandmother coming in 1888 from Lithuania, near Kovno, or Odessa, the daughter of a strict rabbi and a violin player. There are details I'd forgotten about, like her not marrying a Marty Melnick, a name I half wonder if I made up. There are notes about her two sisters, her sister's death in the 1919 flu outbreak. I planned to link three generations and had penciled in in the margin, "The theme of betrayals." In the chapter about my mother I started with her feeling hated because she'd been born a girl, something she stressed again in part of an interview I did with her less than two weeks ago. In her early memories of the deaths of grandmothers, the left-out feelings when other children hung up stockings, loved Jesus, sang carols up and down North Pleasant Street, and later of being followed by a father who didn't trust her, are clues to our tangled closeness.

One afternoon when my mother was in her early teens in Middlebury, Vermont, the kind of small town *Life* magazine used to come and photograph after snowstorms, a calendar village, white clapboard houses, village green, Episcopal church, a town where everyone is Protestant, possibly Catholic, and there were few ethnic names, no pizza, no Chinese food, my mother had a feeling of being pulled into her father's store. It was as if against her will, she told her friend Peggy, a magnet, a leash, a lasso. As I write this, I'm thinking how in my poetry and prose there's a quality, often, of interruptions, sidetracks, parenthetical descriptions, roads that go where I hadn't expected, a breathless run-on, convoluted style, stories that move, no, leapfrog and vault between the past and the present, which is really the way my mother talks. Maybe it's the way our family related. That afternoon she found out her mother had been so badly hurt in a car accident the next days the papers reported her dead. Gramp's hair turned white overnight. My grandmother was rushed to the Bishop de Gosbriand Hospital, a Catholic hospital in Burlington. For years I heard how the nuns brought her candles on Friday night, said you pray in your way and we'll pray in ours. In what seemed to many a miracle, my grandmother recovered, never to stop worrying, to such an extent we gave her worry beads. She expected disaster, picked up the phone, as my mother does, with a "Is something wrong?" Everyone was so grateful to the sisters and doctors my mother decided to have her first child at that hospital, even when her doctor tried to talk her out of it. All they care about is the baby and the father, she told me later, remembering the pain they gave her nothing for and how when she groaned or complained they were more concerned about the suffering, poor father. I still want to know what songs were on the radio, if there was one the morning she woke up and said she felt funny and they drove the thirty miles from Barre to Burlington. I'd like to know what my mother wore. Just this summer I put on a white and royal blue two-piece summer dress she had, wrote a poem about that. I have a black-velvet and fox cape she was given at eighteen by a man who still sees her as she was, in pleated skirt, giggling on bleachers in Boston.

*

After two weeks flat on her back, the day my mother brought me home my father was late picking her up and she didn't have any formula. "My insides," she said, "from being in bed so long, felt they were about to slide out." It must have been strange for her to have me howling, hungry. In the apartment she yelped, was in awe, and dragged her mother to see, not sure what to do with the first evidence I'd do more than howl in the diaper that would have to be hand-washed, boiled on the stove, hung from long lines that broke twice, plunging forty cotton diaper squares into mud.

The first baby, I was photographed it seems on the hour. August 11, four weeks less one day, wrapped in a blanket in tall grass, a house on the hill behind my mother and me. Six months and a day, January 13, against wallpaper with oriental trees I can't bring back to mean anything, tho in the hall of my mother's present apartment the wallpaper is something like that. In group photos, many of birthday parties, most people seem to be looking at me. The baby photos are labeled Rosalynn, my real name, a name my mother thought she'd made up, theatrical, good for an actress. Rosalynn Diane—a name I've used on and off. Even today, going for a new passport, I see it's the name I used on my expired one. Raisel Devora was my Hebrew name, I think. I've given myself that name anyway, liking it, finding it exotic. I wish I had some of the photographs still tied up and with the filmmaker for the documentary. In the early ones my mother's hair is dark and curly, her teeth, which wouldn't hold up well, a dentist told her ten years before, still very white.

Someone gave me a *Newsweek* from July of that first week with gas masks on the cover. On the first page, a Studebaker ad. Franco has just sentenced one hundred to death. Quaker Chemical announces a crystalline compound to make fabrics flameproof as Governor Long is rolling up his sleeves and someone looks back at Mussolini and Hitler. Stalin holds the balance, trouble brews. There's a photo of Goebbels patting blond braided young girls in Danzig as Winston Churchill's still smiling and Georges Braque and Kuniyoshi win awards. NBC resurrects the lost hit plays. I remember the ritual of curling close to my mother and father in their bed, a special treat on Fridays with cocoa and marshmallow fluff, listening to some radio program, and how at six I went into a mournful depression at the loss of a radio voice, Santa Claus, when my mother said, after the ritual and baths, and then listening to the radio reading of letters, he'd be gone for a year. I didn't believe I'd get thru that, much as I was sure I couldn't make it, losing the touch of others, on and off the radio now. *Newsweek* says portable radios are a find, about the size of a beach bag, light enough, finally, to carry. People drink Schlitz. My mother did, I bet, or Miller's, when she and my father went out for a big night at the Brown Derby. I see "Alan Carter," the father of a boy I'd have a crush on, "has created the 67 piece Vermont State Orchestra, Plain Folks Symphony." Esperanto looks good. Knox gelatin reduces fatigue. Books on the best-seller list have to do with those with Jewish blood being sadistically treated. No wonder my mother at times wished she'd brought us up as Christians, told us we had to be careful, being Jewish in a small town. Part of what always made me feel outside things, an onlooker, someone looking thru glass, as I did in the dark hail with stained glass and a black creaking grandfather clock, the stucco filling in my grandmother's house. Or, as a writer, I still feel.

When I was born, bicycles were big, and ocean liners. You could go for twenty-eight days for 127 dollars and up. Pepsodent sweetens breath. I wonder if I still use it for nostalgia. A lovesick man says, "I'll be holding my breath till I see you again," as the woman glad to get away shrugs, "Swell, dear." Skirts were just below the knees, a style not unlike this summer's. The dress my mother is wearing in one photograph could have come off this summer's Macy's rack. Except she would, having recently lost so much weight, after years of trying to, swim in it.

I said my first word at six months, "cig," for cigarette. And, before I was three, driving to Middlebury in a bumpy car on a back road over Lincoln Mountain, before the cigar a man smoked made me sick, said, "It looks like the trees are dancing," as we drove past. My mother wanted to write that down, an omen. If I wasn't to be an actress, I'd be a writer. Trees became a recurring image, and wood and women who, Daphnelike, run into trees. The first poem I wrote when I skipped and slid from first grade to third was about apple trees, and apples have been in the titles of at least three books, *Black Apples, Paper Apples* and *Forty Days, Apple Nights.* I live in a house on Appletree, and branches, hearts of wood, are inside and outside me.

We lived in Barre, a granite-mining town, where what I remember is a bench in a park where you could whisper anything and it would circle, come back to you. As some poems do. My father worked in his brother's store. Wearing a clown suit, I beat up the boy next door, and my mother defended me as she has and does, said I didn't do it, couldn't, was too sweet, rosebud mouth, huge eyes, plump but not fat. Yet. Maybe there was a song that had "Are you happy?" in it as a refrain. My mother, I heard, asked me that so

often that my father frowned, growled, "Don't keep asking her that. She might think she's not."

My deepest emotions are so tangled with my mother, sometimes in rage and anger—times I've felt suffocated, choked, sometimes with joy, often with the terror of losing her, something I felt as early as six, hearing stories of bad children playing with matches who start fires, burn their mother up. If I didn't write this piece now, with her thin, fragile, smaller, but still alive, it would be hard for years to, later.

She must have been fairly happy in Barre. There were a number of other young women having new babies, sharing terrors of war. It was before my mother and father started fighting as much as they would. Bridge games, mah-jongg, costume parties, suppers, birthday parties with those delicate crepe-paper baskets filled with jelly beans, gumdrops, peppermint patties, and a flower in a stem. Still in Barre, I'm naked in the grass, about one, with a boy who'd later invite me to Boston University. Close to three, I had my tonsils out, remember the bright-colored gum balls in the globe of glass, like stained glass I'd find magical later in Tiffany-style lamps and old stained-glass windows, bring back to my house to turn light less green. For years, perhaps because of the strangeness of ether, I was afraid to sleep on my back.

Ice cream after the hospital might have made up for the time there if November hadn't been fragmented by a rushed move my mother never wanted to make back to Middlebury. The town she was always ready to leave. Her brothers were in the army or at college or about to be, and tho she dreaded it, as if she knew once there she would never leave, reluctantly she and my father packed the white jigsaw horse that fit into a turquoise back and the Lindbergh doll I'd break in one of my tantrums, packed the black stuffed animal, ruby punch bowl, a wedding gift still on my mother's dining-room buffet, and the blond Heywood-Wakefield furniture, scorched with Marlboro and Camel and Herbert Tareyton burns, the locket with Rosalynn on it that I chewed, my first teeth marks on it, and my navy suspender skirt, my mother's camel-hair coat I never saw. And what, I wonder, of my father's did we bring with us?

They put sheets over the blue velvet sofa, still in the living room on Main Street covered over with the twentieth or thirtieth pair of sofa throws, three or four years before the small fluffy grey kitten peed on it and my mother splashed Clorox all over, turned the royal to bluish mud. They packed the gold chair my father left the stain of his head on, now a nubby yellow, and the chair I'd remember curling into the deepest curves of just before we'd move to the third house I'd live in, a night my father told me if you rubbed marbles long enough and hard enough they'd dissolve, loaded it in a van, a draped ghost in November snow, the leaves gone already.

The last thing my mother brought in the car could have been the red plaid carriage blanket downstairs, or the white and gold dishes last weekend she wanted to give me and I said, "Later." In the backseat, evening dresses my mother had many of before her marriage, now rarely needed, or the album of photographs of me, the windup Victrola, as much as they could fit into the black Plymouth my grandparents gave them that they couldn't afford, the pots and pans, and headed one and a half hours southeast for a stretch that wouldn't be anything like what my mother ever wanted.

Cold, raw, leafless. The weather a metaphor for the next many years, tho my mother might have told friends at the goodby parties, "It won't be as bad as I'm expecting."

\*

In spite of a fairly successful department store, Lazarus Department Store, a Middlebury landmark until the January after JFK died, when it burned down and, as if the store was a part of him, my grandfather died a few months later, my grandparents' house, even with company coming and staying for weeks, wasn't without its own darkness. By the time I got married, I expected marriage to be gloomy. Both grandparents came from Russia; Kovno and Odessa are the cities I heard. My grandfather had worked as a peddler, met my grandmother, married her, and started a small store in Granville, New York, and Witherbee, where my mother was born, before they moved to Vermont, Middlebury, an unlikely place for someone Jewish to bring up four children. He was supposed to be very religious, but my mother and I, later, caught him eating candy on Passover. As a young girl my mother was aware something peculiar was going on when her father brought the young Polish girl who worked for

them into the bed in the den where my mother, sick, was sleeping and she heard them grunting in the sheets and something about "nice pussy." Later my grandmother heard about her husband's exploits, fainted out on the front lawn, then moved into her own room. Maybe this was when she began to write poems she never showed anybody, perhaps because her older brother, Hyman, was known as the family poet, coming up with rhymed couplets for family events. I don't remember them, but do remember how he'd say before he died he wished he could see me with my hair cut. Now my uncle sleeps in the mahogany bed, near the elephant statues my grandmother collected, where she watched hemlocks, shadows the moon made on mirrors years of nights she couldn't sleep. When my grandfather died she showed no emotion. His room, never entered all the years he lurked there, was padlocked. My mother knew nothing good could grow of moving her own family closer to what she had left, braiding her life up with her parents again, bringing along this man who they hardly knew, was hard to know.

My grandmother was in many ways independent. She ran much of the business of the store. At different times we all worked there, muggy Julys before air-conditioning, folding Ship & Shore blouses, watching the clock that seemed to go slower as it reached into the eighties. After her accident my grandmother was sick often. I'm sure my mother felt trapped by the afternoon ritual: from the time I was three, and for years after my sister was born, she packed us each afternoon and brought us when my grandmother was sick or depressed there, where my mother tried to cajole her, read to her, told stories. She tried to be silly, make my grandmother laugh before hurrying back to the Emilo house, a brown and white two-story with blue grapes in the backyard, where once I was told, playing in a tub of water, I tore off my clothes and ran naked in front of two stuffy, aging schoolteachers. Miss Hincks, fortunately retired before I got there and Mrs. McCormack, a woman I never saw smile. My father withdrew more and more. Behind his back, my grandfather complained to my mother about him. She and my father, who even that early I began to call Ben, began to fight. Most of the fights had to do with money and houses. "Merle doesn't have to live like this," something I heard my mother say about my father's brother's wife, who had a beautiful home with a lawn, is in several poems.

Most Sundays we went to my grandmother's, a pattern that continued even when I was in high school. Grownups slapped cards and ate my grandmother's brownies while I read or daydreamed in the front living room, dark with an exotic black shiny dragon of a Chinese chair and a green water-lily rug surrounded by dusky roses. Before the uncles came home to stay, they were mostly scratchy uniforms. For a while I was the only grandchild, my hair piled on top of my head as I clutched a white elephant. I outgrew a pink, itchy snowsuit, plump, still not quite fat. My mother smoked more. My grandmother peeled tinfoil from gum wrappers, Black Jack and Pepsin, rolled and stored them in an elephant-shaped vase. My mother must have been waiting for something to begin or get over. In a few years we moved from the house around the corner from her mother's. In Vermont last weekend I could see that house on a postcard with an aerial view of the town. Set back from the street, pointed roof, slanted ceilings, on Seminary Street near the Methodist church where Patty Bissette, whose adopted parents never let her go out without a prissy dress, tight tight curls, was buried after she became one of the Boston strangler's choices.

The more I think about it, the more horrid those early years back in Middlebury must have been for my mother. Soon she was pregnant with my sister. This time tho with all-day morning sickness, a mother she felt obligated to rush to see, and no circle of friends. She lost weight, and when it seemed the baby was coming early, was rushed to Burlington. My grandmother hurried to take care of me. I was four, had measles. I clearly remember delicious hours in a darkened room my mother brought fruit juices to with a glass straw. Suddenly she wasn't there and my grandmother was flushing false teeth down the toilet in a wad of Kleenex and nothing seemed quiet or still.

In photographs of me and what turned out to be my sister, Joy, I seem happy, proud, grown up, and big sisterly. But much of waiting for her to be born was awful. I missed my mother, desperately. Over measles, I was sent to play-school, where, too unhappy to play, to distract me or make me laugh, I was hosed with icy water. I was enraged, had to go home and change, and have resisted, since then, organized play. All I liked of the playground was a house tall enough to stand up in and a vat of water we made oil and water prints in, globs of paint swirling plum, mango, and jade on meat-wrap paper.

I remember my loneliness, staying at my grandmother's. An uncle told me if I ate the small candy

pellets in glass ships on the piano, worms would crawl into my belly. The bedroom I slept in seemed icy, even in July with wasps in the shades. Nothing, not making clay men in the driveway or the smell of Yardley's Lavender in the orchid and green-tile bathroom, helped. When I fell off my tricycle, riding over cut-up cement, and bruised my leg and crotch and belly, I was furious. It was my new sister's fault. I wouldn't have been on that street if she hadn't been born.

Within months, we moved again. Not to our own house but the Zeno house, a stucco house I drove by last week. Sinks, motors, and mowers were in the front yard, the stucco almost guava. It was the end of the street then, near Battell Woods and a pine forest. Still as a church, carpeted with red needles. The house was surrounded by wildness. Queen Anne's lace in a clump of stones and, behind the house, rhubarb a baby-sitter once told us panthers lurked in, the night we put candles in halved walnut shells and floated them in pans of water. They made eerie shadows anything could have lurked in. Upstairs the bedrooms had wide boards painted grey, with enough room between them for dead bugs to pile up, and heat grates where I could lie on my stomach listening. Eavesdropping. As I still do, spying. I learned to read early, before first grade. *Jack and Jill* magazine had stories of soldiers and dentists and a stone that would glow red and rose in a closet and transformed itself if you held it close and tight.

I painted Cheerios into rainbow beads, longed for a kitten. On the night before my sixth birthday, after my parents had tried to get one, a scraggly kitten appeared at the door, and within months she had kittens she was too young to take care of. My mother thought the kittens would die, until another pregnant cat appeared, gave birth in a coal bin, and when water rose, my father and one of the bigger cats carried many mewling, wet, scrawny bags of fur to the top stair. The boxes of cats in the kitchen near the old white and grey stove on legs is one of my warmest memories. It's cats, not dolls, I hold in most photos.

My sister was born dark with a birthmark. I was appalled, sure people would think because she had blue eyes she didn't belong in our family. She got blond, slowly became someone to play with. One uncle was still at Fort Devon. My mother made him brownies, one of the few recipes handed down to me, and

*Lyn, her father, and her sister, Joy*

listened to the brown Zenith. Across the street in a dark house with coves and a spiral teak staircase, a house that smelled of lemon, oil, polished wood, a smell that pulled me to the house I now live in and know it probably meant the heat-vents exchanger was about to go, a Baptist minister who was always trying to convert us lived, with his two daughters, Geraldine and Priscilla, who once lured me to steal some matches from their stove and bring them out to the club we were making in chickory and wild carrot.

That last summer on Seminary my mother rented a cottage at Mallets Bay on Lake Champlain. Inside, ceilings were low and the rooms smelled of oilcloth, linoleum, and citronella. Louis Armstrong played near a roller-skating rink across the way, where I found a girl with one blue eye and one green eye riveting. All these images haunted when I wrote about them, leaving Vermont for good. Until writing this tho, I hadn't realized how many scary memories are connected to baby-sitters. At the lake, the baby-sitter filled us with stories of atrocities in Germany and Poland, "what they did to young girls," and she painted the smoke from bodies in tunnels, said you could smell scorched hair. This may be where over a year of nightmares about fires began. And where two other obsessions got a start: wanting to be thin and wanting to have straight, not curly, wavy hair. It was the summer before school began I started to see myself as fat and ugly, and having to wear glasses very soon didn't help. A cousin, Elaine, was skinny and pretty and snotty and always had her way. I thought the two went together. In a photograph from that summer I'm standing on the wharf looking unhappy in what seems like an old lady's two-piece bathing suit, my sister is cute and blond and skinny. A poem I often read, "Fat," deals with the loathing I had/have if I step on the scale and weigh more than I expected. I especially hated having legs I thought fat, especially thighs, and in one photo it looks like I'm trying to hide them. The first five years I took ballet, I'd only wear black tights. Until this past year I've had long hair that wasn't straight without help. I can smell the dampness of leaves near the lake, wet wooden stairs. Night smells, wild roses opening. My mother's cigarette on the next screened porch was a beacon. We washed our hair in the lake, just mothers and children, except for Saturday nights. When I combed my wet hair sleek and straight I prayed it would stay that way, horrified to find it curly in the morning.

For my mother, being at the lake meant seeing her women friends from Barre for the summer. In Middlebury, weeks before school started, we moved again, and again, not to our own house. I'm sure my mother never expected that this many years later she'd still be in those rooms.

Thirty-eight Main Street. An apartment.

\*

We had to give the kittens and cats away. Later I'd say I got married to give my cat a home. In my own homes, I'm never catless. The first poems I sold, wrote, and made money on, were a blue book of cat poems.

The Main Street apartment, run down now and getting that way a long time, never was fixed, because my mother hoped, wanted, longed, begged, argued, demanded, but never got, a house of her own. Finally my grandfather bought the building so we wouldn't have to move again. With low or no rent, my father seemed even less interested in a house and grew increasingly distant, like too many men I've tried to know. In their louder, more frequent fights, my mother yelled that if he cared for any of us, he'd want a house. Not wanting that translated into not caring about us.

The flat jutted out over Otter Creek, rushing, falling in the spring and a trickle in summer. From the room that became my last bedroom, a whirlpool of branches, old marble mill, the Alibi, a bowling alley where I

remember on a New Year's I had a date wearing a blue dress with rhinestones, hoping my hips didn't look enormous, then a bar, and Middlebury College Chapel spire slicing the last blood and purple sun. In the back of the house, the falls shut out fighting. Since then, I've run from confrontations, arguing, proving, combating. Except on paper.

*Upstate Madonna* has a series of poems based on the history of Middlebury, some of the haunting bits of the past I read about took place along Otter River and the river recurs in poems. And the images of water, things that flow and blur, take something important away. To this day I often put the dishwasher on before I go to sleep. The apartment still haunts when I go there, in spite of what I've brought back with me: velvet boxes of fraternity pins, rhinestone earrings I can still connect with the first Iranian man I had a crush on, who pulled me upstairs at the Middlebury Inn onto his bed. Each inch in the house is a museum. The rooms could be elegant, people usually say, but they aren't. The August we moved in my mother stayed up all night spraying, painting everything with Clorox. In dampness, hideous fuzzy bugs waddle over the grey rug that gets thinner. It was like being fat or Jewish to not have a yard: different, separate, outside what mattered.

I suppose most artists feel they didn't or don't fit in, are on the outside. That they observe carefully and redo much in a way that feels better. Another scary baby-sitter incident happened not long after we moved in. Lela, who may have stayed with us before, asked me on a night it was still light and the creek was roaring if I wanted to play doctor, pulled off my underpants, put her tongue in and all over. I didn't fight her, but when she took off her clothes and tried to push my head and mouth into what seemed a scary mess of hair I pulled away.

My mother's living room faces Main Street. I'd watch, for hours, listening, imagining. Read, draw, dream. Thru glass. At a distance. On Main Street I often ducked into store doorways if there was someone I didn't want to see, not unlike the way now I almost never answer the door unless I expect someone, keep an answering machine on.

I loved reading, and it was knowing how to, at four or five, that catapulted me quickly out of Mrs. Butterfield's first grade into second then third grade when there weren't enough chairs. What I remember of second grade is Miss Everts, skinny, ostrichlike in black silk, and that we made clay animals in a room full of lilac and lilies of the valley and that I wore a black embroidered wool jumper that was pretty but itched. Then I was in third grade with Mrs. Flag. This is where writing poems seriously started, probably because I never learned much long division. Shoved thru those first grades, words were what I grabbed and held on to. Especially words in poems Mrs. Flag had us read, poets like Blake, Milton, Wordsworth. I loved the *Children's Hour,* the mystery and magical sensuousness, and had read *Now We Are Six* a bit earlier, judging by the pencil stabs in the margins and drawings of horses. I especially liked "I had a little beetle, Alexander was his name," "Buttercup Days," "Where is Anne? Close to her man. Brown head, gold head, in and out the buttercups," and "Binker."

Mrs. Flag had us write a lot of poems. 1 wrote about apples, apple blossoms, umbrellas. A packet of handwritten early poems is now in Temple University's archives. One Saturday I copied a poem of William Blake's out from *Songs of Innocence,* showed it to my mother. Since Middlebury, then, had a population of about three thousand, it's not surprising she ran into this teacher, said how thrilling, wonderful it was she'd inspired me to write this poem full of words like "rill" and "descending." So I had to write my own poem by the next Monday.

I don't know how old I was when I saw the film *Bambi* but I was horrified that a mother could just burn up. That, and stories of Germany and a terror that began on a school trip, kept me dreaming of fires and death at least two years. My father drove four of us, one of the few times I remember him being involved with anything I was doing, to Ticonderoga, a day trip my mother still has the postcard we sent her from. What the postcard doesn't say is how I was intrigued and terrified by what was thought to be the mummy of a six-year-old Indian child. Each night I imagined turning to stone, how people could lose each other. What dissolves, disappears, can't be held or touched long enough, haunts what I write.

Maybe I wanted to pare as much of myself as I could away, like a Shaker chair, so there wouldn't be more to lose, have taken from me. I wanted to be skinny but heard relatives suggest I try Chubbettes. I'm sure there really was, as in "Fat," a man in a furniture store in

Rutland who said my sister was blond and pretty, and then, looking at me with disgust, asked my mother if it was hard, having this *other* child. I'm sure he sneered or growled. I curled in the brown chair and ate M & M's, read, listened to "Let's Pretend." Friday nights I'd curl up with my mother and father in their bed with hot chocolate. In the back of an autograph book I kept from the age of nine to when I was fourteen (with its recipes for Man Ketchup and puns) I drew a ballet dancer on pointe with my name under it: Rosalynn. Legs longer and thinner than I thought mine would be. I lost myself in painting, took ballet, longed for tall thin legs like Sally Smith's, who was "discovered" on a ferry, became a model, was on *Today* and *Tonight,* then was ditched at nineteen, as old. Louise, one of my closest friends, lived in a wonderful old brick house with window seats where we dreamed of boys, of how to get them to ask us out, walked to the river, made a clubhouse one winter in an uprooted tree. Everyone I knew went to Pilgrim Fellowship or Catholic Youth. My sister got blonder, cuter, more popular with boys, I got A's, dreamed of being an actress. Or airline hostess. I took violin lessons and baton and once, after a hurricane, walked thru broken wires to Mrs. Russo's house, tho warned not to, as obsessive about not missing those lessons as I am about ballet lately. I rode horses, painted black stallions against flame and mango sky, gypsies dancing around camp fires. I wanted to be a gypsy, to change my name to Gitana. For a while I went from Rosalynn to Lyn, was mortified when told Lyn was a boy's name. I didn't rebel much until twenty-six or twenty-eight. But I did once, with a group of other girls, leave Girl Scouts, leave Mrs. Drake, who I later wrote of as "elephantine in khaki," to form a more adventurous club. One initiation trial was to jump into an open grave. It sounded like jumping on tin. Once in, I couldn't get out, was sure I'd be left. Still, a leitmotif.

In fifth grade, Miss Hogan, a favorite teacher, had us write how we could change ourselves. Thinner, I said, taller, no glasses, no curly hair. In sixth grade, Ginny, the prettiest girl in school, and one of the thinnest, who later would be badly hurt and scarred in a car accident, did a term paper on "Scotland, England, Whales." Blushing wildly when she realized her mistake seemed only to make her more attractive to the boys. Tho I'd skipped several grades and was younger than the other kids, I got my period too fast and wasn't happy. At twelve I was sure I didn't want children, used Kotex not with pride, like the other girls, but with resentment. I was sure I could tell by the way a woman walked if she had this nuisance. Pregnant women seemed even worse.

During grade-school years my family would go to Maine for a week or two, dolls of rubber turned brown in the backseat car window. Packing the doll clothes was more fun than going. That "looking forward" may be what Hugh Fox called the "tantalization" in my poems. I had crushes on movie stars, read about Valentino, decided dark men were for me. Men like Tony Dexter, who looked like Valentino in a movie, or Mario Lanza, kept scrapbooks on both. I loved the sadness and drama of Valentino's early death, of Pola Negri's veiled visit to his grave each year with white roses. Polio was still a fear tho hardly anybody I knew got it. I rarely felt pretty during this time. Once I remember thinking it was stupid for me to be able to get clothes from my grandfather's store (which later became my uncle's) when there were other girls they'd look better on. My mother said I was pretty but I didn't believe her.

On one trip to Maine, after eating glazed donuts on an especially hot day, my father had pains and we left suddenly, drove to Maiden where his relatives still stayed. I was ten or eleven when this new, scary symbol of loss and uncertainty jammed itself into our lives. For two weeks my sister and I stayed with one of my father's sisters in a cold house we felt lonely and scared in. Especially when mystery programs on TV slithered up under the door where we were supposed to be sleeping. My sister and I felt abandoned, that things had changed. After that, my father became more depressed, quiet. He'd climb the thirty or forty steep stairs to the apartment slowly. Often, driving, he'd stop and put a white pill under his tongue. Many nights he got up with pain and sat in a chair. My mother got up with him, stayed up weeks with no sleep. One doctor, Dr. Paul White, thought he'd worried himself into a heart condition. He stopped smoking right away. My mother smoked twice as much.

Since my father couldn't play softball anymore (I'm not actually sure he ever had), my uncles, who had girlfriends, many of them, but didn't marry until late, taught me to pitch and catch and hit a ball. In photographs, the living room is still wallpapered with a design that looks like feathers. On the dusty piano, in that room, my sister and I and, somewhere in a drawer, my mother are caught in matching caramel, butterscotch, and snow pinafore dresses. My sister's

long blond hair had to be curled. One uncle had a store, United Five to Dollar, with thread, buttons, and odd joke cards under the counter. One had a woman who squirted from between her knees when anyone opened the cover. There were fires in the A & P under us, as if the dreams of fire and smoke were omens, and we ran out twice in the middle of the night, in nightgowns. Summers it was often too hot to stay upstairs. We went for rides to Lake Dunmore or made tents with poles and army blankets in the front yard on North Pleasant. Or sat on my grandmother's screened-in porch. I'd wish I was still light enough to be carried back home, upstairs, sleeping. Spirea, red spirea, peonies, and yellow roses crawled toward my grandparents' house.

The summer I was eight I went to Camp Hochelaga. Two days in the top bunk with bratty Birdie Rothman, the sting of homesickness, the devastating separation from my family, my mother especially, made me so despondent that nothing, not swimming, archery, stories around a camp fire, not the smell of fresh-cut pine or apricot jam could soothe. After two days my parents were called to come for me. I wondered even then if I could ever not feel pain leaving. The pull and stranglehold of Middlebury, in spite of ambivalent feelings, makes the town a character in itself. The ache each time I left for school, or even now, started then. In "The Visit" the silences, unanswered questions, tensions, losses, separations, and deaths haunt, are that "heavy love," images that can never be unified or undone. When I came back from camp, quickly, I found *Love without Fear* in the bathroom and, reading thru it, was fascinated by the words "If a girl lets a man put his tongue in her teeth, she'll let him do anything," leaving me astonished, curious, wondering.

As early as grade school I felt even if I was fat and shy and wore glasses, was too serious, later, maybe, it would be different. In one of those red five-year diaries I wrote, "I want to be an actress," and pages later, "I want to be a ballerina." Recently I've put together a group of dance poems, and doing readings is a way of performing, of acting. Bob Peters called one book something like "Madonna as Boardwalk Tease," and there is an undercurrent in many poems, a feeling of a speaker who would and could turn herself inside out to startle and stun, an actress trying on costumes: mad girl, madonna, "blond vamp," "rock star," Hugh Fox says in his book about me, Indian woman, Plymouth woman, women who are seductive, reclusive, Holocaust survivors, women married to six-hundred-pound men, women who were Houdini. It's a way of looking in, thru glass, a way to, as Fox says, "be in the world but not part of it."

People rarely see I have a temper. That rage and anger are transformed into poems. Perhaps when I saw "kike" on the blackboard I started storing barbs: my strongest poems have been triggered by rejection or rage. I wish I had, in a December 6 diary entry, written when I was about thirteen, detailed what the black mood flowered from when I wrote, "Oh God, there's only one thing I want. I want to die."

Few got divorced. In spite of a lot of fights, in photographs my parents still have their arms around each other, and there's one picture, near the Morgan Horse Farm, where my father is holding both my sister and me close; in many photographs tho, he seems to touch us cautiously, lightly, as if not sure we are real. On the way home from those nightly rides to watch the colts, watch the elms and maples leafing out, we drove thru a wooden bridge, Pulpmill Bridge, held our breath, closed our eyes, made a wish.

I wish I'd written in that sketchy diary what more of those wishes were. By seventh and eighth grade, still in the same brick elementary school with rickety fire escapes and the smell of floor wax, halved apples, they focused on boys. Pancho Gonzalez, who'd hold his hand over the lump in his crotch and jiggle it at Paula and me, grinning, taunting us to touch it. For two years Mr. Dewey taught, flirted, punished, and in subtle ways lured and manipulated. A lot of us had crushes on him. A compliment from him and we'd be floating over the wooden chairs, a snide look or sarcastic "Oh Rosalynn, a dress today? What's the special occasion?" and I'd blush. I especially hated being weighed in front of everyone, the offensive number blurted out for everyone. We still played marbles, kick the can, red rover, but what boys were thinking and wanting and saying began to mesmerize us and we'd focus on what we could do to lure those who were worth luring.

Christmas was the holiday I remember clearest. Tho we had a Christmas tree sometimes, it was usually rather small, portable enough to be shoved into a closet when my grandfather clomped up the stairs. Christmas Eve my mother and father worked in the store. Snow

*The author (bottom right) as a gypsy in a high-school talent contest*

turned Main Street white, lights stretched from the Battell Block. We may have had Hanukkah candles but I remember the red and green lights more clearly, smell of holly. The best presents were books to curl back with under the quilts with a half-eaten maple-sugar man. One Valentine's Day I ran thru the hall, broke a thumb that had to be bandaged in a thick clumsy cast. I had a new green dress for that Valentine's party, but along with pink plastic glasses, this clunky bracelet made me feel even less lovely.

In my diary, I see notes about skating. I was never good at that. The beauty and chill of nature came to me mostly thru overnight camping hikes, lying in pine beds listening to stories, and the nearly clear blue light starting like the blue light in a painting on velvet in my grandmother's dining room.

\*

For the first day of high school I carefully selected a black and red striped dress I hoped would hide what I wanted it to. I'd have given anything those years to have been popular, not on the dean's list, to be slutty, a cheerleader, like Joyce Menard, someone boys wanted to take across the state line, or exotic as Jo Ann, whose father came to open a funeral parlor with his daughter, who danced, who even tho she said she weighed a hundred and thirty pounds was tan, firm, flashed a white-toothed smile so many found irresistible. It wasn't until the second month of high school, October 9 or 10, that I realized I wasn't popular, sexy, grabbable, or longed for, and the pain and rage of sitting with socks like absurd cotton fluffy rabbit blimps on the gym bleachers, only slightly camouflaged, slammed me. It's one of the most vivid, unpleasant images, and it carved such nightmarish anguish that, as so many poems suggest or scream, "some part of me would never stop waiting to be asked to dance." I learned that if I couldn't get attention wiggling my hips, if I had to pretend I wasn't all that studious to boys like Doug, who I never liked, but, since he was on the football team, was relieved to have ask me to dances, games, and parties closed to me before this, I could get attention drawing and painting and getting awards for that.

Three years I worked alone, like a poet, often waiting for the phone to ring, in agony, or ecstasy about some boy, on science projects that always won prizes on the local, state, and national level and gave me the chance, as with poetry readings, to be in another town, where boys didn't know I was really shy, serious, and scared. At least for a short time, in the dazzle of models, posters, newspaper reporters, I could fool them. I did an exhibit on dentistry, one on carbon, and the biggest one, complete with huge papier-mâché model of the eye using about twenty bottles of vaseline for the aqueous humor and twelve bottles of clear glue for the vitreous, a display that took up six or seven tables and quite literally was "The Eye" screaming, look at me! In my diary from then: For each of these three exhibits, three different years, the comments squeezed into those tiny allotted four lines had little to do with the science fair but were mostly the reactions of others. "Ed Foote thought I was good," one year. Another year, "Went to Morrisville and won first prize," with four exclamation points, followed by "Met Dick Frenier." And another year, "Went to Springfield Science Fair, won second. Met Bobby Jones, a doll," and finally, "Lots of congrats. Even from Mark (the intellectual macho heartthrob), at music David and Hilton said congratulations. This afternoon *Rutland Herald* took my picture for the paper. He made such a fuss over me." Only in another town, I was sure, could someone as moody, wild, hoody as Cat Callahan have found me someone he could write "To my sweet brown eyed baby" and sign it, "The Cat," on the back of the rather punk photo of him holding a Fats Domino record. When I saw the recent Sylvia Plath documentary I couldn't help but think of a similar need, a passion to win, prove, startle, lure, be alluring.

I won United Nations Poster contests, was the first Miss Middlebury High in *Tiger's Tale,* and wrote, usu-

ally with polysyllabic Latinate words from *Word Wealth,* poems, won art contests, designed dance programs for proms I was in agony I wouldn't even get asked to, did the high-school yearbook drawings. One fall I was sent to New York City to the Columbia University yearbook conference and fell in love with New York, the Rockettes, Hitchcock films, lights, crowds of people. Carmelina, the girl I went with, who I thought would later be a nun, and I were so innocent, so sheltered, that a flasher across the way captivated us, had us giggling, unbuttoning the top buttons of leather jackets. Somehow we gave him our phone number at the Plymouth Hotel so the phone rang all night in the adjoining room, where the teacher we came with grew increasingly puzzled and annoyed.

In an English class I wrote one story that showed me the power of words. I watched Mrs. Cunningham cringe and frown as she read of the speaker being petted and stroked. Then I saw her relief, at the end, discovering it was from a dog's point of view. I loved how I could hold students on the edge of their seats. At twelve or thirteen, when I saw a poem in a Middlebury College literary magazine about trading freedom for a ring of gold, I felt the same way.

I never thought of marriage and children as a goal or dream. Important as attention from boys was, I often preferred reading alone, knew clearly I didn't want to be just someone's mother. I didn't want to run down for nylons, as my mother did, rush out for those bottles of vaseline for any daughter's science projects. The ambivalence and longing and running to and away from the same thing with equal wildness that gives my best work its intensity, I'm sure began in high school. To not get a phone call from some boy, to feel someone I wanted didn't want me, was as devastating as later being thought of as someone's wife would be.

Summers after my father's heart attack were spent on Cape Cod, where the water was warmer than in Maine. I loved Hyannis Music Tent. *Brigadoon* and *Countess Maritza* were favorites, and being in summer stock a daydream. I wanted to write, too, remember trying on a rainy day in a cabin, the Henry House, to find something worth writing about, wondering if I'd ever have anything to say.

The cliché about bad love making good songs applies to poems too. The January I was fourteen or fifteen, David Lane, a rather strange, tall, aloof, dark-haired, difficult senior on the brink of a navy career called me and began the pull, the attraction, of a string of similar men, adept at the yo-yo technique: slam you in and slam you away, something I've often been too vulnerable to, the agony-ecstasy poem trigger. If I had written poems then, I'd probably have churned out orange crates full. Instead, I worked on those science projects. Waited, refused other boys. Waited for the phone too often, bought sheer blouses, not unlike some recent contortions, lace this time. Now there's a number of poems with blue lace in them. At fourteen, it took weeks to feel fingers inch toward plastic and rhinestone buttons, towards bra straps. I agonized when he didn't talk in study hall or on the Middlebury College campus, where for months, after a fire burned the high school down the night I saw *Giselle,* we had classes. When he left, not even saying goodby, I felt my life at fourteen or fifteen was over. Those feelings, even so many years later, are not at all unfamiliar. That July my parents took me to Saratoga, perhaps to distract me. Groucho Marx, after a play where he came out onstage and answered questions, motioned to me, pointed out what he called my "astonishing hair." I was too despondent to bother noting it in my diary. When I saw David in the fall he wrote on a photograph, "To my dearest from her swabby in his brother's civvies—to you Ros with all my fondest thoughts and deepest affections I love you." I wasn't prepared for him to disappear again. Wordlessly. Something to this day I hate. I think it was the impetus to lose enough weight to finally become pretty. "You'd better start eating," Ginny Lafayette wrote in the yearbook, and Linda Goulash wrote, "To the girl with the biggest waist," by then a joke.

Like my mother I looked forward to leaving Middlebury in my new body, leaving high school, letting those Junior Women's Club dances and hayrides women had to invite men to, wait for them to "decide," and then often get no for an answer, fade. Even the best of those events, even when Ron Agassipour pulled me up to his room at Middlebury Inn and peeled rhinestone spray earrings from where they were making holes in my ears. I was looking forward to leaving even Dick Wood, who died before he was twenty-eight, Fitzi, brazen and charming but difficult at the Drive Inn, tho a great subject for poems, like a beached whale in a poem just published in *Deep Down* and a prose piece forthcoming. It was goodby to Annette, who had two babies, came back to school, walked the babies up and down Frog Alley, and to Paula, whose sister lured Leo Durocher back to Middlebury years

later, only to have him run off with Paula's and Carolyn's mother, their father's wife, end up with an alienation-of-affections lawsuit, and even to Martha with her iris torn—enough characters, like callers on local nighttime talk radio, to write a Spoon Riverish unending play.

At graduation, tho I had, like no one else, won local, state, and national science contests, the school opted not to give a prize for outstanding science work that year, as if there was no one worthy. I don't remember graduation night. My mother probably does, she was always there, remembers better than I do what I wore to each dance, how I'd change my clothes sometimes for two hours "to be right." I don't know if we had what's now called a disfunctional family; my father rode the *Wall Street Journal.* In an early poem, "Traveling," I saw him "riding the *Wall Street Journal* / leaving with a brown bag of loss" and wondered, "How do we learn to be whole." That he'd never told me I was pretty stung and comes back years later. To my mother, I was always a beauty. Just yesterday, an incident I've spit out in poems, of being in that furniture store in Rutland, couldn't, she insists, have happened.

                              *

Brandeis was my first choice for college. I was drawn to the political and artistic energy, a rebellious, counterculture mood I found exciting when I went there for my first college weekend, a sophomore in high school. People in Boston smirked, "You can tell they're from Brandeis." Instead I began at Syracuse University as a drama major. Within the first week everyone I met had exotic names like Neela Dunay and it seemed years of summer stock or off-Broadway experience. I switched to English with a minor in radio and TV and art history. The closest I got to theater was teaching drama and ballet Saturday mornings with two other students, including Frank Langella.

Moving into Mt. Olympus that first September afternoon, the image of my roommate: cigarette-smoking woman in a tight orange-striped sheath, twisting to some music in her head. Mementos from that uneasy alliance surfaced the other day. In a box of photographs, handwritten notes this woman left me— one ended up triggering a poem in one workshop when I smelled fruit and remembered a box of oranges and grapefruit mailed me that winter, delivered on the floor outside my door, since Fran insisted on the whole green stucco room being dark early. Scrawled at the end of a Hemingway quote was "Lyn I'm trying to sleep so please be a little careful the door doesn't slam and the light is at a minimum." I drew her in crayon first as a black stick, a dead figure on the floor in a black room with everything bright as fruit a long distance from her.

The whirl of being social was overwhelming. I was informed, by an empty-headed handsome jerk who four years later appeared at another school and said, since he was leaving to serve Uncle Sam, I should, tho I hadn't talked to him for years, for my country, do him *the* service, he wouldn't date a woman who wasn't in a sorority and the sorority had to be one of three. During rushing, sorority sisters would touch your shoulder to see if your sweater was lamb's wool or cashmere. Or just Orlon or wool. I have those lilac, pink, blue, and white Dalton cashmeres with me. Still. Football was as important as cashmere. We learned placard cheering the first week. I had six dates—including a flasher who did it on one of the seventy-seven steps up to Mt. Olympus so quickly I thought perhaps a few teeth on his zipper just broke, until two years later at a sorority coffee he pulled me off into a corner and did the same thing again. One afternoon of that frantic, exhausting, confused orientation week I thought maybe marriage would be easier. But soon I was swept up in what must have been like the fervor Americans felt going to France or what artists felt in the twenties and thirties in Greenwich Village. I got a C- or D+ on my first college English composition, "purple" was written on it, crammed as it must have been with all those polysyllabic words. "Commingling," I remember the professor wrote, isn't a word. It was, I later gloated. Maybe this was when I began to pare down my writing, as well as my hips, and be drawn to things Shaker. The next semester a professor made poetry magical, Mr. Marx. I was transfixed by Dylan Thomas. Only a few poems in an anthology, but enough to make me want to do my master's thesis on him. And Garcia Lorca.

By my sophomore year I discovered the man who in an odd way, in his strange courses, most touched something that made feelings and urgency and experiences and excesses justifiable, made being aware of living in the moment, not in some vague future, what really mattered. Leonard Stanley Brown died over

Christmas vacation. It was rumored to be suicide or severe alcoholism. He'd taught a number of three-figure courses: Lawrence, Nietzsche, and Dinesen, or Mann, Joyce, and Nabokov. He knew Pasternak and would come in late saying he'd just been talking to Nabokov. When we studied Joyce, he'd read, over and over, the Molly Bloom speech, half in our world, half in his, with "I got him to propose to me yes first I gave him the bit of seed cake out of my mouth and it was leapyear like now yes 16 years ago my God after that long kiss I near lost my breath yes he said I was a flower of the mountain yes so we are flowers all a womans body yes that was the one true thing he said in his life and the sun shines for you today yes that was why I liked him because I saw he understood or felt what a woman is and I knew I could always get round him and I gave him all the pleasure I could . . ." When I asked him for a reference he said, why don't you just leave school, travel, see people, I wanted to.

Art-history classes were a drug. I could barely wait to have the room darken, the slides go up. I longed to live in Athens or Florence. Some of the guest artists I remember were Lipshitz, Herbert Marcuse, Robert Frost, Aaron Copland. I was fascinated by talks on *On the Road* and Kerouac and the Beats. I joined a sorority, thought I ought to. A Jewish one, since I'd never quite belonged in Vermont, with one friend's father an Episcopal minister, most of my other friends Congregationalists. I envied the dark stained-glass quiet of the church we'd play in during the week and the socials, parties. But I felt different, too, with these Jewish women. An outsider there, too. I never knew the Jewish or Yiddish phrases, so my roommate for the last years of college, Dorothy, tried to teach me a few needed phrases, like "drop dead," with her Rochester accent. I never fit into the sorority tho I was social chairman, found the counterculture more interesting than sororities or fraternities. I heard Emlyn Williams do his Dylan Thomas performance, Segovia, Pablo Casals; and I applied for Syracuse in Italy, only to have my parents come up, as they had one summer when I was accepted for a summer program in England, with too many reasons I shouldn't and couldn't. Somehow I got into an intermediate painting course. The first assignment was a collage. Not sure just what that was, I ended up with a still-wet purple oil and lavender, lilac, orchid, violet thing that my professor's dog tracked over her white wall-to-wall. Years later, at Yaddo, a painter, Susan Criele, said at Bennington she'd been told she couldn't be a poet and became a painter. I, told I'd never paint, didn't.

My second or third year, I wrote and directed an hour-long skit for a sorority dance that took place in Greenwich Village with artists, beatniks, and a poet. I played the poet and did a song to the tune of *South Pacific*'s "We Ain't Got Dames" about having "anapests and dactyls, sentiment so true, onomatopoeia but the thing that makes me blue is this sacrilegious habit, it happens all the time, I can't for the life of me stop making these damn words rhyme." The production was a hit. A sorority sister I admired, in law school, said one image, of carbon-copy lives, impressed her. University of Texas at Austin or Temple University, where many of my papers are, have those original scripts. I was drawn to radio and television classes, where we listened to Norman Corwin and wrote our own children's radio and television shows. Tho I wanted to write, I was terrified of taking a real creative-writing course. What if I couldn't write enough? What if no one liked any of it? An intermediate composition course was as close as I got. I've written little, really, about college, but the poem "Writing Class, Syracuse Winter" catches a lot of what was going on. And what wasn't.

I wanted to slam into life, not be, as a romantic-lit professor chided us for being, conformist, silent, nonpolitical. In an interview I said I'd choose Iran or Greece to live and work in. I wanted to move to Greenwich Village. Unlike others in the sorority, I couldn't stand the thought of being engaged or married and I didn't want children. I couldn't imagine not dying to travel, taste everything, see and feel what I felt a marriage and children would only stifle, suffocate. I wanted to be wilder than I was. (Someone sent me a "wild women don't get the blues" button. I think, then, I believed that.) But I ran when a man who would later publish notes he had near his bed that he drew me to said he wanted to show me, and win a Pulitzer prize for denying death and then dying, wanted me to wriggle out of my lavender clothes. He wouldn't let me go until I promised I'd come back, spend the night lying near him. I did, to get out. Still I did want to taste everything, be open, say yes. But if my period was late, even if I'd just danced close, upstairs in a fraternity house, I was sure I was knocked up. Once I even changed my name to Sherri Liane Russell and went, with a sweaty fist of wadded up dollar bills, to make sure.

Spring in Syracuse was wet branches heavy with rose flowers dripping, the lushness of sitting in the music room with rain bending lilacs in two, a new Wagner or

*With roommate, Dorothy Yellen Appel (left), at Syracuse University*

Mozart record on as water beaded. I walked to have skirts I was thrilled were too big—they had to fit tight—made smaller to show how much of me I was paring away. I got contact lenses, let my hair grow longer, even pared part of my name away and went from Rosalynn to Lynn then Lyn. When a coffeehouse opened off Marshall Street where people sat on the floor and talked about books, films, art, and poetry as candles dripped turquoise, lemon, and violet wax down Chianti bottles, anything seemed possible.

Summers I went back to Middlebury, worked in my uncle's store or at the library at Middlebury College, where instead of pasting envelopes in the backs of books, as I was supposed to, I read them and tried to guess, as someone approached the desk, if they'd speak Italian, German, Russian, Spanish, or French. I wrote some of the first poems since high school one summer, triggered by a small argument I'd had with my sister over a woman in my sorority. One of these, "Disillusions," was the one my father showed Robert Frost, as mysterious to me an act still as everything about my father. I'd love to know what they talked about, how they started to talk, since neither was friendly. But from sometime in the fifties until Frost's death they stayed in touch. This summer I brought back a number of signed books and poems and cards he sent to my father, as well as my father's collection of newspaper articles, magazine clips about Frost, notices, especially around the time of Frost's death, when my father must have been more alone than ever, since he and my mother were separated and on the verge of divorce. Since my mother had the car, my father would hitchhike or take the bus to memorial services in Amherst, Boston, Maine, check out schedules to towns he didn't make it to. But that summer he showed my poem to Frost we were still all in the apartment and I can remember how thrilled I felt opening the blue and white magazine. Frost's words were staggering, much more overwhelming to me than silver dollars once filling my hand from a carnival's scooping claw machine. I wish I had had more poems to show Frost, that he hadn't died before I could. I suspect those comments were part of what made several schools give me excellent graduate scholarships, made me, even tho I didn't really write much for years, feel maybe I could.

(The cover is falling off the *Syracuse Review*—I hadn't noticed that the only two prominent ads are for Sylvania, where it says, "At Sylvania a man may choose from 67 plants and labs . . . will find tough, but challenging problems, salaries are excellent . . ." and then, on the back cover for Wamsutta Supercale, two whispering coeds in front of a college bulletin board where there's only a man's face tacked up. One woman, her legs demurely crossed, says, "If anybody asks you what I want for my trousseau . . . just be sure you mention lots of Wamsutta sheets . . . our first home may not be exactly a palace . . . but we do want everything to be just right . . . beige for complete heaven and of course, white with *his* monogram" I'm not sure what I was thinking about when I wrote about what dissolves, what would melt like snow in a palm, be "elusive, as his shadow to a child / When a storm-cloud breaks the spell / And his dreammate disappears," in that first published poem, but it could have been the fantasy of living with just the dream of a trousseau and sheets that would last till I was sixty, or why, when I did get married, the rituals of choosing patterns of silver and china always made me cringe.)

\*

Unlike leaving high school, I hated to leave Syracuse. I knew I didn't want to get married. I'd collected several fraternity pins but didn't "feel" pinned. I wish I'd collected more photographs from then. There are some bathing-suit photos a la Natalie Wood and shots of my roommate and me in front of bulletin boards in

baby-doll pajamas I still have, a poster of Quebec, banners, mugs, a Belafonte record of mine in the background, a Sinatra album (hers)—I never cared much for him, once shocked a fiancée because I preferred Elvis to Frank. In other photos we are wearing slinky cocktail dresses, our hair long and sleek. I wish I could make out the photo on the bulletin board behind me, or the card. One might have been from a deaf doctor I couldn't imagine wouldn't call but didn't after I fainted in the elevator from flu I caught from him. (Writing this, I felt so close, tho we hadn't talked for years, to my college roommate, I tracked her down, five addresses from the one listed in the Syracuse directory. We have talked, plan to meet.)

I wish I'd saved more letters, especially from my family, before phone calls became easier, too frequent. Then obsessive. In one I was warned I might be kidnapped and sold to the white-slave market.

Robert Kennedy spoke at graduation and I said goodby for a month or two, until Bread Loaf, to a boy I found myself pinned to, and went to an all-night party with someone I hardly knew: proud I'd finally done something that wasn't expected, safe. I was excited that I'd missed curfew tho the night was totally innocent: no drugs, no booze, no sex. I showed up at my parents' motel at dawn giggling and then heard I was a slut as we drove past Bomoseen quietly home.

After Syracuse, that feeling of being outside things, not fitting, seemed outlined in a kohl black I'd begun liking my brown eyes exaggerated in. Tho I was pinned, the idea of marriage or engagement still seemed scary. There wasn't an urgent need for English majors with radio-TV and fine arts as a minor. Grad school seemed the only alternative that summer, so with the English major whose pin I never wore (I just found a photograph of us, the morning after I accepted the little TEP pearl bar)—an odd college weekend really. I'd agreed to sign out for the weekend, naively believing I would be sharing a room with one of his fraternity brothers' dates. Yet it must have occurred to me that there could be more expected, because I did buy a filmy lavender and a filmy white negligee—something I'd have no need for in the dorm or sorority house, where flannel and cotton were more cuddly. Suddenly I was with this boy in a motel room and I felt about twelve—insisted we spend the night walking on the highway someplace outside Syracuse. After that weekend, at least three TEP couples rushed into marriage, pregnant.

It was a six-week course at Bread Loaf. We'd drive up every morning early. William Meredith taught a poetry course and couldn't imagine why I'd picked the subject I did: Jungian imagery in Yeats. There was a fascinating course on the American novel. Later I found all the lectures in another book not written by the man who taught it. Especially impressive was Moses Hadas, whose blue eyes were as riveting as his talks. And there was Donald Davidson, who I liked, who graciously wrote me a recommendation that I'm sure helped get me a scholarship to Vanderbilt. As a commuter at Bread Loaf, I felt outside things, there too. Felt restless, peeled off nail polish on the white clapboard chairs as writers I never got to know well played croquet and something in the air glued my eyelids together. My friend enrolled for the writers' conference in August. I went up for a number of the readings but, to my astonishment, remember none.

In the fall, I went to the University of Vermont. I felt more isolated, more outside things, very unconnected. I lived in a room in a house where the husband of a woman I was sure didn't want him coughed all night. I almost went to Boston University but at the last minute, frustrated with trying to find an apartment, didn't. "Why are you here?" a professor asked and, rather shakily I suppose, I said, "I want to write." I had little to say when he barked, "Then why don't you?"

I decided to write my master's thesis on Dylan Thomas. Frances and Gladys Colburn, a painter and poet in Burlington, knew Thomas, I was told, and I called them to talk about the poet whose reputation and mythic tours intrigued me almost as much as his poetry. Their son David edited a small college literary magazine, *Centaur,* and for that year and longer was another of those cool, elusive, hardly available men who've fascinated me more than is comfortable and have for so long triggered poems. Long icy walks and bittersweet exploding in an iced raw wind from Champlain started a few poems. It was there the first poem I published, "Jonathan," in *Kauri* got its start.

By next fall, with straight A's, course work finished for a master's degree, and the choice of several full scholarships, I chose Brandeis and moved into a pink room an Armenian woman with glass animals on fragile shelves was renting. It was the first time I ate baklava or artichokes—a Princeton med student who had taken a year off for an English degree made them

for me, and that the first day in Waltham I wore hoop earrings and a corduroy orange mini still in my closet. Instead of *Beowulf* which I had loved at UVM, it was *Piers Plowman.*

Early September I began to juggle something I couldn't: weekends I'd drive to Providence to see Bob, an English major at Brown and someone new, who, tho his family thought I was wrong for their son, I'd marry. J. V. Cunningham taught a course required of all graduate students. At any dreaded four o'clock Tuesday, your "exam" question could be sprung on you. No one could hear him, he whispered so, but no one dared sit up close because so often he lashed out, ridiculed. I audited a creative-writing class a few times. I've no photographs from then, no diary. Only the lamb's wool and cashmere sweaters I wore then, connect with a walk up Mount Auburn, or the Chinese restaurant I went to after the man I'd marry asked if we had school on Columbus Day.

As a child visiting relatives around Boston, Normbega Park, with its caterpillar ride, had been my favorite, that dark cave of a bug my sister and I were small enough to have my father still draw us close to him in. At Brandeis I wanted to go back there, try to remember. One weekend in Providence I threw tin cans thru a window, to my surprise: I'd always been too nice to. Another weekend I brought back the palm-sized black kitten, Othello, I'd get married to give a home to. It's astonishing how much doesn't stay. I've just read "Cabbages, Leaves, and Morphine," a poem loosely about those weekends I'd drive to Providence, but it doesn't tell me much about then. The man I married liked cats better than the one I didn't. When anyone asked what we had in common, I'd say cats and folk music. Seeing both men, I worked less than I needed to. I'm best at working full tilt on one thing: science contests, an anthology, writing. I hadn't finished my master's thesis on Dylan Thomas. Maybe I'd been in school too long without a break. In February, just after I registered for second semester, for reasons that aren't very clear, I left, as the man I'd marry less than a year later did, less than a year after he kissed me in his father's borrowed Chrysler, smelling of cinnamon Life Savers near midnight the same time of year I'm writing this.

I can't remember my feelings leaving Brandeis. I just let it go. I was exhausted from juggling the two relationships, remember nights I'd stay up in the pink room until three or four while my cat slept on the pillow. I'm surprised, with that scholarship, my parents didn't press me to stay.

Back in Middlebury that winter, nights seemed endless. Eric, the man I would marry, got a job and then took the bus to Vermont on weekends. His family feared and mistrusted, probably hated, me. They thought I'd seduced their son from an engineering career, so they took his Daimler, his coin collection. I was finishing my master's degree and my parents were finishing their marriage. My college roommate married, and on the way back from Rochester my family met Eric's family. My enthusiasm for Peter, Paul, and Mary made them think I was rather odd, as almost everything I did or felt or cared for would, and at two a.m., Eric appeared at the motel I was at with my parents, never wanting to be in his family's house again.

I boarded my cat at the vet's, noticed how much nicer this man was to him than the Brown boyfriend who seemed to think since I'd left school I could shrivel into a wife. After a Josh White concert I learned the guitar-playing poet I'd been so drawn to was marrying too. My parents weren't living in the same house by spring, and my sister, mother, and I moved for a few weeks in with my grandmother. By June we took a cottage on Lake Dunmore, where I could keep the cat. When we drove into town, we were told to keep the car windows up, not to stop on the street if we saw our father. Bob came up one weekend, Eric the next. Bob was edgy, didn't want me to wear a bikini, and one weekend had a rock in the car he wouldn't throw away, and at that moment I decided I couldn't marry him. With so little full of light, the idea of a wedding, something to not think of what was dying, seemed a cove, and that July, with only a month or two to plan the wedding, I stopped saying no and said OK. Those weeks were a giddy swirl. Still living at my grandmother's, my mother and I drove daily to Burlington or Rutland, checked out gowns, flowers, invitations, clothes. We were too busy to eat. Early in August I called my father to invite him, let him know, and he told me he didn't want to be involved. I got off the phone in my grandmother's dining room, where the stucco had pulled away, and went into the cluttered second living room, where ferns were already dying, sat quietly with my head in my hands and cried. I saw my father only one more time, days before the wedding in the post office, where all he said to me was, "Never do what you don't want to do."

"Get all the attention you can today," the rabbi said, "After this it will be your husband and your child." The motel we'd had reservations for gave the room away by mistake, definitely an omen. After a trip to Canada we picked up my black cat, guitar, and headed west for a fall that would be difficult. I'd never taught, never taken an education course, and was about three years younger than some of my students. Ten days after the wedding I began teaching at Wilbur Lynch High in Amsterdam, New York.

Nothing was as I'd expected: marriage, teaching, living in a new town. The college-prep students were fine; the others, called "terminal," were challenges I was in no way prepared for. There were thirty-six or more in most classes. I knew nothing about discipline. Most of the teachers were nearing retirement, were lifelong residents of Amsterdam. It was a nightmare. Later I wrote "Ramona Lake" about one black-haired student with her 70 IQ I can still see in a sea of chatter and noises and spitballs like a startled deer, dazed, about to be hit by a car, pleading for what I couldn't give her.

\*

I couldn't wait to escape school in my dusty rose Plymouth convertible that the top, after putting it up while driving in a storm, didn't still go up and down automatically on. Past Division Street there were lilac rooms I could take my hair out of pins in and wonder how I'd gotten myself in all this. There were moments, as I described in "Hair," when I put my hair up and sprayed it by mistake with Raid "as if it was a living, flying thing." Two months into the marriage I began having devastatingly unsettling anxiety attacks. When I heard tachycardia I thought of my father's heart attack. At a teachers' meeting around then I passed out in a crowd of three hundred in downtown Schenectady. I felt corners go black, windows and lights blur. We'd rush to the emergency room. I felt I was someone else in clothes that just looked like mine. Downstairs in the apartment, a retired cop said he'd kill the cat. I don't remember his reason. In December, after a horrendous Friday, dressed in a gold wool suit I'd worn about two hours after the wedding, someone came up to me, said, that looks like a going-away outfit, and I thought, yes, it is. I never entered that high school again.

Snowdrifts were up to my waist that winter, panic slithered into depression. Other wives seemed to like cooking, talked of babies. I'd focus on years before to not feel the rooms go licorice. Everything seemed over. I couldn't even read. I'd hold *One Flew over the Cuckoo's Nest* and read the same page over and over. I never dreamed I'd be in residence, giving workshops and readings with Ken Kesey for a week in Virginia, sharing screwdrivers from his thermos, driving thru catalpa and live oak, red bud starting. Since I was no longer teaching, there was no reason to live in such a dreary, isolated town, and we moved into my husband's parents' in Albany to look for an apartment. I was so depressed I began to sleep until one in the afternoon. Running the water for a long, lulling bath, I could hear his mother whimper, whisper to her friends how weird I was. "No More Apologizing," perhaps one of the most autobiographical poems I've written, spits some of those afternoons out. I sat in the small guest room, the only room without a rug, feeling January wind thru panes, and tried to write poems, waited for my husband to come back. By April we moved to Schenectady into a flat where lilacs were about to bloom, and I got into SUNY grad school. We repainted the walls, got a couch, marble tables, and began to feel life wasn't really done. I was about nineteen.

I've no photographs of the apartment on Jackson Avenue, nothing from there except for a series of poems with the address for a title, "222 Jackson Ave." There's not one shot I can find of those first years, tho later my husband got into photography and took hundreds of shots. In the closet are negatives never even developed. In that first Schenectady place if you opened the back door and the front living room, the lilac breeze changed the afternoon. I sat at a marble coffee table eavesdropping on the couple with the organ whose family kept having heart attacks, who wanted oriental furniture, or on fights the couple with a poodle and underground connections had much of the day, and tried a few poems. Weekends we'd listen to folk music at Cafe Lena, where I got into theater, considered just doing that, forgetting grad school. Or we went to foreign films, *Black Orpheus, The Joker.* The black cat I brought from Providence to Waltham, then to Vermont, rescued from the vet's, brought with me when I got married to give it a home, to Amsterdam and then Schenectady, ran away, and we got a grey one that had kittens and more kittens, some that had to be cut out of the bedsprings. In the summer we drove to Newport, saw Dylan and Baez, and in September I plunged back into graduate school. Again I was asked why and again, when I said I wanted to be a writer, was sneered at, asked why if I wanted to I

didn't. Being an extremist, I made everything second to graduate school. Nothing else mattered. I attacked weekly papers fiercely. Spenser, eighteenth-century lit, Elizabethan theater. It was a new doctoral program.

SUNY, formerly, the State Teachers' College of New York, was planning to move to a bigger campus and was hiring professors with reputations, trying to be as traditional as possible, as if to get an instant reputation. I got all A's. Tho I'd never studied Italian, with flash cards and a few random books, managed to be the only one of several to pass the Italian exam the first time. I'd written a hundred pages of what would be my doctoral dissertation on a comparison of the Psalms of Wyatt, who I really liked, and those of Sidney, who I didn't. I loved the ragged, explosive, jagged thought-in-process of Wyatt, the darkness, surprise, how his poems were colloquial, not polished and polished so smooth nothing caught and startled and snagged. It was, I thought, exciting to be the first Ph.D. candidate. I'd be the youngest, I was sure, to get a degree, just over twenty. I didn't pick up on one or two omens: even with the best academic record, when I talked about getting an instructorship I was told, "You aren't a man with a family to support," and during the first year with a teaching fellowship I got a note suggesting "I dress in a way that's more professional, wear my hair up," a note in my mailbox that became part of the second most anthologized poem, "You Understand the Requirements." No wonder hair has been a recurring image, the subject of two long poems, one a *New York Quarterly* Sadin Award.

"Energetic" was the way the head of the graduate department described me. Within weeks I was simply too involved in, too excited by, the literature I was studying to imagine I'd not be a professor. In early readings I often went over the experience of those written and oral Ph.D. exams. The poem "Orals" is pretty much a true account. Because I was the first candidate and many were new to the Ph.D. program, they actually asked me how many days, how long, the exams should be. I did go and buy special suits to wear for this, masks. And I was asked, perhaps the first question, what I thought of adultery, bedbugs, by Edward Le Comte, the newly hired respected Milton scholar. The exam clearly embarrassed the other professors: it was so sexist and shoddy, and it was because of that cut short. They decided I should have a written exam. I'd passed exams in other fields and was anxious to get this last written one over. The exam had two parts: first, fifty quotes from seventeenth-century poetry, all slightly misquoted. I was to identify the poet, make the corrections, and say why the original was better. The second half was to explicate a section from Herbert's *The Temple.* I knew seventeenth-century poetry and after the exam went out to celebrate, sure I'd passed. That night I got a call saying, "You have identified the poems correctly, and the poets," then added, "but in your explication it seems you do not have the religious background to work sympathetically in the seventeenth century. You don't have enough affiliation or sympathy for seventeenth-century English Anglicanism."

The department still had confidence in me, said there seemed to be a personality conflict, decided I should take a last exam from someone else. I was drained, wiped out. But I had to take it two weeks from that day, December 15. Unable to concentrate, tho it was a fair, actually easy exam, I slammed out of the room onto Central Avenue, without a coat, hoped, I think, I'd get hit by a car.

I wanted to get a Ph.D. so I could write and then wrote because I didn't get one. When I cleared out my desk in the English Annex, the hundred pages on Wyatt had disappeared. I should thank some of the department for pushing me, finally, to write. But for years I couldn't go near the university. The first time I did, nervously, to a party, I got a flat tire in the lot and then, somehow, managed to be in the elevator when it got stuck. Stuck with me was Dr. Le Comte. Many of the professors could recognize themselves in some prose pieces in an upcoming book from Applezaba, *Doctors.* As I left, to be nice one man said, "Well, why don't you just have a baby."

For months after that, I painted, did oils, abstracts, watercolors. A small gallery wanted to show them, and a few people asked if they could buy some of the stormy dark landscapes that disappeared in a move. That April I took a job at a local public-television station editing their program guide and got a copy of the *International Directory of Little Magazines* that Len Fulton published, and I began writing for sample copies. It was thrilling to see magazines I'd no idea existed. I was drawn to the more startling titles: *Marijuana Quarterly, Blitz, Earth Rose, Ole, Lung Socket, Wormwood,* as well as the beautifully produced ones, like the *Outsider, Choice, Folio, El Corno Emplumado,* and the political mimeos, like *Kauri,*

*Outcast, Work, New.* I learned magazines, like the *Caller,* might be published by funeral parlors, want only poems on death. At Channel 17 I began to type up the few poems I'd written. In June or July I left town for a weekend, came back to find there'd been trouble with typesetting, and tho I had nothing to do with this, I was fired.

\*

The photographs on the back of my first book, *Why Is the House Dissolving,* show me with my arms wrapped around myself, sunglasses, sitting in what looks like a beach. It's the sand in back of 92 Rapple, the raised ranch we moved into when the landlord said the cats couldn't stay. It was one of ninety houses we saw go up, board by board. Having lived since six in apartments, a house suggested roots, belonging, not being on the run. The back of the house faced onto this lake of sand that stretched into woods a lover could hide in. And did. I discovered poetry on the radio and at noon on Tuesdays took the phone off the hook to listen, spellbound to whoever was reading. In an interview I was quoted saying, "I wrote like a hippy but was living like a nun." I was more isolated than ever. The few friends I'd had in grad school were in their own world. We no longer had what we had had in common. The other hundred raised ranches were families whose only interest (except for a strange Scientologist husband and wife with glazed eyes) seemed having 2.3 kids and keeping their lawns manicured and shaved like crewcuts. Tho the houses were modest, often the shrubbery was not. Weekdays from eight to five I was alone. Gas and oil were still inexpensive and I'd open the windows, let chiffon and gauzey long veil-like drapes blow from the bed as if I was trying to air the house of some dreary night spirits, and write. I wrote standing up at the kitchen counter. In one photograph you can see the postage scale near a jar of beans. The kitchen there was white, new, with brown delft tiles. Spotless, bright, as few other kitchens I've lived in since have been. A white wrought-iron glass-covered table is rotting outside the house I live in now, a ghost of itself. It was usually piled with little magazines and blue, turquoise, and lavender, lilac, and purple candies in the candelabra I cherished for years. Bamboo, rubber trees, huge begonias, ivy, and fuchsia pulled green into the house, and thick plush wall-to-wall carpet turned the room, in bright light, into a beach. When I took any job, I used the pay to buy paintings, and large oils and prints and etchings covered the white walls along with psychedelic posters, dried leaves, books, and, after one summer when I think more than ever I wanted to twist and change and transform what I saw, rows of colored glass bottles.

First I wrote on yellow lined paper, folded into four pieces and put into a red bag. When the bag was filled, I typed them up, threw many of the handwritten manuscripts away. Except for poems in books, I have only some carbons of the first few years I wrote. Most were sold and are in the archives at the University of Texas at Austin. Each week I discovered a new poet; like a drug addict I'd float high on that. Or a new magazine. I planted red tulips, watched tumbleweed blow toward the house, watched blood maples turn fire. Maybe the women in poems running into and disappearing in trees, the Daphne images so prevalent, come from leaning against the glass, feeling the branches move nearer.

I was drawn to the most wild, direct poems, still felt torn, burnt by my graduate-school whirl, and devoured poems of writers like Bukowski, D. R. Wagner, Steve Richmond, and also the surrealistic dream landscapes of poets who later I realized had read Bly. I remember discovering Anne Sexton while sitting in a car in a snowstorm glued to "The Double Image." The only thing I can compare to the excitement of discovering so many unique, strange, bizarre, weird, and wonderful images and poets and poetry and magazines is the feeling I get now going to international film festivals, an obsession.

During that time, I lived in the past and in my imagination. My most erotic, shocking to some, poems (I was pleased to find, since I'd rarely done anything not well-behaved) were fantasy. "Nice," a poem I wrote when asked for something erotic, something that was to be published in some popular erotic magazine, was written at Union College on a piece of Spearmint gum wrapper while I watched a Bergman film. I hadn't been political but, hearing news and TV coverage of Vietnam, began writing poems about society and published many of them in *Outcast* and *Kauri* and *Win.* And I began to see my growing up in Vermont, my family, in a way I hadn't.

I felt again the outsider in the neighborhood I lived in, the setting for many poems in *Why Is the House Dissolving?* where "people wonder should they plant identical hedges, put the same screens on windows of their very similar heads." I was seen as strange, not a good daughter-in-law, since I couldn't goo and coo, call my father-in-law Daddy, didn't cook dinner for my in-laws often enough, have the right friends. But as bad, I wore my hair long and straight, gypsily free, tho I'd been told after twenty "a lady cuts it or wears it up." And most horrid, I hadn't had babies. I don't think I ever told my in-laws part of the reason, out of my control, why.

Much of that time, in memory, seems peaceful, sheltered, safe. The wildness and danger was in what I wrote. Somewhere else, women, including a woman I mentioned earlier I'd known in high school, were getting strangled or marching on Selma. But the poems knew a lot more than I did, even the early titles: "What We Grow Away From," "The Way Sun Falls Away from Every Window," and images of loss and leaving stud that first book, so many images of dissolving, a word that recurs, was a map to what was ahead.

*Why Is the House Dissolving* was published in 1968. It came from a probably too-large submission of poems to *Ole* magazine, just folding. Brown Miller had worked on it and picked a couple for *Lung Socket* magazine, then edited the manuscript for Open Skull Press. I'd wanted strong poems: nothing academic, prissy, safe. Now I can see there's a lot of bottled-up rage and anger I didn't see then, tho others reacted to what they felt was violence. It was odd to see the poems printed in mimeo, a few at odd angles. Unsettling maybe, like the first reaction to the birth of a child. The street language in the book is a mask, "knocked up" in the poem "She Sigh Happy," almost a costume I was trying on as I tried out surrealism in lines like "Lace grows in her eyes like fat weddings." The book was stapled together with a nice bright white and black square cover. Many of the poems less pared down, more imagistic, than a lot of what I write now. With the tone often mysterious, the subjects are often hard or tough: rape, castration, the brutalities of war and marriage.

Probably as important to me as Frost's encouraging words was a review of this book in *Works,* an issue that first had an article from Blazek, the publisher of Open Skull Press, saying he wanted "poetry that is dangerous." That would by itself have pleased me. But it was the review, by John Hopper, who said, "The most exciting poems published by any of the presses I covered were in Lyn Lifshin's *Why Is the House Dissolving?* There is an unmistakable—and yet undisguised—femininity at work here that reminds of Sylvia Plath and yet stands very much on its own gorgeous legs. There is not the mordant urgency of the *Ariel* poems, that despair so often overpowering, but encountering the woman alone generates such touching felicities I was sorry the poems ran out so soon." He closed saying, "I do not know what attempt the established houses make to scan small press poets, but here is an excellent example of a fine strong voice whose book, the reverse title page tells us is 'published in a limited edition of roughly five hundred copies.' I know nothing of Miss Lifshin's attitudes toward making it in the Big Time, but somebody with international distribution has a real obligation to give her a lot of bread and a wider audience. She well deserves it" (*Works* 11, no. 1, spring 1969). The review made me show people the book. Before I hadn't.

One wall in my garage is lined with notebooks, diaries I've kept since October of 1976, copies of letters, too many to go thru. If I'd kept a diary or journal or even copies of letters those first years of writing, I might remember what I did besides writing. I worked briefly at the New York State Mental Health Department, where "Office" and "Thaw" grew out of talks with the secretaries about weddings and silver or just being outside those first early March days. Writing an autobiography reminds me how memory really is like a kaleidoscope, how it shifts, rearranges, lets different patterns thru. Writing this, I hear glass explode. The cat tears thru a sill of colored glass bottles, there at least ten years. Maybe it was a sparrow hot for the last red berries that lured him, and now an old and fragile white demitasse cup, a wedding or shower present from the sister I haven't talked to the last two and a half years, is splintered in pieces. One glue doesn't work and I try another, foul smelling. It's old and has to be mixed. It takes forever to dry or to piece what's broken together, find all the fragments, as with poems or something remembered.

I'm sure I'd have remembered different triggers, different faces, if I had written this ten years before or even next year. When I reread some early interviews some of what I meant dissolves. In my master's thesis on Dylan Thomas I explored how he made a religion almost out of poetry and I think I started doing something like that too. I'd drive to NYC, a two-and-a-half or three-hour drive, to go to poetry readings in

East Village lofts, just bought poetry volumes. Long before I wrote, I saw and was fascinated by Beat poetry readings in the Village, readings I'd change any plans to go to.

\*

I'd been writing to a few poets and wasn't surprised when one arrogant, taunting, challenging note came from a poet in California who said he'd seen my photo in a clump of poems in a rather bad magazine. He said my poems needed work and I probably chewed gum but he'd like to take me down the Mississippi on a raft, hollering poems and blowing weed. It was outlandish. I answered. He began calling, I think from houses he broke into, sent outrageous letters, photographs of himself, including one of Dylan Thomas with his name inked on the side. I *had* been living like a nun. Suddenly wild letters from this man who looked like a cross between Clint Eastwood and Robert Redford, an ex-con poet with a pet water beetle, came daily along with bottles of Château Ausone from Pacific Grove. He sent luscious dreams, slivers of Puerto Vallerto nights he wanted to show me that were like ruby glass, twisting what was. But I wasn't prepared, never quite believed he'd actually come to Albany. In letters to him I'd been flamboyant, open, free, the mask I used in some poems but had never, not even in the house alone in front of a mirror, tried on. Even later flirtatious phone calls, one from a man in a rock group after he'd seen my photograph in *Rolling Stone,* would flatter rather than insult me. It was still such a new experience. I didn't know how to be coy or seductive or sexy, and being called wholesome in high school had convinced me I'd never haunt any man. It was one thing to respond to his letters. California seemed planets away. And safe. Even when he said he was coming, was on his way, I didn't think he would and was astonished that March afternoon, or maybe it was April, that he was real, tall, gorgeous. I gulped cognac to not show how terrified I was, something for a while I'd do other times I felt scared, with someone new or with someone special. And, for a while, at poetry readings.

I'd imagined this ex-con poet had been jailed for something like drugs, but it was armed robbery. He was still married to a woman who'd seen his smile, fell for him, drove seven hundred miles up the coast for two years, and with influence, got him released early. Probably it was his stories, his charm, something

I've also had a weakness for, that got her. And so many women. East, in "Aaaaaalbaeney," as he pronounced it, he'd con motel owners (and then walk out), priests, and a number of famous poets. He was adept at conning everyone. I can never not think of him, passing the Arcadia Motel, where I walked, still not (tho I had my license at fifteen) driving since the year after I was married. When he ran out of his wife's money he started living in the trees in back of my raised ranch. Nights he'd scavenge backyards for lawn chairs, melons, beer, beach towels, and built himself a lean-to past where sand and tumbleweed ended. Every night at an appointed time, 9 p.m. or 10, he'd light a match under the white-tiled bathroom window and I'd flick the switch. Mornings when my husband's green Healy pulled away, this man came in full of leaves to make eggs Benedict, tell outrageous stories of making love in coffins, running drugs across the border. I'd been totally innocent, something he was astonished to find. Little besides his fantasies seemed real. But he was often on the verge of suicide. I expected to find his six-foot-two-inch corpse dangling or across the top front stair. He scrounged around, lifted bottles of beer. We'd laugh and he'd read while I sorted laundry. A Mary McCarthy story was one of his favorites and he loved Plath and Louise Gluck. Once John Dos Passos was talking at Union College—since I couldn't see the poet after 5 or 6 p.m., I wrote a huge note in the tumbleweed and sand. I gave him money for beer, but when I wasn't looking he stole Kennedy silver dollars, opened my mail, including one of my first invitations to read. Later I found library books in the weeds, Katherine Mansfield, letters he'd written to James Dickey and Ed Field.

It was a juggling act, a situation I found myself in more and more. He went back and forth to Carmel. Once, when I was on the west coast, I was sure I'd see him on the roof of a house, screaming at stars. In Albany he lived near where Legs Diamond had when it got too cold to live in the trees. Women were always after him. If he needed a typewriter he'd suck up to a warmhearted priest, pretending he wanted to go dry out. He even stuck it out a few months in Utica at a clinic where a woman gave him her car and a watch with her name on it, somehow now in my drawer. When he wasn't here, he wrote hilarious letters. I just took boxes of them out of the cellar to leave in between the screen door and the main door like a charm, or to get the musty smell out of them. I'd forgotten how clever, bawdy, touching, and sad they were. He thought we'd live somewhere in Big Sur,

and in one envelope, a key fell out to a house where I was to meet him. He published several poems. I often found them stilted. But his letters were wild, endearing, funny, enraging, strange. He was the opposite of my husband, a split I've found myself torn between again and again.

Once, when my mother was visiting, since I couldn't feed this poet-con man in the trees, I cooked large vats of lasagna and put them in Maxwell House coffee tins so the cats wouldn't get them and left them under the window. Hearing a noise when he came thru the grass to get it, my mother was about to call the police. Once, knowing nothing about where anyone got drugs locally, when he said in jail they used nutmeg and mace, we poured A & P ground nutmeg powder into a glass of water. In two hours was totally and unpleasantly stoned. I avoided all drugs after that. Once he brought a man who'd been a journalist and had been drinking a long time, looked as if he'd been living on the streets, over. I was sure they'd both pass out in the living room on the plush pile wall-to-wall carpet. It's still hard for me to resist men who tell good stories, especially if their eyes are blue, and they've a sense of life being a joke, often absurd. I'm drawn to them and really know they (or I) can't stay, that I need someone very unlike that, too. I knew I'd never leave to tramp around Big Sur or mooch off others, live in other people's attics or caves in the leaves. But I couldn't tear myself away from such an intense periscope on an alien life.

He lived on the edge, fearlessly, taunting death because he really didn't care; poems were all that mattered. I'm not sure which of his stories were lies. About two years after we met, he, and a new wife, he said, went off to Majorca, said they were getting rich writing porn and living in Graves's castle. Not long after that, I got a phone call and then a letter I just came across saying that on Good Friday he'd collided with a school bus. In keeping with the strangeness of knowing him, a woman later called me from California, said while she was trying to paint, this man's ghost came to her, pleading that she call me, tho he didn't want her, she said, to tell me how he'd been, before the suicide, half himself, so worn out with cirrhosis, sick. Her story was as weird as his, but she said she'd met him in Spain, seen an aura around him that meant he was extraordinary, and had fallen for him. She got extremely close and involved with him and his wife and went on about a woman in Graves's castle shooting up and bathing in vitamin E, a story I borrowed for "I Don't Want Diana in the Palace." That Good Friday she said there was to be a gross-out party, everyone trying to outdo the others in coming up with something bizarre. He had sheets of blood for a tablecloth, fruit. But he outdid the others by killing himself before it began, crashing his car head-on into a school bus on an embankment. The woman who called me suggested she and I and his wife collaborate on a play or film, catch our views of him. Often she called from California, or suggested we go to Paris for lunch or into his Majorca tomb. The oddest thing was that she sent me a box of poems he'd written about me I'd never seen. They're in the door now, losing the smell of what held them too.

*

I thought I'd write the past up to the spring of 1986, when something I can't write about yet started, am astonished, since I thought I left so much out, that I've typed only two and a half of six notebooks up and I've only come to the publishing of the first of around eighty books and chapbooks. For someone apt to write twenty-seven jealousy poems, twenty "The Thud of Not Seeing You"s, as if to exorcise or catch what can't stay, maybe it's not strange that some sidetracks, these parenthetical, jagged detours, not just the way my mother and I often talk, but part of the rushed breathless slam of many of my poems, is also the way memory swirls and braids and discovers.

It's February 1, 1989. I started pulling the past back last October and, tho I hadn't planned to, did go back to the diaries, some letters; it was like dragging nets, coming up with jewels and driftwood, bones, barbwire, ghosts. This turns out to be a beginning of autobiography. It stops before separations, divorce, and just before *Black Apples,* before I edited three anthologies—one of mother and daughter poems, *Tangled Vines;* and *Ariadne's Thread,* women's diaries and journals; and *Unsealed Lips,* women's memoirs and autobiography—before I went to Europe, filled a green notebook, Appunti, with slices of Frascati, the tombs of Cecilia Metalla, catacombs, before I thought twenty-six was the end of an exciting life, as I had felt at thirteen, before Yaddo, Millay, MacDowell and Bread Loaf, and readings in towns with rivers I'd never heard of, Winona, Sangre de Cristo; it's before this house on Appletree with polished cherry that goes amber and guava in honey light, before Abyssinian

cats, the first, when it seemed everyone was leaving, before I let my hair go curly, my hair lighten in sun to fire. It will take at least as long a piece as this to get to what happened before and during the eighty chapbooks and books, all this before my black T Bird, my night radio adventure, or the September a car slashed my forehead. It stops before I went from worrying I couldn't write enough to worrying I wrote more than I should, before the documentary film *Not Made of Glass* some years after I threw glass, as if to get it out of me, before so many poems became real after I wrote them and what was real dissolved and ghosts got more stubborn, before this ruby and cobalt velvet quilt I'm writing under, that I hope some no longer feeling it will remember got less thick. Now no one left still calls me Rosalynn. This stops before spaceships exploded on TV; it was when my mother could still open jars nobody else could and bolt up stairs, or up Boylston in three-and-a-half-inch heels. Vietnam moved from television to my arms and left scars there as red wood fades and the tulip trees I planted in a house I left are about to flower, before plum and quince here lost their leaves and those sticks of crab apple and elderberry I stuck in spread, tangle with black walnuts. I've left out the desert, Arizona, 1984, when I'd fill forty spiral diaries in one year, feel blue stain many nights, the blues gnaw like ants. Now blue lace means more than blue lace; diamonds and teeth chip. This ends before I wrote poems about houses of sawdust or blue towels, before *Rolling Stone* called me for poems, before my mother gave up cigarettes and began calling and calling. In the house I lived in when *Why Is the House Dissolving* was published, the ferns have doubled. This stops way before so many mad girls and madonnas. Later it seemed I was either running toward or away from men. I'd use "exhausted" and "drained" and "rushing" more and more in letters and diaries. This stops before I thought anyone would write a Ph.D. on me or a book of criticism or say, "The mask goes up, the mask down, the mask is hard irony, sarcasm and when it comes down the Lifshin behind it is the soft vulnerable Outsider" (Hugh Fox's *Lyn Lifshin: A Critical Study*). I couldn't have dreamed then I'd be packing boxes of poems and galleys and posters for archives at U of Texas, Austin, and Temple U, or read with writers I idolized in California, Illinois, Boston, Virginia, or imagined Reagan's visit to Bitburg or how I'd be haunted by Kent State or have Kristallnacht flood poems. Before skimming bits of this I realize I put in so little about my father's death, how on the way to his lawyer's, just before I was supposed to testify against him in court, he fell on the snow, left a stain of rose spreading, a story I told in one of the earliest, longest poems, "How It Happened," in *Mad Windows.* After I wrote *Why Is the House Dissolving* the roof really did dissolve. This was before I even imagined so much of what would matter. There were no videotapes of readings then, and when there were it would take years to have them or play them. I'd never heard of Emerald Lake, Diamond Head, Lerchi, or being stranded midwinter in a blue cabin in Maine. Later, Montreal in August for films made the summer ending more bearable, and I'd do workshops I'd never even thought of: mothers and daughters, diaries and journals, memoirs, publishing, creativity workshops. At the point this ends, I couldn't have imagined writing so many poems with war and nuclear landscapes, or that two and a half years would go by without talking to my sister. Some fantasies became reality; more would be roller coasters of spun glass in 250-mile-per-hour winds that shattered, left a hole, before I'd have any clue, like reading even three words, seemingly harmless, in a November 85 diary, "A delight, warmth, humanness," how they'd turn ghosts, sting.

Unstapling letters in these last years of diaries is a bit like walking on mine fields. Once I was told I had a layer of fat missing so I bruised when anyone touched me. Some of that dark spreading that didn't get into poems will I hope grow into stories. Because of some eye-muscle imbalance an eye doctor said it's hard for me to look at what's near, like much these past wild, funny, impossible years. I'll keep it for later like news clips, photos, a T-shirt someone gone away once wore.

I started finishing this on January 16 with salmon light falling thru cracked walnut branches on the red velvet quilt. Orange peels, Memento, my Abyssinian cat, 4:20 light thru lime and raspberry stained glass falling on leather, candles, just-stitched ribbons on new pointe shoes. "Tangled Up in Blue" on the air, roses in the lowest room, parched lily of the valley. Downstairs, prisms, polished bronze, mortar and pestle my grandmother brought from Russia. Silver horse yanked from the crushed grill of my torn Mustang, near the "wild women don't get the blues" button I wore to a reading where no one could hear, a wreath of diaries bulge with letters, rages, horrors, jealousies, and highs, nights I'll never let go of, hips and lips, blue eyes, lace.

I didn't finish tho, ran off to a ballet class. Now, Feb 2, a day I still remember not as Ground Hog Day but as Janice Burby's birthday, when there were always

*Lyn and her mother*

red crepe-paper baskets full of hearts and we played pin the tail on the donkey; it's grey, and after a day it hit sixty-five it's sleet and ice, the blue stones glazed over. I'm looking not just backward but forward to the film, finally coming out, new books—*Rubbed Silk, Blood Road, Skin Divers, Reading Lips, Doctors*—to an interview in *New York Quarterly,* reading in England, my anthology of women's memoirs, *Unsealed Lips,* and more.

Lifshin contributed the following update to *CA* in 2002:

### *"ON THE OUTSIDE: LIPS, BLUES, BLUE LACE"*

In mid-winter, 1989, in cold, upstate New York, I finished "On the Outside: Lips, Blues, Blue Lace." It was an icy late afternoon with wild tangerine light falling through glass, turning the cherry wood flame. Memento, my seven-year-old Abyssinian cat was on the bed, kneading the velvet quilt, intrigued by pink ribbons I had just sewed on new pointe shoes. Now when I look at the last page of what I called "the beginning of autobiography," I'm stunned at both the wild changes and also what is unchanged as the house on Appletree Lane with its stained glass, prisms, boxed diaries, my black 1986 Thunderbird with about 20,000 miles on it. The house, which I have enjoyed less time in since the summer of 1992, is full of old blues records, blue leaves, reflections of lips. Ghosts fill the house in photographs, things left in a closet as if still waiting for the ones who wore them to fill them: pocket books, glasses, gold dresses. Early contributor copies of my first published poems, and yellowing copies of *Rolling Stone* are in my small study from when magazines I published in could still fit on shelves, not have to be boxed. The ruby, jade, and sapphire squares of velvet have not faded. The same plants trail on wooden bricks in the cold room near leaves from the film set of *Billy Bathgate*. Tempted to leave the asparagus ferns from a house I lived in during the early 1970s outside, finally let them go. They looked so good in mid-October. I brought them back inside where they are probably tempting mice with their orange berries.

When I began "On the Outside," I thought I'd capture the past to the spring of 1988 but was "astonished since I thought I left so much out that I'd typed only two and a half of the six notebooks of memoir and only covered the first of around eighty (now over one hundred) books and chapbooks." I ended the memoir with a tantalizing litany of all I didn't include from the publication of *Why Is the House Dissolving* in 1968 to that winter. Though changes were starting, they were as camouflaged as road signs masked behind drifting snow. The notebooks I never typed up then seem mysterious, like jewel boxes, as past words often do. But they hardly suggest the enormous changes that came so soon after "On the Outside" appeared.

Of several wrenching changes, the first was my mother's terminal illness and her death five months later, just as "On the Outside" was published. I remember commenting in 1989 how difficult it would have been to write a memoir if she were no longer alive. Our closeness was extreme. Some would complain there were no boundaries. I was glad she was able, in October of 1989, to go the premiere of a documentary film about me. For months before it she talked about a purple dress she'd bought, hoped she'd "be there to wear," and then returned before Mary Ann Lynch's award-winning documentary, *Lyn Lifshin: Not Made of Glass,* was first shown in the New

York State capitol building. I'm pleased to have the documentary but regret we listened to my mother and did not shoot in Middlebury, Vermont, in the apartment I grew up in because my mother wanted to "fix it up first." We did not even go to the small town where each walk, each street is filled with memories. The event was video taped and I can still watch her beaming at everything (almost) I did. I can see how thin she already looked but remember that when we all went out to eat afterward, she ordered coquille St. Jacques and ate it all.

That October the film premiered at the Denver Film Festival, a truly exciting happening, especially for someone as addicted to films as I am. Even living much of the time in Virginia, I get up to the Montreal Film Festival every summer. In contrast to poetry conferences and festivals, at the Denver Film Festival the director and I were awed at how we were treated like celebrities! We were taken by limousine to formal events and cocktail parties and had a chance to mingle with many well know directors and actors, including Seymour Cassels, Robert Wise (who wrote the screen play for *Citizen Kane* and so many other films), as well as the stars of the opening film, *Crimes and Misdemeanors.* Some other films opening were *My Left Foot, Sex, Lies, and Video Tapes,* several films of Krzysztof's, *Roger and Me,* and *Cinema Paradisio.* There were tributes to Jack Clayton, John Cassavetes, and Stockard Channing. We were thrilled when my documentary was so popular it was shown twice. On one of the loveliest days, there was a side trip to see the aspens north of Denver with Robert Wise, Seymour Cassels, and Michael Wilson, who appeared in one of my favorite filmmaker's, Alan Rudolph's, *The Moderns.* After Denver, Mary Ann and I toured the states and prepared for a nearly month-long tour of southern California, Hawaii, and then northern California, where the film had its commercial opening at the Roxy Theater in the Mission District, along with a documentary on Alice Walker. We did readings, workshops, and parties up and down the coast of California as we did those weeks in Hawaii. We had tremendous crowds in Honolulu at the museum and university and in Maui at the Hui Noeau Arts Center, a beautiful old estate, where we planned to stay overnight. The others thought it seemed haunted and left. I woke up to a circle of ants around the bed and breathtaking flowers in the courtyard, bu I couldn't shut out the thought that just before I left my mother had sounded strange on the phone, said she couldn't eat anything much on New Year's, couldn't swallow

*With filmmaker Mary Ann Lynch (left) at the commercial premiere of*
**Lyn Lifshin: Not Made of Glass** *at the Roxie Theater in San Francisco*

salmon. That nothing tasted good. This was unlike her, and I was relieved she would be staying at my sister and brother-in-law's while I was traveling. Even so, she remained a constant worry, and with the filmmaker's mother ill, too, each day we were greeted by the hotel desk clerk's questions about our mothers' health. I had visions of bringing my mother to Hawaii, out of the cold mountains in Vermont, supposing the ocean and light and the smells of Plumeria, Pikake, Fragomeni, and wild ginger would heal her.

The trip was such a high, with many wonderful hosts and great audiences. Only a week ago this year, I learned of the death of Bill Packard, editor of *New York Quarterly,* who was interviewed in the film. Seeing him on the screen, I always felt I had just seen him, just been interviewed by him. And the February 11, 2002, death of my twenty-year-old cat (who I wrote six notebooks of poems about after that) made me sad when I saw the film soon after that.

Slamming back to reality was a shock. Snow in Niskayuna, and then dashing up to Stowe, Vermont, where I found my mother needy, frail. She was always the one who took care of everyone else. Even in that last year she was still sure she could. There was something suspicious in her throat, the doctor said. I stayed with her in Stowe since that was the only way she would agree to additional tests. I had to promise a trip to my house after that. I think she hoped that, as in the past, having fun shopping and eating out in New York would help her regain her strength. From April to August 1990, I pretty much dropped all readings, film showings, workshops to stay with her. Two of my strongest, prize-winning essays are about that experience; "August Wind," a memoir published in *Response* and "On Writing Mind Leaves at Yaddo," a non-fiction essay that was published in *Writer's Digest* and won several awards, including the best piece about writing, were about those four months. Instead of traveling to promote the new documentary, I was with her twenty-three hours a day, writing while she dozed. She shriveled. As if to keep up with her, I lost weight, too. The poems I wrote in the small, half-underground room where we slept and in the upstairs TV room are among my strongest. Many appear in two recent Black Sparrow books, *Cold Comfort* and *Before It's Light,* as well as in many magazines. I continued taping her words until she was too tired, have ten tapes I have not yet been able to play. My mother and I talked, I wrote, we looked at old films. I took photographs. Such a contrast to the film tour. The big outing was a trip to the Grand Union with my sister to buy paper towels or try to find some delicacy to tempt my mother, who ate less and less. It seemed there was no summer, no spring that year, just winter until July 4, when the roads washed out.

When I edited *Tangled Vines* in 1978 I had no mother-and-daughter poems until I wrote some then. That spring, summer, and fall I wrote little else. Afterwards there were years, there *are* years, of letters to her. Many sprawling, long, loose poems without the tightness of the daily poems I wrote between getting her ice chips, strawberries and cream, pills she never took easily. When the tension grew in Stowe, my mother, never a woman to be quietly polite or passive (as I wrote in "My Mother and the Lampchops, Steak, Lobster Roast Beef" in *Cold Comfort,* "My mother who never was namby pamby, never held her tongue") bolted up in the doctor's office, all sixty or seventy pounds of her, and insisted she wanted to leave my sister and brother in law's and come to my house. As I write this, twelve and a half years later, every detail is clear. The words, the terror, the exhaustion. One poem in *Cold Comfort,* "Nichols Lodge in the Rain," I wrote my last night in Stowe, there to pick up my mother and bring her by ambulance to my house on August 6. I can feel the damp musk, damp air of gladiolas, tiger lilies, roses. And the last words hurled at me as the ambulance door closed still sting. Just yesterday I typed and printed a poem about the ambulance ride through black-eyed susans to my house, sitting sideways in the ambulance, not sorry I could not "look ahead." That last night I knew the end of the story but not how we'd get there.

At my house, the luxury to sit with my mother and write dissolved. It was IV needles, syringes, angiocaths. Demerol disguised in beet juice. Laundry. One day trying to get my mother to the commode in time (which I didn't) and then trying to get her back up into the hospital bed (which I couldn't), the phone man, who came to install a personal line for my mother at my sister's insistence, lifted her up into the bed as if this were a normal part of his job, while I cleaned up. Most nights I was too drained to write. With all the hospital supplies,—wheel chair, hospital stands, IV stands, tables for medicines and lotions—the rooms were transformed. Bookshelves were beyond reach with the regular bed stuffed into my study. When the night aid came, I collapsed. But I could be with my mother, watch films with the cat on the TV (which went green on her last day). I stayed with her until August 20 at 9:40 when she became very quiet, the line between living and dying so muted. When my twenty-year-old cat died (also on a Monday night at 9:40, also in my arms in my house) last February, it was so similar, so hard to know exactly when death came. With both losses, writing in those first days seemed the best therapy.

My mother's presence had been so tangled in mine: the phone calls in her last years, the worrying, the support, the pride, the tension, the love. Editing *Tangled Vines,* a collection of mother-and-daughter poems, intensity and ambivalence were central to the poems as they often are to that relationship. When I went to clean out her house, it was like digging through forty years of "treasures" buried in baby powder. I carried a notebook and almost everything seemed a poem, from drawers of sexy satin underwear from the 1920s to boxes of Depends. There were the dishes she wanted to give me, and I always said "later," as if agreeing to take them while she was alive meant I knew she might not be soon. Everything seemed to trigger memories and feelings: phone books

my mother collected from cities she had visited and ones she hadn't in enormous stacks. There were collections of batteries, old radios, 1920s jewelry, boxes of every letter I sent her, every drawing and postcard, report cards, old magazines like *Pageant,* and paperbacks. Only my books were in a new glass case. Often it was like excavating a buried city: coins, lipsticks, jewelry, all hidden under Johnson's baby talc. Some days I wanted to keep everything for poems and memories: a dotted Swiss baby dress, chipped original Fiestaware, old evening gowns. Other days, exhausted from filling plastic bags with what clearly had to be tossed, I wanted everything out of the house immediately. A used book dealer took all my mother's books, one of the saddest things to see leave her house. It reminded me of her body, wrapped in purple velvet and carried out of the house as I watched, against the funeral director's advice. I spent weeks at the apartment on Main Street drowning in the past, jotting notes. I was dazed and amazed at some things I found, like a box of handwritten letters, small, blue-inked words on blue paper from the man my mother really loved but couldn't marry because they came from different religious backgrounds. Incredible letters that shape a series of poems in *Before It's Light* called "Stories That Could be True."

Little escaped being recorded for a possible poem: her red metal stool, her old TV, the comedy and tragedy lamps, pins, plaques, and earrings. Many of the finished poems are in *Cold Comfort* and *Before It's Light.* Lost was my favorite "sweet sixteen" rose dress. Friends "helping" apparently dumped it at a Good Will. Being gone, it became a focus of several Rose Dress poems, published in the spring 2003 issue of the *Paterson Literary Review.*

That first fall without my mother, I wrote many more mother-and-daughter poems, many more letter poems to her. By winter 1991 Desert Storm was going on in Iraq, and I wrote poems about that. In January of 1991, I was asked to teach a workshop at New York State Museum to coincide with a June exhibit: "Traveling with Daniel," a Holocaust story. Not having relatives connected to WWII or the Holocaust, I began to read voraciously: diaries, memoirs, histories, novels. I watched films and videos, took many notes for the course I'd teach. Many images, dreams, nightmares melted into poems and became in 1995 a big part of *Blue Tattoo.* Event Horizon, knowing the fiftieth anniversary of the Holocaust was coming up, wanted to do something to commemorate it. To explain how and why I wrote that book of Holocaust poems, I wrote a piece about my creative process. I began the article, now included with copies of *Blue Tattoo* by explaining, "As many know, I am not a survivor, nor am I a child of survivors. Growing up Jewish, I heard my mother's accounts of roommates in the mostly non-Jewish college from which she graduated. The roommates would say such things as, 'Hitler is right, Frieda, but you are different.'" One summer when I was six, a baby-sitter told me stories of what happened in tunnels to Jewish children during World War II. She told me of the tortures, the ovens, and those nightmares kept me waking up screaming. I gave my publisher and editor permission to alter my lines, which I often carried over with a syncopated rhythms. He made the lines end-stopped, more like newspaper clippings, more straightforward. And to add to the newspaper feeling, he printed the poems in columns.

Though I worked from January to June to be sure I would know a lot about the Holocaust, my workshop consisted almost entirely of non-Jewish young students who knew very little about Hitler or the atrocities. As usual, I had overprepared.

That year an expanded version of *Tangled Vines* came out with about forty additional pages of new poems. When I gave readings and did workshops it seemed especially sad doing them for the first time motherless. *Lips Unsealed,* a new collection of women's confidences, was out, too. I wondered if I had been right in not showing it to my mother as I always did when something was published, because it had contained a memoir about a Jewish mother dying and about the burial ritual, knowing it anticipated what was ahead.

When I planned for a garage sale, I took photographs of the rooms and the things I was going to sell. Several "Garage Sale" poems are in a chap book Wormwood published in *Parade* in 1994. It was hard to let go of many things. Still feeling tied to the past, my fantasies of sleeping forever in my old purple room over Otter Falls continued. Within a year, however, I was packing my mother's Heywood Wakefield furniture to be refinished and then trucked down to Washington, D.C., where I was going to spend much of my time in the Pennsylvania Quarter. It was a total change. I was in The Lansburgh. In weeks, Janet Reno moved in next door (she got up at 10 of 7 every morning—I could hear the water running). There was a drug dealer

across the hall. On the other side of the apartment, young, leather-clad men who ran a night club, brought in Cirque de Soleil to perform and stay in our apartment building. The night club owners played loud music at 4 AM. Nothing could have been more wildly different from Vermont or upstate New York. I was resistant, kept my house, and still have it. My cat was ten, and she adored dashing through boxes. The apartment was about two minutes from National Archives, five from the Portrait Gallery and National Museum of American Art, and ten from the National Gallery, National History Museum, and National Natural History Museum. The first afternoon I went to an exhibit of photographs of Jews in Wyoming, which became another series; several poems from it were published in *Wormwood Review.* August is hot in D.C., but that August was lovely. Drinking a cup of Cappuccino in Navy Memorial Park, I thought maybe this wouldn't be as bad as I feared, though D.C. was still considered the murder capital of the country. I went back to my house the day Hurricane Andrew hit and for some odd reason remember it was the last day my cat, Memento, caught a mouse. She left feet, blood, hair, and gristle in a disgusting smear. While the floors were being sanded, all planned before D.C. was in the picture, one of the men gashed an artery. I grabbed a once favorite orange and pink madras dress for a tourniquet. His blood must still be dried under the floor.

The first week in D.C. I bought a passport bag to use instead of a pocketbook, counted the steps from Archives metro to the apartment, especially at night. By June 12, 1994, packing for Virginia, I hated to leave. In two years I had become attached to the apartment (in spite of seeing roaches for the first time) and loved never having to drive. The last day at 486 Eighth Street NW were excruciating: all the goodbyes, taking photographs of each room. I loved the round window where I could dream with the cat, though she usually took up most of it. Virginia seemed the last place I should end up. It seemed farther from everything. The week I moved in, the same week of Simpson's white bronco chase, I was being audited by the IRS, in a year I'd lived in three places and had paperwork scattered all over. My basement in NY had flooded, receipts I needed had been sitting in water and had glued themselves to each other, and the ink blurred, dissolved. I had just begun a series of dentist appointments, and had a deadline for an article for *Writer's Digest.* I was sure I could never finish on time, never do the job I wanted to, and was supposed to be going out to Glenwood Springs, Colorado to teach for two

*At the Eiffel Tower, June 2002*

weeks. From there I had a reading in Cleveland. Nothing was unpacked in Virginia, but I loaded some books and clothes (half slipping from me since I hadn't been able to eat for weeks). It ended up being great. The staff, the rainbows in the mountains, sage. On this icy black December night it warms me thinking of then, shocks me how long ago it was, how long since I felt as I did then.

Walking distance from my D.C. apartment to the metro was about 200 steps. In Virginia, it is only a five-minute walk but somehow the first weeks I felt very far from everything, isolated. The best part was the pond behind the townhouse. Though I grew up over Otter Falls in Vermont, I had never lived so close to the water. In 1994 no trees had grown up yet to block the view, so it was as if the pond was in the living room. Water birds, herons, gulls, ducks, geese, snow geese, hawks, beavers, muskrats, water rats, deer on

one side, the metro and beltway on the other. Before summer becomes too hot, I like to take my notebook and coffee out on the deck and let the green leaves, birds, the sounds of goose music (as in a poem I published in Yankee) move into poems. I know Canada geese are now supposed to be "common," but I had never seen many close up. A neighbor and I were at the edge of the pond most days and having the birds stay all winter seemed wonderful since the pond was often frozen over. One day I saw a bird with a band, and I jotted the day down, the times and hours it came, and the band number. Then another banded bird came. Someone told me it meant nothing, probably just there to show there were too many geese. I tried to read more about wild birds but didn't find much. When *Fly Away Home,* the film about the sculptor-inventor Bill Lishman teaching motherless geese to migrate following an Ultralite plane, came out, I wanted to see it. A few days after the movie, the *Washington Post* had an article about the "real life" experience of the movie, with a photograph of Dr. William Sladen (who runs Operation Migration) and some of the geese he had trained, as well as his plans to bring endangered swans to the Chesapeake. I wasn't sure where in Virginia Airlie Center was, but noticing the band on the goose in the photograph looked familiar, I checked it out. I was amazed I could find the notes. When I looked, the numbers were close. I wrote Dr. Sladen, wondering if he gave lectures and could recommend some books. A few days later, my phone rang non-stop: biologists, environmentalists calling to say to call back at any time of the day or night.

It turned out I had seen one of the original geese from Lishman's experiments. I'm not sure how well known this story is, but between the film and his book *Father Goose,* and some appearances on places like *20/20,* the story has charmed many. Of the fifteen geese that followed that plane in the shape of a goose from Canada over New York, Pennsylvania, Maryland, and Virginia and then on to North Carolina, thirteen of the fifteen geese that were never seen again in United States were reported seen returning to Canada. "My goose" came back separately. But no one had ever been able to find any of the original geese in the United States. So they wanted to see the pond and invited me to spend the day at Airlie when Lishman came down from Canada to talk about the film. He circled a goose on the inside cover of his book, wrote "Lyn's goose." The movie was much closer to truth than I would have guessed. Now I have many goose poems and a group of poems about birds that are half-swan, half-woman. For several years I watched for my goose, wrote about lost birds. When the moon is in the same position, I still look.

On New Year's Eve 1990 in Albany, I said the new decade felt like the decade of death. It was. By accident I learned of the death of someone I had been, or thought I'd been, close to. Poems based on his stories are liberally scattered through my new book from March Street, *A New Film about a Woman in Love with the Dead.* This book, published in fall 2002, came accidentally from a huge submission of poems to Parting Gifts. Robert Bixby found a narrative in it that seems to have touched some recent reviewers. Writing about relationships or a relationship is much harder in a memoir than in poems where what is true is always tempered, shaped, twisted, sculpted, and controlled by the writer, so it's both less true and more true than what happened.

Internet presses began to publish my poems in books, sometimes with my knowledge, often without. I think it was in 1995 that Michael McNeilly, who had published many of my poems in his magazines, asked if I'd be interested in having him do a Web site. I was excited, and within a short time, he had my site up and running (http://www.lynlifshin.com). I began to get more requests to critique poems, send submissions, do more readings. There were some book orders. When I gave readings, before Black Sparrow, I usually found I was known by the magazines and anthology publications, not by my hundred books, which were harder it seemed for readers to find. As I write this, I can barely imagine researching without the internet. Today, looking for a certain poem of mine (living between two places I'm often hunting for some poem or photograph) with a few clicks I learned five poems of mine had been set to music and performed by a quartet in Chicago (http://www.rbgmusic.com/pieces_of_some_dream.htm) and found a panel discussion and interpretation of a poem of mine. There was beautiful broadside from Santa Fe Poetry Broadside with my poem, "Moonrise, Hernandez, New Mexico, 1944" and an interview I had not seen. Both surprises and all in minutes while the ice is glazing trees, branches snapping, the new kitten amazed by what looks like thick slabs of liquid glass blurring the screens. Suddenly a poem not even "accepted" is out there. Anything in a book can be turned into music, theater, dance. If I go to Google and type in my name, there are so many poems and interviews I've forgotten about or never seen. It's great. But there are the fake e-mails—someone taking part of my name and writing vile notes to and about other writers as if the e-mail, sounding like me, really is me. But the ease of finding information, even if there's too much at times, still astonishes me and is so much easier on this no-ballet morning to do it in a thick fleece sweatshirt and jeans and a cup of red tea.

A perfect day to stay inside. Certainly not one on which I'd want to be traveling to do readings. I still do them, not as many as in the past. It's not only that I don't want to read and not be paid. For all the readings I've done, I still have stage fright before a reading. Unlike some poets who love to perform anywhere at anytime, it's hard for me, though I'm known as an excellent reader. About a November 16, 2002 reading for the *Utne Reader,* Catherine Savoy McCormack wrote "she's a fantastic reader, with a strong voice and animated delivery. . . . her delivery engaged the audience from beginning to end." I try to include a variety of poems, including those that might be called lighter like "The Condom Chain Letter Poem" and poems about Barbie, Marilyn Monroe, and Lorena Bobbit. I keep planning to read some of the Jesus poems, but so far I haven't. I think they'd be good reading poems. Some editors think they are my best. Several are in *Cold Comfort, Before It's Light,* and the forthcoming *Another Woman Who Looks Like Me.* In them I might meet Jesus at Starbucks the night I've fought with my boyfriend or find Jesus trying out for a part as an extra in *Godspell* only to be told he looks too much like a hippie. (An odd synchronicity: when I took the mail in after my last sentence, there was a note from a small press that said "I have spent months trying to figure out how to deal with the Jesus Poems. They are simply magnificent. I can't for the life of me figure out why you would send them to some little magazine. Do you mean there are no major publishers who would take these?") Some Jesus poems did appear in a small chap book but I never thought of sending them to a major press and this seems a good transition to why.

In the four years before 2002, my Abyssinian, Memento, seventeen in 1988, had a series of problems that tied me even closer to her: she needed prednisone pills and insulin shots. With no children and little family she became a bigger part of my life and my poems. When she wouldn't eat, it was like when my mother wouldn't eat. Each time something went wrong, it reminded me of my mother's decline. Memento loved to travel, and I took her to my Niskayuna house often, to the film festival in Montreal. Suddenly many women were telling me stories of their cats, it seemed, and I began writing about that. "Cat Women," appears in *Before It's Light.* Some women I am in touch with I seem to have become close to because of our interest in cats. Men, too, though I was wrong in judging one man's kindness to cats as something that extended to people.

Since the 1990s, especially with e-mail and the internet, I have done endless interviews. I always agree to do them, hoping something will inspire someone to look at my books. Strange to know what helps sales. I read a Barbie poem on *Talk of the Nation:* not a single person told me they heard me. It was great that anyone who reads poetry knows Black Sparrow. When I needed books shipped to a reading, I knew they would get there, that Black Sparrow would quickly respond to any question. I began to submit poems again, to let

*Before ballet class, Paris, June 2002*

people know I had a new book coming. As I said, Martin wanted my third book, *Another Woman Who Looks Like Me,* by mid-fall 2001. As I was selecting poems, I wasn't sure how September 11 affected that. A more sober tone maybe? I had written some poems of the disaster but not typed them up yet. Many recently came out in the anthology *An Eye for an Eye and We Will All Be Blind.* I had considered including prose in *Another Woman.* People had asked me to reprint some of my Madonna poems, since those books were out of print. But the mood of Washington seemed too sad for those poems. I made some changes I imagine came from the mood of the country.

I was on my way to a ballet class that bright blue morning. I knew there had been an accident but I assumed it was a small plane hitting the building. As more dancers arrived at the studio and more was known, there was panic. Classes were cancelled. Someone gave me a ride home. We could see smoke from the Pentagon. Then the anthrax scares made each metro trip a little tense, each bit of mail suspicious. I continued going to ballet. Nobody used talcum powder. When I flew to St. Louis for a series of readings,

National Airport, which had just opened, was deserted. It was a relief to be away from one of the two prime targets.

Along with the general under-the-surface-but-always-there unease, there were other problems. A friend was sick. New Year's Eve was horrible. With the house full of people staying days, sleeping bags tangling with old newspaper, dirty dishes, a house of people coming and going, I got news that my last uncle had died, the last of two in less than four years. While the people crowding the house were drinking champagne, I was packing dark clothes, booking a flight. At the funeral, I realized it was goodbye not only to my uncle but, in a startling, shocking, ugly scene, to another once-close relative.

Back in Virginia, preparing for a day in a hospital waiting room, I began to read *Savage Beauty,* the recently published book by Nancy Milford about Edna St. Vincent Millay, saved for what I knew would be a stressful day. I had been at the Millay Colony in September 1979. Norma Millay was still alive, but we were told to keep out of her way unless she spoke to us. On the last night of my stay, all the colonists were invited to her house, the main house of Steepletop, for a concert and drinks. My stay at the colony was with a small group and I spent most of my time alone, wandering the same fields Millay did, reading the edition of her letters Norma had chosen for the library. Walking past one field into a clump of trees past an old weathered bar and bar stools, I came face to face with myself in a tall mirror in the trees. It was like a walking into a dream. I was fascinated by what I knew of Edna's life, the information carefully controlled by Norma, and wrote a group of Millay poems that appeared in an issue of *Greenfield Review.* Millay's feelings about giving readings, her poems of loss and nature, resonated. I had no idea how much I would identify with her feelings and actions reading more. I hated to have *Savage Beauty* end. So much seemed to parallel my life: her closeness with her mother, an absent father, the feelings of being unpopular through high school, of needing to retreat from having to perform, to be "on," for too many people, from having to be a poet. Just recently I read that she, too, had written her first poem about birds. Next I read *What Lips These Lips Have Kissed* with a lot more of the letters Norma had kept from the public. Apparently Norma had burned many nude photos. I wonder what else she destroyed. I coaxed a friend to read these two

*The author's beloved Abyssinian, Memento*

books, and we talked a lot about Millay's independence, sexually freedom, drive, how braided her life continued to be to her mother's and sisters'. I think I was in a Millay daze, did things I might not have, half expected all men to be Eugen, her husband. Though I knew the earlier books on Millay were always in some way scrutinized by Norma, I had to have them, got every out-of-print book I could, and always found something new, something contradictory. "You should channel Millay," someone told me.

Thinking of the turbulence in Millay's life, I go back over some of the most painful parts of last year, as well as the highs. The February night the Olympics were beginning, I noticed my twenty-and-a-half-year-old cat seemed to hardly eat. Yes, I'd had other scares with her, but something seemed different. Saturday I knew it was more than a stretch when I'd opened five or six tins before she finally ate something. Rushing to the vet, though my cat sitter had seen her a week before and found her in good shape, they found she was anemic. That seemed the worst news. Her kidney function was slowing down. she was over twenty and had lost weight. The vet, always trying to keep her, had me bring her to a weekend emergency care center. Sunday she rallied. I was thrilled. By Monday, her test results were worse. She was not looking good. With my regular vet gone, a simply hideous man took over. He was very insensitive. He harangued me: either put her in an extraordinary, extreme measure program or put her to sleep. I wanted to bring her home for the night. He was horrendous, said I was torturing her. Just writing this I feel as horrified as I did that afternoon with him. I brought my cat home and kept her on the bed. I could see her slipping away, and as I held her, almost in the same way as earlier my mother had, she died peacefully, so gently it was never possible to tell the line between being alive and dying. Like my mother, she died on a Monday at 9:40.

Afraid to show my grief, I stayed home a week, didn't go out, just wrote about her, and didn't stop writing until I had filled many notebooks. I wasn't ready for a new cat, but one breeder who had been so helpful and sympathetic during the ordeal the day of Memento's death told me to call when I was. I now have a seven-month-old beauty, Jetè Pentimento, born April 10. She is not a replacement for my sweet, timid, cautious but adorable Aby, Memento, but a fearless, long, wild beauty. She's so much fun. Between cats, after traveling mostly for readings, I spent time in Paris and Berlin in June, and now am working notes from that brief visit into poems.

Deaths, not only of relatives, but friends and editors and publishers have colored recent years. The death of Bill Packard, one of the most supportive editors, as well as a novelist and friend, Maxine Combs, whom I had recently read with and shared a publicity party with the year before, darkened this year. Another enormous loss and shock came after a week at the Austin Poetry Festival. I came back to terrible news May 2, an e-mail titled IMPORTANT ANNOUNCE-MENT, which began, "I want to be the first to let you know about an important development at Black Sparrow Press. This relates to a press release issued today by Harper Collins Publishers." Even without details I realized that something that seemed central and so important, so comforting was no longer going to be. Even though the e-mail said "Black Sparrow will now go forward as usual with the business at hand and at the same time continue to evaluate where we stand as a publishing company," I had a sinking feeling. John Martin, an editor to whom I owe so much thanks, had decided to sell Black Sparrow authors Bukowski, Bowles, and Fante. I was devastated. My book was slated for months from then, fall 2002. I had just passed out *Another Woman* flyers at my recent readings, arranged publication readings. Another Black Sparrow writer thought all contracted works would certainly be published, but I'm always pessimistic. Someone said about the other writer, "She's an easy-going country girl. You're intense, a city woman." John Martin, I'm sure, felt loyal to his writers and was upset at how some of us would feel. He told me he would be talking to another press, that I should do

*Reading from* **Cold Comfort**

nothing until I heard back from him, June 7. On June 4, I left for Paris. To my amazement I was able to love being there, walking in the rain, imagining Millay there for her first time, listening to the bells from Notre Dame. I could see the church and the Seine from the balcony. I took ballet class at Danse du Maurais, and loved it—the trip was a perfect escape. When I got back, there was news that David Godine, Inc., would be continuing the Black Sparrow imprint, would distribute already published Black Sparrow books, and would publish the planned Black Sparrow titles. It is all very new, and of course the books will be delayed while everything is in transition. In so many ways this past year, so much seems less certain.

One good thing is that Temple University will continue to collect my archives. Since their last acquisition was in 1986 and I have continued to write and publish prolifically, you can imagine how magazines, handwritten spiral notebooks, posters, flyers, tapes, and videos have accumulated. Besides the material I collected for the Holocaust workshop at New York State Museum, I have boxes full of workshop material designed to go with many exhibits, as well as the poems that came from them: "Mother and Daughters," "the Changing Urban Scene," "Mirrors Inside and Outside," "Feelings about War." I've spent less time lately in museums even though many wonderful ones are only a metro ride away. When I went to the Portrait Gallery talks, poems were triggered about gipsies, Asian immigrants, poems from Inuit drawings and sculptures, Native American masks and clothing. It will be hard to pack off all the flyers and pamphlets from D.C. museums. Though I've kept some contributor copies, even those should be packed and shipped. I've joked that I'd like to include my wedding gown, 1970s Betsey Johnson dresses still in my closet, and all the cashmere sweaters I had in college. I'm terrible at getting rid of clothes. With one box of old clothes, first I had to write a goodbye poem for each dress. After my mother died I bought tons of stretch leggings and leather jackets. For comfort? To hold me? After the news of Black Sparrow no longer being Black Sparrow, I bought too many suede and leather jackets. But the urge to pare poems and closets down, turn lines and drawers to something Shaker is always colliding with my velvet coats and scarves. It's a pattern in poems, too, stripped down, spare, only the essentials side by side with what flows and grows like a Vermont house. Part of me wants to hang on to everything from the sheet music my mother saved, stored in a closet, to the baby teeth she kept in a jar (all in poems so I'll always have them). I will keep the letters I wrote to her from the time I was six, which she kept, and letters from men who were good enough or bad enough for whole books. Photographs. There's a part of me that wants to pack up even autographed copies of poetry books and all the posters, but I then wonder: What if there is another film?

When I did the first autobiography for Gale series, I went through every diary, every letter. But I don't keep a diary now, only a diary of my new cat. My letters are no longer in folders or stapled into diaries but on disks. It seemed for "On the Outside" that letters were more useful in pulling back the past, the details, the feelings, better than diaries. I doubt I will box up photographs, the first thing I took clearing out my mother's house and what I wanted, but found gone, in my grandmother's and uncle's house. Knowing what to get rid of and what to keep—with objects, relationships, memories, feelings, always a mystery.

I'm writing this at the kitchen table, a postcard of the Black Angel from a graveyard in Iowa, something else I would never have written about unless someone was doing an anthology on her. There's a stack of e-mails in a clip I've done a series of poems based on. Also on the refrigerator, Iroquois words about avoiding doctors, removable rose tattoos. There are Marilyn Monroe postcards and a Plath card, cat magnets, a photo of a close friend in a skirt I gave her, almost forgetting her birthday that year. There's less stained glass in this house though, and since I rarely wear necklaces, I've thought of hanging glass beads near the light. Upstairs, on the vanity once in my mother's house, the same barrettes I used to spread out on the blue quilt at Appletree. In Hawaii I found hair danglers made of old crystals, perfect since I don't wear earrings. The beads glow in my still-long blond hair. Rushing off to ballet so often, I rarely change the crystal or diamond drop necklaces I love but rarely get to wear. But the rhinestone and crystal barrettes glisten wildly in the sun on the wood my mother's Johnson's baby talc and a musical jewel box once covered. By chance, I brought the yellow, spiral, handwritten notebooks with the first part of my autobiography down to Virginia over half a year ago and noticed they started in October 1988 and went to February 1999. The title, "On the Outside: Lips, Blues, Blue Lace" still seems right. Maybe I'd add velvet, or leather, burnt velvet, burn-out velvet, that lushness when something is taken away.

So many of my books are out of print. I see some at very high prices on the Web. Yet I've still not written in this autobiography about so much of the time when all but the last of my books in print and my first book were published. In 1989 I wrote that I was "astonished, since I thought I left so much out that I've typed only two and a half of six notebooks up and I've only come to the publishing of the first of around eighty (now over one hundred) books and chap books." On the metro now, where I do more writing lately, I'm wondering about those still untyped notebooks. I couldn't just add them because memory changes through time, would reshape reality differently.

Or could I?

*BIOGRAPHICAL AND CRITICAL SOURCES:*

BOOKS

*Contemporary Poets,* 6th edition, St. James Press (Detroit, MI), 1996.
*Contemporary Women Poets,* St. James Press (Detroit, MI), 1998.
Fox, Hugh, *Lifshin: A Critical Study,* Whitiston Press (Troy, NY), 1985.

PERIODICALS

*Albany,* December, 1986.
*Booklist,* April 1, 1978; July 15, 1978; April 15, 1990; January 1, 1991.
*Bookwatch,* January, 1991.
*Choice,* March, 1977; December, 1978.
*Greenfield Review,* summer-fall, 1983.
*Library Journal,* June, 1971; December, 1972; June 1, 1976.
*Little Magazine,* summer-fall, 1972.
*Los Angeles Times,* October 18, 1982.
*Los Angeles Times Book Review,* September 23, 1984; October 13, 1985.
*Minneapolis Star,* April 18, 1972.
*Ms.,* September, 1976; July, 1978; July, 1983.
*New York Times Book Review,* December 17, 1978.
*North American Review,* fall, 1978; March, 1985.
*Northeast,* fall-winter, 1971-72.
*Poetry Now,* spring, 1980.
*Review of Contemporary Fiction,* fall, 1990.
*Road Apple Review,* summer-fall, 1971.
*San Francisco Review of Books,* spring, 1985; fall, 1985.
*Small Press Book Review,* March, 1991.
*Small Press Review,* September, 1983; March, 1984; January, 1985; May, 1990.
*Southwest Review,* winter, 1983.
*Utne Reader,* spring, 1990.
*Village Voice,* September 24, 1979.
*Windless Orchard,* summer, 1972.
*Wormwood Review,* Volume XII, number 3, 1971.
*Writers Digest,* September, 1994.

OTHER

*Lyn Lifshin Web site,* http://www.lynlifshin.com (June 3, 2003).
Lynch, Mary Ann, *Lyn Lifshin: Not Made of Glass* (film), Women Make Movies, 1990.

## LILLY, John F. 1954-

*PERSONAL:* Born November 3, 1954, in Chicago, IL; son of George P., Sr. (an insurance actuary) and Myrtle (a homemaker; maiden name, Sheber) Lilly; married Catherine Carpenter, October 7, 1989; children: John Mason, George Stuart. *Ethnicity:* "Caucasian." *Education:* Attended University of Illinois, 1972-75, and Arizona State University, 1976; Davis and Elkins College, B.A., 1996.

*ADDRESSES: Home*—P.O. Box 5402, Charleston, WV 25361. *Office—Goldenseal,* Cultural Center, West Virginia Division of Culture and History, 1900 Kanawha Blvd. E., Charleston, WV 25305; fax: 304-558-2779. *E-mail*—john.lilly@wvculture.org.

*CAREER:* Editor and author. Country Music Foundation, Nashville, TN, tour guide at Country Music Hall of Fame and Museum, 1988-91; Davis and Elkins College, Elkins, WV, publicist for Augusta Heritage Center, 1992-97; West Virginia Division of Culture and History, Charleston, WV, editor, 1997—.

*MEMBER:* North American Folk Music and Dance Alliance, Americana Music Association, West Virginia Library Association.

*AWARDS, HONORS:* Spirit of West Virginia Award, West Virginia Division of Tourism, 2000, for *Goldenseal.*

*WRITINGS:*

(Editor) *Mountains of Music: West Virginia Traditional Music from "Goldenseal,"* University of Illinois Press (Champaign, IL), 1999.

Contributor to periodicals. Associate editor, *Old-Time Herald,* 1991-96; editor, *Goldenseal,* 1997—.

\*     \*     \*

## LIN, Henry B.

*PERSONAL:* Born in China; son of John H. (a professor) and Mary C. (a professor) Lin. *Ethnicity:* "Chinese." *Education:* Earned M.B.A.

*ADDRESSES: Agent*—c/o Llewellyn Publications, P.O. Box 64383, St. Paul, MN 55164. *E-mail*—hlin6@ excite.com.

*CAREER:* Writer.

*WRITINGS:*

*What Your Face Reveals,* Llewellyn Publications (St. Paul, MN), 1999.
*Chinese Health Care Secrets,* Llewellyn Publications (St. Paul, MN), 2000.
*The Art and Science of Feng Shui,* Llewellyn Publications (St. Paul, MN), 2000.

*SIDELIGHTS:* Henry B. Lin told *CA:* "My primary motivation for writing is to serve as a bridge between Chinese culture and Western societies. The ancient Chinese culture and Dr. Wan Laishen, my late teacher who was a great martial artist, philosopher, and doctor, have major influences on my works.

"Typically, I learn the subject matter and practice it for years. Then I summarize the knowledge and findings, do extensive literary research, and put the information down on paper. I organize and revise my writing as much as I can before I submit it to my publisher.

"The reasons I chose the subjects of my books are that I am very familiar with them, and I feel the books will be very useful to Western readers."

\*   \*   \*

**LINTON, Calvin D(arlington) 1914-2002**

*OBITUARY NOTICE*—See index for *CA* sketch: Born June 11, 1914, in Kensington, MD; died after a heart attack July 19, 2002, in Washington, DC. Educator and author. Linton was an authority on seventeenth- and twentieth-century British literature, as well as a biblical scholar. He received his doctorate from Johns Hopkins University in 1940. After brief teaching stints with Johns Hopkins University and at Queens College in Charlotte, North Carolina, Linton served in the Office of Naval Intelligence during World War II. He spent the balance of his academic career at George Washington University where he rapidly rose from assistant professor in 1945 to professor of English literature in 1948. He was made dean of the Columbia College of Arts and Sciences in 1957, a position he held until his retirement in 1984. However, even after retirement Linton's interest in the Christian faith led him to continue to teach the course "Christianity and Literature." In related work, he served as editor-at-large for the magazine *Christianity Today,* contributed articles to *Christianity and Literature,* was director of the Institute of Advanced Christian Studies, and served as president and co-organizer of the Conference on Christianity and Literature. In addition to his work as professor and dean, Linton often taught writing classes to government employees and was the author of *How to Write Reports* (1954) and *Effective Writing* (1958; revised edition, 1962). Active in numerous literary and educational organizations, he was a one-time president of the Literary Society of Washington, the Eastern Association of Deans and Advisors, and the Cosmos Club, as well as U.S. chairman of England's Modern Humanities Research Association. His other publication work includes writing *Educated Gullibility* (1961), editing *The Bicentennial Almanac* (1975; revised as *The American Almanac,* 1977), and co-editing *Quick Reference Encyclopedia: The Complete Reference Handbook of Basic Knowledge for Home, School, and Office* (1978; revised edition, 1980).

*OBITUARIES AND OTHER SOURCES:*

BOOKS

*Directory of American Scholars,* ninth edition, Gale (Detroit, MI), 1999.

*PERIODICALS*

*Washington Post,* July 22, 2002, p. B4.

\*   \*   \*

**LIU, Wu-chi 1907-2002**

*OBITUARY NOTICE*—See index for *CA* sketch: Born July 27, 1907, in Wu-chiang, Kiangsu, China; died October 3, 2002, in Menlo Park, CA. Educator and author. Liu was a noted expert on Chinese literature and helped build awareness of Chinese works in the

United States. He moved to Wisconsin in 1927 to attend Lawrence College (now Lawrence University), where he earned his B.A. in 1928; he graduated with a Ph.D. in English literature from Yale University in 1931, and also did postdoctoral work at the University of London. Returning to China, Liu taught English at Nankai University before World War II and was a professor of foreign languages at National Central University during the war. In the late 1940s he decided to return to the United States and teach Chinese languages and culture. He was a visiting professor at Rollins College and Yale University, and during the early 1950s was also chairman of the department of Chinese studies at Hartwick College. This was followed by a one-year stint at the University of Pittsburgh before he joined Indiana University at Bloomington as professor of East Asian languages and literature, where he remained until his retirement as emeritus professor in 1976. Liu wrote and edited over two dozen books during his career, one of the most notable of which is his edited work *Sunflower Splendor: Three Thousand Years of Chinese Poetry* (1975),

which was hailed as the best collection of translated Chinese poetry at the time. Other works by Liu include *An Introduction to Chinese Literature* (1966) and *Selected Essays by Liu Wu-chi* (1984). He was also a former editor of the journal *International Southern Society.*

*OBITUARIES AND OTHER SOURCES:*

*BOOKS*

*Writers Directory,* 12th edition, Gale (Detroit, MI), 1998.

*PERIODICALS*

*Los Angeles Times,* October 19, 2002, p. B18.
*Washington Post,* October 21, 2002, p. B7.

# M

## MADIGAN, Tim(othy S.) 1957-

*PERSONAL:* Born December 16, 1957, in Crookston, MN; son of Myke and Lois Madigan; married; wife's name, Catherine; children: Melanie, Patrick. *Education:* University of North Dakota, B.A., 1980.

*ADDRESSES: Office*—c/o Fort Worth *Star-Telegram*, 400 West 7th Street, Fort Worth, TX 76101. *E-mail*—tmadigan@star-telegram.com.

*CAREER:* Worked variously for newspapers in Williston, ND and in Odessa, TX, and for the *Chicago Tribune;* Fort Worth *Star-Telegram,* journalist, 1984—; writer.

*AWARDS, HONORS:* Texas Reporter of the Year, 1996, 1997.

*WRITINGS:*

*See No Evil: Blind Devotion and Bloodshed in David Koresh's Holy War,* Summit Publishers Group, 1993.
*The Burning: Massacre, Destruction, and the Tulsa Race Riot of 1921,* Thomas Dunne Books/St. Martin's Press (New York, NY), 2001.

*SIDELIGHTS:* Ever since graduating from college, Tim Madigan has been working for newspapers. In the 1990s, as a journalist for the Fort Worth *Star-Telegram,* he's made a name for himself and twice was named Texas Reporter of the Year. His abilities to gather facts and write a compelling story are evidenced not only in his articles for the newspapers but also in two books he has published. While his subject matter varies, Madigan's writing, as *New York Times* book reviewer Adam Nossiter described it, is "skillful, clear-eyed telling."

In 1993, while the U.S. citizens were riveted to their television sets as the story of David Koresh and the Branch Davidians unfolded, Madigan stood, for three days, witnessing the standoff between the FBI and Koresh's group outside the Waco, Texas, compound. A week later, according to Courtenay Thompson in the *Columbia Journalism Review,* Madigan was "offered a book contract and he took a month's leave to report and write it." Thompson wrote that throughout the whole Waco tragedy there was a mad rush by television and movie producers, as well as book publishers, to dramatize this story and get it out to the public. Madigan was aware of the publisher's desire to be the first to have a book in the stores. He told Thompson thay he had a different motive. His "goal as a journalist was, given those ground rules, to write a good book." His focus was to "help advance the story rather than sensationalize it." Julia Null, a reviewer for the *Texas Monthly,* liked Madigan's efforts, and noted that the book that resulted from them, *See No Evil: Blind Devotion and Bloodshed in David Koresh's Holy War,* "reads well."

The circumstances surrounding Madigan's second book, *The Burning: Massacre, Destruction, and the Tulsa Race Riot of 1921,* are a little different. This story is based on that the city of Tulsa managed to keep a secret from the rest of the world for almost eight decades. Not until the Tulsa Race Riot Commission (1998-2000) was formed did people living outside of the city know that on May 31, 1921, mobs formed in the streets of Tulsa, demanding the lynching of Dick Rowland, an African American, whom the local papers had falsely accused of raping Sarah Page, a white woman. Street fights ensued and by the end of the week, a prosperous section of town inhabited mostly by African Americans had been completely destroyed.

The mobs that ruled Tulsa's streets that night included both white and black people. In the crowd was a black war veteran carrying a gun. He was determined, according to Jim Morris of *CNN.com,* to protect his friend Rowland, whom he was afraid the white mob would lynch. When a white man confronted the armed veteran and tried to take his gun away from him, "the gun went off, the white man was dead, the riot was on," wrote Morris.

No one knows for sure how many people were killed before the riots ended, but most people agree that the majority killed were African Americans. Some estimates state that one hundred people died; other estimates are much higher, some reaching as high as three thousand. Many were killed by gunfire. Other people had their homes burned. Some survivors of the riots claim that explosive devices were dropped on their homes from airplanes flying overhead. The riots lasted two days. In the end, thirty-four blocks of the black community called Greenwood had been burnt to the ground.

In a review of Madigan's book, Chris Patsilelis, writing for the *Houston Chronicle,* called the riots, "the deadliest domestic outbreak of barbarism since the Civil War." Calling *The Burning* "engrossing and revealing," Patsilelis added, "Madigan does an excellent job of tracing events leading up to the riot and of evoking the dense atmosphere of racial hatred that pervaded post-Civil War America: the hardships of emancipation, the murderous rides of the Ku Klux Klan, the oppression of Jim Crow laws and the thousands of lynchings of blacks, usually for imagined crimes."

Although reading the accounts of what Margaret Flanagan, for *Booklist,* described as "the most shameful episodes in the troubled history of race relations in

the U.S." is difficult, Flanagan referred to Madigan's research and subsequent writing as "compelling" and "riveting." Other reviewers also used the word "compelling" in describing Madigan's second book. According to a reviewer for *Publishers Weekly,* Madigan shows "how the riot touched individual lives." Madigan does this "by creating full-scale portraits of black and white citizens" and creating "absorbing narratives" from the stories of those he has interviewed.

Adam Nossiter, commending Madigan's efforts, noted in the *New York Times Book Review,* that "You won't find any mention" of the Tulsa Race Riot "in a number of standard histories of the 1920's."

## BIOGRAPHICAL AND CRITICAL SOURCES:

*PERIODICALS*

*Booklist,* November 1, 2001, Margaret Flanagan, review of *The Burning: Massacre, Destruction, and the Tulsa Race Riot of 1921,* pp. 458-459.

*Essence,* November, 2001, review of *The Burning,* p. 86.

*Kirkus Reviews,* September 1, 2001, review of *The Burning,* p. 1269.

*Library Journal,* September 1, 2001, Robert Flatley, review of *The Burning,* p. 203.

*New York Times Book Review,* November 11, 2001, Adam Nossiter, "Something Tulsa Forgot," p. 33.

*Publishers Weekly,* September 10, 2001, review of *The Burning,* p. 70.

*Texas Monthly,* February, 1994, Julia Null, review of *See No Evil: Blind Devotion and Bloodshed in David Koresh's Holy War,* p. 70.

*OTHER*

*CNN.com,* http://www.cnn.com/ (June 17, 2002), Jim Morris, "Tulsa Panel Seeks Truth from 1921 Race Riot."

*Columbia Journalism Review,* http://www.cjr.org/ (June 15, 2002), Courtenay Thompson, "Apocalypse Now, Waco and the Lure of Instant Books."

*HoustonChronicle.com,* http://www.chron.com/ (May 20, 2002), Chris Patsilelis, "Tulsa's Bloody Riot Detailed in Compelling Work."*

## MAHARAJ, Mac (Sathyandranath R.) 1935-

*PERSONAL:* Born April 22, 1935, in Newcastle, Kwa-ZuluNatal; married: wife's name, Zarina (a lecturer, researcher, and columnist); children: Amilcar, Sekai. *Education:* St. Oswald's High School, Newcastle, 1952; UNNE, B.A., 1956; Studied law at London School of Economics, 1959-61; University of South Africa, B.A., and two years towards a B.Sc.

*ADDRESSES: Home*—Private Bag X9129, Cape Town 8000, South Africa.

*CAREER: New Age,* editor, 1956; ANC Headquarters, Lusaka, Zambia, secretary of Underground Section, 1977; Commander, Operation Vula, South Africa for three years; Codesa secretary; Minister of Transportation, 1994—. FirstRand Bank Holdings, member, board of directors; Softline Limited, member, board of directors. Served on three cabinet committees: Economic Affairs, Committee for Office Bearers, and Inter-ministerial Cabinet Committee (IMCC); Chairperson of the transport sector of the National Framework Agreement (NFA). Member of Revolutionary Council, Politico Military Council, National Executive Council, National Executive Committee (1985-90, and 1991—), Political Bureau and Central Committee, Government of National Unity, and Transitional Executive Council (joint secretary).

*WRITINGS:*

(Editor) *Reflections in Prison,* Zebra and the Robben Island Museum (Cape Town, South Africa), 2001, University of Massachusetts Press (Amherst, MA), 2002.

*SIDELIGHTS:* Mac Maharaj has had a tumultuous life, going from an activist, to political prisoner, then on to a government official. Maharaj is now a non-executive director for Softline Limited Board of Directors, as well as director of FirstRand Ltd. and FirstRand Bank Holdings. A writer for the *African National Congress* stated, "Mac Maharaj's political life uniquely brings together all the strands of the struggle for democracy in South Africa." The same writer detailed Maharaj's arrest with "Wilton Mkwayi and four others on 177 counts of sabotage under the Sabotage Act and the Unlawful Organisations Act, and in 1965 began his 12 years of imprisonment on Robben Island." He was released in 1976, and with him he took the essays that he encouraged other activists to write. Twenty-five years later, Maharaj was able to publish the writings.

*Reflections in Prison* "reflected the determination of Nelson Mandela, Walter Sisulu, Govan Mbeki, Herman Toivo ya Toivo, John Pokela, Eddie Daniels and Billy Niar to provide a political context for themselves and those who would follow in their footsteps," according to Mandla Langa of the *Sunday Times.* Langa commented on the eerie knowledge those men must have had in knowing "that tragedy was stalking the children," when they had little idea of what was going on outside of the hallowed halls of their prison. Langa continued, "The defiant act of writing was a determination of an authority that was increasingly slipping away from the jailer. . . . the essays are an analysis of power gone mad." *Business Day* critic Cara Bouwer described the book as "a revealing glimpse into the psyches and strengths of many of the men who personify the struggle against apartheid. . . . secretly written, under the fear of reprisal, each word is a defiance against apartheid and a reaffirmation of the beliefs and freedom these men strove to achieve."

*BIOGRAPHICAL AND CRITICAL SOURCES:*

*PERIODICALS*

*African News Service,* July 15, 1999, "Maharaj Moves to World of Finance"; November 28, 2000, "Ellerine, Maharaj Join Softline Board"; November 30, 2000, "Bolt from Blue Strikes Heath Unit."
*Financial Times,* July 15, 1999, "Big Mac," p. 15; July 16, 1999, "Red Flag," p. 13.

*OTHER*

*African National Congress Web site,* http://www.anc.org.za/ (April 16, 2002).
*Business Day,* http://www.bday.co.za/ (July 1, 2002), Cara Bouwer, "Secret thoughts of apartheid captives,".
*Sunday Times,* http://www.suntimes.co.za (July 1, 2002), Mandla Langa, "Lessons from the Past for a Present Perfect,".*

## MARSHALL, Teresa 1962-

*PERSONAL:* Born 1962, in Truro, Nova Scotia, Canada. *Education:* Nova Scotia College of Art and Design, B.F.A., 1990.

*ADDRESSES: Office*—Marshall Art Studio, 272 East Fourth Ave., Vancouver, British Columbia, Canada V5T 1G5.

*CAREER:* Poet and artist. Installation and mixed-media artist based in Vancouver, British Columbia, Canada. Affiliated with theater department at Dalhousie University; visiting artist; public speaker; juror of art competitions. Est Nord Est, artist-in-residence; Banff Centre for the Arts, artist-in-residence and George Watchorn Memorial Scholar. Singer and poet. *Exhibitions:* Solo exhibitions include shows at Other Art Gallery, Art Gallery of Mount Saint Vincent, and Anna Leonowens Gallery, all Halifax, Nova Scotia, Canada, Gallery 101, Ottawa, Ontario, Canada, Connection Gallery, Fredericton, New Brunswick, Canada, and Thunder Bay Art Gallery; solo traveling exhibition through Department of Indian Affairs, 1994-95; work also represented in numerous group exhibitions; work in collections throughout Canada, including Canadian Native Arts Foundation, Confederacy of Mainland Micmacs, Native Council of Nova Scotia, Royal Ontario Museum, and Vancouver Art Gallery.

*AWARDS, HONORS:* Award from Peace Hill Trust; grants from Nova Scotia Tourism and Culture, Micmac Association of Cultural Studies, Canada Council, and British Columbia Cultural Alliance; Canadian Native Arts Foundation award.

*WRITINGS:*

Poetry represented in anthologies, including *Gatherings: The En'Owkin Journal of First North American Peoples,* Volume 4, Theytus Books (Penticton, British Columbia, Canada), 1993; *Kelusultiek: Original Women's Voices of Atlantic Canada,* Institute for the Study of Women, Mount St. Vincent University Press (Halifax, Nova Scotia, Canada), 1994; *Steal My Rage: New Native Voices,* Douglas & McIntyre (Vancouver, British Columbia, Canada), 1995; and *Native Women in the Arts: In a Vast Dreaming,* Native Women in the Arts (Toronto, Ontario, Canada), 1995. Contributor of

poetry to periodicals, including *Fireweed Feminist Quarterly* and *Absinthe Literary Journal: Writings by Women of Color and Aboriginal Women.*

*BIOGRAPHICAL AND CRITICAL SOURCES:*

*BOOKS*

*St. James Guide to Native North American Artists,* St. James Press (Detroit, MI), 1998, pp. 350-354.

*PERIODICALS*

*Aboriginal Peoples and Canada,* fall, 1995, Anne Whitelaw, "Land Spirit Power: First Nations Cultural Production and Canadian Nationhood."
*Aboriginal Voices,* July, 1995, Michael Huppe, "Indian Acts."
*Arts Atlantic,* fall, 1992, J. Murchie, "Subject Matter, Contemporary Sculpture and Painting in Nova Scotia"; fall, 1994, Brigid Toole Grant, "Re-Search"; winter, 1995, R. Rosenfield, "The Deportment of Indian Affairs."
*Artscraft,* winter, 1991, Lee Parpart, "Concrete Statements."
*Border Crossings,* December, 1993, Joseph Christianson, "Spirit Landing."
*C,* winter, 1993, Carol Podedworney, "Indigena and Land Spirit Power."
*Canadian Art,* spring, 1993, Scott Watson, "Whose Nation"; fall, 1994, Oliver Girling, "Fast Forward."
*Espace,* fall, 1995, Debbie O'Rourke, "Confrontation and Redemption."
*Fuse,* summer, 1995, "Monopoly Artist Project."
*Healthsharing,* fall-winter, 1992, E. Paul, "Teresa Marshall."
*Matriart,* Volume 3, number 2, 1992, Mary Ann Barkhouse, "Land, Spirit, Power"; Volume 4, number 4, 1994.
*Mix,* fall, 1995, Jane Ash Poitras and Clint Buehler, "Undressing Victim Art."
*New Art Examiner,* March, 1993, W. Jackson Rushing, "Canada's 'Indigena' and 'Land, Spirit, Power': Contingent Histories, Aesthetic Politics."
*Parachute,* number 70, 1992, Anne Whitelaw, "Land Spirit Power."

*Parallelogramme Magazine of Contemporary Art,* Volume 19, number 3, 1993-94, Cheryl L'Hirondelle, "It's a Cultural Thing"; Volume 19, number 4, 1993, Lance Belanger, "Mora's Armour."*

\*       \*       \*

**MARTINSON, Janis**
   **See HERBERT, Janis**

\*       \*       \*

**McALARY, Mike 1957-1998**

*PERSONAL:* Born 1957; died of colon cancer, December 25, 1998.

*CAREER:* Journalist and author. Sports writer for *Boston Herald* and *ABC Sports;* reporter with the *New York Daily News* and *New York Post.*

*AWARDS, HONORS:* Pulitzer Prize for journalism coverage in the *New York Daily News* of a Haitian immigrant's brutalization at a New York police station, 1998.

*WRITINGS:*

*Buddy Boys: When Good Cops Turn Bad,* Putnam (New York, NY), 1987.
*Cop Shot: The Murder of Edward Byrne,* Putnam (New York, NY), 1990.
*Good Cop, Bad Cop: Detective Joe Trimboli's Heroic Pursuit of NYPD Officer Michael Dowd,* Pocket (New York, NY) 1994.
*Cop Land (screenplay),* Miramax (New York, NY), 1997.
*Sore Loser,* William Morrow (New York, NY), 1998.

*SIDELIGHTS:* Mike McAlary was a journalist who began his career as a sports writer with the *Boston Herald,* later working for *ABC Sports.* McAlary wrote for several New York City papers and became a columnist with the *Daily News* in 1988. His articles often reflected the heroism of the police, but he also exposed the failures within the system. In 1997, he broke the story of the police beating of a Haitian immigrant.

McAlary's *Buddy Boys: When Good Cops Turn Bad* is an account of the 1986 scandal in the seventy-seventh precinct, referred to as the Alamo, in Brooklyn's Bedford-Stuyvesant and Crown Heights neighborhoods. McAlary first broke the story in *Newsday.* Although the precinct commander suspected corruption as early as 1982, the guilty were protected, and no action was taken until the internal affairs unit came down on Officer Henry Winter. Winter's history before joining the force was soiled. He had stolen from the cash register at his first job, collected unemployment while working, and cheated at the police academy.

Winter and Officer Anthony Magno were the first to be caught. McAlary wrote of the beginning of their corrupt practices. They started by taking bribes and stealing from the dead. When they went to crime scenes, they pocketed valuables burglars had missed. Banding together with other officers, they committed burglaries, drug deals, and armed robberies. The officers carried burglary tools and other equipment in their squad cars. Winter and Magno escaped prosecution by becoming informants. They wore wires as they continued committing crimes and exposing fellow officers, including one who shot himself in the head as a result. Edna Buchanan wrote in the *New York Times Book Review* that McAlary "constructs his narrative from interviews with Officers Winter and Magno and others. He does no moralizing, points no fingers, reaches no conclusions. He lets the officers tell the tale in their own words. He stays out of it. He does not need to bash the reader over the skull to make his point. The officers do it themselves." Buchanan wrote that when the officers were caught, they had "a reason for everything. When they stole turkeys and cheese intended for the poor they reasoned that people who receive free food often sell it themselves. And the ultimate excuse: everybody's doing it."

Thirteen officers were charged. Buchanan wrote, "The state appears to have given a break to the worst of the lot." As of April 1998, two of the officers had been convicted, one acquitted, and four had their charges dismissed. Two had entered guilty pleas, one had committed suicide, and three cases were pending. Buchanan concluded that "the voices in this book are pure cop. *Buddy Boys* is searing, outrageous, and painful." A *Publishers Weekly* reviewer wrote, "Written in a momentous style that is often overdone, this shocking probe of the seamy world of police corruption reads like a thriller." "Well-crafted, fast paced, and thorough," was Sandra K. Lindheimer's description in *Library Journal.*

*Cop Shot: The Murder of Edward Byrne* is McAlary's account of the killing of a young police officer while he was guarding the home of a witness in a Queens drug case. The four crack dealers who executed Byrne were caught, tried, found guilty, and sentenced to long prison terms. McAlary is critical of former mayor Edward Koch and former police commissioner Benjamin Ward. "The murder outraged cops not because it broke the law . . . but because it broke the rules," wrote David Gates in *Newsweek.* "Journalistic writing of a high order, the book tells a grim story with streetwise cynicism and telegraphic urgency," concluded a *Publishers Weekly* reviewer.

In *Good Cop, Bad Cop: Detective Joe Trimboli's Heroic Pursuit of NYPD Officer Michael Dowd,* McAlary recounts the events that led to Dowd's conviction in 1992. McAlary broke the story in the *New York Post.* Dorothy Uhnak wrote in the *New York Times Book Review* that McAlary "knows his city, its streets, its precincts, its politics, and its characters, good and bad. His account has all the ingredients of an exciting novel." McAlary wrote that for many years prior to Dowd's arrest he and other officers were dealing drugs and involved in a variety of criminal activities. McAlary said Dowd was linked to drug lords in the Dominican Republic and cocaine dealers in New York City, and that Dowd was well compensated. He owned a Corvette, four houses on Long Island, and was purported to be pulling in eight thousand dollars a week over and above his police salary.

Joseph Trimboli worked in internal affairs, on a promise that he would get his longed-for detective's shield after a couple of years. He hadn't planned on making waves for the short time he would be with the unit. "But a funny thing happened on Joseph Trimboli's road to that gold shield," wrote Uhnak. "Crack hit the streets of New York, particularly in Brooklyn, where he was assigned. And the cop whose name kept turning up in reports to Internal Affairs was Michael Dowd." Trimboli began his investigation of Dowd in 1986, but in spite of the mounting evidence, his attempts to have more men assigned to the case and his requests for telephone taps and Dowd's financial records were rejected. McAlary wrote that "the department was in no hurry for another police scandal."

Dowd was caught when he and his cohorts expanded into Suffolk County. The police there began an investigation that led to fifty arrests. Dowd was arrested and convicted on federal racketeering charges. McAlary said Milton Mollen, head of Mayor David Dinkins's police corruption commission made a deal with Dowd. Dowd was not required to name names. When Trimboli testified, he was not asked to name the officials who had failed to take action. In a plea bargain, Dowd was sentenced to fourteen years in prison.

Uhnak questioned how these criminal activities could have gone on for so long "without the complicity of higher-ups . . . open, contemptuously. . . . Why were so few superior officers penalized for their failure to act? Three police commissioners—Benjamin Ward, Lee Brown, and Raymond Kelly—were in place, yet no one acted until newspaper headlines forced their hand." Uhnak wrote that McAlary "has told a disturbing and frightening story well, but there are some major missing pieces." A *Kirkus Reviews* reviewer called *Good Cop, Bad Cop* "a gritty if tasteless and overblown recounting." Michael Sawyer described the book in *Library Journal* as "a sad story of a problem that continues to plague the NYPD."

A *Publishers Weekly* reviewer described McAlary's *Sore Loser* as "bedecked with humor, shiv-sharp dialogue, and a surfeit of urban lore," and added that "this surreal fiction debut . . . crackles from the first page." Tennis player Ginny Glade gets a bad call from an umpire and slugs him with a tire iron. She becomes involved with police inspector Mickey Donovan and his junkie daughter, Dillon. Other bad calls lead to the demise of more umpires, who begin making safe calls rather than put their lives on the line. "In manic overdrive, the hyperkinetic style eventually sends the story swerving off into total fantasy," wrote Marilyn Stasio in the *New York Times Book Review.* "McAlary is fun to read."

*Sore Loser* is McAlary's first and only novel. He died of colon cancer, at age forty-one, on December 25, 1998.

*BIOGRAPHICAL AND CRITICAL SOURCES:*

*PERIODICALS*

*Advertising Age,* April 15, 1991, p. 30.
*Editor & Publisher,* May 14, 1994, p. 17; May 30, 1998, p. 8.

*Esquire,* December, 1997, p. 118.

*Kirkus Reviews,* October 15, 1994, review of *Good Cop, Bad Cop,* p. 1389.

*Library Journal,* June 1, 1988, Sandra K. Lindheimer, review of *Buddy Boys,* p. 132; December, 1994, Michael Sawyer, review of *Good Cop, Bad Cop,* p. 112.

*Newsweek,* July 2, 1990, David Gates, review of *Cop Shot,* p. 53.

*New York,* January 7, 1991, p. 12; October 11, 1993, p. 46; July 25, 1994, p. 22; October 2, 1995, p. 17.

*New York Times Book Review,* April 10, 1988, Edna Buchanan, review of *Buddy Boys,* p. 22; February 5, 1995, Dorothy Uhnak, review of *Good Cop, Bad Cop,* p. 10; June 11, 1995, p. 29; November 29, 1998, Marilyn Stasio, review of *Sore Loser,* p. 24.

*People's Weekly,* September 15, 1997, p. 46.

*Publishers Weekly,* December 25, 1987, review of *Buddy Boys,* p. 66; April 20, 1990, review of *Cop Shot,* p. 65; November 7, 1994, p. 60; October 26, 1998, Review of *Sore Loser,* p. 46.

*Sports Illustrated,* September 19, 1988, p. 36.

*Vanity Fair,* October, 1995, p. 184.

OBITUARIES:

PERIODICALS

*Time,* January 11, 1999, p. 25.*

\* \* \*

## McKERN, Leo
### See McKERN, Reginald

\* \* \*

## McKERN, Reginald 1920-2002
### (Leo McKern)

OBITUARY NOTICE—See index for *CA* sketch: Born March 16, 1920, in Sydney, Australia; died July 23, 2002, in Bath, England. Actor and author. McKern was a character actor who is often remembered for his role as the barrister Horace Rumpole in episodes of the British television series "Rumpole of the Bailey,"

which ran from 1975 to 1992. His childhood ended somewhat tragically when, at the age of fifteen, he lost an eye while working at a refrigerator factory to help support his family during the Great Depression. He then abandoned work as an apprentice engineer to study commercial art at Sydney Technical High School. It was while there that he took the name Leo because his classmates made fun of his given name. When Australia entered World War II, McKern joined the Corps of Engineers, serving from 1940 to 1942. In the military he discovered he had a talent for acting when he realized he could get out of trouble with his superior officers by lying to them convincingly. As an actor, he struggled at first to earn a living; his glass eye made it difficult for him to get acting jobs, but he managed to make his stage debut in Sydney in 1944. In 1946 he moved to England and joined the actors at the Old Vic Theater, followed by work at the Shakespeare Memorial Theater, where he earned bigger and bigger parts, including Iago in *Macbeth*. In 1955 McKern made his West End debut playing the part of Toad of Toad Hall in *The Wind in the Willows* and later had parts in plays such as *Cat on a Hot Tin Roof* and *A Man for All Seasons*. The early 1950s also saw McKern make his film debut in *Murder in the Cathedral* (1952), followed by appearances in such films as *The Mouse That Roared* (1959) and the Beatle's movie *Help!* (1965). More recent films in which McKern had parts include *The Omen* (1976) and *The French Lieutenant's Woman* (1981). In 1975 he appeared as Rumpole for the first time in a *BBC Play of the Month* television production. He liked the part so much—and won an award from Radio Industries for it—that he suggested a series be made based on the character. Despite his aversion to being typecast, McKern appeared as Rumpole in forty-four episodes of *Rumpole of the Bailey*, making it his most famous role. Although he did become most recognizable for this part, McKern continued to show his diversity as an actor through the late 1980s and 1990s on stage in *Uncle Vanya* and *Crime and Punishment* and in the films *A Foreign Field* (1993) and *Molokai: The Story of Father Damien* (1999). In 1983 McKern published his memoirs, *Just Resting*. That same year he was made an officer of the Australian Order.

OBITUARIES AND OTHER SOURCES:

BOOKS

*Debrett's People of Today,* Debrett's Peerage, 2002.

*PERIODICALS*

*New York Times,* July 24, 2002, p. A17.
*Times* (London, England), July 24, 2002.
*Washington Post,* July 24, 2002, p. B5.

\*  \*  \*

## McNAIR, Sylvia 1924-2002

*OBITUARY NOTICE*—See index for *CA* sketch: Born April 13, 1924, in Haiju, Korea (now North Korea); died of cancer August 9, 2002, in Evanston, IL. Editor and author. McNair is best remembered as an editor and author of travel guides. She was a graduate of Oberlin College, where she received a bachelor's degree in economics in 1945. After getting married, she worked with her husband negotiating labor contracts until her love for books and travel led her into a publishing career. Beginning with work as a production editor for the American Hospital Association in the mid-1950s, she then became a partner at Editorial and Research Service in 1958, while also working for several other companies, including Herman Smith Associates. McNair was a senior editor of travel guides and editor-in-chief of the "Mobil Travel Guide" series for Rand McNally from 1968 to 1978. While at Rand McNally she also developed the *Vacation and Travel Guide.* After writing the travel guides *Florida and the Southeast* (1984; third edition, 1986) and *New England* (1985; second edition, 1986), McNair achieved bestseller status with her book *Vacation Places Rated* (1986). Much of the rest of her career was spent writing books about U.S. states and foreign countries for younger audiences, including *Thailand* (1987), *Chile* (2000), and *Arkansas* (2001), and she was involved in editing the Great Lakes edition of *America on Wheels* for Arthur Frommer. For her achievements in travel writing, McNair was the recipient of Mark Twain awards for *Vacation Places Rated* (1986), *Kentucky* (1988), and *Finland* (1997).

*OBITUARIES AND OTHER SOURCES:*

*BOOKS*

*Who's Who of American Women,* 22nd edition, Marquis (New Providence, NJ), 2000.

*PERIODICALS*

*Chicago Tribune,* August 23, 2002, section 2, p. 11.

\*  \*  \*

## McNEESE, Tim 1953-

*PERSONAL:* Born January 25, 1953, in Bellvue, NE; son of Willard (a contractor and real estate agent) and Norma Jean (a homemaker; maiden name, Kelly) McNeese; married Beverly Diane Doty (an English instructor), August 12, 1972; children: Noah Michael, Summer Elizabeth. *Education:* York College, A.A., 1973; Harding University, B.A. (history) and social studies teaching certification, 1976; Southwest Missouri State University, M.A. (history), 1981, English and journalism teaching certification, 1988. *Politics:* Republican. *Religion:* Church of Christ.

*ADDRESSES: Home*—5 Arbor Ct., York, NE 68467. *Office*—York College, 1125 East 8th St., York, NE 68467. *E-mail*—tdmcneese@york.edu.

*CAREER:* Seymour Public Schools, Seymour, MO, instructor, 1976-85; Logan-Rogersville Public Schools, Rogersville, MO, 1985-92; York College, York, NE, associate professor, history department chair, 1992—, director, Old Main Archaeology Excavation, 1999-2000.

*MEMBER:* Phi Alpha Theta, Phi Delta Kappa.

*AWARDS, HONORS:* All-Missouri Honors, *Wildfire* sponsor, 1991; Man of the Year, Alpha Chi Epsilon, 1999; Second Miler Award, 1999; Dale Larsen Teacher of Achievement Award, 2002.

*WRITINGS:*

*American Timeline,* seven volumes, Milliken Publishing (St. Louis, MO), 1986.
*The Illustrated Myths of Native America,* two volumes, Cassell Books (London, England), 1998-1999.
*A History of the United States,* ten volumes, Milliken Publishing (St. Louis, MO), 2001-2003.

*George W. Bush: The First President of the New Century,* Morgan Reynolds (Greensboro, NC), 2002.

*The Attack on Pearl Harbor: America Enters World War II,* Morgan Reynolds (Greensboro, NC), 2002.

*Remember the Maine: The Spanish War Begins,* Morgan Reynolds (Greensboro, NC), 2002.

*The Space Race,* Children's Press (Danbury, CT), 2003.

*The Challenger Disaster,* Children's Press (Danbury, CT), 2003.

Contributor to *Christian Chronicle,* 2001-02.

*"AMERICANS ON THE MOVE" SERIES*

*America's First Railroads,* Crestwood House (New York, NY), 1993.

*Clippers and Whaling Ships,* Crestwood House (New York, NY), 1993.

*Conestogas and Stagecoaches,* Crestwood House (New York, NY), 1993.

*West by Steamboat,* Crestwood House (New York, NY), 1993.

*America's Early Canals,* Crestwood House (New York, NY), 1993.

*Early River Travel,* Crestwood House (New York, NY), 1993.

*From Trails to Turnpikes,* Crestwood House (New York, NY), 1993.

*Western Wagon Trains,* Crestwood House (New York, NY), 1993.

*"BUILDING HISTORY" SERIES*

*The Panama Canal,* Lucent Books (San Diego, CA), 1997.

*The Great Wall of China,* Lucent Books (San Diego, CA), 1997.

*The New York Subway System,* Lucent Books (San Diego, CA), 1997.

*The Pyramids at Giza,* Lucent Books (San Diego, CA), 1997.

*"THE HISTORY OF CIVILIZATION" SERIES*

*The Renaissance,* Milliken Publishing (St. Louis MO), 1999.

*The Modern World,* Milliken Publishing (St. Louis MO), 1999.

*The Greeks,* Milliken Publishing (St. Louis MO), 1999.

*The Ancient World,* Milliken Publishing (St. Louis MO), 1999.

*The Middle Ages,* Milliken Publishing (St. Louis MO), 1999.

*The Romans,* Milliken Publishing (St. Louis MO), 1999.

*The Industrial Revolution,* illustrated by Bob Cass, Milliken Publishing (St. Louis MO), 2000.

*The Age of Progress,* illustrated by Bob Althage, Milliken Publishing (St. Louis MO), 2000.

*The Reformation,* Milliken Publishing (St. Louis MO), 2000.

*The Age of Absolutism,* Milliken Publishing (St. Louis MO), 2000.

*The Age of Progress,* Milliken Publishing (St. Louis MO), 2000.

*The Age of Napoleon,* Milliken Publishing (St. Louis MO), 2000.

*The World at War,* Milliken Publishing (St. Louis MO), 2000.

*"SIEGES THAT CHANGED HISTORY" SERIES*

*Masada,* Chelsea House (Philadelphia, PA), 2002.

*Constantinople,* Chelsea House (Philadelphia, PA), 2003.

*The Alamo,* Chelsea House (Philadelphia, PA), 2003.

*Stalingrad,* Chelsea House (Philadelphia, PA), 2003.

*WORK IN PROGRESS:* A book on building the Erie Canal, for Children's Press; series editor of Chelsea House's "Sieges that Changed History" series; biographies of General John J. Pershing and General H. Norman Schwarzkopf, for Chelsea House; *Battle of the Bulge,* for Chelsea House; "Rivers in America's Life and Times" series, including books on the Mississippi, Missouri, Ohio, and Colorado rivers; an overview of black slavery in America for Enslow.

*SIDELIGHTS:* The author of over fifty books for children and middle-grade readers, Tim McNeese focuses on historical themes ranging from American history to the history of Western civilization. Written to enhance the classroom learning experience, McNeese's books deal with elements of history from battles to presidents, as well as methods of transport and construction. His seven-volume "American Timeline" books, thirteen-volume "A History of Civilization," books, and ten-volume "A History of the United

States" books are all published by Milliken and represent over half of his publications to date. A teacher of history at the middle school, high school, and college levels, McNeese brings the training of a professional researcher and educator to his books, which are known for their accuracy of detail and use of contemporary materials and eyewitness accounts.

"I have formed a career around both teaching and writing," McNeese told *CA*. "Though sometimes requiring a tricky balance of time, energy, and resources, I enjoy both profoundly and receive a great deal of satisfaction from each. It has provided many payoffs for me, especially personal. Although I am currently teaching college students, writing for a younger audience has remained important to me. I found my niche writing for the upper elementary and middle grade crowd a long time ago, and I have no intention of abandoning them any time soon. I get a personal kick out of knowing I am writing books that introduce young, eager students to their first taste of subjects ranging from the Great Wall of China to nineteenth-century stagecoaches."

McNeese was born in Nebraska in 1953, and received his college education at Harding University in Arkansas, and at Southwest Missouri State University, where he earned a master's degree in history in 1981. He began his teaching career in 1976; ten years later he wrote his first history books for young readers, the "American Timeline" books, targeted at grades seven to nine, including individual titles such as *Settlements, 1607-1755*. In 1993, after he had begun teaching at the college level, he produced eight titles in the "Americans on the Move" series for Crestwood House. This middle grade series traces the development of different modes of eighteenth- and nineteenth-century transport in the United States, from canal traffic and stagecoaches to turnpikes. Blending black-and-white illustration with informative text, McNeese is "especially good at choosing incidents and anecdotes to illustrate these brief histories," according to Joyce Adams Burner in a *School Library Journal* review of *America's First Railroads* and other books in the series. Burner further praised the books as "well organized, and . . . useful for reports." In *America's Early Canals*, McNeese serves up an introduction to several of these, such as the Potomac Canal, the Chesapeake and Ohio Canal, and the Erie Canal, providing interesting facts about who built the passageways and how boats moved along their waters.

Reviewing both *America's Early Canals* and *From Trails to Turnpikes, Booklist*'s Carolyn Phelan found that both titles "offer useful information about aspects of early American travel."

Similarly, McNeese investigates great feats of construction through the ages in the "Building History" series, including the titles *The Panama Canal, The Great Wall of China, The New York Subway System,* and *The Pyramids at Gaza*. While many history books for younger readers focus on the political machinations behind such monuments, McNeese concentrates on the actual building and construction, "providing much more depth in his treatment of that era," as Sally Estes noted in a *Booklist* review of *The Panama Canal*. In addition to such concerns, McNeese also examines some of the social and political issues, employing illustrations and sidebars with bits of information on topics from feeding the workers to the operation of the locks on the canal. Elaine Lesh Morgan noted in *School Library Journal* that the author "describes in detail the great effort that was required to complete this project," and praised the book as a "solid choice."

McNeese applies a similar treatment to other wonders of the ancient and not so ancient worlds in *The Pyramids at Giza* and *The Great Wall of China*. Cathryn A. Camper, writing in *School Library Journal,* commented that both titles "are dense with information" and that they answer "many questions of building techniques" that young readers may have. Camper concluded that McNeese's *Great Wall of China* is a "substantial volume." Reviewing that title, as well as *The New York Subway,* in *Booklist,* Frances Bradburn called the entire "Building History" series "fascinating," and concluded that both books "illuminate humankind's problem-solving brilliance and its ability to carry out long-term projects." John Peters remarked in a *School Library Journal* review of *The New York Subway* that McNeese presents a "detailed, if haphazard account" of the construction of the New York Subway system, selecting "plenty of incidents, accidents, and anecdotes for human-interest sidebars."

Working in the "First Battles" series for Morgan Reynolds publishers, McNeese has also tackled famous battles in American history in titles such as *The Attack on Pearl Harbor* and *Remember the Maine: The Spanish-American War Begins*. In the former title, McNeese offers a useful background to the cultural and societal situation inside Japan on the eve of war with the United States, according to Carolyn Phelan in a *Booklist* review. Phelan also went on to note that McNeese "describes events clearly, with vivid details that bring historical scenes to life." Heather Hepler, reviewing the same title in *Voice of Youth Advocates,* wrote that McNeese takes an "in-depth look at the events and their players," providing an "excellent" source of information for young readers. Reviewing *Remember the Maine* in *Booklist,* Todd Morning praised McNeese for recounting events in the mysterious sinking of that battleship in Havana harbor "in a detailed yet concise manner that adults as well as young people will find informative." Writing in *School Library Journal,* William McLoughlin felt that though McNeese's "journalistic prose is occasionally awkward . . . , his research is thorough." McLoughlin further praised this "seamless chronicle," drawn from genuine articles of the day, including newspaper accounts, letters, and eyewitness accounts.

With the 2002 title *George W. Bush: First President of the New Century,* McNeese provides a "warts and all" look at Bush as a young man, according to Mary R. Hofmann, reviewing the title in *School Library Journal.* He follows Bush from childhood through the controversial 2000 elections in an account that is "balanced with enough empathy to maintain reader interest and dodge any questions of bias," Hofmann maintained.

"I hope I continue writing and publishing for many years to come," McNeese told *CA.* "I would encourage young readers who are interested in writing to read as much as they can. This will help them gain exposure to the various rhythms of the written word. Reading is fundamental to becoming a good writer. Also, patience is always a virtue, especially for writers. Do not expect to make lots of money writing; few of us do. So, if you want to write, put words on paper and keep doing that until you have penned something someone is willing to pay you to publish."

*BIOGRAPHICAL AND CRITICAL SOURCES:*

PERIODICALS

*Booklist,* November 15, 1993, Carolyn Phelan, review of *America's Early Canals* and *From Trails to Turnpikes,* p. 821; August, 1997, Sally Estes, review of *The Panama Canal,* p. 1895; December 1, 1997, Frances Bradburn, review of *The Great Wall of China* and *The New York Subway System,* p. 622; October 1, 2001, Carolyn Phelan, review of *The Attack on Pearl Harbor,* p. 308; November 1, 2001, Todd Morning, review of *Remember the Maine: The Spanish-American Begins,* p. 450.

*Horn Book Guide,* fall, 1993, Bridget Bennett, review of *West by Steamboat,* p. 354; spring, 1994, Bridget Bennett, review of *From Trails to Turnpikes,* p. 135.

*School Library Journal,* August, 1993, Joyce Adams Burner, review of *America's First Railroads, Clippers and Whaling Ships,* and *West by Steamboat,* p. 178; July, 1997, Elaine Lesh Morgan, review of *The Panama Canal,* pp. 108-109; August, 1997, Cathryn A. Camper, review of *The Great Wall of China* and *The Pyramids at Giza,* p. 172; November, 1997, John Peters, review of *The New York Subway System,* p. 130; January, 2002, Andrew Medlar, review of *The Attack on Pearl Harbor,* p. 161; April, 2002, William McLoughlin, review of *Remember the Maine,* pp. 176-177; April, 2002, Mary R. Hofmann, review of *George W. Bush: First President of the New Century,* p. 176.

*Voice of Youth Advocates,* December, 2001, Heather Hepler, review of *The Attack on Pearl Harbor,* p. 383.

*        *        *

## MERENDINO, James 1967-

*PERSONAL:* Born 1967, in New Jersey.

*ADDRESSES: Home*—Los Angeles, CA. *Agent*—c/o Sony Pictures Classics, 10202 West Washington Blvd., Culver City, CA 90232.

*CAREER:* Director, producer, writer, and actor. Work as film director includes *Witchcraft IV: The Virgin Heart,* Academy Entertainment, 1992; *The Upstairs Neighbour,* 1994; *Hard Drive,* Triboro Entertainment Group, 1994; *Terrified,* A-pix Entertainment, 1995; *Livers Ain't Cheap,* Trimark, 1997; *A River Made to Drown In,* Showcase Entertainment, 1997; *S.L.C. Punk!,* Sony Pictures Classics, 1999; *Magicians,* 2000; and *Amerikana,* AppolloMedia, 2001. Film appearances include *Ivansxtc,* 2000. Television work includes (producer and director) *Alexandria Hotel,* 1998.

*WRITINGS:*

SCREENPLAYS

*Witchcraft IV: The Virgin Heart,* Academy Entertainment, 1992.
*Witchcraft V: Dance with the Devil,* Academy Entertainment, 1993.
*Hard Drive,* Triboro Entertainment Group, 1994.
*Terrified* (also known as *Evil Never Sleeps* and *Tough Guy*), A-pix Entertainment, 1995.
*Livers Ain't Cheap* (also known as *The Real Thing*), Trimark, 1997.
*SLC Punk!,* Sony Pictures Classics, 1999.

Other screenplays include *The Upstairs Neighbour,* 1994; *Alexandria Hotel* (TV script), 1998; and *Magicians,* 2000.

*SIDELIGHTS:* Attempting to provide a genre under which to classify James Merendino's independent film *SLC Punk!,* John Petkovic of the Cleveland, Ohio, *Plain Dealer* identified it as "rebel nostalgia." In such films, of which other examples (according to Petkovic) are *Goodfellas, 54, Boogie Nights,* and *Velvet Goldmine,* "well-adjusted characters revisit wild, bygone days only to realize that 'Yes, it was crazy, but I'm not that person anymore.'"

Petkovic concluded that "Merendino is no tourist when it comes to the scene: The lingo is dead-on, and the soundtrack, by Generation X, the Vandals, Dead Kennedys, and the Ramones, is authentic and excellent." The story comes from Merendino's own experience as a teen, when circumstances cast him in the unlikely role of a punk rocker in the famously conservative, heavily Mormon, Utah capital. "To be an anarchist in Salt Lake City in 1985 was no easy task," proclaims his protagonist, Stevo, perhaps speaking for Merendino himself.

Dennis Harvey and Todd McCarthy of *Variety* criticized the film for what they viewed as insincerity, maintaining that "what we [the viewers] see looks a lot more like a suburban fashion statement, for all the voiceover railing against just such 'posers'." Most reviewers, however, were less inclined to doubt the authenticity, and treated *SLC Punk!* as an engaging, if sometimes chaotic, experience. Joanna Connors of the

*Plain Dealer* called *SLC Punk!* an "exuberant and oddly sweet film [that] pays tribute to the punks, freaks, and assorted outcasts who dared to be different in a time and place when being different was a dangerous occupation."

"Like a guy at a raucous party, scarfing munchies at the hors d'oeuvres table," wrote Lisa Schwarzbaum in *Entertainment Weekly,* "Merendino freely samples current filmmaking styles." In the words of Ed Masley in the *Pittsburgh Post-Gazette,* Merendino's work "is a stylish, quirky, oddly moving coming-of-age-in-Manic-Panic-hair-dye film about the greater truths that lie beyond 'No future.'"

*BIOGRAPHICAL AND CRITICAL SOURCES:*

BOOKS

*Contemporary Theatre, Film, and Television,* Gale (Detroit, MI), Volume 34, 2001.

PERIODICALS

*Chicago Sun-Times,* May 14, 1999, Roger Ebert, review of *SLC Punk!,* p. 33.
*Entertainment Weekly,* April 23, 1999, Lisa Schwarzbaum, review of *SLC Punk!,* p. 41.
*New Yorker,* April 19, 1999, review of *SLC Punk!,* pp. 106-109.
*Pittsburgh Post-Gazette,* November 13, 1999, Ed Masley, review of *SLC Punk!,* p. B6.
*Plain Dealer* (Cleveland, OH), June 18, 1999, Joanna Connors, review of *SLC Punk!,* p. 7; June 21, 1999, John Petkovic, review of *SLC Punk!,* p. E1.
*San Francisco Chronicle,* April 27, 1999, James Sullivan, "*SLC Punk!* Director Likes Wit with His Anarchy," p. C1.
*Sight and Sound,* May, 2000, Charlotte O'Sullivan, review of *SLC Punk!,* p. 61.
*Variety,* February 26, 1996, Todd McCarthy, review of *Livers Ain't Cheap,* p. 82; February 8, 1999, Dennis Harvey and Todd McCarthy, review of *SLC Punk!,* p. 81.*

*          *          *

## MITCHELL, David 1969-

*PERSONAL:* Born January, 1969, in Southport, Lancashire, England; married. *Education:* University of Kent, B.A., 1990, also received M.A.

*ADDRESSES: Office*—c/o Random House Publicity, 299 Park Ave., New York, NY 10171.

*CAREER:* Writer and teacher. Taught English at Hiroshima Kokusai University for four years.

*AWARDS, HONORS: Mail on Sunday*/John Llewellyn Rhys prize, and *Guardian* First Book Award shortlist, both 1999, both for *Ghostwritten;* Booker Prize shortlist, 2001, for *Number9dream.*

*WRITINGS:*

*Ghostwritten,* Random House (New York, NY), 1999.
*Number9dream,* Random House (New York, NY), 2001.

*WORK IN PROGRESS: Cloud Atlas,* due for publication in 2004.

*SIDELIGHTS:* Having spent his childhood in England, writer David Mitchell moved to Hiroshima, Japan, where he lived and worked as an English teacher for eight years. In 2001, he returned to his homeland. During his stay in Japan, he wrote two novels, the first of which was published *Ghostwritten.*

*Ghostwritten* is a collection of nine separate tales that take place all over the world. Each has its own distinct narrative voice, but each voice is somehow connected to and has influence on the other eight tales. Each chapter, or tale, is named after a different physical place, beginning in the East and traveling westward. As the reader becomes involved in the stories, an underlying thread emerges, one involving a manmade-yet-uncontrollable superintelligence grappling with humanity's tendency toward self-destruction.

Critics have commented on the debut novel's episodic structure. In her review for *Salon.com,* Laura Miller observed that "some of the chapters in *Ghostwritten* do work on their own, for Mitchell has a genuine aptitude for storytelling. Too often, though, even the enjoyable segments of *Ghostwritten* bring to mind other writers who tend to be more accomplished with the sort of writing at hand. . . . The result is often readable, but never inspired, a peculiar effect considering the project is the kind of thing usually only at-

tempted by eccentric geniuses following fiercely individual visions." Critic Nicholas Blincoe noted in the *Guardian* that while "several of the episodes are outstanding pieces of prose," other portions "fall flat." As the critic explained: "By rejecting the novel's tradition form, Mitchell forces me to judge him entirely on his prose: on the quality of his sentences, line-by-line, and on their content, fact by fact. This is harsh, but it is his own fault." Blincoe nevertheless recognized the book's strengths as well. "Although *Ghostwritten* suffers because of its episodic structure, Mitchell is never guilty of a creative abdication. The book hangs together through its own hard work, not because it relies on ideas supplied from the outside."

Brian Kenney, in his review for *Booklist,* was effusive in his praise. "It is a thrill to read a piece of fiction this engrossing, challenging, urgent, and, ultimately, so very new." The critic compared Mitchell's writing to that of American novelist Don DeLillo and Japanese novelist Haruki Murakami, and noted its science fictional influences: "Especially in its continual probing of what is real and what is not, this book remains very much its own thing: a novel of the twenty-first century." As a *Publishers Weekly* reviewer concluded: "Mitchell's wildly variegated story can be abstruse and elusive in its larger themes, but the gorgeous prose and vibrant, original construction make this an accomplishment not to be missed."

Mitchell's second novel, *Number9dream,* is the story of twenty-year-old Eiji Miyake and his search for the father he never knew. It takes place in modern day Tokyo, and Eiji's search takes him far from home, where he encounters nothing less than the god of thunder, John Lennon, and organ harvesters. The book is a surreal treatment of a very realistic event—the search for identity. It begins with multiple openings and ends with a missing dream. Critics in general gave a warmer welcome to Mitchell's second novel, which was shortlisted for Britain's prestigious Booker Prize. Calling *Number9dream* a "terrific book," *Booklist* contributor Keir Graff added: "Flexing his considerable stylistic muscle, [Mitchell] plays with form while hewing true to a tightly plotted tale that pulls you along." In *Time International,* reviewer Neil Gough observed that "Unlike Mitchell's first book, a loosely connected collection of stories, *Number9dream* is a more fully fleshed-out tale, and reaffirms what many had already suspected: the arrival of a vastly talented and imaginative novelist." *Newsweek* critic Malcolm

Jones likewise remarked that "Mitchell has produced a novel as accomplished as anything being written. Funny, tenderhearted and horrifying, often all at once, it refashions the rudiments of the coming-of-age novel into something completely original."

James Urquhart of the *Independent* interviewed Mitchell just after *Number9dream* was published. When asked about the similar structures of his two novels, Mitchell admitted, "I didn't really plan the recurrent theme of power and control in *Ghostwritten,* but it does seem to be there. Throughout the novel, events happen because of different levels of power, rather like the inevitable effect of different levels of water in a lock." He further explained how his writing process changed as the manuscript for *Ghostwritten* progressed. "The first two or three chapters began as discrete stories until I had the idea of linking them together. From then on there was more of a master plan. Each chapter addresses why things happen, and how different forces—from surrender, greed, and love to history and quantum physics—shape the course of events." Similarly, in *Number9dream* "each chapter is about a different mode of the mind, and it is written as far as I could in that mode." Even if the reader doesn't notice the structure, Mitchell told Urquhart, "it provides a strong force that helps to stop the book from flying off in all directions."

## BIOGRAPHICAL AND CRITICAL SOURCES:

*PERIODICALS*

*Book,* September, 2000, Tom LeClair, review of *Ghostwritten,* p. 69.

*Booklist,* August, 2000, Brian Kenney, review of *Ghostwritten,* p. 2112; November 15, 2000, Bonnie Smothers, review of *Ghostwritten,* p. 615; March 1, 2002, Keir Graff, review of *Number9dream,* p. 1093.

*Guardian* (London, England), August 21, 1999, Nicholas Blincoe, "Spirit That Speaks"; March 10, 2001, Steven Poole, "I Think I'm Turning Japanese"; April 6, 2002, Carrie O'Grady and Veronica Horwell, "Stories from the City."

*Independent,* March 24, 2001, James Urquhart, "David Mitchell: You May Say He's a Dreamer," p. WR11.

*Library Journal,* August, 2000, Ann Kim, review of *Ghostwritten,* p. 160.

*New Statesmen,* March 12, 2001, Hugo Barnacle, "Novel of the Week," p. 55.

*Newsweek,* September 18, 2000, p. 82; March 25, 2002, Malcolm Jones, "A Samurai in Sneakers: English Novelist David Mitchell Delivers a Deft, Scary and Often Funny Adventure—about Modern Japan," p. 58.

*New Yorker,* March 18, 2002, review of *Number9dream,* p. 145.

*New York Times,* September 12, 2000, Michiko Kakutani, "When Lives, and Worlds, Converge," p. B8; March 15, 2002, Kakutani, "Wandering along the Border between Reality and Fantasy," p. B40.

*New York Times Book Review,* September 17, 2000, Richard Eder, "Caller No. 1: These Linked Tales Feature a Deity That Phones a Radio Show for Advice," p. 18; March 24, 2002, Daniel Zalewski, "Zombie Spawn Descend to Earth: In This Novel, a Japanese Youth's Surreal Fantasies Are Inspired by Pop Culture," p. 7.

*Observer* (London, England), March 11, 2001, Robert MacFarlane, "When Blade Runner Meets Jack Kerouac."

*Publishers Weekly,* July 3, 2000, review of *Ghostwritten,* p. 46; January 28, 2002, review of *Number9dream,* p. 268.

*Review of Contemporary Fiction,* spring, 2001, Jason Picone, review of *Ghostwritten,* p. 193; summer, 2002, Picone, review of *Number9dream,* p. 226.

*San Francisco Chronicle,* February 17, 2002, Andrew Roe, "Daydreaming in Tokyo: David Mitchell's Surrealistic Coming-of-Age Novel Was a Finalist for the Booker Prize."

*Spectator,* July 24, 2002, Robert Edric, "One Hand Clapping."

*Time International,* April 1, 2002, Neil Gough, "Looking for Reality: David Mitchell's Second Book Is a Dreamy Journey," p. 54.

*Times Literary Supplement,* March 2, 2001, Shomit Dutta, review of *Number9dream,* p. 22.

*Village Voice,* February 25, 2002, Joy Press, "The Literary Show-Off."

*Yale Review,* July, 2002, Meghan O'Rourke, "Fiction in Review," p. 159.

*OTHER*

*BBC Arts,* http://www.bbc.co.uk/arts/ (September 19, 2001), "David Mitchell: Dream Weaver"; (July 24, 2002), review of *Number9dream.*

*Beatrice,* http://www.beatrice.com/ (July 29, 2002), Ron Hogan, "David Mitchell" (interview).

*Bold Type,* http://www.randomhouse.com/ (June 6, 2002), synopsis and reviews of *Number9dream* and *Ghostwritten,* author interviews.

*Bookpage,* http://www.bookpage.com/ (June 6, 2002), Lynn Hamilton, "Not All Dreams Are Sweet."

*Bookreporter,* http://www.bookreporter.com/ (October 20, 2000), interview with author.

*Get Hiroshima,* http://www.gethiroshima.com/ (July 24, 2002), Nihongo, interview with author.

*Greenwoods,* http://www.greenwoods.com/ review of *Number9dream.*

*Hackwriters,* http://www.hackwriters.com/ (June 6, 2002), review of *Number9dream.*

*Salon.com,* http://www.salon.com/ (October 10, 2000), Laura Miller, review of "*Ghostwritten.*"

\*     \*     \*

## MONSON-BURTON, Marianne 1975-

*PERSONAL:* Born September 12, 1975, in Boston, MA; daughter of Dwight E. (a business consultant) and Marilynn (a homemaker; maiden name, Allred) Monson; married Keith B. Burton (a computer analyst), June 22, 1996; children: Nathanael Monson Burton. *Education:* Attended Lewis & Clark College; Brigham Young University, B.A. (English, with honors); graduate work at Vermont College. *Religion:* Church of Jesus Christ of Latter-day Saints. *Hobbies and other interests:* Reading, painting, hiking, swimming, playing with my son.

*ADDRESSES: Home*—2005 Northeast 51st Ave., Hillsboro, OR 97124. *E-mail*—marianne_monson@hotmail.com.

*CAREER:* Writer, editor, and teacher. Beyond Words Publishing, Hillsboro, OR, managing editor, 1997-2000; freelance editor and author, 1999—; writing teacher at a Portland, OR, community college, 2000-02.

*MEMBER:* Society of Children's Book Writers and Illustrators.

*WRITINGS:*

(Compiler) *Girls Know Best Two: Tips on Life and Fun Stuff to Do* (young adult nonfiction), Beyond Words Publishing (Hillsboro, OR), 1998.

(Compiler) *Girls Know Best Three: Your Words, Your World* (young adult nonfiction), Beyond Words Publishing (Hillsboro, OR), 1999.

(With Michelle Roehm McCann) *Finding Fairies: Secrets for Attracting Little People from around the World,* illustrated by David Hohn, Beyond Words Publishing (Hillsboro, OR), 2001.

*WORK IN PROGRESS: Latter-day Passover,* adult nonfiction, due in 2003; *Abby Embers,* young-adult fiction, due in 2005.

*SIDELIGHTS:* Marianne Monson-Burton's first two books for children are compilations of advice from American girls ranging from ages ten to seventeen. Reviewers noted that the topics extend from the superficial, such as tips on hosting a successful slumber party or redecorating your bedroom, to more serious advice on how to cope with loss. "An excellent chapter is devoted to friendship and how to handle getting dumped by friends," observed Katie O'Dell Madison in a *School Library Journal* review of *Girls Know Best Two.* Each contributor is identified by name and photo, and a short biography, listing hobbies and future plans, for example, helps readers identify with the advice-givers, Madison added. Topics covered in *Girls Know Best Three,* which follows the same format, include exercise, religion, simplifying your life, and being an only child. Though not all entries are of equal quality, remarked Anita L. Burkam in a *Horn Book Guide* review of this edition, "the good ones are original and intriguing."

Monson-Burton told *CA:* "In writing for children, I try to create books that I wanted to read when I was a child. *Girls Know Best Two & Three* affirms that you can become a published author at a very young age—my life-long dream. *Finding Fairies* is the book that my best friend and I always wanted to own. I spent my childhood tromping through the woods looking for fairies, building them houses, and writing poems for them. I want to give life to books that help children feel powerful and know they can make their dreams come true."

*BIOGRAPHICAL AND CRITICAL SOURCES:*

*PERIODICALS*

*Horn Book Guide,* fall, 2001, Anita L. Burkam, review of *Girls Know Best Three,* p. 334.

*Publishers Weekly,* November 22, 1999, "More Where
    That Came From," p. 57.
*School Library Journal,* January, 1999, Katie O'Dell
    Madison, review of *Girls Know Best Two,* p. 148.

*       *       *

## MOORE, Lenard D(uane) 1958-

*PERSONAL:* Born February 13, 1958, in Jacksonville,
NC; son of Rogers Edward (a career veteran of the
U.S. Marine Corps) and Mary Louise (a club supervisor; maiden name, Pearson) Moore; married Marcille
Lynn Gardner (a poet), October 15, 1985; children:
Maiisha L. *Ethnicity:* "African American." *Education:*
Shaw University, B.A., 1995; North Carolina Agricultural and Technical State University, M.A., 1997. *Politics:* Democrat. *Religion:* Baptist. *Hobbies and other
interests:* Reading, music, sports, gardening, family
events.

*ADDRESSES: Home*—5625 Continental Way, Raleigh,
NC 27610. *E-mail*—PoetLDM@aol.com.

*CAREER:* North Carolina Department of Public
Instruction, Raleigh, media technician, 1984-95; high
school English teacher in Raleigh, NC, 1995-96; North
Carolina Agricultural and Technical State University,
Greensboro, editorial assistant, 1995-96; Shaw
University, Raleigh, NC, adjunct instructor in English,
1998—. North Carolina State University, visiting
lecturer, 1997-2001. International Black Writers'
Conference, regional director, 1982-83; North Carolina
Writers' Network, member of board of directors, 1990-
92; Carolina African American Writers' Collective,
founder and executive director, 1992—; Washington
Streets Group, cofounder. Mira Mesa Branch Library,
San Diego, CA, poet-in-residence, 1983-84; United
Arts Council of Raleigh and Wake County, writer-in-
residence, 1987-93; North Carolina Literary Hall of
Fame, committee member; also affiliated with Artist
Housing Task Force, City of Raleigh Arts Commis-
sion; workshop presenter; gives readings from his
works at poetry festivals, colleges, and cultural centers,
and on television and radio programs. *Military service:*
U.S. Army, 1978-81.

*MEMBER:* World Poetry Society, International Plat-
form Association, National Federation of State Poetry
Societies, Poetry Society of America, Academy of
American Poets, Haiku Society of America, Tanka
Society of America, National Book Critics Circle, Col-
lege Language Association, North Carolina Poetry
Society, North Carolina Haiku Society (executive
chair, 1995-97 and 1998-2001), Poetry Council of
North Carolina, Haiku Poets of Northern California,
Raleigh Writing Alliance, Poetry Study Club of Terre
Haute.

*AWARDS, HONORS:* Emerging artist grant, City of
Raleigh Arts Commission, 1989; American Book
Award nomination, 1993; awards from Haiku Museum
of Tokyo, 1993 and 1994; Indies Arts Award, *Indepen-
dent Weekly,* 1996; Margaret Walker Creative Writing
Award, College Language Association, 1997; named
Tar Heel of the Week, 1998; scholarships for Cave
Canem Poets Workshop, 1998, 1999, and 2000; grant
from North Carolina Haiku Press; Dr. Antonio J. War-
ing, Jr. Prize; winner of annual Black Writer's
Competition, North Carolina Writers' Network.

*WRITINGS:*

*The Open Eye,* North Carolina Haiku Society Press
    (Raleigh, NC), 1985.
*Forever Home,* St. Andrews College Press (Laurinburg,
    NC), 1992.
*Desert Storm: A Brief History,* Los Hombres Press
    (San Diego, CA), 1993.

Work represented in anthologies, including *Father-
songs,* Beacon Press (Boston, MA), 1997; *In Daddy's
Arms I Am Tall,* Lee & Low (New York, NY), 1997;
*Catch the Fire,* Putnam (New York, NY), 1998; *Home:
A Collection of Poetry and Art,* Abrams (New York,
NY), 1999; and *Step into a World: A Global Anthol-
ogy of the New Black Literature,* Wiley (New York,
NY), 2000. Contributor of more than 300 poems, es-
says, and reviews to periodicals, including *Colorado
Review, Dragonfly, Langston Hughes Review, Griot,
Kentucky Poetry Review, Cold Mountain Review,
Painted Bride Quarterly, Callaloo, Black American
Literature Forum,* and *New Directions.* Coeditor-in-
chief, *Shawensis,* 1993-94; associate editor, *Pine
Needles,* 1988-90; contributing editor, *Small Press
Book Review,* 1987-93; guest editor, *BMa: Sonia
Sanchez Literary Review,* 1999; guest contributing edi-
tor, *Drumvoices Revue,* 2000. Moore's writings have
been translated into Spanish, Italian, Japanese,
Chinese, Romanian, and Croatian.

*WORK IN PROGRESS:* Three volumes of poetry, *A Point of Light, A Million Shadows at Noon,* and *A Temple Looming: Photographic Memory;* research on African-American literature and African-American haiku.

\* \* \*

## MOSELEY, James W(illett) 1931-
### (Fred Broman, Oiseau, Agent Orange)

*PERSONAL:* Born August 4, 1931, in New York, NY; son of George Van Horn (a general in the army) and Florence Barber Moseley (a homemaker); married Sandra Swendsen, September 15, 1962 (divorced); children: Elizabeth Rich. *Ethnicity:* "Caucasian." *Education:* Attended Princeton University. *Politics:* Liberal. *Religion:* Agnostic.

*ADDRESSES: Home*—P.O. Box 1709, Key West, FL 33041. *Agent*—Cherry Weiner, 28 Kipling Way, Manalapan, NJ 07726.

*CAREER:* Amateur archeologist and art collector, lecturer, and author. President of Moseley Industries, Inc., (personal holding company); owner of Rose Lane Antiques, Key West, FL, c. 1980s; International UFO Conference, permanent chairman, 1971—. Lectures on UFOs, treasure hunting, and archeology on television and radio shows, as well as personal presentations.

*MEMBER:* Mel Fisher Maritime Heritage Society, Key West Art and Historical Society, International UFO Museum and Research Center, Key West Chamber of Commerce, Graves Museum of Archeology and Natural History, Key West Business Guild, Broward County Archeological Society.

*WRITINGS:*

(Editor) *Jim Moseley's Book of Saucer News,* Saucerian Books (Clarksburg, WV), 1967.
*The Wright Field Story,* Saucerian Books (Clarksburg, WV), 1971.
*UFO Crash Secrets at Wright Patterson Air Force Base,* Abelard Productions, 1991.

(With Karl T. Pflock) *Shockingly Close to the Truth: Confessions of a Grave-Robbing Ufologist,* Prometheus Books (Amherst, NY), 2002.

Contributor to periodicals, including *Argosy, Fate, Real,* and others. Editor of *Saucer News,* 1954-68, and *Saucer Smear,* 1981—. Works sometimes published under names Fred Broman, Oiseau, and Agent Orange.

*SIDELIGHTS:* James W. Moseley is a well-known and often controversial figure in the UFO community. Editor of *Saucer Smear* and *Saucer News,* two famous newsletters in the world of ufology, Moseley has also written a few books on the subject. His other abiding interest is archeology, and for many years, he owned an antique store in Florida that featured some of his own discoveries from his time in Peru, as well as various other South American artifacts. In his book *Shockingly Close to the Truth: Confessions of a Grave-Robbing Ufologist,* Moseley worked with coauthor Karl T. Pflock to chronicle major players in the UFO field, including an index of other sources that might provide information on the subject.

Moseley told *CA:* "I am looking forward to writing my second major book (the other being *Shockingly Close to the Truth*) with Karl T. Pflock. This will be a lighthearted account of my treasure-hunting adventures in Peru back in the 1950s, and also a discussion of the moral and legal aspects of the field of archeology, and the international antique trade. When this book is published, I will have said all I want to say that would be of interest to the general public. Like anyone, I have opinions on many different subjects, but UFOs and 'amateur archeology' are the only areas I have explored that are worthy of a major book on the same. I will mercifully keep my other opinions to myself."

About his work *Shockingly Close to the Truth,* Moseley wrote: "All I can say is that there has never been a UFO book remotely like this one. The perspective is unique. If we can get the attention of the major media—which is not unlikely—this book will take off. I love to travel and to massage my ego by lecturing and/or doing media appearances. I am semi-retired and have plenty of free time for this kind of activity."

*BIOGRAPHICAL AND CRITICAL SOURCES:*

*PERIODICALS*

*Booklist,* February 15, 2002, George Eberhart, review of *Shockingly Close to the Truth: Confessions of a Grave-Robbing Ufologist,* 972.

*Caveat Emptor,* spring, 1972, "What I Really Believe," pp. 5-6, 21-22; winter, 1988, Gene Steinberg, "The *Caveat Emptor* Interview: James W. Moseley," pp. 7-14.

*Publishers Weekly,* February 4, 2002, "Of This Earth?," p. 73.

*School Library Journal,* September, 2002, Christine C. Menefee, review of *Shockingly Close to the Truth,* p. 258.

*Skeptical Inquirer,* July-August, 2002, Kendrick Frazier, review of *Shockingly Close to the Truth,* p. 59.

\*     \*     \*

## MULLAN, Pat 1939-

*PERSONAL:* Born April 19, 1939, in County Derry, Northern Ireland; married Jean Custer Watson (a director of a language school). *Ethnicity:* "Irish." *Education:* State University of New York, B.Sc., 1975; Northwestern University, graduate diploma, 1977.

*ADDRESSES: Agent*—c/o Author Mail, 1stBooks Library, 2595 Vernal Pike, Bloomington, IN 47404. *E-mail*—mullan@iol.ie.

*CAREER:* Writer. Formerly worked in finance. *Military service:* U.S. Army, 1963-65; served in Korea.

*WRITINGS:*

*Childhood Hills* (poetry), Universe, 2000.
*The Circle of Sodom* (suspense novel), 1stBooks Library (Bloomington, IN), 2002.
*Mullan: A Writer and His Art* (paintings and photographs), xlibris, 2002.

Contributor of articles, short stories, poetry, and reviews to periodicals, including *Buffalo Spree, National Hibernian Digest,* and *Dublin Writers.*

*WORK IN PROGRESS: Blood Red Square: Who Killed Dag Hammarskjold?,* a suspense novel; *Awakening,* a poetry collection; research on the death of Dag Hammarskjold in the Congo in 1961, the G8 conference in Birmingham in 2000, Stalin's Jewish autonomous homeland of Birobidzhan, Siberia, Che Guevara and his Irish heritage, and technical topics related to satellites, videophones, fuzzy logic, artificial intelligence systems, bulletproof vests, and sniper rifles.

*SIDELIGHTS:* Pat Mullan told *CA:* "I was born in County Derry, Northern Ireland, but I have lived much of my life in the United States. I believe that my book *Childhood Hills* is very definitely colored by my experience growing up in the divided society of my birthplace. I was born into a Catholic family, but one branch of my family was Presbyterian. Now there's some hope with the Unionists and the Nationalists agreeing to share power in their new Assembly and the Irish Republican Army declaring that they will put their weapons 'beyond use.' Many people have worked hard and with great patience to get to this stage. Two Americans are especially owed a debt for their efforts: former President Bill Clinton and Senator George Mitchell.

"There's no way that one can grow up in Ireland without being surrounded by writers. Everybody writes! And, if they don't, they tell stories. The Celtic oral tradition is alive and well. When I was a little boy in our country farmhouse, people would come in of an evening, sit around the fire, and tell stories till the wee hours of the morning.

"I have always had a desire to write. Putting words together seems to be an innate ability. Over the years I exercised that (or maybe I should say exorcized) in my business life by writing papers and other creative documents while my scribbled poems ended up in the sock drawer. Six years ago I left a senior position in finance in the United States and returned to live in Connemara in the west of Ireland. I had always wanted to write, but I never had the time. Of course, that was a convenient excuse. I was afraid that, if I ever sat down to write, I'd discover that I couldn't. So, I forced myself to write, reserving three or four hours each day for writing. The weeks and months passed, and one page turned into ten, and then fifty. Soon I realized that I had written 25,000 words of my first novel and that I had created a family of characters.

"When I finished my novel *The Circle of Sodom,* I drafted the best query letter that I could and sent it out to agents in batches of about fifteen at a time. I spent a year doing that and collected a range of rejection letters. After a year I acquired a New York agent who loved my novel, and who also garnered a number of personal rejection letters from the major publishers. At the end of the year I did not renew my contract with the New York agent.

"My advice to anyone who wants to (who must) write is write, write, write! And read, read, read! Don't worry about getting published. Concentrate on your writing. Find some readers who will give you critical feedback. And remember: stamina and fortitude are even more important than the art and skill of writing."

\*   \*   \*

## MURRAY, Sabina

*PERSONAL:* Female; married John Hennessey (a poet); children: Two. *Education:* Mt. Holyoke College, B.A.; University of Texas, M.A.

*ADDRESSES: Office*—Department of English, University of Massachusetts, Amherst, MA 01002.

*CAREER:* Author and educator. Phillips Academy, Andover, MA, Roger Murray writer-in-residence, 2000-03; University of Massachusetts, Amherst, instructor in M.F.A. program, beginning 2003.

*AWARDS, HONORS:* Michener fellow, University of Texas; Bunting fellow, Radcliffe Institute, Harvard University; PEN/Faulkner Award, 2003, for *The Caprices.*

*WRITINGS:*

*Slow Burn* (novel), Ballantine Books (New York, NY), 1990.
*The Caprices* (stories), Houghton Mifflin (Boston, MA), 2002.

Author of screenplay *Beautiful Country.* Contributor to periodicals and literary journals, including *Ploughshares, New England Review,* and *Ontario Review.*

*WORK IN PROGRESS: A Carnivore's Inquiry,* a novel.

*SIDELIGHTS:* Sabina Murray is a novelist and short story writer whose first collection, *The Caprices,* was honored with the 2003 PEN/Faulkner Award. Murray was raised in Australia and the Philippines, and her work springs from her past. Her first novel, *Slow Burn,* is set in contemporary Manila, and is the story of the beautiful Isobel della Fortuna, a drug-addicted young woman who pairs up with Paul Aguilar, son of the Philippine opposition leader.

Murray's mother was a child at the time of the Japanese occupation of Manila during World War II, and Murray's paternal grandfather and uncle were imprisoned, never to be heard from again. The nine stories in *The Caprices* are set during that period, and take place in Southeast Asia, the United States, and Australia. Murray was moved to write them to define war and the people who suffer from it.

*Ploughshares* contributor Debra Spark wrote that the stories in *The Caprices* "are first and foremost about the ironies, humiliations, and brutalities of war. Murray is unsparing in her vision of starvation, death, and disease. . . . And yet, Murray's tight writing, her powerful sense of story, and her passionate urgency prevent tragedy from subsuming art, from making the book too lugubrious to press on." A *Publishers Weekly* reviewer commented that Murray "also handles humor with laudable finesse, using it to separate those characters who can still appreciate it from those who now find laughter unfamiliar and awkward."

In the story "Guinea," an Italian-American soldier and an Irish Bostonian struggle to survive in the jungle with their Japanese prisoner, while in "Order of Precedence," Harry Gillen, a Scottish-Indian prisoner, recalls his polo-playing days in Calcutta, and how his superior, Major Berystede, blocked his admission for membership in a gentlemen's club. Claire Messud, who called "Order of Precedence" "one of the strongest" in her review of *The Caprices* for the *New York Times Book Review,* added that "the ambiguities and snobberies of the prewar Raj are recreated as vividly as the equalizing deprivation of the prison camp where Harry and Berystede are reunited. . . . Murray leaps from past to present, conveying a great deal of experience and emotion . . . with an intriguingly ragged efficiency."

The final days of Amelia Earhart are envisioned in "Folly," while in "Colossus" an aging American veteran recalls the Japanese invasion of the Philippines and the death march of 1941. In her foreword to *The Caprices,* Murray notes that the title story could be set in peacetime. It's characters include a young girl named Trinidad and Shori, a Japanese servant, along with the clubfooted Jose, a deranged woman locked away in the basement, and a ghost that visits Trinidad's grandmother.

In her fiction, concluded Messud, Murray "illuminates in dark, at times near gothic, splendor her unsparing vision. . . . Unflinching, these brimming, sometimes jagged stories endure powerfully in the reader's memory as they reach across continents and time with precision and—in the heart of darkness—a measure of grace."

*BIOGRAPHICAL AND CRITICAL SOURCES:*

*PERIODICALS*

*Los Angeles Times Book Review,* January 12, 2003, Gloria Emerson, review of *The Caprices,* p. R13.

*New York Times Book Review,* Claire Messud, review of *The Caprices,* p. 16.

*Ploughshares,* spring, 2002, Debra Spark, review of *The Caprices,* p. 202.

*Publishers Weekly,* June 15, 1990, Penny Kaganoff, review of *Slow Burn,* p. 65; January 7, 2002, review of *The Caprices,* p. 49.*

## NAIR, Meera 1963-

*PERSONAL:* Born 1963, in India; immigrated to United States, 1997; children: one daughter. *Education:* Temple University, M.A.; New York University, M.F.A.

*ADDRESSES: Agent*—c/o Author Mail, Random House 299 Park Avenue, New York, NY 10171.

*CAREER:* Author.

*AWARDS, HONORS: New York Times* fellow.

*WRITINGS:*

*Video* (stories), Pantheon Books (New York, NY), 2002.

Contributor to periodicals and journals, including the *New York Times Magazine, Threepenny Review,* and *Calyx.*

*WORK IN PROGRESS:* A novel.

*SIDELIGHTS:* Meera Nair, who was born and raised in India, immigrated to the United States in 1997 to study creative writing. Her short story, "Video," which is the title story of her first collection, was the winner of the 2000 PEN/*Amazon.com* short story contest, but the honor was almost immediately withdrawn when it was discovered that Nair had published another story in the *Threepenny Review.* Because that journal has a circulation over 5,000, Nair was deemed ineligible under the conditions of the contest, but she was allowed to keep the prize money.

"Video" is about an Indian couple whose marriage flounders after the husband sees a pornographic film and asks his wife to engage in a sexual act performed on the video. According to an article in *Book,* Nair developed this story after reading a newspaper article about Western pornography's effect on Indian villagers. Another of the stories in *Video* was generated after former president Bill Clinton visited India. In "A Warm Welcome to the President, Insh'Allah!," the residents of a small village in Bangladesh build a new toilet so that it will be available should the president desire to use it. There are ten stories in all, with some taking place in India and others in the United States. In "Curry Leaf Tree," Dilip, who left his village to take a job with Motorola in Arizona, acquires a wife through an arranged marriage but is disappointed when she sheds their traditions for American ways. Dilip, who has an extraordinary sense of smell, is also unfortunate in that his new wife is unable to cook.

In "Sculptor of Sands," a young man makes incredible artistic progress after finding the body of a young woman buried on a beach. In "Summer," a young girl who is sexually molested by a cousin can no longer play the part of the princess in the family play. The fifteen-year-old-boy of "My Grandfather Dreams of Fences" watches helplessly as his grandfather is exploited.

Carlin Romano of the *Philadelphia Inquirer* compared Nair's work with that of successful Indian authors

Arundhati Roy (*The God of Small Things*) and Jhumpa Lahiri (*Interpreter of Maladies*) and the Indian writers who followed them, saying that *Video* "shares the pluses and minuses of much Indian/Indian American fiction." Romano praised Nair's use of authentic detail but felt a glossary would have helped non-Indians. "On the other hand," wrote Romano, "*Video* shares with Lahiri's overpraised work a stilted, passive, uninventive English that would win many non-Indian MFA candidates a trip to the active-verb woodshed. One can't fault Nair or any Indian-born writer for keeping to the rhythms and diction of her country's prose, which sometimes resembles a creaky form of British English in which passive syntax reinforces static ideas. But it tires the American ear, eager for fresh images, zippy metaphors, and ironic wordplay, rather than unmagical realism."

*Booklist*'s Bonnie Johnston, who called the stories in *Video* "vibrant," said that Nair "searches for cross-cultural differences at the personal level." Peter Gordon, who reviewed *Video* for *Asian Review of Books* online, felt that "Nair's sympathy for her subjects is apparent. Sometimes it is apparent in gentle self-mockery . . . other stories are moving treatments of families, death, and aging. The word *sensitive* comes to mind." A *Publishers Weekly* contributor wrote that "throughout, Nair's ear for dialogue is spot-on, and varying degrees of rage, exhilaration, or confusion are crisply expressed."

"Observation and experience, as Faulkner noted, are only two of an author's tools," commented Jeffery Paine in *Washington Post Book World,* "and Nair excels in using the third tool Faulkner named—the imagination. Her stories are so inventive that they make many of her predecessors' fictions look like sociological studies. Nair can imagine magical things—say a boy's nose sensitive enough to identify every aroma, or beach-sand sculptures that cause their viewers unnameable longings—and then so imagine the consequent details that the wondrous becomes reality."

*USA Today*'s Whitney Matheson said that Nair "creates passionate, distinctive characters, establishing herself as a writer to watch. From 'The Sculptor of Sands,' a timeless fable, to the more modern 'Curry Leaf Tree,' her work pulsates with captivating, varied subject matter that all types of readers can appreciate."

*BIOGRAPHICAL AND CRITICAL SOURCES:*

PERIODICALS

*Book,* January-February, 2002, "The New Commuter: Meera Nair," p. 39.

*Booklist,* March 1, 2002, Bonnie Johnston, review of *Video.*

*New York Times,* May 23, 2000, Dinitia Smith, "First Winner Is Ruled Out of Story Prize; Eligibility Mix-up in Amazon Contest," p. C8.

*Philadelphia Inquirer,* April 7, 2002, Carlin Romano, review of *Video.*

*Publishers Weekly,* January 21, 2002, review of *Video,* p. 60.

*USA Today,* May 5, 2002, Whitney Matheson, "Vivid *Video* Images Capture Indian Life."

*Washington Post Book World,* June 2, 2002, Jeffery Paine, review of *Video,* p. 15.

OTHER

*Asian Review of Books,* http://www.asianreview ofbooks.com/ (November 6, 2002), Peter Gordon, review of *Video.**

\*　　\*　　\*

**NELSON, Maggie**
    **See NELSON, Margaret**

\*　　\*　　\*

**NELSON, Margaret 1973-**
  (Maggie Nelson)

*PERSONAL:* Born March 12, 1973, in San Francisco, CA; daughter of Bruce Arthur (a lawyer) and Barbara Jo (a business writer and consultant; maiden name, Mixer) Nelson. *Ethnicity:* "White." *Education:* Wesleyan University, Middletown, CT, B.A., 1994; Graduate Center of the City University of New York, doctoral study, 1998—.

*ADDRESSES: Home*—151 Smith St., No. 4R, Brooklyn, NY 11201. *E-mail*—mixnelson@aol.com.

*CAREER:* Wesleyan University, Middletown, CT, visiting lecturer in poetry, 2001-02; New School University, New York, NY, visiting faculty member, 2002.

*WRITINGS:*

POETRY; UNDER NAME MAGGIE NELSON

(With Cynthia Nelson) *Not Sisters,* Soft Skull Press, 1996.
*The Scratch-Scratch Diaries,* Graywolf Press (Minneapolis, MN), 1998.
*Shiner,* Hanging Loose Press, 2001.
*The Latest Winter,* Hanging Loose Press, 2003.

*WORK IN PROGRESS: Jane,* a novel in verse based on the life of the author's aunt, who was murdered in 1969; research for a book on women poets and painters of "the so-called New York School."

*SIDELIGHTS:* Margaret Nelson, who publishes her poetry under the name Maggie Nelson, told *CA:* "Though I write all kinds of things, generally speaking, my first two books consist of poems that draw on daily happenstance and 'ordinary' language. It is not that I don't struggle, but I keep on writing poems because it has been, thus far, my most natural way of being in the world.

"When I was in eighth grade I won a poetry contest sponsored by the rock band the Cure. The poem was called 'Shame' and, while it was probably terrible, I was quite energized by this early success. I left California for the East Coast in 1990 and moved to New York City shortly thereafter to find out what the poets were doing. In New York I studied with the brilliant writer Eileen Myles, whose informal workshops constituted most of my poetic education. Robert Creeley has also been a great inspiration. I have always felt an equal (if not somewhat opposite) affinity with the drama, stringency, and terseness of poets such as Sylvia Plath, Paul Celan, and George Oppen, on the one hand, and the irreverence, openness, and long-windedness of so-called New York School poets such as James Schuyler and Frank O'Hara, on the other. I am deeply impressed by Alice Notley's writing, especially her exploration of the possibility of 'feminine epic.'

"As for motivation, I usually write when I am overwhelmed, and when I feel convinced that writing will elucidate the core of the matter—make an intimacy or an abstraction utterly clear. Knowing full well, however, that language can both clarify and mystify (and often does both at the same time), I have come to enjoy the perversity of the process."

\* \* \*

## NEWLYN, Walter T(essier) 1915-2002

*OBITUARY NOTICE*—See index for *CA* sketch: Born July 26, 1915, in London, England; died October 4, 2002, in Leeds, England. Economist, educator, and author. Specializing in development economics, Newlyn was interested in the economies of African nations. After working as a clerk and then chartering broker for a grain merchant company in London, he joined the Royal Corps of Signals during World War II, serving in India and attaining the rank of major. His interest in economics, which had been sparked after visiting a coal field in Wales in 1939, led him to apply to the London School of Economics, from which he received his B.Sc. in 1948. It was while a student that Newlyn met and became friends with Bill Phillips. Both students were interested in macroeconomics, and they decided to develop what became known as the Phillips hydraulic machine, which calculated money circulation based on Keynesian theories of economic systems. After university, Newlyn pursued a growing interest in developing economies by going to Africa. He was a research fellow at the West African Institute of Social and Economic Research from 1953 to 1954, an economic advisor for the government of Uganda in the late 1950s, and, during the mid-1960s, director of economic research at the East African Institute of Social Research, director of the Bank of Uganda, and consultant to the government of Bechuanaland. These experiences made him eminently qualified to become a teacher of development economics at the University of Leeds, where he was a professor until his retirement in 1978. While teaching, Newlyn wrote such useful books for his students as *Theory of Money* (1962; third edition, 1978) and *Finance for Development* (1968). He was also the author of *Money in an African Context* (1966) and coauthor of *The Financing of Economic Development* (1977). In addition to his work as an economist, Newlyn loved the theater; he and his wife established the Uganda Pilgrim Players, made donations to Uganda's national theater, and, in England, helped found the Leeds Playhouse.

*OBITUARIES AND OTHER SOURCES:*

*PERIODICALS*

*Guardian* (London, England), October 16, 2002, p. 24.
*Herald* (Glasgow, Scotland), October 23, 2002, p. 22.
*Times* (London, England), October 19, 2002, p. 48.

\*   \*   \*

**NICHOLS, Nadia**
  **See GRAY, Penny**

\*   \*   \*

**NOBLE, Jeanne L(aveta) 1926-2002**

*OBITUARY NOTICE*—See index for *CA* sketch: Born July 18, 1926, in Palm Beach, FL; died of congestive heart failure October 17, 2002, in New York, NY. Educator, historian, and author. Noble was an expert on education who served on a number of government commissions under three different U.S. presidents. She received her B.A. from Howard University in 1946 and a doctorate in educational psychology and counseling from Columbia University in 1955; she also attended graduate courses at the University of Birmingham, England. From 1948 to 1950 she was a teacher at Albany State College, and then became dean of women at Langston University in Oklahoma where she worked until 1952. Joining New York University's faculty in 1959, she was an instructor at that school's Center for Human Relations; she later became a professor at the Graduate Center, retiring as professor emeritus. Among Noble's other accomplishments in the field of education was her work in 1964 on the Women's Job Corps under the Lyndon Johnson administration, and on national educational commissions during the presidencies of Richard Nixon and Gerald Ford. In 1967 she was director of training for the Harlem Domestic Peace Corps, and she also served as a member of the board of the Urban League in New York City and for the Girl Scouts of America. Noble was the author of two books about education: *The Negro Woman as College Graduate* (1956) and *College Education as Personal Development* (1960), the latter which she cowrote with Margaret Fisher. Her work as an authority on education issues and as a champion of minority rights led her to be consulted on school desegregation issues and hired by corporations such as Exxon and Mutual of New York Insurance to help develop affirmative action plans. Besides her interest in promoting education for black women, Noble was also interested in black history in general, and toward this end she wrote *Beautiful, Also, Are the Souls of My Black Sisters: A History of the Black Woman in America* (1976). She was also active in the media, producing the record album *Roses and Revolutions* (1973), the video *Seventy-five Years in Retrospect,* and moderating and writing the television program *The Learning Experience,* for which she earned an Emmy award in 1970. Noble was named "one of the 100 most influential Negroes of the Emancipation Year" in 1963 by *Ebony* magazine; she also won the Bethune-Roosevelt Award for service in the field of education in 1965; the Lifetime Achievement Award from the National Association of Black Women in Higher Education in 1989; the Award of Perseverance from the Consortium of Doctors in 1993; and several honorary doctorates.

*OBITUARIES AND OTHER SOURCES:*

*BOOKS*

*Notable Black American Women,* Gale (Detroit, MI), 1996.

*PERIODICALS*

*New York Times,* November 2, 2002, p. A15.

\*   \*   \*

**OCHS-OAKES, George Washington 1861-1931**

*PERSONAL:* Original name, George Washington Ochs; name legally changed, 1917; born October 27, 1861, in Cincinnati, OH; died of an embolism October 26, 1931; son of Julius and Bertha Ochs; married Bertie Gans, 1907 (died 1913); children: John Bertram, George Washington. *Education:* University of Tennessee, B.A., 1880; studied history at Columbia University, 1925-31. *Religion:* Jewish. *Hobbies and other interests:* Civic leadership.

*CAREER: Knoxville Chronicle,* Knoxville, TN, newspaper boy, 1868-80; *Chattanooga Daily Times,* Chattanooga, TN, reporter, 1878-91, general manager, 1896; city of Chattanooga, TN, police commissioner, 1891, mayor, 1893-97; Democratic National Convention, Chicago, IL, delegate, 1892; *Tradesman,* Chattanooga, TN, manager, 1891-96; Chattanooga Board of Education, Chattanooga, TN, member, 1896-1900; Chattanooga Chamber of Commerce, Chattanooga, TN, president, 1899-1900; *Philadelphia Times* (later *Public Ledger*), Philadelphia, PA, general manager, 1901-15; *New York Times Current History* and *Mid-Week Pictorial,* New York, NY, manager, 1915. *Military service:* National Guard; served during World War I; became private.

*MEMBER:* Civitan Club of New York (president, three terms), Chattanooga Society in New York (president), Tennessee Society in New York (president), Camp of Sons of Confederate Veterans (historian).

*AWARDS, HONORS:* Cross of the Chevalier of the Legion of Honor, 1900.

*WRITINGS:*

*Hamilton County, Tennessee, Together with a Brief Resume of the Growth and Resources of Chattanooga, Tenn.,* Times Printing (Chattanooga, TN), 1889.
*Chattanooga and Hamilton County, Tennessee,* Committee of Chattanooga and Hamilton County (Chattanooga, TN), 1897.
*The Life and Letters of George Washington Ochs-Oakes,* arranged and edited by William M. Schuyler, privately printed (New York, NY), 1933.

Also contributor to periodicals *Annals of the American Academy of Political and Social Sciences, Current History,* and *Congressional Digest.*

*SIDELIGHTS:* George Washington Ochs-Oakes is probably best known as the brother of newspaper magnate Adolph Ochs, but he was himself an able editor, civic leader, and historian. Ochs-Oakes' management helped improve the quality of his brother's newspaper and magazine empire. He also spent considerable time in politics. U.S. Senator Cordell

Hull from Tennessee, as quoted by Whitney R. Mundt in the *Dictionary of Literary Biography,* said at Ochs-Oakes's death: "No person cherished a more intense devotion to his fellow-men, nor worshiped at the shrine of unalloyed patriotism more devotedly than he."

Ochs-Oakes' parents, Julius and Bertha Ochs, were German immigrants fiercely loyal to America; Ochs-Oakes' name, George Washington, reflects his father's patriotism. During World War I, in fact, Ochs-Oakes, against his family's desires, legally changed his German name so his children could take the Anglicized surname Oakes.

Julius Ochs fought for the Union in the Civil War during Ochs-Oakes' infancy, but after the war he and his family moved from Cincinnati, Ohio to Knoxville, Tennessee. Ochs-Oakes took on a *Knoxville Chronicle* delivery route at age seven. He continued this work until one year before he graduated from the University of Tennessee; he had become an impressive scholar, and he knew newspapers well.

By 1880, Adolph Ochs, Ochs-Oakes' older brother, had already acquired the *Chattanooga Daily Times.* Ochs-Oakes joined the *Times* as a reporter immediately after graduation, laboring in a tough job to build up the newspaper's name. Mundt explained, "In his memoirs he relates that newspaper life in Chattanooga was a rough-and-tumble affair in those post-Civil War days when the town's population numbered only twelve thousand or so, about one-third black. Twice he was forced to draw his weapon in self-defense, and on one of those occasions he shot his assailant." Ochs-Oakes, however, thrived in Chattanooga. In 1891, he was appointed police commissioner, and one year later was a delegate to the Democratic National Convention in Chicago. The following year, Ochs-Oakes was elected mayor of Chattanooga.

While Ochs-Oakes was flourishing as a local politician and civic leader, he moved from the *Chattanooga Times* to a bi-weekly industrial magazine, the *Tradesman,* which Ochs also owned. Reportedly, Ochs disapproved of his brother's political career, but Ochs-Oakes persevered. He served two mayoral terms, but having rejoined the *Chattanooga Times* as general manager, declined to run for a third. He continued, however, as president of the Chattanooga Chamber of Commerce.

While Ochs-Oakes was running the *Chattanooga Times,* his brother Adolph was attempting to turn around a new acquisition, a failing newspaper Ochs thought had potential. The *New York Times* was being held in escrow for Ochs: If he could turn a profit on the paper in four years, he could have it. In the down-and-dirty world of New York news, where only sensational headlines seemed to captivate readers, Ochs took the high road. He captioned the paper "All the News That's Fit to Print," and lowered the price from three pennies to one. The *Times* began to sell eight times as many papers, and Ochs was in the black.

Ochs, with plans for the *Times,* now enlisted Ochs-Oakes' help. To further establish the *Times* as a top-of-the-line newspaper, Ochs-Oakes traveled to the Paris Exposition of 1900, where he printed a daily edition of the *Times* at the American pavilion. Mundt wrote, "For eight months that year, six days each week, George [Ochs-Oakes] published a ten- to fourteen-page edition of the paper in the American Pavilion, in full view of thousands of visitors each day. He used an octuple Goss press, the largest on the continent, and six Linotypes, mechanical marvels which had been invented by Ottmar Mergenthaler only four years earlier." The plan worked; the *Times* became known worldwide as America's top paper and French President Emile Loubet nominated Ochs-Oakes for the Cross of the Chevalier of the Legion of Honor.

Back in the United States, Ochs-Oakes helped his brother again, serving as general manager of the *Philadelphia Times* (later the *Philadelphia Public Ledger*). Mundt noted, "In his memoirs [Ochs-Oakes] relates, with apparent pride, that during his fourteen years with the newspapers in Philadelphia he refrained from political activity. Considering George's extensive political involvement in Chattanooga and the intensity of Adolph's opposition to it (he reportedly refused to vote for George in the mayoral election), it is probably that Adolph offered the position in Philadelphia to George on the condition that he stay out of politics." Ochs saw political involvement as compromising newspaper excellence, but for Ochs-Oakes, newspaper work was part of his political involvement. In Philadelphia, then, Ochs-Oakes continued to speak out politically, even as he declined to run for office. He married Bertie Gans and they had two sons. After Gans died in 1913, Ochs-Oakes' older sister, Nannie, became the children's caretaker.

Ochs-Oakes stayed at the *Public Ledger* until 1915, two years after Ochs sold the paper. He then moved with his family to New York, where he began to manage two of his brother's journals, *New York Times Current History* and *Mid-Week Pictorial.* Both magazines commenced in 1914 to chronicle the war in Europe. *Current History* was styled "a repository for the official and authentic records of the War." *Mid-Week Pictorial,* too, provided a weekly accounting of the war, though it emphasized maps, cartoons, and photographs. The war affected Ochs-Oakes deeply. Mundt wrote: "It was especially traumatic to him because of his German descent; he was filled with revulsion that Germans were committing such barbarities as the sinking of the *Lusitania.*"

Ochs-Oakes continued to oversee the two journals after the war, successfully shifting their emphasis to more general world events. Mundt explained, "Ochs enlarged the scope of the publication so that the magazine became a more comprehensive contemporary historical record, including articles on international politics, sociology, economics, and literature." Circulation increased, and contributors included the likes of H. G. Wells, Rudyard Kipling, John Galsworthy, Arthur Conan Doyle, Bruce Bliven, Ernest K. Lindley, and Raymond B. Clapper. Ochs-Oakes, though less visible politically, returned to civic leadership, serving as president and historian of several organizations. He also completed significant work toward a Ph.D. in history at Columbia University, but on the day before Ochs-Oakes' seventieth birthday, he died of an embolism after surgery. President Herbert Hoover called him "a splendid American."

## BIOGRAPHICAL AND CRITICAL SOURCES:

### BOOKS

*Dictionary of Literary Biography,* Volume 137: *American Magazine Journalists, 1900-1960,* Gale (Detroit, MI), 1994.
Talese, Gay, *The Kingdom and the Power,* World (New York, NY), 1969.

### PERIODICALS

*Current History,* December, 1931.*

\*    \*    \*

**OISEAU**
**See MOSELEY, James W(illett)**

# P

## PAGE, Willie F. 1929-

*PERSONAL:* Born January 2, 1929, in Dothan, AL; *Education:* Wayne State University, B.S., 1961; Adelphi University, M.B.A., 1970; New York University, Ph.D., 1975.

*ADDRESSES: Office*—Dept. of Africana Studies, Brooklyn College, City University of New York, 2901 Bedford Ave., Brooklyn, NY 11210-2813. *E-mail*—wpage@brooklyn.cuny.edu.

*CAREER:* Boeing Corporation, Seattle, WA, engineer, 1961-63; Grumman Aerospace, assistant to the director of production, 1967-70; Glen Cove Cooperative College Center, State University of New York, Glen Cove, NY, director, lecturer, 1971-72; CHES, Nassau-Suffolk Counties, NY, executive director, 1972-74; Brooklyn College, City University of New York, Brooklyn, NY, associate professor, 1974—, chairman of Department. of Africana Studies, 1974-79. Consultant to the Head Start Regional Training Center, New York, NY, 1975-79, National Endowment for the Humanities, 1977-78, and the New York State Department of Education, 1977-79.

*MEMBER:* Phi Delta Kappa.

*AWARDS, HONORS:* Fellowships from New York University, 1973, Fund Atlanta, 1975, and National Endowment for the Humanities, 1978; Henry Messner Research Award, New York University, 1975.

*WRITINGS:*

*The Dutch Triangle: The Netherlands and the Atlantic Slave Trade, 1621-1664* (revised edition of 1975 thesis), Garland Publishing (New York, NY), 1997.

*The Encyclopedia of African History and Culture,* Volume 1: *Ancient Africa,* Volume 2: *African Kingdoms,* Volume 3: *From Conquest to Colonization,* Facts on File (New York, NY), 2001.

*SIDELIGHTS:* Willie F. Page is a black studies scholar and the author of *The Dutch Triangle: The Netherlands and the Atlantic Slave Trade, 1621-1664,* his updated 1975 thesis. Page studies European rivalries for dominance of West Africa, the creation of the West India Company in 1621 and how it first became involved in the slave trade in 1636, the control of territories on both sides of the Atlantic, the suffering of black slaves and Native Americans, and the fate and struggles of Africans in the colonies. The first chapter covers the early history of the Netherlands prior to 1621, and the second discusses Dutch and Portuguese activities in West and West Central Africa. Dutch control of Brazil is discussed in the third chapter, along with the colonization of Guiana and the origins of the slave colonies on Curacao and Bonaire. The final two chapters are devoted to New Netherland, as New York was know from 1609 to 1664.

Adam Jones of the *Journal of African History* wrote that Page draws largely on two books written for schoolchildren and one by a non-Africanist. Jones wrote that "few of the standard works written since the 1970s are even mentioned" and that most of the statistical updates consist of tables "copied directly from published works. . . . More critical, perhaps, is the fact that Page's book represents an extreme case of the common tendency for historians to choose topics for which they lack the necessary language. skills."

Dennis R. Hidalgo, who reviewed *The Dutch Triangle* for *H-Net* online, wrote that Page "comes across as well-versed on Dutch slave trade documents, and from his experience with the subject, he has shared information relevant to the comprehension of the Dutch treatment of Africans in their American colonies. He achieved his goal of providing a conscientious coverage of the Dutch Atlantic slave trade in a book organized fairly well. . . . The author's use of satisfactory amounts of endnotes assures that students will easily find the references they need."

Page's three-volume *Encyclopedia of African History and Culture* covers three periods. The first volume, *Ancient Africa,* covers prehistory to 500 C.E., including the histories and cultures of the Egyptian, Nubian, Bantu, and San peoples, as well as archaeology, legends and myths, and religions. The second volume, titled *African Kingdoms,* looks at the medieval period from 500 to 1500 C.E., the spread of Islam, the Bantu migration, the development of states, and the expansion of trade. In the third volume, *From Conquest to Colonization,* Page covers the tumultuous period from 1500 to 1850 C.E., a time that saw civil wars, exchanges of power, the beginning of the transatlantic slave trade, and a surge in European exploration and colonization.

Within each volume, entries are arranged alphabetically, and each includes a timeline, glossary, and index. *Choice* reviewer G. Walsh felt that the work suffers from repetition and said the chronological approach disrupts the encyclopedic format. Walsh, who wrote that "use of ancient and modern geographic names is inconsistent" and "names of ethnic and linguistic groups are confusing and misleading," felt the encyclopedia to be "seriously flawed."

A *Booklist* contributor noted that the chronological arrangement is useful for historical purposes, but felt that "it also creates challenges for the reader. Some topics, such as Ancestor worship, Body adornment, and Family structure, are addressed only in Volume One, although they also have relevance for Volumes Two and Three. Coverage of other topics can be disjointed. . . . Fortunately, the index and extensive cross-references do a good job of referring readers to content in all three volumes." *Library Journal*'s Edward McCormack called the set "valuable as a time-saving reference tool for its accessible prose and easy-to-use format."

BIOGRAPHICAL AND CRITICAL SOURCES:

PERIODICALS

*Booklist,* January 1, 2002, review of *The Encyclopedia of African History and Culture,* p. 888.
*Choice,* April, 2002, G. Walsh, review of *The Encyclopedia of African History and Culture,* p. 1404.
*Journal of African History,* October, 1998, Adam Jones, review of *The Dutch Triangle: The Netherlands and the Atlantic Slave Trade, 1621-1664,* p. 482.
*Library Journal,* March 15, 2002, Edward McCormack, review of *The Encyclopedia of African History and Culture,* p. 74.
*Reference & Research Book News,* November, 1997, review of *The Dutch Triangle,* p. 96.

OTHER

*H-Net,* http://www2.h-net.msu.edu/ (August, 1998), Dennis R. Hidalgo, review of *The Dutch Triangle.**

\*          \*          \*

## PARDECK, John T. 1947-

*PERSONAL:* Born January 30, 1947; son of Kenneth C. (a telephone worker) and Ruth M. (a service worker; maiden name, Nieemann) Pardeck; married Jean A. Musick, August 18, 1973; children: Jonathan T., James K. *Ethnicity:* "German." *Education:* Central Missouri State University, B.A., 1970, M.A., 1972; Saint Louis University, Ph.D., 1982. *Politics:* Democrat. *Religion:* Lutheran.

*ADDRESSES: Home*—2022 East Barataria, Springfield, MO 65804. *Office*—School of Social Work, Southwest Missouri State University, Springfield, MO 65804; fax: 417-836-7688. *E-mail*—jtp121f@smsu. edu.

*CAREER:* Tulane University, New Orleans, LA, assistant professor and researcher, 1980-82; Arkansas State University, Jonesboro, AR, associate professor and director of social-work program, 1982-87; Southeast Missouri State University, Cape Girardeau,

MO, professor of social-work policy and research, 1987-91; Southwest Missouri State University, Springfield, MO, professor of social-work policy and research, 1991—, research fellow, 2001—. Licensed clinical social worker; Missouri Protection and Advocacy, member of board of directors, 1994-2000; Springfield Commission on Human Rights, member, 1997-2000. *Military service:* Served in U.S. Army.

*MEMBER:* Missouri Association for Social Welfare (member of board of directors, 1991-2001), Phi Kappa Phi.

*WRITINGS:*

*The Forgotten Children: A Study of the Stability and Continuity of Foster Care,* University Press of America (Washington, DC), 1983.

(With wife, Jean A. Pardeck) *Young People with Problems: A Guide to Bibliotherapy,* Greenwood Press (Westport, CT), 1984.

(With Jean A. Pardeck) *Books for Early Childhood: A Developmental Perspective,* Greenwood Press (Westport, CT), 1986.

(With John W. Murphy) *Computerization of Human Services Agencies: A Critical Appraisal,* Auburn House (Westport, CT), 1991.

(With Jean A. Pardeck) *Bibliotherapy: A Guide to Using Books in Clinical Practice,* Mellen Research University Press, 1992.

(With Jean A. Pardeck) *Bibliotherapy: A Clinical Approach for Helping Children,* Gordon & Breach Science Publishers (New York, NY), 1992.

*Bibliotherapy in Clinical Practice,* Greenwood Press (Westport, CT), 1993.

*Social Work Practice: An Ecological Approach,* Auburn House (Westport, CT), 1996.

*Using Books in Clinical Social Work Practice: A Guide to Bibliotherapy,* Haworth Social Work Practice Press (New York, NY), 1998.

*Social Work after the Americans with Disabilities Act: New Challenges and Opportunities for Social Services Professionals,* Auburn House (Westport, CT), 1998.

*Children's Rights: Policy and Practice,* Haworth Social Work Practice Press (New York, NY), 2002.

(With Roland Meinert and Larry L. Kreuger) *Social Work: Seeking Relevancy in the Twenty-first Century,* Haworth Social Work Practice Press (New York, NY), 2000.

*EDITOR*

(With Kathy Nance, Rebecca Hegar, and Cynthia Christy Baker) *Child Welfare Training and Practice: An Annotated Bibliography,* Greenwood Press (Westport, CT), 1982.

(With John W. Murphy) *Technology and Human Productivity: Challenges for the Future,* Quorum Press (Westport, CT), 1986.

(With John W. Murphy) *Computers and Social Service Delivery,* Haworth Social Work Practice Press (New York, NY), 1988.

*Child Abuse and Neglect: Theory, Practice, and Research,* Gordon & Breach Science Publishers (New York, NY), 1989.

(With John W. Murphy) *Microcomputers in Early Childhood Education,* Gordon & Breach Science Publishers (New York, NY), 1989.

(With John W. Murphy) *Computers in Human Services: An Overview for Clinical and Welfare Services,* 1990.

(With John W. Murphy) *Social and Psychological Issues during Adolescence and Youth: An International Perspective,* Academic Publishers, 1991.

(With Roland Meinert and William P. Sullivan) *Issues in Social Work: A Critical Analysis,* Auburn House (Westport, CT), 1994.

(With Martha J. Markward) *Re-assessing Social Work Practice with Children: A Book of Readings,* Gordon & Breach Science Publishers (New York, NY), 1996.

(With Roland Meinert and John W. Murphy) *Postmodernism, Religion, and the Future of Social Work,* Haworth Social Work Practice Press (New York, NY), 1998.

(With Charles F. Longino and John W. Murphy) *Reason and Rationality in Health and Human Services Delivery,* Haworth Social Work Practice Press (New York, NY), 1998.

(With Francis Yuen) *Family Health in Social Work Practice: A Holistic Approach,* Auburn House (Westport, CT), 1999.

*Family Health: A Macro Level Approach to Social Work Practice,* Auburn House (Westport, CT), 2002.

(With others) *Family Health Social Work Practice: A Knowledge and Skills Casebook,* Haworth Social Work Practice Press, 2003.

Also editor, *Journal of Social Work in Disability and Rehabilitation.*

*WORK IN PROGRESS: Social Work for the Twenty-first Century: A Critical Analysis,* for Praeger Press (Westport, CT); research on the scholarly productivity of social work faculty.

*SIDELIGHTS:* John T. Pardeck told *CA:* "My primary motivation for writing is to explore areas related to social work and the social sciences in general. I particularly enjoy writing on civil rights, with emphasis on the rights of children and persons with disabilities. The greatest influence on my work was the academic education I received in my doctoral program at Saint Louis University. I am presently writing a book on the profession of social work in the twenty-first century. The work is a critical analysis of the profession. I plan to continue writing on the social work profession and to explore areas critical to the human condition."

*BIOGRAPHICAL AND CRITICAL SOURCES:*

PERIODICALS

*Adolescence,* summer, 1998, review of *Social Work after the Americans with Disabilities Act: New Challenges and Opportunities for Social Service Professionals,* p. 500.

\*     \*     \*

**PETRI, György 1943-2000**

*PERSONAL:* Born December 22, 1943, in Budapest, Hungary; died of cancer of the larynx, July 16, 2000, in Budapest, Hungary; son of a book trader and an office worker; married twice; children: (first marriage) one daughter; (second marriage) one son. *Education:* Studied philosophy and literature at Eötvös Loránd University, Budapest, 1966-71.

*CAREER:* Freelance writer, 1974-2000. Also worked as a shop assistant, journalist, nurse in a mental hospital, actor, and translator. Founding editor of *Beszélő,* and founding member of Fund for Supporting the Poor (SZETA) and the Alliance of Free Democrats (SZDSZ).

*AWARDS, HONORS:* József Atilla Prize, 1990; Kossuth Prize, 1996.

*WRITINGS:*

*Magyarázatok M. számára* (title means "Explanations for M."), Szépirodalmi (Budapest, Hungary), 1971.
*Körülírt zuhanás* (title means "Circumscribed Falling"), Szépirodalmi Kiadó (Budapest, Hungary), 1974.
*ÖrökhétfO* (title means "Eternal Monday"), AB Független Kiadó (Budapest, Hungary), 1980.
*Hólabda a kézben* (poems; title means "Snowball in the Hand"), HHRF/CHRR (New York, NY), 1984.
*Azt hiszik* (title means "They Think So"), AB Független Kiadó (Budapest, Hungary), 1985.
*Valahol megvan* (title means "Its There Somewhere"), Szépirodalmi Kiadó (Budapest, Hungary), 1989.
*Ami kimaradt* (title means "What Was Left Out"), Aura Kiadó (Budapest, Hungary), 1989.
*Valami ismeretlen* (title means "Something Unknown"), Pécs (Jelenkor, Hungary), 1990.
*Night Song of the Personal Shadow: Selected Poems,* translated by Clive Wilmer and George Gömöri, Bloodaxe Books (Newcastle upon Tyne, England), 1991.
*Petri György versei* (title means "Collected Verse"), Szépirodalmi Kiadó (Budapest, Hungary), 1991.
*Sár* (title means "Mud"), Pécs (Jelenkor, Hungary), 1993.
*Versek: 1971-1995* (title means "Verses: 1971-1995"), Pécs (Jelenkor, Hungary), 1996.
*Eternal Monday: New & Selected Poems,* translated by Clive Wilmer and George Gömöri, Bloodaxe Books (Newcastle upon Tyne, England), 1999.

Petri's work has also been translated into German and French.

*SIDELIGHTS:* György Petri was "to his fellow Hungarians, the most original poet of his generation and something of a national hero," observed Clive Wilmer in an obituary for Petri in the London *Guardian.* He rejected "inflated language," Wilmer stated, and instead "wrote in a style that was harsh, spare and colloquial, sometimes to the point of coarseness." Whether he wrote about politics or about love, his language was always very frank and truthful.

Petri was born in Budapest to Jewish Serbian refugee parents. His father was a book trader and his mother held a civilian job with the Hungarian army. As a teenager, Petri worked as a journalist and a psychiatric nurse. Later, he attended college to study philosophy and Hungarian literature, but did not stay long enough to complete his degree. It was during his college studies that he made important contacts, especially his connection with philosopher Jano Kis, who would greatly influence his work.

Petri published his first poem when he was seventeen, but stopped writing a few years later because he thought his poetry was too conventional. He did not resume writing for six years. In 1971 his first collection of poetry was published and was well received. From that time on, he was able to earn enough money on which to live through his writing.

Petri's poetry, in his later years, was anything but conventional. He was not a typical Hungarian poet. As a writer for the London *Times* stated in the poet's obituary, Petri's "use of irony was at odds with the Hungarian romantic tradition, which he considered compromised, and his taste for the raw meat of street language rubbed up against the precise minutiae of political and sexual life in a way that his contemporaries found wholly convincing."

During his lifetime Petri enjoyed a wide readership. He wrote about politics and love with "irony" and "biting honesty" observed a *Times* obituary writer, sometimes offending and embarrassing conservatives by writing about political events considered taboo, such as the Hungarian Revolution of 1956 and the invasion of Czechoslovakia. He was often identified with the "liberal left-wing of the dissident movement," Wilmer noted.

Petri's dislike of the conventional language of most of his fellow poets caused Petri's work to be banned in Hungary between 1975 and 1989. He refused to write abstractly, refused to use language that skirted important issues, especially in the political arena. During the years that his writing was banned, when communist leaders controlled Hungary, he relinquished the concept of reaching a large audience and had his work published by an independent illegal press, then passed out copies of his work to friends.

*Night Song of the Personal Shadow: Selected Poems*, one of two of Petri's collections to be published in English, contains political and love poems, both types

written, according to Andras Sandow in a review of the book for *World Literature Today*, in a "tone and temper" that have been "forged by experiences both public and private. The liberties, often amusing, often appalling, that Petri's true-to-life persona takes with women, language, and God, we can see now, are of the same nature as the liberties he has taken with regard to a raped public life."

Critics who read both the Hungarian and English versions of *Night Song of the Personal Shadow* commented on the difficulty in translating Petri, who, as Wilmer noted in his introduction to the book, loved word play. Writing for the *Times Literary Supplement*, George Szirtes commented on the "Sartrean existentialism" of Petri's vocabulary, making reference to a line in one of the poems contained in *Night Song of the Personal Shadow*: "I could do with an autumn free of humans." In this line, Szirtes sees Petri not just as a man alienated from his society, but rather as alienation itself. Commenting further on Petri's existential tone, Szirtes wrote: "In a four-line poem called 'Me,' published in 1982, he refers to himself as 'God's only-begotten / rotten grape.'" Despite Petri's alienation, and maybe because of it, Petri's is the voice of his times, Szirtes contended. "To understand him is to understand the declining years of European Communism and to sharpen our eyes for intimate half-truths of our own."

In 1999 a second collection of Petri's poems was published in English. *Eternal Monday: New & Selected Poems* contains some of the poems from the first collection plus thirty-six new ones, many of them written earlier than the poems in *Night Song of the Personal Shadow*. The tone of the whole collection shows how the poet's outlook has changed, as the majority of Petri's earlier poems were more personal and less political. As George Szirtes stated in a review of *Eternal Monday* for the *Times Literary Supplement*: "What makes Petri a marvelous and gripping poet is . . . the humour, courage, honesty and astringency of his oeuvre, his poetic persona."

The title of *Eternal Monday* comes from the concept that Hungarian communism, as Petri experienced it, was not to be trusted. As Ray Olson described it for *Booklist*, "what was allowed or ignored on Monday might be actionable on Tuesday." Petri despised the hypocrisy of the Communist regime in his country and, according to Olson, "turned his natural lyricism to satirical purposes."

One of Petri's recurring themes was that of death. "Some of the best poems . . . were inspired by funerals of writers; and when contemplating the possibility of his own death, Petri grows philosophical," wrote George Gömöri in his review of *Versek: 1971-1995* for *World Literature Today.* Petri died July 16, 2000, of cancer of the larynx. At the time of his death, he was living in Budapest, just a short distance from the house in which he had been born.

### BIOGRAPHICAL AND CRITICAL SOURCES:

*PERIODICALS*

*Booklist,* April 1, 2000, Ray Olson, review of *Eternal Monday,* p. 1426.

*Encounter,* March, 1990, Clive Wilmer, "Daily Bread: On György Petri," pp. 42-45.

*Kirkus Reviews,* May 1, 2000, review of *Eternal Monday,* p. 604.

*Stand Magazine,* autumn, 1992, Lawrence Sail, review of *Night Song of the Personal Shadow,* pp. 52-60.

*Times Literary Supplement,* January 17, 1992, George Szirtes, review of *Night Song of the Personal Shadow,* p. 26; January 28, 2000, George Szirtes, review of *Eternal Monday,* p. 25.

*World Literature Today,* spring, 1983, George Gömöri, review of *Orokhetfo,* p. 325; summer, 1986, George Gömöri, review of *Azt hiszik,* p. 497; winter, 1987, Andras Sandor, review of *Zur Hoffnung Verkommen,* pp. 133-134; summer, 1991, George Gömöri, review of *Valami ismeretlen,* pp. 523-534; winter, 1993, Andras Sandor, review of *Night Song of the Personal Shadow,* p. 216; summer, 1997, George Gömöri, review of *Versek,* pp. 624-625; spring, 1999, George Gömöri, review of *Hungarian,* p. 367; summer, 2000, Thomas Kabdebo, review of *Eternal Monday,* p. 615.

### OBITUARIES:

*PERIODICALS*

*Guardian* (London, England), August 8, 2000, Clive Wilmer, p. 17.

*Times* (London, England), August 16, 2000, p. 19.*

## POCKNELL, Pauline

*PERSONAL:* Born in Heptonstall, Yorkshire, England; citizenship British and Canadian; daughter of John and Annie Reed; divorced; children: Ann Pocknell, Oliver Pocknell. *Education:* University of Manchester, B.A. (with honors); McMaster University, M.A.; Ontario Institute for Studies in Education, B.Ed. *Hobbies and other interests:* Music, reading, walking, travel, visiting art galleries.

*ADDRESSES: Home*—1797 Main St. W., No. 27, Hamilton, Ontario, Canada L8S 1H6; fax: 905-570-0014. *E-mail*—pocknelp@mcmail.cis.mcmaster.ca.

*CAREER:* McMaster University, Hamilton, Ontario, Canada, sessional lecturer in French, 1979—. Freelance translator from French into English. Great Romantics (annual festival), committee member, 1994—.

*MEMBER:* American Liszt Society, Istituto Liszt (Italy; corresponding member).

*WRITINGS:*

(Translator, editor, annotator, and author of introduction) *Franz Liszt and Agnes Street-Klindworth: A Correspondence, 1854-1886,* Pendragon Press (Hillsdale, NY), 2000.

Contributor to books, including *Analecta Lisztiana II: Liszt and His World,* edited by Michael Saffle, Pendragon Press, 1997; *Liszt 2000: The Great Hungarian and European Master at the Threshold of the Twenty-first Century,* edited by Klára Hamburger, Liszt Ferenc Társaság (Budapest, Hungary), 2000; and *Analecta Lisztiana III: Liszt and the Birth of Modern Europe; Music as a Mirror of Religious, Political, Social, and Aesthetic Transformation,* edited by Michael Saffle and Rossana Dalmonte, Pendragon Press, 2002. Contributor to periodicals, including *Liszt Society Journal, Journal of the American Liszt Society,* and *Liszt Saeculum.*

*WORK IN PROGRESS:* Editing *Franz Liszt et la Princesse Marie Von Sayn-Wittgenstein: une correspondance, 1848-1886,* completion expected in 2003; editing Liszt's pocket diaries.

*SIDELIGHTS:* Pauline Pocknell told *CA:* "My primary motivation for writing is curiosity—a great wish to 'get things right,' particularly in biographies of nineteenth-century figures who can no longer speak for themselves, but get spoken about anyway. Their letters are the closest thing to an autobiography, and it is the letters in French of nineteenth-century musicians, especially Franz Liszt, for whom no general correspondence exists, on which I have concentrated.

"My master's thesis was on Arthur Rimbaud. Afterward I worked as a research assistant and translator for Dr. Alan Walker, author of a biography of Franz Liszt, because of my French and my research skills. It was not hard to move focus from writers to musicians in that century; what was a revelation was the enormous amount of *primary* material in archives worldwide, written in French, never published, which changed entirely the myths about these musicians and their world. My field of research switched in 1985, thanks to my years of part-time work for Dr. Walker.

"I get curious about a detail that doesn't fit—a person close to a musician about whom little is known, a batch of unpublished correspondence in an obscure archive. I throw anything that I discover about it into a big envelope or bag. Eventually I empty it all out, search very actively for still-missing details, and write it up. My footnotes make me notorious, but if I don't say the obscure details, pertinent for a letter, who will? Big people get lots of write-up (often faulty because of the lack of these details); little people, important in their time, often disappear from all reference books. I put them in footnotes."

\*   \*   \*

### POLLARD, Jann Lawrence 1942-

*PERSONAL:* Born April 11, 1942, in Mount Pleasant, IA; daughter of Don R. (a farmer) and Mary E. (a homemaker) Lawrence; married Gene A. Pollard (a financial advisor), April 25, 1970; children: Brittany, Natalie. *Education:* University of Colorado—Boulder, B.F.A., 1963; also attended College of San Mateo. *Politics:* Republican. *Hobbies and other interests:* Computers, graphic design.

*ADDRESSES: Home and office*—105 La Mesa Dr., Burlingame, CA 94010. *E-mail*—pollardart@attbi.com.

*CAREER:* Interior designer, author, and artist. Self-employed interior designer, 1959-87; painter in watercolors, acrylics, and oils. Teacher of watercolor workshops; juror of competitions; work represented in group and solo exhibitions throughout California and in galleries. National Kidney Foundation, member of authors' committee, 1994-2002.

*MEMBER:* National Watercolor Society (Signature member), American Watercolor Society (associate member), California Watercolor Association (Signature member).

*AWARDS, HONORS:* First-place award, Burlingame Art Society, 1971; Outstanding Achievement Award, California Watercolor Association, 2002; other art awards.

*WRITINGS:*

(With Jerry Little) *Creative Computer Tools for Artists: Using Software to Develop Drawings and Paintings,* Watson-Guptill Publications (New York, NY), 2001.

Contributor to periodicals, including *International Artist.* Newsletter editor, California Watercolor Association, 1998-99.

*SIDELIGHTS:* Jann Lawrence Pollard told *CA:* "As a painter, my passion to travel gives me an endless supply of subjects and emotions. How the atmosphere and light affect old-world architecture is my particular interest. In my travels, I return with hundreds of photographs and sketches from which to work.

"I started using the computer with Adobe Photoshop software to redesign the photographs and sketches into new compositions. Eventually, from input of my students, I felt I should share my knowledge with other artists. There are hardly any books on the subject written especially for artists. I compare artists and the use of computers as a new tool in their work with the introduction of the camera in the Impressionist era. The Impressionists hid from the public the fact that they were using the camera. Today an artist doesn't think twice about using the camera with his work. We are at such a crossroads today with the computer.

"Because this concept was new for artists, my coauthor and I invited several well-known artists to my studio. They were told to bring their photographs or sketches. I put their photographs into the computer and acted as their technician as they described their creative process in redesigning the composition. They went home with the 'computer sketches,' made paintings from the sketches, and sent us back photographs. All of the steps and the completed painting are shown in our book. Several artists' styles and media are included."

*BIOGRAPHICAL AND CRITICAL SOURCES:*

*PERIODICALS*

*Library Journal,* March 15, 2002, Daniel Lombardo, review of *Creative Computer Tools for Artists: Using Software to Develop Drawings and Paintings,* p. 78.

# R

**RITER, A. W.**
   See **ROLFE, Frederick (William Serafino Austin Lewis Mary)**

\*     \*     \*

**ROBERTS, Sam**

*PERSONAL:* Male.

*ADDRESSES: Office*—New York Times, 229 West 43rd St., New York, NY 10036.

*CAREER:* Journalist. *New York Times,* editor.

*WRITINGS:*

(With Michael Kramer) *"I Never Wanted to Be Vice President of Anything!": An Investigative Biography of Nelson Rockefeller,* Basic Books (New York, NY), 1976.

*Who We Are: A Portrait of America Based on the Latest U.S. Census,* Times Books (New York, NY), 1993.

*The Brother: The Untold Story of Atomic Spy David Greenglass and How He Sent His Sister, Ethel Rosenberg, to the Electric Chair,* Random House (New York, NY), 2001.

*SIDELIGHTS:* Sam Roberts is an editor at the *New York Times,* and the author of several books. *Who We Are: A Portrait of America Based on the Latest U.S. Census* presents the vast amount of data collected by the 1990 census in narrative format. Roberts compares this data to that from previous years and analyzes how the United States is changing. In the *New York Times Book Review,* Cullen Murphy wrote, "Roberts has probably done as good a job as can be done in making the results of the 1990 census accessible to the general public."

*The Brother: The Untold Story of Atomic Spy David Greenglass and How He Sent His Sister, Ethel Rosenberg, to the Electric Chair* tells the story of Ethel and Julius Rosenberg, who were convicted of spying for the Soviet Union and executed in 1954 in the electric chair at Sing Sing Prison. The key prosecution witness was Ethel's younger brother, David Greenglass. In researching the book, Roberts convinced Greenglass to grant him interviews and access to Greenglass's version of the story. In exchange, Greenglass would receive a share of the profits from the book. Although Roberts does not offer a great deal of new information on the case, according to Ronald Radosh in the *New Republic,* "His accomplishment . . . is to have opened a window on the character of the Rosenberg and Greenglass families" and what led them to spy for the Soviet Union.

*BIOGRAPHICAL AND CRITICAL SOURCES:*

*PERIODICALS*

*American Legion,* December, 1994, "Who Is America?," p. 26.

*Booklist,* February 1, 1994, Denise Perry Donavin, review of *Who We Are: A Portrait of America Based on the Latest U.S. Census,* p. 985; February 1, 2002, Brad Hooper, review of *The Brother: The Untold Story of Atomic Spy David Greenglass and How He Sent His Sister, Ethel Rosenberg, to the Electric Chair,* p. 907.

*Choice,* September, 1994, J. de Vries, review of *Who We Are,* p. 216.

*Library Journal,* March 1, 1994, Suzanne Wood, review of *Who We Are,* p. 106.

*National Review,* October 24, 1994, Peter Brimelow, review of *Who We Are,* p. 64.

*New Republic,* December 24, 2001, Ronald Radosh, "The Untrue Believer," p. 39.

*New York Law Journal,* November 20, 2001, Sam Reynolds, review of *The Brother,* p. 1.

*New York Times,* June 16, 1994, Dick Kirschten, review of *Who We Are,* p. C15; September 18, 2001, James Bamfod, "Of Atomic Secrets, Loyalty, and Bitter Deceit," p. E6.

*New York Times Book Review,* March 20, 1994, Cullen Murphy, "Here's Looking at Us," p. 6; October 28, 2001, David Oshinsky, "The Informer," p. 11.

*Publishers Weekly,* January 31, 1994, review of *Who We Are,* p. 70.

*Wall Street Journal,* October 1, 2001, Michael J. Ybarra, "When Espionage Was All in the Family, and Loyalty Was Not" p. A22.

*Washington Post,* September 23, 2001, Robert Sherrill, "Blood Relation," pp. 3-4.*

\* \* \*

# ROCHE, Judith

*PERSONAL:* Female.

*ADDRESSES: Agent*—c/o Author Mail, University of Washington Press, P.O. Box 50096 Seattle, WA 98145-5096. *E-mail*—judith@onereel.org.

*CAREER:* Writer; artist-in-residence, Washington State Arts Commission, Seattle, WA, and Seattle Arts and Lectures. Instructor at colleges, universities, and prisons in the United States. Literary arts director, One Reel; literary manager of the Bumbershoot Arts Festival, Seattle, WA.

*AWARDS, HONORS:* American Book Award, Before Columbus Foundation, 1999.

*WRITINGS:*

*Ghosts* (poems), Empty Bowl, 1984.

*Myrrh/My Life as a Screamer* (poems), Black Heron Press, 1996.

(Editor, with Meg McHutchison) *First Fish, First People: Salmon Tales of the North Pacific Rim,* University of Washington Press (Seattle, WA), 1998.

Also editor of two creative-writing textbooks.

*SIDELIGHTS:* Writing instructor Judith Roche is a recognized poet, and the author of the poetry collections *Myrrh/My Life as a Screamer* and *Ghosts.* Of the latter, Sibyl James of *Women's Review of Books* found that "the ghosts of *Ghosts* operate on three levels: the ghosts of the poet's personal past; mythic ghosts—Persephone, Undine, Morganna Le Fay; and ghosts less specific than these, not gathered up into a label or name. These are fears, desires, wisdoms that take on human or animal form or the shape of natural things—wind, water, lightning. All of them haunt or taunt or aid the poet. All are forces she must open to and deal with."

Roche's writings took a different path in 1998 with *First Fish, First People: Salmon Tales of the North Pacific Rim.* As editor with Meg McHutchison, Roche collected stories from such ancient fishing cultures as the Ainu of Japan, the Nyvkh from Sakhalin, and the Coastal Salish of Canada. The authors, said Emmett Wright in a *Science Books & Films* article, "paint both a historical and a contemporary perspective about their peoples' relationship with the wild salmon, while alerting us to current dangers and conditions facing the declining wild population." In the view of Edna Boardman, a contributor in *Kliatt,* "readers and student researchers jaded by the diatribes and charts of ecologists and harbingers of disaster will be informed and moved by this blend of environmental science, political plea, and cultural evocation."

*BIOGRAPHICAL AND CRITICAL SOURCES:*

*PERIODICALS*

*Kliatt,* March, 1999, Edna Boardman, review of *First Fish, First People: Salmon Tales of the North Pacific Rim,* p. 31.

*Reference & Research Book News,* February, 1999, review of *First Fish, First People,* p. 37.

*Science Books & Films,* May, 1999, Emmett Wright, review of *First Fish, First People,* p. 117.

*Women's Review of Books,* December, 1984, Sibyl James, "Voyages of Discovery," p. 17.

\*     \*     \*

## ROLFE, Frederick (William Serafino Austin Lewis Mary) 1860-1913

(Baron Corvo, Frederick Austin, A. W. Riter, Al Siddik, Uriele de Ricardi, May Chester, Vincenza, Duchess of Deira, Ifor Williams)

*PERSONAL:* Born July 22, 1860, in Cheapside, London, England; died October 23, 1913, in Venice, Italy; son of James (a piano manufacturer and agent) and Ellen Elizabeth Rolfe. *Education:* Attended North London Collegiate School until 1874; spent several months at Oxford as a non-matriculated student; trained as a cleric at Oscott Seminary and Scots College, 1887-90. *Religion:* Catholic.

*CAREER:* Novelist and short story writer. Taught at various schools, 1874-86.

*WRITINGS:*

*Tarcissus: The Boy Martyr of Rome,* Boardman (Essex, England), 1880.

*Stories Toto Told Me,* John Lane (New York, NY), 1898.

*The Attack on St. Winefride's Well; or, Holywell Gone Mad,* c. 1898.

*In His Own Image,* John Lane (New York, NY), 1901.

*Chronicles of the House of Borgia,* Dutton (New York, NY), 1901, published as *A History of the Borgias,* Modern Library (New York, NY), 1931.

(Translator) *The Rubaiyat of Umar Khaiyam,* John Lane (New York, NY), 1903.

(Ghostwriter) *Owen Thomas, Agricultural and Pastoral Prospects of South Africa,* Constable (London, England), 1904.

*Hadrian the Seventh: A Romance,* Chatto & Windus (London, England), 1904, Knopf (New York, NY), 1925.

*Don Tarquinio: A Kataleptic Phantasmatic Romance,* Chatto & Windus (London, England), 1905.

*Don Renato: An Ideal Content Historical Romance,* Griffiths (London, England), 1909.

(With Harry Pirie-Gordon) *The Weird of the Wanderer: Being the Papyrus Records of Some Incidents in One of the Previous Lives of Mr. Nicholas Crabbe, by Rolfe and Harry Pirie-Gordon as Prospero and Caliban,* Rider (London, England), 1912.

*The Bull against the Enemy of the Anglican Race,* privately printed (London, England), 1929.

*The Desire and Pursuit of the Whole: A Romance of Modern Venice,* Cassell (London, England), 1934, New Directions (New York, NY), 1953.

(With Harry Pirie-Gordon) *Hubert's Arthur: Being Certain Curious Documents Found among the Literary Remains of Mr. N.C., by Rolfe and Pirie-Gordon as Prospero and Caliban,* Cassell (London, England), 1935.

(Translator) *The Songs of Meleager,* First Edition Club (London, England), 1937.

*Three Tales of Venice,* Corvine Press (Thames Ditton, England), 1950.

*Amico di Sandro: A Fragment of a Novel,* privately printed (Harrow, England), 1951.

*The Cardinal Prefect of Propaganda and Other Stories,* Vane (London, England), 1957.

*Nicholas Crabbe; or, The One and the Many: A Romance,* Chatto & Windus (London, England), 1958.

*The Armed Hands and Other Stories and Pieces,* edited by Cecil Woolf, Woolf (London, England), 1972.

*Collected Poems,* edited by Cecil Woolf, Woolf (London, England), 1972.

Also contributor to periodical *Holywell Record.* Author of works published under pseudonyms, including Baron Corvo, Frederick Austin, A. W. Riter, Al Siddik, Uriele de Ricardi, May Chester, Vincenza Duchess of Deira, and Ifor Williams.

*SIDELIGHTS:* Frederick Rolfe is remembered less for his literary output than for the quirky qualities, eccentricities, and paranoid behavior that he exhibited throughout his writing life. His fiction contains many of the elements that personify the decadent movement, most notably a distinct perverse morality and extreme self-consciousness. Rolfe's work was usually very self-involved, used as a way to denounce and offend the friends and patrons whom Rolfe believed slighted him; yet, with lush language and provocative descriptions,

Rolfe was often able to transform his personal experiences into mythically significant events. His work never achieved the recognition that Rolfe felt was deserved, and it was largely overshadowed by the interest that his life and psyche generated. Rolfe's short stories and novels, with the exception of *Hadrian the Seventh,* have mostly been forgotten.

Rolfe was born in 1860 to Ellen Elizabeth Pilcher and James Rolfe. The Rolfe family had a relatively successful piano-making business since 1784, yet by the time Frederick was born the business had deteriorated profoundly. Rolfe attended North London Collegiate School until 1874, when he was fourteen years old. He spent some months at Oxford, though he was not a matriculated student, and he returned there regularly to read for a friend, one of the few he retained for life. His modest upbringing was largely at odds with the ambitions and airs to class that Rolfe developed. Maureen Modlish, writing in *Dictionary of Literary Biography,* noted that "Indeed [Rolfe] seemed to want desperately to belong to the elite, but his class background precluded the possibility."

Rolfe went on to teach at various schools, and in 1886, he converted to Roman Catholicism, soon latching on to the idea that he had a calling to the priesthood. He entered Oscott Seminary in 1887, but soon left it; then he joined Scots College in Rome, only to be expelled in mid-1890. Commentators believe that Rolfe was led to the seminary not through some noble vocation, but in pursuit of status and power. Pamela Hansford Johnson, in *New Quests for Corvo,* wrote that Rolfe "wanted less to be priest than to be Pope." Following his ill-fated quest to join the clergy, Rolfe resided in Rome with the Sforza-Cesarini family for several months. Rolfe claims that the Duchess Sforza-Cesarini bestowed on Rolfe the title of Baron Corvo, and became his patron, providing an allowance that lasted throughout Rolfe's stay in Rome and some time after he returned to England. Several critics claim that the title had dubious origins; some speculate that Rolfe himself came up with it, to compensate for his failings and attempts at becoming a priest.

Rolfe's literary career began with the publication of some short fictional pieces. Prevalent in several early stories was the theme of being buried alive. (Much of Rolfe's work, in fact, refers to his feelings that he has been metaphorically buried alive, in loneliness, poverty, and obscurity; he once wrote in a letter "All I want is to be picked out of this hole where I am buried.") In "An Unforgettable Experience" (1894) a poor woman who lives in a crowded slum is pronounced dead of a fever and is sent home to be buried. The priest, Father Serafico, conducts his service over her open coffin, but he cannot believe she is dead. The narrator, Baron Corvo, repeatedly tries to revive her and finally succeeds. This story is different from most of Rolfe's other fiction, as the environment described reflects the poverty and desperate lives of the urban poor. "Rolfe was no socialist," wrote Jeffrey Parker in *Dictionary of Literary Biography,* "even though he spent most of his life in poverty as an outcast." Parker added, "In fact, after reading Edward Carpenter's *Towards Democracy* (1833-1902) Rolfe drafted a reply titled 'Towards Aristocracy.'"

Another work that deals directly with premature burial is "How I was Buried Alive" (1896). But this short piece, like much of Rolfe's work, is largely autobiographical and seems to have been based on an incident in Rolfe's life that involved his fear of reptiles. The story commences when a man is expelled from the seminary for lacking a vocation, and an Italian family invites him into their household to recover. When a lizard leaps onto his arm, the protagonist, Baron Corvo, falls into a trance. After Corvo awakens, he discovers that he has been placed in a coffin. When he kicks free the nailed-down lid, Corvo re-enters the world.

The bulk of Rolfe's books and stories, penned between 1898 and 1908, are retellings of perceived attacks and slights on Rolfe. Modlish commented that "Rolfe was so convinced of the reality of his delusions about himself that he was not only able to convince others of their reality, but was able to make business agreements on the basis of them." Rolfe promised that when he became successful, he would repay his lenders. When the books failed and lenders and patrons tired of him, he mounted elaborate campaigns against them, claiming breach of faith, often ridiculing and vengefully exposing them in his stories. One of his early stories "The Saint, the Priest, the Nowt, the Devil" (1897), written under the name A. W. Riter, was created in response to Rolfe's perception that he had been duped and swindled by a Catholic priest, Father Beauclerk. In exchange for lodging and attempts by the priest to procure commissions for Rolfe, the writer was to paint banners for the church. When Rolfe found that the priest sold one of his designs, Rolfe demanded an exorbitant amount of money. The priest refused, and Rolfe drafted the story from his distinct and highly subjective perspective. This story is but one of many, many examples where Rolfe denounced and scandalized people—including priests, literary peers, and patrons—through his writings.

*Stories Toto Told Me,* a collection of stories published in 1898 and considered by critics to be based on real-life events, attracted considerable attention and critical discussion. Toto Maidalchini is the storyteller, and as Parker wrote, the "beautiful leader of a group of boys with whom he spent the summer." Parker added that "Toto is variously described as an example of unquestioning faith, and uneducated peasant, and the triumph of oral tradition over literature." Parker noted, paraphrasing Miriam Benkovitz from her *Frederick Rolfe, Baron Corvo: A Biography,* that in Toto "one finds a combination of all the complex tendencies in Rolfe's personality, including his hostilities and his fidelity to a benign and humble Christianity based on spontaneous charity." These tales, a rich and colorful tapestry of saints, sinners, theology, and legend, won Rolfe some admirers. Parker said that these stories "reveal [Rolfe's] talents at their most imaginative, humorous, and vindictive." But Parker also mentioned how they also call attention to another side of Rolfe's complex personality, his homoerotic tendencies: "When Toto is described as a 'slim faun in the forest' or is said to have 'undulated deliciously,' another aspect of Rolfe's personality surfaces, calling to mind . . . his penchant for photographing young boys in the nude."

Much of Rolfe's work seemed to provide a forum for the writer to portray his own life as heroic and mythical. His self-absorption and delusions are particularly emphasized in *Hadrian the Seventh* (1904), the book for which Rolfe is most remembered. The protagonist of the tale, George Rose, like Rolfe, was rejected for the priesthood. But Rolfe re-creates his story, elevating Rose to a position of grandeur and glory. The Church recalls Rose and acknowledges their mistake, finally appointing him pope. Then, as pope, he conducts his role scandalously, even selling Vatican jewels to raise funds for the poor. The story's mythical dimensions are heightened by Rolfe's use of arcane punctuation and idiosyncratic spellings.

The very same eccentricities, idiosyncrasies, and peccadilloes that alienate many of Rolfe's readers serve to strongly attract others. As Modlish pointed out, "his

[Rolfe's] intensity, his peculiarities which were initially part of his charm, and his ability, in his conversation as well as in his stories, to give events from his life the aura of mythological significance, drew friends and patrons no less ardent in their attention than the 'Corvinists' among his readers." Yet Corvo was unable to sustain that appeal, and some people, mentioned Modlish, "came to feel that he was more a con artist than a literary artist."

Rolfe deserves credit for his experimentation with language and narrative perspective, yet "his technical ability is overshadowed by his penchant for the unusual, which is largely responsible for his individuality as a writer," concluded Modlish.

## BIOGRAPHICAL AND CRITICAL SOURCES:

*BOOKS*

Benkovitz, Miriam J., *Frederic Rolfe, Baron, Corvo: A Biography,* Putnam (New York, NY), 1977.
*Dictionary of Literary Biography,* Gale (Detroit, Mi), Volume 34: *British Novelists, 1890-1929: Traditionalists,* 1984, Volume 156: *British Short-Fiction Writers, 1880-1914: The Romantic Tradition,* 1996.
Johnson, Pamela Hansford, *New Quests for Corvo,* Icon Books, 1965.
Luke, Peter, *Hadrian VII,* Knopf (New York, NY), 1969.
Mix, Katherine Lynn, *A Study in Yellow: The Yellow Book and Its Contributors,* University Press of Kansas, 1960.
Symons, A. J. A., *The Quest for Corvo: An Experiment in Biography,* Michigan State University Press (East Lansing, MI), 1955.
Weeks, Donald, *Corvo,* Joseph, 1971.
Woolf, Cecil, *A Bibliography of Frederick Rolfe, Baron Corvo,* Hart-Davis, 1972.

*PERIODICALS*

*Atlantic Monthly,* August, 1953.
*Nation,* September 5, 1953.
*New Statesman,* October 25, 1958.
*New York Times,* July 19, 1953.

*Time,* February 2, 1959.
*Times Literary Supplement,* September 4, 1959.*

\* \* \*

## ROSEMAN, Mark 1958-

*PERSONAL:* Born September 7, 1958, in London, England; son of Nathan Stephen and Joan Lillian (Hyames) Roseman; married (separated); children: three. *Education:* Christ's College, Cambridge, B.A. (honors), 1979; University of Warwick, Ph.D., 1987.

*ADDRESSES: Office*—Department of History, Room 2081, University of Southampton, Southampton S017 1BJ, England. *E-mail*—m.roseman@soton.ac.uk.

*CAREER:* Warwick University, Coventry, England, seminar teacher in modern German history, 1980-81; Department of Modern Languages, Aston University, Birmingham, England, lecturer, 1984-89; Department of History, Keele University, Keele, Staffordshire, England, lecturer, 1989-94, senior lecturer, 1994-2000; University of Southampton, Southampton, England, professor of modern history, 2000—.

*MEMBER:* German History Society, (committee member, 1988-93; treasurer, 1989-93).

*AWARDS, HONORS:* German Academic Exchange Service Award, 1980, 1981-82; Leverhulme Trust Studentship, 1982-83; German Historical Institute grant, 1983-84; British Academy award, 1989; Goethe Institute grant, 1991, 1993; British Academy grant, 1991, 1995; DAAD research grant, 1991; Keele Research Award, 1994; French Embassy Grant, 1995; Royal Historical Society grant, 1995; History 2000 Award, 1997; Nuffield research grant, 1998; Alexander von Humboldt fellowship, 1998; Arts and Humanities Research Board grant, 2000; Frankel Prize, 2000, Wingate Literary Prize, 2000, and Mark Lynton History Prize, 2002, all for *A Past in Hiding: Memory and Survival in Nazi Germany.*

*WRITINGS:*

*Recasting the Ruhr 1945-1958: Manpower, Economic Recovery and Labour Relations,* Berg, (New York, NY), 1992

(Editor and author of introductory essays) *Generations in Conflict: Youth Rebellion and Generation Formation in Modern Germany 1770-1968,* Cambridge University Press (Cambridge, England), 1995.

*The Past in Hiding: Memory and Survival in Nazi Germany,* Metropolitan Books (New York, NY), 2001.

(Editor, with Carl Levy) *Three Post-War Eras in Comparison: Western Europe, 1918-1945-1989,* Palgrave (New York, NY), 2001.

*The Wannsee Conference and the Final Solution: A Reconsideration,* Metropolitan Books (New York, NY), 2002.

Contributor to books and periodicals.

*SIDELIGHTS:* Historian Mark Roseman's career as a teacher and scholar has led him to specialize in twentieth century German history, with emphasis on the Holocaust and the impact of war on society. He has published extensively on these topics and has gained a reputation for his ability to put a human face on the facts of history. His work has gained favorable critical attention from scholars in the field and is also accessible to the general reader. Roseman's book, *A Past in Hiding: Memorial and Survival in Nazi Germany* has won awards internationally. He is currently professor of modern history at the University of Southampton in England.

*Recasting the Ruhr, 1945-1958: Manpower, Economic Recovery and Labour Relations,* published in 1992, grew out of Roseman's dissertation work directed by Volker Berghan at the University of Warwick. This book is a close examination, divided into two parts, of the history of labor policies designed to restore the coal industry in the Ruhr mining district in Germany. Through extensive use of political and social archival material both in Germany and England, Roseman has revealed, in detail, aspects of the miners' lives as well as the progress of labor relations. The first part of the book is concerned with the period immediately following the end of the war in 1945 until 1948. The mistrust that existed between German and British forces in addition to the competing plans of the other occupying nations is described, providing a full picture of the times. The second half of the book deals with the period from 1948 to 1958, the era of Ludwig Erhard's economic policies. Roseman analyzes and evaluates what he labels the "social engineering" efforts to recruit and retain miners. Housing, entertainment and social values all were scrutinized by the authorities, and attempts were made to re-shape the miners' lives in hopes of retaining a stable workforce. Traditional home designs were rejected and replaced with buildings that the authorities hoped would have more appeal to the miners. There were also attempts to instill attitudes that would increase greater productivity. It was a general effort to re-engineer the miners' culture. The reasons for the failure of this experiment are clearly delineated.

*Generations in Conflict: Youth Revolt and Generation Formation in Germany, 1770-1968* is a collection of essays that grew out of a conference held in 1991 that was formed around the study of generational conflict in Germany. As the editor, Roseman, has put together and introduced a collection of essays from an international group of scholars that addresses various aspects of this topic. The majority of the essays are concerned with the period after 1918, with an emphasis on the generation educated in the Nazi era and their response to the allied occupation. Such titles as "The Ideal of Youth in Eighteenth-Century Germany," "The Generation Conflict That Never Was: Young Labor in the Ruhr Mining Industry 1945-1957," and "German Kriegskinder: Origins and Impact of the Generation of 1968," demonstrate the scope of this collection devoted to the examination of the conflict of German youth and the established order.

The 2002 winner of the Mark Lynton History Prize, *A Past in Hiding: Memorial and Survival in Nazi Germany* is the story of Marianne Strauss, a young German Jew, who escaped being transported to a concentration camp with her family and then lived in Germany, aided by an underground resistance group, until the end of World War II. The story of how her experiences came to light is intriguing and forms an important part of the book. She remained virtually silent about her wartime experiences until the early 1980s when she wrote an article for a German periodical. Roseman saw the article, was interested, and met with her in 1989. Her reluctance to speak at any length remained intact, however, and Roseman left the interview with little information. He contacted her again five years later and this time she was more forthcoming. In the course of three interviews Roseman learned much of the painful, complex story that was to become the book. Marianne Strauss died in

December of 1996. Upon her death Roseman, accompanied by her son, Vivian Ellenbogen, discovered an extensive collection of documents, including postcards, letters, diaries and official papers from her underground life. This is more than an account of her dramatic life during World War II. Through her diaries, letters and the interviews Roseman had with her, he shows the development of this complex woman. *Booklist* reviewer George Cohen called *A Past in Hiding* "an eloquent account of surviving the holocaust."

In *The Wannsee Conference and the Final Solution: A Reconsideration,* Roseman traces the path of discussions between officials in the Nazi government that led to the Holocaust of World War II. The conference held at Wannsee on January 20, 1942 was attended by important figures in the Nazi regime, including chief of police Reinhold Heydrich. Hitler, himself, was absent. Roseman asserts that the meeting was organized to give Heydrich's police complete power in the formation and execution of policies regarding the Jews and to assure the cooperation of the rest of the government departments. The author reminds us that in the beginning Hitler's policies of harassment and discrimination were aimed at promoting Jewish emigration. In the course of the Wannsee conference, Heydrich presented a plan designed to eliminate all Jews by working them to death and killing those who did not succumb to the extreme conditions of forced labor. Roseman points out that although this conference was not the precise "moment of decision," it was the first formal step toward genocide. The minutes of the conference are included at the end of the book. A *Kirkus Reviews* contributor called *The Wannsee Conference and the Final Solution* "A chilling keyhole glimpse of Nazi evil's bureaucratic banality."

## BIOGRAPHICAL AND CRITICAL SOURCES:

*PERIODICALS*

*American Historical Review,* June, 1993, Raymond G. Stokes, review of *Recasting the Ruhr, 1945-1958: Manpower, Economic Recovery and Labour Relations,* pp. 899-900.
*Booklist,* February 15, 2001, George Cohen, review of *The Past in Hiding: Memory and Survival in Nazi Germany,* p. 1113; April 15, 2002 Jay Freeman, review of *The Wannsee Conference and the Final Solution: A Reconsideration,* p. 1379.

*Business History,* July 1993, Frances M. B. Lynch, review of *Recasting the Ruhr, 1945-1958: Manpower, Economic Recovery and Labour Relations,* p. 122.

*Central European History,* 1992, John Gillingham, review of *Recasting the Ruhr, 1945-1958: Manpower, Economic Recovery and Labour Relations,* pp. 484-485.

*English Historical Review,* June, 1997, Bob Moore, review of *Generations in Conflict: Youth Revolt and Generation Formation in Germany, 1770-1968,* p. 809.

*Journal of Modern History,* March, 1995, Diethelm Prowe, review of *Recasting the Ruhr, 1945-1958: Manpower, Economic Recovery and Labour Relations,* pp. 230-234; March, 1998, Michael H. Kater, review of *Generations in Conflict: Youth Revolt and Generation Formation in Germany, 1770-1968,* p. 224.

*Journal of Social History,* summer, 1997, Robert Wegs, review of *Generations in Conflict: Youth Revolt and Generation Formation in Germany, 1770-1968,* p. 1004.

*Kirkus Reviews,* March 1, 2002, review of *The Wannsee Conference and the Final Solution: A Reconsideration,* p. 31.

*Library Journal,* February 1, 2001, Randall L. Schroeder, review of *A Past in Hiding: Memory and Survival in Nazi Germany,* p. 108; April 1, 2002, Barbara Walden, review of *The Wannsee Conference and the Final Solution: A Reconsideration,* p. 125.

*New Statesman,* January 21, 2002, Joanna Bourke, review of *The Wannsee Conference and the Final Solution: A Reconsideration,* p. 52.

*Publishers Weekly,* November 27, 2000, review of *A Past in Hiding: Memory and Survival in Nazi Germany,* p. 61; March 4, 2002, review of *The Wannsee Conference and the Final Solution: A Reconsideration,* p. 65.

OTHER

*University of Southampton Web site,* http://www.soton.ac.uk/~mr5/ (June 6, 2002).*

*       *       *

## RUSSELL, Joan Plummer 1930-

*PERSONAL:* Born February 24, 1930; daughter of Thomas F. and Sibyl Fahnestock Plummer; married Robert M. V. Russell (in sales), 1952; children: Mary-Sibyl, Virginia, Sheridan, Beth, Margy, Kate, Rob, John, Tom. *Education:* Graduated Chevy Chase Junior College, 1950. *Politics:* Conservative. *Religion:* Catholic.

*ADDRESSES: Home*—Northern OH. *Agent*—c/o Author's Mail, Boyd's Mills Press, 815 Church St., Honesdale, PA 18431. *E-mail*—sjprq@yahoo.com.

*CAREER:* Author and full-time mother. Worked as a member of the Pastoral Care Team at St. Alexis Hospital.

*MEMBER:* Police Writers Association (associate member), U.S. Police Canine Association, Shaker Heights Citizens Police Alumni (secretary).

*AWARDS, HONORS:* Children's Book Award (primary nonfiction category), International Reading Association, 2002, for *Aero and Officer Mike, Police Partners.*

*WRITINGS:*

*Aero and Officer Mike, Police Partners,* photographs by Kris Turner Sinnenberg, Boyds Mills Press (Honesdale, PA), 2001.

*WORK IN PROGRESS:* A children's book on firefighters; an adult book on law enforcement.

*SIDELIGHTS:* Joan Plummer Russell told *CA:* "My grandmother wrote a bestseller (with a *New York Times* listing) when she was fifty. I have been encouraged to write, always. I never felt I had a subject I was interested in enough to put it on paper.

"I joined our local Citizens Police Academy, a ten-week course of three hours each week. Different police departments gave talks on their duties, gave demonstrations, and let us take part in shooting on the range and riding on patrol.

"On patrol I met Corporal Mike Matsik and his handsome K9 partner, Aero. Mike invited me to ride on several patrols with him. I was fascinated with what this team could do. I asked Mike if he was interested in working on a book with me. He did not hesitate, but said, 'If the Chief okays it, yes.'

"Our Chief of Police immediately gave me permission to ride with Mike for two shifts a month for two years as I collected dozens of photos and many, many taped conversations, some filled with Aero barking!

"By some magic, I found a lovely editor who helped me make changes. Boyds Mills Press published my book. They did a wonderful layout. I am very proud of my book. I was often invited to observe many training days when officers and their dogs met twice a month for extra training, for me a great joy to see a well-trained team at work.

"Mike and I are often asked to give talks locally in libraries and schools, and of course, Aero steals the show, letting kids pet him. My aim was to show that K9s are not aggressive biting dogs unless you are the bad guy! They are gentle pets who love to have their tummy scratched when they are not on duty. I did get my book approved by our local Law Department before submitting for publication. The success of my book continues to surprise and delight me! I am now working on another children's book and one for adults, concerning law enforcement. They are my heroes."

*BIOGRAPHICAL AND CRITICAL SOURCES:*

*PERIODICALS*

*Booklist,* Shelley Townsend-Hudson, review of *Aero and Mike: Police Partners,* p. 229.
*Childhood Education,* spring, 2002, Linda Gibbs, review of *Aero and Officer Mike: Police Partners,* p. 172.
*School Library Journal,* December, 2001, Lynn Dye, review of *Aero and Officer Mike,* p. 128; June, 2002, "Book Awards," p. 22.

\*     \*     \*

**RYLANDS, Enriqueta Augustina Tennant 1843-1908**

*PERSONAL:* Born May 31, 1843, in Cuba; died February 4, 1908; daughter of a merchant; married John Rylands (an industrialist and book collector), October 6, 1875 (died 1888).

*CAREER:* Worked at John Rylands Library, Manchester University, Manchester, England, 1889-1908.

*AWARDS, HONORS:* Freedom of the City of Manchester, 1899; L.L.D., Victoria University of Manchester.

*WRITINGS:*

*Catalogue of the Printed Books and Manuscripts in the John Rylands Library, Manchester,* three volumes, edited by Edward Gordon Duff, J. E. Cornish (Manchester, England), 1899.
*Catalogue of the Manuscripts, Books, and Bookbindings Exhibited at the Opening of the John Rylands Library, Manchester, October 6th,* [Manchester, England], 1899.

*SIDELIGHTS:* Enriqueta Augustina Tennant Rylands established in her late husband's name one of the most impressive collections of medieval manuscripts and theological rarities in England. Her legacy to English literature, the John Rylands Library, opened in Manchester, England, in 1900. Rylands had been married to one of Britain's most dedicated book collectors for just over a dozen years, but she continued John Rylands' passion for acquiring sacred music, early printed Bibles and other religious-themed treasures until her own death.

Little is known about Rylands' early life. Cuba then was a colony of the Spanish empire, with vast sugar plantations and many slaves. Her father, a merchant whose business profited from ships that ferried cargo on the trade route between Havana and Liverpool, England, died when Rylands was five. Her mother remarried, and Rylands was sent abroad to schools in New York, Paris, and London. She was thirty-two when she married and had abandoned her Roman Catholic faith. Little else is known of Rylands' life before she wed John Rylands, partly because she ordered that all her personal papers and effects be destroyed when she died.

John Rylands, an English industrialist, derived his wealth from a family textile firm in Manchester, England that he guided to prosperity during the nineteenth century. Twice widowed, he was seventy-four when he married Enriqueta Tennant; the third Mrs. Rylands had been the companion of his ailing second wife for several years. The couple lived at his large manor house outside Manchester called Longford Hall, at which her husband had already spent part of his fortune in filling it with art. His true passion, however, was acquiring rare books and manuscripts, particularly religious ones. A devout Congregationalist, John Rylands generously donated to charities.

With her husband, Rylands became involved in these activities. He paid to print Bibles, for instance, and distributed them to the public; he did the same with hymnals, such as *The Cavendish Hymnal* from 1864 and *Hymns of the Church Universal. In Two Parts. I. The Spirit of the Psalms. II. General Hymns,* printed in 1885 with her name on the title page. After her husband's death she kept donating copies of this hymnal to the poor. Rylands took interest in her husband's collection of sacred music, some of it rare. His library at Longford Hall contained collections of hymns translated from the early Greek and Latin, others dating from the Middle Ages, and still others that were significant to the early years of the Protestant Reformation in Germany.

Scholars assume Rylands contributed to her husband's bibliophile activities, and likely helped compile a two-volume catalogue of his manuscript that dates from 1881. After he died, she wished to honor him and his interest in theology and religious philanthropy. She acquired a parcel of land in the city of Manchester and commissioned a leading architect to create a grand library in the Gothic style. The John Rylands Library, which opened to the public in 1900, took nearly a decade to build. It was fireproof, and one of the first public buildings lit by electricity. Its original wiring remained until 1994.

Rylands also continued her husband's manuscript acquisitions, boosting the library's collection. Advised by the Reverend Samuel Gosnell Green and his son, John Arnold Green, she began to purchase many books on theology. The younger Green helped arrange the transactions with English booksellers and dealers in antiquities, since Rylands wished to conceal her identity. "Mrs. Rylands did not always approve of Green's purchases," wrote Brenda J. Scragg in the *Dictionary of Literary Biography.* "He had a broader view of the library's purpose than his client, and from early in his association with her he viewed the Rylands Library as an important national institution."

The one acquisition on which they agreed was the Althorp Library. The sale of this treasure in 1892 to Rylands by the fifth Earl Spencer, John Poyntz Spencer (the ninth earl, Charles Spencer, is the brother of the late Diana, Princess of Wales), was a coup for the Rylands Library. George John Spencer, the second Earl Spencer, had founded the Althorp Library and its 43,000 volumes included a great collection of very early printed Bibles.

An American collector had reportedly offered 300,000 pounds, but Rylands and Green paid 210,000 pounds and the treasure remained in England. It was shipped in 600 special boxes over three months from Northamptonshire to Manchester on farm wagons and railroad cars. The transaction was ultimately leaked to the media, and the *Manchester Guardian* identified Rylands as the Althorp Library buyer.

Rylands hired Edward Gordon Duff in 1893 as its librarian. Duff issued *The Catalogue of the Printed Books and Manuscripts in the John Rylands Library, Manchester* in 1899. That same year, Henry Guppy became partner to Duff for the job, but as Scragg explained, "increasing differences of opinion with Mrs. Rylands caused Duff to resign shortly after the opening of the Rylands Library, and Guppy was then the sole librarian." The building opened with a grand ceremony on October 6, 1899, what would have been the Rylands' twenty-fourth wedding anniversary. More than 600 invitees attended, and Rylands that day became the first female to receive the honor of Freedom of the City from Manchester civic authorities. That evening, she hosted a lavish fete at the library for a thousand guests. Many of the Rylands Library's rarities were on display, including ten bibles in Latin, Greek and Hebrew, and a collection of seventy-four different types of bookbindings.

Rylands planned for a board to run the library, and its mission statement read, in part, that the "Rylands Library is intended to afford free access for Scholars, Authors, Students and serious readers generally, to the best Literature of the ancient and modern world, especially in the departments of Theology, Philosophy, the Moral Sciences and Universal History." In 1901, she and her agents acquired a second significant collection, that of the Earl of Crawford, from a manor house called Haigh Hall.

Extant correspondence shows Rylands an astute purchaser of the Rylands Library rarities and an apparent bargainer. "It has often been said that Mrs. Rylands relied heavily on her advisers in the choice of books for the library," Scragg said. "This assertion is certainly true, but it should not be forgotten that she had an excellent education and was a good linguist, speaking Spanish and French and perhaps Italian." After her death, another 3,000 rarities came to the Rylands Library from her home at Longford Hall. The John Rylands Library became part of Manchester University in 1972.

*BIOGRAPHICAL AND CRITICAL SOURCES:*

*BOOKS*

*Dictionary of Literary Biography,* Volume 184: *Nineteenth-Century British Book Collectors and Bibliographers,* Gale (Detroit, MI), 1997, pp. 388-398.

Guppy, Henry, *The John Rylands Library, Manchester: 1899-1935. A Brief Record of Its History with Descriptions of the Building and Its Contents,* Manchester University Press (Manchester, England), 1935.*

# S

## SALTUS, Edgar 1855-1921
### (Myndart Verelst)

PERSONAL: Born October 8, 1855, in New York, NY; died July 31, 1921; buried in Tarrytown, NY; son of Francis Henry (a businessman and an inventor) and Eliza (Howe) Evertson; married Helen Sturges Read, 1883 (divorced); married Elsie Walsh Smith (divorced); married Marie Giles, 1911; children: (second marriage) Elsie. *Education:* Attended Yale University, 1875; attended schools in Heidelberg, Munich, and Paris; Columbia University, LL.D., 1880.

CAREER: Writer.

WRITINGS:

*Balzac,* Houghton, Mifflin (Boston, MA), 1884.

*The Philosophy of Disenchantment,* Houghton, Mifflin (Boston, MA), 1885.

*The Anatomy of Negation,* Scribner & Welford (New York, NY), 1886, revised edition, Belford, Clarke (Chicago, IL), 1889.

*Mr. Incoul's Misadventure,* Benjamin & Bell (New York, NY), 1887.

*The Truth about Tristrem Varick,* Belford, Clarke (Chicago, IL), 1888.

*Eden: An Episode,* Belford, Clarke (Chicago, IL), 1888.

*A Transaction in Hearts: An Episode,* Belford, Clarke (Chicago, IL), 1889.

*The Pace That Kills: A Chronicle,* Belford, Clarke (Chicago, IL), 1889.

*A Transient Guest and Other Episodes,* Belford, Clarke (Chicago, IL), 1889.

*Love and Lore,* Belford (New York, NY), 1890.

*Mary Magdalen: A Chronicle,* Belford (New York, NY), 1891, published as *Mary of Magdala: A Chronicle,* Osgood & McIlvaine (London, England), 1891.

*Imperial Purple,* Morrill, Higgins (Chicago, IL), 1892.

*The Facts in the Curious Case of H. Hyrtl, Esq.,* Collier (New York, NY), 1892.

*Madam Sapphira: A Fifth Avenue Story,* Neely (New York, NY), 1893.

*Enthralled: A Story of International Life Setting Forth the Curious Circumstances Concerning Lord Cloden and Oswald Quain,* Tudor (London, England), 1894, AMS Press (New York, NY), 1969.

*When Dreams Come True: A Story of Emotional Life,* Collier (New York, NY), 1894.

*The Lovers of the World,* 3 volumes, Collier (New York, NY), 1896-1897.

*Purple and Fine Women,* Ainslee (New York, NY), 1903.

*Wit and Wisdom from Edgar Saltus,* edited by G. F. Monkshood and George Gamble, Greening (London, England), 1903.

*The Pomps of Satan,* Greening (London, England), 1904, Kennerley (New York, NY), 1906.

*The Perfume of Eros: A Fifth Avenue Incident,* Wessels (New York, NY), 1905.

*Vanity Square: A Story of Fifth Avenue Life,* Lippincott (Philadelphia, PA), 1906.

*Historia Amoris: A History of Love, Ancient and Modern,* Kennerley (New York, NY), 1906, republished as *Love throughout the Ages,* Sisley (London, England), 1908.

*The Lords of the Ghostland: A History of the Ideal,* Kennerley (New York, NY), 1907.

*Daughters of the Rich,* Kennerley (New York, NY), 1909.

*The Monster,* Pulitzer (New York, NY), 1912.

*Oscar Wilde: An Idler's Impression,* Brothers of the Book (Chicago, IL), 1917.

*The Paliser Case,* Boni & Liveright (New York, NY), 1919.

*The Imperial Orgy: An Account of the Tsars from the First to the Last,* Boni & Liveright (New York, NY), 1920.

*The Gardens of Aphrodite,* Pennell Club (Philadelphia, PA), 1920.

*The Ghost Girl,* Boni & Liveright (New York, NY), 1922.

*Parnassians Personally Encountered,* Torch Press (Cedar Rapids, Iowa), 1923.

*The Uplands of Dream,* edited, with an introduction by Charles Honce, Covici (Chicago, IL), 1925.

*Victor Hugo and Golgotha,* Covici (Chicago, IL), 1925.

(With Marie Saltus) *Poppies and Mandragora,* Vinal (New York, NY), 1926.

*OTHER*

(Contributor and translator, under pseudonym Myndart Verelst) *Honoré de Balzac, After-Dinner Stories from Balzac,* Coombes (New York, NY), 1886.

(Contributor and translator, under pseudonym Myndart Verelst) Théophile Gautier and Mérimée Prosper, *Tales before Supper from Théophile Gautier and Mérimée Prosper,* Brentano's (New York, NY), 1887.

(Contributor) Jules Amédée Barbey d'Aurevilly, *The Story without a Name,* Belford (Chicago, IL), 1891.

(Contributor) Wolfgang Menzel, *Germany from the Earliest Period,* translation by Mrs. George Horrocks, Collier (New York, NY), 1898.

Alfred Rambaud, *Russia,* translation by Leonora B. Lang, Collier (New York, NY), 1898.

(Contributor) J. Talboys Wheeler, *India and the Frontier States of Afghanistan, Nipal and Burma,* Collier (New York, NY), 1899.

(Contributor) W. L. George, *A Bed of Roses,* Boni & Liveright (New York, NY), 1919.

(Contributor) Oscar Wilde, *Salomé, The Importance of Being Earnest, Lady Windermere's Fan,* Boni & Liveright (New York, NY), 1919.

Contributor to periodical publications, including *Ainslee's* and *The Smart Set.*

*SIDELIGHTS:* Edgar Saltus is known for his staunch rejection of the sentimentality of late-nineteenth-century literature. Instead, he countered the optimism and false spirituality with a hedonism, pessimism, eroticism, and melodrama that pervaded his novels, essays, and short stories. Arthur Symons, writing in his *Dramatis Personae,* found that Saltus' writings "exhale a kind of exotic and often abnormal perfume of colors, colors of sensations, of heats, of crowded atmospheres." W. L. George, in his introduction to Saltus' collection *Purple and Fine Women,* called the author's style "essentially oriental and fantastic. . . . He makes a world about him, sensuous and aesthetic, a world of chinchilla, emeralds, and Malines lace, where evolve only people to whom work is an incident, and perhaps love an accident." In addition to his fiction, Saltus also wrote several philosophical studies of pessimism and disenchantment.

Saltus' most acclaimed works include *Imperial Purple,* a collection of essays on Roman historical figures; the companion volumes *The Philosophy of Disenchantment* and *The Anatomy of Negation,* Saltus' treatises on decadence and nihilism; and his novels, *Mr. Incoul's Misadventure* and *The Truth about Tristrem Varick.*

Although Saltus initially earned high praise for his clever phrasing and urbane wit, many critics claim the writer eventually sacrificed meaning for style. H. L. Mencken, in his *Prejudices: Fifth Series,* described Saltus as "simply a bright young fellow who succumbed to his own cleverness. The goady glittering phrase enchanted him." Saltus' work continues to attract a small cult following of readers, yet his lurid eroticism, sensationalism, and cynicism have generally kept him outside the literary mainstream.

Born into a wealthy family in New York society, Saltus traveled and studied in Europe. When Saltus was seven, his parents separated and he remained with his mother, Eliza. According to Saltus' third wife, Marie, as noted in her biography of her husband, Eliza lavished money and attention on Edgar. Saltus attended Yale University for two semesters and then studied in Paris, Heidelberg and Munich. While he was abroad, the pessimistic philosophy of Arthur Schopenhauer and the aesthetics and mood of French writers captivated him. Saltus returned to the United States and received a law degree from Columbia University, though he never practiced law.

Saltus' literary career began with *Balzac,* a biography highly praised for its graceful and lively treatment. Honoré de Balzac, Victor Hugo, and Gustave Flaubert were among Saltus' favorite writers—from them he learned precision and craftsmanship. In his second book, *The Philosophy of Disenchantment,* Saltus established his trademark pessimistic philosophy and themes. The essays in this book, along with those in its companion volume, *The Anatomy of Negation,* illuminate Schopenhauer's philosophy that life is nothing but despair and suffering. Saltus believed, as Carol Sue Hubbell noted in the *Dictionary of Literary Biography,* that "the prospects for contentment are greater for the pessimist who expects suffering . . . than for [someone] with high expectations." Speaking of *The Anatomy of Negation,* Carl Van Vechten, in his *Excavations: A Book of Advocacies,* said: "Never was any book, so full of erudition and ideas, written by a true sceptic so easy to read."

Saltus' first novel, *Mr. Incoul's Misadventure,* became an immediate sensation. As Percival Pollard noted in *Their Day in Court,* "Mr. Saltus was of those who spurred the general interest in sex stories." When the protagonist, Mr. Incoul, suspects his wife of being unfaithful, murder and suicide follow. This melodramatic story of the diabolical Incoul reveals how Saltus can construct a suspenseful, entertaining tale, yet criticisms varied. Although a critic in the *Literary World* noted that Saltus "has a style of his own, and this style, while not free from affectations, is brilliant, subtle, abounding in color," the same critic concluded that the novel "is not an agreeable novel to read, and it leaves a bad taste in the mouth." Other reviewers cited *Mr. Incoul's Misadventure* as one of Saltus' best novels. Van Wyck Brooks, in his *The Confident Years: 1885-1915,* called Saltus' style "translucent and restrained," and Van Vechten saw "pages permeated with suspense, horror, information, cynicism, and an icy charm."

Many of Saltus' other fifteen novels also deal with unrequited love and the pursuit of the ideal, yet most observers viewed his second novel, *The Truth of Tristrem Varick,* as a noteworthy example of Saltus' stylistics and storytelling. The story follows Tristrem Varick's quest for the love of the gorgeous Viola Rari-

tan—a pursuit, really, of "the chimera of his imagination," as Symons noted. The hero obsesses with this pursuit. Hubbell wrote: "He rationalizes her signals of disinterest to suit his dream and continues to pursue her, eventually assuming the role of her protector to the point of murdering her dishonorable lover." Hubbell added: "Confusion develops between illusion and reality, emotion and reason, and . . . virtue and vice. Tristrem mistakes his emotional vision for truth and pursues a dream as if it were reality." The plot is rife with bizarre incidents and crises culminating when Varick is sent to the electric chair. Although the themes are unmistakably pessimistic, Saltus infuses playfulness. The tightly woven plot, suspense and clever irony make *The Truth of Tristrem Varick* one of Saltus' most highly acclaimed works.

*Imperial Purple,* a collection of essays on historic Roman personalities, is generally considered Saltus' finest work. This lyrical, even outrageous account of the excesses and decadence of powerful Roman emperors, involves malicious characters that are not entirely fictional. Hubbell explained: "A picture of the caesars of Imperial Rome in a luxuriously draped parade of corruption, it [*Imperial Purple*] may be read as a study in the corruptibility of human nature and the insatiability of power." Symons said the book shows "the zenith of Saltus's talent." Eric McKitrick, writing in the *American Quarterly,* claimed *Imperial Purple* was "undoubtedly Edgar Saltus' masterpiece. Nothing he ever did, before or after, quite came up to it." Mencken found *Imperial Purple* holds up. "A certain fine glow is still in it; it has gusto if not profundity." Saltus' detractors, however, saw *Imperial Purple* as another opportunity for Saltus to revel in depravity. The book, according to Hubbell, "reinforced the aura of wickedness imputed to him by his popular 'erotic' novels, tame by today's standards, and his troubled marriages."

Many readers found Saltus' cynicism, hedonism, and luridness unpalatable. Many others admired the writer, yet found Saltus lacking substance, commitment, and conviction. McKitrick praised much of Saltus' work, yet he said there is within them "a gnawing fear of involvement, a terrible unwillingness to be spiritually, morally, or intellectually engaged, even in the simplest way." Regardless, Saltus earned a reputation for seeing through the sentimental, superficial society of his time, and providing a brave alternative.

*BIOGRAPHICAL AND CRITICAL SOURCES:*

*BOOKS*

Brooks, Van Wyck, *The Confident Years: 1885-1915,* Dutton (New York, NY), 1952.
De Casseres, Benjamin, *Forty Immortals,* Joseph Lawren (New York, NY), 1926.
*Dictionary of Literary Biography,* Volume 202: *Nineteenth-Century American Fiction Writers,* Gale (Detroit, MI), 1999.
Mencken, H. L., *Prejudices: Fifth Series,* Knopf (New York, NY), 1926.
Pollard, Percival, *Their Day in Court,* Neale (New York, NY), 1909.
Saltus, Edgar, *Purple and Fine Women,* Covici (Chicago, IL), 1925.
Saltus, Marie, *Edgar Saltus, the Man,* Covici (Chicago, IL), 1925.
Sprague, Claire, *Edgar Saltus,* Twayne (New York, NY), 1968.
Symons, Arthur, *Dramatis Personae,* Bobbs-Merrill (Indianapolis, IN), 1923.
Van Vechten, Carl, *Excavations: A Book of Advocacies,* Knopf (New York, NY), 1926.

*PERIODICALS*

*American Quarterly,* spring, 1951, pp. 22-35.
*Broom,* June, 1922, pp. 250-60.
*Literary World,* October 15, 1887, p. 347.
*New Englander and Yale Review,* June, 1888, pp. 432-442.
*New Republic,* November 29, 1922, pp. 23-24.
*New York Review of Books,* November 5, 1970, pp. 41-42.
*New York Times,* June 9, 1906, p. 365.
*Philistine,* October, 1907, pp. 129-143.
*Tulane Studies in English,* Volume 23, 1978, pp. 61-69.
*Westminster Review,* October, 1904, pp. 463-174.*

\*            \*            \*

## SCHMIDT, Michael 1945-

*PERSONAL:* Born October 6, 1945, in Berlin, Germany; married Angelika Miersch, 1968 (divorced, 1974); married Karin Kopto, 1982; children: Olivia. *Education:* Self-taught in photography; passed external examination as graduate photo-designer at Fachhochschule, Dortmund, 1980.

*ADDRESSES: Agent*—Galerie Rudolf Springer, Fasanenstrasse 13, 1000 Berlin 12, Germany.

*CAREER:* Freelance photographer, Berlin, Germany, 1965—. Volkhochschule, Berlin-Kreuzberg, instructor in photography, 1969—; Pädagogische Hochschule, Berlin, Germany, instructor, 1976-78; Universität FB4, Essen, Germany, instructor, 1979-80. Member, Deutsche Gesellschaft für Photographie, and Gesellschaft Deutsche Lichtbildner. *Exhibitions:* Individual exhibitions include Berlin Museum, West Berlin, Germany, 1973; Galerie Springer, West Berlin, 1975; Landesbildstelle, Hamburg, Germany, 1977; Kunstamt Wedding, West Berlin, 1978; Galerie Springer, West Berlin; Forum Stadtpakr, Graz, Austria, 1982; Poll Studio, West Berlin, 1983; Dryphoto Prato, Italy, 1984; Museuo di Rimini, Italy, 1985; *U-ni-ty,* Museum of Modern Art, New York, NY, 1996. Group exhibitions include *Aspekte Deutscher Landschaftsfotografie,* Stadtmuseum Munich, Germany, 1978; *In Deutschland,* Rheinisches Landesmuseum, Bonn, Germany, 1979; *Michael Schumidt und Schüler,* Werkstatt für Fotografie der VHS Kreuzberg, West Berlin, 1980; *Larry Fink/Andreas Müller-Pohle/Michael Schmidt,* Künstmuseum, Dusseldorf, Germany, 1981; *Photographie en Allemagne 1920-82,* Musée de Besançon, France, 1982; *Photography from Berlin,* Castelli Graphics, New York, NY, 1984; *Das fotografische Selbstporträt,* Künstverein, Stuttgart, Germany, 1985; *Reste des Authentischen,* Museum Folkwang, Essen, West Germany, 1986; and *New Photography 4,* Museum of Modern Art, New York, NY, 1988. Work included permanent collections including Berlinische Galerie, Berlin; Stadtmuseum Munich; Musée d'Art et d'Histoire, Frebourg, Switzerland; Bibliothèque Nationale, Paris; and Museum für Kunst und Gwerbe, Hamburg.

*WRITINGS:*

*Berlin-Kreuzberg,* [West Berlin, Germany], 1973.
*Michael Schmidt Photographien,* [West Berlin, Germany], 1975.
(Photographer) Heinz Ohff, *Berlin: Stadtlandschaft und Menschen,* [West Berlin, Germany], 1978.
(Photographer) Heinz Ohff, *Berlin-Wedding,* [West Berlin, Germany], 1978.
*Michael Schmidt: Stadtslandschaften,* [Essen, West Germany], 1981.
(Photographer) Ernst Klee, *Benachteiligt,* [West Berlin, Germany], 1982.

*Michael Schmidt: Berlin-Kreuzbert Stadtbilder,* [West Berlin, Germany], 1983.

(Photographer) Einar Schleef, *Waffenruhe* (title means "Cease-Fire"), D. Nishen (Berlin, Germany), 1987.

(Photographer) Paolo Costantini, *Correggio,* translated by Leslie Morrow, Arcadia Edizioni (Rubiera, Italy), 1991.

(Photographer) *U-ni-ty,* Scalo Publishers, 1995.


*EXHIBITION CATALOGUES*


(Photographer) Klaus Honnef, *In Deutschland,* [Bonn, Germany], 1979.

(Photographer) *Michael Schmidt und Schüler,* [West Berlin, Germany], 1980.

(Photographer) *Museum Folkwang: Die Fotografische Sammlung,* introduction by Ute Eskildsen, [Essen, West Germany], 1983.

(Photographer) *Michael Schmidt, Bilder 1979-86,* edited by Peter Gauditz and others, [Hanover, Germany], 1987.

(Photographer) *Frauen,* König (Cologne, Germany), 2000.


Also contributed articles to *Camera,* 1979; wrote article in exhibition catalogue, *Thomas Leuner: Notizen aus einer Stadt,* West Berlin, 1980.


*SIDELIGHTS:* At first, photography was a hobby for Michael Schmidt that he pursued as he worked at his job as a city official in Berlin, Germany. When he was twenty years old, with no training in the medium, he started using a miniature camera. Five years later, in 1969, he was teaching a course in photography at the Volkhochschulse in Berlin-Dreuzberg, and he eventually organized photography seminars and workshops. Schmidt has gone on to publish books of photography and exhibit his work throughout Europe and the United States. "Working in a style that is impressionistic and seemingly casual, he fashions images that are simultaneously personal and political. . . . [and] imbues his art with a sense of foreboding," noted *New York Times* reviewer Andy Grundberg.

Schmidt quit his city job in 1973, the same year his first book, *Berlin-Kreuzberg,* was published and an exhibit of the same name was held in the Berlin Museum. The focus of the project is Berlin: its streets and houses and its residents. "It is a forceful and thrill-ing small format photography concentrating more on subject than on faultless reproduction. The social tendency is obvious, and a certain ruggedness of style is evidence of the photographer's temperament," observed a *Contemporary Photographers* writer. Schmidt continued to examine the landscape and people of Berlin subsequent other projects. In *Berlin: Stadtlandschaft und Menschen,* his next book, the images of the city are separate from those of the people. There is a lot to see in the pictures, but they do not tell stories as much as record reality. Described the *Contemporary Photographers* writer, "Instead of 'interesting' or picturesque detail, there are now views where many details are to be seen, which the eye is asked to discover. Neither focus nor lighting is accentuated." *Berlin-Wedding* also focuses on the city as its subject, dividing the photos of people into a separate section. The pictures are somber and sunless, shot in refracted daylight in full focus with a 9 x 12 mm camera. "His people offer themselves in icy seriousness," remarked the *Contemporary Photographers* writer. "They appear sterile, and their rooms, in general, are no less sterile. It is a terrifying analysis of modern uniformity."

Schmidt participated in a group exhibition at the Museum of Modern Art in New York City called *New Photography 4* in 1988, his photographs for this show taken from his book *Waffenruhe.* Images of the Berlin Wall are prominent, as is fitting of the book's subject of cease-fire, and Schmidt also included shots of the city's decaying infrastructure and its toughened denizens. Reflected *New York Times* reviewer Grundberg, Shmidt's "portraits of his contemporaries and of a younger generation modeling itself after punk culture have a chilling effect. The expressions are hard-edged, the eyes as obdurate as metal. It is as if cynicism were the price of survival."

*U-ni-ty,* Schmidt's exhibit and related book project that explores the question of what it means to be German, is composed both of his own black-and-white photographs and of those from the mass media. The pictures are displayed with no captions or titles, making time periods ambiguous so it is difficult to tell if images, such as those of parading gymnasts or troops of soldiers, are from Nazi Germany, Communist Germany, or unified Germany. Schmidt also offers contrasts between nostalgic clichés of German life, such as sweeping mountain scenes and traveling musicians, and harsh shots of polluted landscapes and gloomy barracks-style apartments. "Mr. Schmidt creates a kind of meditation on history and identity by juxtaposing painfully familiar images from Germany's troubled past with scenes from its uncertain present. The results raise more questions than they answer, which is undoubtedly [his] intention," said Charles Hagen in the *New York Times*.

*BIOGRAPHICAL AND CRITICAL SOURCES:*

*BOOKS*

*Contemporary Photographers,* 3rd edition, St. James Press (Detroit, MI), 1996.

*PERIODICALS*

*New York Times,* December 2, 1988, Andy Grundberg, "Urbane Images of Alienation and Voyeurism," p. C1, C30; January 26, 1996, Charles Hagen, "Seeking the Meaning of Being German Today," p. C3.*

\*  \*  \*

### SCOTT, J. K(eith) L. 1966-

*PERSONAL:* Born September 30, 1966, in Lurgan, Northern Ireland. *Education:* Jesus College, Oxford University, B.A., 1989; University of Wales College of Cardiff, Ph.D., 1993. *Hobbies and other interests:* "Strong coffee, Portishead, Neil Gaiman's 'Sandman', and raccoons."

*ADDRESSES: Office*—Department of Modern Languages, De Montfort University, The Gateway, Leicester LE1 9BH, England. *E-mail*—jklscott@dmu.ac.uk.

*CAREER:* Lecturer in French, University of Wales College of Cardiff, 1993-99; senior lecturer in French, De Montfort University, Leicester, England, 1999—.

*WRITINGS:*

*From Dreams to Despair: An Integrated Reading of the Novels of Boris Vian,* Rodopi BV Editions (Amsterdam, Netherlands), 1998.

Contributor to reference volumes, including *Encyclopedia of Literary Translations into English,* Fitzroy Dearborn, 2000, and *On Translating French Literature and Film,* edited by G. Harris, Rodopi, 1996. Contributor to various scholarly journals, including *French Cultural Studies, French Studies Bulletin,* and *Cincinnati Romance Review.*

*SIDELIGHTS:* J. K. L. Scott, who teaches in the Department of Modern Languages at De Montfort University in Leicester, England, is the author of the definitive study of twentieth-century French novelist, poet, and existentialist playwright Boris Vian (1920-1959). Although he wrote under the pen name Vernan Sullivan, Vian is best remembered as the author of a series of crime novels in the hardboiled tradition of American writers such as Mickey Spillane and James M. Cain.

Writing in *American Book Review,* reviewer Bart Plantenga described Scott's book *From Dreams to Despair* as "a meticulous bookworm's textual analysis of Vian's novels." Plantenga added, "[The book] attempts to 'read' Vian's life through a close reading of his novels. This commendable effort, cobbled together with perspiration/admiration, is, however, like any travel guide, best called upon as one journeys through Vian's own writings."

*BIOGRAPHICAL AND CRITICAL SOURCES:*

*PERIODICALS*

*American Book Review,* January-February, 2000, Bert Plantenga, "Pataphysical Anarchist," pp. 21-22.

*OTHER*

*DeMontfort University Web site,* http://www.cta.dmu.ac.uk/ (February 8, 2002).*

\*  \*  \*

### SEARS, Martha 1945-

*PERSONAL:* Born Martha Vivian McMenamy, January 24, 1945, in St. Louis, MO; married William Sears, 1966; children: eight. *Education:* DePaul School of Nursing, St. Louis, MO, 1965; Postgraduate fellowship, St. Louis University, St. Louis, MO, 1966; study at the International Childbirth Education Association, 1975; Lactation Institute of Los Angeles, Los Angeles, CA, certified as a breastfeeding consultant, 1983. *Religion:* Baptist.

*ADDRESSES: Office*—Sears Family Pediatric Practice, 655 Camino de los Mares, Suite 117, San Clemente, CA 92672.

*CAREER:* Author, lecturer, and childbirth educator. Breastfeeding Center, San Clemente, CA, director; numerous appearances on news and talk shows, including *Good Morning America* and *Oprah.*

*MEMBER:* LaLeche League International.

*WRITINGS:*

WITH HUSBAND, WILLIAM SEARS

*The Ministry of Parenting Your Baby,* Life Journey Books (Elgin, IL), 1990.

*Keys to Breastfeeding,* Barrons (New York, NY), 1991.

*Preparing for Your New Baby,* Life Journey Books, (Elgin, IL), 1991.

*300 Questions New Parents Ask: About Pregnancy, Childbirth and Infant & Child Care,* Plume, (New York, NY), 1991.

*The Baby Book: Everything You Need to Know About Your Baby—from Birth to Age Two,* Little, Brown, (Boston, MA), 1993, revised, 2003.

*The Birth Book: Everything You Need to Know to Have a Safe and Satisfying Birth,* Little, Brown (Boston, MA), 1994.

*The New Baby Planner,* Thomas Nelson (Nashville, TN), 1994.

*Twenty-five Things Every New Mother Should Know,* Harvard Common Press, (Boston, MA), 1995.

*The Discipline Book: Everything You Need to Know to Have a Better-Behaved Child—from Birth to Age Ten,* Little Brown (Boston, MA), 1995.

*Parenting the Fussy Baby and High-Need Child: Everything You Need to Know—from Birth to Age Five,* Little, Brown (Boston, MA), 1996.

*The Complete Book of Christian Parenting,* Broadman & Holman Publishers (Nashville, TN), 1997.

(With Linda H. Holt) *The Pregnancy Book: A Month-by-Month Guide,* Little, Brown (Boston, MA), 1997.

*The Growing Years,* Thomas Nelson (Nashville, TN), 1998.

*Now That Baby is Home,* Thomas Nelson (Nashville, TN), 1998.

*So You're Going to be a Parent,* Thomas Nelson (Nashville, TN), 1998.

*The Family Nutrition Book: Everything You Need to Know about Feeding Your Children—from Birth through Adolescence* Little, Brown (Boston, MA), 1999.

*The Breastfeeding Book: Everything You Need to Know Nursing Your Child from Birth through Weaning,* Little Brown, (Boston, MA), 2000.

*The Attachment Parenting Book: A Commonsense Guide to Understanding and Nurturing Your Child,* Little, Brown, (Boston, MA), 2001.

*Feeding the Picky Eater,* Little, Brown (Boston, MA), 2001.

*The First Three Months,* Little, Brown (Boston, MA), 2001.

*Baby on the Way,* Little, Brown (Boston, MA), 2001.

*How to Get Your Baby to Sleep,* Little, Brown (Boston, MA), 2001.

*Keeping Your Baby Healthy,* Little, Brown (Boston, MA), 2001.

(With Christie Watts Kelly) *What Baby Needs,* illustrated by Renee Andriani, Little, Brown (Boston, MA), 2001.

*Eat Healthy, Feel Great: A Kid's Guide to Nutrition,* Little, Brown (Boston, MA), 2002.

(With Elizabeth Pantley) *The Successful Child: What Parents Can Do to Help Kids Turn Out Well,* Little, Brown (Boston, MA), 2002.

(With Christie Watts Kelly) *You Can Go to the Potty,* illustrated by Renee Andriani, Little, Brown (Boston, MA), 2002.

*SIDELIGHTS:* Martha Sears, usually in conjunction with her husband, pediatrician William Sears, is best known for her well-regarded advice on parenting, through a series of books covering a range of issues, including the fussy eater, the high-need child, pregnancy and toilet training. Together, they have developed the method of parenting known as "attachment parenting." Emphasized is the formation of a close physical bond that leads to an intuitive understanding of the child's individual needs. The Sears assert that this is not a system of rigid rules. Rather, parents are offered a selection of practices to try, such as the "family bed" or carrying the infant in a baby sling as a means to form the desired intimate bond with the child. The Sears, through attachment parenting, also counsel parents to become acquainted with each child's unique traits and avoid raising children according to timetables. Understanding the child's uniqueness makes it possible to set realistic expectations for behavior and decreases the anxiety of parents. Much of the writing the two have done addresses various aspects of attachment parenting at different stages of the child's development.

In *The Baby Book: Everything You Need to Know About Your Baby from Birth to Age Two* Martha and William Sears cover all aspects of child care. As people with long careers in the area of children's health and as experienced parents of eight, they take a reasonable, non-dogmatic approach to childrearing. Advice is given on birthing, changes in the parents' relationship, baby care, and development. This book is considered by many to be the heir to the classic by Benjamin Spock.

Not all of the Sears' books are written for adults. *Baby on the Way* is aimed at an audience of children ages two through the fourth grade. The book is a preparation of the elder siblings for the changes that will occur in the family and also for the new roles they will be called upon to play. The Sears suggest that each member of the family has something of value to contribute and much stress is laid on the competence of the siblings to help make this transition. Additionally, factual information is given about pregnancy and the effects on the mother. Illustrations give this book a broad appeal. For the parents, the authors have included a information about "attachment parenting" and describe the fundamental elements such as breastfeeding, the family bed, and birth bonding.

Although the Sears have spent much of their time writing about the first few years of a child's life, they have also pondered the task of raising emotionally intelligent, responsible, productive individuals to adulthood. *The Successful Child: What Parents Can Do to Help Kids Turn Out Well* addresses the challenges of this long process. They take their approach of "attachment parenting" and make it viable for older children. Most of the emphasis is on the emotional and psychological development of the child, but there is also advice on diet and nutrition and health. The authors are known for their calm and reassuring attitude and the accessibility of their writing.

*BIOGRAPHICAL AND CRITICAL SOURCES:*

*PERIODICALS*

*Booklist,* February 1, 1993, Denise Perry Donavin, review of *The Baby Book,* p. 961; January 15, 1994, Jo Peer-Haas, review of *The Birth Book,* p. 886; September 1, 1996, Kathryn Carpenter, review of *Parenting the Fussy Baby and High-Need Child: Everything You Need to Know from Birth to Age Five,* p. 104; April 1, 2002, Douglas C. Lord, review of *The Successful Child* p. 49.

*Library Journal,* March 1, 1991, Kathryn Hammell Carpenter, review of *300 Questions New Parents Ask about Pregnancy, Childbirth, and Infant & Child Care,* p. 110; February 1, 1993, Mary J. Jarvis, review of *The Baby Book,* p.104; January, 1994, Mary J. Jarvis, review of *The Birth Book: Everything You Need to Know to Have a Safe and Satisfying Birth,* p. 153; August, 1996, Mary J. Jarvis, review of *Parenting the Fussy Baby and High-Need Child,* p. 132.

*Publishers Weekly,* January 31, 1994, review of *The Birth Book,* p. 86; February 4, 2002, review of *The Successful Child: What Parents can do to Help Kids Turn out Well* p.74.

*School Library Journal,* October, 2001, Kathie Meizner, *Baby on the Way,* p. 147.

*Whole Earth,* spring, 2002, review of *The Baby Book,* p. 30.

*OTHER*

*iParenting.com,* http://iparenting.com/sears/ (June 6, 2002).*

\*        \*        \*

## SELL, Louis (D.) 1947-

*PERSONAL:* Born 1947. *Education:* Franklin Marshall College, B.A., 1969; Johns Hopkins University, M.A., 1973.

*ADDRESSES: Office*—University of Maine, Farmington, Department of Social Services and Business, 270 Main Street, Farmington, ME 04938. *E-mail*—louis. sell@maine.edu.

*CAREER:* Official with United States Department of State, 1974-2000, including postings in Yugoslavia; political deputy to first high representative for Bosnian peace implementation, 1995-96; Kosovo director of International Crisis Group, 2000; University of Maine, Farmington, lecturer in Russian History.

*AWARDS, HONORS:* Fellow, Woodrow Wilson International Center for Scholars.

*WRITINGS:*

*Slobodan Milosevic and the Destruction of Yugoslavia,* Duke University Press (Durham, NC), 2002.

Contributor to periodicals, including *Wilson Quarterly,* and *East European Politics and Societies*

*SIDELIGHTS:* Louis Sell's career in the Department of State and his long involvement in Yugoslavia have put him in a unique position to write about the conflict that destroyed that nation. His postings to Yugoslavia began in 1974 and ended in 2000. His presence in the region, fluency in Serbo-Croatian, easy access to intelligence material and network of colleagues in diplomatic circles contributed to the fullness of the picture he was able to form for readers.

*Slobodan Milosevic and the Destruction of Yugoslavia* is more than a biography of the controversial Yugoslav leader. Although Milosevic does hold the center stage position, it is also a detailed picture of the complete unraveling of the country. The author places particular emphasis on the rise to power of Milosevic and the confluence of personal and social conditions that allowed this to happen. The book is noted for its detailed account of the circumstances that enabled him to gain prominence, as well as his inevitable downfall. Sell pays particular attention to the complexities of both Yugoslav and Serbian party politics to give a rich description of this portion of history. The effects of international interventions are laid out, with much attention given to the delineation of the motivations for Milosevic's actions, his style of negotiation, relationships with his family, the military, and subordinates. The author makes the point that Milosevic was, for a time a dedicated socialist, but switched to Serbian nationalism when this seemed the surer path to power.

It is Sell's opinion that in the end, the sole motivating force for Milosevic was personal power. Sell wrote, "Take away Slobodan Milosevic's interest in power and the man was pretty much a cipher." Time and time again Milosevic demonstrated that he was a man who believed that the truth was whatever he said it was and any and all ways of working his will were acceptable. The combination of the total self-confidence and willingness to do anything to maintain his superior position goes far in explaining how Milosevic was able to do what he did. Sell also describes the roles and effects of Milosevic's rivals; such men as Franjo Tudjman, the Croatian nationalist, and Bosnia's Alija Izetbegovic. These men also had a devastating impact on the region, but Milosevic was by far the most destructive. Much time is spent detailing the West's ambiguous response to the violence. The portrait Sell paints of Milosevic is of a man single-mindedly and madly in pursuit of power to the destruction of all.

A *Kirkus Reviews* contributor found the book "An important contribution to the literature surrounding the disintegration of Yugoslavia and the ethnic wars that followed." Sell states that, "A major motivation for this book is an effort to understand how the Yugoslavia that I and many other foreign observers knew and loved could have so quickly succumbed to barbarism."

*BIOGRAPHICAL AND CRITICAL SOURCES:*

*BOOKS*

Sell, Louis, *Slobodan Milosevic and the Destruction of Yugoslavia,* Duke University Press (Durham, NC), 2002.

*PERIODICALS*

*Foreign Affairs,* March/April, 2002, Robert Legvold, review of *Slobodan Milosevic and the Destruction of Yugoslavia.*
*Kirkus Reviews,* January 15, 2002, review of *Slobodan Milosevic and the Destruction of Yugoslavia,* p. 93.
*Library Journal,* March 15, 2002, Marcia L. Sprules, review of *Slobodan Milosevic and the Destruction of Yugoslavia,* p. 89.

*Nation,* May 27, 2002, Dusko Doder, review of *Slobodan Milosevic and the Destruction of Yugoslavia,* p.25.

*Washington Post,* April 28, 2002, Andrew Nagorski, review of *Slobodan Milosevic and the Destruction of Yugoslavia,* p. BW05.

OTHER

*Duke University Press Web site,* http://www.dukeu press.edu./ (May 15, 2003), "Louis Sell."*

\*    \*    \*

**SENED, Yonat 1926-**

*PERSONAL:* Born August 11, 1926, in Czestochowa, Poland; moved to Israel, 1948; daughter of Joseph and Helena (Dawidowicz) Sack; married Alexander Sened, June 1, 1948; children: Joav, Itai, Daniel. *Education:* Attended University of Geneva, Switzerland, 1946-48.

*ADDRESSES: Agent*—c/o Author Mail, Hakibbutz Hameuchad Publishing House, Ltd., Hayarkon 23 (P.O. Box 1432), Bnei Brak 51114, Israel.

*CAREER:* Novelist.

*AWARDS, HONORS:* Ussishkin, Jerusalem, 1951; Kugel, Holong, 1956; Brenner award, 1965; Pras Haizira, 1975.

*WRITINGS:*

(With Alexander Sened) *Adamah le-lo tsel* (novel, title means "Earth without Shadow" or "Land without Shade"), Hotsa'at ha-Kibuts ha-me'uhad (Tel Aviv, Israel), 1951, new edition, Tsaha, Mifkedet Ketsin hinukh rashi, Misrad ha-bitahon (Tel Aviv, Israel), 1985.

(With Alexander Sened) *Erd on Shotn* (novel), Hotsa'at Po'alim (Tel Aviv, Israel), 1953.

(With Alexander Sened) *ha-Kitah ha-hamishit* (novel), ha-Kibuts ha-me'uhad (Tel Aviv, Israel), 1954.

(With Alexander Sened) *Yemehem ha-perutsim la-ruah* (novel), ha-Kibuts ha-me'uhad (Tel Aviv, Israel), 1958.

(With Alexander Sened) *Ben ha-metim u-ven ha-hayim* (title means "Between the Dead and the Living"), ha-Kibuts ha-me'uhad (Tel Aviv, Israel), 1964.

(With Alexander Sened) *ha-Nisayon ha-nosaf,* ha-Kibuts ha-me'uhad (Tel Aviv, Israel), 1968, published as *Another Attempt,* translation by Noel Canin, Institute for the Translation of Hebrew Literature (Tel Aviv, Israel), 1981.

(With Alexander Sened), *Tandu,* ha-Kibuts ha-me'uhad (Tel Aviv, Israel), 1964.

(With Alexander Sened) *Le-an ume-ayin: mivhar,* ha-Kibuts ha-me'uhad (Tel Aviv, Israel), 1974.

(Translator) Choderlos de Laclos, *Les Liaisons Dangerous,* translated as *Yehasim mesukanim,* (title means "Dangerous Liasons"), ha-Kibuts ha-me'uhad (Tel Aviv, Israel), 1975.

(Translator) Jean Paul Sartre, *L'Âge de reason,* translated as *Gil ha-tevunah* (title means "The Age of Reason"), ha-Kibuts ha-me'uhad, (Tel Aviv, Israel), 1978.

(Translator) Jean Paul Sartre, *La mort dans l'ame* (translated as *Mavet ba-lev),* Sifriyat Po'alim (Tel Aviv, Israel), 1978.

(With Alexander Sened) *Kevar erets noshevet* (title means "The Land Inhabited"), ha-Kibuts ha-me'uhad (Tel Aviv, Israel), 1981.

*Arkah,* ha-Kibuts ha-me'uhad: ha-Mo'atsah ha-tsibunit le-tarbut ule-omanut, ha-Mif'al le-tirgum sifre mofet (Tel Aviv, Israel), 1981.

(With Alexander Sened) *Nikra Lo le'on* (title means "We'll Call Him Leon"), ha-Kibuts ha-me'uhad (Tel Aviv, Israel), 1985.

(With Alexander Sened) *O'azis* (title means "Oasis"), ha-Kibuts ha-me'uhad (Tel Aviv, Israel), 1985.

(Translator) Nathalie Sarraute, *Les fruits d'or,* translated as *Perot ha-zahav,* Sifriyat Ma'ariv (Tel Aviv, Israel), 1991.

(With Alexander Sened), *Yoman shel zug me'ohav* (title means "Diary of a Couple in Love"), ha-Kibuts ha-me'uhad (Tel Aviv, Israel), 1992.

(Translator, with Alexander Sened) Janusz Korczak, *Jak Kochac Dziecko, Momenty Wychowawcze and Prawo Dziecka do Szacunku,* translated as *Keh le-ehov yeled; Rega'im hinukhiyim; Zekhut ha-yeled le-khavod,* ha-Kibuts ha-me'uhad (Tel Aviv, Jerusalem, Israel), 1996.

(Translator, with Alexander Sened) Janusz Korczak, *Ketavim,* Yad va-shem; ha-Agudah 'a.sh. Yanush Korts'ak be-Yisra'el: Bet Lohame ha-geta'ot 'a.

sh. Yitshak Katsenelson: ha-Kibuts ha-me'uhad (Tel Aviv, Israel), 1996.

(With Alexander Sened), *Ba-midbar melon orhim* (title means "In the Desert a Lodging Place"), ha-Kibuts ha-me'uhad (Tel Aviv, Israel), 1998.

*Adamah le-lo tsel* was published in Yiddish and Portuguese; and *Ben ha-metim u-ven ha-hayim* was published in German.

*SIDELIGHTS:* Yonat Sened has written numerous novels with her husband Alexander Sened. Born in Poland, Sened spent most of World War II in the Warsaw ghetto. She met her husband when he went to Europe to help organize the immigration of Jewish refugees after the war. Sened first went to study at the University of Geneva but then she and Alexander made their way across the Israeli border in 1948 during the Israeli War of Independence.

In their 1981 novel, *Kevar erets noshevet,* the Seneds tell a story partly based on their own experience as parents who have lost a son. During a radio show, transribed in *Modern Hebrew Literature,* Dan Miron and Menahem Perry pointed out that the book does not deal with the classic story of bereavement in the normal fashion of Israeli literature and society. Perry noted, "The question of the sequence of events leading up to the death is ignored, as is its significance, whether social, national or mythic. On the other hand, there is very direct confrontation with the experience of bereavement: what it does to the people close to it, how they think about it, dream it, how they build an existence around it, stressing that the world, the objective world, has not changed." Miron pointed out that, in many ways, the death of the son, happenings on the kibbutz, and other aspects of the book are more important as metaphors that describe "the failure to understand reality; in other words, the failure to come to terms with it directly and completely."

*BIOGRAPHICAL AND CRITICAL SOURCES:*

*PERIODICALS*

*Modern Hebrew Literature,* spring-summer, 1982, Dan Miron and Perry Manahem, "Yonat and Alexander Sened's *The Land Inhabited:* A Radio Talk," pp. 87-90.*

## SEWELL, Winifred 1917-2002

*OBITUARY NOTICE*—See index for *CA* sketch: Born August 12, 1917, in Newport, WA; died of congestive heart failure October 23, 2002, in Cabin John, MD. Librarian, educator, and author. Sewell specialized in medical library science and worked for the National Library of Medicine. She was educated at Washington State University, where she earned her B.S. in 1938 before attending Columbia University for her master's degree, which she received in 1940; she also attended graduate-level classes at universities in New York City from 1940 to 1946. Sewell's first position was as a librarian for Welcome Research Laboratories from 1942 to 1946, which led to a job at the Squibb Institute for Medical Research, where she was senior librarian until 1961. At the National Library of Medicine in Bethesda, Maryland she was a subject-heading specialist and deputy chief of the Bibliographic Services division during the early 1960s and headed the drug literature program from 1965 to 1970. The remainder of Sewell's career was spent at the University of Maryland's School of Pharmacy, where she was adjunct professor of pharmacy from 1970 until her retirement in 1992; she also was an adjunct lecturer at the university. Sewell was a member of several scientific and medical organizations, including the International Federation of Pharmacy and the National Academy of Sciences. For her work in the field, she was honored with several awards, including the Ida and George Eliot Prize from the Medical Library Association and an honorary doctorate from the Philadelphia College of Pharmacy and Science. She was the author of three books: *Using MeSH for Effective Searching: A Programmed Guide* (1975), which she wrote with Mere Harrison, *Guide to Drug Information* (1976), and *Micromanual for Casual Users of National Library of Medicine Databases* (1986), the last written with Sandra D. Teitelbaum. Sewell was also an editor of the journal *Unlisted Drugs* and editor of the "Gale Information Guides: Health Affairs" series from 1971 to 1980.

*OBITUARIES AND OTHER SOURCES:*

*BOOKS*

*Who's Who in Medicine and Health Care,* third edition, Marquis (New Providence, NJ), 2000.

*PERIODICALS*

*Washington Post*, November 9, 2002, p. B6.

\*   \*   \*

## SEYMOUR, Jane 1951-

*PERSONAL:* Born Joyce Penelope Wilhelmina Frankenberg, February 15, 1951, in Wimbledon, England; immigrated to the United States, 1976; daughter of John (an obstetrician) and Mieke (a Red Cross nurse) Frankenberg; married Michael Attenborough, 1971 (divorced, 1973); married Geoffrey "Jeep" Planer, 1977 (divorced, 1978); married David Flynn, 1981 (divorced, May, 1992); married James Keach, May, 1993; children: (third marriage) Katie, Sean; (fourth marriage) John, Kristopher (twins); (stepchildren) Jennifer, Kalen. *Education:* Attended Arts Educational School (London, England)

*ADDRESSES: Office*—c/o Guttman Associates, 118 South Beverly Dr., Beverly Hills, CA, 90212.

*CAREER:* Made debut as dancer with London Festival Ballet, 1964; also formerly affiliated with the Kirov Ballet; principal film appearances include *Young Winston*, 1972; *Live and Let Die*, 1973; *Sinbad and the Eye of the Tiger*, 1977; *Oh! Heavenly Dog*, 1980; *Somewhere in Time*, 1980; *Lassiter*, 1984; *Head Office*, 1986; *El Tunel (The Tunnel)*, 1988; *The New Swiss Family Robinson*, 1998, and *Toughing Wild Horses*, 2002; also appeared in *Oh! What a Lovely War*, 1969, and *The Only Way*, 1970. Principal stage appearances include *Macbeth*, *A Doll's House*, and *Amadeus* (originated role of Constanze Weber, Broadhurst Theater, NY, 1980). Principal television appearances include *The Onedin Line*, 1976; *Captains and the Kings* (miniseries), NBC, 1976; *The Awakening Land* (miniseries), NBC, 1978; *Our Mutual Friend* (miniseries), PBS, 1978; *Battlestar Galactica*, 1979; *John Steinbeck's "East of Eden"* (miniseries), ABC, 1981; *Ernest Hemingway's "The Sun Also Rises"* (miniseries), 1984; *War and Remembrance* (miniseries), ABC, 1988; and *Jack the Ripper*, CBS, 1988; television movies include *Frankenstein: The True Story*, *Killer on Board*, *Seventh Avenue*, *The Story of David*, *Love's Dark Ride*, *The Four Feathers*, *The*

*Dallas Cowboys Cheerleaders*, *The Scarlett Pimpernel*, *Phantom of the Opera*, *The Haunting Passion*, *The Dark Mirror*, *Obsessed With a Married Woman*, *Jamaica Inn*, *Crossings*, *The Woman He Loved*, *Onassis: The Richest Man in the World*, *Sunstroke*, *Angel of Death*, *Matters of the Heart*, *Heidi*, and *Heart of a Stranger*. Also appeared in television specials *Battle of the Network Stars* (ABC), *On Top All Over the World*, and *M&W, Men and Women*. Host of *Japan*, PBS, 1988, *Break the Silence*, CBS, 1994, *A Passion for Justice: The Hazel Brannon Smith Story*, ABC, 1994, *The Absolute Truth*, 1997, and *Dr. Quinn: The Movie*, 1999. Star of television series *Dr. Quinn, Medicine Woman*, 1993-1998. Copartner of Catfish Productions. Painter. Designer of the Jane Seymour Signature Collection clothing line. Also active in ChildHelp USA and City Hearts charities.

*MEMBER:* Actors' Equity, British Actors' Equity Association, Screen Actors Guild, American Federation of Television and Radio Artists.

*AWARDS, HONORS:* Outstanding Lead Actress in a Miniseries or Special nomination, Emmy Awards, 1977, for *Captains and the Kings;* Best Performance by an Actress in a Miniseries or Motion Picture Made for TV, Golden Globe Awards, 1982, for *John Steinbeck's "East of Eden";* Outstanding Supporting Actress in a Miniseries or Special, Emmy Awards, 1988, for portrayal of Maria Callas in ABC-TV's *Onassis: The Richest Man Alive;* Best Performance by an Actress in a Miniseries or Motion Picture Made for TV nomination, Golden Globe Awards, 1989, for performance as the Duchess of Windsor in the CBS-TV movie *The Woman He Loved;* Distinguished Service Award, Simon Wiesenthal Center for the Performing Arts, 1989; Outstanding Lead Actress in a Miniseries or Special nomination, Emmy Awards, and Best Performance by an Actress in a Miniseries or Motion Picture Made for TV nomination, Golden Globe Awards, both 1989, both for her portrayal of a concentration camp survivor in *War and Remembrance;* Woman of the Year Award, 1992, from ChildHelp USA; Best Performance by an Actress in a TV Series—Drama nominations, Golden Globe Awards, 1994, 1995, and 1997, Outstanding Lead Actress in a Drama Series nomination, Emmy Awards, 1994 and 1998, Outstanding Performance by a Female Actor in a Drama Series nominations, Screen Actors Guild Awards, 1995 and 1997, Best Performance by an Actress in a TV Series—Drama, Golden Globe

Awards, 1996, and Viewers for Quality Television Award nomination, Best Actress in a Quality Drama Series, 1998, all for *Dr. Quinn, Medicine Woman;* Outstanding Classical Music-Dance Program nomination (with others), Emmy Awards, 1999, for *A Streetcar Named Desire;* Hollywood Walk of Fame Star, 1999; Order of the British Empire, 2000.

*WRITINGS:*

*Jane Seymour's Guide to Romantic Living,* Atheneum (New York, NY), 1986.
(With Pamela Patrick Novotny) *Two at a Time: Having Twins: The Journey Through Pregnancy and Birth,* Simon and Schuster (New York, NY), 2001.
(With Pamela Patrick Novotny) *Remarkable Changes: Turing Life's Challenges into Opportunities,* Regan Books (New York, NY), 2003.

*FOR CHILDREN; WITH HUSBAND JAMES KEACH*

*Splat!: The Tale of a Colorful Cat,* illustrated by Geoffrey Planer, Putnam (New York, NY), 1998.
*Yum!: A Tale of Two Cookies,* illustrated by Geoffrey Planer, Putnam (New York, NY), 1998.
*Boing!: No Bouncing on the Bed,* illustrated by Geoffrey Planer, Putnam (New York, NY), 1999.

*"THIS ONE 'N' THAT ONE" SERIES; WITH HUSBAND JAMES KEACH*

*Me and Me,* illustrated by Geoffrey Planer, Putnam (New York, NY), 1999.
*Eat,* illustrated by Geoffrey Planer, Putnam (New York, NY), 1999.
*Play,* illustrated by Geoffrey Planer, Putnam (New York, NY), 1999.
*Talk,* illustrated by Geoffrey Planer, Putnam (New York, NY), 1999.

Author of foreword to *Homeopathic Remedies,* written by Asa Hershoff, Avery Publishers (Garden City Park, NY), 2000.

*SIDELIGHTS:* Jane Seymour is famed for her years of acting in movies and on television. Once dubbed the "Queen of the Miniseries" for all the work she did in such productions during the 1980s, Seymour also starred for six seasons on *Dr. Quinn, Medicine Woman,* the series about a Boston physician who puts out her medical shingle in the Colorado frontier during the nineteenth century. In addition to her acting career, Seymour began her professional life as a dancer, and has also added painting and clothes design to her lengthy resume. Giving birth to twins at age forty-five, however, set her on yet another career, this one as a children's author, penning books for young readers in the "This One 'n That One" series of picture books and board books.

Seymour was born in England, in 1951, and was raised on the outskirts of London, the daughter of a doctor of Polish descent and a Dutch Red Cross nurse who had been held in a Japanese prisoner-of-war camp until 1945. Seymour has noted that her childhood was not that of the typical English girl, as she was introduced to the theater at an early age—an experience that changed her life. Her father had many opera singers among his patients, so the family paid frequent trips to London's Covent Garden theater. One of three daughters, Seymour was called Joyce Frankenberg until she finally changed her name at age seventeen because she thought Jane Seymour was less cumbersome as a stage name. By that time Seymour had opted for a career in the stage, beginning ballet lessons as a youngster, despite the fact that, as she told Cork Millner in the *Saturday Evening Post,* she knew her build was "totally wrong" for ballet. She was not tall enough, but consoled herself with having a long neck. "I was told early on that I was not built for classical ballet," she told Millner, "but I was such a high achiever, I made my body do more than it could tolerate." Eventually her body rebelled. At seventeen, dancing professionally with the Kirov Ballet at Covent Garden, Seymour sustained a knee injury that ended her ballet-dancing career. "As a dancer, I was never technically very brilliant," Seymour further explained to Millner. Her reviewers mostly commented on the fact that she acted better than she danced, so with her career-ending injury, Seymour decided to give acting a try.

In England, Seymour performed on the stage, in films, and on television, getting her film debut in *Oh! What a Lovely War.* Her breakthrough came in 1973 with the role of Solitaire in the James Bond film *Live and Let Die.* With that role under her belt, Seymour was well on her way to a film and television career in the

United States, as well, and moved from England to California in 1976. She earned her first Emmy Award nomination for her role in the television miniseries *Captains and the Kings.* This was only the first of a number of such nominations and awards for Seymour, and also the first of a long line of performances in miniseries. Throughout the 1980s, she was also active in film, starring opposite Christopher Reeves in *Somewhere in Time,* and originating the role of Constanze Weber, Mozart's wife, in the Broadway production of *Amadeus.* More recognition came her way with her portrayal of a concentration camp survivor in the miniseries *War and Remembrance,* and for her portrayal of the opera diva Maria Callas in *Onassis: The Richest Man Alive.* Explaining her success in a wide variety of roles, Seymour told Millner, "I have a lot of people inside me . . . and I am so blessed to be in a profession where they pay me to discover these people!"

It was also in the 1980s when Seymour began her career as a writer, penning the adult title *Jane Seymour's Guide to Romantic Living.* "I'm not a writer," she told Millner. "I wrote the book for the person who wants to live romantically." With little writing experience or not, Seymour's first book project was a success, both financially and critically.

Seymour suffered a near-death experience in 1988 that changed her life, as she explained to Susan Schindehette in *People.* After suffering an allergic reaction to a dose of antibiotics, she realized that "the only things that mattered were my children or the love of my life," as she told Schindehette. "I wasn't thinking about my career, having a new car or a house I might have owned." As a result, she began focusing more on her family life. She also worked in the 1990s in the popular television series *Dr. Quinn, Medicine Woman,* winning awards and millions of fans weekly to the adventures of the plucky doctor from Boston. When her third marriage ended in 1992, she married for a fourth time and decided to have children again in her forties. Undergoing infertility treatment, she gave birth to twin boys at age forty-five, and this inspired her to devote more time to writing.

In 1998, working with her husband James Keach, Seymour published the first in a series of books which are directly related to that birth. She named the central characters of the book "This One and That One, because . . . my doctors used to call them that" when she was pregnant, as Seymour told a contributor for

*People.* She and her husband even began referring to the twin boys when they were born as This One and That One, the nicknames becoming a family joke. As the boys grew into toddlers, Seymour began to see how their energetic tumbling and play could be adapted to a series of books about a very different set of twins, the youngest members of a cat family in Malibu, California. In *Splat!: The Tale of a Colorful Cat,* mother cat Lady Jane goes shopping and leaves the pair of kittens in the charge of her husband, Big Jim. The young kittens want to use their mother's paints and brushes, but they cannot decide what to paint. Big Jim suggests they paint him, and when he dozes off, the twins take the suggestion literally, turning him into a rainbow of color. In a companion volume *Yum!: A Tale of Two Cookies,* the twins are again up to their antics. Lady Jane bakes some cookies, taking a basket full of them to her husband, who is fishing. Meanwhile, the twin kittens, This One and That One, are presumably sleeping soundly back at the house. Not so; they have instead sneaked into the basket and devoured all the cookies. A contributor for *Publishers Weekly* found the two books "slaphappy stories" and "cheerful little capers," and Peggy Muntz, reviewing the two titles in *Children's Book Review Service,* called them "just plain fun."

A third picture book in the series, *Boing!: No Bouncing on the Bed,* finds the frisky twin kittens circumventing parental advice. When their parents tell them not bounce on chairs, they take to the sofa. When commanded not to jump on the sofa, they opt for the bed. Soon the mother gives in to her kittens and is found happily joining her two offspring kittens bouncing on the bed. When Big Jim decides to join in, however, he breaks the bed. Roxanne Burg, reviewing the title in *School Library Journal,* noted that the kittens "are having a hopping good time."

Seymour and her husband have also teamed up on four smaller board books with simplified text featuring the twin kittens. Concepts are presented in each of the four titles, *Eat, Me and Me, Play,* and *Talk.* Colorful artwork is combined with a few descriptive words for each layout. In *Play,* for example, This One and That One climb trees, dance, crawl, catch a ball, and finally go to rest. Body parts are featured in *Me and Me,* and talking and eating are featured in the other two titles in the series.

Seymour's late-in-life birth of twins also inspired her 2001 adult title, *Two at a Time: Having Twins: The*

*Journey Through Pregnancy and Birth.* Annette V. Janes, writing in *Library Journal,* felt that Seymour's "voice is compelling and reaches out to comfort and assist anyone expecting twins." Seymour also combines charity work in her busy life, working for organizations such as ChildHelp USA and UNICEF. ChildHelp named her their Woman of the Year in 1992, and UNICEF commissioned Christmas cards from Seymour's brush. In downtown Los Angeles, she helps to run City Hearts, a program for children at risk.

## BIOGRAPHICAL AND CRITICAL SOURCES:

*BOOKS*

*Contemporary Theatre, Film, and Television,* Volume 22, Gale (Detroit, MI), 1999.
*Newsmakers 1994,* Gale (Detroit, MI), 1994.

*PERIODICALS*

*Booklist,* October 15, 1986, review of *Jane Seymour's Guide to Romantic Living,* pp. 311-312.
*Children's Book Review Service,* October, 1998, Peggy Muntz, review of *Splat!: The Tale of a Colorful Cat* and *Yum!: A Tale of Two Cookies,* p. 17.
*Entertainment Weekly,* April 8, 1994; December 15, 1995, p. 24.
*Horn Book Guide,* spring, 1999, Peter D. Sieruta, review of *Splat!: The Tale of a Colorful Cat* and *Yum!: A Tale of Two Cookies,* p. 43; spring, 2000, Peter D. Sieruta, review of *Boing!: No Bouncing on the Bed,* p. 54.
*Kirkus Reviews,* September 1, 1986, review of *Jane Seymour's Guide to Romantic Living,* p. 1359; September 1, 1999, review of *Boing!: No Bouncing on the Bed,* p. 1422.
*Ladies' Home Journal,* May, 1994, pp. 163, 215-217.
*Lear's,* October, 1993.
*Library Journal,* March 1, 2001, Annette V. Janes, review of *Two at a Time: Having Twins: The Journey Through Pregnancy and Birth,* p. 124.
*People,* February 15, 1993, Susan Schindehette, "What's Up Doc?," pp. 75-78, 80; April 21, 1997, p. 58; September 29, 1997, p. 172; May 18, 1998, "One-Upmanship," p. 198; June 15, 1998, p. 11.
*Prevention,* July, 1998, Heidi Parker, "Meet the Alternative Medicine Woman," p. 94.

*Psychology Today,* September-October, 2001, Cybi Ma, "See Jane Run," pp. 36-40.
*Publishers Weekly,* September 28, 1998, review of *Splat!* and *Yum!,* p. 100; March 19, 2001, review of *Two at a Time,* p. 97.
*Saturday Evening Post,* May-June, 1989, Cork Millner, "Not-So-Plain-Jane Seymour," pp. 42-46.
*School Library Journal,* February, 1999, Blair Christolon, review of *Splat!* and *Yum!,* pp. 88-89; November, 1999, Roxanne Burg, review of *Boing!,* p. 130.
*Teen,* January, 1993.
*TV Guide,* February 20, 1993.
*Village Voice,* March 31, 1987, Michael Covino, "Rich and Shameless," p. 52.

*OTHER*

*Friends of Jane* (official Jane Seymour Web site) http://www.friendsofjane.com (June 5, 2002).

\*    \*    \*

## SHACKLEY, Theodore (George), Jr. 1927-2002

*OBITUARY NOTICE*—See index for *CA* sketch: Born July 16, 1927, in Springfield, MA; died December 9, 2002, in Bethesda, MD. Intelligence agent and author. Shackley was a renowned Central Intelligence Agency agent and director who was involved in several important counterinsurgency operations during the cold war. After serving in the U.S. Army, he earned a degree in politics and government from the University of Maryland in 1951. The Korean War led to his being recalled into the army, but he was assigned to the C.I.A. instead of being sent to Korea. His first post was in West Berlin, and he became heavily involved in espionage intrigue against the USSR and communist East Germany. Next, while station chief in Miami in 1962 he worked with anti-Castro rebels to try to overthrow the dictator in Cuba. It was during this time that he earned the nickname "the Blond Ghost" because of his blond hair, pale skin, cool efficiency, and mysterious ways. During the 1960s Shackley supervised Hmong insurgents against the North Vietnamese and was made station chief in Saigon during the height of the Vietnam conflict. He returned to Washington, D.C. in 1972 to head clandestine operations in the western hemisphere, and in 1976 was promoted to associate deputy director at C.I.A. headquarters in Langley, Virginia, where he worked on all international covert operations, including the overthrow of Chilean President Salvador Allende. Shackley ran into controversy in the late 1970s, however, when a close friend of his was caught selling illegal arms to Libyan leader Muammar al-Qaddafi. This, along with the gradual replacement of secret agents with spy satellites and other technology, led to his retirement from the C.I.A. in 1979. Shackley went on to found Research Associates International, Ltd., a business risk-analysis consulting firm in Bethesda. Throughout his career in the C.I.A., Shackley believed that counterinsurgency techniques were an effective weapon against foreign enemies. He wrote about his views in the book *The Third Option: An American View of Counterinsurgency Operations* (1981); he was also the author, with Robert Oatland, of *You're the Target* and of *Still the Target: Coping with Terror and Crime.* Shackley, who was sometimes called "the godfather of secret wars," became a legend in the C.I.A., earning three Distinguished Intelligence medals; he was also the subject of the David Corn book *Blond Ghost: Ted Shackley and the C.I.A.'s Crusades* (1994).

*OBITUARIES AND OTHER SOURCES:*

*BOOKS*

O'Toole, G. J. A., *The Encyclopedia of American Intelligence and Espionage: From the Revolutionary War to the Present,* Facts on File (New York, NY), 1988.

*PERIODICALS*

*Chicago Tribune,* December 16, 2002, section 1, p. 13.
*Los Angeles Times,* December 14, 2002, p. B21.
*New York Times,* December 14, 2002, p. B18.
*Times* (London, England), December 13, 2002.
*Washington Post,* December 13, 2002, p. B9.

\*          \*          \*

## SHALEV, Meir 1948-

*PERSONAL:* Born 1948 in Nahalal, Israel; son of Itzhak (a poet) and Batia Shalev; married; children: two sons. *Education:* Attended Hebrew University. *Religion:* Jewish. *Hobbies and other interests:* Motorcycle and Jeep enthusiast.

*ADDRESSES: Home*—Jerusalem, Israel. *Agent*—c/o Author Mail, HarperCollins, 10 East 53rd St., 7th Fl., New York, NY 10022.

*CAREER: Yediot Aharonot* (Israeli daily newspaper), journalist/columnist.

*WRITINGS:*

*ha-Yeled Hayim veha-mifletset mi-Yerushalayim,* ha-Kibuts ha-me'uhad (Tel Aviv, Israel), 1981.
*Mishkav letsim,* D. Peled (Hertsliyah, Israel), 1982.
*Gumot ha-hen shel Zohar* (title means "Zohar's Dimples"), Keter (Jerusalem, Israel), 1985.
*Tanakj 'akhshav,* Shoken (Jerusalem, Israel), 1985.
*Ha-Kinah Nechama* (title means "Nehama the Louse"), Am Oved (Tel Aviv, Israel), 1988.
*Rewriting History in the Bible: the Book of Ruth vs. the Book of Chronicles,* Harvard University Library (Cambridge, MA), 1988.
*Aba 'oseh bushot,* Keter (Jerusalem, Israel), 1988.
*Roman Rusi* (title means "Russian Novel"), Am Oved (Tel Aviv, Israel), 1988, translated as *The Blue Mountain,* HarperCollins (New York, NY), 2002.
*Michael and the Monster of Jerusalem,* Tower of David—Museum of the History of Jerusalem (Jerusalem, Israel), 1989.
*My Father Always Embarrasses Me* (translation), Wellington Publishers (Chicago, IL), 1990.
*ha-Kinah Nehamah,* Am Oved (Tel Aviv, Israel), 1990.
*'Esav* (title means "Esau"), Am Oved (Tel Aviv, Israel), 1991.
*Ekh ha-adam ha-kadmon himtsi le-gamre be-mikreh et ha-kabab ha-Romani: sipur li-yeladim* (voice recording), Am Oved (Tel Aviv, Israel), 1993.
*Ke-yamim ahadim,* (title means "As a Few Days"), Am Oved (Tel Aviv, Israel), 1994, translated by Barbara Harshav as *The Loves of Judith,* Ecco Press (Hopewell, NJ), 1999; published as *Four Meals,* Canongate (Edinburgh, Scotland), 1999.
*Mabul, nahash u-shete tevot: sipure Tanakh li-yeladim,* (title means "A Snake, a Flood and Two Arks") Keter (Jerusalem, Israel), 1994.
*Be-'ikar 'al ahavah* (title means "Mainly About Love"), Am Oved (Tel Aviv, Israel), 1995.
*Sod ahizat ha-'enayim* (title means "Elements of Conjuration"), Am Oved (Tel Aviv, Israel), 1999.
*Hozrim la-shetah: maslule tiyulim le-g'ipim, traktorim ve-ofno'im,* A. Barkai (Israel), 1997.

*Be-veto ba-midbar* (title means "In His House in the Wilderness"), Am Oved (Tel Aviv, Israel), 1998.

*Ha-traktor be-argaz-ha-hol: sipur 'al traktor gadol li-yeladim* ketanim (title means "The Tractor in the Sandbox"), Am Oved (Tel Aviv, Israel), 1998.

Author's works have also been translated into Japanese, Dutch, Polish, Swedish, Danish, Norwegian, Italian, and German.

*ADAPTATIONS: The Blue Mountain* was adapted for audiocassette.

*SIDELIGHTS:* Israeli-born Meir Shalev is hailed as one of the greatest modern-day writers of his country and has even been called the Hebrew Gabriél Garcia Marquez for his use of magic realism. Shalev has written for both juvenile and adult audiences, and his work has been praised for its larger-than-life characters.

Perhaps Shalev's best-known juvenile book is *My Father Always Embarrasses Me.* In it, Mortimer Dunne speaks of his mother, a TV journalist, with pride. But when it comes to his father, Mortimer sings a different tune. His dad never gets him to school on time, wears horribly inappropriate clothing, and—worst of all—tries to kiss him in front of his classmates. When Mortimer's school hosts a baking contest, it's Dad who shows up with a plain brown cake, and Mortimer is sure he's in for the ultimate humiliation. What happens next is, instead, what allows Mortimer to learn that his father, a writer, was embarrassed by his own father because he was only a baker. *My Father Always Embarrasses Me* is a humorous twist on role-reversal, and a *Publishers Weekly* review wrote, "[Shalev] uses liberal portions of humor to serve up some splendid points about the intricates of father-son relationships."

*A Snake, a Flood and Two Arks* spent months in the Number One spot on children's bestseller lists, and critics raved about the stories and drawings by Italian artist Emanuel Luzzati. In an interview with Knight-Ridder/Tribune News Service reporter John Donnelly, Shalev explained why he created this collection of six Biblical stories. "The Bible is stingy with descriptions," he said. As a young boy, Shalev's father took him to the exact river bed where David and Goliath battled. Shalev was given a slingshot and five pebbles,

which he systematically embedded into a rusty oil barrel. "I learned that day what was written in the Bible—that the stone sank into Goliath's forehead—was literally true." And with that, the Bible had come alive for the youthful Shalev.

*A Snake, a Flood and Two Arks* contains simplified versions of some of the best-known Biblical stories, including the Garden of Eden, Joseph and his coat of many colors, and the Tower of Babel. Newspaper reviewer Yael Dar said, "The language has been simplified without sacrificing the complexity of the plots. He has added bits of his own: descriptions of nature, character traits, concealed thoughts and even humor." Shalev told Donnelly, "Kids love Bible stories if presented in the right way—if they are not presented with all this holiness and importance."

Not everyone was impressed with the book. The religious right criticized the author for the liberties he took, going so far as to recommend banning the book because it was written by an anti-religious person. Shalev wrote an adult version of the children's book titled *The Bible Now.*

Shalev's first novel for adult audiences was *The Blue Mountain,* originally published in Hebrew and eventually translated into ten languages. The first English edition was published in 1991 by HarperCollins. The story takes place in a socialist kibbutz in Palestine that was established by a group of Ukrainian immigrants. Baruch, grandson of one of the founders, narrates the book by drawing on anecdote, family history and legend, and pure rumor. The characters are uniquely individual—from an uncle who disappears along with his bull, to a gifted horticulturalist who is unlucky in love—yet remain believable. Reviewer Peter Whittaker wrote in the *New Internationalist,* "It makes good use of folk history, humor, and a dash of magical realism. Its humanistic message that ordinary people, in all their glory and confusions, are worthy of respect and dignity, is one that we should surely heed." Paul Berman reviewed *The Blue Mountain* for *New Republic* and wrote, "Can Shalev tell a story! He spins his yarn very adroitly, alternately pulling the thread taut and letting it play out. The many amazing things that happen in this novel are related with an utter absence of amazement, as if they were simply inscribed in the being of the world."

Shalev's next adult novel, *Esau,* was written in Hebrew and translated into six languages. It is a contemporary treatment of the traditional Biblical tale of lost inheritance and sibling rivalry. Esau, the protagonist, grows up in Palestine in the late 1920s, early 1930s where his highly critical father runs a bakery. Esau's brother, Jacob, marries Leah, the woman Esau loves, and inherits the bakery. A resentful Esau immigrates to America and becomes a gourmet food columnist who is unable to sustain a meaningful relationship. A *Publishers Weekly* reviewer gave the novel an "A" and said in a review, "Shalev weaves three seemingly unrelated tales . . . that eventually intersect with the main plot in surprising and ingenious ways." A write-up in *Kirkus Reviews* was not so kind. "For all its bravado and braggadocio, this novel never quite goes mano a mano with its subject. Arm wrestling without the table."

*The Loves of Judith* was also published under the alternate title of *Four Meals.* During the lull between the two World Wars, Judith comes to a Palestinian village, mourning the disappearance of her daughter. Three village men find themselves hopelessly in love with Judith; Moshe Rabinovitch is Judith's employer and a widower; Globerman is a deceptive cattle dealer who spends his afternoons socializing with Judith; and Jacob Sheinfeld is a shy canary breeder whose wife leaves him over his intense love for Judith. When Judith gives birth to her son Zayde, she is determined to raise him alone in a cowshed, and so she does. Fiercely independent, she refuses to confirm the identity of the boy's father.

*The Loves of Judith* is structured around four meals Zayde shares with Jacob over a period of three decades. As with previous novels, this one has been praised for its quirky-but-believable characters. The name Zayde means "grandfather," a name Judith intentionally gave her only son so as to ward off the angel of death. Because of this and other oddities, Zayde, over the length of the novel, spends his time trying to discover and uncover the mysteries his mother left behind after her untimely death. Andrea MacPherson, a reviewer for *January Magazine,* wrote, "Shalev has created a strange, lovely world where anything is possible: where a boy may be raised as a girl until puberty; where cows, canaries and crows all act as emissaries of fate; where three men may collectively be the father of a child who, miraculously, resembles all three." A reviewer for *The Source Israel. com* wrote, "*The Loves of Judith* is a novel that reads like a Chagall painting. The mystical qualities of the characters make the novel a visual reading experience."

Shalev lives with his family in Israel, where he works as a newspaper columnist and television presenter.

*BIOGRAPHICAL AND CRITICAL SOURCES:*

*PERIODICALS*

*Atlantic,* August, 1991, Phoebe-Lou Adams, review of *The Blue Mountain,* pp. 103-104.

*Booklist,* February 15, 1999, GraceAnne A. DeCandido, review of *The Loves of Judith,* p. 1042.

*Kirkus Reviews,* January 15, 1999, review of *The Loves of Judith,* p. 96.

*Knight-Ridder News/Tribune News Service,* March 8, 1995, John Donnelly, "Israeli Writer Adds Kid Appeal to stories in Bible."

*Library Journal,* June 1, 1991, Beth Ann Mills, review of *The Blue Mountain,* p. 196; October 1, 1992, Sheldon Kaye, review of *The Blue Mountain* (sound recording), pp. 130-131; December, 1994, Molly Abramowitz, review of *Esau,* p. 134; February 15, 1999, Lisa Rohrbaugh, review of *The Loves of Judith,* p. 186.

*New Internationalist,* January-February, 2002, Peter Whittaker, review of *The Blue Mountain,* p. 47.

*New Republic,* September 9, 1991, Paul Berman, review of *The Blue Mountain,* pp. 39-42.

*New York Times,* August 14, 1991, Herbert Mitgang, review of *The Blue Mountain,* p. B2.

*New York Times Book Review,* August 18, 1991, Barbara Finkelstein, review of *The Blue Mountain,* p. 14; January 1, 1995, Cathy A. Colman, review of *Esau,* p. 16.

*Observer* (London, England), April 16, 2000, Joanna Griffiths, "Three Men and a Baby." p. 13.

*Publishers Weekly,* May 3, 1991, Sybil Steinberg, review of *The Blue Mountain,* p. 65; October 17, 1994, review of *Esau,* pp. 62-63; January 25, 1999, review of *The Loves of Judith,* p. 70.

*School Library Journal,* June 8, 1990, Diane Roback and Richard Donahue, review of *My Father Always Embarrasses Me,* p. 53; February, 1991, review of *My Father Always Embarrasses Me,* p. 74.

*Times Literary Supplement,* August 4, 2000, Eleanor Birne, review of *Four Meals,* p. 21.

*World Literature Today,* spring, 1989, Dov Vardi, review of *Roman Russi,* p. 362; winter, 1995, Dov Vardi, review of *Keyamim ahadim,* pp. 217-218.

*OTHER*

*American-Israel Cooperative Enterprise,* http://www. us-israel.org/ (March 4, 2002), Jewish Virtual Library.

*January Magazine,* http://www.januarymagazine.com/ (July, 2000), Andrea MacPherson, "Judith's Loves."

*The Source Israel.com,* http://www.thesourceisrael. com/ (July 12, 2002), review of *The Loves of Judith.*\*

\*    \*    \*

**SHAMIR, Moshe 1921-**

*PERSONAL:* Born September 15, 1921, in Safed, Israel; son of Arie and Ella (Aronshohn) Shamir; married Zvia Frumkin, June 6, 1946; children: Ennula, Yael, Elyahu.

*ADDRESSES: Home*—3 Rosanis St. Tel Aviv, Israel.

*CAREER:* Novelist, playwright, and writer. Israeli Defense Force, founding editor of *Bamaheneh,* 1948-50. Coeditor of *BaShaar, Omer, Massa.* Elected to the Knesset as a member of the Likud, 1977-81. *Nativ,* (publication of the Ariel Center for Policy Research), member of advisory council. *Military service:* Iraeli Defense Force, captain, 1948.

*MEMBER:* Land of Israel Movement, Tehiya Party (founder).

*AWARDS, HONORS:* Ussishkin prize, 1949; Brenner prize, 1953; Bialik prize, 1955; Neumann Literary Award, New York University, 1981; Israel Prize, 1988, for contribution to Israeli literature.

*WRITINGS:*

*Hu halakh ba-sadot* (novel), Sifriyat Po'alim (Merhavyah, Israel), 1947, published as *He Walked Through the Fields,* translation by Aubrey Hodes, World Zionist Organization, Department for Edu-

cation and Culture in the Diaspora (Jerusalem, Israel), 1959, reprinted (as a play), Or-'am (Tel Aviv, Israel), 1989.

*Yedidav ha-gedolim shel Gadi: ve-sipurim aherimu* (short stories) Sifriyat Po'alim (Merhavyah, Israel), 1947.

(With Aryeh Navon)*Portsei derekh Yerushlalayim: pirk 'alilat Nahshon,* Yotse le-or 'al yede Mahleket ha-tarbut shel Tseva haganah le-Yisra'el (Tel Aviv, Israel), 1948, translated as *Taking the Mountains: The Story of the Nahshon Operation,* Lion the Printer for the Keren Hayesod, Youth Department (Jerusalem, Israel), 1949.

*Kilometer 56* (play), Sifriyat Po'alim (Merhavyah, Israel), 1949.

(With Aryeh Navon) *'Ad Elat,* Sifriyat Po'alim (Merhavyah, Israel), 1950.

*Tahat ha-shemesh* (novel; title means "Under the Sun"), Sifnyat Po'alim (Merhavyah, Israel), 1950, reprinted, Am Oved (Tel Aviv, Israel), 1975.

*Be-mo yadav: Pirtkei Elik,* Sifriyat Po'alim (Merhavyah, Israel), 1951, reprinted, Am Oved (Tel Aviv, Israel), 1990, translation by Joseph Shacter published as *With His Own Hands,* Institute for the Translation of Hebrew Literature (Jerusalem, Israel), 1970.

*Bet hilel: Mahazeh be-shalosh ma'arakhot,* N. Tverski (Tel Aviv, Israel), 1951.

(With Shemuel Katz), *ehad efes le-tovatenu: sipurim,* N. Tverski (Tel Aviv, Israel), 1951.

*The Call of the Land,* translation by Shemuel Lowensohn and Yitchak Avrahami, Education Department of the Jewish National Fund (London, England), 1951.

*Nashim mehakot ba-huts: 13* sipurim (short stories), Sifriyat Po'alim (Merhavyah, Israel), 1952.

*Eleh pene Yisra'el,* photographs by Zoltan Kluger, English commentary by Leo Rissin, Le'on hamadpis (Tel Aviv, Israel), 1952.

*Melekh basar va-dam: roman histori* (historical novel) Sifriyat Po'alim (Merhavyah, Israel), 1954, reprinted, 'Am 'oved (Tel Aviv, Israel), 1983, published as *The King of Flesh and Blood,* translation by David Patterson, East and West Library (London, England), 1956.

*Sof ha-'olam: komedyah me-haye ha-arets be-shalosh ma'arakhot,* Hotsa'at ha-sefarim veha-tavim shel ha-Merkaz le-tarbut ule hinukh (Tel Aviv, Israel), 1954.

*Ha-Hut ha-meshulash: sipurim* (short stories), Mo'etset po'ale hefah, Va'adat ha-Tarbut (Hefah, Israel), 1955.

*Milhemet Bene Or: mahazeh hisotir mi-yeme Yanai ha-melekh,* Sifriyat Po'alim (Merhavyah, Israel), 1955, reprinted, Am Oved (Tel Aviv, Israel), 1989.

*Kivsat ha-rash: sipur Uriyah ha-Hiti,* Davar (Tel Aviv, Israel), 1956, reprinted, 'Am oved (Tel Aviv, Israel) 1974, translation by M. Benaya published as *David's Stranger,* Abelard-Schuman (New York, NY), 1965, also published as *The Hittite Must Die,* East and West Library (New York, NY), 1978.

*Me-agadot Lod: sipur u-mahazeh,* Sifriyat Po'alim (Merhavyah, Israel), 1958.

*Kulam be-yahad: sipurim le-yeladim be-shenai kolot* (short stories), Sifriyat Po'alim (Merhavyah, Israel), 1959.

*Hamishah ma'arkhonim,* ha-Merkaz le-tarbut ule-hinukh (Tel Aviv, Israel), 1959.

*Be-kulmos manhir,* Sifriyat Po'alim (Merhavyah, Israel), 1960.

*On the Sabbath He Rode His Horse (Astride His Horse on the Sabbath),* translated by Rabbi Zalman M. Schacter, 1960.

*Why Ziva Cried on the Feast of the First Fruits* (juvenile fiction), translated by Tamara Kahana, illustrated by Cyril Satorsky, Abelard-Schuman (New York, NY), 1960.

*Ha-galgal ha-hamishi* (juvenile), [Tel Aviv, Israel], 1961, reprinted, 'Am 'oved (Tel Aviv, Israel), 1990, published as *The Fifth Wheel,* illustrated by Shemuel Katz, Benmir Books (Berkeley, CA), 1986.

*ha-Gevul,* (novel; title means "The Border: A Novel"), Sifriyat Po'alim (Merhavyah, Israel), 1966, reprinted, Zemorah-Bitan (Tel Aviv, Israel), 1997.

(With Shemuel Katz) *Be-'ikvot Iohame Sinai: anashim ve-nofim be-mivtsa' Kadesh,* ha-Hotsa'ah le-or shel Misrad ha-bitahon (Tel Aviv, Israel), 1966.

*Hu halakh ba-sadot: nosah 1966-1967,* (Tel Aviv, Israel), 1967.

*Nes lo karah lanu,* Lewin-Epstein (Tel Aviv, Israel), 1968.

*Hayai 'im Yishma'el,* Sifriyat Ma'ariv (Tel Aviv, Israel), 1968, translation by Rose Kirson published as *My Life with Ishmael,* Valentine, Mitchell (London, England), 1970.

*Sipurah shel Hefah; 'ir ha-Karmel,* (title means "The Saga of Haifa; City of Carmel"), illustrated by Reuben R. Hecht, Shikmonah (Hefah, Israel),1968.

(Translator) Samuel Beckett *Mehakim le-Godo,* (translation of means *Waiting for Godot*), Tarshish (Jerusalem, Israel), 1968.

*The Heir: A Play in Two Acts* (produced in Haifa at the Haifa Municipal Theatre, 1963), translated by Joseph Bahral, Mortonplay (Paris, France), 1968.

*Manhigim ve-shoftim: mi-Yehoshu'a 'ad Sha'ul* (juvenile), Amir (Israel), 1970.

*Yonah me-hatser zarah* (novel; title means "From a Different Yard"), 'Am 'oved (Tel Aviv, Israel), 1973.

*El mul pene ha-milhamah ha-hazakah,* Shikmonah (Jerusalem, Israel), 1974.

*Sipurim* (short stories), Misrad ha-bitahon ha-hotsa'ah le-or (Tel Aviv, Israel), 1974.

*Ha-Mamlakhah ha-me'uihedet: David u-Shelomoh,* Amir hotsa'ah le-'or (Tel Aviv, Israel), 1976.

*Malkhe bet-David: mi-Rehav'am 'ad Hizyahu,* Sifriyat ma'ariv (Tel Aviv, Israel), 1977.

*Sipurim bi-sheloshah kolot* (title means "Stories in Three Voices"), Devir (Tel Aviv, Israel), 1977, reprinted, ha-Mahlakah le-hinukh ule-tarbut Yehudiyim ba-golah, ha-Rashut ha-meshutefet le-hinukh Yehudi Tsiyoni (Jerusalem, Israel), 1996.

*Malkhe Yisra'el: mi-pilug 'ad galut,* Sifriyat Ma'ariv (Tel Aviv, Israel), 1978.

*Lo rehokim min ha-'ets: korot bayit ehad be-Yisra'el,* Devir (Jerusalem, Israel), 1983.

*Hinumat ha-kalah* (novel; title means "The Bridal Veil"), 'Am 'oved (Tel Aviv, Israel), 1984.

*Yalde ha-sha'ashu'im* (title means "Playboys"), 'Am 'oved (Tel Aviv, Israel), 1986.

*Hut ha-shani: 'al Tsiyonut ve-sotsyalizm (nisayon le-ma'azan histori)* (title means "The Red Thread"), Devir (Tel Aviv, Israel), 1986.

*'Inyan ishi: 'im sheloshim va-hamishah meshorerim* (title means "Personal View"), Devir (Tel Aviv, Israel), 1987.

*Ki 'erom atah: romanuu* (novel), 'Am 'Oved (Tel Aviv, Israel), 1988.

*Natan Alterman: ha-meshorer ke-manhig,* Devir (Tel Aviv, Israel), 1988.

*Ha-Be'ad veha-neged: 'im bene dori: sofrim, sefarim, sugyot ba-sifrut ha-'Ivrit bat yamenu* (title means "For and Against: Literature and Society in Contemporary Israel"), Devir (Tel Aviv, Israel), 1989.

*Nos'e ha-meshekh: 'al gedole ha-sifrut ha'Ivrit veha-'olamit: pulmus, bikoret, bikoret 'atsmitu* (title means "The Seed Carriers"), Devir (Tel Aviv, Israel), 1989.

*Ha-Yoresh: mahazeh bi-shete ma'arakhot* (play), Or'am (Tel Aviv, Israel), 1989.

*Yehudit shel ha-metsora'im: mahzeh bi-shene halakim,* Or'am (Ramat Gan, Israel), 1989.

*Ki-me'at: Kol shire Mosheh Shamir,* (poetry) Sifriyat po'alim (Tel Aviv, Israel), 1991.

*Protokol shel mapolet: 'im Begin ve-negdo, 737-742, 1976-1982,* Sifriyat Bet-El (Bet-El, Israel), 1991.

*Ha-Makom ha-yarok: beli Tsiyonut zeh lo yelekh* (title means "The Green Place"), Devir (Tel Aviv, Israel), 1991.

*Ad ha-sof* (novel; title means "To the End"), 'Am'oved (Tel Aviv, Israel), 1991.

*Va-afilu li-re'ot kokhavim: sipurimu* (title means "And Even To See the Stars: Short Stories"), 'Am 'oved (Tel Aviv, Israel), 1993.

*Re'uven Hekht: agadat hayim,* Hadar (Haifah, Israel), 1994, translation by Carl Alpert published as *Reuben Hect: Vision and Fulfillment,* Hadar Publishing House (Tel Aviv, Israel), 1995.

*Avraham ba-boker,* Even hoshen (Ra'ananah, Israel), 1995.

*Zarkor la-'omek: zehutenu ha-Yehudit, moreshet ve-etgar* (title means "Searchlight to the Depth: Our Jewish Identity, Heritage and Challenge"), Devir (Tel Aviv, Israel), 1996.

*Ha-'Omdim ba-pirtsah: 'al sifrut ve-sofrim,* Sifre bit-saron (Jerusalem, Israel), 1999.

*Ya'ir, Avraham Shtern: hayav, milhamto, moto: roman bioygrafi* (title means "Yair, a Biographical Novel"), Zemorah-Bitan (Lod, Israel), 2001.

*EDITOR*

(With Shlomo Tanny), *Yalkut ha-re'im,* Mosad Byalik (Jerusalem, Israel), 1943.

(With Hayim Glikshtain and Shlomo Tanny) *Daf ha-dash: le-sifrut, omanut u-vikoret,* Defus Lidor (Tel Aviv, Israel), 1947.

(With Azriel Ukhamani and Shlomo Tanny, *Dor ba-arets; antologyah shel sifrut Yisre'elit,* Sifriyat Po'alim (Merhavyah, Israel), 1958.

(With Shlomo Tanny) *Sefer 'Yalkut ha-re'im,* Mosad Byalik (Jerusalem, Israel), 1992.

(With Nathan Shaham and Haim Gouri) *Dor ha-Palmah ba-sifrut uva-shirah: bi-melot 50 shanim le-dor ha-Palmah* (title mans "Palmach, Literature and Poetry"), Tag (Israel), 1994.

Short stories have appeared in anthologies, including *Shiv'ah mesaprim,* Misrad ha-hinukh veha-tarbut be-shituf Yahdav (Tel Aviv, Israel), 1973. Author's works have also been translated into Spanish, Russian, Chinese, Bulgarian, German, Portuguese, and Dutch.

Also author of plays, including *Meagadot Lod, Gam Zu Letova, Halayla leish, A Home in Good Condition, Judith of the Lepers, The Strong Hand,* and *Carnival in Venice.*

*SIDELIGHTS:* Moshe Shamir is a prolific writer in Hebrew whose works include fiction, children's literature, poetry, essays, plays, and literary criticism. He is most widely known for his fiction, which includes historical novels and numerous short stories. Shamir, who lived for six years on the Kibbutz Mishmar Ha'emek, has long been a proponent of the "Greater Land of Israel" ideology, which focuses on Jewish sovereignty over the entire Israeli territories occupied after 1967 and the idea of further settling the land. In his early fiction, Shamir wrote about the important issues and themes that preoccupied Israelis before the official establishment of the State of Israel and then about the issues facing a growing nation.

Shamir's first novel, *He Walked Through the Fields,* takes place on a kibbutz in the 1940s and tells the story of a native-born kibbutznik and his family. Within the context of the story is the Jewish theme of the *aqedah,* the biblical story in which Abraham, at the request of God, is going to sacrifice his son Isaac. Writing in *Backgrounds for the Bible,* Edna Amir Coffin noted, "This theme has emerged as central in Modern Hebrew literature at least partly in response to historical events which have affected the Jewish community in the twentieth century." Shamir's handling of them takes both an idealistic view of Israeli society and a realistic view. The story focuses on a family in a kibbutz and ends tragically with the death of a son during military training and the breakup of a family—both serve as metaphors for the larger notion of the kibbutz and the Jewish community. "The novel reflects a structural affinity to the *aqedah,*" wrote Coffin, "but unlike the biblical story and like many other modern works of fiction which have used this theme, in this *aqedah* the sacrifice is carried out, and there is no divine presence or interference." Rather, as Coffin pointed out, the "responsibility for the outcome" lies with "individuals and their community." The novel's central issue, noted Coffin, is "whether ideological commitment to national goals supersedes the needs of individuals."

By the late 1950s, Shamir's work was less idealistic in terms of how he viewed the Israeli world. Even his historical novels about past leaders of the Jewish people contain strong metaphorical elements relating to the modern issues of Israeli leadership. In *The King of Flesh and Blood* Shamir presents a fictionalized account of Alexander Yannai, a Jewish leader during the Hasmonean era. The book focuses on the first five years after Yannai becomes king of Judea (c. 103 B.C.). Writing in, *Israeli Writers Consider the "Outsider,"* Shamir says that *The King of Flesh and Blood* "reflects my basic attitude to the subject of time: the notion of total identification with the past, denial of a rupture between past and present, and active awareness of our national existence, so encompassing and significant that it embraces everything from our forefather Abraham until the messianic age." David Patterson, who translated *The King of Flesh and Blood* from the Hebrew, also noted in an essay in *Israeli Writers Consider the "Outsider,"* that Shamir was "faced with the formidable problem of writing convincingly about ancient periods in Israel's history," especially in terms of "attempting to create a stratum of language strikingly reminiscent of postbiblical Hebrew." Patterson went on to note that "Shamir achieved a veritable linguistic tour de force" with the novel.

In *David's Stranger,* Shamir focuses on a period one thousand years before the time of *The King of Flesh and Blood.* Shamir, once again writing in *Israeli Writers Consider the "Outsider"* notes that "this is a highly subjective book, with no proclivity or pretense whatever of being a historical account." In the book, Shamir addresses the issue of the reader as the judge when the first-person narrator says to the reader, "I can't render judgment. You're the clever one who knows. You can judge." The story focuses on Uriah, a man torn between the love for his wife and the love for his king. Shamir describes him as a "sacrificial victim in every sense of the word." Shamir also says about the novel's character, "Sometimes, there is a personal pain which no justification or explanation can wish away. The wound, like a scream, always remains open."

In the same essay, Shamir also discusses his work *Hinumat ha-kalah,* noting that it "belongs to the realm of family memory" and, as such, deals with "recent past." In essence, Shamir calls the book "a debate" in which the "author argues with his heroine" about the "basic question of our existence, of our humanity and our Jewishness, the essence of life, the purpose of life, the sanctity of life." As for writing a historical novel of the recent past, Shamir said it was "a most difficult and complex challenge" to tie it "to the present." He concludes, "Perhaps it is for this reason that I only came to it after I had experience dealing with subjects from the distant past." The story takes place in Russia at the beginning of the twentieth century and focuses on Leah Berman, a woman born to the middle class who becomes a radical crusader who spends time in prison, is eventually smuggled out of the country and finally gives up all hopes of personal happiness to devote her life to others. Dov Vardi, reviewing the book in *World Literature Today,* noted that Leah is like many of Shamir's working-class heroes who are "less paralyzed in their actions by deliberation and soul-searching, are ready to sacrifice themselves for the cause, and are brave."

Shamir has received many awards for his novels, which have also focused on such issues as Israeli social class and structure, kibbutz life, and the problems associated with some Israeli values. Based on the volume of his work and its willingness to confront the issues of Israeli society, Shamir is viewed as one of the most important Israeli writers. Advancing age has not slowed down his prolific output. At about the age of eighty, Shamir saw the publication of his 2001 biographical novel *Ya'ir, Avraham Shtern.*

In the conclusion of his *Israeli Writers Consider the "Outsider"* essay, Shamir says, "I will be glad if the readers of all my books . . . will find in them a reflection on the past while moving forward. It was not nostalgia that has motivated the writer, nor was the glorification of some figure the objective of these books. They were written, and others are still being written, so that we may have strength, and knowledge of where we are going, as we sense and know from whence we have come."

## BIOGRAPHICAL AND CRITICAL SOURCES:

### BOOKS

O'Connor, Michael Patrick, and David Noel Freeman, *Backgrounds for the Bible,* Eisenbrauns (Winona Lake, IN), 1987, pp. 293-308.

Yudkin Leon, I., editor, *Israeli Writers Consider the "Outsider."* pp. 100-111.

### PERIODICALS

*Booklist,* May 15, 1975, Sylvia S. Goldberg, brief review of Kivsat ha-rash, p. 944.

*Iton 77,* 1988, S. Alonim, "Alterman: Haim ve-politkah," pp. 103-104.

*Modern Hebrew Literature,* fall-winter, 1995, Nurit Gertz, "The Book and the Film: A Case Study of *He Walked through the Fields,*" pp. 22-26.

*New Statesman,* October 30, 1970, review of *My Life with Ishmael,* p. 568.

*World Literature Today,* winter, 1986, Dov Vardi, review of *Hinumat Kala,* pp. 173-174.

\*   \*   \*

## SHARP, Adrienne

*PERSONAL:* Daughter of Norman and Rona Subotnik; children: two. *Education:* Attended Brandeis University; University of California, San Diego; Johns Hopkins University, M.A.; University of Southern California, M.A.; University of Virginia. *Religion:* Jewish.

*ADDRESSES: Home*—Redondo Beach, CA. *Agent*—c/o Author Mail, Random House, Inc., 1540 Broadway, New York, NY 10036.

*CAREER:* Writer. Former dancer with Harkness Ballet in New York, NY.

*AWARDS, HONORS:* Henry Hoyns Fellow, University of Virginia graduate writing program.

*WRITINGS:*

*White Swan, Black Swan: Stories,* Random House (New York, NY), 2001.

*SIDELIGHTS:* Former ballet dancer Adrienne Sharp drew upon her knowledge of the profession in her writing debut, the short story collection *White Swan, Black Swan.* The title refers to the plot of the ballet *Swan Lake* and is also the name of one of the twelve tales within it. The book reveals the off-stage existence of real and fictional ballet dancers; the stories show the often dark side of life that contrasts with the excitement of performing. Sharp began dancing at the age of seven and left her dancing career in New York City to study creative writing at Johns Hopkins and the University of Virginia.

Sharp's stories are dark, peopled by characters struggling with ruined love affairs, alcohol and drug problems, AIDS, and anorexia. Some of the fictional characters include the trio of dancers in "White Swan, Black Swan": wife Lexa, husband Robbie, and his young dance partner and mistress, Sandra. Robbie uses Sandra and drugs to gratify his urge for the unattainable. Other fictional characters find themselves turning to or from ballet according to the influence of their personal relationships. Many stories also feature famous dance figures. Using information found in biographies and popular publications, Sharp created fictionalized accounts of episodes in their lives. "Don Quixote," for example, has an aging George Balanchine describing his past obsession with eighteen-year-old dancer Suzanne Farrell. Furious at her refusal to leave her lover, he risked ruining his dance company by firing her. The widely publicized romance between stars Margot Fonteyn and Rudolf Nureyev is expanded on in "The Immortals: Margot + Rudolph 4 Ever."

Reviewers responded to *White Swan, Black Swan* with widely disparate judgments. The book was both praised and condemned strongly. Negative remarks included commentary from Susie Linfield in the *Los Angeles Times.* After noting that the realm of classical ballet is extremely difficult to capture in literature, Linfield said that Sharp follows in the footsteps of many others who have failed in the attempt. Linfield was most impressed with "In the Kingdom of the Shades," a story about a depressed dancer who is on leave of absence from her company after taking an overdose of Valium. The critic found valuable insight into the woman's relationship with her father. In a review for the *Washington Post Book World,* Laura Jacobs expressed disappointment with the author's use of famous names and ballet companies and saw a too-heavy emphasis on sex. "Sharp understands that there is a mind-body dichotomy locked into the heart of every dancer. . . . Unfortunately, it's the blunt body that fills these pages, often to the point of prurience," she objected.

Several other reviewers, however, were charmed with Sharp's knowledge of the dance world and applauded her work as a strong first effort. A writer for *Kirkus Reviews* called *White Swan, Black Swan* a "luminous debut collection" in which all the stories are "dark in mood, more like reports from a war zone." Donna Seaman commented in *Booklist* that it is a "breathtaking" collection that "adroitly captures the elegance, magic, sexuality, obsession, ambition, sacrifice, vulnerability, and pain that define dancers' lives." Seaman enjoyed Sharp's writing skills and ability to probe "the deeper implications" of this art form. Further praise was found in *Publishers Weekly,* where a critic wrote that "the dance world becomes palpably real in this accomplished debut collection." In contrast to some of the negative criticism, this writer deemed that the use of real figures made the stories "resonate with realism for readers who recognize the first-name references." The *Publishers Weekly* contributor recommended the stories to readers familiar with ballet, who would have a "full appreciation" of their significance.

*BIOGRAPHICAL AND CRITICAL SOURCES:*

*PERIODICALS*

*Booklist,* June 1, 2001, Donna Seaman, review of *White Swan, Black Swan,* p. 1849.
*Kirkus Reviews,* May 1, 2001, review of *White Swan, Black Swan.*
*Los Angeles Times,* July 20, 2001, Susie Linfield, "Dancers of 'White Swan, Black Swan' Drown in a Lake of Cliches," p. E3.
*Publishers Weekly,* May 28, 2001, review of *White Swan, Black Swan,* p. 47.
*Washington Post Book World,* July 1, 2001, Laura Jacobs, review of *White Swan, Black Swan,* p. T09.*

\*   \*.   \*

## SHAULL, (Millard) Richard 1919-2002

*OBITUARY NOTICE*—See index for *CA* sketch: Born November 24, 1919, in Felton, PA; died October 25, 2002, in Ardmore, PA. Missionary, educator, and author. Shaull was a Princeton Theological Seminary professor of ecumenics who worked for many years as a missionary in Latin America. An alumnus of Elizabeth Town College, where he earned a B.A. in 1938, and of Princeton Theological Seminary, where he earned a Th.B. in 1941 and a Th.D. in 1959, Shaull was a Presbyterian missionary in Colombia during the 1940s. He then moved to Brazil, where he was a professor of church history at Campinas Theological Seminary during the 1950s and vice president of the Mackenzie Institute in São Paulo from 1960 to 1962.

Returning to his alma mater, Shaull taught ecumenics there until his retirement as professor emeritus in 1980. In addition to his teaching, he was active in Christian organizations such as the World Student Christian Federation, for which he served as a chairperson and consultant in Latin America and in Germany, France, India, Japan, and Korea. Shaull was the author of several books, some in Portuguese and German, including *Heralds of a New Reformation: The Poor of South and North America* (1984), *The Reformation and Liberation Theology: Insights for the Challenges Today* (1991), and the cowritten work *Pentecostalism and the Future of the Christian Churches: Promises, Limitations, Challenges* (2000).

*OBITUARIES AND OTHER SOURCES:*

*BOOKS*

*Who's Who in America,* 53rd edition, Marquis (New Providence, NJ), 1999.

*PERIODICALS*

*New York Times,* November 4, 2002, p. A23.

\*   \*   \*

## SHEPHERD, Naomi

*PERSONAL:* Born in England. *Education:* Oxford University.

*ADDRESSES: Home*—Israel. *Agent*—c/o Author Mail, Peter Halban Ltd., 22 Golden Square, London W1F 9JW, England.

*CAREER:* Journalist. *New Statesman,* London, England, former Israeli correspondent; Hebrew University, Jerusalem, Israel, former teacher; Jewish Agency, script writer.

*WRITINGS:*

*Health and Medical Care,* Israel Digest (Jerusalem, Israel), 1973.
*A Refuge from Darkness: Wilfrid Israel and the Rescue of the Jews,* Pantheon Books (New York, NY), 1984.

*The Zealous Intruders: The Western Rediscovery of Palestine,* Harper and Row (San Francisco, CA), 1987.

*Teddy Kollek, Mayor of Jerusalem,* Harper and Row (New York, NY), 1988.

*Alarms and Excursions: Thirty Years in Israel,* Collins (London, England), 1990.

*A Price Below Rubies: Jewish Women as Rebels and Radicals,* Harvard University Press (Cambridge, MA), 1993.

*The Russians in Israel: The Ordeal of Freedom,* Simon and Schuster (New York, NY), 1994.

*Ploughing Sand: British Rule in Palestine,* Rutgers University Press (New Brunswick, NJ), 2000.

*Ashes* (story collection), Peter Halban (London, England), 2001.


*SIDELIGHTS:* In *Ploughing Sand: British Rule in Palestine,* Naomi Shepherd examines the British attempt to rule Palestine before Israel was established. This area has been under contention since before the British had the area mandated to their rule by the League of Nations at the end of World War I, and it remains torn by conflict today. Shepherd views the mandate from the British point of view, relying on British documents, but she steers away from political discussions and emphasizes the mandate's effects on the daily lives of Arabs and Jews who lived in Palestine at the time. The book begins with a description of the British conquest of Palestine during World War I, the military government that lasted there until 1920, and the subsequent civilian government, run by Sir Herbert Samuel. Later chapters discuss immigration, land ownership, health, and education. In the last chapter, Shepherd discusses the British reaction to Arab and Jewish violence. The book includes character portraits of the ruling British administrators, as well as many details of government and culture of the time that are not widely known. In the *Middle East Journal,* John L. McTague wrote, "Although [Shepherd] lives in Israel, she has taken an unbiased approach to an extremely emotional topic." In *Contemporary Review,* George Evans called the book "instructive" and "well-researched."


*The Russians in Israel: The Ordeal of Freedom* discusses the problems of Russians who emigrated from Russia to Israel between 1989 and 1993, and their "attempts to understand a free society and come to terms with their own lack of modern skills," according to Geoffrey Heptonstall in *Contemporary Review.*

In *The Zealous Intruders: The Western Rediscovery of Palestine,* Shepherd examines the history of Palestine, focusing on the resurgence of interest in the area by European Jews in the nineteenth century. In the *Times Literary Supplement,* Robert Irwin remarked, "In general, Shepherd aims to entertain. She tells lots of good tales."


*A Price Below Rubies: Jewish Women as Rebels and Radicals* examines traditional restrictive expectations of Jewish women, and women who broke out of those bonds. As Ruth Brandon wrote in *New Statesman,* "They were an extraordinary and violent lot. Their implacability perhaps reflected the emotional violence they inflicted on themselves when first they broke the bond that chained them to their families and communities." Shepherd writes about Anna Kuliscioff, Rosa Luxemburg, Esther Frumkin, Manya Shochat, Rose Pesotta, Emma Goldman, and Bertha Pappenheim. Some of these women were anarchists, others violent political activists. Brandon commented, "Naomi Shepherd, setting them in the background they so vehemently rejected, enables us to see these extraordinary lives from a new angle." In *Kirkus Reviews,* a writer called the book a "fastidiously researched explanation for the emergence of Jewish women as radicals."


*BIOGRAPHICAL AND CRITICAL SOURCES:*


*PERIODICALS*

*American Jewish History,* June, 1995, Pamela S. Nadell, review of *A Price Below Rubies: Jewish Women as Rebels and Radicals,* p. 321.

*Biblical Archaeologist,* December, 1989, M. Patrick Graham, review of *The Zealous Intruders: The Western Rediscovery of Palestine,* p. 231.

*Choice,* April, 1994, J. Zimmerman, review of *A Price Below Rubies,* p. 1343; September, 2000, B. Harris, Jr., review of *Ploughing Sand: British Rule in Palestine,* p. 1971.

*Church History,* December, 1989, James H. Glassman, review of *The Zealous Intruders,* p. 523.

*Contemporary Review,* March, 1994, Geoffrey Heptonstall and Michael L. Nash, review of *The Russians in Israel: The Ordeal of Freedom,* p. 168; April, 2000, George Evans, review of *Ploughing Sand,* p. 211.

*Economist,* January 20, 2001, Tom Segev, "To have and To Hold; Britain's Mandate in Palestine," p. 4.

*English Historical Review,* January, 1991, C. G. Smith, review of *The Zealous Intruders,* p. 221.

*Foreign Affairs,* fall, 1988, John C. Campbell, review of *Teddy Kollek, Mayor of Jerusalem,* p. 196.

*Journal of Military History,* October, 2000, Kenneth Perkins, review of *Ploughing Sand,* p. 1186.

*Journal of Palestine Studies,* spring, 2001, Ann M. Lesch, "Governing the Mandate," p. 108.

*Judaism,* winter, 1989, p. 128.

*Kirkus Reviews,* February 1, 1988, review of *Teddy Kollek,* p. 188; July 15, 1993, review of *A Price Below Rubies,* p. 921.

*Library Journal,* October 15, 1984, Nancy C. Cridland, review of *A Refuge from Darkness: Wilfrid Israel and the Rescue of the Jews,* p. 1940; October 15, 1988, David P. Snider, review of *Teddy Kollek,* p. 159.

*Middle Eastern Studies,* April, 1989, p. 277.

*Middle East Journal,* winter, 2001, John J. McTague, review of *Ploughing Sand,* p. 157.

*New Statesman,* June 29, 1984, Brian Martin, "Wilfrid Israel: German Jewry's Secret Ambassador," p. 107; October 8, 1993, Ruth Brandon, review of *A Price Below Rubies,* p. 37; October 25, 1999, Frank McLynn, review of *Ploughing Sand,* p. 55.

*New York Times Book Review,* August 7, Alison Knopf, review of *Teddy Kollek,* 1988, p. 21; November 14, 1993, Dorothy Gallagher, review of *A Price Below Rubies,* p. 13.

*Publishers Weekly,* June 15, 1984, p. 68; March 11, 1988, review of *Teddy Kollek,* p. 93.

*Shofar,* summer, 2001, "Israel," p. 179.

*Signs,* autumn, 1995, Paula Rabinowitz, review of *A Price Below Rubies,* p. 180.

*Slavic Review,* winter, 1994, Ann Hibner Koblitz, review of *A Price Below Rubies,* p. 1123.

*Times Literary Supplement,* July 13, 1984, A. J. Sherman, "Help for the Hunted," p. 793; October 9, 1987, Robert Irwin, "Barging into the Bible," p. 1102; July 6, 2001, Bryan Cheyette, "The State's Foundations," p. 21.

*Wilson Library Bulletin,* April, 1994, Judith M. Amory, review of *A Price Below Rubies,* p. 106.

*Women and Politics,* spring, 1996, Martha A. Ackelsberg, review of *A Price Below Rubies,* p. 83.

*Women's Review of Books,* December, 1993, Lillian S. Robinson, review of *A Price Below Rubies,* p. 16.*

## SHINEBERG, Dorothy (Lois) 1927-

*PERSONAL:* Born February 5, 1927, in Melbourne, Australia; married; children: two. *Education:* University of Melbourne, B.A., Ph.D., 1965; Smith College, M.A., 1952.

*ADDRESSES: Home*—28 Getting Crescent, Campbell, Australian Capital Territory, Australia. *Office*—Division of Pacific and Asian History, Research School of Pacific and Asian Studies, H. C. Coombs Building No. 9, Australian National University, Canberra, Australian Capital Territory 0200, Australia. *E-mail*—dorothy. shineberg@anu.edu.au; or barrysh.@webone.com.au.

*CAREER:* Professor and scholar of Pacific studies. Australian School of Pacific Administration, Sydney, lecturer in history, 1948-50; University of Melbourne, Melbourne, Australia, lecturer in history, 1953-56; Australian National University, Canberra, research fellow, 1964-70, senior lecturer, 1970-74, reader, 1974-88, visiting professor of Pacific and Asian history, 1988—. Brown University, Providence, RI, research associate, 1972. Member of editorial board, *Journal of Pacific History,* 1966-97.

*AWARDS, HONORS:* Fulbright traveling scholarship, 1950-52.

*WRITINGS:*

*They Came for Sandalwood: A Study of the Sandalwood Trade in the South-West Pacific, 1830-1865,* Melbourne University Press (Carlton, Australia), 1967.

(Editor) *The Trading Voyages of Andrew Cheyne, 1841-1844* Australian National University Press (Canberra, Australia), 1971.

*The People Trade: Pacific Island Laborers and New Caledonia, 1865-1930,* University of Hawaii Press (Manoa, Hawaii), 1999.

Coeditor, *Journal of Pacific History,* 1987-90. Contributor of articles to academic journals and anthologies.

Shineberg's works have been translated into French.

*SIDELIGHTS:* Australian historian Dorothy Shineberg's *They Came for Sandalwood: A Study of the Sandalwood Trade in the South-West Pacific, 1830-1865* is an extended version of her Ph.D. dissertation at the University of Melbourne. The book is a detailed study of many facets of the sandalwood trade, including its economic logic and the effects arising from the fact that this was in most cases the earliest regular contact between Europeans and Melanesians. The trade brought an "iron revolution" to an area which had not known metals before, cutting the labor required for many tedious tasks. Many other changes resulted from the new knowledge of the outside world, particularly for those natives employed on ships and in sandalwood stations run by Australian traders.

*They Came for Sandalwood* is notable as the first modern study of this trade in the South Pacific. Prior to its publication, the primary anthropological sources for the history of the Pacific commerce in sandalwood were the often-biased accounts of Christian missionaries in the region. These missionaries generally presented the sandalwood trade as pure Western exploitation. They claimed that the traders used their superior weaponry to force the native Melanesians into cutting the wood to be traded, and that the occasional massacres of Westerners by the Melanesians were justified reactions to previous Western offenses. Shineberg, through a detailed examination of such primary sources as traders' diaries and logs, contemporary newspaper and magazine articles, and the records of Australian businesses engaged in the sandalwood trade, presents a more nuanced picture of the interactions between the two groups. She shows that the Melanesians were skilled traders themselves who often profited as much if not more than the Westerners with whom they traded. Shineberg also presents evidence that the Melanesians' various weapons were more effective than the traders' flintlock firearms in the situations in which they found themselves, particularly when they were attacked from ambush while walking through the bush.

Shineberg's *The People Trade: Pacific Island Laborers and New Caledonia, 1865-1930* is a history of the indentured laborers who worked in the French Pacific colony of New Caledonia. Like *They Came for Sandalwood, The People Trade* is largely a close analysis of varied primary sources. These sources are used to create a detailed portrait of the lives of the workers who left their homes, mostly on the islands of the New He-

brides (now Vanuatu), to live and work in New Caledonia. New Caledonia's labor trade was the third largest in the Pacific, behind Fiji and Queensland. Very little has been published on the labor history of the French Territories of the Pacific, and *The People Trade* helps to address this lack. As well as providing a detailed account of the recruitment, life, and all-too-frequent death at the workplace, the work addresses the controversy over whether indentured labor is simply slavery under another name, and the degree to which recruits signed on willingly or were "pressed" into service.

*BIOGRAPHICAL AND CRITICAL SOURCES:*

PERIODICALS

*American Anthropologist,* June, 1969, Marianne L. Stoller, review of *They Came for Sandalwood,* pp. 574-575.
*Australian Historical Studies,* Volume 116, 2002, Donald Denoon, review of *The People Trade,* pp. 159-160.
*Australian Journal of Anthropology,* Volume 12, number 1, Steve Mullins, review of *The People Trade,* pp. 116-118.
*Business History Review,* autumn, 1973, Jacques M. Dowas, review of *They Came for Sandalwood,* pp. 405-407.
*Choice,* January, 1970, review of *They Came for Sandalwood,* p. 1641; January, 2000, Michael J. O'Brien and R. Lee Lyman, review of *The People Trade,* p. 977.
*Contemporary Pacific,* spring, 2002, Jacqueline Leckie, review of *The People Trade,* pp. 253-254.
*International History Review,* December, 2001, Doug Munro, review of *The People Trade,* pp. 932-934.
*Journal of Pacific History,* Volume 35, number 2, 2002, Isabelle Merle, review of *The People Trade,* pp. 228-229.

OTHER

*Research School of Pacific and Asian Studies,* http://rspas.anu.edu.au/ (August 21, 2001).

\*　　\*　　\*

**SHIRINIAN, Lorne 1945-**

*PERSONAL:* Born 1945, in Toronto, Ontario, Canada. *Education:* University of Toronto, BA., Carleton University, M.A., University of Montreal, Ph.D. *Hobbies and other interests:* Filmmaking, film noir.

*ADDRESSES: Home*—P.O. Box 17000, Kingston, Ontario, K7K 7B4 Canada. *Office*—Department of English, Royal Military College of Canada, Kingston, Ontario K7K 5L0 Canada; Blue Heron Press, 160 Greenlees Dr., Kingston, Ontario K7K 6P4 Canada. *E-mail*—shirinian-l@rmc.ca.

*CAREER:* Royal Military College of Canada, Kingston, Ontario, professor of comparative literature and head of department of English, 1994—; Blue Heron Press, Kingston, Ontario, founder, c. 1999. *Manna*, founder and editor, 1971-74.

*WRITINGS:*

*Manuscript: Tom Sturgess* (poems), Abbey (Toronto, Ontario, Canada), 1971.

*Armenian-North American Poets: An Anthology,* Manna Publishing (St. Jean, Quebec, Canada), 1974.

*Poems of Dispersion and Other Rites of Movement,* Manna Publishing (St. Jean, Quebec, Canada), 1977.

*Armenian-North American Literature: A Critical Introduction: Genocide, Diaspora, and Symbols,* Edwin Mellen Press (Lewiston, NY), 1990.

*Earthquake,* Edwin Mellen Press (Lewiston, NY), 1991.

*Beginnings and Ends,* Zoryan Institute (Toronto, Ontario, Canada), 1991.

*The Republic of Armenia and the Rethinking of the North-American Diaspora in Literature,* Mellen Press (Lewiston, NY), 1992.

*History of Armenia, and Other Fiction,* Blue Heron Press (Kingston, Ontario, Canada), 1999.

*Quest for Closure: The Armenian Genocide and the Search for Justice in Canada,* Blue Heron Press (Kingston, Ontario, Canada), 1999.

*Rough Landing* (poetry), Blue Heron Press (Kingston, Ontario, Canada), 1999.

*Survivor Memoirs of the Armenian Genocide,* Taderon Press (Reading, England), 1999.

*Writing Memory: The Search for Home in Armenian Literature as Cultural Practice,* Blue Heron Press, (Kingston, Ontario, Canada), 2000.

(With Alan Whitehorn) *The Armenian Genocide: Resisting the Inertia of Indifference,* Blue Heron Press (Kingston, Ontario, Canada), 2001.

Author of two screenplays, including *Extras.*

*WORK IN PROGRESS: In a Dark Light: David Goodis and Film Noir, Ripe for Shaking* (a novel).

*SIDELIGHTS:* Lorne Shirinian's area of expertise is Armenian-North American literature and issues pertaining to the Armenian genocide and diaspora of the early twentieth century. More broadly, his interest translates into the study of ethnicity and multiculturalism in literature. Shirinian has published works of scholarly criticism as well as short stories, poetry, and nonfiction works about film noir and detective fiction. A life-long resident of Canada, Shirinian lived and taught in Montreal for twenty years before assuming the leadership of the English department at Canada's Royal Military College in Kingston, Ontario. He is also the founder of Blue Heron Press, which publishes many of his books.

In *Armenian-North American Literature: A Critical Introduction: Genocide, Diaspora, and Symbols,* Shirinian chronicles nearly one hundred years of Armenian literature created after the genocide and diaspora of 1915 and concludes that the specter of the holocaust looms large in the symbolism of Armenian authors, whether or not they were present during the time of the tragedy. It is "a study that has important implications for scholars interested in the ethnic, minority, and diaspora literatures of North America," wrote K. Tololyan in *Choice.*

Shirinian's fiction is also concerned with the Armenian genocide; his poems and stories consistently reflect upon mass murder, displacement, dispossession, and rootlessness. Michael Hurley, writing in *Books in Canada,* noted that the poems in Shirinian's collection *Rough Landing* have an "edgy intensity" and that "Shirinian continues the journey begun by his Armenian ancestors so many years ago: an impassioned quest to create a space where their tragically abbreviated lives may complete themselves and issue into coherence and significance." Hurley concluded that "Shirinian manages to register a deeply personal response to tragedy and catastrophe, rooting his vision in the suffering of a particular people while lifting his gaze to embrace all peoples."

In addition to his scholarly work, Shirinian is also a screenwriter and has had one of his scripts filmed in Montreal in 1997. He has also completed a novel and a nonfiction manuscript about film noir.

*BIOGRAPHICAL AND CRITICAL SOURCES:*

PERIODICALS

*American Literature,* March, 1991, review of *Armenian-North American Literature,* p. 178.
*Books in Canada,* winter, 2002, Michael Hurley, "Poems and Stories to Place on Graves," p. 27.
*Choice,* December, 1990, K. Tololyan, review of *Armenian-North American Literature,* p. 632.

OTHER

*Blue Heron Press Web site,* http://www.blueheronpress. ca/ (July 19, 2002).*

\*　　\*　　\*

**SIDDIK, Al**
　　**See ROLFE, Frederick (William Serafino Austin Lewis Mary)**

\*　　\*　　\*

**SIFRY, Micah L.**

*PERSONAL:* Male.

*ADDRESSES: Office*—Public Campaign, 1320 19th St., NW, Suite M-1, Washington, DC 20036; fax: 202-293-0202. *Agent*—c/o Routledge, 29 West 35th Street, New York, NY 10001.

*CAREER:* Journalist and author. *Nation,* New York, NY, former editor; Public Campaign, Washington, DC, senior analyst; freelance writer.

*WRITINGS:*

(Editor, with Christopher Cerf) *The Gulf War Reader: History, Documents, Opinions,* Times Books (New York, NY), 1991.
*Spoiling for a Fight: Third-Party Politics in America,* Routledge (New York, NY), 2002.

Contributor to periodicals, including the *New York Times, Nation, American Prospect, Progressive, Salon, Wired,* and *Tikkun.*

*SIDELIGHTS:* Micah L. Sifry is a former editor for *Nation,* and has contributed to numerous periodicals. He is currently a senior analyst at Public Campaign, a nonpartisan campaign finance reform group.

Described by Tim Kelsey in the *San Francisco Review of Books* as "a comprehensive collection of documents and essays," *The Gulf War Reader: History, Documents, Opinions* presents a variety of perspectives on the Gulf War, including those of former president George Bush, Saddam Hussein, and commentators William Safire and Walter Cronkite. In the *Washington Post Book World,* William F. Powers, Jr. wrote that the coeditors "have produced a remarkably interesting collection of . . . articles, official transcripts and other documents from the war." Powers also found the book "highly valuable."

In *Spoiling for a Fight: Third-Party Politics in America,* Sifry examines the history of third parties in American politics, focusing mainly on Ralph Nader's 2000 bid for the presidency. Sifry researched the book by attending national conventions of third parties, interviewing party leaders, and attending rallies, presidential debates, and hearings of the U.S. Supreme Court on third-party issues. According to Sifry, the current U.S. political system is a "duopoly" that prevents most other parties from successfully running for office. In *Publishers Weekly,* a reviewer commented that Sifry "presents a balanced, important and enlightened new way to think through the political process." The book is "enriched with quotes and insights from candidates and key players," wrote Thomas J. Baldino in *Library Journal.*

*BIOGRAPHICAL AND CRITICAL SOURCES:*

PERIODICALS

*Booklist,* September 1, 1991, review of *The Gulf War Reader: History, Documents, Opinions,* p. 36.
*Library Journal,* February 15, 2002, Thomas J. Baldino, review of *Spoiling for a Fight: Third-Party Politics in America,* p. 165.

*Progressive,* November, 1991, Linda Rocawich, "Gulf War History: Off the Mark," pp. 38-43.

*Publishers Weekly,* January 28, 2002, review of *Spoiling for a Fight,* p. 282.

*San Francisco Review of Books,* February, 1991, Tim Kelsey, "The Facts of War," pp. 20-23.

*Washington Post Book World,* William F. Powers, Jr., review of *The Gulf War Reader,* p. 8.*

\*     \*     \*

## SILVERGLATE, Harvey A. 1942-

*PERSONAL:* Born 1942. *Education:* Princeton University, 1964; Harvard Law School, 1967.

*ADDRESSES: Office*—Boston, MA. *Agent*—c/o Author Mail, Simon & Schuster, 1230 Avenue of the Americas, New York, NY 10020.

*CAREER:* Attorney, author, lecturer, and teacher.

*MEMBER:* American Civil Liberties Union.

*WRITINGS:*

(With Alan Charles Kors) *The Shadow University: The Betrayal of Liberty on America's Campuses,* Free Press (New York), 1998.

Contributor of articles to various periodicals.

*SIDELIGHTS:* Harvey A. Silverglate is a trial lawyer in Boston who specializes in civil liberties cases. Along with Alan Charles Kors, a professor of history at the University of Pennsylvania, he has written a book titled *The Shadow University: The Betrayal of Liberty on America's Campuses.* Silverglate and Kors explore what they see as threats to the right of free speech on college campuses. They believe that all people have the right to express their viewpoints, whether it is a popular opinion or not, guaranteed by the First Amendment to the Constitution. This right extends to conservatives, moderates, and radicals alike. Silverglate, in his practice, has defended members of the American Nazi party as well as anti-war protesters.

Many college campuses have adopted speech codes and other rules they feel protect the rights of the students enrolled at these institutions. In addition to speech codes, many universities mandate freshmen orientation, sensitivity training, and diversity workshops. Silverglate and Kors view some of this instruction as commendable, but in reality, they say, instead of encouraging discussion, the universities use these opportunities to tell students exactly what is and what is not acceptable behavior. According to Silverglate and Kors, this is intimidation against the right to free speech, stifling all freedom of expression, mandating conformity, and encouraging groupthink and censorship.

*The Shadow University* explores a case in which Kors himself made headlines for the defense of a student at the University of Pennsylvania who shouted out his window at a group of noisy African-American sorority sisters, calling them "water buffalo." Kors adamantly defended this student, saying that even though the student's words were not very likable, it was still his right to express them.

In addition to the University of Pennsylvania occurrence, *The Shadow University* describes similar incidents at other universities and discusses how these matters were settled. At one conservative Baptist school, a sociology professor was dismissed after he wrote an article that defended patriarchy, maintaining that it was biological. The article angered a feminist colleague and, subsequently, the professor and a dean who defended him both lost their jobs. Kors and Silverglate wonder why the more radical viewpoint is tolerated, while the conservative is not. The authors have found that many college campuses, while aggressively attacking any would-be offenders to their codes, often do not allow the accused to put on any sort of defense. They are judged guilty without being able to tell their side, question their accuser, or bring in others who may refute the attacker's claims.

Silverglate and Kors also note in *The Shadow University* that many of the heterosexual, conservative, white men on campus are watched very carefully for any violation of free speech rules, while feminists, homosexuals, and people of different races and color are allowed to speak out on anything they want. Silverglate and Kors strongly support the idea that all people should be allowed to express all views and not be monitored so closely for infractions. They also believe that sometimes what is viewed as offensive speech is often the very idea that bring about social change.

*The Shadow University* maintains that many students on college campus want exposure to more diverse viewpoints. Students are tired of being so politically correct and sheltered, say Silverglate and Kors, who also warn against what will happen if universities continue to mandate what students' must think. Silverglate and Kors see a generation of timid conservatives being produced, instead of freethinking individuals capable of bringing about change in society.

*The Shadow University* met with tempered praise. Many critics noted a glut of books being marketed that lead attacks on everything that is wrong with college universities, but at the same time recognized that *The Shadow University* is a well-written work with a different take on the subject of free speech.

*BIOGRAPHICAL AND CRITICAL SOURCES:*

PERIODICALS

*Booklist,* September 1, 1998, p. 40.
*Library Journal,* September 1, 1998, p. 14.
*Stanford Daily,* October 22, 1998.
*Wall Street Journal,* September 28, 1998, Daniel J. Silver, review of *The Shadow University: The Betrayal of Liberty on America's Campuses,* p. A26.*

\*    \*    \*

## SIMON, William L(eonard) 1930-

*PERSONAL:* Born December 3, 1930, in Washington, DC; son of Isaac B. (a teacher) and Marjorie (a social worker, maiden name Felsteiner) Simon; married Arynne Lucy Abeles, September 18, 1966; children: Victoria Marie, Sheldon M. Bermont (stepson). *Education:* Cornell University, Ithaca, New York, B.E.E., 1954; Golden State University, San Diego, CA, M.A., 1982, Ph.D., 1983. *Politics:* Republican. *Hobbies and other interests:* Tennis, serving the crew of the square-

rigged brigantine ship *Pilgrim,* Orange County Maritime Museum, and also the *Star of India,* San Diego Museum.

*ADDRESSES: Home*—6150 Paseo, P.O. Box 2048, Rancho Sante Fe, CA 92067-2048. *Agent*—Waterside Productions, 2191 San Elijo Avenue, Cardiff-by-the-Sea, CA 92007.

*CAREER:* Author; writer-producer of film and television projects; lecturer at George Washington University, Washington, DC, 1968-70. *Military service:* United States Navy, 1954-58.

*MEMBER:* National Academy of Television Arts and Sciences, Silver Circle, Writers Guild of America, American Film Institute, International Documentary Association, Rotary International, Eta Kappa Nu, Tau Beta Pi.

*AWARDS, HONORS:* Recipient of twelve Golden Eagle Film Awards from the Cine Film Festival; gold medal, New York International Festivals for Freedom Found; IFPA Gold Cindy; awards from the Berlin, Belgrade, and Venice film festivals, and numerous others.

*WRITINGS:*

(With Gil Amelio) *Profit From Experience: The National Semiconductor of Transformation Management,* Van Nostrand Reinhold (New York, NY), 1996.
*Beyond the Numbers: How Leading Companies Measure and Drive Success,* Van Nostrand Reinhold (New York, NY) 1997.
(With Rob Lebow) *Lasting Change: Building the Shared Values That Make Companies Great,* Van Nostrand Reinhold (New York, NY), 1997.
(With Gil Amelio) *On the Firing Line: My 500 Days at Apple,* HarperBusiness (New York, NY), 1998.
(With Brian K. Muirhead) *High Velocity Leadership: The Mars Pathfinder Approach to Faster, Better, Cheaper,* HarperBusiness (New York, NY), 1999.
(With Robert L. McDowell) *Driving Digital: Microsoft and Its Customers Speak About Thriving in the E-Business Era,* HarperBusiness (New York, NY), 2001.

(With Gary E. Schwartz) *The Afterlife Experiments: Breakthrough Scientific Evidence of Life After Death,* foreword vy Deepak Chopra Pocket Books (New York, NY), 2002.

(With Kevin Mitnick) *The Art of Deception,* John Wiley and Sons (New York, NY), 2002.

Also the author of more than six hundred film scripts and screenplays. Contributor of articles to numerous newspapers and periodicals.

*WORK IN PROGRESS: The Accidental Pornographer.*

*SIDELIGHTS:* Washington-born William L. Simon enjoyed a highly successful literary career writing more than six hundred scripts and screenplays for the film and television industry before he wrote his first book, a collaborative effort that was published in 1996, when he was already sixty-six years old. In the years since, Simon has continued his hectic pace, in the process achieving a reputation as one of America's most successful ghostwriters and compiling impressive sales for his writings about business and corporate subjects.

Simon was born in Washington, D.C., on December 3, 1930. His father was a high school teacher and his mother a social worker. Simon was an excellent student to whom learning "came naturally," as he recalled in an interview with *CA.* After graduating from high school, Simon attended Cornell University in Ithaca, New York, where he studied for a Bachelor of electrical engineering (B.E.E.) degree. "I had a talent in math and sciences, but it soon became apparent to me that I was in the wrong program," Simon told *CA.* "It was one of those mistakes young people make."

Despite his misgivings, Simon pressed ahead. He earned his B.E.E. in 1954, and then joined the United States Navy for a four-year hitch. It was while he was in the military that Simon got involved in making instructional films. He wrote scripts, learned the basics of directing and producing, and made many important contacts in the film industry. As a result, when Simon completed his Navy service he launched into a successful career working as a freelance writer for film and television. Being dedicated and disciplined to his craft, he has always found work. Among the many projects he has been involved in over the years are the award-winning documentaries *A Touch of Love,* which deals with "poor people and kids in need" and *Setting Sail* a documentary about tall ships that is narrated by legendary television newsman Walter Cronkite, a series of documentaries called *Combat Vietnam,* and the feature films *Fair Woman Without Discretion, Majorca,* and *A Touch of Love.* The list of prizes Simon received for his work includes twelve Golden Eagle Awards as well as honors from film festivals in the United States and Europe.

Being ever ready to tackle new challenges, Simon changed tack in his career in the early 1980s. "As you grow older and wiser, you realize there are things that you'd like to know more about," he told *CA.* As a result, Simon returned to university as a mature student, enrolling in graduate studies at Golden State University in San Diego, California. There he earned a Master of Arts in educational psychology in 1982 and his Ph.D. in communications the following year. Throughout this period, Simon continued to work in the film industry, and he wrote freelance articles for such publications as the *Washington Post* and *USA Today.* However, he began another phase in his career one day after high-tech industry executive Gil Amelio invited him to attend one of his lectures. Amelio was doing some teaching at the Stanford Business School. Simon recalled in his *CA* interview, "As I listened I thought to myself, 'This could be the basis for a book.' In fact, Amelio was thinking the same thing. That was why he had invited me to listen to him."

The two men collaborated on a business self-help book called *Profit From Experience: The National Semiconductor of Transformation Management.* Reviewer Peter Burrows of *Business Week* described *Profit From Experience* as a "pedantic . . . management tome," but the text met a clear need and became a bestseller. It also gave Simon his first taste of what it takes to write a book. His next effort, *Beyond the Numbers: How Leading Companies Measure and Drive Success,* was Simon's only solo work.

His third book, *Lasting Change: Building The Shared Values That Make Companies Great* was another collaborative effort. He worked with businessman Rob Lebow, the founder and chair of Lebow Company, on the 1997 book that recounted Lebow's secrets for management success—Lebow's Shared Values Process. Reviewing *Lasting Change* for *Library Journal,* Peggy

D. Odom observed that the work "neatly summarizes management principles in recent years."

Simon teamed with Amelio again the following year to write *On the Firing Line: My 500 Days at Apple.* This 1998 bestseller is a candid, revealing, and fast-paced account of Amelio's turbulent tenure as head of the Apple Computer company. *Business Week* reviewer Peter Burrows described *On the Firing Line* as a "compelling, if flawed memoir" in which "the ousted Apple boss gathers all the ammo he can find and fires back—taking aim at everyone from reporters . . . to such powerful figures as Microsoft Corp[oration] Chairman William H. Gates III and current Apple CEO Steven P. Jobs." Reviewer Rick Tetzeli of *Fortune* (which Amelio skewered in his narrative) derided *On the Firing Line,* however, he concluded that the book "offers a vivid picture of what it's like when a manager tries to tame an unruly culture—Apple's is the most chaotic."

Having mastered the art of working quickly and effectively, Simon completed four more books over the next four years. Apart from the breakneck pace at which he writes, what is particularly striking about Simon's output is the extraordinary range of subject matter he has covered. *High Velocity Leadership: The Mars Pathfinder Approach to Faster, Better, Cheaper,* written in collaboration with project manager Brian Muirhead, tells the story of how the National Aeronautics and Space Administration managed to achieve a stunning success in its 1997 Pathfinder Mission to Mars while coping with limited budgets and a tight schedule. *Booklist* reviewer David Rouse praised *High Velocity Leadership* as "a dramatic account of the enterprise as it evolved and unfolded."

Writing on his Web site *Global Future Report,* futurist Terry J. van der Werff offered similar comments and praised Simon's abilities as both a writer and a storyteller. "This is a gripping story from the first page," ven der Werff wrote. "*High Velocity Leadership* is filled with technological wonder, superb engineering design, conflict, and drama." The reviewer went on to point out, "This nook opens new ground by introducing 'VideoNotes on the Web' . . . where fifteen movie clips for parts of the mission can be seen, conveying considerably more information than a simple photo can."

Simon stuck with high-tech themes when in 2001 he and Microsoft executive Robert L. McDowell wrote *Driving Digital: Microsoft and Its Customers Speak About Thriving in the E-Business Era.* A *Publishers Weekly* reviewer observed that while this primer on how businesses can adapt to today's Internet-based technology does not have a lot of new information for younger readers, "old-school management may find this clear, helpful advice." Reviewer Steven Silkunas of *Library Journal* lamented that "given the rapidity of change within the computer industry, the book will have a relatively short shelf life." However, he also noted that much of the information offered "transcend[s] the current issues and practices" in industry.

The 2002 book *The Afterlife Experiments: Breakthrough Scientific Evidence of Life After Death* is, as the name suggests, an examination of the latest experiments to determine whether or not human consciousness survives death. Simon worked with Dr. Gary Schwartz, the director of the Human Energy Systems Laboratory at the University of Arizona, to recount and explain the scientific experiments Schwartz and his research team were conducting. "Armed with consummate authority . . . the book progresses through the lab's findings," a *Publishers Weekly* reviewer noted. Meanwhile, William Beatty, writing in *Booklist,* concluded, "The Afterlife Experiments should provoke considerable discussions which . . . should be of value for further investigations in this controversial field."

The fourth book Simon wrote in the years 1998-2002 is *The Art of Deception: Controlling the Human Element of Security,* which was published in late 2002. Simon sat down for a "tell-all" session with cyber-desperado Kevin Mitnick, one of the world's most notorious computer hackers. Mitnick, who at one time was among the Federal Bureau of Investigation's "most wanted men" and served time in prison for his crimes, explains how he breached computer security at some of America's best known companies and even gained access to sensitive government databanks.

Asked what advice he could offer to other writers who might seek to emulate his success, Simon told *CA,* "I have a rather uncommon attitude that applies to my freelance work. I've learned that mastering the craft of writing is important, but the real thing that is far more important than that, the thing that distinguishes the successful person in the field from those who don't succeed is the dedication to get up every morning and do the work. It's this commitment to work that's essential."

*BIOGRAPHICAL AND CRITICAL SOURCES:*

*PERIODICALS*

*Booklist,* April 1, 1999, David Rouse, review of *High Velocity Leadership,* p. 1372; March 1, 2001, David Rouse, review of *Digital Driving,* p. 1214; February 15, 2002, William Beatty, review of *The Afterlife Experience,* p. 973.

*Business Week,* May 4, 1998, Peter Burrows, "From Sour Grapes to Sour Apples," pp. 22-23.

*Corporate Board,* January 2000, review of *Lasting Change,* p. 29.

*Fortune,* April 27, 1998, Rick Tetzeli, review of *On the Firing Line,* pp. 414-415.

*Journal of Business Strategy,* January, 2000, William L. Simon and Bob McDowell, "Business Re-Process Engineering: Microsoft and Its Customers Speak Out About Thriving in the E-Business Era," p. 5.

*Library Journal,* October 15, 1997, Peggy D. Odom, review of *Lasting Change,* p. 72; February 15, 2001, Steven Silkunas, review of *Driving Digital,* p. 179.

*Publishers Weekly,* February 26, 2001, review of *Digital Driving,* p. 70; February 25, 2002, review of *The Afterlife Experience,* p. 52.

*St. Louis Post Dispatch,* April 26, 1998, "Amelio Says He Met His Match At Apple: The Company Humbled a Man Who Once Had the Swagger to Ask for $30 Million in Compensation," p. E2.

*Washington Times,* May 4, 1998, Mark A. Kellner, "Having Apple on Media Menu Healthy for Bottom Line," p. 7.

*OTHER*

*Global Future Reports,* http://www.globalfuture.com (July 22, 2002), Dr. Terry van der Werff, review of High *Velocity Leadership.*

*National Institute for Discovery Science Web site,* http://www.nidsci.org (July 22, 2002), John Alexander, review of *The Afterlife Experiments.**

*       *       *

## SKAINE, Rosemarie 1936-

*PERSONAL:* Born June 11, 1936, in Grand Island, NE; daughter of Warren V. (a meter reader and bill collector) and Marie (a homemaker; maiden name, Kuehner) Keller; married James C. Skaine (a pro-fessor), June 4, 1957; children: James, Todd. *Ethnicity:* "American/Caucasian." *Education:* Attended Sioux Falls College, 1954-57; University of South Dakota, B.A., 1958; University of Northern Iowa, M.A., 1977. *Politics:* Democrat. *Religion:* Methodist.

*ADDRESSES: Home*—2215 Clay St., Cedar Falls, IA 50613; fax: 319-266-1406. *E-mail*—rskaine@cfu.net.

*CAREER:* Sociologist and writer.

*MEMBER:* Pi Kappa Delta, Alpha Kappa Delta.

*AWARDS, HONORS:* Citation for "outstanding book on the subject of human rights in North America," Gustavus Myers Center for the Study of Human Rights in North America, 1997, for *Power and Gender: Issues in Sexual Dominance and Harassment.*

*WRITINGS:*

*Power and Gender: Issues in Sexual Dominance and Harassment,* McFarland & Co. (Jefferson, NC), 1996.

(With James C. Skaine) *A Man of the Twentieth Century: A Collection of Memories of Warren V. Keller, a Nebraskan,* 1999.

*Women at War: Gender Issues of Americans in Combat,* McFarland & Co. (Jefferson, NC), 1999.

*Women College Basketball Coaches,* McFarland & Co. (Jefferson, NC), 2001.

*The Women of Afghanistan under the Taliban,* McFarland & Co. (Jefferson, NC), 2001.

*Paternity and the Law,* McFarland & Co. (Jefferson, NC), 2002.

Contributor to periodicals, including *Ethnicities, Des Moines Register, Personal Romance,* and *Iowan.*

*BIOGRAPHICAL AND CRITICAL SOURCES:*

*OTHER*

*Rosemarie Skaine Web site,* http://www.authorsden.com/rosemarieskaine/ (February 27, 2002).

## SKAU, Michael 1944-

*PERSONAL:* Born January 6, 1944, in Chicago, IL; son of Walter F. and Martha (Marich) Skau. *Ethnicity:* "Caucasian." *Education:* University of Illinois at Urbana-Champaign, B.A., 1965, M.A., 1967, Ph.D, 1967. *Hobbies and other interests:* Poetry, softball, pinballs.

*ADDRESSES: Home*—4913 Chicago St., Omaha, NE 68132-2914. *Office*—Department of English, University of Nebraska at Omaha, 60th and Dodge Sts., Omaha, NE 68182. *E-mail*—michael_skau@unomaha. edu.

*CAREER:* University of Illinois at Urbana, research/ teaching assistant, 1965-73; University of Nebraska at Omaha, assistant professor, 1973-78, associate professor, 1978-85, professor of English, 1985—.

*MEMBER:* Modern Language Association, American Association of University Professors.

*AWARDS, HONORS:* Jefferis Chair in English, University of Nebraska at Omaha, 1997-2000.

*WRITINGS:*

(With J. N. Hook) *A Map of Illinois Authors,* Illinois Association of Teachers of English (Urbana, IL), 1966.
*"Constantly Risking Absurdity": The Writings of Lawrence Ferlinghetti,* Whitston (Troy, NY), 1989.
*Me and God Poems* (chapbook), bradypress (Omaha, NE), 1990.
*"A Clown in a Grave": Complexities and Tensions in the Works of Gregory Corso,* Southern Illinois University Press (Carbondale, IL), 1999.

Contributor to *Dictionary of Literary Themes and Motifs,* edited by Jean-Charles Seigneuret, Greenwood Press, 1988; and *Right Brain Vacation Photos: Omaha Magic Theatre New Plays and Production Photographs, 1972-1992,* edited by Jo Ann Schmidman, Sora Kimberlain, and Megan Terry, Omaha Magic Theatre (Omaha, NE), 1992. Poems published in *Echoes of Yesterday,* edited by Cynthia A. Stevens, National Library of Poetry (Owings Mill, MD), 1994,

and in periodicals, including *Green Feather, Earthwise Poetry Journal, Short Fuse, Red Owl, Parnassus, Prairie Winds, Tucumcari Literary Review, Pikeville Review, Piedmont Literary Review, Atom Mind, Romantist, New Press Literary Quarterly, Old Red Kimono, Poetry Motel, Midwest Quarterly, Kumquat Meringue, Skylark, Midland Review, Cumberland Poetry Review, Northwest Review, Kentucky Poetry Review, Prophetic Voices, Sequoia, Galley Sail Review, Carolina Quarterly, Paintbrush, Great River Review, Illuminations, Passaic Review, Blue Unicorn, Minotaur, Clock Radio, Metropolitan, Orphic Lute, Long Pond Review, Elkhorn Review, Yet Another Small Magazine, Kansas Quarterly, Separate Doors, Images, American Poetry Anthology, Pteranodon, Laurel Review, Axletree, Spectacle Arts Magazine, Shadows, Lunch, Periodical of Art in Nebraska, Grain of Sand,* and *Voyeur.* Fiction published in *Illinois Technograph* and *Bouillabaisse.* Articles published in *McNeese Review, University of Dayton Review, Concerning Poetry, Polish Review, Style, Portland Review, Modern Drama, Critique, Periodical of Art in Nebraska, Explicator, American Notes & Queries,* and *Illinois Technograph.*

*WORK IN PROGRESS:* Numerous poems. Researching articles on the teaching of Beat literature, William Blake's prosody, and Farina's *Been down so Long It Looks like Up to Me.*

*SIDELIGHTS:* Michael Skau told *CA:* "My interest in writing literary criticism on the Beat Generation stems essentially from my teaching of courses on Beat writers and from discovering a paucity of valuable analysis of their works. Instead, most writers about the Beats seem enchanted by their lives rather than by their literature. Through my publications, I hope to show that traditional critical approaches, particularly New Criticism, can provide valuable insights about this literature. In 1973 I completed my dissertation on 'Themes and Movements in the Literature of the Beat Generation,' and I have continued to investigate the works of these writers for about thirty years.

"For my creative writing, my poetry splits almost equally between poems which are formal and those which are free. In terms of my themes, my poems focus on the emotional responses of ordinary people, on the complexities of human needs, on the refusal of people to accept what too often seems the inevitability of a perverse and unfriendly fate, and on their crippled triumphs in dragging themselves above these obstacles. As a result, my poems frequently tremble on the edge of sentiment (without, I hope, leaping off that edge)."

"For both my critical and creative writing, I see literature as a window: first, we can look through the window to see the topic of the literature and its characters; second, we can draw back our vision to look at the window itself, its shape and form; and finally, we can see ourselves reflected in the window's glass. This may possibly seem simplistic, but it has deep significance for me as a critic, a writer, and a teacher."*

\*   \*   \*

## SMITH, Jaune Quick-to-See 1940-

*PERSONAL:* Born January 15, 1940, in St. Ignatius, Indian Mission Flathead Reservation, MT; daughter of Arthur (a trader and horseman) Smith. *Education:* Framingham State College, MA, B.A., 1976; University of New Mexico, M.A., 1980.

*ADDRESSES: Office*—c/o Steinbaum Krauss Gallery, 132 Greene Street, New York, NY 10012.

*CAREER:* Collage artist. Public commissions, including Terazzo Floor, Denver Airport, Cultural Museum, Flathead Reservation, and Yerba Buena Park, Sculpture Garden, San Francisco, 1991, and National Museum of the American Indian, Smithsonian Institution, Washington, DC (artist on design team), 1993; Ken Phillips Gallery, Denver, CO, curator, including "Contemporary Native American Art," 1980, "Women of Sweetgrass, Cedar and Sage" (co-curator, traveling, catalog), 1985, "The Submuloc Show/Columbus Wohs" (traveling), 1990, "Positives and Negatives: Native American Photographers," (traveling; Europe), 1995; juror, including New Mexico Women Artists Exhibition, 1983, National Endowments for the Arts, 1986, Millay County for the Arts, 1995-96; trustee, including Atlati, 1984-94, American Indian Community Arts, 1984-88, Institute of American Indian Arts, 1986-90, College Art Association, 1989-95; and Salish Kostenai College Foundation, board member, 1995; printmaker, Tamarind Lithography Workshop, Albuquerque, New Mexico, 1978-82,1988-89, 1995-96. Lecturer, catalog contributor, editor, and producer; writer.

*AWARDS, HONORS:* Several fellowships; honorary doctorate, Minneapolis College of Art and Design, 1992; master artist-in-residence, Santa Fe Institute of Fine Arts, 1994; Wallace Stegner Award, Center of the American West, University of Colorado, 1995; Joan Mitchell Foundation Award for Painting, 1996; Women's Caucus for Art Award for Outstanding Achievement in the Visual Arts, 1997.

*WRITINGS:*

*Jaune Quick-to-See Smith, Modern Times,* New Mexico State University (Las Cruces, NM), 1997.

Contributor of text to exhibition catalogs.

*SIDELIGHTS:* Jaune Quick-to-See Smith is a member of the Flathead Reservation in Montana and an accomplished artist. She is also a political activist for Native American rights, and her life story and artwork has been the subject of three Public Broadcasting System documentaries. As a child, she led a rather nomadic lifestyle, constantly moving around the Pacific Northwest. She developed a relationship with and love for nature and land that heavily influences her artwork as an adult.

Smith's art often takes the form of collage, or mixed media paintings. Her style has been called post-modern and involves newsprint, fabrics, advertisements and paint. She also works with superimposed images. The artist often focuses on political themes that surround the Native American community, such as land rights and destruction of the earth. Her artwork often examines modern Native American identity and questions historical narratives. One of her goals is to portray herself as both a modern artist and an artist of the Native American community.

Smith travels to areas both Indian and non-Indian, using her art to educate people about the history of Native people. She has also been the curator of many Native art shows, and has written several curator catalogs to accompany the shows. In addition, she is the author of the book *Jaune Quick-to-see Smith, Modern Times.*

*BIOGRAPHICAL AND CRITICAL SOURCES:*

*BOOKS*

*Native North American Artists,* St. James Press (Detroit, MI), 1998.

*PERIODICALS*

*Artforum International,* January, 1993, Jenifer P. Borum, "Jaune Quick-to-see Smith," p. 87.

*Art in America,* November, 2001, Gerrit Henry, "Jaune Quick-to-see Smith at the Neuberger Museum," p. 155.

*School Arts,* May-June, 1996, Marilyn Stewart, "Jaune Quick-to-see Smith," p. 23.*

\*   \*   \*

## SPAZIANI, Maria Luisa 1924-

*PERSONAL:* Born December 7, 1924, in Turin, Italy. *Education:* Earned advanced degree.

*ADDRESSES: Home*—Rome, Italy. *Agent*—c/o Mondadori, via Ponti, 10, 20143, Milan, Italy.

*CAREER:* Poet and educator. Founder, *Il dado* (journal), 1942-43. University of Messina, Messina, Italy, professor of French language and literature, 1964—.

*AWARDS, HONORS:* Byron Award, 1954; Premio Firenze, 1962, for *Il gong;* Saint-Vincent Great Prize, 1962, for short stories; Premio Carducci, 1966, for *Utilità della memoria;* Premio Cittadella, and Premio Trieste, both 1970, both for *L'occhio del ciclone;* Premio Viareggio, 1981, for *Geometria del disordine;* Premio Pescara-Flaiano, Premio Citta di Adelphia, and Premio Citta di Catazaro, all 1986, all for *La stella del libero arbitrio;* Premio Gian Carlo Fusco, and Premio Fondi-la Pastora, both 1992, both for *L'Isola Tiberina.*

*WRITINGS:*

*Primavera a Parigi* (poetry; title means "Springtime in Paris"), Scheiwiller (Milan, Italy), 1954.

*Le acque del Sabato* (poetry; title means "The Sabbath's Waters"), Mondadori (Milan, Italy), 1954.

*Luna lombardo* (poetry; title means "Lombard Moon"), Neri Pozza (Venice, Italy), 1959.

*Il gong* (poetry; title means "The Gong"), Mondadori (Milan, Italy), 1962.

(Translator) Marguerite Yourcenar, *Il colpo di grazia* [and] *Alexis,* Feltrinelli (Milan, Italy), 1962.

*Utilità della memoria* (poetry; title means "The Usefulness of Memory"), Mondadori (Milan, Italy), 1966.

*L'occhio del ciclone* (poetry; title means "The Eye of the Cyclone"), Mondadori (Milan, Italy), 1970.

*La Pléiade,* Genal (Messina, Italy), 1972.

*Ronsard fra gli astri della Pléiade* (criticism), ERI (Turin, Italy), 1972.

*Il teatro francese del Settecento* (criticism), Faro/Nuova Biblioteca Universitaria (Rome, Italy), 1974.

*Il teatro francese dell'Ottocento* (criticism), Faro/Nuova Biblioteca Universitaria (Rome, Italy), 1975.

*Il teatro francese del Novecento* (criticism), EDAS (Messina, Italy), 1976.

*Ultrasuoni,* Munt (Samedan, Italy), 1976.

*Storia dell'Alessandrino,* EDAS (Messina, Italy), 1977.

*Transito con catene* (poetry; title means "Passage with Chains"), Mondadori (Milan, Italy), 1977.

*Alessandrino e altri versi fra Ottocento e Novecento,* EDAS (Messina, Italy), 1978.

*Poesia,* edited by Luigi Baldacci, Mondadori (Milan, Italy), 1979.

*Geometria del disordine* (poetry; title means "Geometry of Disorder"), Mondadori (Milan, Italy), 1981.

*Racine* (criticism), Garzanti (Milan, Italy), 1986.

*La stella del libero arbitrio* (poetry), Mondadori (Milan, Italy), 1986, translation by Irene Marchegiani Jones and Carol Lettieri published as *Star of Free Will,* Guernica, 1996.

*Giovanna d'Arco* (poetry; title means "Joan of Arc"), Mondadori (Milan, Italy), 1990.

*All'America* (poetry; title means "To America"), La Bautta (Ferrara, Italy), 1990.

*Donne in poesia* (criticism and interviews; title means "Women in Poetry"), Marsilio (Venice, Italy), 1992.

*L'Isola Tiberina* (play; title means "The Tiberine Island"), produced 1992.

*Torri di vedetta* (poetry), Crocetti (Milan, Italy), 1992, translation by Laura Stortoni published as *Sentry Towers,* introduction by Natalia Costa-Zalessow, Hesperia Press (Berkeley, CA), 1995.

*I fasti dell'ortica,* Mondadori (Milan, Italy), 1996.

(With others) *Trash,* Studio S. (Rome, Italy), 1996.

*Epiphanie de l'alphabet: choix de poèmes, 1954-1992 = Epifania dell'alfabeto,* French translation by Maria Luisa Caldognetto and Jean Portante, Ecrits de Forges (Trois-Rivières, Québec, Canada), 1997.

*La védova Goldoni = La Veuve Goldoni* (one-act play), French translation by Maria Luisa Caldognetto and Jean Portante, Echternach (Luxembourg), 1997.

*La radice del mare,* T. Pironti (Naples, Italy), 1999.

*La freccia,* Marsilio (Venice, Italy), 2000.

*Poesie: 1954-1996,* Mondadori (Milan, Italy), 2000.

*La traversata dell'oasi: poesie d'amore 1998-2001,* Mondadori (Milan, Italy), 2002.

Contributor to periodicals, including *La Stampa.* Work represented in anthologies, including *Ritratti su misura,* edited by Elio Filippo Accrocca, Sodalizio del Libro, 1960; *Donne in poesie: Antologia della poesia femminile in Italia dal dopoguerra ad oggi,* edited by Biancamaria Frabotta, Savelli, 1976; *Italian Poetry Today: Currents and Trends,* edited by Ruth Feldman and Brian Swann, New Rivers, 1979; and *The Defiant Muse: Italian Feminist Poems from the Middle Ages to the Present: A Bilingual Anthology,* edited by Beverly Allen, Muriel Kittel, and Keala Jane Jewell, Feminist Press, 1986.

Spaziani's work has been translated into French.

*TRANSLATOR*

Winston Clewes, *Amacizie violente,* Mondadori (Milan, Italy), 1951.

E. H. Gombrich, *Il mondo dell'arte,* Mondadori (Milan, Italy), 1952.

Jacques Audiberti, *Il padrone di Milano,* Bompiani (Milan, Italy), 1956.

Langston Moffet, *Il diavolo e la sua coda,* Clug Degli (Milan, Italy), 1962.

George Sand, *Francesco il trovatello,* ERI (Turin, Italy), 1963.

Sally Prudhomme, *Poesie,* Fratelli Fabbri (Milan, Italy), 1965.

Paul-Jean Toulet, *Poesie,* Einaudi (Turin, Italy), 1966.

Conte di Gobineau, *Sull'ineguaglianza delle razze,* Longanesi (Milan, Italy), 1968.

Saul Bellow, *La vittima,* Feltrinelli (Milan, Italy), 1968.

Jean Racine, *Bajazet,* Faro/Nuova Biblioteca Universitaria (Rome, Italy), 1973.

Michel Tournier, *Le Meteore,* Mondadori (Milan, Italy), 1979.

André Gide, *Oscar Wilde,* Giusti (Florence, Italy), 1979.

Marguerite Yourcenar, *Alexis,* Feltrinelli (Milan, Italy), 1983.

Marguerite Yourcenar, *Novelle orientali,* Rizzoli (Milan, Italy), 1989.

Also author of additional translations.

*SIDELIGHTS:* Maria Luisa Spaziani is a prolific Italian writer who has won acclaim for her numerous volumes of poetry. Barbara Zecchi, writing in *Italian Women Writers,* affirmed that "Spaziani is considered one of the most captivating and relevant poets" of twentieth-century Italy, an "idiosyncratic and powerful voice in the firmament of modern Italian poetry." Another writer, Rebecca West, declared in the *Dictionary of Literary Biography* that Spaziani's poetry "stands as an important contribution to the achievements of the modern Italian lyric."

Spaziani was born in 1924 in Turin. In her youth she traveled to Paris and Cologne, two cities that proved, as West noted, to be "compatible with [Spaziani's] inner sense of an ideal poetic landscape." West added that Spaziani's "future poetry was to be dominated by the wintry, more austere ambience of this ideal north, which conditions her verse both psychologically and rhetorically."

In 1942, when she was still in her late teens, Spaziani began her literary career by founding the periodical *Il dado,* which lasted into the following year. In *Il dado* Spaziani published original writings as well as translations from works in French, English, and German. After the journal ceased publication, Spaziani pursued academic studies and in 1948 produced a dissertation on Marcel Proust. Five years later she returned to Paris, where she found poetic inspiration. In 1954 she published her first two poetry volumes, *Primavera a Parigi* and *Le acque del Sabato,* both of which show the influence of Eugenio Montale. In these early works Spaziani readily established herself as a somber, contemplative artist. According to Zecchi, Spaziani "goes back to a Jewish tradition whereby poetry is conceived as the time of contemplation, a concept maintained in the rest of her books . . . where poetry is defined as a static moment, a place of observation." Zecchi added that Spaziani's "recurrent themes are solitude, memory, fame, and death."

In the 1960s Spaziani produced *Il gong* and *Utilità della memoria,* two prize-winning collections that served to solidify her status among Italy's prominent poets. In the ensuing decade, however, she began demonstrating an increasing inclination to consider both the limitations of poetic expression and the more insidious aspects of human experience. "More and more," wrote West, "the cruel ironies of experience are the subject of Spaziani's verse, and the limits and dangers of poetic re-creation that relies on rationality and control are emphasized." With regard to *Transito con catene,* West contended that the title itself serves to indicate "Spaziani's continued interest in the contradictory and ultimately unknowable aspects of experience." Cecilia Rose declared in *World Literature Today* that in *Transito con catene,* Spaziani expresses "a concern for the eternal dilemmas of mankind: whether it is worthwhile to be born; whether there is an afterlife." Rose asserted that "Spaziani shows herself to be the creature of a Christian civilization."

Although Spaziani questions the nature of human existence, she also continues to value poetry as what Lucia Marino, writing in *World Literature Today,* called "the incantation that wards off external chaos and darkness." Marino, in a review of *Geometria del disordine,* declared that poetry serves Spaziani as "both a refuge and a sacred palm to exorcise the harsh sounds and Babelic confusion that assail us, penetrating even our dreams." Marino concluded her review of *Geometria del disordine* by assuring that the book "should amply reward its reader."

*Giovanna d'Arco* is a volume comprised of nearly 14,000 verses about Joan of Arc, the French mystic and warrior who was condemned as a heretic and burned at the stake. Writing in *World Literature Today,* Michela Montante observed that the "point that Spaziani seems to be making is that each of us must follow our own destiny. In fact, if we turn away from it, we are doomed to boredom and despair." Montante concluded, "For its form and subject matter, [*Giovanna d'Arco*] will find a multitude of readers in the decades to come." Among Spaziani's other writings are plays, including *La védova Goldoni,* wherein a prostitute and Maria Nicoletta Connio, widow of famed playwright Carlo Goldoni, discuss their sexual experiences. As Montante observed, "In *La védova Goldoni,* as in much of Spaziani's other work, we find a passion for the lives and accomplishments of women."

Spaziani's writings in English translation include the poetry collections *Star of Free Will* and *Sentry Towers.* In a *Translation Review Supplement* appraisal of *Star of Free Will,* a critic noted the work's "striking imagery," and in *Choice* J. Shreve concluded that the volume "is full of original and valuable insights." Melinda Emmons, meanwhile, wrote in *Chelsea* that *Star of Free Will* constitutes "a lament for those of us who live catatonically." In the same review, the critic perceived *Sentry Towers* as a collection of "pulsing insistence, still decrying the forces that menace our artistic imagination and self-expression, but also now more actively defending against them."

## BIOGRAPHICAL AND CRITICAL SOURCES:

*BOOKS*

*Dictionary of Literary Biography,* Volume 128: *Twentieth-Century Italian Poets, Second Series,* Gale (Detroit, MI), 1993.

*PERIODICALS*

*Chelsea,* Volume 33, 1997, Melinda Emmons, review of *Star of Free Will* and *Sentry Towers,* pp. 151-161.
*Choice,* October, 1996, J. Shreve, review of *Star of Free Will,* p. 287.
*Translation Review Supplement,* Volume 2, number 2, 1996, review of *Star of Free Will;* Volume 5, 1999, review of *Sentry Towers,* p. 17.
*World Literature Today,* winter, 1979, Michela Montante, review of *Transito con catene,* pp. 98-99; winter, 1983, Lucia Marino, review of *Geometria del disordine,* p. 86; winter, 1991, Michel Montante, review of *Giovanna d'Arco,* p. 98; autumn, 1998, Michela Montante, review of *La védova Goldoni,* p. 812.*

*        *        *

## STEPHENSON, Fred, Jr.

*PERSONAL:* Male. *Education:* Elon College, B.A.; University of Minnesota, M.S., Ph.D.

ADDRESSES: *Office*—University of Georgia, 137 Brooks Hall, Athens, GA 30602-6258.

CAREER: University of Georgia, Terry College of Business, Athens, GA, associate professor.

AWARDS, HONORS: Josiah Meigs Award, University of Georgia, 1988, 1997.

WRITINGS:

(Editor) *Extraordinary Teachers: The Essence of Excellent Teaching,* Andrews McMeel (Kansas City, MO), 2001.

SIDELIGHTS: A long-time professor of business at the University of Georgia, Fred Stephenson Jr. has twice won that school's highest teaching award, the Josiah Meigs Award. After his second award, Stephenson got an inspiration: to draw on the experiences of other Meigs Award winners and compile their advice and experience for the benefit of other teachers. The result was *Extraordinary Teachers: The Essence of Excellent Teaching,* a series of thirty-six essays edited with short introductions by Stephenson. The wide-ranging essays cover a number of perspectives from "Helping Students Find Joy in Learning" to "Tough Love in the Classroom." Some emphasize the importance of preparation, while others focus on the importance of enthusiasm in the classroom. Perhaps inevitably, the essays are by older, more experienced teachers, and one reviewer questioned this. "While older teachers surely have much to say about their profession, wouldn't fresh young teachers have new views on how teaching is changing, and challenging, in 2001?" asked Charity Vogel in the *Buffalo News,* although she acknowledged that the essays do "include anecdotes that are so wonderful, or so funny, that they almost make the book worth it." Others were more enthusiastic. A *Publishers Weekly* reviewer called the book "a first-class inspiring primer on how and what to teach while generating excitement and creativity among pupils."

BIOGRAPHICAL AND CRITICAL SOURCES:

PERIODICALS

*Buffalo News* (Buffalo, NY), December 23, 2001, Charity Vogel, "'Essence of Excellent Teaching' Gets a Failing Grade," p. E5.

*Publishers Weekly,* October 1, 2001, review of *Extraordinary Teachers: The Essence of Excellent Teaching,* p. 52.*

\*    \*    \*

## STERELNY, Kim 1950-

PERSONAL: Surname is pronounced "stir-ell-nee"; born November 11, 1950; son of Igor Alexander and Joyce Irons (Lawrence) Sterelny; partner of Melanie Claire Nolan (a historian); children: one. *Education:* Sydney University, B.A., 1972, Ph.D., 1977. *Politics:* "Ex-leftie, no active political engagement." *Hobbies and other interests:* "Eating curries, drinking red wine, bushwalking, and birding."

ADDRESSES: *Office*—Department of Philosophy, Rm. 101, 22 Kelburn Parade, Victoria University of Wellington, Wellington, New Zealand; Philosophy Program, RSSS, Australian National University, Canberra, Australian Capital Territory 0200, Australia. *E-mail*—Kim.Sterelny@vuw.ac.nz.

CAREER: Sydney University, Sydney, Australia, part-time tutor and research student in philosophy department, 1973-75; New South Wales University of Technology, Sydney, Australia, part-time lecturer in philosophy department, 1976; La Trobe University, Melbourne, Australia, tutor in philosophy department, 1978, lecturer in linguistics division, 1979-81; Sydney University, Sydney, Australia, lecturer in traditional and modern philosophy department, 1982, tutor, 1983; Australian National University, Canberra, research fellow, then senior research fellow in philosophy department, Research School of the Social Sciences, 1983-87, part-time senior research fellow, 2000-01, full professor, 2002—. University of Maryland, College Park, visiting professor in philosophy department, 1986-87; Victoria University of Wellington, New Zealand, reader, 1988-99, personal chair in philosophy department, 2000—; Simon Fraser University, Burnaby, British Columbia, Canada, visiting professor in philosophy department, 1990; California Institute of Technology, Pasadena, visiting professor in philosophy, humanities, and social sciences department, 1996, 2002. Member of editorial board, *Philosophy of Science,* 2001—, and *Australasian Journal of Philosophy.*

MEMBER: Australian Association of Philosophy (president, 2000-01).

*AWARDS, HONORS:* Fellow, Australian Academy of Humanities.

*WRITINGS:*

(With Michael Devitt) *Language and Reality: An Introduction to the Philosophy of Language,* MIT Press (Cambridge, MA), 1987.

*The Representational Theory of Mind: An Introduction,* B. Blackwell (Cambridge, MA), 1991.

(With Paul E. Griffiths) *Sex and Death: An Introduction to Philosophy of Biology,* University of Chicago Press (Chicago, IL), 1999.

*The Evolution of Agency and Other Essays,* Cambridge University Press (New York, NY), 2001.

*Dawkins vs. Gould: The Survival of the Fittest,* edited by Jon Turney, Icon Books (Cambridge, England), 2001.

Contributor to textbooks including *Developmental Mechanisms in Language,* edited by R. Harris and C. J. Bailey, Pergamon, 1984; *Encyclopedia of Language and Linguistics,* edited by P. Lamarque, Pergamon, 1994; *The Evolution of Cognition,* edited by C. Heyes and L. Huber, MIT Press, 2000; and *Cycles of Contingency,* edited by Russell Gray, Paul Griffiths, and Susan Oyama, MIT Press, 2001.

Contributor to scholarly journals, including *Journal of Philosophy, Australasian Journal of Philosophy, Biology and Philosophy, Philosophical Studies, Philosophy of Science, New Zealand Science Review,* and *Philosophical Quarterly.* Editor of *Monist,* special issue on philosophy of biology; editor of *Biology and Philosophy,* 2001—; coeditor, with Rob Wilson, of MIT series on philosophy of psychology and biology.

*SIDELIGHTS:* Australian educator Kim Sterelny is a specialist in the study of this discipline as it relates to biology, psychology, and the development of the mind. A "physicalist," he takes a pragmatic, functional approach to the evolution and development of the human species. Sterelny, who divides his time between teaching positions at Victoria University of Wellington in New Zealand and the Australian National University in Canberra, has articulated his sometimes-controversial theories in his many writings. He is the author or coauthor of scholarly books, and since 1981 has contributed scores of papers to learned journals in Australia, New Zealand, and the United States.

Assessing *The Representational Theory of Mind: An Introduction* for *Choice,* reviewer C. J. Shields hailed the work as "an excellent introduction for the serious student" and noted that "unlike more standard introductions to mind-body relations . . . [*The Representational Theory of Mind*] pushes a partisan line. (In this sense, it is very much like Sterelny's earlier work with Michael Devitt.)"

Sterelny and University of Sydney colleague Paul E. Griffiths applied a physicalist rationale in the writing of their provocatively titled textbook, *Sex and Death: An Introduction to the Philosophy of Biology.* Reviewer J. E. Platz, writing in *Choice,* observed that the authors "introduce the reader to numerous controversial areas of biology containing evolutionary content; each has philosophical or sociological implications." Platz went on to recommend *Sex and Death* as a "starting point for an advanced readings course." Reviewing the same book in *Science,* Ernst Mayr described it as "a helpful first introduction into the philosophical problems of biology." Reviewer Daniel Albert, writing in the journal *Perspectives in Biology and Medicine,* commented that *Sex and Death* is "an engaging and relatively accessible version of modern philosophy of biology told by two philosophers steeped in their discipline and knowledgeable about a wide range of interesting avenues in the modern science of biology."

*Dawkins vs. Gould: Survival of the Fittest* attempts to explain the roots of the intellectual "punch-up" between star biologists Richard Dawkins and Stephen Jay Gould. Dawkins, an "ethologist" and the author of such books as *The Selfish Gene* and *The Blind Watchmaker,* espouses a view of human evolution as a struggle between competing genes. "Ethology aims to understand the adaptive significance of particular behavioural patterns," Sterelny explained. Meanwhile, paleontologist Gould, who is known for his popular books, for example, *Rock of Ages* and *Wonderful Life,* takes a wider view, explaining evolution as a competition between competing organisms. "[The two men] have different views on evolution, and they and their allies have engaged in an increasingly public, and increasingly polemical, exchange," Sterelny wrote.

Reviewing *Dawkins vs. Gould* for *Science,* Michael Goldman wrote that "Sterelny explains the conflict between Dawkins and Gould in terms of two distinct ideologies." While praising the book's readability, the reviewer lamented that Sterelny ultimately fails to "[bring] us any closer to a resolution," or to explain "why the controversy may never be resolved."

*BIOGRAPHICAL AND CRITICAL SOURCES:*

PERIODICALS

*Books and Culture,* July, 2000, p. 33.

*Choice,* C. J. Shields, September, 1991, review of *The Representational Theory of Mind,* p. 120; January, 2000, J. E. Platz, review of *Sex and Death: An Introduction to the Philosophy of Biology,* p. 959; July, 2001, pp. 845-853.

*Nature,* September 20, 2001, Michael Goldman, "Spandrels of Selection," pp. 252-253.

*Perspective in Biology and Medicine,* summer, 2000, Daniel Albert, review of *Sex and Death: An Introduction to the Philosophy of Biology,* pp. 622-623.

*Philosophy and Phenomenological Research,* July, 2000, pp. 207-215.

*Philosophy in Review,* June, 2000, p. 227.

*Philosophy of Science,* Supplement, September, 2000, pp. 369-387.

*Science,* Ernst Mayr, September 17, 1999, review of *Sex and Death: An Introduction to the Philosophy of Biology,* p. 1856.

*Science Books and Films,* September, 2000, p. 210.

\*　　\*　　\*

**STERN, Lesley**

*PERSONAL:* Born in Rhodesia (now Zimbabwe).

*ADDRESSES: Office*—University of New South Wales, Sydney, Australia, 2052. *E-mail*—lfstern@ucsd.edu.

*CAREER:* Filmmaker. Professor at University of New South Wales.

*AWARDS, HONORS:* Named "Writer on the Verge," *Village Voice,* 1999.

*WRITINGS:*

*The Scorsese Connection,* Indiana University Press/ British Film Institute (Bloomington, IN), 1995.

*The Smoking Book,* University of Chicago Press (Chicago, IL), 1999.

(Editor, with George Kouvaros) *Falling For You: Essays on Cinema and Performance,* Power Publications (Sydney, New South Wales, Australia), 1999.

*SIDELIGHTS:* A filmmaker and faculty member at the University of New South Wales in Australia, Lesley Stern is noted for writing that combines critical and personal perspectives. In her first book, *The Scorsese Connection,* Stern traced relationships among the various films of Martin Scorsese, and between these works and those of several other filmmakers. Although *Library Journal* critic Thomas J. Wiener found Stern's writing "impenetrable" and her "impressionistic takes" of the material unconvincing, other reviewers enjoyed her fusion of criticism and personal response. A. Hirsh, writing in *Choice,* considered *The Scorsese Connection* a "useful" study and credited Stern with being "alive in her usage of myth and symbolism from both historical myth and intertextual source." *Australian Book Review* critic Jose Borghino applauded Stern's critical acumen and the "adventurous" relationships she drew between Scorsese's work and other films. Borghino especially admired her linking of Scorsese's *Raging Bull,* a film about boxing star Jake La Motta, with the 1950s melodrama *The Red Shoes.* The critic deemed Stern's chapter on the connections between Scorsese's *Taxi Driver* and John Ford's *The Searchers* a "tour de force," praising Stern's "meticulous" analysis here but adding that "it is Stern's insistence in reading these films emotionally, as a viewer and participant in their narratives, that stands out."

Stern again combines personal and analytical approaches in *The Smoking Book,* a collection of fifty-four short pieces on the rituals, economics, cultural significance, and individual pleasures of smoking. A *Publishers Weekly* reviewer appreciated Stern's "often stunning and always intriguing" perspective, noting that her mix of fiction, criticism, history, and memoir "puts a new twist on the discussion of the delicious passion, and equally delicious irony, of smoking in a nonsmoking world." Similar enthusiasm marked the response of other reviewers. In *Booklist* Frank Caso noted that Stern's "engrossing panegyric to nicotine" is often witty but also "painful" and "poignant." Pam Kingsbury, writing in *Library Journal,* found *The Smoking Book* "sexy and provocative" and "an homage to sensual addiction."

## BIOGRAPHICAL AND CRITICAL SOURCES:

*PERIODICALS*

*Australian Book Review,* May, 1996, pp. 42-43.
*Booklist,* November 1, 1999, p. 503.
*Choice,* October, 1996, pp. 288-289.
*Library Journal,* March 15, 1996, p. 74; November 1, 1999, p. 82.
*Publishers Weekly,* October 11, 1999, p. 53.*

*       *       *

## STRATE, Grant 1927-

*PERSONAL:* Born December 7, 1927, in Cardston, Alberta, Canada; son of Alfred and Mable (Wilson) Strate. *Education:* University of Alberta, B.A., 1949, LL.B., 1950; studied modern dance with Laine Metz. *Hobbies and other interests:* Reading, film, music.

*ADDRESSES: Home*—128 West Thirteenth Avenue, Vancouver, BC V5Y 1V7, Canada. *E-mail*—gstrate@ sfu.ca.

*CAREER:* National Ballet of Canada, charter member, 1951, charter dancer, assistant to the artistic director, 1951-70, resident choreographer, 1953-70, emissary; Julliard School of Music and Dance, New York, NY, teacher, choreographer, 1962-63; York University, Ontario, dance department founding chairman, member of fine arts faculty, 1970-76, dance department acting chairman, 1977-78, choreographic seminar organizer and administrator, 197; Center for the Arts, Simon Fraser University, Burnaby, BC, director, 1980-89, dance program coordinator, 1991-92, Contemporary Arts Summer Institute director, 1989-94, choreographic seminar organizer and administrator, 1985, 1991; Studio Ballet, Antwerp, Belgium, choreographer; Royal Swedish Ballet, Stockholm, Sweden, choreographer. Dance in Canada Association, founding chairman and board member, 1973-78; Vancouver Dance Centre, board member, 1985-95; World Dance Alliance Americas Center Third Assembly, chairman, 1997.

*AWARDS, HONORS:* Centennial Medal, 1967; Queen's Silver Jubilee Medal, 1978; Ontario Dance Award, 1979; Dance in Canada Award, 1984; Canada Dance Award, 1988; Jean R. Chalmers Award for Creativity in Dance, 1993; Order of Canada, 1994; Governor General's Performing Arts Award, 1996.

*WRITINGS:*

*China Dance Journal: September 5-October 12, 1996,* Dance Collection Danse (Toronto, Ontario, Canada), 1997.

Contributor to *Canadian Dance Studies* and *Dance in Canada.*

*SIDELIGHTS:* A pioneer in dance and choreography in Canada, Grant Strate is a founding member of the National Ballet of Canada, which began in 1951. Strate had little dance experience in 1951 at the age of twenty-three when he met Celia Fanca, who was touring Canada to recruit members for the ballet company. In fact, his only dance education was tap dance lessons as a child and a few recreational dance classes in college. She saw some promise in him, and recruited him as a dancer; he later became choreographer for the National Ballet of Canada. Over the course of Strate's career he has choreographed more than fifty ballets. In the *Simon Fraser News,* Strate commented, "The development of dance as an art form is my most cherished achievement in Canada."

## BIOGRAPHICAL AND CRITICAL SOURCES:

*BOOKS*

*International Dictionary of Modern Dance,* St. James Press (Detroit, MI), 1998.

*OTHER*

*Harbour Dance Centre Web site,* http://harbourdance. bc.ca/ (April 15, 2002), "Grant Strate."
*Simon Frasier News Online,* http://www.sfu.ca/ (April 15, 2002), "1999 Honorary Degree Recipient,"; "List of Mentors 2001/2002."*

*       *       *

## STROHMEYER, Sarah

*PERSONAL:* Born in Bethlehem, PA; married Charles Merriman (a lawyer); children: Anna, Sam. *Education:* Tufts University, B.A., 1984; attended Case Western University.

*ADDRESSES: Agent*—Author Mail, c/o Dutton, 375 Hudson St., New York, NY 10014. *E-mail*—Bubbles Yablonsky@yahoo.com.

*CAREER: Home News,* New Brunswick, NJ, former reporter; *Plain Dealer,* Cleveland, OH, former reporter; *Valley News,* Lebanon, NH, former reporter.

*WRITINGS:*

*Barbie Unbound: A Parody of the Barbie Obsession,* photographs by Geoff Hanson, New Victoria (Norwich, VT), 1997.
*Bubbles Unbound,* Dutton (New York, NY), 2001.
*Bubbles in Trouble,* Dutton (New York, NY), 2002.

*SIDELIGHTS:* Sarah Strohmeyer wrote *Bubbles Unbound,* a mystery novel about a beautician-reporter-detective named Bubbles Yablonsky, following an interview she conducted with mystery novelist Janet Evanovich. The similarities between Evanovich's work and Strohmeyer's creation were noted by GraceAnne A. DeCandido in *Booklist,* who said that "having studied at the feet of the Master Evanovich, first-novelist Strohmeyer unleashes Lehigh, Pennsylvania's Bubbles Yablonsky." Similarly, Bob Hahn noted on *Bookbrowser.com* that "Strohmeyer's comical cozy should find a comfortable niche on the shelf alongside her mentor's Stephanie Plum novels."

Strohmeyer's second installment of the "Bubbles Yablonsky" series, *Bubbles in Trouble,* follows Bubbles into Amish country as she searches for her friend who disappeared on her wedding day. The investigation is made even more interesting by Bubbles's sacrifice of make-up and spandex in order to be accepted into the Amish community. With a cast of characters that range from a neo-Nazi chocolatier to Bubbles's crazy mother Lulu, *Bubbles in Trouble* continues the same level of enjoyment to Bubbles fans the first novel offered. GraceAnne A. DeCandido in *Booklist* found that "Bubbles 'Plain' doesn't really work"; however, "Bubbles' relationship to her brilliant teen daughter and to the elusive but hunky photographer Stiletto helps carry one through." A critic in *Publishers Weekly* wrote that Strohmeyer "successfully navigates the fine line between humorous stereotype and sympathetic amateur investigator."

*BIOGRAPHICAL AND CRITICAL SOURCES:*

*PERIODICALS*

*Booklist,* January 1, 2001, GraceAnne A. DeCandido, review of *Bubbles Unbound,* p. 927; May 15, 2002, GraceAnne A. DeCandido, review of *Bubbles in Trouble.*
*Publishers Weekly,* June 3, 2002, review of *Bubbles in Trouble.*

*OTHER*

*Bookbrowser.com,* http://www.bookbrowser.com/ (November 12, 2000), Bob Hahn, review of *Bubbles Unbound.*
*Sarah Strohmeyer Web site,* http://www.sarah strohmeyer.com (August 26, 2002).
*Whitestone Books,* http://www.whitestone.com/reviews (March 2001), Harriet Klausner, review of *Bubbles Unbound.**

\*    \*    \*

## SWEATMAN, Margaret (Lisa) 1953-

*PERSONAL:* Born May 13, 1953, in Winnipeg, Manitoba, Canada; daughter of Alan and Lorraine Mary (MacDonald) Sweatman; children: Bailey, Hillery. *Education:* University of Winnipeg, B.A.; Concordia University, postgraduate diploma in communication arts, 1976; Simon Fraser University, M.A., 1985.

*ADDRESSES: Home*—Winnipeg, Manitoba, Canada. *Agent*—c/o Author Mail, Knopf Canada, Suite 210, 33 Yonge St., Toronto, Ontario, Canada M5E 1G4. *E-mail*—sweatman@mbnet.mb.ca.

*CAREER:* Author, playwright, and lyricist; teaches creative writing workshops for young people; performs with the Broken Songs Band.

*MEMBER:* Manitoba Writers Guild.

*AWARDS, HONORS:* McNally Robinson Book of the Year, 1991, and the John Hirsch Award for Most Promising Manitoba Writer, 1992, both for *Fox;* Rogers Writers' Trust Fiction Prize, Writers' Trust of Canada, 2002.

*WRITINGS:*

*Private Property,* Turnstone Press (Winnipeg, Manitoba, Canada), 1988.

*Fox,* Turnstone Press (Winnipeg, Manitoba, Canada), 1991.

*Sam and Angie,* Turnstone Press (Winnipeg, Manitoba, Canada), 1996.

*When Alice Lay Down with Peter,* Knopf Canada (Toronto, Ontario), 2001.

*SIDELIGHTS:* Author of the award-winning novel, *Fox,* Margaret Sweatman is a Manitoba resident who often uses the history and environment of her surroundings as backdrops for her fiction. For example, *Fox* is set in Winnipeg, during the 1919 General Strike, and blends historical fact with fiction to tell the story about Canada's largest strike after the end of World War I. The novel was well received, earning Sweatman both the McNally Robinson Book of the Year Award as well as the inaugural John Hirsch Award. Reviewing the work for *Quill & Quire,* Roderick W. Harvey called *Fox* a "complicated novel" with qualities that would fascinate readers particularly interested in Canadian history. Characterizing the work as "metafiction" because of Sweatman's blending of historical events with "multiple historical perspectives and multilayered narration" Harvey also recommended the book for those interested in "literary post-modernism." Writing for *Canadian Forum,* Ormond McKague remarked on the duality of *Fox,* calling it a work of "breathtaking poetic beauty" as well as one that throws the conflict and pain of the strike into sharp focus. And although McKague felt that Sweatman's focus on language and characterization leads her to distance the reader from the harsh realities of the strike against which the story is set, the overall effect is a "beautiful book."

Sweatman's second novel was titled *Sam and Angie,* and it tells the story of a couple's failing marriage. The book did not garner the praise received by *Fox,* and critics remarked on the difficulty of connecting with the characters, primarily due to Sweatman's complicated writing style. In her most recent work, *When Alice Lay Down with Peter,* Sweatman returns to Manitoba as the canvass on which she paints her story. The epic tale begins with the story of Alice and Peter, who arrive in Canada from Orkney, England. Once there, the two lovers become involved in the fight to keep Manitoba free from Canadian acquisition. Beginning in the mid-1800s, the novel blends actual events with characters created by Sweatman, following the stories of Alice and Peter, their daughter Blondie McCormack, and her daughter, Helen, until the story ends, in the 1930s.

*BIOGRAPHICAL AND CRITICAL SOURCES:*

*PERIODICALS*

*Canadian Book Review Annual,* 1997, Virginia Gillham, review of *Sam and Angie,* p. 201.

*Canadian Dimension,* July-August, 1991, Brenda Austin-Smith, review of *Fox,* p. 34.

*Canadian Forum,* April, 1992, Ormond Mckague, "Language Languid, History Hidden," p. 28.

*Choice,* March, 1992, R. H. Solomon, review of *Fox,* p. 1081.

*Maclean's,* November 26, 2001, "A River Runs Through It," p. 47.

*Quill & Quire,* April, 1991, Roderick W. Harvey, review of *Fox,* p. 31; August, 1996, Patty Osborne, review of *Sam and Angie,* p. 36.*

\* \* \*

## SWETNAM, Michael S.

*PERSONAL:* Born in Espanola, NM.

*ADDRESSES: Office*—Potomac Institute for Policy Studies, 901 North Stuart St., Suite 200, Arlington, VA 22203. *E-mail*—mswetman@potomacinstitute.org.

*CAREER:* Potomac Institute for Policy Studies, founder and chairman of the board, 1994—, president, 1994-2001; member of technical advisory group to U.S Senate Special Select Committee on Intelligence; program monitor on intelligence community staff for director of central intelligence agency (CIA); intelligence positions in the U.S. Navy, the National Security Agency and the CIA; foreign intelligence advisory board, member, 1990-1992. Pacific-Sierra Research Corporation, vice president of engineering; GTE, director of information processing systems, GTE Government Systems, manager of strategic planning. *Military service:* U.S. Navy, 1972-1996.

*WRITINGS:*

(Editor, with Yonah Alexander) *Cyber Terrorism and Information Warfare,* Oceana Publications (Dobbs Ferry, NY), 1999.
(With Yonah Alexander and Herbert M. Levine) *ETA: Profile of a Terrorist Group,* Transnational Publishers (Ardsley, NY), 2001.
(With Yonah Alexander) *Usama bin Laden's al-Qaida: Profile of a Terrorist Network,* Transnational Publishers (Ardsley, NY), 2001.

*SIDELIGHTS:* Michael S. Swetnam, along with colleague Yonah Alexander, is the author of a four-volume set on cyber terrorism titled *Cyber Terrorism and Information Warfare,* which talks extensively about the growing threat to U.S. intelligence from terrorists. The work does not focus on groups affiliated with any one country, but several nations who are now capable of attacking other countries without risking their own lives.

Each volume presents a series of documents that detail the threat to the U.S. information infrastructure from such sources. The threat is increased by American society's reliance on information infrastructure. Swetnam substantiates his thesis with documents from multiple sources, including the CIA, the FBI, the Department of Defense, the U.S. Congress, as well as from the Attorney General's office. There is also mention of several existing regulations and laws to deal with the threat of cyber terrorism and the U.S. government's state of readiness. In his review of *Cyber Terrorism and Information Warfare,* John P. Joergensen in *Legal Information Alert,* noted that one of the volumes contains a series of reports that set "out a road map for research and development efforts to protect a specific area of the economy that is vulnerable to electronic terrorism." Essential services such as banking, finance, communications, and health services are particularly at risk since any breakdown in services would create large-scale panic in society.

In a review of Swetnam's other offering, *Usama bin Laden's al-Qaida: Profile of a Terrorist Network,* James T. Dunne commented in *Security Management* that it is a concise compilation of "all relevant, significant, and publicly available documents pertaining to the multimillionaire militant, his men, and his munitions." It is a detailed reference source for all information on al-Qaida, its principles and ideologies, the structure of the terrorist organization headed by bin Laden, and its hierarchical leadership. Also covered in the discussion are sources of funding for al-Qaida, its supporters, its sphere of influence, and area of operations. A chronological chart of events provides a timeline of the rise and growth of al-Qaida. The book aims at increasing an understanding of the growth, development, and expansion of the terrorist organization.

*BIOGRAPHICAL AND CRITICAL SOURCES:*

*PERIODICALS*

*Albuquerque Journal,* October 12, 2001, Diane Velasco, review of *Usama bin Laden's al-Qaida: Profile of a Terrorist Network,* p. A1.
*Legal Information Alert,* July-August, 2000, John P. Joergenson, review of *Cyber Terrorism and Information Warfare,* p. 9.
*Security Management,* November, 2001, James T. Dunne, review of *Usama bin Laden's al-Qaida,* p. 106.

*OTHER*

*Usama bin Laden's al-Qaida,* http://www.potomacinstitute.org/ (May 09, 2002), review of *Usama bin Laden's al-Qaida: Profile of a Terrorist Network.**

# T

## TAS, Filip (Josef) 1918-

PERSONAL: Born March 11, 1918, in London, England . Education: Attended Academy of Fine Arts, Antwerp, Belgium, 1935-39; School of Industry, Antwerp, Belgium, 1939-46, Dip.Chim., 1946.

ADDRESSES: Home—Kleine Beerstraat 42, 2000 Antwerp, Belgium. Agent—Galerij Paule Pia, Kammenstraat 57, 2000 Antwerp, Belgium.

CAREER: Freelance photographer. Gevaert Photo Products, Mortsel, Belgium, chemist, 1937-44; G 58-Hessenhuis plastic arts group, Antwerp, Belgium, member and founder, beginning 1958; Flemish television, Antwerp, Belgium, film director, 1960—; De Standaard (newspaper), Brussels, Belgium, photography editor, 1965—; National Higher Institute for Architecture and Town Planning, Antwerp, Belgium, professor of photography, 1968—.

AWARDS, HONORS: Gold medal for photography, San Sebastian, Spain, 1948; first prize for photography, Province of Antwerp, 1951, and Province of Limburg, Belgium, 1952; gold workshop prize, Belgian Government, 1977; state award for the arts, Brussels, 1983; award for special merit, Province of Antwerp, 1983.

WRITINGS:

Antwerp: City on the River, [Tielt, Belgium], 1965.
De Keygnaert: A Residence in the Polder, [Tielt, Belgium], 1975.

The Catholic University of Louvain-Kortrijk, [Tielt, Belgium], 1975.
South America: People and Tribes, Amsterdam Boek (Amsterdam, Netherlands), 1977.
Filip Tas: Portfolio, [Antwerp, Belgium], 1980.
(Coauthor with Raoul van den Boom) Antwerpen Provincie: Fotos, Lanoo (Amsterdam, Netherlands), 1980.
Filip Tas: Portfolio, Internationaal Cultureel Centrum (Antwerp, Belgium), 1983.
Antwerp behind the Scenes, [Tielt, Belgium], 1986.
Antwerpen, [Mortsel, Belgium], 1986.
Portfolio: Maastricht, [Maastricht, Netherlands], 1988.
Kunstenaars in Antwerpen, [Antwerp, Belgium], 1993.
Architectuur, Leon Stijnen, [Antwerp, Belgium], 1993.*

\* \* \*

## TAYLOR, Timothy 1963(?)-

PERSONAL: Born 1963 (one source lists 1964), in Venezuela; married; wife's name, Jane. Education: Attended University of Alberta; Queens University, Toronto, Canada, M.B.A.

ADDRESSES: Home—Vancouver, British Columbia, Canada. Agent—c/o Author Mail, Counterpoint Press/ Perseus Books Group, 5500 Central Ave., Boulder, CO 80301.

CAREER: Writer. Toronto Dominion Bank, commercial banker, 1987-91.

*AWARDS, HONORS:* National Magazine Award; Journey Prize.

*WRITINGS:*

*Stanley Park,* Counterpoint (Washington, DC), 2002.
*Silent Cruise and Other Stories,* Counterpoint (Washington, DC), 2002.

*WORK IN PROGRESS: El Primero,* a novel.

*SIDELIGHTS:* Not many fiction writers have an M.B.A. to their credit, but Timothy Taylor actually began his career as a commercial banker. While this career offered security, it left him dissatisfied, and he gave it up in favor of a new career as a full-time freelance writer. In time he supplemented his freelance income with consulting work that still left him plenty of time to write. He has emerged as a well-respected short story writer and was the first writer ever to have three stories published in a single edition of the *Journey Prize Anthology.*

In 2000, Taylor published his first novel, *Stanley Park,* about an eccentric chef named Jeremy who decides to open a restaurant in Vancouver dedicated to local produce and ingredients. At the same time, Jeremy's father, an anthropologist, is attempting to go local a different way, by living with and studying the homeless population living in Vancouver's Stanley Park. At first hostile to his father's project, Jeremy gradually gets closer to him and even winds up cooking for the homeless, learning to prepare squirrel and raccoon and other park animals. Gradually, Jeremy is drawn into a mystery that his father has come across, involving the murder of two children in the park thirty years previously. "Carefully nuanced characters, an intriguing plot, and thematic explorations of the relationships of people to their environment and food combine to make *Stanley Park* a rich and satisfying read," wrote *Resource Links* reviewer Jill Kedersha McClay. "Taylor has written a sort of cook's version of the anti-WTO protests, striking a heartfelt and entertaining blow against conformity," a *Publishers Weekly* review remarked. For *Booklist* reviewer Dennis Dodge, the mystery subplot pales in comparison to Jeremy's struggles with his restaurant, "and the greater pleasure derives from the deliciously detailed descriptions of his culinary creations."

*BIOGRAPHICAL AND CRITICAL SOURCES:*

PERIODICALS

*Booklist,* March 1, 2002, Dennis Dodge, review of *Stanley Park,* p. 1097.
*Publishers Weekly,* March 18, 2002, review of *Stanley Park,* p. 72.
*Resource Links,* October, 2001, Jill Kedersha McClay, review of *Stanley Park,* p. 56.*

*     *     *

## TEILHARD de CHARDIN, (Marie Joseph) Pierre 1881-1955

*PERSONAL:* Born May 1, 1881, in Sarcenat, France; died April 10, 1955, in New York, NY. *Education:* Attended Jesuit college of Mongré in Vellefranche; studied philosophy at a Jewish training center; studied theology near Hastings, England; Institut Catholique and the Museum d'Histoire, received degree, 1922; further Jesuit training in Canterbury. *Religion:* Roman Catholic. *Hobbies and other interests:* Paleontology.

*CAREER:* Jesuit priest, philosopher, and paleontologist. *Military service:* Served in the military during World War I; earned French Croix de Guèrre, 1915, Médaille Militaire, 1917, and Légion d'honneur, 1920.

*WRITINGS:*

*Les Mammifères de l'éocène inférieur français et leurs gisements,* 1922.
*Etude géologique sur la région du Dalai-Noor,* 1926.
*Les Mammifères de l'éocène inférieur de la Belgique,* 1927.
(With Jean Piveteau) *Les Mammifères fossiles de Nihowan* [China], 1930.
(With others) *Etudes géologiques en Ethiopie, Somalie, et Arabie méridionale,* 1930.
(With C. C. Young) *Fossil Mammals from the Late Cenozoic of Northern China,* 1931.
(With others) *Fossil Man in China,* 1933
*Fossil Mammals from Locality 9 of Choukoutien,* 1936.

(With C. C. Young) *On the Mammalian Remains from the Archaeological Site of Anyang*, 1936.

*The Fossils from Locality 12 of Choukoutien*, 1938.

*The Fossils from Locality 18, Near Peking*, 1940.

(With Pei Wen-Ching) *The Fossil Mammals from Locality 13 of Choukoutien*, 1941.

*Early Man in China*, 1941.

*New Rodents of the Pliocene and Lower Pleistocene*, 1942.

(With Pierre Leroy) *Chinese Fossil Mammals*, 1942.

*Fossil Men: Recent Discoveries and Present Problems* (lecture), 1943.

(With Pei Wen-Ching) *Le Néolithique de la Chine*, 1944.

(With Pierre Leroy) *Les Félides de Chine*, 1945.

(With Pierre Leroy) *Les Mustelides de Chine*, 1945.

*Le Groupe zoologique: Structure et directions evolutives*, 1956, translated as *Man's Place in Nature: The Human Zoological Group*, 1966.

*Le Phénomene humain*, 1955, translated as *The Phenomenon of Man*, 1959, revised edition, 1965.

*Science et Christ*, 1955, translated as *Science and Christ*, 1968.

*L'Apparition de l'homme*, 1956, translated as *The Appearance of Man*, 1965.

*La Vision du passé*, 1957, translated as *The Vision of the Past*, 1966.

*Le Milieu divin: Essai de vie intérieure*, 1957, translated as *The Divine Milieu: An Essay on the Inner Life*, 1960.

*Construire la terre*, 1958, translated as *Building the Earth*, 1965.

*L'Avenir de l'homme*, 1959, translated as *The Future of Man*, 1964.

*Pensées*, edited by Fernande Tardivel, 1961.

*L'Energie humaine*, 1962, translated as *Human Energy*, 1969.

*Hymne de l'univers*, 1962, translated as *Hymn of the Universe*, 1965.

*La Messe sur le monde*, 1962.

*L'Activation de l'energie*, 1963, translated as *Activation of Energy*, 1970.

*Le Christ évoluteur: Socialisation et religion; Carriere scientifique*, 1965.

*Mon univers*, 1965.

*Le Prêtre*, 1965.

*Sur le bonheur*, 1966, translated as *On Happiness*, 1973.

*Je m'explique*, edited by Jean-Pierre Demoulin, 1966, translated as *Let Me Explain*, 1970.

*Sur l'amour*, 1967, translated as *On Love*, 1972.

*Comment je crois*, 1969, translated as *Christianity and Evolution*, 1971.

*Toujours en avant*, edited by Cahrlotte Engles, 1970.

*Réflexions et prières dans l'espace-temps*, edited by Édouard and Suzanne Bret, 1972.

*Les Directions de l'avenir*, 1973, translated as *Towards the Future*, 1975.

*Sur la souffrance*, 1974, translated as *On Suffering*, 1975.

*Le Coeur de la matière*, 1976, translated as *The Heart of the Matter*, 1978.

*On Love and Happiness* (includes *On Love* and *On Happiness*), 1984.


OTHER


*Lettres de voyage (1923-1939); Nouvelles lettres de voyage (1939-1955)*, two volumes, edited by Claude Aragonnes, 1956, 1957, translated as *Letters from a Traveler*, 1962.

*Genèse d'une pensée: lettres 1914-1919*, edited by Alice Teilhard-Chambron and Max Henri Begouen, 1961, translated as *The Making of a Mind: Letters from a Soldier-Priest, 1914-1919*, 1965.

*Lettres d'Egypte, 1905-1908*, 1963, translated as *Letters from Egypt, 1905-1908*, 1965.

*Ecrits du temps de la guerre (1916-1919)*, 1965, translated as *Writings in Time of War*, 1968.

*Lettres à Léontine Zanta*, 1965, translated as *Letters to Leontine Zanta*, 1969.

*Lettres d'Hastings et de Paris 1908-1914*, 1965, translated edition published in two volumes as *Letters from Paris 1912-1914* and *Letters from Hastings 1908-1912*, 1968.

*Pierre Teilhard de Chardin and Maurice Blondel: Correspondence*, 1967.

*Etre plus: Directives extraites des Ecrits publiés ou inédits du père, de sa correspondance et de ses notes*, 1968.

*Lettres to Two Friends, 1926-1952*, 1968.

*Dans le sillage des sinanthropes: lettres inédites de Pierre Teilhard de Chardin et Johan Gunnar Andersson, 1926-1934*, 1971.

*L'Oeuvre scientifique 1905-1955*, ten volumes, edited by Nicole and Karl Schmitz-Moorman, 1971.

*Lettres intimes à Auguste Valensin, Bruno de solages, Henri de Lubac, 1919-1955*, 1972.

*Journal*, edited by Nicole and Karl Schmitz-Moormann, 1975.

*Lettres familières de Pierre Teilhard de Chardin, mon ami: les dernières années, 1948-1955*, 1975, translated as *Lettres from My Friend, Pierre Teilhard de Chardin, 1948-1955, Including Letters Written during His Final Years in America*, 1980.

SIDELIGHTS: Jesuit priest and paleontologist Pierre Teilhard de Chardin merged his Christian faith with his beliefs in evolution to form a mystical philosophy to which other paleontologists or strict Catholics objected, but which enlightened many intellectual and scientifically minded Christians. By his death, basic Catholic principles such as original sin, redemption, the immortality of the human soul and monogenesis (the belief that one God created the world and its inhabitants) were reaffirmed in the papal encyclical *Humani generis*. From the statement issued at the First Vatican Council of 1869-70, "Not all the dogmas of faith can be understood and demonstrated from natural principles," the Catholic leadership had been fighting the perceived threats of new scientific findings and the growing modernism. Though the church encouraged Teilhard de Chardin in his scientific studies, they found his findings incompatible with Catholic dogma. But Teilhard de Chardin could no more abandon his commitment to scientific integrity than he could renounce his faith in the Church. He did agree to publish only scientific papers, not popular articles or books. His synthesis of his Catholic faith and evolutionary theory was not published until after his death. Those writings shaped his reputation.

Teilhard de Chardin grew up the fourth of eleven children in a devout middle-class family. His father owned farms and dabbled in natural history. The children were raised amid learning and faith. Teilhard de Chardin attended the Jesuit college of Mongré in Vellefranche, and after a two-year novitiate, entered the Jesuit order in 1899. By 1902 the Jesuits had been forced to move their training centers outside of France because of the French Combes administration. Teilhard studied philosophy for three years, and collected and wrote about prehistoric plants and animals in his free time. He continued his scientific studies during his regency in a French Jesuit school in Cairo. He taught chemistry and physics and oversaw a museum and then began his four-year study of theology. Near his theology house by Hastings he discovered the tooth of a new species of a small mammal. He participated in digs whenever he could. During his third year in theological studies he took the anti-modernist oath required for ordination as a priest.

Teilhard de Chardin based his evolutionary concepts on Henri Bergson's *L'Evolution créatrice* (1907). From the key concepts of complexification and convergence, he developed his own religious interpretation of "unanimization" in the "noonsphere," or self-consciousness, and "Christification." He studied for his doctorate at the Institut Catholique and at the Museum d'Histoire Naturelle in Paris. At the Museum he befriended another influential figure, Édouard Le Roy. Together they discussed Bergson, whom the Catholic church had recently disavowed. The church put Le Roy's own writings on a list of forbidden books in 1931. Teilhard de Chardin also befriended Maurice Blondel, who defended the orthodox position against modernism. When Teilhard de Chardin sent his writings to Blondel for his comments, Blondel, cautioning against an embrace of modernism, urged his friend to revolve all his theories around Christ.

Teilhard de Chardin completed his spiritual training as a Jesuit at Canterbury, England, just before World War I began. He served as a stretcher-bearer during the war and received three medals for bravery. He turned down a commission to spend three years as a geology professor at the Institut Catholique in Paris. Though he was humorous and genial on the surface, his letters to friends reflect strain over the conflict between his holy orders and scientific inquiry. This strain motivated him to develop his spiritual and scientific philosophy on humanity's development and destiny. His 1921 paper on evolutionary transformism, published in *La Vision du passé*, got him excluded from the Institut Catholique and essentially banished to China. He wrote on mammals in the lower Eocene for his doctorate dissertation.

Teilhard de Chardin began teaching at the Jesuit college of higher education in Tientsin, China, in 1923, remaining there until 1946. He wrote his major philosophical work, *La Messe sur le monde,* during a 1923 journey between Peking and Ordos, and wrote his religious meditation, *Le Milieu divin,* in 1926 and 1927. In 1929 he published his first paper on the finding of Sinanthropus; by the following year, he had reconciled his scientific findings with his faith in Christ as central to all creation, concluding that "Evolutionism can give to the universe the grandeur, profundity, and unity which are the natural atmosphere of the Christian faith."

Teilhard de Chardin returned to France in 1924, and then traveled throughout the East and Africa. In the 1930s he spent nine months on the Yellow River, toured Shansi by cart and followed the Yangtze River nearly to Tibet. In 1938 he was allowed to take a post at the Institut de la Paléontologies Humaine in France. Through World War II he remained in China under Japanese occupation. Teilhard de Chardin suffered a severe heart attack in 1947. While recovering at his brother's house in the Auvergn he wrote his intimate apologia, *Le Coeur de la matiere.* Upon recovering, he visited South Africa and South America. While in New York he accepted a position with the Wenner-Gren Foundation, and was then offered a chair at the Collège de France. Having written *Le Phénomene Humain* and *Le Milieu divin,* he was forbidden to publish either, and could not accept the chair. Publishing these works during his lifetime would have been considered an act of defiance.

For the rest of his life, Teilhard de Chardin studied geology, and committed himself to the study of human community and the influence of Christ on humanity. After further travels to New York and South Africa, he died on Easter Sunday, 1955. At the advice of friends, he had left his philosophical writings to literary executors. At the time of his death, he was perceived as a failure, an obscure priest restrained by the Catholic Church who published only a smattering of minor scientific works. Yet within four years, after his seven major philosophical works were published, he was internationally known as a provocative thinker. His books sold more than 300,000 copies in five years and inspired liberalizing theologians and Christian intellectuals worldwide. Karl Stern wrote in *Phenomenon of Man* in *Commonwealth,* "Here, one feels, the concept of biological evolution . . . has found its crowning and, at the same time, its antithesis. Father Teilhard possessed that extremely rare combination . . . of scientific and contemplative genius . . . there is no doubt that later, when people will look back at our times as the dark ages of positivism, Father Teilhard's search will stand out like a flashing beam."

*BIOGRAPHICAL AND CRITICAL SOURCES:*

*BOOKS*

Cuénot, Claude, *Teilhard de Chardin: A Biographical Study* (includes bibliography), Burns & Oates (London, England), 1965.

*Dictionary of Twentieth Century Culture,* Volume 2: *French Culture 1900-1975,* Gale (Detroit, MI), 1995.

Dodson, Edward O., *The Phenomenon of Man Revisited: A Biological Viewpoint on Teilhard de Chardin,* Columbia University Press (New York, NY), 1984.

Faricy, Robert, *All Things in Christ: Teilhard de Chardin's Spirituality,* Collins (London, England), 1981.

*Guide to French Literature, 1789 to the Present,* St. James (Detroit, MI), 1992.

King, Thomas M., *Teilhard's Mysticism of Knowing,* Seabury Press (New York, NY), 1981.

King, Thomas M., and James F. Salmon, editors, *Teilhard and the Unity of Knowledge: The Georgetown University Centennial Symposium,* Paulist Press (New York, NY), 1983.

Lubac, Henri de, *The Religion of Teilhard de Chardin,* Desclee (New York, NY), 1967.

McCarthy, Joseph M., *Teilhard de Chardin; A Comprehensive Bibliography,* Garland (New York, NY), 1981.

Perlinski, Jerome, editor, *The Spirit of the Earth: A Teilhard Centenary Celebration,* Seabury (New York, NY), 1981.

*PERIODICALS*

*Commonwealth,* January 1, 1960.*

*       *       *

**THARP, Twyla 1941-**

*PERSONAL:* Born July 1, 1941, in Portland, IN; daughter of William and Lecile Tharp; married Peter Young (divorced); married Robert Huot (Divorced); children: Jesse. *Education:* Attended Pomona College; attended American Ballet Theatre School; Barnard College, B.A., 1963; Indiana University, L.H.D., 1987; Pomona College, D.F.A. 1987; studied dance with Richard Thomas, Merce Cunningham, Igor Schwezoff, Louis Mattox, Paul Taylor, Margaret Craske, Erick Hawkins.

*ADDRESSES: Office*—Twyla Tharp Dance Foundation, 336 Central Park West, Flat 17B, New York, NY 10025. *E-mail*—mk@twylatharp.org.

*CAREER:* Dancer and choreographer. Paul Taylor Dance Company, dancer, 1963-65; Twyla Tharp Dance Foundation, New York, NY, founder, director, 1965-88, 2000—; American Ballet Theatre, New York, NY, artistic associate, resident choreographer, 1987-91, 1995—; Tharp!, founder, 1996; John Curry, Olympic skater, choreographer; White Oak Dance Project, choreographer. Choreographer for films, including *Hair*, directed by Milos Forman, 1979; *Ragtime*, directed by Milos Forman, 1981; *Amadeus*, directed by Milos Forman, 1984; *White Nights*, directed by Taylor Hackford, 1985; and *I'll Do Anything*, directed by James Brooks, 1992. Television work includes *Eight Jelly Rolls* produced for London Weekend Television, 1974, *The Bix Pieces*, produced for CBS *Camera Three*, 1973; *Sue's Leg, Remembering the Thirties'*, produced for PBS *Dance in America* series, 1976; *The Catherine Wheel*, produced for BBC and PBS, for *Dance in America* series; *Confessions of a Corner-maker*, featuring *Baker's Dozen, Short Stories,* and *Duet* from the *Third Suite,* produced for CBS, 1981. Co-producer and director of *Making Television Dance;* co-director of *Baryshnikov by Tharp* (television special). Toured new works and repertoire with companies including *Cutting Up* with Mikhail Baryshnikov, 1991-94; freelance choreography for American Ballet Theatre, Australian Ballet, Boston Ballet, Hubbard Street Dance Chicago, Joffrey Ballet, New York City Ballet, Paris Opera Ballet, Royal Ballet, and Twyla Tharp Dance Foundation, 1965-87; directed and choreographed Broadway production of *Singin' in the Rain.* Has taught at colleges and universities including University of Massachusetts, Oberlin College, Walker Art Center, and Boston University.

*AWARDS, HONORS:* Guggenheim fellowship, John S. Guggenheim Memorial Foundation, 1971; Creative Arts citation, Brandeis University, 1972; challenge grant, National Endowment for the Arts, 1977, 1985; honorary degree, California Institute of Arts, 1978; honorary degree, Bucknell University, 1979; Silver Satellite Award, American Women in Radio and Television, for *Making Television Dance*, 1978; honorary degree, Bates College, 1980; Dance Educators of America Award, 1980, for *Making Television Dance; Dance* magazine award, 1981; honorary degree, Brown University, 1981; honorary degree, Barnard College, 1981: Dance Film Award, Chicago International Film Festival, 1981; for *Making Television Dance;* New York Mayor's Award of Honor for Arts and Culture, 1984; two Emmy Awards, 1985, for *Baryshnikov by Tharp;* Directors Guild of America Award for Out-

standing Director Achievement, 1985, for *Baryshnikov by Tharp;* honorary degrees from Indiana University, 1987, Ponoma College, 1987, Hamilton College, 1988, Skidmore College, 1988, and Marymount Manhattan College, 1989; University Excellence Medal, Columbia University, and Lions of the Performing Arts Award, New York Public Library, both 1989; Samuel M. Scripps Award, American Dance Festival, 1990; Laurence Olivier Award, Laurence Olivier Foundation, 1991, for *In the Upper Room;* Wexner Foundation Award, Ohio State University Wexner Center for the Arts, 1992; MacArthur Foundation fellowship, 1992; Golden Plate Award, American Academy of Achievement, 1993; Woman of Achievement, Barnard College, 1993; Inductee, American Academy of the Arts and Sciences, 1993.

*WRITINGS:*

*Push Comes to Shove,* Bantam Books (New York, NY), 1992.
(Director) *Scrapbook Tape,* (video anthology), PBS, 1982.
*Twyla Tharp: Oppositions, Dance in America,* (television series), PBS, 1996.

*WORK IN PROGRESS: The Creative Habit,* a book about being an artist.

*SIDELIGHTS:* When Twyla Tharp was born her mother told people that "She'll grow up to be famous," according to *Wisconsin State Journal* contributor Nadine Goff. Her mother's predictions proved correct, and Tharp is now well known for her choreography. She founded her own dance company, Twyla Tharp Dance Foundation, in New York in 1965—the first U.S. dance company to pay dancers to work the entire year. Her dance style is a combination of modern dance and ballet and is set to a variety of music types, including classical and popular. A contributor to the *International Dictionary of Modern Dance* described Tharp as "One of the most eclectic choreographers of the twentieth century."

Thorpe has choreographed dances for companies such as American Ballet Theatre, Australian Ballet, Boston Ballet, Joffrey Ballet, New York City Ballet, Paris Opera Ballet, and the Royal Ballet. Since 1965 she has choreographed more than 120 ballets, and has choreographed for television and for film.

*Push Comes to Shove* Tharp's autobiography, includes information about her childhood, dance education, dance and choreography career, family life, relationships, and the hardships she has endured. A *Publishers Weekly* contributor noted, "The wit and drive of Tharpe's dances also feed her life story."

*BIOGRAPHICAL AND CRITICAL SOURCES:*

BOOKS

*International Dictionary of Modern Dance,* St. James Press (Detroit, MI), 1998.

PERIODICALS

*Dance,* March, 2001, Wendy Perron, "Twyla Tharp," p. 44.
*Entertainment Weekly,* November 27, 1992, Suzanne Ruta, review of *Push Comes to Shove,* p. 74; November 16, 2001, Matthew Flamm, "Between the Lines: The Inside Scoop on the Book World," p. 165.
*New Republic,* May 31, 1993, Mindy Aloff, review of *Push Comes to Shove,* p. 31.
*People,* March 15, 1993, Pam Lambert, review of *Push Comes to Shove,* p. 32.
*Publishers Weekly,* November 2, 1992, review of *Push Comes to Shove,* p. 63.
*Wisconsin State Journal,* January 27, 2002, "For the People Twyla Tharp a Trendsetter without the Elitism," p. E1.

OTHER

*American Ballet Theatre Web site,* http://www.abt.org/ (April 16, 2002), "Twyla Tharp."
*American Dance Festival Web site,* http://www. americandancefestival.org/ (April 16, 2002), "Twyla Tharp."
*New York Public Library Web site,* http://digilib.nypl. org/ (April 16, 2002), "Biographical Sketch of Twyla Tharp."
*Twyla Tharp Web site,* http://www.twylatharp.org/ (April 16, 2002).*

*       *       *

**TIMMERMANS, Stefan 1968-**

*PERSONAL:* Born March 15, 1968. *Education:* University of Illinois at Urbana-Champaign, Ph.D.

*ADDRESSES: Office*—Department of Sociology, MS 071, Brandeis University, Waltham, MA 02454-9110.

*CAREER:* Educator and author. Brandeis University, Waltham, MA, assistant professor of sociology, 1995—.

*WRITINGS:*

*Sudden Death and the Myth of CPR,* Temple University Press (Philadelphia, PA), 1999.

*       *       *

**TOMASZEWSKI, Tomasz 1953-**

*PERSONAL:* Born May 6, 1953, in Warsaw, Poland; married Malgorzata Niezbitowska (a journalist), 1978; children: Maryna. *Education:* Attended Warsaw University, 1973-74, and Warsaw Technical University, 1974-78.

*ADDRESSES: Home*—05-510 Konstancin-Jeziorna, ul Batorego #19, Poland.

*CAREER:* Photojournalist and educator. *ITD,* Warsaw, Poland, photojournalist, 1976-76; *Razem,* Warsaw, staff photographer, 1976-77; *Perspektywy,* Warsaw, staff photographer, 1977-81; freelance photographer, 1981—. Lecturer, Film and Television College, Katowice, Poland, 1985, Film and Television School, Poland, 1988-90, and International Photographic Workshops, 1991 and 1992. *Exhibitions:* Works included in permanent collection of Museum of Art, Lodz, Poland, and National Library, Warsaw. Solo exhibitions include *Pokoje na godziny,* Warsaw Technical University, 1975; *Sytuacje rodzinne,* Klub Mechanik, Warsaw, 1976; Prince Gallery, Detroit, MI, 1987; and Canon Gallery, Amsterdam, Netherlands, 1990. Group exhibitions include *Press Photography,* ZPAF Gallery, Warsaw, 1976; *Polish Photography,* Polish Cultural Institute, Stockholm, Sweden, 1980; and *Contemporary Polish Art Photography,* Zacheta Gallery, Warsaw, 1985.

*MEMBER:* Union of Polish Art Photographers (deputy chairman, 1985—), German Photo Agency.

*AWARDS, HONORS:* First prize, Twentieth Press Photography Competition (Warsaw), 1977; Solidarity Award, 1985 and 1986; honorable mention, *Washington Journalism Review* photojournalism competition, 1992.

*WRITINGS:*

PHOTOGRAPHER

*Cofni wskazowe zegara* (title means "Put the Clock Back"), text by A. Rowinski, [Warsaw, Poland], 1980.

*Die verbannten Dichter,* text by J. Serke, [Hamburg, Germany], 1982.

*Cyganie Polscy* (title means "Polish Gypsies"), text by J. Ficowski, [Warsaw, Poland], 1985.

*The Last Jews of Poland—Remnants,* text by Malgorzata Niezbitowska, [New York, NY], 1986.

*Day in the Life of America,* [New York, NY], 1987.

*Day in the Life of Spain,* [New York, NY], 1988.

*Day in the Life of Soviet Union,* [New York, NY], 1988.

*Odyssey, the Art of Photography,* [Washington, DC], 1989.

*Power to Heal,* [New York, NY], 1990.

*In Search of America,* [Warsaw, Poland], 1994.

Contributor of photographs to periodicals, including *National Geographic, Paris Match, Perspektywy,* and *Razem.* Photography editor, *Przeglad Katolicki,* 1984-85.

*SIDELIGHTS:* Tomasz Tomaszewski is a notable Polish photographer who is probably best known for his depictions of Polish Jews. "The subject is not an easy one," declared a *Contemporary Photographers* contributor. "The relationship between Poles and Jews has a long and difficult history. It is drenched . . . in bitterness and accusation." Tomaszewski—accompanied by his wife, journalist Malgorzata Niezbitowska—devoted five years of his life to the photographing of Polish Jews, whose numbers had declined dramatically as a consequence of the anti-Semitic genocide that raged across Europe from the 1930s to the end of World War II. The project, which he described in *Contemporary Photographers* as "a history of absence," resulted in more than seven thousand photographs, including those works exhibited as *The Last Jews of Poland—Remnants* in 1985. "It must be emphasized that Tomaszewski portrays this history with exceptional honesty and objectivity," acknowledged the *Contemporary Photographers* writer. "In no way is his photography photography with a message."

Tomaszewski began his career as a photographer in the mid-1970s, when he worked for Polish publications such as *Razem* and *Perspektywy.* After becoming a freelance photographer in 1981, he began providing pictures to publications such as *National Geographic* and *Paris Match.* In the ensuing years he showed his photographs in various solo exhibitions and group works, and he published further collections, including *Odyssey, the Art of Photography* and *In Search of America.*

*BIOGRAPHICAL AND CRITICAL SOURCES:*

BOOKS

*Contemporary Photographers,* 3rd edition, St. James Press (Detroit, MI), 1996.

PERIODICALS

*Chicago Tribune,* December 6, 1985, Mathew Vita, "Remnants of Polish Jewry Sit for a Bleak Portrait."*

\*     \*     \*

**TORODE, Sam 1976-**

*PERSONAL:* Born February 29, 1976, in Kalamazoo, MI; son of Eugene and Mary (Conner) Torode; married Bethany Patchin, November 24, 2000; children: Gideon. *Education:* Hillsdale College, B.A. (art), 1998. *Religion:* Christian. *Hobbies and other interests:* Painting, fine arts.

*ADDRESSES: Home*—P.O. Box 65, South Wayne, WI 53587.

*CAREER:* Freelance book designer, 1999—; Philokalia Books, South Wayne, WI, editorial director, 2002—. *Touchstone,* art director, 1999—.

*WRITINGS:*

(With Bethany Torode) *Open Embrace: A Protestant Couple Rethinks Contraception,* William B. Eerdmans Publishing (Grand Rapids, MI), 2002.

(Editor) *Pope John Paul II's Theology of the Body in Simple Language,* four volumes, Philokalia Books (South Wayne, WI), in press.

Contributor to books, including *Best Christian Writing 2002.* Contributor to periodicals, including *Books and Culture, Boundless Webzine, Touchstone, World,* and *American Enterprise.*

*SIDELIGHTS:* Sam Torode told *CA:* "My current project is *Pope John Paul II's Theology of the Body in Simple Language,* a four-book series for which I'm adapting the pope's theology of sex, marriage, celibacy, and the body into everyday English. I am motivated by the desire to put a beautiful vision for love and marriage within the reach of all readers—especially those in the late teens and early twenties."

*BIOGRAPHICAL AND CRITICAL SOURCES:*

PERIODICALS

*Publishers Weekly,* May 6, 2002, review of *Open Embrace: A Protestant Couple Rethinks Contraception,* p. 55.

OTHER

*Torode Design,* http://www.torodedesign.com/ (January 20, 2003).

\*     \*     \*

## TORRES, Daniel 1961-

*PERSONAL:* Born March 9, 1961, in Caguas, PR. *Ethnicity:* "Puerto Rican." *Education:* Universidad de Puerto Rico, B.A., 1984; State University of New York—Stony Brook, M.A., 1986; University of Cincinnati, Ph.D., 1990. *Politics:* "Independentista."

*ADDRESSES: Home*—320 West Union St., Athens, OH 45701. *Office*—283 Gordy Hall, Ohio University, Athens, OH 45701. *E-mail*—torres@ohio.edu.

*CAREER:* Ohio University, Athens, OH, associate professor of Spanish literature, 1990—.

*AWARDS, HONORS:* PEN Club Award, 1990; Letras de Oro Award, 1991-92.

*WRITINGS:*

*Los versos del coronel Buendia,* Maiten (Chile), 1985.

*La identidad cultural de Hispanoamerica,* Maiten (Chile), 1986.

*Jose Emilio Pacheco: Poesia y poetica del prosaismo,* Pliegos (Spain), 1990.

*Moriras si da una primavera,* Iberian Studies Institute (Miami, FL), 1993.

*El palimpsesto del calco aparente: una poetica del Barroco de Indias,* Peter Lang (New York, NY), 1993.

*Cabronerias: historias de tres cuerpor,* Isla Negra (Puerto Rico), 1995.

*Siete poemas de carinho* (poetry), Candelaria, 1995.

*Fusilado dios* (poetry), Isla Negra (Puerto Rico), 2000.

Contributor of articles to professional journals.

*WORK IN PROGRESS: Conversacion con Aurelia,* a novel "about drag queens in Puerto Rico"; *Mariconerias: Historias del amor pueril,* a collection of short stories "about growing up gay in Puerto Rico"; *Y el verbo se hizo carne: La lirica homoerotica en Hispanoamerica,* a "book-length project on homoerotic poetry in Latin America."

*SIDELIGHTS:* Daniel Torres told *CA:* "In my scholarly work I write about Latin American poetry (colonial and contemporary periods). In my creative writing I have developed a vision of male homoeroticism from AIDS to love triangles. I am interested in decoding gender and understanding desire and pleasure."

\*     \*     \*

## TREITEL, Jonathan 1959-

*PERSONAL:* Born 1959, in London, England.

*ADDRESSES: Agent*—c/o Author Mail, Bloomsbury Publishing PLC, 38 Soho Square, London W1D 3HB, England.

*CAREER:* Novelist, poet, short story writer, and physicist.

*WRITINGS:*

*Red Cabbage Café,* Pantheon Books (New York, NY) 1990.
*Emma Smart,* Bloomsbury Publishing (London, England), 1992.

Author of ten short stories read on BBC Radio; contributed stories to periodicals; work collected in anthologies *New Yorker, New Writing 6,* and *New Writing 8.*

*SIDELIGHTS:* British-born writer Jonathan Treitel is best known as the author of *Red Cabbage Café,* a critically acclaimed novel set in Moscow in the years just after the 1917 Russian Revolution. The book is the story of Humphrey Veil, a left-leaning Anglo-German-American engineer who has been hired to design a new subway system for the capital of the Soviet Union. Humphrey falls in love with a young woman named Sophia, the curator of a wax museum. It is Sophia who introduces Humphrey to the Red Cabbage Café, the seedy bohemian saloon from which the novel draws its name. Sophia also involves Humphrey in a spy ring and a love triangle with a pretentious Russian artist-poet named Gritz as the third party.

*Library Journal* reviewer Dean Willms praised Treitel's first novel as "intelligent, creative, and entertaining." Writing in the British newspaper *Observer,* reviewer Valentine Cunningham commented, "History, in Treitel's book, is all faking, dodgy substitutions, [and] lies. Historiography is wacky and iconoclastic, keen to live up to [Karl] Marx's dictum about history returning first as tragedy then as farce. The result is pleasant, low-budget Magic Realism." Writing in the *Los Angeles Times Book Review,* Michael Harris observed, "This is a novel that shouldn't work but does. . . . Treitel, for a first novel-

ist, has an unusually delicate sense of tone. He tells outrageous lies but remains true to the underlying reality." Reviewing *Red Cabbage Café* for the *Spectator,* Beatrice Wilson described the book as "remarkable" in its "surrealist black humor, with the power to make death seem funny and falsehoods true. In an era when so many people prize worthiness above entertainment in literature, that makes a refreshing change."

Reviewer Mason Buck of the *New York Times Book Review* was among the minority of critics who turned thumbs down on *Red Cabbage Café.* Buck wrote: "Although Mr. Treitel has some valid points to make about the manipulation involved in political image making, his protagonist's personality and narrative voice just aren't powerful enough to sustain interest in the proceedings."

Treitel's second novel, *Emma Smart,* is the story of an English child-prodigy mathematician who is the book's title character. On a visit to New York, Emma meets a slippery character named Frank, who recruits her to work on a book project that turns out to be not quite what Emma anticipated. Treitel has also written short stories published in the *New Yorker* magazine and various British "best-stories-of-the-year" anthologies.

*BIOGRAPHICAL AND CRITICAL SOURCES:*

*PERIODICALS*

*Library Journal,* November 1, 1990, Dean Willms, review of *Red Cabbage Café.*
*Los Angeles Times Book Review,* January 20, 1991, Michael Harris, review of *Red Cabbage Café,* p. 6.
*New York Times Book Review,* February 3, 1991, Mason Buck, review of *Red Cabbage Café,* p. 18.
*Observer* (London, England), July 15, 1990, Valentine Cunningham, "From Russia with Love and Lies," p. 52.
*Spectator,* July 28, 1990, Beatrice Wilson, "Waxworks in Moscow," p. 32.
*Tribune Books* (Chicago, IL), March 3, 1991, Gary Houston, "A Naïve Engineer Stumbles into the Illusory World of 1920s Moscow," pp. 6-7.*

# U-V

## UELSMANN, Jerry N(orman) 1934-

*PERSONAL:* Born June 11, 1934, in Detroit, MI; married Marilyn Kamischke, 1957 (divorced, 1974); married Diane Farris, 1975; children: (second marriage) Andrew. *Education:* Rochester Institute of Technology, B.F.A., 1957; Indiana University Graduate School, M.S., 1958, M.F.A., 1960.

*ADDRESSES: Home*—5701 South West 17th Drive, Gainesville, FL 32608. *Agent*—Witkin Gallery, 415 West Broadway, New York, NY 10012.

*CAREER:* Photographer, 1953—; University of Florida, Gainesville, FL, interim instructor in photography, 1960-62; instructor, 1962-64, assistant professor, 1964-66, associate professor, 1966-69, professor, 1969-74, graduate research professor, 1974—. Nihon University College of Art, Tokyo, Japan, visiting professor, October, 1979. *Exhibitions:* Works included in permanent collections at the Museum of Modern Art, New York, NY; International Museum of Photography, George Eastman House, Rochester, NY; Philadelphia Museum of Art; Art Institute of Chicago; Center for Creative Photography, University of Arizona, Tucson, AZ; San Francisco Museum of Modern Art; National Gallery of Canada, Ottawa; National Museum of American Art, Washington, DC; Boston Museum of Fine Arts; Victoria and Albert Museum, London, England; Bibliotheque Nationale, Paris, France; and Moderna Museet, Stockholm, Sweden.

*MEMBER:* Society for Photographic Education (founding member, 1962; member of the board of directors, 1966); Friends of Photography (advisory trustee).

*AWARDS, HONORS:* Guggenheim fellowship, 1967; faculty development grant, 1971; Teacher/Scholar of the Year Award, University of Florida, 1975; National Endowment for the Arts fellowship, 1972; City of Arles Medal, France, 1973; Royal Photographic Society fellow, 1973; Bronze Medal, International Exhibition of Photography, 1979.

*WRITINGS:*

*PHOTOGRAPHER*

*Eight Photographs: Jerry Uelsmann,* text by William E. Parker, Doubleday (New York, NY), 1970.

*Jerry N. Uelsmann,* introduction by Peter C. Bunnell, fables by Russell Edson, Aperture (New York, NY), 1970.

*Jerry Uelsmann: Silver Meditations,* introduction by Peter C. Bunnell, Morgan & Morgan, (Dobbs Ferry, NY), 1975.

William Everson, *The Mate-Flight of Eagles: Two Poems on the Love-Death of the Cross,* afterword by Allan Campo, illustrated by Richard Hotchkiss, Blue Oak Press (Newcastle, CA), 1977.

*Jerry N. Uelsmann: Photographs from 1975-1979,* edited and introduction by Steven Klindt, essay by Jim Enyeart, Columbia College (Chicago, IL), 1980.

*Jerry N. Uelsmann: Twenty-Five Years, a Retrospective,* text by James L. Enyeart, Little, Brown (Boston, MA), 1982.

*Uelsmann: Process and Perception,* text by John Ames, University Press of Florida (Gainesville, FL), 1985.

*Jerry Uelsmann: Photo Synthesis,* foreword by A. D. Coleman, University Press of Florida (Gainesville, FL), 1992.

*Uelsmann/Yosemite: Photographs,* University Press of Florida (Gainesville, FL), 1996.

*SIDELIGHTS:* Jerry N. Uelsmann became interested in photography as a career while in high school. He went on to study photography at Rochester Institute of Technology and was influenced by instructors such as Minor White and Ralph Hattersley. His first publication of a photograph came in 1957, the year he graduated, in *Photography Annual.* His photographs have been on exhibit in more than one hundred shows around the world and permanent collections of his work are on display at major museums.

Ueslmann is known for photomontage, the making of one photograph by superimposing parts of different photographs. He produces all his photographs by using techniques in a darkroom, not by working minutes at a computer, resulting in images that look more like paintings than photographs. *Florida Times Union* contributor Charlie Patton quoted Uelsmann as commenting, "I used multiple printing techniques to make my images look like paintings. . . . This kind of challenged what the critics and historians said photography was."

*Uelsmann/Yosemite: Photographs* is a collection of Uelsmann's photographs of Yosemite National Park. Each photograph is a combination of two photographs, one is a scene from Yosemite and another of a different subject. The photographs appear to be altered by a computer, but they are not. *Petersen's Photographic* contributor Donald Robertson commented, "Uelsmann is the best-known artist in his field in the world, and there's not one bit of computer work here."

*BIOGRAPHICAL AND CRITICAL SOURCES:*

BOOKS

*Contemporary Photographers,* 3rd edition, St. James Press (Detroit, MI), 1996.

PERIODICALS

*Albuquerque Journal,* November 23, 2001, Michael More, "Surrealist Photographs Fascinating," p. 6.

*Florida Times Union,* September 23, 1999, Charlie Patton, "Photographer a Pioneer in 'Altered States' Approach," p. D-1.

*Peterson's Photographic,* Donald Robertson, "Jerry Uelsmann's Yosemite," of p. 58.

*PSA Journal,* November, 1992, Donald Robertson, review of *Jerry Uelsmann: Photosynthesis,* p. 7.

*Publishers Weekly,* September 28, 1992, review of *Jerry Uelsmann: Photosynthesis,* p. 63.

*School Arts,* January, 1997, Bay Hallowell, "Hot Dog for the PMA," p. 23.*

\*                    \*                    \*

## URBAN, Joao Aristeu 1943-

*PERSONAL:* Born April 21, 1943, in Curitiba, Brazil; married Adelaide Fortes, 1969 (divorced, 1980); children: Dora, Vladimir. *Education:* Attended Colegio Santa Maria, 1954-56; attended Colegio Estaduel do Parana, 1956-63.

*ADDRESSES: Home*—Rua Angelo Zeni, 1048, 80520 Curitiba, Parana, Brazil.

*CAREER:* Urban Ltd., Curitiba, Parana, Brazil, store clerk, 1957-59; Bamerindus, Curitiba, Parana, Brazil, bank teller, 1959-67; Photon Photos Ltd, Curitiba, Parana, Brazil, owner, 1967-69; Phototecnica, Curitiba, Parana, Brazil, photographer, 1969—. *Exhibitions:* Works included in permanent collections at Fundacion Nacional de Bellas Artes, Rio de Janeiro, Brazil; Casa Romario Martins, Curitiba, Brazil; Culture Foundation of Curitiba, Parana, Brazil; Brazilian Art and Culture Institute, Rio de Janiero, Brazil; Art Museum of São Paulo; French Museum of Photography, Paris, France; Künsthaus, Zurich, Switzerland; Collection Joaquim Paila, Brasil; and Collection Lili Sverner, São Paulo.

*AWARDS, HONORS:* Bienal de São Paulo Prize, 1977; Banco de Brasil Prize, 1978.

*WRITINGS:*

PHOTOGRAPHER

(With others) *Hencho en Latino-America,* edited by Consejo Mexicano de Fotografia, [Mexico City, Mexico], 1978.

(With others) *O Espaco Habitado,* edited by the Institute de Arquitetos do Brasil, [Brazil], 1979.

(With others) *Our People,* [Rio de Janeiro, Brazil], 1979.

(With others) *The Child in Latin America,* edited by Unicef, [Santiago, Chile], 1980.

*Hecho en Latino-America II,* [Mexico], 1981.

*1a Fotosul 83,* [Brazil], 1983.

*Boias-Frias, Tagelohner in Suden Brasiliens,* text by Tereza Urban, [Switzerland], 1984.

*Boias-Frias—Vista Parcial,* Culture Foundation of Curitiba (Curitiba, Brazil), 1988.

*Tropeiros,* 1992.

*OTHER*

Contributor of a series of articles in *Grafia, O Jornal da Foto,* 1978-79.

*SIDELIGHTS:* Know mainly for his photography, Joao Aristeu Urban specializes in photography as social documentary. A *Contemporary Photographers* contributor noted, "He has not only recorded facts, events and conditions; he has also been able to represent that mass of feelings—hopes and sorrows—that are the inward nature of man."

*BIOGRAPHICAL AND CRITICAL SOURCES:*

*BOOKS*

*Contemporary Photographers,* 3rd edition, St. James Press (Detroit, MI), 1996.*

\*      \*      \*

## VALDUGA, Patrizia 1953-

*PERSONAL:* Born May 20, 1953, in Castelfranco Vento, Italy. *Education:* University of Venice, degree in French literature.

*ADDRESSES: Home*—Milan, Italy. *Agent*—c/o Giulio Einaudi Editore SpA, Via Biancamano 2, 10121, Turin, Italy.

*CAREER:* Poet. Editor, Einaudi (publishing house), Turin, Italy; director, *Poesie* (monthly journal).

*AWARDS, HONORS:* Premio Viareggio, 1982, for *Medicamenta.*

*WRITINGS:*

*POETRY*

*Medicamenta* (title means "Medicine"), Guanda (Milan, Italy), 1982.

*La tentazione* (title means "Temptation"), Crocetti (Milan, Italy), 1985.

*Medicamenta e altri medicamenta,* Einaudi (Turin, Italy), 1989.

*Donna di dolori* (title means "Lady of Suffering"), Mondadori (Milan, Italy), 1991.

*Requiem: per mio padre morto il 2 dicembre 1991,* Marsilio (Venice, Italy), 1994.

(With others) *Il cimitero marino,* Mondadori (Milan, Italy), 1995.

*Corsia degli incurabili* (title means "Terminal Ward"), Garzanti (Milan, Italy), 1996.

*Cento quartine e altre storie d'amore,* Einaudi (Turin, Italy), 1997.

*Prima antologia,* Einaudi (Turin, Italy), 1998.

*Quartine: seconda centuria,* Einaudi (Turin, Italy), 2001.

*TRANSLATIONS*

John Donne, *Canzoni e sonetti,* Studio Editoriale, 1985

Stéphan Mallarmé, *Poesie,* Mondadori (Milan, Italy), 1991.

Tadeusz Kantor, *Stille Nacht,* Ubulibri, 1991.

Paul Valéry, *Il Cimitero marino,* Mondadori (Milan, Italy), 1995.

Molière, *Il Misantropo,* Giunti, 1995.

Maurice Blanchot, *L'istante della mi morte,* "Aut Aut," 1995.

Molière, *Il Malato immaginario,* Giunti, 1995

William Shakespeare, *Riccardo III,* Einaudi (Turin, Italy), 1998.

Also translator of works for the theater, including Louis-Ferdinand Celine, *Féerie* (part one, performed at Spoloto Festival, 1989); Molière, *L'Avaro;* Crébillon the Elder, *Gli imprevisti accanto al fuoco;* Cocteau, *La voce umana;* Molière, *Tartuffe;* William Shakespeare, *Macbeth;* and Samuel Beckett, *Mica io, Monologo e Dondonanna,* and *Aspettando Godot.*

*SIDELIGHTS:* Patrizia Valduga "is a woman of definite cultural views," declared Guido Mascagni in a *Dictionary of Literary Biography* entry. "Her love for poetry began when she was only seven. She prefers Dante—with his 'pluralingualism'—to Petrarch, and [Renaissance-era poet] Torquato Tasso to Ludovico Ariosoto." Among her contemporaries, Valduga cites the playwright Tadeusz Kantor as a major influence. "Her musical tastes runs to baroque music and the works of Richard Wagner," Mascagni continued. "She prefers the poetry and prose of the seventeenth and eighteenth centuries over twentieth-century fiction." Valduga, Mascagni concluded, "is one of the most prominent and characteristic personalities of the new generation of Italian poets."

According to Mascagni, Valduga has rejected the "freedom of the free verse" in favor of a traditional poetic forms. In the critic's view, Valduga brings to mind one of her influences by using the sonnet form in much of her *Medicamenta,* "in which ottava rima appears throughout a whole section. She also uses the triplet. La tentazione comprises ten cantos of thirty-three triplets and one hendecasyllable each, a scheme that unmistakably recalls Dante's poetry." As for Valduga's vocabulary, that "is rich, too—the fruit of diligent linguistic studies and research, even in antiquarian dictionaries—and it includes neologisms. The product is always the result of long reflection and intense, constant work and research."

Reviewing *Corsia degli incurabili,* a theatrical-style monologue, *Times Literary Supplement* writer Margaret Hall found that Valduga "aims at the kind of writing whose legitimacy comes from acknowledging its own falseness. Her speaker, who may be male or female and seems to symbolize poetry or the poet, is dying in a decayed hospital, lonely and unloved, railing against the horrors of the modern world, lamenting her (or his) state and finally asking for forgiveness and mercy." Hall described the work as "a thoroughly over-the-top and sometimes touching performance which is held together by the formal pressures of *terza rima* and a degraded but still recognizable version of traditional poetic language."

As Mascagni observed, "Without poetry, according to Valduga, life is nothing but a blind transit through meaningless banalities, an absurd routine, unintelligible daily repetitions, and above all a renunciation of the present for a futile illusion of a fully true life in the future."

Valduga has also translated a wide variety of poetic and theatrical material into Italian, including works by Shakespeare, Beckett, and Molière.

*BIOGRAPHICAL AND CRITICAL SOURCES:*

*BOOKS*

*Dictionary of Literary Biography,* Volume 128: *Twentieth-Century Italian Poets,* Gale (Detroit MI), 1993.

*PERIODICALS*

*Times Literary Supplement,* August 11, 1989, Patrick McCarthy, "Body Language," p. 874; July 19, 1996, Margaret Hall, "Honeycomb, Bees, and Honey," p. 12.

\*     \*     \*

## VAN DEVANTER, Lynda (Margaret) 1947-2002

*OBITUARY NOTICE*—See index for *CA* sketch: Born May 27, 1947, in Washington, DC; died November 15, 2002, in Herndon, VA. Nurse, activist, and author. Van Devanter became a controversial figure with the publication of her autobiography *Home before Morning: The Story of an Army Nurse in Vietnam* (1983), in which she reported that many doctors and nurses operated on patients while under the influence of drugs and alcohol. Soon after graduating with her medical degree in nursing from Mercy Hospital School of Nursing in 1968, Van Devanter went to Vietnam to serve at the 71st Evacuation Hospital in Pleiku. The horrors she experienced there left a scar on her psyche that would last for the rest of her life. Her tour of duty lasted a year, and she left the army in 1970 as a first lieutenant. During the 1970s Van Devanter worked as a nurse at several California hospitals, but she continued to suffer psychologically from Vietnam and underwent therapy for several years. Finally, she resolved to face her fears and do something to help women nurses who, like herself, were Vietnam veterans who had their problems ignored by both the American public and the U.S. government. She established the Women's Project of the Vietnam Veterans of America in Washington, D.C., and wrote her autobiography. Her book caused many nurses who had been in the war to protest that Van Devanter's revelations about doctor and nurse behavior were highly exaggerated. On the other hand, many others came out in support of the author, some even claiming that the problems addressed in *Home before Morning* are actually understated. Regardless, the book brought considerable attention to the suffering of American women vets, and it was later adapted as the television series *China Beach,* which ran from 1988 to 1991. Van Devanter received a number of honors for her work, including being named Woman of the Year by the American Association of Minority Veteran Program Administrators in 1982. Tragically, her pain from Vietnam was not only psychological but physical, and she claimed her body had been poisoned by Agent Orange, leading to vascular disease. After her death, Van Devanter's attorneys continued to press her case on behalf of her daughter, Molly.

*OBITUARIES AND OTHER SOURCES:*

BOOKS

*War and American Popular Culture: A Historical Encyclopedia,* Greenwood (Westport, CT), 1999.
*Women and the Military: An Encyclopedia,* ABC-CLIO (Santa Barbara, CA), 1996.

PERIODICALS

*Chicago Tribune,* November 24, 2002, section 4, p. 9.
*Los Angeles Times,* November 25, 2002, p. B9.
*New York Times,* November 23, 2002, p. A17.
*Washington Post,* November 21, 2002, p. B7.

\*     \*     \*

## van de WAARSENBURG, Hans 1943-

*PERSONAL:* Born 1943.

*ADDRESSES: Home*—Maastricht, Netherlands. *Office*—c/o Author Mail, J. M. Meulenhoff, P.O. Box 100, 1000, AC Amsterdam, Netherlands. *E-mail*—hvdwaarsenburg@compuserve.com.

*CAREER:* Poet.

*AWARDS, HONORS:* Jan Campertprijs, 1974.

*WRITINGS:*

*Met innige deelneming,* 1968.
*Niet dat powesie nu zo belangrijk is,* Sijthoff (Leiden, Netherlands), 1969.
*Powesie 69,* 1971.
*De vergrijzing,* Nijgh & Van Ditmar (The Hague, Netherlands), 1972.
*Tussen nat mos en een begrafenis,* Nijgh & Van Ditmar (The Hague, Netherlands), 1973.
*Verschrikkelijke Winter,* Nijgh & Van Ditmar (The Hague/Rotterdam, Netherlands), 1975.
*Het sleutelbeen van Napoleon,* Nijgh & Van Ditmar (The Hague/Rotterdam, Netherlands), 1977.
*De dag van de witte chrysanten,* Nijgh & Van Ditmar (The Hague/Rotterdam, Netherlands), 1979
*Zeelandschappen,* Bonnefant, 1979.
*Avondlandschappen,* Meulenhoff (Amsterdam, Netherlands), 1982.
*Van de aanvaller geen spoor, gedichten 1973-1983* (poems), Meulenhoff (Amsterdam, Netherlands), 1983.
*De dorst der havensteden,* Meulenhoff (Amsterdam, Netherlands), 1990.
*Avond val* (poems), Meulenhoff (Amsterdam, Netherlands), 1993.
*Zuidwal* (poems), Meulenhoff (Amsterdam, Netherlands), 1995.
*Maastrickt in verhalen en gedichten: schrijvers en dichters over de zuidelijkste stad van Nederland,* Meulenhoff (Amsterdam, Netherlands), 1996.
*Beschrijvingen van het meer,* Bèta Press, 2000.

*SIDELIGHTS:* In the 1960s Dutch poet Hans van de Waarsenburg was a voice for the idealistic generation that was intent upon overthrowing the old and creating a new society. His poetry of that period is full of optimism for the unlimited possibilities of the revolution that would overthrow twentieth-century Western society. He also wrote passionate anti-Vietnam pieces and other angry protest poems. He even turned against poetry itself, since publishing collections of paper poetry was not in tune with his desire to shout out his anger at the world.

When the revolution never came, and his generation could not end injustice and violence, van de Waarsenburg's poetry lost some of its fervor, reflecting his disappointment through an increasingly melancholic and bitter tone. He felt that because poetry had lost its power, human existence had become inauthentic. Drawn into the apathetic mood of the time, he distanced himself from society more and more in his later work. In the writing he did undertake, van de Waarsenburg focused on new subject matter, including some observations about his grandfather's decline.

Van de Waarsenburg's poetry largely lacks rhyme and meter, creating internal tension and rhythm by instead breaking the sentences in certain places. His tone fluctuates between tender and aggressive, giving his poetry a unique character and intensity.

*BIOGRAPHICAL AND CRITICAL SOURCES:*

*PERIODICALS*

*Ons erfdeel,* Volume 18, number 1, 1975, Jan van der Vegt, "Tegen de spoelmachine van de tijd," pp. 103-106; January, 1977, Frans Deschoenmaeker, "De tijd van de grote moeheid," pp. 130-132.

*OTHER*

*Antiqbook,* http://www.antiqbook.nl/ (May, 2001).
*Poetry International Rotterdam,* http://www.poetry.nl/ (October 7, 2001).*

\*      \*      \*

# VANDO, Gloria 1936-

*PERSONAL:* Born May 21, 1936, in New York, NY; daughter of Erasmo and Anita (Velez-Mitchell) Vando; married William M. Hickok October 4, 1980. *Education:* Attended New York University, 1951-56; attended University of Amsterdam, 1953-54; Texas A & I University, B.A., 1975; Long Island University, postgraduate study, 1982-83. *Hobbies and other interests:* Photography.

*ADDRESSES: Office*—Helicon Nine Editions, 3607 Pennsylvania Avenue, Kansas City, MO 64111-2820. *E-mail*—helicon9@aol.com.

*CAREER:* Helicon Nine Editions, Kansas City, MO, publisher and editor, 1977—; *North American Review,* Cedar Falls, IA, contributing editor, 1996—. Mayor's Special School Task Force, New York, NY, educational ombudsman, 1969-70; Youth Diversion project, Mayor's Office, Kansas City, MO, educational consultant, 1977-79.

*MEMBER:* PEN International, Poetry Society of America, Academy of American Poets, Council of Literary Magazines and Presses, Missouri Citizens for Arts.

*AWARDS, HONORS:* Billee Murray Denny prize for poetry, 1991; Governor's Arts award, state of Kansas, 1991.

*WRITINGS:*

*Promesas: Geography of the Impossible,* Arté Público Press (Houston, TX), 1993.
(Editor, with Robert Stewart) *Spud Songs: An Anthology of Potato Poems—To Benefit Hunger Relief,* Helicon Nine Editions (Kansas City, MO), 1999.
*Shadows & Supposes,* Arté Público Press (Houston, TX), 2002.

*SIDELIGHTS:* An accomplished poet and a publisher of others' poetry through Helicon Nine Editions, Gloria Vando published her first poetry collection, *Promesas: Geography of the Impossible,* in 1993. Through childhood memories of her Puerto Rican family, explorations of historical events, and discussions of contemporary topics, Vando claims her joint legacy, both American and Puerto Rican. "Vando's poems revel in the triumph of one woman, yet, as the book's title portends, they unselfishly offer promise to those who still seek their nation," in the words of Emily Dunlap, a contributor to *Belles Lettres.* The first poems are told in a child's voice, a child trying to make sense of her father's abandonment of the family and her consignment to a religious boarding school. "Vando's is a universal voice expressing childhood anguish and passion," wrote a *Publishers Weekly* reviewer, who felt, "The volume loses some of its impact when the speakers mature." Others found vitality throughout the collection. *Library Journal* reviewer Frank Allen wrote, "these intense poems explode like flares above a battlefield of the heart to reveal a 'geography of the impossible.'"

Vando's next book, *Spud Songs: An Anthology of Potato Poems—To Benefit Hunger Relief,* may seem somewhat lighter in tone, but there is a seriousness of purpose. With her coeditor Robert Stewart, Vando collected various poets' odes to the humble potato, a food that has actually staved off starvation in two world wars and other times of stress among European populations. A *Publishers Weekly* reviewer noted that "like its namesake, the book works to fight hunger," with all proceeds going to Share Our Strength.

"On Hearing that a Potato Costs $70 in Sarajevo," Vando's poem from *Spud Songs,* also appeared in her next collection, *Shadows & Supposes.* A wide-ranging series of poems, topics include impressions of different cities, poetic odes to various artists and writers, and small dramas, such as a boy lost in the Museum of Natural History or a Black-shirt trying to seduce a blonde Jew. "The clarity of voice in Vando's second collection feels deliberate in its desire to convey basic information about the world," wrote a *Publishers Weekly* reviewer.

*BIOGRAPHICAL AND CRITICAL SOURCES:*

PERIODICALS

*Belles Lettres,* spring, 1994, Emily Dunlap, review of *Promesas: Geography of the Impossible,* p. 83.
*Library Journal,* April 1, 1993, Frank Allen, review of *Promesas: Geography of the Impossible,* p. 102.
*Publishers Weekly,* March 8, 1993, review of *Promesas: Geography of the Impossible,* p. 74; November 30, 1998, review of *Spud Songs,* p. 69; February 25, 2002, review of *Shadows & Supposes,* p. 58.*

\*          \*          \*

**VANESCH, Jean (Louis) 1950-**

*PERSONAL:* Born May 28, 1950, in Liege, Belgium; married Lucia Radochonska, 1974; children: Carole. *Education:* Studied photography at the Saint-Luc Fine Arts Institute.

*ADDRESSES: Home*—57 Rue des 3 Chenes, 4621 Retinne, Belgium. *E-mail*—jean-louis.vanesch@skynet.be.

*CAREER:* Photographer. *Exhibitions:* Work included in permanent collections at the Musée de la Photographie, Charleroi, Belgium; Musée de la Phtographie de l'Elysee, Lausanne, Switzerland; Chateau d'Eau, Toulouse, France; FRAC, Aix en Provence, France; Bibliotheque Nationale, Paris, France; and Arthoteque de Lyon, France. Individual exhibitions include Galerie Sogno di Carta, Liege, Belgium, 1983; Galerie Pennings, Eindhoven, Holland; and Galerie J. P. Lambert, Paris, France, 1994.

*WRITINGS:*

PHOTOGRAPHER

*Ce Sentiment a la Fois d'Exil et d'Ivresse,* (portfolio), text by J.P. Otte.

Contributor of photographs to *Cliche, Art Press, La Photographie Europeenne, Sogno di Carta, Contretype,* and *L'Histoire Continue.*

*SIDELIGHTS:* Jean Vanesch studied photography at the Saint-Luc Fine Arts Institute. He has never worked as an industrial or commercial photographer, and his photographs can only be seen in exhibits or portfolios. His photographic interests have changed over the years, ranging from suburban areas, the countryside, nature, and the textures found in nature.

*BIOGRAPHICAL AND CRITICAL SOURCES:*

BOOKS

*Contemporary Photographers,* 3rd edition, St. James Press (Detroit, MI), 1996.*

\*          \*          \*

**VERELST, Myndart**
**See SALTUS, Edgar**

# VILLAS BÔAS, Orlando 1914-2002

*OBITUARY NOTICE*—See index for *CA* sketch: Born January 12, 1914, in Santa Cruz do Rio Pardo, Brazil; died of multiple organ failure from an intestinal infection December 12, 2002, in São Paolo, Brazil. Explorer, activist, and author. Along with his two brothers, Cláudio and Leonardo, Villas Bôas helped explore the Brazilian interior, where he encountered numerous undiscovered indigenous tribes and helped find uncharted rivers. Exploring their country's interior from 1943 to 1960, all three brothers had a tremendous respect for the native peoples; this led to Villas Bôas's role in helping to establish the Xingu Indigenous National Park, which preserved 46,000 square miles of forest for use by native tribes alone. Under pressure from development throughout the region, the tribes were brought together at Xingu to preserve their culture. Despite some initial friction between these people due to the fact of their suddenly being thrust together, they eventually learned to live in harmony and share the preserve. Beginning in 1963, Villas Bôas also helped build airplane landing strips and set up hospitals to treat tribal members for illnesses such as influenza. Toward the end of his career, friction with the Brazilian government caused Villas Bôas to be dismissed from his work at the Indian Affairs Bureau, though he was later given an official apology for the unjust firing. For their work, he and Cláudio Villas Bôas—Leonardo died in 1961—were nominated for the Nobel Peace Prize in 1971 and 1975. Though they did not win this prize, they did receive a Founders Gold Medal from the Royal Geographical Society. Villas-Bôas was the author of several books about his work in the Amazon jungle, including two in English translation: *Xingu: The Indians, Their Myths* (1973), coauthored with brother Cláudio, and *Xingu: Tribal Territory* (1979).

## OBITUARIES AND OTHER SOURCES:

### BOOKS

*International Who's Who,* 65th edition, Europa Publications (London, England), 2002.

### PERIODICALS

*Los Angeles Times,* December 13, 2002, p. B16.
*New York Times* December 13, 2002, p. C16.
*Times* (London, England), December 14, 2002.
*Washington Post,* December 15, 2002, p. C11.

# VINCENZA, DUCHESS OF DEIRA
## See ROLFE, Frederick (William Serafino Austin Lewis Mary)

\*    \*    \*

# VITERITTI, Joseph P. 1946-

*PERSONAL:* Born 1946.

*ADDRESSES: Office*—Program on Education and Civil Society, Robert F. Wagner Graduate School of Public Service, 269 Mercer St., #207, New York, NY 10819. *E-mail*—jpv1@nyu.edu.

*CAREER:* Robert F. Wagner Graduate School of Public Service, Program on Education and Civil Society, co-chair and director, 1996—; New York University, New York, NY, professor of public administration. Served as special assistant to the chancellor of New York City public school system, 1978-81, and senior advisor to the superintendent of schools in Boston and San Francisco.

*WRITINGS:*

*Police, Politics, and Pluralism in New York City: A Comparative Case Study,* Sage (Beverly Hills, CA), 1973.
*Bureaucracy and Social Justice: The Allocation of Jobs and Services to Minority Groups,* Kennikat (Port Washington, NY), 1979.
*Across the River: Politics and Education in the City,* Holmes & Meier (New York, NY), 1983.
(Editor, with Diane Ravitch) *New Schools for a New Century: The Redesign of Urban Education,* Yale University (New Haven, CT), 1997.
*Choosing Equality: School Choice, the Constitution, and Civil Society,* Brookings Institution (Washington, DC), 1999.
(Editor, with Diane Ravitch) *City Schools: Lessons from New York,* Johns Hopkins University Press (Baltimore, MD), 2000.
(Editor, with Diane Ravitch) *Making Good Citizens: Education and Civil Society,* Yale University Press (New Haven, CT), 2001.
(Editor, with Diane Ravitch) *Kid Stuff: Marketing Sex and Violence to America's Children,* Johns Hopkins University Press (Baltimore, MD), 2003.

*SIDELIGHTS:* Educator and administrator Joseph P. Viteritti has written and edited a number of books dealing with the bureaucratic structures of both government and public school systems, particularly those in urban areas. A professor of public administration at New York University's Wagner School of Public Service and director of the Program on Education and Civil Society, Viteritti has also served as a special assistant to the chancellor of the New York public schools, and was once an assistant for the school superintendents of Boston and San Francisco. He utilized this inside knowledge of how public school systems operate to pen a number of volumes, including *Across the River: Politics and Education in the City* and *Choosing Equality: School Choice, the Constitution, and Civil Society.* Viteritti has also edited four books with Diane Ravitch. Two of them, *New Schools for A New Century: The Redesign of Urban Education* and *City Schools: Lessons from New York,* focus on the plight of urban schools. Each of the books addresses various social and political reasons behind failing urban schools. One of Viteritti's conclusions is that administrators who want to reform a failing school system or district are often deterred by external influences. Reviewer Jewel Bellush of the *National Civic Review* quoted Viteritti as saying that he has "a very deep-seated conviction that the major obstacles to change in a large urban school system like New York's are not found within the internal administrative structure but exist in the very complex and turbulent external environment." Bellush thought that "the study is exceptionally well organized and offers a good deal of material for extensive discussion of how to make things better." Critic Arnold L. Goren of the *New York Times Book Review* praised *Across the River* as a "useful and informative book."

In 1979 Viteritti published *Bureaucracy and Social Justice: The Allocation of Jobs and Services to Minority Groups,* a critically praised effort that details his research into governmental service inequities received by minority groups, such as blacks and Hispanics. He gives an overview of developments in the municipal government of New York City during the course of a decade, as well as discussing important changes that have taken place in public administration in other locales. Viteritti concludes that, because of the way bureaucracy is set up, government works best for the more affluent segments of society, even when reforms are enacted to help minorities and other traditionally impoverished groups attain more benefits. He suggests

that one of the reasons for this is voter apathy among those groups. Literary critics lauded the book for providing an accurate look at how government actually functions. "The subject . . . is of considerable importance, and it is to be hoped that others will pursue this line of inquiry, building on this useful first step," wrote Thomas A. Clark in *Social Science Quarterly.*

*New Schools for a New Century* is a collection of ten essays, edited by Viteritti and Ravitch, detailing innovations being applied in various school systems around the United States. Ravitch contributes an essay that explores the need to provide parents, particularly those in inner cities, with vouchers so they can choose the school, public or private, they want their children to attend. "*New Schools for a New Century* is both an enormously hopeful book and, at least for liberals, a very uncomfortable one," wrote critic James Traub of the *New York Times,* who added, "Taken together, the essays constitute a powerful argument that the schools will never change . . . unless they are challenged from the outside."

Viteritti revisits the topic of school choice in *Choosing Equality,* in which he also advocates a voucher system. In the book he details how such projects, including magnet schools and black independent schools, which benefit from voucher systems, have worked in recent history. "If there is a more thorough and thoughtful argument for school choice, I am unaware of it," critic Christopher Rapp of the *National Review* wrote of the book. A contributor for *Publishers Weekly* called *Choosing Equality* a "scholarly manifesto."

In another book coedited with Ravitch, titled *Making Good Citizens: Education and Civil Society,* Viteritti presents a group of essays which question the idea that public education is important to the health of the nation. Essays selected by Viteritti and Ravitch argue that private schools do a better job of producing the critical thinkers who are so important to the success of a society. The authors cite as one of the many causes for the downward direction of public schools the economic and racial segregation that still exists. *Library Journal*'s Terry Christner wrote that in *Making Good Citizens,* "there's something here for everyone," adding that the "essays are well written and thought-provoking."

*BIOGRAPHICAL AND CRITICAL SOURCES:*

*PERIODICALS*

*American Political Science Review,* March, 2001, Jerome J. Hanus, review of *Choosing Equality: School Choice, the Constitution, and Civil Society,* p. 224.

*American Prospect,* March 25, 2002, Richard D. Kahlenberg, review of *Making Good Citizens: Education and Civil Society,* p. 37.

*Choice,* May, 1984, p. 1358; January, 2001, N. L. Arnez, review of *City Schools: Lessons from New York,* p. 954; April, 2002, J. L. DeVitis, review of *Making Good Citizens,* p. 1472.

*Journal of Politics,* February, 1981, pp. 287-288.

*Library Journal,* September 15, 2001, Terry Christner, review of *Making Good Citizens,* p. 91.

*National Civic Review,* June, 1980, p. 362; March, 1984, p. 161.

*National Review,* March 20, 2000, p. 60.

*New York Times Book Review,* November 25, 1984, p. 27; November 9, 1997, p.13; November 18, 2001, Gary Rosen, review of *Making Good Citizens,* p. 64.

*Publishers Weekly,* January 3, 2000, p. 67.

*Social Science Quarterly,* December, 1980, p. 684.*

* * *

## VIVIANI, Cesare 1947-

*PERSONAL:* Born April 22, 1947, Siena, Italy; son of Antonio Viviani (a lawyer) and Biancamaria Viviani; married; wife's name, Francesca, 1976. *Education:* University of Siena, degree in law; University of Florence, degree in education.

*ADDRESSES: Agent*—c/o Author Mail, Arnoldo Mondadori Editore, via Monadori 20090, Segrate, Milan, Italy.

*CAREER:* Psychologist in Milan, Italy, beginning 1973; poet.

*WRITINGS:*

*Confidenza a parole* (title means "Confidence in Words"), Nuovi Quaderni di Poesia (Parma, Italy), 1971.

*L'ostrabismo cara* (neologism; title means "The Ostracized-cross-eyed-ism, Dear"), Feltrinelli (Milan, Italy), 1973.

*Psicanalisi interrotta,* Sugarco (Milan, Italy), 1975.

*La pazzia spiegata dai bambini,* Formichiere (Milan, Italy), 1976.

*Piumana,* Guanda (Milan, Italy), 1977.

(Editor, translator, and author of introduction) Paul Verlaine, *Feste galanti,* Guanda (Milan, Italy), 1979, expanded as *Feste galanti, La buona canzone,* Mondadori (Milan, Italy), 1988.

(Editor, with Tomaso Kemeny, and author of introduction and contributor) *Il movimento della poesia italiana degli anni settanta,* Dedalo (Bari), 1979.

*Papa linguaggio mamma paura,* Emme (Milan, Italy), 1980.

(Editor, with Tomaso Kemeny, and author of introduction and contributor) *I percorsi della nuova poesia italiana,* Guida (Naples, Italy), 1980.

*L'amore delle parti* (title means "The Love of the Parts"), Mondadori (Milan, Italy), 1981.

*Summulae, 1966-1972* (title means "Summaries"), All'Insegna del Pesce d'Oro (Milan, Italy), 1983.

*La scena prove di poetica* (title means "The Scene: Attempts at a Poetics"), Barbablu (Siena, Italy), 1985.

*Merisi,* Mondadori (Milan, Italy), 1986.

*Folle avena,* Studio Tesi (Pordenone, Italy), 1987.

*Pensieri per una poetica della veste,* Crocetti (Milan, Italy), 1988.

*Il sogno dell'interpretazione una critica radicale all'ideologia psicanalitica,* Costa & Nolan (Genoa, Italy), 1989.

*Preghiera del nome* (title means "The Prayer of the Name"), Mondadori (Milan, Italy), 1990.

*L'opera lasciata sola,* Mondadori (Milan, Italy), 1993.

*Cori non io (1975-1977),* Crocetti (Milan, Italy), 1994.

*Una comunita degli animi,* Mondadori (Milan, Italy), 1997.

Also contributor to *Il pubblico della poesia,* edited by Alfonso Berardinelli and Franco Cordelli, Lerici (Cosenza, Italy), 1975. Contributor to periodicals, including *Almanacco dello specchio* and *Verri.*

*SIDELIGHTS:* Cesare Viviani is an Italian poet and psychoanalyst known for developing the experimental Italian poetry of the 1960s. He recognized that the cultural changes from the radicalism of the 1960s forced a new look at poetry, and focused on the formal development of a new subjectivity. In his introduction to *Il movimento della poesia italiana degli anni settanta,* which he co-edited, Viviani writes, "The I lives and perceives itself in a new way, remembers and acts, believes and looks ahead in a new way. It reads and writes, realizes its fantasies and establishes relationships in a new way. . . . Therefore today the subject has a different relationship also with poetic experience. And, therefore, poetic writing has changed . . . the I is decentered." John P. Welle wrote in *Dictionary of Literary Biography,* "After the culmination of the polemics of the 'novissimi' (newest ones)—poets such as Edoardo Sanguinetti, Antonio Porta, Alfredo Giuliani, Nanni Balestrini, and others who wanted to destabilize the traditional codes of Italian poetry in the interest of a new experimentalism—Viviani has been able to benefit from the groundbreaking efforts of his predecessors while finding his own distinctive voice." In addition to penning several works on psychoanalysis, Viviani also has edited books on Italian poetry and translated the work of French poet Paul Verlaine. Welle asserted that Viviani is "an avid explorer and bold creator of metalanguage."

Viviani's first poem was published in 1970 in the periodical *Bimestre,* and he published his second the following year in *Quasi.* In 1971 he published his first book, *Confidenza a parole,* which displays his interest in the connection between states of the mind and body, a theme he will later develop. When Viviani writes "Between being/and nonbeing," he displays not only meditative and quixotic wonderment, but also an interest in exploring states of consciousness, important for ontological, as well as psychoanalytical study. Critics have noted that his early, minimalist work parallels the classical hermeticism of the 1930s and 1940s and the neohermeticism of the 1950s. Welle noted that in the poet's early work "spare diction and bare minimalism recall his predecessors' attempts to recharge the vitality of the poetic word." Welle added, however, "Viviani soon developed a more distinct and complex poetic style."

His second volume, *L'ostrabismo cara,* also exhibits the tendency to sustain the syntactical examinations that occupied the neo-avant-garde Italian poets of the 1960s, but pushes the experimentation firmly into Sasurrean linguistics and Lacanian psychoanalysis, using various modern techniques as wordplay, lapses and substitution. A neoteric hybrid of styles and influences, *L'ostrabismo cara* displays Viviani's interest in exploring morphology, syntax and self-reflexivity, and shows

influences of the critical studies of such theorists as Roland Barthes, Jacques Derrida and Michel Foucault. Welle wrote, "*L'ostrabismo cara* forms part of the writerly tradition in contemporary literature—literary works that explore the nature of writing itself. At the same time, his voice distinguishes itself with a certain poetic bravado, a gift for comedy, and a sense of humor that, at times, bring to mind the futurists."

Viviani continued his linguistic and psychoanalytic investigations of *L'ostrabismo cara* in his 1977 work, *Piumana.* This work uses extended narratives and a light, lyrical flow to delve into subjectivity and the mind-body relationship. Welle noted that "In gathering fragments from the flux of experience, Viviani gives birth to dreamlike fantasies." Viviani, with longer verse, attained a critical awareness lacking earlier. Several critics also found this work an exciting, fresh development in contemporary poetry.

Four years later, in *L'amore delle parti* Viviani returned to traditional poetic forms, but in a modern way. While the poems have some epic quality, Viviani still maintains an experimental and self-conscious voice. He reflects on his own text, writing, "approaching the long story or poem/how the two of them closed their day!" Also, he further explores the decentered subject of his earlier works. Viviani's prose, organized into twelve sections, seems more coherent and displays a new originality. This collection, with a postmodern, epic form, has the essence of a non-traditional love story. Welle said, "Viviani's multiple points of view, the succession of voices, and the frequent interruption of the narrative are held together by an elusive approximation of the address to the reader in classical poetry," adding, "The originality of Viviani's poetry becomes more apparent in *L'amore delle parti.* Psychoanalysis and the eruption of desire into poetic language continue to provide the main focus, as he seeks to name desire."

In 1983 Viviani published a selection of his work titled *Summulae,* which features poetry he wrote before the publication of *L'ostrabismo cara* and some amended early work he thought may have been published prematurely. In a note in *Summulae,* Viviani writes, "the more the new physiognomy of my language grew the greater was my embarrassment at my first attempts. . . . Therefore with the mind of today, I thought I would make a selection of the work that preceded *L'ostrabismo cara,* eliminating the weaker parts, and overlooking the prudent concept by which a revision such as this can only be done by a poet after the age of fifty."

In 1986 he published *Merisi,* a collection of twenty-nine poems that investigate Viviani's self-reflexive human perception through his continuing use of traditional styles. These verses, fiercely lyrical, have some of the epic quality of much Italian poetry. Welle noted that this work features "brief scenes, miniature dramas, and lyrical spectacles with a minimalist-epic style." He added, "The Italy sung about by great poets in the past is celebrated here by a decentered, polycentric I. The poetic text is no longer rigidly controlled by an egomaniacal lyric presence that sees and knows all. Rather, the changing points of view create surprising twists and turns connected by frequent enjambments."

Viviani has emphasized the experimental, pushed traditional poetry boundaries and explored new ground. His interest in rediscovering the potential of the subject, and his commitment to investigating theoretical and linguistic poetic possibilities, have given him a unique style that extends previous experimentation. Adept at re-fashioning morphology and syntax, Viviani has presented a challenging new voice to Italian poetry.

*BIOGRAPHICAL AND CRITICAL SOURCES:*

*BOOKS*

*Dictionary of Literary Biography,* Volume 128: *Twentieth-Century Italian Poets,* Gale (Detroit, MI), 1993.*

# W-Y

**WAARSENBURG, Hans van de**
See van de WAARSENBURG, Hans

\* \* \*

**WADMAN, Anne Sijbe 1919-**

*PERSONAL:* Born November 30, 1919, in Langweer, Netherlands. *Education:* University of Amsterdam, Ph. D., 1955.

*ADDRESSES: Home*—Sneek, Friesland, Netherlands. *Office*—c/o Fryske Akademy, P.O. Box 54, 8900 AB, Leeuwarden/Ljouwert, Netherlands.

*CAREER:* Frisian writer and educator, c. 1945—.

*MEMBER:* PEN (Dutch center).

*AWARDS, HONORS:* Gysbert Japiks Prize for Frisian literature.

*WRITINGS:*

*Fan tsien wallen,* De Torenlaan (Assen, Netherlands), 1945.
*Op koart front: fersen,* Kamminga (Dokkum, Netherlands), 1946.
*Fiole en faem: roman,* Arbeiderspers (Amsterdam, Netherlands), 1948.

*1880 met vertalingen in het Nederlands,* L. Stafleu (Leiden, Netherlands), 1949.
*Reedridder: novelle,* Laverman (Drachten, Netherlands), 1949.
*Kleine keur uit Firese dichters sinds 1880: met vertalingen in het Nederlands,* L. Stafleu (Lieden, Netherlands), 1950.
(With Wybren Jan Buma and Pieter Gervenzon) *Trijeresom: ynliedeingen halden yn de Fryske seksje fan it Nederlands Philologekongres 1950,* J. B. Wolter (Grins, Netherlands), 1950.
(Editor) *De Friese kwestie: wat neit-Friesen er van zeggen in kranten en tijdschriften,* Drukkerij Laverman (Drachten, Netherlands), 1951.
*Kritysk konfoai: Essays,* Laverman (Drachten, Netherlands), 1951.
*Fryske fersleare,* Laverman (Drachten, Netherlands), 1953.
*In skoalmaster yn 'e dokkumerwalden: libbensgong fan Hjerre Gjerrits van der Veen,* Laverman (Drachten, Netherlands), 1955.
*Schola Alvini: lotgevallen van de Latijnse School en het Gymnasium te Sneek,* A. J. Osinga (Bolsward, Netherlands), 1958.
*Yn'e lytse loege: forhalen,* Laverman (Drachten, Netherlands), 1960.
*Hoe moat dat nou, Mirijke?,* Laverman (Drachten, Netherlands), 1960.
*Fries verhaelen in het Netherlands,* Nijgh & Van Ditmar ('s Gravenhage, Netherlands), 1960.
*Kugels foar in labbekak: roman,* Laverman (Drachten, Netherlands), 1964.
*Handdruk en handgemeen, leesavonturen met Simon Vestdijk,* A.W. Bruna and Zoon (Utrecht, Netherlands), 1965.
*De oerwinning fan Bjinse Houtsma: roman,* A. W. Bruna & Zoon (Utretcht, Netherlands), 1965.

*De smeerlappen: boerenroman,* A. W. Bruna & Zoon (Utrecht, Netherlands), 1965.

*By de duvel to bycht: roman,* Laverman (Drachten, Netherlands), 1966.

*De Feestgongers,* Laverman (Drachten, Netherlands), 1968.

*Mei Abraham fustkje,* Laverman (Drachten, Netherlands), 1969.

*It rammeljen fan de pels: damesroman,* Friese Pers (Ljouwert, Netherlands), 1970.

*De feestgangers,* A. W. Bruna & Zoon (Utrecht, Netherlands), 1971.

*Yn Adams harnas,* Friese Pers (Ljouwert, Netherlands), 1982.

*Een hartversterking: de reacties op Vestdijks eerste dichtbundel,* Stabo/All-Round (Gröningen, Netherlands), 1984.

*Biografisch bijwerk,* Stabo (Gröningen, Netherlands), 1984.

*Tinke oan alde tiden,* Friese Pers Boekerij (Ljouwert, Netherlands), 1985.

*In bolle yn'e reak,* Friese Pers Boekerij (Ljouwert, Netherlands), 1986.

*De grote explosie: snuffelen in de marge van Vestdijks gedichten 1930-1932,* Servo (Garrelsweer, Netherlands), 1987.

*De terechtstelling: roman,* Servo (Garrelsweer, Netherlands), 1987.

*De frou yn'e flesse: roman fan Janneke en Jip,* Osinga (Drachten/Ljouwert, Netherlands), 1988.

*Fjoer 'ut in döve hurd: roman,* Utjouwerij Fryslan (Ljouwert, Netherlands), 1990.

*De fearren fan de wikel,* Wimpel (Amsterdam, Netherlands), 1990.

*It kritysk kerwei: resinsjes en skogingen, 1950-1970,* Fryske Akademy (Ljouwert, Netherlands), 1990.

*In unbetelle rekken,* Stichting It Fryske Boek (Grou, Netherlands), 1992.

*In okse nei de slachtbank: roman,* Koperative Utjouwerij (Boalsert, Netherlands), 1994.

*Oer oarmans en eigen: essayistysk en kritysk ferskaat (mei bibliografy 1972-1994),* Fryske Akademy (Ljouwert, Netherlands), 1994.

SIDELIGHTS: Frisian writer and educator Anne Sijbe Wadman is noted for his poetry, fiction, and literary criticism. Wadman's novels include *De oerwinning fan Bjinse Houtsma* and *Kugels foar in labbekak,* both published in the mid-1960s. Of Wadman's nineteenth novel *De frou yn'e flesse,* Henry J. Baron, a reviewer in *World Literature Today,* commented, "Here too there is a strong psychological dimension: a study of the interplay of wounded human psyches and energetic libidos, of íd and ego, of reason and emotion." Baron called Wadman "an accomplished novelist, essayist, and literary critic whose intelligence and craftsmanship always lend their distinguished touches to his fiction."

Baron noted that Wadman's characters "suffer invariably from a failed quest for achievement and fulfillment." Froukje, the protagonist in Wadman's novella *De fearren fan de wikel,* is one such character. A victim of violence, Fourkje searches for justice but rejects assistance when offered. Baron noted *De fearren fan de wikel*'s "superb dialogue and excellent characterization" but commented that there seemed to be "no clear thematic center." An initiated quest is at the heart of Wadman's novel *Fjoer 'ut in döve hurd.* Baron commended Wadman's "intelligent staging of the human dilemma and skillful use of language" as "amply reward[ing] the reader's efforts."

Written in the seventh decade of Wadman's life, *In okse nei de slachtbank* is a novel of sensuality and soul-searching. Baron, reviewing the novel in *World Literature Today,* called the work "one of the most satisfying [Wadman] has written." Baron commented, "The intersecting plot lines are skillfully integrated, the characters . . . vividly individualized, and the main character is memorably rendered as a quester for spiritual fullness."

BIOGRAPHICAL AND CRITICAL SOURCES:

BOOKS

*Cassell's Encyclopedia of World Literature,* William Morrow and Co. (New York, NY), 1973.

PERIODICALS

*World Literature Today,* autumn, 1989, Henry J. Baron, review of *De frou yn'e flesse,* p. 690; winter, 1993, Henry J. Baron, review of *De fearren fan de sikel* and *Fjoer 'ut in döve hurd,* p. 194; autumn, 1995, Henry J. Baron, review of *In okse nei de slachtbank,* p. 801.

OTHER

*Anne Sybe Wadman,* http://www.flmd.nl/wadman.htm/ (November 12, 2000), "Frysk Letterkundich Museum en Dokumintaasjesintrum."*

\* \* \*

## WAINWRIGHT, J(ohn) A(ndrew) 1946-

*PERSONAL:* Born May 12, 1946, in Toronto, Ontario, Canada; married Marjorie Stone; children: Michael, Eric. *Education:* University of Toronto, B.A., 1969; Dalhousie University, M.A., 1973, Ph.D. (cum laude), 1978.

*ADDRESSES: Office*—c/o Department of English, Dalhousie University, Halifax, Nova Scotia, Canada. *E-mail*—andrew.wainwright@dal.ca.

*CAREER:* Poet, educator, and writer. Dalhousie University, Halifax, Nova Scotia, Canada, associate professor of English literature.

*MEMBER:* Writers' Federation of Nova Scotia.

*WRITINGS:*

*Notes for a Native Land: A New Encounter with Canada,* Oberon Press (Ottawa, Ontario, Canada), 1969.
*Charles Bruce: A Literary Biography,* Formac Pub. Co. (Halifax, Nova Scotia, Canada), 1988.
(Editor) *A Very Large Soul: Selected Letters from Margaret Laurence to Canadian Writers,* Cormorant Books (Dunvegan, Ontario, Canada), 1995.
*A Deathful Ridge: A Novel of Everest,* Mosaic Press (Oakville, Ontario, Canada), 1997.
*A Far Time,* Mosaic Press (Oakville, Ontario, Canada), 2001.

POETRY

*Moving Outward,* New Press (Toronto, Ontario, Canada), 1970.
*The Requiem Journals,* Fiddlehead Poetry Books (Fredericton, New Brunswick, Canada), 1976.

*After the War,* Mosaic Press (Oakville, Ontario, Canada), 1981.
(Editor, with Lesley Choyce) *The Mulgrave Road: Selected Poems of Charles Bruce, Pottersfield Press* (Porters Lake, Nova Scotia, Canada), 1985.
*Flight of the Falcon: Scott's Journey to the South Pole 1910-1912,* Mosaic Press (Oakville, Ontario, Canada), 1987.
*Landscape and Desire: Poems Selected and New,* Mosaic Press (Oakville, Ontario, Canada), 1992.
*Border Lines: Contemporary Poems in English,* Copp Clark (Toronto, Ontario, Canada), 1995.

*SIDELIGHTS:* An accomplished poet, with a number of poetry collections already published, in 1987 J. A. Wainwright published a poetic treatment of Captain Robert Scott's final expedition. In *Flight of the Falcon: Scott's Journey to the South Pole 1910-1912,* Wainwright tells the story of Scott's race to be the first to reach the Pole, his heartbreaking loss to Norwegian Roald Amundsen, and the return trip that finished off Scott and his four fellow explorers. Told through poems, diary entries, photographs, and a map, *Flight of the Falcon* "not only produces in magnificent collage the stark details of the Antarctic drama but also provides for the reader the opportunity to seek answers to questions about failure, tragedy, heroism and the far reaches of human endeavor," wrote *Dalhousie Review* contributor Douglas Lockhead. In this sense, the book is a history lesson, a poetic meditation, and a character study, "and although such an imaginative treatment of the traces of the expedition falters and drags at times, it remains a worthy effort at capturing the essence of Scott's expedition," according to I. S. MacLaren in *Essays on Canadian Writing. Choice* reviewer B. Almon felt that "Wainwright might have explored Scott's character further; he is a controversial figure. Still, this book is a good acquisition at any level." Going somewhat further, Pat Bolger wrote in *Canadian Materials,* "Like his subject, Wainwright is exploring new territory, and his book will be compelling reading for adults who like poetry (and probably for some who don't), and for mature teenagers who are interested in its theme of survival."

In *A Deathful Ridge: A Novel of Everest,* Wainwright's first novel, he takes up the theme of another doomed adventurer, George Herbert Leigh-Mallory, who died in 1924 on the slopes of Mount Everest in his third attempt to reach the summit. In Wainwright's retelling, Mallory survives, but kills his traveling partner,

Andrew Irvine (who actually died with him). To save his heroic reputation, he and the surviving members of the expedition concoct the story of his death, and he returns in secret to live out his days in a small Welsh town. Told from the point of view of a narrator who discovers Mallory's secret, the book "explores the nature of the biographical quest in all its complexity—illusive, elusive, allusive—and comes to acknowledge that there is no one true story of a life," Eva Tihanyi wrote in *Books in Canada*. Some were not entirely pleased with the results. A *Publishers Weekly* reviewer felt that "Wainwright has a strong, literate voice . . . but his failure to maintain the momentum of the action on the mountain itself sometimes turns this novel into its own long, slow climb." Others were much more satisfied. "Wainwright, whose poet's eye view of the hazards, failures, and achievements in polar exploration was memorably expressed in his *Flight of the Falcon* . . . has clearly staked a strong claim for himself in the realm of poetically reconstructed history," concluded *Dalhousie Review* contributor James Grey.

In *A Very Large Soul: Selected Letters from Margaret Laurence to Canadian Writers*, Wainwright gives a glimpse of a different kind of pioneer. As a writer and a mentor, Margaret Laurence not only set a standard for excellence in her fiction, she also launched a sort of renaissance for Anglophone Canadian writers, including Margaret Atwood, Alice Munro, and Wainwright himself, many of whom drew inspiration from her works and from personal contact with her. "Wainwright's collection of letters offers valuable insight into Laurence's relations with other Canadian writers," wrote Susan J. Warwick in the *Journal of Canadian Studies*. For *Canadian Literature* contributor Deborah Dudek, "Reading *A Very Large Soul* translates into a conversation with Margaret Laurence. She is warm and funny and astonishingly insightful." Janice Kulyk Keefer concluded in *Books of Canada* that Lawrences' "private efforts to encourage all those writers lucky enough to come within her ken cannot be separated from her public services to the writing community in general. All this *A Very Large Soul* recalls, and in this way it serves as both a memorial and as a timely reminder."

*BIOGRAPHICAL AND CRITICAL SOURCES:*

PERIODICALS

*Books in Canada*, September, 1995, Janice Kulyk Keefer, review of *A Very Large Soul*, p. 36;

December, 1997, Eva Tihanyi, review of *A Deathful Ridge*, pp. 39-40.
*Canadian Literature*, winter, 1996, Deborah Dudek, review of *A Very Large Soul*, p. 135.
*Canadian Materials*, May, 1988, Pat Bolger, review of *Flight of the Falcon*, p. 104.
*Choice*, January, 1988, B. Almon, review of *Flight of the Falcon*, p. 7.
*Dalhousie Review*, spring, 1987, Douglas Lochhead, review of *Flight of the Falcon*, pp. 138-140; autumn, 1996, James Gray, review of *A Deathful Ridge*, pp. 449-451.
*Essays on Canadian Writing*, spring, 1990, I. S. MacLaren, "Hauling at the Traces," pp. 25-31.
*Journal of Canadian Studies*, winter, 1996, Susan J. Warwick, "Between the Dancer and the Dance: Reading the Life and Work of Margaret Laurence," pp. 177-187.
*Publishers Weekly*, August 25, 1997, review of *A Dreadful Ridge*, p. 47.*

\*     \*     \*

## WALSH, Robert L. 1933-

*PERSONAL:* Born April 6, 1933, in Beverly, MA; married Sandra Holben (an appraiser), October 15, 1988. *Education:* University of Vermont, M.Ed., 1979; Colgate University, B.A. (English), 1955. *Religion:* Catholic. *Hobbies and other interests:* Tennis, biking, reading.

*ADDRESSES: Home and office*—Walsh & Burrell Associates, LLC, 17 Mountain View Blvd., South Burlington, VT 05403. *E-mail*—walshburrell@cs.com.

*CAREER:* South Burlington High School, South Burlington, VT, teacher, 1977-95; University of Vermont, Burlington, VT, adjunct faculty, 1999—; Walsh & Burrell Associates, South Burlington, president, 2001—. Served in Vermont House of Representatives, 1983-89. *Military service:* U.S. Marie Corps, 1955-76; became lieutenant colonel; received Bronze Star.

*WRITINGS:*

(With Leon F. Burrell) *The Other America: The African American Experience*, Walsh & Burrell Associates (South Burlington, VT), 2001.

*WORK IN PROGRESS:* Examining the subject of reparations as they pertain to slavery.

*SIDELIGHTS:* Robert L. Walsh told *CA:* "I have written on the African-American experience, because as a teacher I am appalled that this subject is rarely discussed in the public school system. Most secondary text books barely address African-American history in a meaningful manner. Understanding of the African-American experience is basic to any effort directed at eliminating racism in the United States."

\* \* \*

## WALVOORD, John F(lipse) 1910-2002

*OBITUARY NOTICE*—See index for *CA* sketch: Born May 1, 1910, in Sheboygan, WI; died December 20, 2002, in Dallas, TX. Minister, educator, and author. Walvoord was a theology professor, seminary president, and authority on Bible prophecies. After receiving his undergraduate degree from Wheaton College in 1931, he earned a doctorate in theology from Dallas Theological Seminary in 1936, as well as a master's degree from Texas Christian University in 1945. A minister associated with the Independent Fundamental Churches of America, Walvoord spent his entire academic career at Dallas Theological Seminary, beginning as a registrar and associate professor during the 1930s and 1940s; he was also assistant to the president from 1945 to 1952. Made a professor of systematic theology in 1952, he was also named president of Dallas Theological Seminary and held that position until his retirement in 1986. During his early years in academia Walvoord was asked to teach a course about the Apocalypse. This sparked his interest in the subject and in biblical prophecies, eventually leading him to write several books on the subject. The most influential of these among the general public was his bestselling 1974 work, *Armageddon, Oil, and the Middle East Crisis: What the Bible Says about the Future of the Middle East and the End of Western Civilization,* which he wrote with his son John E. Walvoord. This book, which predicts that the world will see the rise of a powerful government headed by an atheist leader in league with Satan and will enter into a great war centered in the Middle East, was revised in 1990 during the Persian Gulf War. Walvoord was subsequently asked to appear on a number of television and radio programs about his ideas, although he came short of asserting that Armageddon was imminent because of U.S. actions in the Middle East. In addition to *Armageddon, Oil, and the Middle East Crisis,* Walvoord wrote or edited over thirty other works, including *Israel and Prophecy* (1962), *Matthew: Thy Kingdom Come* (1974), *The Prophecy Knowledge Handbook* (1990), and *Prophecy in the New Millennium: A Fresh Look at Future Events* (2001).

*OBITUARIES AND OTHER SOURCES:*

*BOOKS*

*Who's Who in America,* 53rd edition, Marquis (New Providence, NJ), 1998.

*PERIODICALS*

*Los Angeles Times,* January 10, 2003, p. B15.
*Washington Post,* December 25, 2002, p. B7.

*OTHER*

*Dallas Theological Seminary,* http://www.dts.edu/ (February 10, 2003).

\* \* \*

## WARRAQ, Ibn

*PERSONAL:* Male.

*ADDRESSES: Agent*—c/o Prometheus Books, 59 John Glenn Dr., Amherst, NY 14228-2197.

*CAREER:* Writer. Former primary school teacher, tour guide, and restaurateur.

*WRITINGS:*

*Why I Am Not a Muslim,* Prometheus Books (Amherst, NY), 1995.
(Editor) *The Origins of the Koran: Classic Essays on Islam's Holy Book,* Prometheus Books (Amherst, NY), 1998.

(Editor) *The Quest for the Historical Muhammad,* Prometheus Books (Amherst, NY), 2000.

(Editor) *What the Koran Really Says: Language, Text, and Commentary,* Prometheus Books (Amherst, NY), 2003.

*SIDELIGHTS:* Ibn Warraq, which means "son of a copyist" in Arabic, is a pseudonym. According to a biography at the Web site *Secular Web,* Warraq was born and raised "in an extremist Islamic society on the Indian subcontinent." He moved to "a Western nation," where he was educated, and as a result he renounced his Islamic faith, as well as all other religions, becoming a secular humanist and freethinker. Warraq has written several books about Middle Eastern politics and religion.

In the *American Prospect,* Chris Mooney wrote that Warraq might seem like an unlikely fighter against Islam. Before becoming a writer, he worked variously as a primary school teacher, a tour guide, and a restaurateur. Warraq told Mooney, "I really do not wish to spend my life being a professional Islam basher."

In *Why I Am Not a Muslim,* Warraq describes his experiences and the reasons he left Islam. Noting that his work was inspired by Bertrand Russell's *Why I Am Not a Christian,* Warraq examines the strict faith of his childhood and the culture in which he lived, discusses inconsistencies in the Muslim holy book, the Koran, and the errors and evils that have been committed under the name of Islam through history. He also presents arguments against Christianity and the idea of God and established religions in general. Kenneth C. W. Leiter wrote in *Middle East Quarterly* that despite the book's "anger," it is "serious and thought-provoking" and "calls . . . [for] an equally compelling response from a believing Muslim."

In *Free Inquiry,* G. A. Wells wrote, "One truth that [*Why I Am Not a Muslim*] brings home very forcibly is that religion has so often been made the basis for perpetuating social injustices." At the *Institute for the Secularisation of Islamic Society* Web site, Maxime Rodinson also noted this, but wrote that some of Warraq's criticisms of what he perceives as Muslim beliefs or practices should rightly be directed at particular cultures that promote them, rather than the Islamic religion as a whole. Rodinson also commented,

"The work is very learned and organised in a rather chaotic fashion. In addition to the reflections and reactions of the author, it is a kind of compilation and encyclopaedia of all the objections . . . [raised against Islam] during fourteen centuries."

In *The Quest for the Historical Muhammad,* Warraq presents studies taken from academic journals from the past 150 years in order to reconstruct the life of Muhammad, the founder of Islam. Most of the essays consider the question of whether it is possible to reconstruct Muhammad's life, given the small amount of source material about it, and most of the authors represented in the book believe that it is an impossible undertaking. In the *Journal of the American Oriental Society,* Asma Afsaruddin wrote that although the book can be viewed as "courting controversy," the authors whose work it includes "have raised pertinent and provocative questions that have been and continue to be debated by scholars in the field." In *Middle East Journal,* a reviewer wrote that *The Quest for the Historical Muhammad* "gathers some of the best studies of Muhammad and early Islam produced by scholars since the 19th century." A *Publishers Weekly* reviewer commented, "Under the guise of scholarly objectivity, Warraq wages a vigorous attack on the traditions of Islam."

*BIOGRAPHICAL AND CRITICAL SOURCES:*

*PERIODICALS*

*American Prospect,* December 17, 2001, Chris Mooney, "Holy War: Republicans Woo an Ex-Muslim Blasphemer in the Fight to Separate Mosque and State," p. 15.

*Booklist,* February 15, 2000, Jay Freeman, review of *The Quest for the Historical Muhammad,* p. 1055.

*Free Inquiry,* winter, 1995, G. A. Wells, review of *Why I Am Not a Muslim,* p. 54; summer, 2000, Robert M. Price, review of *The Origins of the Koran: Classic Essays on Islam's Holy Book,* p. 62.

*Journal of the American Oriental Society,* October-December, 2001, Asma Afsaruddin, review of *The Quest for the Historical Muhammad,* p. 728.

*Library Journal,* February 15, 2000, Michael W. Ellis, review of *The Quest for the Historical Muhammad,* p. 170.

*Middle East Journal,* summer, 2000, review of *The Quest for the Historical Muhammad,* p. 494.

*Middle East Quarterly,* March, 1996, Kenneth C. W. Leiter, review of *Why I Am Not a Muslim,* p. 86.

*National Catholic Reporter,* November 17, 1995, Robert Obach, review of *Why I Am Not a Muslim,* p. 30.

*Publishers Weekly,* March 6, 2000, review of *The Quest for the Historical Muhammad,* p. 102.

OTHER

*Institute for the Secularisation of Islamic Society Web site,* http://www.secularislam.org/ (February, 2000), Maxime Rodinson, review of *Why I Am Not a Muslim.*

*Secular Web,* http://www.secweb.org/ (April 22, 2002), review of *Why I Am Not a Muslim.*\*

\*      \*      \*

## WARREN, Doug(las) 1935-2002

*OBITUARY NOTICE*—See index for *CA* sketch: Born January 28, 1935, in Oberlin, OH; died from complications after heart surgery September 28, 2002, in Burbank, CA. Journalist and author. Warren was a noted author of biographies about film stars and Hollywood celebrities. After attending Kent State University he worked at a Houston, Texas television station during the early 1960s. He then worked as a Sunday magazine writer for the *Akron Beacon Journal* and the *Albany Times Union.* Joining United Press International in 1967, he became a field reporter in Vietnam during the war, later becoming Saigon bureau chief for Multimedia-Asia, Inc. Returning to the United States, Warren went back to his work as a Sunday magazine writer, this time for the *Cleveland Plain Dealer,* until 1973, when he became a full-time freelancer. Warren, who was interested in acting and was, for a time, an actor himself in New York City, was also employed as a photographer for the Hollywood publications *Silver Screen* and *Screenland.* His fascination with actors led him to write the biography *Betty Grable: The Reluctant Movie Queen* (1981), and the authorized autobiographies *James Cagney* (1983) and *Yvonne* (1987), about Yvonne De Carlo. He was also author of the books *Walking Tall* (1974), *Demonic Possession* (1975), and *A Case of Rape* (1975).

OBITUARIES AND OTHER SOURCES:

PERIODICALS

*Los Angeles Times,* October 12, 2002, p. B23.

\*      \*      \*

## WATSON, Graham (Angus) 1913-2002

*OBITUARY NOTICE*—See index for *CA* sketch: Born June 8, 1913, in Newcastle upon Tyne, England; died November 14, 2002, in Rye, England. Literary agent and author. Watson was well known through his affiliation with London-based Curtis Brown Ltd., the world's largest literary agency. After graduating from Cambridge University with a bachelor's degree in 1934, he worked at a printing shop for a year before being hired by his grandfather's publishing house Nicholas & Watson. During World War II Watson was in the Royal Artillery, and after the war he joined the staff of the *Spectator* as a writer. In 1947 he made the move to Curtis Brown, where he was director from 1947 to 1967 and managing director from 1967 until he retired in 1976. Watson became an integral part of the agency, and he worked with such famous authors as C. P. Snow, Antonia Fraser, Malcolm Bradbury, Wilfred Thesiger, and Daphne du Maurier. He wrote about his publishing-house experiences in his autobiography, *Book Society* (1979), and was also the author of *A Guide to the Fishing Inns of Scotland* (1977).

OBITUARIES AND OTHER SOURCES:

PERIODICALS

*Los Angeles Times,* November 21, 2002, p. B21.
*New York Times,* November 21, 2002, p. A29.
*Times* (London, England), November 18, 2002.

\*      \*      \*

## WELPOTT, Jack (Warren) 1923-

*PERSONAL:* Born April 27, 1923, in Kansas City, KS; married Doris Jean Franklin, 1949 (divorced, 1968); married Judy Dater (a photographer), 1971 (divorced, 1977); children (first marriage): Jan Marie, Matthew David. *Education:* University of Indiana, Bloomington, B.S., 1949, M.S., 1955, M.F.A., 1959.

*ADDRESSES: Office*—28 Precita Avenue, San Francisco, CA 94110.

*CAREER:* Independent photographer, 1959—. Indiana University, Bloomington, Audio-Visual Center, Bloomington, IN, production supervisor, 1949-59; San Francisco State University, San Francisco, CA, assistant professor, 1959-60, associate professor, 1961-70, professor of photography, 1971—; University of California Extension, San Francisco, CA, lecturer, 1966-69. Friends of Photography, Carmel, CA, member of board of trustees. *Military service:* U.S. Air Force, intelligence unit, 1943-46, staff sergeant, three combat stars.

*MEMBER:* Society for Photgraphic Education.

*AWARDS, HONORS:* Medal of Arles, France, 1973; National Endowment for the Arts grant, 1979.

*WRITINGS:*

*Women and Other Visions: Photographs by Judy Dater and Jack Welpott,* Morgan & Morgan (New York, NY), 1975.
*The Artist as Teacher, the Teacher as Artist: Photographs 1950-1975,* San Francisco Museum of Art, (San Francisco, CA), 1975.*

\*    \*    \*

**WHATMORE, Richard 1968-**

*PERSONAL:* Born January 19, 1968, in Newcastle upon Tyne, England. *Education:* University of Cambridge, read history, 1986-89, Ph.D., 1995.

*ADDRESSES: Office*—Arts B, University of Sussex, Falmer, Brighton BN1 9QN, England. *E-mail*—r.whatmore@sussex.ac.uk.

*CAREER:* University of Sussex, Brighton, England, senior lecturer in intellectual history, 1993—.

*WRITINGS:*

(Editor, with Stefan Collini and Brian Young) *British Intellectual History, 1750-1950,* Volume I: *Economy, Polity, and Society,* Volume II: *History, Religion, and Culture,* Cambridge University Press (New York, NY), 2000.

*Republicanism and the French Revolution: An Intellectual History of Jean-Baptiste Say's Political Economy,* Oxford University Press (New York, NY), 2000.

*SIDELIGHTS:* An historian and lecturer at the University of Sussex, Richard Whatmore joined with colleagues Stefan Collini and Brian Young in editing and publishing *British Intellectual History, 1750-1950,* a two-volume collection of essays by historians in the "Sussex School of Intellectual History." A loose term, largely rejected even by Collini in his introduction, the Sussex school "consists of an openness to the attractions and advantages of a 'thickly textured' sense of the intellectual past, in which the full range of ideas, idioms, and audiences that goes into making a piece of writing and its reputation are given proper consideration," according to David Runciman in the *Times Higher Education Supplement.* The twenty-two essays in these volumes address such topics as Edmund Gibbons' religious feelings, the Victorians' newfound admiration of Oliver Cromwell, and the growth of Adam Smith's reputation in the early nineteenth century. For Runciman, "The best essays here are the ones that seek to rescue people or ideas from acquired reputations that are unmerited without presuming to suppose that this is for their sakes rather than for ours." A *History Today* reviewer found that "there are very few weak entries, and even when one disagrees with a piece, there is usually something substantial to disagree with." "As to the Sussex School," wrote John Vincent in the *Times Literary Supplement,* "as far as institutions go, it clearly has not wasted its time. Most universities can only regard it with some envy."

The same year as *British Intellectual History, 1750-1950* came out, Whatmore published *Republicanism and the French Revolution: An Intellectual History of Jean-Baptiste Say's Political Economy.* "Those deterred by the thought of 200 pages on a largely forgotten ideologue will miss an important contribution to a much bigger field," wrote William Doyle in the *Times Literary Supplement.* In addition to exploring Say's economic prescriptions, Whatmore delves into their intellectual root and ultimately into the entire background to French republicanism, which seemed to emerge so suddenly in 1791. In doing so, "Whatmore provides a new understanding of the intellectual movements of one of the most turbulent periods of European history," concluded *Choice* reviewer D. J. Heimmermann.

*BIOGRAPHICAL AND CRITICAL SOURCES:*

*PERIODICALS*

*Choice,* October, 2001, D. J. Heimmermann, review of *Republicanism and the French Revolution,* p. 382.

*History Today,* October, 2000, review of *British Intellectual History, 1750-1950,* p. 55.

*Times Higher Education Supplement,* July 13, 2001, David Runciman, "Conversation with the Past Acquires an Ironic Twist, p. 28."

*Times Literary Supplement,* November 3, 2000, John R. Vincent, "Thickness Has Its Price," p. 26; September 21, 2001, William Doyle, "Father of the Republic," p. 26.

\*   \*   \*

## WICKS, Robert S(igfrid) 1954-

*PERSONAL:* Born 1954. *Education:* University of Washington, B.S., 1975; Cornell University, Ph.D., 1983.

*ADDRESSES: Office*—124 Art Building, Miami University, Oxford, OH 45056. *E-mail*—wicksrs@muohio.edu.

*CAREER:* University of Miami, Oxford, OH, professor of art, 1983—, interim director. Silpakorn University, fulbright lecturer, 1987; Kansai Gaidai University, visiting professor, 1992.

*WRITINGS:*

*Gandharan Sculpture,* Miami University Art Museum (Oxford, OH), 1985.

*Money, Markets, and Trade in Early Southeast Asia: The Development of Indigenous Monetary Systems to AD 1400,* Southeast Asia Program, Cornell University (Ithaca, NY), 1992, revised edition, 1996.

(With Roland H. Harrison) *Buried Cities, Forgotten Gods: William Niven's Life of Discovery and Revolution in Mexico and the American Southwest,* Texas Tech University (Lubbock, TX), 1999.

*WORK IN PROGRESS:* An examination of the 1844 political murder of the first Mormon prophet, Joseph Smith, to be completed in late 2002.

*SIDELIGHTS:* In *Money, Markets, and Trade in Early Southeast Asia: The Development of Indigenous Monetary Systems to AD 1400,* Robert S. Wicks, a specialist in art history, provides his research on the history of money in Southeast Asia up to the fifteenth century. He discusses the materials used to make the money, and also its various uses in the different areas of Southeast Asia. *Journal of the American Oriental Society* contributor Michael W. Charney called the book, "A highly valuable study."

Wicks became interested in William Nivin when he was a high school student. Nivin was a mineralogist, businessman, archeologist, and explorer, among other things. His explorations included ruins in the Mexican state of Guerrero, and his finding of twenty-six hundred inscribed stone tablets in the Valley of Mexico. Many of the areas he explored were later destroyed by neglect, robbers, and the Mexican Revolution in 1911. Wicks' interest in Nivin continued into adulthood, and he wrote *Buried Cities, Forgotten Gods: William Niven's Life of Discovery and Revolution in Mexico and the American Southwest* with Nivin's grandson, Roland H. Harrison. *Buried Cities, Forgotten Gods* is a biography on Nivin and his explorations, based on Nevin's manuscripts, papers, and personal letters to his family.

*BIOGRAPHICAL AND CRITICAL SOURCES:*

*PERIODICALS*

*Choice,* January, 2000, review of *Buried Cities, Forgotten Gods: William Niven's Life of Discovery and Revolution in Mexico and the American Southwest,* p. 1000.

*Journal of the American Oriental Society,* January-March, 1996, Michael W. Charney, review of *Money, Markets, and Trade in Early Southeast Asia: The Development of Indigenous Monetary Systems to AD 1400,* p. 179.

*OTHER*

*Miami University School of Fine Arts Web site,* http://www.fna.muohio.edu/ (May 8, 2002), "Robert Wicks Biography."

*Newsletter of the Katherine Anne Porter Society,* http://www.lib.umd.edu/ (May 8, 2002), Beth Alvarez, "Katherine Anne Porter in Recent Biography of William Niven."

*Texas Tech University Press Web site,* http://www.ttup.ttu.edu/ (May 8, 2002), review of *Buried Cities, Forgotten Gods.*

*Weekly Wire,* http://www.weeklywire.com/ (May 8, 2002), Randall Holdrige, "The Wanderer: Fortune-Seeker William Niven Grew Rich in Tales of Adventure."*

\*        \*        \*

## WILBURN, Reudene E.

*PERSONAL:* Born in New York, NY; married Ralph A. Wilburn, 1970; children: Renee, Ralph Jr., Raymond. *Ethnicity:* "African-American." *Education:* Fordham University, Ph.D. (education), 1997. *Religion:* Baptist. *Hobbies and other interests:* Writing mysteries.

*ADDRESSES: Agent*—c/o Peter Lang Publishing Inc., 275 Seventh Ave., 28th Fl., New York, NY 10001. *E-mail*—jahydah@msn.com.

*CAREER:* Holy Cross School, Bronx, NY, director of early childhood, 1977—; Fordham University, New York, NY, adjunct instructor, 1991.

*WRITINGS:*

*Understanding the Preschooler* (nonfiction), Peter Lang Publishing (New York, NY), 2000.

*WORK IN PROGRESS:* The mystery novels *View from the Floor, Shu-Bop and the Teddy Bear Factory, In the Name of God the Merciful,* and *Ramblings of a Midnight Guilty Woman.*

*SIDELIGHTS:* Reudene E. Wilburn told *CA:* "I wrote *Understanding the Preschooler* as an outgrowth of my Ph.D. dissertation. I wanted to share the data I collected with people who were beginning their careers in education.

"I found some of the information convoluted and esoteric to a degree and that motivated me to write a clear, concise book with references for further reading and explanation.

"I am currently fully engaged in writing mystery novels. I need an agent."

\*        \*        \*

## WILLIAMS, Ifor
    See ROLFE, Frederick (William Serafino Austin Lewis Mary)

\*        \*        \*

## WIRTH, Louis 1897-1952

*PERSONAL:* Born August 28, 1897, in Gemunden, Germany; immigrated to the United States in 1911; died of a heart attack, May 3, 1952, in Buffalo, NY; son of Joseph Wirth (a cattle dealer) and Rosalie Lorig; married Mary Bolton (a social worker), February 14, 1923; children: Elizabeth, Alice. *Education:* University of Chicago, A.B., 1919, M.A., 1925, and Ph.D., 1926. *Politics:* "Anti-capitalist."

*CAREER:* Jewish Charities of Chicago, Bureau of Personal Service, director of the division of delinquent boys, 1919; University of Chicago, IL, instructor, 1925-28, professor of sociology, 1931-52; Tulane University, New Orleans, LA, instructor, 1928-30; Illinois Post War Planning Commission, director of planning, 1944. Managing editor, *American Journal of Sociology,* 1931.

*MEMBER:* American Sociological Association (president, 1946), International Sociological Association (founding member and first president, 1950), Urban League, American Jewish Committee, Society for Social Research (president), Public Administration Clearing House, American Society of Planning Officials, National Association of Inter-group Relations, American Council on Race Relations (founder and director), University of Chicago Quandrangle Club (president).

*AWARDS, HONORS:* Social Science Research Council fellowship, 1931.

*WRITINGS:*

*The Ghetto,* University of Chicago Press (Chicago, IL), 1928, reprinted with a new introduction by Hasia R. Diner, Transaction (New Brunswick, NJ), 1998.

(Author of introduction and translator, with Edward Shils) *Ideology and Utopia: An Introduction to the Sociology of Knowledge,* Harcourt (New York, NY), 1936.

(Editor, and author of introduction) *Contemporary Social Problems: A Tentative Formulation for Teachers of Social Studies,* University of Chicago Press (Chicago, IL), 1940.

(Editor) *Eleven Twenty-Six: A Decade of Social Science Research,* University of Chicago Press (Chicago, IL), 1940.

*Community Life and Social Policy: Selected Papers,* University of Chicago Press (Chicago, IL), 1956.

*Louis Wirth on Cities and Social Life: Selected Papers,* University of Chicago Press (Chicago, IL), 1964.

Contributor to books, including *The City,* by Robert E. Park, Ernest W. Burgess, and Roderick D. McKenzie, University of Chicago Press, 1925. Contributor to periodicals, including *American Journal of Sociology.*

*SIDELIGHTS:* Louis Wirth was a sociologist who rose to prominence in the 1930s as part of the "Chicago school" of social scientists at the University of Chicago and who developed the theory of "new urbanism." In his most prominent book, *The Ghetto,* Wirth traced the history of Jewish communities in large cities from antiquity to 1920s Chicago, thereby becoming one of the first social scientists to explore the relationship between cultural identity and population patterns. In his landmark 1938 essay "Urbanism as a Way of Life," Wirth accepted the growing notion that urban life alienates individuals from one another and fosters homogenous communities, but he also claimed that such communities ultimately allow for greater personal freedom than traditional, rural communities. Wirth remained at the University of Chicago for most of his career, and his output, though small, proved influential to later generations of urban sociologists. He lectured widely and was active in many organizations, particularly those that sought to understand race relations in urban society.

Wirth was born into a prominent Jewish family in the farming community of Gemunden, Germany, in 1897. His mother valued education highly, and in 1911 she sent him to Omaha, Nebraska, to live with relatives in order to learn English and go to high school—an option not readily available in their small town. In Nebraska, Wirth excelled in academics and won a scholarship to the University of Chicago, where he developed an interest in sociology shortly after his arrival. He was influenced by the founders of the "Chicago school" of sociology, including Albion Small, Robert Park, Ernest Burgess, and George Mead, who were developing new ideas about how communities and individuals function within cities. Wirth was fascinated by their studies of urban life, particularly those that focused on how immigration and assimilation of different ethnic groups characterized American cities of the early twentieth century. Wirth was particularly interested in the concept of Jewish life as it played out in major cities and how Jews become assimilated into American culture. Historically, Jews had been segregated from other city populations in ghettos, a trend that continued in the United States despite the absence of legal segregation. His doctoral dissertation, *The Ghetto,* published in 1928, traces the segregation of the Jews from ancient times, when segregation was self-selective, to the Middle Ages, when it was mandated by law. Characterizing the Jewish ghetto throughout history as a "city within a city," he outlines how these practices carried over to the modern-day Chicago Jewish community.

In "Urbanism as a Way of Life," Wirth defines cities as large areas populated densely by heterogeneous people. He views urbanism, the growth of cities at the expense of rural areas, to be a continuing trend in modern society. Moreover, as his theory of "new urbanism" states, the process of living in a large city changes the way people relate to one another. Primary relationships are not as important as secondary relationships, and secondary relationships tend to be superficial and revolve around the limited roles people assume: banker, cashier, doorman, mail carrier, etc. Wirth explains how and why people tend to group themselves together—by religion or race—based on the laws of homogeneity, a fact that leads to segmentation of urban life, which although it may be detrimental to community involvement, often leads to a satisfactory measure of personal freedom.

Wirth was an early supporter of urban planning and advocated the regulation of housing development, zoning, and land use. Not content to remain an academic, Wirth became the director of planning for the Illinois

Post War Planning Commission in 1944, an era in which it was recognized that sociologists, as well as architects and engineers, were necessary to create successful communities. Wirth conducted little sociological research on his own and never fully developed his concept of "new urbanism," preferring instead to practice applied sociology and spread his influence through his involvement in professional organizations. He founded many sociological organizations, including the International Sociological Association and the American Council on Race Relations. In 1931 he returned to Germany to study on a Social Science Research Council fellowship and was alarmed at the country's growing anti-Semitism. Over the course of the next few years, he worked to bring to America his remaining family members—eleven in all—in advance of the Nazi Party's assumption of power. According to Zane L. Miller of the *Journal of Urban History,* "Wirth was convinced that the fate of society depended on the determined efforts of men to harness cultural differences to bring about a harmonious and progressive world order."

*BIOGRAPHICAL AND CRITICAL SOURCES:*

BOOKS

*Encyclopedia of World Biography Supplement,* Volume 21, Gale (Detroit, MI), 2001.
*Twentieth-Century Literary Criticism,* Volume 92, Gale (Detroit, MI), 2000, pp. 357-399.
*World of Sociology,* Volume 2, Gale (Detroit, MI), 2001, p. 714.

PERIODICALS

*American Prospect,* May 22, 2000.
*Journal of Urban History,* May, 1992, Zane L. Miller, "Pluralism, Chicago School Style: Louis Wirth, the Ghetto, the City, and 'Integration', " p. 251.*

\*     \*     \*

## WOOD, Jamie (Martinez) 1967-

*PERSONAL:* Born December 23, 1967, in Santa Ana, CA; daughter of John (a landscaper) and Cathi (a teacher) Budd; married Kevin Wood (a sales manager), August 21, 1994; children: Skyler, Kobe. *Ethnicity:* "Latina/Anglo." *Education:* California State University—Fresno, B.A., 1991; also studied Reiki and massage therapy. *Politics:* Green Party. *Religion:* Wicca.

*ADDRESSES: Agent*—Julie Castiglia, Castiglia Literary Agency, 1155 Camino del Mar, Suite 510, Del Mar, CA 92014. *E-mail*—jarlagency@aol.com.

*CAREER:* Orange County/Anaheim Visitor and Convention Bureau, Anaheim, CA, member of communication staff, 1988-92; Orange City Performing Arts Center, Costa Mesa, CA, group sales manager, 1992-95; Castiglia Literary Agency, Del Mar, CA, agent assistant, 1995-98; writer, 1998—.

*MEMBER:* Authors League, Authors Guild.

*WRITINGS:*

(With Tara Seefeldt) *The Wicca Cookbook: Recipes, Rituals, and Lore,* Ten Speed Press (Berkeley, CA), 2000.
*The Hispanic Baby Name Book: Como te llamas, Baby,* Berkeley Publishing, 2001.
*The Teen Spell Book: Magick for Young Witches,* Ten Speed Press (Berkeley, CA), 2001.

*WORK IN PROGRESS:* Historical fiction set in California, 1769-1776.

*SIDELIGHTS:* Jamie Wood told *CA:* "I write because it is my truest and easiest form of communication. Through the medium of words I can express myself at deep-rooted, multifaceted levels. The power of words transports me to an illimitable world of self-discovery while it transforms and raises my fears to ideas of love and connectedness. The paper or computer does not judge me but implores me to dig deeper.

"I have been writing stories since I was nine years old and still have every one of my diaries. I believe that to write well authors must be willing to viscerally feel the emotions and situations they are describing. So I use these older pieces as well as current journals as reference points to my simple, candid self. I endeavor to turn the maudlin entries into self-healing journeys that resonate with another's pain or triumphs. In researching *The Teen Spell Book: Magick for Young Witches,* I referenced my first diary—written from the time I was eleven until I was fourteen—to excavate the old pain and angst and transform these negative emotions into forgiveness and self-empowerment.

"My favorite time to write is at 10:00 p.m., although I do find myself writing at any chance I get. My usual process is getting the thoughts down on paper, using a pencil. I allow the stream of consciousness to flow, often saving the editing for another day. I prefer to separate the creator from the critic. When I have a block of time, I set a creative atmosphere with candles, incense, and instrumental music."

## BIOGRAPHICAL AND CRITICAL SOURCES:

### PERIODICALS

*Booklist,* January 1, 2001, Mark Knoblauch, review of *The Wicca Cookbook: Recipes, Rituals, and Lore,* p. 894.

*Publishers Weekly,* July 26, 1999, "Wiccan Wisdom," p. 44.

\* \* \*

## WOOD, Joanna E. 1867-1927
### (Jean d'Arc)

*PERSONAL:* Born December 28, 1867, in Lesmahagow, Lanarkshire, Scotland; died May 1, 1927, in Detroit, MI; daughter of Robert (a farmer) and Agnes (a homemaker; maiden name, Tod) Wood. *Education:* Attended St. Catharines Collegiate Institute.

*CAREER:* Fiction writer, c. 1894-1927.

*WRITINGS:*

*The Untempered Wind,* Tait (New York, NY), 1894.
*Judith Moore; or, Fashioning a Pipe,* Ontario Publishing (Toronto, Ontario, Canada), 1898.
*A Daughter of Witches,* Gage (Toronto, Ontario, Canada), 1900.
*Farden Ha',* Hurst & Blackett (London, England), 1902.

Also author of short stories, sometimes under pseudonym Jean d'Arc, including "Mahalla's Revenge," "A Martyr to Love," "The Mystery of the Carved Coconut," "The Last Cock Fight at San Mateo," and "Where Waters Beckon."

*SIDELIGHTS:* Researchers have had difficulty over the years in locating information about the life and works of Canadian author Joanna Wood. A writer of popular fiction in the late nineteenth and early twentieth centuries, Wood published several novels and short stories. She was featured frequently in *Canadian Magazine.* Born in Scotland, Wood lived with her family on a farm at Queenston, near Niagara Falls, New York. Under the pen name Jean d'Arc, she first published short stories in American magazines.

She reportedly won several literary awards in New York, but no evidence supports this claim. Critics compared Wood's first novel, *The Untempered Wind,* to Thomas Hardy stories in how it depicts small-town life. In the fictional Jamestown, people are intolerant of an unwed mother, "with all the single-mindedness of the Puritans in Nathaniel Hawthorne's *The Scarlet Letter,*" Carole Gerson wrote in *Dictionary of Literary Biography.*

The narrow-minded Jamestown citizens make the woman promise to reveal her secret to everyone when she leaves the town. Gerson said that although the "social satire is undermined by [Wood's] penchant for melodrama," the book is noteworthy because it was the first to deal with the "puritan ethos" of Canadian small towns.

Wood's novel *Judith Moore; or, Fashioning a Pipe* is about a famous singer who falls in love with a Canadian farmer. After much soul-searching, Judith renounces her career and moves to the farm with her new husband. Canadian reviewers praised this novel, while others in the United States were less complimentary. *A Daughter of Witches,* which also appeared in book form, was serialized in the *Canadian Magazine.* This story, set in New England, concerns two cousins, the innocent Mabella, and the evil-natured Vashti, who reflects her witch ancestor as she tries to take revenge against her husband.

Some of Wood's notable short stories, according to Gerson, "indicate her mastery of many different forms of popular fiction." "The Last Cock Fight in San Mateo" is set in the Southwest; "A Martyr to Love" is a potboiler about a New York courtesan; her last known story, "Where Waters Beckon," takes place near the Niagara River and the falls, and exalts romantic love. Only one copy of *Farden Ha',* set in the border country of northern England, is known to exist in the British Library in London.

Details about Wood's later life are sketchy. She reportedly spent some time in France and the United States and may have been presented at the English court, where she met the poet Algernon Charles Swinburne. In 1907 she was living with her mother in Niagara-on-the-Lake, Ontario and in 1908, lectured to the Niagara Historical Society. She may have left Canada after 1910. She died at her sister's home in Detroit in 1927.

*BIOGRAPHICAL AND CRITICAL SOURCES:*

BOOKS

*Dictionary of Literary Biography*, Volume 92: *Canadian Writers, 1890-1920*, Gale (Detroit, MI), 1990, pp. 388-390.

PERIODICALS

*Early Canadian Life*, April, 1980, Elsie M. Stevens, "She's Canada's Charlotte Brontë," p. B3, B15.
*Literary Criterion*, numbers 3-4, 1984, Barbara Godard, "A Portrait with Three Faces: The New Woman in Fiction by Canadian Women, 1880-1920," pp. 72-92.

OTHER

*Government of Canada*, http://collections.ic.gc.ca/ (May 26, 2002), "Joanne E. Wood, 1867-1927: Canada's Charlotte Brontë."*

\*     \*     \*

**WOODBRIDGE, (Barbara) Patricia 1946-**

*PERSONAL:* Born August 9, 1946, in Philadelphia, PA; daughter of J. Eliot (a scientist) and Carol (a homemaker; maiden name, Coburn) Woodbridge; married Robert G. Dunn (a writer), August 24, 1988. *Ethnicity:* "Caucasian." *Education:* Bennington College, B.A.; New York University, M.F.A. *Politics:* Democrat. *Religion:* Unitarian-Universalist.

*ADDRESSES: Home*—530 West End Ave., New York, NY 10024. *Agent*—Rita Rosenkranz, 440 West End Ave., New York, NY 10024. *E-mail*—patrwoodbr@aol.com.

*CAREER:* Production designer, art director, and set designer. New York University, New York, NY, teacher at Tisch School of the Arts, 1977-91; Tulane University, master teacher, spring, 1991. Set designer for theatrical productions, including *The Other Half*, produced in New York City at Manhattan Theater Club; *Dispatches* and *Fishing*, both for New York Shakespeare Festival; *Nightclub Cantata; How I Got That Story; The Runner Stumbles;* and *Faith, Hope, and Charity;* regional work includes plays at McCarter Theater, Cincinnati Playhouse, Philadelphia Drama Guild, Goodman Theater, and Arena Stage, Washington, DC; also designer for ballets and operas. Production designer for film *Johnny Suede;* art director for films *Cadillac Man*, Orion Releasing; *My Father, the Hero*, Walt Disney Pictures; *The Object of My Affection*, Twentieth Century-Fox; *A Perfect Murder*, Warner Bros.; *The Hurricane*, Beacon Communications; *Company Man*, Greenstreet Films; *Bait*, Castle Rock Pictures; *Down*, Gun for Hire Productions; and *City by the Sea*, Seabreeze Productions; also worked as assistant art director for films.

*MEMBER:* United Scenic Artists (Local 829), League of Professional Theater Women (New York, NY), New York Women in Film.

*AWARDS, HONORS:* Helen Hayes Award nomination for outstanding set design, 1986.

*WRITINGS:*

*Designer Drafting for the Entertainment World*, Focal Press (Woburn, MA), 2000.

\*     \*     \*

**YOUNG, Josh(ua D.)**

*PERSONAL:* Male.

*ADDRESSES: Agent*—c/o Pocket Books, 1230 Avenue of the Americas, New York, NY 10020.

*CAREER:* Freelance writer.

*WRITINGS:*

(With Mike Medavoy) *You're Only as Good as Your Next One: 100 Great Films, 100 Good Films and 100 for Which I Should Be Shot*, Pocket Books (New York, NY), 2002.

Contributor to periodicals, including *Entertainment Weekly, George, Talk, Esquire,* and the *New York Times.*

*SIDELIGHTS:* Writer Josh Young teamed up with Mike Medavoy, chair of Sony's TriStar Pictures, and spent two years writing *You're Only as Good as Your Next One: 100 Great Films, 100 Good Films and 100 for Which I Should Be Shot.* The book, which covers four decades of American film history, describes Medavoy's career, beginning with his birth in Shanghai, China, through his childhood in Chile and his first Hollywood job in the mailroom of Universal Studios. Young and Medavoy also discuss the films Medavoy ultimately went on to produce.

At the *Calendarlive on latimes.com* Web site, film critic Kenneth Turan wrote that *You're Only as Good as Your Next One* is "a decent, intelligent book about a business that is often neither." In *Library Journal,* Richard W. Grefrath commented that the book is "a refreshing departure" from the run-of-the-mill Hollywood memoir. Mike Tribby, writing in *Booklist,* called the work a "breezy, confident memoir."

Medavoy told B. Alan Orange in an interview at *MovieWeb* that Young spent many hours conversing with him, reading memos and books, and organizing material. Then, Medavoy said, "We'd talk about it, and he'd write up a chapter." Medavoy praised Young, saying, "He did a really good job of putting it together."

*BIOGRAPHICAL AND CRITICAL SOURCES:*

*PERIODICALS*

*Booklist,* February 1, 2002, Mike Tribby, review of *You're Only as Good as Your Next One: 100 Great Films, 100 Good Films and 100 for Which I Should Be Shot,* p. 915.
*Library Journal,* February 1, 2002, Richard W. Grefrath, review of *You're Only as Good as Your Next One,* p. 101.
*Publishers Weekly,* January 28, 2002, review of *You're Only as Good as Your Next One,* p. 282.

*OTHER*

*Calendarlive on latimes.com,* http://www.calendarlive.com/ (March 10, 2002), Kenneth Turan, "Executive Privilege."
*MovieWeb,* http://www.movieweb.com/ (July 1, 2002), B. Alan Orange, interview with Mike Medavoy.*